John Steinbeck, 1902–1968
Countee Cullen, 1903–1946
Frank O'Connor, 1903–1966
Earle Birney, b. 1904
Richard Eberhart, b. 1904
C. Day Lewis, 1904–1972
Robert Penn Warren, b. 1905
W. H. Auden, 1907–1973
Theodore Roethke, 1907–1963
Walter Van Tilburg Clark, 1909–1971
Stephen Spender, 1909–1986
Eudora Welty, b. 1909
Elizabeth Bishop, 1911–1979
J. V. Cunningham, b. 1911
Tennessee Williams, 1911–1983
John Cheever, 1912–1982
Irving Layton, b. 1912
Robert Hayden, b. 1913
Tillie Olsen, b. 1913
Muriel Rukeyser, b. 1913
Karl Shapiro, b. 1913
Irwin Shaw, 1913–1984
Ralph Ellison, b. 1914
Barbara Howes, b. 1914
Randall Jarrell, 1914–1965
Dudley Randall, b. 1914
Henry Reed, b. 1914
William Stafford, b. 1914
Dylan Thomas, 1914–1953
Tom Whitecloud, 1914–1972
Isabella Gardner, 1915–1981
Arthur Miller, b. 1915
Américo Parédes, b. 1915
Margaret Walker, b. 1915
Gwendolyn Brooks, b. 1917
Robert Lowell, 1917–1977
Margaret Avison, b. 1918
Shirley Jackson, 1919–1965
Doris Lessing, b. 1919
May Swenson, b. 1919
Edwin Morgan, b. 1920
Mary Ellen Solt, b. 1920
James Emanuel, b. 1921
Mona Van Duyn, b. 1921
Richard Wilbur, b. 1921
Philip Larkin, 1922–1985
Grace Paley, b. 1922
James Dickey, b. 1923
Richard Hugo, 1923–1982
Edward Field, b. 1924
Vassar Miller, b. 1924
John Fandel, b. 1925
Donald Justice, b. 1925
Carolyn Kizer, b. 1925
Maxine Kumin, b. 1925
Flannery O'Connor, 1925–1964
Gerald Stern, b. 1925
A. R. Ammons, b. 1926
Robert Bly, b. 1926
Allen Ginsberg, b. 1926
James Merrill, b. 1926
Frank O'Hara, 1926–1966

W.
David Wagoner, b. 1926
W. S. Merwin, b. 1927
James Wright, 1927–1980
Edward Albee, b. 1928
Maya Angelou, b. 1928
Anne Sexton, 1928–1974
Gabriel García Márquez, b. 1928
John Hollander, b. 1929
Adrienne Rich, b. 1929
Jon Silkin, b. 1930
John Engels, b. 1931
Alice Munro, b. 1931
Linda Pastan, b. 1932
Sylvia Plath, 1932–1963
John Updike, b. 1932
Etheridge Knight, b. 1933
Imamu Amiri Baraka (LeRoi Jones), b. 1934
Marge Piercy, b. 1934
Sonia Sanchez, b. 1934
Mark Strand, b. 1934
Paul Zimmer, b. 1934
Betty Keller, b. 1935
Lucille Clifton, b. 1936
Marvin Bell, b. 1937
Judith Minty, b. 1937
Luis Omar Salinas, b. 1937
Diane Wakoski, b. 1937
Michael S. Harper, b. 1938
Virginia Scott, b. 1938
Margaret Atwood, b. 1939
Toni Cade Bambara, b. 1939
Seamus Heaney, b. 1939
Billy Collins, b. 1941
Simon Ortiz, b. 1941
Tino Villanueva, b. 1941
Isabel Allende, b. 1942
Marilyn Hacker, b. 1942
Don L. Leee, b. 1942
Sharon Olds, b. 1942
Dave Smith, b. 1942
Nikki Giovanni, b. 1943
Thomas Rabbitt, b. 1943
James Tate, b. 1943
Alice Walker, b. 1944
Daniel Halpern, b. 1945
Carol Muske, b. 1945
Maura Stanton, b. 1946
Leonard Adamé, b. 1947
Roberta Hill, b. 1947
Leslie Marmon Silko, b. 1948
Olga Broumas, b. 1949
Bruce Weigl, b. 1949
Carolyn Forché, b. 1950
Chase Twichell, b. 1950
Rita Dove, b. 1952
Beth Henley, b. 1952
Naomi Shihab Nye, b. 1952
Cathy Song, b. 1955
Mari Evans, 20th century
Cynthia MacDonald, 20th century
Arthur W. Monks, 20th century

LITERATURE

An Introduction to Reading and Writing

LITERATURE

An Introduction to Reading and Writing

SECOND EDITION

EDGAR V. ROBERTS

Lehman College,
The City University of New York

HENRY E. JACOBS

PRENTICE HALL, ENGLEWOOD CLIFFS, NEW JERSEY 07632

Library of Congress Cataloging-in-Publication Data

ROBERTS, EDGAR V.
  Literature: an introduction to reading and writing / Edgar
V. Roberts, Henry E. Jacobs.

    p.   cm.
  Includes index.
  ISBN 0-13-537648-3
  1. Literature.   2. Literature—Collections.   3. Exposition
(Rhetoric)   4. College readers.   I. Jacobs, Henry E.   II. Title.
  PN45.R575 1989   808.3—dc19   88-19504 CIP

Editorial and production supervision: **Hilda Tauber**
Cover design: **Karen A. Stephens**
Manufacturing buyer: **Ray Keating**
Development editor: **Virginia Feury-Gagnon**

Cover photo: Frank Whitney/The Image Bank

Credits and copyright acknowledgments appear on pp. 1653–1659,
which constitute an extension of the copyright page.

© 1989, 1987 by Prentice-Hall, Inc.
A Division of Simon & Schuster, Inc.
Englewood Cliffs, New Jersey 07632

Printed in the United States of America

10 9 8 7 6 5 4 3 2

ISBN 0-13-537648-3

Prentice-Hall International (UK) Limited, *London*
Prentice-Hall of Australia Pty. Limited, *Sydney*
Prentice-Hall Canada Inc., *Toronto*
Prentice-Hall Hispanoamericana, S.A., *Mexico*
Prentice-Hall of India Private Limited, *New Delhi*
Prentice-Hall of Japan, Inc., *Tokyo*
Simon & Schuster Asia Pte. Ltd., *Singapore*
Editora Prentice-Hall do Brasil, Ltda., *Rio de Janeiro*

Brief Contents

Drama

Contents

3   PLOT AND STRUCTURE

4   CHARACTERS: THE PEOPLE IN FICTION

5   POINT OF VIEW

10   IDEA OR THEME: THE MEANING AND THE MESSAGE IN FICTION

11   ADDITIONAL STORIES

Poetry

12   MEETING POETRY: SIMPLE THEME AND FORM

15   IMAGERY: THE POEM'S LINK TO THE SENSES   *603*

16   RHETORICAL FIGURES: A SOURCE OF DEPTH AND RANGE IN POETRY   *623*

17   TONE: THE CREATION OF ATTITUDE IN POETRY   *656*

Tone, Choice, and Reader Response, 657 • *Tone and the Need for Control*, 659 • *Common Grounds of Assent, 661*
Tone and Irony, 661 • *Satire*, 664 • *Reading for Tone in Poetry*, 665

Writing About Tone in Poetry, 673 • *Sample Essay: The Tone of Confidence in "Theme for English B" by Langston Hughes*, 676

20   SYMBOLISM AND ALLUSION: WINDOWS TO A WIDE EXPANSE OF MEANING   **772**

24   ADDITIONAL POEMS   898

Drama

Preface

The second edition of *Literature: An Introduction to Reading and Writing* is a unique book. Not only an excellent anthology, the book is also a comprehensive guide to writing essays about literature. It therefore has a broader sense of mission than do most anthologies. Indeed, we began with the aim of incorporating literary selections within a context of writing, and we now reaffirm this aim.

The integration of reading literature and writing essays begins in Chapter 1, which has been revised to highlight this goal. Guy de Maupassant's famous story "The Necklace" is printed along with sample marginal comments to illustrate the process of active reading. These active reading notes guide students toward further thinking, and therefore toward writing. The notes are embodied within an expanding set of prewriting activities: general observations, selected details focusing on one major aspect for consideration in an essay, an essay outline, and finally, two versions of a sample essay based on the foregoing planning and drafting. The first essay is finished but in need of more work, while the second is revised, expanded, and more sharply pointed. The chapter concludes with general principles about focus, evidence, and language. Thus Chapter 1 emphasizes the principle on which the book is based: the integration of reading, drafting, writing, and revising.

Organization

We have arranged the sections of the book in the commonly accepted order of fiction, poetry, and drama, for these genres form a natural progression from the less difficult to the more difficult, although instructors are free to make assignments from any section, as they wish. We have also sought to provide a broad range of authors from a variety of cultural and ethnic groups, reflecting the current critical trends of reexamining and widening the literary canon. Thus, there are works by men and women, blacks and whites, Hispanics and Native Americans, conservatives and liberals, people with strong religious convictions and others who are indifferent. We have included works by writers with secure places in the history of literature as well as by writers who are less well known.

In the sections on Fiction and Poetry, the chapters cover elements such as character, setting, tone, imagery, theme, and symbolism. In the Drama section, the chapters deal with major categories such as tragedy and comedy. We have chosen this approach, rather than thematic or historical arrangements, because it permits students to analyze various aspects of literature one at a time and in depth. The chapters begin with general discussions of the particular elements or techniques, and include analyses—some brief, some more extensive—of works selected for the chapter. References are also freely made to relevant works in other chapters. The intention of these analyses is not to preempt the student's own reading, but rather to provide specimens, or models, of how the precepts in the chapter may be realized in reading and analysis. Key terms and concepts are highlighted in boldface type, and are all gathered together in a comprehensive Glossary/Index at the back of the book.

The introductory material in each chapter is followed by selections to be read and studied in the context of the chapter, and also to be considered fully and independently for their content, mode, and style. When necessary for understanding, we provide brief marginal glosses and longer explanatory footnotes. Words that are defined or explained are highlighted by a small degree sign (°) in the text. Following each selection are study questions designed to help students explore and understand the selection. Some questions are factual and may be easily answered; others provoke extended thought, classroom discussion, and shorter or longer writing assignments.

The Selections and the Reading Apparatus

In the Fiction section the number of stories has been expanded to a total of 48, compared with 39 in the first edition; 17 of the stories here are entirely new. Most of the stories are by authors from the United States, England, and Canada, but there are also stories by authors from South America, France, and Russia. In addition, we have selected stories by 20 women writers, making this anthology one of the most balanced to be found in any comprehensive anthology.

Of particular note, to strengthen the connection between reading and dramatization, we have selected a number of stories not only because they are good, but also because they are available on videocassettes which may be used in the classroom as teaching tools for support and interpretation (but not as substitutes for reading). In addition, for unique comparison we include two versions of the same subject matter—a short story and a one-act play—by the same author: Susan Glaspell's "A Jury of Her Peers" and *Trifles*. The result of these changes is to provide a wide, interesting, and challenging selection of fiction for both beginning and also more advanced students. As in the first edition, the last chapter of the section contains a selection of stories for further study. Also, as in the first edition, the paragraphs are numbered for easy reference.

The Poetry section is confined to poems in original English, written by men and women alike, from all areas of English-speaking culture. There are 337 poems, many by "standard" poets such as Shakespeare, Wordsworth, Frost, Donne, Dickinson, Roethke, Bogan, Bishop, and Plath, and many by recent poets such as Van Duyn, Giovanni, Angelou, Adamé, Song, and Forché. The chapters are arranged according to particular characteristics or techniques (e.g., words, form, prosody), in the expectation that the book will be used to teach important aspects of poetry, but the selections are also comprehensive enough to permit observations about the history of poetry in England and the United States.

In this second edition our goal has been to enhance the usefulness of these poetry chapters. Thus, for example, the three chapters on rhythm, segments, and rhyme in the first edition have been condensed into one, because lack of time did not permit instructors to assign all three of them. Other compressions and revisions, both in our introductory materials and in the selections, were done for greater focus on the chapter topics and for better understanding and discussion. Any student who studies the new poetry section should be able to handle poetry assignments with skill, knowledge, and confidence. For further study, a final chapter contains many additional poems from all periods of poetry, in alphabetical order by author's name. For convenient references, every fifth line of all poems is numbered.

The Drama section, which includes 14 plays, has also been changed to be more useful for students. The longer and most important plays have been retained (*Oedipus the King*, *Hamlet*, *A Midsummer Night's Dream*, *A Doll's House*, *Death of a Salesman*, and *The Glass Menagerie*). Among the shorter plays, we have added Betty Keller's *Tea Party*, Beth Henley's *Am I Blue*, and Molière's *Love Is the Doctor* (*L'Amour Médecin*), which replaces *The Misanthrope*.

One-act plays have the great advantage that they may be covered within a classroom period, and also can be made especially vivid by the assignment of acting parts to students for complete readings within a relatively short time. The possibilities for these shorter plays are extensive. As in the first edition, the poetic dramas are line numbered every fifth line. New in this edition is that prose dramas now have reference numbers, with every fifth speech being numbered. This system of references makes the plays consistent with the stories.

To place the various works in their historical context, we include the life dates for all authors, together with a chronological list on the inside front covers. In addition, we give the date of publication for each work in the text, along with a date of composition, when known, in parentheses.

Writing as a Major Goal of the Second Edition

For us, writing about literature is not a minor topic that can be addressed in a separate section at the back of the book. It is a coequal concern, and therefore we stress the study and preparation needed for good writing about the topics of all chapters. These approaches to writing, developed from tested principles of studying literature together with our own classroom experience, have been presented for more than twenty-five years in *Writing Themes About Literature* by Edgar V. Roberts.

The skills needed for writing effective essays about literature do not represent a distinct body of knowledge. Rather, careful reading and effective writing are integrated. Both ask that students make important discoveries and decisions about the work being considered, and both require that students be able to point to specific features to justify their conclusions.

To this end, we have supplied "road maps" that show the way to move from reading to responding and thinking, and then to planning and writing. These discussions on writing about literature focus on the topic or element presented in each chapter. They are carefully designed to help students write confidently. Each writing section contains suggestions and questions for planning an essay, developing a central idea, selecting supporting details from the work at hand, organizing thoughts effectively, and beginning the writing process and bringing it to a conclusion.

In these writing sections we do not simply *say* what can be done with a topic of literary study, but we also *show* ways in which it might be done. Each writing section concludes with a sample essay (sometimes more than one) to exemplify the methods and strategies discussed. Thus, the general guidelines are combined with specific essay-length examples to make the writing process as open and clear as possible. Following each essay is a brief commentary showing how the principles of writing presented in the discussion have been carried out. Thus, the sample essays may be combined with the brief exemplary discussions in the introductory sections to provide comprehensive guidance for students with papers to write.

In addition, at the end of each chapter is a set of questions, new in this edition, designed for writing assignments. Many of these questions involve comparison-contrast, and for help the student may consult the discussion of this technique in Appendix B, which has been expanded in this edition. In addition, some of these end-of-chapter assignments provide students with ideas with which to write their own creative works (for example, "Write a poem," or "Compose a short scene"). The objective of these is not to require superb poems, scenes, or stories, but rather to give students a "hands on" experience with the literary techniques discussed in the chapters. The assignments are hence designed to help students understand through their own experiences as writers.

Major Goals of This Book

Reading and writing skills are useful beyond the study of literature. Effective techniques acquired in the methodical use of this book will help students in virtually every course they ever take, and in whatever profession they follow when they leave school. Students may not have many future occasions to read the authors anthologized here, but they will always *read*—if not these authors, then other authors, and certainly always newspapers, legal documents, magazine articles, technical reports, business proposals, and much more. Although students may never need to write again about specific literary topics like setting, structure, or metaphor, they will certainly find future situations requiring them to *write*. Indeed, the more effectively students learn to write about literature during their introduction to literature courses, the better they will be able to write—no matter what the topic—in later days. And, we may add, it is increasingly clear that the power to analyze problems and make convincing written and oral presentations is a major quality of excellence and leadership.

While we stress the value of our book as a teaching tool, we also emphasize that literature is to be *enjoyed*. Sometimes we overlook the truth that study and delight are complementary processes, and that intellectual and emotional enjoyment develops not only from the immediate responses of amusement, involvement, and sympathy, but also from increasing depths of understanding, assimilation, and contemplation. We therefore hope that the literature in the text will teach students about humanity, about their own lives, perceptions, and feelings, and about the timeless patterns of human existence. We hope they will take delight in such discoveries, and grow as they make them. We see the book, then, not as an end, but rather as the beginning of lifelong understanding and joy in great literature.

ACKNOWLEDGMENTS

This book has been a long time in the making and revising, and many people have offered helpful advice and suggestions. For help with the first edition we thank particularly Professors Robert Halli, Claudia Johnson, Matthew Marino, and Matthew Winston, and also Christel Bell, Linda Bridgers, Catherine Davis, Edward Hoeppner, Anna F. Jacobs, and Eleanor Tubbs. In addition, we thank Professors David Bady, Alice Griffin, Gerhard Joseph, Francis Kearns, Ruth Milberg-Kaye, Michael Paull, and Dan Rubey, and also Nanette Roberts and Eve Zarin. The assistance of Jonathan Roberts has been invaluable at virtually every stage of both the first and second editions.

A number of other people have provided invaluable guidance for the preparation of the second edition. To name them, as Dryden said in *Absalom and Achitophel*, is to praise them. They are: Donald G. Anderson, Bemidji State University; Christopher Baker, Lamar University; Shirley A. Curtis, Polk Community College; Adam Fischer, Coastal Carolina Community College; John C. Freeman, El Paso Community College; Judy Kidd, North Carolina State University; Alexander J. Kucsma, County College of Morris; J. Michael Matthews, Tarrant County Junior College; John M. Thomson, U. S. Air Force Academy; Ralph F. Voss, University of Alabama; and Nancy Walker, Southwest Missouri State University.

A word of special thanks goes to Bill Oliver, former Prentice Hall English editor, and to Phil Miller, Editor-in-chief, Humanities, for their imagination, foresight, support, and patience in the development and revision of this project. Of particular importance has been the work of Virginia Feury-Gagnon, development editor of this edition. She has been a cheerful, helpful, understanding, and patient guide during the writing and revising of many chapters. In addition, Ray Mullaney, Editor-in-chief, Development, offered constant guidance and support on the first edition. To Hilda Tauber, the production and copy editor of the second edition, we offer thanks for insight, exactness, and creativity. Additional thanks are due to Jane Bauman and Carol Carter.

The saddest acknowledgment I make is to my associate on this project, Professor Henry E. Jacobs of the University of Alabama. His death in July, 1986 was a stunning blow. Without him, there would have been no book, for his vision, energy, and intelligence were essential in the planning and writing of the first edition. The second edition represents, as it were, a continued collaboration, even though the version that I now present is surely different in detail, though I hope not in general outline, from what we would have presented together. His untimely passing is cause of regret and the deepest sorrow.

EDGAR V. ROBERTS

1

Introduction: Reading, Responding, and Writing about Literature

WHAT IS LITERATURE?

Literature, broadly defined, can refer to just about everything written, from a grocery list to a Shakespearean sonnet. In this book when we use the word *literature*, we exclude things like grocery lists, and confine ourselves to *imaginative literature*. Imaginative literature, which we will call simply *literature*, refers to written (and also spoken) compositions designed to tell stories, dramatize situations, and reveal thoughts and emotions, and also, more importantly, to interest, entertain, stimulate, broaden, and ennoble readers.

There are many ways in which these ends are gained. Some writers, wishing to move us deeply, may describe a great person undergoing misfortune, or more happily may show us people becoming successful in forming human relationships. Other writers, wishing to tell us about new ways of thought and feeling, may speak about wide ranges of experience and emotion. Still other writers, to involve us in some kind of action, may inform us and also try to inspire us to copy the examples which they tell us about. Much literature is designed only for the printed page and is assimilated by readers reading silently, but a great deal of literature is also designed to be read aloud, and some is designed to be spoken and acted out by live actors.

Whatever the form, all literature has much to offer, and the final word on the value of literary study has not been written. Often, in fact, people read books and poems without explaining, even to themselves, why they enjoy it, because goals and ideals are not easily articulated. There are, however, areas of general agreement about some of the things that reading great literature can do, if it is done systematically over a long period of time.

1

Literature helps us grow, both personally and intellectually; it provides an objective base for our knowledge and understanding; it helps us connect ourselves to the broader cultural, philosophic, and religious world of which we are a part; it enables us to recognize human dreams and struggles in different places and times that we would never otherwise know. Literature helps us develop mature sensibility and compassion for the condition of *all* living things—human, animal, and vegetable; it gives us the knowledge and perception needed to appreciate the beauty of order and arrangement, just as a well-structured song or a beautifully done painting can; it provides the comparative basis from which we can see worthiness in the aims of all people, and it therefore helps us see beauty in the world around us; it exercises our emotions through interest, concern, tension, excitement, hope, fear, regret, laughter, and sympathy. Through cumulative experience in reading, great literature shapes our goals and values by helping us clarify our own identities, both positively, through acceptance of the admirable in human beings, and negatively, through rejection of the sinister. It helps us shape our judgments through the comparison of the good and the bad. Literature enables us to develop a perspective on the events that occur around us and in the world at large, and thereby it enables us to gain understanding and control. It is one of the shaping influences of life. It helps to make us human.

TYPES OF LITERATURE: THE GENRES

We usually classify literature—imaginative literature (excluding nonfiction prose)—into the following genres or classes: (1) prose fiction, (2) poetry, and (3) drama. These three genres have many common characteristics. All are art forms, each with its own requirements of structure and style. In varying degrees, all the genres are dramatic and imaginative; they have at least some degree of action, or are based in part on dramatic situations.

Imaginative literature differs from textbooks, historical and biographical works, and news articles, all of which describe or interpret facts. While literature is related to the truths of human life, it may be based on situations that have never occurred, and which may never occur. This is not to say that imaginative literature is not truthful, but rather that its truth is to life and human nature, not necessarily to the detailed world of reportorial, scientific, and historical facts in which we all live.

Although the three main genres have much in common, they also differ in many ways. **Prose fiction,** or **narrative fiction,** is in prose form and includes *novels, short stories, myths, parables, romances*, and *epics*. These works generally focus on one or a few major characters who undergo some kind of change as they meet other characters or deal with problems or difficulties in their lives. **Poetry,** in contrast to prose fiction, is much more economical in the use of words, and it relies heavily on *imagery, figurative language, rhythm*, and *sound*. **Drama** (or **plays**) is the form of literature designed to be performed by actors. Like fiction, drama may focus on a single character or a small number of characters, and it presents fictional events as if they were happening in the present, to be witnessed by a group of people composing an audience. Some dramas employ much of the imagery, rhythm, and sound of poetry.

READING A WORK AND RESPONDING TO IT ACTIVELY

Sometimes students confuse a cursory reading with an active reading. A quick reading of a work is little more than that; for example, you might read an entire story and not be able to say anything about it at all. A more careful, active reading, however, enables you to understand and respond to questions about meaning and organization. The reading we are encouraging here is this active sort—a reading in which we engage the work and interact with it. Obviously, we must first follow the work and understand its details. At the same time we must respond to the words, get at the ideas, understand the implications of what is happening, and apply our own experiences to verify the accuracy and truth of the situation and incidents, to appreciate the characters and their solutions to the problems they face, and to articulate our own emotional responses. In short, as active, participating readers, we should assimilate the work into our minds and spirits.

To illustrate the process of active reading, we present below "The Necklace," a story by the French writer Guy de Maupassant, with marginal comments representing a possible set of reader responses. Many of these comments, particularly at the beginning, do no more than record the factual details of the story. But as the story progresses, a number of comments are responsive and interpretive; that is, they indicate reactions and observations about the meaning of the incidents. These comments reflect not just a first reading, but the fuller responses of second and third readings. The responses are general rather than specific. That is, they are not concentrated around a central point of inquiry, but rather are broad in scope, to show reading responses as an ongoing process.

GUY DE MAUPASSANT (1850–1893)

The Necklace   *1884*

Translated by Edgar V. Roberts

She was one of those pretty and charming women, born, as if by an error of destiny, into a family of clerks and copyists. She had no dowry, no prospects, no way of getting known, courted, loved, married by a rich and distinguished

"She" is pretty but poor. Apparently there is no other life for her than marriage. Without connections, she has no man. She finally settled for a marriage with a minor clerk in the Ministry of Education.

She was a simple person, without the money to dress well, but she was as unhappy as if she had gone through bankruptcy, for women have neither rank nor race. In place of high birth or important family connections, they can rely only on their beauty, their grace, and their charm. Their inborn finesse, their elegant taste, their engaging personalities, which are their only power, make working-class women the equals of the grandest duchesses.

She suffered constantly, feeling herself destined for all delicacies and luxuries. She suffered because of her grim apartment with its drab walls, threadbare furniture, ugly curtains. All such things, which most other women in her situation would not even have noticed, tortured her and filled her with despair. The sight of the young country girl who did her simple housework awakened in her only a sense of desolation and lost hopes. She daydreamed of large, silent anterooms, decorated with oriental tapestries and lighted by high bronze floor lamps, with two elegant valets in short culottes dozing in large armchairs under the effects of forced-air heaters. She visualized large drawing rooms draped in the most expensive silks, with fine end tables on which were placed knickknacks of inestimable value. She dreamed of the perfume of dainty private rooms, which were designed only for intimate tête-à-têtes with the closest friends, who because of their achievements and fame would make her the envy of all other women.

When she sat down to dinner at her round little table covered with a cloth that had not been washed for three days, in front of her husband who opened the kettle while declaring ecstatically, "Oh boy, beef stew, my favorite," she dreamed of expensive banquets with shining placesettings, and wall hangings depicting ancient heroes and exotic birds in an enchanted forest. She imagined a gourmet-prepared main course carried on the most exquisite trays and served on the most beautiful dishes, with whispered gallantries which she would hear with a sphinxlike smile as she dined on the pink meat of a trout or the delicate wing of a quail.

5   She had no decent dresses, no jewels, nothing. And she loved nothing but these; she believed herself born only for these. She burned with the desire to please, to be envied, to be attractive and sought after.

She had a rich friend, a comrade from convent days, whom she did not want to see anymore because she suffered so much when she returned home. She would weep for the entire day afterward with sorrow, regret, despair, and misery.

---

entry into high society, and marries an insignificant clerk.

She is unhappy.

A view of women that excludes the possibility of a career. In 1884, women had little else than their personalities to get ahead.

She suffers because of her cheap belongings, wanting expensive things. She dreams of wealth and of how other women would envy her if she had all these fine things. But these luxuries are unrealistic and unattainable for her.

Her husband's taste is for plain things, while she dreams of expensive gourmet food. He has adjusted to his status. She has not.

She lives for her unrealistic dreams, and these increase her frustration.

She even thinks of giving up a rich friend because she is so depressed after visiting her.

Well, one evening, her husband came home glowing and carrying a large envelope.

"Here," he said, "this is something for you."

She quickly tore open the envelope and took out a card engraved with these words:

The Chancellor of Education and Mrs. George Ramponneau request that Mr. and Mrs. Loisel do them the honor of coming to dinner at the Ministry of Education on the evening of January 8.

10 Instead of being delighted, as her husband had hoped, she threw the invitation spitefully on the table, muttering:

"What do you expect me to do with this?"

"But honey, I thought you'd be glad. You never get to go out, and this is a special occasion! I had a lot of trouble getting the invitation. Everyone wants one; the demand is high and not many clerks get invited. Everyone important will be there."

She looked at him angrily and stated impatiently:

"What do you want me to wear to go there?"

15 He had not thought of that. He stammered:

"But your theater dress. That seems nice to me . . ."

He stopped, amazed and bewildered, as his wife began to cry. Large tears fell slowly from the corners of her eyes to her mouth. He said falteringly:

"What's wrong? What's wrong?"

But with a strong effort she had recovered, and she answered calmly as she wiped her damp cheeks:

20 "Nothing, except that I have nothing to wear and therefore can't go to the party. Give your invitation to someone else at the office whose wife will have nicer clothes than mine."

Distressed, he responded:

"Well, all right, Mathilde. How much would a new dress cost, something you could use at other times, but not anything fancy?"

She thought for a few moments, adding things up and thinking also of an amount that she could ask without getting an immediate refusal and a frightened outcry from the frugal clerk.

25 Finally she responded tentatively:

"I don't know exactly, but it seems to me that I could get by on four hundred francs."

He blanched slightly at this, because he had set aside just that amount to buy a shotgun and go with a few friends to Nanterre on Sundays the next summer to shoot larks.

(Marginal notes)

A new section in the story.

An invitation to dinner at the Ministry of Education. A big plum.

It only upsets her.

She declares that she hasn't anything to wear. He tries to persuade her that her theater dress might do for the occasion.

Her name is Mathilde.

He volunteers to pay for a new dress.

She is manipulating him.

The dress will cost him his next summer's vacation. (He doesn't seem to have included her in his plans.)

folds of the shawl, in the pockets, everywhere. They found nothing.

He asked:

70 "You're sure you still had it when you left the party?"

"Yes. I checked it in the vestibule of the Ministry." · They can't find it.

"But if you had lost it in the street, we would have heard it fall. It must be in the cab."

"Yes, probably. Did you notice the number?"

"No. Did you see it?"

75 "No."

Overwhelmed, they looked at each other. Finally, Loisel got dressed again:

"I'm going out to retrace all our steps," he said, "to see if I can find the necklace that way."

And he went out. She stayed in her evening dress, · He goes out to search for without the energy to get ready for bed, stretched out in · the necklace. a chair, drained of strength and thought.

Her husband came back at about seven o'clock. He · But is unsuccessful. had found nothing.

80 He went to Police Headquarters and to the newspapers · He really tries. He is doing to announce a reward. He went to the small cab compa- · his best. nies, and finally he followed up even the slightest hopeful lead.

She waited the entire day, in the same enervated state, in the face of this frightful disaster.

Loisel came back in the evening, his face pale and haggard. He had found nothing.

"You'll have to write to your friend," he said, "that · Loisel's plan to explain you broke a clasp on her necklace and that you are having · delaying the return. He it fixed. That will give us time to look around." · takes charge, is · resourceful.

She wrote as he dictated.

85 At the end of a week they had lost all hope. · Things are hopeless.

And Loisel, looking five years older, declared:

"We'll have to see about replacing the jewels."

The next day they took the case which had contained · They hunt for a the necklace and went to the jeweler whose name was inside. · replacement. He looked at his books:

"I wasn't the one, Madam, who sold the necklace. I only made the case."

90 Then they went from jeweler to jeweler, searching for a necklace like the other one, racking their memories, both of them sick with the worry and anguish.

In a shop in the Palais-Royal, they found a necklace · A new diamond necklace of diamonds that seemed to them exactly like the one they · will cost 36,000 francs. were looking for. It was priced at forty thousand francs. They could buy it for thirty-six thousand.

They got the jeweler to promise not to sell it for three · They make a deal with the days. And they made an agreement that he would buy it · jeweler. (Is Maupassant back for thirty-four thousand francs if the original was recovered before the end of February.

Loisel had saved eighteen thousand francs that his father had left him. He would have to borrow the rest.

He borrowed, asking a thousand francs from one, five hundred from another, five louis° here, three louis there. He wrote promissory notes, undertook ruinous obligations, did business with finance companies and the whole tribe of loan sharks. He compromised himself for the remainder of his days, risked his signature without knowing whether he would be able to honor it, and, terrified by anguish over the future, by the black misery that was about to descend on him, by the prospect of all kinds of physical deprivations and moral tortures, he went to get the new necklace, and put down thirty-six thousand francs on the jeweler's counter.

95   Mrs. Loisel took the necklace back to Mrs. Forrestier, who said with an offended tone:

"You should have brought it back sooner; I might have needed it."

She did not open the case, as her friend feared she might. If she had noticed the substitution, what would she have thought? What would she have said? Would she not have taken her for a thief?

Mrs. Loisel soon discovered the horrible life of the needy. She did her share, however, completely, heroically. That horrifying debt had to be paid. She would pay. They dismissed the maid; they changed their address; they rented an attic flat.

She learned to do heavy housework, dirty kitchen jobs. She washed the dishes, wearing away her manicured fingernails on greasy pots and encrusted baking dishes. She handwashed dirty linen, shirts, and dish towels that she hung out on the line to dry. Each morning, she took the garbage down to the street, and she carried up water, stopping at each floor to catch her breath. And, dressed in cheap house dresses, she went to the fruit dealer, the grocer, the butchers, with her basket under her arms, haggling, insulting, defending her measly cash penny by penny.

100   They had to make installment payments every month, and, to buy more time, to refinance loans.

The husband worked evenings to make fair copies of tradesmen's accounts, and late into the night he made copies at five cents a page.

And this life lasted ten years.

louis: a gold coin worth twenty francs.

---

hinting that things might work out for them?)

It will take all of Loisel's inheritance plus another 18,000 francs that must be borrowed at enormous rates of interest.

Mrs. Forrestier complains about the delay.

Is this enough justification for not telling the truth? It seems to be for the Loisels.

A new section, the fifth.

They suffer to repay their debts. Loisel works late at night. Mathilde accepts a cheap attic flat, and does all the heavy housework herself to save on domestic help.

She pinches pennies, and haggles with the local tradesmen.

They struggle to meet payments.

Mr. Loisel moonlights to make extra money.

For ten years they endure all this.

At the end of ten years, they had paid back everything—everything—including the extra charges imposed by loan sharks and the accumulation of compound interest.

The last section. They have finally paid back the entire debt.

Mrs. Loisel looked old now. She had become the strong, hard, and rude woman of poor households. Her hair unkempt, with uneven skirts and rough, red hands, she spoke loudly, washed floors with large buckets of water. But sometimes, when her husband was at work, she sat down near the window, and she dreamed of that evening so long ago, of that party, where she had been so beautiful and so admired.

Mrs. Loisel (how come the narrator does not say "Mathilde"?) is roughened and aged by the work. But she has behaved "heroically" (¶ 98), and has shown her mettle.

105   What would life have been like if she had not lost that necklace? Who knows? Who knows? Life is so peculiar, so uncertain. How little a thing it takes to destroy you or to save you!

A moral? Our lives are shaped by small, uncertain things; we hang by a thread.

Well, one Sunday, when she had gone for a stroll along the Champs-Elysées to relax from the cares of the week, she suddenly noticed a woman walking with a child. It was Mrs. Forrestier, still youthful, still beautiful, still attractive.

A scene on the Champs-Elysées. She sees Jeanne Forrestier, after ten years.

Mrs. Loisel felt moved. Would she speak to her? Yes, certainly. And now that she had paid, she could tell all. Why not?

She walked closer.

"Hello, Jeanne."

110   The other gave no sign of recognition and was astonished to be addressed so familiarly by this working-class woman. She stammered:

"But . . . Madam! . . . I don't know. . . . You must have made a mistake."

"No. I'm Mathilde Loisel."

Her friend cried out:

"Oh! . . . My poor Mathilde, you've changed so much."

Jeanne notes Mathilde's changed appearance.

115   "Yes. I've had some hard times since I saw you last; in fact miseries . . . and all because of you! . . .

"Of me . . . how so?"

"You remember the diamond necklace that you lent me to go to the party at the Ministry of Education?"

"Yes. What then?"

"Well, I lost it."

She tells Jeanne everything.

120   "How, since you gave it back to me?"

"I returned another exactly like it. And for ten years we've been paying for it. You understand that this wasn't easy for us, who have nothing. . . . Finally it's over, and I'm mighty glad."

Mrs. Forrestier stopped her.

125

"You say that you bought a diamond necklace to replace mine?"

"Yes, you didn't notice it, eh? It was exactly like yours."

And she smiled with proud and childish joy.

Mrs. Forrestier, deeply moved, took both her hands.

"Oh, my poor Mathilde! But mine was only costume jewelry. At most, it was worth only five hundred francs! . . ."

SURPRISE! The lost necklace was not real diamonds, and the Loisels slaved for no reason at all. But hard work and sacrifice probably brought out better qualities in Mathilde than she otherwise might have shown. Is this the moral of the story?

STUDYING THROUGH USE OF A NOTEBOOK

The marginal comments alongside the story above demonstrate the active reading–responding process you should apply with everything you read as a student. Once you make this process methodical, with an emphasis on specific topics and assignments, you are no longer just reading, but are studying. A widely accepted assumption is that students should spend two hours of study out of class for every period spent in class. This number may seem arbitrary, but if you devote that much time, on average, you will be well on the way to being a successful student.

An efficient way to reinforce your reading is by writing down your observations and other details. If you are in the habit of underlining important passages and making marginal comments (as we did in "The Necklace"), you should continue to do so. But it is also very helpful to keep a notebook as a study aid and a resource for your writing assignments.

It is not difficult to keep such a notebook. Your objective should be to learn an assigned work inside and out, and to be able to say perceptive things about it. If you have developed your own notational methods, just keep following these. In all likelihood, however, your comments will take the shape of first observations followed by more searching ones, as in the study plans suggested below. Use the notebook systematically as a "memory bank" of your knowledge and ideas about a work, from which you can draw when you go through the process of writing.

Whether you are studying for a particular assignment or not, you should keep your notebook in the manner described below. Follow the Guidelines for the First Reading of a Work for everything you read, to obtain your first impressions and basic understanding. Follow the Guidelines for Further Study for a more searching study of the work.

GUIDELINES FOR THE FIRST READING OF A WORK

1. *Observations for basic understanding*
   a. Determine what is happening in the work. For a story or play, where do the actions take place? What do the actions show? Who is involved? Who is the major figure? Why is he/she major? What relationships do the characters have with each other? What concerns do the characters

have? What do they do? Who says what to whom? What do the speeches do to advance the action, and to advance your understanding of the characters? For a poem, who seems to be doing the talking, and to whom? What is the situation, and what does the speaker think about the characters and say about them? Why does the poem end as it does and where it does?

    b.   Record things that you do not understand, or that you think need explaining. Write down and try to remember words that are new or not totally familiar. Whenever you run across a passage that you do not quickly understand, decide whether the problem arises from words you do not know. Use your dictionary and write the relevant meanings in your notebook, but be sure that these meanings clarify your understanding of the passages in which the words appear. Make note of special difficulties so that you may ask your instructor about them.

2.   *Notes on your first impressions*

    a.   Make a record of your reactions and responses to the work. Is there anything funny, memorable, noteworthy, or otherwise striking? Did you laugh, smile, worry, get scared, feel a thrill, learn a great deal, feel proud, find a lot to think about?

    b.   Make notes on interesting characterizations, events, techniques, and ideas. If you like a character or idea, try to describe what you like, and do the same for characters and ideas you don't like. Is there anything else in the work that you especially like or dislike? Are parts particularly easy or difficult to understand? Why? Are there any surprises? What was your reaction to them? Be sure to use *your own* words for these observations.

GUIDELINES FOR FURTHER STUDY OF THE WORK

3.   *Development of ideas and enlargement of responses*

    a.   Examine your marginal notations and underlinings. In your notebook (or on separate cards if more convenient), write out in full some of the passages you think most important. Carry the passages with you, and when riding public transportation, walking to class, or otherwise not occupying your time, try to memorize phrases, sentences, or lines.

    b.   Come to grips with words and/or concepts that need special emphasis. What explanations need to be made about the characters? Beyond obvious first conclusions, do the events and statements seem to invite more extensive interpretation? Why so? What assumptions do the actors and speakers say and show about life and humanity generally, about themselves, the people around them, their families, their friends, and about work, the economy, religion, politics, and the state of the world? What manners or customs do they exhibit? Do these habits magnify or inhibit their responses? To what degree? What sort of language do they use: formal or informal words, slang or profanity? What literary devices or features seem to be operating in the work? A literary device or **convention** is a feature that is usual and expected by the reader in the story. For example, you would expect to find an obvious moral when you read a fable. Can you determine any particular characteristics resulting from these literary conventions?

c.   Trace developing patterns in the work. Make an outline or scheme for the story or main idea. What conflicts appear in the work? Do these conflicts exist between people, groups, or ideas? How does the author resolve them? Is one force, idea, or side the winner? Why? How do you respond to the winner, or loser?

d.   Make a practice of writing a paragraph, or several paragraphs, describing your reactions and thoughts after reading and considering the work. If you are reading the work to prepare for a specific type of essay, your paragraphs may become useful for you later, for they may be directly transferable to the essay. Even if you are making only a general preparation, however, always continue the practice of writing down your thoughts.

e.   Always, whenever questions occur to you, make a note of them for use in class and also in your own further study.

Specimen Notebook Entries

Following are some sample notes on the topic of "The Necklace." These notes follow the suggestions for notebook entries listed under Guidelines 1 and 2 for a first reading, and they are also related to the marginal responses placed beside the story on pp. 3–11. Since the notebook is not to be a composition, however, the ordering of remarks is random, more or less as the observations occur as a result of reading. What is important is that the notebook should record enough observations and responses to be useful later, both for additional study and also for a developing essay.

NOTES ON MAUPASSANT'S "THE NECKLACE"

Early in the story, Mathilde seems spoiled. She is poor, or at least lower middle class, but she seems unable to face her own situation.

As a dreamer, she seems harmless. Her daydreams about a fancy home, with all the expensive belongings, are not unusual. Most people dream of being well off, and therefore indulge their wishes for better things.

She seems not to like her husband, and is apparently embarrassed by his taste for plain food. The story contrasts her taste for trout and quail with Loisel's cheaper favorites.

Only when the Loisels get the invitation does Mathilde seem difficult. Her wish for an expensive dress (the cost of Loisel's entire vacation), and then her wanting the jewelry, make real difficulty for her husband.

Her success at the party shows that she has the true charm the speaker talks about in paragraph 2. She seems never to have had any other chances in life to exert her power.

The worst part of her personality is her hurrying away from the party because she is ashamed of her everyday shawl. Therefore, it is Mathilde's unhappiness and unwillingness to adjust to her modest means that cause the financial downfall of the Loisels. It is clearly her fault.

The borrowing of the money to replace the necklace shows that both Loisel and Mathilde have a strong sense of honor. Making up for the loss is a good thing, even if it is going to destroy them economically.

There are some nice touches in the story, such as Loisel's seeming to be five years older (paragraph 86), and his staying with the other husbands of women enjoying themselves at the party (paragraph 54). These are done quickly but tellingly.

It's too bad that Loisel and Mathilde don't tell Jeanne directly that the jewels have been lost. Their pride stops them—or perhaps a fear of being accused of theft.

Their ten years of slavish work (paragraphs 98–102) show how they have come down in life. Mathilde's work must all be done by hand, without any labor-saving machines, so she really does pitch in, and is heroic.

The life in the attic flat (paragraph 98) shows Mathilde's strength as it also shows her becoming loud and frumpy. She does what she has to. In the same way, the earlier places on the Street of Martyrs and in her imagination bring out the limitations of her character.

The setting of the Champs-Elysées also reflects her character, for she feels free there to confess the disastrous loss and sacrifice to Jeanne (paragraph 107), and it is this that produces the surprise ending.

The narrator's thought about how "little a thing it takes to destroy you or save you" (paragraph 105) is likely true, although the point is made only briefly. The necklace is a little thing, but the problem is that it seems very large financially. This makes for the story's irony.

Questions: Is this story more about the surprise ending or about the character of Mathilde? Are we expected to admire her or condemn her? Is the outcome dependent on little things that make or break us, as the speaker suggests, or on the difficulty of rising above one's economic class, which certainly seems true, or both? What is to be made of the speaker's opening remarks about the status of women? (Remember that the story was published in 1884.) This probably isn't relevant, but wouldn't Jeanne, after hearing about the substitution, give the full value of the necklace to the Loisels, and wouldn't they then be pretty well off?

These are reasonable notebook responses and observations to "The Necklace." For our present purposes they are in the form of complete sentences, and they have been fairly well unified, but on the whole, they represent what can be done for most reading tasks. For all assignments, you should make a similar use of a notebook. You may judge how far your notes should go by the nature of what is expected. For example, if the assignment is simply to read a work, general notes like those taken here should be sufficient. Such entries would prepare you for study with fellow students and also for classroom discussion. If you are preparing for a test, you might do more with your discussions and observations, and also answer some of the questions that you raise while taking your notes. The same holds true if you are preparing for a writing assignment, for you would then focus your notes on matters specifically related to your topic. Whatever your purpose, you should always use a notebook as you read, and put into it as much detail as you can. Your detailed notebook will be a valuable aid in refreshing your memory as you prepare to write and as you study for exams.

WRITING ESSAYS ABOUT LITERATURE

Writing is the sharpened, focused expression of thought and study. As you develop your writing skills, you also improve your perceptions and increase your critical faculties. Although few people ever achieve perfection in writing—a state in which words and ideas blend perfectly together— everyone can work hard to improve.

The subject of this book is literature: studying it, asking questions about it, and writing about it. The development of your ability to think and to write about literature will also prepare you to write about other topics. Literature itself contains the subject material, though not in a systematic way, of philosophy, religion, psychology, sociology, and politics. Learning to analyze literature and to write about it will also improve your perception of these and other disciplines. Developing your capacity for analysis will also enable you to analyze and reach conclusions about issues and problems that affect your life.

Writing begins with the search for something to say—an idea. Not all ideas are equal; some are better than others. You will discover that your ability to acquire good ideas will improve the longer you engage in the analysis of literature (or the analysis of any topic). In the same way, the quality of your thought will improve as you go through the process of originating ideas, seeing the flaws in some of your thinking processes, proposing new avenues of development, securing new data to support ideas, and creating new aspects of ideas in the course of diligent and applied thought. Your objective always will be to persuade your reader that your details are correct and that your conclusions are both valid and interesting.

Unlike ordinary conversation and classroom discussion, writing must stick with great determination to a specific point. Ordinary conversation is usually random and disorganized; it frequently shifts from topic to topic, often without any apparent cause, and it is needlessly repetitive. Classroom discussion is a form of formal, organized talk, but it is free and spontaneous, and irrelevant digressions may occur. By contrast, writing is the most concise and highly organized form of expression that you will ever create.

WHAT IS AN ESSAY?

Writing demands tight organization and control. The first requirement of the organized and finished essay—although it is not the first requirement in the writing *process*—is that it have a **central idea**. In fact, an **essay** may be defined as a fully developed set of paragraphs that grow systematically out of a central idea. Everything in the essay should be directly connected to the idea or should contribute to the reader's understanding of the idea. The central idea is central to your control over your writing.

Let us consider this definition in relation to essays about literature. A successful essay should be a brief but thorough examination, not an exhaustive treatment, of a particular subject. It might be a character study, an analysis of the point of view of a story or poem, or a comparison-contrast. Unity is achieved through the consistent reference to the central idea, and completeness is achieved through the demonstration of how a selected number of details relate to and support the idea. Typical central ideas might be (1) that a character is strong and tenacious (Maupassant's "The Necklace"), (2) that the point of view makes the action seem up close and personal (O'Connor's "First Confession"),* or (3) that one work is different from or better than another. All details introduced into essays on these topics should be tied to these ideas. Thus, it is a fact that Mathilde Loisel in "The Necklace" spends ten years in slavish work and sacrifice. This fact is not relevant to an essay on her character, however, unless you *connect* the fact by showing how it illustrates two of her major traits—in this case, her strength and tenacity. Similarly, it is not important in an essay about idea or theme in O'Connor's "First Confession" to say that Nora insults Jackie (though it is essential in the story itself) unless you relate her speeches to an idea—for example, the idea that family life may be filled with tension and rivalry. By the same token, any attempt to show that "First Confession" reveals more about character than "The Necklace" must be introduced as part of an argument that O'Connor's story is different from or superior to Maupassant's, at least as regards the development of character.

These principles of *unity*, *connection*, and *development* should be your goal when you plan and write your essay. Here they are again:

1. The essay should cover the assigned topic (for example, character, point of view, and others.)
2. The essay should have a central idea that governs its development.
3. The essay should be organized so that every part contributes something to the reader's understanding of the central idea.

---

* This story is in Chapter 11, pp. 490–495.

them as the basis for "brainstorming"; that is, a free play of mind concentrated to fit details from the work to the subject of the developing essay. Not everything in your notes will be relevant, for notes by definition are disorganized and unfocused. However, the notes are a starting point. Since our assignment concerns character (rather than plot, imagery, symbolism, or the like), you should go over the notes to develop observations that relate specifically to Mathilde's character traits. You need to ensure that these sentences focus on the subject at hand—character—and do not lead toward plot summary or other digressions. A reformulated list of sentences about Mathilde might look like this:

Mathilde begins the story as a kind of fish out of water. She dreams of wealth but is confined to a drab existence with her ordinary husband.

Her fantasies about lavish rooms make her even more dissatisfied. She is almost punishing herself.

Her character can be related to the real places where she lives and moves (the first place on the Street of Martyrs, the scene of the dinner, the attic flat), and also the imaginary place which she fills with expensive things.

Her initial response to the invitation causes discomfort to her husband, but no real harm. She, however, is aggressively cranky, and manipulates her husband into buying her an expensive dress.

Her dream world hurts her real life when her desire for wealth causes the borrowing of the necklace. The loss of the necklace is just bad luck.

The attic flat brings out her potential coarseness, but it also develops her potential for sacrifice and cooperation. That she is a loser makes her, in effect, a winner.

are all observations that might or might not turn out to be worth in your essay. You cannot tell until you do some further thinking them. These basic ideas, however, are worth working up further, ith additional substantiating details.

VELOPING YOUR OBSERVATIONS AS PARAGRAPHS.   To develop these ideas you should begin to create paragraphs, all the time checking with ginal notebook entries and also with the work (to get all details The object of writing paragraphs is to explore what you know efore to catch important ideas for your developing essay. Until things down, you will not know which way your mind is directing e are four paragraphs done in a "brainstorming" attempt to find ssay materials:

lde comes to life as a character. She is a dreamer, but that is not at all al. Her thoughts of unreachable wealth are like those that cause people

THE PROCESS OF WRITING AN ESSAY

Essays do not organize themselves magically as they are written. *Writing is a process*. It often begins in vagueness and uncertainty, and ends in something finished. But when students look at a complete, polished, well-formed essay written by someone else, they may at first believe that it was perfect just as it flowed from the writer's pen, typewriter, or word processor.

This assumption—that an essay must be perfect the first time—is false. If you could see the early drafts of writing you admire, you would be surprised—and encouraged—to see how messy, uncertain, and incomplete they are. In final drafts, early ideas are discarded and others added; new facts are introduced; early paragraphs are cut in half and assembled elsewhere with parts of other paragraphs; words are changed and misspellings corrected; sentences are revised or completely rewritten, and new writing is added to tie together the reassembled materials and make them flow smoothly together.

All this is normal. In fact, for your own purposes, you should use the finished essay not as something to begin with, but rather as something to achieve—a goal or ideal. How you reach your goal is up to you, because everyone has unique work habits. But you should always remember that writing is a process in which you try to overcome not only the difficulties of reading and interpreting the literary work, but also the natural resistance of your own mind.

The pathway towards a finished essay may sometimes seem halting, digressive, and purposeless. Many of these ordinary difficulties in writing can be overcome if you continue to remind yourself that writing cannot be perfect the first time. It is important just to start writing—no matter how unacceptable the first products seem—to create a beginning, to force yourself to lock horns with the materials. You are not committed to anything you first put down on paper or on the screen of a word processor. You may throw it out and write something else, or you may write over it, or move it around, as you wish. But if you keep it locked in your mind by not beginning to write anything at all, you will have nothing to work with, and then your frustration will be justified. Accept the uncertainties in the writing process and use them to work *for* you rather than *against* you.

INVENTION AND PREWRITING

The intentional, systematic, and also accidental processes that take place in the development of a piece of writing are called invention and prewriting. **Invention** is the process of uncovering, discovering, and dragging out of your mind some of the things that need to be said on a particular topic.

Prewriting is the process of studying, thinking, raising and answering questions, planning, developing tentative ideas and first drafts, crossing out, erasing, changing, rearranging, and adding. In a way, prewriting and invention are different words for the process of planning and thinking. They both acknowledge the mysterious and uncertain but also the exciting and stimulating ways in which minds work, and also the fact that ideas are not always known and shaped until they are written. *Writing, at any stage, should always be thought of as a process of discovery as well as creation.*

To describe the invention and prewriting process, we will use as our topic The Character of Mathilde in Maupassant's "The Necklace." When you carry out writing assignments, you may change the order and skip some of the steps given below, but on the whole you will probably stay within the pattern.

Not every step in the writing process can be detailed here. Although we present an early draft of the essay printed at the end of this chapter, there is not enough space to show the development of all the early drafts. If you compare the original notes and marginal observations, however (see pp. 13–14, above) with early drafts of observations and paragraphs, you can see that many changes take place and that one step really merges with another.

INVENTION AND PREWRITING STEPS

1. *Read the work through at least once for general understanding.* It is important to have general knowledge of the work before you develop your central idea. Be sure, in this first reading, to use your notebook, and to follow all the general principles of studying listed on pages 11–13.

2. *Take notes that direct you into your assignment.* Remember the third principle of unity and organization mentioned on page 16. Because our subject is the character of Mathilde in "The Necklace," our notes will be centered about her—her traits as they are disclosed by her actions, thoughts, speeches, and reactions to the things around her. The same focus would apply if your assignment were on metaphor, ideas, or another aspect. By focusing your notes in this way, and by excluding other approaches to the work, you are already concentrating on your writing assignment.

3. *Use the questions that follow the specific work on which the assignment is based.* Your answers to these questions, together with your notes and ideas, can often be used directly in parts of your developing essay.

4. *Use a pen, pencil, typewriter, or word processor as an extension of your thought.* Writing, together with actually *seeing* and *reflecting about* the things written, is for most people a vital part of thinking. Therefore it is essential to get thoughts into a visible form so that you may develop them further. For many people, the hand is a psychological necessity in this process. In noting, sketching out, and drafting the things that may go into the developing essay, be sure to write on only one side of the cards or paper you are using. With everything on only one may spread out, and in this way may get an overview as you plan and

A special word seems in order about word processors, which ar increasingly important for many students in the composition proces can handle the keyboard—the same as for a typewriter—the word help you in developing ideas, for you can eliminate unworkable put others in their places. You may move sentences and paragra into new contexts, test out how they look, and move them somewh prefer. You can more readily see misspelling and typographical have shown that many errors and awkward sentences can be found of pages prepared with a conventional typewriter. One explanatio hesitate to make improvements once they reach the bottom of t of the resulting messiness or because of their reluctance to typ The word processor eliminates this difficulty completely. Chan anywhere in the draft, at any time, without damage to the final draft.

In addition, with the rapid printers commonly available to out drafts even in the initial and tentative stages. With a com use your pen or pencil to make additional notes, marginal lines indicating new spots for a particular passage to go, and su development. With the draft in your hands for guidance, yo word processor and carry out the instructions you have give repeat this process once, twice, or more times. The machine incentive for improvement, right up until the moment of

However, no matter what method of writing you use, that unwritten thought is still incomplete thought. Theref composing process, it is vital to prepare a complete draft of Even with the word processor's screen, you cannot lay but can see only a small part. A clean, readable draft pern together and to make even more improvements.

5. *Once you have put everything together in this way,* central idea will serve as the focus of your planning an

FINDING A CENTRAL IDEA OR THESIS

You cannot find a central idea in a hat. It com steps just described. In a way, you might thir idea as one of the major goals in prewriting. (idea, you have a guide for accepting some others, rearranging, changing, and rewordir to see how the central idea may be develope

WRITING OBSERVATIONS FROM YOUR NO you make a set of notes on the work, like th

to make bets or buy lottery tickets. She really thinks of a life better than the one she is living.

2. The original apartment in the Street of Martyrs, and the dream world of wealthy places, both show aspects of her character. The real-life apartment, though livable, is shabby. The furnishings all bring out her capacity for discontentment. The shabbiness makes her think only of luxuriousness, and her one servant girl makes her dream of many servants. The luxury of her dream life thus heightens her unhappiness with what she actually has.

3. Mathilde becomes coarsened during the ten-year period of repayment. She gives up her domestic help, and takes on all the heavy housework herself. She climbs stairs carrying heavy pails of water, and throws the water around to clean floors. She washes greasy and encrusted pots and pans, takes out the garbage, and does the clothes and dishes by hand. She gives up caring for her hair and hands, and wears the cheapest clothing possible. She becomes loud and argumentative, and spends a good deal of time haggling with the local shopkeepers in order to save as much money as she can. Whatever delicacy and attractiveness she had, she loses.

4. Her Sunday walk to the Champs-Elysées is in character. This is a fashionable street, and her walk to it is similar to her earlier daydreams about wealth, for it is on this wide street that the wealthy stroll. Her meeting with Jeanne there is accidental, but it also brings out her sense of pride; that is, she confesses now to the loss of the necklace, having seen things through to the complete repayment of all indebtedness. The Champs-Elysées thus brings out the surprise and irony of the story, and Mathilde's going there is totally in character, in keeping with her earlier dreams of a luxurious life.

DETERMINING YOUR CENTRAL IDEA. Once you have written such paragraphs, you are ready to form a central idea. Look for a common thread or term that you use in your notes and paragraphs. In the materials we have been developing here, a common thread is the relationship of various settings to Mathilde's character. Both her weaknesses and her strengths may be connected to the real and imaginary places that are described in the story. Once you have found such a common thread, you can use it as your central idea to accelerate your thinking further.

Because the central idea is so vital in shaping an essay, you should formulate it as a complete sentence. Just the topic of setting and character alone (or any other topic) cannot help shape thoughts as much as a sentence, which will move from the topic outward into the areas to be discovered and explored in the essay. You might tinker with the topic, and make several different sentences. For instance:

1. The setting is related to Mathilde's character.
2. The settings seem to determine Mathilde's character.
3. Mathilde is fated not to rise above her shabby surroundings.
4. If she had been truthful, Mathilde could have overcome her bad luck.

Each of these sentences would give us unique guidance for an essay. The first is the simplest, for it would require no more than an exemplification of how the setting relates to Mathilde's character. The second would do much the same, but would also stress how Mathilde is a prisoner of where she lives. The third suggests something like the second, but also indicates the possible development of an economic-political argument about the place of people like Mathilde. The fourth suggests an analysis of Mathilde's weaknesses and an argument about how her own limitations have held her down.

Once you have your central idea (let us use the first one), you can use it to bring your observations and conclusions into focus. Let us reshape the third paragraph that we developed while brainstorming.

ORIGINAL PARAGRAPH

Mathilde becomes coarsened during the ten-year period of repayment. She gives up her domestic help, and takes on all the heavy housework herself. She climbs stairs carrying heavy pails of water, and throws the water around to clean floors. She washes greasy and encrusted pots and pans, takes out the garbage, and does the clothes and dishes by hand. She gives up caring for her hair and hands, and wears the cheapest clothing possible. She becomes loud and argumentative, and spends a good deal of time haggling with the local shopkeepers in order to save as much money as she can. Whatever delicacy and attractiveness she had, she loses.

RESHAPED PARAGRAPH

The attic flat reflects the coarsening of Mathilde's character. Maupassant emphasizes the strain she endures to keep up the flat, such as throwing around heavy pails of water to clean the floors, cleaning greasy and encrusted pots and pans, taking out the garbage, and washing clothes and dishes by hand. This makes her rough and coarse, a fact also shown by her giving up care of her hair and hands, her wearing of the cheapest dresses possible, and her becoming loud and penny-pinching in haggling with the local shopkeepers. If at the beginning she is delicate and attractive, at the end she is unpleasant and coarse.

Notice that the story materials are just about the same in each paragraph, but that the central idea has been used to focus the right-hand paragraph. The left-hand column provides details from the story without making many connections with the beginning topic sentence, while the one on the right connects the coarsening to Mathilde's work in the attic flat. The right-hand paragraph thus leads to a discovery: It shows how details from a work may be fitted to a pattern of substantiation of a topic idea, how the work may be linked to interpretation. When we first read the story, we follow the details and appreciate the story's movement. When we think about the story, however, and begin to write about it, we uncover ways of seeing and assimilating it. The process of writing thus leads us to broaden our understanding and appreciate the author's thoughts.

The Thesis Sentence

Using the central idea for guidance, we can now go back to our earlier notes and paragraphs to select materials to include in our developing essay. Our goal is to establish a number of major topics to support the central idea. We may use the paragraph we have just shaped substantially as it is. We can next work with the reshaped paragraph above. This paragraph has two topics which we can entitle "real-life apartment" and "dream surroundings." Our list of topics has grown to include:

1. Real-life apartment
2. Dream surroundings
3. Attic flat

We may use this list as the order of topics for the development of our essay.

For our reader's benefit, however, we should also use this ordering for the writing of our **thesis sentence.** When writing your essay use the following general plan.

Tell what you are going to say.
Say it.
Tell what you've said.

The thesis sentence is a plan or groundwork for our essay; it connects the central idea and the list of topics in the order of presentation. Thus, if we put the central idea at the left, and our list of topics at the right, we have the shape of our thesis sentence:

CENTRAL IDEA	TOPICS
The setting of "The Necklace" reflects Mathilde's character.	1. Real-life apartment 2. Dream surroundings 3. Attic flat

From this arrangement we can write the following thesis sentence, which should usually be arranged to conclude the introductory paragraph of an essay (and thus to tell the reader what to find in the body of the essay):

Mathilde's character development is related to her first apartment, her dream-life mansion rooms, and her attic flat.

With whatever changes may be made necessary by the finishing touches of the final essay, this thesis sentence, along with the central idea, can go directly into our introduction. The central idea, as we have seen, is the glue. The thesis sentence lists the parts to be fastened together; that is, the topics in which the central idea is to be demonstrated and argued.

The Body of the Essay: Topic Sentences

The term regularly used in this book for the development section of the central idea is *body*. The **body** is where you fit together the materials you have been working up in your prewriting to bolster the point made in your thesis sentence. You may alter, reject, and rearrange things, as you wish, as long as you change your thesis sentence to account for your changes. Since the thesis sentence we have generated contains three topics (it could be two, or four, or more), we will use these to form the body.

Just as the organization of the entire essay is based on the thesis sentence, the form of each paragraph is based on its **topic sentence.** You make up the topic sentence by combining one of the topics from the thesis sentence with an assertion about how the topic is to support the central idea. The first topic in our example is the relationship of Mathilde's character to her first apartment, and our topic should emphasize this relationship. Suppose we choose her trait of being constantly dissatisfied. We can then put together the topic and that trait, to form the following topic sentence:

Details about the first apartment explain her dissatisfaction and depression.

With this sentence as a beginning, we would fill out the paragraph by showing how things in the apartment, such as the furniture, the curtains, and the unwashed tablecloth, feed Mathilde's capacity for dissatisfaction.

You should follow the same process in forming other topic sentences, so that when you finish them you can use them in developing unified paragraphs to be included in the body.

The Outline

All along we have been developing an **outline** to shape and organize the essay. Some writers never use formal outlines at all, while others rely on them constantly in shaping their writing. Still other writers insist that they cannot write an outline until they have finished their essays. All these views can be reconciled if you realize that finished essays should have a tight structure. At some point, therefore, you should create a guiding outline. It may be early in your prewriting, or it may be late. What is important is that your final essay follow an outline form.

The kind of outline we have been developing here is the **analytical sentence outline.** This type is easier to create than it sounds, for it is nothing more than a graphic form, a skeleton, of the essay. It consists of the following:

1. TITLE: How Setting in "The Necklace" Is Related to the Character of Mathilde

2. INTRODUCTION:
   a. *Central Idea*: Setting is used to bring out the change and development of Mathilde.
   b. *Thesis Sentence*: Her character development is related to her first apartment, her dream-life mansion rooms, and her attic flat.

3. BODY: *Topic sentences* a, b, and c (d, e, f, and so on)
   a. Details about her first apartment explain her dissatisfaction and depression.
   b. Her dream-life images of wealth are like the apartment because they too make her unhappy.
   c. The attic flat reflects the coarsening of her character.

4. CONCLUSION:
   Topic sentence: Everything in the story, particularly the setting, is focused on the character of Mathilde.

In this outline, the conclusion is optional. Because it is a separate item, it is technically independent of the body, but it is part of the thematic organization and hence should be closely tied to the central idea. It may be a summary of the main points in the body (that is, "Tell what you've said."); it may evaluate the main idea; it may suggest further points of discussion; or it may (as is suggested by the topic sentence here) be a reflection on the details of the body. Each of the writing sections in the various chapters of this book will offer suggestions to help you develop materials for your conclusions.

By the time you have created an outline, you will have been planning and drafting your essay for quite some time. The outline should thus be a guide for *finishing* and *polishing* your essay, not for actually developing it from scratch. Throughout the discussion of the writing process, we have seen that writing is discovery. At the right point, the outline can speed your discovery, for it will help you reshape, reposition, and rephrase some of your ideas. In short, it may help you to finish some ideas and create still others, for the needs of filling out the form itself will prove an incentive to discovery and development.

Using the Outline

Briefly, here is how to use the outline:

1. Include both the central idea and the thesis sentence in your introduction. (Some instructors require a fusion of the two in the final draft. Therefore, make sure you ask what your instructor expects.) Use the suggestions in the writing sections to determine what else might go into the introduction.

2. Include the various topic sentences at the beginning of your paragraphs, changing them as necessary to provide transitions. Throughout this book the various topics are generally confined to single paragraphs. However, it is also acceptable to divide the topic into two or more subtopics, each devoted to a number of paragraphs, particularly if the topic is difficult or heavily detailed. Should you make this division, your topic then is really a *section*, and paragraphs in the section should each have their own topic sentences.

In paragraphs designed to demonstrate the validity of an assertion, the topic sentence usually begins the paragraph. The details then illustrate the truth of the assertion made by the topic sentence. (The use of literary material as evidence is discussed on pp. 31–33.) It is also acceptable to include the topic sentence elsewhere in the paragraph, particularly if you use details to lead up to your topic idea.

Throughout this book, for illustrative purposes, all the thesis and topic sentences in sample essays are underlined so that you may distinguish them clearly as guides for your own writing.

THE SAMPLE ESSAY

To show you the processes we have been discussing, we provide two draft essays of the same assignment. The first is an early draft on the topic of the relationship of setting to the character of Mathilde Loisel. The organizing sentences are underlined in this essay and in all subsequent essays in this book. Draft 1 shows how even working from an outline may still leave a good deal yet to do in the process of writing a finished essay. Some minor details are not included, and one major topic is not treated. Some details need re-ordering, some ideas need sharpening, and some materials may need revision in order to highlight the central idea. You may assume that all sample essays in this book began in a somewhat similar way. There were many good starts, and many false ones. Much was changed and rearranged in the prewriting stages, and much was redone and repositioned once the outline for the essay was established. The first draft, then, represents an early stage of composition, which we all go through in the process of developing an acceptable piece of writing.

SAMPLE ESSAY: DRAFT 1

How Setting in "The Necklace"* Is Related to the Character of Mathilde Loisel

[1]   In "The Necklace," Maupassant does not give much detail about the setting. He does not even describe the necklace itself, which is the central object in his plot, but he says only that it is "superb." Rather he uses the setting to reflect the character of the central figure, Mathilde Loisel.° All his details are presented to bring out her traits. Her character development is related to her first apartment, her dream-life mansion rooms, and her attic flat.°

[2]   Details about her first apartment explain her dissatisfaction and depression. The walls are "drab," the furniture "threadbare," and the curtains "ugly." There is only a single country girl to do the housework. The tablecloth is not cleaned daily, and the best dinner dish is beef stew boiled in a kettle. Mathilde has no pretty dresses, but only a theater dress which she does not like. These details show her dissatisfaction about life with her low-salaried husband.

[3]   Her dream-life images of wealth are like the apartment because they too make her unhappy. In her daydreams, the rooms are large, filled with expensive furniture and bric-a-brac, and draped in silk. She imagines private rooms for intimate talks, and big dinners with delicacies like trout and quail. With dreams of such a rich home, she feels even more despair about her modest apartment on the Street of Martyrs.

[4]   The attic flat reflects the coarsening of Mathilde's character. Maupassant emphasizes the strain she endures to keep up the flat, such as throwing around heavy pails of water to clean the floors, cleaning greasy and encrusted pots and pans, taking out the garbage, and doing dishes and washing by hand. This makes her rough and coarse, a fact also shown by her giving up care of her hair and hands, her wearing of the cheapest dresses possible, and her becoming loud and penny-pinching in haggling with the local shopkeepers. If at the beginning she is delicate and attractive, at the end she is unpleasant and coarse.

[5]   In summary, Maupassant focuses everything in the story, including the setting, on the character of Mathilde. Anything extra is not needed, and he does not include it. Thus he says little about the big party scene, but emphasizes the necessary detail that Mathilde was a great "success," because this detail brings out some of her early attractiveness and charm (despite her more normal unhappiness). In "The Necklace," Maupassant uses setting as a means to his end—the story of Mathilde and her needless sacrifice.

* See pp. 3–11 for this story.
° Central idea.
□ Thesis sentence.

This first draft is adequate, but it needs improving. While the details from the story are all relevant to the various topic sentences, they are not tied in strongly enough.

The second essay, on the other hand, creates more introductory detail, leading to the topic and thesis sentences, and it reshapes each of the paragraphs to stress the particular topics. Even so, it leaves much more that might be done by way of expansion and development. Within the limits of a short assignment, however, the essay illustrates all the principles of organization and unity that we have been discussing.

SAMPLE ESSAY: DRAFT 2

Maupassant's Use of Setting in "The Necklace" to Show the Character of Mathilde

[1] In "The Necklace," Maupassant uses setting to reflect the character and development in the major figure, Mathilde Loisel.° As a result, his setting is not particularly vivid or detailed. He does not even provide a description of the ill-fated necklace—the central object in the story—but states only that it is "superb." He includes only enough description to illuminate his central character, Mathilde. Her traits and her change may be related to the first apartment, the dream-life mansion rooms, the attic flat, and the public street.°

[2] Details about the modest apartment of the Loisels on the Street of Martyrs indicate Mathilde's peevish lack of adjustment to life. Though everything is serviceable, she is dissatisfied with the "drab" walls, "threadbare" furniture, and "ugly" curtains. She has domestic help, but wants more servants than the simple country girl who does the household chores. Her dissatisfaction is also shown by details of her irregularly cleaned tablecloth and the plain and inelegant beef stew that her husband adores. Even her best dress, which she wears for the theater, provokes her unhappiness. All these details of the apartment establish that Mathilde's dominant character trait at the start of the story is maladjustment. She therefore seems unpleasant and unsympathetic.

[3] Like the real-life apartment, the impossibly expensive setting of her daydreams provokes her unhappiness and enables her to avoid reality. As she indulges in her fantasies, all her rooms are large and expensive, being draped in silk and filled with nothing but the best furniture and bric-a-brac. Within this unreal setting, she imagines private rooms for intimate talks, and big dinners with delicacies like trout and quail. With dreams of such a rich home, she feels even more despair about her own condition of life. Ironically,

° Central idea.
° Thesis sentence.

this despair, together with her inability to live with reality, is the cause of her economic and social undoing. It is the root cause of her borrowing the necklace (which is just as unreal as her daydreams of wealth), and it is the loss of the necklace that forces her to recognize truth and accept reality through the loss of her apartment and the move into poverty in the attic flat.

[4] Also ironically, the attic flat is related to the coarsening of her character while at the same time it enables her to bring out her best qualities of cooperativeness, pride, and honesty. Maupassant emphasizes the drudgery of the work she must endure to maintain the flat, such as walking up many stairs, washing floors with large pails of water, doing greasy and encrusted pots and pans, taking out the garbage, handwashing clothes, and haggling loudly about prices with local tradespeople. All this reflects her coarsening and loss of sensibility, also shown by her giving up hair and hand care, and wearing the cheapest dresses. The things she does, however, make her heroic. As she cooperates to help her husband pay back the loans, her dreams of a mansion fade and all she has left is the memory of that one happy evening at the Minister of Education's reception. Thus the attic flat brings out her physical change for the worse at the same time that it also brings out her psychological and moral change for the better.

[5] Her walk on the Champs-Elysées illustrates a similar combination of her traits—in this case self-indulgence and also frankness. The Champs-Elysées is a fashionable street, and her walk to it is similar to her earlier daydreams about wealth; she is, in effect, seeing how the upper-class people are living. But it is on this street where she meets Jeanne, however accidentally, and it is her frankness in confessing the loss and replacement to Jeanne that makes her, finally, completely honest with her friend. While the walk thus serves as the occasion for the concluding surprise and irony of the story, Mathilde's being on the Champs-Elysées is totally in character, in keeping with her earlier reveries about a life of luxury.

[6] Other details in the story also have a similar bearing on Mathilde's character. For example, the story mentions little about the party scene, but emphasizes only that she was a great "success"—a judgment that shows her ability to shine if given the chance. After she and Loisel determine that the necklace cannot be found, Maupassant includes details about the Parisian streets, the visits to loan sharks, and the jewelry and jewelry-case shops, in order to bring out Mathilde's sense of honesty and pride as she "heroically" prepares to live the life of the poor. Thus, in "The Necklace," Maupassant uses setting as a means to highlight Mathilde's maladjustment, her needless misfortune, her loss of youth and beauty, and finally her growth as a responsible human being.

Essay Commentaries

Throughout this book, a short commentary follows each sample essay at the end of the chapter. Each commentary points out how the assignment is handled and how the instruction and guidelines in the first part of the chapter are applied to the essay. For essays in which several approaches are suggested, the commentary points out which one is employed. When a sample essay uses two or more approaches, the commentary makes this fact clear. The commentaries are there to help you develop the insight necessary to use the sample essays as aids in your own study and writing.

SOME COMMON PROBLEMS IN WRITING ESSAYS

The fact that you understand the early stages of the composing process and can apply the principles of developing a central idea and organizing with an outline does not mean that you will have no problems in writing. It is not hard to recognize good writing when you see it, but it can be difficult to explain why it is superior.

The most difficult and perplexing questions you will ask as you write are: (1) "How can I improve my writing?" (2) "If I got a C on my last essay, why wasn't the grade a B or an A? How can I get higher grades?" These are really the same question, but each has a different emphasis. Another way to ask the question is: "When I first read a work, I have a hard time following it. Yet when my instructor explains it, my understanding is greatly increased. How can I develop the ability to understand the work and write about it well without my instructor's help? How can I become an independent, confident reader and writer?"

The discussions accompanying the readings in this book are designed to help you do just that. Many students, when writing about literature, commit a major error and do no more than retell a story or reword an idea, despite their best intentions. Retelling a story shows only that you have read it, not that you have thought about it. Writing a good essay, however, shows that you have digested the work and arranged it into a pattern of thought.

Using Your Own Order of References

There are a number of ways in which you may set up patterns of development to show your understanding of a work. One is to stress your own order when referring to parts of the work. Do not treat things as they occur in the work, but change them around to suit your own thematic plans. Rarely, if ever, should you begin an essay by speaking about a work's opening; it is better to talk about the conclusion or middle first. Beginning your essay by referring to later parts of the work will help you to stress your own central idea rather than to get caught up in the chronological order of the work. If you look back at the fourth paragraph of the second draft of the essay on "The Necklace," you will see that this technique has been used. The references there are introduced as a means of stressing the essay writer's thoughts, and hence they do not follow the order in the story exactly. The principle is that you, also, should introduce references from the text as they support the point you are making.

Addressing Your Audience or "Mythical Reader"

In preparing to write, you will need to consider how much detail to select and discuss. This task can be easier if you consider that your audience is another student, like yourself, who has read the work but who has not thought about it. Such a reader knows the events, and knows who says what and when. As a result, you need not retell everything, but should regard your role as that of explainer or interpreter. Thus, you should concentrate on what things in the work mean only as they have a bearing on your central idea, and you may omit references to things that are not relevant, even if they are important in the work.

To look at your writing situation in still another way, you might remember that Sherlock Holmes, in the famous stories by A. Conan Doyle, always points out to Dr. Watson that all the facts in a case are available to both of them. Watson, however, does not *observe* things as Holmes does, and therefore he cannot produce solutions to the mysteries the two men go about solving. If you look at the sample essays on "The Necklace," you will observe that everywhere *the assumption has been made that readers already know the story.* References to the work are thus made only to cause readers to think about details they already know, as part of the emphasis in the essays on drawing conclusions and developing arguments.

Using Literary Material as Evidence

The comparison with Sherlock Holmes should remind you that whenever you write, your position is like that of a detective using clues as evidence for building a case, or of a lawyer using evidence as support for arguments. For practical purposes only, when you write, you may conveniently regard the work as a part of your own discourse. Your goal should be to convince your readers of your own knowledge and the reasonableness of your conclusions.

It is vital to use evidence convincingly so that your readers may follow your ideas. Let us look briefly at two new examples to see how writing may be improved by the pointed use of details. These are from longer essays on the character of Mathilde.

PARAGRAPH 1

The major extenuating thing about Mathilde is that she seems to be isolated, locked away from other people. She and her husband do not speak to each other much, except about things. He speaks about his liking for beef stew, and she states that she cannot accept the big invitation because she has no nice dresses. Once she gets the dress, she complains because she has no jewelry. Even when borrowing the necklace from Jeanne Forrestier, she does not say much. When she and her husband discover that the necklace is lost, they simply go over the details, and Loisel dictates a letter of explanation, which she writes in her own hand. Even when she meets Jeanne on the Champs-Elysées, she does not say a great deal about her life, but only goes through enough details about the loss and replacement of the necklace to make Jeanne exclaim about the needlessness of the ten-year sacrifice.

PARAGRAPH 2

Perhaps the major flaw of Mathilde's character is that she is withdrawn and uncommunicative, apparently unwilling or unable to form an intimate relationship. For example, she and her husband do not speak to each other much, except about things, such as his taste for beef stew and her lack of a party dress and jewelry. With such a marriage, one might suppose that she might be more open with her close friend, Jeanne Forrestier, but even here Mathilde does not say much. This flaw hurts her greatly, because if she were more open she might have explained the loss and avoided the horrible sacrifice. This lack of openness, along with her self-indulgent dreaminess, is her biggest defect.

The answer to the difficult question of how to turn C writing into an A grade is to be found in conclusions that we may draw about these two paragraphs. In general, superior writers always allow their minds to play on the materials. They give readers the results of their thinking. They dare to trust their responses, and are not afraid to make judgments about the literary work they are considering. Their principal aim in referring to actions, scenes, and characters in a work is to develop their own thematic pattern. Inferior writers do none of these things.

A close comparison of the two paragraphs bears out these assertions. Although the first paragraph has more words than the second (155 to 117), it is not adequate, for it shows that the writer is simply restating things that the readers already know. The paragraph is cluttered with details that do not support any conclusions. If you judge it for what you might learn about Maupassant's actual *use* of Mathilde's withdrawn, solitary traits in "The Necklace," you cannot avoid concluding that it gives you no help at all. The writer did not have to think much to write the paragraph.

On the other hand, the details introduced into the second paragraph all support the declared topic. Phrases like "for example," "but even here," and "this lack" show that the writer of paragraph 2 has assumed that the audience knows the story and now wants help in interpretation. Paragraph 2 therefore *guides readers by connecting the details to the topic*. It uses these details *only* as evidence, not as a recounting of actions. By contrast, paragraph 1 recounts a number of actions from the story, and, even though these actions are relevant to the topic sentence, the paragraph does not *show* how they are connected. More details, of course, could have been added to paragraph 2, but they are unnecessary because the paragraph demonstrates the point with the details used. There are many things that make good writing good, and one of the most important is evident here: *In good writing details are used only as evidence in an original pattern of thought.*

Keeping to Your Point

Whenever you write an essay about literature, then, you must pay great attention to organization and to the correct use of references to the work assigned. As you write, you should try constantly to keep your material unified, for should you go off on a tangent, you are no longer controlling but are being controlled. It is all too easy to start with your point but then wander off into a retelling of the story. Once again, resist the tendency to be a narrator rather than an interpreter.

To show these distinctions, let us consider a third example. The following paragraph is drawn from an essay on The Idea of Economic Determinism in "The Necklace." In this paragraph the writer discusses the theme as it is brought out in a number of incidents from the story. The idea is to assert that Mathilde's difficulties result not from her character but rather from her financial restrictions:

> More important than chance in governing life is the idea that people are controlled by economic circumstances. Mathilde, as is shown right at the start, is born poor. Therefore she doesn't get the right doors opened for her, and her marriage is to a minor clerk. With a vivid imagination and a burning desire for luxury, seeming to be born only for the wealthy life, her poor home brings out her daydreams of expensive surroundings. She taunts her husband, Loisel, when he brings the big invitation, because she does not have a suitable (read "expensive") dress. Once she gets the dress it is jewelry that she lacks, and she borrows that and loses it. The loss of the necklace is the greatest trouble, because it forces the Loisels to borrow deeply and to lead an impoverished life for ten years.

This paragraph shows how easily writers may be diverted from their objective. The first sentence is an effective topic sentence, indicating that the writer begins with a good plan. The remaining part, however, does not follow through. The flaw is that the material of the paragraph, while an accurate account of what happens in the story itself, is not tied to the topic. Once the second sentence is under way, the paragraph gets lost in a retelling of events, and the fine opening sentence is left behind. From the example of this paragraph, we may conclude that writers should not rely on detail alone to make meanings clear. Instead they must make the connections of detail and conclusions needed to make all relationships *explicitly* clear.

How can the problem of writing shown in the paragraph above be addressed? If we drew a diagram of the ideal paragraph, the paragraph's topic would be a straight line moving toward and reaching a specific goal (explicit meaning), with an exemplifying line moving away from the straight line briefly to bring in evidence, but returning to the line after each new fact to demonstrate the relevance of the fact. Thus, the ideal scheme would look like this:

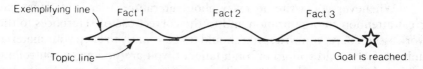

Notice that the exemplifying line, which illustrates how documentation or exemplification should be used, *always returns to the topic line.* A diagram of the faulty paragraph, however, would look like this, with the line never returning, but flying out into space:

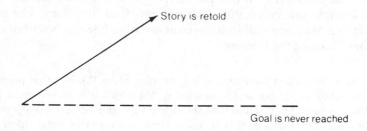

How might the faulty paragraph be improved? The best way is to remind the reader again and again of the topic, and to bring in examples from the text only to support the topic. Consistently with our diagram, each time the topic is mentioned, the undulating line merges with the straight line, or central-idea line. This image of the relationship of topic to illustrative examples should prevail no matter what subject you write about. If you are analyzing point of view, for example, you should keep pointing out the relevance of your material to the speaker, or narrator, of the work, and the same applies to a study of character or whatever aspect of literature you are studying. According to this principle, we might revise the paragraph on the idea of economic determinism in "The Necklace" as follows, keeping as much of the original wording as we can. (Parts of sentences stressing the relationship of the examples to the topic of the paragraph are in italics.)

> More important than chance in governing life is the idea that people are controlled by economic circumstances. *As illustration*, the narrator emphasizes right at the start that Mathilde, the major character, is born poor. Therefore she doesn't get the right doors opened for her, and her marriage is to a minor clerk. *In keeping with the idea*, her vivid imagination and burning desire for luxury (she seems to have been born only for the wealthy life) feed on her weakness of character as she feels deep unhappiness and depression because of the contrast between her daydreams of expensive surroundings and the poor home she actually has. *The straightened economic circumstances* inhibit her relationship with her husband, and she taunts him when he brings the big invitation because she does not have a suitable (read "expensive") dress. As a merging of her unrealistic dream life with actual reality, *her borrowing of the necklace suggests the impossibility, according to the idea, of overcoming economic restrictions. In the context of the idea*, the ten-year impoverishment following the disastrous borrowing to replace the lost necklace *symbolizes how economic circumstances keep people in their place, destroying their dreams of a better life.*

The original paragraph has been improved so that now it reaches the goal of the topic sentence. While it has also been lengthened, the length has been caused not by inessential detail but by phrases and sentences that give form and direction. You might object that if you lengthened all your paragraphs in this way, your essays would grow too bulky. You can avoid this problem if you reduce the total number of major points and paragraphs in your essays, on the theory that *it is better to develop a few topics pointedly than many pointlessly*. Revision done to strengthen central and topic ideas requires that you throw out some topics or else incorporate them as sub-points in the topics you keep. This assertion of your own control can result only in improvement.

Insight, Newness, Growth

Sticking to a point is therefore one of the first requirements of a good essay, for you will not be successful unless you thoroughly exemplify and support your central idea. Another major quality of excellence is not only to be well organized, but also to make the central idea expand and grow. The word *growth* is a metaphor for development, the creation of new insights, the disclosure of ideas that were not at first noticeable, the expression of new, fresh, and original interpretations.

A student might argue that it is difficult to be original when you are writing about someone else's work. "The author has said everything," might go the argument, "and therefore I can do little more than follow the story (poem, or play)." This claim assumes that you have no choice in selecting material for an essay, and no opportunity to make individual thoughts and original contributions. But you have. The author has presented the work to you, and you can, if you look hard, find layer upon layer of meaning. One obvious area where you can exert your power of originality is the development and formulation of your central idea. For example, an obvious first thought about "The Necklace" is that it is about a woman who loses a borrowed necklace and endures hardship to pay for replacing it. This topic alone does not go very far, however, and an additional idea might be developed from the observation that the hardship is "needless." This idea is regrettably not very original either. But a more original insight can be provided if the topic is related directly to the relationship in the story between the dreamy, withdrawn traits of the major character and her misfortune. Thus, an idea might be that the story demonstrates that "People themselves bring about their own misfortunes." With such an idea, it is possible to do more in creating a fresh, original essay analyzing the story's development than the first proposed topic could do.

You can also develop your ability to treat your subject freshly and originally if you plan the body of the essay to build up to what you think is your most important, incisive, and well-conceived idea. As examples of such planning, the following brief topic outlines suggest how a central idea may be widened and expanded (relevant chapters in this book are shown in parentheses).

A. Mathilde as a growing character (*Character*, Chapter 4)
   1. Mathilde as a person with normal daydreams
   2. Mathilde as a taker of risks to make her daydreams seem real.
   3. Mathilde as a person who faces up to mistakes and works hard to right them and to shoulder responsibility

B. The idea of economic determinism (*Idea or Theme*, Chapter 10)
   1. Mathilde's economic class as an inhibition on her wishes
   2. Her economically poor married life as a damper on her character
   3. The ten-year penance as a literal punishment for trying to move above economic circumstances

C. The development of irony in the story (*Tone*, Chapter 8)
   1. The situation of Mathilde's dissatisfaction as a contrast with her dreams and hopes
   2. The irony of the loss of the necklace
   3. The needless waste produced by Mathilde's failure to confess the loss to Jeanne

D. The symbolic value of the necklace (*Symbolism and Allegory*, Chapter 9)
   1. As a symbol of economic wealth and ease
   2. As a symbol of reality versus appearance
   3. As a symbol of the value of sacrifice and work

These outlines all indicate a way in which topics may be treated in an increasing order of importance, which we may equate with growth or development—the idea being not only to illustrate a topic, but to enlarge it. Both the first and last outlines, for example, move toward ideas about moral values, while the second moves toward a broad consideration of the story, and the third, similarly, suggests a climax based on the story's situational irony. Details in essays guided by the outlines would all be included as a part of the developing pattern of growth, and in no way would they be introduced simply to retell the major events in the story. These suggested patterns show how two primary standards of excellence in writing—organization and growth—can be met. Without these qualities, there is no totally successful thinking, and there can certainly be no successful writing.

Whenever you write, an important goal should be the development of your central idea. Constantly adhere to your topic, and constantly develop it. Nurture it and make it grow. Admittedly, in a short essay you will be able to move only a short distance with an idea, but you should never be satisfied to leave the idea exactly where you found it. To the degree that you can learn to develop your ideas, you will receive recognition for increasingly superior writing. Your grades, in short, will go higher.

Using Accurate and Forceful Language

In addition to the qualities of organization and development we have just discussed, the best writing has the qualities of accuracy, precision, and force. Quite often the first sentences and paragraphs we write are weak, and they need to be rethought, recast, and reworded. Sometimes this process cannot be carried out immediately, for it may take days or even weeks for us to gain objectivity about what we say. As a student you usually do not have that kind of time, and thus you must acquire the habit of challenging your own statements almost as soon as you write them. Ask yourself whether they really *mean* what you intend, or if you can make a stronger statement than the one you first write.

As an example, consider the following sentence, put forward as a central idea about "The Necklace":

> The central idea in this story is how Mathilde and her husband respond to the loss of the necklace.

This sentence could not carry a writer very far in the development of an essay. Because it promises nothing more than simple retelling of the story's events, it needs further thought and rephrasing. Here are two possible new central ideas (revisions of the sentence) that would go farther as the basis of an essay:

In the story Maupassant exemplifies the idea that hard work and responsibility are basic and necessary in life.

Maupassant makes the surprise ending of the story a symbol of the need for always being truthful.

Although both new sentences deal substantially with the same story materials, they imply differences of treatment. The first would be built up out of the virtue shown by the Loisels in shouldering the costs of replacing the necklace and in bearing the full effects of sacrifice. Since the second sentence contains the word "symbol," an essay to be developed from it would stress the mistake made by the Loisels in not reporting truthfully that they had lost the necklace. In dealing with the general, broadly symbolic meaning of their failure, such an essay would focus on the negative aspects of their characters, while the essay developed from the first sentence would stress their positive aspects. Whatever the final essay, however, either of the two revised sentences is more accurate as a guide than the original sentence, and would move an essay writer toward a superior composition.

Quite important—and also quite challenging—is to make sure that you really say exactly what you mean. If you do not keep your eyes steadily on your subjects, you may wind up saying nothing. For example, consider these two sentences from essays about "The Necklace":

1. It seems as though the major character's dreams of luxury cause her to respond as she does in the story.
2. This incident, although it may seem trivial or unimportant, has substantial significance in the creation of the story; by this I mean the incident which occurred is essentially what the story is all about.

The vagueness of sentences like these must be resisted. A sentence should not end up in limbo the way these do. The first sentence is satisfactory up to the verb "cause," but then it falls apart because the writer has lost sight of the meaning. It is best to describe *what* that response is, rather than to state vaguely that there *is* a response. A more accurate and forceful revision may be made as follows:

Mathilde's dreams of luxury make it impossible for her to accept her own possessions, and therefore she goes beyond her means to attend the party.

With this revision, the writer could go on to consider the meaning of the early pages of the story, and could contrast the ideas there with those in the latter part. Without the revision, it is not clear where the writer might go.

The second sentence is so vague that it confuses rather than informs. Such sentences hint at an idea, and claim importance for it, but they never directly define what that idea is. The cause, again, is that the writer has lost sight of the topic. If we adopt the principle that we need to aim directly at the specific things we are talking about, however, we may see how to recover from the grips of such unfortunate vagueness:

> The accidental loss of the necklace, which in truth is trivial, in practice serves as the basis for the narrator's claim that the major turns in people's lives are produced not by earthshaking events, but rather by minor ones.

When you write your own sentences, you might test them in a similar way. Are you referring to an idea? State the idea directly. Are you mentioning a response or impression? Do not say simply, "The poem (play, story) left me with a definite impression," but *state* what the impression is, like this: "The poem left me with an impression of sympathy," or "The story deepened my understanding of the hard lot of the migrant farmer." Similarly, do not rest with a statement such as "I found Maupassant's 'The Necklace' interesting," but try to describe *what* was interesting and *why*: "I found Maupassant's 'The Necklace' interesting because of its focus on how the forces of chance may make or destroy the prosperity of people." If you always confront your impressions and responses by naming them and pinning them down, no matter how elusive they seem, your sentences will take on the force that comes from exactness. Naturally, your instructor will let you know how you are doing—both what you have accomplished and failed to accomplish. Good writing habits that you develop from these criticisms of your work, and also from discussions with your instructor, will help you to write more accurately and forcefully.

To sum up, these are the guidelines to follow whenever you write an essay: (1) Keep returning to the points you intend to make. (2) Regard the material in the work you have read as evidence to support your argument, not as a story to be retold or as an idea to be summarized. (3) Demonstrate that all exemplifying detail is relevant to your main point. (4) Constantly try to develop your topic; make it bigger than it was when you began writing. (5) Constantly try to make your statements accurate, complete, and forceful. If you observe these precepts, you should be well on the way toward successfully handling any of the study questions and writing assignments in this book.

RESPONDING TO LITERATURE: LIKES AND DISLIKES

As you read any work of literature, you will also respond to it emotionally. Emotional responses, reduced to their simplest level, take the form of pleasure or pain: we like or dislike a specific piece of literature. There are, of course, many degrees and expressions of approval or disapproval; we might like one work very much indeed, be unmoved by another, and be thoroughly repulsed by a third. Usually, these are first reactions and they do not convey much information about the work itself. Your goal, instead, should be to relate your responses to things in the work that caused them. In other words, you should present responses that are *informed* and *informative* rather than *uninformed* and *unexplained*.

Sometimes the first response readers express about a work is that it is "boring." This reaction is usually a mask to cover an incomplete and superficial first reading; it is neither informative nor informed. As you study most works, however, you will discover that you invariably get drawn into them. One word that describes this process is *interest*; that is, the reader is taken right into the work emotionally. *Involvement*, another word that describes the process, occurs when the reader's emotions become almost rolled into the work, and get taken up by the characters, problems, and outcomes. Sometimes both words are used defensively, just like the word *boring*. It is easy to say that something you read is "interesting," or that you get "involved" in it, and you might say just these things with a hope that no one will ask you what you mean. Both interest and involvement do indeed describe genuine responses to reading, however. Once you become interested, your reading becomes more a pleasure than a task and, although you may do some of the detailed assignments grudgingly because of the needed time and effort, your deepening appreciation will be its own reward.

Using Your Notebook to Record Responses

No one can tell you what you should or should not like; liking is your own concern. While your experience of reading is still fresh, therefore, you should use your notebook (discussed earlier) to record not only your observations about a work, but also your responses. Be absolutely frank in your judgment. Write down your likes and dislikes, and try to explain the reasons for your response, even if these are brief and not completely thought through. If, with later thought and fuller understanding, you change or modify your first impressions, record these changes too. Here is such a notebook entry about "The Necklace":

> I like "The Necklace" because of the surprise ending. It isn't that I like Mathilde's bad luck, but I like the way Maupassant hides the most important fact in the story until the end. Mathilde thus does all that work and sacrifice for no reason at all, and the surprise ending makes this point strongly.

This paragraph could easily be expanded as a part of a developing essay. It is a clear statement of the student's liking, followed by the major details in the work that prompt this response. The pattern, which might best be phrased as "I like [dislike] this work *because* . . . ," can be quite helpful in your notebook entries.

The challenge in considering positive or negative reactions to literature is that you must eventually consider some of the "because" areas more fully. For this reason it is essential to pinpoint some of the specific things to which you have responded. If at first you cannot put into your notebook any full sentences detailing the causes of your responses, at least make a brief list of those things that you like or dislike. If you write nothing, you will probably forget your reactions; and recovering them at a later time, either for discussion or writing, will be difficult.

Responding Favorably

Often you can equate your interest in a work with liking it. But you can be more specific about your favorable responses by using the following as possible reasons:

You like and admire the characters and approve of what they do and stand for.

You learn more about topics very important to you.

You learn something you had never known or thought before.

You gain new or fresh insights into things you had already known.

You learn about characters from different ways of life.

You are involved and interested in the outcome of the action or ideas, and do not want to put the work down until you have finished it.

You feel happy because of reading the work.

You are amused and laugh often as you read.

You like the author's presentation.

You find that some of the ideas and expressions are beautiful and worth remembering.

Obviously, if you find none of these things in the work, or find something that is distasteful, you will not like the work.

Responding Unfavorably

Although so far we have dismissed *boring* and stressed *interest, involvement,* and *liking,* it is important to know that disliking an entire work, or something in it, is normal and acceptable. You do not need to hide this response. Here, for example, are two short notebook responses expressing dislike for "The Necklace":

1. I do not like "The Necklace" because Mathilde seems spoiled, and I don't think she is worth reading about.
2. "The Necklace" is not an adventure story, and I like reading only adventure stories.

These are both legitimate responses because they are based on a clear standard of judgment. The first stems out of a distaste for an unlikable trait shown by the main character; the second, on a preference for mystery or adventure stories, which contain rapid action to evoke interest in the dangers faced and overcome by main characters.

Here is a notebook-type entry that might be developed from the first response. What is important is that the reasons for dislike are explained. They would need only slightly more development to be expressed later in classroom discussion or in an essay form:

> I do not like "The Necklace" because Mathilde seems spoiled and I do not think she is worth reading about. She is a phony. She nags her husband because he is not rich. She never tells the truth. I especially dislike her hurrying away from the party because she is afraid of being seen in her shabby coat. It is foolish and dishonest of her not to tell Jeanne Forrestier about losing the necklace. It is true that she works hard to pay the debt, but she also puts her husband through ten years of unnecessary hardship and misery. If Mathilde had faced facts, she might have had a better life. I do not like her and cannot like the story because of her.

As long as you explain *why* you dislike something, you can use your reasons for further study and consideration. You might even change your mind. However, it is better to record your honest responses of dislike than to force yourself to say you like something which you do not.

Putting Dislikes into a Larger Context

While it is important to be truthful about a negative response, it is equally important to broaden your perspective and expand your taste. For example, the dislike based on a preference for only mystery or adventure stories, if it is applied generally, would cause a person to dislike most works of literature. This seems unnecessarily self-limiting.

By putting negative responses into a larger context, it is possible to expand one's likes in line with personal responses. One reader might be deeply involved in personal concerns and therefore be uninterested in seemingly remote literary figures. However, if by reading about literary characters he can gain insight into general problems of life, and therefore his own concerns, he can find something to like in just about any work of literature. Another reader might care only for sports events and therefore not read anything but sports magazines. But what probably interests that reader in sports is competition, so if competition, or conflict, can be found in a work of literature, she or he can like that work. By looking at works of literature from different perspectives (for example, competition for the sports enthusiast), a reader may find a work more enjoyable than he or she did at first reading.

As an example, let us consider again the dislike based on a preference for adventure stories, and see if this preference can be analyzed. Here are some reasons for liking adventures:

1. Adventure has fast action.
2. Adventure has danger and tension, and therefore interest.
3. Adventure has daring, active characters.
4. Adventure has obstacles that the characters work hard to overcome.

No one could claim that the first three points are relevant to "The Necklace," but the fourth point is promising. Mathilde, the major character, works hard to overcome an obstacle—paying off the large debt. If our student likes adventures because the characters try to gain worthy goals, then he or she can also like "The Necklace" for the same reason. The principle here is clear: If a reason for liking a favorite work or type of work can be found in another work, then there is reason to like that new work. The problem is that the student must first be able to articulate responses to the favorite work. Thought and analogy will then do the rest, and therefore such a comparative method can become the basis for analyzing and developing responses to newly encountered works of literature.

The following paragraph shows a possible operation of this "bridging" process of extending preferences. (The sample essay at the end of this chapter is also developed along these lines.)

> I usually like only adventure stories, and therefore I disliked "The Necklace" at first because it is not adventure. But one of my reasons for liking adventure is that the characters work hard to overcome difficult obstacles, like finding buried treasure or exploring new places. Mathilde, Maupassant's main character in "The Necklace," also works hard to overcome an obstacle—helping to pay back the money and interest for the borrowed 18,000 francs used as part of the payment for the replacement necklace. I like adventure characters because they stick to things and win out. I see the same toughness in Mathilde. Her problems therefore get more interesting as the story moves on after a slow beginning. I came to like the story.

Thus an accepted principle of liking can be applied to another work where it also applies. A person who adapts principles in this open-minded way can redefine dislikes, no matter how slowly, and may consequently expand the ability to like and appreciate many kinds of literature.

An equally open-minded way to develop understanding and to widen taste is to put dislikes in the following light: An author's creation of an unlikable character, situation, attitude, or expression may be deliberate. Your dislike might then result from the author's *intentions*. A first task of study is therefore to understand and explain the intention or plan. As you put the plan into your own words, you may find that you can like a work with unlikable things in it. Here is a paragraph that traces this pattern of thinking, based again on "The Necklace":

> Maupassant apparently wants the reader to dislike Mathilde, and I do. At first, he shows her being unrealistic and spoiled. She lies to everyone and nags her husband. Her rushing away from the party so that no one can see her shabby coat is a form of lying. But I like the story itself because Maupassant makes another kind of point. He does not hide her bad qualities, but makes it clear that she herself is the cause of her trouble. If people like Mathilde never face the truth, they will get into bad situations. This is a good point, and I like the way the author makes it. The entire story is therefore worth liking even though I still do not like Mathilde.

Neither of these two ways of broadening the contexts of response is dishonest to the original negative reactions. In the first example, the writer applies one of his principles of liking to include "The Necklace." In the second, the writer considers her initial dislike in the context of the work, and discovers a basis of liking the story as a whole while still disliking the main character. The main concern in both responses is to keep an open mind despite initial dislike, and then to see if the unfavorable response can be more fully and broadly considered.

If, after consideration, you decide that your dislike overbalances any reasons you can find for liking, then you should be prepared to describe and defend your dislike of the work. As long as you relate your response accurately to the work, and measure it by a clear standard of judgment, your dislike of even a commonly liked work is acceptable.

WRITING ABOUT RESPONSES: LIKES AND DISLIKES

In writing about your responses, you should rely on your initial informed reactions to the work assigned. It is not easy to reconstruct your first responses after a lapse of time, so you will need your notebook observations as your guide in the prewriting stage. Develop your essay by stressing what interests you (or does not interest you) in the work.

A major difficulty in such an essay is to relate the details of the work to the point you are making about your ongoing responses. That is, it might be easy to begin by indicating that you like the work, and then, in describing what it is that you like, you might forget your responses as you enumerate details. It is therefore necessary to keep stressing your involvement in the work as you bring out evidence from it. You can show your attitudes by indicating approval (or disapproval), by commenting favorably (or unfavorably) on the details, by indicating things that seem new (or shopworn) and particularly instructive (or wrong), and by giving assent to (or dissent from) ideas or expressions of feeling.

Organizing Your Essay

INTRODUCTION.   Begin by describing briefly the conditions that influence your response. Your central idea should be whether you like or dislike the work. The thesis sentence should list the major causes of your response, which are to be developed in the body of your essay.

BODY.   The most common approach is to consider the thing or things about the work that you like or dislike (for a list of possible reasons for liking a work, see Responding Favorably, p. 41). You may have admired a particular character, or maybe you got so interested in the story that you could not put it down. Also, it may be that a major idea, a new or fresh insight, or a particular outcome is the major point that you wish to develop. The sample notebook paragraph on page 40 shows a "surprise ending" as the cause of a favorable response.

Another approach is to give details about how your responses either developed or changed in your reading of the work. This development requires that you pinpoint, in order, the various good (or bad) parts of the work and your responses to them. Because of the orderly introduction of details, you should avoid the pitfall of simply retelling a story or summarizing an argument.

Two additional approaches (described in detail above, pp. 41–44) bring out a shift or development of response, either from negative to positive (most common) or vice versa. The first approach allows the writer to show that a principle for liking one kind of literature may be applied to the assigned work. (This approach is illustrated in the sample essay at the end of this chapter). The second suggests that a writer may first respond unfavorably to something about the work, but on further consideration be able to establish a larger context which permits a more favorable response.

CONCLUSION.   Here you might briefly summarize the reasons for your major response. You might also try to face any issues brought up by a change in or modification of your first reactions. That is, if you have always held certain assumptions about your taste but like the work despite these assumptions, you may wish to talk about your own change or development.

This topic is personal, but in an essay about likes or dislikes, discovery about yourself is something you should aim for.

SAMPLE ESSAY

Some Reasons for Liking Guy de Maupassant's "The Necklace"*

[1]
To me, the most likable reading is adventure. Although there are many reasons for my preference, an important one is that adventure characters work hard to overcome obstacles. Because "The Necklace" is not adventure, I did not like it at first. But in one respect the story is like adventure: Mathilde, with her husband Loisel, works hard for ten years to overcome a difficult obstacle. Thus, because Mathilde does what adventure characters also do, the story is likable.° Mathilde's appeal results from her hard work, strong character, sad fate, and also from the way our view of her changes.□

[2]
Mathilde's hard work makes her seem good. Once she and her husband are faced with the huge debt of 18,000 francs with interest, she works like a slave to pay it back. She gives up her servant and moves to a cheaper place. She does the household drudgery, wears cheap clothes, and bargains with shopkeepers for the lowest prices and greatest savings. Just like the characters in adventure stories, who sometimes must do hard and unpleasant things, she does what she has to do, and this makes her admirable.

[3]
Her strong character makes her endure—a likable trait. To do the bad jobs, she needs toughness. At first she is a nagging, spoiled person, always dreaming about wealth and telling lies, but she changes and gets better. She recognizes her blame in losing the necklace, and she has the strength to help her husband redeem the debt. She sacrifices "heroically" (Maupassant's word) by giving up her comfortable way of life, and in the process she also loses her youth and beauty. Her jobs are not the exotic and glamorous ones of adventure stories, but her force of character makes her as likable as an adventure heroine.

[4]
Her sad fate also makes her likable. In adventure stories the characters often suffer as they do their jobs. Mathilde also suffers, but in a different way, because her suffering is permanent while the hardships of adventure characters are temporary. This fact makes her pitiable, and even more so because all her sacrifices are not necessary. This unfairness about her life invites the reader to take her side.

[5]
Another quality of Mathilde's sad fate which promotes admiration is the way Maupassant shifts our view of her. As Mathilde goes deeper into her hard life, Maupassant does not let the reader into her innermost thoughts, as he does at the beginning. In other words, the view into her character at the start, when she dreams about wealth, invites dislike, while the view at

* See pp. 3–11 for this story.
° Central idea.
□ Thesis sentence.

the end is focused on her achievements, with no mention of unhappiness and complaint except for a moment of fond memory at one point (paragraph 104). This shift in focus, from Mathilde's inward dissatisfaction to her outward strength, encourages the reader to like her.

[6] "The Necklace" is not an adventure story, but some of the good qualities of adventure characters are present in Mathilde. Also, the surprise revelation that the lost necklace was false is an unforgettable twist which makes her more deserving than she seems at first. Maupassant has arranged the story so that the reader finally admires Mathilde. "The Necklace" is a skillful and likable story.

Commentary on the Essay

The argument in this essay is that "The Necklace," which the writer did not enjoy at first, can be enjoyed because Mathilde, the main character, has many of the qualities that make adventure-story characters likable. The writer enumerates the qualities of Mathilde that connect her to adventure characters. In this way the writer's liking for adventure stories serves as a bridge to liking "The Necklace." Some other reasons are also brought out in the conclusion of the essay.

In the introduction the writer uses as a central idea the common bonds that make Mathilde as likable as characters in adventure stories. The thesis sentence lists four topics which are to be developed in the body of the essay.

Paragraph 2 gives instances of Mathilde's hard work as a cause for liking, and concludes by comparing Mathilde and adventure characters as workers. Paragraph 3 gives examples of Mathilde's toughness of character and also compares her strength with the strength of adventure characters. In paragraph 4 a comparison is made between Mathilde's sacrifices and the hardship experienced by adventure characters, and the pity and sympathy evoked by Mathilde are claimed as causes for liking her. The paragraph most independent of the bridge from adventure stories is paragraph 5, in which the idea is advanced that a shift in the mode of narration focuses on Mathilde's strength as a character. Paragraph 5, however, is closely connected to the ideas of sacrifice mentioned in paragraph 4. Paragraph 6, the conclusion, restates the comparison and also lists the surprise ending and the development of the story as reasons for liking "The Necklace."

Throughout the essay, the central idea that the story is liked is brought out in words and expressions such as "likable," "Mathilde's appeal," "strong character," "she does what she has to," "pitiable," and "take her side." These expressions, mixed as they are with references to many details from the story, create thematic continuity that shapes and develops the essay. This thematic development, together with the use of responses to details from the story as supporting evidence, shows how an essay on the responses of liking and disliking may be both informed and informative.

FICTION

2

The Elements of Fiction

Fiction originally meant anything made up, crafted, or shaped. As we understand the word today, it means a prose story based in the imagination of the author, not in literal facts. In English the first recorded use of the word in this sense was in the year 1599. The original meaning of the word in reference to things made up or crafted is helpful to us in focusing on the fact that we distinguish fiction from works that it has often imitated, such as reports, historical accounts, biographies, autobiographies, collections of letters, and personal memoirs and meditations. While writers of fiction may deliberately design their works to resemble these forms, fiction has a separate identity because of its origin in the creative, shaping powers. Writers of fiction may include true and historically accurate details in their works, but they create their main stories not because of a wish to be faithful to history but rather because of a hope to say something significant about life.

The essence of fiction, as opposed to drama, is **narration,** the relating or recounting of a sequence of events or actions. The earliest works of fiction relied almost exclusively on narration, with speeches and dialogue being reported rather than quoted directly. Many recent works of fiction include extended passages of dialogue, thereby rendering the works more dramatic even though narration is still the primary mode.

Fiction had its roots in ancient myths and folk tales. In primitive civilizations, stories were circulated by word of mouth, and often traveling storytellers would appear in a court or village to entertain eager listeners with tales based on the exploits of heroes and gods. Although many of these were heavily fictionalized accounts of events and people who may or may not ever have existed, they were largely accepted by the people as fact or history. An especially long tale, an **epic,** was recited over a period of days, and to aid their memories the storytellers delivered these works in poetic lines, perhaps also impressing and entertaining their listeners by playing stringed instruments.

Although the retelling of myths and legends was meant in part to be entertainment, these stories made a point or taught a lesson considered important either for the local religion or the dominant power structure. Myths of gods like Zeus and Athena (Greece), or Jupiter and Minerva (Rome) abounded, together with stories of famous men and women like Jason, Helen of Troy, Agamemnon, Hercules, Andromeda, Achilles, Odysseus, and Penelope. The ancient Macedonian king and conqueror Alexander the Great (356–323 B.C.) developed many of his ideas about nobility and valor from his boyhood learning of Homer's epic *The Iliad,* which told of the Trojan War. Perhaps nowhere is the moralistic-argumentative aspect of storytelling better illustrated than in the **fables** of Aesop, a Greek who wrote in the sixth century, B.C., and in the **parables** of Jesus as told in the Gospels of the New Testament. In these works, a short narrative is clearly directed to a religious, philosophic, or psychological conclusion, as in "The Fox and the Grapes" and "The Parable of the Prodigal Son."

Beginning about 800 years ago, storytelling in Western civilization was developed to a fine art by writers such as Marie de France, a Frenchwoman who wrote in England near the end of the twelfth century, Giovanni Boccaccio (Italian, 1313–1375), and Geoffrey Chaucer (English, c. 1340–1400). William Shakespeare (1564–1616) drew heavily on history and legend for the stories and characters in his plays.

MODERN FICTION

Fiction in the modern sense of the word did not begin to flourish until the late seventeenth and eighteenth centuries, when human beings of all social stations and ways of life became important literary topics. As one writer put it in 1709, human nature could not be explained simply, but only with reference to many complex motives like "passion, humor, caprice, zeal, faction, and a thousand other springs."[1] Thus fiction moved toward the characteristic concerns that it has today—the psychological and the highly individual. Indeed, fiction gains its strength from being grounded in the real and personal. Most characters have both first and last names; the cities and villages in which they live and move are modeled on real places; and the events and responses recounted are like those that readers themselves have experienced, could experience, or could easily imagine themselves experiencing.

The first true works of fiction in the Western world were the lengthy

---

[1] Anthony Ashley Cooper, Third Earl of Shaftesbury, *Sensus Communis*, pt. III, sec. iii.

Spanish and French **romances** written in the sixteenth and seventeenth centuries. (The French word for "novel" is still *roman*.) In English the word **novel** was borrowed from French and Italian to describe these works and to distinguish them from medieval and classical romances as something that was *new* (the meaning of *novel*). In England the word *story* was used along with *novel* in reference to this new literary form.

It was natural that increased levels of general education and literacy in the eighteenth century would make possible the further development of fiction. In the time of Shakespeare and shortly later the only way a writer could make money out of writing was to write a play and then receive either a percentage of the admissions or the proceeds from an "author's benefit" performance. The audiences, however, were limited to people who lived within a short distance of the theater (or who could afford the cost of travel to a performance) and who had the leisure time to attend a play. Once great numbers of people could read, the paying audience for literature expanded. A writer could write a novel and have it printed by a publisher, who could then sell it widely to many people, giving a portion of the proceeds to the writer. Readers could pick up the book at their leisure and finish it as they chose. Reading a novel could even be a social event: people read to each other as a means of sharing the experience. With this wider audience, authors could make a career out of writing. Fiction had arrived as a major genre of literature.

THE SHORT STORY

Most novels were long, and reading them required many hours. It took an American writer, Edgar Allan Poe (1809–1849), to develop a theory of the **short story,** which he described in a review of Nathaniel Hawthorne's *Twice-Told Tales*. Poe was convinced that "worldly interests" prevented most readers from concentrating on their reading, and that as a result they lost the "totality" of comprehension and emotional reaction that careful reading should permit. He added to this practical consideration the belief that a short, concentrated story (which he called "a brief prose tale") could create a powerful, single impression on the reader. Thus he concluded that the best work of fiction was the short story that could be read at a single sitting of not more than an hour.

Once Poe had established a taste among his readers for short fiction, many later writers began working extensively in the short story form. Today, innumerable short stories are printed in weekly and monthly periodicals and in collections. Many writers who publish stories over a long period of time collect their works for inclusion in single volumes. Writers like William Faulkner, F. Scott Fitzgerald, Ernest Hemingway, Shirley Jackson, Guy de Maupassant, Flannery O'Connor, Frank O'Connor, Alice Walker, and Eudora Welty, to name only a small number, have had their works collected in this way.

ELEMENTS OF FICTION

Modern fiction is in a sense similar to myth and epic in that it may teach a lesson or make a point that the writer views as important. Even works purportedly written with a goal of simply entertaining are based in an idea or position. Thus, writers of comic works are usually committed to the belief that human difficulties can be ironed out by discussion and humor. More serious works may instruct by involving characters in difficult moral choices, with the underlying assumption that in losing situations the only winner is the one who can maintain honor and self-respect. Works designed to create mystery and suspense are based in the belief that problems have solutions, even if they may not at first seem apparent. In the creation of stories, writers may deal with the triumphs and defeats of life, the admirable and the despicable, the humorous and the pathetic, but whatever their goal, they always have something to say about the human experience. If they are successful as writers, they will communicate their vision directly to us through their stories.

As a first aspect of this vision, fiction, along with drama, has a basis in **realism** or **verisimilitude.** That is, the situations or characters, though they are the **invention** of writers, are similar to those that many human beings know or experience in their lives. Even **fantasy,** the creation of events that are dreamlike or fantastic (and in this sense a counter to realism), is derived from a perception of life and action that is ultimately real. This similarity of art to life has led some critics to label fiction, and also drama, as an art of **imitation.** Shakespeare's Hamlet states that an actor attempts to portray real human beings in realistic situations (to "hold a mirror up to Nature"). That might also be said of the writer of fiction.

In accord with the idea of verisimilitude or imitation, everything in fiction is related in one way or another to the reality of everyday life. Some stories are told as though they actually occurred in life, not unlike reports of actual news events in a newspaper. Eudora Welty's "A Worn Path" is such a story. It recounts a woman's walking journey through a wooded area, to the streets of a town, and then to the interior of a building. The events of the story are on the level of the real: They could actually happen in life just as Welty tells about them.

Other levels of reality may also be offered in fiction. Shirley Jackson's "The Lottery," for example, seems at first to be happening on a plane of absolute, small-town reality. By the story's end, however, it is apparent that something else is happening, that the realistic level has changed into a more symbolic one. Such a story suggests that fiction may have many kinds of connections with reality. This link with reality in "The Lottery" may be regarded as a **postulate,** a given **premise,** what Henry James called a *donnée* (something given). Here the premise is this: "What would happen if a small, ordinary town held a lottery in which the 'winner' would be ritually stoned to death?" Everything follows from this given idea. The connection with reality can become remote, or fanciful, as in Poe's "The Masque of the Red Death," in which the given idea is, "What would happen if Death could actually attend a party in person and claim all the partygoers?" The connection can become symbolic or even miraculous, as in Marjorie Pickthall's "The Worker in Sandalwood," in which Jesus, who in life had worked as a carpenter, returns to earth and builds a masterly piece of furniture. In Walter Clark's "A Portable Phonograph" the events occur in a possible future after much of the world's civilization has been destroyed in a global war. As you read works such as these, in which the actions and scenes do not seem realistic in our ordinary sense of the word, you should not dismiss the works as unreal. Instead, you should seek meaning in the actions as caused by the given situation. Always, you may judge a work by the standard of whether it is true if one grants the premises, or the *données,* created by the writer.

Indeed, you may accurately say that in fiction there is always some element of control that shapes the actions the author depicts. Even an apparently everyday level of reality disguises the craft and selectivity of the author. This control may be an occasion (such as the social worker calling the mother and expressing concern about the daughter in Tillie Olsen's "I Stand Here Ironing"). It may be a level of behavior (the boy's reactions to the people around him in O'Connor's "First Confession"). It may be an environment and a social situation, as in Anderson's "I'm a Fool." Some controls apply to particular types of fiction. There are, for example, "love stories." In the simplest love story two people meet and overcome an obstacle of some sort (usually not a really serious one) on the way to falling in love. Interesting variations on this type may be seen in D. H. Lawrence's "The Horse Dealer's Daughter" and Anton Chekhov's "Lady with Lapdog." In James Joyce's "Araby" only one of the major characters is in love; this is the narrator, who is telling about his boyhood crush on the sister of a friend. In another type of story, the "detective story," a mysterious event is posited, and then the detective draws conclusions based on the available evidence. A variation on the detective story may be seen in Susan Glaspell's "A Jury of Her Peers," in which the detective work is done by two women, and not by the investigator who has come to find evidence of a murder. Most stories, however, resist classification into types like these. They are simply stories about characters like those you find in real life, characters who undergo experiences that are sometimes difficult and painful, other times happy and successful, sometimes a mixture of many emotions. In short, stories represent the full range of human experience.

CHARACTER, PLOT, AND STRUCTURE

All works of fiction share a number of common elements which will be discussed in detail in the various chapters. The more apparent ones, for reference here, are *character, plot,* and *structure.*

Character

Stories, like drama, are about characters—characters who, though not real people, are drawn from life. A character, as defined in Chapter 4, is a reasonable facsimile of a human being, with all the good and bad traits of being human.[2] A story is usually concerned with a major problem that a character must face. This may involve interaction with another character, with a difficult situation, or with an idea or general circumstances that force action. The character may win, lose, or tie. He or she may learn and be the better for the experience or may miss the point and be unchanged despite what has happened.

Earlier we mentioned that modern fiction rose coincidentally with the development of a psychological interest in human beings. Psychology itself has grown out of the philosophical and religious idea that people are not necessarily evil, but rather that they have an inborn capacity for goodness. They are not free of problems, and they make many mistakes in their lives, but they nevertheless are of independent interest and they are therefore worth writing about in literature, whether they are male or female; white, black, tan, or yellow; rich or poor; worker or industrialist; farmer, secretary, shepherd, clerk, or salesperson.

It would therefore seem that there is virtually nothing in the modern world that is beyond the scope of fiction. The plight of a married couple struggling under an enormous debt, the meditation of a woman about the growth of her daughter, the experience of a boy learning about sin and forgiveness, the regrets of a young man afraid to admit a lie, the pathos of a woman surrounded by insensitive and self-seeking men, the humor that develops because a true hero does not fit the public conception of what a hero should be—all of these are important because human beings are important. In fiction you may expect characters from every area of life, and, because we all share the same human capacities for concern, involvement, sympathy, happiness, sorrow, exhilaration, and disappoint-

---

[2] Even the beings from other worlds and the lifelike robots and computers that we meet in science fiction, along with animals who populate beast fables and modern comics and films, interest us only as they exhibit human characteristics. Thus, Yogi Bear prefers honey to berries; a supremely intelligent computer with a conflicting program turns destructive; and an alien of superhuman strength riding on a spaceship tries to destroy all the human passengers. But we all know human beings with a sweet tooth; we all know that internal conflicts can produce unpredictable and sometimes destructive results; and who would say that the desire for power is not human?

ment, you should be able to become interested in the plights of characters and in how they try to handle the world around them.

Plot

Fictional characters, imitated from life, must go through a series of lifelike **actions,** or **incidents,** which in total make up the story. The interrelationship of incidents and character within a total design is the **plot** of the story. Plot has been compared to a map, scheme, or blueprint. In a carefully worked plot, all the actions, speeches, thoughts, and observations are inextricably linked to make up an entirety, sometimes called an **organic unity.** The essence of this unity of plot is the development and resolution of a **conflict,** in which a **protagonist,** or central character, is engaged in a struggle of some sort. Often this struggle is directed against another character, an **antagonist,** or group of antagonists. Just as often, however, the struggle may occur between opposing forces, ideas, and choices. The conflict may be carried out wherever human beings spend their lives, such as in open nature, communities, houses, courts of law, or mountain resorts. The conflict may also take place internally, within the mind of the protagonist.

Plot in its simplest stage is worked out in a pattern of **cause and effect** that can be traced in a **sequence** or **chronology.** That is, the incidents happen over a period of time, but chronology alone is not the cause of the sequence of actions. Instead, time enters into the cause-and-effect pattern to give the opportunity for effects to follow causes.

Structure

Whereas a plot is related to chronology, the **structure** of a story may be different because authors often choose to present their stories in something other than direct chronological order. If a story is told in straightforward narrative from beginning to end, then plot and structure are virtually identical. If, however, the story gets pieced together through out-of-sequence events, speeches, remembrances, fragments of letters, descriptions of actions, overheard conversations, and the like, then the actual arrangement or structure of the story may diverge from the plot. Also, whereas the plot refers to the entire pattern of conflict as evidenced through cause and effect in the story, the study of structure may be directed toward a smaller aspect of arrangement. Structure, in other words, refers to the way in which the plot is assembled, either in whole or in part.

Theme

We have said that writers write because they have things to say about life. One of the elements unifying a story is the existence of an underlying **theme** or **central idea,** which is present throughout the work. The theme is somewhat comparable to a scaffold that is used by workers in the construction of a large building; once the building is complete, it is removed, but the effect of the scaffold is still apparent.

The comparison is not totally valid, however, because authors may sometimes leave some of the "scaffolding" in their stories in the form of a direct statement. Thus Maupassant in "The Necklace" indicates that people may be destroyed or made fortunate by the most insignificant of events. The accidental loss of the necklace is just such an event; this misfortune ruins the lives of both Mathilde and her husband for the following ten years. Here the author has presented us with a direct statement of an idea, as it were, a part of his scaffold. There are many other ideas, however, that we might also locate in the story, such as that adversity may bring out worth, or that good fortune is never recognized until it is lost. With each of these alternatives, the story can be seen as being a consistent embodiment of an idea.

The process of determining and describing ideas in stories is probably never complete; there is always another idea that is equally valid and applicable. Such wide opportunity for discussion and interpretation is one of the things that makes fiction interesting and valuable.

THE WRITER'S TOOLS

Narration

Writers have a number of modes of presentation, or "tools," with which they may create their stories. The principal of these tools (and the heart of fiction) is **narration,** the reporting of actions in chronological sequence. The object of narration is, as much as possible, to *render* the story, to make it clear and to bring it alive to the reader's imagination.

Style

The medium of fiction and of all literature is language, and the manipulation of language—the **style**—is a primary skill of the writer of fiction. A mark of a good writer's style is the use of *active verbs*, and the use of nouns that are *specific* and *concrete*. Even with the most active and graphic diction possible, writers can never make an exact rendering of their incidents and scenes, but they can indeed be judged on the extent to which they make their narration vivid.

Point of View

One of the most important ways in which writers knit their stories together, and also an important way in which they try to interest and engage readers, is the careful control of **point of view** (see Chapter 5). Point of view is the voice of the story, the speaker who is doing the narration. It is the means by which the reality and truthfulness of a story are made to seem authentic. It may be regarded as the *focus* of the story, the *angle of vision* from which things are not only seen and reported but also judged.

A story may be told by a fictitious "observer" who tells us what he or she saw, heard, concluded, and thought. This **speaker** or observer may sometimes seem to be the author speaking directly using an authorial voice, but just as often the speaker is a **persona** with characteristics that separate him or her from the author. Sometimes the speaker is a fictitious actor or participant in the story. Stories told in either of these ways have **first-person** points of view, for the speaker usually uses the "I" personal pronoun in referring to his or her position as an observer or commentator.

The other point of view is the **third person.**[3] The third-person point of view may be (1) **limited,** with the focus being on one particular character and what he or she does, says, hears, thinks, and otherwise experiences, (2) **omniscient,** with the thoughts and behaviors of all the characters being open and fully known by the speaker, and (3) **dramatic,** or **objective,** with the story being confined *only* to essential reporting of actions and speeches, with no commentary and no revelation of the thoughts of any of the characters.

Point of view is often quite subtle—indeed, it may be one of the most difficult of all concepts in the study of literature. In fuller perspective, therefore, it may be considered as the position from which things are viewed, understood, and then communicated. It is point of view that makes fiction lifelike, although the author arranges the point of view so that the reader may be properly guided to learn of actions and dialogue. But point of view raises some of the same questions that are found in life. For example, we cannot always be sure of the reliability of what people tell us; we often need to know what their position is. In life, all people have their own limitations, attitudes, and opinions, so that their description of any event, and their attributions or conclusions about such events, will invariably be colored by these attitudes. For example, would the testimony of a near-sighted person who witnessed a distant incident while not wearing glasses be accurate? Would someone's report be reliable if the person were interpreting an activity of someone he or she did not like? The same applies to the speakers that we encounter in fiction. For readers, the perception of a fictional point of view can be as complex as life itself, and it may be as difficult—in fiction as in life—to find and rely upon proper sources of information.

Description

Together with narration, an important aspect of fiction is the use of **description,** which brings scenes and feelings to the imagination of readers. Description can be both physical (places and persons) and psychological

---

[3] The possibilities of a second-person point of view are discussed in Chapter 5.

(an emotion or set of emotions). As an end in itself, description can interrupt action, so that many writers include only as much as is necessary for the highlighting of important actions. In Tillie Olsen's "I Stand Here Ironing," for example, there is a minimum of physical description, although all of us can imagine where a woman doing the week's ironing might be and what she might look like. Other writers may make lavish descriptions in their works. Joseph Conrad, for example, provides extensive descriptions in his novels and stories. His scenes are not only places in which the characters act, but are so evocative that they provide a backdrop designed to give philosophical and even a semireligious perspective to the actions. Edgar Allan Poe uses descriptions extensively. In "The Fall of the House of Usher" he attempted to evoke an impression of decay and doom; in "The Masque of the Red Death" his descriptions suggest a mood of macabre festivity.

Mood and **atmosphere** are important adjuncts of descriptive writing, and to the degree that descriptions evoke ideas and actions beyond those they stand for on the surface, they may reach the level of **metaphor** and **symbolism.** These characteristics of fiction are a property of all literature, and you will also encounter them in your considerations of poetry and drama.

Dialogue

Another major tool of the writer of fiction is the creation of **dialogue.** At its simplest, dialogue is the conversation of two people, but more characters may participate, depending on their importance, the number present, and also the circumstances of the scene and action. The major medium of the dramatist, dialogue is just one of the means by which the fiction writer makes a story vivid and dramatic. Straight narration and description can do no more than say that a character's thoughts and responses exist, but dialogue makes everything real and firsthand. Dialogue is hence a means of *rendering* rather than presenting. If characters feel pain or declare love, their speeches can be the exact expressions (or inexact, depending on the degree of their articulateness) of what is on their minds, in their own words. Some dialogue may be terse and minimal, like that found in Hemingway. Other dialogue may be expanded, depending on the situation, the personalities of the characters, and the author's intent. Dialogue may be about virtually anything, including future plans and goals, reactions, indications of emotion, and political, social, philosophical, or religious ideas.

The language of dialogue indicates the intelligence, articulateness, educational levels, or emotional states of the speakers. Hence the author might use *grammatical mistakes, faulty pronunciation,* or *slang* to show a character of limited or disadvantaged background or a character who is trying to be seen in that light. *Dialect* clearly shows the regional location from which the speaker comes, just as an accent indicates the place of national origin. *Jargon* and *cliché* suggest a person who is pretentious—usually an infallible directive for the reader's laughter. The use of *private, intimate expressions* might show people who are close to each other emotionally. Speech that is interrupted with *voiced pauses* ("er," "ah," "um," "you know," and so on) and speech that is characterized by *inappropriate words* might show a character who is unsure or is not in control. There are many possibilities in dialogue, but no matter what specific qualities you observe, writers include dialogue in order to enable you better to know the characters peopling the scenes and the experiences they face.

Commentary

Writers may also include **commentary, analysis,** or **interpretation** in the expectation that readers need at least some insight or illumination about the characters and actions. We have already spoken of "scaffolding" in relation to the ideas in fiction. Commentary is the use of scaffolding as a means of showing how things are put together. When fiction was new, authors often expressed such commentary. Henry Fielding (1707–1754), for example, divided his novels into "books" and included a chapter of philosophical or artistic commentary at the beginning of each book. In the next century, George Eliot (1819–1880) included many extensive passages of commentary in her novels.

Later writers have kept commentary at a minimum, preferring instead to concentrate on direct action and dialogue. They have left it to readers to draw their own conclusions about meaning—to erect their own scaffolding, as it were. One is likely, however, to encounter something like interpretive observations in first-person narrations, particularly where the speaker not only is a storyteller but also has been a participant. Joseph Conrad's "Youth" is such a work, as is Olsen's "I Stand Here Ironing." Observations made by dramatic speakers in works like these may be accepted at face value, but you should recognize that anything the speakers say is also a mode of character disclosure. Such commentary is therefore just as much a part of the story as the narrative incidents.

Tone and Irony

In every story one may consider **tone,** that is, an attitude or attitudes that the author conveys about the material in the story and also toward the readers of the story. In "The Necklace," for example, Maupassant presents the bitter plight of Mathilde and her husband. Pity is thus an appropriate way of describing the attitude that the author conveys in this section of the story, and pity is indeed an appropriate response for the reader. Maupassant also shows that to a great degree Mathilde has brought her misfortune directly on herself, so the attitude is one of at least partial satisfaction that justice has been done. But Mathilde works hard and unself-ishly; hence admiration tempers any inclination that the reader might have had to condemn her. Finally, the story's conclusion shows that Mathilde's virtual enslavement was unnecessary. Hence regret enters into the response. In a discussion of the tone of the story, it would be necessary to describe this mixture or complexity of attitudes. Usually, tone is complex in this way.

Because Mathilde's sacrifice for a period of ten years is unnecessary, her situation is ironic. **Irony** is the use of language and situations that are widely inappropriate or opposite from what might be ordinarily expected. **Situational irony** is a means by which authors create a strong emotional impact by presenting circumstances in which punishments do not fit crimes, or in which rewards are not earned. Forces, in other words, are beyond human control or comprehension. The characteristic of **dramatic irony** is that a character may perceive his or her situation in a limited way while the reader sees things more broadly and comprehensively. In John Collier's "The Chaser," for example, the main character believes that he is about to embark upon lifelong ecstasy and romance, but Collier makes the reader aware that the character's life will be sinister and not ecstatic. In **verbal irony,** which applies to language, what is *meant* is different from, or opposite to, what is *said*. Thus Maupassant in "The Necklace" does not directly say that Mathilde's husband is a crashing bore during the big party, but by asserting ironically that he had been sleeping "in a little empty room with three other men whose wives had also been enjoying themselves," Maupassant conveys this idea with amusing force.

Symbolism and Allegory

Because fiction impresses itself upon the human imagination, it is almost a necessary consequence that the incidents, speeches, and characters acquire an underlying idea or value. To this degree, even an apparently ordinary thing may be construed as a **symbol;** that is, it may be understood to mean something beyond itself, something bigger than itself. Because Sammy in Updike's "A & P" walks out on his job in protest against the way the girls in swimsuits are treated, he might easily serve as a symbol standing for freedom of personal behavior. To consider Sammy as a symbol, however, depends on the reader's willingness to make the necessary connection and justification. Many other symbols do not need such explanation, for sometimes writers deliberately create symbols. The cane in Hawthorne's "Young Goodman Brown" is such an example, for Hawthorne describes it as resembling the serpent associated with Satan. The cane therefore is a symbol showing that Brown's woodland companion is actually the Devil himself.

When a story, in addition to maintaining its own narrative integrity, may be clearly applied to another, parallel, set of situations, it is an **allegory.**

"Young Goodman Brown" may be considered as an allegory of the development of hatred, distrust, and paranoia. Stories are usually not like "Young Goodman Brown," however, even though they may contain sections that have allegorical parallels. Thus, the narrative of Mathilde's long servitude in Maupassant's "The Necklace" is similar to the lives and activities of many people who carry out tasks for reasons that are incorrect or even meaningless. For this reason, "The Necklace" may be considered allegorically, even though it is not a complete allegory.

These, then, are the major tools of writers of fiction. For analytical purposes, one or another of them may be discussed so that the artistic achievement of a particular author may be recognized. It is important to realize, however, that in a story everything is happening at once. The story may be told by a character who is a witness, and thus there is a *first-person point of view*. The major *character*, the *protagonist*, goes through a series of *actions* as a result of a carefully arranged *plot*. Because of this plot, together with the author's chosen method of narration, the story will exhibit an organization, or *structure*. One of the things that the actions may demonstrate will be the *theme* or *central idea* of the story. The writer's *style* may be manifested in *ironic* expressions. The description of the character's activity may reveal *irony of situation*, while at the same time this situation is made vivid through *dialogue* in which the character is a participant. Because the plight of the character is like the plight of many persons in the world, it may be considered as an *allegory*, and the character herself or himself may be a *symbol*.

Throughout the story, no matter what characteristics one is considering at the moment, it is most important to realize that a work of fiction is an entirety, a unity. Any reading of a story should be undertaken not to break things down into parts, but to understand and assimilate the work as a whole. The separate analysis of various topics, to which this book is committed, is thus the means to that end, not the end itself. Finally, the study of fiction, like the study of all literature, is designed to foster growth and understanding and to encourage the ultimate improvement of life.

JOHN UPDIKE   (b. 1932)

A & P°   *1961*

In walks these three girls in nothing but bathing suits. I'm in the third checkout slot, with my back to the door, so I don't see them until they're over by the bread.

A & P: "The Great Atlantic and Pacific Tea Company," a large grocery chain still operating in many states.

The one that caught my eye first was the one in the plaid green two-piece. She was a chunky kid, with a good tan and a sweet broad soft-looking can with those two crescents of white just under it, where the sun never seems to hit, at the top of the backs of her legs. I stood there with my hand on a box of HiHo crackers trying to remember if I rang it up or not. I ring it up again and the customer starts giving me hell. She's one of these cash-register-watchers, a witch about fifty with rouge on her cheekbones and no eyebrows, and I know it made her day to trip me up. She'd been watching cash registers for fifty years and probably never seen a mistake before.

By the time I got her feathers smoothed and her goodies into a bag—she gives me a little snort in passing, if she'd been born at the right time they would have burned her over in Salem—by the time I get her on her way the girls had circled around the bread and were coming back, without a pushcart, back my way along the counters, in the aisle between the checkouts and the Special bins. They didn't even have shoes on. There was this chunky one, with the two-piece— it was bright green and the seams on the bra were still sharp and her belly was still pretty pale so I guessed she just got it (the suit)—there was this one, with one of those chubby berry-faces, the lips all bunched together under her nose, this one, and a tall one, with black hair that hadn't quite frizzed right, and one of these sunburns right across under the eyes, and a chin that was too long—you know, the kind of girl other girls think is very "striking" and "attractive" but never quite makes it, as they very well know, which is why they like her so much—and then the third one, that wasn't quite so tall. She was the queen. She kind of led them, the other two peeking around and making their shoulders round. She didn't look around, not this queen, she just walked straight on slowly, on these long white prima-donna legs. She came down a little hard on her heels, as if she didn't walk in her bare feet that much, putting down her heels and then letting the weight move along to her toes as if she was testing the floor with every step, putting a little deliberate extra action into it. You never know for sure how girls' minds work (do you really think it's a mind in there or just a little buzz like a bee in a glass jar?) but you got the idea she had talked the other two into coming in here with her, and now she was showing them how to do it, walk slow and hold yourself straight.

She had on a kind of dirty-pink—beige, maybe, I don't know—bathing suit with a little nubble all over it and, what got me, the straps were down. They were off her shoulders looped loose around the cool tops of her arms, and I guess as a result the suit had slipped a little on her, so all around the top of the cloth there was this shining rim. If it hadn't been there you wouldn't have known there could have been anything whiter than those shoulders. With the straps pushed off, there was nothing between the top of the suit and the top of her head except just *her*, this clean bare plane of the top of her chest down from the shoulder bones like a dented sheet of metal tilted in the light. I mean, it was more than pretty.

She had sort of oaky hair that the sun and salt had bleached, done up in a bun that was unraveling, and a kind of prim face. Walking into the A & P with your straps down, I suppose it's the only kind of face you *can* have. She held her head so high her neck, coming up out of those white shoulders, looked kind of stretched, but I didn't mind. The longer her neck was, the more of her there was.

   She must have felt in the corner of her eye me and over my shoulder Stokesie in the second slot watching, but she didn't tip. Not this queen. She kept her eyes moving across the racks, and stopped, and turned so slow it made my stomach rub the inside of my apron, and buzzed to the other two, who kind of huddled against her for relief, and then they all three of them went up the cat-and-dog-food-breakfast-cereal-macaroni-rice-raisins-seasonings-spreads-spaghetti-soft-drinks-crackers-and-cookies aisle. From the third slot I look straight up this aisle to the meat counter, and I watched them all the way. The fat one with the tan sort of fumbled with the cookies, but on second thought she put the package back. The sheep pushing their carts down the aisle—the girls were walking against the usual traffic (not that we have one-way signs or anything)—were pretty hilarious. You could see them, when Queenie's white shoulders dawned on them, kind of jerk, or hop, or hiccup, but their eyes snapped back to their own baskets and on they pushed. I bet you could set off dynamite in an A & P and the people would by and large keep reaching and checking oatmeal off their lists and muttering "Let me see, there was a third thing, began with A, asparagus, no ah, yes, applesauce!" or whatever it is they do mutter. But there was no doubt, this jiggled them. A few houseslaves in pin curlers even looked around after pushing their carts past to make sure what they had seen was correct.

   You know, it's one thing to have a girl in a bathing suit down on the beach, where what with the glare nobody can look at each other much anyway, and another thing in the cool of the A & P, under the fluorescent lights, against all those stacked packages, with her feet paddling along naked over our checkerboard green-and-cream rubber-tile floor.

   "Oh Daddy," Stokesie said beside me. "I feel so faint."

   "Darling," I said. "Hold me tight." Stokesie's married, with two babies chalked up on his fuselage already, but as far as I can tell that's the only difference. He's twenty-two, and I was nineteen this April.

   "Is it done?" he asks, the responsible married man finding his voice. I forgot to say he thinks he's going to be manager some sunny day, maybe in 1990 when it's called the Great Alexandrov and Petrooshki° Tea Company or something.

   What he meant was, our town is five miles from the beach, with a big summer colony out on the Point, but we're right in the middle of town, and the women generally put on a shirt or shorts or something before they get out of the car into the street. And anyway these are usually women with six children and varicose veins mapping their legs and nobody, including them, could care less. As I say, we're right in the middle of town, and if you stand at our front doors you can see two banks and the Congregational church and the newspaper store and three real-estate offices and about twenty-seven old freeloaders tearing up Central Street because the sewer broke again. It's not as if we're on the Cape;° we're north of Boston and there's people in this town haven't seen the ocean for twenty years.

   The girls had reached the meat counter and were asking McMahon something.

   Great Alexandrov and Petrooshki: Apparently a reference to the possibility that someday Russia might rule the United States.
   the Cape: Cape Cod, the southeastern area of Massachusetts, a place of many resorts and beaches.

He pointed, they pointed, and they shuffled out of sight behind a pyramid of Diet Delight peaches. All that was left for us to see was old McMahon patting his mouth and looking after them sizing up their joints. Poor kids, I began to feel sorry for them, they couldn't help it.

Now here comes the sad part of the story, at least my family says it's sad, but I don't think it's so sad myself. The store's pretty empty, it being Thursday afternoon, so there was nothing much to do except lean on the register and wait for the girls to show up again. The whole store was like a pinball machine and I didn't know which tunnel they'd come out of. After a while they come around out of the far aisle, around the light bulbs, records at discount of the Caribbean Six or Tony Martin Sings or some such gunk you wonder they waste the wax on, sixpacks of candy bars, and plastic toys done up in cellophane that fall apart when a kid looks at them anyway. Around they come, Queenie still leading the way, and holding a little gray jar in her hand. Slots Three through Seven are unmanned and I could see her wondering between Stokes and me, but Stokesie with his usual luck draws an old party in baggy gray pants who stumbles up with four giant cans of pineapple juice (what do these bums *do* with all that pineapple juice? I've often asked myself) so the girls come to me. Queenie puts down the jar and I take it into my fingers icy cold. Kingfish Fancy Herring Snacks in Pure Sour Cream: 49¢. Now her hands are empty, not a ring or a bracelet, bare as God made them, and I wonder where the money's coming from. Still with that prim look she lifts a folded dollar bill out of the hollow at the center of her nubbed pink top. The jar went heavy in my hand. Really, I thought that was so cute.

Then everybody's luck begins to run out. Lengel comes in from haggling with a truck full of cabbages on the lot and is about to scuttle into that door marked MANAGER behind which he hides all day when the girls touch his eye. Lengel's pretty dreary, teaches Sunday school and the rest, but he doesn't miss that much. He comes over and says, "Girls, this isn't the beach."

Queenie blushes, though maybe it's just a brush of sunburn I was noticing for the first time, now that she was so close. "My mother asked me to pick up a jar of herring snacks." Her voice kind of startled me, the way voices do when you see the people first, coming out so flat and dumb yet kind of tony, too, the way it ticked over "pick up" and "snacks." All of a sudden I slid right down her voice into her living room. Her father and the other men were standing around in ice-cream coats and bow ties and the women were in sandals picking up herring snacks on toothpicks off a big glass plate and they were all holding drinks the color of water with olives and sprigs of mint in them. When my parents have somebody over they get lemonade and if it's a real racy affair Schlitz in tall glasses with "They'll Do It Every Time"° cartoons stenciled on.

"That's all right," Lengel said. "But this isn't the beach." His repeating this   15 struck me as funny, as if it had just occurred to him, and he had been thinking all these years the A & P was a great big dune and he was the head lifeguard. He didn't like my smiling—as I say he doesn't miss much—but he concentrates on giving the girls that sad Sunday-school-superintendent stare.

"They'll Do It Every Time": A syndicated daily and Sunday cartoon created by Jimmy Hatlo.

Queenie's blush is no sunburn now, and the plump one in plaid, that I liked better from the back—a really sweet can—pipes up, "We weren't doing any shopping. We just came in for the one thing."

"That makes no difference," Lengel tells her, and I could see from the way his eyes went that he hadn't noticed she was wearing a two-piece before. "We want you decently dressed when you come in here."

"We *are* decent," Queenie says suddenly, her lower lip pushing, getting sore now that she remembers her place, a place from which the crowd that runs the A & P must look pretty crummy. Fancy Herring Snacks flashed in her very blue eyes.

"Girls, I don't want to argue with you. After this come in here with your shoulders covered. It's our policy." He turns his back. That's policy for you. Policy is what the kingpins want. What the others want is juvenile delinquency.

All this while, the customers had been showing up with their carts but, you know, sheep, seeing a scene, they had all bunched up on Stokesie, who shook open a paper bag as gently as peeling a peach, not wanting to miss a word. I could feel in the silence everybody getting nervous, most of all Lengel, who asks me, "Sammy, have you rung up their purchase?"

I thought and said "No" but it wasn't about that I was thinking. I go through the punches, 4, 9, GROC, TOT—it's more complicated than you think, and after you do it often enough, it begins to make a little song, that you hear words to, in my case "Hello (*bing*) there, you (*gung*) hap-py *pee*-pul (*splat*)!"—the *splat* being the drawer flying out. I uncrease the bill, tenderly as you may imagine, it just having come from between the two smoothest scoops of vanilla I had ever known were there, and pass a half and a penny into her narrow pink palm, and nestle the herrings in a bag and twist its neck and hand it over, all the time thinking.

The girls, and who'd blame them, are in a hurry to get out, so I say "I quit" to Lengel quick enough for them to hear, hoping they'll stop and watch me, their unsuspected hero. They keep right on going, into the electric eye; the door flies open and they flicker across the lot to their car, Queenie and Plaid and Big Tall Goony-Goony (not that as raw material she was so bad), leaving me with Lengel and a kink in his eyebrow.

"Did you say something, Sammy?"

"I said I quit."

"I thought you did."

"You didn't have to embarrass them."

"It was they who were embarrassing us."

I started to say something that came out "Fiddle-de-doo." It's a saying of my grandmother's, and I know she would have been pleased.

"I don't think you know what you're saying," Lengel said.

"I know you don't," I said. "But I do." I pull the bow at the back of my apron and start shrugging it off my shoulders. A couple customers that had been heading for my slot begin to knock against each other, like scared pigs in a chute.

Lengel sighs and begins to look very patient and old and gray. He's been a friend of my parents for years. "Sammy, you don't want to do this to your Mom and Dad," he tells me. It's true, I don't. But it seems to me that once you begin a gesture it's fatal not to go through with it. I fold the apron, "Sammy" stitched in red on the pocket, and put it on the counter, and drop the bow tie on top of it.

20

25

30

The bow tie is theirs, if you've ever wondered. "You'll feel this for the rest of your life," Lengel says, and I know that's true, too, but remembering how he made that pretty girl blush makes me so scrunchy inside I punch the No Sale tab and the machine whirs "pee-pul" and the drawer splats out. One advantage to this scene taking place in summer, I can follow this up with a clean exit, there's no fumbling around getting your coat and galoshes, I just saunter into the electric eye in my white shirt that my mother ironed the night before, and the door heaves itself open, and outside the sunshine is skating around on the asphalt.

I look around for my girls, but they're gone, of course. There wasn't anybody but some young married screaming with her children about some candy they didn't get by the door of a powder-blue Falcon° station wagon. Looking back in the big windows, over the bags of peat moss and aluminum lawn furniture stacked on the pavement, I could see Lengel in my place in the slot, checking the sheep through. His face was dark gray and his back stiff, as if he'd just had an injection of iron, and my stomach kind of fell as I felt how hard the world was going to be to me hereafter.

Falcon: A small car that had recently been introduced by the Ford Motor Company.

QUESTIONS

1. Consider the first eleven paragraphs as exposition, in which you learn about the location, the issues, and the participants of the conflict in the story. Is there anything inessential? Do you learn enough to understand the story? On the basis of your conclusions, consider the nature of exposition in a work of fiction.

2. From Sammy's language what do you learn about his view of himself? About his educational and class level? The first sentence, for example, is grammatically incorrect in Standard English but not uncommon in colloquial English. Point out similar passages. Do they suggest that he violates Standard English deliberately or unwittingly?

3. Indicate evidence in the narration that Sammy is an experienced "girl watcher." What is his estimation of the intelligence of most girls? Is this judgment consistent with what he finally does?

4. Why does Sammy say "I quit" so abruptly? Does it seem to him at the time that his gesture is meaningful? What do you think he means at the end by saying that the world is going to be hard to him afterwards?

SUSAN GLASPELL   (1882–1948)

A Jury of Her Peers   *1917*

When Martha Hale opened the storm-door and got a cut of the north wind, she ran back for her big woolen scarf. As she hurriedly wound that round her head her eye made a scandalized sweep of her kitchen. It was no ordinary thing that called her away—it was probably further from ordinary than anything that had ever happened in Dickson County. But what her eye took in was that her kitchen was in no shape for leaving: her bread all ready for mixing, half the flour sifted and half unsifted.

She hated to see things half done; but she had been at that when the team from town stopped to get Mr. Hale, and then the sheriff came running in to say his wife wished Mrs. Hale would come too—adding, with a grin, that he guessed she was getting scary and wanted another woman along. So she had dropped everything right where it was.

"Martha!" now came her husband's impatient voice. "Don't keep folks waiting out here in the cold."

She again opened the storm-door, and this time joined the three men and the one woman waiting for her in the big two-seated buggy.

After she had the robes tucked around her she took another look at the woman who sat beside her on the back seat. She had met Mrs. Peters the year before at the county fair, and the thing she remembered about her was that she didn't seem like a sheriff's wife. She was small and thin and didn't have a strong voice. Mrs. Gorman, sheriff's wife before Gorman went out and Peters came in, had a voice that somehow seemed to be backing up the law with every word. But if Mrs. Peters didn't look like a sheriff's wife, Peters made it up in looking like a sheriff. He was to a dot the kind of man who could get himself elected sheriff—a heavy man with a big voice, who was particularly genial with the law-abiding, as if to make it plain that he knew the difference between criminals and non-criminals. And right there it came into Mrs. Hale's mind, with a stab, that this man who was so pleasant and lively with all of them was going to the Wrights' now as a sheriff. 5

"The country's not very pleasant this time of year," Mrs. Peters at last ventured, as if she felt they ought to be talking as well as the men.

Mrs. Hale scarcely finished her reply, for they had gone up a little hill and could see the Wright place now, and seeing it did not make her feel like talking. It looked very lonesome this cold March morning. It had always been a lonesome-looking place. It was down in a hollow, and the poplar trees around it were lonesome-looking trees. The men were looking at it and talking about what had happened. The county attorney was bending to one side of the buggy, and kept looking steadily at the place as they drew up to it.

"I'm glad you came with me," Mrs. Peters said nervously, as the two women were about to follow the men in through the kitchen door.

Even after she had her foot on the door-step, her hand on the knob, Martha Hale had a moment of feeling she could not cross that threshold. And the reason it seemed she couldn't cross it now was simply because she hadn't crossed it before. Time and time again it had been in her mind, "I ought to go over and see Minnie Foster"—she still thought of her as Minnie Foster, though for twenty years she had been Mrs. Wright. And then there was always something to do and Minnie Foster would go from her mind. But *now* she could come.

The men went over to the stove. The women stood close together by the door. Young Henderson, the county attorney, turned around and said, "Come up to the fire, ladies." 10

Mrs. Peters took a step forward, then stopped. "I'm not—cold," she said.

And so the two women stood by the door, at first not even so much as looking around the kitchen.

The men talked for a minute about what a good thing it was the sheriff had sent his deputy out that morning to make a fire for them, and then Sheriff Peters stepped back from the stove, unbuttoned his outer coat, and leaned his hands on the kitchen table in a way that seemed to mark the beginning of official business. "Now, Mr. Hale," he said in a sort of semi-official voice, "before we move things about, you tell Mr. Henderson just what it was you saw when you came here yesterday morning."

The county attorney was looking around the kitchen.

"By the way," he said, "has anything been moved?" He turned to the sheriff. "Are things just as you left them yesterday?"   15

Peters looked from cupboard to sink; from that to a small worn rocker a little to one side of the kitchen table.

"It's just the same."

"Somebody should have been left here yesterday," said the county attorney.

"Oh—yesterday," returned the sheriff, with a little gesture as of yesterday having been more than he could bear to think of. "When I had to send Frank to Morris Center for that man who went crazy—let me tell you, I had my hands full *yesterday*. I knew you could get back from Omaha by today, George, and as long as I went over everything here myself—"

"Well, Mr. Hale," said the county attorney, in a way of letting what was past and gone go, "tell just what happened when you came here yesterday morning."   20

Mrs. Hale, still leaning against the door, had that sinking feeling of the mother whose child is about to speak a piece. Lewis often wandered along and got things mixed up in a story. She hoped he would tell this straight and plain, and not say unnecessary things that would just make things harder for Minnie Foster. He didn't begin at once, and she noticed that he looked queer—as if standing in that kitchen and having to tell what he had seen there yesterday morning made him almost sick.

"Yes, Mr. Hale?" the county attorney reminded.

"Harry and I had started to town with a load of potatoes," Mrs. Hale's husband began.

Harry was Mrs. Hale's oldest boy. He wasn't with them now, for the very good reason that those potatoes never got to town yesterday and he was taking them this morning, so he hadn't been home when the sheriff stopped to say he wanted Mr. Hale to come over to the Wright place and tell the county attorney his story there, where he could point it all out. With all Mrs. Hale's other emotions came the fear now that maybe Harry wasn't dressed warm enough—they hadn't any of them realized how that north wind did bite.

"We come along this road," Hale was going on, with a motion of his hand   25
to the road over which they had just come, "and as we got in sight of the house I says to Harry, 'I'm goin' to see if I can't get John Wright to take a telephone.' You see," he explained to Henderson, "unless I can get somebody to go in with me they won't come out this branch road except for a price *I* can't pay. I'd spoke to Wright about it once before; but he put me off, saying folks talked too much anyway, and all he asked was peace and quiet—guess you know about how much

he talked himself. But I thought maybe if I went to the house and talked about it before his wife, and said all the women-folks liked the telephones, and that in this lonesome stretch of road it would be a good thing—well, I said to Harry that that was what I was going to say—though I said at the same time that I didn't know as what his wife wanted made much difference to John—"

Now there he was!—saying things he didn't need to say. Mrs. Hale tried to catch her husband's eye, but fortunately the county attorney interrupted with:

"Let's talk about that a little later, Mr. Hale. I do want to talk about that, but I'm anxious now to get along to just what happened when you got here."

When he began this time, it was very deliberately and carefully:

"I didn't see or hear anything. I knocked at the door. And still it was all quiet inside. I knew they must be up—it was past eight o'clock. So I knocked again, louder, and I thought I heard somebody say, 'Come in.' I wasn't sure—I'm not sure yet. But I opened the door—this door," jerking a hand toward the door by which the two women stood, "and there, in that rocker"—pointing to it—"sat Mrs. Wright."

Everyone in the kitchen looked at the rocker. It came into Mrs. Hale's mind 30
that that rocker didn't look in the least like Minnie Foster—the Minnie Foster of twenty years before. It was a dingy red, with wooden rungs up the back, and the middle rung was gone, and the chair sagged to one side.

"How did she—look?" the county attorney was inquiring.

"Well," said Hale, "she looked—queer."

"How do you mean—queer?"

As he asked it he took out a note-book and pencil. Mrs. Hale did not like the sight of that pencil. She kept her eye fixed on her husband, as if to keep him from saying unnecessary things that would go into that note-book and make trouble.

Hale did speak guardedly, as if the pencil had affected him too. 35

"Well, as if she didn't know what she was going to do next. And kind of—done up."

"How did she seem to feel about your coming?"

"Why, I don't think she minded—one way or other. She didn't pay much attention. I said, 'Ho' do, Mrs. Wright? It's cold, ain't it?' And she said, 'Is it?'—and went on pleatin' at her apron.

"Well, I was surprised. She didn't ask me to come up to the stove, or to sit down, but just set there, not even lookin' at me. And so I said: 'I want to see John.'

"And then she—laughed. I guess you would call it a laugh. 40

"I thought of Harry and the team outside, so I said, a little sharp, 'Can I see John?' 'No,' says she—kind of dull like. 'Ain't he home?' says I. Then she looked at me. 'Yes,' says she, 'he's home.' 'Then why can't I see him?' I asked her, out of patience with her now. ' 'Cause he's dead,' says she, just as quiet and dull—and fell to pleatin' her apron. 'Dead?' says I, like you do when you can't take in what you've heard.

"She just nodded her head, not getting a bit excited, but rockin' back and forth.

" 'Why—where is he?' says I, not knowing *what* to say.

"She just pointed upstairs—like this"—pointing to the room above.

"I got up, with the idea of going up there myself. By this time I—didn't   45
know what to do. I walked from there to here; then I says: 'Why, what did he die
of?'

" 'He died of a rope around his neck,' says she; and just went on pleatin at
her apron."

Hale stopped speaking, and stood staring at the rocker, as if he were still
seeing the woman who had sat there the morning before. Nobody spoke; it was
as if every one were seeing the woman who had sat there the morning before.

"And what did you do then?" the county attorney at last broke the silence.

"I went out and called Harry. I thought I might—need help. I got Harry
in, and we went upstairs." His voice fell almost to a whisper. "There he was—
lying over the—"

"I think I'd rather have you go into that upstairs," the county attorney in-   50
terrupted, "where you can point it all out. Just go on now with the rest of the
story."

"Well, my first thought was to get that rope off. It looked—"

He stopped, his face twitching.

"But Harry, he went up to him, and he said, 'No, he's dead all right, and
we'd better not touch anything.' So we went downstairs.

"She was still sitting that same way. 'Has anybody been notified?' I asked.
'No,' says she, unconcerned.

" 'Who did this, Mrs. Wright?' said Harry. He said it businesslike, and she   55
stopped pleatin' at her apron. 'I don't know,' she says. 'You don't *know*?' says
Harry. 'Weren't you sleepin' in the bed with him?' 'Yes,' says she, 'but I was on
the inside.' 'Somebody slipped a rope round his neck and strangled him, and,
you didn't wake up?' says Harry. 'I didn't wake up,' she said after him.

"We may have looked as if we didn't see how that could be, for after a
minute she said, 'I sleep sound.'

"Harry was going to ask her more questions, but I said maybe that weren't
our business; maybe we ought to let her tell her story first to the coroner or the
sheriff. So Harry went fast as he could over to High Road—the Rivers' place,
where there's a telephone."

"And what did she do when she knew you had gone for the coroner?" The
attorney got his pencil in his hand all ready for writing.

"She moved from that chair to this one over here"—Hale pointed to a small
chair in the corner—"and just sat there with her hands held together and looking
down. I got a feeling that I ought to make some conversation, so I said I had
come in to see if John wanted to put in a telephone; and at that she started to
laugh, and then she stopped and looked at me—scared."

At sound of a moving pencil the man who was telling the story looked up.   60

"I dunno—maybe it wasn't scared," he hastened; "I wouldn't like to say it
was. Soon Harry got back, and then Dr. Lloyd came, and you, Mr. Peters, and so
I guess that's all I know that you don't."

He said that last with relief, and moved a little, as if relaxing. Everyone
moved a little. The county attorney walked toward the stair door.

"I guess we'll go upstairs first—then out to the barn and around there."

He paused and looked around the kitchen.

"You're convinced there was nothing important here?" he asked the sheriff. 65
"Nothing that would—point to any motive?"

The sheriff too looked all around, as if to re-convince himself.

"Nothing here but kitchen things," he said, with a little laugh for the insignificance of kitchen things.

The county attorney was looking at the cupboard—a peculiar, ungainly structure, half closet and half cupboard, the upper part of it being built in the wall, and the lower part just the old-fashioned kitchen cupboard. As if its queerness attracted him, he got a chair and opened the upper part and looked in. After a moment he drew his hand away sticky.

"Here's a nice mess," he said resentfully.

The two women had drawn nearer, and now the sheriff's wife spoke. 70

"Oh—her fruit," she said, looking to Mrs. Hale for sympathetic understanding. She turned back to the county attorney and explained: "She worried about that when it turned so cold last night. She said the fire would go out and her jars might burst."

Mrs. Peters' husband broke into a laugh.

"Well, can you beat the women! Held for murder, and worrying about her preserves!"

The young attorney set his lips.

"I guess before we're through with her she may have something more serious 75
than preserves to worry about."

"Oh, well," said Mrs. Hale's husband, with good-natured superiority, "women are used to worrying over trifles."

The two women moved a little closer together. Neither of them spoke. The county attorney seemed suddenly to remember his manners—and think of his future.

"And yet," said he, with the gallantry of a young politician, "for all their worries, what would we do without the ladies?"

The women did not speak, did not unbend. He went to the sink and began washing his hands. He turned to wipe them on the roller towel—whirled it for a cleaner place.

"Dirty towels! Not much of a housekeeper, would you say, ladies?" 80

He kicked his foot against some dirty pans under the sink.

"There's a great deal of work to be done on a farm," said Mrs. Hale stiffly.

"To be sure. And yet"—with a little bow to her—"I know there are some Dickson County farm-houses that do not have such roller towels." He gave it a pull to expose its full length again.

"Those towels get dirty awful quick. Men's hands aren't always as clean as they might be."

"Ah, loyal to your sex, I see," he laughed. He stopped and gave her a keen 85
look. "But you and Mrs. Wright were neighbors. I suppose you were friends, too."

Martha Hale shook her head.

"I've seen little enough of her of late years. I've not been in this house—it's more than a year."

"And why was that? You didn't like her?"

"I liked her well enough," she replied with spirit. "Farmers' wives have their hands full, Mr. Henderson. And then—" She looked around the kitchen.

"Yes?" he encouraged.   90

"It never seemed a very cheerful place," said she, more to herself than to him.

"No," he agreed; "I don't think anyone would call it cheerful. I shouldn't say she had the home-making instinct."

"Well, I don't know as Wright had, either," she muttered.

"You mean they didn't get on very well?" he was quick to ask.

"No; I don't mean anything," she answered, with decision. As she turned a   95
little away from him, she added: "But I don't think a place would be any the cheerfuler for John Wright's bein' in it."

"I'd like to talk to you about that a little later, Mrs. Hale," he said. "I'm anxious to get the lay of things upstairs now."

He moved toward the stair door, followed by the two men.

"I suppose anything Mrs. Peters does'll be all right?" the sheriff inquired. "She was to take in some clothes for her, you know—and a few little things. We left in such a hurry yesterday."

The county attorney looked at the two women whom they were leaving alone there among the kitchen things.

"Yes—Mrs. Peters," he said, his glance resting on the woman who was not   100
Mrs. Peters, the big farmer woman who stood behind the sheriff's wife. "Of course Mrs. Peters is one of us," he said, in a manner of entrusting responsibility. "And keep your eye out, Mrs. Peters, for anything that might be of use. No telling; you women might come upon a clue to the motive—and that's the thing we need."

Mr. Hale rubbed his face after the fashion of a showman getting ready for a pleasantry.

"But would the women know a clue if they did come upon it?" he said; and, having delivered himself of this, he followed the others through the stair door.

The women stood motionless and silent, listening to the footsteps, first upon the stairs, then in the room above them.

Then, as if releasing herself from something strange, Mrs. Hale began to arrange the dirty pans under the sink, which the county attorney's disdainful push of the foot had deranged.

"I'd hate to have men comin' into my kitchen," she said testily—"snoopin'   105
round and criticizin'."

"Of course it's no more than their duty," said the sheriff's wife, in her manner of timid acquiescence.

"Duty's all right," replied Mrs. Hale bluffly; "but I guess that deputy sheriff that come out to make the fire might have got a little of this on." She gave the roller towel a pull. "Wish I'd thought of that sooner! Seems mean to talk about her for not having things slicked up, when she had to come away in such a hurry."

She looked around the kitchen. Certainly it was not "slicked up." Her eye was held by a bucket of sugar on a low shelf. The cover was off the wooden bucket, and beside it was a paper bag—half full.

Mrs. Hale moved toward it.

"She was putting this in there," she said to herself—slowly.   110

She thought of the flour in her kitchen at home—half sifted, half not sifted. She had been interrupted, and had left things half done. What had interrupted Minnie Foster? Why had that work been left half done? She made a move as if to finish it,—unfinished things always bothered her,—and then she glanced around and saw that Mrs. Peters was watching her—and she didn't want Mrs. Peters to get that feeling she had got of work begun and then—for some reason—not finished.

"It's a shame about her fruit," she said, and walked toward the cupboard that the county attorney had opened, and got on the chair, murmuring: "I wonder if it's all gone."

It was a sorry enough looking sight, but "Here's one that's all right," she said at last. She held it toward the light. "This is cherries, too." She looked again. "I declare I believe that's the only one."

With a sigh, she got down from the chair, went to the sink, and wiped off the bottle.

"She'll feel awful bad, after all her hard work in the hot weather. I remember   115
the afternoon I put up my cherries last summer."

She set the bottle on the table, and, with another sigh, started to sit down in the rocker. But she did not sit down. Something kept her from sitting down in that chair. She straightened—stepped back—and, half turned away, stood looking at it, seeing the woman who had sat there "pleatin' at her apron."

The thin voice of the sheriff's wife broke in upon her: "I must be getting those things from the front-room closet." She opened the door into the other room, started in, stepped back. "You coming with me, Mrs. Hale?" she asked nervously. "You—you could help me get them."

They were soon back—the stark coldness of that shut-up room was not a thing to linger in.

"My!" said Mrs. Peters, dropping the things on the table and hurrying to the stove.

Mrs. Hale stood examining the clothes the woman who was being detained   120
in town had said she wanted.

"Wright was close!"° she exclaimed, holding up a shabby black skirt that bore the marks of much making over. "I think maybe that's why she kept so much to herself. I s'pose she felt she couldn't do her part; and then, you don't enjoy things when you feel shabby. She used to wear pretty clothes and be lively—when she was Minnie Foster, one of the town girls, singing in the choir. But that—oh, that was twenty years ago."

With a carefulness in which there was something tender, she folded the shabby clothes and piled them at one corner of the table. She looked up at Mrs. Peters, and there was something in the other woman's look that irritated her.

"She don't care," she said to herself. "Much difference it makes to her whether Minnie Foster had pretty clothes when she was a girl."

Then she looked again, and she wasn't so sure; in fact, she hadn't at any time been perfectly sure about Mrs. Peters. She had that shrinking manner, and yet her eyes looked as if they could see a long way into things.

close: that is, frugal, tight-fisted.

"This all you was to take in?" asked Mrs. Hale.

"No," said the sheriff's wife; "she said she wanted an apron. Funny thing to want," she ventured in her nervous little way, "for there's not much to get you dirty in jail, goodness knows. But I suppose just to make her feel more natural. If you're used to wearing an apron—. She said they were in the bottom drawer of this cupboard. Yes—here they are. And then her little shawl that always hung on the stair door."

She took the small gray shawl from behind the door leading upstairs, and stood a minute looking at it.

Suddenly Mrs. Hale took a quick step toward the other woman.

"Mrs. Peters!"

"Yes, Mrs. Hale?"   130

"Do you think she—did it?"

A frightened look blurred the other thing in Mrs. Peters' eyes.

"Oh, I don't know," she said, in a voice that seemed to shrink away from the subject.

"Well, I don't think she did," affirmed Mrs. Hale stoutly. "Asking for an apron, and her little shawl. Worryin' about her fruit."

"Mr. Peters says—." Footsteps were heard in the room above; she stopped, looked up, then went on in a lowered voice: "Mr. Peters says—it looks bad for her. Mr. Henderson is awful sarcastic in a speech, and he's going to make fun of her saying she didn't—wake up."

For a moment Mrs. Hale had no answer. Then, "Well, I guess John Wright   135 didn't wake up—when they was slippin' that rope under his neck," she muttered.

"No, it's *strange*," breathed Mrs. Peters. "They think it was such a—funny way to kill a man."

She began to laugh; at sound of the laugh, abruptly stopped.

"That's just what Mr. Hale said," said Mrs. Hale, in a resolutely natural voice. "There was a gun in the house. He says that's what he can't understand."

"Mr. Henderson said, coming out, that what was needed for the case was a motive. Something to show anger—or sudden feeling."

"Well, I don't see any signs of anger around here," said Mrs. Hale. "I don't—"   140

She stopped. It was as if her mind tripped on something. Her eye was caught by a dish-towel in the middle of the kitchen table. Slowly she moved toward the table. One half of it was wiped clean, the other half messy. Her eyes made a slow, almost unwilling turn to the bucket of sugar and the half empty bag beside it. Things begun—and not finished.

After a moment she stepped back, and said, in that manner of releasing herself:

"Wonder how they're finding things upstairs? I hope she had it a little more red up° up there. You know,"—she paused, and feeling gathered,—"it seems kind of *sneaking*: locking her up in town and coming out here to get her own house to turn against her!"

"But, Mrs. Hale," said the sheriff's wife, "the law is the law."

"I s'pose 'tis," answered Mrs. Hale shortly.   145

She turned to the stove, saying something about that fire not being much

red up: neat.

to brag of. She worked with it a minute, and when she straightened up she said aggressively:

"The law is the law—and a bad stove is a bad stove. How'd you like to cook on this?"—pointing with the poker to the broken lining. She opened the oven door and started to express her opinion of the oven; but she was swept into her own thoughts, thinking of what it would mean, year after year, to have that stove to wrestle with. The thought of Minnie Foster trying to bake in that oven—and the thought of her never going over to see Minnie Foster—.

She was startled by hearing Mrs. Peters say: "A person gets discouraged—and loses heart."

The sheriff's wife had looked from the stove to the sink—to the pail of water which had been carried in from outside. The two women stood there silent, above them the footsteps of the men who were looking for evidence against the woman who had worked in that kitchen. That look of seeing into things, of seeing through a thing to something else, was in the eyes of the sheriff's wife now. When Mrs. Hale next spoke to her, it was gently:

"Better loosen up your things, Mrs. Peters. We'll not feel them when we go out." 150

Mrs. Peters went to the back of the room to hang up the fur tippet she was wearing. A moment later she exclaimed, "Why, she was piecing a quilt," and held up a large sewing basket piled high with quilt pieces.

Mrs. Hale spread some of the blocks on the table.

"It's log-cabin pattern," she said, putting several of them together. "Pretty, isn't it?"

They were so engaged with the quilt that they did not hear the footsteps on the stairs. Just as the stair door opened Mrs. Hale was saying:

"Do you suppose she was going to quilt it or just knot it?" 155

The sheriff threw up his hands.

"They wonder whether she was going to quilt it or just knot it!"

There was a laugh for the ways of women, a warming of hands over the stove, and then the county attorney said briskly:

"Well, let's go right out to the barn and get that cleared up."

"I don't see as there's anything so strange," Mrs. Hale said resentfully, after 160 the outside door had closed on the three men—"our taking up our time with little things while we're waiting for them to get the evidence. I don't see as it's anything to laugh about."

"Of course they've got awful important things on their minds," said the sheriff's wife apologetically.

They returned to an inspection of the block for the quilt. Mrs. Hale was looking at the fine, even sewing, and preoccupied with thoughts of the woman who had done that sewing, when she heard the sheriff's wife say, in a queer tone:

"Why, look at this one."

She turned to take the block held out to her.

"The sewing," said Mrs. Peters, in a troubled way. "All the rest of them 165 have been so nice and even—but—this one. Why, it looks as if she didn't know what she was about!"

Their eyes met—something flashed to life, passed between them; then, as if with an effort, they seemed to pull away from each other. A moment Mrs. Hale sat there, her hands folded over that sewing which was so unlike all the rest of the sewing. Then she had pulled a knot and drawn the threads.

"Oh, what are you doing, Mrs. Hale?" asked the sheriff's wife, startled.

"Just pulling out a stitch or two that's not sewed very good," said Mrs. Hale mildly.

"I don't think we ought to touch things," Mrs. Peters said, a little helplessly.

"I'll just finish up this end," answered Mrs. Hale, still in that mild, matter-of-fact fashion.   170

She threaded a needle and started to replace bad sewing with good. For a little while she sewed in silence. Then, in that thin, timid voice, she heard:

"Mrs. Hale!"

"Yes, Mrs. Peters?"

"What do you suppose she was so—nervous about?"

"Oh, *I* don't know," said Mrs. Hale, as if dismissing a thing not important   175
enough to spend much time on. "I don't know as she was—nervous. I sew awful queer sometimes when I'm just tired."

She cut a thread, and out of the corner of her eye looked up at Mrs. Peters. The small, lean face of the sheriff's wife seemed to have tightened up. Her eyes had that look of peering into something. But next moment she moved, and said in her thin, indecisive way:

"Well, I must get those clothes wrapped. They may be through sooner than we think. I wonder where I could find a piece of paper—and string."

"In that cupboard, maybe," suggested Mrs. Hale, after a glance around.

One piece of the crazy sewing remained unripped. Mrs. Peters' back turned, Martha Hale now scrutinized that piece, compared it with the dainty, accurate sewing of the other blocks. The difference was startling. Holding this block made her feel queer, as if the distracted thoughts of the woman who had perhaps turned to it to try and quiet herself were communicating themselves to her.

Mrs. Peters' voice roused her.   180

"Here's a bird-cage," she said. "Did she have a bird, Mrs. Hale?"

"Why, I don't know whether she did or not." She turned to look at the cage Mrs. Peters was holding up. "I've not been here in so long." She sighed. "There was a man round last year selling canaries cheap—but I don't know as she took one. Maybe she did. She used to sing real pretty herself."

Mrs. Peters looked around the kitchen.

"Seems kind of funny to think of a bird here." She half laughed—an attempt to put up a barrier. "But she must have had one—or why would she have a cage? I wonder what happened to it."

"I suppose maybe the cat got it," suggested Mrs. Hale, resuming her sewing.   185

"No; she didn't have a cat. She's got that feeling some people have about cats—being afraid of them. When they brought her to our house yesterday, my cat got in the room, and she was real upset and asked me to take it out."

"My sister Bessie was like that," laughed Mrs. Hale.

The sheriff's wife did not reply. The silence made Mrs. Hale turn round. Mrs. Peters was examining the bird-cage.

"Look at this door," she said slowly. "It's broke. One hinge has been pulled apart."

Mrs. Hale came nearer.

"Looks as if someone must have been—rough with it."

Again their eyes met—startled, questioning, apprehensive. For a moment neither spoke nor stirred. Then Mrs. Hale, turning away, said brusquely:

"If they're going to find any evidence, I wish they'd be about it. I don't like this place."

"But I'm awful glad you came with me, Mrs. Hale." Mrs. Peters put the bird-cage on the table and sat down. "It would be lonesome for me—sitting here alone."

"Yes, it would, wouldn't it?" agreed Mrs. Hale, a certain determined natural- 195 ness in her voice. She had picked up the sewing, but now it dropped in her lap, and she murmured in a different voice: "But I tell you what I *do* wish, Mrs. Peters. I wish I had come over sometimes when she was here. I wish—I had."

"But of course you were awful busy, Mrs. Hale. Your house—and your children."

"I could've come," retorted Mrs. Hale shortly. "I stayed away because it weren't cheerful—and that's why I ought to have come. I"—she looked around—"I've never liked this place. Maybe because it's down in a hollow and you don't see the road. I don't know what it is, but it's a lonesome place, and always was. I wish I had come over to see Minnie Foster sometimes. I can see now—" She did not put it into words.

"Well, you mustn't reproach yourself," counseled Mrs. Peters. "Somehow, we just don't see how it is with other folks till—something comes up."

"Not having children makes less work," mused Mrs. Hale, after a silence, "but it makes a quiet house—and Wright out to work all day—and no company when he did come in. Did you know John Wright, Mrs. Peters?"

"Not to know him. I've seen him in town. They say he was a good man." 200

"Yes—good," conceded John Wright's neighbor grimly. "He didn't drink, and kept his word as well as most, I guess, and paid his debts. But he was a hard man, Mrs. Peters. Just to pass the time of day with him—." She stopped, shivered a little. "Like a raw wind that gets to the bone." Her eye fell upon the cage on the table before her, and she added, almost bitterly: "I should think she would've wanted a bird!"

Suddenly she leaned forward, looking intently at the cage. "But what do you s'pose went wrong with it?"

"I don't know," returned Mrs. Peters; "unless it got sick and died."

But after she said it she reached over and swung the broken door. Both women watched it as if somehow held by it.

"You didn't know—her?" Mrs. Hale asked, a gentler note in her voice. 205

"Not till they brought her yesterday," said the sheriff's wife.

"She—come to think of it, she was kind of like a bird herself. Real sweet and pretty, but kind of timid and—fluttery. How—she—did—change."

That held her for a long time. Finally, as if struck with a happy thought and relieved to get back to everyday things, she exclaimed:

"Tell you what, Mrs. Peters, why don't you take the quilt in with you? It might take up her mind."

"Why, I think that's a real nice idea, Mrs. Hale," agreed the sheriff's wife, 210 as if she too were glad to come into the atmosphere of a simple kindness. "There couldn't possibly be any objection to that, could there? Now, just what will I take? I wonder if her patches are in here—and her things?"

They turned to the sewing basket.

"Here's some red," said Mrs. Hale, bringing out a roll of cloth. Underneath that was a box. "Here, maybe her scissors are in here—and her things." She held it up. "What a pretty box! I'll warrant that was something she had a long time ago—when she was a girl."

She held it in her hand a moment; then, with a little sigh, opened it.

Instantly her hand went to her nose.

"Why—!"

Mrs. Peters drew nearer—then turned away.

"There's something wrapped up in this piece of silk," faltered Mrs. Hale.

"This isn't her scissors," said Mrs. Peters, in a shrinking voice.

Her hand not steady, Mrs. Hale raised the piece of silk. "Oh, Mrs. Peters!" she cried. "It's—"

Mrs. Peters bent closer.

"It's the bird," she whispered.

"But, Mrs. Peters!" cried Mrs. Hale. "*Look* at it! Its *neck*—look at its neck! It's all—other side *to*."

She held the box away from her.

The sheriff's wife again bent closer.

"Somebody wrung its neck," said she, in a voice that was slow and deep.

And then again the eyes of the two women met—this time clung together in a look of dawning comprehension, of growing horror. Mrs. Peters looked from the dead bird to the broken door of the cage. Again their eyes met. And just then there was a sound at the outside door.

Mrs. Hale slipped the box under the quilt pieces in the basket, and sank into the chair before it. Mrs. Peters stood holding to the table. The county attorney and the sheriff came in from outside.

"Well, ladies," said the county attorney, as one turning from serious things to little pleasantries, "have you decided whether she was going to quilt it or knot it?"

"We think," began the sheriff's wife in a flurried voice, "that she was going to—knot it."

He was too preoccupied to notice the change that came in her voice on that last.

"Well, that's very interesting, I'm sure," he said tolerantly. "He caught sight of the bird-cage. "Has the bird flown?"

"We think the cat got it," said Mrs. Hale in a voice curiously even.

He was walking up and down, as if thinking something out.

"Is there a cat?" he asked absently.

Mrs. Hale shot a look up at the sheriff's wife.

"Well, not *now*," said Mrs. Peters. "They're superstitious, you know; they leave."

She sank into her chair.

The county attorney did not heed her. "No sign at all of anyone having come in from the outside," he said to Peters, in the manner of continuing an interrupted conversation. "Their own rope. Now let's go upstairs again and go

215

220

225

230

235

over it, piece by piece. It would have to have been someone who knew just the—"

The stair door closed behind them and their voices were lost.

The two women sat motionless, not looking at each other, but as if peering   240
into something and at the same time holding back. When they spoke now it was
as if they were afraid of what they were saying, but as if they could not help
saying it.

"She liked the bird," said Martha Hale, low and slowly. "She was going to
bury it in that pretty box."

"When I was a girl," said Mrs. Peters, under her breath, "my kitten—there
was a boy took a hatchet, and before my eyes—before I could get there—" She
covered her face an instant. "If they hadn't held me back I would have"—she
caught herself, looked upstairs where footsteps were heard, and finished weakly—
"hurt him."

Then they sat without speaking or moving.

"I wonder how it would seem," Mrs. Hale at last began, as if feeling her
way over strange ground—"never to have had any children around?" Her eyes
made a slow sweep of the kitchen, as if seeing what that kitchen had meant through
all the years. "No, Wright wouldn't like the bird," she said after that—"a thing
that sang. She used to sing. He killed that too." Her voice tightened.

Mrs. Peters moved uneasily.   245

"Of course we don't know who killed the bird."

"I knew John Wright," was Mrs. Hale's answer.

"It was an awful thing was done in this house that night, Mrs. Hale," said
the sheriff's wife. "Killing a man while he slept—slipping a thing round his neck
that choked the life out of him."

Mrs. Hale's hand went out to the bird cage.

"His neck. Choked the life out of him."   250

"We don't *know* who killed him," whispered Mrs. Peters wildly. "We don't
know."

Mrs. Hale had not moved. "If there had been years and years of—nothing,
then a bird to sing to you, it would be awful—still—after the bird was still."

It was as if something within her not herself had spoken, and it found in
Mrs. Peters something she did not know as herself.

"I know what stillness is," she said, in a queer, monotonous voice. "When
we homesteaded in Dakota, and my first baby died—after he was two years old—
and me with no other then—"

Mrs. Hale stirred.   255

"How soon do you suppose they'll be through looking for the evidence?"

"I know what stillness is," repeated Mrs. Peters, in just that same way. Then
she too pulled back. "The law has got to punish crime, Mrs. Hale," she said in
her tight little way.

"I wish you'd seen Minnie Foster," was the answer, "when she wore a white
dress with blue ribbons, and stood up there in the choir and sang."

The picture of that girl, the fact that she had lived neighbor to that girl for
twenty years, and had let her die for lack of life, was suddenly more than she
could bear.

"Oh, I *wish* I'd come over here once in a while!" she cried. "That was a   260
crime! Who's going to punish that?"

"We mustn't take on," said Mrs. Peters, with a frightened look toward the stairs.

"I might 'a' *known* she needed help! I tell you, it's *queer*, Mrs. Peters. We live close together, and we live far apart. We all go through the same things—it's all just a different kind of the same thing! If it weren't—why do you and I *understand?* Why do we *know*—what we know this minute?"

She dashed her hand across her eyes. Then, seeing the jar of fruit on the table, she reached for it and choked out:

"If I was you I wouldn't *tell* her her fruit was gone! Tell her it *ain't*. Tell her it's all right—all of it. Here—take this in to prove it to her! She—she may never know whether it was broke or not."

She turned away.   265

Mrs. Peters reached out for the bottle of fruit as if she were glad to take it—as if touching a familiar thing, having something to do, could keep her from something else. She got up, looked about for something to wrap the fruit in, took a petticoat from the pile of clothes she had brought from the front room, and nervously started winding that round the bottle.

"My!" she began, in a high, false voice, "it's a good thing the men couldn't hear us! Getting all stirred up over a little thing like a—dead canary." She hurried over that. "As if that could have anything to do with—with— My, wouldn't they *laugh?*"

Footsteps were heard on the stairs.

"Maybe they would," muttered Mrs. Hale—"maybe they wouldn't."

"No, Peters," said the county attorney incisively; "it's all perfectly clear, except   270
the reason for doing it. But you know juries when it comes to women. If there was some definite thing—something to show. Something to make a story about. A thing that would connect up with this clumsy way of doing it."

In a covert way Mrs. Hale looked at Mrs. Peters. Mrs. Peters was looking at her. Quickly they looked away from each other. The outer door opened and Mr. Hale came in.

"I've got the team round now," he said. "Pretty cold out there."

"I'm going to stay here awhile by myself," the county attorney suddenly announced. "You can send Frank out for me, can't you?" he asked the sheriff. "I want to go over everything. I'm not satisfied we can't do better."

Again, for one brief moment, the two women's eyes found one another.

The sheriff came up to the table.   275

"Did you want to see what Mrs. Peters was going to take in?"

The county attorney picked up the apron. He laughed.

"Oh, I guess they're not very dangerous things the ladies have picked out."

Mrs. Hale's hand was on the sewing basket in which the box was concealed. She felt that she ought to take her hand off the basket. She did not seem able to. He picked up one of the quilt blocks which she had piled on to cover the box. Her eyes felt like fire. She had a feeling that if he took up the basket she would snatch it from him.

But he did not take it up. With another little laugh, he turned away, saying: 280

"No; Mrs. Peters doesn't need supervising. For that matter, a sheriff's wife is married to the law. Ever think of it that way, Mrs. Peters?"

Mrs. Peters was standing beside the table. Mrs. Hale shot a look up at her;

but she could not see her face. Mrs. Peters had turned away. When she spoke, her voice was muffled.

"Not—just that way," she said.

"Married to the law!" chuckled Mrs. Peters' husband. He moved toward the door into the front room, and said to the county attorney:

"I just want you to come in here a minute, George. We ought to take a look at these windows."   285

"Oh—windows," said the county attorney scoffingly.

"We'll be right out, Mr. Hale," said the sheriff to the farmer, who was still waiting by the door.

Hale went to look after the horses. The sheriff followed the county attorney into the other room. Again—for one final moment—the two women were alone in that kitchen.

Martha Hale sprang up, her hands tight together, looking at that other woman, with whom it rested. At first she could not see her eyes, for the sheriff's wife had not turned back since she turned away at that suggestion of being married to the law. But now Mrs. Hale made her turn back. Her eyes made her turn back. Slowly, unwillingly, Mrs. Peters turned her head until her eyes met the eyes of the other woman. There was a moment when they held each other in a steady, burning look in which there was no evasion nor flinching. Then Martha Hale's eyes pointed the way to the basket in which was hidden the thing that would make certain the conviction of the other woman—that woman who was not there and yet who had been there with them all through that hour.

For a moment Mrs. Peters did not move. And then she did it. With a rush   290
forward, she threw back the quilt pieces, got the box, tried to put it in her handbag. It was too big. Desperately she opened it, started to take the bird out. But there she broke—she could not touch the bird. She stood there helpless, foolish.

There was the sound of a knob turning in the inner door. Martha Hale snatched the box from the sheriff's wife, and got it in the pocket of her big coat just as the sheriff and the county attorney came back into the kitchen.

"Well, Henry," said the county attorney facetiously, "at least we found out that she was not going to quilt it. She was going to—what is it you call it, ladies?"

Mrs. Hale's hand was against the pocket of her coat.

"We call it—knot it, Mr. Henderson."

QUESTIONS

1. From the materials in the story, describe the character of Minnie Wright in a brief essay of 3 to 4 paragraphs.

2. Who is the major character in the story itself? That is, on whom does the story focus as it unfolds?

3. Describe the differences between Mrs. Hale and Mrs. Peters, in terms of their present status, their backgrounds, and their comparative strengths of character.

4. Why do the two ladies not voice their conclusions about the identity of the murderer? How does Glaspell show that they both know the identity of the murderer, the reasons, and the method? Why do they both assent to the rapid "cover-up" at the story's conclusion?

ALICE WALKER   (b. 1944)

Everyday Use   *1973*

for your grandmama

I will wait for her in the yard that Maggie and I made so clean and wavy yesterday afternoon. A yard like this is more comfortable than most people know. It is not just a yard. It is like an extended living room. When the hard clay is swept clean as a floor and the fine sand around the edges lined with tiny, irregular grooves, anyone can come and sit and look up into the elm tree and wait for the breezes that never come inside the house.

Maggie will be nervous until after her sister goes: she will stand hopelessly in corners, homely and ashamed of the burn scars down her arms and legs, eying her sister with a mixture of envy and awe. She thinks her sister has held life always in the palm of one hand, that "no" is a word the world never learned to say to her.

You've no doubt seen those TV shows° where the child who has "made it" is confronted, as a surprise, by her own mother and father, tottering in weakly from backstage. (A pleasant surprise, of course: What would they do if parent and child came on the show only to curse out and insult each other?) On TV mother and child embrace and smile into each other's faces. Sometimes the mother and father weep, the child wraps them in her arms and leans across the table to tell how she would not have made it without their help. I have seen these programs.

Sometimes I dream a dream in which Dee and I are suddenly brought together on a TV program of this sort. Out of a dark and soft-seated limousine I am ushered into a bright room filled with many people. There I meet a smiling, gray, sporty man like Johnny Carson who shakes my hand and tells me what a fine girl I have. Then we are on the stage and Dee is embracing me with tears in her eyes. She pins on my dress a large orchid, even though she has told me once that she thinks orchids are tacky flowers.

In real life I am a large, big-boned woman with rough, man-working hands. In the winter I wear flannel nightgowns to bed and overalls during the day. I can kill and clean a hog as mercilessly as a man. My fat keeps me hot in zero weather. I can work outside all day, breaking ice to get water for washing; I can eat pork liver cooked over the open fire minutes after it comes steaming from the hog. One winter I knocked a bull calf straight in the brain between the eyes with a sledge hammer and had the meat hung up to chill before nightfall. But of course all this does not show on television. I am the way my daughter would want me to be: a hundred pounds lighter, my skin like an uncooked barley pancake. My hair glistens in the hot bright lights. Johnny Carson has much to do to keep up with my quick and witty tongue. 5

But that is a mistake. I know even before I wake up. Who ever knew a

---

°*TV shows*: In the early days of television, a popular show was "This Is Your Life," which the narrator describes exactly here.

Johnson with a quick tongue? Who can even imagine me looking a strange white man in the eye? It seems to me I have talked to them always with one foot raised in flight, with my head turned in whichever way is farthest from them. Dee, though. She would always look anyone in the eye. Hesitation was no part of her nature.

"How do I look, Mama?" Maggie says, showing just enough of her thin body enveloped in pink skirt and red blouse for me to know she's there, almost hidden by the door.

"Come out into the yard," I say.

Have you ever seen a lame animal, perhaps a dog run over by some careless person rich enough to own a car, sidle up to someone who is ignorant enough to be kind to him? That is the way my Maggie walks. She has been like this, chin on chest, eyes on ground, feet in shuffle, ever since the fire that burned the other house to the ground.

Dee is lighter than Maggie, with nicer hair and a fuller figure. She's a woman now, though sometimes I forget. How long ago was it that the other house burned? Ten, twelve years? Sometimes I can still hear the flames and feel Maggie's arms sticking to me, her hair smoking and her dress falling off her in little black papery flakes. Her eyes seemed stretched open, blazed open by the flames reflected in them. And Dee. I see her standing off under the sweet gum tree she used to dig gum out of; a look of concentration on her face as she watched the last dingy gray board of the house fall in toward the red-hot brick chimney. Why don't you do a dance around the ashes? I'd wanted to ask her. She had hated the house that much.

I used to think she hated Maggie, too. But that was before we raised the money, the church and me, to send her to Augusta° to school. She used to read to us without pity; forcing words, lies, other folks' habits, whole lives upon us two, sitting trapped and ignorant underneath her voice. She washed us in a river of make-believe, burned us with a lot of knowledge we didn't necessarily need to know. Pressed us to her with the serious way she read, to shove us away at just the moment, like dimwits, we seemed about to understand.

Dee wanted nice things. A yellow organdy dress to wear to her graduation from high school; black pumps to match a green suit she'd made from an old suit somebody gave me. She was determined to stare down any disaster in her efforts. Her eyelids would not flicker for minutes at a time. Often I fought off the temptation to shake her. At sixteen she had a style of her own: and knew what style was.

I never had an education myself. After second grade the school was closed down. Don't ask me why: in 1927 colored asked fewer questions than they do now. Sometimes Maggie reads to me. She stumbles along good-naturedly, but can't see well. She knows she is not bright. Like good looks and money, quickness passed her by. She will marry John Thomas (who has mossy teeth in an earnest face) and then I'll be free to sit here and I guess just sing church songs to myself. Although I never was a good singer. Never could carry a tune. I was always better

Augusta: City in eastern Georgia, the location of Paine College.

at a man's job. I used to love to milk till I was hooked in the side° in '49. Cows are soothing and slow and don't bother you, unless you try to milk them the wrong way.

I have deliberately turned my back on the house. It is three rooms, just like the one that burned, except the roof is tin; they don't make shingle roofs any more. There are no real windows, just some holes cut in the sides, like the portholes on a ship, but not round and not square, with rawhide holding the shutters up on the outside. This house is in a pasture, too, like the other one. No doubt when Dee sees it she will want to tear it down. She wrote me once that no matter where we "choose" to live, she will manage to come see us. But she will never bring her friends. Maggie and I thought about this and Maggie asked me, "Mama, when did Dee ever *have* any friends?"

She had a few. Furtive boys in pink shirts hanging about on washday after   15
school. Nervous girls who never laughed. Impressed with her they worshiped the well-turned phrase, the cute shape, the scalding humor that erupted like bubbles in lye. She read to them.

When she was courting Jimmy T she didn't have much time to pay to us, but turned all her faultfinding power on him. He *flew* to marry a cheap city girl from a family of ignorant flashy people. She hardly had time to recompose herself.

When she comes I will meet—but there they are!

Maggie attempts to make a dash for the house, in her shuffling way, but I stay her with my hand. "Come back here," I say. And she stops and tries to dig a well in the sand with her toe.

It is hard to see them clearly through the strong sun. But even the first glimpse of leg out of the car tells me it is Dee. Her feet were always neat-looking, as if God himself had shaped them with a certain style. From the other side of the car comes a short, stocky man. Hair is all over his head a foot long and hanging from his chin like a kinky mule tail. I hear Maggie suck in her breath. "Uhnnnh," is what it sounds like. Like when you see the wriggling end of a snake just in front of your foot on the road. "Uhnnnh."

Dee next. A dress down to the ground, in this hot weather. A dress so loud   20
it hurts my eyes. There are yellows and oranges enough to throw back the light of the sun. I feel my whole face warming from the heat waves it throws out. Earrings gold, too, and hanging down to her shoulders. Bracelets dangling and making noises when she moves her arm up to shake the folds of the dress out of her armpits. The dress is loose and flows, and as she walks closer, I like it. I hear Maggie go "Uhnnnh" again. It is her sister's hair. It stands straight up like the wool on a sheep. It is black as night and around the edges are two long pigtails that rope about like small lizards disappearing behind her ears.

"Wa-su-zo-Tean-o!"° she says, coming on in that gliding way the dress makes her move. The short stocky fellow with the hair to his navel is all grinning and he follows up with "Asalamalakim,° my mother and my sister!" He moves to hug

---

hooked in the side: Kicked by a cow.
Wa-su-zo-Tean-o: A greeting used by American Black Muslims.
Asalamalakim: A Muslim salutation meaning "Peace be with you."

Maggie but she falls back, right up against the back of my chair. I feel her trembling there and when I look up I see the perspiration falling off her chin.

"Don't get up," says Dee. Since I am stout it takes something of a push. You can see me trying to move a second or two before I make it. She turns, showing white heels through her sandals, and goes back to the car. Out she peeks next with a Polaroid. She stoops down quickly and lines up picture after picture of me sitting there in front of the house with Maggie cowering behind me. She never takes a shot without making sure the house is included. When a cow comes nibbling around the edge of the yard she snaps it and me and Maggie *and* the house. Then she puts the Polaroid in the back seat of the car, and comes up and kisses me on the forehead.

Meanwhile Asalamalakim is going through motions with Maggie's hand. Maggie's hand is as limp as a fish, and probably as cold, despite the sweat, and she keeps trying to pull it back. It looks like Asalamalakim wants to shake hands but wants to do it fancy. Or maybe he don't know how people shake hands. Anyhow, he soon gives up on Maggie.

"Well," I say. "Dee."

"No, Mama," she says. "Not 'Dee,' Wangero Leewanika Kemanjo!"   25

"What happened to 'Dee'?" I wanted to know.

"She's dead," Wangero said. "I couldn't bear it any longer, being named after the people who oppress me."

"You know as well as me you was named after your aunt Dicie," I said. Dicie is my sister. She named Dee. We called her "Big Dee" after Dee was born.

"But who was *she* named after?" asked Wangero.

"I guess after Grandma Dee," I said.   30

"And who was she named after?" asked Wangero.

"Her mother," I said, and saw Wangero was getting tired. "That's about as far back as I can trace it," I said. Though, in fact, I probably could have carried it back beyond the Civil War through the branches.

"Well," said Asalamalakim, "there you are."

"Uhnnnh," I heard Maggie say.

"There I was not," I said, "before 'Dicie' cropped up in our family, so why   35 should I try to trace it that far back?"

He just stood there grinning, looking down on me like somebody inspecting a Model A car.° Every once in a while he and Wangero sent eye signals over my head.

"How do you pronounce this name?" I asked.

"You don't have to call me by it if you don't want to," said Wangero.

"Why shouldn't I?" I asked. "If that's what you want us to call you, we'll call you."

"I know it might sound awkward at first," said Wangero.   40

"I'll get used to it," I said. "Ream it out again."

Well, soon we got the name out of the way. Asalamalakim had a name twice as long and three times as hard. After I tripped over it two or three times he told

---

Model A car: The Ford car that replaced the Model T in 1930. The Model A was almost proverbial for its quality and durability.

me to just call him Hakim-a-barber. I wanted to ask him was he a barber, but I didn't really think he was, so I didn't ask.

"You must belong to those beef-cattle peoples down the road," I said. They said "Asalamalakim" when they met you, too, but they didn't shake hands. Always too busy: feeding the cattle, fixing the fences, putting up salt-lick shelters,° throwing down hay. When the white folks poisoned some of the herd the men stayed up all night with rifles in their hands. I walked a mile and a half just to see the sight.

Hakim-a-barber said, "I accept some of their doctrines, but farming and raising cattle is not my style." (They didn't tell me, and I didn't ask, whether Wangero (Dee) had really gone and married him.)

We sat down to eat and right away he said he didn't eat collards and pork   45 was unclean. Wangero, though, went on through the chitlins and corn bread, the greens and everything else. She talked a blue streak over the sweet potatoes. Everything delighted her. Even the fact that we still used the benches her daddy made for the table when we couldn't afford to buy chairs.

"Oh, Mama!" she cried. Then turned to Hakim-a-barber. "I never knew how lovely these benches are. You can feel the rump prints," she said, running her hands underneath her and along the bench. Then she gave a sigh and her hand closed over Grandma Dee's butter dish. "That's it!" she said. "I knew there was something I wanted to ask you if I could have." She jumped up from the table and went over in the corner where the churn stood, the milk in it clabber° by now. She looked at the churn and looked at it.

"This churn top is what I need," she said. "Didn't Uncle Buddy whittle it out of a tree you all used to have?"

"Yes," I said.

"Uh huh," she said happily. "And I want the dasher, too."

"Uncle Buddy whittle that, too?" asked the barber.   50

Dee (Wangero) looked up at me.

"Aunt Dee's first husband whittled the dash," said Maggie so low you almost couldn't hear her. "His name was Henry, but they called him Stash."

"Maggie's brain is like an elephant's," Wangero said, laughing. "I can use the churn top as a centerpiece for the alcove table," she said, sliding a plate over the churn, "and I'll think of something artistic to do with the dasher."

When she finished wrapping the dasher the handle stuck out. I took it for a moment in my hands. You didn't even have to look close to see where hands pushing the dasher up and down to make butter had left a kind of sink in the wood. In fact, there were a lot of small sinks; you could see where thumbs and fingers had sunk into the wood. It was beautiful light yellow wood, from a tree that grew in the yard where Big Dee and Stash had lived.

After dinner Dee (Wangero) went to the trunk at the foot of my bed and   55 started rifling through it. Maggie hung back in the kitchen over the dishpan. Out came Wangero with two quilts. They had been pieced by Grandma Dee and then Big Dee and me had hung them on the quilt frames on the front porch and

----

salt-lick shelters: Shelters built to prevent rain from dissolving the large blocks of rock salt set up on poles for cattle.

clabber: curdled, turned sour.

quilted them. One was in the Lone Star pattern. The other was Walk Around the Mountain. In both of them were scraps of dresses Grandma Dee had worn fifty and more years ago. Bits and pieces of Grandpa Jarrell's Paisley shirts. And one teeny faded blue piece, about the size of a penny matchbox, that was from Great Grandpa Ezra's uniform that he wore in the Civil War.

"Mama," Wangero said sweet as a bird. "Can I have these old quilts?"

I heard something fall in the kitchen, and a minute later the kitchen door slammed.

"Why don't you take one or two of the others?" I asked. "These old things was just done by me and Big Dee from some tops your grandma pieced before she died."

"No," said Wangero. "I don't want those. They are stitched around the borders by machine."

"That'll make them last better," I said.   60

"That's not the point," said Wangero. "These are all pieces of dresses Grandma used to wear. She did all this stitching by hand. Imagine!" She held the quilts securely in her arms, stroking them.

"Some of the pieces, like those lavender ones, come from old clothes her mother handed down to her," I said, moving up to touch the quilts. Dee (Wangero) moved back just enough so that I couldn't reach the quilts. They already belonged to her.

"Imagine!" she breathed again, clutching them closely to her bosom.

"The truth is," I said, "I promised to give them quilts to Maggie, for when she marries John Thomas."

She gasped like a bee had stung her.   65

"Maggie can't appreciate these quilts!" she said. "She'd probably be backward enough to put them to everyday use."

"I reckon she would," I said. "God knows I been saving 'em for long enough with nobody using 'em. I hope she will!" I didn't want to bring up how I had offered Dee (Wangero) a quilt when she went away to college. Then she had told me they were old-fashioned, out of style.

"But they're *priceless*!" she was saying now, furiously; for she has a temper. "Maggie would put them on the bed and in five years they'd be in rags. Less than that!"

"She can always make some more," I said. "Maggie knows how to quilt."

Dee (Wangero) looked at me with hatred. "You just will not understand.   70
The point is these quilts, *these* quilts!"

"Well," I said, stumped. "What would *you* do with them?"

"Hang them," she said. As if that was the only thing you *could* do with quilts.

Maggie by now was standing in the door. I could almost hear the sound her feet made as they scraped over each other.

"She can have them, Mama," she said, like somebody used to never winning anything, or having anything reserved for her. "I can 'member Grandma Dee without the quilts."

I looked at her hard. She had filled her bottom lip with checkerberry snuff   75
and it gave her face a kind of dopey, hangdog look. It was Grandma Dee and Big Dee who taught her how to quilt herself. She stood there with her scarred hands hidden in the folds of her skirt. She looked at her sister with something

like fear but she wasn't mad at her. This was Maggie's portion. This was the way she knew God to work.

When I looked at her like that something hit me in the top of my head and ran down to the soles of my feet. Just like when I'm in church and the spirit of God touches me and I get happy and shout. I did something I never had done before: hugged Maggie to me, then dragged her on into the room, snatched the quilts out of Miss Wangero's hands and dumped them into Maggie's lap. Maggie just sat there on my bed with her mouth open.

"Take one or two of the others," I said to Dee.

But she turned without a word and went out to Hakim-a-barber.

"You just don't understand," she said, as Maggie and I came out to the car.

"What don't I understand?" I wanted to know.

"Your heritage," she said. And then she turned to Maggie, kissed her, and said, "You ought to try to make something of yourself, too, Maggie. It's really a new day for us. But from the way you and Mama still live you'd never know it."

She put on some sunglasses that hid everything above the tip of her nose and her chin.

Maggie smiled; maybe at the sunglasses. But a real smile, not scared. After we watched the car dust settle I asked Maggie to bring me a dip of snuff. And then the two of us sat there just enjoying, until it was time to go in the house and go to bed.

80

QUESTIONS

1. Describe the mixture of narration and dialogue in the story. Why do you think there is a great deal of dialogue from paragraph 24 to the end? On the basis of the use of narration and dialogue, what conclusions can you draw about the use that fiction makes of these elements?

2. Describe the narrator. Who is she? What is she like? Where and how does she live? What kind of life has she had? How does the story bring out her judgments about her two daughters?

3. Describe the narrator's daughters. How are they different physically and mentally? How have their lives been different?

4. Why did Dee change her name to "Wangero?" How is this change important, and how is it reflected in her attitude toward the family artifacts in the narrator's house?

5. Describe the importance of the phrase "everyday use" (paragraph 66). How does this phrase highlight the conflicting values in the story?

HOW TO WRITE A PRÉCIS OR ABRIDGMENT

A **précis** is a shortening, in your own words, of the text of a written work. The words *précis* and *precise* are closely related, and this connection is helpful in enabling an understanding of the nature of a précis—namely, a cutting down of a story into its *precise*, essential parts. The object is to make a short—**short**—encapsulation of the most significant details. Other words describing the précis are *abridgment, paraphrase, abstract, condensation,* and *epitome*. *Epitome* is particularly helpful as a description for a précis, for an epitome is a *cutting away,* so that only the important, most vital parts remain.

Uses of the Précis

Beyond the service of enabling you to follow a story with accuracy, the précis is important in study, research, and speaking and writing. One of the best ways to study any work is to write a précis of it, for by so doing you force yourself to grasp each of the parts. Précis writing can be used in note taking, preparation for exams, establishment and clarification of facts for any body of discourse, study for classroom discussion, and the reinforcement of things learned in the past. The object of a précis should not be to tell *everything*, but only as much as will give the highlights, so that any reader would be able to know the main points of the work about which the précis has been written.

When you do research, you must take notes on the material you find. Here the ability to shorten and paraphrase is essential, for it is impossible to reproduce everything in your notes. The better you are able to write a précis, the better will be your grasp of details for research.

In discussions, you will improve your arguments if you refer briefly but accurately to sections of the work being discussed. When you are writing an essay, particularly a longer one, it is necessary to support your conclusions by referring to events or facts in a particular work. In an argumentative or persuasive speech or essay, when you are trying to convince your listeners or readers, it is necessary to present a common understanding of the facts, so that you may eliminate possible objections that may be raised about your use of detail. Although you may sometimes need to condense an entire plot or epitomize an entire argument, most often you will refer to no more than parts of works, because your arguments will depend on a number of separate interpretations.

GUIDELINES FOR PRÉCIS WRITING

Below are guidelines to follow in the development of a précis.

1. **SELECTION.** Only essential details belong in a précis. For example, at the opening of the story "Everyday Use," Walker describes the narrator as a large woman who has lived a very hard life. We learn that she can kill animals for food and survival. She is fully capable of taking care of herself and her family. Writing about all these details, however, would

needlessly lengthen a précis of "Everyday Use." Instead, it is sufficient to say something like "Mrs. Johnson is a strong black woman," because this description gets at the vital facts about her.

Concentration on only essentials enables you to achieve the shortening required of a précis. Thus a 5,000-word story might be epitomized in 100, 200, or 400 words. Of course more details might be selected for inclusion in a longer précis than in shorter ones. Whatever the length of the final précis, however, selection of detail is to be based on the importance of the material in the work being considered.

2. ACCURACY. All details in a précis should be both correct and accurate. It is important to avoid factual misstatement, but also to avoid using words that might give a misleading impression of the original. In "The Necklace," for example, Mathilde cooperates with her husband for ten years to repay their 18,000-franc debt. In a précis it would be possible to say no more than that she "works" during this time. The word "works" is misleading, however, for it may be interpreted to mean that Mathilde gets paid for outside employment. In fact she does not. What Maupassant tells us is that Mathilde gives up her servant girl and then does all the heavy housework herself as a part of her general economizing in her *own* household, not in the houses of others.

In the same way, the need to condense long sections of a work necessarily produces the need not only for accuracy but also for comprehensiveness. In reference to Walker's "Everyday Use," there is a concluding dispute between the mother (the narrator) and her visiting daughter about the daughter's request for the two homemade quilts which contain patches of cloth that were contributed by important members of the family. The daughter wants them to adorn a wall, while the mother refuses on the grounds that she has promised them to her other daughter for "everyday use" during her approaching marriage. These details are complex, and they represent the climax of the major conflict in the story. In a précis about the episode, it is important not just to explain the claims but also to present language comprehensive enough to get at the conflict (without, however, resorting to a detailed analysis). Thus, accurate and comprehensive language might be the following: "Mrs. Johnson hesitates, having already promised the quilts to Maggie for use when she gets married. Though Maggie generously offers to give Wangero the quilts, Mrs. Johnson insists on her original promise. Wangero then objects, claiming that the quilts will be spoiled by 'everyday use' and that her mother misunderstands the value of the family heritage." This language explains the details accurately and comprehensively—the goal of précis writing.

3. DICTION. A précis should be an original essay, to be judged as original, and therefore it should be written in your own words, not those

of the work you are abridging. The best way to ensure original wording is to read the work, record the major things that happen, and then put the work out of sight during the writing process. That way the temptation to borrow words can be avoided.

However, if a number of words from the text find their ways into the précis even after you have tried conscientiously to be original, then it is important to put these words into quotation marks. As long as direct quotations are kept at a minimum, they are satisfactory. Too many quoted words, however, indicate that your précis is not original.

4. OBJECTIVITY. A précis should be scrupulously factual. Avoid explanatory or introductory material unless it is a true part of the story. As much effort should be made to *avoid* conclusions in a précis as is exerted to *include* them in other kinds of writing about literature. Here is a comparative example of what to do and what to avoid:

WHAT TO DO

Mrs. Johnson, a strong black woman living on her Southern farm with her younger daughter, Maggie, is waiting for a visit by her elder daughter, Dee. Dee is returning from her home in the city, and the mother has cleaned and swept the house and yard in order to make a good impression.

WHAT TO AVOID

Walker opens the story by building up the contrast that will soon be made apparent. Her narrator, Mrs. Johnson, is a plain, down-to-earth black woman who has worked hard all her life and whose basic value is her home and possessions. By contrast, she is waiting for a visit from her elder daughter, Dee, who has left home and lived a more sophisticated life in the city. Mrs. Johnson takes pride in her home, while Dee will regard the home and her mother's belongings as being of no more use than to be put on display.

The right-hand column contains a guiding topic sentence, to which the following sentences adhere. Such writing is commendable everywhere else, but not in a précis. The left-hand column is better writing *as a précis*, for it presents a selection of details only as they appear in the story, without introductory sentences, because in the story there are no such introductions.

5. SENTENCES. Because a précis should be concise and factual, it is tempting to write sentences that are like short bursts of machine-gun fire. Sentences of this kind are often called "choppy," or "bumpy." Here is an example of choppy sentences:

Dee comes in a car. She is dressed flamboyantly. She is with a strange man. He is short and bearded. She greets her mother and sister with foreign phrases. The man does, too. She immediately begins taking pictures. She snaps her mother with her sister in the background. She also takes pictures of wandering cows. She makes sure to get the house in all the shots. She kisses her mother then, on the forehead.

An entire essay consisting of sentences like these might make readers feel as though they actually have been machine-gunned. The problem is to include detail but also to remember to shape and organize your sentences. Here is a more acceptable set of sentences revised to contain the same information:

> When Dee comes, she is flamboyantly dressed, and gets out of the car with a strange, short, and bearded man. Both Dee and the man greet Mrs. Johnson and Maggie with foreign phrases. Before embracing her mother, Dee gets her Polaroid camera and takes pictures of her mother, her sister, and wandering cows, taking care to include the house in all her shots. Only then does she kiss her mother, and then only on the forehead.

This revision blends the shorter sentences together while still attempting to cover the essential details from the story. Starting the last sentence with "Only then," gets at Dee's ridiculous behavior without calling it ridiculous. Even though sentences in a précis must be almost rigidly factual, you should try to make them as graceful as possible.

WRITING A PRÉCIS

Your writing task is to condense the original work with the least possible distortion. Thus it is necessary to keep intact the arrangement and sequence of the original. For example, let us suppose that a work has a surprise ending, like that in "The Necklace." In a précis, it is important to keep the same order and withhold the conclusion until the very end. It is proper, however, to introduce essential details of circumstance, such as names and places, at the beginning of the précis, even though these details are not brought out immediately in the story. For example, Maupassant does not name Mathilde right away, and he never says that she is French, but a précis of "The Necklace" would be obscure without these details.

If your assignment is a very short précis, say 100 to 150 words, you might confine everything to only one paragraph. For a longer précis, the normal principle of devoting a separate paragraph to each topic applies. If each major division, episode, scene, action, or section of the story (or play) is considered a topic, then the précis may be divided into paragraphs devoted to each of the divisions.

Sometimes the author may number these divisions or scenes, or else may use spaces on the page to separate the parts or scenes of the work.

The paragraphing in the sample essay below recognizes such divisions, although for brevity some of the spaced sections are combined into one paragraph. The first two paragraphs, for example, include the first three spaced divisions, leading up to the daughter's return. Because "Everyday Use" contains a lengthy concluding section, however, the précis devotes three paragraphs to it, more or less confined to internal divisions of material in this section. Some works have no such divisions, but run continuously. For these you may need to create your own topics, such as (1) the events leading up to the main action, (2) the action itself, and (3) the consequences of the action. Or you may be able to determine sections for paragraphing according to the entrances or exits of some of the characters. Use your own judgment about paragraphing, and let the work itself be your guide.

SAMPLE ESSAY

A Précis of Alice Walker's "Everyday Use"*

[1] Mrs. Johnson, a strong black woman living on her Southern farm with her younger daughter, Maggie, is waiting for a visit by her elder daughter, Dee. Dee is returning from her home in the city, and the mother has cleaned and swept the house and yard in order to make a good impression.

[2] As she waits, she thinks of how independent Dee has been in the past, and of how self-confident and sophisticated she may be now. She contrasts Dee with Maggie, who is awkward, homely, and burn-scarred, and who has never left home. She also contrasts Dee with herself, thinking of Dee's many opportunities for self-improvement while she herself has never had any opportunities at all.

[3] When Dee comes, she is flamboyantly dressed, and gets out of the car with a strange, short, and bearded man. Both Dee and the man greet Mrs. Johnson and Maggie with foreign phrases. Before embracing her mother, Dee gets her Polaroid camera, and takes pictures of her mother, her sister, and wandering cows, taking care to get the house in all her shots. Only then does she kiss her mother, and then only on the forehead.

[4] Dee soon explains that she no longer wishes to be called "Dee," but that she has taken a new name, "Wangero Leewanika Kemanjo," which she regards as her own, and not the name that previous oppressors had given her. The man she is with has an incomprehensible name, which the family understands as "Hakim-a-Barber," which he has also taken in keeping with his present philosophy.

[5] Once greetings are past, the family sits down to eat. Wangero (Dee) is impressed with the artistic qualities of the homemade furniture, and asks for the family butter churn and dasher for display in her present home. After dinner, Wangero also asks for two homemade quilts that had been in the

* See p. 84 for this story.

family for years. Mrs. Johnson hesitates, having already promised the quilts to Maggie for use when she gets married. Though Maggie generously offers to give Wangero the quilts, Mrs. Johnson insists on her original promise. Wangero then objects, claiming that the quilts will be spoiled by "everyday use" and that her mother misunderstands the value of the family heritage. Wangero hurriedly leaves with Hakim, while Mrs. Johnson and Maggie remain together, enjoying their snuff, until bedtime.

Commentary on the Essay

This précis, about 400 words long, illustrates the selection of major actions and the omission of interesting but inessential detail. Thus, the phrase "a strong black woman" contains four words, and it condenses more than 150 words of detailed description in paragraph 5 of the story. By contrast, paragraph 3 of the sample essay deals with a relatively short paragraph of the story (paragraph 22). This amount of detail, however, is important because it indicates, right at Dee's entrance, her confused attitudes about her mother and the farm; the farm seems more to her like something for a scrapbook or for a wall than for real living. It is this confusion on Dee's part that underlies the major conflict of the story.

To demonstrate omissions, some materials that disclose things about Hakim's character and philosophy, to be found in paragraphs 43–45 of the story, are left out entirely from the précis, because they are not essential to the main characters—namely, the three women.

Each of the five paragraphs in the précis is devoted to comparable sections of "Everyday Use." Paragraphs 1 and 2 describe the story up to the appearance of Dee and her man. Paragraph 3 details Dee's activity at her entrance. Paragraph 4 treats the conversation and narrative from paragraphs 24–44 of the story. The last paragraph condenses the dinner and post-dinner scene, featuring Dee's requests to take away family heirlooms, including the vitally important quilts.

The basis in the précis for determining the content of paragraphs is not only fidelity to the narrative development of the story, but also unity of subject matter. Thus, paragraph 1 is unified by the speaker's expectations, while paragraph 2 is unified by her contrast of her two daughters and also her contrast of herself with her returning daughter. Each of the other paragraphs is similarly unified—paragraph 3 by Dee's photography, paragraph 4 by the use of new names, and paragraph 5 by the conflicting attitudes about the disposal of family heirlooms. In any précis, similar attempts should be made to unify paragraphs.

WRITING TOPICS FOR CHAPTER 2

1. Assuming that Sammy in "A & P" is speaking to a friend or at least to a sympathetic listener, and not to us as the readers, write an essay on his

conversational style. What evidence do you find in the story that his formal or written style may be different from his conversation? What does his speech indicate about his character?

2. Consider the action of "Everyday Use" from the standpoint of the visiting daughter, Wangero. How might she describe her mother's responses, say, if she were discussing it with Hakim-a-barber on the way back after the episodes of the story? You might wish to rewrite the story entirely as though Wangero were telling it.

3. Write an essay on the comparative competence of the women and the men in "A Jury of Her Peers." What might be expected from each group, and how completely does each group live up to these expectations? To what extent is there a role reversal in the story?

3

Plot and Structure

Fictional people or characters are derived from life, as are the things they do. These **actions** or **incidents,** occur in sequence, or in chronological order. Once we have established the narrative or sequential order, however, there is still more to be considered. This is **plot,** or the plan of development of the actions.

WHAT IS PLOT?

Without a plot, we do not have a story or drama. A plot is a plan or groundwork of human motivations, with the actions resulting from believable and realistic human responses. In a well-plotted work, nothing is irrelevant; everything is related. The British novelist E. M. Forster, in *Aspects of the Novel*, presents a memorable illustration of plot. As a bare minimum narration of actions in contrast to a story with a plot, he uses the following: "The king died, and then the queen died." This sentence describes a sequence, a chronological order, but it is no more. To have a plot, a sequence must be integrated with human motivation. Thus Forster's following sentence contains a plot: "The king died, and then the queen died of grief." Once the narrative introduces the operative element "of grief," which shows that one thing (grief over the king's death) produces or overcomes another (the normal human desire to live), there is a plot. Stories and plays take place in time or chronological order. Time is important not because one thing happens *after* another, but because one thing happens *because* of another. It is response, interaction, causation, and conflict that make a plot out of a simple series of actions.

Conflict

The most significant element, the essence, of plot is **conflict.** In conflict, human responses are brought out to their highest degree. In its most elemental form, a conflict is the opposition of two people. They may fight, argue, enlist help against each other, and otherwise carry on their opposition. Conflicts may also exist between larger groups, although in imaginative literature, conflicts between individuals are more identifiable and therefore more interesting. Conflict may also exist between an individual and larger forces, such as natural objects, ideas, modes of behavior, public opinion, and the like. The existence of difficult *choices* that a character must make may also be presented as a conflict, or **dilemma.** In addition, the conflict may occur not necessarily as direct opposition, but rather as contrasting ideas or values. In short, there are many ways to bring out a conflict in fictional works.

CONFLICT, DOUBT, TENSION, AND INTEREST.   The reason that conflict is the major ingredient in a plot is that once two forces are in opposition, there may be doubt about the outcome. The doubt, if the reader becomes interested and engaged with the characters, produces curiosity and also tension. The same concern is the lifeblood of athletic competition. For just a moment, consider which kind of football game is more interesting: (1) one in which the score goes back and forth and there is doubt about the outcome right up to the last second, or (2) one in which one of the teams gets so far ahead in the first quarter that there is no doubt about who will win. The interest of a highly contested game is also generated by a conflict in a story. The conflict should be a contest, an engagement between characters or forces of approximately equal strength. It should never be a "walkaway," "mismatch," "rout," or "laugher," as the terminology from the sports world goes. The reason is that unless there is doubt there is no tension, and unless there is tension there is no interest.

CONFLICT IN PLOT.   To see a plot in operation, let us build on Forster's description. Here is a bare plot for a story: "John and Jane meet, fall in love, and get married." This plot has no apparent conflict and therefore only minimal interest, and it probably would get very few readers. Let us, however, try the same essential narrative of "boy meets girl" and introduce some conflicting elements:

> John and Jane meet at school and fall in love. They go together for two years, and they plan to marry, but a problem arises. Jane wants to develop a career first, and after marriage she wants to be an equal contributor to

the family. John understands Jane's desire for a career, but he wants to marry first and let her continue her studies afterward in preparation for her goal. Jane believes that this solution will not work, insisting that it is a trap from which she will never escape. This conflict interrupts their plans, and they part in regret and anger. Going in different ways even though they still love each other, both marry other people and build separate lives and careers. Neither is completely happy even though they like and respect their spouses. Many years later, after children and grandchildren, they meet again. John is now a widower and Jane has divorced. Their earlier conflict no longer being a barrier, they marry and live successfully together. During their marriage, however, even their new happiness is tinged with regret and self-reproach because of their earlier conflict, their increasing age, and the lost years that they might have spent with each other.

Here we have a true plot, with a conflict that takes a number of shapes. The (1) initial difference in plans and hopes is resolved by (2) a parting of the characters, leading them to separate lives that are (3) not totally happy. The final marriage produces (4) not unqualified happiness, but a note of regret and (5) a sense of time lost that cannot be restored. It is the establishment of these contrasting or conflicting situations and responses that produces the interest our short-short story contains. The situation is lifelike; the conflict stems out of realistic values; the outcome is true to life. The imposition of the various conflicts and contrasts has made an interesting plot out of what could have been a common "boy meets girl" sequence.

THE STRUCTURE OF FICTION

Structure describes the arrangement and placement of materials within a narrative or drama. While *plot* describes the confict or conflicts, *structure* concerns the way in which the work is laid out and given form or shape to bring out the conflict. The word belongs to a whole family of common words that are concerned with spreading and ordering, including *instruct*, *construct*, *street*, *stratagem*, and, pleasantly, *streusel* (a pastry topping).

The study of structure in fiction is about the causes and reasons (*stratagem* here is the most helpful related word) behind matters such as placement, balance, recurring themes, juxtapositions, true and misleading conclusions, suspense, and the imitation of models or forms like letters, conversations, confessions, and the like. Thus a story may be divided into parts, or it might develop according to a pattern of movement from country-side to city, or according to the developing relationships between two people from their first introduction to their falling in love. The study of structure is about these arrangements and the purposes for which they are made.

FORMAL CATEGORIES OF STRUCTURE

Many aspects of structure are common to all genres of literature, and often the structure of fiction is parallel to that of drama. In any story, the following five elements are present and form the backbone, skeleton, or pattern of development.

(1) EXPOSITION. **Exposition** is the *laying out*, the putting forth, of the materials in the work: the main characters, their backgrounds, characteristics, basic assumptions about life, goals, limitations, and potentials. It presents everything that is going to be important in the pattern of actions. Exposition may appear at the beginning of the work, where it is most expected, but it may be found anywhere. Thus, there may be intricacies, twists, turns, false leads, blind alleys, surprises, and other quirks introduced in order to perplex, intrigue, please, and otherwise interest readers. Whenever something new arises, to the degree that it is new it is a part of exposition. Eventually, however, the introduction of new materials must cease and the story must end with only those elements of exposition that have already been included.

(2) COMPLICATION. The **complication** marks the onset of the major conflict in the story—the onset of the plot. The participants are the protagonist and the antagonist, together with whatever ideas and values they represent, such as good and evil, individualism and collectivization, childhood and age, love and hate, intelligence and stupidity, knowledge and ignorance, freedom and slavery, desire and resistance, and the like.

(3) CRISIS. The **crisis** is the turning point, the separation between what has gone before and what will come after. In practice, the crisis is usually a decision or action undertaken to resolve the conflict. It is important to stress, however, that the crisis, through a result of operating forces and decisions, may not produce the intended results. That aspect is the next part of the formal structure, the climax.

(4) CLIMAX. The **climax** (a Greek word meaning "ladder") is the *high point* in the action, in which the conflict and the consequent tension are brought out to the fullest extent. Another way to think of climax is as the point when all the rest of the action becomes firmly set—the point of inevitability and no return. For example, in Stephen Crane's "The Blue Hotel," the climax is the Swede's attempt to use physical action in persuading the card players to drink with him. The forces of self-preservation and primitive "honor" set in motion by his action makes it inevitable that a disastrous outcome will result. It is this inevitability that marks the Swede's action as the climax, or the beginning of the end, of the story.

(5) **RESOLUTION, OR DÉNOUEMENT.**   The **resolution** (releasing, untying) or **dénouement** (untying) is the set of actions bringing the story to its conclusion. The resolution of "The Blue Hotel" is composed of the retreat of the gambler, the focus on the dead Swede, the news of the gambler's sentence, and the concluding conversation between the Cowboy and the Easterner. The "untying" is usually managed as quickly as possible, for the conflict or conflicts are over, and readers would lose interest if things were to drag on too long. Thus the final section of "The Blue Hotel" is quite short, as are the endings of Eudora Welty's "A Worn Path," Frank O'Connor's "First Confession," and John Collier's "The Chaser," all of which describe characters walking away. Once the major conflicts are resolved, in other words, a brief action of this sort underscores the note of finality.

FORMAL AND ACTUAL STRUCTURE

The formal structure just described is an ideal one, a pattern that takes place in straightforward, chronological order and which is almost identical to the plot. In practice, however, most narratives vary the ideal structure, even though all the elements are present. Mystery stories, for example, postpone climaxes until the last moment, and also necessarily delay crucial exposition, inasmuch as the goal is to mystify. In a story where the exposition allows readers to know who a wrongdoer is, by contrast, the goal of the story is often to create suspense about whether the protagonist can maintain life while seeking the wrongdoer out.

More realistic, less "artificial" stories might also embody structural variations. For example, in Welty's "A Worn Path" a memorable variation is produced by the information introduced at the very end. During most of the story, the complication seems to be that Phoenix Jackson's major problem or conflict is with (1) her age, and (2) the natural environment. At the end, however, we learn the additional detail that she is the sole guardian and caretaker of an invalid grandson. Thus, even at the end, we get exposition and complication, so much so that our previous understanding of the conflict must be rethought and revised. The anguish of our response is made more acute, for Phoenix's antagonist is not just age and environment but also hopeless illness. The *structure* of the story, in other words, is designed to withhold an essential detail to maximize impact. The resolution of the story, coming as it does at the same moment as this crucial complication, points toward the final, inevitable defeat of Phoenix, while it also demonstrates her determined character.

Other variants in structure are almost as numerous as the works you will encounter. There might be a "flashback" method, for example: The moment at which the flashback is introduced may be a part of the resolution of the plot, and the flashback might lead you into a moment of climax, but then go from there to develop the details that are more properly part of the exposition. Let us again consider our brief plot about John and Jane, and develop a possible flashback way of structuring the story.

Jane is now old, and a noise outside causes her to think of the argument that forced her to part with John many years before. Then she thinks of the years she and John have spent happily together after they married. She then contrasts her happiness with her earlier, less happy marriage, and from there she reflects on her years of courtship with John before their conflict over career plans developed. Then she looks over at John, reading in a chair, and smiles. John smiles back, and the story ends.

This structure is only one way of shaping the story. There might be others. Let us suppose that John is in a sickbed at the time Jane thinks about their past, or perhaps he might be dead in his coffin. These variations would produce different stories. Additionally, let us suppose that Jane is a widow of many years, either thinking about her past or giving advice to a son or daughter. Then, too, she might be looking back as a divorcée from her first marriage, having just met John again, with the final action being their wedding. The years of happiness might then be introduced as anticipation, or as a resolution described by a narrator, who might have heard about things later from a friend. The possibilities of structuring our little story, in short, are great. Using the flashback method like the one demonstrated here, we would necessarily bring out all the formal elements of plot, but the actual arrangement—the real structure—would be unique.

There are many other ways to structure a story. A plot might be developed by a group of persons, each one knowing no more than a part of the details; by the time all finish making their contributions, all the necessary complications and resolutions would be clear. Parts or sections of a story might be carried on through conversation, as in "The Blue Hotel" and "Everyday Use," or through a ceremony witnessed by a major character, as in "Young Goodman Brown," or through an announcement of a party, as in "The Necklace." Another work might develop mostly with narration but partially with dialogue, as in "The Lottery," and still another might be almost totally dialogue, as in "The Chaser." There might be dreamlike sequences, as in "The Worker in Sandalwood," "The Demon Lover," and "Young Goodman Brown." The possibilities for variation are endless.

Questions for the Study of Structure

In determining the structure of any work, there are a number of recurrent questions that might be asked: What does the reader need to know in order to understand the actions? Are all these things actually included? How are they arranged? Do they come at a point when they might be expected, in the light of the plot? What comes first, and why? What comes afterward, and why? If the order were changed, how would the story be different? How does the present ordering of actions, scenes, speeches, and narration contribute to the completion of the story? How are these placements influential in the effect produced by the story?

STEPHEN CRANE   (1871–1900)

The Blue Hotel   *1898*

I

The Palace Hotel at Fort Romper was painted a light blue, a shade that is on the legs of a kind of heron, causing the bird to declare its position against any background. The Palace Hotel, then, was always screaming and howling in a way that made the dazzling winter landscape of Nebraska seem only a grey swampish hush. It stood alone on the prairie, and when the snow was falling the town two hundred yards away was not visible. But when the traveller alighted at the railway station he was obliged to pass the Palace Hotel before he could come upon the company of low clapboard houses which composed Fort Romper, and it was not to be thought that any traveller could pass the Palace Hotel without looking at it. Pat Scully, the proprietor, has proved himself a master of strategy when he chose his paints. It is true that on clear days, when the great transcontinental expresses, long lines of swaying Pullmans, swept through Fort Romper, passengers were overcome at the sight, and the cult that knows the brown-reds and the subdivisions of the dark greens of the East expressed shame, pity, horror, in a laugh. But to the citizens of this prairie town and to the people who would naturally stop there, Pat Scully had performed a feat. With this opulence and splendour, these creeds, classes, egotisms, that streamed through Romper on the rails day after day, they had no colour in common.

As if the displayed delights of such a blue hotel were not sufficiently enticing, it was Scully's habit to go every morning and evening to meet the leisurely trains that stopped at Romper and work his seductions upon any man that he might see wavering, gripsack in hand.

One morning, when a snow-crusted engine dragged its long string of freight cars and its one passenger coach to the station, Scully performed the marvel of catching three men. One was a shaky and quick-eyed Swede, with a great shining cheap valise; one was a tall bronzed cowboy, who was on his way to a ranch near the Dakota line; one was a little silent man from the East, who didn't look it, and didn't announce it. Scully practically made them prisoners. He was so nimble and merry and kindly that each probably felt it would be the height of brutality to try to escape. They trudged off over the creaking board sidewalks in the wake of the eager little Irishman. He wore a heavy fur cap squeezed tightly down on his head. It caused his two red ears to stick out stiffly, as if they were made of tin.

At last, Scully, elaborately, with boisterous hospitality, conducted them through the portals of the blue hotel. The room which they entered was small. It seemed to be merely a proper temple for an enormous stove, which, in the centre, was humming with godlike violence. At various points on its surface the iron had become luminous and glowed yellow from the heat. Beside the stove Scully's son Johnnie was playing High-Five° with an old farmer who had whiskers both grey and sandy. They were quarrelling. Frequently the old farmer turned his face toward a box of sawdust—coloured brown from tobacco juice—that was behind the stove, and spat with an air of great impatience and irritation. With a loud flourish of words Scully destroyed the game of cards, and bustled his son upstairs with part of the baggage of the new guests. He himself conducted them to three basins of the coldest water in the world. The cowboy and the Easterner burnished themselves fiery red with this water, until it seemed to be some kind of metal-polish. The Swede, however, merely dipped his fingers gingerly and with trepidation. It was notable that throughout this series of small ceremonies the three travellers were made to feel that Scully was very benevolent. He was conferring great favours upon them. He handed the towel from one to another with an air of philanthropic impulse.

Afterward they went to the first room, and, sitting about the stove, listened to Scully's officious clamour at his daughters, who were preparing the midday meal. They reflected in the silence of experienced men who tread carefully amid new people. Nevertheless, the old farmer, stationary, invincible in his chair near the warmest part of the stove, turned his face from the sawdust-box frequently and addressed a glowing commonplace to the strangers. Usually he was answered in short but adequate sentences by either the cowboy or the Easterner. The Swede said nothing. He seemed to be occupied in making furtive estimates of each man in the room. One might have thought that he had the sense of silly suspicion which comes to guilt. He resembled a badly frightened man. 5

Later, at dinner, he spoke a little, addressing his conversation entirely to Scully. He volunteered that he had come from New York, where for ten years he had worked as a tailor. These facts seemed to strike Scully as fascinating, and afterward he volunteered that he had lived at Romper for fourteen years. The Swede asked about the crops and the price of labour. He seemed barely to listen to Scully's extended replies. His eyes continued to rove from man to man.

Finally, with a laugh and a wink, he said that some of these Western communities were very dangerous; and after his statement he straightened his legs under the table, tilted his head, and laughed again, loudly. It was plain that the demonstration had no meaning to the others. They looked at him wondering and in silence.

II

As the men trooped heavily back into the front room, the two little windows presented views of a turmoiling sea of snow. The huge arms of the wind were making attempts—mighty, circular, futile—to embrace the flakes as they sped. A

High-Five: The most commonly played cardgame in the United States before it was replaced in popularity by poker.

gate-post like a still man with a blanched face stood aghast amid this profligate fury. In a hearty voice Scully announced the presence of a blizzard. The guests of the blue hotel, lighting their pipes, assented with grunts of lazy masculine content-ment. No island of the sea could be exempt in the degree of this little room with its humming stove. Johnnie, son of Scully, in a tone which defined his opinion of his ability as a card-player, challenged the old farmer of both grey and sandy whiskers to a game of High-Five. The farmer agreed with a contemptuous and bitter scoff. They sat close to the stove, and squared their knees under a wide board. The cowboy and the Easterner watched the game with interest. The Swede remained near the window, aloof, but with a countenance that showed signs of an inexplicable excitement.

The play of Johnnie and the grey-beard was suddenly ended by another quarrel. The old man arose while casting a look of heated scorn at his adversary. He slowly buttoned his coat, and then stalked with fabulous dignity from the room. In the discreet silence of all other men the Swede laughed. His laughter rang somehow childish. Men by this time had begun to look at him askance, as if they wished to inquire what ailed him.

A new game was formed jocosely. The cowboy volunteered to become the   10
partner of Johnnie, and they all then turned to ask the Swede to throw in his lot with the little Easterner. He asked some questions about the game, and, learning that it wore many names, and that he had played it when it was under an alias, he accepted the invitation. He strode toward the men nervously, as if he expected to be assaulted. Finally, seated, he gazed from face to face and laughed shrilly. This laugh was so strange that the Easterner looked up quickly, the cowboy sat intent and with his mouth open, and Johnnie paused, holding the cards with still fingers.

Afterward there was a short silence. Then Johnnie said, "Well, let's get at it. Come on now!" They pulled their chairs forward until their knees were bunched under the board. They began to play, and their interest in the game caused the others to forget the manner of the Swede.

The cowboy was a board-whacker. Each time that he held superior cards he whanged them, one by one, with exceeding force, down upon the improvised table, and took the tricks with a glowing air of prowess and pride that sent thrills of indignation into the hearts of his opponents. A game with a boardwhacker in it is sure to become intense. The countenances of the Easterner and the Swede were miserable whenever the cowboy thundered down his aces and kings, while Johnnie, his eyes gleaming with joy, chuckled and chuckled.

Because of the absorbing play none considered the strange ways of the Swede. They paid strict heed to the game. Finally, during a lull caused by a new deal, the Swede suddenly addressed Johnnie: "I suppose there have been a good many men killed in this room." The jaws of the others dropped and they looked at him.

"What in hell are you talking about?" said Johnnie.

The Swede laughed again his blatant laugh, full of a kind of false courage   15
and defiance. "Oh, you know what I mean all right," he answered.

"I'm a liar if I do!" Johnnie protested. The card was halted, and the men stared at the Swede. Johnnie evidently felt that as the son of the proprietor he should make a direct inquiry. "Now, what might you be drivin' at, mister?" he asked. The Swede winked at him. It was a wink full of cunning. His fingers shook on the edge of the board. "Oh, maybe you think I have been to nowheres. Maybe you think I'm a tenderfoot?"

"I don't know nothin' about you," answered Johnnie, "and I don't give a damn where you've been. All I got to say is that I don't know what you're driving at. There hain't never been nobody killed in this room."

The cowboy who had been steadily gazing at the Swede, then spoke: "What's wrong with you, mister?"

Apparently it seemed to the Swede that he was formidably menaced. He shivered and turned white near the corners of his mouth. He sent an appealing glance in the direction of the little Easterner. During these moments he did not forget to wear his air of advanced pot-valour. "They say they don't know what I mean," he remarked mockingly to the Easterner.

The latter answered after prolonged and cautious reflection. "I don't under-   20
stand you," he said, impassively.

The Swede made a movement then which announced that he thought he had encountered treachery from the only quarter where he had expected sympathy, if not help. "Oh, I see you are all against me. I see———"

The cowboy was in a state of deep stupefaction. "Say," he cried, as he tumbled the deck violently down upon the board, "say, what are you gittin' at, hey?"

The Swede sprang up with the celerity of a man escaping from a snake on the floor. "I don't want to fight!" he shouted. "I don't want to fight!"

The cowboy stretched his long legs indolently and deliberately. His hands were in his pockets. He spat into the sawdust-box. "Well, who the hell thought you did?" he inquired.

The Swede backed rapidly toward a corner of the room. His hands were   25
out protectingly in front of his chest, but he was making an obvious struggle to control his fright. "Gentlemen," he quavered. "I suppose I am going to be killed before I can leave this house! I suppose I am going to be killed before I can leave this house!" In his eyes was the dying-swan° look. Through the windows could be seen the snow turning blue in the shadow of dusk. The wind tore at the house, and some loose thing beat regularly against the clapboards like a spirit tapping.

A door opened, and Scully himself entered. He paused in surprise as he noted the tragic attitude of the Swede. Then he said, "What's the matter here?"

The Swede answered him swiftly and eagerly: "These men are going to kill me."

"Kill you!" ejaculated Scully. "Kill you! What are you talkin'?"

The Swede made the gesture of a martyr.

Scully wheeled sternly upon his son. "What is this, Johnnie?"   30

The lad had grown sullen. "Damned if I know," he answered. "I can't make no sense of it." He began to shuffle the cards, fluttering them together with an angry snap. "He says a good many men have been killed in this room, or something like that. And he says he's goin' to be killed here too. I don't know what ails him. He's crazy, I shouldn't wonder."

---

dying swan: Proverbially, a swan sings its most beautiful notes when it is about to die.

Scully then looked for explanation to the cowboy, but the cowboy simply shrugged his shoulders.

"Kill you?" said Scully again to the Swede. "Kill you? Man, you're off your nut."

"Oh, I know," burst out the Swede. "I know what will happen. Yes, I'm crazy—yes. Yes, of course, I'm crazy—yes. But I know one thing—" There was a sort of sweat of misery and terror upon his face. "I know I won't get out of here alive."

The cowboy drew a deep breath, as if his mind was passing into the last   35
stages of dissolution. "Well, I'm doggoned," he whispered to himself.

Scully wheeled suddenly and faced his son. "You've been troublin' this man!"

Johnnie's voice was loud with its burden of grievance. "Why, good Gawd, I ain't done nothin' to 'im."

The Swede broke in. "Gentlemen, do not disturb yourselves. I will leave this house. I will go away, because"—he accused them dramatically with his glance—"because I do not want to be killed."

Scully was furious with his son. "Will you tell me what is the matter, you young divil? What's the matter, anyhow? Speak out!"

"Blame it!" cried Johnnie in despair, "don't I tell you I don't know? He—he says we want to kill him, and that's all I know. I can't tell what ails him."

The Swede continued to repeat: "Never mind, Mr. Scully; never mind. I will leave this house. I will go away, because I do not wish to be killed. Yes, of course, I am crazy—yes. But I know one thing! I will go away. I will leave this house. Never mind, Mr. Scully; never mind. I will go away."

"You will not go 'way," said Scully. "You will not go 'way until I hear the reason of this business. If anybody has troubled you I will take care of him. This is my house. You are under my roof, and I will not allow any peaceable man to be troubled here." He cast a terrible eye upon Johnnie, the cowboy, and the Easterner.

"Never mind, Mr. Scully; never mind. I will go away. I do not wish to be killed." The Swede moved toward the door which opened upon the stairs. It was evidently his intention to go at once for his baggage.

"No, no," shouted Scully peremptorily; but the white-faced man slid by him and disappeared. "Now," said Scully severely, "what does this mane?"°

Johnnie and the cowboy cried together: "Why, we didn't do nothin' to 'im!"   45
Scully's eyes were cold. "No," he said, "you didn't?"

Johnnie swore a deep oath. "Why, this is the wildest loon I ever see. We didn't do nothin' at all. We were just sittin' here playin' cards, and he———"

The father suddenly spoke to the Easterner. "Mr. Blanc," he asked, "what has these boys been doin'?"

The Easterner reflected again. "I didn't see anything wrong at all," he said at last, slowly.

Scully began to howl. "But what does it mane?" He stared ferociously at his   50
son. "I have a mind to lather you for this, me boy."

Johnnie was frantic. "Well, what have I done?" he bawled at his father.

---

mane: mean. Scully speaks with a slight Irish brogue (see paragraph 114).

III

"I think you are tongue-tied," said Scully finally to his son, the cowboy, and the Easterner; and at the end of this scornful sentence he left the room.

Upstairs the Swede was swiftly fastening the straps of his great valise. Once his back happened to be half turned toward the door, and, hearing a noise there, he wheeled and sprang up, uttering a loud cry. Scully's wrinkled visage showed grimly in the light of the small lamp he carried. This yellow effulgence, streaming upward, coloured only his prominent features, and left his eyes, for instance, in mysterious shadow. He resembled a murderer.

"Man! man!" he exclaimed, "have you gone daffy?"

"Oh, no! Oh, no!" rejoined the other. "There are people in this world who know pretty nearly as much as you do—understand?" 55

For a moment they stood gazing at each other. Upon the Swede's deathly pale cheeks were two spots brightly crimson and sharply edged, as if they had been carefully painted. Scully placed the light on the table and sat himself on the edge of the bed. He spoke ruminatively. "By cracky, I never heard of such a thing in my life. It's a complete muddle. I can't, for the soul of me, think how you ever got this idea into your head." Presently he lifted his eyes and asked: "And did you sure think they were going to kill you?"

The Swede scanned the old man as if he wished to see into his mind. "I did," he said at last. He obviously suspected that this answer might precipitate an outbreak. As he pulled on a strap his whole arm shook, the elbow wavering like a bit of paper.

Scully banged his hand impressively on the footboard of the bed. "Why, man, we're goin' to have a line of ilictric street-cars in this town next spring."

" 'A line of electric street-cars,' " repeated the Swede, stupidly.

"And," said Scully, "there's a new railroad goin' to be built down from Broken 60 Arm to here. Not to mintion the four churches and the smashin' big brick school-house. Then there's the big factory, too. Why, in two years Romper'll be a met-tro-*pol*-is."

Having finished the preparation of his baggage, the Swede straightened him-self. "Mr. Scully," he said, with sudden hardihood, "how much do I owe you?"

"You don't owe me anythin'," said the old man, angrily.

"Yes, I do," retorted the Swede. He took seventy-five cents from his pocket and tendered it to Scully; but the latter snapped his fingers in disdainful refusal. However, it happened that they both stood gazing in a strange fashion at three silver pieces on the Swede's open palm.

"I'll not take your money," said Scully at last. "Not after what's been goin' on here." Then a plan seemed to strike him. "Here," he cried, picking up his lamp and moving toward the door. "Here! Come with me a minute."

"No," said the Swede, in overwhelming alarm. 65

"Yes," urged the old man. "Come on! I want you to come and see a picter—just across the hall—in my room."

The Swede must have concluded that his hour was come. His jaw dropped and his teeth showed like a dead man's. He ultimately followed Scully across the corridor, but he had the step of one hung in chains.

Scully flashed the light high on the wall of his own chamber. There was revealed a ridiculous photograph of a little girl. She was leaning against a balustrade of gorgeous decoration, and the formidable bang to her hair was prominent. The figure was as graceful as an upright sled-stake, and, withal, it was of the hue of lead. "There," said Scully, tenderly, "that's the picter of my little girl that died. Her name was Carrie. She had the purtiest hair you ever saw! I was that fond of her, she————"

Turning then, he saw that the Swede was not contemplating the picture at all, but, instead, was keeping keen watch on the gloom in the rear.

"Look, man!" cried Scully, heartily. "That's the picter of my little gal that died. Her name was Carrie. And then here's the picter of my oldest boy, Michael. He's a lawyer in Lincoln, an' doin' well. I gave that boy a grand eddication, and I'm glad for it now. He's a fine boy. Look at 'im now. Ain't he bold as blazes, him there in Lincoln, an honoured an' respicted gintleman! An honoured and respicted gintleman," concluded Scully with a flourish. And, so saying, he smote the Swede jovially on the back. 70

The Swede faintly smiled.

"Now," said the old man, "there's only one more thing." He dropped suddenly to the floor and thrust his head beneath the bed. The Swede could hear his muffled voice. "I'd keep it under me piller if it wasn't for that boy Johnnie. Then there's the old woman————Where is it now? I never put it twice in the same place. Ah, now come out with you!"

Presently he backed clumsily from under the bed, dragging with him an old coat rolled into a bundle. "I've fetched him," he muttered. Kneeling on the floor, he unrolled the coat and extracted from its heart a large yellow-brown whiskey-bottle.

His first maneuver was to hold the bottle up to the light. Reassured, apparently, that nobody had been tampering with it, he thrust it with a generous movement toward the Swede.

The weak-kneed Swede was about to eagerly clutch this element of strength, but he suddenly jerked his hand away and cast a look of horror upon Scully. 75

"Drink," said the old man affectionately. He had risen to his feet, and now stood facing the Swede.

There was a silence. Then again Scully said: "Drink!"

The Swede laughed wildly. He grabbed the bottle, put it to his mouth; and as his lips curled absurdly around the opening and his throat worked, he kept his glance, burning with hatred, upon the old man's face.

IV

After the departure of Scully the three men, with the card-board still upon their knees, preserved for a long time an astounded silence. Then Johnnie said: "That's the dod-dangedest Swede I ever see."

"He ain't no Swede," said the cowboy, scornfully. 80

"Well, what is he then?" cried Johnnie. "What is he then?"

"It's my opinion," replied the cowboy deliberately, "he's some kind of a Dutchman." It was a venerable custom of the country to entitle as Swedes all light-haired men who spoke with a heavy tongue. In consequence the idea of the cowboy was not without its daring. "Yes, sir," he repeated. "It's my opinion this feller is some kind of Dutchman."

"Well, he says he's a Swede, anyhow," muttered Johnnie, sulkily. He turned to the Easterner: "What do you think, Mr. Blanc?"

"Oh, I don't know," replied the Easterner.

"Well, what do you think makes him act that way?" asked the cowboy.   85

"Why, he's frightened." The Easterner knocked his pipe against the rim of the stove. "He's clear frightened out of his boots."

"What at?" cried Johnnie, and the cowboy together.

The Easterner reflected over his answer.

"What at?" cried the others again.

"Oh, I don't know, but it seems to me this man has been reading dime   90
novels, and he thinks he's right out in the middle of it—the shootin' and stabbin' and all."

"But," said the cowboy, deeply scandalized, "this ain't Wyoming, ner none of them places. This is Nebrasker."

"Yes," added Johnnie, "an' why don't he wait till he gits *out West?*"

The travelled Easterner laughed. "It isn't different there even—not in these days. But he thinks he's right in the middle of hell."

Johnnie and the cowboy mused long.

"It's awful funny," remarked Johnnie at last.   95

"Yes," said the cowboy. "This is a queer game. I hope we don't git snowed in, because then we'd have to stand this here man bein' around with us all the time. That wouldn't be no good."

"I wish pop would throw him out," said Johnnie.

Presently they heard a loud stamping on the stairs, accompanied by ringing jokes in the voice of old Scully, and laughter, evidently from the Swede. The men around the stove stared vacantly at each other. "Gosh!" said the cowboy. The door flew open, and old Scully, flushed and anecdotal, came into the room. He was jabbering at the Swede, who followed him, laughing bravely. It was the entry of two roisterers from a banquet hall.

"Come now," said Scully sharply to the three seated men, "move up and give us a chance at the stove." The cowboy and the Easterner obediently sidled their chairs to make room for the new-comers. Johnnie, however, simply arranged himself in a more indolent attitude, and then remained motionless.

"Come! Git over, there," said Scully.   100

"Plenty of room on the other side of the stove," said Johnnie.

"Do you think we want to sit in the draught?" roared the father.

But the Swede here interposed with a grandeur of confidence. "No, no. Let the boy sit where he likes," he cried in a bullying voice to the father.

"All right! All right!" said Scully, deferentially. The cowboy and the Easterner exchanged glances of wonder.

The five chairs were formed in a crescent about one side of the stove. The   105
Swede began to talk; he talked arrogantly, profanely, angrily. Johnnie, the cowboy, and the Easterner maintained a morose silence, while old Scully appeared to be receptive and eager, breaking in constantly with sympathetic ejaculations.

Finally the Swede announced that he was thirsty. He moved in his chair, and said that he would go for a drink of water.

"I'll git it for you," cried Scully at once.

"No," said the Swede contemptuously. "I'll get it for myself." He arose and stalked with the air of an owner off into the executive parts of the hotel.

As soon as the Swede was out of hearing Scully sprang to his feet and whispered intensely to the others: "Upstairs he thought I was tryin' to poison 'im."

"Say," said Johnnie, "this makes me sick. Why don't you throw 'im out in the snow?"

"Why, he's all right now," declared Scully. "It was only that he was from the East, and he thought this was a tough place. That's all. He's all right now."

The cowboy looked with admiration upon the Easterner. "You were straight," he said. "You were on to that there Dutchman."

"Well," said Johnnie to his father, "he may be all right now, but I don't see it. Other time he was scared, but now he's too fresh."

Scully's speech was always a combination of Irish brogue and idiom, Western twang and idiom, and scraps of curiously formal diction taken from the storybooks and newspapers. He now hurled a strange mass of language at the head of his son. "What do I keep? What do I keep? What do I keep?" he demanded, in a voice of thunder. He slapped his knee impressively, to indicate that he himself was going to make reply, and that all should heed. "I keep a hotel," he shouted. "A hotel, do you mind? A guest under my roof has sacred privileges. He is to be intimidated by none. Not one word shall he hear that would prijudice him in favor of goin' away. I'll not have it. There's no place in this here town where they can say they iver took in a guest of mine because he was afraid to stay here." He wheeled suddenly upon the cowboy and the Easterner. "Am I right?"

"Yes, Mr. Scully," said the cowboy, "I think you're right."

"Yes, Mr. Scully," said the Easterner, "I think you're right."

V

At six-o'clock supper, the Swede fizzed like a fire-wheel. He sometimes seemed on the point of bursting into riotous song, and in all his madness he was encouraged by old Scully. The Easterner was encased in reserve; the cowboy sat in wide-mouthed amazement, forgetting to eat, while Johnnie wrathily demolished great plates of food. The daughters of the house, when they were obliged to replenish the biscuits, approached as warily as Indians, and, having succeeded in their purpose, fled with ill-concealed trepidation. The Swede domineered the whole feast, and he gave it the appearance of a cruel bacchanal. He seemed to have grown suddenly taller; he gazed, brutally disdainful, into every face. His voice rang through the room. Once when he jabbed out harpoon-fashion with his fork to pinion a biscuit, the weapon nearly impaled the hand of the Easterner, which had been stretched quietly out for the same biscuit.

After supper, as the men filed toward the other room, the Swede smote Scully ruthlessly on the shoulder. "Well, old boy, that was a good, square meal." Johnnie looked hopefully at his father; he knew that shoulder was tender from an old fall; and, indeed, it appeared for a moment as if Scully was going to flame out over the matter, but in the end he smiled a sickly smile and remained silent. The others understood from his manner that he was admitting his responsibility for the Swede's new view-point.

Johnnie, however, addressed his parent in an aside. "Why don't you license somebody to kick you downstairs?" Scully scowled darkly by way of reply.

When they were gathered about the stove, the Swede insisted on another   120
game of High-Five. Scully gently deprecated the plan at first, but the Swede turned
a wolfish glare upon him. The old man subsided, and the Swede canvassed the
others. In his tone there was always a great threat. The cowboy and the Easterner
both remarked indifferently that they would play. Scully said that he would presently
have to go to meet the 6.58 train, and so the Swede turned menacingly upon
Johnnie. For a moment their glances crossed like blades, and then Johnnie smiled
and said, "Yes, I'll play."

They formed a square, with the little board on their knees. The Easterner
and the Swede were again partners. As the play went on, it was noticeable that
the cowboy was not board-whacking as usual. Meanwhile, Scully, near the lamp,
had put on his spectacles and, with an appearance curiously like an old priest,
was reading a newspaper. In time he went out to meet the 6.58 train, and, despite
his precautions, a gust of polar wind whirled into the room as he opened the
door. Besides scattering the cards, it chilled the players to the marrow. The Swede
cursed frightfully. When Scully returned, his entrance disturbed a cosy and friendly
scene. The Swede again cursed. But presently they were once more intent, their
heads bent forward and their hands moving swiftly. The Swede had adopted the
fashion of board-whacking.

Scully took up his paper and for a long time remained immersed in matters
which were extraordinarily remote from him. The lamp burned badly, and once
he stopped to adjust the wick. The newspaper, as he turned from page to page,
rustled with a slow and comfortable sound. Then suddenly he heard three terrible
words: "You are cheatin'!"

Such scenes often prove that there can be little of dramatic import in environment. Any room can present a tragic front; any room can be comic. This little
den was now hideous as a torture-chamber. The new faces of the men themselves
had changed it upon the instant. The Swede held a huge fist in front of Johnnie's
face, while the latter looked steadily over it into the blazing orbs of his accuser.
The Easterner had grown pallid; the cowboy's jaw had dropped in that expression
of bovine amazement which was one of his important mannerisms. After the three
words, the first sound in the room was made by Scully's paper as it floated forgotten
to his feet. His spectacles had also fallen from his nose, but by a clutch he had
saved them in air. His hand, grasping the spectacles, now remained poised awkwardly
and near his shoulder. He stared at the card-players.

Probably the silence was while a second elapsed. Then, if the floor had been
suddenly twitched out from under the men they could not have moved quicker.
The five had projected themselves headlong toward a common point. It happened
that Johnnie, in rising to hurl himself upon the Swede, had stumbled slightly
because of his curiously instinctive care for the cards and the board. The loss of
the moment allowed time for the arrival of Scully, and also allowed the cowboy time to give the Swede a great push which sent him staggering back. The
men found tongue together, and hoarse shouts of rage, appeal, or fear burst
from every throat. The cowboy pushed and jostled feverishly at the Swede, and
the Easterner and Scully clung wildly to Johnnie; but through the smoky air,
above the swaying bodies of the peace-compellers, the eyes of the two warriors ever sought each other in glances of challenge that were at once hot and
steely.

Of course the board had been overturned, and now the whole company of   125
cards was scattered over the floor, where the boots of the men trampled the fat
and painted kings and queens as they gazed with their silly eyes at the war that
was waging above them.

Scully's voice was dominating the yells. "Stop now! Stop, I say! Stop, now—"

Johnnie, as he struggled to burst through the rank formed by Scully and
the Easterner, was crying. "Well, he says I cheated! He says I cheated! I won't
allow no man to say I cheated! If he says I cheated, he's a—— ——!"

The cowboy was telling the Swede, "Quit, now! Quit, d'ye hear——"

The screams of the Swede never ceased: "He did cheat! I saw him! I saw
him——"

As for the Easterner, he was importuning in a voice that was not heeded: 130
"Wait a moment, can't you? Oh, wait a moment. What's the good of a fight over
a game of cards? Wait a moment——"

In this tumult no complete sentences were clear. "Cheat"—"Quit"—"He
says"—these fragments pierced the uproar and rang out sharply. It was remarkable
that, whereas Scully undoubtedly made the most noise, he was the least heard of
any of the riotous band.

Then suddenly there was a great cessation. It was as if each man had paused
for breath; and although the room was still lighted with the anger of men, it
could be seen that there was no danger of immediate conflict, and at once Johnnie,
shouldering his way forward, almost succeeded in confronting the Swede. "What
did you say I cheated for? What did you say I cheated for? I don't cheat, and I
won't let no man say I do!"

The Swede said, "I saw you! I saw you!"

"Well," cried Johnnie, "I'll fight any man what says I cheat!"

"No, you won't," said the cowboy. "Not here."   135

"Ah, be still, can't you?" said Scully, coming between them.

The quiet was sufficient to allow the Easterner's voice to be heard. He was
repeating, "Oh, wait a moment, can't you? What's the good of a fight over a game
of cards? Wait a moment!"

Johnnie, his red face appearing above his father's shoulder, hailed the Swede
again. "Did you say I cheated?"

The Swede showed his teeth. "Yes."

"Then," said Johnnie, "we must fight."   140

"Yes, fight," roared the Swede. He was like a demoniac. "Yes, fight! I'll show
you what kind of a man I am! I'll show you who you want to fight! Maybe you
think I can't fight! Maybe you think I can't! I'll show you, you skin, you card-
sharp! Yes, you cheated! You cheated! You cheated!"

"Well, let's go at it, then, mister," said Johnnie coolly.

The cowboy's brow was beaded with sweat from his efforts in intercept-
ing all sorts of raids. He turned in despair to Scully. "What are you goin' to do
now?"

A change had come over the Celtic visage of the old man. He now seemed
all eagerness; his eyes glowed.

"We'll let them fight," he answered stalwartly. "I can't put up with it any   145
longer. I've stood this damned Swede till I'm sick. We'll let them fight."

VI

The men prepared to go out of doors. The Easterner was so nervous that he had great difficulty in getting his arms into the sleeves of his new leather coat. As the cowboy drew his fur cap down over his ears his hands trembled. In fact, Johnnie and old Scully were the only ones who displayed no agitation. These preliminaries were conducted without words.

Scully threw open the door. "Well, come on," he said. Instantly a terrific wind caused the flame of the lamp to struggle at its wick, while a puff of black smoke sprang from the chimney-top. The stove was in mid-current of the blast, and its voice swelled to equal the roar of the storm. Some of the scarred and bedabbled cards were caught up from the floor and dashed helplessly against the farther wall. The men lowered their heads and plunged into the tempest as into a sea.

No snow was falling, but great whirls and clouds of flakes, swept up from the ground by the frantic winds, were streaming southward with the speed of bullets. The covered land was blue with the sheen of an unearthly satin, and there was no other hue save where, at the low, black railway station—which seemed incredibly distant—one light gleamed like a tiny jewel. As the men floundered into a thigh-deep drift, it was known that the Swede was bawling out something. Scully went to him, put a hand on his shoulder, and projected an ear. "What's that you say?" he shouted.

"I say," bawled the Swede again. "I won't stand much show against this gang. I know you'll all pitch on me."

Scully smote him reproachfully on the arm. "Tut, man!" he yelled. The   150
wind tore the words from Scully's lips and scattered them far alee.

"You are all a gang of———" boomed the Swede, but the storm also seized the remainder of the sentence.

Immediately turning their backs upon the wind, the men had swung around a corner to the sheltered side of the hotel. It was the function of the little house to preserve here, amid this great devastation of snow, an irregular V-shape of heavily encrusted grass, which crackled beneath the feet. One could imagine the great drifts piled against the windward side. When the party reached the comparative peace of this spot it was found that the Swede was still bellowing.

"Oh, I know what kind of a thing this is! I know you'll all pitch on me. I can't lick you all!"

Scully turned upon him panther-fashion. "You'll not have to whip all of us. You'll have to whip my son Johnnie. An' the man what troubles you durin' that time will have me to dale with."

The arrangements were swiftly made. The two men faced each other, obedient   155
to the harsh commands of Scully, whose face, in the subtly luminous gloom, could be seen set in the austere impersonal lines that are pictured on the countenances of the Roman veterans. The Easterner's teeth were chattering, and he was hopping up and down like a mechanical toy. The cowboy stood rock-like.

The contestants had not stripped off any clothing. Each was in his ordinary attire. Their fists were up, and they eyed each other in a calm that had the elements of leonine cruelty in it.

During this pause, the Easterner's mind, like a film, took lasting impressions of three men—the iron-nerved master of the ceremony; the Swede, pale, motionless, terrible; and Johnnie, serene yet ferocious, brutish yet heroic. The entire prelude had in it a tragedy greater than the tragedy of action, and this aspect was accentuated by the long, mellow cry of the blizzard, as it sped the tumbling and wailing flakes into the black abyss of the south.

"Now!" said Scully.

The two combatants leaped forward and crashed together like bullocks. There was heard the cushioned sound of blows, and of a curse squeezing out from between the tight teeth of one.

As for the spectators, the Easterner's pent-up breath exploded from him   160
with a pop of relief, absolute relief from the tension of the preliminaries. The cowboy bounded into the air with a yowl. Scully was immovable as from supreme amazement and fear at the fury of the fight which he himself had permitted and arranged.

For a time the encounter in the darkness was such a perplexity of flying arms that it presented no more detail than would a swiftly revolving wheel. Occasionally a face, as if illumined by a flash of light, would shine out, ghastly and marked with pink spots. A moment later, the men might have been known as shadows, if it were not for the involuntary utterance of oaths that came from them in whispers.

Suddenly a holocaust of warlike desire caught the cowboy, and he bolted forward with the speed of a broncho. "Go it, Johnnie! go it! Kill him! Kill him!"

Scully confronted him. "Kape back," he said; and by his glance the cowboy could tell that this man was Johnnie's father.

To the Easterner there was a monotony of unchangeable fighting that was an abomination. This confused mingling was eternal to his sense, which was concentrated in a longing for the end, the priceless end. Once the fighters lurched near him, and as he scrambled hastily backward he heard them breathe like men on the rack.

"Kill him, Johnnie! Kill him! Kill him! Kill him!" The cowboy's face was   165
contorted like one of those agony masks in museums.

"Keep still," said Scully, icily.

Then there was a sudden loud grunt, incomplete, cut short, and Johnnie's body swung away from Swede and fell with sickening heaviness to the grass. The cowboy was barely in time to prevent the mad Swede from flinging himself upon his prone adversary. "No, you don't," said the cowboy, interposing an arm. "Wait a second."

Scully was at his son's side. "Johnnie! Johnnie, me boy!" His voice had a quality of melancholy tenderness. "Johnnie! Can you go on with it?" He looked anxiously down into the bloody, pulpy face of his son.

There was a moment of silence, and then Johnnie answered in his ordinary voice, "Yes, I—it—yes."

Assisted by his father he struggled to his feet. "Wait a bit now till you git   170
your wind," said the old man.

A few paces away the cowboy was lecturing the Swede. "No, you don't! Wait a second!"

The Easterner was plucking at Scully's sleeve. "Oh, this is enough," he pleaded. "This is enough! Let it go as it stands. This is enough!"

"Bill," said Scully, "git out of the road." The cowboy stepped aside. "Now." The combatants were actuated by a new caution as they advanced toward collision. They glared at each other, and then the Swede aimed a lightning blow that carried with it his entire weight. Johnnie was evidently half stupid from weakness, but he miraculously dodged, and his fist sent the over-balanced Swede sprawling.

The cowboy, Scully, and the Easterner burst into a cheer that was like a chorus of triumphant soldiery, but before its conclusion the Swede has scuffed agilely to his feet and come in berserk abandon at his foe. There was another perplexity of flying arms, and Johnnie's body again swung away and fell, even as a bundle might fall from a roof. The Swede instantly staggered to a little wind-waved tree and leaned upon it, breathing like an engine, while his savage and flamelit eyes roamed from face to face as the men bent over Johnnie. There was a splendour of isolation in his situation at this time which the Easterner felt once when, lifting his eyes from the man on the ground, he beheld that mysterious and lonely figure, waiting.

"Are you any good yet, Johnnie?" asked Scully in a broken voice.   175

The son gasped and opened his eyes languidly. After a moment he answered, "No—I ain't—any good—any—more." Then, from shame and bodily ill, he began to weep, the tears furrowing down through the blood-stains on his face. "He was too—too—too heavy for me."

Scully straightened and addressed the waiting figure.

"Stranger," he said, evenly, "it's all up with our side." Then his voice changed into that vibrant huskiness which is commonly the tone of the most simple and deadly announcements. "Johnnie is whipped."

Without replying, the victor moved off on the route to the front door of the hotel.

The cowboy was formulating new and unspellable blasphemies. The Easterner   180 was startled to find that they were out in a wind that seemed to come direct from the shadowed arctic floes. He heard again the wail of the snow as it was flung to its grave in the south. He knew now that all this time the cold had been sinking into him deeper and deeper, and he wondered that he had not perished. He felt indifferent to the condition of the vanquished man.

"Johnnie, can you walk?" asked Scully.

"Did I hurt—hurt him any?" asked the son.

"Can you walk, boy? Can you walk?"

Johnnie's voice was suddenly strong. There was a robust impatience in it. "I asked you whether I hurt him any!"

"Yes, yes, Johnnie," answered the cowboy, consolingly; "he's hurt a good   185 deal."

They raised him from the ground, and as soon as he was on his feet he went tottering off, rebuffing all attempts at assistance. When the party rounded the corner they were fairly blinded by the pelting of the snow. It burned their faces like fire. The cowboy carried Johnnie through the drift to the door. As they entered, some cards again rose from the floor and beat against the wall.

The Easterner rushed to the stove. He was so profoundly chilled that he almost dared to embrace the glowing iron. The Swede was not in the room. Johnnie sank into a chair and, folding his arms on his knees, buried his face in them. Scully, warming one foot and then the other at a rim of the stove, muttered to himself with Celtic mournfulness. The cowboy had removed his fur cap, and with a dazed and rueful air he was running one hand through his tousled locks. From overhead they could hear the creaking of boards, as the Swede tramped here and there in his room.

The sad quiet was broken by the sudden flinging open of a door that led toward the kitchen. It was instantly followed by an inrush of women. They precipitated themselves upon Johnnie amid a chorus of lamentation. Before they carried their prey off to the kitchen, there to be bathed and harangued with that mixture of sympathy and abuse which is a feat of their sex, the mother straightened herself and fixed old Scully with an eye of stern reproach, "Shame be upon you, Patrick Scully!" she cried. "Your own son, too. Shame be upon you!"

"There, now! Be quiet, now!" said the old man, weakly.

"Shame be upon you, Patrick Scully!" The girls, rallying to this slogan, sniffed   190
disdainfully in the direction of those trembling accomplices, the cowboy and the Easterner. Presently they bore Johnnie away, and left the three men to dismal reflection.

VII

"I'd like to fight this here Dutchman myself," said the cowboy, breaking a long silence.

Scully wagged his head sadly. "No, that wouldn't do. It wouldn't be right. It wouldn't be right."

"Well, why wouldn't it?" argued the cowboy. "I don't see no harm in it."

"No," answered Scully, with mournful heroism. "It wouldn't be right. It was Johnnie's fight, and now we mustn't whip the man just because he whipped Johnnie."

"Yes, that's true enough," said the cowboy; "but—he better not get fresh   195
with me, because I couldn't stand no more of it."

"You'll not say a word to him," commanded Sully, and even then they heard the tread of the Swede on the stairs. His entrance was made theatric. He swept the door back with a bang and swaggered to the middle of the room. No one looked at him. "Well," he cried, insolently, at Scully, "I s'pose you'll tell me now how much I owe you?"

The old man remained stolid. "You don't owe me nothin'."

"Huh!" said the Swede, "huh! Don't owe 'im nothin'."

The cowboy addressed the Swede. "Stranger, I don't see how you come to be so gay around here."

Old Scully was instantly alert. "Stop!" he shouted, holding his hand forth,   200
fingers upward. "Bill, you shut up!"

The cowboy spat carelessly into the sawdust-box. "I didn't say a word, did I?" he asked.

"Mr. Scully," called the Swede, "how much do I owe you?" It was seen that he was attired for departure, and that he had his valise in his hand.

"You don't owe me nothin'," repeated Scully in the same imperturbable way.

"Huh!" said the Swede. "I guess you're right. I guess if it was any way at all, you'd owe me somethin'. That's what I guess." He turned to the cowboy. "'Kill him! Kill him! Kill him!'" he mimicked, and then guffawed victoriously. "'Kill him!'" He was convulsed with ironical humour.

But he might have been jeering the dead. The three men immovable and   205
silent, staring with glassy eyes at the stove.

The Swede opened the door and passed into the storm, giving one derisive
glance backward at the still group.

As soon as the door was closed, Scully and the cowboy leaped to their feet
and began to curse. They trampled to and fro, waving their arms and smashing
into the air with their fists. "Oh, but that was a hard minute!" wailed Scully. "That
was a hard minute! Him there leerin' and scoffin'! One bang at his nose was
worth forty dollars to me that minute! How did you stand it, Bill?"

"How did I stand it?" cried the cowboy in a quivering voice. "How did I
stand it? Oh!"

The old man burst into sudden brogue. "I'd loike to take that Swade,"
he wailed, "and hould 'im down on a shtone flure and bate 'im to a jelly wid a
shtick!"

The cowboy groaned in sympathy. "I'd like to git him by the neck and hammer   210
him"—he brought his hand down on a chair with a noise like a pistol-shot—"hammer
that there Dutchman until he couldn't tell himself from a dead coyote!"

"I'd bate 'im until he———"

"I'd show *him* some things———"

And then together they raised a yearning, fanatic cry—"Oh-o-oh! if we only
could———"

"Yes!"

"Yes!"   215

"And then I'd———"

"O-o-oh!"

VIII

The Swede, tightly gripping his valise, tacked across the face of the storm
as if he carried sails. He was following a line of little naked, gasping trees which,
he knew, must mark the way of the road. His face, fresh from the pounding of
Johnnie's fists, felt more pleasure than pain in the wind and the driving snow. A
number of square shapes loomed upon him finally, and he knew them as the
houses of the main body of the town. He found a street and made travel along
it, leaning heavily upon the wind whenever, at a corner, a terrific blast caught
him.

He might have been in a deserted village. We picture the world as thick
with conquering and elate humanity, but here, with the bugles of the tempest
pealing, it was hard to imagine a peopled earth. One viewed the existence of
man then as a marvel, and conceded a glamour of wonder to these lice which
were caused to cling to a whirling, fire-smitten, ice-locked, disease-stricken, space-
lost bulb. The conceit of man was explained by this storm to be the very engine
of life. One was a coxcomb not to die in it. However, the Swede found a saloon.

In front of it an indomitable red light was burning, and the snowflakes were   220
made blood-colour as they flew through the circumscribed territory of the lamp's
shining. The Swede pushed open the door of the saloon and entered. A sanded
expanse was before him, and at the end of it four men sat about a table drinking.
Down one side of the room extended a radiant bar, and its guardian was leaning

upon his elbows listening to the talk of the men at the table. The Swede dropped his valise upon the floor and, smiling fraternally upon the barkeeper, said, "Gimme some whisky, will you?" The man placed a bottle, a whisky-glass, and a glass of ice-thick water upon the bar. The Swede poured himself an abnormal portion of whisky and drank it in three gulps. "Pretty bad night," remarked the bartender, indifferently. He was making the pretension of blindness which is usually a distinction of his class; but it could have been seen that he was furtively studying the half-erased blood-stains on the face of the Swede. "Bad night," he said again.

"Oh, it's good enough for me," replied the Swede, hardily, as he poured himself some more whisky. The barkeeper took his coin and manoeuvred it through its reception by the highly nickelled cash-machine. A bell rang; a card labelled "20 cts." had appeared.

"No," continued the Swede, "this isn't too bad weather. It's good enough for me."

"So?" murmured the barkeeper, languidly.

The copious drams made the Swede's eyes swim, and he breathed a trifle heavier. "Yes, I like this weather. I like it. It suits me." It was apparently his design to impart a deep significance to these words.

"So?" murmured the bartender again. He turned to gaze dreamily at the   225
scroll-like birds and bird-like scrolls which had been drawn with soap upon the mirrors in back of the bar.

"Well, I guess I'll take another drink," said the Swede, presently. "Have something?"

"No, thanks; I'm not drinkin'," answered the bartender. Afterward he asked, "How did you hurt your face?"

The Swede immediately began to boast loudly. "Why, in a fight. I thumped the soul out of a man down here at Scully's hotel."

The interest of the four men at the table was at last aroused.

"Who was it?" said one.   230

"Johnnie Scully," blustered the Swede. "Son of the man what runs it. He will be pretty near dead for some weeks, I can tell you. I made a nice thing of him, I did. He couldn't get up. They carried him in the house. Have a drink?"

Instantly the men in some subtle way encased themselves in reserve. "No, thanks," said one. The group was of curious formation. Two were prominent local business men; one was the district attorney; and one was a professional gambler of the kind known as "square." But a scrutiny of the group would not have enabled an observer to pick the gambler from the men of more reputable pursuits. He was, in fact, a man so delicate in manner, when among people of fair class, and so judicious in his choice of victims, that in the strictly masculine part of the town's life he had come to be explicitly trusted and admired. People called him a thorough-bred. The fear and contempt with which his craft was regarded were undoubtedly the reason why his quiet dignity shone conspicuous above the quiet dignity of men who might be merely hatters, billiard-markers, or grocery clerks. Beyond an occasional unwary traveller who came by rail, this gambler was supposed to prey solely upon reckless and senile farmers, who, when flush with good crops, drove into town in all the pride and confidence of an absolutely invulnerable stupidity. Hearing at times in circuitous fashion of the despoilment of such a farmer, the important men of Romper invariably laughed in contempt of the victim, and if they thought of the wolf at all, it was with a kind of pride at the knowledge that he would ever dare think of attacking their wisdom and courage. Besides, it was popular that this gambler had a real wife and two real children in a neat cottage in a suburb, where he led an exemplary home life; and when any one even suggested a discrepancy in his character, the crowd immediately vociferated descriptions of this virtuous family circle. Then men who led exemplary home lives, and men who did not lead exemplary home lives, all subsided in a bunch, remarking that there was nothing more to be said.

However, when a restriction was placed upon him—as, for instance, when a strong clique of members of the new Pollywog Club refused to permit him, even as a spectator, to appear in the rooms of the organization—the candour and gentleness with which he accepted the judgment disarmed many of his foes and made his friends more desperately partisan. He invariably distinguished between himself and a respectable Romper man so quickly and frankly that his manner actually appeared to be a continual broadcast compliment.

And one must not forget to declare the fundamental fact of his entire position in Romper. It is irrefutable that in all affairs outside his business, in all matters that occur eternally and commonly between man and man, this thieving cardplayer was so generous, so just, so moral, that, in a contest, he could have put to flight the consciences of nine tenths of the citizens of Romper.

And so it happened that he was seated in this saloon with the two prominent local merchants and the district attorney.   235

The Swede continued to drink raw whisky, meanwhile babbling at the barkeeper and trying to induce him to indulge in potations. "Come on. Have a drink. Come on. What—no? Well, have a little one, then. By gawd, I've whipped a man to-night, and I want to celebrate. I whipped him good, too. Gentlemen," the Swede cried to the men at the table, "have a drink?"

"Ssh!" said the barkeeper.

The group at the table, although furtively attentive, had been pretending to be deep in talk, but now a man lifted his eyes toward the Swede and said, shortly, "Thanks. We don't want any more."

At this reply the Swede ruffled out his chest like a rooster. "Well," he exploded, "it seems I can't get anybody to drink with me in this town. Seems so, don't it? Well!"

"Ssh!" said the barkeeper.   240

"Say," snarled the Swede, "don't you try to shut me up. I won't have it. I'm a gentleman, and I want people to drink with me. And I want 'em to drink with me now. *Now*—do you understand?" He rapped the bar with his knuckles.

Years of experience had calloused the bartender. He merely grew sulky. "I hear you," he answered.

"Well," cried the Swede, "listen hard then. See those men over there? Well, they're going to drink with me, and don't you forget it. Now you watch."

"Hi!" yelled the barkeeper, "this won't do!"

"Why won't it?" demanded the Swede. He stalked over to the table, and by   245
chance laid his hand upon the shoulder of the gambler. "How about this?" he asked wrathfully. "I asked you to drink with me."

The gambler simply twisted his head and spoke over his shoulder. "My friend, I don't know you."

"Oh, hell!" answered the Swede, "come and have a drink."

"Now, my boy," advised the gambler, kindly, "take your hand off my shoulder and go 'way and mind you own business." He was a little, slim man, and it seemed strange to hear him use this tone of heroic patronage to the burly Swede. The other men at the table said nothing.

"What! You won't drink with me, you little dude? I'll make you, then! I'll make you!" The Swede had grasped the gambler frenziedly at the throat, and was dragging him from his chair. The other men sprang up. The barkeeper dashed around the corner of his bar. There was a great tumult, and then was seen a long blade in the hand of the gambler. It shot forward, and a human body, this citadel of virtue, wisdom, power, was pierced as easily as if it had been a melon. The Swede fell with a cry of supreme astonishment.

The prominent merchants and the district attorney must have at once tumbled out of the place backward. The bartender found himself hanging limply to the arm of a chair and gazing into the eyes of a murderer.   250

"Henry," said the latter, as he wiped his knife on one of the towels that hung beneath the bar rail, "you tell 'em where to find me. I'll be home, waiting for 'em." Then he vanished. A moment afterward the barkeeper was in the street dinning through the storm for help and, moreover, companionship.

The corpse of the Swede, alone in the saloon, had its eyes fixed upon a dreadful legend that dwelt atop the cash-machine: "This registers the amount of your purchase."

IX

Months later, the cowboy was frying pork over the stove of a little ranch near the Dakota line, when there was a quick thud of hoofs outside, and presently the Easterner entered with the letters and the papers.

"Well," said the Easterner at once, "the chap that killed the Swede has got three years. Wasn't much, was it?"

"He has? Three years?" The cowboy poised his pan of pork, while he ruminated upon the news. "Three years. That ain't much."   255

"No. It was a light sentence," replied the Easterner as he unbuckled his spurs. "Seems there was a good deal of sympathy for him in Romper."

"If the bartender had been any good," observed the cowboy, thoughtfully, "he would have gone in and cracked that there Dutchman on the head with a bottle in the beginnin' of it and stopped all this here murderin'."

"Yes, a thousand things might have happened," said the Easterner, tartly.

The cowboy returned his pan of pork to the fire, but his philosophy continued. "It's funny, ain't it? If he hadn't said Johnnie was cheatin' he'd be alive this minute. He was an awful fool. Game played for fun, too. Not for money. I believe he was crazy."

"I feel sorry for that gambler," said the Easterner.   260

"Oh, so do I," said the cowboy. "He don't deserve none of it for killin' who he did."

"The Swede might not have been killed if everything had been square."

"Might not have been killed?" exclaimed the cowboy. "Everythin' square? Why, when he said that Johnnie was cheatin' and acted like such a jackass? And then in the saloon he fairly walked up to git hurt?" With these arguments the cowboy browbeat the Easterner and reduced him to rage.

"You're a fool!" cried the Easterner, viciously. "You're a bigger jackass than the Swede by a million majority. Now let me tell you one thing. Let me tell you something. Listen! Johnnie *was* cheating!"

"'Johnnie,'" said the cowboy, blankly. There was a minute of silence, and then he said, robustly, "Why, no. The game was only for fun."   265

"Fun or not," said the Easterner, "Johnnie was cheating. I saw him. I know it. I saw him. And I refused to stand up and be a man. I let the Swede fight it out alone. And you—you were simply puffing around the place wanting to fight. And then old Scully himself! We are all in it! This poor gambler isn't even a noun. He is a kind of an adverb. Every sin is the result of a collaboration. We, five of us, have collaborated in the murder of this Swede. Usually there are from a dozen to forty women really involved in every murder, but in this case it seems to be only five men—you, I, Johnnie, old Scully; and that fool of an unfortunate gambler came merely as a culmination, the apex of a human movement, and gets all the punishment."

The cowboy, injured and rebellious, cried out blindly into this fog of mysterious theory: "Well, I didn't do anythin', did I?"

QUESTIONS

1. Describe the conflict in the story. Why is the Swede the major antagonist? How could he be seen as protagonist, instead of antagonist? Why do the others stress his identity as a Swede, and why is he never named, as the other guests in the hotel are?

2. Consider the Easterner's analysis (paragraph 90) as a plausible explanation of the Swede's strange behavior before the confrontation and the fight. How fully does this analysis explain these actions? How could the analysis be used in an argument that "The Blue Hotel" is a critique of conventional, dime-store views of the wild west?

3. Analyze the structure of the story. What relationship do the parts of abstract formal structure (described on pp. 101–102) have to the part divisions marked by Crane himself? Why is most of the story about events at the Blue Hotel, and why do events at the saloon, where the murder occurs, occupy only a small section? Explain, in relation to the story's structure, why we do not learn until the very end that Johnny actually *was* cheating.

4. What codes of male conduct and "honor" underlie the major actions of the story (e.g., the need to fight when affronted)? To what extent are they made to seem serious in the story? How are they ridiculed?

5. How adequately does the Easterner's "noun-adverb" analysis in the concluding paragraphs explain the events of the story? Could such events be stopped at a certain point, or are they inevitable regardless of the Easterner's theory about collaborative control and responsibility?

6. Describe the characters of the Swede, Pat Scully, the Easterner, and the Cowboy.

EUDORA WELTY   (b. 1909)

A Worn Path   *1941*

It was December—a bright frozen day in the early morning. Far out in the country there was an old Negro woman with her head tied in a red rag, coming along a path through the pinewoods. Her name was Phoenix Jackson. She was very old and small and she walked slowly in the dark pine shadows, moving a little from side to side in her steps, with the balanced heaviness and lightness of a pendulum in a grandfather clock. She carried a thin, small cane made from an umbrella, and with this she kept tapping the frozen earth in front of her. This made a grave and persistent noise in the still air, that seemed meditative like the chirping of a solitary little bird.

She wore a dark striped dress reaching down to her shoe tops, and an equally long apron of bleached sugar sacks, with a full pocket: all neat and tidy, but every time she took a step she might have fallen over her shoelaces, which dragged from her unlaced shoes. She looked straight ahead. Her eyes were blue with age. Her skin had a pattern all its own of numberless branching wrinkles and as though a whole little tree stood in the middle of her forehead, but a golden color ran underneath, and the two knobs of her cheeks were illumined by a yellow burning under the dark. Under the rag her hair came down on her neck in the frailest of ringlets, still black, and with an odor like copper.

Now and then there was a quivering in the thicket. Old Phoenix said, "Out of my way, all you foxes, owls, beetles, jack rabbits, coons and wild animals! . . . Keep out from under these feet, little bob-whites. . . . Keep the big wild hogs out of my path. Don't let none of those come running my direction. I got a long way." Under her small black-freckled hand her cane, limber as a buggy whip, would switch at the brush as if to rouse up any hiding things.

On she went. The woods were deep and still. The sun made the pine needles almost too bright to look at, up where the wind rocked. The cones dropped as light as feathers. Down in the hollow was the mourning dove—it was not too late for him.

The path ran up a hill. "Seem like there is chains about my feet, time I get this far," she said, in the voice of argument old people keep to use with themselves. "Something always take a hold of me on this hill—pleads I should stay."

After she got to the top she turned and gave a full, severe look behind her where she had come. "Up through pines," she said at length. "Now down through oaks."

Her eyes opened their widest, and she started down gently. But before she got to the bottom of the hill a bush caught her dress.

Her fingers were busy and intent, but her skirts were full and long, so that before she could pull them free in one place they were caught in another. It was not possible to allow the dress to tear. "I in the thorny bush," she said. "Thorns, you doing your appointed work. Never want to let folks pass, no sir. Old eyes thought you was a pretty little *green* bush."

Finally, trembling all over, she stood free, and after a moment dared to stoop for her cane.

"Sun so high!" she cried, leaning back and looking, while the thick tears   10
went over her eyes. "The time getting all gone here."

At the foot of this hill was a place where a log was laid across the creek.

"Now comes the trial," said Phoenix.

Putting her right foot out, she mounted the log and shut her eyes. Lifting
her skirt, leveling her cane fiercely before her, like a festival figure in some parade,
she began to march across. Then she opened her eyes and she was safe on the
other side.

"I wasn't as old as I thought," she said.

But she sat down to rest. She spread her skirts on the bank around her and   15
folded her hands over her knees. Up above her was a tree in a pearly cloud of
mistletoe. She did not dare to close her eyes, and when a little boy brought her a
plate with a slice of marble-cake on it she spoke to him. "That would be acceptable,"
she said. But when she went to take it there was just her own hand in the air.

So she left that tree, and had to go through a barbed-wire fence. There she
had to creep and crawl, spreading her knees and stretching her fingers like a
baby trying to climb the steps. But she talked loudly to herself: she could not let
her dress be torn now, so late in the day, and she could not pay for having her
arm or her leg sawed off if she got caught fast where she was.

At last she was safe through the fence and risen up out in the clearing. Big
dead trees, like black men with one arm, were standing in the purple stalks of
the withered cotton field. There sat a buzzard.

"Who you watching?"

In the furrow she made her way along.

"Glad this not the season for bulls," she said, looking sideways, "and the   20
good Lord made his snakes to curl up and sleep in the winter. A pleasure I don't
see no two-headed snake coming around that tree, where it come once. It took a
while to get by him, back in the summer.

She passed through the old cotton and went into a field of dead corn. It
whispered and shook and was taller than her head. "Through the maze now,"
she said, for there was no path.

Then there was something tall, black, and skinny there, moving before her.

At first she took it for a man. It could have been a man dancing in the
field. But she stood still and listened, and it did not make a sound. It was as
silent as a ghost.

"Ghost," she said sharply, "who be you the ghost of? For I have heard of
nary death close by."

But there was no answer—only the ragged dancing in the wind.   25

She shut her eyes, reached out her hand, and touched a sleeve. She found
a coat and inside that an emptiness, cold as ice.

"You scarecrow," she said. Her face lighted. "I ought to be shut up for
good," she said with laughter. "My senses is gone. I too old. I the oldest people I
ever know. Dance, old scarecrow," she said, "while I dancing with you."

She kicked her foot over the furrow, and with mouth drawn down, shook
her head once or twice in a little strutting way. Some husks blew down and whirled
in steamers about her skirts.

Then she went on, parting her way from side to side with the cane, through
the whispering field. At last she came to the end, to a wagon track where the

silver grass blew between the red ruts. The quail were walking around like pullets, seeming all dainty and unseen.

"Walk pretty," she said. "This is the easy place. This the easy going."   30

She followed the track, swaying through the quiet bare fields, through the little strings of trees silver in their dead leaves, past cabins silver from weather, with the doors and windows boarded shut, all like old women under a spell sitting there. "I walking in their sleep," she said, nodding her head vigorously.

In a ravine she went where a spring was silently flowing through a hollow log. Old Phoenix bent and drank. "Sweet-gum makes the water sweet," she said, and drank more. "Nobody know who made this well, for it was here when I was born."

The track crossed a swampy part where the moss hung as white as lace from every limb. "Sleep on, alligators, and blow your bubbles." Then the track went into the road.

Deep, deep the road went down between the high green-colored banks. Overhead the live-oaks met, and it was as dark as a cave.

A black dog with a lolling tongue came up out of the weeds by the ditch.   35
She was meditating, and not ready, and when he came at her she only hit him a little with her cane. Over she went in the ditch, like a little puff of milkweed.

Down there, her sense drifted away. A dream visited her, and she reached her hand up, but nothing reached down and gave her a pull. So she lay there and presently went to talking. "Old woman," she said to herself, "that black dog come up out of the weeds to stall you off, and now there he sitting on his fine tail smiling at you."

A white man finally came along and found her—a hunter, a young man, with his dog on a chain.

"Well, Granny!" he laughed. "What are you doing there?"

"Lying on my back like a June-bug waiting to be turned over, mister," she said, reaching up her hand.

He lifted her up, gave her a swing in the air, and set her down. "Anything   40
broken, Granny?"

"No sir, them old dead weeds is springy enough," said Phoenix, when she had got her breath. "I thank you for your trouble."

"Where do you live, Granny?" he asked, while the two dogs were growling at each other.

"Away back yonder, sir, behind the ridge. You can't even see it from here."

"On your way home?"

"No sir, I goin to town."   45

"Why, that's too far! That's as far as I walk when I come out myself, and I get something for my trouble." He patted the stuffed bag he carried, and there hung down a little closed claw. It was one of the bob-whites, with its beak hooked bitterly to show it was dead. "Now you go on home, Granny!"

"I bound to go to town, mister," said Phoenix. "The time come around."

He gave another laugh, filling the whole landscape. "I know you old colored people! Wouldn't miss going to town to see Santa Claus!"

But something held old Phoenix very still. The deep lines in her face went into a fierce and different radiation. Without warning, she had seen with her own eyes a flashing nickel fall out of the man's pocket onto the ground.

"How old are you, Granny?" he was saying.   50
"There is no telling, mister," she said, "no telling."
Then she gave a little cry and clapped her hands and said, "Git on away
from here, dog! Look! Look at that dog!" She laughed as if in admiration. "He
ain't scared of nobody. He a big black dog." She whispered, "Sic him!"
"Watch me get rid of that cur," said the man. "Sic him, Pete! Sic him!"
Phoenix heard the dogs fighting, and heard the man running and throwing
sticks. She even heard a gunshot. But she was slowly bending forward by that
time, further and further forward, the lids stretched down over her eyes, as if
she were doing this in her sleep. Her chin was lowered almost to her knees. The
yellow palm of her hand came out from the fold of her apron. Her fingers slid
down and along the ground under the piece of money with the grace and care
they would have in lifting an egg from under a setting hen. Then she slowly
straightened up, she stood erect, and the nickel was in her apron pocket. A bird
flew by. Her lips moved. "God watching me the whole time. I come to stealing."
The man came back, and his own dog panted about them. "Well, I scared   55
him off that time," he said, and then he laughed and lifted his gun and pointed
it at Phoenix.
She stood straight and faced him.
"Doesn't the gun scare you?" he said, still pointing it.
"No, sir, I seen plenty go off closer by, in my day, and for less than what I
done," she said, holding utterly still.
He smiled, and shouldered the gun. "Well, Granny," he said, "you must be
a hundred years old, and scared of nothing. I'd give you a dime if I had any
money with me. But you take my advice and stay home, and nothing will happen
to you."
"I bound to go on my way, mister," said Phoenix. She inclined her head in   60
the red rag. Then they went in different directions, but she could hear the gun
shooting again and again over the hill.
She walked on. The shadows hung from the oak trees to the road like curtains.
Then she smelled wood-smoke, and smelled the river, and she saw a steeple and
the cabins on their steep steps. Dozens of little black children whirled around
her. There ahead was Natchez shining. Bells were ringing. She walked on.
In the paved city it was Christmas time. There were red and green electric
lights strung and crisscrossed everywhere, and all turned on in the daytime. Old
Phoenix would have been lost if she had not distrusted her eyesight and depended
on her feet to know where to take her.
She paused quietly on the sidewalk where people were passing by. A lady
came along in the crowd, carrying an armful of red-, green- and silver-wrapped
presents; she gave off perfume like the red roses in hot summer, and Phoenix
stopped her.
"Please, missy, will you lace up my shoe?" She held up her foot.
"What do you want, Grandma?"   65
"See my shoe," said Phoenix. "Do all right for out in the country, but wouldn't
look right to go in a big building."
"Stand still then, Grandma," said the lady. She put her packages down on
the sidewalk beside her and laced and tied both shoes tightly.

"Can't lace 'em with a cane," said Phoenix. "Thank you, missy. I doesn't mind asking a nice lady to tie up my shoe, when I gets out on the street."

Moving slowly and from side to side, she went into the big building, and into a tower of steps, where she walked up and around and around until her feet knew to stop.

She entered a door, and there she saw nailed up on the wall the document   70
that had been stamped with the gold seal and framed in the gold frame, which matched the dream that was hung up in her head.

"Here I be," she said. There was a fixed and ceremonial stiffness over her body.

"A charity case, I suppose," said an attendant who sat at the desk before her.

But Phoenix only looked above her head. There was sweat on her face, the wrinkles in her skin shone like a bright net.

"Speak up, Grandma," the woman said. "What's your name? We must have your history, you know. Have you been here before? What seems to be the trouble with you?"

Old Phoenix only gave a twitch to her face as if a fly were bothering her.   75

"Are you deaf?" cried the attendant.

But then the nurse came in.

"Oh, that's just old Aunt Phoenix," she said. "She doesn't come for herself— she has a little grandson. She makes these trips just as regular as clockwork. She lives away back off the Old Natchez Trace." She bent down. "Well, Aunt Phoenix, why don't you just take a seat? We won't keep you standing after your long trip." She pointed.

The old woman sat down, bolt upright in the chair.

"Now, how is the boy?" asked the nurse.   80

Old Phoenix did not speak.

"I said, how is the boy?"

But Phoenix only waited and stared straight ahead, her face very solemn and withdrawn into rigidity.

"Is his throat any better?" asked the nurse. "Aunt Phoenix, don't you hear me? Is your grandson's throat any better since the last time you came for the medicine?"

With her hands on her knees, the old woman waited, silent, erect and motion-   85
less, just as if she were in armor.

"You mustn't take up our time this way, Aunt Phoenix," the nurse said. "Tell us quickly about your grandson, and get it over. He isn't dead, is he?"

At last there came a flicker and then a flame of comprehension across her face, and she spoke.

"My grandson. It was my memory had left me. There I sat and forgot why I made my long trip."

"Forgot?" the nurse frowned. "After you came so far?"

Then Phoenix was like an old woman begging a dignified forgiveness for   90
waking up frightened in the night. "I never did go to school, I was too old at the Surrender," she said in a soft voice. "I'm an old woman without an education. It was my memory fail me. My little grandson, he is just the same, and I forgot it in the coming."

"Throat never heals, does it?" said the nurse, speaking in a loud, sure voice to old Phoenix. By now she had a card with something written on it, a little list. "Yes. Swallowed lye. When was it—January—two, three years ago—"

Phoenix spoke unasked now. "No, missy, he not dead, he just the same. Every little while his throat begin to close up again, and he not able to swallow. He not get his breath. He not able to help himself. So the time come around, and I go on another trip for the soothing medicine."

"All right. The doctor said as long as you came to get it, you could have it," said the nurse. "But it's an obstinate case."

"My little grandson, he sit up there in the house all wrapped up, waiting by himself," Phoenix went on. "We is the only two left in the world. He suffer and it don't seem to put him back at all. He got a sweet look. He going to last. He wear a little patch quilt and peep out holding his mouth open like a little bird. I remembers so plain now. I not going to forget him again, no, the whole enduring time. I could tell him from all the others in creation."

"All right." The nurse was trying to hush her now. She brought her a bottle of medicine. "Charity," she said, making a check mark in a book.   95

Old Phoenix held the bottle close to her eyes, and then carefully put it into her pocket.

"I thank you," she said.

"It's Christmas time, Grandma," said the attendant. "Could I give you a few pennies out of my purse?"

"Five pennies is a nickel," said Phoenix stiffly.

"Here's a nickel," said the attendant.   100

Phoenix rose carefully and held out her hand. She received the nickel and then fished the other nickel out of her pocket and laid it beside the new one. She stared at her palm closely, with her head on one side.

Then she gave a tap with her cane on the floor.

"This is what come to me to do," she said. "I going to the store and buy my child a little windmill they sells, made out of paper. He going to find it hard to believe there such a thing in the world. I'll march myself back where he waiting, holding it straight up in this hand."

She lifted her free hand, gave a little nod, turned around, and walked out of the doctor's office. Then her slow step began on the stairs, going down.

QUESTIONS

1. From the description of her physical appearance, what do you conclude about Phoenix's economic condition? Has she taken the path through the woods before? How do you know? Is she accustomed to being alone? What do you make of her speaking to animals, and of her imagining a boy offering her a piece of cake? What does her speech show about her education and general background?

2. Describe the plot of the story. With Phoenix as the protagonist, what are the antagonisms ranged against her? Are they malevolent to any degree? How might Phoenix be considered to be in the grip of large and indifferent social and political forces?

3. Describe the structure of the story according to exposition, complication, crisis, climax, and resolution. Does the actual structure correspond to this orderly arrangement? Wherein does it depart? Why?

4. Comment on the meaning of this dialogue between Phoenix and the hunter:

"Doesn't the gun scare you?" he said, still pointing it.

"No, sir, I seen plenty go off closer by, in my day, and for less than what I done," she said, holding utterly still.

5. A number of responses might be made to this story, among them admiration for Phoenix, pity for her and her grandson and for the downtrodden generally, anger at her impoverished condition, and apprehension about her approaching senility. Do you share in any of these responses? Do you have any others?

TOM WHITECLOUD (1914–1972)

Blue Winds Dancing   *1938*

There is a moon out tonight. Moon and stars and clouds tipped with moonlight. And there is a fall wind blowing in my heart. Ever since this evening, when against a fading sky I saw geese wedge southward. They were going home. . . . Now I try to study, but against the pages I see them again, driving southward. Going home.

Across the valley there are heavy mountains holding up the night sky, and beyond the mountains there is home. Home, and peace, and the beat of drums, and blue winds dancing over snow fields. The Indian lodge will fill with my people, and our gods will come and sit among them. I should be there then. I should be at home.

But home is beyond the mountains, and I am here. Here where fall hides in the valleys, and winter never comes down from the mountains. Here where all the trees grow in rows; the palms stand stiffly by the roadsides, and in the groves the orange trees line in military rows, and endlessly bear fruit. Beautiful, yes; there is always beauty in order, in rows of growing things! But it is the beauty of captivity. A pine fighting for existence on a windy knoll is much more beautiful.

In my Wisconsin, the leaves change before the snows come. In the air there is the smell of wild rice and venison cooking; and when the winds come whispering through the forests, they carry the smell of rotting leaves. In the evenings, the loon calls, lonely; and birds sing their last songs before leaving. Bears dig roots and eat late fall berries, fattening for their long winter sleep. Later, when the first snows fall, one awakens in the morning to find the world white and beautiful and clean. Then one can look back over his trail and see the tracks following. In the woods there are tracks of deer and snowshoe rabbits, and long streaks where partridges slide to alight. Chipmunks make tiny footprints on the limbs and one can hear squirrels busy in hollow trees, sorting acorns. Soft lake waves wash the shores, and sunsets burst each evening over the lakes, and make them look as if they were afire.

That land which is my home! Beautiful, calm—where there is no hurry to get anywhere, no driving to keep up in a race that knows no ending and no goal. No classes where men talk and talk and then stop now and then to hear their own words come back to them from the students. No constant peering into the maelstrom of one's mind; no worries about grades and honors; no hysterical preparing for life until that life is half over; no anxiety about one's place in the thing they call Society.

I hear again the ring of axes in deep woods, the crunch of snow beneath my feet. I feel again the smooth velvet of ghost-birch bark. I hear the rhythm of the drums. . . . I am tired. I am weary of trying to keep up this bluff of being civilized. Being civilized means trying to do everything you don't want to, never doing anything you want to. It means dancing to the strings of custom and tradition; it means living in houses and never knowing or caring who is next door. These civilized white men want us to be like them—always dissatisfied—getting a hill and wanting a mountain.

Then again, maybe I am not tired. Maybe I'm licked. Maybe I am just not smart enough to grasp these things that go to make up civilization. Maybe I am just too lazy to think hard enough to keep up.

Still, I know my people have many things that civilization has taken from the whites. They know how to give; how to tear one's piece of meat in two and share it with one's brother. They know how to sing—how to make each man his own songs and sing them; for their music they do not have to listen to other men singing over a radio. They know how to make things with their hands, how to shape beads into design and make a thing of beauty from a piece of birch bark.

But we are inferior. It is terrible to have to feel inferior; to have to read reports of intelligence tests, and learn that one's race is behind. It is terrible to sit in classes and hear men tell you that your people worship sticks of wood—that your gods are all false, that the Manitou forgot your people and did not write them a book.

I am tired. I want to walk again among the ghost-birches. I want to see the leaves turn in autumn, the smoke rise from the lodgehouses, and to feel the blue winds. I want to hear the drums; I want to hear the drums and feel the blue whispering winds. 10

There is a train wailing into the night. The trains go across the mountains. It would be easy to catch a freight. They will say he has gone back to the blanket; I don't care. The dance at Christmas. . . .

A bunch of bums warming at a tiny fire talk politics and women and joke about the Relief and the WPA and smoke cigarettes. These men in caps and overcoats and dirty overalls living on the outskirts of civilization are free, but they pay the price of being free in civilization. They are outcasts. I remember a sociology professor lecturing on adjustment to society; hobos and prostitutes and criminals are individuals who never adjusted, he said. He could learn a lot if he came and listened to a bunch of bums talk. He would learn that work and a woman and a place to hang his hat are all the ordinary man wants. These are all he wants, but other men are not content to let him want only these. He must be taught to want radios and automobiles and a new suit every spring. Progress would stop if he did not want these things. I listen to hear if there is any talk of communism or socialism in the hobo jungles. There is none. At best there is a sort of disgusted philosophy about life. They seem to think there should be a better distribution of wealth, or more work, or something. But they are not rabid about it. The radicals live in the cities.

I find a fellow headed for Albuquerque, and talk road-talk with him. "It is hard to ride fruit cars. Bums break in. Better to wait for a cattle car going back to the Middle West, and ride that." We catch the next east-bound and walk the tops until we find a cattle car. Inside, we crouch near the forward wall, huddle, and try to sleep. I feel peaceful and content at last. I am going home. The cattle car rocks. I sleep.

Morning and the desert. Noon and the Salton Sea, lying more lifeless than a mirage under a somber sun in a pale sky. Skeleton mountains rearing on the skyline, thrusting out of the desert floor, all rock and shadow and edges. Desert. Good country for an Indian reservation. . . .

Yuma and the muddy Colorado. Night again, and I wait shivering for the dawn.   15

Phoenix. Pima country. Mountains that look like cardboard sets on a forgotten stage. Tucson. Papago country. Giant cacti that look like petrified hitchhikers along the highways. Apache country. At El Paso my road-buddy decides to go on to Houston. I leave him, and head north to the mesa country. Las Cruces and the terrible Organ Mountains, jagged peaks that instill fear and wondering. Albuquerque. Pueblos along the Rio Grande. On the boardwalk there are some Indian women in colored sashes selling bits of pottery. The stone age offering its art to the twentieth century. They hold up a piece and fix the tourist with black eyes until, embarrassed, he buys or turns away. I feel suddenly angry that my people should have to do such things for a living. . . .

Santa Fe trains are fast, and they keep them pretty clean of bums. I decide to hurry and ride passenger coaltenders. Hide in the dark, judge the speed of the train as it leaves, and then dash out, and catch it. I hug the cold steel wall of the tender and think of the roaring fire in the engine ahead, and of the passengers back in the dining car reading their papers over hot coffee. Beneath me there is a blur of rails. Death would come quick if my hands should freeze and I fall. Up over the Sangre De Cristo range, around cliffs and through canyons to Denver. Bitter cold here, and I must watch out for Denver Bob. He is a railroad bull who has thrown bums from fast freights. I miss him. It is too cold, I suppose. On north to the Sioux country.

Small towns lit for the coming Christmas. On the streets of one I see a beam-shouldered young farmer gazing into a window filled with shining silver toasters. He is tall and wears a blue shirt buttoned, with no tie. His young wife by his side looks at him hopefully. He wants decorations for his place to hang his hat to please his woman. . . .

Northward again. Minnesota, and great white fields of snow; frozen lakes, and dawn running into dusk without noon. Long forests wearing white. Bitter cold, and one night the northern lights. I am nearing home.

I reach Woodruff at midnight. Suddenly I am afraid, now that I am but   20
twenty miles from home. Afraid of what my father will say, afraid of being looked on as a stranger by my own people. I sit by a fire and think about myself and all other young Indians. We just don't seem to fit in anywhere—certainly not among the whites, and not among the older people. I think again about the learned sociology professor and his professing. So many things seem to be clear now that I am away from school and do not have to worry about some man's opinion of my ideas. It is easy to think while looking at dancing flames.

Morning. I spend the day cleaning up, and buying some presents for my family with what is left of my money. Nothing much, but a gift is a gift, if a man buys it with his last quarter. I wait until evening, then start up the track toward home.

Christmas Eve comes in on a north wind. Snow clouds hang over the pines, and the night comes early. Walking along the railroad bed, I feel the calm peace of snowbound forests on either side of me. I take my time; I am back in a world where time does not mean so much now. I am alone; alone but not nearly so lonely as I was back on the campus at school. Those are never lonely who love the snow and the pines; never lonely when the pines are wearing white shawls and snow crunches coldly underfoot. In the woods I know there are the tracks of deer and rabbit; I know that if I leave the rails and go into the woods I shall find them. I walk along feeling glad because my legs are light and my feet seem to know that they are home. A deer comes out of the woods ahead of me, and stands silhouetted on the rails. The North, I feel, has welcomed me home. I watch him and am glad that I do not wish for a gun. He goes into the woods quietly, leaving only the design of his tracks in the snow. I walk on. Now and then I pass a field, white under the night sky, with houses at the far end. Smoke comes from the chimneys of the houses, and I try to tell what sort of wood each is burning by the smoke; some burn pine, others aspen, others tamarack. There is one from which comes black coal smoke that rises lazily and drifts out over the tops of the trees. I like to watch houses and try to imagine what might be happening in them.

Just as a light snow begins to fall I cross the reservation boundary; somehow it seems as though I have stepped into another world. Deep woods in a white-and-black winter night. A faint trail leading to the village.

The railroad on which I stand comes from a city sprawled by a lake—a city with a million people who walk around without seeing one another; a city sucking the life from all the country around; a city with stores and police and intellectuals and criminals and movies and apartment houses; a city with its politics and libraries and zoos.

Laughing, I go into the woods. As I cross a frozen lake I begin to hear the drums. Soft in the night the drums beat. It is like the pulse beat of the world. The white line of the lake ends at a black forest, and above the trees the blue winds are dancing.

I come to the outlying houses of the village. Simple box houses, etched black in the night. From one or two windows soft lamplight falls on the snow. Christmas here, too, but it does not mean much; not much in the way of parties and presents. Joe Sky will get drunk. Alex Bodidash will buy his children red mittens and a new sled. Alex is a Carlisle man, and tries to keep his home up to white standards. White standards. Funny that my people should be ever falling farther behind. The more they try to imitate whites the more tragic the result. Yet they want us to be imitation white men. About all we imitate well are their vices.

The village is not a sight to instill pride, yet I am not ashamed; one can never be ashamed of his own people when he knows they have dreams as beautiful as white snow on a tall pine.

Father and my brother and sister are seated around the table as I walk in. Father stares at me for a moment, then I am in his arms, crying on his shoulder.

I give them the presents I have brought, and my throat tightens as I watch my sister save carefully bits of red string from the packages. I hide my feelings by wrestling with my brother when he strikes my shoulder in token of affection. Father looks at me, and I know he has many questions, but he seems to know why I have come. He tells me to go alone to the lodge, and he will follow.

I walk along the trail to the lodge, watching the northern lights forming in the heavens. White waving ribbons that seem to pulsate with the rhythm of the drums. Clean snow creaks beneath my feet, and a soft wind sighs through the trees, singing to me. Everything seems to say, "Be happy! You are home now— you are free. You are among friends—we are your friends; we, the trees, and the snow, and the lights." I follow the trail to the lodge. My feet are light, my heart seems to sing to the music, and I hold my head high. Across white snow fields blue winds are dancing.

Before the lodge door I stop, afraid, I wonder if my people will remember   30
me. I wonder—"Am I Indian, or am I white?" I stand before the door a long time. I hear the ice groan on the lake, and remember the story of the old woman who is under the ice, trying to get out, so she can punish some runaway lovers. I think to myself, "If I am white I will not believe that story; If I am Indian, I will know that there is an old woman under the ice." I listen for a while, and I know that there is an old woman under the ice. I look again at the lights, and go in.

Inside the lodge there are many Indians. Some sit on benches around the walls, others dance in the center of the floor around a drum. Nobody seems to notice me. It seems as though I were among a people I have never seen before. Heavy women with long hair. Women with children on their knees—small children that watch with intent black eyes the movements of the dancers, whose small faces are solemn and serene. The faces of the old people are serene, too, and their eyes are merry and bright. I look at the old men. Straight, dressed in dark trousers and beaded velvet vests, wearing soft moccasins. Dark, lined faces intent on the music. I wonder if I am at all like them. They dance on, lifting their feet to the rhythm of the drums swaying lightly, looking upward. I look at their eyes, and am startled at the rapt attention to the rhythm of the music.

The dance stops. The men walk back to the walls, and talk in low tones or with their hands. There is little conversation, yet everyone seems to be sharing some secret. A woman looks at a small boy wandering away, and he comes back to her.

Strange, I think and then remember. These people are not sharing words— they are sharing a mood. Everyone is happy. I am so used to white people that it seems strange so many people could be together without someone talking. These Indians are happy because they are together, and because the night is beautiful outside, and the music is beautiful. I try hard to forget school and white people, and be one of these—my people. I try to forget everything but the night, and it is a part of me that I am one with my people and we are all a part of something universal. I watch eyes, and see now that the old people are speaking to me. They nod slightly, imperceptibly, and their eyes laugh into mine. I look around the room. All the eyes are friendly; they all laugh. No one questions my being here. The drums begin to beat again, and I catch the invitation in the eyes of the old men. My feet begin to lift to the rhythm, and I look out beyond the walls into the night and see the lights. I am happy. It is beautiful. I am home.

QUESTIONS

1. Describe the first section of the story in terms of the plot. How much is exposition? How much complication? Could a case be made that this first section contains its own crisis and climax and that the rest of the story is really a resolution?

2. What do you learn in the first section about the conflict in the attitudes of the young Indian narrator? What is his attitude about "civilization"? What values derived from his home make him think this way? If he is the protagonist, who or what is the antagonist?

3. What does the narrator mean by saying, "I am alone; alone but not nearly so lonely as I was back on the campus at school"?

4. What is meant by the dancing of the blue winds? What kind of wisdom is represented by this perception? What is the place for such wisdom in a computerized, industrialized society?

5. The narrator claims that the only things about whites that Indians imitate well are their vices. Are there roles in the mainstream society that Indians could successfully manage while preserving the Indian identity and integrity?

WRITING ABOUT THE PLOT OF A STORY

When you compose an essay about plot, you should describe and analyze the conflict and the developments and routes it takes. Just a straightforward chronological listing, as in the précis theme (see Chapter 2), is not the goal. The organization of an essay about plot is not based on parts of the story or principal events, because these would invite a chronological summary. Instead, the organization is to be developed out of the important elements of the conflict or conflicts.

Organizing Your Essay

INTRODUCTION. The introduction contains brief references to the principal characters, circumstances, and issues of the plot. The introduction also contains, as a central idea for the essay, a sentence describing the plot, or principal conflict. The thesis sentence contains the topics to be developed and usually concludes the introduction.

BODY. The body focuses on the major elements of the plot, brought out to emphasize the plan of conflict in the story. Who is the main character? What qualities of this character are important in the conflict? What strengths and weaknesses does the character have? What is the conflict? How is it embodied in the work? Who are the antagonists, and how do their characteristics and interests involve them in the conflict? If the conflict stems out of contrasting ideas or values, what are these, and how are they brought out? Does the major character face a difficult decision of any sort? (In our model short-short story, for example, Mary faces the decision of choosing a career and losing John, or accepting John on his terms and losing her career.) Are the effects of any decision the intended ones? In terms of success by personal, occupational, or political standards, does the conflict make the principal character successful or unsuccessful, happy or dissatisfied? Does the character emerge from the conflict in triumph, defeat, or somewhere in the middle?

Because a description of elements in a plot can easily become long, it is necessary to be selective and also to decide on a particular approach. Rather than detail everything point by point, for example, you should stress the major character and his or her involvement in the conflict. Such an essay on Eudora Welty's "A Worn Path" might emphasize Phoenix as she encounters the various obstacles that she must meet and overcome. When there is a conflict between two major characters, the most obvious approach is to focus equally on both. For brevity, however, the emphasis might be placed on just one. Thus, an essay on the plot of "The Blue Hotel" might stress the things we learn about the Swede that are important to his being a major participant in the conflict.

In addition, the plot may be analyzed more broadly in terms of things such as impulses, goals, ideas, values, issues, and historical perspectives. In "Blue Winds Dancing," for example, such an essay would stress the narrator's resentment, homesickness, and desire for an Indian identity. It might be possible, too, to emphasize more broadly the values of the Indian culture to which the narrator is returning, as a contrast to the values of the predominant "civilized" culture which he is leaving. It would also be possible to make the same treatment for the antagonistic side of the plot.

CONCLUSION.   The conclusion may contain a brief summary of the points in the body. Also, this is an appropriate place to include a consideration of the *impact* of the plot and its effect on the reader. Additional comments might concentrate on an evaluation of the plot, such as whether the author has contrived it in any way to tip the balance toward one side or the other, or whether it is realistic, true to life, fair, and impartial.

SAMPLE ESSAY

The Plot of Eudora Welty's "A Worn Path"*

[1]   At first, the complexity of Eudora Welty's plot in "A Worn Path" is not clear. The main character is Phoenix Jackson, an old, poor, and frail black

* See p. 124 for this story.

woman; the story seems to be no more than a record of her walk to Natchez through the woods from her rural home. By the story's end, however, the plot is clear: It consists of the brave attempts of a courageous, valiant woman to carry on normally despite overwhelming negative forces.° The gap between her determination and the odds against her gives the story its impact. The powers she opposes in the story are environment, poverty, and old age.□

[2] Environment is shown, during that portion of the story when Phoenix walks to town, as almost an active opponent. Thus she must contend against a long hill, a thornbush, a log across a creek that poses a threat of falling, and a barbed-wire fence. Also a part of the force against her is the dog which attacks her. Against these obstacles, Phoenix asserts her determination by carrying on a cheerful monologue. She prevails, for the moment at least, because she finally reaches her destination, the city of Natchez.

[3] The poverty against which Phoenix must contend is evident not in any one spot, but is shown throughout. She cannot take her trip to town by car, for example, but must walk alone on the long "worn path" wearing only tennis shoes. She has no money, and keeps the nickel dropped by the hunter; at the medical office she asks for and gets another nickel. She is the recipient of charity, and is given the "soothing syrup" for her grandson as a free service. Despite the boy's obvious need for advanced medical care, she does not have the means to provide it, and the story therefore shows that her guardianship is doomed.

[4] Old age as an opponent is shown in signs of Phoenix's increasing senility. As she walks, she speaks to the unreponsive things around her. When she falls into the ditch, she cannot get out without help. When she needs to tie her shoe, she asks a passing stranger for help because she is unable to bend down to make the tie herself.

[5] These signs of age reach a sort of crisis when she pursues her mission in Natchez. Not her mind but her feet tell her where to find the medical office. Despite her quiet inner strength, she is unable to tell the nursing attendant why she is there, but instead she sits dumbly and unknowingly for a time. Perhaps the strongest sign of age is that she does not tell about her errand at all, with the nurse being the one to tell the attendant about the infirm grandson. All these suggest that she is losing against the power of advancing age. The implication is that she soon will lose entirely.

[6] This brief description of the elements of conflict in the plot can only hint at the final power of the story. Phoenix is strong and admirable, but with everything against her, she can never win. The story itself is layered to bring out the full range of the conditions against her. Welty saves the most hopeless fact, the condition of the invalid grandson, to the very end. It is the delayed final revelation of the plot that creates almost overwhelmingly sympathy for Phoenix. The plot is powerful because it is so real, and Phoenix is a pathetic but memorable protagonist struggling against overwhelming odds.

° Central idea.
□ Thesis sentence.

Commentary on the Essay

In this essay on plot, emphasis is given to the major aspects of the conflict in "A Worn Path." The plot involves the protagonist, Phoenix, who is opposed by the forces of environment, poverty, and old age. The introduction points out how these forces cumulatively account for the story's impact. Paragraph 2 details the environmental obstacles of the conflict, the sheer physical difficulties that she must experience. Paragraph 3 examines Phoenix's poverty, and paragraphs 4 and 5 consider her old age. The concluding paragraph introduces another major conflict—the invalid condition of the grandson—as another of the forces she must contend with. This paragraph also points out that in this set of conflicts the protagonist cannot win, except as she lives out her duty and her devotion to help her grandson. Continuing the theme of the introduction, the last paragraph also accounts for the power of the plot: By building up to Phoenix's personal affirmation against unbeatable forces, the story evokes both strong sympathy and great admiration.

WRITING ABOUT STRUCTURE IN A STORY

An essay about structure is concerned with arrangement and shape. In form, the essay does not need to follow the pattern of the story part by part. Rather it explains why things are where they are: "Why is this here and not there?" is the fundamental question you should answer in your prewriting and planning. Thus it is possible to begin with the dénouement of the work, and in your explanation to consider how the author's manipulation of the previous sections have built up to it. A vital piece of information, for example, might have been withheld early in the story (as in "The Blue Hotel" and "A Worn Path"), but delayed until the very end; the dénouement might thereby be heightened because there would have been less suspense if the detail had been introduced earlier. Another thing to consider is the effect or impact of the work, and then to analyze how the structuring produces this effect.

Organizing Your Essay

INTRODUCTION. The introduction first presents a general overview of the work, and then centers on the aspect or aspects of structure to be emphasized in the body. The central idea is a succinct statement about the structure, such as that it is built up to reveal the desperate nature of a character's situation, or that it is designed to create surprise, or that it is arranged to bring out maximum humor. The thesis sentence points out the various main headings of the body.

BODY. The body is best developed in concert or agreement with what the story contains. There may be a number of separate scenes, or settings, such as the countryside, city, and building in "A Worn Path." An essay based on the structural importance of these locations would explain the relationship of each to the development of the plot. Similarly, both "Blue Winds Dancing" and "The Blue Hotel" involve characters riding trains and then arriving at their destination. A structural study of these stories might stem out of these locations and their relationship to the resolution of the plot.

Other ways to consider structure would also necessarily be developed from noteworthy characteristics of the story. In "A Worn Path" a vital piece of exposition, as has been emphasized already, is withheld until the conclusion. An essay on structure might consider what effects this delay produces in the story, and therefore the benefit (or detriment) of this kind of mystery or suspense.

You might also devote the body not to the entire structure of the story, but to a major part, character, or action. For example, the climax of a story might be the principal subject. Questions to be explored would be these: Where does the climax begin? What events are included in it? Is any new piece of information, or any new interpretation of existing details, introduced in the climax? Why then and not earlier? What is the expected, or logical way in which the climax is resolved? Is this resolution indeed the one created by the author? How and how soon does the reader learn what the resolution is going to be? Similar questions might be posed and answered if the topic of the essay is, say, the complication or the crisis. With such a concentration on only one aspect of structure, you would need in your introduction to explain why you are analyzing a part of the work rather than the whole.

If you should decide to write about the author's structuring of particular characters, it would be important to establish how the characters are introduced, how information is brought out about them, how they figure in the plot, and how they are treated in the resolution. With an action, it might be that one little event is introduced to demonstrate the importance of fate, chance, or casual happenings in life. Or it might be that the outcome is not the one intended by the character or by a group. Thus the event could be seen in a perspective of irony, or of bad luck.

CONCLUSION. Here you may highlight the main parts of your essay, or deal briefly with the relationship of structure to the plot. If the work you have analyzed departs in any way from strict chronology, you might emphasize the effects of the variations. Your aim should be to focus on the success of the work as it has been brought about by the author's choices in development.

SAMPLE ESSAY

The Structure of Eudora Welty's "A Worn Path"*

[1]   On the surface, Eudora Welty's "A Worn Path" is structured simply. The narrative is easy to follow, and things move chronologically. The main character is Phoenix Jackson, an old, poor black woman. She walks from her rural home in Mississippi through the woods to Natchez to get a free bottle of medicine for her grandson, who is a hopeless invalid. Everything takes place in just a few hours. This action is only the frame, however, for a skillfully and powerfully structured plot.° The masterly control of structure is shown in the story's locations, and in the way in which the delayed revelation produces both mystery and complexity.□

[2]   The locations in the story are arranged to coincide with the increasing difficulties faced by Phoenix. The first and most obvious "worn path" is the rural woods with all its physical difficulties. For most people the obstacles would not be challenging, but for an old woman they are formidable. In Natchez, the location of the final section of the story, Phoenix's inability to bend over to tie her shoe demonstrates the lack of flexibility of old age. In the medical office, where the final scene takes place, two major difficulties of the plot are brought out. One is Phoenix's increasing senility, and the other is the disclosure that her grandson is an incurable invalid. This set of oppositions, the major conflicts in the plot, thus coincide with locations, or scenes, that highlight the power of the conditions against Phoenix.

[3]   The most powerful of these conditions, the revelation about the grandson, makes the story something like a mystery. Because this detail is not known until the end, the reader is left in the dark to wonder what might happen next to Phoenix. For this reason, some parts of the story are false leads. For example, the episode with the dog is threatening, but it leads nowhere; Phoenix, with the aid of the hunter, is unharmed by the animal. Her theft of the nickel might seem at first to be cause for punishment, but the young hunter is ignorant of the missing coin, and he makes no accusations against her. Right up to the moment of her entering the medical building, therefore, there is no apparent pending resolution. The reader is still wondering what might happen.

[4]   Hence the details about the grandson, carefully concealed until the end, make the story much more complex than it at first seems. Because of this concluding revelation, the reader must do a double-take, a reconsideration of what has gone on before. Phoenix's difficult walk into town must be seen not as an ordinary errand but as a hopeless mission of mercy. Phoenix's character also bears reevaluation: She is not just a funny old woman who speaks to the objects and animals around her, but she is an amazingly brave woman carrying on normally against crushing odds. The complexity of the story also produces a complex response, for many readers may feel a degree

---

* See p. 124 for this story.
° Central idea.
□ Thesis sentence.

of shame for earlier uncomplimentary judgments, just as they feel admiration as they learn of their valor.

Thus the parts of "A Worn Path," while seemingly simple, are skillfully arranged. The key to the double-take and reevaluation is that Welty withholds, up to the very end, the most important detail of exposition. As it were, parts of the exposition and complication merge with the climax at just about the same point near the end of the story, in the speeches of the attendant and the nurse. One might claim that the nurse's disclosure makes it seem that Phoenix's entire existence is a crisis, although she is characteristically unaware of this condition as she leaves the office to buy the paper windmill. It is this complex buildup and emotional peaking that mark "A Worn Path" as the creation of a master writer.

[5]

Commentary on the Essay

To highlight the differences between essays on plot and structure, the topic of this sample essay is Welty's "A Worn Path," the same story analyzed in the sample essay on plot. While both essays are concerned with the conflicts of the story, the essay on plot concentrates on the opposing forces, while the essay of structure focuses on the placement and arrangement of the plot elements. Please note that neither essay retells the story, point by point, like a précis. Instead, these are analytical essays which explain the conflict (for plot) and the purposes of arrangement and layout (for structure). In both, the assumption is made that the reader has read the work and already knows the details, whereas in the précis the assumption is that the reader has not done the reading and therefore needs the details.

The introduction of the essay asserts that the masterly structure accounts for the story's power. Paragraph 2 develops the topic that the geographical locations are arranged climactically to demonstrate the forces against the major character. Paragraph 3 concerns the delayed revelation about the invalid grandson, pointing out that the suspended detail leaves the reader concerned but baffled about the ultimate climax and resolution of the plot. Paragraph 4, an extension of paragraph 3, deals with the complexity resulting from the delayed information: The necessary reevaluation of Phoenix's character and her mission to town, and the consequent development of reader response. The last paragraph accounts for the story's power by pointing out how the merging of plot elements near the end makes the conclusion both swift and forceful.

WRITING TOPICS FOR CHAPTER 3

1. Write an essay on the celebration of Phoenix's strength as she opposes poverty, old age, and illness in "A Worn Path."

2. Write an essay on the structuring of the formal elements in "The Blue Hotel." To what degree is the plot arranged to provide a surprise ending? How

is the material presented, and also withheld, to enable the conclusion to come out as it does?

3. Write an essay on the plot of "Blue Winds Dancing" as a conflict between Indian and White values.

4. Read "Everyday Use" (in Chapter 2) and write an essay comparing it to "Blue Winds Dancing" as a study in the clashing of values. How are the two stories similar? Different?

5. Select an event in your life in which you experienced doubt, difficulty, and conflict. Making yourself anonymous (use another name and place), write a brief story about the event, stressing the conflict and how it was resolved.

4

Characters:
The People in Fiction

Character in literature generally, and in fiction specifically, is an extended verbal representation of a human being, the inner self that determines thought, speech, and behavior. Through dialogue, action, and commentary, authors capture some of the interactions of character and circumstance. Fiction makes these interactions interesting by portraying characters who are worth caring about, rooting for, and even loving, although there are also characters at whom you may laugh or whom you may dislike or even hate.

CHOICE AND CHARACTER

The choices that people make indicate their characters, if we assume they have freedom of choice. We always make silent comparisons with the choices made or rejected. Thus, if you know that John works twelve hours a day, while Tom puts in five, and Jim sleeps under a tree, you have a number of separate facts, but you do not conclude anything about their characters unless you have a basis for comparison. This basis is easy: The usual, average number of working hours is eight. With no more than this knowledge for comparison, you might conclude that John is a workaholic, Tom lazy, and Jim either unwell or a dropout. To be fair, you would need to know much more about the life of each person before you could make your conclusions definite.

In fiction you may expect such completeness of context. You may think of each action or speech, no matter how small or seemingly unusual, as an accumulating part of a total portrait. Whereas in life things may "just happen," in literature all the actions, interactions, speeches, and observations are arranged to give you the details you need for conclusions about character. Thus, you read about important events like a child's first confession (O'Connor's "First Confession"), a long period of work and sacrifice (Maupassant's "The Necklace"), the first nonstop airplane trip around the earth (Thurber's "The Greatest Man in the World"), the murder of a husband by a wife (Glaspell's "A Jury of Her Peers"), or an act of defiance (Faulkner's "Barn Burning"). From these events in their contexts you draw conclusions about the characters involved.

MAJOR CHARACTER TRAITS

In studying a literary character, you should determine the character's major trait or traits. A **trait** is a typical or habitual mode of behavior, such as acting first and thinking afterwards, crowding another person closely while talking, looking directly into a person's eyes or avoiding eye contact completely, and borrowing money and not repaying it. If we learn about a person's traits, we can develop an understanding of that person. Sometimes a particular trait may be the primary characteristic of a person, not only in literature but also in life. Thus, characters may be lazy or ambitious, anxious or serene, aggressive or fearful, assertive or bashful, negligent or compulsive, open or secretive, confident or self-doubting, adventurous or timid, noisy or quiet, visionary or practical, reasonable or hot-headed, careful or careless, impartial or biased, straightforward or underhanded, a "winner" or a "loser," and so on.

With this sort of list, to which you may add according to need, you can analyze and develop conclusions about character. For example, in studying Sarty, the major character in Faulkner's "Barn Burning," you would note that though he is a child and therefore subject to his father's will, he is also guided by the idea of truth. When he learns that his father is going to commit criminal arson, he is forced to make a decision, and as a result of his choice he leaves home. It is out of such conflict and reactions that you can get a "handle" on characters.

APPEARANCE, ACTION, AND CHARACTER

When you study character, be sure to consider physical descriptions, but also be sure to relate the physical to the mental or psychological. Suppose your author stresses the neatness of one character and the sloppiness of another. Most likely, these descriptions can be related to your character study. The same also applies to your examination of what a character *does*. Go beyond the actions themselves and try to determine what they show *about* the character. Always try to get from the outside to the inside, for it is on the inside that character resides.

TYPES OF CHARACTERS: ROUND AND FLAT

In literature you will encounter two types of characters, which E. M. Forster (in *Aspects of the Novel*) calls "round" and "flat." The basic requirement for a **round character,** usually one of the major figures in the work, is that he or she profits from experience and undergoes a change of some sort. Round characters have many realistic traits and are relatively fully developed. For this reason they are often given the names **hero** or **heroine.** Because many major characters are anything but heroic, however, it is probably best to use the more neutral word **protagonist,** which implies only that a character is a center of attention, not a moral or physical giant. The protagonist is central to the action, moves against an **antagonist,** and usually exhibits the human attributes we expect of round characters.

To the degree that round characters have many individual and unpredictable human traits, and because they undergo change or growth as a result of their experiences, they may be considered **dynamic.** In Faulkner's "Barn Burning," for example, Sarty is a dynamic character. He begins the story as an ordinary child, but events demonstrate that he is thinking and developing as a person of conscience and honor. By the story's end, though still a child in years, he has taken on the self-awareness and commitment of an independent adult. These changes show that he is capable of development and growth—in short, that he is dynamic.

In considering a round character, you may decide for yourself whether alterations indicate *change* or *growth.* Do human beings develop new traits as circumstances bring them out, or do circumstances draw out traits that are already present, though hidden? Paul, of Willa Cather's "Paul's Case," is a young man whose imagination takes him beyond the drab circumstances of his life. There is much good in Paul, but he is also quite haughty, he lies, and he shows little concern for his own immediate welfare at home and at school. When he commits grand larceny and finally commits suicide, do these actions show that he has suddenly become self-destructive, or is self-destructiveness his major trait all along? With round or full characters, this sort of question is appropriate, for round characters are just as complex and as difficult to understand as living people. A round character therefore stands out, totally identifiable within the class, occupation, or circumstances of which she or he is a part. Obviously, in a brief story we cannot learn everything there is to know about a character, but if the author is skillful, there will be enough detail in the work to add up to a dynamic character. Indeed, you may judge an author by how fully he or she can bring characters to life-like roundness or completeness.

As contrasted with the round character, the **flat character** is undistinguishable from other persons in a particular group or class. Therefore the flat character is not individual, but representative. Flat characters are usually minor, although not all minor characters are flat. They may be the parent or the brother or sister of a major character, may walk along a street and greet a major character, may be contrasted in some way with a major character, and may provide a service for a major character; they may poke around in rooms in a house, explain a procedure or custom that would otherwise not be explained, and perform the other important tasks in the development of a story. We learn little if anything about their traits and their lives, and they are in truth peripheral to the main plot. Because they do not change or grow, they are **static,** not dynamic like round characters.

Sometimes flat characters are prominent in certain types of fiction, such as cowboy, police, and detective stories, where the main characters must be strong, tough, steadfast, and clever enough to overcome the obstacles before them or solve the crime. These and other types of stories feature recurring situations and require characters to perform similar roles. The term **stock character** refers to characters in these repeating situations. Obviously, names, ages, and sexes are often changed, and places and offices may vary slightly, but stock characters have many common traits. Some of the many stock characters are the clown, the revenger, the foolish boss, the bewildered parent, the overbearing husband or the henpecked husband, the servile wife or the henpecking wife, the angry police captain, the lovable drunk, the younger or older sister or brother, and the town do-gooder.

As long as they perform only their functions, exhibit conventional and unindividual traits, and then disappear from the story and from your memory these characters are flat. When stock characters express no attitudes except those to be expected, they are often given the label **stereotype,** because they all seem to be cast in the same mold. Often in highly conventionalized works like cowboy and police stories, and in romances, even the major characters are flat and stereotypical although they occupy center stage throughout as protagonists.

Complications occur when round characters are in stock roles and exceed their expected stereotypical behavior. Thus John Wright, the murdered husband in Glaspell's "A Jury of Her Peers," is described has having been in life a typically insensitive and bluntly overbearing and even cruel husband—a flat, stock character. The plot of the story develops, however, because his wife, Minnie, having accepted a servile and unimportant role for twenty years—in other words, having been a flat, stock servile wife—has been provoked to move out of this role and destroy her oppressor, her husband. Because of this complication, we know that she is a round character, even though we never see her firsthand, but only hear about her actions and draw our conclusions about her through the discoveries of the two women in the kitchen. Had she continued to acquiesce in her dreary lot with her husband, even to the point of accepting his deliberate cruelty, she would have continued to be flat, representative, and stereotypical, and there would have been no story. Thurber's "The Greatest Man in the World" contains an amusing situation involving stock characteristics: Jacky Smurch is a stereotypical cigar-smoking macho male who performs an act of extraordinary difficulty and heroism. Because he refuses to transfer stereotypes by conforming to the expected image of a modest, self-effacing, gracious public hero, however, he dooms himself.

HOW IS CHARACTER DISCLOSED IN FICTION?

Authors use four distinct ways to present information about characters. Remember that you must use your own knowledge and experience with human beings to make judgments about the qualities—the flatness or roundness—of the characters being revealed.

1. *What the characters themselves say (and think, if the author expresses their thoughts).* On the whole, speeches may be accepted at face value to indicate the character of a speaker. Sometimes, however, a speech may be made offhand, or it may reflect a momentary emotional or intellectual state. Thus, if characters in deep despair say that life is worthless, you must balance this speech with what the same characters say when they are happy. You must also consider the situation or total context of a statement. Macbeth's despair at the end of Shakespeare's play *Macbeth* is voiced after he has shown himself to be guilty of ruthless political suppression and assassination. In fact, his brooding self-condemnation indicates that he is at heart a good person, but that he has taken the wrong path. He would not feel guilt otherwise. You should also consider whether speeches show change or development. A despairing character might say depressing things at the start but happy things at the end. Your analysis of such speeches should indicate how they reflect change or development.

2. *What the characters do.* You have heard that "actions speak louder than words," and you should interpret actions as signs of character. Thus you might consider Phoenix's trip through the woods (Welty's "A Worn Path") as a sign of a loving, responsible character, even though Phoenix herself nowhere claims to be loving and responsible. The difficulty and hardship she goes through on the walk, however, justify such a conclusion about her.

Often you will find that action is inconsistent with logic or expectation. Such behaviors may signal naiveté, weakness, deceit, or a scheming personality; they may also signalize strong inner conflicts, and also change or growth. The old man in Collier's "The Chaser" is a schemer. He is planning eventually to make the big sale of the death potion, the "chaser," and hence he speaks to Alan Austen indirectly and manipulatively; he is ostensibly selling love, but he is really selling death. A strong inner conflict and almost immediate growth may be found in the two women in Glaspell's "A Jury of Her Peers." They have the obligation to the law and to legal justice that we all have, but they develop an even stronger obligation to the accused killer, Mrs. Wright, because they understand her situation so well. Hence they remain silent even though they discover incriminating evidence against her.

3. *What other characters say about them.* In stories and in plays, as in life, people often talk about other people. If the speakers are honest, you may accept their opinions as accurate descriptions of other characters. However, sometimes a person's prejudices and interests distort what that person says. You know, for example, that the word of a person's enemy is likely to be prejudicial and untrue. Therefore an author may give you a good impression of characters by having a bad or negative character say negative things about them (see, for example, Nora's comments about her brother Jackie in O'Connor's "First Confession"). Similarly, the word of a close friend may be biased in favor of a particular character, and thus may exaggerate that character's good qualities. You must always consider the context and source of all remarks before you draw conclusions about character.

4. *What the author says about them, speaking as storyteller or observer.* What the author, speaking with the authorial voice, says about a character is to be accepted as accurate. However, when the authorial voice *interprets* actions and characteristics, the author himself or herself assumes the role of a reader or critic, and any opinions may be either right or wrong. For this reason, authors frequently avoid interpretations and devote their skill instead to arranging events and speeches so that only readers themselves draw conclusions.

REALITY AND PROBABILITY: VERISIMILITUDE

You are entitled to expect characters in literature to be true to life. That is, their actions, statements, and thoughts must all be what human beings are *likely* to do, say, and think under the conditions presented in the work. This expectation is often called the standard of **verisimilitude** ("similar to truth"), **probability,** or **plausibility.** That is, there are persons *in life* who do seemingly impossible tasks (such as singlehandedly capturing 200 enemy soldiers, or giving away a fortune). Such characters *in literature* would ordinarily not be true to life, however, because they exceed *normal* or *usual* human behavior. They are not probable or believable (unless they appear in adventure works, fantasies, or fairy tales).

One should therefore distinguish between what can *possibly* happen and what would frequently or *most usually* happen. Some reactions do not belong in a work featuring full, round characters. Thus, for example, in Maupassant's "The Necklace" it is possible that Mathilde could be truthful and tell her friend Jeanne Forrestier that she has lost the necklace. In light of the sense of pride, honor, shame, and respectability of Mathilde and her husband, however, it is more normal, more believable, for her to hide the fact, borrow money to buy a replacement necklace, and endure the ten-year penance to pay back the loans. The probable, here, has overshadowed the possible.

Nevertheless, probability does not rule out exceptional behavior, surprise, or even exaggeration. It is not unreasonable that young Sarty would try to inform on his father, because he has been developing a sense of morality throughout "Barn Burning." Nor do the monumental accomplishments of Granny, in "The Jilting of Granny Weatherall," seem impossible, such as her having done all the manual labor involved in fencing 100 acres of farming land. We learn that when she was young, she developed a strong sense of determination and obligation to lead a normal life despite having been betrayed by her unfaithful fiancé. It is therefore not improbable that she would do anything that would further this goal. In short, her achievements, though formidable indeed, meet the standard of verisimilitude, or probability.

There are many ways of rendering the probable in literature. Fiction that attempts to mirror life—the realistic, naturalistic, or "slice of life" types of fiction like Welty's "A Worn Path"—sets up conditions and raises expectations about the characters that are different from those of works that attempt to portray a romantic, fanciful world. A character's behavior and speech in the "realistic" setting would be out of place in the romantic setting.

But the situation is more complex than this, for within the romantic setting a character might reasonably be *expected* to behave and speak in a fanciful, dreamlike way. Speech and action under both conditions are therefore *probable* as we understand the word, although different aspects of human character are presented in these two different types of works.

It is also possible that within the same work you might find some characters who are realistic and others who are not. In such works you have contrasting systems of reality. Mathilde in "The Necklace" exhibits such a contrast. Her dream world at the beginning is so powerful that she makes unrealistic demands on her husband. When the borrowed necklace is lost, her character as a dreamer has effectively destroyed her life in the real world.

You might also encounter works where there are *mythical* and *supernatural* personages, like the woodland guide in Hawthorne's "Young Goodman Brown." You may wonder how you should interpret the character of such figures. Usually, gods and goddesses embody qualities of the best and most moral human beings, and devils like Hawthorne's guide take on attributes of the worst. However, you might remember that the devil is often imagined as a character with many dashing and engaging traits, the easier to deceive poor sinners and lead them into hell. In judging characters of this or any type, your best guide is probability, consistency, and believability.

WILLA CATHER   (1873–1947)

Paul's Case   1905 (1904)
A Study in Temperament

It was Paul's afternoon to appear before the faculty of the Pittsburgh High School
to account for his various misdemeanors. He had been suspended a week ago,
and his father had called at the Principal's office and confessed his perplexity
about his son. Paul entered the faculty room suave and smiling. His clothes were
a trifle outgrown, and the tan velvet on the collar of his open overcoat was frayed
and worn; but for all that there was something of the dandy about him, and he
wore an opal pin in his neatly knotted black four-in-hand, and a red carnation in
his buttonhole. This latter adornment the faculty somehow felt was not properly
significant of the contrite spirit befitting a boy under the ban of suspension.

Paul was tall for his age and very thin, with high, cramped shoulders and a
narrow chest. His eyes were remarkable for a certain hysterical brilliancy, and he
continually used them in a conscious, theatrical sort of way, peculiarly offensive
in a boy. The pupils were abnormally large, as though he were addicted to bella-
donna, but there was a glassy glitter about them which that drug does not produce.

When questioned by the Principal as to why he was there, Paul stated, politely
enough, that he wanted to come back to school. This was a lie, but Paul was
quite accustomed to lying; found it, indeed, indispensable for overcoming friction.
His teachers were asked to state their respective charges against him, which they
did with such a rancor and aggrievedness as evinced that this was not a usual
case. Disorder and impertinence were among the offenses named, yet each of his
instructors felt that it was scarcely possible to put into words the real cause of the
trouble, which lay in a sort of hysterically defiant manner of the boy's; in the
contempt which they all knew he felt for them, and which he seemingly made
not the least effort to conceal. Once, when he had been making a synopsis of a
paragraph at the blackboard, his English teacher had stepped to his side and attempted to guide his hand. Paul had started back with a shudder and thrust his
hands violently behind him. The astonished woman could scarcely have been more
hurt and embarrassed had he struck at her. The insult was so involuntary and
definitely personal as to be unforgettable. In one way and another, he had made
all his teachers, men and women alike, conscious of the same feeling of physical
aversion. In one class he habitually sat with his hand shading his eyes; in another
he always looked out of the window during the recitation; in another he made a
running commentary on the lecture, with humorous intent.

His teachers felt this afternoon that his whole attitude was symbolized by
his shrug and his flippantly red carnation flower, and they fell upon him without
mercy, his English teacher leading the pack. He stood through it smiling, his pale
lips parted over his white teeth. (His lips were continually twitching, and he had
a habit of raising his eyebrows that was contemptuous and irritating to the last
degree.) Older boys than Paul had broken down and shed tears under that ordeal,
but his set smile did not once desert him, and his only sign of discomfort was the
nervous trembling of the fingers that toyed with the buttons of his overcoat, and
an occasional jerking of the other hand which held his hat. Paul was always smiling,

always glancing about him, seeming to feel that people might be watching him and trying to detect something. This conscious expression, since it was as far as possible from boyish mirthfulness, was usually attributed to insolence or "smartness."

As the inquisition proceeded, one of his instructors repeated an impertinent remark of the boy's, and the Principal asked him whether he thought that a courteous speech to make to a woman. Paul shrugged his shoulders slightly and his eyebrows twitched.

"I don't know," he replied. "I didn't mean to be polite or impolite, either. I guess it's a sort of way I have, of saying things regardless."

The Principal asked him whether he didn't think that a way it would be well to get rid of. Paul grinned and said he guessed so. When he was told that he could go, he bowed gracefully and went out. His bow was like a repetition of the scandalous red carnation.

His teachers were in despair, and his drawing master voiced the feeling of them all when he declared there was something about the boy which none of them understood. He added "I don't really believe that smile of his comes altogether from insolence; there's something sort of haunted about it. The boy is not strong, for one thing. There is something wrong about the fellow."

The drawing master had come to realize that, in looking at Paul, one saw only his white teeth and the forced animation of his eyes. One warm afternoon the boy had gone to sleep at his drawing board, and his master had noted with amazement what a white, blue-veined face it was; drawn and wrinkled like an old man's about the eyes, the lips twitching even in his sleep.

His teachers left the building dissatisfied and unhappy; humiliated to have felt so vindictive toward a mere boy, to have uttered this feeling in cutting terms, and to have set each other on, as it were, in the gruesome game of intemperate reproach. One of them remembered having seen a miserable street cat set at bay by a ring of tormentors.

As for Paul, he ran down the hill whistling the Soldiers' Chorus from *Faust*,° looking wildly behind him now and then to see whether some of his teachers were not there to witness his light-heartedness. As it was now late in the afternoon and Paul was on duty that evening as usher at Carnegie Hall,° he decided that he would not go home to supper.

When he reached the concert hall the doors were not yet open. It was chilly outside, and he decided to go up into the picture gallery—always deserted at this hour—where there were some of Raffaëlli's° gay studies of Paris streets and an airy blue Venetian scene or two that always exhilarated him. He was delighted to find no one in the gallery but the old guard, who sat in the corner, a newspaper on his knee, a black patch over one eye and the other closed. Paul possessed himself of the place and walked confidently up and down, whistling under his breath. After a while he sat down before a blue Rico° and lost himself. When he bethought him to look at his watch, it was after seven o'clock, and he rose with a

Faust: The most popular opera of Charles Gounod (1818–1893), first produced in 1859.
Carnegie Hall: in Pittsburgh, not the more famous one in New York.
Raffaëlli: Jean-François Rafaëlli (1850–1924), impressionist painter and sculptor, known for his scenes of Parisian life.
Rico: Martin Rico (1833–1908), Spanish painter, known for his landscapes.

start and ran downstairs, making a face at Augustus Caesar,° peering out from the cast-room, and an evil gesture at the Venus of Milo° as he passed her on the stairway.

When Paul reached the ushers' dressing-room half a dozen boys were there already, and he began excitedly to tumble into his uniform. It was one of the few that at all approached fitting, and Paul thought it very becoming—though he knew the tight, straight coat accentuated his narrow chest, about which he was exceedingly sensitive. He was always excited while he dressed, twanging all over to the tuning of the strings and preliminary flourishes of the horns in the music-room; but tonight he seemed quite beside himself, and he teased and plagued the boys until, telling him that he was crazy, they put him down on the floor and sat on him.

Somewhat calmed by his suppression, Paul dashed out to the front of the house to seat the early comers. He was a model usher. Gracious and smiling he ran up and down the aisles. Nothing was too much trouble for him; he carried messages and brought programs as though it were his greatest pleasure in life, and all the people in his section thought him a charming boy, feeling that he remembered and admired them. As the house filled, he grew more and more vivacious and animated, and the color came to his cheeks and lips. It was very much as though this were a great reception and Paul were the host. Just as the musicians came out to take their places, his English teacher arrived with checks for the seat which a prominent manufacturer had taken for the season. She betrayed some embarrassment when she handed Paul the tickets, and a *hauteur* which subsequently made her feel very foolish. Paul was startled for a moment and had the feeling of wanting to put her out; what business had she here among all these fine people and gay colors? He looked her over and decided that she was not appropriately dressed and must be a fool to sit downstairs in such togs. The tickets had probably been sent her out of kindness, he reflected, as he put down a seat for her, and she had about as much right to sit there as he had.

When the symphony began Paul sank into one of the rear seats with a long   15
sigh of relief, and lost himself as he had done before the Rico. It was not that symphonies, as such, meant anything in particular to Paul, but the first sigh of the instruments seemed to free some hilarious spirit within him; something that struggled there like the Genius in the bottle found by the Arab fisherman.° He felt a sudden zest of life; the lights danced before his eyes and the concert hall blazed into unimaginable splendor. When the soprano soloist came on, Paul forgot even the nastiness of his teacher's being there, and gave himself up to the peculiar intoxication such personages always had for him. The soloist chanced to be a German woman, by no means in her first youth, and the mother of many children; but she wore a satin gown and a tiara, and she had that indefinable air of achievement, that world-shine upon her, which always blinded Paul to any possible defects.

After a concert was over, Paul was often irritable and wretched until he got to sleep,—and tonight he was even more than usually restless. He had the feeling of not being able to let down; of its being impossible to give up this delicious excitement which was the only thing that could be called living at all. During the

---

Caesar . . . Milo: copies of the famous statues of Augustus in the Vatican Museum and the Venus de Milo in the Louvre.

Arab fisherman: A reference to the tale of "The Fisherman and the Jinni" from *The Arabian Nights*.

last number he withdrew and, after hastily changing his clothes in the dressing-room, slipped out to the side door where the singer's carriage stood. Here he began pacing rapidly up and down the walk, waiting to see her come out.

Over yonder the Schenley, in its vacant stretch, loomed big and square through the fine rain, the windows of its twelve stories glowing like those of a lighted cardboard house under a Christmas tree. All the actors and singers of any importance stayed there when they were in the city, and a number of the big manufacturers of the place lived there in the winter. Paul had often hung about the hotel, watching the people go in and out, longing to enter and leave schoolmasters and dull care° behind him forever.

At last the singer came out, accompanied by the conductor, who helped her into her carriage and closed the door with a cordial *auf Wiedersehen*,—which set Paul to wondering whether she were not an old sweetheart of his. Paul followed the carriage over to the hotel, walking so rapidly as not to be far from the entrance when the singer alighted and disappeared behind the swinging glass doors which were opened by a Negro in a tall hat and a long coat. In the moment that the door was ajar, it seemed to Paul that he, too, entered. He seemed to feel himself go after her up the steps, into the warm, lighted building, into an exotic, a tropical world of shiny, glistening surfaces and basking ease. He reflected upon the mysterious dishes that were brought into the dining-room, the green bottles in buckets of ice, as he had seen them in the supper party pictures of the Sunday supplement. A quick gust of wind brought the rain down with sudden vehemence, and Paul was startled to find that he was still outside in the slush of the gravel driveway; that his boots were letting in the water and his scanty overcoat was clinging wet about him; that the lights in front of the concert hall were out, and that the rain was driving in sheets between him and the orange glow of the windows above him. There it was, what he wanted—tangibly before him, like the fairy world of Christmas pantomime; as the rain beat in his face, Paul wondered whether he were destined always to shiver in the black night outside, looking up at it.

He turned and walked reluctantly toward the car tracks. The end had to come some time; his father in his night-clothes at the top of the stairs, explanations that did not explain, hastily improvised fictions that were forever tripping him up, his upstairs room and its horrible yellow wallpaper, the creaking bureau with the greasy plush collar-box, and over his painted wooden bed the pictures of George Washington and John Calvin,° and the framed motto, "Feed my Lambs,"° which had been worked in red worsted by his mother, whom Paul could not remember.

Half an hour later, Paul alighted from the Negley Avenue car and went slowly down one of the side streets off the main thoroughfare. It was a highly respectable street, where all the houses were exactly alike, and where business men of moderate means begot and reared large families of children, all of whom went to Sabbath-school and learned the shorter catechism, and were interested in arithmetic; all of whom were as exactly alike as their homes, and of a piece with the monotony in which they lived. Paul never went up Cordelia Street without a shudder of loathing. His home was next to the house of the Cumberland minister. He approached it tonight with the nerveless sense of defeat, the hopeless feeling

20

---

dull care: A phrase from the popular seventeenth-century song "Begone, Dull Care."
John Calvin: John Calvin (1509–1564), a major theologian of the early Reformation in Switzerland.
"*Feed my Lambs:*" see John 21:15–17.

of sinking back forever into ugliness and commonness that he had always had when he came home. The moment he turned into Cordelia Street he felt the waters close above his head. After each of these orgies of living, he experienced all the physical depression which follows a debauch; the loathing of respectable beds, of common food, of those permeated by kitchen odors; a shuddering repulsion for the flavorless, colorless mass of everyday existence; a morbid desire for cool things and soft lights and fresh flowers.

The nearer he approached the house, the more absolutely unequal Paul felt to the sight of it all; his ugly sleeping chamber, the cold bathroom with the grimy zinc tub, the cracked mirror, the dripping spiggots; his father, at the top of the stairs, his hairy legs sticking out from his nightshirt, his feet thrust into carpet slippers. He was so much later than usual that there would certainly be inquiries and reproaches. Paul stopped short before the door. He felt that he could not be accosted by his father tonight; that he could not toss again on that miserable bed. He would not go in. He would tell his father that he had no car fare, and it was raining so hard he had gone home with one of the boys and stayed all night.

Meanwhile, he was wet and cold. He went around to the back of the house and tried one of the basement windows, found it open, raised it cautiously, and scrambled down the cellar wall to the floor. There he stood, holding his breath, terrified by the noise he had made; but the floor above him was silent, and there was no creak on the stairs. He found a soap-box, and carried it over to the soft ring of light that streamed from the furnace door, and sat down. He was horribly afraid of rats, so he did not try to sleep, but sat looking distrustfully at the dark, still terrified lest he might have awakened his father. In such reactions, after one of the experiences which made days and nights out of the dreary blanks of the calendar, when his senses were deadened, Paul's head was always singularly clear. Suppose his father had heard him getting in at the window and had come down and shot him for a burglar? Then, again, suppose his father had come down, pistol in hand, and he had cried out in time to save himself, and his father had been horrified to think how nearly he had killed him? Then, again, suppose a day should come when his father would remember that night, and wish there had been no warning cry to stay his hand? With this last supposition Paul entertained himself until daybreak.

The following Sunday was fine; the sodden November chill was broken by the last flash of autumnal summer. In the morning Paul had to go to church and Sabbath-school, as always. On seasonable Sunday afternoons the burghers of Cordelia Street usually sat out on their front "stoops," and talked to their neighbors on the next stoop, or called to those across the street in neighborly fashion. The men sat placidly on gay cushions placed upon the steps that led down to the sidewalk, while the women, in their Sunday "waists," sat in rockers on the cramped porches, pretending to be greatly at their ease. The children played in the streets; there were so many of them that the place resembled the recreation grounds of a kindergarten. The men on the steps—all in their shirt sleeves, their vests unbuttoned—sat with their legs well apart, their stomachs comfortably protruding, and talked of the prices of things, or told anecdotes of the sagacity of their various chiefs and overlords. They occasionally looked over the multitude of squabbling children, listened affectionately to their high-pitched, nasal voices, smiling to see their own proclivities reproduced in their offspring, and interspersed their legends of the iron kings with remarks about their sons's progress at school, their grades in arithmetic, and the amounts they had saved in their toy banks. On this last Sunday of November, Paul sat all the afternoon on the lowest step of his "stoop," staring into the street, while his sisters, in their rockers, were talking to the minister's daughters next door about how many shirtwaists they had made in the last week, and how many waffles someone had eaten at the last church supper. When the weather was warm, and his father was in a particularly jovial frame of mind, the girls made lemonade, which was always brought out in a red-glass pitcher, ornamented with forget-me-nots in blue enamel. This the girls thought very fine, and the neighbors joked about the suspicious color of the pitcher.

Today Paul's father, on the top step, was talking to a young man who shifted a restless baby from knee to knee. He happened to be the young man who was daily held up to Paul as a model, and after whom it was his father's dearest hope that he would pattern. This young man was of a ruddy complexion, with a compressed, red mouth, and faded, near-sighted eyes, over which he wore thick spectacles, with gold bows that curved about his ears. He was clerk to one of the magnates of a great steel corporation, and was looked upon in Cordelia Street as a young man with a future. There was a story that, come five years ago—he was now barely twenty-six—he had been a trifle 'dissipated,' but in order to curb his appetites and save the loss of time and strength that a sowing of wild oats might have entailed, he had taken his chief's advice, oft reiterated to his employees, and at twenty-one had married the first woman whom he could persuade to share his fortunes. She happened to be an angular school mistress, much older than he, who also wore thick glasses, and who had now borne him four children, all nearsighted, like herself.

The young man was relating how his chief, now cruising in the Mediterranean,   25
kept in touch with all the details of the business, arranging his office hours on his yacht just as though he were at home, and "knocking off work enough to keep two stenographers busy." His father told, in turn, the plan his corporation was considering, of putting in an electric railway plant at Cairo. Paul snapped his teeth; he had an awful apprehension that they might spoil it all before he got there. Yet he rather liked to hear these legends of the iron kings, that were told and retold on Sundays and holidays; these stories of palaces in Venice, yachts on the Mediterranean, and high play at Monte Carlo appealed to his fancy, and he was interested in the triumphs of cash boys° who had become famous, though he had no mind for the cash-boy stage.

After supper was over, and he had helped to dry the dishes, Paul nervously asked his father whether he could go to George's to get some help in his geometry, and still more nervously asked for car fare. This latter request he had to repeat, as his father, on principle, did not like to hear requests for money, whether much or little. He asked Paul whether he could not go to some boy who lived nearer, and told him that he ought not to leave his school work until Sunday; but he gave him the dime. He was not a poor man, but he had a worthy ambition to come up in the world. His only reason for allowing Paul to usher was that he thought a boy ought to be earning a little.

---

cash boys: *The Cash Boy*, a novel by Horatio Alger (1832–1899), tells about the progress of a young boy from a $156 a year "cash boy" position to the inheritance of a million dollars.

Paul bounded upstairs, scrubbed the greasy odor of the dishwater from his hands with the ill-smelling soap he hated, and the shook over his fingers a few drops of violet water from the bottle he kept hidden in his drawer. He left the house with his geometry conspicuously under his arm, and the moment he got out of Cordelia Street and boarded a downtown car, he shook off the lethargy of two deadening days, and began to live again.

The leading juvenile of the permanent stock company which played at one of the downtown theaters was an acquaintance of Paul's, and the boy had been invited to drop in at the Sunday night rehearsals whenever he could. For more than a year Paul had spent every available moment loitering about Charley Edwards's dressing-room. He had won a place among Edwards's following not only because the young actor, who could not afford to employ a dresser, often found him useful, but because he recognized in Paul something akin to what churchmen term "vocation."

It was at the theater and at Carnegie Hall that Paul really lived; the rest was but a sleep and a forgetting.° This was Paul's fairy tale, and it had for him all the allurement of a secret love. The moment he inhaled the gassy, painty, dusty odor behind the scenes, he breathed like a prisoner set free, and felt within him the possibility of doing or saying splendid, brilliant things. The moment the cracked orchestra beat out the overture from *Martha*,° or jerked at the serenade from *Rigoletto*,° all stupid and ugly things slid from him, and his senses were deliciously, yet delicately fired.

Perhaps it was because, in Paul's world, the natural nearly always wore the guise of ugliness, that a certain element of artificiality seemed to him necessary in beauty. Perhaps it was because his experience of life elsewhere was so full of Sabbath-school picnics, petty economies, wholesome advice as to how to succeed in life, and the unescapable odors of cooking, that he found this existence so alluring, these smartly-clad men and women so attractive, that he was so moved by these starry apple orchards that bloomed perennially under the limelight.   30

It would be difficult to put it strongly enough how convincingly the stage entrance of that theater was for Paul the actual portal of Romance. Certainly none of the company ever suspected it, least of all Charley Edwards. It was very like the old stories that used to float about London of fabulously rich Jews, who had subterranean halls, with palms, and fountains, and soft lamps and richly apparelled women who never saw the disenchanting light of London day. So, in the midst of that smoke-palled city, enamored of figures and grimy toil, Paul had his secret temple, his wishing-carpet, his bit of blue-and-white Mediterranean shore bathed in perpetual sunshine.

Several of Paul's teachers had a theory that his imagination had been perverted by garish fiction; but the truth was, he scarcely ever read at all. The books at home were not such as would either tempt or corrupt a youthful mind, and as for reading the novels that some of his friends urged upon him—well, he got

a sleep and a forgetting: From "Intimations of Immortality," an ode by William Wordsworth (1770–1850), published in 1807.
Martha: An opera by Friedrich von Flotow (1812–1883), first performed in 1847, the source of "The Last Rose of Summer."
Rigoletto: One of the best known operas of Giuseppe Verdi (1813–1901), first performed in 1851.

what he wanted much more quickly from music; any sort of music, from an orchestra to a barrel organ. He needed only the spark, the indescribable thrill that made his imagination master of his senses, and he could make plots and pictures enough of his own. It was equally true that he was not stage-struck—not, at any rate, in the usual acceptation of that expression. He had no desire to become an actor, any more than he had to become a musician. He felt no necessity to do any of these things; what he wanted was to see, to be in the atmosphere, float on the wave of it, to be carried out, blue league after blue league, away from everything.

After a night behind the scenes, Paul found the school-room more than ever repulsive; the bare floors and naked walls; the prosy men who never wore frock coats, or violets in their buttonholes; the women with their dull gowns, shrill voices, and pitiful seriousness about prepositions that govern the dative. He could not bear to have the other pupils think, for a moment, that he took these people seriously; he must convey to them that he considered it all trivial, and was there only by way of a joke, anyway. He had autograph pictures of all the members of the stock company which he showed to classmates, telling them the most incredible stories of his familiarity with these people, of his acquaintance with the soloists who came to Carnegie Hall, his suppers with them and the flowers he sent them. When these stories lost their effect, and his audience grew listless, he would bid all the boys good-by, announcing that he was going to travel for a while; going to Naples, to California, to Egypt. Then, next Monday, he would slip back, conscious and nervously smiling; his sister was ill, and he would have to defer his voyage until spring.

Matters went steadily worse with Paul at school. In the itch to let his instructors know how heartily he despised them, and how thoroughly he was appreciated elsewhere, he mentioned once or twice that he had no time to fool with theorems; adding—with a twitch of the eyebrows and a touch of that nervous bravado which so perplexed them—that he was helping the people down at the stock company; they were old friends of his.

The upshot of the matter was, that the Principal went to Paul's father, and Paul was taken out of school and put to work. The manager at Carnegie Hall was told to get another usher in his stead; the door-keeper at the theater was warned not to admit him to the house; and Charley Edwards remorsefully promised the boy's father not to see him again.   35

The members of the stock company were vastly amused when some of Paul's stories reached them—especially the women. They were hard-working women, most of them supporting indolent husbands or brothers, and they laughed rather bitterly at having stirred the boy to such fervid and florid inventions. They agreed with the faculty and with his father, that Paul's was a bad case.

The east-bound train was plowing through a January snowstorm; the dull dawn was beginning to show gray when the engine whistled a mile out of Newark. Paul started up from the seat where he had lain curled in uneasy slumber, rubbed the breath-misted window glass with his hand, and peered out. The snow was whirling in curling eddies above the white bottom lands, and the drifts lay already deep in the fields and along the fences, while here and there the long dead grass and dried weed stalks protruded black above it. Lights shone from the scattered houses, and a gang of laborers who stood beside the track waved their lanterns.

Paul had slept very little, and he felt grimy and uncomfortable. He had made the all-night journey in a day coach because he was afraid if he took a Pullman he might be seen by some Pittsburgh business man who had noticed him in Denny & Carson's office. When the whistle woke him, he clutched quickly at his breast pocket, glancing about him with an uncertain smile. But the little, clay-bespattered Italians were still sleeping, the slatternly women across the aisle were in open-mouthed oblivion, and even the crumby, crying babies were for the nonce stilled. Paul settled back to struggle with his impatience as best he could.

When he arrived at the Jersey City station, he hurried through his breakfast, manifestly ill at ease and keeping a sharp eye about him. After he reached the Twenty-third Street station, he consulted a cabman, and had himself driven to a men's furnishing establishment which was just opening for the day. He spent upward of two hours there, buying with endless reconsidering and great care. His new street suit he put on in the fitting-room; the frock coat and dress clothes he had bundled into the cab with his new shirts. Then he drove to a hatter's and a shoe house. His next errand was at Tiffany's, where he selected silver-mounted brushes and a scarf-pin. He would not wait to have his silver marked, he said. Lastly, he stopped at a trunk shop on Broadway, and had his purchases packed into various traveling bags.

It was a little after one o'clock when he drove up to the Waldorf, and, after 40 settling with the cabman, went into the office. He registered from Washington; said his mother and father had been abroad, and that he had come down to await the arrival of their steamer. He told his story plausibly and had no trouble, since he offered to pay for them in advance, in engaging his rooms; a sleeping-room, sitting room and bath.

Not once, but a hundred times Paul had planned this entry into New York. He had gone over every detail of it with Charley Edwards, and in his scrap book at home there were pages of description about New York hotels, cut from the Sunday papers.

When he was shown to his sitting room on the eighth floor, he saw at a glance that everything was as it should be; there was but one detail in his mental picture that the place did not realize, so he rang for the bell boy and sent him down for flowers. He moved about nervously until the boy returned, putting away his new linen and fingering it delightedly as he did so. When the flowers came, he put them hastily into water, and them tumbled into a hot bath. Presently he came out of his white bathroom, resplendent in his new silk underwear, and playing with the tassels of his red robe. The snow was whirling so fiercely outside his windows that he could scarcely see across the street; but within, the air was deliciously soft and fragrant. He put the violets and jonquils on the tabouret beside the couch, and threw himself down with a long sigh, covering himself with a Roman blanket. He was thoroughly tired; he had been in such haste, he had stood up to such a strain, covered so much ground in the last twenty-four hours, that he wanted to think how it had all come about. Lulled by the sound of the wind, the warm air, and the cool fragrance of the flowers, he sank into deep, drowsy retrospection.

It had been wonderfully simple; when they had shut him out of the theater and concert hall, when they had taken away his bone, the whole thing was virtually determined. The rest was a mere matter of opportunity. The only thing that at all surprised him was his own courage—for he realized well enough that he had always been tormented by fear, a sort of apprehensive dread that, of late years, as the meshes of the lies he had told closed about him, had been pulling the muscles of his body tighter and tighter. Until now, he could not remember a time when he had not been dreading something. Even when he was a little boy, it was always there—behind him, or before, or on either side. There had always been the shadowed corner, the dark place into which he dared not look, but from which something seemed always to be watching him—and Paul had done things that were not pretty to watch, he knew.

But now he had a curious sense of relief, as though he had at last thrown down the gauntlet to the thing in the corner.

Yet it was but a day since he had been sulking in the traces; but yesterday afternoon that he had been sent to the bank with Denny & Carson's deposit, as usual—but this time he was instructed to leave the book to be balanced. There was above two thousand dollars in checks, and nearly a thousand in the bank notes which he had taken from the book and quietly transferred to his pocket. At the bank he had made out a new deposit slip. His nerves had been steady enough to permit of his returning to the office, where he had finished his work and asked for a full day's holiday tomorrow, Saturday, giving a perfectly reasonable pretext. The bank book, he knew, would not be returned before Monday or Tuesday, and his father would be out of town for the next week. From the time he slipped the bank notes into his pocket until he boarded the night train for New York, he had not known a moment's hesitation. 45

How astonishingly easy it had all been; here he was, the thing done; and this time there would be no awakening, no figure at the top of the stairs. He watched the snowflakes whirling by his window until he fell asleep.

When he awoke, it was four o'clock in the afternoon. He bounded up with a start; one of his precious days gone already! He spent nearly an hour in dressing, watching every stage of his toilet carefully in the mirror. Everything was quite perfect; he was exactly the kind of boy he had always wanted to be.

When he went downstairs, Paul took a carriage and drove up Fifth avenue toward the Park. The snow had somewhat abated; carriages and tradesmen's wagons were hurrying soundlessly to and fro in the winter twilight; boys in woolen mufflers were shoveling off the doorsteps; the avenue stages made fine spots of color against the white street. Here and there on the corners whole flower gardens blooming behind glass windows, against which the snow flakes stuck and melted; violets, roses, carnations, lilies of the valley—somehow vastly more lovely and alluring that they blossomed thus unnaturally in the snow. The Park itself was a wonderful stage winter-piece.

When he returned, the pause of the twilight had ceased, and the tune of the streets had changed. The snow was falling faster, lights streamed from the hotels that reared their many stories fearlessly up into the storm, defying the raging Atlantic winds. A long, black stream of carriages poured down the avenue, intersected here and there by other streams, tending horizontally. There were a score of cabs about the entrance of his hotel, and his driver had to wait. Boys in livery were running in and out of the awning stretched across the sidewalk, up and down the red velvet carpet laid from the door to the street. Above, about, within it all, was the rumble and roar, the hurry and toss of thousands of human beings as hot for pleasure as himself, and on every side of him towered the glaring affirmation of the omnipotence of wealth.

The boy set his teeth and drew his shoulders together in a spasm of realiza- 50 tion; the plot of all dramas, the text of all romances, the nerve-stuff of all sensations was whirling about him like the snowflakes. He burnt like a faggot in a tempest.

When Paul came down to dinner, the music of the orchestra floated up the elevator shaft to greet him. As he stepped into the thronged corridor, he sank back into one of the chairs against the wall to get his breath. The lights, the chatter, the perfumes, the bewildering medley of color—he had, for a moment, the feeling of not being able to stand it. But only for a moment; these were his own people, he told himself. He went slowly about the corridors, through the writing-rooms, smoking-rooms, reception-rooms, as though he were exploring the chambers of an enchanted palace, built and peopled for him alone.

When he reached the dining room he sat down at a table near a window. The flowers, the white linen, the many-colored wine glasses, the gay toilettes of the women, the low popping of corks, the undulating repetitions of the *Blue Danube*° from the orchestra, all flooded Paul's dream with bewildering radiance. When the roseate tinge of his champagne was added—that cold, precious, bubbling stuff that creamed and foamed in his glass—Paul wondered that there were honest men in the world at all. This was what all the world was fighting for, he reflected; this was what all the struggle was about. He doubted the reality of his past. Had he ever known a place called Cordelia Street, a place where fagged-looking business men boarded the early car? Mere rivets in a machine they seemed to Paul,—sickening men, with combings of children's hair always hanging to their coats, and the smell of cooking in their clothes. Cordelia Street—Ah, that belonged to another time and country! Had he not always been thus, had he not sat here night after night, from as far back as he could remember, looking pensively over just such shimmering textures, and slowly twirling the stem of a glass like this one between his thumb and middle finger? He rather thought he had.

He was not in the least abashed or lonely. He had no special desire to meet or to know any of these people; all he demanded was the right to look on and conjecture, to watch the pageant. The mere stage properties were all he contended for. Nor was he lonely later in the evening, in his loge at the Opera. He was entirely rid of his nervous misgivings, of his forced aggressiveness, of the imperative desire to show himself different from his surroundings. He felt now that his surroundings explained him. Nobody questioned the purple; he had only to wear it passively. He had only to glance down at his dress coat to reassure himself that here it would be impossible for anyone to humiliate him.

He found it hard to leave his beautiful sitting room to go to bed that night, and sat long watching the raging storm from his turret window. When he went to sleep, it was with the lights turned on in his bedroom; partly because of his old timidity, and partly so that, if he should wake in the night, there would be no wretched moment of doubt, no horrible suspicion of yellow wall-paper, or of Washington and Calvin above his bed.

On Sunday morning the city was practically snow-bound. Paul breakfasted   55
late, and in the afternoon he fell in with a wild San Francisco boy, a freshman at Yale, who said he had run down for a "little flyer" over Sunday. The young man

---

Blue Danube: Composed in 1866, "The Blue Danube" is perhaps the best-known waltz of Johann Strauss (1825–1899).

offered to show Paul the night side of the town, and the two boys went off together after dinner, not returning to the hotel until seven o'clock the next morning. They had started out in the confiding warmth of a champagne friendship, but their parting in the elevator was singularly cool. The freshman pulled himself together to make his train, and Paul went to bed. He woke at two o'clock in the afternoon, very thirsty and dizzy, and rang for ice water, coffee, and the Pittsburgh papers.

On the part of the hotel management, Paul excited no suspicion. There was this to be said for him, that he wore his spoils with dignity and in no way made himself conspicuous. His chief greediness lay in his ears and eyes, and his excesses were not offensive ones. His dearest pleasures were the gray winter twilights in his sitting room; his quiet enjoyment of his flowers, his clothes, his wide divan, his cigarette and his sense of power. He could not remember a time when he had felt so at peace with himself. The mere release from the necessity of petty lying, lying every day and every day, restored his self-respect. He had never lied for pleasure, even at school; but to make himself noticed and admired, to assert his difference from other Cordelia Street boys; and he felt a good deal more manly, more honest, even, now that he had no need for boastful pretensions, now that he could, as his actor friends used to say, "dress the part." It was characteristic that remorse did not occur to him. His golden days went by without a shadow, and he made each as perfect as he could.

On the eighth day after his arrival in New York, he found the whole affair exploited in the Pittsburgh papers, exploited with a wealth of detail which indicated that local news of a sensational nature was at a low ebb. The firm of Denny & Carson announced that the boy's father had refunded the full amount of his theft, and that they had no intention of prosecuting. The Cumberland minister had been interviewed, and expressed his hope of yet reclaiming the motherless lad, and Paul's Sabbath-school teacher declared that she would spare no effort to that end. The rumor had reached Pittsburgh that the boy had been seen in a New York hotel, and his father had gone East to find him and bring him home.

Paul had just come in to dress for dinner; he sank into a chair, weak in the knees, and clasped his head in his hands. It was to be worse than jail, even; the tepid waters of Cordelia Street were to close over him finally and forever. The gray monotony stretched before him in hopeless, unrelieved years; Sabbath-school, Young People's Meeting, the yellow-papered room, the damp dish-towels; it all rushed back upon him with sickening vividness. He had the old feeling that the orchestra had suddenly stopped, the sinking sensation that the play was over. The sweat broke out on his face, and he sprang to his feet, looked about him with his white, conscious smile, and winked at himself in the mirror. With something of the childish belief in miracles with which he had so often gone to class, all his lessons unlearned, Paul dressed and dashed whistling down the corridor to the elevator.

He had no sooner entered the dining room and caught the measure of the music, than his remembrance was lightened by his old elastic power of claiming the moment, mounting with it, and finding it all sufficient. The glare and glitter about him, the mere scenic accessories had again, and for the last time, their old potency. He would show himself that he was game, he would finish the thing splendidly. He doubted, more than ever, the existence of Cordelia Street, and for the first time he drank his wine recklessly. Was he not, after all, one of these fortunate beings? Was he not still himself, and in his own place? He drummed a nervous accompaniment to the music and looked about him, telling himself over and over that it had paid.

He reflected drowsily, to the swell of the violin and the chill sweetness of his wine, that he might have done it more wisely. He might have caught an outbound steamer and been well out of their clutches before now. But the other side of the world had seemed too far away and too uncertain then; he could not have waited for it; his need had been too sharp. If he had to choose over again, he would do the same thing tomorrow. He looked affectionately about the dining room, now gilded with a soft mist. Ah, it had paid indeed!

60

Paul was awakened the next morning by a painful throbbing in his head and feet. He had thrown himself across the bed without undressing, and had slept with his shoes on. His limbs and hands were lead heavy, and his tongue and throat were parched. There came upon him one of those fateful attacks of clear-headedness that never occurred except when he was physically exhausted and his nerves hung loose. He lay still and closed his eyes and let the tide of realities wash over him.

His father was in New York; "stopping at some joint or other," he told himself. The memory of successive summers on the front stoop fell upon him like a weight of black water. He had not a hundred dollars left, and he knew now, more than ever, that money was everything, the wall that stood between all he loathed and all he wanted. The thing was winding itself up; he had thought of that on his first glorious day in New York, and had even provided a way to snap the thread. It lay on his dressing-table now; he had got it out last night when he came blindly up from dinner,—but the shiny metal hurt his eyes, and he disliked the look of it, anyway.

He rose and moved about with a painful effort, succumbing now and again to attacks of nausea. It was the old depression exaggerated; all the world had become Cordelia Street. Yet somehow he was not afraid of anything, was absolutely calm; perhaps because he had looked into the dark corner at last, and knew. It was bad enough, what he saw there; but somehow not so bad as his long fear of it had been. He saw everything clearly now. He had a feeling that he had made the best of it, that he had lived the sort of life he was meant to live, and for half an hour he sat staring at the revolver. But he told himself that was not the way, so he went downstairs and took a cab to the ferry.

When Paul arrived at Newark, he got off the train and took another cab, directing the driver to follow the Pennsylvania tracks out of the town. The snow lay heavy on the roadways and had drifted deep in the open fields. Only here and there the dead grass or dried weed stalks projected, singularly black, above it. Once well into the country, Paul dismissed the carriage and walked, floundering along the tracks, his mind a medley of irrelevant things. He seemed to hold in his brain an actual picture of everything he had seen that morning. He remembered every feature of both his drivers, the toothless old woman from whom he had bought the red flowers in his coat, the agent from whom he had got his ticket, and all of his fellow-passengers on the ferry. His mind, unable to cope with vital matters near at hand, worked feverishly and deftly at sorting and grouping these images. They made for him a part of the ugliness of the world, of the ache in his head, and the bitter burning on his tongue. He stooped and put a handful of snow into his mouth as he walked, but that, too, seemed hot. When he reached a little hillside, where the tracks ran through a cut some twenty feet below him, he stopped and sat down.

The carnations in his coat were drooping with the cold, he noticed; all their red glory over. It occurred to him that all the flowers he had seen in the show windows that first night must have gone the same way, long before this. It was only one splendid breath they had, in spite of their brave mockery at the winter outside the glass. It was a losing game in the end, it seemed, this revolt against the homilies by which the world is run. Paul took one of the blossoms carefully from his coat and scooped a little hole in the snow, where he covered it up. Then he dozed a while, from his weak condition, seeming insensible to the cold.

The sound of an approaching train woke him, and he started to his feet, remembering only his resolution, and afraid lest he should be too late. He stood watching the approaching locomotive, his teeth chattering, his lips drawn away from them in a frightened smile; once or twice he glanced nervously sidewise, as though he were being watched. When the right moment came, he jumped. As he fell, the folly of his haste occurred to him with merciless clearness, the vastness of what he had left undone. There flashed through his brain, clearer than ever before, the blue of Adriatic water, the yellow of Algerian sands.

He felt something strike his chest,—his body was being thrown swiftly through the air, on and on, immeasurably far and fast, while his limbs gently relaxed. Then, because the picture-making mechanism was crushed, the disturbing visions flashed into black, and Paul dropped back into the immense design of things.

QUESTIONS

1. Why is the story called "Paul's Case?" What about it makes it a case?

2. What sort of speaker is telling the story? What concerns does the speaker show to Paul? How does the speaker describe the other characters? At what point does the speaker shift attention exclusively to Paul? Why does this shift occur?

3. Decribe the plot of the story and also the structure. Do the two coincide? Where is the crisis of the story? The climax?

4. Describe the character of Paul. What means does Cather use to give us information about him? In what ways does he seem to be physically or mentally ill? How does he grow or change? What strengths and skills or abilities does he have? What weaknesses? What do his preferences and annoyances show about him? Why does he enjoy the concerts and the theater so? What does his meeting with the college boy in New York show about him?

5. Why does it seem to Paul that forgiveness and subsequent correction would be worse punishments for his theft than outright imprisonment?

6. What elements in the story could make it be construed as a criticism not of Paul but of early twentieth-century society at large? What opportunities does Paul see for himself in the future? What sorts of lives are being led around him by the people of Cordelia Street? To what degree is Paul's judgment of this life justified?

7. What is the meaning of the final sentence, particularly the word "design?" How can it be claimed that Paul has been part of a design? How can the final sentence be interpreted as ironic?

KATHERINE ANNE PORTER (1890–1980)

The Jilting of Granny Weatherall   1930

She flicked her wrist neatly out of Doctor Harry's pudgy careful fingers and pulled the sheet up to her chin. The brat ought to be in knee breeches. Doctoring around the country with spectacles on his nose! "Get along now, take your schoolbooks and go. There's nothing wrong with me."

Doctor Harry spread a warm paw like a cushion on her forehead where the forked green vein danced and made her eyelids twitch. "Now, now, be a good girl, and we'll have you up in no time."

"That's no way to speak to a woman nearly eighty years old just because she's down. I'd have you respect your elders, young man."

"Well, Missy, excuse me." Doctor Harry patted her cheek. "But I've got to warn you, haven't I? You're a marvel, but you must be careful or you're going to be good and sorry."

"Don't tell me what I'm going to be. I'm on my feet now, morally speaking. 5 It's Cornelia. I had to go to bed to get rid of her."

Her bones felt loose, and floated around in her skin, and Doctor Harry floated like a balloon around the foot of the bed. He floated and pulled down his waistcoat and swung his glasses on a cord. "Well, stay where you are, it certainly can't hurt you."

"Get along and doctor your sick." said Granny Weatherall. "Leave a well woman alone. I'll call for you when I want you. . . . Where were you forty years ago when I pulled through milk-leg and double pneumonia? You weren't even born. Don't let Cornelia lead you on," she shouted, because Doctor Harry appeared to float up to the ceiling and out. "I pay my own bills, and I don't throw my money away on nonsense!"

She meant to wave good-by, but it was too much trouble. Her eyes closed of themselves, it was like a dark curtain drawn around the bed. The pillow rose and floated under her, pleasant as a hammock in a light wind. She listened to the leaves rustling outside the window. No, somebody was swishing newspapers: no, Cornelia and Doctor Harry were whispering together. She leaped broad awake, thinking they whispered in her ear.

"She was never like this, *never* like this!" "Well, what can we expect?" "Yes, eighty years old. . . ."

Well, and what if she was? She still had ears. It was like Cornelia to whisper 10 around doors. She always kept things secret in such a public way. She was always being tactful and kind. Cornelia was dutiful; that was the trouble with her. Dutiful and good: "So good and dutiful," said Granny, "that I'd like to spank her." She saw herself spanking Cornelia and making a fine job of it.

"What'd you say, Mother?"

Granny felt her face tying up in hard knots.

"Can't a body think, I'd like to know?"

"I thought you might want something."

"I do. I want a lot of things. First off, go away and don't whisper."   15

She lay and drowsed, hoping in her sleep that the children would keep out and let her rest a minute. It had been a long day. Not that she was tired. It was always pleasant to snatch a minute now and then. There was always so much to be done, let me see: tomorrow.

Tomorrow was far away and there was nothing to trouble about. Things were finished somehow when the time came; thank God there was always a little margin over for peace: then a person could spread out the plan of life and tuck in the edges orderly. It was good to have everything clean and folded away, with the hair brushes and tonic bottles sitting straight on the white embroidered linen: the day started without fuss and the pantry shelves laid out with rows of jelly glasses and brown jugs and white stone-china jars with blue whirligigs and words painted on them: coffee, tea, sugar, ginger, cinnamon, allspice: and the bronze clock with the lion on top nicely dusted off. The dust that lion could collect in twenty-four hours! The box in the attic with all those letters tied up, well she'd have to go through that tomorrow. All those letters—George's letters and John's letters and her letters to them both—lying around for the children to find afterwards made her uneasy. Yes, that would be tomorrow's business. No use to let them know how silly she had been once.

While she was rummaging around she found death in her mind and it felt clammy and unfamiliar. She had spent so much time preparing for death there was no need for bringing it up again. Let it take care of itself now. When she was sixty she had felt very old, finished, and went around making farewell trips to see her children and grandchildren, with a secret in her mind: This is the very last of your mother, children! Then she made her will and came down with a long fever. That was all just a notion like a lot of other things, but it was lucky too, for she had once for all got over the idea of dying for a long time. Now she couldn't be worried. She hoped she had better sense now. Her father had lived to be one hundred and two years old and had drunk a noggin of strong hot toddy on his last birthday. He told the reporters it was his daily habit, and he owed his long life to that. He had made quite a scandal and was very pleased about it. She believed she'd just plague Cornelia a little.

"Cornelia! Cornelia!" No footsteps, but a sudden hand on her cheek. "Bless you, where have you been?"

"Here, mother."   20

"Well, Cornelia, I want a noggin of hot toddy."

"Are you cold, darling?"

"I'm chilly, Cornelia. Lying in bed stops the circulation. I must have told you that a thousand times."

Well, she could just hear Cornelia telling her husband that Mother was getting childish and they'd have to humor her. The thing that most annoyed her was that Cornelia thought she was deaf, dumb, and blind. Little hasty glances and tiny gestures tossed around her and over her head saying, "Don't cross her, let her have her way, she's eighty years old," and she sitting there as if she lived in a thin glass cage. Sometimes Granny almost made up her mind to pack up and move back to her own house where nobody could remind her every minute that she was old. Wait, wait, Cornelia, till your own children whisper behind your back!

In her day she had kept a better house and had got more work done. She wasn't too old yet for Lydia to be driving eighty miles for advice when one of the children jumped the track, and Jimmy still dropped in and talked things over: "Now, Mammy, you've a good business head, I want to know what you think of this? . . ." Old Cornelia couldn't change the furniture around without asking. Little things, little things! They had been so sweet when they were little. Granny wished the old days were back again with the children young and everything to be done over. It had been a hard pull, but not too much for her. When she thought of all the food she had cooked, and all the clothes she had cut and sewed, and all the gardens she had made—well, the children showed it. There they were, made out of her, and they couldn't get away from that. Sometimes she wanted to see John again and point to them and say, Well, I didn't do so badly, did I? But that would have to wait. That was for tomorrow. She used to think of him as a man, but now all the children were older than their father, and he would be a child beside her if she saw him now. It seemed strange and there was something wrong in the idea. Why, he couldn't possibly recognize her. She had fenced in a hundred acres once, digging the post holes herself and clamping the wires with just a negro boy to help. That changed a woman. John would be looking for a young woman with the peaked Spanish comb in her hair and the painted fan. Digging post holes changed a woman. Riding country roads in the winter when women had their babies was another thing: sitting up nights with sick horses and sick negroes and sick children and hardly ever losing one. John, I hardly ever lost one of them! John would see that in a minute, that would be something he could understand, she wouldn't have to explain anything!

It made her feel like rolling up her sleeves and putting the whole place to rights again. No matter if Cornelia was determined to be everywhere at once, there were a great many things left undone on this place. She would start tomorrow and do them. It was good to be strong enough for everything, even if all you made melted and changed and slipped under your hands, so that by the time you finished you almost forgot what you were working for. What was it I set out to do? she asked herself intently, but she could not remember. A fog rose over the valley, she saw it marching across the creek swallowing the trees and moving up the hill like an army of ghosts. Soon it would be at the near edge of the orchard, and then it was time to go in and light the lamps. Come in, children, don't stay out in the night air.

Lighting the lamps had been beautiful. The children huddled up to her and breathed like little calves waiting at the bars in the twilight. Their eyes followed the match and watched the flame rise and settle in a blue curve, then they moved away from her. The lamp was lit, they didn't have to be scared and hang on to mother any more. Never, never, never more. God, for all my life I thank Thee. Without Thee, my God, I could never have done it. Hail, Mary, full of grace.

I want you to pick all the fruit this year and see that nothing is wasted.

There's always someone who can use it. Don't let good things rot for want of using. You waste life when you waste good food. Don't let things get lost. It's bitter to lose things. Now, don't let me get to thinking, not when I am tired and taking a little nap before supper. . . .

The pillow rose about her shoulders and pressed against her heart and the memory was being squeezed out of it: oh, push down the pillow, somebody: it would smother her if she tried to hold it. Such a fresh breeze blowing and such a green day with no threats in it. But he had not come, just the same. What does a woman do when she has put on the white veil and set out the white cake for a man and he doesn't come? She tried to remember. No, I swear he never harmed me but in that. He never harmed me but in that . . . and what if he did? There was the day, the day, but a whirl of dark smoke rose and covered it, crept up and over into the bright field where everything was planted so carefully in orderly rows. That was hell, she knew hell when she saw it. For sixty years she had prayed against remembering him and against losing her soul in the deep pit of hell, and now the two things were mingled in one and the thought of him was a smoky cloud from hell that moved and crept in her head when she had just got rid of Doctor Harry and was trying to rest a minute. Wounded vanity, Ellen, said a sharp voice in the top of her mind. Don't let your wounded vanity get the upper hand of you. Plenty of girls get jilted. You were jilted, weren't you. Then stand up to it. Her eyelids wavered and let in streamers of blue-gray light like tissue paper over her eyes. She must get up and pull the shades down or she'd never sleep. She was in bed again and the shades were not down. How could that happen? Better turn over, hide from the light, sleeping in the light gave you nightmares. "Mother, how do you feel now?" and a stinging wetness on her forehead. But I don't like having my face washed in cold water!

Hapsy? George? Lydia? Jimmy? No, Cornelia, and her features were swollen   30
and full of little puddles. "They're coming, darling, they'll all be here soon." Go wash your face, child, you look funny.

Instead of obeying, Cornelia knelt down and put her head on the pillow. She seemed to be talking but there was no sound. "Well, are you tongue-tied? Whose birthday is it? Are you going to give a party?"

Cornelia's mouth moved urgently in strange shapes. "Don't do that, you bother me, daughter."

"Oh, no, Mother, Oh, no. . . ."

Nonsense. It was strange about children. They disputed your every word. "No what, Cornelia?"

"Here's Doctor Harry."   35

"I won't see that boy again. He just left five minutes ago."

"That was this morning, Mother. It's night now. Here's the nurse."

"This is Doctor Harry, Mrs. Weatherall. I never saw you look so young and happy!"

"Ah, I'll never be young again—but I'd be happy if they'd let me lie in peace and get rested."

She thought she spoke up loudly, but no one answered. A warm weight on   40
her forehead, a warm bracelet on her wrist, and a breeze went on whispering,

trying to tell her something. A shuffle of leaves in the everlasting hand of God. He blew on them and they danced and rattled. "Mother, don't mind, we're going to give you a little hypodermic." "Look here, daughter, how do ants get in this bed? I saw sugar ants yesterday." Did you send for Hapsy too?

It was Hapsy she really wanted. She had to go a long way back through a great many rooms to find Hapsy standing with a baby on her arm. She seemed to herself to be Hapsy also, and the baby on Hapsy's arm was Hapsy and himself and herself, all at once, and there was no surprise in the meeting. Then Hapsy melted from within and turned flimsy as gray gauze and the baby was a gauzy shadow, and Hapsy came up close and said, "I thought you'd never come," and looked at her very searchingly and said, "You haven't changed a bit!" They leaned forward to kiss, when Cornelia began whispering from a long way off, "Oh, is there anything you want to tell me? Is there anything I can do for you?"

Yes, she had changed her mind after sixty years and she would like to see George. I want you to find George. Find him and be sure to tell him I forgot him. I want him to know I had my husband just the same and my children and my house like any other woman. A good house too and a good husband that I loved and fine children out of him. Better than I hoped for even. Tell him I was given back everything he took away and more. Oh, no, oh, God, no, there was something else besides the house and the man and the children. Oh, surely they were not all? What was it? Something not given back. . . . Her breath crowded down under her ribs and grew into a monstrous frightening shape with cutting edges; it bored up into her head, and the agony was unbelievable: Yes, John, get the doctor now, no more talk, my time has come.

When this one was born it should be the last. The last. It should have been born first, for it was the one she had truly wanted. Everything came in good time. Nothing left out, left over. She was strong, in three days she would be as well as ever. Better. A woman needed milk in her to have her full health.

"Mother, do you hear me?"

"I've been telling you—"   45

"Mother, Father Connolly's here."

"I went to Holy Communion only last week. Tell him I'm not so sinful as all that."

"Father just wants to speak to you."

He could speak as much as he pleased. It was like him to drop in and inquire about her soul as if it were a teething baby, and then stay on for a cup of tea and a round of cards and gossip. He always had a funny story of some sort, usually about an Irishman who made his little mistakes and confessed them, and the point lay in some absurd thing he would blurt out in the confessional showing his struggles between native piety and original sin. Granny felt easy about her soul. Cornelia, where are your manners? Give Father Connolly a chair. She had her secret comfortable understanding with a few favorite saints who cleared a straight road to God for her. All as surely signed and sealed as the papers for the new Forty Acres. Forever . . . heirs and assigns forever. Since the day the wedding cake was not cut, but thrown out and wasted. The whole bottom dropped out of the world, and there she was blind and sweating with nothing under her feet and the walls falling away. His hand had caught her under the breast, she had not fallen, there was the freshly polished floor with the green rug on it, just as before. He had cursed like a sailor's parrot and said, "I'll kill him for you." Don't lay a hand on him, for my sake leave something to God. "Now, Ellen, you must believe what I tell you. . . ."

So there was nothing, nothing to worry about any more, except sometimes   50
in the night one of the children screamed in a nightmare, and they both hustled out shaking and hunting for the matches and calling, "There, wait a minute, here we are!" John, get the doctor now. Hapsy's time has come. But there was Hapsy standing by the bed in a white cap. "Cornelia, tell Hapsy to take off her cap. I can't see her plain."

Her eyes opened very wide and the room stood out like a picture she had seen somewhere. Dark colors with the shadows rising towards the ceiling in long angles. The tall black dresser gleamed with nothing on it but John's picture, enlarged from a little one, with John's eyes very black when they should have been blue. You never saw him, so how do you know how he looked? But the man insisted the copy was perfect, it was very rich and handsome. For a picture, yes, but it's not my husband. The table by the bed had a linen cover and a candle and a crucifix. The light was blue from Cornelia's silk lampshades. No sort of light at all, just frippery. You had to live forty years with kerosene lamps to appreciate honest electricity. She felt very strong and she saw Doctor Harry with a rosy nimbus around him.

"You look like a saint, Doctor Harry, and I vow that's as near as you'll ever come to it."

"She's saying something."

"I heard you, Cornelia. What's all this carrying-on?"

"Father Connolly's saying—"   55

Cornelia's voice staggered and bumped like a cart in a bad road. It rounded corners and turned back again and arrived nowhere. Granny stepped up in the cart very lightly and reached for the reins, but a man sat beside her and she knew him by his hands, driving the cart. She did not look in his face, for she knew without seeing, but looked instead down the road where the trees leaned over and bowed to each other and a thousand birds were singing a Mass. She felt like singing too, but she put her hand in the bosom of her dress and pulled out a rosary, and Father Connolly murmured Latin in a very solemn voice and tickled her feet. My God, will you stop that nonsense? I'm a married woman. What if he did run away and leave me to face the priest by myself? I found another a whole world better. I wouldn't have exchanged my husband for anybody except St. Michael himself, and you may tell him that for me with a thank you in the bargain.

Light flashed on her closed eyelids, and a deep roaring shook her. Cornelia, is that lightning? I hear thunder. There's going to be a storm. Close all the windows. Call the children in. . . . "Mother, here we are, all of us." "Is that you, Hapsy?" "Oh, no, I'm Lydia. We drove as fast as we could." Their faces drifted above her, drifted away. The rosary fell out of her hands and Lydia put it back. Jimmy tried to help, their hands fumbled together, and Granny closed two fingers around Jimmy's thumb. Beads wouldn't do, it must be something alive. She was so amazed her thoughts ran round and round. So, my dear Lord, this is my death and I wasn't even thinking about it. My children have come to see me die. But I can't, it's not time. Oh, I always hated surprises. I wanted to give Cornelia the amethyst set—Cornelia, you're to have the amethyset set, but Hapsy's to wear it when she wants, and, Doctor Harry, do shut up. Nobody sent for you. Oh, my dear Lord, do wait a minute. I meant to do something about the Forty Acres, Jimmy doesn't need it and Lydia will later on, with that worthless husband of hers. I meant to finish the alter cloth and send six bottles of wine to Sister Borgia for her dyspepsia. I want to send six bottles of wine to Sister Borgia, Father Connolly, now don't let me forget.

Cornelia's voice made short turns and tilted over and crashed. "Oh, Mother, oh, Mother, oh, Mother. . . ."

"I'm not going, Cornelia. I'm taken by surprise. I can't go."

You'll see Hapsy again. What about her? "I thought you'd never come."   60 Granny made a long journey outward, looking for Hapsy. What if I don't find her? What then? Her heart sank down and down, there was no bottom to death, she couldn't come to the end of it. The blue light from Cornelia's lampshade drew into a tiny point in the center of her brain, it flickered and winked like an eye, quietly it fluttered and dwindled. Granny lay curled down within herself, amazed and watchful, staring at the point of light that was herself; her body was now only a deeper mass of shadow in an endless darkness and this darkness would curl around the light and swallow it up. God, give a sign!

For the second time there was no sign. Again no bridegroom and the priest in the house. She could not remember any other sorrow because this grief wiped them all away. Oh, no, there's nothing more cruel than this—I'll never forgive it. She stretched herself with a deep breath and blew out the light.

QUESTIONS

1. Describe the method of narration. Who is talking, and under what circumstances? By what specific means (e.g., recollection, reflection, conversation) do we learn the specific details that make up the story?

2. Describe the character of Granny Weatherall. Is she round or flat, static or dynamic? What changes has she undergone throughout her life, and why did she go through them? What strengths has she developed? What weaknesses does she retain? What relationships has she had with her children, and what do these show about her? How accurate are her recollections of the things going through her consciousness?

3. Who is George? Why does Granny remember him so vividly after so long a time? Why might she wish to speak to him now? What would she want to say? Why does she want to say it? What does her concern with George indicate about her?

4. Describe the plot of the story. What is the conflict? How is the conflict resolved?

5. Describe the parallels between the earthly bridegroom and the heavenly one (paragraphs 29, 60–61). How are they linked in Granny's mind? How does her failure to receive a heavenly sign parallel her jilting? Contrast her disappointments at having been "jilted" twice. Explain how her life contradicts her dying unhappiness.

6. References to light and darkness are made in the story. What do these references indicate about the character of Granny?

JAMES THURBER   (1894–1961)

The Greatest Man in the World   *1935*

Looking back on it now, from the vantage point of 1950, one can only marvel that it hadn't happened long before it did. The United States of America had been, ever since Kitty Hawk,° blindly constructing the elaborate petard by which, sooner or later, it must be hoist.° It was inevitable that some day there would come roaring out of the skies a national hero of insufficient intelligence, background, and character successfully to endure the mounting orgies of glory prepared for aviators who stayed up a long time or flew a great distance. Both Lindbergh° and Byrd,° fortunately for national decorum and international amity, had been gentlemen; so had our other famous aviators. They wore their laurels gracefully, withstood the awful weather of publicity, married excellent women, usually of fine family, and quietly retired to private life and the enjoyment of their varying fortunes. No untoward incidents, on a worldwide scale, marred the perfection of their conduct on the perilous heights of fame. The exception to the rule was, however, bound to occur and it did, in July, 1937, when Jack ("Pal") Smurch, erstwhile mechanics' helper in a small garage in Westfield, Iowa, flew a second-hand, single-motored Bresthaven Dragon-Fly III monoplane all the way around the world, without stopping.

Never before in the history of aviation had such a flight as Smurch's ever been dreamed of. No one had even taken seriously the weird floating auxiliary gas tanks, invention of the mad New Hampshire professor of astronomy, Dr. Charles Lewis Gresham, upon which Smurch placed full reliance. When the garage worker, a slightly built, surly, unprepossessing young man of twenty-two appeared at Roosevelt Field in early July, 1937, slowly chewing a great quid of scrap tobacco, and announced "Nobody ain't seen no flyin' yet," the newspapers touched briefly and satirically upon his projected twenty-five-thousand-mile flight. Aeronautical and automotive experts dismissed the idea curtly, implying that it was a hoax, a publicity stunt. The rusty, battered, second-hand plane wouldn't go. The Gresham auxiliary tanks wouldn't work. It was simply a cheap joke.

Smurch, however, after calling on a girl in Brooklyn who worked in the flap-folding department of a large paper-box factory, a girl whom he later described as his "sweet patootie," climbed nonchalantly into his ridiculous plane at dawn of the memorable seventh of July, 1937, spat a curve of tobacco juice into the still air, and took off, carrying with him only a gallon of bootleg gin and six pounds of salami.

When the garage boy thundered out over the ocean the papers were forced to record, in all seriousness, that a mad, unknown young man—his name was

---

Kitty Hawk: In North Carolina, the location of the first heavier-than-air flight by the Wright brothers in 1903.
petard . . . hoist: i.e., to be destroyed by one's own cleverness. See *Hamlet*, act III, scene iv, lines 206–207.
Lindbergh: Charles A. Lindbergh (1902–1974), considered to be America's greatest aviation hero, made the first solo trans-Atlantic flight in May, 1927.
Byrd: Richard E. Byrd, "Admiral Byrd" (1888–1957), made the first flight to the North Pole in 1926, and the first airmail flight to France in June, 1927.

variously misspelled—had actually set out upon a preposterous attempt to span the world in a rickety, one-engined contraption, trusting to the long-distance refueling device of a crazy schoolmaster. When, nine days later, without having stopped once, the tiny plane appeared above San Francisco Bay, headed for New York, spluttering and choking, to be sure, but still magnificently and miraculously aloft, the headlines, which long since had crowded everything else off the front page— even the shooting of the Governor of Illinois by the Vileti gang—swelled to unprecedented size, and the news stories began to run to twenty-five and thirty columns. It was noticeable, however, that the accounts of the epoch-making flight touched rather lightly upon the aviator himself. This was not because facts about the hero as a man were too meagre, but because they were too complete.

Reporters, who had been rushed out to Iowa when Smurch's plane was first sighted over the little French coast town of Serly-le-Mar, to dig up the story of the great man's life, had promptly discovered that the story of his life could not be printed. His mother, a sullen short-order cook in a shack restaurant on the edge of a tourists' camping ground near Westfield, met all enquiries as to her son with an angry, "Ah, the hell with him; I hope he drowns." His father appeared to be in jail somewhere for stealing spotlights and laprobes from tourists' automobiles; his younger brother, a weak-minded lad, had but recently escaped from the Preston, Iowa Reformatory and was already wanted in several Western towns for the theft of money-order blanks from post offices. These alarming discoveries were still piling up at the very time that Pal Smurch, the greatest hero of the twentieth century, blear-eyed, dead for sleep, half-starved, was piloting his crazy junk-heap high above the region in which the lamentable story of his private life was being unearthed, headed for New York under greater glory than any man of his time had ever known.

The necessity for printing some account in the papers of the young man's career and personality had led to a remarkable predicament. It was of course impossible to reveal the facts, for a tremendous popular feeling in favor of the young hero had sprung up, like a grass fire, when he was halfway across Europe on his flight around the globe. He was, therefore, described as a modest chap, taciturn, blond, popular with his friends, popular with girls. The only available snapshot of Smurch, taken at the wheel of a phony automobile in a cheap photo studio at an amusement park, was touched up so that the little vulgarian looked quite handsome. His twisted leer was smoothed into a pleasant smile. The truth was, in this way, kept from the youth's ecstatic compatriots; they did not dream that the Smurch family was despised and feared by its neighbors in the obscure Iowa town, nor that the hero himself, because of numerous unsavory exploits, had come to be regarded in Westfield as a nuisance and a menace. He had, the reporters discovered, once knifed the principal of his high school—not mortally, to be sure, but he had knifed him; and on another occasion, surprised in the act of stealing an altar-cloth from a church, he had bashed the sacristan over the head with a pot of Easter lilies; for each of these offences he had served a sentence in the reformatory.

Inwardly, the authorities, both in New York and in Washington, prayed that an understanding Providence might, however awful such a thing seemed, bring disaster to the rusty, battered plane and its illustrious pilot, whose unheard-of flight had aroused the civilized world to hosannas of hysterical praise. The authorities were convinced that the character of the renowned aviator was such that the limelight of adulation was bound to reveal him to all the world, as a congenital hooligan mentally and morally unequipped to cope with his own prodigious fame. "I trust," said the Secretary of State, at one of many secret Cabinet meetings called to consider the national dilemma, "I trust that his mother's prayer will be answered," by which he referred to Mrs. Emma Smurch's wish that her son might be drowned. It was, however, too late for that—Smurch had leaped the Atlantic and then the Pacific as if they were millponds. At three minutes after two o'clock in the afternoon of 17 July, 1937, the garage boy brought his idiotic plane into Roosevelt Field for a perfect three-point landing.

It had, of course, been out of the question to arrange a modest little reception for the greatest flier in the history of the world. He was received at Roosevelt Field with such elaborate and pretentious ceremonies as rocked the world. Fortunately, however, the worn and spent hero promptly swooned, had to be removed bodily from his plane, and was spirited from the field without having opened his mouth once. Thus he did not jeopardize the dignity of this first reception, a reception illumined by the presence of the Secretaries of War and the Navy, Mayor Michael J. Moriarity of New York, the Premier of Canada, Governors Fanniman, Groves, McFeely, and Critchfield, and a brilliant array of European diplomats. Smurch did not, in fact, come to in time to take part in the gigantic hullabaloo arranged at City Hall for the next day. He was rushed to a secluded nursing home and confined to bed. It was nine days before he was able to get up, or to be more exact, before he was permitted to get up. Meanwhile the greatest minds in the country, in solemn assembly, had arranged a secret conference of city, state and government officials, which Smurch was to attend for the purpose of being instructed in the ethics and behavior of heroism.

On the day that the little mechanic was finally allowed to get up and dress and, for the first time in two weeks, took a great chew of tobacco, he was permitted to receive the newspapermen—this by way of testing him out. Smurch did not wait for questions. "Youse guys," he said—and the *Times* man winced—"youse guys can tell the cock-eyed world dat I put it over on Lindbergh, see? Yeh—an' made an ass o' them two frogs." The "two frogs" was a reference to a pair of gallant French fliers who, in attempting a flight only halfway round the world, had, two weeks before, unhappily been lost at sea. The *Times* man was bold enough, at this point, to sketch out for Smurch the accepted formula for interviews in cases of this kind; he explained that there should be no arrogant statements belittling the achievements of other heroes, particularly heroes of foreign nations. "Ah, the hell with that," said Smurch. "I did it, see? I did it, an' I'm talkin' about it." And he did talk about it.

None of this extraordinary interview was, of course, printed. On the contrary, the newspapers, already under the disciplined direction of a secret directorate created for the occasion and composed of statesmen and editors, gave out to a panting and restless world that "Jacky," as he had been arbitrarily nicknamed, would consent to say only that he was very happy and that anyone could have done what he did. "My achievement has been, I fear, slightly exaggerated," the *Times* man's article had him protest, with a modest smile. These newspaper stories were kept from the hero, a restriction which did not serve to abate the rising malevolence of his temper. The situation was, indeed, extremely grave, for Pal

10

Smurch was, as he kept insisting, "rarin' to go." He could not much longer be kept from a nation clamorous to lionize him. It was the most desperate crisis the United States of America had faced since the sinking of the *Lusitania*.°

On the afternoon of the twenty-seventh of July, Smurch was spirited away to a conference-room in which were gathered mayors, governors, government officials, behaviorist psychologists, and editors. He gave them each a limp, moist paw and a brief unlovely grin. "Hah ya?"° he said. When Smurch was seated, the Mayor of New York arose and, with obvious pessimism, attempted to explain what he must say and how he must act when presented to the world, ending his talk with a high tribute to the hero's courage and integrity. The Mayor was followed by Governor Fanniman of New York, who, after a touching declaration of faith, introduced Cameron Spottiswood, Second Secretary of the American Embassy in Paris, the gentlemen selected to coach Smurch in the amenities of public ceremonies. Sitting in a chair, with a soiled yellow tie in his hand and his shirt open at the throat, unshaved, smoking a rolled cigarette, Jack Smurch listened with a leer on his lips. "I get ya, I get ya," he cut in nastily. "Ya want me to ack like a softy, huh? Ya want me to ack like that—baby-faced Lindbergh, huh? Well, nuts to that, see?" Everyone took in his breath sharply; it was a sigh and a hiss. "Mr. Lindbergh," began a United States Senator, purple with rage, "and Mr. Byrd—" Smurch, who was paring his nails with a jacknife, cut in again, "Byrd!" he exclaimed. "Aw fa God's sake, dat big—" Somebody shut off his blasphemies with a sharp word. A newcomer had entered the room. Everyone stood up, except Smurch, who, still busy with his nails, did not even glance up. "Mr. Smurch," said someone sternly, "the President of the United States!" It had been thought that the presence of the Chief Executive might have a chastening effect upon the young hero, and the former had been, thanks to the remarkable co-operation of the press, secretly brought to the obscure conference-room.

A great, painful silence fell. Smurch looked up, waved a hand at the President. "How ya comin'?" he asked, and began rolling a fresh cigarette. The silence deepened. Someone coughed in a strained way. "Geez, it's hot, ain't it?" said Smurch. He loosened two more shirt buttons, revealing a hairy chest and the tattooed word "Sadie" enclosed in a stenciled heart. The great and important men in the room, faced by the most serious crisis in recent American history, exchanged worried frowns. Nobody seemed to know how to proceed. "Come awn, come awn," said Smurch. "Let's get the hell out of here! When do I start cuttin' in on de parties, huh? And what's they goin' to be *in* it?" He rubbed a thumb and a forefinger together meaningly. "Money!" exclaimed a state senator, shocked, pale. "Yeh, money," said Pal, flipping his cigarette out of a window, "an' big money." He began rolling a fresh cigarette. "Big money," he repeated, frowning over the rice paper. He tilted back in his chair, and leered at each gentleman, separately, the leer of an animal that knows its power, the leer of a leopard loose in a bird-and-dog shop. "Aw, fa God's sake, let's get some place where it's cooler," he said. "I been cooped up plenty for three weeks!"

Smurch stood up and walked over to an open window, where he stood staring down into the street, nine floors below. The faint shouting of newsboys floated

---

Lusitania: A British liner sunk by a German submarine in 1915. More than a thousand people were killed, including 128 Americans.

Hah ya: "How are you?"

up to him. He made out his name. "Hot dog!" he cried, grinning, ecstatic. He
leaned out over the sill. "You tell 'em, babies!" he shouted down. "Hot diggity
dog!" In the tense little knot of men standing behind him, a quick, mad impulse
flared up. An unspoken word of appeal, of command, seemed to ring through
the room. Yet it was deadly silent. Charles K. L. Brand, secretary to the Mayor of
New York City, happened to be standing nearest Smurch; he looked inquiringly
at the President of the United States. The President, pale, grim, nodded shortly.
Brand, a tall, powerfully built man, once a tackle at Rutgers, stepped forward,
seized the greatest man in the world by his left shoulder and the seat of his pants,
and pushed him out of the window.

"My God, he's fallen out the window!" cried a quick-witted editor.

"Get me out of here!" cried the President. Several men sprang to his side   15
and he was hurriedly escorted out of a door toward a side-entrance of the building.
The editor of the Associated Press took charge, being used to such things. Crisply
he ordered certain men to leave, others to stay; quickly he outlined a story which
all the papers were to agree on, sent two men to the street to handle that end of
the tragedy, commanded a Senator to sob and two Congressmen to go to pieces
nervously. In a word, he skillfully set the stage for the gigantic task that was to
follow, the task of breaking to a grief-stricken world the sad story of the untimely,
accidental death of its most illustrious and spectacular figure.

The funeral was, as you know, the most elaborate, the finest, the solemnest,
and the saddest ever held in the United States of America. The monument in
Arlington Cemetery, with its clean white shaft of marble and the simple device of
a tiny plane on its base, is a place for pilgrims, in deep reverence, to visit. The
nations of the world paid lofty tributes to little Jacky Smurch, America's greatest
hero. At a given hour there were two minutes of silence throughout the nation.
Even the inhabitants of the small, bewildered town of Westfield, Iowa, observed
this touching ceremony; agents of the Department of Justice saw to that. One of
them was especially assigned to stand grimly in the doorway of a little shack restaurant on the edge of the tourists' camping ground just outside the town. There,
under his stern scrutiny, Mrs. Emma Smurch bowed her head above two ham-
burger steaks sizzling on her grill—bowed her head and turned away, so that
the Secret Service man could not see the twisted, strangely familiar, leer on her
lips.

QUESTIONS

1. Describe the character of Jacky Smurch. What do you learn about him from
   his actions, from the words of others, from his statements? Is he flat or
   round, static or dynamic?

2. How does Thurber develop the plot? What is the basic conflict in the story?
   How is it resolved? Who is the protagonist, the antagonist? What values are
   brought out through the conflict?

3. How probable is it that a person in Smurch's position would refuse to undergo
   the changes required of his new success? How probable is it that someone
   would push him out the window if he didn't? From your answers to these
   questions, what conclusions can you make about the level of realism in the
   story?

4. Describe the humor of the story. What does Thurber ask you to laugh at? How is the laughter produced? How is the conflict linked to the humor?

5. What serious purpose underlies the story? To what degree is it true that public relations require people to adjust their character to what is expected of them because of their station and achievements? What might happen if politicians, for example, did not scrupulously control the "image" they project before the public?

WILLIAM FAULKNER   (1897–1962)

Barn Burning   *1939*

The store in which the Justice of the Peace's court was sitting smelled of cheese. The boy, crouched on his nail keg at the back of the crowded room, knew he smelled cheese, and more: from where he sat he could see the ranked shelves close-packed with the solid, squat, dynamic shapes of tin cans whose labels his stomach read, not from the lettering which meant nothing to his mind but from the scarlet devils and the silver curve of fish—this, the cheese which he knew he smelled and the hermetic meat which his intestines believed he smelled coming in intermittent gusts momentary and brief between the other constant one, the smell and sense just a little of fear because mostly of despair and grief, the old fierce pull of blood. He could not see the table where the Justice sat and before which his father and his father's enemy (*our enemy* he thought in that despair; *ourn! mine and his both! He's my father!*) stood, but he could hear them, the two of them that is, because his father had said no word yet:

"But what proof have you, Mr. Harris?"

"I told you. The hog got into my corn. I caught it up and sent it back to him. He had no fence that would hold it. I told him so, warned him. The next time I put the hog in my pen. When he came to get it I gave him enough wire to patch up his pen. The next time I put the hog up and kept it. I rode down to his house and saw the wire I gave him still rolled on to the spool in his yard. I told him he could have the hog when he paid me a dollar pound fee. That evening a nigger came with the dollar and got the hog. He was a strange nigger. He said, 'He say to tell you wood and hay kin burn.' I said, 'What?' 'That whut he say to tell you,' the nigger said. 'Wood and hay kin burn.' That night my barn burned. I got the stock out but I lost the barn."

"Where is the nigger? Have you got him?"

"He was a strange nigger, I tell you. I don't know what became of him."   5

"But that's not proof. Don't you see that's not proof?"

"Get that boy up here. He knows." For a moment the boy thought too that the man meant his older brother until Harris said, "Not him. The little one. The boy," and, crouching, small for his age, small and wiry like his father, in patched and faded jeans even too small for him, with straight, uncombed, brown hair and eyes gray and wild as storm scud, he saw the men between himself and the table part and become a lane of grim faces, at the end of which he saw the Justice, a shabby, collarless, graying man in spectacles, beckoning him. He felt no floor under his bare feet; he seemed to walk beneath the palpable weight of the grim turning faces. His father, stiff in his black Sunday coat donned not for the trial but for the moving, did not even look at him. *He aims for me to lie*, he thought, again with that frantic grief and despair. *And I will have to do hit.*

"What's your name, boy?" the Justice said.

"Colonel Sartoris Snopes," the boy whispered.

"Hey?" the Justice said. "Talk louder, Colonel Sartoris? I reckon anybody   10
named for Colonel Sartoris in this country can't help but tell the truth, can they?" The boy said nothing. *Enemy! Enemy!* he thought; for a moment he could not even see, could not see that the Justice's face was kindly nor discern that his voice was troubled when he spoke to the man named Harris: "Do you want me to question this boy?" But he could hear, and during those subsequent long seconds while there was absolutely no sound in the crowded little room save that of quiet and intent breathing it was as if he had swung outward at the end of a grape vine, over a ravine, and at the top of the swing had been caught in a prolonged instant of mesmerized gravity, weightless in time.

"No!" Harris said violently, explosively. "Damnation! Send him out of here!" Now time, the fluid world, rushed beneath him again, the voices coming to him again through the smell of cheese and sealed meat, the fear and despair and the old grief of blood:

"This case is closed. I can't find against you, Snopes, but I can give you advice. Leave this country and don't come back to it."

His father spoke for the first time, his voice cold and harsh, level, without emphasis: "I aim to. I don't figure to stay in a country among people who . . ." he said something unprintable and vile, addressed to no one.

"That'll do," the Justice said, "Take your wagon and get out of this country before dark. Case dismissed."

His father turned, and he followed the stiff black coat, the wiry figure walking   15
a little stiffly from where a Confederate provost's man's musket ball had taken him in the heel on a stolen horse thirty years ago, followed the two backs now, since his older brother had appeared from somewhere in the crowd, no taller than the father but thicker, chewing tobacco steadily, between the two lines of grim-faced men and out of the store and across the worn gallery and down the sagging steps and among the dogs and half-grown boys in the mild May dust, where as he passed a voice hissed:

"Barn burner!"

Again he could not see, whirling; there was a face in a red haze, moonlike, bigger than the full moon, the owner of it half again his size, he leaping in the red haze toward the face, feeling no blow, feeling no shock when his head struck the earth, scrabbling up and leaping again, feeling no blow this time either and tasting no blood, scrabbling up to see the other boy in full flight and himself already leaping into pursuit as his father's hand jerked him back, the harsh, cold voice speaking above him: "Go get in the wagon."

It stood in a grove of locusts and mulberries across the road. His two hulking sisters in their Sunday dresses and his mother and her sister in calico and sunbonnets were already in it, sitting on and among the sorry residue of the dozen and more movings which even the boy could remember—the battered stove, the broken beds and chairs, the clock inlaid with mother-of-pearl, which would not run, stopped at some fourteen minutes past two o'clock of a dead and forgotten day and time, which had been his mother's dowry. She was crying, though when she saw him she drew her sleeve across her face and began to descend from the wagon. "Get back," the father said.

"He's hurt. I got to get some water and wash his . . . ."

"Get back in the wagon," his father said. He got in too, over the tail-gate.   20
His father mounted to the seat where the older brother already sat and struck the gaunt mules two savage blows with the peeled willow, but without heat. It was not even sadistic; it was exactly that same quality which in later years would cause his descendants to over-run the engine before putting a motor car into motion, striking and reining back in the same movement. The wagon went on, the store with its quiet crowd of grimly watching men dropped behind; a curve in the road hid it. *Forever* he thought. *Maybe he's done satisfied now, now that he has . . .* stopping himself, not to say it aloud even to himself. His mother's hand touched his shoulder.

"Does hit hurt?" she said.

"Naw," he said. "Hit don't hurt. Lemme be."

"Can't you wipe some of the blood off before hit dries?"

"I'll wash tonight," he said. "Lemme be, I tell you."

The wagon went on. He did not know where they were going. None of   25
them ever did or ever asked, because it was always somewhere, always a house of sorts waiting for them a day or two days or even three days away. Likely his father had already arranged to make a crop on another farm before he . . . Again he had to stop himself. He (the father) always did. There was something about his wolflike independence and even courage when the advantage was at least neutral which impressed strangers, as if they got from his latent ravening ferocity not so much a sense of dependability as a feeling that his ferocious conviction in the rightness of his own actions would be of advantage to all whose interest lay with his.

That night they camped, in a grove of oaks and beeches where a spring ran. The nights were still cool and they had a fire against it, of a rail lifted from a nearby fence and cut into lengths—a small fire, neat, niggard almost, a shrewd fire; such fires were his father's habit and custom always, even in freezing weather. Older, the boy might have remarked this and wondered why not a big one; why should not a man who had not only seen the waste and extravagance of war, but who had in his blood an inherent prodigality with material not his own, have burned everything in sight? Then he might have gone a step farther and thought that that was the reason: that niggard blaze was the living fruits of nights passed during those four years in the woods hiding from all men, blue or gray, with his strings of horses (captured horses, he called them). And older still, he might have divined the true reason: that the element of fire spoke to some deep mainspring of his father's being, as the element of steel or of powder spoke to other men, as the one weapon for the preservation of integrity, else breath were not worth the breathing, and hence to be regarded with respect and used with discretion.

But he did not think this now and he had seen those same niggard blazes all his life. He merely ate his supper beside it and was already half asleep over his iron plate when his father called him, and once more he followed the stiff back, the stiff and ruthless limp, up the slope and on to the starlit road where, turning, he could see his father against the stars but without face or depth—a shape black, flat, and bloodless as though cut from tin in the iron folds of the frockcoat which had not been made for him, the voice harsh like tin and without heat like tin:

"You were fixing to tell them. You would have told him." He didn't answer. His father struck him with the flat of his hand on the side of the head, hard but without heat, exactly as he had struck the two mules at the store, exactly as he would strike either of them with any stick in order to kill a horse fly, his voice still without heat or anger: "You're getting to be a man. You got to learn. You got to learn to stick to your own blood or you ain't going to have any blood to stick to you. Do you think either of them, any man there this morning, would? Don't you know all they wanted was a chance to get at me because they knew I had them beat? Eh?" Later, twenty years later, he was to tell himself, "If I had said they wanted only truth, justice, he would have hit me again." But now he said nothing. He was not crying. He just stood there. "Answer me," his father said.

"Yes," he whispered. His father turned.

"Get on to bed. We'll be there tomorrow." 30

Tomorrow they were there. In the early afternoon the wagon stopped before a paintless two-room house identical almost with the dozen others it had stopped before even in the boy's ten years, and again, as on the other dozen occasions, his mother and aunt got down and began to unload the wagon, although his two sisters and his father and brother had not moved.

"Likely hit ain't fitten for hawgs," one of the sisters said.

"Nevertheless, fit it will and you'll hog it and like it," his father said. "Get out of them chairs and help your Ma unload."

The two sisters got down, big, bovine, in a flutter of cheap ribbons; one of them drew from the jumbled wagon bed a battered lantern, the other a worn broom. His father handed the reins to the older son and began to climb stiffly over the wheel. "When they get unloaded, take the team to the barn and feed them." Then he said, and at first the boy thought he was still speaking to his brother: "Come with me."

"Me?" he said.

"Yes," his father said. "You." 35

"Abner," his mother said. His father paused and looked back—the harsh level stare beneath the shaggy, graying, irascible brows.

"I reckon I'll have a word with the man that aims to begin tomorrow owning me body and soul for the next eight months."

They went back up the road. A week ago—or before last night, that is—he would have asked where they were going, but not now. His father had struck him before last night but never before had he paused afterward to explain why; it was as if the blow and the following calm, outrageous voice still rang, repercussed, divulging nothing to him save the terrible handicap of being young, the light weight of his few years, just heavy enough to prevent his soaring free of the world as it seemed to be ordered but not heavy enough to keep him footed solid in it, to resist it and try to change the course of its events.

Presently he could see the grove of oaks and cedars and the other flowering 40 trees and shrubs where the house would be, though not the house yet. They walked beside a fence massed with honeysuckle and Cherokee roses and came to a gate swinging open between two brick pillars, and now, beyond a sweep of drive, he saw the house for the first time and at that instant he forgot his father and the terror and despair both, and even when he remembered his father again (who had not stopped) the terror and despair did not return. Because, for all the twelve movings, they had sojourned until now in a poor country, a land of small farms and fields and houses, and he had never seen a house like this before. *Hit's big as a courthouse* he thought quietly, with a surge of peace and joy whose reason he could not have thought into words, being too young for that: *They are safe from him. People whose lives are a part of this peace and dignity are beyond his touch, he no more to them than a buzzing wasp: capable of stinging for a little moment but that's all; the spell of this peace and dignity rendering even the barns and stable and cribs which belong to it impervious to the puny flames he might contrive . . .* this, the peace and joy, ebbing for an instant as he looked again at the stiff black back, the stiff and implacable limp of the figure which was not dwarfed by the house, for the reason that it had never looked big anywhere and which now, against the serene columned backdrop, had more than ever that impervious quality of something cut ruthlessly from tin, depthless, as though, sidewise to the sun, it would cast no shadow. Watching him, the boy remarked the absolutely undeviating course which his father held and saw the stiff foot come squarely down in a pile of fresh droppings where a horse had stood in the drive and which his father could have avoided by a simple change of stride. But it ebbed only for a moment, though he could not have thought this into words either, walking on in the spell of the house, which he could even want but without envy, without sorrow, certainly never with that ravening and jealous rage which unknown to him walked in the ironlike black coat before him: *Maybe he will feel it too. Maybe it will even change him now from what maybe he couldn't help but be.*

They crossed the portico. Now he could hear his father's stiff foot as it came down on the boards with clocklike finality, a sound out of all proportion to the displacement of the body it bore and which was not dwarfed either by the white door before it, as though it had attained to a sort of vicious and ravening minimum not to be dwarfed by anything—the flat, wide, black hat, the formal coat of broadcloth which had once been black but which had now that friction-glazed greenish cast of the bodies of old house flies, the lifted sleeve which was too large, the lifted hand like a curled claw. The door opened so promptly that the boy knew the Negro must have been watching them all the time, an old man with neat grizzled hair, in a linen jacket, who stood barring the door with his body, saying "Wipe yo foots, white man, fo you come in here. Major ain't home nohow."

"Get out of my way, nigger," his father said, without heat too, flinging the door back and the Negro also and entering, his hat still on his head. And now the boy saw the prints of the stiff foot on the doorsill and saw them appear on the pale rug behind the machinelike deliberation of the foot which seemed to bear (or transmit) twice the weight which the body compassed. The Negro was shouting "Miss Lula! Miss Lula!" somewhere behind them, then the boy, deluged as though by a warm wave by a suave turn of carpeted stair and a pendant glitter of chandeliers and a mute gleam of gold frames, heard the swift feet and saw her too, a lady—perhaps he had never seen her like before either—in a gray, smooth gown with lace at the throat and an apron tied at the waist and the sleeves turned back, wiping cake or biscuit dough from her hands with a towel as she came up the hall, looking not at his father at all but at the tracks on the blond rug with an expression of incredulous amazement.

"I tried," the Negro cried. "I tole him to . . ."

"Will you please go away?" she said in a shaking voice. "Major de Spain is not at home. Will you please go away?"

His father had not spoken again. He did not speak again. He did not even 45 look at her. He just stood stiff in the center of the rug, in his hat, the shaggy iron-gray brows twitching slightly above the pebble-colored eyes as he appeared to examine the house with brief deliberation. Then with the same deliberation he turned; the boy watched him pivot on the good leg and saw the stiff foot drag round the arc of the turning, leaving a final long and fading smear. His father never looked at it, he never once looked down at the rug. The Negro held the door. It closed behind them, upon the hysteric and indistinguishable woman-wail. His father stopped at the top of the steps and scraped his boot clean on the edge of it. At the gate he stopped again. He stood for a moment, planted stiffly on the stiff foot, looking back at the house. "Pretty and white, ain't it?" he said. "That's sweat. Nigger sweat. Maybe it ain't white enough yet to suit him. Maybe he wants to mix some white sweat with it."

Two hours later the boy was chopping wood behind the house within which his mother and aunt and the two sisters (the mother and aunt, not the two girls, he knew that; even at this distance and muffled by walls the flat loud voices of the two girls emanated an incorrigible idle inertia) were setting up the stove to prepare a meal, when he heard the hooves and saw the linen-clad man on a fine sorrel mare, whom he recognized even before he saw the rolled rug in front of the Negro youth following on a fat bay carriage horse—a suffused, angry face vanishing, still at full gallop, beyond the corner of the house where his father and brother were sitting in the two tilted chairs; and a moment later, almost before he could have put the axe down, he heard the hooves again and watched the sorrel mare go back out of the yard, already galloping again. Then his father began to shout one of the sisters' names, who presently emerged backward from the kitchen door dragging the rolled rug along the ground by one end while the other sister walked behind it.

"If you ain't going to tote, go on and set up the wash pot," the first said.

"You, Sarty!" the second shouted. "Set up the wash pot!" His father appeared at the door, framed against that shabbiness, as he had been against that other bland perfection, impervious to either, the mother's anxious face at his shoulder.

"Go on," the father said. "Pick it up." The two sisters stooped, broad, lethargic; stooping, they presented an incredible expanse of pale cloth and a flutter of tawdry ribbons.

"If I thought enough of a rug to have to git hit all the way from France I 50 wouldn't keep hit where folks coming in would have to tromp on hit," the first said. They raised the rug.

"Abner," the mother said. "Let me do it."

"You go back and git dinner," his father said. "I'll tend to this."

From the woodpile through the rest of the afternoon the boy watched them, the rug spread flat in the dust beside the bubbling wash pot, the two sisters stooping over it with that profound and lethargic reluctance, while the father stood over them in turn, implacable and grim, driving them though never raising his voice again. He could smell the harsh homemade lye they were using; he saw his mother come to the door once and look toward them with an expression not anxious now but very like despair; he saw his father turn, and he fell to with the axe and saw from the corner of his eye his father raise from the ground a flattish fragment of field stone and examine it and return to the pot, and this time his mother actually spoke: "Abner. Abner. Please don't. Please, Abner."

Then he was done too. It was dusk; the whippoorwills had already begun. He could smell coffee from the room where they would presently eat the cold food remaining from the mid-afternoon meal, though when he entered the house he realized they were having coffee again probably because there was a fire on the hearth, before which the rug now lay spread over the backs of the two chairs. The tracks of his father's foot were gone. Where they had been were now long, water-cloudy scoriations resembling the sporadic course of a Lilliputian mowing machine.

It still hung there while they ate the cold food and then went to bed, scattered   55
without order or claim up and down the two rooms, his mother in one bed, where his father would later lie, the older brother in the other, himself, the aunt, and the two sisters on pallets on the floor. But his father was not in bed yet. The last thing the boy remembered was the depthless, harsh silhouette of the hat and coat bending over the rug and it seemed to him that he had not even closed his eyes when the silhouette was standing over him, the fire almost dead behind it, the stiff foot prodding him awake. "Catch up the mule," his father said.

When he returned with the mule his father was standing in the black door, the rolled rug over his shoulder. "Ain't you going to ride?" he said.

"No. Give me your foot."

He bent his knee into his father's hand, the wiry, surprising power flowed smoothly, rising, he rising with it, on to the mule's bare back (they had owned a saddle once; the boy could remember it though not when or where) and with the same effortlessness his father swung the rug up in front of him. Now in the starlight they retraced the afternoon's path, up the dusty road rife with honeysuckle, through the gate and up the black tunnel of the drive to the lightless house, where he sat on the mule and felt the rough warp of the rug drag across his thighs and vanish.

"Don't you want me to help?" he whispered. His father did not answer and now he heard again that stiff foot striking the hollow portico with that wooden and clocklike deliberation, that outrageous overstatement of the weight it carried. The rug, hunched, not flung (the boy could tell that even in the darkness) from his father's shoulder, struck the angle of wall and floor with a sound unbelievably loud, thunderous, then the foot again, unhurried and enormous; a light came on in the house and the boy sat, tense, breathing steadily and quietly and just a little fast, though the foot itself did not increase its beat at all, descending the steps now; now the boy could see him.

"Don't you want to ride now?" he whispered. "We kin both ride now," the   60
light within the house altering now, flaring up and sinking. *He's coming down the stairs now*, he thought. He had already ridden the mule up beside the horse block; presently his father was up behind him and he doubled the reins over and slashed the mule across the neck, but before the animal could begin to trot the hard,

thin arm came round him, the hard, knotted hand jerking the mule back to a walk.

In the first red rays of the sun they were in the lot, putting plow gear on the mules. This time the sorrel mare was in the lot before he heard it at all, the rider collarless and even bareheaded, trembling, speaking in a shaking voice as the woman in the house had done, his father merely looking up once before stooping again to the hame he was buckling, so that the man on the mare spoke to his stooping back:

"You must realize you have ruined that rug. Wasn't there anybody here, any of your women . . ." He ceased, shaking, the boy watching him, the older brother leaning now in the stable door, chewing, blinking slowly and steadily at nothing apparently. "It cost a hundred dollars. But you never had a hundred dollars. You never will. So I'm going to charge you twenty bushels of corn against your crop. I'll add it in your contract and when you come to the commissary you can sign it. That won't keep Mrs. de Spain quiet but maybe it will teach you to wipe your feet off before you enter her house again."

Then he was gone. The boy looked at his father, who still had not spoken or even looked up again, who was now adjusting the logger-head in the hame.

"Pap," he said. His father looked at him—the inscrutable face, the shaggy brows beneath which the gray eyes glinted coldly. Suddenly the boy went toward him, fast, stopping as suddenly. "You done the best you could!" he cried. "If he wanted hit done different why didn't he wait and tell you how? He won't git no twenty bushels! He won't git none! We'll get hit and hide hit! I kin watch . . ."

"Did you put the cutter back in that straight stock like I told you?"   65

"No, sir," he said.

"Then go do it."

That was Wednesday. During the rest of that week he worked steadily, at what was within his scope and some which was beyond it, with an industry that did not need to be driven nor even commanded twice; he had this from his mother, with the difference that some at least of what he did he liked to do, such as splitting wood with the half-size axe which his mother and aunt had earned, or saved money somehow, to present him with at Christmas. In company with the two older women (and on one afternoon even one of the sisters), he built pens for the shoat and the cow which were a part of his father's contract with the landlord, and one afternoon, his father being absent, gone somewhere on one of the mules, he went to the field.

They were running a middle buster now, his brother holding the plow straight while he handled the reins, and walking beside the straining mule, the rich black soil shearing cool and damp against his bare ankles, he thought *Maybe this is the end of it. Maybe even that twenty bushels that seems hard to have to pay for just a rug will be a cheap price for him to stop forever and always from being what he used to be*; thinking, dreaming now, so that his brother had to speak sharply to him to mind the mule: *Maybe he even won't collect the twenty bushels. Maybe it will all add up and balance and vanish—corn, rug, fire; the terror and grief, the being pulled two ways like between two teams of horses—gone, done with forever and ever.*

Then it was Saturday; he looked up from beneath the mule he was harnessing   70
and saw his father in the black coat and hat. "Not that," his father said. "The wagon gear." And then, two hours later, sitting in the wagon bed behind his father

and brother on the seat, the wagon accomplished a final curve, and he saw the weathered paintless store with its tattered tobacco- and patent-medicine posters and the tethered wagons and saddle animals below the gallery. He mounted the gnawed steps behind his father and brother, and there again was the lane of quiet, watching faces for the three of them to walk through. He saw the man in spectacles sitting at the plank table and he did not need to be told this was a Justice of the Peace; he sent one glare of fierce, exultant, partisan defiance at the man in collar and cravat now, whom he had seen but twice in his life, and that on a galloping horse, who now wore on his face an expression not of rage but of amazed unbelief which the boy could not have known was at the incredible circumstance of being sued by one of his own tenants, and came and stood against his father and cried at the Justice: "He ain't done it! He ain't burnt . . ."

"Go back to the wagon," his father said.

"Burnt?" the Justice said. "Do I understand this rug was burned too?"

"Does anybody here claim it was?" his father said. "Go back to the wagon." But he did not, he merely retreated to the rear of the room, crowded as that other had been, but not to sit down this time, instead, to stand pressing among the motionless bodies, listening to the voices:

"And you claim twenty bushels of corn is too high for the damage you did to the rug?"

"He brought the rug to me and said he wanted the tracks washed out of it. I washed the tracks out and took the rug back to him." 75

"But you didn't carry the rug back to him in the same condition it was in before you made the tracks on it."

His father did not answer, and now for perhaps half a minute there was no sound at all save that of breathing, the faint, steady suspiration of complete and intent listening.

"You decline to answer that, Mr. Snopes?" Again his father did not answer. "I'm going to find against you, Mr. Snopes. I'm going to find that you were responsible for the injury to Major de Spain's rug and hold you liable for it. But twenty bushels of corn seems a little high for a man in your circumstances to have to pay. Major de Spain claims it cost a hundred dollars. October corn will be worth about fifty cents. I figure that if Major de Spain can stand a ninety-five-dollar loss on something he paid cash for, you can stand a five-dollar loss you haven't earned yet. I hold you in damages to Major de Spain to the amount of ten bushels of corn over and above your contract with him, to be paid to him out of your crop at gathering time. Court adjourned."

It had taken no time hardly, the morning was but half begun. He thought they would return home and perhaps back to the field, since they were late, far behind all other farmers. But instead his father passed on behind the wagon, merely indicating with his hand for the older brother to follow with it, and crossed the road toward the blacksmith shop opposite, pressing on after his father, overtaking him, speaking, whispering up at the harsh, calm face beneath the weathered hat: "He won't git no ten bushels neither. He won't git one. We'll . . ." until his father glanced for an instant down on him, the face absolutely calm, the grizzled eyebrows tangled above the cold eyes, the voice almost pleasant, almost gentle:

"You think so? Well, we'll wait till October anyway." 80

The matter of the wagon—the setting of a spoke or two and the tightening of the tires—did not take long either, the business of the tires accomplished by driving the wagon into the spring branch behind the shop and letting it stand there, the mules nuzzling into the water from time to time, and the boy on the seat with the idle reins, looking up the slope and through the sooty tunnel of the shed where the slow hammer rang and where his father sat on an upended cypress bolt, easily, either talking or listening, still sitting there when the boy brought the dripping wagon up out of the branch and halted it before the door.

"Take them on to the shade and hitch," his father said. He did so and returned. His father and the smith and a third man squatting on his heels inside the door were talking, about crops and animals; the boy, squatting too in the ammoniac dust and hoof-parings and scales of rust, heard his father tell a long and unhurried story out of the time before the birth of the older brother even when he had been a professional horsetrader. And then his father came up beside him where he stood before a tattered last year's circus poster on the other side of the store, gazing rapt and quiet at the scarlet horses, the incredible poisings and convolutions of tulle and tights and the painted leers of comedians, and said, "It's time to eat."

But not at home. Squatting beside his brother against the front wall, he watched his father emerge from the store and produce from a paper sack a segment of cheese and divided it carefully and deliberately into three with his pocket knife and produce crackers from the same sack. They all three squatted on the gallery and ate slowly, without talking; then in the store again, they drank from a tin dipper tepid water smelling of the cedar bucket and of living beech trees. And still they did not go home. It was a horse lot this time, a tall rail fence upon and along which men stood and sat and out of which one by one horses were led, to be walked and trotted and then cantered back and forth along the road while the slow swapping and buying went on and the sun began to slant westward, they— the three of them—watching and listening, the older brother with his muddy eyes and his steady, inevitable tobacco, the father commenting now and then on certain of the animals, to no one in particular.

It was after sundown when they reached home. They ate supper by lamplight, then, sitting on the doorstep, the boy watched the night fully accomplish, listening to the whippoorwills and the frogs, when he heard his mother's voice: "Abner! No! No! Oh, God. Oh, God. Abner!" and he rose, whirled, and saw the altered light through the door where a candle stub now burned in a bottle neck on the table and his father, still in the hat and coat, at once formal and burlesque as though dressed carefully for some shabby and ceremonial violence, emptying the reservoir of the lamp back into the five-gallon kerosene can from which it had been filled, while the mother tugged at his arm until he shifted the lamp to the other hand and flung her back, not savagely or viciously, just hard, into the wall, her hands flung out against the wall for balance, her mouth open and in her face the same quality of hopeless despair as had been in her voice. Then his father saw him standing in the door.

"Go to the barn and get that can of oil we were oiling the wagon with," he said. The boy did not move. Then he could speak.

"What . . ." he cried. "What are you . . ."

"Go get that oil," his father said. "Go."

Then he was moving, running, outside the house, toward the stable: this the old habit, the old blood which he had not been permitted to choose for himself,

85

which had been bequeathed him willy nilly and which had run for so long (and who knew where, battening on what of outrage and savagery and lust) before it came to him. *I could keep on*, he thought. *I could run on and on and never look back, never need to see his face again. Only I can't.* I can't, the rusted can in his hand now, the liquid sloshing in it as he ran back to the house and into it, into the sound of his mother's weeping in the next room, and handed the can to his father.

"Ain't you going to even send a nigger?" he cried. "At least you sent a nigger before!"

This time his father didn't strike him. The hand came even faster than the   90
blow had, the same hand which had set the can on the table with almost excruciating care flashing from the can toward him too quick for him to follow it, gripping him by the back of his shirt and on to tiptoe before he had seen it quit the can, the face stooping at him in breathless and frozen ferocity, the cold, dead voice speaking over him to the older brother who leaned against the table, chewing with that steady, curious, sidewise motion of cows:

"Empty the can into the big one and go on. I'll catch up with you."

"Better tie him up to the bedpost," the brother said.

"Do like I told you," the father said. Then the boy was moving, his bunched shirt and the hard, bony hand between his shoulder-blades, his toes just touching the floor, across the room and into the other one, past the sisters sitting with spread heavy thighs in the two chairs over the cold hearth, and to where his mother and aunt sat side by side on the bed, the aunt's arms about his mother's shoulders.

"Hold him," the father said. The aunt made a startled movement. "Not you," the father said. "Lennie. Take hold of him. I want to see you do it." His mother took him by the wrist. "You'll hold him better than that. If he gets loose don't you know what he is going to do? He will go up yonder." He jerked his head toward the road. "Maybe I'd better tie him."

"I'll hold him," his mother whispered.   95

"See you do then." Then his father was gone, the stiff foot heavy and measured upon the boards, ceasing at last.

Then he began to struggle. His mother caught him in both arms, he jerking and wrenching at them. He would be stronger in the end, he knew that. But he had no time to wait for it. "Lemme go!" he cried. "I don't want to have to hit you!"

"Let him go!" the aunt said. "If he don't go, before God, I am going up there myself!"

"Don't you see I can't?" his mother cried. "Sarty! Sarty! No! No! Help me, Lizzie!"

Then he was free. His aunt grasped at him but it was too late. He whirled,   100
running, his mother stumbled forward on to her knees behind him, crying to the nearer sister: "Catch him, Net! Catch him!" But that was too late too, the sister (the sisters were twins, born at the same time, yet either of them now gave the impression of being, encompassing as much living meat and volume and weight as any other two of the family) not yet having begun to rise from the chair, her head, face, alone merely turned, presenting to him in the flying instant an astonishing expanse of young female features untroubled by any surprise even, wearing only an expression of bovine interest. Then he was out of the room, out of the house, in the mild dust of the starlit road and the heavy rifeness of honeysuckle, the

pale ribbon unspooling with terrific slowness under his running feet, reaching the gate at last and turning in, running, his heart and lungs drumming, on up the drive toward the lighted house, the lighted door. He did not knock, he burst in, sobbing for breath, incapable for the moment of speech; he saw the astonished face of the Negro in the linen jacket without knowing when the Negro had appeared.

"De Spain!" he cried, panted. "Where's . . ." then he saw the white man too emerging from a white door down the hall. "Barn!" he cried. "Barn!"

"What?" the white man said. "Barn?"

"Yes!" the boy cried. "Barn!"

"Catch him!" the white man shouted.

But it was too late this time too. The Negro grasped his shirt, but the entire   105
sleeve, rotten with washing, carried away, and he was out that door too and in the drive again, and had actually never ceased to run even while he was screaming into the white man's face.

Behind him the white man was shouting. "My horse! Fetch my horse!" and he thought for an instant of cutting across the park and climbing the fence into the road, but he did not know the park nor how high the vine-massed fence might be and he dared not risk it. So he ran on down the drive, blood and breath roaring; presently he was in the road again though he could not see it. He could not hear either: the galloping mare was almost upon him before he heard her, and even then he held his course, as if the very urgency of his wild grief and need must in a moment more find him wings, waiting until the ultimate instant to hurl himself aside and into the weed-choked roadside ditch as the horse thundered past and on, for an instant in furious silhouette against the stars, the tranquil early summer night sky which, even before the shape of the horse and rider vanished, strained abruptly and violently upward: a long, swirling roar incredible and sound- less, blotting the stars, and he springing up and into the road again, running again, knowing it was too late yet still running even after he heard the shot and, an instant later, two shots, pausing now without knowing he had ceased to run, crying "Pap! Pap!," running again before he knew he had begun to run, stumbling, tripping over something and scrabbling up again without ceasing to run, looking backward over his shoulder at the glare as he got up, running on among the invisible trees, panting, sobbing, "Father! Father!"

At midnight he was sitting on the crest of a hill. He did not know it was midnight and he did not know how far he had come. But there was no glare behind him now and he sat now, his back toward what he had called home for four days anyhow, his face toward the dark woods which he would enter when breath was strong again, small, shaking steadily in the chill darkness, hugging himself into the remainder of his thin, rotten shirt, the grief and despair now no longer terror and fear but just grief and despair. *Father. My father*, he thought. "He was brave!" he cried suddenly, aloud but not loud, no more than a whisper: "He was! He was in the war! He was in Colonel Sartoris' cav'ry!" not knowing that his father had gone to that war a private in the fine old European sense, wearing no uniform, admitting the authority of and giving fidelity to no man or army or flag, going to war as Malbrouck° himself did: for booty—it meant nothing and less than nothing to him if it were enemy booty or his own.

Malbrouck: The hero of an old French ballad ("Malbrouck s'en va-t-en guerre") about the uncertain fate of soldiers going to war.

The slow constellations wheeled on. It would be dawn and then sun-up after a while and he would be hungry. But that would be tomorrow and now he was only cold, and walking would cure that. His breathing was easier now and he decided to get up and go on, and then he found that he had been asleep because he knew it was almost dawn, the night almost over. He could tell that from the whippoorwills. They were everywhere now among the dark trees below him, constant and inflectioned and ceaseless, so that, as the instant for giving over to the day birds drew nearer and nearer, there was no interval at all between them. He got up. He was a little stiff, but walking would cure that too as it would the cold, and soon there would be the sun. He went on down the hill, toward the dark woods within which the liquid silver voices of the birds called unceasing—the rapid and urgent beating of the urgent and quiring heart of the late spring night. He did not look back.

QUESTIONS

1. What is the story's setting (time and place)? How does Faulkner convey this information to the reader?

2. Who is telling the story? Why are the boy and his father in court?

3. Describe the Snopes family. How does Faulkner let us know that they have moved often from place to place? What does this tell us about the family? Are the mother and sisters round or flat? Explain.

4. What is Abner Snopes like as a character? How does his behavior in court help define his character? To what extent does his Civil War experience contribute to this definition? What is his attitude toward the de Spain family? To what extent does his behavior with the rug illustrate his attitude and help define his character?

5. What is Sarty (Colonel Sartoris Snopes) like? What is his attitude toward his father? Toward his father's decision to act against the de Spains? Why does Sarty leave and "not look back" at the end of the story?

6. What conflicts are developed in the story? What is the central conflict? To what extent is this conflict resolved in the climax? To what extent does this resolution help us identify the protagonist of the story?

7. For what reasons might we argue that Sarty is a round (rather than flat) character and a dynamic (rather than static) character? In what ways does Sarty change and grow in the story? What does he learn?

8. In the Old Testament, 2 Samuel, chapters 2 and 3, Abner, the cousin of King Saul, was a powerful commander, warrior, and king maker. He was loyal to the son of Saul and fought against the supporters of King David. When Abner died, it became possible for David to become uncontested king over the ancient holy land. Do you see any significance in Faulkner's choosing the name *Abner* for the father of the Snopes family? What aspects of Abner's character make him heroic? What aspects make him antiheroic?

9. At the climax, who is the rider of the horse? Who fires the three shots?

Why does Faulkner not tell us the result of the shooting? (In Book I of Faulkner's *The Hamlet*, we learn that Abner and his other son, Flem, escape.)

WRITING ABOUT CHARACTER

Most likely your essay assignment will be to write about a major character, although you might be assigned a minor character or characters. Either way, your prewriting procedures will be much the same. After your overview, take notes directed toward your assignment. Determine as many traits as you can, and also determine how the author has presented information about the character. When comments are made by other characters or by the authorial voice, determine whether these are true. When characters go into action, consider what these actions tell about their natures. If there are unusual traits, determine what they show.

Try to answer questions like these: Does the character come to life? What change or changes does he or she undergo? Is he or she "round" or "flat," lifelike or wooden? Are there admirable qualities, or are there many shortcomings? What are they? Is the character central to the action, and therefore the hero or protagonist of the story? What traits make the character genuinely major? Do you like him or her? Why? Who or what is the antagonist? How does reaction to the antagonist bring out qualities in the character? What are they? Does the character exhibit stock or stereotypical qualities? If so, does he or she rise above them, and how? What is the relationship of the character to the other characters? What do the others say or think about him, or her? How accurate are their observations?

Once you have gathered materials in response to these and other questions, you will be able to do the classifying and sorting necessary for the composition of the essay.

Organizing Your Essay

INTRODUCTION. The introduction may begin with a brief identification of the character to be analyzed, which may be followed by reference to noteworthy problems about the character's qualities. The central idea is a statement about the major trait or quality of the character. The thesis sentence links the central idea to the main sections to be covered in the body.

BODY. The organization is designed to illustrate the central idea to make it convincing. There is much freedom in the approach to take, such as the following:

1. *Organization around central traits or major habits and characteristics.* Examples might be "kindness, gentleness, generosity, firmness," or "resoluteness of will frustrated by inopportune moments for action, resulting

in despondency, doubt, and melancholy." A body containing this sort of structure would demonstrate how these qualities are exhibited in the work. For example, a particularly strong quality might be shown in speeches that one character makes about the major character, or in the speeches and actions of the major character. Emphasizing the quality thus enables you to study the different ways in which the author presents the character, and it also enables you to focus on separate parts of the work irrespective of the narrative or chronological development of the plot.

2. *Organization around the growth or change of a character.* The beginning of such a body would establish the traits that the character possesses at the start of the story, and then describe the changes or developments that occur. It is important here to avoid retelling a narrative, and to stress the alterations as they emerge from the circumstances of the story. It is also important to determine whether the growth or change is genuine; do the traits belong clearly to the character, and are they logically produced, or are they manufactured as needed by the events of the story?

3. *Organization around central actions, objects, or quotations.* Certain key actions may stand out in a work, along with objects closely associated with the character being analyzed, together with several key quotations spoken by the character or by someone else in the work. The body of an essay on character study might effectively be structured using these as signposts. As with the second organization, it is important to stress in the topic sentences that the purpose is to illuminate the character, to show how the topics are keys or wedges to opening up an understanding of the character, not just to expand on the incidents, things, or quotations as separate topics themselves.

4. *Organization around qualities of a flat character or characters.* If the essay is assigned on a character who is not round but flat, the body might treat topics like the function and relative significance of the character, the group of which the character is representative, the relationship of the flat character to the round ones and the importance of this relationship, and any additional qualities or traits discoverable in the work.

CONCLUSION.   The conclusion is the place for statements about how the discussed characteristics are related to the story as a whole. If the person was good but came to a bad end, does this discrepancy elevate him or her to tragic stature? If the person was a nobody and came to a bad end, does this fact suggest any authorial attitudes about the class or type to which the character belongs? Or does it seem to illustrate the author's general view of human life? Or both? Do the characteristics explain why the person helps or hinders other characters? Does the essay help in the clearing up of any misunderstandings that might have been present on a first reading? Questions like these may be raised and answered in the conclusion.

SAMPLE ESSAY

The Character of Granny Weatherall*

[1]
    Granny Weatherall is the major character in Katherine Anne Porter's "The Jilting of Granny Weatherall." She is a woman of eighty, and is on her deathbed during the narrative. The story moves forward as she responds to concerned people around her and also as she thinks about the previous sixty years of her life. We learn that the deepest pain in her life was that a lover named George jilted her on her wedding day; the pain returns during her final recollections and thoughts. We also learn that she overcame her grief, that she married and had four children and a number of grandchildren, that she became widowed early, and that she had a hard life but nevertheless a loving and successful one. All the story's details show a poignant and rounded portrait of her as a person of determination, liveliness, nobility, and resilience.° These qualities are apparent in her confidence, responsibility, perceptiveness, and vulnerability.□

[2]
    Her confidence results from a healthy sense of accomplishment and self identity. She is confident of her status with others, and speaks to her daughter and to the doctor as though she has earned their respect. In her life she has overcome great difficulty: The two major blows we learn about— the jilting by George and the early death of her husband John—might have rendered a less resilient person unable to cope. But cope Granny did, managing the children and the family farm all by herself, and doing quite well at it. Readers may share her quiet pride in her recollections of moments with the children, the beginnings of each new day with things in order, and the trips around the local countryside to attend to the needs of neighbors in various midwifing and veterinarian duties. Granny sees her life as a record of work and achievement, and her self-confidence shows the honesty of her judgment.

[3]
    The quality justifying this confidence is her sense of dedicated responsibility. She is the kind who gets things done herself, a self-starter and also a finisher. As she says to the doctor, she remembers a time forty years before, when she recovered from disease without a doctor's aid (paragraph 7). Even on her deathbed, her belief in her own strength causes her to try dismissing the doctor with the claim "There's nothing wrong with me" (paragraph 1). This quality of being responsible for getting things done is shown in her having fenced 100 acres, digging the post holes and stretching the wires herself with the aid of only one other person. Constantly, even on her deathbed, she thinks that she has many things to do—a habitual response to life even as she is leaving it (paragraph 16).

[4]
    To accompany her sense of performance she possesses great perceptiveness and insight. It seems natural to her to see needs, for it is her vision that has enabled her to be a doer. Her thoughts about her belongings, for example, indicate that she sees a need for continued helpfulness even beyond

* See p. 164 for this story.
° Central idea.
□ Thesis sentence.

death (paragraph 57). She therefore wants to leave "Sister Borgia" six bottles of wine for a stomach ailment, but more significantly, she thinks that her daughter Lydia will benefit from receiving the "Forty Acres" as a hedge against the shiftlessness of her husband. A touching illustration of her capacity for insight, even on her deathbed, is her recollection of her husband; she remembers him as a man, but in fact he was younger than their children now. Thus she concludes that he would seem like "a child beside her if she saw him now" (paragraph 25). Her insight into these differences, and the irony of her perspective, seems remarkable.

[5] Unless the reader thinks of Granny Weatherall as nothing more than a doing and accomplishing machine, however, the completeness of the portrait is brought out in her very human vulnerability. This is the inner side of her life, when she was "Ellen" and not "Granny"—the side that remains hurt even sixty years after having been jilted on her wedding day, and the side that makes her slightly uneasy because some of her youthful love letters might be discovered after her death. That she is able to claim, with great justification, that she had a life of fulfilment despite her great humiliation (paragraphs 29, 42), does not change her responses. The very conclusion of the story touches this theme of her vulnerability, except that the issue moves from the romantic to the religious. In her darkening consciousness, she asks God for a sign, which does not appear to her (paragraph 60). In effect, her perception is that the bridegroom has rejected her a second time, and so she thinks, in her dying moments, that "there's nothing more cruel than this—I'll never forgive it" (paragraph 61). This, coming at the end as it does, reveals the depth of her sensitivity to hurt, and it also explains how strong she needed to be to overcome her lifelong disappointment.

[6] Porter's story about Granny is remarkably full; it presents a portrait of a character who grows from sensitive youth to strong and self-sufficient age. One of the major marks of Granny's character is Porter's use of references to lightness and darkness. Throughout her life, it is clear, Granny has been a bringer of light, and she has had faith in the biblical promise that the bridegroom would come. Because in dying she feels betrayed a second time, she blows out the light of life in bitterness (paragraph 61). Her own character, however, has been a tribute to light (paragraphs 26, 27). She is an example of the power and strength of the human spirit (light) to overcome disappointments, sorrows, and obstacles (darkness). Surely the reader would agree that with such a string of accomplishments behind her, her life does not end in darkness. She has been weighed in the balance and has not been found wanting. She is strong, giving, resilient, and noble—a genuinely inspiring character.

Commentary on the Essay

For illustration, the opening paragraph begins by stressing how readers learn about Granny Weatherall, the character being analyzed. The purpose is to establish that the narrative method moves readers back and forth from the present to the past; therefore, current perceptions, memories, and reflections supply the materials for a rounded character portrait. The central idea stresses Granny's strong qualities. The thesis sentence describes an organization for the body of the essay stemming out of a number of particular traits; this illustrates the first approach described above (see Organizing Your Essay, pp. 189–190). Another possible approach would be an organization stressing Granny's growth from her youthful hurt to life spent in overcoming it (approach 2), or else an organization based on a number of actions, such as her having been jilted, her duties as a single mother, and her death (approach 3).

In the body of the essay the goal is to show how the traits total up to a rounded portrait. Thus paragraphs 2 and 3 illustrate the closely related qualities of self-confidence and the acceptance of the responsibility to work and to do. Paragraph 4 is tied to these through its stress on how Granny's perceptiveness has given her both insight into life and the knowledge to achieve. Paragraph 5 is a climax of the body; it deals with the human, vulnerable side of Granny. Because this vulnerability accounts for Granny's strength of character through her capacity to adjust to the hurts of life, and also because it "rounds" the portrait of Granny, paragraph 5 is vital in the essay. The last paragraph, 6, deals with some of the religious implications of Granny's story and character. The conclusion is that Granny's character is far more positive than might be indicated by her concluding disappointment or disillusionment.

WRITING TOPICS FOR CHAPTER 4

1. Write an essay discussing how the story "Barn Burning" embodies the idea that culture and civilization in the American South have declined since the Civil War.

2. From one of the stories in this chapter, select a character whom you considered to be dynamic. Write a brief essay demonstrating how this character changed or developed, with supporting evidence from the story. For example, you might select Paul of "Paul's Case," Sarty of "Barn Burning," or Granny Weatherall of "The Jilting of Granny Weatherall."

3. Topics for brief papers (3 to 5 pages):
    a. Why does Jacky Smurch not fit the role of "The Greatest Man in the World?" How honest and genuine can anyone be who is trying to fit such a role?
    b. Why does Abner Snopes go about burning barns? What satisfaction might he get from doing so? What might Abner say to himself about his own activities?
    c. Does the narrator of "Paul's Case" actually "get inside" Paul? To what degree, if any, does the narrator seem baffled by what happens to him?

4. Using the first person, write a brief narrative about an important decision you have made (e.g., declaring a major, complaining about a bad grade, etc.). Show how qualities of your character are brought out by the decision and by the events before and after it.

5
Point of View

Point of view is the position from which details in a narrative are perceived and related to the reader. It is a method of rendering, a means by which authors create a speaking **voice, persona,** or **narrator,** a centralizing intelligence, a narrative personality, an intellectual filter through which you understand the story. Other terms describing point of view are *viewpoint*, *perspective, angle of vision, mask, center of attention,* and *focus.* Another helpful term is *coign of vantage*, which implies a high spot or corner—a vantage point—from which things below may be seen and described.

In practice, you can think of point of view as the character or **speaker** who does the talking. To study point of view is to determine the effect of the speaker's traits, motives, circumstances, and limitations on the literary work.

Does this definition mean that authors do not use their own "voice" when they write, but somehow change themselves into another character who may be a totally separate creation? This is an important question to raise. It is true that authors, as writers of their own works, control what gets written, but it does not follow that they always use *their own* voice as they write. It is not easy to determine exactly what one's "own voice" is. Test yourself: When you speak to your instructor, to your friend, to a child, to a person you love, or to a distant relative, your voice always sounds the same, but the personality—or persona—that you employ changes according to the person you are talking to.

Authors create not only stories and ideas, then, but also their speakers or voices. The situation is very much like that of actors on stage. The actors are always themselves, but the roles they play are not those of their own identities or personal lives. Actors imitate characters like Hamlet or Othello, Desdemona or Lady Macbeth. Authors, too, may create separate roles for the speakers you hear in their works, such as Sammy in "A & P," Rosie in "Goodbye and Good Luck," and Jackie in "First Confession.

POINT OF VIEW AND "THROWING THE VOICE"

A helpful way to consider point of view is to think of the speaker as a ventriloquist's dummy and the author not as the speaker but the ventriloquist. The author "throws" the voice into the dummy, or speaker, whose words you read. Although the speaker is doing the talking, the author is the one who makes the speaker believable and consistent. Consider the relationship as illustrated here:

Often this speaker, or voice, is separate and totally independent, a character who is imagined and made consistent by the author. A problem of identifying the voice occurs when the speaker seems to be the author in person. To claim that authors are also speakers, however, assumes that we have absolute biographical and psychological knowledge about them. Authors, like all people, change; they may have been changing even as they were writing the stories you are reading. In addition, they may have been creating a separate personality, or aspect of themselves, as the voice they used when they wrote. Beyond all that, there is the general problem that human personality is elusive. For all these reasons, in works where the author seems to be talking directly, it is more proper to refer to the author's **authorial voice** as the speaker rather than the author himself or herself.

It is most important to understand the potential complexity of these details. As an exercise, suppose for a moment that you are an author and are planning a set of stories. Try to imagine the speakers you would create to make stories out of the following situations:

A happy niece who has just inherited $25 million from an uncle recalls a childhood experience with the uncle years ago.

A disappointed nephew who was cut off without a cent describes a childhood experience with the same uncle.

A ship's captain who is filled with ideas of personal honor, integrity, and responsibility describes the life of a sailor who has committed a cowardly act.

A young man filled with regret and self-reproach describes the episode in which he made his mistakes.

A woman on her deathbed, in the last hours before dying, considers the events of her life.

An economist looks at problems of unemployment.

A person who has just lost a job looks at problems of unemployment.

In creating voices and stories for the various situations, you will recognize the importance of your *imagination* in the selection of point of view. You are always yourself, but your imagination enables you to speak like a person totally distinct from yourself. Point of view is hence an imaginative creation, just as much a part of the author's work as the events narrated or the ideas discussed.

POINT OF VIEW AS A PHYSICAL POSITION

Thus far we have considered point of view as an interaction of personality and circumstance. There are also purely physical aspects, specifically (1) the speaker as one who sees and reports actions and statements, and (2) the speaker as one who receives and passes on information from others. If narrators have been at the "scene" of an action, this position gives them credibility because they are reporting events they actually saw or heard. Some speakers may have been direct participants in the action; others may have been bystanders. It is possible that a speaker may have overheard a conversation, or may have witnessed a scene through a keyhole. If the speakers were not "on the spot," they must have learned the "facts" in a believable way. They could get them from someone else who was a witness or participant. They could receive letters, read newspaper articles, go through old papers in an attic or library, or hear things on a radio or television program. Sometimes the unidentified voice of the author comes from a person who seems to be hovering somehow right above the characters as they move and speak. Such a speaker, being present everywhere without being noticed, is a reliable source of all information presented in the narrative.

DISTINGUISH POINT OF VIEW FROM OPINION

It should be clear that point of view is not the same as opinion or idea. It is true that a person's opinions (most obviously, about politics or religion) influence what that person says about a social issue or personal behavior. As a result, many students conclude that point of view is just another way of defining opinions. But this is not true. In examining point of view, therefore, you should try to draw as many conclusions as possible about the voice you are hearing, about the speaker who remains invisible but who nevertheless is doing the talking. Opinions are no more important in this discussion than closeness or distance from the events, capacities of understanding, personal or ideological involvement in the situation, and general personality. A discussion of point of view requires you to analyze the character and circumstances of the speaker who is relating the events of the story or poem.

KINDS OF POINTS OF VIEW

The kinds of points of view are easy to identify and remember. You may detect the point of view in any work by determining the grammatical voice of the speaker. Then, of course, you should go on to all the other considerations thus far discussed.

First Person

If the story is told by an "I," the author is using the **first-person** point of view—the voice of a fictional narrator and not the author's own voice. First-person speakers report significant things that they see, hear, and think and, as they do, they convey not only the action of the work, but also some of their own background, thinking, attitudes, and prejudices. Jackie, in O'Connor's "First Confession," is a first-person narrator who tells about events that occurred to him as a child. As he speaks he not only tells the story but also tells a good deal about both his childhood angers and adult prejudices.

Depending upon the involvement imagined for the events being narrated, first-person speakers disclose information either firsthand or secondhand. One kind of speaker has acquired information because he or she has been a direct participant in the action as a major character (or "major mover"). Sammy in "A & P" is a deeply involved major mover. The story "I'm a Fool" is told by another major mover, an unnamed young man. He tells about having fallen in love but also having destroyed the possibility of a relationship by having told foolish lies.

Sometimes speakers may not have been present at the actions, and so they tell us what they have learned from others, as in "The Worker in Sandalwood," which is told by a narrator who pieces things together from the stories of people directly involved. Similarly, the initial narrators of "Luck" and "Youth" have not been involved in the action at all, but merely quote the speaker, and thus they are not so much narrators themselves as transmitters of the words of another.

In a first-person narration, the speaker's background and educational level greatly affect content and mode of presentation. A mature adult, like Marlow in "Youth," and the unnamed narrator in "I'm a Fool," presents his or her recollections and also provides reflective commentary on the experience. These reflections are worth considering. A less aware narrator, like the speaker in Américo Parédes's "The Hammon and the Beans," may similarly recount what happens, but may supply less valuable comments. Some narrators have reached adulthood, but may not yet have reached adult understanding of the events, as in Joyce's "Araby" and O'Connor's "First Confession." The comments made by the narrators of these works indicate that they have not grown out of the problems they describe in the stories, and hence they indicate their own shortcomings as they speak. With first-person points of view like these, the reader must sort out details and also judge the quality of whatever observations the narrators make.

One thing is clear about stories and poems containing the first-person point of view: The speaker telling the story is often just as important as the story. Because everything we read is reported by the speaker, that speaker's abilities, position as an observer, character, attitudes, and possible prejudices or self-interests are to be considered along with everything that is said. The speaker of Tillie Olsen's "I Stand Here Ironing," for example, not only tells the story of her daughter's growth, but also reveals the misfortunes, doubts, and uncertainties that have underlain her own growth. Therefore, like virtually all first-person narrators, she is as much a focus of interest as the story itself.

Second Person

In a **second-person** narration, the narrator tells a listener, using the personal pronoun "you," what the listener has done and said at some time in the past. This kind of point of view is rarely used because it requires a first-person speaker who addresses the "you" of the narrative. Thus a parent might tell a child what the child did during infancy; or people having an argument might review a past action as a way of strengthening their real or supposed grievances; or a doctor might tell a patient with amnesia about the patient's earlier life before the loss of memory; or a lawyer, while making an accusation, might describe a defendant's crime directly to the defendant. In practice you will rarely encounter the second-person point of view. A. A. Milne uses it briefly at the beginning of his children's story *Winnie the Pooh*, but drops it as soon as the events of Pooh Bear and the rest of the animals get under way. In *Bright Lights, Big City*, Jay MacInerny uses the "you" narrative, but it is clear that the "you" being addressed really means "I" and "me," so this is actually first person.

Third Person

If the narrator is not introduced as a character, and if everything in the work is described in the third person (that is, "he," "she," "it," "they"), the author is using the **third-person** point of view. There are three variants: dramatic or objective, omniscient, and limited omniscient.

DRAMATIC or OBJECTIVE. The basic mode of describing action and recording conversation or dialogue is the dramatic or objective point of view (also called **third-person objective**). The objective point of view is characteristic of plays, for which dramatists present speeches, descriptions of scenes, and stage directions or actions. Similarly, writers of fiction using the dramatic point of view try simply to "report the facts" scrupulously and objectively, without comment. They avoid saying that certain characters thought this or felt that, but instead allow the characters themselves to state what is on their minds. Shirley Jackson's "The Lottery" (the subject of the sample essay) is a prime example of the dramatic point of view. The narrator of the dramatic point of view perceives things and reports them in a way that is analogous to a hovering or tracking motion-picture camera. Thus, characters in the out of doors may be seen and heard at a distance or up close, and when they move indoors or into a conveyance of some sort, the speaker continues to observe and report their activities and record their dialogue.

Though actions and dialogue are the main substance of the dramatic point of view, authors may allow certain characters to express their own attitudes and feelings, which then also become a part of the story. Old Man Warner in "The Lottery" is an example of the commentator who represents a conservative voice in favor of the institution of the lottery, even as he recognizes that persons in nearby communities want to give it up.

The key to the dramatic point of view is that the writer presents actions and dialogue, and leaves conclusions and interpretations to the readers. Naturally, however, the author does not relinquish his or her shaping spirit with the choice of the dramatic viewpoint. Hence the reader's conclusions are shaped by the author's ordering of the materials of the story.

OMNISCIENT.   The third-person point of view is called **omniscient** (all-knowing) when the speaker not only presents the action and dialogue of the work, but also knows and reports how the characters are responding and thinking. In the third-person omniscient point of view, authors take great responsibility: By delving into the minds of their characters, they assume a stance that exceeds our ordinary experience with other persons. The result is that an omniscient story is not realistic according to our present way of seeing things. On some occasions, however, authors present the thoughts and goals of characters as a convenient way of adding explanations to actions.

LIMITED, or LIMITED OMNISCIENT.   More common than the omniscient point of view, therefore, is the limited, or limited omniscient point of view, in which the author describes actions and records dialogue objectively while confining or *limiting* your attention to what a major character does, says, hears, sees, and thinks. Because this character is the center about whom events in the work turn, he or she may be called the **point of view character,** as in "Paul's Case" by Cather, "Young Goodman Brown" by Hawthorne, and "Miss Brill" by Mansfield. Everything in these stories is there because Paul, Brown, and Miss Brill see it, hear it, imagine or dream it, respond to it, do it or share in it, try to control it, are controlled by it, or are victimized by it. Often the limited omniscient mode of presentation is so focused on the major character that it brings out particular words and expressions that the point-of-view character might use, as in "Miss Brill" and Porter's "The Jilting of Granny Weatherall." Obviously there are variations on how deeply the limited omniscience may extend. Thus, we learn more about the minds of Miss Brill and Granny Weatherall than we do about the mind of Mathilde, another point-of-view character (in "The Necklace") because Mansfield and Porter present more responses and thoughts than does Maupassant.

MINGLING POINTS OF VIEW

In most stories and narratives you will find a mingling of viewpoints. Hence a point of view may be limited omniscient when focused on the thoughts of a major character, but dramatic when focused on the actions and dialogue. The writer may tell most of the story in one type of point of view but then shift at an important moment in order to sustain interest, create suspense, or put the burden of response entirely upon readers. For example, Hawthorne in "Young Goodman Brown" shifts the narrative in such a way that Brown becomes distanced from the reader, and therefore more fitting for the condemnatory judgments made about him at the end of the story. Thus Brown is seen less personally and therefore less sympathetically.

When analyzing point of view in a literary work you may find the following guidelines helpful.

POINTS OF VIEW

1. First person ("I"). First-person narrators may have (1) complete understanding, (2) partial or incorrect understanding, or (3) no understanding at all.
    a. Major participant
        i.   telling his or her own story as a major mover.
        ii. telling a story about others and also about herself or himself as one of the major inter-actors.
        iii. telling a story mainly about others; this narrator is on the spot and completely involved but is not a major mover.
    b. Minor participant, telling a story about events experienced and/or witnessed.
    c. Uninvolved character, telling a story not witnessed but reported to the narrator by other means.

2. Second person ("you"). A second-person narrator has more authority over a character's actions than the character himself or herself; for example, parent, psychologist, lawyer. This point of view cannot be sustained easily, and therefore it is used only in brief passages when necessary.

3. Third person ("she," "he," "it," "they").
    a. Dramatic or third-person objective. Speaker reports only actions and speeches. Thoughts of characters can be expressed only as dialogue.
    b. Omniscient. Omniscient speaker sees all, reports all, knows and explains the inner workings of the minds of any or all characters.
    c. Limited, or limited omniscient. Attention is focused on a major character, and his or her thoughts and responses may be reported.

POINT OF VIEW AND "EVIDENCE"

In considering point of view, you should analyze all aspects that bear on the presentation of the material. You may imagine yourself somewhat like a member of a jury. Jury members cannot accept testimony uncritically, because some witnesses may have much to gain by misstatements, distortions, "failures" of memory, and outright lies. Before rendering a verdict, jury members must consider all these possibilities. Speakers in literary works are usually to be accepted as reliable witnesses, but it is true that their characters, interests, capacities, personal involvements, and positions to view action may have a bearing on the material they present. An interesting example is Anderson's "I'm a Fool," in which the narrator tells about his own self-defeating lies even though the lies have cost him the possible love of the most compatible woman he has ever met. Because he passes strongly negative judgments upon himself, we are inclined to believe that he is being honest about his experiences. By contrast, a rejection of statements made dramatically is invited in Kate Chopin's "The Story of an Hour." Here, the cause of the protagonist's death is attributed to a weak heart having succumbed to the shock of delight. Because of the limited omniscient point of view in the earlier part of the story, however, we know that the doctor describing the cause of death is dead wrong. While few stories will direct you to reject information provided by speakers, you should always consider the circumstances, interests, and character of the storyteller before drawing conclusions and making judgments.

DOROTHY RICHARDSON (1873–1957)

Death   1924

This was death this time, no mistake. Her cheeks flushed at the indecency of being seen, dying and then dead. If only she could get it over and lay herself out decent before anyone came in to see and meddle. Mrs. Gworsh winning, left out there in the easy world, coming in to see her dead and lay her out and talk about her. . . . While there's life there's hope. Perhaps she wasn't dying. Only afraid. People can be so mighty bad and get better. But no. Not after that feeling rolling up within, telling her in words, her whom it knew, that this time she was going to be overwhelmed. That was the beginning, the warning and the certainty. To be more and more next time, any minute, increasing till her life flowed out for all to see. Her head thumped. The rush of life beating against the walls of her body, making her head spin, numbed the pain and brought a mist before her eyes. Death. What she'd always feared so shocking, and put away. But no one knows what it is, how awful beyond everything, till they're in for it. Nobody knows death is this rush of life in all your parts.

The mist cleared. Her face was damp. The spinning in her head had ceased. She drew a careful breath. Without pain. Some of the pain had driven through her without feeling. But she was heavier. It wasn't gone either. Only waiting. She saw the doctor on his way. Scorn twisted her lips against her empty gums. Scores of times she'd waited for him. Felt him drive fear away. Joked. This time he'd say nothing. Watch, for her secret life to come up and out. When his turn came he'd know what it was like letting your life out; and all of them out there. No good telling. You can't know till you're in for it. They're all in for it, rich and poor alike. No help. The great enormous creature driving your innards up, what nobody knows. What *you* don't know. . . . Life ain't worth death.

It's got to be stuck, shame or no . . . but how do you do it?

She lay still and listened for footsteps. They knew next door by now. That piece° would never milk Snowdrop dry. Less cream, less butter. Everything going back. Slip-slop, go as you please, and never done. Where'd us be to now if I

piece: no-account woman, tart.

hadn't? That's it. What they don't think of. Slip-slop. Grinning and singing enough
to turn the milk. I've got a tongue. I know it. You've got to keep on and keep on
at them. Or nothing done. I been young, but never them silly ways. Snowdrop'll
go back; for certain. . . .

But I shan't ever *see* it no more . . . the thought flew lifting through her   5
mind. See no more. Work no more. Worry no more. Then what had been the
good of it? Why had she gone on year in year out since Tom died and she began
ailing, tramping all weathers up to the field, toiling and aching, and black as thunder
most times. What was the good? Nobody knew her. Tom never had. And now
there was only that piece downstairs, and what she did didn't matter any more.
Except to herself, and she'd go on being slip-slop; not knowing she was in for
death that makes it all one whatever you do. Good and bad they're all dying and
don't know it's the most they've got to do.

Her mind looked back up and down her life. Tom. What a fool she'd been
to think him any different. Then when he died she'd thought him the same as at
first, and cried because she'd let it all slip in the worries. Little Joe. Tearing her
open, then snuggled in her arms, sucking. And all outside bright and peaceful;
better than the beginning with Tom. But they'd all stop if they knew where it
led. Joe, and his wife, and his little ones, in for all of it, getting the hard of it
now, and death waiting for them. She could tell them all now what it was like, all
of them, the squire, all the same. All going the same way, rich and poor.

The Bible was right, "Remember now thy Creator in the days of thy youth."°
What she had always wanted. She had always wanted to be good. Now it was too
late. Nothing mattering, having it all lifted away, made the inside of you come
back as it was at the first, ready to begin. Too late. Shocking she had thought it
when parson said prepare for death, live as if you were going to die tonight. But
it's true. If every moment was your last on earth you could be yourself. You'd
dare. Everybody would dare. People is themselves when they are children, and
not again till they know they'm dying. But conscience knows all the time. I've a
heavy bill for all my tempers. God forgive me. But why should He? He was having
his turn now, anyhow, with all this dying to do. Death must be got through as
life had been, just somehow. But how?

When the doctor had gone she knew she was left to do it alone. While
there's life there's hope. But the life in her was too much smaller than the great
weight and pain. He made her easier, numb. Trying to think and not thinking.
Everything unreal. The piece coming up and downstairs like something in another
world. Perhaps God would let her go easy. Then it was all over? Just fading to
nothing with everything still to do. . . .

The struggle came unexpectedly. She heard her cries, and then the world
leapt upon her and grappled, and even in the midst of the agony of pain was the
surprise of her immense strength. The strength that struggled against the huge
stifling, the body that leapt and twisted against the heavy darkness, a shape within
her shape, that she had not known. Her unknown self rushing forward through
all her limbs to fight. Leaping out and curving in a great sweep away from where
she lay to the open sill, yet pinned back, unwrenchable from the bed. Back and
back she slid, down a long tunnel at terrific speed, cool, her brow cool and wet,

Remember . . . youth: Ecclesiastes 12:1.

with wind blowing upon it. Darkness in front. Back and back into her own young body, alone. In front on the darkness came the garden, the old garden in April, the crab-apple blossom, all as it was before she began, but brighter. . . .

QUESTIONS

1. Describe the way in which the story is narrated. What is achieved by the shifts from third person limited omniscient to first person? How do these shifts occur without any inconsistency in the narrative about the dying woman?

2. What kind of life has the protagonist led? From what economic level does she come? How old is she? What do we learn about her son? From the language of the story, particularly from certain words and phrases, what do you learn about her educational and cultural level?

3. Compare "Death" with "The Jilting of Granny Weatherall" (Chapter 4). What similarities and differences do you find in the points of view of the stories? In their topics, character developments, and background information?

4. What does the protagonist mean by saying "they'd all stop if they knew where it led"? What would it mean to "stop?" Where does "it" lead? How adequate and comprehensive is the knowledge and perspective that the protagonist brings to her dying judgment about life?

SHERWOOD ANDERSON   (1876–1941)

I'm a Fool   *1924*

It was a hard jolt for me, one of the most bitterest I ever had to face. And it all came about through my own foolishness, too. Even yet sometimes, when I think of it, I want to cry or swear or kick myself. Perhaps, even now, after all this time, there will be a kind of satisfaction in making myself look cheap by telling of it.

It began at three o'clock one October afternoon as I sat in the grand stand at the fall trotting and pacing meet at Sandusky, Ohio.

To tell the truth, I felt a little foolish that I should be sitting in the grand stand at all. During the summer before I had left my home town with Harry Whitehead and, with a nigger named Burt, had taken a job as swipe° with one of the two horses Harry was campaigning through the fall race meets that year. Mother cried and my sister Mildred, who wanted to get a job as a schoolteacher in our town that fall, stormed and scolded about the house all during the week before I left. They both thought it something disgraceful that one of our family should take a place as a swipe with race horses. I've an idea Mildred thought my taking the place would stand in the way of her getting the job she'd been working so long for.

---

swipe: A groom and general handyman; the narrator describes a swipe's duties in paragraph 6.

But after all I had to work, and there was no other work to be got. A big lumbering fellow of nineteen couldn't just hang around the house and I had got too big to mow people's lawns and sell newspapers. Little chaps who could get next to people's sympathies by their sizes were always getting jobs away from me. There was one fellow who kept saying to everyone who wanted a lawn mowed or a cistern cleaned that he was saving money to work his way through college, and I used to lay awake nights thinking up ways to injure him without being found out. I kept thinking of wagons running over him and bricks falling on his head as he walked along the street. But never mind him.

I got the place with Harry and I liked Burt fine. We got along splendid   5
together. He was a big nigger with a lazy sprawling body and soft, kind eyes, and when it came to a fight he could hit like Jack Johnson.° He had Bucephalus, a big black pacing stallion that could do 2.09 or 2.10 if he had to, and I had a little gelding named Doctor Fritz that never lost a race all fall when Harry wanted him to win.

We set out from home late in July, in a box car with the two horses and after that, until late November, we kept moving along to the race meets and the fairs. It was a peachy time for me, I'll say that. Sometimes now I think that boys who are raised regular in houses, and never have a fine nigger like Burt for best friend, and go to high schools and college, and never steal anything, or get drunk a little, or learn to swear from fellows who know how, or come walking up in front of a grand stand in their shirt sleeves and with dirty horsy pants on when the races are going on and the grand stand is full of people all dressed up— What's the use of talking about it? Such fellows don't know nothing at all. They've never had no opportunity.

But I did. Burt taught me how to rub down a horse and put the bandages on after a race and steam a horse out and a lot of valuable things for any man to know. He could wrap a bandage on a horse's leg so smooth that if it had been the same color you would think it was his skin, and I guess he'd have been a big driver, too, and got to the top like Murphy and Walter Cox and the others if he hadn't been black.

Gee whizz! it was fun. You got to a county-seat town, maybe say on a Saturday or Sunday, and the fair began the next Tuesday and lasted until Friday afternoon. Doctor Fritz would be, say, in the 2.25 trot on Tuesday afternoon and on Thursday afternoon Bucephalus would knock 'em cold in the "free-for-all" pace. It left you a lot of time to hang around and listen to horse talk, and see Burt knock some yap cold that got too gay,° and you'd find out about horses and men and pick up a lot of stuff you could use all the rest of your life, if you had some sense and salted down what you heard and felt and saw.

And then at the end of the week when the race meet was over, and Harry had run home to tend up to his livery-stable business, you and Burt hitched the two horses to carts and drove slow and steady across country, to the place for the next meeting, so as to not overheat the horses, etc., etc., you know.

Gee whizz! Gosh amighty! the nice hickory-nut and beechnut and oaks and   10
other kinds of trees along the roads, all brown and red, and the good smells, and

---

Jack Johnson: (1878–1946). The first black heavyweight champion, 1910–1915.
gay: High spirited, a state frequently induced by alcoholic spirits.

Burt singing a song called "Deep River,"° and the country girls at the windows of houses and everything. You can stick your colleges up your nose for all me. I guess I know where I got my education.

Why, one of those little burgs of towns you came to on the way, say now on a Saturday afternoon, and Burt says, "Let's lay up here." And you did.

And you took the horses to a livery stable and fed them, and you got your good clothes out of a box and put them on.

And the town was full of farmers gaping, because they could see you were racehorse people, and the kids maybe never see a nigger before and was afraid and run away when the two of us walked down their main street.

And that was before prohibition and all that foolishness, and so you went into a saloon, the two of you, and all the yaps come and stood around, and there was always some one pretended he was horsy and knew things and spoke up and began asking questions, and all you did was to lie and lie all you could about what horses you had, and I said I owned them, and then some fellow said, "Will you have a drink of whisky?" and Burt knocked his eye out the way he could say, offhand like, "Oh, well, all right, I'm agreeable to a little nip. I'll split a quart with you." Gee whizz!

But that isn't what I want to tell my story about. We got home late in November and I promised mother I'd quit the race horses for good. There's a lot of things you've got to promise a mother because she don't know any better.

And so, there not being any work in our town any more than when I left there to go to the races, I went off to Sandusky and got a pretty good place taking care of horses for a man who owned a teaming and delivery and storage and coal and real-estate business there. It was a pretty good place with good eats, and a day off each week, and sleeping on a cot in a big barn, and mostly just shoveling in hay, and oats to a lot of big good-enough skates of horses that couldn't have trotted a race with a toad. I wasn't dissatisfied and I could send money home.

And then, as I started to tell you, the fall races come to Sandusky and I got the day off and I went. I left the job at noon and had on my good clothes and my new brown derby hat I'd bought the Saturday before, and a stand-up collar.

First of all I went downtown and walked about with the dudes. I've always thought to myself, "Put up a good front," and so I did it. I had forty dollars in my pockets and so I went into the West House, a big hotel, and walked up to the cigar stand. "Give me three twenty-five cent cigars," I said. There was a lot of horsemen and strangers and dressed-up people from other towns standing around in the lobby and in the bar, and I mingled amongst them. In the bar there was a fellow with a cane and a Windsor tie on, that it made me sick to look at him. I like a man to be a man and dressed up, but not to go put on that kind of airs. So I pushed him aside, kind of rough, and had me a drink of whisky. And then he looked at me, as though he thought maybe he'd get gay, but he changed his mind and didn't say anything. And then I had another drink of whisky, just to show him something, and went out and had a hack out to the races, all to myself, and when I got there I bought myself the best seat I could get up in the grand stand, but didn't go in for any of these boxes. That's putting on too many airs.

"*Deep River*": A well-known Spiritual.

And so there I was, sitting up in the grand stand as gay as you please and looking down on the swipes coming out with their horses, and with their dirty horsy pants on and the horseblankets swung over their shoulders, same as I had been doing all the year before. I liked one thing about the same as the other, sitting up there and feeling grand and being down there and looking up at the yaps and feeling grander and more important, too.

One thing's about as good as another, if you take it just right. I've often said that.

Well, right in front of me, in the grand stand that day, there was a fellow with a couple of girls and they was about my age. The young fellow was a nice guy, all right. He was the kind maybe that goes to college and then comes to be a lawyer or maybe a newspaper editor or something like that, but he wasn't stuck on himself. There are some of that kind are all right and he was one of the ones.

He had his sister with him and another girl and the sister looked around over his shoulder, accidental at first, not intending to start anything—she wasn't that kind—and her eyes and mine happened to meet.

You know how it is. Gee, she was a peach! She had on a soft dress, kind of a blue stuff and it looked carelessly made, but was well sewed and made and everything. I knew that much. I blushed when she looked right at me and so did she. She was the nicest girl I've ever seen in my life. She wasn't stuck on herself and she could talk proper grammar without being like a schoolteacher or something like that. What I mean is, she was O.K. I think maybe her father was well-to-do, but not rich to make her chesty because she was his daughter, as some are. Maybe he owned a drug store or a dry-goods store in their home town, or something like that. She never told me and I never asked.

My own people are all O.K. too, when you come to that. My grandfather was Welsh and over in the old country, in Wales he was— But never mind that.

The first heat of the first race come off and the young fellow setting there with the two girls left them and went down to make a bet. I knew what he was up to, but he didn't talk big and noisy and let everyone around know he was a sport, as some do. He wasn't that kind. Well, he come back and I heard him tell the two girls what horse he'd bet on, and when the heat trotted they all half got to their feet and acted in the excited, sweaty way people do when they've got money down on a race, and the horse they bet on is up there pretty close at the end, and they think maybe he'll come on with a rush, but he never does because he hasn't got the old juice in him, come right down to it.

And then, pretty soon, the horses came out for the 2.18 pace and there was a horse in it I knew. He was a horse Bob French had in his string but Bob didn't own him. He was a horse owned by a Mr. Mathers down at Marietta, Ohio.

This Mr. Mathers had a lot of money and owned some coal mines or something and he had a swell place out in the country, and he was stuck on race horses, but was a Presbyterian or something, and I think more than likely his wife was one, too, maybe a stiffer one than himself. So he never raced his horses hisself, and the story round the Ohio race tracks was that when one of his horses got ready to go to the races he turned him over to Bob French and pretended to his wife he was sold.

So Bob had the horses and he did pretty much as he pleased and you can't blame Bob, at least, I never did. Sometimes he was out to win and sometimes he

20

25

wasn't. I never cared much about that when I was swiping a horse. What I did want to know was that my horse had the speed and could go out in front, if you wanted him to.

And, as I'm telling you, there was Bob in this race with one of Mr. Mathers' horses, was named "About Ben Ahem"° or something like that, and was fast as a streak. He was a gelding and had a mark of 2.21, but could step in .08 or .09.

Because when Burt and I were out, as I've told you, the year before, there   30 was a nigger Burt knew, worked for Mr. Mathers and we went out there one day when we didn't have no race on at the Marietta Fair and our boss Harry was gone home.

And so everyone was gone to the fair but just this one nigger and he took us all through Mr. Mathers' swell house and he and Burt tapped a bottle of wine Mr. Mathers had hid in his bedroom, back in a closet, without his wife knowing, and he showed us this Ahem horse. Burt was always stuck on being a driver but didn't have much chance to get to the top, being a nigger, and he and the other nigger gulped the whole bottle of wine and Burt got a little lit up.

So the nigger let Burt take this About Ben Ahem and step him a mile in a track Mr. Mathers had all to himself, right there on the farm. And Mr. Mathers had one child, a daughter, kinda sick and not very good looking, and she came home and we had to hustle to get About Ben Ahem stuck back in the barn.

I'm only telling you to get everything straight. At Sandusky, that afternoon I was at the fair, this young fellow with the two girls was fussed, being with the girls and losing his bet. You know how a fellow is that way. One of them was his girl and the other his sister. I had figured that out.

"Gee whizz," I says to myself, "I'm going to give him the dope."

He was mighty nice when I touched him on the shoulder. He and the girls   35 were nice to me right from the start and clear to the end. I'm not blaming them.

And so he leaned back and I give him the dope on About Ben Ahem. "Don't bet a cent on this first heat because he'll go like an oxen hitched to a plow, but when the first heat is over go right down and lay on your pile." That's what I told him.

Well, I never saw a fellow treat any one sweller. There was a fat man sitting beside the little girl, that had looked at me twice by this time, and I at her, and both blushing, and what did he do but have the nerve to turn and ask the fat man to get up and change places with me so I could set with his crowd.

Gee whizz, craps amighty. There I was. What a chump I was to go and get gay up there in the West House bar, and just because that dude was standing there with a cane and that kind of a necktie on, to go and get all balled up and drink that whisky, just to show off.

Of course she would know, me setting right beside her and letting her smell of my breath. I could have kicked myself right down out of that grand stand and all around that race track and made a faster record than most of the skates of horses they had there that year.

Because that girl wasn't any mutt of a girl. What wouldn't I have give right   40 then for a stick of chewing gum to chew, or a lozenger, or some licorice, or most

---

"*About Ben Ahem*": more likely "Abou Ben Adhem," from the poem "Abou Ben Adhem and the Angel" (1834) by Leigh Hunt (1784–1859).

anything. I was glad I had those twenty-five cent cigars in my pocket and right away I give that fellow one and lit one myself. Then that fat man got up and we changed places and there I was, plunked right down beside her.

They introduced themselves and the fellow's best girl, he had with him, was named Miss Elinor Woodbury, and her father was a manufacturer of barrels from a place called Tiffin, Ohio. And the fellow himself was named Wilbur Wessen and his sister was Miss Lucy Wessen.

I suppose it was their having such swell names that got me off my trolley. A fellow, just because he has been a swipe with a race horse, and works taking care of horses for a man in the teaming, delivery, and storage business isn't any better or worse than any one else. I've often thought that, and said it too.

But you know how a fellow is. There's something in that kind of nice clothes, and the kind of nice eyes she had, and the way she had looked at me, awhile before, over her brother's shoulder, and me looking back at her, and both of us blushing.

I couldn't show her up for a boob, could I?

I made a fool of myself, that's what I did. I said my name was Walter Mathers   45
from Marietta, Ohio, and then I told all three of them the smashingest lie you ever heard. What I said was that my father owned the horse About Ben Ahem and that he had let him out to this Bob French for racing purposes, because our family was proud and had never gone into racing that way, in our own name, I mean, and Miss Lucy Wessen's eyes were shining, and I went the whole hog.

I told about our place down at Marietta, and about the big stables and the grand brick house we had on a hill, up above the Ohio River, but I knew enough not to do it in no bragging way. What I did was to start things and then let them drag the rest out of me. I acted just as reluctant to tell as I could. Our family hasn't got any barrel factory, and since I've known us, we've always been pretty poor, but not asking anything of any one at that, and my grandfather, over in Wales—but never mind that.

We set there talking like we had known each other for years and years, and I went and told them that my father had been expecting maybe this Bob French wasn't on the square, and had sent me up to Sandusky on the sly to find out what I could.

And I bluffed it through I had found out all about the 2.18 pace, in which About Ben Ahem was to start.

I said he would lose the first heat by pacing like a lame cow and then he would come back and skin 'em alive after that. And to back up what I said I took thirty dollars out of my pocket and handed it to Mr. Wilbur Wessen and asked him, would he mind, after the first heat, to go down and place it on About Ben Ahem for whatever odds he could get. What I said was that I didn't want Bob French to see me and none of the swipes.

Sure enough the first heat come off and About Ben Ahem went off his   50
stride, up the back stretch, and looked like a wooden horse or a sick one, and come in to be last. Then this Wilbur Wessen went down to the betting place under the grand stand and there I was with the two girls, and when that Miss Woodbury was looking the other way once, Lucy Wessen kinda, with her shoulder you know, kinda touched me. Not just tucking down, I don't mean. You know how a woman

can do. They get close, but not getting gay either. You know what they do. Gee whizz.

And then they give me a jolt. What they had done, when I didn't know, was to get together, and they had decided Wilbur Wessen would bet fifty dollars, and the two girls had gone and put in ten dollars each, of their own money, too. I was sick then, but I was sicker later.

About the gelding, About Ben Ahem, and their winning their money, I wasn't worried a lot about that. It came out O.K. Ahem stepped the next three heats like a bushel of spoiled eggs going to market before they could be found out, and Wilbur Wessen had got nine to two for the money. There was something else eating at me.

Because Wilbur come back, after he had bet the money, and after that he spent most of his time talking to that Miss Woodbury, and Lucy Wessen and I was left alone together like on a desert island. Gee, if I'd only been on the square or if there had been any way of getting myself on the square. There ain't any Walter Mathers, like I said to her and them, and there hasn't ever been one, but if there was, I bet I'd go to Marietta, Ohio, and shoot him tomorrow.

There I was, big boob that I am. Pretty soon the race was over, and Wilbur had gone down and collected our money, and we had a hack downtown, and he stood us a swell supper at the West House, and a bottle of champagne beside.

And I was with the girl and she wasn't saying much, and I wasn't saying   5 much either. One thing I know. She wasn't stuck on me because of the lie about my father being rich and all that. There's a way you know . . . Craps amighty. There's a kind of girl you see just once in your life, and if you don't get busy and make hay, then you're gone for good and all, and might as well go jump off a bridge. They give you a look from inside of them somewhere, and it ain't no vamping, and what it means is—you want that girl to be your wife, and you want nice things around her like flowers and swell clothes, and you want her to have the kids you're going to have, and you want good music played and no ragtime. Gee whizz.

There's a place over near Sandusky, across a kind of bay, and it's called Cedar Point. And after we had supper we went over to it in a launch, all by ourselves. Wilbur and Miss Lucy and that Miss Woodbury had to catch a ten o'clock train back to Tiffin, Ohio, because, when you're out with girls like that you can't get careless and miss any trains and stay out all night, like you can with some kinds of Janes.

And Wilbur blowed himself to the launch and it cost him fifteen cold plunks, but I wouldn't never have knew if I hadn't listened. He wasn't no tin horn kind of a sport.

Over at the Cedar Point place, we didn't stay around where there was a gang of common kind of cattle at all.

There was big dance halls and dining places for yaps, and there was a beach you could walk along and get where it was dark, and we went there.

She didn't talk hardly at all and neither did I, and I was thinking how glad   6 I was my mother was all right, and always made us kids learn to eat with a fork at the table, and not swill soup, and not be noisy and rough like a gang you see around a race track that way.

Then Wilbur and his girl went away up the beach and Lucy and I sat down in a dark place, where there was some roots of old trees the water had washed up, and after that the time, till we had to go back in the launch and they had to catch their trains, wasn't nothing at all. It went like winking your eye.

Here's how it was. The place we were setting in was dark, like I said, and there was the roots from that old stump sticking up like arms, and there was a watery smell, and the night was like—as if you could put your hand out and feel it—so warm and soft and dark and sweet like an orange.

I most cried and I most swore and I most jumped up and danced, I was so mad and happy and sad.

When Wilbur come back from being alone with his girl, and she saw him coming, Lucy she says, "We got to go to the train now," and she was most crying too, but she never knew nothing I knew, and she couldn't be so all busted up. And then, before Wilbur and Miss Woodbury got up to where we was, she put her face up and kissed me quick and put her head up against me and she was all quivering and—Gee whizz.

Sometimes I hope I have cancer and die. I guess you know what I mean.   65
We went in the launch across the bay to the train like that, and it was dark, too. She whispered and said it was like she and I could get out of the boat and walk on water, and it sounded foolish, but I knew what she meant.

And then quick we were right at the depot, and there was a big gang of yaps, the kind that goes to the fairs, and crowded and milling around like cattle, and how could I tell her? "It won't be long because you'll write and I'll write you." That's all she said.

I got a chance like a hay barn afire. A swell chance I got.

And maybe she would write me, down at Marietta that way, and the letter would come back, and stamped on the front of it by the U.S.A. "there ain't any such guy," or something like that, whatever they stamp on a letter that way.

And me trying to pass myself off for a big-bug and a swell—to her, as decent a little body as God ever made. Craps amighty—swell chance I got!

And then the train come in, and she got on it, and Wilbur Wessen, he   70
come and shook hands with me, and that Miss Woodbury was nice too and bowed to me, and I at her, and the train went and I busted out and cried like a kid.

Gee, I could have run after the train and made Dan Patch° look like a freight train after a wreck but, socks amighty, what was the use? Did you ever see such a fool?

I'll bet you what—if I had an arm broke right now or a train had run over my foot—I wouldn't go to no doctor at all. I'd go set down and let her hurt and hurt—that's what I'd do.

I'll bet you what—if I hadn't a drunk that booze I'd never been such a boob as to go tell such a lie—that couldn't never be made straight to a lady like her.

I wish I had that fellow right here that had on a Windsor tie and carried a cane. I'd smash him for fair. Gosh darn his eyes. He's a big fool—that's what he is.

And if I'm not another you just go find me one and I'll quit working and   75

Dan Patch: One of the fastest pace horses, Dan Patch still held records at the time of the story. Proverbial for his speed, his records were not broken until well into the 1930s.

be a bum and give him my job. I don't care nothing for working, and earning money, and saving it for no such boob as myself.

QUESTIONS

1. Describe the point of view of "I'm a Fool." Who is the narrator? How completely does he describe himself? What level of diction does the narrator use, and what is the effect of this diction on the story? Why does the narrator, in paragraphs 8 and 11–14, shift to "you" as the apparent point of view?

2. Describe the character of the speaker. Is he flat or round? How intelligent is he? What is his background? How does he evaluate his own experience as opposed to the experience of becoming educated? Does he seem likable? What changes does he undergo during the story?

3. Describe the plot of the story. If the narrator is the protagonist, who or what is the antagonist? Where is the crisis, the climax? What values are brought out by the outcome of the plot?

4. Compare the character of Lucy Wessen with that of the narrator. How does he feel about her? How accurate is his belief that she is deeply interested in him? How successful might a match have been between the two if the narrator had not made things impossible by his false stories about himself?

5. Describe the importance of location and background in the development of the story. How authentic are the locations? How does the narrator's familiarity with horses and racing enable him to impress Lucy and her brother?

KATHERINE MANSFIELD   (1888–1923)

Miss Brill°   1920

Although it was so brilliantly fine—the blue sky powdered with gold and great spots of light like white wine splashed over the Jardins Publiques° —Miss Brill was glad that she had decided on her fur. The air was motionless, but when you opened your mouth there was just a faint chill, like a chill from a glass of iced water before you sip, and now and again a leaf came drifting—from nowhere, from the sky. Miss Brill put up her hand and touched her fur. Dear little thing! It was nice to feel it again. She had taken it out of its box that afternoon, shaken out the moth-powder, given it a good brush, and rubbed the life back into the dim little eyes. "What has been happening to me?" said the sad little eyes. Oh, how sweet it was to see them snap at her again from the red eiderdown! . . . But the nose, which was of some black composition, wasn't at all firm. It must have had a knock, somehow. Never mind—a little dab of black sealing-wax when the time came—when it was absolutely necessary. . . . Little rogue! Yes, she really felt like that about it. Little rogue biting its tail just by her left ear. She could

---

Miss Brill: Brill is the name of a common deep-sea flatfish.
   Jardins Publiques: public gardens or park. The setting of the story is apparently a French seaside town.

have taken it off and laid it on her lap and stroked it. She felt a tingling in her hands and arms, but that came from walking, she supposed. And when she breathed, something light and sad—no, not sad, exactly—something gentle seemed to move in her bosom.

There were a number of people out this afternoon, far more than last Sunday. And the band sounded louder and gayer. That was because the Season had begun. For although the band played all the year round on Sundays, out of season it was never the same. It was like some one playing with only the family to listen; it didn't care how it played if there weren't any strangers present. Wasn't the conductor wearing a new coat, too? She was sure it was new. He scraped with his foot and flapped his arms like a rooster about to crow, and the bandsmen sitting in the green rotunda blew out their cheeks and glared at the music. Now there came a little "flutey" bit—very pretty!—a little chain of bright drops. She was sure it would be repeated. It was; she lifted her head and smiled.

Only two people shared her "special" seat: a fine old man in a velvet coat, his hands clasped over a huge carved walking-stick, and a big old woman, sitting upright, with a roll of knitting on her embroidered apron. They did not speak. This was disappointing, for Miss Brill always looked forward to the conversation. She had become really quite expert, she thought, at listening as though she didn't listen, at sitting in other people's lives just for a minute while they talked round her.

She glanced, sideways, at the old couple. Perhaps they would go soon. Last Sunday, too, hadn't been as interesting as usual. An Englishman and his wife, he wearing a dreadful Panama hat and she button boots. And she'd gone on the whole time about how she ought to wear spectacles; she knew she needed them; but that it was no good getting any; they'd be sure to break and they'd never keep on. And he'd been so patient. He'd suggested everything—gold rims, the kind that curved round your ears, little pads inside the bridge. No, nothing would please her. "They'll always be sliding down my nose!" Miss Brill had wanted to shake her.

The old people sat on the bench, still as statues. Never mind, there was always the crowd to watch. To and fro, in front of the flower-beds and the band rotunda, the couples and groups paraded, stopped to talk, to greet, to buy a handful of flowers from the old beggar who had his tray fixed to the railings. Little children ran among them, swooping and laughing; little boys with big white silk bows under their chins, little girls, little French dolls, dressed up in velvet and lace. And sometimes a tiny staggerer came suddenly rocking into the open from under the trees, stopped, stared, as suddenly sat down "flop," until its small high-stepping mother, like a young hen, rushed scolding to its rescue. Other people sat on the benches and green chairs, but they were nearly always the same, Sunday after Sunday, and—Miss Brill had often noticed—there was something funny about nearly all of them. They were odd, silent, nearly all old, and from the way they stared they looked as though they'd just come from dark little rooms or even—even cupboards!

Behind the rotunda the slender trees with yellow leaves down drooping, and through them just a line of sea, and beyond the blue sky with gold-veined clouds.

Tum-tum-tum tiddle-um! tiddle-um! tum tiddle-um tum ta! blew the band.

Two young girls in red came by and two young soldiers in blue met them,

5

and they laughed and paired and went off arm-in-arm. Two peasant women with funny straw hats passed, gravely, leading beautiful smoke-coloured donkeys. A cold, pale nun hurried by. A beautiful woman came along and dropped her bunch of violets, and a little boy ran after to hand them to her, and she took them and threw them away as if they'd been poisoned. Dear me! Miss Brill didn't know whether to admire that or not! And now an ermine toque° and a gentleman in grey met just in front of her. He was tall, stiff, dignified, and she was wearing the ermine toque she'd bought when her hair was yellow. Now everything, her hair, her face, even her eyes, was the same colour as the shabby ermine, and her hand, in its cleaned glove, lifted to dab her lips, was a tiny yellowish paw. Oh, she was so pleased to see him—delighted! She rather thought they were going to meet that afternoon. She described where she'd been—everywhere, here, there, along by the sea. The day was so charming—didn't he agree? And wouldn't he, perhaps? . . . But he shook his head, lighted a cigarette, slowly breathed a great deep puff into her face, and, even while she was still talking and laughing, flicked the match away and walked on. The ermine toque was alone; she smiled more brightly than ever. But even the band seemed to know what she was feeling and played more softly, played tenderly, and the drum beat, "The Brute! The Brute!" over and over. What would she do? What was going to happen now? But as Miss Brill wondered, the ermine toque turned, raised her hand as though she'd seen some one else, much nicer, just over there, and pattered away. And the band changed again and played more quickly, more gaily than ever, and the old couple on Miss Brill's seat got up and marched away, and such a funny old man with long whiskers hobbled along in time to the music and was nearly knocked over by four girls walking abreast.

Oh, how fascinating it was! How she enjoyed it! How she loved sitting here, watching it all! It was like a play. It was exactly like a play. Who could believe the sky at the back wasn't painted? But it wasn't till a little brown dog trotted on solemn and then slowly trotted off, like a little "theatre" dog, a little dog that had been drugged, that Miss Brill discovered what it was that made it so exciting. They were all on the stage. They weren't only the audience, not only looking on; they were acting. Even she had a part and came every Sunday. No doubt somebody would have noticed if she hadn't been there; she was part of the performance after all. How strange she'd never thought of it like that before! And yet it explained why she made such a point of starting from home at just the same time each week—so as not to be late for the performance—and it also explained why she had quite a queer, shy feeling at telling her English pupils how she spent her Sunday afternoons. No wonder! Miss Brill nearly laughed out loud. She was on the stage. She thought of the old invalid gentleman to whom she read the newspaper four afternoons a week while he slept in the garden. She had got quite used to the frail head on the cotton pillow, the hollowed eyes, the open mouth and the high pinched nose. If he'd been dead she mightn't have noticed for weeks; she wouldn't have minded. But suddenly he knew he was having the paper read to him by an actress! "An actress!" The old head lifted; two points of light quivered in the old eyes. "An actress—are ye?" And Miss Brill smoothed the newspaper as

---

ermine toque: A closefitting hat made of the white fur of an ermine; here the phrase stands for the woman wearing the hat.

though it were the manuscript of her part and said gently: "Yes, I have been an actress for a long time."

The band had been having a rest. Now they started again. And what they played was warm, sunny, yet there was just a faint chill—a something, what was it?—not sadness—no, not sadness—a something that made you want to sing. The tune lifted, lifted, the light shone; and it seemed to Miss Brill that in another moment all of them, all the whole company, would begin singing. The young ones, the laughing ones who were moving together, they would begin, and the men's voices, very resolute and brave, would join them. And then she too, she too, and the others on the benches—they would come in with a kind of accompaniment—something low, that scarcely rose or fell, something so beautiful—moving. . . . And Miss Brill's eyes filled with tears and she looked smiling at all the other members of the company. Yes, we understand, we understand, she thought—though what they understood she didn't know.

Just at that moment a boy and a girl came and sat down where the old couple had been. They were beautifully dressed; they were in love. The hero and heroine, of course, just arrived from his father's yacht. And still soundlessly singing, still with that trembling smile, Miss Brill prepared to listen.

"No, not now," said the girl, "Not here, I can't."

"But why? Because of that stupid old thing at the end there?" asked the boy. "Why does she come here at all—who wants her? Why doesn't she keep her silly old mug at home?"

"It's her fu-fur which is so funny," giggled the girl. "It's exactly like a fried whiting."

"Ah, be off with you!" said the boy in an angry whisper. Then: "Tell me, ma petite chérie—"

"No, not here," said the girl. "Not *yet*."

On her way home she usually bought a slice of honeycake at the baker's. It was her Sunday treat. Sometimes there was an almond in her slice, sometimes not. It made a great difference. If there was an almond it was like carrying home a tiny present—a surprise—something that might very well not have been there. She hurried on the almond Sundays and struck the match for the kettle in quite a dashing way.

But to-day she passed the baker's by, climbed the stairs, went into the little dark room—her room like a cupboard—and sat down on the red eiderdown. She sat there for a long time. The box that the fur came out of was on the bed. She unclasped the necklet quickly; quickly, without looking, laid it inside. But when she put the lid on she thought she heard something crying.

QUESTIONS

1. Describe the point of view of "Miss Brill." Is it in the third-person limited, omniscient, or dramatic? Who says, in paragraph 1, "Dear little thing!" about the fur? How do you justify your conclusion about the source of this and similar insights that appear throughout the story?

2. Would this story be possible if told in the first person by Miss Brill herself? What might it have been like if told by a walker in the park who observed Miss Brill and overheard the conversation about her by the boy and girl?

3. A shift in the point of view occurs when the boy and girl sit down and Miss Brill overhears them. Describe the nature of this shift. Why do you think Mansfield made the change at this point?

4. In relation to the point of view, explain the last sentence of the story: "But when she put the lid on she thought she heard something crying." Is this sentence consistent with the point of view of the preceding seven paragraphs or with the bulk of the story before that?

5. Briefly describe the things that happen in the story. Are there many genuine actions? On the basis of your answers to these questions, would you say that "Miss Brill" is mainly active, or mainly reflective and psychological?

6. What is illustrated in the description of the woman wearing the ermine toque? Is there any parallel with the life of Miss Brill herself?

SHIRLEY JACKSON   (1919–1965)

The Lottery   *1948*

The morning of June 27th was clear and sunny, with the fresh warmth of a full summer day; the flowers were blossoming profusely and the grass was richly green. The people of the village began to gather in the square, between the post office and the bank, around ten o'clock; in some towns there were so many people that the lottery took two days and had to be started on June 26th, but in this village, where there were only about three hundred people, the whole lottery took less than two hours, so it could begin at ten o'clock in the morning and still be through in time to allow the villagers to get home for noon dinner.

The children assembled first, of course. School was recently over for the summer, and the feeling of liberty sat uneasily on most of them; they tended to gather together quietly for a while before they broke into boisterous play, and their talk was still of the classroom and the teacher, of books and reprimands. Bobby Martin had already stuffed his pockets full of stones, and the other boys soon followed his example, selecting the smoothest and roundest stones; Bobby and Harry Jones and Dickie Delacroix—the villagers pronounced this name "Delacroy"—eventually made a great pile of stones in one corner of the square and guarded it against the raids of the other boys. The girls stood aside, talking among themselves, looking over their shoulders at the boys, and the very small children rolled in the dust or clung to the hands of their older brothers or sisters.

Soon the men began to gather, surveying their own children, speaking of planting and rain, tractors and taxes. They stood together, away from the pile of stones in the corner, and their jokes were quiet and they smiled rather than laughed. The women, wearing faded house dresses and sweaters, came shortly after their menfolk. They greeted one another and exchanged bits of gossip as they went to join their husbands. Soon the women, standing by their husbands, began to call to their children, and the children came reluctantly, having to be called four or five times. Bobby Martin ducked under his mother's grasping hand and ran, laughing, back to the pile of stones. His father spoke up sharply, and Bobby came quickly and took his place between his father and his oldest brother.

The lottery was conducted—as were the square dances, the teen-age club, the Halloween program—by Mr. Summers, who had time and energy to devote to civic activities. He was a round-faced, jovial man and he ran the coal business, and people were sorry for him, because he had no children and his wife was a scold. When he arrived in the square, carrying the black wooden box, there was a murmur of conversation among the villagers, and he waved and called, "Little late today, folks." The postmaster, Mr. Graves, followed him, carrying a three-legged stool, and the stool was put in the center of the square and Mr. Summers set the black box down on it. The villagers kept their distance, leaving a space between themselves and the stool, and when Mr. Summers said, "Some of you fellows want to give me a hand?" there was a hesitation before two men, Mr. Martin and his oldest son, Baxter, came forward to hold the box steady on the stool while Mr. Summers stirred up the papers inside it.

The original paraphernalia for the lottery had been lost long ago, and the   5
black box now resting on the stool had been put into use even before Old Man Warner, the oldest man in town, was born. Mr. Summers spoke frequently to the villagers about making a new box, but no one liked to upset even as much tradition as was represented by the black box. There was a story that the present box had been made with some pieces of the box that had preceded it, the one that had been constructed when the first people settled down to make a village here. Every year, after the lottery, Mr. Summers began talking again about a new box, but every year the subject was allowed to fade off without anything's being done. The black box grew shabbier each year; by now it was no longer completely black but splintered badly along one side to show the original wood color, and in some places faded or stained.

Mr. Martin and his oldest son, Baxter, held the black box securely on the stool until Mr. Summers had stirred the papers thoroughly with his hand. Because so much of the ritual had been forgotten or discarded, Mr. Summers had been successful in having slips of paper substituted for the chips of wood that had been used for generations. Chips of wood, Mr. Summers had argued, had been all very well when the village was tiny, but now that the population was more than three hundred and likely to keep on growing, it was necessary to use something that would fit more easily into the black box. The night before the lottery, Mr. Summers and Mr. Graves made up the slips of paper and put them in the box, and it was then taken to the safe of Mr. Summers' coal company and locked up until Mr. Summers was ready to take it to the square next morning. The rest of the year, the box was put away, sometimes one place, sometimes another; it had spent one year in Mr. Graves's barn and another year underfoot in the post office, and sometimes it was set on a shelf in the Martin grocery and left there.

There was a great deal of fussing to be done before Mr. Summers declared the lottery open. There were the lists to make up—of heads of families, heads of households in each family, members of each household in each family. There was the proper swearing-in of Mr. Summers by the postmaster, as the official of the lottery; at one time, some people remembered, there had been a recital of some sort, performed by the official of the lottery, a perfunctory, tuneless chant that had been rattled off duly each year; some people believed that the official of the lottery used to stand just so when he said or sang it, others believed that he was supposed to walk among the people, but years and years ago this part of the ritual had been allowed to lapse. There had been, also, a ritual salute, which the official of the lottery had had to use in addressing each person who came up to draw from the box, but this also had changed with time, until now it was felt necessary only for the official to speak to each person approaching. Mr. Summers was very good at all this; in his clean white shirt and blue jeans, with one hand resting carelessly on the black box, he seemed very proper and important as he talked interminably to Mr. Graves and the Martins.

Just as Mr. Summers finally left off talking and turned to the assembled villagers, Mrs. Hutchinson came hurriedly along the path to the square, her sweater thrown over her shoulders, and slid into place in the back of the crowd. "Clean forgot what day it was," she said to Mrs. Delacroix, who stood next to her, and they both laughed softly. "Thought my old man was out back stacking wood," Mrs. Hutchinson went on, "and then I looked out the window and the kids was gone, and then I remembered it was the twenty-seventh and came a-running." She dried her hands on her apron, and Mrs. Delacroix said, "You're in time, though. They're still talking away up there."

Mrs. Hutchinson craned her neck to see through the crowd and found her husband and children standing near the front. She tapped Mrs. Delacroix on the arm as a farewell and began to make her way through the crowd. The people separated good-humoredly to let her through; two or three people said, in voices just loud enough to be heard across the crowd, "Here comes your Missus, Hutchinson," and "Bill, she made it after all." Mrs. Hutchinson reached her husband, and Mr. Summers, who had been waiting, said cheerfully, "Thought we were going to have to get on without you, Tessie." Mrs. Hutchinson said, grinning, "Wouldn't have me leave m'dishes in the sink, now, would you, Joe?," and soft laughter ran through the crowd as the people stirred back into position after Mrs. Hutchinson's arrival.

"Well, now," Mr. Summers said soberly, "guess we better get started, get   10
this over with, so's we can go back to work. Anybody ain't here?"

"Dunbar," several people said. "Dunbar, Dunbar."

Mr. Summers consulted his list. "Clyde Dunbar," he said. "That's right. He's broke his leg, hasn't he? Who's drawing for him?"

"Me, I guess," a woman said, and Mr. Summers turned to look at her. "Wife draws for her husband," Mr. Summers said. "Don't you have a grown boy to do it for you, Janey?" Although Mr. Summers and everyone else in the village knew the answer perfectly well, it was the business of the official of the lottery to ask such questions formally. Mr. Summers waited with an expression of polite interest while Mrs. Dunbar answered.

"Horace's not but sixteen yet," Mrs. Dunbar said regretfully. "Guess I gotta fill in for the old man this year."

"Right," Mr. Summers said. He made a note on the list he was holding.   15
Then he asked, "Watson boy drawing this year?"

A tall boy in the crowd raised his hand. "Here," he said. "I'm drawing for m'mother and me." He blinked his eyes nervously and ducked his head as several voices in the crowd said things like "Good fellow, Jack," and "Glad to see your mother's got a man to do it."

"Well," Mr. Summers said, "guess that's everyone. Old Man Warner make it?"

"Here," a voice said, and Mr. Summers nodded.

A sudden hush fell on the crowd as Mr. Summers cleared his throat and looked at the list. "All ready?" he called. "Now, I'll read the names—heads of families first—and the men come up and take a paper out of the box. Keep the paper folded in your hand without looking at it until everyone has had a turn. Everything clear?"

The people had done it so many times that they only half listened to the directions; most of them were quiet, wetting their lips, not looking around. Then Mr. Summers raised one hand high and said, "Adams." A man disengaged himself from the crowd and came forward. "Hi, Steve," Mr. Summers said, and Mr. Adams said, "Hi, Joe." They grinned at one another humorlessly and nervously. Then Mr. Adams reached into the black box and took out a folded paper. He held it firmly by one corner as he turned and went hastily back to his place in the crowd, where he stood a little apart from his family, not looking down at his hand. 20

"Allen," Mr. Summers said. "Anderson. . . . Bentham."

"Seems like there's no time at all between lotteries any more," Mrs. Delacroix said to Mrs. Graves in the back row. "Seems like we got through with the last one only last week."

"Time sure goes fast," Mrs. Graves said.

"Clark. . . . Delacroix."

"There goes my old man," Mrs. Delacroix said. She held her breath while her husband went forward. 25

"Dunbar," Mr. Summers said, and Mrs. Dunbar went steadily to the box while one of the women said, "Go on, Janey," and another said, "There she goes."

"We're next," Mrs. Graves said. She watched while Mr. Graves came around from the side of the box, greeted Mr. Summers gravely, and selected a slip of paper from the box. By now, all through the crowd there were men holding the small folded papers in their large hands, turning them over and over nervously. Mrs. Dunbar and her two sons stood together, Mrs. Dunbar holding the slip of paper.

"Harburt. . . . Hutchinson."

"Get up there, Bill," Mrs. Hutchinson said, and the people near her laughed.

"Jones." 30

"They do say," Mr. Adams said to Old Man Warner, who stood next to him, "that over in the north village they're talking of giving up the lottery."

Old Man Warner snorted. "Pack of crazy fools," he said. "Listening to the young folks, nothing's good enough for *them*. Next thing you know, they'll be wanting to go back to living in caves, nobody work any more, live *that* way for a while. Used to be a saying about 'Lottery in June, corn be heavy soon.' First thing you know, we'd all be eating stewed chickweed and acorns. There's *always* been a lottery," he added petulantly. "Bad enough to see young Joe Summers up there joking with everybody."

"Some places have already quit lotteries," Mrs. Adams said.

"Nothing but trouble in *that*," Old Man Warner said stoutly. "Pack of young fools."

"Martin." And Bobby Martin watched his father go forward. "Overdyke. . . . Percy." 35

"I wish they'd hurry," Mrs. Dunbar said to her older son. "I wish they'd hurry."

"They're almost through," her son said.

"You get ready to run tell Dad," Mrs. Dunbar said.

Mr. Summers called his own name and then stepped forward precisely and selected a slip from the box. Then he called, "Warner."

"Seventy-seventh year I been in the lottery," Old Man Warner said as he   40
went through the crowd. "Seventy-seventh time."

"Watson." The tall boy came awkwardly through the crowd. Someone said, "Don't be nervous, Jack," and Mr. Summers said, "Take your time, son."

"Zanini."

After that, there was a long pause, a breathless pause, until Mr. Summers, holding his slip of paper in the air, said, "All right, fellows." For a minute, no one moved, and then all the slips of paper were opened. Suddenly, all the women began to speak at once, saying, "Who is it?" "Who's got it?" "Is it the Dunbars?" "Is it the Watsons?" Then the voices began to say, "It's Hutchinson. It's Bill," "Bill Hutchinson's got it."

"Go tell your father," Mrs. Dunbar said to her older son.

People began to look around to see the Hutchinsons. Bill Hutchinson was   45
standing quiet, staring down at the paper in his hand. Suddenly, Tessie Hutchinson shouted to Mr. Summers, "You didn't give him time enough to take any paper he wanted. I saw you. It wasn't fair!"

"Be a good sport, Tessie," Mrs. Delacroix called, and Mrs. Graves said, "All of us took the same chance."

"Shut up, Tessie," Bill Hutchinson said.

"Well, everyone," Mr. Summers said, "that was done pretty fast, and now we've got to be hurrying a little more to get done in time." He consulted his next list. "Bill," he said, "you draw for the Hutchinson family. You got any other households in the Hutchinsons?"

"There's Don and Eva," Mrs. Hutchinson yelled. "Make *them* take their chance!"

"Daughters draw with their husbands' families, Tessie," Mr. Summers said   50
gently. "You know that as well as anyone else."

"It wasn't *fair*," Tessie said.

"I guess not, Joe," Bill Hutchinson said regretfully. "My daughter draws with her husband's family, that's only fair. And I've got no other family except the kids."

"Then, as far as drawing for families is concerned, it's you," Mr. Summers said in explanation, "and as far as drawing for households is concerned, that's you, too. Right?"

"Right," Bill Hutchinson said.

"How many kids, Bill?" Mr. Summers asked formally.   55

"Three," Bill Hutchinson said. "There's Bill, Jr., and Nancy, and little Dave. And Tessie and me."

"All right, then," Mr. Summers said. "Harry, you got their tickets back?"

Mr. Graves nodded and held up the slips of paper. "Put them in the box, then," Mr. Summers directed. "Take Bill's and put it in."

"I think we ought to start over," Mrs. Hutchinson said, as quietly as she could. "I tell you it wasn't *fair*. You didn't give him time enough to choose. *Every-body* saw that."

Mr. Graves had selected the five slips and put them in the box, and he   60
dropped all the papers but those onto the ground, where the breeze caught them
and lifted them off.

"Listen, everybody," Mrs. Hutchinson was saying to the people around her.

"Ready, Bill?" Mr. Summers asked, and Bill Hutchinson, with one quick
glance around at his wife and children, nodded.

"Remember," Mr. Summers said, "take the slips and keep them folded until
each person has taken one. Harry, you help little Dave." Mr. Graves took the
hand of the little boy, who came willingly with him up to the box. "Take a paper
out of the box, Davy," Mr. Summers said. Davy put his hand into the box and
laughed. "Take just *one* paper," Mr. Summers said. "Harry, you hold it for him."
Mr. Graves took the child's hand and removed the folded paper from the tight
fist and held it while little Dave stood next to him and looked up at him wonderingly.

"Nancy next," Mr. Summers said. Nancy was twelve, and her school friends
breathed heavily as she went forward, switching her skirt, and took a slip daintily
from the box. "Bill, Jr.," Mr. Summers said, and Billy, his face red and his feet
over-large, nearly knocked the box over as he got a paper out. "Tessie," Mr. Summers
said. She hesitated for a minute, looking around defiantly, and then set her lips
and went up to the box. She snatched a paper out and held it behind her.

"Bill," Mr. Summers said, and Bill Hutchinson reached into the box and   65
felt around, bringing his hand out at last with the slip of paper in it.

The crowd was quiet. A girl whispered, "I hope it's not Nancy," and the
sound of the whisper reached the edges of the crowd.

"It's not the way it used to be," Old Man Warner said clearly. "People ain't
the way they used to be."

"All right," Mr. Summers said. "Open the papers. Harry, you open little
Dave's."

Mr. Graves opened the slip of paper and there was a general sigh through
the crowd as he held it up and everyone could see that it was blank. Nancy and
Bill, Jr., opened theirs at the same time, and both beamed and laughed, turning
around to the crowd and holding their slips of paper above their heads.

"Tessie," Mr. Summers said. There was a pause, and then Mr. Summers   70
looked at Bill Hutchinson, and Bill unfolded his paper and showed it. It was blank.

"It's Tessie," Mr. Summers said, and his voice was hushed. "Show us her
paper, Bill."

Bill Hutchinson went over to his wife and forced the slip of paper out of
her hand. It had a black spot on it, the black spot Mr. Summers had made the
night before with the heavy pencil in the coal-company office. Bill Hutchinson
held it up, and there was a stir in the crowd.

"All right, folks," Mr. Summers said. "Let's finish quickly."

Although the villagers had forgotten the ritual and lost the original black
box, they still remembered to use stones. The pile of stones the boys had made
earlier was ready; there were stones on the ground with the blowing scraps of
paper that had come out of the box. Mrs. Delacroix selected a stone so large she
had to pick it up with both hands and turned to Mrs. Dunbar. "Come on," she
said. "Hurry up."

Mrs. Dunbar had small stones in both hands, and she said, gasping for breath,   75
"I can't run at all. You'll have to go ahead and I'll catch up with you."

The children had stones already, and someone gave little Davy Hutchinson a few pebbles.

Tessie Hutchinson was in the center of a cleared space by now, and she held her hands out desperately as the villagers moved in on her. "It isn't fair," she said. A stone hit her on the side of the head.

Old Man Warner was saying, "Come on, come on, everyone." Steve Adams was in the front of the crowd of villagers with Mrs. Graves beside him.

"It isn't fair, it isn't right," Mrs. Hutchinson screamed, and then they were upon her.

QUESTIONS

1. Describe the point of view of the story. Is it best described as third-person limited, omniscient, or dramatic? What seems to be the position from which the narrator sees and describes the events? How much extra information does the narrator provide? Does the narrator anywhere express any opinion about the events connected with the lottery?

2. What would the story be like if it were attempted with an omniscient point of view? What if first person? Could the story be as suspenseful as it is? Would it be necessary to provide more information than is now present about the lottery? Why so? In what other ways might the story be different with a different point of view?

3. Does the conclusion of "The Lottery" seem to come as a surprise? In retrospect, are there hints earlier in the story about what is to come? Discuss how you perceived these hints before and after you read the conclusion.

4. A scapegoat, in the ritual of purification described in the Old Testament (Leviticus 16), was an actual goat that was released into the wilderness after having been ceremonially heaped with the "iniquities" of the people (Leviticus 16:22). What traces of such a ritual are suggested in "The Lottery" by references to things like the abandoned salute and the recital, and also the jingle "Lottery in June, corn be heavy soon"? Can you think of any other kinds of rituals that are retained today even though their basis of belief is now remote or even nonexistent?

5. Is the story a horror story or a surprise story, or neither or both?

6. What idea or ideas do you think Jackson is asserting by making the characters in "The Lottery" seem to be just plain, ordinary folks? What would the story have been like if the people had been criminals? If they had all been devil worshippers?

WRITING ABOUT POINT OF VIEW

In prewriting activity for an essay on point of view, you must consider things like language, authority and opportunity for observation, selection of detail, characterization, interpretive commentaries, and narrative development. You might plan an analysis of one, a few, or all of these elements.

Generally the essay should explain how the point of view has contributed to making the work unique. One of the major purposes in your study and preparation is to determine ways in which the narration is made to seem real and probable: Are the actions and speeches reported authentically, as they might be seen and reported in life? As you sketch out materials for your essay, try to apply this question to various parts of the work you are studying, so that you can determine whether the actual narration is just as "true" as the story itself.

Organizing Your Essay

INTRODUCTION.   In your introduction you should get at the matters that you plan to develop. Which point of view is used in the work? What is the major influence of this point of view on the work? (For example, "The omniscient point of view enables us to gain insights into all the characters," or "The first-person point of view focuses all the attention on the limitations of the speaker.") To what extent does the selected point of view make the work particularly interesting and effective, or uninteresting and ineffective? What particular aspects of the work (action, dialogue, characters, description, narration, analysis) do you wish to analyze in support of your central idea?

BODY.   The questions you raise here depend on the work you have studied. It is impossible to answer all the following questions in your analysis, but going through them should help you determine what to include in the body.

If you have read a work with a first-person point of view, your analysis concerns the speaker. Who is she (supposing, for the moment, it's a woman)? Is she a major or minor character? How reliable is she as an observer? What is her background? What is her relationship to the person listening to her (if there is a listener)? Does this situation make you, the reader, an eavesdropper on something private? Does she speak directly to you, the reader, and if so, do you feel cast in the role of a listener? How does the speaker describe the various situations? Is her method uniquely a function of her character? How did she acquire the information she is presenting? How much does she disclose or seem to hide? Why? Does she ever rely on the information of others for her material? How reliable are these other witnesses? Or (supposing it's a man), does the speaker undergo any changes that affect his presentation of material? Do his recollections and descriptions show strengths or limitations? Does he notice one kind of thing (for example, discussion) but miss others (for example, natural scenery)? What might have escaped him, if anything? Does the author put the speaker into situations that he describes but does not understand? Why? Is the speaker ever confused? Is he close to the action or distant from it? Does he show emotional involvement in any situations? Are you sympathetic to his concerns or are you put off by them? If the speaker makes comments, are his thoughts valid? To what extent, if any, is the speaker of as much interest as the material he presents?

If you encounter any of the third-person points of view, try to determine the characteristics of the voice employed by the author. Does it seem that the author is speaking in an authorial voice, or that the narrator has a special voice? You can approach this problem by answering many of the questions relevant to the first-person point of view. Also try to determine the distance of the narrator to the action. How is the action described? How is the dialogue recorded? Is there any background information given? Do the descriptions reveal any bias toward any of the characters? Are the descriptions full or bare? Does the author include descriptions or analyses of a character's thoughts? What are these like? Do you see evidence of what you take to be the author's own philosophy? Does the choice of words direct you toward any particular interpretations? What limitations or freedoms devolve upon the story as a result of the point of view?

CONCLUSION.   In your conclusion you should evaluate the success of the point of view: Was it consistent, effective, truthful? What did the writer gain (if anything) by choosing this point of view? What was lost (if anything)? How might a less skillful writer have handled similar material? After answering questions like these, you may end your essay.

Problems

1. In considering point of view, you will encounter the problem of whether to discuss the author or the speaker as the originator of attitudes and ideas. If the author is employing the first-person point of view, there is no problem. Use the speaker's name, if he or she is given one (for example, Jackie from "First Confession"), or else talk about the "speaker" or "persona" if there is no name (for example, the speaker of Jackson's "The Lottery"). You face a greater problem with the third-person points of view, but even here it is safe for you to discuss the "speaker" rather than the "author," remembering always that the author is manipulating the narrative voice. Sometimes authors emphasize a certain phase of their own personalities in their authorial voices. Many ideas are therefore common to both the author and the speaker, but your statements about these must be inferential, not absolute.

2. Be careful not to wander away from point of view into retelling the story or discussing the ideas. To keep on the topic, emphasize the presentation of the events and ideas and the causes for this presentation. Do not emphasize the subject material itself, but use it only as it bears on your consideration of point of view. Your object is not just to interpret

the work, but also to show how the point of view *enables* you to interpret the work.

Obviously you must talk about the material in the work, but use it only to illustrate your assertions about point of view. Avoid the following pattern of statement, which will always lead you astray: "The speaker says this, which means this." Instead, adhere to the following pattern, which will keep your emphasis always on your central idea: "The speaker says this, which shows this about her and her attitudes." If a particular idea is difficult, you might need to explain it, but do not do so unless it illustrates your central idea.

3. Remember that you are dealing with point of view in the *entire* work and not simply in single narrations and conversations. For example, an individual character has her own way of seeing things when she states something, but in relation to the entire work her speech is a function of the dramatic point of view. Thus, you should not talk about Character A's point of view, and Character B's, but instead should state that "using the dramatic point of view, Author Z allows the various characters to argue their cases, in their own words and with their own limitations."

4. Once again, be particularly careful to distinguish between point of view and opinions or beliefs. Point of view refers to the total position from which things are seen, heard, and reported, whereas an opinion is a thought about something. In this essay, you are to describe not the ideas, but the method of narration of an author.

SAMPLE ESSAY

Shirley Jackson's Dramatic Point of View in "The Lottery"*

[1]   The dramatic point of view in Shirley Jackson's "The Lottery" is essential to the success with which the story renders horror in the midst of the ordinary.° But the story does not deal just with horror: It could also be called a surprise story, an allegory, or a portrayal of human obtuseness, passivity, and cruelty. But the validity of all other claims for "The Lottery" hinges on the author's control over point of view to make the events develop out of a seemingly everyday, matter-of-fact situation—a situation that could not be easily maintained if another point of view were used. The success of Jackson's point of view is achieved through her characterization, selection of details, and diction.°

Because of the dramatic point of view, the story presents the villagers as ordinary folks attending a normal, festive event—in contrast to the horror of their real purpose. This characterization depends upon a speaker who is

---

* See p. 216 for this story.
° Central idea.
□ Thesis sentence.

remote and emotionally uninvolved. The speaker thus records only enough details about the villagers to permit the understanding that they are ordinary people, but not enough to give them life as round human beings. Similarly, Mr. Summers is presented as not much more than a middle-aged, pillar-of-society type. Tessie Hutchinson is the principal character in the story, but the speaker presents little more about her than that she is friendly, ordinary,

[2]   and relatively inarticulate—all details that are essential to her behavior at the end of the story when she objects not to the lottery itself but to the "unfairness" of the drawing. So it is also with the other characters. Their brief conversations are recorded but no more. Because of the objective, remote point of view, we see them from a distance, as we would likely see any typical people at a public gathering. This detached, reportorial method of illustrating character is fundamental to the dramatic point of view, and the twist of cruelty at the end depends on the method.

While there could be much description, Jackson's speaker concentrates on only those details that bring out the horror of the lottery drawing. At the beginning of the story, the speaker presents enough information about the lottery to make sense of it, but does not tell that the prize for winning is instant death. Thus, the speaker establishes that the villagers are gathering

[3]   rocks, but includes no mention of why. The short saying "Lottery in June, corn be heavy soon" is mentioned as a remnant of an earlier but forgotten ritual, but the speaker either does not know the meaning or chooses not to go into it (paragraph 32). All such references seem innocent as first presented by the speaker, and it is only after the ending is known that they are made to seem sinister.

Without exaggeration, another point of view would have required more detail, and therefore would have spoiled Jackson's doubletake of horror. A first-person speaker, for example, could not have been credible without explaining the situation in advance. (As an example, an "I" would need to say something like "The little boys gathered rocks without thinking about their forthcoming

[4]   use in an execution.") An omniscient narrator would necessarily have expressed some commentary on the reactions of the townsfolk (otherwise, how could he or she be omniscient?). By contrast, the dramatic point of view can point out that characters hesitated, or looked worried, but can keep us from learning why. Thus we get information, but not enough to give away the ending.

Appropriate both to the ending, and to the simple and unquestioning nature of the villagers, is the speaker's language. The speaker uses uncolored and unemotional words which are accurate and descriptive but not elaborate. When Tessie Hutchinson appears, she dries "her hands on her apron" (para-

[5]   graph 8)—words that are common and not suggestive. Most of these simple, bare words may be seen as a means by which Jackson uses point of view to delay the reader's understanding of what is happening. The piles of stones, for example, are to be used in the stoning of Tessie Hutchinson, yet one does not draw this conclusion when they are first described (paragraph 2):

Bobby Martin had already stuffed his pockets full of stones, and the other boys soon followed his example, selecting the smoothest and roundest stones; Bobby and Harry Jones and Dickie Delacroix—the villagers pronounced this name "Dellacroy"—eventually made a great pile of stones in one corner of the square and guarded it against the raids of other boys.

The speaker's references to the nicknames, and to the association of the stones with apparently normal boyhood games, both divert the reader's attention and obscure the horror that in just a short time the stones will be used in a ritual death. Even at the end, the speaker uses the word "pebbles" to describe the stones given to Tessie Hutchinson's son Davy. The implication is that the boy is going to a game, not to the killing of his own mother!

[6]   <u>Such masterly control over point of view is a major cause of Jackson's success in "The Lottery."</u> Her objective is to establish a superficial appearance of everyday, harmless reality, which she maintains up to the last few paragraphs. Indeed, she is so successful that a possible response to the stoning is that "such a killing could not take place among the ordinary, earthy folks in this story." Yet it is because of this reality that a reader sees the validity of Jackson's vision. Horror is not to be found on moors and in haunted castles, but among everyday people like the villagers in Tessie Hutchinson's home town. Without Jackson's skill in controlling point of view, there could be little of this power of suggestion, and it would not be possible to claim such success for the story.

Commentary on the Essay

For illustrative purposes, this essay analyzes Jackson's choice of the dramatic or objective point of view as it affects characterization, description, and diction. In your essay you might wish to consider all these aspects or only one, depending on the length of your assignment.

The introductory paragraph develops the relationship of the dramatic point of view to the success of the work both as horror story and suspense story. The thesis sentence points out the areas to be developed in the body.

In the second paragraph, the aim is *not* to present a full character study (since the essay is not about character but point of view), but rather to discuss the ways in which the dramatic point of view *enables* the character to be rendered. The only idea about the characters that is needed for the paragraph is that they are to be judged not as complete human beings but as "ordinary folks." Once this idea is established, then the thrust of the paragraph is to show how the point of view is used to keep the reader at a distance sufficient to permit this conclusion.

In the same way, the paragraphs about detail (3 and 4) emphasize the sparseness of detail in keeping with the conception that the speaker is distant and relatively uninvolved. Note that in paragraph 4 the dramatic point of view is contrasted with other points of view that might have been used. This way of developing a discussion might be helpful for you to adapt, for by imagining how the events might be described in another way you may develop a better understanding of the method used in the work you are studying.

The third section of the body (paragraph 5) emphasizes the idea that the flat, colorless diction defers the reader's awareness of what is happening in the story. Therefore the point of view is vital in the development of horror and surprise. The concluding paragraph emphasizes the way in which general response to the story, and also its success, are conditioned by the detached, dramatic point of view.

WRITING TOPICS FOR CHAPTER 5

1. Write an essay on the influence of the point of view (third-person limited) on your perception of Miss Brill in the story "Miss Brill."

2. Imagine how the events in "The Lottery" might be described if a different point of view were used. How would such a change affect the story? Would the conclusion be more or less effective with such a change? Write some sample paragraphs with an omniscient point of view or with a limited point of view.

3. Write a short narrative from the point of view of one of these characters:
   a. Lucy Wessen in "I'm a Fool." "How I met and lost the most wonderful man."
   b. The Baker in "Miss Brill." "My favorite customer."
   c. Grandmother in "First Confession." "Jackie seems to be bound for Hell."

4. How would the story "Death" be affected if told by the narrator of "The Lottery" or the narrator of "Miss Brill?"

5. Write a brief story using one of the situations listed on p. 196. Write from the first-person point of view, as though you are describing things that actually happened to you. Then write an analysis explaining how your point of view governs you, as a story writer, in your descriptions and word choices.

6

Setting: Place and Objects in Fiction

Setting refers to the natural and artificial scenery or environment in which characters in literature live and move, together with the things they use. Times of day, conditions of sun and clouds, weather, hills and valleys, trees and animals, sounds both outside and inside, and smells—all these may go into the setting of a work. Setting may also include artifacts like walking sticks, paper windmills, duelling pistols, birdcages, breadknives, necklaces, furpieces, park benches, hair ribbons, and many other items. The setting of a work may also extend to references to clothing, descriptions of physical appearance, and spatial relationships. In short, the setting of a work is the total of references to physical and temporal objects and artifacts.

The setting of stories and novels is much like the sets and properties of the stage or the location for a motion picture. The dramatist writing for the theater is physically limited by what can be put on a stage. Writers of fiction, however, are limited only by their imaginations. It is possible for them to include details of many places without the slightest external restraint.

The action of a story, while often taking place in one city, countryside, or house, may shift within an area or location as characters move about to perform their tasks. In a novel, the author may shift the characters to many different locations. Whether there is one location or many, however, the term *setting* refers to all the places and objects that are important in the work, whether natural or manufactured.

TYPES OF SETTINGS

Natural

The setting for a great number of works is the out-of-doors, and, as one might expect, Nature herself is seen as a force that shapes action and therefore directs and redirects lives. A deep woods may make walking difficult or dangerous, or may be a place for a sinister meeting of devil worshippers. A park bench on a sunny afternoon may be the place where a person feels the deepest joy and also begins a descent into misery. A brackish lake may mark an end of hopelessness and the beginning of commitment. The ocean may be the location of a test of youth but also may provide the environment for the memory of vanished dreams. Nature, in short, is one of the major forces governing the circumstances of characters who experience life and try to resolve their conflicts.

Manufactured

Manufactured things always reflect the people who made them. A building or a room tells about the people who built it and live in it, and ultimately about the social and political orders that maintain it. A richly decorated house shows the expensive tastes and resources of the characters owning it. A few cracks in the plaster and some chips in the paint may show a declining neighborhood, or even a declining nation. Ugly and impoverished surroundings may contribute to the weariness, insensitivity, negligence, or even hostility of the characters living in them.

Possessions may enter into character motivation and development. A bottle of medicine may cause a woman to take a journey of mercy, while a bottle of beer may embarrass a sensitive young boy. The loss of a borrowed but cheap necklace may plunge a young married couple into indebtedness and a life of drudgery, and the destruction of a prized canary may produce uncontrollable rage in the bird's owner. The drawing of a lottery "prize" may unleash a collective, community horror. As in life, literature includes all the forces that may be generated among people by objects of value and convenience.

STUDYING THE USES OF SETTING

In studying the setting of a story, your first concern should be to discover all the details that form a part of setting, and then to determine how the author has used them. For example, as writers stress character, plot, or action, they may emphasize or minimize setting. At times a setting may be no more than a roughly sketched place where events occur. In other stories, the setting may be so prominent that it may almost be considered as a participant in the action. An instance of such "participation" is Welty's "A Worn Path," where the woods and roadway are almost active antagonists against Phoenix as she walks on her worn path toward Natchez.

Setting and Credibility

One of the major purposes of setting is to lend realism or verisimilitude. As the description of setting is made more particular and detailed, the events of the work become more believable. Irwin Shaw's "Act of Faith" presents the realistic conditions of rural France as a background in which authentic soldiers plan an actual trip to Paris so that they may enjoy their weekend leave. The more detailed the description of setting, the more believable the events of the story become. For example, because the details of the woodworking shop in Marjorie Pickthall's "The Worker in Sandalwood" are well delineated, they lend authenticity to the miracle that occurs there. Even futuristic, unrealistic, symbolic, and fantastic stories, as well as ghost stories, take on authenticity if the setting is presented as though the world of these stories is the one we normally see and experience. Clark's "The Portable Phonograph," Kafka's "A Hunger Artist," Hawthorne's "Young Goodman Brown," and Poe's "The Masque of the Red Death" are such stories. Without a basis in detailed settings, such works would lose credibility, even though they make no pretenses at everyday realism.

Setting and Statement

Setting may be a kind of pictorial language, a means by which the author makes statements much as a painter uses certain images as ideas in a painting. Thus the paths in both "Young Goodman Brown" and "A Worn Path" may be understood as visual equivalents of the solitude, obstacles, and uncertainties of life, which all persons must face, for better or worse. The dwelling place of Dr. Jenkins in "The Portable Phonograph" is compared to the "mouth of a mine tunnel;" that is, a cave. Because the setting of the story is the dark, bleak, cold world after a catastrophic war, the idea conveyed is that warfare sends all of us back to the primitive caves we lived in during the Stone Ages.

Setting and Character

In the same vein, setting may intersect with character as a means by which authors underscore the importance of place, circumstances, and time upon human growth and change. In "A Jury of Her Peers," Susan Glaspell creates the scene in the kitchen of the lonely, dreary Wright farm. The setting is a place of nothing but hard work, joylessness, oppression, and cruelty, so that we realize that Mrs. Wright, however bright and promising she had been as a young woman, was also vulnerable, so much so that her outburst of anger in murdering her husband is made to seem understandable. Here the setting is dominant in helping us shape our ideas of her character. A similar blending of the setting and the major character is explored in the sample essay about Maupassant's "The Necklace" (p. 3). In virtually every work where place and objects are important, comparable relationships may be found and studied.

Setting and Organization

Authors might also use setting as a means of organization. The various actions in Jackson's "The Lottery" are all related to the place of the lottery drawing in the village square, "between the post office and the bank;" the story begins at ten o'clock in the morning and ends almost exactly at noon—in other words, according to a time sequence of before, during, and immediately after the drawing. In Maupassant's "The Necklace," the action removes Mathilde and her husband from a pleasant though not lavish apartment on the Street of Martyrs in Paris to an attic flat in a poor neighborhood. The final scene of the story is believable only because Mathilde leaves her poor neighborhood to take a nostalgic walk on one of the most fashionable streets in Paris, the Champs Elysées. Without this shift of scene, she could not have met Jeanne again, for their ways of life could otherwise never intersect.

Another organizational application of place, time, and object is the **framing** or **enclosing method.** An author frames a story by opening with a description of a setting, and then returning to the same setting at the end. Like a picture frame, the setting affects the reader's perceptions. An example is Shaw's "Act of Faith," which is set in France immediately after World War II. The story begins with two soldiers slogging through the mud with the hope of getting enough money for a weekend in Paris. At the end, the same two soldiers, together with a third, are walking in "damp, dead grass"—the same activity over similar ground. Their intention to go to town has not changed, but the stakes have escalated dramatically, from the simple intention of having a good time to a major commitment about the future of Jews in postwar America. Shaw's setting of muddy and slippery ground, in short, frames a story of serious importance. In the same way, Hawthorne's "Young Goodman Brown" is framed by Brown's leaving Salem. When alive, at the beginning, he leaves home on his walk in the woods; when dead, at the end, he is carried in a funeral procession to his grave. In such ways, the framing or enclosing setting emphasizes that many things about life remain the same even though people undergo constant growth and change.

Setting and Atmosphere

Setting also affects the **atmosphere** or **mood** of stories. You might note that a typical action usually requires no more than a functional description of setting. Thus, an action in a forest needs just the statement that the forest is there. However, if you read descriptions of the trees, the shapes, the light and shadows, the animals, the wind, and the sounds, you may be sure that the author is working to create an atmosphere or mood for the action (as in Hawthorne's "Young Goodman Brown"). There are many ways of creating moods. Descriptions of "warm" colors (red, orange, yellow) may contribute to a mood of happiness. "Cooler" colors may suggest gloom. References to smells and sounds bring the setting even more to life by asking additional sensory responses from the reader. The setting of a story on a farm or in a city apartment may evoke a response to these habitats that may contribute to a story's atmosphere.

Setting and Irony

Just as setting is present as an element of agreement, reinforcement, and strengthening of character and theme, so may it work ironically—as an environment that is the opposite of what actually occurs in the work. For example, in "The Lottery" Jackson describes the local townsfolk to set up the expectation that the winner of the small-town lottery will receive a valuable prize. This location in normal, rural America makes the conclusion grimly ironic, for it is just real, everyday folks who cast the stones of ritual execution. Glaspell uses setting ironically in "A Jury of Her Peers," where the two women examine the personal effects in the kitchen of the major character. While their husbands dismiss their activities and look for solutions to the crime in other places in the farmhouse, the women uncover the background, the causes, and the method of the crime themselves. A bizarre irony is created by Poe in "The Masque of the Red Death," when Prince Prospero seals off his palace to prevent the entry of plague, but at the same moment he seals the "Red Death" within his own walls, and thereby he ensures the end of all the revelers. The irony is that closed doors may as easily prevent escape as attack.

EDGAR ALLAN POE (1809–1849)

The Masque of the Red Death   *1842*

The "Red Death" had long devastated the country. No pestilence had ever been so fatal, or so hideous. Blood was its Avatar° and its seal—the redness and the horror of blood. There were sharp pains, and sudden dizziness, and then profuse bleeding at the pores, with dissolution. The scarlet stains upon the body and especially upon the face of the victim, were the pest ban which shut him out from the aid and from the sympathy of his fellow-men. And the whole seizure, progress, and termination of the disease, were the incidents of half an hour.

Avatar: model, incarnation, manifestation.

But the Prince Prospero° was happy and dauntless and sagacious. When his dominions were half depopulated, he summoned to his presence a thousand hale and light-hearted friends from among the knights and dames of his court, and with these retired to the deep seclusion of one of his castellated abbeys. This was an extensive and magnificent structure, the creation of the prince's own eccentric yet august taste. A strong and lofty wall girdled it in. This wall had gates of iron. The courtiers, having entered, brought furnaces and massy hammers and welded the bolts. They resolved to leave means neither of ingress nor egress to the sudden impulses of despair or of frenzy from within. The abbey was amply provisioned. With such precautions the courtiers might bid defiance to contagion. The external world could take care of itself. In the meantime it was folly to grieve, or to think. The prince had provided all the appliances of pleasure. There were buffoons, there were improvisatori, there were ballet-dancers, there were musicians, there was Beauty, there was wine. All these and security were within. Without was the "Red Death."

It was toward the close of the fifth or sixth month of his seclusion, and while the pestilence raged most furiously abroad, that the Prince Prospero entertained his thousand friends at a masked ball of the most unusual magnificence.

It was a voluptuous scene, that masquerade. But first let me tell of the rooms in which it was held. There were seven—an imperial suite. In many palaces, however, such suites form a long and straight vista, while the folding doors slide back nearly to the walls on either hand, so that the view of the whole extent is scarcely impeded. Here the case was very different; as might have been expected from the duke's love of the *bizarre*. The apartments were so irregularly disposed that the vision embraced but little more than one at a time. There was a sharp turn at every twenty or thirty yards, and at each turn a novel effect. To the right and left, in the middle of each wall, a tall and narrow Gothic window looked out upon a closed corridor which pursued the windings of the suite. These windows were of stained glass whose color varied in accordance with the prevailing hue of the decorations of the chamber into which it opened. That at the eastern extremity was hung, for example, in blue—and vividly blue were its windows. The second chamber was purple in its ornaments and tapestries, and here the panes were purple. The third was green throughout, and so were the casements. The fourth was furnished and lighted with orange—the fifth with white—the sixth with violet. The seventh apartment was closely shrouded in black velvet tapestries that hung all over the ceiling and down the walls, falling in heavy folds upon a carpet of the same material and hue. But in this chamber only, the color of the windows failed to correspond with the decorations. The panes here were scarlet—a deep blood color. Now in no one of the seven apartments was there any lamp or candelabrum, amid the profusion of golden ornaments that lay scattered to and fro or depended from the roof. There was no light of any kind emanating from lamp or candle within the suite of chambers. But in the corridors that followed the suite, there stood, opposite to each window, a heavy tripod, bearing a brazier of fire, that projected its rays through the tinted glass and so glaringly illumined the room. And thus were produced a multitude of gaudy and fantastic appearances. But in the western

---

Prospero: that is, "prosperous." In Shakespeare's play *The Tempest*, the principal character is Prospero.

or black chamber the effect of the fire-light that streamed upon the dark hangings through the blood-tinted panes was ghastly in the extreme, and produced so wild a look upon the countenances of those who entered, that there were few of the company bold enough to set foot within its precincts at all.

It was in this apartment, also, that there stood against the western wall, a gigantic clock of ebony. Its pendulum swung to and fro with a dull, heavy, monotonous clang; and when the minute-hand made the circuit of the face, and the hour was to be stricken, there came from the brazen lungs of the clock a sound which was clear and loud and deep and exceedingly musical, but of so peculiar a note and emphasis that, at each lapse of an hour, the musicians of the orchestra were constrained to pause, momentarily, in their performance, to hearken to the sound; and thus the waltzers perforce ceased their evolutions; and there was a brief disconcert of the whole gay company; and, while the chimes of the clock yet rang, it was observed that the giddiest grew pale, and the more aged and sedate passed their hands over their brows as if in confused revery or meditation. But when the echoes had fully ceased, a light laughter at once pervaded the assembly; the musicians looked at each other and smiled as if at their own nervousness and folly, and made whispering vows, each to the other, that the next chiming of the clock should produce in them no similar emotion; and then, after the lapse of sixty minutes (which embrace three thousand and six hundred seconds of the Time that flies), there came yet another chiming of the clock, and then were the same disconcert and tremulousness and meditation as before.

But, in spite of these things, it was a gay and magnificent revel. The tastes of the duke were peculiar. He had a fine eye for colors and effects. He disregarded the *decora*° of mere fashion. His plans were bold and fiery, and his conceptions glowed with barbaric lustre. There are some who would have thought him mad. His followers felt that he was not. It was necessary to hear and see and touch him to be *sure* that he was not.

He had directed, in great part, the movable embellishments of the seven chambers, upon occasion of this great fête,° and it was his own guiding taste which had given character to the masqueraders. Be sure they were grotesque. There were much glare and glitter and piquancy and phantasm—much of what has been since seen in "Hernani."° There were arabesque figures with unsuited limbs and appointments. There were delirious fancies such as the madman fashions. There were much of the beautiful, much of the wanton, much of the *bizarre*, something of the terrible, and not a little of that which might have excited disgust. To and fro in the seven chambers there stalked, in fact, a multitude of dreams. And these— the dreams—writhed in and about, taking hue from the rooms, and causing the wild music of the orchestra to seem as the echo of their steps. And, anon, there strikes the ebony clock which stands in the hall of the velvet. And then, for a moment, all is still, and all is silent save the voice of the clock. The dreams are stiff-frozen as they stand. But the echoes of the chime die away—they have endured but an instant—and a light, half-subdued laughter floats after them as they depart.

decora: schemes, patterns.
fête: party, revel.
Hernani: a tragedy by Victor Hugo (1802–1885), featuring elaborate scenes and costumes.

And now again the music swells, and the dreams live, and writhe to and fro more merrily than ever, taking hue from the many-tinted windows through which stream the rays from the tripods. But to the chamber which lies most westwardly of the seven there are now none of the maskers who venture; for the night is waning away; and there flows a ruddier light through the blood-colored panes; and the blackness of the sable drapery appalls; and to him whose foot falls upon the sable carpet, there comes from the near clock of ebony a muffled peal more solemnly emphatic than any which reaches *their* ears who indulge in the more remote gaieties of the other apartments.

But these other apartments were densely crowded, and in them beat feverishly the heart of life. And the revel went whirlingly on, until at length there commenced the sounding of midnight upon the clock. And then the music ceased, as I have told; and the evolutions of the waltzers were quieted; and there was an uneasy cessation of all things as before. But now there were twelve strokes to be sounded by the bell of the clock; and thus it happened, perhaps that more of thought crept, with more of time, into the meditations of the thoughtful among those who revelled. And thus too, it happened, perhaps, that before the last echoes of the last chime had utterly sunk into silence, there were many individuals in the crowd who had found leisure to become aware of the presence of a masked figure which had arrested the attention of no single individual before. And the rumor of this new presence having spread itself whisperingly around, there arose at length from the whole company a buzz, or murmur, expressive of disapprobation and surprise—then, finally, of terror, of horror, and of disgust.

In an assembly of phantasms such as I have painted, it may well be supposed that no ordinary appearance could have excited such sensation. In truth the masquerade license of the night was nearly unlimited; but the figure in question had out-Heroded Herod,° and gone beyond the bounds of even the prince's indefinite decorum. There are chords in the hearts of the most reckless which cannot be touched without emotion. Even with the utterly lost, to whom life and death are equally jests, there are matters of which no jest can be made. The whole company, indeed, seemed now deeply to feel that in the costume and bearing of the stranger neither wit nor propriety existed. The figure was tall and gaunt, and shrouded from head to foot in the habiliments of the grave. The mask which concealed the visage was made so nearly to resemble the countenance of a stiffened corpse that the closest scrutiny must have had difficulty in detecting the cheat. And yet all this might have been endured, if not approved, by the mad revellers around. But the mummer had gone so far as to assume the type of the Red Death. His vesture was dabbled in *blood*—and his broad brow, with all the features of the face, was besprinkled with the scarlet horror.

When the eyes of Prince Prospero fell upon this spectral image (which, with   10
a slow and solemn movement, as if more fully to sustain its *rôle*, stalked to and fro among the waltzers) he was seen to be convulsed, in the first moment with a strong shudder either of terror or distaste; but, in the next, his brow reddened with rage.

"Who dares"—he demanded hoarsely of the courtiers who stood near him—

out-Heroded Herod: quoted from Shakespeare's *Hamlet*, act 3, scene 2, line 13, in reference to extreme overacting.

"who dares insult us with this blasphemous mockery? Seize him and unmask him—that we may know whom we have to hang, at sunrise, from the battlements!"

It was in the eastern or blue chamber in which stood the Prince Prospero as he uttered these words. They rang throughout the seven rooms loudly and clearly, for the prince was a bold and robust man, and the music had become hushed at the waving of his hand.

It was in the blue room where stood the prince, with a group of pale courtiers by his side. At first, as he spoke, there was a slight rushing movement of this group in the direction of the intruder, who, at the moment was also near at hand, and now, with deliberate and stately step, made closer approach to the speaker. But from a certain nameless awe with which the mad assumptions of the mummer had inspired the whole party, there were found none who put forth hand to seize him; so that, unimpeded, he passed within a yard of the prince's person; and, while the vast assembly, as if with one impulse, shrank from the centres of the rooms to the walls, he made his way uninterruptedly, but with the same solemn and measured step which had distinguished him from the first, through the blue chamber to the purple—through the purple to the green—through the green to the orange—through this again to the white—and even thence to the violet, ere a decided movement had been made to arrest him. It was then, however, that the Prince Prospero, maddening with rage and the shame of his own momentary cowardice, rushed hurriedly through the six chambers, while none followed him on account of a deadly terror that had seized upon all. He bore aloft a drawn dagger, and had approached, in rapid impetuosity, to within three or four feet of the retreating figure, when the latter, having attained the extremity of the velvet apartment, turned suddenly and confronted his pursuer. There was a sharp cry—and the dagger dropped gleaming upon the sable carpet, upon which, instantly afterward, fell prostrate in death the Prince Prospero. Then, summoning the wild courage of despair, a throng of the revellers at once threw themselves into the black apartment, and, seizing the mummer, whose tall figure stood erect and motionless within the shadow of the ebony clock, gasped in unutterable horror at finding the grave cerements and corpse-like mask, which they handled with so violent a rudeness, untenanted by any tangible form.

And now was acknowledged the presence of the Red Death. He had come like a thief in the night.° And one by one dropped the revellers in the blood-bedewed halls of their revel, and died each in the despairing posture of his fall. And the life of the ebony clock went out with that of the last of the gay. And the flames of the tripods expired. And Darkness and Decay and the Red Death held illimitable dominion over all.

QUESTIONS

1. What is happening throughout the country in Poe's "Masque of the Red Death"? How does Prince Prospero react to these events? What does the Prince's reaction tell us about him?

thief in the night: 2 Peter 3:10.

2. How is the building in which Prince Prospero and his thousand nobles take shelter described? To what extent does the description of this "abbey" help us form an opinion of Prince Prospero?

3. How many rooms are used in the masquerade ball or revel in the story? In what ways might this number be significant? What is the dominant color of each room? How are the rooms lighted? How do these details help create the atmosphere and mood of the story?

4. What color is the last room? What color is its window? Why does this room make the revellers nervous? To what extent does this last room reflect the plot and ideas of the story?

5. What single object is located in this last room? How is this object described? What effect does it have on the revellers when it sounds? How might you explain this effect? What do you think Poe is suggesting symbolically with this object and its effects?

6. How are the nobles dressed for the masquerade? Why does the "masked figure" introduced near the end of the story stand out as remarkable? How does Prospero react to this masked figure? Can you explain Prospero's reaction? What does this figure represent?

7. What is the central conflict in this story? Who is the protagonist? The antagonist? Where is the climax of the story? How is the central conflict resolved at the climax?

WALTER VAN TILBURG CLARK   (1909–1971)

The Portable Phonograph   1942

The red sunset, with narrow, black cloud strips like threats across it, lay on the curved horizon of the prairie. The air was still and cold, and in it settled the mute darkness and greater cold of night. High in the air there was wind, for through the veil of the dusk the clouds could be seen gliding rapidly south and changing shapes. A sensation of torment, of two-sided, unpredictable nature, arose from the stillness of the earth air beneath the violence of the upper air. Out of the sunset, through the dead, matted grass and isolated weed stalks of the prairie, crept the narrow and deeply rutted remains of a road. In the road, in places, there were crusts of shallow, brittle ice. There were little islands of an old oiled pavement in the road too, but most of it was mud, now frozen rigid. The frozen mud still bore the toothed impress of great tanks, and a wanderer on the neighboring undulations might have stumbled, in this light, into large, partially filled-in and weed-grown cavities, their banks channeled and beginning to spread into badlands. These pits were such as might have been made by falling meteors, but they were not. They were the scars of gigantic bombs, their rawness already made a little natural by rain, seed and time. Along the road there were rakish remnants of fence. There was also, just visible, one portion of tangled and multiple barbed wire still erect, behind which was a shelving ditch with small caves, now very quiet and empty, at intervals in its back wall. Otherwise there was no structure or remnant of a structure visible over the dome of the darkling earth, but only, in sheltered hollows, the darker shadows of young trees trying again.

Under the wuthering arch of the high wind a V of wild geese fled south. The rush of their pinions sounded briefly, and the faint, plaintive notes of their expeditionary talk. Then they left a still greater vacancy. There was the smell and expectation of snow, as there is likely to be when the wild geese fly south. From the remote distance, toward the red sky, came faintly the protracted howl and quick yap-yap of a prairie wolf.

North of the road, perhaps a hundred yards, lay the parallel and deeply intrenched course of a small creek, lined with leafless alders and willows. The creek was already silent under ice. Into the bank above it was dug a sort of cell, with a single opening, like the mouth of a mine tunnel. Within the cell there was a little red of fire, which showed dully through the opening, like a reflection or a deception of the imagination. The light came from the chary burning of four blocks of poorly aged peat, which gave off a petty warmth and much acrid smoke. But the precious remnants of wood, old fence posts and timbers from the long-deserted dugouts, had to be saved from the real cold, for the time when a man's breath blew white, the moisture in his nostrils stiffened at once when he stepped out, and the expansive blizzards paraded for days over the vast open, swirling and settling and thickening, till the dawn of the cleared day when the sky was a thin blue-green and the terrible cold, in which a man could not live for three hours unwarmed, lay over the uniformly drifted swell of the plain.

Around the smoldering peat four men were seated cross-legged. Behind them, traversed by their shadows, was the earth bench, with two old and dirty army blankets, where the owner of the cell slept. In a niche in the opposite wall were a few tin utensils which caught the glint of the coals. The host was rewrapping in a piece of daubed burlap, four fine, leather-bound books. He worked slowly and very carefully, and at last tied the bundle securely with a piece of grass-woven cord. The other three looked intently upon the process, as if a great significance lay in it. As the host tied the cord, he spoke. He was an old man, his long, matted beard and hair gray to nearly white. The shadows made his brows and cheekbones appear gnarled, his eyes and cheeks deeply sunken. His big hands, rough with frost and swollen by rheumatism, were awkward but gentle at their task. He was like a prehistoric priest performing a fateful ceremonial rite. Also his voice had in it a suitable quality of deep, reverent despair, yet perhaps, at the moment, a sharpness of selfish satisfaction.

"When I perceived what was happening," he said, "I told myself, 'It is the end. I cannot take much; I will take these.'"   5

"Perhaps I was impractical," he continued. "But for myself, I do not regret, and what do we know of those who will come after us? We are the doddering remnant of a race of mechanical fools. I have saved what I love; the soul of what was good in us here; perhaps the new ones will make a strong enough beginning not to fall behind when they become clever."

He rose with slow pain and placed the wrapped volumes in the niche with his utensils. The others watched him with the same ritualistic gaze.

"Shakespeare, the Bible, *Moby Dick*,° *The Divine Comedy*,"° one of them said
softly. "You might have done worse; much worse."

"You will have a little soul left until you die," said another harshly. "That is
more than is true of us. My brain becomes thick, like my hands." He held the
big, battered hands, with their black nails, in the glow to be seen.

"I want paper to write on," he said. "And there is none."   10

The fourth man said nothing. He sat in the shadow farthest from the fire,
and sometimes his body jerked in its rags from the cold. Although he was still
young, he was sick, and coughed often. Writing implied a greater future than he
now felt able to consider.

The old man seated himself laboriously, and reached out, groaning at the
movement, to put another block of peat on the fire. With bowed heads and averted
eyes, his three guests acknowledged his magnanimity.

"We thank you, Doctor Jenkins, for the reading," said the man who had
named the books.

They seemed then to be waiting for something. Doctor Jenkins understood,
but was loath to comply. In an ordinary moment he would have said nothing.
But the words of *The Tempest*,° which he had been reading, and the religious attention
of the three, made this an unusual occasion.

"You wish to hear the phonograph,"° he said grudgingly.   15

The two middle-aged men stared into the fire, unable to formulate and expose
the enormity of their desire.

The young man, however, said anxiously, between suppressed coughs, "Oh,
please," like an excited child.

The old man rose again in his difficult way, and went to the back of the
cell. He returned and placed tenderly upon the packed floor, where the firelight
might fall upon it, an old, portable phonograph in a black case. He smoothed
the top with his hand, then opened it. The lovely green-felt-covered disk became
visible.

"I have been using thorns as needles," he said. "But tonight, because we
have a musician among us"—he bent his head to the young man, almost invisible
in the shadow—"I will use a steel needle. There are only three left."

The two middle-aged men stared at him in speechless adoration. The one   20
with the big hands, who wanted to write, moved his lips, but the whisper was not
audible.

"Oh, don't," cried the young man, as if he were hurt. "The thorns will do
beautifully."

"No," the old man said. "I have become accustomed to the thorns—but they
are not really good. For you, my young friend, we will have good music tonight.

Moby Dick: By Herman Melville (1819–1891), a classic American novel published in
1851.
    The Divine Comedy: By Dante (1265–1321), regarded as the supreme poem of the
Italian Renaissance, circulated about 1300.
    The Tempest: Shakespeare's last play, first performed about 1611.
    phonograph: Early phonographs, in use before electrically driven record players, had
to be wound up by hand. They played records at a speed of 78 revolutions per minute,
and used steel needles that had to be changed very often. The phonograph is especially
valuable to the characters in this story because they have no electricity.

"After all," he added generously, and beginning to wind the phonograph, which creaked, "they can't last forever."

"No, nor we," the man who needed to write said harshly. "The needle, by all means."

"Oh, thanks," said the young man. "Thanks," he said again, in a low, excited   25
voice, and then stifled his coughing with a bowed head.

"The records, though," said the old man when he had finished winding, "are a different matter. Already they are very worn. I do not play them more than once a week. One, once a week, that is what I allow myself."

"More than a week I cannot stand it; not to hear them," he apologized.

"No, how could you?" cried the young man. "And with them here like this."

"A man can stand anything," said the man who wanted to write, in his harsh, antagonistic voice.

"Please, the music," said the young man.   30

"Only the one," said the old man. "In the long run we will remember more that way."

He had a dozen records with luxuriant gold and red seals. Even in that light the others could see that the threads of the records were becoming worn. Slowly he read out the titles, and the tremendous, dead names of the composers and the artists and the orchestras. The three worked upon the names in their minds, carefully. It was difficult to select from such a wealth what they would at once most like to remember. Finally the man who wanted to write named Gershwin's "New York."°

"Oh, no," cried the sick young man, and then could say nothing more because he had to cough. The others understood him, and the harsh man withdrew his selection and waited for the musician to choose.

The musician begged Doctor Jenkins to read the titles again, very slowly, so that he could remember the sounds. While they were read, he lay back against the wall, his eyes closed, his thin, horny hand pulling at his light beard, and listened to the voices and the orchestras and the single instruments in his mind.

When the reading was done he spoke despairingly. "I have forgotten," he   35
complained. "I cannot hear them clearly."

"There are things missing," he explained.

"I know," said Doctor Jenkins. "I thought that I knew all of Shelley° by heart. I should have brought Shelley."

"That's more soul than we can use," said the harsh man. "*Moby Dick* is better. "By God, we can understand that," he emphasized.

The doctor nodded.   40

"Still," said the man who had admired the books, "we need the absolute if we are to keep a grasp on anything."

"Anything but these sticks and peat clods and rabbit snares," he said bitterly.

"Shelley desired an ultimate absolute," said the harsh man. "It's too much," he said. "It's no good; no earthly good."

George Gershwin (1898–1937): American composer who wrote in the jazz idiom, not in the classical manner.

Percy Bysshe Shelley (1792–1822): English poet who wrote poems about the soul, intellectual beauty, and mutability.

The musician selected a Debussy° nocturne. The others considered and approved. They rose to their knees to watch the doctor prepare for the playing, so that they appeared to be actually in an attitude of worship. The peat glow showed the thinness of their bearded faces, and the deep lines in them, and revealed the condition of their garments. The other two continued to kneel as the old man carefully lowered the needle onto the spinning disk, but the musician suddenly drew back against the wall again, with his knees up, and buried his face in his hands.

At the first notes of the piano the listeners were startled. They stared at each other. Even the musician lifted his head in amazement, but then quickly bowed it again, strainingly, as if he were suffering from a pain he might not be able to endure. They were all listening deeply, without movement. The wet, blue-green notes tinkled forth from the old machine, and were individual, delectable presences in the cell. The individual, delectable presences swept into a sudden tide of unbearably beautiful dissonance, and then continued fully the swelling and ebbing of that tide, the dissonant inpourings, and the resolutions, and the diminishments, and the little, quiet wavelets of interlude lapping between. Every sound was piercing and singularly sweet. In all the men except the musician, there occurred rapid sequences of tragically heightened recollection. He heard nothing but what was there. At the final, whispering disappearance, but moving quietly, so that the others would not hear him and look at him, he let his head fall back in agony, as if it were drawn there by the hair, and clenched the fingers of one hand over his teeth. He sat that way while the others were silent, and until they began to breathe again normally. His drawn-up legs were trembling violently.

Quickly Doctor Jenkins lifted the needle off, to save it, and not to spoil the recollection with scraping. When he had stopped the whirling of the sacred disk, he courteously left the phonograph open and by the fire, in sight.

The others, however, understood. The musician rose last, but then abruptly, and went quickly out at the door without saying anything. The others stopped at the door and gave their thanks in low voices. The doctor nodded magnificently.

"Come again," he invited, "in a week. We will have the 'New York.' "

When the two had gone together, out toward the rimmed road, he stood in the entrance, peering and listening. At first there was only the resonant boom of the wind overhead, and then, far over the dome of the dead, dark plain, the wolf cry lamenting. In the rifts of clouds the doctor saw four stars flying. It impressed the doctor that one of them had just been obscured by the beginning of a flying cloud at the very moment he heard what he had been listening for, a sound of suppressed coughing. It was not near by, however. He believed that down against the pale alders he could see the moving shadow.

With nervous hands he lowered the piece of canvas which served as his door, and pegged it at the bottom. Then quickly and quietly, looking at the piece of canvas frequently, he slipped the records into the case, snapped the lid shut, and carried the phonograph to his couch. There, pausing often to stare at the canvas and listen, he dug earth from the wall and disclosed a piece of board. Behind this there was a deep hole in the wall, into which he put the phonograph. After a moment's consideration, he went over and reached down his bundle of

45

50

Claude Debussy (1862–1918): French composer. A "nocturne" is a "night piece."

books and inserted it also. Then, guardedly, he once more sealed up the hole with the board and the earth. He also changed his blankets, and the grass-stuffed sack which served as a pillow, so that he could lie facing the entrance. After carefully placing two more blocks of peat on the fire, he stood for a long time watching the stretched canvas, but it seemed to billow naturally with the first gusts of a lowering wind. At last he prayed, and got in under his blankets, and closed his smoke-smarting eyes. On the inside of the bed, next the wall, he could feel with his hand, the comfortable piece of lead pipe.

QUESTIONS

1. Clark devotes the first three paragraphs of this story completely to description, thus establishing the general setting. What kind of environment is described? How would you characterize the scene? What has obviously happened before the story opens? To what extent do these paragraphs establish the tone and atmosphere of the entire story?

2. The first three descriptive paragraphs are loaded with adjectives. In the first, for example, we find *narrow, black, still, cold, mute, dead, isolated, shallow, brittle, old, frozen, tangled, quiet,* and *empty.* What do most of these adjectives have in common? How do they contribute to the establishment of setting and, in turn, mood?

3. How is "the host's" home described? What adjectives and comparisons are employed? What objects and utensils are described? What do these specific details tell us about humanity and existence in the world of the story?

4. Who is "the host"? What was his profession? What things does he seem to value most highly? What do his valued possessions tell us about him?

5. What record do the men choose to hear? How do the listeners react to it? What do the phonograph and the music represent to these men?

6. What does Dr. Jenkins do with the books, the phonograph, and records after the men leave? How does he readjust his bed? Why does he do these things? What do these actions imply?

7. Who is the protagonist in this story? Who or what is the antagonist? What are the conflicts here? Which is the central conflict? To what extent is it resolved in the story?

IRWIN SHAW (1913–1984)

Act of Faith   *1946*

"Present it in a pitiful light," Olson was saying, as they picked their way through the mud toward the orderly room° tent. "Three combat-scarred veterans, who fought their way from Omaha Beach to—what was the name of the town we fought our way to?"

"Konigstein," Seeger said.

---

orderly room: administrative headquarters of an army unit.

"Konigstein." Olsen lifted his right foot heavily out of a puddle and stared admiringly at the three pounds of mud clinging to his overshoe. "The backbone of the army. The noncommissioned officer. We deserve better of our country. Mention our decorations in passing."

"What decorations should I mention?" Seeger asked. "The marksman's medal?"

"Never quite made it," Olson said. "I had a cross-eyed scorer at the butts.°   5
Mention the Bronze Star, the Silver Star, the Croix de Guerre, with palms, the unit citation, the Congressional Medal of Honor."

"I'll mention them all." Seeger grinned. "You don't think the CO° 'll notice that we haven't won most of them, do you?"

"Gad, sir," Olson said with dignity, "do you think that one southern military gentleman will dare doubt the word of another southern military gentleman in the hour of victory?"

"I come from Ohio," Seeger said.

"Welch comes from Kansas," Olson said, coolly staring down a second lieutenant who was passing. The lieutenant made a nervous little jerk with his hand as though he expected a salute, then kept it rigid, as a slight superior smile of scorn twisted at the corner of Olson's mouth. The lieutenant dropped his eyes and splashed on through the mud. "You've heard of Kansas," Olson said. "Magnolia-scented Kansas."

"Of course," said Seeger. "I'm no fool."   10

"Do your duty by your men, Sergeant." Olson stopped to wipe the rain off his face and lectured him. "Highest ranking noncom° present took the initiative and saved his comrades, at great personal risk, above and beyond the call of you-know-what, in the best traditions of the American army."

"I will throw myself in the breach,"° Seeger said.

"Welch and I can't ask more," said Olson, approvingly.

They walked heavily through the mud on the streets between the rows of tents. The camp stretched drearily over the Rheims plain, with the rain beating on the sagging tents. The division had been there over three weeks by now, waiting to be shipped home, and all the meager diversions of the neighborhood had been sampled and exhausted, and there was an air of watchful suspicion and impatience with the military life hanging over the camp now, and there was even reputed to be a staff sergeant in C Company who was laying odds they would not get back to America before July Fourth.

"I'm redeployable," Olson sang. "It's so enjoyable . . ." It was a jingle he   15
had composed to no recognizable melody in the early days after the victory in Europe, when he had added up his points and found they only came to 63. "Tokyo, wait for me . . ."

They were going to be discharged as soon as they got back to the States, but Olson persisted in singing the song, occasionally adding a mournful stanza

butts: mound of dirt used as a backstop on a target range.
CO: abbreviation for "Commanding Officer."
noncom: a noncommissioned officer (corporal and above), distinguished from a commissioned officer (second lieutenant and above).
"I . . . breach": quoted from Shakespeare, *Henry V*, act 3, scene 1, line 1.

about dengue fever° and brown girls with venereal disease. He was a short, round boy who had been flunked out of air cadets' school and transferred to the infantry, but whose spirits had not been damaged in the process. He had a high, childish voice and a pretty baby face. He was very good-natured, and had a girl waiting for him at the University of California, where he intended to finish his course at government expense when he got out of the army, and he was just the type who is killed off early and predictably and sadly in motion pictures about the war, but he had gone through four campaigns and six major battles without a scratch.

Seeger was a large lanky boy, with a big nose, who had been wounded at Saint Lô, but had come back to his outfit in the Siegfried Line,° quite unchanged. He was cheerful and dependable, and he knew his business and had broken in five or six second lieutenants who had been killed or wounded and the CO had tried to get him commissioned in the field, but the war had ended while the paper-work was being fumbled over at headquarters.

They reached the door of the orderly tent and stopped. "Be brave, Sergeant," Olson said. "Welch and I are depending on you."

"O.K." Seeger said, and went in.

The tent had the dank, army-canvas smell that had been so much a part of   20
Seeger's life in the past three years. The company clerk was reading a July, 1945, issue of the *Buffalo Courier-Express*, which had just reached him, and Captain Taney, the company CO, was seated at a sawbuck table he used as a desk, writing a letter to his wife, his lips pursed with effort. He was a small, fussy man, with sandy hair that was falling out. While the fighting had been going on, he had been lean and tense and his small voice had been cold and full of authority. But now he had relaxed, and a little pot belly was creeping up under his belt and he kept the top button of his trousers open when he could do it without too public loss of dignity. During the war Seeger had thought of him as a natural soldier, tireless, fanatic about detail, aggressive, severely anxious to kill Germans. But in the past few months Seeger had seen him relapsing gradually and pleasantly into a small-town wholesale hardware merchant, which he had been before the war, sedentary and a little shy, and, as he had once told Seeger, worried, here in the bleak champagne fields of France, about his daughter, who had just turned twelve and had a tendency to go after the boys and had been caught by her mother kissing a fifteen-year-old neighbor in the hammock after school.

"Hello, Seeger," he said, returning the salute in a mild, offhand gesture. "What's on your mind?"

"Am I disturbing you, sir?"

"Oh, no. Just writing a letter to my wife. You married, Seeger?" He peered at the tall boy standing before him.

"No, sir."

"It's very difficult," Taney sighed, pushing dissatisfiedly at the letter before   25
him. "My wife complains I don't tell her I love her often enough. Been married fifteen years. You'd think she'd know by now." He smiled at Seeger. "I thought you were going to Paris," he said. "I signed the passes yesterday."

"That's what I came to see you about, sir."

---

dengue fever: a tropical disease, spread by mosquitoes.
Siegfried Line: a German line of fortifications against France.

"I suppose something's wrong with the passes." Taney spoke resignedly, like a man who has never quite got the hang of army regulations and has had requisitions, furloughs, requests for court-martial returned for correction in a baffling flood.

"No, sir," Seeger said. "The passes're fine. They start tomorrow. Well, it's just . . ." He looked around at the company clerk, who was on the sports page.

"This confidential?" Taney asked.

"If you don't mind, sir."   30

"Johnny," Taney said to the clerk, "go stand in the rain some place."

"Yes, sir," the clerk said, and slowly got up and walked out.

Taney looked shrewdly at Seeger, spoke in a secret whisper. "You pick up anything?" he asked.

Seeger grinned. "No, sir, haven't had my hands on a girl since Strasbourg."

"Ah, that's good." Taney leaned back, relieved, happy he didn't have to   35
cope with the disapproval of the Medical Corps.

"It's—well," said Seeger, embarrassed, "it's hard to say—but it's money."

Taney shook his head sadly. "I know."

"We haven't been paid for three months, sir, and . . ."

"Damn it!" Taney stood up and shouted furiously. "I would like to take every bloody chair-warming old lady in the Finance Department and wring their necks."

The clerk stuck his head into the tent. "Anything wrong? You call for me, sir?"   40

"No," Taney shouted. "Get out of here."

The clerk ducked out.

Taney sat down again. "I suppose," he said, in a more normal voice, "they have their problems. Outfits being broken up, being moved all over the place. But it is rugged."

"It wouldn't be so bad," Seeger said. "But we're going to Paris tomorrow, Olson, Welch and myself. And you need money in Paris."

"Don't I know it." Taney wagged his head. "Do you know what I paid for a   45
bottle of champagne on the Place Pigalle° in September . . . ?" He paused significantly. "I won't tell you. You won't have any respect for me the rest of your life."

Seeger laughed. "Hanging," he said, "is too good for the guy who thought up the rate of exchange."

"I don't care if I never see another franc as long as I live." Taney waved his letter in the air, although it had been dry° for a long time.

There was silence in the tent and Seeger swallowed a little embarrassedly, watching the CO wave the flimsy sheet of paper in regular sweeping movements. "Sir," he said, "the truth is, I've come to borrow some money for Welch, Olson and myself. We'll pay it back out of the first pay we get, and that can't be too long from now. If you don't want to give it to us, just tell me and I'll understand and get the hell out of here. We don't like to ask, but you might just as well be dead as be in Paris broke."

Place Pigalle: A notorious district in Paris, mispronounced as "pig alley" by many American soldiers. Whiskey and prostitutes were plentiful there.

dry: Taney is using a fountain pen with liquid ink. Ball-point pens were not in common use in 1945.

Taney stopped waving his letter and put it down thoughtfully. He peered at it, wrinkling his brow, looking like an aged bookkeeper in the single gloomy light that hung in the middle of the tent.

"Just say the word, Captain," Seeger said, "and I'll blow . . ."   50

"Stay where you are, son," said Taney. He dug in his shirt pocket and took out a worn, sweat-stained wallet. He looked at it for a moment. "Alligator," he said, with automatic, absent pride. "My wife sent it to me when we were in England. Pounds don't fit in it. However . . ." He opened it and took out all the contents. There was a small pile of francs on the table in front of him. He counted them. "Four hundred francs," he said. "Eight bucks."

"Excuse me," Seeger said humbly. "I shouldn't have asked."

"Delighted," Taney said vigorously. "Absolutely delighted." He started dividing the francs into two piles. "Truth is, Seeger, most of my money goes home in allotments. And the truth is, I lost eleven hundred francs in a poker game three nights ago, and I ought to be ashamed of myself. Here . . ." he shoved one pile toward Seeger. "Two hundred francs."

Seeger looked down at the frayed, meretricious paper, which always seemed to him like stage money, anyway. "No, sir," he said, "I can't take it."

"Take it," Taney said. "That's a direct order."   55

Seeger slowly picked up the money, not looking at Taney. "Some time, sir," he said, "after we get out, you have to come over to my house and you and my father and my brother and I'll go on a real drunk."

"I'll regard that," Taney said, gravely, "as a solemn commitment."

They smiled at each other and Seeger started out.

"Have a drink for me," said Taney, "at the Café de la Paix.° A small drink." He was sitting down to write his wife he loved her when Seeger went out of the tent.

Olson fell into step with Seeger and they walked silently through the mud   60
between the tents.

"Well, *mon vieux*?"° Olson said finally.

"Two hundred francs," said Seeger.

Olson groaned. "Two hundred francs! We won't be able to pinch a whore's behind on the Boulevard des Capucines° for two hundred francs. That miserable, penny-loving Yankee!"

"He only had four hundred," Seeger said.

"I revise my opinion," said Olson.   65

They walked disconsolately and heavily back toward their tent.

Olson spoke only once before they got there. "These raincoats," he said, patting his. "Most ingenious invention of the war. Highest saturation point of any modern fabric. Collect more water per square inch, and hold it, than any material known to man. All hail the quartermaster!"

Welch was waiting at the entrance of their tent. He was standing there peering excitedly and short-sightedly out at the rain through his glasses, looking angry

---

Café de la Paix: One of the best-known Parisian restaurants, on the Boulevard des Capucines, which Olson mentions a few moments later.

mon vieux: French for "old boy," "old friend," "old fellow," "buddy."

Boulevard des Capucines: A street near the business district, extending from the Madeleine to the Opéra.

and tough, like a big-city hack driver, individual and incorruptible even in the ten-million colored uniform. Every time Seeger came upon Welch unexpectedly, he couldn't help smiling at the belligerent stance, the harsh stare through the steel-rimmed GI glasses, which had nothing at all to do with the way Welch really was. "It's a family inheritance," Welch had once explained. "My whole family stands as though we were getting ready to rap a drunk with a beer glass. Even my old lady." Welch had six brothers, all devout, according to Welch, and Seeger from time to time idly pictured them standing in a row, on Sunday mornings in church, seemingly on the verge of general violence, amid the hushed Latin and Sabbath millinery.

"How much?" Welch asked loudly.

"Don't make us laugh," Olson said, pushing past him into the tent. 70

"What do you think I could get from the French for my combat jacket?" Seeger said. He went into the tent and lay down on his cot.

Welch followed them in and stood between the two of them, a superior smile on his face. "Boys," he said, "on a man's errand."

"I can just see us now," Olson murmured, lying on his cot with his hands clasped behind his head, "painting Montmartre red. Please bring on the naked dancing girls. Four bucks worth."

"I am not worried," Welch announced.

"Get out of here." Olson turned over on his stomach. 75

"I know where we can put our hands on sixty-five bucks." Welch looked triumphantly first at Olson, then at Seeger.

Olson turned over slowly and sat up. "I'll kill you," he said, "if you're kidding."

"While you guys are wasting your time," Welch said, "fooling around with the infantry, I used my head. I went into Reems° and used my head."

"Rance," Olson said automatically. He had had two years of French in college and he felt, now that the war was over, that he had to introduce his friends to some of his culture.

"I got to talking to a captain in the air force," Welch said eagerly. "A little 80 fat old paddle-footed captain that never got higher off the ground than the second floor of the Com Z headquarters, and he told me that what he would admire to do more than anything else is to take home a nice shiny German Luger pistol with him to show to the boys back in Pacific Grove, California."

Silence fell on the tent and Welch and Olson looked tentatively at Seeger.

"Sixty-five bucks for a Luger, these days," Olson said, "is a very good figure."

"They've been sellin' for as low as thirty-five," said Welch hesitantly. "I'll bet," he said to Seeger, "you could sell yours now and buy another one back when you get some dough and make a clear twenty-five on the deal."

Seeger didn't say anything. He had killed the owner of the Luger, an enormous SS° major, in Coblenz, behind some paper bales in a warehouse, and the major had fired at Seeger three times with it, once knicking his helmet, before Seeger hit him in the face at twenty feet. Seeger had kept the Luger, a long, heavy, well-balanced gun, very carefully since then, lugging it with him, hiding it at the bottom

---

Reems: Welch mispronounces *Reims*; Olson corrects him.

SS: The Schutzstaffel, a German military unit led by Heinrich Himmler, dreaded for its ruthlessness and atrocities.

of his bedroll, oiling it three times a week, avoiding all opportunities of selling it, although he had been offered as much as a hundred dollars for it and several times eighty and ninety, while the war was still on, before German weapons became a glut on the market.

"Well," said Welch, "there's no hurry. I told the captain I'd see him tonight around 8 o'clock in front of the Lion d'Or Hotel. You got five hours to make up your mind. Plenty of time."   85

"Me," said Olson, after a pause. "I won't say anything."

Seeger looked reflectively at his feet and the other two men avoided looking at him. Welch dug in his pocket. "I forgot," he said. "I picked up a letter for you." He handed it to Seeger.

"Thanks," Seeger said. He opened it absently, thinking about the Luger.

"Me," said Olson, "I won't say a bloody word. I'm just going to lie here and think about that nice fat air force captain."

Seeger grinned a little at him and went to the tent opening to read the letter in the light. The letter was from his father, and even from one glance at the handwriting, scrawly and hurried and spotted, so different from his father's usual steady, handsome, professorial script, he knew that something was wrong.   90

"Dear Norman," it read, "sometime in the future, you must forgive me for writing this letter. But I have been holding this in so long, and there is no one here I can talk to, and because of your brother's condition I must pretend to be cheerful and optimistic all the time at home, both with him and your mother, who has never been the same since Leonard was killed. You're the oldest now, and although I know we've never talked very seriously about anything before, you have been through a great deal by now, and I imagine you must have matured considerably, and you've seen so many different places and people. . . . Norman, I need help. While the war was on and you were fighting, I kept this to myself. It wouldn't have been fair to burden you with this. But now the war is over, and I no longer feel I can stand up under this alone. And you will have to face it some time when you get home, if you haven't faced it already, and perhaps we can help each other by facing it together. . . ."

"I'm redeployable," Olson was singing softly, on his cot. "It's so enjoyable, In the Pelilu° mud, With the tropical crud . . ." He fell silent after his burst of song.

Seeger blinked his eyes, at the entrance of the tent, in the wan rainy light, and went on reading his father's letter, on the stiff white stationery with the University letterhead in polite engraving at the top of each page.

"I've been feeling this coming on for a long time," the letter continued, "but it wasn't until last Sunday morning that something happened to make me feel it in its full force. I don't know how much you've guessed about the reason for Jacob's discharge from the army. It's true he was pretty badly wounded in the leg at Metz, but I've asked around, and I know that men with worse wounds were returned to duty after hospitalization. Jacob got a medical discharge, but I don't think it was for the shrapnel wound in his thigh. He is suffering now from what I suppose you call combat fatigue, and he is subject to fits of depression

Pelilu: Peleliu Island, in the Palau chain, part of the Caroline Islands, in the South Pacific.

and hallucinations. Your mother and I thought that as time went by and the war and the army receded, he would grow better. Instead, he is growing worse. Last Sunday morning when I came down into the living room from upstairs he was crouched in his old uniform, next to the window, peering out . . ."

"What the hell," Olson was saying, "if we don't get the sixty-five bucks we can always go to the Louvre. I understand the Mona Lisa is back."   95

"I asked Jacob what he was doing," the letter went on. "He didn't turn around. 'I'm observing,' he said. 'V-1's and V-2's.° Buzz-bombs and rockets. They're coming in by the hundreds.' I tried to reason with him and he told me to crouch and save myself from flying glass. To humor him I got down on the floor beside him and tried to tell him the war was over, that we were in Ohio, 4,000 miles away from the nearest spot where bombs had fallen, that America had never been touched. He wouldn't listen. 'These're the new rocket bombs,' he said, 'for the Jews.' "

"Did you ever hear of the Pantheon?" Olson asked loudly.

"No," said Welch.

"It's free."

"I'll go," said Welch.   100

Seeger shook his head a little and blinked his eyes before he went back to the letter.

"After that," his father went on, "Jacob seemed to forget about the bombs from time to time, but he kept saying that the mobs were coming up the street armed with bazookas and Browning automatic rifles. He mumbled incoherently a good deal of the time and kept walking back and forth saying, 'What's the situation? Do you know what the situation is?' And he told me he wasn't worried about himself, he was a soldier and he expected to be killed, but he was worried about Mother and myself and Leonard and you. He seemed to forget that Leonard was dead. I tried to calm him and get him back to bed before your mother came down, but he refused and wanted to set out immediately to rejoin his division. It was all terribly disjointed and at one time he took the ribbon he got for winning the Bronze Star and threw it in the fireplace, then he got down on his hands and knees and picked it out of the ashes and made me pin it on him again, and he kept repeating, 'This is when they are coming for the Jews.' "

"The next war I'm in," said Olson, "they don't get me under the rank of colonel."

It had stopped raining by now and Seeger folded the unfinished letter and went outside. He walked slowly down to the end of the company street, and facing out across the empty, soaked French fields, scarred and neglected by various armies, he stopped and opened the letter again.

"I don't know what Jacob went through in the army," his father wrote, "that   105
has done this to him. He never talks to me about the war and he refuses to go to a psychoanalyst, and from time to time he is his own bouncing, cheerful self, playing in tennis tournaments, and going around with a large group of girls. But he has devoured all the concentration camp reports, and I have found him weeping when the newspapers reported that a hundred Jews were killed in Tripoli some time ago.

V-1's and V-2's: The first rocket weapons, developed by the Germans near the end of World War II, and used against England.

"The terrible thing is, Norman, that I find myself coming to believe that it is not neurotic for a Jew to behave like this today. Perhaps Jacob is the normal one, and I, going about my business, teaching economics in a quiet classroom, pretending to understand that the world is comprehensible and orderly, am really the mad one. I ask you once more to forgive me for writing you a letter like this, so different from any letter or any conversation I've ever had with you. But it is crowding me, too. I do not see rockets and bombs, but I see other things.

"Wherever you go these days—restaurants, hotels, clubs, trains—you seem to hear talk about the Jews, mean, hateful, murderous talk. Whatever page you turn to in the newspapers you seem to find an article about Jews being killed somewhere on the face of the globe. And there are large, influential newspapers and well-known columnists who each day are growing more and more outspoken and more popular. The day that Roosevelt died I heard a drunken man yelling outside a bar, 'Finally, they got the Jew out of the White House.' And some of the people who heard him merely laughed and nobody stopped him. And on V-E Day,° in celebration, hoodlums in Los Angeles savagely beat a Jewish writer. It's difficult to know what to do, whom to fight, where to look for allies.

"Three months ago, for example, I stopped my Thursday night poker game, after playing with the same men for over ten years. John Reilly happened to say that the Jews were getting rich out of this war, and when I demanded an apology, he refused, and when I looked around at the faces of the men who had been my friends for so long, I could see they were not with me. And when I left the house no one said good night to me. I know the poison was spreading from Germany before the war and during it, but I had not realized it had come so close.

"And in my economics class, I find myself idiotically hedging in my lectures. I discover that I am loath to praise any liberal writer or any liberal act and find myself somehow annoyed and frightened to see an article of criticism of existing abuses signed by a Jewish name. And I hate to see Jewish names on important committees, and hate to read of Jews fighting for the poor, the oppressed, the cheated and hungry. Somehow, even in a country where my family has lived a hundred years, the enemy has won this subtle victory over me—he has made me disfranchise myself from honest causes by calling them foreign, Communist, using Jewish names connected with them as ammunition against them.

"And, most hateful of all, I find myself looking for Jewish names in the $\quad$ 110 casualty lists and secretly being glad when I discover them there, to prove that there at least, among the dead and wounded, we belong. Three times, thanks to you and your brothers, I have found our name there, and, may God forgive me, at the expense of your blood and your brother's life, through my tears, I have felt the same twitch of satisfaction. . . .

"When I read the newspapers and see another story that Jews are still being killed in Poland, or Jews are requesting that they be given back their homes in France, or that they be allowed to enter some country where they will not be murdered, I am annoyed with them, I feel they are boring the rest of the world with their problems, they are making demands upon the rest of the world by being killed, they are disturbing everyone by being hungry and asking for the return of their property. If we could all fall through the crust of the earth and

V-E Day: May 8, 1945, the day of Victory in Europe.

vanish in one hour, with our heroes and poets and prophets and martyrs, perhaps
we would be doing the memory of the Jewish race a service. . . .

"This is how I feel today, son. I need some help. You've been to the war,
you've fought and killed men, you've seen the people of other countries. Maybe
you understand things that I don't understand. Maybe you see some hope somewhere. Help me. Your loving father."

Seeger folded the letter slowly, not seeing what he was doing because the
tears were burning his eyes. He walked slowly and aimlessly across the dead autumn
grass of the empty field, away from the camp.

He tried to wipe away his tears, because with his eyes full and dark, he
kept seeing his father and brother crouched in the old-fashioned living room in
Ohio and hearing his brother, dressed in the old, discarded uniform, saying,
"These're the new rocket bombs. For the Jews."

He sighed; looking out over the bleak, wasted land. Now, he thought, now   115
I have to think about it. He felt a slight, unreasonable twinge of anger at his
father for presenting him with the necessity of thinking about it. The army was
good about serious problems. While you were fighting, you were too busy and
frightened and weary to think about anything, and at other times you were relaxing,
putting your brain on a shelf, postponing everything to that impossible time of
clarity and beauty after the war. Well, now, here was the impossible, clear, beautiful
time, and here was his father, demanding that he think. There are all sorts of
Jews, he thought, there are the sort whose every waking moment is ridden by the
knowledge of Jewishness, who see signs against the Jew in every smile on a streetcar,
every whisper, who see pogroms° in every newspaper article, threats in every change
of the weather, scorn in every handshake, death behind each closed door. He
had not been like that. He was young, he was big and healthy and easy-going
and people of all kinds had seemed to like him all his life, in the army and out.
In America, especially, what was going on in Europe had seemed remote, unreal,
unrelated to him. The chanting, bearded old men burning in the Nazi furnaces,
and the dark-eyed women screaming prayers in Polish and Russian and German
as they were pushed naked into the gas chambers had seemed as shadowy and
almost as unrelated to him as he trotted out onto the Stadium field for a football
game, as they must have been to the men named O'Dwyer and Wickersham and
Poole who played in the line beside him.

They had seemed more related in Europe. Again and again in the towns
that had been taken from the Germans, gaunt, gray-faced men had stopped him
humbly, looking searchingly at him, and had asked, peering at his long, lined,
grimy face, under the anonymous helmet, "Are you a Jew?" Sometimes they asked
it in English, sometimes French, or Yiddish. He didn't know French or Yiddish,
but he learned to recognize the phrase. He had never understood exactly why
they had asked the question, since they never demanded anything from him, rarely
even could speak to him, until, one day in Strasbourg, a little bent old man and a
small, shapeless woman had stopped him, and asked, in English, if he was Jewish.

"Yes," he said, smiling at them.

The two old people had smiled widely, like children. "Look," the old man
had said to his wife. "A young American soldier. A Jew. And so large and strong."

pogrom: an organized massacre of a minority, specifically Jews.

He had touched Seeger's arm reverently with the tips of his fingers, then had touched the Garand° he was carrying. "And such a beautiful rifle . . ."

And there, for a moment, although he was not particularly sensitive, Seeger got an inkling of why he had been stopped and questioned by so many before. Here, to these bent, exhausted old people, ravaged of their families, familiar with flight and death for so many years, was a symbol of continuing life. A large young man in the uniform of the liberator, blood, as they thought, of their blood, but not in hiding, not quivering in fear and helplessness, but striding secure and victorious down the street, armed and capable of inflicting terrible destruction on his enemies.

Seeger had kissed the old lady on the cheek and she had wept and the old man had scolded her for it, while shaking Seeger's hand fervently and thankfully before saying good-bye.

And, thinking back on it, it was silly to pretend that, even before his father's letter, he had been like any other American soldier going through the war. When he had stood over the huge dead SS major with the face blown in by his bullets in the warehouse in Coblenz, and taken the pistol from the dead hand, he had tasted a strange little extra flavor of triumph. How many Jews, he'd thought, has this man killed, how fitting it is that I've killed him. Neither Olson nor Welch, who were like his brothers, would have felt that in picking up the Luger, its barrel still hot from the last shots its owner had fired before dying. And he had resolved that he was going to make sure to take this gun back with him to America, and plug it and keep it on his desk at home, as a kind of vague, half-understood sign to himself that justice had once been done and he had been its instrument.

Maybe, he thought, maybe I'd better take it back with me, but not as a memento. Not plugged, but loaded. America by now was a strange country for him. He had been away a long time and he wasn't sure what was waiting for him when he got home. If the mobs were coming down the street toward his house, he was not going to die singing and praying.

When he was taking basic training he'd heard a scrawny, clerklike-looking soldier from Boston talking at the other end of the PX° bar, over the watered beer. "The boys at the office," the scratchy voice was saying, "gave me a party before I left. And they told me one thing. 'Charlie,' they said, 'hold onto your bayonet. We're going to be able to use it when you get back. On the Yids.' "°

He hadn't said anything then, because he'd felt it was neither possible nor desirable to fight against every random overheard voice raised against the Jews from one end of the world to another. But again and again, at odd moments, lying on a barracks cot, or stretched out trying to sleep on the floor of a ruined French farmhouse, he had heard that voice, harsh, satisfied, heavy with hate and ignorance, saying above the beery grumble of apprentice soldiers at the bar, "Hold onto your bayonet. . . ."

And the other stories—Jews collected stories of hatred and injustice and inklings of doom like a special, lunatic kind of miser. The story of the naval officer, commander of a small vessel off the Aleutians, who, in the officers' wardroom,

Garand: an American standard infantry rifle.
PX: Post Exchange, where military personnel may buy at cost.
Yids: A snide name for Jews, derived from the word *Yiddish*.

had complained that he hated the Jews because it was the Jews who had demanded
that the Germans be beaten first and the forces in the Pacific had been starved in
consequence. And when one of his junior officers, who had just come aboard,
had objected and told the commander that he was a Jew, the commander had
risen from the table and said, "Mister, the Constitution of the United States says
I have to serve in the same navy with Jews, but it doesn't say I have to eat at the
same table with them." In the fogs and the cold, swelling Arctic seas off the Aleutians,
in a small boat, subject to sudden, mortal attack at any moment . . .

And the two young combat engineers in an attached company on D Day,°
when they were lying off the coast right before climbing down into the landing
barges. "There's France," one of them had said.

"What's it like?" the second one had asked, peering out across the miles of
water toward the smoking coast.

"Like every place else," the first one had answered. "The Jews've made all
the dough during the war."

"Shut up!" Seeger had said, helplessly thinking of the dead, destroyed, wandering, starving Jews of France. The engineers had shut up, and they'd climbed down
together into the heaving boat, and gone into the beach together.

And the million other stories. Jews, even the most normal and best adjusted   130
of them, became living treasuries of them, scraps of malice and bloodthirstiness,
clever and confusing and cunningly twisted so that every act by every Jew became
suspect and blameworthy and hateful. Seeger had heard the stories, and had made
an almost conscious effort to forget them. Now, holding his father's letter in his
hand, he remembered them all.

He stared unseeingly out in front of him. Maybe, he thought, maybe it would've
been better to have been killed in the war, like Leonard. Simpler. Leonard would
never have to face a crowd coming for his mother and father. Leonard would
not have to listen and collect these hideous, fascinating little stories that made of
every Jew a stranger in any town, on any field, on the face of the earth. He had
come so close to being killed so many times, it would have been so easy, so neat
and final.

Seeger shook his head. It was ridiculous to feel like that, and he was ashamed
of himself for the weak moment. At the age of twenty-one, death was not an
answer.

"Seeger!" It was Olson's voice. He and Welch had sloshed silently up behind
Seeger, standing in the open field. "Seeger, *mon vieux*, what're you doing—grazing?"

Seeger turned slowly to them. "I wanted to read my letter," he said.

Olson looked closely at him. They had been together so long, through so   135
many things, that flickers and hints of expression on each other's face were recognized and acted upon. "Anything wrong?" Olson asked.

"No," said Seeger. "Nothing much."

"Norman," Welch said, his voice young and solemn. "Norman, we've been
talking. Olson and me. We decided—you're pretty attached to that Luger, and
maybe—if you—well . . ."

"What he's trying to say," said Olson, "is we withdraw the request. If you
want to sell it, O.K. If you don't, don't do it for our sake. Honest."

D Day: June 6, 1944, the day on which the allied forces invaded France from the sea.

Seeger looked at them, standing there, disreputable and tough and familiar. "I haven't made up my mind yet," he said.

"Anything you decide," Welch said oratorically, "is perfectly all right with   140
us. Perfectly."

They walked aimlessly and silently across the field, away from camp. As they walked, their shoes making a wet, sliding sound in the damp, dead grass, Seeger thought of the time Olson had covered him in the little town outside Cherbourg, when Seeger had been caught going down the side of a street by four Germans with a machine gun on the second story of a house on the corner and Olson had had to stand out in the middle of the street with no cover at all for more than a minute, firing continuously, so that Seeger could get away alive. And he thought of the time outside Saint Lô when he had been wounded and had lain in a mine field for three hours and Welch and Captain Taney had come looking for him in the darkness and found him and picked him up and run for it, all of them expecting to get blown up any second.

And he thought of all the drinks they'd had together and the long marches and the cold winter together, and all the girls they'd gone out with together, and he thought of his father and brother crouching behind the window in Ohio waiting for the rockets and the crowds armed with Browning automatic rifles.

"Say," he stopped and stood facing them. "Say, what do you guys think of the Jews?"

Welch and Olson looked at each other, and Olson glanced down at the letter in Seeger's hand.

"Jews?" Olson said finally. "What're they? Welch, you ever heard of the   145
Jews?"

Welch looked thoughtfully at the gray sky. "No," he said. "But remember, I'm an uneducated fellow."

"Sorry, Bud," Olson said, turning to Seeger. "We can't help you. Ask us another question. Maybe we'll do better."

Seeger peered at the faces of his friends. He would have to rely upon them, later on, out of uniform, on their native streets, more than he had ever relied on them on the bullet-swept street and in the dark mine field in France. Welch and Olson stared back at him, troubled, their faces candid and tough and dependable.

"What time," Seeger asked, "did you tell that captain you'd meet him?"

"Eight o'clock," Welch said. "But we don't have to go. If you have any feeling   150
about that gun . . ."

"We'll meet him," Seeger said. "We can use that sixty-five bucks."

"Listen," Olson said, "I know how much you like that gun and I'll feel like a heel if you sell it."

"Forget it," Seeger said, starting to walk again. "What could I use it for in America?"

QUESTIONS

1. Why is it important to the story to include at the beginning the details about the states from which the various characters come? Even though the immediate setting is just after World War II, can a case be made that the setting is the entire United States?

2. How many separate scenes are introduced as places for action in the story? What function and importance might these have as bases of organization?

3. Why is the mud of the streets mentioned early in the story, and why is the wet grass mentioned at the end? Can you perceive any contrast between this drab setting and the ideas in the minds of the soldiers about the streets of Paris?

4. Describe the significance of the German Luger in the story. How is it a source of possible conflict among the soldiers? In what way is it the cause of the story's resolution?

5. What is the immediate central conflict in the story? How does the larger fear that Seeger has about the future figure into this conflict? How is the immediate conflict resolved?

6. Describe the point of view of the story. How does it begin? At what point does it shift to become limited to Seeger? What issue becomes prominent with this shift?

7. What stories does Seeger recall about prejudice toward Jews? What does he recall about his associations with Welch, Taney, and Olson? What is his act of faith? Does his question at the end, "What could I use it [the Luger] for in America?" seem to be an accurate assessment on which to base his decision?

8. In what ways do Welch, Taney, and Olson all make acts of faith?

WRITING ABOUT SETTING

In prewriting activity for an essay about setting, you should take notes directed toward the locations and artifacts that figure prominently in the work. Generally you should determine if there is one location of action or more. Raise questions about how much detail is included: Are things described visually so that you can make a sketch or draw a plan (such a sketch might help you to organize your essay), or are the locations left vague? Why? What influence do the locations have upon the characters in the story, if any? Do the locations bring characters together, push them apart, make it easy for them to be private, make intimacy and conversation difficult? What artifacts are important in the action, and how important are they? Are they well described? Are they vital to the action? Are shapes, colors, times of day, locations of the sun, conditions of light, seasons of the year, and conditions of vegetation described? Do characters respect or mistreat the environment around them?

With answers to questions like these, you can formulate ideas for your essay. Remember to develop a central idea to enable you to avoid writing no more than a description of scenes and objects (such an essay is analogous to simply retelling the story). Emphasize the connection between setting and whatever aspect or aspects you choose about the story. A possible central idea might thus be, "The normal, everyday setting (of

"The Lottery") not only is plainly described, but in retrospect it demonstrates that human evil is also common and ordinary," or "The dreary kitchen underscores the long-suffering ordeal of Mrs. Wright (of "A Jury of Her Peers") and helps readers to understand her violent act of self-assertion." Emphasis on such ideas would encourage you to use description only as illustration and evidence, and not as an end in itself.

Organizing Your Essay

INTRODUCTION.　The introduction should give a brief description of the setting or scenes of the story, with a characterization of the degree of detail presented by the author (that is, a little, a lot; visual, auditory; colorful, monochromatic, and so on). The central idea explains the relationship to be explored in the essay, and the thesis sentence determines the major topics in which the central idea will be traced.

BODY.　Following are five possible approaches to essays about setting. Which one you choose is your decision, but you may find that some works almost invite you to pick one approach over the others. Although each approach outlines a major emphasis for an essay, you may bring in details from one of the others if they seem important.

1. *Setting and action.* Here you explore the use of setting in the various actions of the work. Among the questions to be answered are these: How detailed and extensive are the descriptions of the setting? Are the scenes related to the action? (Are they essential or incidental?) Does the setting serve as part of the action (places of flight or concealment; public places where people meet openly or out-of-the-way places where they meet privately; natural or environmental obstacles; sociological obstacles; seasonal conditions such as searing heat or numbing cold, and so on)? Are details of setting used regularly, or are they mentioned only when they are necessary to an action? Do any physical objects figure into the story as causes of inspiration or conflict (for example, a walking stick, a pretty necklace, a coin, a dog, a horse, a toy windmill, a piece of candy, a pistol, a dead bird)?

2. *Setting and organization.* A closely related way of writing about setting is to connect it to the organization of the work. Some questions to help you get started with this approach are these: Is the setting a frame, an enclosure? Is it mentioned at various points, or at shifts in the action? Does the setting undergo any expected or unexpected changes as the action changes? Do any parts of the setting have greater direct importance in shaping the action than other parts? Do any objects, such as money or property, figure into the developing or changing motivation of the characters? Do descriptions made at the start become important in the action later on? If so, in what order?

3. *Setting and character.* Here you pick those details important to your understanding of character, and write about their effects. The major question is the degree to which the setting interacts with or influences character. You might get at this topic through additional questions: Are the characters happy or unhappy where they live? Do they express their feelings, or get into discussions or arguments about them? Do they seem adjusted? Do they want to stay or leave? Does the economic, cultural, or ethnic level of the setting make the characters think in any unique ways? What jobs do the characters perform because of their ways of life? What freedoms or restraints do these jobs cause? How does the setting influence their decisions, transportation, speech habits, eating habits, attitudes about love and honor, and general folkways?

4. *Setting and atmosphere.* The concern here is the relationship of setting to mood. Some questions are: Does the detail of setting go beyond the minimum needed for action or character? Do details clarify the conflicts in the story, or do vague and amorphous details make these conflicts problematic? Are descriptive words used mainly to paint verbal pictures? To evoke a mood through references to colors, shapes, sounds, smells, or tastes? Does the setting establish a mood, say, of joy or hopelessness, lushness or spareness, sobriety or hilarity? Do things happen in daylight or at night? Do motions and actions suggest constantly recurring, typical human patterns (such as missions of mercy, actions of futility, and conversations leading to love). Does anything about the setting suggest impermanence (like footsteps in the sand, movement through water, or the procession for a funeral)? If temperatures are mentioned, are things warm and pleasant, or cold and harsh? For any details of setting suggesting mood, what are the implications for life generally?

5. *Other aspects.* Two other important uses of setting that were discussed in this chapter are "Setting and Statement" and "Setting and Irony." Not all stories lend themselves to either treatment, but for stories that do, you could create an interesting essay. If the author uses setting as a means of underscoring the circumstances and ideas in the work, you might refer to the section on setting and statement as a guide for the body of your paper. If you see a contrast between setting and content, that might be the basis of an essay like those described under setting and irony.

CONCLUSION.   You may summarize your major points in your conclusion, but you might also write about anything you have neglected in the body. Thus, you might have been treating the relationship of the setting to the action, and may wish to mention something about any noticeable connections that the setting has with character or atmosphere. You might also point out whether your central idea about the setting also applies to other major aspects of the work.

SAMPLE ESSAY

Poe's Use of Interior Setting to Evoke Mood in "The Masque of the Red Death"*

[1]
In "The Masque of the Red Death," Poe uses setting to bring out a mood of eeriness. The story is about how people are powerless before death, regardless of their attempts to avoid it. Poe's Prince Prospero is the example of this idea; he believes that he can lock himself away in his castle, with a thousand people, and get off scott free from the plague of the red death raging outside. At the end, however, Death wins. Poe uses interior setting to underscore this irony, and also to make Prospero's pride seem pointless, bizarre, and insane.° These moods are brought out through° Poe's use of graphic description, geographical direction, evocative color, and sepulchral sound.□

[2]
In the extensive fourth paragraph of the story, Poe provides a graphic description of the suite of seven rooms. The reader may trace this description easily. The blue room is the easternmost, and the adjoining rooms are, in order, purple, green, orange, white, violet, and finally, black. The narrator explains that the rooms are maintained in these colors by a "brazier of fire" throwing light through stained glass, which imparts a glaring, grisly light and awesome mood.

[3]
These rooms are not only graphically described, but they are spatially arranged to complement the certainty of death. The direction of east to west suggests a movement away from life. One might note that the blue room, in the east, suggests the direction of the rising sun, new day, blue sky, and optimism, while the westernmost room, the black one, suggests the setting sun and the end of time at midnight, when Death takes over. If one has doubt about Poe's use of these geographical directions, it is important to note that Prospero's final challenge to the figure of the Red Death takes him directly from east to west on his charge toward doom.

[4]
Of greatest importance is this westernmost room, the black one, on which Poe devotes the most evocative of his descriptions. The room is hung with black velvet tapestries, and its glow is made lurid by the scarlet, "deep blood" light (for suggestiveness, Poe clearly avoids the more neutral word "red" here). This room is the most weird of the seven. The narrator notes that the room is "ghastly in the extreme" and that it produces "a wild look." Visually, this room evokes feelings of darkness, wildness, evil, and an almost ghoulish delight in blood. It is a sinister room, designed not to relax but to disturb and distress.

[5]
This room, as the major part of the evocative setting, is made even more bizarre by the large, ominous, "ebony" clock that Poe puts in it (paragraph 5). The clock stands "against" the western wall, and it is both loud and disturbing. On the hour it gongs out the time, as though announcing to everyone

---

* See p. 233 for this story.
° Central idea.
□ Thesis sentence.

that another period of life has gone by. The narrator points out that these eerie, tomblike sounds stop all music, all merriment, and create a disturbed silence in the people in the rooms. Clearly, this use of sound, along with the bizarre color and light, is designed to make readers uneasy and unsettled.

[6]   Thus Poe's use of interior setting combines usefulness with mood. In fact, the major action of the story takes place in the rooms—the costume party attended by all Prospero's friends, except the one uninvited guest, the Red Death itself, who instantly kills all the revelers. Prospero's last movement takes him through all the rooms. More importantly, however, Poe centers this setting on an idea—the folly of trying to escape death—and also focuses the setting to evoke a mood—that not only is the escape attempt folly, but it is outrightly bizarre and insane. The unity of the story, the sustained mood, the consistent idea, are all tied together by Poe's masterly control of setting.

Commentary on the Essay

Because it deals with the topic of setting and mood or atmosphere, this essay illustrates the fourth approach described above. The essay considers those aspects of setting that are needed for the story, and then stresses how Poe's mode of presentation brings out the eerie mood, the irony of the major character's pretentions, and the folly of his pride. The thesis sentence announces four topics to be developed in the body.

Paragraph 2, the first in the body, describes the physical layout of Prospero's suite of rooms, and it also points out the eerie suggestiveness of Poe's descriptions of how the rooms are lighted. Paragraph 3 deals with the implications of Poe's geographical arrangement of the rooms, with the idea being that this arrangement complements the story's movement from life to death. Paragraphs 4 and 5 treat the last room of the suite, the most sinister of them all. Paragraph 4 stresses the mood suggested by the colors black and scarlet or "deep blood," and paragraph 5 stresses the somber sounds of the huge clock in the room. The central idea about Poe's use of setting to augment mood is thus brought out in the body by the consideration of those descriptions in the story that are strongly suggestive and emotive.

The concluding paragraph of the essay summarizes the main thought, stressing once again that Poe goes beyond simple description in order to heighten the eerie, macabre atmosphere of his story.

WRITING TOPICS FOR CHAPTER 6

1. Write an essay describing how setting serves as a frame for the actions in "Act of Faith."
2. What role does the setting of "The Portable Phonograph" play in your perception of the characters of Dr. Jenkins and the Musician?

3. Choose a story from this chapter and, first, rewrite a page or two, taking the characters out of their setting and placing them in the setting of another story or in another setting of your choosing. Write an essay answering the question "What did you learn about the uses of setting in a story?" Were your characters out of place in their new setting, or did they seem at home? Why?

4. Write a short scene that might be included in a longer story. Choose (a) or (b) or both.
   a. Relate a natural setting or type of day to a mood (for example, a nice day to happiness and satisfaction; or a cold, cloudy, rainy day to sadness).
   b. Indicate how an object might become the cause of conflict or reconciliation (compare the books and records of "The Portable Phonograph" or the German luger in "Act of Faith").

7

Style: The Words That Tell the Story

The word **style,** derived from the Latin word *stilus* (a writing instrument), is understood to mean the way in which writers assemble words to tell the story, develop the argument, dramatize the play, or compose the poem. Often the definition is extended to distinguish style from content. It is probably wiser, however, not to make this separation but to consider style as the placement of words in the *service* of content. The way a thing is said, in other words, cannot be separated from the thing itself.

Style is also highly individualistic. It is a matter of the way in which specific authors put words together under specific conditions in specific works. It is therefore possible to speak of the style of Ernest Hemingway, for example, and of Mark Twain, even though both writers at any time are adapting their words to the situations imagined in their works. Thus authors may actually have a separate style for narrative and descriptive passages, and their style in dialogue is likely different from either of these. Indeed, it would be a mark of an inferior style if a writer were to use the same manner for all the varying purposes that must exist in a story. It must therefore be emphasized that style is to be judged on the degree of its adaptability. The better the writer, the more that writer's words will fit the precise situation called for in the story. Jonathan Swift defined style as the right words in the right places. We may add to this definition that style is also the right words at the right time and in the right circumstances.

DICTION: CHOICE OF WORDS

The study of style begins with words, and **diction** refers to a writer's selection of specific words. The selection should be accurate and explicit, so that all actions and ideas are clear. It is perhaps difficult to judge accuracy and completeness, inasmuch as often we do not have any basis of comparison. Nevertheless, if a passage comes across as effective, if it conveys an ideal well or gets at the essence of an action vividly and powerfully, we may confidently say that the words have been the right ones. In a passage describing action, for example, there should be active verbs, whereas in a description of a place there should be nouns and adjectives that provide locations, relationships, colors, and shapes. An explanatory or reflective passage should probably include a number of words that convey thoughts, states of mind and emotion, and various conditions of human relationships.

Formal, Neutral, and Informal Diction

Words fall naturally into three basic groups, or classes, that may be called **formal** or *high*, **neutral** or *middle*, and **informal** or *low*. Formal or high diction consists of standard and often elegant words (frequently polysyllabic), the retention of correct word order, and the absence of contractions. The sentence "It is I," for example, is formal. The following sentences from Poe's "The Masque of the Red Death" use formal language:

> They resolved to leave means neither of ingress nor egress to the sudden impulses of despair or of frenzy from within. The abbey was amply provisioned. With such precautions the courtiers might bid defiance to contagion.

Note here words like *ingress, egress, provisioned, bid defiance*, and *contagion*. These words are not in ordinary, everyday vocabulary and have what we may call elegance. Though they are used accurately and aptly, and though the sentences are brief and simple, the diction is high.

Neutral or middle diction is ordinary, everyday, but still standard vocabulary, with a shunning of longer words but with the use of contractions when necessary. The sentence "It's me," for example, is neutral, the sort of thing many people say in preference to "It is I" when identifying themselves on the telephone. The following passage from Alice Munro's "The Found Boat" illustrates middle, neutral diction:

> What surprised them in the second place was that when the boys did actually see what boat was meant, this old flood-smashed wreck held up in the branches, they did not understand that they had been fooled, that a joke had been played on them. They did not show a moment's disappointment, but seemed as pleased at the discovery as if the boat had been whole and new. They were already barefoot, because they had been wading in the water to get lumber, and they waded in here without a stop, surrounding the boat and appraising it and paying no attention even of an insulting kind to Eva and Carol who bobbed up and down on their log. Eva and Carol had to call to them.

In this passage the words are ordinary and easy. Even the longer words, like *surprised, disappointment, surrounding, appraising,* and *insulting,* are not beyond the level of conversation, although *appraising* and *surrounding* would not be out of place in a more formal passage. Essentially, however, the words do not draw attention to themselves but are centered on the topic. In a way, such words in the neutral style are designed to be like clear windows, while words of the high style are more like stained glass.

Informal or low diction may range from colloquial—the language used by people in relaxed, common activities—to the level of substandard or slang expressions. A person speaking to a very close friend is likely to use diction and idiom that would not be appropriate in public and formal situations, and even in some social situations. Low language is thus appropriate for dialogue in stories, depending on the characters speaking, and for stories told in the first-person point of view as though the speaker is talking directly to a group of sympathetic and relaxed close friends. For example, Sammy's opening sentence in John Updike's "A & P" illustrates the informal, low style:

> In walks these three girls in nothing but bathing suits.

Note the idiomatic "In walks," a singular verb, followed by a plural subject. Note also the use of "these" girls, an idiom used indefinitely to refer to specific people. In Grace Paley's story "Goodbye and Good Luck" the diction is informal; the uniqueness is caused by the omission of certain key words and the unusual positioning of phrases, as in this passage:

> Nowadays you could find me any time in a hotel, uptown or downtown. Who needs an apartment to live like a maid with a dustrag in the hand, sneezing?

Note here the misuse of *could* for *can,* the omission of *at* which more formally would begin the phrase *any time.* The second sentence is almost impossible to analyze except to note that it has been arranged with masterly skill to duplicate exactly the idiomatic speech of the Jewish woman who is the speaker.

Specific–General and Concrete–Abstract Language

Specific refers to a real thing or things that may be readily perceived or imagined; "my pet dog" is specific. **General** statements refer to broad classes of persons or things. "Dogs make good pets" is a generalization. **Concrete** refers to words that describe qualities or conditions; in the phrase "a cold day" the word *cold* is concrete. You cannot see cold, but you know the exact difference between cold and hot, and therefore you understand the word readily in reference to the external temperature. **Abstract** refers to qualities that are more removed from the concrete, and abstract words can therefore refer to many classes of separate things. On a continuum of qualities, ice cream may be noted as being cold, sweet, and creamy. If we go on to say that it is *good*, however, this word is abstract because it is far removed from ice cream itself and conveys little if any information about it. A wide number of things may be good, just as they may be *bad*, *fine*, "*cool*," *excellent*, and so on. Abstract words like these are difficult to apply specifically, and thus if we use them we express more about ourselves than the topic we are discussing.

Usually, narrative and descriptive writing features specific and concrete words in preference to general and abstract ones. It stands to reason: When we confront many vague words that may mean a number of things at once, we become uncertain and confused. Usually, therefore, such words are out of place in stories and novels. On the other hand, we can visualize and understand passages containing words about specific things and actions, for with more specificity and concreteness there is less ambiguity. Because vividness is a goal of most fiction, specific and concrete words are the writer's basic tool.

The point, however, is not that abstract and general words do not belong, but that words should be *appropriate in the context*. Good writers manipulate style to match their narrative and descriptive purposes. As an example, we may observe Hemingway's diction in "Soldier's Home." This story concerns the aftereffects of war on a sensitive young man who, fresh from the excitement and danger he has experienced abroad, cannot adjust to the humdrum life back home. By combining specific and abstract language to get these ideas across, Hemingway fits style to subject exactly. Thus, in paragraph 6 (p. 275), Hemingway uses abstract terms to describe the mental state of Krebs, the young veteran. We read that Krebs feels "nausea in regard to experience that is the result of untruth or exaggeration," that he goes into the "easy pose of the old soldier" when he meets another veteran, and that he has "lost everything" as a result of his malaise. It is not easy to understand these words.

In contrast, however, Hemingway's next paragraph describes Krebs's typical daily activities: getting out of bed, walking to the library, eating lunch, reading on the front porch, and drifting down to the local pool room. These details are specific; although Hemingway does not elaborate further on them, we know from the passage that Krebs is bogged down in aimless boredom. The two paragraphs together reflect on each other, with the specific examples in paragraph 7 helping to explain the abstract descriptions of paragraph 6. In short, Hemingway skillfully combines specific and abstract words to build up his portrait of a young man who has not developed a vision of what to do with his life.

Denotation and Connotation

Another way of understanding style is to study the author's management of denotation and connotation. **Denotation** refers to what a word means, and **connotation** to what the word suggests. It is one thing to call a person *skinny*, for example, another to use the words *thin* or *gaunt*, and still something else to say *svelte* or *shapely*. Similarly, both *cat* and *kitten* are close to each other denotatively, but *kitten* connotes more playfulness and cuteness than *cat*. If a person in a social situation behaves in ways that are *friendly, warm, polite,* or *correct*, these words all suggest slight differences in behavior, not because the words are not close in meaning, but because they have different connotations.

Through the careful choice of words, not only for denotation but also for connotation, authors control their meaning and prod our imaginative responses. In Bowen's "The Demon Lover," (p. 282) for example, paragraph 15 describes Kathleen's walk to her house, as a girl of 19, after meeting her soldier lover and promising fidelity to him. The paragraph contains a number of highly connotative words and phrases, which are italicized here:

1. She is "*free* to run up the *silent* lawn."
2. She feels "that *unnatural* promise drive down between her and the rest of all human kind."
3. She is made to feel "*apart, lost and forsworn.*"
4. She "could not have plighted a more *sinister* troth."

These italicized words seem not only evocative, but right and accurate. "Free," for example, implies that there has been something confining, not liberating, about Kathleen's early relationship with her lover. The word "silent" does not describe anything about the lawn, but the word's connotation suggests stillness and solemnity—conditions more appropriate for a cemetery than for happy lovers. "Apart" is not unusual, describing only a degree of solitude, but both "lost" and "forsworn" connote self-condemnation along with alienation. "Unnatural promise" and "sinister troth" are both negative. We infer from them that Kathleen is making promises, but connotatively the adjectives go beyond vows of fidelity, or even sexual invitation, and suggest instead that something vaguely occultish is going on. Admittedly, at this point in the story, the implications are puzzling more than frightening, but the passage cumulatively tugs at the imagination. The examples show that Bowen's control over connotation contributes to the mysterious, haunting horror of Kathleen's fate.

RHETORIC

Broadly, **rhetoric** refers to the art of persuasive writing and, even more broadly, to the general art of writing. Any passage can be studied for its rhetorical qualities. For this reason it is necessary to develop both the methods and the descriptive vocabulary with which to carry out an analysis. Some things that may easily be done involve counting various elements in a passage and analyzing the types of sentences the author uses.

Counting

Doing a count of the number of words in a sentence; or the number of verbs, adjectives, prepositions, and adverbs; or the number of syllables in relation to the total number of words can often lead to valuable conclusions about style, especially if the count is related to other aspects of the passage. The virtue of counting is that it is easy to do and therefore it provides a "quick opening" into at least one aspect of style. Always remember that conclusions based on a count will provide *tendencies* of a particular author rather than absolutes. For illustration, let us say that Author *A* uses words mainly of 1 or 2 syllables, while Author *B* includes many words of 3, 4, and 5 syllables. Going further, let us say that *A* uses an average of 12 words per sentence while *B* uses 35. It would be fair to conclude that Author *A* is brief while Author *B* is more expansive. This is not to say that Author *A*'s passage would be easier or superior, however, for a long string of short sentences with short words might become choppy and tiresome and might cause your mind to wander.

Sentence Types

You can often learn much about a passage by determining the sorts of sentences it contains. Though you have probably learned the basic sentence types at one time or another, let's review them here:

1. **Simple sentences** contain one subject and one verb, together with modifiers and complements. They are often short and are most appropriate for actions and declarations. Often they are idiomatic, particularly in dialogue.

2. **Compound sentences** contain two simple sentences joined by a conjunction (*and, but, for, or, nor,* and so on) and a comma, or by a semicolon without a conjunction. Frequently, compound sentences are strung together as a series of three or four or more simple sentences.

3. **Complex sentences** contain a main clause and a subordinate clause. Because of the subordinate clause, the complex sentence is often suitable for describing cause-and-effect relationships in narrative, and also for analysis and reflection.

4. **Compound-complex sentences** contain two main clauses and a dependent clause. In practice many authors produce sentences that may contain a number of subordinate clauses together with many more than two main clauses. Usually, the more clauses, the more difficult the sentence.

Loose and Periodic Sentences

A major way to describe sentences is to use the terms *loose* and *periodic*. A **loose sentence** unfolds easily, with no surprises. Because it is predictable, it is the most commonly used sentence in stories. Here is an example:

> In America, the idea of equality was first applied only to white males.

Periodic sentences are arranged as much as possible in an order of climax, with the concluding information or thought being withheld to make the sentence especially interesting or surprising. Usually the periodic sentence begins with a dependent clause so that the content may be built up to the final detail, as in this sentence:

> Although in America the idea of equality was first applied only to males of European ancestry, in this century, despite the reluctance and even the opposition of many men who have regarded equality as a mark of their own status and not as a right for everyone, it has been extended to women and to persons of all races.

In narrative prose, sentences of this type are usually carefully placed in spots of crucial importance. Often the sentence alone might be said to contain the crisis and resolution at the same moment, as in this sentence from Poe's "The Fall of the House of Usher":

> For a moment she remained trembling and reeling to and fro upon the threshold, then, with a low moaning cry, fell heavily inward upon the person of her brother, and in her violent and now final death-agonies, bore him to the floor a corpse, and a victim to the terrors he had anticipated.

Parallelism

To create interest, authors often rely on the rhetorical device called *parallelism*, which is common and easily recognized. **Parallelism** is the repetition of the same grammatical form (nouns, verbs, phrases, clauses) to balance expressions, conserve words, and build up to climaxes. Here, for example, is another sentence from Poe, which occurs in the story "The Black Cat":

> I grew, day by day, more moody, more irritable, more regardless of the feelings of others.

Arrangements like this are called *parallel* because they can actually be laid out graphically, according to parts of speech, in parallel lines, as in the following (with the phrase "day to day" left out):

I grew
{
more moody
more irritable
more regardless of the feelings of others
}

Poe's sentence achieves an order of increasing severity of psychological depression developing from the personal to the social. Such an ascending order marks a deliberate attempt at climax, unlike the parallelism in the following sentence from the concluding paragraph of Clark's "The Portable Phonograph" (p. 242):

1   2   1

Then quickly and quietly, looking at the piece of canvas frequently, he slipped

2   3

the records into the case, snapped the lid shut, and carried the phonograph to his couch.

Here there are two parallel adverbs at the beginning, both ending in *-ly*, and three past tense verbs ending in *-ed*, all of which have direct objects. The order here is time. In a short sentence, Clark conveys a great deal of information.

The same parallel arrangements may be seen also in individual sentences within a paragraph or longer unit. In the following passage from Alice Munro's "The Found Boat," for example, there are a number of sentences of identical structure which sum up the exhilaration of young people dashing naked to swim in a river. Parallel sentences begin "They felt," "They felt," "They thought," "They went running," and finally "They dipped and floated and separated":

> Nobody said a word this time, they all bent and stripped themselves. Eva, naked first, started running across the field, and then all the others ran, all five of them running bare through the knee-high hot grass, running towards the river. Not caring now about being caught but in fact leaping and yelling to call attention to themselves, if there was anybody to hear or see. They felt as if they were going to jump off a cliff and fly. They felt that something was happening to them different from anything that had happened before, and it had to do with the boat, the water, the sunlight, the dark ruined station, and each other. They thought of each other now hardly as names or people, but as echoing shrieks, reflections, all bold and white and loud and scandalous, and as fast as arrows. They went running without a break into the cold water and when it came almost to the tops of their legs they

fell on it and swam. It stopped their noise. Silence, amazement, came over them in a rush. They dipped and floated and separated, sleek as mink.

CUMULATIO OR ACCUMULATION.   The paragraph from "The Found Boat" also illustrates another rhetorical device much used by writers, namely **cumulatio** or **accumulation.** While parallelism refers to grammatical constructions, cumulatio refers to the building up of details, such as the materials in the "they" sentences in Munro's paragraph. The device is therefore a brief way of introducing much information, for once the parallel rhythm of the buildup begins, readers will readily accept new material directly into the pattern. The device thus acts as a series of quick glimpses, or vignettes, and vividness is established through the parallel repetition.

CHIASMUS OR ANTIMETABOLE.   Also fitting into the pattern of parallelism is a favorite device called **chiasmus** or **antimetabole.** This pattern is designed to create vividness through memorable repetition. The pattern is *A B B A*, which can be arranged graphically at the ends of an *X* (from the Greek letter *chi*):

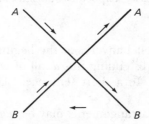

Mark Twain, in the story "Luck," creates a sentence that shows the pattern:

> *A*   *B*   *B*   *A*
> I drilled him and crammed him, and crammed him and drilled him.

You may not always encounter such easily observed patterns, but you should always be alert to positions and arrangements that you think are particularly noticeable or effective. Even though you may not be able to use a technically correct name, your analysis should go well as long as you focus your attention on important aspects of effective writing in the stories that you read.

STYLE IN GENERAL

If the work is successful, you probably will not think of the style as you read, for clear expressions and easy reading are marks of a writer's success. On consideration, however, you can begin to understand the author's achievement through a study of style. The action described in a particular passage, the relationship of the passage to the entire work, the level of the diction, the vividness of the descriptions—all these can enter into an assessment of the passage.

In the paragraph quoted above from Munro's "The Found Boat," for example, great stylistic mastery can be perceived beyond the parallelism that we noted. The passage could readily be considered the climax of the story, which is, among other things, about emerging sexuality. In an almost ritualistic way, the paragraph describes young people running impetuously toward a river and diving in—an action that may be construed as having symbolic sexual overtones. Note that after the first two sentences describing action, Munro's narrator shifts the focus with four sentences of omniscient analysis describing the feelings of the young people. If her intention had been to create searching psychological scrutiny here, she might have selected words from the language of psychology (*libido, urge, sublimation*, and so on). Instead, Munro uses words that could genuinely have been in the vocabularies of the characters. Hence the young people feel "as if they were going to jump off a cliff and fly" and feel "that something was happening to them different from anything that had happened before." With these neutral words, the passage focuses on the excitement of the situation rather than upon any hidden psychological significance. In light of all these considerations, the style of the paragraph seems just right. Munro describes the actions adequately but not extensively, she objectivizes the feelings of the characters, and she avoids the sort of psychological analysis that here would interrupt rather than instruct.

Observations of this kind may not occur on first reading, but on reflection you will find that the style of just about any passage will yield relatively full material for study. As long as the focus is on the content and also on the relationship of words to content, fruitful analysis of style will result.

MARK TWAIN (1835–1910)
[SAMUEL LANGHORNE CLEMENS]

Luck[1]   *1891*

It was at a banquet in London in honor of one of the two or three conspicuously illustrious English military names of this generation. For reasons which will presently appear, I will withhold his real name and titles and call him Lieutenant-General Lord Arthur Scoresby, Y.C., K.C.B., etc., etc. What a fascination there is in a renowned name! There sat the man, in actual flesh, whom I had heard of so

---

[1] This is not a fancy sketch. I got it from a clergyman who was an instructor at Woolwich forty years ago, and who vouched for its truth. [Twain's note.]

many thousands of times since that day, thirty years before, when his name shot suddenly to the zenith from a Crimean battlefield,° to remain forever celebrated. It was food and drink to me to look, and look, and look at that demi-god; scanning, searching, noting: the quietness, the reserve, the noble gravity of his countenance; the simple honesty that expressed itself all over him; the sweet unconsciousness of his greatness—unconsciousness of the hundreds of admiring eyes fastened upon him, unconsciousness of the deep, loving, sincere worship welling out of the breasts of those people and flowing toward him.

The clergyman at my left was an old acquaintance of mine—clergyman now, but had spent the first half of his life in the camp and field and as an instructor in the military school at Woolwich. Just at the moment I have been talking about a veiled and singular light glimmered in his eyes and he leaned down and muttered confidentially to me—indicating the hero of the banquet with a gesture:

"Privately—he's an absolute fool."

This verdict was a great surprise to me. If its subject had been Napoleon, or Socrates, or Solomon, my astonishment could not have been greater. Two things I was well aware of: that the Reverend was a man of strict veracity and that his judgment of men was good. Therefore I knew, beyond doubt or question, that the world was mistaken about this hero: he *was* a fool. So I meant to find out, at a convenient moment, how the Reverend, all solitary and alone, had discovered the secret.

Some days later the opportunity came, and this is what the Reverend told me: 5

About forty years ago I was an instructor in the military academy at Woolwich. I was present in one of the sections when young Scoresby underwent his preliminary examination. I was touched to the quick with pity, for the rest of the class answered up brightly and handsomely, while he—why, dear me, he didn't know *anything*, so to speak. He was evidently good, and sweet, and lovable, and guileless; and so it was exceedingly painful to see him stand there, as serene as a graven image, and deliver himself of answers which were veritably miraculous for stupidity and ignorance. All the compassion in me was aroused in his behalf. I said to myself, when he comes to be examined again he will be flung over, of course; so it will be simply a harmless act of charity to ease his fall as much as I can. I took him aside and found that he knew a little of Caesar's history; and as he didn't know anything else, I went to work and drilled him like a galley-slave on a certain line of stock questions concerning Caesar which I knew would be used. If you'll believe me, he went through with flying colors on examination day! He went through on that purely superficial "cram," and got compliments too, while others, who knew a thousand times more than he, got plucked. By some strangely lucky accident— an accident not likely to happen twice in a century—he was asked no question outside of the narrow limits of his drill.

It was stupefying. Well, all through his course I stood by him, with something of the sentiment which a mother feels for a crippled child; and he always saved himself—just by miracle, apparently.

Now, of course, the thing that would expose him and kill him at last was

Crimean battlefield: In the Crimean War (1853–1856), England was one of the allies that fought against Russia.

mathematics. I resolved to make his death as easy as I could; so I drilled him and crammed him, and crammed him and drilled him, just on the line of questions which the examiners would be most likely to use, and then launched him on his fate. Well, sir, try to conceive of the result: to my consternation, he took the first prize! And with it he got a perfect ovation in the way of compliments.

Sleep? There was no more sleep for me for a week. My conscience tortured me day and night. What I had done I had done purely through charity, and only to ease the poor youth's fall. I never had dreamed of any such preposterous results as the thing that had happened. I felt as guilty and miserable as Frankenstein. Here was a wooden-head whom I had put in the way of glittering promotions and prodigious responsibilities, and but one thing could happen: he and his responsibilities would all go to ruin together at the first opportunity.

The Crimean War had just broken out. Of course there had to be a war, I   10
said to myself. We couldn't have peace and give this donkey a chance to die before he is found out. I waited for the earthquake. It came. And it made me reel when it did come. He was actually gazetted to a captaincy in a marching regiment! Better men grow old and gray in the service before they climb to a sublimity like that. And who could ever have foreseen that they would go and put such a load of responsibility on such green and inadequate shoulders? I could just barely have stood it if they had made him a cornet; but a captain—think of it! I thought my hair would turn white.

Consider what I did—I who so loved repose and inaction. I said to myself, I am responsible to the country for this, and I must go along with him and protect the country against him as far as I can. So I took my poor little capital that I had saved up through years of work and grinding economy, and went with a sigh and bought a cornetcy in his regiment, and away we went to the field.

And there—oh, dear, it was awful. Blunders?—why he never did anything *but* blunder. But, you see, nobody was in the fellow's secret. Everybody had him focused wrong, and necessarily misinterpreted his performance every time. Consequently they took his idiotic blunders for inspirations of genius. They did, honestly! His mildest blunders were enough to make a man in his right mind cry; and they did make me cry—and rage and rave, too, privately. And the thing that kept me always in a sweat of apprehension was the fact that every fresh blunder he made increased the luster of his reputation! I kept saying to myself, he'll get so high that when discovery does finally come it will be like the sun falling out of the sky.

He went right along, up from grade to grade, over the dead bodies of his superiors, until at last, in the hottest moment of the battle of ——— down went our colonel, and my heart jumped into my mouth, for Scoresby was next in rank! Now for it, said I; we'll all land in Sheol in ten minutes, sure.

The battle was awfully hot; the allies were steadily giving way all over the field. Our regiment occupied a position that was vital; a blunder now must be destruction. At this crucial moment, what does this immortal fool do but detach the regiment from its place and order a charge over a neighboring hill where there wasn't a suggestion of an enemy! "There you go!" I said to myself; "this *is* the end at last."

And away we did go, and were over the shoulder of the hill before the   15
insane movement could be discovered and stopped. And what did we find? An entire and unsuspected Russian army in reserve! And what happened? We were eaten up? That is necessarily what would have happened in ninety-nine cases out

of a hundred. But no; those Russians argued that no single regiment would come browsing around there at such a time. It must be the entire English army, and that the sly Russian game was detected and blocked; so they turned tail, and away they went, pell-mell, over the hill and down into the field, in wild confusion, and we after them; they themselves broke the solid Russian center in the field, and tore through, and in no time there was the most tremendous rout you ever saw, and the defeat of the allies was turned into a sweeping and splendid victory! Marshal Canrobert looked on, dizzy with astonishment, admiration, and delight; and sent right off for Scoresby, and hugged him, and decorated him on the field in presence of all the armies!

And what was Scoresby's blunder that time? Merely the mistaking his right hand for his left—that was all. An order had come to him to fall back and support our right; and, instead, he fell *forward* and went over the hill to the left. But the name he won that day as a marvelous military genius filled the world with his glory, and that glory will never fade while history books last.

He is just as good and sweet and lovable and unpretending as a man can be, but he doesn't know enough to come in when it rains. Now that is absolutely true. He is the supremest ass in the universe; and until half an hour ago nobody knew it but himself and me. He has been pursued, day by day and year by year, by a most phenomenal astonishing luckiness. He has been a shining soldier in all our wars for a generation; he has littered his whole military life with blunders, and yet has never committed one that didn't make him a knight or a baronet or a lord or something. Look at his breast; why, he is just clothed in domestic and foreign decorations. Well, sir, every one of them is the record of some shouting stupidity or other; and, taken together, they are proof that the very best thing in all this world that can befall a man is to be born lucky. I say again, as I said at the banquet, Scoresby's an absolute fool.

QUESTIONS

1. Describe Twain's style as a writer of narrative prose. What kinds of detail does he present? Does he give you enough detail about the battle during the Crimean War, for example, to justify an assertion that he describes action vividly? Or does he confine his detail to illuminate the life of Scoresby?

2. What elements in the story are amusing? Does Twain's style have any influence on laughter? If so, how does the development of humor depend on the arrangement of words?

3. Study the first paragraph for rhetorical effect. What does it seem that Twain intended after the "look, and look, and look" phrase? Why do you think that he begins the story with such a description that might even be called heroic? Contrast this paragraph with the rhetoric of paragraph 12, where the word "blunder" is repeated.

4. Who begins telling the story? Who finally tells the story? What is the effect of this change of point of view upon the debunking of Scoresby that is the main subject? How does the clergyman narrator learn about all that Scoresby does? How does he summarize Scoresby's career?

5. How does Twain explain things so as to make it believable that Scoresby

could have passed his exams? Why is it necessary to include this cramming as a first step in the great career?

6. Describe the organization of the story. What is the climax? Where does it occur? What is the relationship of the story's title to the resolution of the plot?

ERNEST HEMINGWAY (1899–1961)

Soldier's Home   1925

Krebs went to the war from a Methodist college in Kansas. There is a picture which shows him among his fraternity brothers, all of them wearing exactly the same height and style collar. He enlisted in the Marines in 1917 and did not return to the United States until the second division returned from the Rhine in the summer of 1919.

There is a picture which shows him on the Rhine with two German girls and another corporal. Krebs and the corporal look too big for their uniforms. The German girls are not beautiful. The Rhine does not show in the picture.

By the time Krebs returned to his home town in Oklahoma the greeting of heroes was over. He came back much too late. The men from the town who had been drafted had all been welcomed elaborately on their return. There had been a great deal of hysteria. Now the reaction had set in. People seemed to think it was rather ridiculous for Krebs to be getting back so late, years after the war was over.

At first Krebs, who had been at Belleau Wood, Soissons, the Champagne, St. Mihiel and in the Argonne did not want to talk about the war at all. Later he felt the need to talk but no one wanted to hear about it. His town had heard too many atrocity stories to be thrilled by actualities. Krebs found that to be listened to at all he had to lie, and after he had done this twice he, too, had a reaction against the war and against talking about it. A distaste for everything that had happened to him in the war set in because of the lies he had told. All of the times that had been able to make him feel cool and clean inside himself when he thought of them; the times so long back when he had done the one thing, the only thing for a man to do, easily and naturally, when he might have done something else, now lost their cool, valuable quality and then were lost themselves.

His lies were quite unimportant lies and consisted in attributing to himself things other men had seen, done or heard of, and stating as facts certain apocryphal incidents familiar to all soldiers. Even his lies were not sensational at the pool room. His acquaintances, who had heard detailed accounts of German women found chained to machine guns in the Argonne forest and who could not comprehend, or were barred by their patriotism from interest in, any German machine gunners who were not chained, were not thrilled by his stories.   5

Krebs acquired the nausea in regard to experience that is the result of untruth or exaggeration, and when he occasionally met another man who had really been a soldier and they talked a few minutes in the dressing room at a dance he fell into the easy pose of the old soldier among other soldiers: that he had been badly, sickeningly frightened all the time. In this way he lost everything.

During this time, it was late summer, he was sleeping late in bed, getting up to walk down town to the library to get a book, eating lunch at home, reading on the front porch until he became bored and then walking down through the town to spend the hottest hours of the day in the cool dark of the pool room. He loved to play pool.

In the evening he practised on his clarinet, strolled down town, read and went to bed. He was still a hero to his two young sisters. His mother would have given him breakfast in bed if he had wanted it. She often came in when he was in bed and asked him to tell her about the war, but her attention always wandered. His father was non-committal.

Before Krebs went away to the war he had never been allowed to drive the family motor car. His father was in the real estate business and always wanted the car to be at his command when he required it to take clients out into the country to show them a piece of farm property. The car always stood outside the First National Bank building where his father had an office on the second floor. Now, after the war, it was still the same car.

Nothing was changed in the town except that the young girls had grown up. But they lived in such a complicated world of already defined alliances and shifting feuds that Krebs did not feel the energy or the courage to break into it. He liked to look at them, though. There were so many good-looking young girls. Most of them had their hair cut short. When he went away only little girls wore their hair like that or girls that were fast. They all wore sweaters and shirt waists with round Dutch collars. It was a pattern. He liked to look at them from the front porch as they walked on the other side of the street. He liked to watch them walking under the shade of the trees. He liked the round Dutch collars above their sweaters. He liked their silk stockings and flat shoes. He liked their bobbed hair and the way they walked.

When he was in town their appeal to him was not very strong. He did not like them when he saw them in the Greek's ice cream parlor. He did not want them themselves really. They were too complicated. There was something else. Vaguely he wanted a girl but he did not want to have to work to get her. He would have liked to have a girl but he did not want to have to spend a long time getting her. He did not want to get into the intrigue and the politics. He did not want to have to do any courting. He did not want to tell any more lies. It wasn't worth it.

He did not want any consequences. He did not want any consequences ever again. He wanted to live along without consequences. Besides he did not really need a girl. The army had taught him that. It was all right to pose as though you had to have a girl. Nearly everybody did that. But it wasn't true. You did not need a girl. That was the funny thing. First a fellow boasted how girls mean nothing to him, that he never thought of them, that they could not touch him. Then a fellow boasted that he could not get along without girls, that he had to have them all the time, that he could not go to sleep without them.

That was all a lie. It was all a lie both ways. You did not need a girl unless you thought about them. He learned that in the army. Then sooner or later you always got one. When you were really ripe for a girl you always got one. You did not have to think about it. Sooner or later it would come. He had learned that in the army.

Now he would have liked a girl if she had come to him and not wanted to talk. But here at home it was all too complicated. He knew he could never get through it all again. It was not worth the trouble. That was the thing about French girls and German girls. There was not all this talking. You couldn't talk much and you did not need to talk. It was simple and you were friends. He thought about France and then he began to think about Germany. On the whole he had liked Germany better. He did not want to leave Germany. He did not want to come home. Still, he had come home. He sat on the front porch.

He liked the girls that were walking along the other side of the street. He liked the look of them much better than the French girls or the German girls. But the world they were in was not the world he was in. He would like to have one of them. But it was not worth it. They were such a nice pattern. He liked the pattern. It was exciting. But he would not go through all the talking. He did not want one badly enough. He liked to look at them all, though. It was not worth it. Not now when things were getting good again.

He sat there on the porch reading a book on the war. It was a history and he was reading about all the engagements he had been in. It was the most interesting reading he had ever done. He wished there were more maps. He looked forward with a good feeling to reading all the really good histories when they would come out with good detail maps. Now he was really learning about the war. He had been a good soldier. That made a difference.

One morning after he had been home about a month his mother came into his bedroom and sat on the bed. She smoothed her apron.

"I had a talk with your father last night, Harold," she said, "and he is willing for you to take the car out in the evenings."

"Yeah?" said Krebs, who was not fully awake. "Take the car out? Yeah?"

"Yes. Your father has felt for some time that you should be able to take the car out in the evenings whenever you wished but we only talked it over last night."

"I'll bet you made him," Krebs said.

"No. It was your father's suggestion that we talk the matter over."

"Yeah. I'll bet you made him," Krebs sat up in bed.

"Will you come down to breakfast, Harold?" his mother said.

"As soon as I get my clothes on," Krebs said.

His mother went out of the room and he could hear her frying something downstairs while he washed, shaved and dressed to go down into the dining-room for breakfast. While he was eating breakfast his sister brought in the mail.

"Well, Hare," she said. "You old sleepy-head. What do you ever get up for?"

Krebs looked at her. He liked her. She was his best sister.

"Have you got the paper?" he asked.

She handed him *The Kansas City Star* and he shucked off its brown wrapper and opened it to the sporting page. He folded *The Star* open and propped it against the water pitcher with his cereal dish to steady it, so he could read while he ate.

"Harold," his mother stood in the kitchen doorway, "Harold, please don't muss up the paper. Your father can't read his *Star* if it's been mussed."

"I won't muss it," Krebs said.

His sister sat down at the table and watched him while he read.

"We're playing indoor° over at school this afternoon," she said. "I'm going to pitch."

indoor: i.e., a softball baseball game.

"Good," said Krebs. "How's the old wing?"   35

"I can pitch better than lots of the boys. I tell them all you taught me. The other girls aren't much good."

"Yeah?" said Krebs.

"I tell them all you're my beau. Aren't you my beau, Hare?"

"You bet."

"Couldn't your brother really be your beau just because he's your brother?"   40

"I don't know."

"Sure you know. Couldn't you be my beau, Hare, if I was old enough and if you wanted to?"

"Sure. You're my girl now."

"Am I really your girl?"

"Sure."   45

"Do you love me?"

"Uh, huh."

"Will you love me always?"

"Sure."

"Will you come over and watch me play indoor?"   50

"Maybe."

"Aw, Hare, you don't love me. If you loved me, you'd want to come over and watch me play indoor."

Kreb's mother came into the dining-room from the kitchen. She carried a plate with two fried eggs and some crisp bacon on it and a plate of buckwheat cakes.

"You run along, Helen," she said. "I want to talk to Harold."

She put eggs and bacon down in front of him and brought in a jug of   55
maple syrup for the buckwheat cakes. Then she sat down across the table from Krebs.

"I wish you'd put down the paper a minute, Harold," she said.

Krebs took down the paper and folded it.

"Have you decided what you are going to do yet, Harold?" his mother said, taking off her glasses.

"No," said Krebs.

"Don't you think it's about time?" His mother did not say this in a mean   60
way. She seemed worried.

"I hadn't thought about it," Krebs said.

"God has some work for every one to do," his mother said. "There can be no idle hands in His Kingdom."

"I'm not in His Kingdom," Krebs said.

"We are all of us in His Kingdom."

Krebs felt embarrassed and resentful as always.   65

"I've worried about you so much, Harold," his mother went on. "I know the temptations you must have been exposed to. I know how weak men are. I know what your own dear grandfather, my own father, told us about the Civil War and I have prayed for you. I pray for you all day long, Harold."

Krebs looked at the bacon fat hardening on his plate.

"Your father is worried, too," his mother went on. "He thinks you have lost your ambition, that you haven't got a definite aim in life. Charley Simmons, who

is just your age, has a good job and is going to be married. The boys are all
settling down; they're all determined to get somewhere; you can see that boys
like Charley Simmons are on their way to being really a credit to the community."
    Krebs said nothing.
    "Don't look that way, Harold," his mother said. "You know we love you   70
and I want to tell you for your own good how matters stand. Your father does
not want to hamper your freedom. He thinks you should be allowed to drive the
car. If you want to take some of the nice girls out riding with you, we are only
too pleased. We want you to enjoy yourself. But you are going to have to settle
down to work, Harold. Your father doesn't care what you start in at. All work is
honorable as he says. But you've got to make a start at something. He asked me
to speak to you this morning and then you can stop in and see him at his office."
    "Is that all?" Krebs said.
    "Yes. Don't you love your mother, dear boy?"
    "No," Krebs said.
    His mother looked at him across the table. Her eyes were shiny. She started
crying.
    "I don't love anybody," Krebs said.   75
    It wasn't any good. He couldn't tell her, he couldn't make her see it. It was
silly to have said it. He had only hurt her. He went over and took hold of her
arm. She was crying with her head in her hands.
    "I didn't mean it," he said. "I was just angry at something. I didn't mean I
didn't love you."
    His mother went on crying. Krebs put his arm on her shoulder.
    "Can't you believe me, mother?"
    His mother shook her head.   80
    "Please, please, mother. Please believe me."
    "All right," his mother said chokily. She looked up at him. "I believe you,
Harold."
    Krebs kissed her hair. She put her face up to him.
    "I'm your mother," she said. "I held you next to my heart when you were a
tiny baby."
    Krebs felt sick and vaguely nauseated.   85
    "I know, Mummy," he said. "I'll try and be a good boy for you."
    "Would you kneel and pray with me, Harold?" his mother asked.
    They knelt down beside the dining-room table and Krebs's mother prayed.
    "Now, you pray, Harold," she said.
    "I can't," Krebs said.   90
    "Try, Harold."
    "I can't."
    "Do you want me to pray for you?"
    "Yes."
    So his mother prayed for him and then they stood up and Krebs kissed his   95
mother and went out of the house. He had tried so to keep his life from being
complicated. Still, none of it had touched him. He had felt sorry for his mother
and she had made him lie. He would go to Kansas City and get a job and she
would feel all right about it. There would be one more scene maybe before he
got away. He would not go down to his father's office. He would miss that one.

He wanted his life to go smoothly. It had just gotten going that way. Well, that was all over now, anyway. He would go over to the schoolyard and watch Helen play indoor baseball.

QUESTIONS

1. Even though Hemingway is often praised for his specific writing, there are a number of vague passages in this story. In relationship to the thematic material, why does Hemingway include them? By what stylistic means does he control the vagueness?

2. Analyze Hemingway's sentences. What relationship is there between the things he describes and the lengths of sentences he uses? What kinds of complexities do you find in the sentences?

3. Analyze Hemingway's descriptive style. What is the level of his diction? What adjectives and adverbs do you find? What do they contribute to the passages containing them? What words does he use for things and actions? How vivid are his descriptions?

4. Describe the character of Harold Krebs. How do we learn about him? What is he like? Is he flat or round? What does his relationship with his sister show about him? What changes, if any, does he undergo in the story?

5. Why does Krebs not wish to be involved? In what senses is he disillusioned? What has disillusioned him? Why does he not go immediately to work? What is illustrated by his disavowal of love for his mother? What are his reactions to the war and to the ways in which people respond to his involvement in it? To what degree is he capable of articulating his feelings?

6. Describe the plot of the story. What is the conflict? Who are the protagonist and the antagonist? What is the crisis of the story? The climax? The resolution?

ELIZABETH BOWEN   (1899–1973)

The Demon Lover   *1945*

Towards the end of her day in London Mrs. Drover went round to her shut-up house to look for several things she wanted to take away. Some belonged to herself, some to her family, who were by now used to their country life. It was late August; it had been a steamy, showery day: at the moment the trees down the pavement glittered in an escape of humid yellow afternoon sun. Against the next batch of clouds, already piling up ink-dark, broken chimneys and parapets stood out. In her once familiar street, as in any unused channel, an unfamiliar queerness had silted up; a cat wove itself in and out of railings, but no human eye watched Mrs. Drover's return. Shifting some parcels under her arm, she slowly forced round her latchkey in an unwilling lock, then gave the door, which had warped, a push with her knee. Dead air came out to meet her as she went in.

The staircase window having been boarded up, no light came down into the hall. But one door, she could just see, stood ajar, so she went quickly through into the room and unshuttered the big window in there. Now the prosaic woman, looking about her, was more perplexed than she knew by everything that she saw, by traces of her long former habit of life—the yellow smoke-stain up the white marble mantelpiece, the ring left by a vase on the top of the escritoire,° the bruise in the wallpaper where, on the door being thrown open widely, the china handle had always hit the wall. The piano, having gone away to be stored, had left what looked like claw-marks on its part of the parquet. Though not much dust had seeped in, each object wore a film of another kind; and, the only ventilation being the chimney, the whole drawing room smelled of the cold hearth. Mrs. Drover put down her parcels on the escritoire and left the room to proceed upstairs; the things she wanted were in the bedroom chest.

She had been anxious to see how the house was—the part-time caretaker she shared with some neighbors was away this week on his holiday, known to be not yet back. At the best of times he did not look in often, and she was never sure that she trusted him. There were some cracks in the structure, left by the last bombing, on which she was anxious to keep an eye. Not that one could do anything—

A shaft of refracted daylight now lay across the hall. She stopped dead and stared at the hall table—on this lay a letter addressed to her.

She thought first—then the caretaker *must* be back. All the same, who, seeing the house shuttered, would have dropped a letter in at the box? It was not a circular, it was not a bill. And the post office redirected, to the address in the country, everything for her that came through the post. The caretaker (even if he *were* back) did not know she was due in London today—her call here had been planned to be a surprise—so his negligence in the matter of this letter, leaving it to wait in the dusk and dust, annoyed her. Annoyed, she picked up the letter, which bore no stamp. But it cannot be important, or they would know. . . . She took the letter rapidly upstairs with her, without a stop to look at the writing till she reached what had been her bedroom, where she let in light. The room looked over the garden and other gardens: the sun had gone in; as the clouds sharpened and lowered, the trees and rank lawns seemed already to smoke with dark. Her reluctance to look again at the letter came from the fact that she felt intruded upon—and by someone contemptuous of her ways. However, in the tenseness preceding the fall of rain she read it: it was a few lines.

5

> Dear Kathleen,
> You will not have forgotten that today is our anniversary, and the day we said. The years have gone by at once slowly and fast. In view of the fact that nothing has changed, I shall rely upon you to keep your promise. I was sorry to see you leave London, but was satisfied that you would be back in time. You may expect me, therefore, at the hour arranged.
>   Until then . . .
>   K.

Mrs. Drover looked for the date: it was today's. She dropped the letter on to the bedsprings, then picked it up to see the writing again—her lips, beneath the remains of lipstick, beginning to go white. She felt so much the change in her own face

---

escritoire: A small, usually decorative desk.

that she went to the mirror, polished a clear patch in it and looked at once urgently and stealthily in. She was confronted by a woman of forty-four, with eyes staring out under a hat brim that had been rather carelessly pulled down. She had not put on any more powder since she left the shop where she ate her solitary tea. The pearls her husband had given her on their marriage hung loose round her now rather thinner throat, slipping into the V of the pink wool jumper her sister knitted last autumn as they sat round the fire. Mrs. Drover's most normal expression was one of controlled worry, but of assent. Since the birth of the third of her little boys, attended by a quite serious illness, she had had an intermittent muscular flicker to the left of her mouth, but in spite of this she could always sustain a manner that was at once energetic and calm.

Turning from her own face as precipitately as she had gone to meet it, she went to the chest where the things were, unlocked it, threw up the lid and knelt to search. But as the rain began to come crashing down she could not keep from looking over her shoulder at the stripped bed on which the letter lay. Behind the blanket of rain the clock of the church that still stood struck six—with rapidly heightening apprehension she counted each of the slow strokes. "The hour arranged. . . . My God," she said, "*what* hour? How should I . . . ? After twenty-five years. . ."

The young girl talking to the soldier in the garden had not ever completely seen his face. It was dark; they were saying goodbye under a tree. Now and then—for it felt, from not seeing him at this intense moment, as though she had never seen him at all—she verified his presence for these few moments longer by putting out a hand, which he each time pressed, without very much kindness, and painfully, on to one of the breast buttons of his uniform. That cut of the button on the palm of her hand was, principally, what she was to carry away. This was so near the end of a leave from France that she could only wish him already gone. It was August 1916. Being not kissed, being drawn away from and looked at intimidated Kathleen till she imagined spectral glitters in the place of his eyes. Turning away and looking back up the lawn she saw, through branches of trees, the drawing room window alight: she caught a breath for the moment when she could go running back there into the safe arms of her mother and sister, and cry: "What shall I do, what shall I do? He has gone."

Hearing her catch her breath, her fiancé said, without feeling: "Cold?"

"You're going away such a long way."

"Not so far as you think."

"I don't understand?"

"You don't have to," he said. "You will. You know what we said."

"But that was—suppose you—I mean, suppose."

"I shall be with you," he said, "sooner or later. You won't forget that. You need do nothing but wait."

Only a little more than a minute later she was free to run up the silent lawn. Looking in through the window at her mother and sister, who did not for the moment perceive her, she already felt that unnatural promise drive down between her and the rest of all human kind. No other way of having given herself could have made her feel so apart, lost and forsworn. She could not have plighted a more sinister troth.

10

15

Kathleen behaved well when, some months later, her fiancé was reported missing, presumed killed. Her family not only supported her but were able to praise her courage without stint because they could not regret, as a husband for her, the man they knew almost nothing about. They hoped she would, in a year or two, console herself—and had it been only a question of consolation things might have gone much straighter ahead. But her trouble, behind just a little grief, was a complete dislocation from everything. She did not reject other lovers, for these failed to appear: for years she failed to attract men—and with the approach of her thirties she became natural enough to share her family's anxiousness on this score. She began to put herself out, to wonder; and at thirty-two she was very greatly relieved to find herself being courted by William Drover. She married him, and the two of them settled down in this quiet, arboreal part of Kensington:° in this house the years piled up, her children were born and they all lived till they were driven out by the bombs of the next war. Her movements as Mrs. Drover were circumscribed, and she dismissed any idea that they were still watched.

As things were—dead or living the letter-writer sent her only a threat. Unable, for some minutes, to go on kneeling with her back exposed to the empty room, Mrs. Drover rose from the chest to sit on an upright chair whose back was firmly against the wall. The desuetude of her former bedroom, her married London home's whole air of being a cracked cup from which memory, with its reassuring power, had either evaporated or leaked away, made a crisis—and at just this crisis the letter-writer had, knowledgeably, struck. The hollowness of the house this evening cancelled years on years of voices, habits and steps. Through the shut windows she only heard rain fall on the roofs around. To rally herself, she said she was in a mood—and, for two or three seconds shutting her eyes, told herself that she had imagined the letter. But she opened them—there it lay on the bed.

On the supernatural side of the letter's entrance she was not permitting her mind to dwell. Who, in London, knew she meant to call at the house today? Evidently, however, this had been known. The caretaker, *had* he come back, had had no cause to expect her: he would have taken the letter in his pocket, to forward it, at his own time, through the post. There was no other sign that the caretaker had been in—but, if not? Letters dropped in at doors at deserted houses do not fly or walk to tables in halls. They do not sit on the dust of empty tables with the air of certainty that they will be found. There is needed some human hand—but nobody but the caretaker had a key. Under circumstances she did not care to consider, a house can be entered without a key. It was possible that she was not alone now. She might be being waited for, downstairs. Waited for—until when? Until "the hour arranged." At least that was not six o'clock: six had struck.

She rose from the chair and went over and locked the door.

The thing was, to get out. To fly? No, not that: she had to catch her train. As a woman whose utter dependability was the keystone of her family life she was not willing to return to the country, to her husband, her little boys and her sister, without the objects she had come up to fetch. Resuming work at the chest she set about making up a number of parcels in a rapid, fumbling-decisive way. These, with her shopping parcels, would be too much to carry; these meant a

20

Kensington: An upwardly mobile district of London.

taxi—at the thought of the taxi her heart went up and her normal breathing resumed. I will ring up the taxi now; the taxi cannot come too soon: I shall hear the taxi out there running its engine, till I walk calmly down to it through the hall. I'll ring up—But no: the telephone is cut off . . . She tugged at a knot she had tied wrong.

The idea of flight . . . He was never kind to me, not really. I don't remember him kind at all. Mother said he never considered me. He was set on me, that was what it was—not love. Not love, not meaning a person well. What did he do, to make me promise like that? I can't remember.—But she found that she could.

She remembered with such dreadful acuteness that the twenty-five years since then dissolved like smoke and she instinctively looked for the weal left by the button on the palm of her hand. She remembered not only all that he said and did but the complete suspension of *her* existence during that August week. I was not myself—they all told me so at the time. She remembered—but with one white burning blank as where acid has dropped on a photograph: *under no conditions could she remember his face.*

So, wherever he may be waiting, I shall not know him. You have no time to run from a face you do not expect.

The thing was to get to the taxi before any clock struck what could be the hour. She would slip down the street and round the side of the square to where the square gave on the main road. She would return in the taxi, safe, to her own door, and bring the solid driver into the house with her to pick up the parcels from room to room. The idea of the taxi driver made her decisive, bold: she unlocked her door, went to the top of the staircase and listened down.

She heard nothing—but while she was hearing nothing the *passé°* air of the staircase was disturbed by a draught that travelled up to her face. It emanated from the basement: down there a door or window was being opened by someone who chose this moment to leave the house.   25

The rain had stopped; the pavements steamily shone as Mrs. Drover let herself out by inches from her own front door into the empty street. The unoccupied houses opposite continued to meet her look with their damaged stare. Making towards the thoroughfare and the taxi, she tried not to keep looking behind. Indeed, the silence was so intense—one of those creeks of London silence exaggerated this summer by the damage of war—that no tread could have gained on hers unheard. Where her street debouched on the square where people went on living she grew conscious of and checked her unnatural pace. Across the open end of the square two buses impassively passed each other; women, a perambulator, cyclists, a man wheeling a barrow signalized, once again, the ordinary flow of life. At the square's most populous corner should be—and was—the short taxi rank. This evening, only one taxi—but this, although it presented its blank rump, appeared already to be alertly waiting for her. Indeed, without looking round the driver started his engine as she panted up from behind and put her hand on the door. As she did so, the clock struck seven. The taxi faced the main road: to make the trip back to her house it would have to turn—she had settled back on the seat and the taxi *had* turned before she, surprised by its knowing movement, recollected that she had not "said where." She leaned forward to scratch at the glass panel that divided the driver's head from her own.

passé: old, stuffy.

The driver braked to what was almost a stop, turned round and slid the glass panel back: the jolt of this flung Mrs. Drover forward till her face was almost into the glass. Through the aperture driver and passenger, not six inches between them, remained for an eternity eye to eye. Mrs. Drover's mouth hung open for some seconds before she could issue her first scream. After that she continued to scream freely and to beat with her gloved hands on the glass all round as the taxi, accelerating without mercy, made off with her into the hinterland of deserted streets.

QUESTIONS

1. When is the story presumably occurring? Why is Bowen so specific about Mrs. Drover's age, and about the time that has elapsed since her meeting with her soldier lover?

2. Describe how the appearance and the content of the letter create suspense. What words are used to describe Mrs. Drover's explanation for the letter, and how does the explanation allay the mystery for a time? What is the effect of the basement noise as Mrs. Drover leaves? How is the taxi described as she approaches it? What is the effect of this description?

3. Analyze the words used to describe Mrs. Drover's soldier lover. What kind of picture are you given? What words contribute to the conclusions you draw about him, and how does the level of diction help to cause your responses?

4. What reasons can you give to explain why Mrs. Drover is sometimes called "Kathleen" and at other times "Mrs. Drover?"

5. How and why does Bowen make the relationship uncertain and unsatisfactory between Mrs. Drover and her soldier lover? Analyze the description of the taxi driver at the very end. Explain the stylistic means by which Bowen is able to produce chills from the concluding paragraph.

6. What is the effect of the references to the death of the soldier in World War I and the bombings of London in World War II? How might the demon lover be considered symbolic of what happens to people as a result of these wars and of all wars?

ALICE MUNRO   (b. 1931)

The Found Boat   *1974*

At the end of Bell Street, McKay Street, Mayo Street, there was the Flood. It was the Wawanash River, which every spring overflowed its banks. Some springs, say one in every five, it covered the roads on that side of town and washed over the fields, creating a shallow choppy lake. Light reflected off the water made everything bright and cold, as it is in a lakeside town, and woke or revived in people certain vague hopes of disaster. Mostly during the late afternoon and early evening, there were people straggling out to look at it, and discuss whether it was still rising, and whether this time it might invade the town. In general, those under fifteen and over sixty-five were most certain that it would.

Eva and Carol rode out on their bicycles. They left the road—it was the end of Mayo Street, past any houses—and rode right into a field, over a wire fence entirely flattened by the weight of the winter's snow. They coasted a little way before the long grass stopped them, then left their bicycles lying down and went to the water.

"We have to find a log and ride on it," Eva said.

"Jesus, we'll freeze our legs off."

"Jesus, we'll freeze our legs off!" said one of the boys who were there too at   5
the water's edge. He spoke in a sour whine, the way boys imitated girls although it was nothing like the way girls talked. These boys—there were three of them—were all in the same class as Eva and Carol at school and were known to them by name (their names being Frank, Bud and Clayton), but Eva and Carol, who had seen and recognized them from the road, had not spoken to them or looked at them or, even yet, given any sign of knowing they were there. The boys seemed to be trying to make a raft, from lumber they had salvaged from the water.

Eva and Carol took off their shoes and socks and waded in. The water was so cold it sent pain up their legs, like blue electric sparks shooting through their veins, but they went on, pulling their skirts high, tight behind and bunched so they could hold them in front.

"Look at the fat-assed ducks in wading."

"Fat-assed fucks."

Eva and Carol, of course, gave no sign of hearing this. They laid hold of a log and climbed on, taking a couple of boards floating in the water for paddles. There were always thing floating around in the Flood—branches, fence-rails, logs, road signs, old lumber; sometimes boilers, washtubs, pots and pans, or even a car seat or stuffed chair, as if somewhere the Flood had got into a dump.

They paddled away from shore, heading out into the cold lake. The water   10
was perfectly clear, they could see the brown grass swimming along the bottom. Suppose it was the sea, thought Eva. She thought of drowned cities and countries. Atlantis. Suppose they were riding in a Viking boat—Viking boats on the Atlantic were more frail and narrow than this log on the Flood—and they had miles of clear sea beneath them, then a spired city, intact as a jewel irretrievable on the ocean floor.

"This is a Viking boat," she said. "I am the carving on the front." She stuck her chest out and stretched her neck, trying to make a curve, and she made a face, putting out her tongue. Then she turned and for the first time took notice of the boys.

"Hey, you sucks!" she yelled at them. "You'd be scared to come out here, this water is ten feet deep!"

"Liar," they answered without interest, and she was.

They steered the log around a row of trees, avoiding floating barbed wire, and got into a little bay created by a natural hollow of the land. Where the bay was now, there would be a pond full of frogs later in the spring, and by the middle of summer there would be no water visible at all, just a low tangle of reeds and bushes, green, to show that mud was still wet around their roots. Larger bushes, willows, grew around the steep bank of this pond and were still partly out of the water. Eva and Carol let the log ride in. They saw a place where something was caught.

It was a boat, or part of one. An old rowboat with most of one side ripped   15
out, the board that had been the seat just dangling. It was pushed up among the
branches, lying on what would have been its side, if it had a side, the prow caught
high.

Their idea came to them without consultation, at the same time:

"You guys! Hey, you guys!"

"We found you a boat!"

"Stop building your stupid raft and come and look at the boat!"

What surprised them in the first place was that the boys really did come,   20
scrambling overland, half running, half sliding down the bank, wanting to see.

"Hey, where?"

"Where is it, I don't see no boat."

What surprised them in the second place was that when the boys did actually
see what boat was meant, this old flood-smashed wreck held up in the branches,
they did not understand that they had been fooled, that a joke had been played
on them. They did not show a moment's disappointment, but seemed as pleased
at the discovery as if the boat had been whole and new. They were already barefoot,
because they had been wading in the water to get lumber, and they waded in
here without a stop, surrounding the boat and appraising it and paying no attention
even of an insulting kind to Eva and Carol who bobbed up and down on their
log. Eva and Carol had to call to them.

"How do you think you're going to get it off?"

"It won't float anyway."   25

"What makes you think it will float?"

"It'll sink. Glub-blub-blub, you'll all be drownded."

The boys did not answer, because they were too busy walking around the
boat, pulling at it in a testing way to see how it could be got off with the least
possible damage. Frank, who was the most literate, talkative and inept of the three,
began referring to the boat as *she*, an affectation which Eva and Carol acknowledged
with fish-mouths of contempt.

"She's caught two places. You got to be careful not to tear a hole in her
bottom. She's heavier than you'd think."

It was Clayton who climbed up and freed the boat, and Bud, a tall fat boy,   30
who got the weight of it on his back to turn it into the water so that they could
half float, half carry it to shore. All this took some time. Eva and Carol abandoned
their log and waded out of the water. They walked overland to get their shoes
and socks and bicycles. They did not need to come back this way but they came.
They stood at the top of the hill, leaning on their bicycles. They did not go on
home, but they did not sit down and frankly watch, either. They stood more or
less facing each other, but glancing down at the water and at the boys struggling
with the boat, as if they had just halted for a moment out of curiosity, and staying
longer than they intended, to see what came of this unpromising project.

About nine o'clock, or when it was nearly dark—dark to people inside the
houses, but not quite dark outside—they all returned to town, going along Mayo
Street in a sort of procession. Frank and Bud and Clayton came carrying the
boat, upside-down, and Eva and Carol walked behind, wheeling their bicycles.
The boys' heads were almost hidden in the darkness of the overturned boat, with
its smell of soaked wood, cold swampy water. The girls could look ahead and see

the street lights in their tin reflectors, a necklace of lights climbing Mayo Street, reaching all the way up to the standpipe. They turned onto Burns Street heading for Clayton's house, the nearest house belonging to any of them. This was not the way home for Eva or for Carol either, but they followed along. The boys were perhaps too busy carrying the boat to tell them to go away. Some younger children were still out playing, playing hopscotch on the sidewalk though they could hardly see. At this time of year the bare sidewalk was still such a novelty and delight. These children cleared out of the way and watched the boat go by with unwilling respect; they shouted questions after it, wanting to know where it came from and what was going to be done with it. No one answered them. Eva and Carol as well as the boys refused to answer or even look at them.

The five of them entered Clayton's yard. The boys shifted weight, as if they were going to put the boat down.

"You better take it round to the back where nobody can see it," Carol said. That was the first thing any of them had said since they came into town.

The boys said nothing but went on, following a mud path between Clayton's house and a leaning board fence. They let the boat down in the back yard.

"It's a stolen boat, you know," said Eva, mainly for the effect. "It must've   35 belonged to somebody. You stole it."

"You was the ones who stole it then," Bud said, short of breath. "It was you seen it first."

"It was you took it."

"It was all of us then. If one of us gets in trouble then all of us does."

"Are you going to tell anybody on them?" said Carol as she and Eva rode home, along the streets which were dark between the lights now and potholed from winter.

"It's up to you. I won't if you won't."   40

"I won't if you won't."

They rode in silence, relinquishing something, but not discontented.

The board fence in Clayton's back yard had every so often a post which supported it, or tried to, and it was on these posts that Eva and Carol spent several evenings sitting, jauntily but not very comfortably. Or else they just leaned against the fence while the boys worked on the boat. During the first couple of evenings neighborhood children attracted by the sound of hammering tried to get into the yard to see what was going on, but Eva and Carol blocked their way.

"Who said you could come in here?"

"Just us can come in this yard."   45

These evenings were getting longer, the air milder. Skipping was starting on the sidewalks. Further along the street there was a row of hard maples that had been tapped. Children drank the sap as fast as it could drip into the buckets. The old man and woman who owned the trees, and who hoped to make syrup, came running out of the house making noises as if they were trying to scare away crows. Finally, every spring, the old man would come out on his porch and fire his shotgun into the air, and then the thieving would stop.

None of those working on the boat bothered about stealing sap, though all had done so last year.

The lumber to repair the boat was picked up here and there, along back lanes. At this time of year things were lying around—old boards and branches, sodden mitts, spoons flung out with the dishwater, lids of pudding pots that had been set in the snow to cool, all the debris that can sift through and survive winter. The tools came from Clayton's cellar—left over, presumably, from the time when his father was alive—and though they had nobody to advise them the boys seemed to figure out more or less the manner in which boats are built, or rebuilt. Frank was the one who showed up with diagrams from books and *Popular Mechanics* magazines. Clayton looked at these diagrams and listened to Frank read the instructions and then went ahead and decided in his own way what was to be done. Bud was best at sawing. Eva and Carol watched everything from the fence and offered criticism and thought up names. The names for the boat that they thought of were: Water Lily, Sea Horse, Flood Queen, and Caro-Eve, after them because they had found it. The boys did not say which, if any, of these names they found satisfactory.

The boat had to be tarred. Clayton heated up a pot of tar on the kitchen stove and brought it out and painted slowly, his thorough way, sitting astride the overturned boat. The other boys were sawing a board to make a new seat. As Clayton worked, the tar cooled and thickened so that finally he could not move the brush any more. He turned to Eva and held out the pot and said, "You can go in and heat this on the stove."

Eva took the pot and went up the back steps. The kitchen seemed black   50
after outside, but it must be light enough to see in, because there was Clayton's mother standing at the ironing board, ironing. She did that for a living, took in wash and ironing.

"Please may I put the tar pot on the stove?" said Eva, who had been brought up to talk politely to parents, even wash-and-iron ladies, and who for some reason especially wanted to make a good impression on Clayton's mother.

"You'll have to poke up the fire then," said Clayton's mother, as if she doubted whether Eva would know how to do that. But Eva could see now, and she picked up the lid with the stove-lifter, and took the poker and poked up a flame. She stirred the tar as it softened. She felt privileged. Then and later. Before she went to sleep a picture of Clayton came to her mind; she saw him sitting astride the boat, tar-painting, with such concentration, delicacy, absorption. She thought of him speaking to her, out of his isolation, in such an ordinary peaceful taking-for-granted voice.

On the twenty-fourth of May, a school holiday in the middle of the week, the boat was carried out of town, a long way now, off the road over fields and fences that had been repaired, to where the river flowed between its normal banks. Eva and Carol, as well as the boys, took turns carrying it. It was launched in the water from a cow-trampled spot between willow bushes that were fresh out in leaf. The boys went first. They yelled with triumph when the boat did float, when it rode amazingly down the river current. The boat was painted black, and green inside, with yellow seats, and a strip of yellow all the way around the outside. There was no name on it, after all. The boys could not imagine that it needed any name to keep it separate from the other boats in the world.

Eva and Carol ran along the bank, carrying bags full of peanut butter-and-jam sandwiches, pickles, bananas, chocolate cake, potato chips, graham crackers stuck together with corn syrup and five bottles of pop to be cooled in the river water. The bottles bumped against their legs. They yelled for a turn.

"If they don't let us they're bastards," Carol said, and they yelled together,   55
"We found it! We found it!"

The boys did not answer, but after a while they brought the boat in, and
Carol and Eva came crashing, panting down the bank.

"Does it leak?"

"It don't leak yet."

"We forgot a bailing can," wailed Carol, but nevertheless she got in, with
Eva, and Frank pushed them off, crying, "Here's to a Watery Grave!"

And the thing about being in a boat was that it was not solidly bobbing,   60
like a log, but was cupped in the water, so that riding in it was not like being on
something in the water, but like being in the water itself. Soon they were all going
out in the boat in mixed-up turns, two boys and a girl, two girls and a boy, a girl
and a boy, until things were so confused it was impossible to tell whose turn came
next, and nobody cared anyway. They went down the river—those who weren't
riding, running along the bank to keep up. They passed under two bridges, one
iron, one cement. Once they saw a big carp just resting, it seemed to smile at
them, in the bridge-shaded water. They did not know how far they had gone on
the river, but things had changed—the water had got shallower, and the land
flatter. Across an open field they saw a building that looked like a house, abandoned.
They dragged the boat up on the bank and tied it and set out across the field.

"That's the old station," Frank said. "That's Pedder Station." The others
had heard this name but he was the one who knew, because his father was the
station agent in town. He said that this was a station on a branch line that had
been torn up, and that there had been a sawmill here, but a long time ago.

Inside the station it was dark, cool. All the windows were broken. Glass lay
in shards and in fairly big pieces on the floor. They walked around finding the
larger pieces of glass and tramping on them, smashing them, it was like cracking
ice on puddles. Some partitions were still in place, you could see where the ticket
window had been. There was a bench lying on its side. People had been here, it
looked as if people came here all the time, though it was so far from anywhere.
Beer bottles and pop bottles were lying around, also cigarette packages, gum and
candy wrappers, the paper from a loaf of bread. The walls were covered with
dim and fresh pencil and chalk writings and carved with knives.

    I LOVE RONNIE COLES

    I WANT TO FUCK

    KILROY WAS HERE

    RONNIE COLES IS AN ASS-HOLE

    WHAT ARE YOU DOING HERE?

    WAITING FOR A TRAIN

    DAWNA   MARY-LOU   BARBARA   JOANNE

It was exciting to be inside this large, dark, empty place, with the loud noise
of breaking glass and their voices ringing back from the underside of the roof.
They tipped the old beer bottles against their mouths. That reminded them that
they were hungry and thirsty and they cleared a place in the middle of the floor
and sat down and ate the lunch. They drank the pop just as it was, lukewarm.
They ate everything there was and licked the smears of peanut butter and jam
off the bread-paper in which the sandwiches had been wrapped.

They played Truth or Dare.

"I dare you to write on the wall, I am a Stupid Ass, and sign your name."   65
"Tell the truth—what is the worst lie you ever told?"
"Did you ever wet the bed?"
"Did you ever dream you were walking down the street without any clothes
on?"
"I dare you to go outside and pee on the railway sign."
It was Frank who had to do that. They could not see him, even his back,   70
but they knew he did it, they heard the hissing sound of his pee. They all sat
still, amazed, unable to think of what the next dare would be.
"I dare everybody," said Frank from the doorway, "I dare—Everybody."
"What?"
"Take off all our clothes."
Eva and Carol screamed.
"Anybody who won't do it has to walk—has to *crawl*—around this floor on   75
their hands and knees."
They were all quiet, till Eva said, almost complacently, "What first?"
"Shoes and socks."
"Then we have to go outside, there's too much glass here."
They pulled off their shoes and socks in the doorway, in the sudden blinding
sun. The field before them was bright as water. They ran across where the tracks
used to go.
That's enough, that's enough," said Carol. "Watch out for thistles!"   80
"Tops! Everybody take off their tops!"
"I won't! We won't, will we, Eva?"
But Eva was whirling round and round in the sun where the track used to
be. "I don't care, I don't care! Truth or Dare! Truth or Dare!"
She unbuttoned her blouse as she whirled, as if she didn't know what her
hand was doing, she flung it off.
Carol took off hers. "I wouldn't have done it, if you hadn't!"   85
"Bottoms!"
Nobody said a word this time, they all bent and stripped themselves. Eva,
naked first, started running across the field, and then all the others ran, all five
of them running bare through the knee-high hot grass, running towards the river.
Not caring now about being caught but in fact leaping and yelling to call attention
to themselves, if there was anybody to hear or see. They felt as if they were going
to jump off a cliff and fly. They felt that something was happening to them different
from anything that had happened before, and it had to do with the boat, the
water, the sunlight, the dark ruined station, and each other. They thought of
each other now hardly as names or people, but as echoing shrieks, reflections,
all bold and white and loud and scandalous, and as fast as arrows. They went running without a break into the cold water and when it came almost to the tops
of their legs they fell on it and swam. It stopped their noise. Silence, amazement, came over them in a rush. They dipped and floated and separated, sleek as
mink.
Eva stood up in the water her hair dripping, water running down her face.
She was waist deep. She stood on smooth stones, her feet fairly wide apart, water
flowing between her legs. About a yard away from her Clayton also stood up,
and they were blinking the water out of their eyes, looking at each other. Eva did

not turn or try to hide; she was quivering from the cold of the water, but also with pride, shame, boldness, and exhilaration.

Clayton shook his head violently, as if he wanted to bang something out of it, then bent over and took a mouthful of river water. He stood up with his cheeks full and made a tight hole of his mouth and shot the water at her as if it was coming out of a hose, hitting her exactly, first one breast and then the other. Water from his mouth ran down her body. He hooted to see it, a loud self-conscious sound that nobody would have expected, from him. The others looked up from wherever they were in the water and closed in to see.

Eva crouched down and slid into the water, letting her head go right under.   90
She swam, and when she let her head out, downstream, Carol was coming after her and the boys were already on the bank, already running into the grass, showing their skinny backs, their white, flat buttocks. They were laughing and saying things to each other but she couldn't hear, for the water in her ears.

"What did he do?" said Carol.

"Nothing."

They crept in to shore. "Let's stay in the bushes till they go," said Eva. "I hate them anyway. I really do. Don't you hate them?"

"Sure," said Carol, and they waited, not very long, until they heard the boys still noisy and excited coming down to the place a bit upriver where they had left the boat. They heard them jump in and start rowing.

"They've got all the hard part, going back," said Eva, hugging herself and   95
shivering violently. "Who cares? Anyway. It never was our boat."

"What if they tell?" said Carol.

"We'll say it's all a lie."

Eva hadn't thought of this solution until she said it, but as soon as she did she felt almost light-hearted again. The ease and scornfulness of it did make them both giggle, and slapping themselves and splashing out of the water they set about developing one of those fits of laughter in which, as soon as one showed signs of exhaustion, the other would snort and start up again, and they would make helpless— soon genuinely helpless—faces at each other and bend over and grab themselves as if they had the worst pain.

QUESTIONS

1. Consider the details used in passages of description in the story. What kinds of details are included? In the first paragraph, for example, what is the focus of interest, the flood or people's reactions to it?

2. What is the level of diction in the dialogue of the story? Do you see contractions? Slang? Grammatical mistakes? Profanity? From the dialogue what do you learn about the various speakers?

3. Study paragraph 10 as an example of the relationship of style to the character Eva as a limited-point-of-view center of interest. What does the paragraph tell you about her? How does it do so?

4. Consider the last paragraph in the story as an example of writing about action. How much action is selected for description? What verbs are used and how well do they help you visualize and imagine the sounds of the

scene? What is the effect of the verb "snort"? How does the paragraph cause you to respond at the story's end?

5. What is "Truth or Dare"? What is the dare that concludes the game? To what degree is the game a guise under which boys and girls may develop their emotions toward each other?

6. What is the plot of the story? Who or what is in conflict? What elements are introduced as complication? What are the climax and resolution of the story?

7. How many details of setting are included? From the lifestyle and artifacts mentioned, what do you learn about the approximate time of the events in the story? About the economic level of the town? How well realized is the town? What is the effect of the facts that it is early springtime, that the water is still cold, but that in May the water is swimmable? What are the implications for summer?

WRITING ABOUT STYLE

In prewriting, you should consider the selected passage in the context of the entire story. What sort of passage is it? Narrative? Descriptive? Does it contain any dialogue? Is there a speaker with clearly established characteristics? How does the passage reflect his or her personality? Try to determine the level of the diction: Did you need to use a dictionary to discover the meaning of any of the words? Are there any unusual words? Any especially difficult or uncommon words? Do any of the words distract you as you read? Is there any slang? Are any words used only in particular occupations or ways of life (such as words used about drink, or automobiles, or horses, words from other languages, and so on)? Are there any contractions? Do they indicate a conversational, intimate level of speech? Are the words the most common ones that might be used? Can you think of more difficult ones? Easier ones? More accurate ones? Are there many short words? Long words?

Can you easily imagine the situations described by the words? If you have difficulty, can you find any reasons that stem out of the level of diction?

Are the sentences long, or short? Is there any variation in length? Can you observe any relationship between length and topic material? Are the sentences simple, compound, or complex? Does one type predominate? Why? Can you describe any noteworthy rhetorical devices? Are there any sentences that may be clearly established to be periodic as opposed to loose? What sort of effect is gained by this sentence or sentences? Are there any other noticeable devices? What are they? How are they used? What is their effect?

With answers to questions like these, you will readily assemble materials for your essay on the style of a passage from a story.

Organizing Your Essay

INTRODUCTION.   In your introduction you should establish the particulars about the passage you are studying and should present a central idea that relates the style to these particulars. You should mention the place of the passage in the work, the general subject matter, any special ideas, the speaker, the apparent audience (if any except the general reader), and the basic method of presentation (that is, monologue, dialogue, or narration, all of which might be interspersed with argument, description, or comparison).

BODY.   In the body of your essay you should describe and evaluate the style of the passage. Always remember to consider the style in relationship to the circumstances of the work. For example, suppose the speaker is in a plane crashing to the ground, or in a racing car just approaching the finish line, or hurrying to meet a sweetheart; or suppose the speaker is recalling the past or considering the future. Such conditions must be kept foremost throughout your analysis.

To focus your essay, you might wish to single out one aspect of style, or to discuss everything, depending on the length of the assignment. Be sure to treat things like levels of diction, categories like specific-general and concrete-abstract, the degree of simplicity or complexity, length, numbers of words (an approach that is relatively easy for a beginning), and denotation-connotation. In discussing rhetorical aspects, go as far as you can with the nomenclature at your command. Consider things like sentence types and any specific rhetorical devices you notice and are able to describe. If you can draw attention to the elements in a parallel structure by using grammatical terms, do so. If you are able to detect the ways in which the sentences are kept simple or made complex, describe these ways. Be sure to use examples from the passage to illustrate your point; indent them and leave spaces between them and your own material.

The sort of essay envisaged here is designed to sharpen your levels of awareness at your own stage of development as a reader. Later, to the degree that you will have gained sharper perceptions and a wider descriptive vocabulary, you will be able to enhance the sophistication of your analyses.

CONCLUSION.   Whereas the body is the place for detailed descriptions and examples, your conclusion is the place where you can make evaluations of the author's style. To what extent have your discoveries in your analysis increased or reinforced your appreciation of the author's technique? Does the passage take on any added importance as a result of your study? Is there anything elsewhere in the work comparable to the content, words, or ideas that you have discussed in the passage?

Numbers for Easy Reference

Include a copy of your passage at the beginning of your essay, as in the example. For your reader's convenience, number the sentences in the passage, and use these numbers as they become relevant in your essay.

SAMPLE ESSAY

Mark Twain's Blending of Style and Purpose in "Luck"*

[1] The battle was awfully hot; the allies were steadily giving way all over the field. [2] Our regiment occupied a position that was vital; a blunder now must be destruction. [3] At this crucial moment, what does this immortal fool do but detach the regiment from its place and order a charge over a neighboring hill where there wasn't a suggestion of an enemy! [4] "There you go!" I said to myself; "this *is* the end at last."

[5] And away we did go, and were over the shoulder of the hill before the insane movement could be discovered and stopped. [6] And what did we find? [7] An entire and unsuspected Russian army in reserve! [8] And what happened? [9] We were eaten up? [10] That is necessarily what would have happened in ninety-nine cases out of a hundred. [11] But no; those Russians argued that no single regiment would come browsing around there at such a time. [12] It must be the entire English army, and that the sly Russian game was detected and blocked; so they turned tail, and away they went, pell-mell, over the hill and down into the field, in wild confusion, and we after them; they themselves broke the solid Russian center in the field, and tore through, and in no time there was the most tremendous rout you ever saw, and the defeat of the allies was turned into a sweeping and splendid victory! [13] Marshal Canrobert looked on, dizzy with astonishment, admiration, and delight; and sent right off for Scoresby, and hugged him, and decorated him on the field in presence of all the armies!

[1] Appearing close to the end of "Luck," these two paragraphs are important in Twain's satiric design to puncture the bubble of Scoresby, a widely recognized and decorated British hero who is nothing more than a lucky boob. In the story, the paragraphs come as a climax. By presenting a brief account of a decisive battle in the Crimean War, in which Scoresby's regiment figures prominently, they bring out his stupidity and luck to the highest degree. Though the passages are narrative, the mark of Twain's style is to underscore how the hero's blundering foolishness is always saved by luck.° In every respect—description, word level, use of general and abstract diction, and the narrator's involvement—the passage embodies Twain's satiric and comic goal.□

The descriptions in the paragraphs are directed toward the idiocy of

* See p. 271 for this story.
° Central idea.
□ Thesis sentence.

the main character. In fact, the descriptions are not about the battle at all. The essential military matter presented in the 13 sentences is that the allies are giving way, that Scoresby orders a charge, and that the Russians turn tail and dash away. There is no report of clashing soldiers and dying men and horses, beyond the claim that the Russians themselves "tore through" their own ranks, and there are no vivid words, beyond these, describing the circumstances of victory. Indeed, the descriptions are minimal, containing just enough to show Scoresby's lucky blunder, but no more. The paragraphs would be unsuccessful as an account of a battle, but as part of this story they are superb.

[2]

In keeping with the exposé, Twain uses a middle, or neutral level of diction. The words are not unusual or difficult. What could be more ordinary, for example, than words like *battle, awfully, steadily, occupied, discovered, stopped, argued,* and *victory*? One may grant that *splendid, astonishment, pell-mell, immortal,* and *crucial* are not common in everyday speech, but in this context they are appropriate, for they fall within the vocabulary of responses to battle. Because of their aptness, they enable the reader to focus entirely on the subject and on the narrator's expressions of humor, and in this respect they fit the middle level of diction.

[3]

Not only is the level neutral, but many words are general and abstract, in accord with the intention of the story to debunk Scoresby. The "allies were steadily giving way," for example, and the "movement" of many individuals is described as "insane." These general words are fitting for groups and mass actions, but not for specific individuals. When the Russians conclude from Scoresby's senseless charge that their "game" is "detected," they turn "tail" and run "pell-mell," dashing in such "wild confusion" that there is "the most tremendous rout you ever saw," resulting in "sweeping and splendid victory"—all general and abstract words. Even the "hero," Scoresby, is not detailed anywhere as a specific leader and fighter; it is as though he is less significant than the blind stupidity he unleashes. Sentence 13 at the end of the passage continues in this mode with the abstract but worshipful responses of the commander, Marshal Canrobert; he is "dizzy with astonishment, admiration, and delight." These abstract words reflect the public renown of Scoresby, which we, as the narrator's listeners, know to be untrue. Both general and abstract words thus jell perfectly with Twain's humor.

[4]

Perhaps the major quality of Twain's style in the passage, however, is the amused, debunking language contributed directly by the narrator. The narrator's words provide the force orchestrating the movements of the battle, as is shown in the first paragraph (sentences 1–4). There, his words and expressions prepare a groundwork of suspense for the anticlimax of Scoresby's victory. He tells us (sentence 3) that the "immortal fool" orders a mistaken charge. His lamenting prediction, "this is the end at last" (sentence 4), is designed for full dramatic and suspenseful effect. The narrator's involvement is also shown by his simply phrased questions just before he tells about the results of the charge: "And what did we find?" "And what happened?" "We were eaten up?" In his reconstruction of the military logic of the Russian command, the narrator's words highlight the English stupidity of having a regiment where it has no intelligent strategic or tactical business. His attitude

[5]

[5] is most amusingly shown by the word "browsing" (sentence 11) which suggests grazing animals, not charging armies. This word emphasizes the utter dimwittedness of Scoresby's command to attack.

[6] In all respects, the passage is a model of the right use of words in the right places. If the writing were about an actual military combat, it would be poor. But because it is part of a comic exposé of a fortunate fool, it is hard to imagine a better way to put things. Twain's speaker gives us what we need to know: namely that Scoresby has a Midas touch in everything he does, no matter how potentially disastrous. The sentences are clear and direct, and convey the facts about Scoresby that show his imbecility. For these reasons, the paragraphs are examples of accurate, purposeful narrative prose.

Commentary on the Essay

This essay shows how separate stylistic topics may be unified. Important in this objective are the transitions from paragraph to paragraph, such as "not only . . . but," "in keeping with the exposé," and "in all respects." These transition phrases enable reader concentration to move smoothly from one topic to the next.

The beginning of the essay demonstrates the importance of relating the passage being studied to the work as a whole. Because the central idea is connected to Mark Twain's debunking objective, the point is made that style and satiric intention are merged and integrated. The thesis sentence indicates four aspects of style to be considered in the essay. Any one of these, if necessary, could be separately developed.

In the body, paragraph 2 treats the absence of specifically descriptive words, explaining this lack by reference to the satiric subject. Paragraph 3 treats the neutral diction, making the point that this language is appropriate because it permits a direct focus on the asinine blunders of the major character. Twain's use of general and abstract language is treated in paragraph 4, the point being that this language is appropriate because the story exposes the emptyheadedness of Scoresby. The major point about the style is brought out in paragraph 5—that the narrator adds his own interpretations to the narration. The intention of placing this topic at the end of the body is to use it as a high point of the discussion. The concluding paragraph, 6, is a tribute to Twain's style, emphasizing again how his satiric objective governs word choices.

Though the emphasis in this sample essay is on the more approachable stylistic topic of diction, an excellent approach might also be the relationship of the control of style and sentence length to the passage. A clear point about the sentences, for example, is that they begin in poise and balance, much in keeping with the way troops are poised before a battle. By contrast, as the battle descends into the chaos caused by the unexpected charge of

Scoresby's regiment, Twain creates sentences that develop in sympathy with the chaos. Sentence 12, for example, containing all the battle details, is 81 words long and is broken up by semicolons and commas into a variety of separate statements and structures describing the pell-mell retreat and victory. The sentence has the same wildness, sweep, and madness as the events being described—here a fitting blending by Twain of grammar and subject.

WRITING TOPICS FOR CHAPTER 7

1. Write an essay on the differences in style between the two narrators in "Luck." What purpose is served in having two narrators?

2. Write an essay which answers the following questions: To what degree are the narrative and descriptive styles of "Soldier's Home" appropriate to the nature of the story? What would be the effect on the story if the style of Faulkner in "Barn Burning" (Chapter 4), or Updike in "A & P" (Chapter 2), or Whitecloud in "Blue Winds Dancing" (Chapter 3) were used?

3. "The Found Boat" is characterized by full descriptions, so that little question is left about what is happening. Would this style be effective in "The Demon Lover?" Why or why not?

4. Write two brief character sketches, or a description of an action, to be included in a longer story. Make the first favorable and glowing, and make the second negative. Analyze your word choices in the contrasting accounts: What kinds of words do you select, and on what principles do you select them? What kinds of words might you select in order to create a neutral or nonjudgmental account? On the basis of your answers, what conclusions might you make about yourself as a literary stylist?

8

Tone: Attitude and Control in Fiction

Tone refers to the methods by which writers convey attitudes, although it is sometimes confused with attitudes themselves. Bear in mind that tone refers not to attitudes but to those techniques and modes of presentation that *reveal* or *create* attitudes.

LITERARY TONE AND SPEAKING TONE OF VOICE

For literary study the word *tone* is borrowed from the phrase *tone of voice* in speech. Tone of voice reflects your attitudes toward a particular thing or situation and also toward your listeners. Let us suppose that Mary has a difficult school assignment on which she expects to work all day. Things go well and she finishes quickly. She happily tells her friend Anne about the work, saying, "I'm so pleased. I needed only two hours for that." Then Mary goes to a theater to buy tickets for a popular play, and the line is long and slow. After she finally gets the tickets and is walking away, she tells a group of people waiting in the back of the line, "I'm so pleased. I needed only two hours for that." The sentences are exactly the same, but by changing her emphasis and vocal inflection, Mary gets the idea across that she is disgusted with the difficulty and slowness of the line, and also that she understands the annoyance of those behind her with the same long wait. By controlling the *tone* of her statements, Mary conveys pleasure at one time, and indignation and anger (and also sympathy) at another.

TONE AS SHOWN BY CHARACTERS WITHIN A WORK

The assumption of a study of tone is that all authors, like our real-life speaker Mary, have a *choice* about what to say and how to say it, and that they make their choices in full consideration of their readers. One obvious authorial judgment is that readers are intelligent, and can perceive the intricacies of both real and fictional human interchanges. As a specific literary example, John Collier, at the beginning of the grim story "The Chaser" (the topic of the sample essay, in this chapter), creates a difficult situation: A young man, Alan Austen, comes to a chemist's shop seeking a love potion. The chemist, an old man, wants to tell Austen about a deadly and untraceable poison. Here the proper tone is essential. Collier must heed the integrity of his characters, which requires that not all things can be directly stated if the aims and goals of each are to be fulfilled. Therefore he has the old man speak indirectly about the poison, as follows:

> "I look at it like this," said the old man. "Please a customer with one article, and he will come back when he needs another. Even if it *is* more costly. He will save up for it, if necessary."

The indirect, veiled style of this speech shows the old chemist's assessment of Austen. If he were to say outright that Austen will eventually come back for the poison to kill the woman whom he now wants so desperately, Austen would flee in horror. So the old man uses the phrase "come back when he needs another" to suggest that in the future Austen may remember these words and fit himself into the category of men wanting the other product, the poison. The speech is right for the circumstances. It shows how an author may judge and control tone by the careful crafting of characters and their speeches within a work.

TONE AND THE AUTHOR'S ATTITUDE
TOWARD READERS

In addition, also by controlling the style of the speech of the old man, Collier demonstrates confidence in the perceptiveness of his readers, who are able to judge whether the dialogue in the story is realistic. Suppose that Collier had written an interchange in which the old man tells Austen that someday he will return for the poison. Could one then expect sophisticated and intelligent readers to believe that Austen would continue his mission to buy the love potion? Obviously Collier's answer is no. The point is that Austen, *at the moment of the story*, is young, romantic, and idealistic, but that *at a future time* he will become cynical, and will grow so weary of his sweetheart that he will want to kill her. He will then remember the old man's poison. The story therefore goes forward as it does, with the old man speaking ambiguously and ominously, and Austen hearing but not understanding. Collier thus shows not only a due regard for the probability of the characters and situation, but also ; a clear acknowledgment of the intelligence and perceptiveness of readers.

This example illustrates that aspect of tone involving the author's attitude toward his or her audience. As it were, the author recognizes that readers are participants in the creative act, and that all elements of a work must take audience response into account. Readers would instantly know that any departures from normally expected behavior—from verisimilitude—would strain credibility, as would any inappropriate language, settings, motivation, chronology, and so on.

LAUGHTER, COMEDY, AND FARCE

A major aspect of tone is laughter and the methods of comedy and farce. Everyone likes to laugh, but not everyone can explain the reasons for laughing. It seems clear that smiles, shared laughter, and good human relationships go together, so that laughter is essential to mental health. Laughter is unplanned, often unpredictable, and sometimes personal and idiosyncratic. It resists close analysis. Despite the difficulty of explaining the causes of laughter, however, it is possible to note that some elements are common. These are:

1. *An object of laughter.* There must be something to laugh at, whether a person, thing, situation, custom, a habit of speech or dialect, or arrangement of words.

2. *Incongruity.* Human beings know what to expect under given conditions, and anything that violates these expectations may cause laughter. When the temperature is 100° F., for example, you reasonably expect people to dress lightly. But if you see a person dressed in a heavy overcoat, a warm hat, a muffler, and large gloves, who is shivering, waving his arms, and stamping his feet as though to keep them warm, this person has violated your expectations. His garments are inappropriate or *incongruous*, and quite likely you laugh at him. If you hear a standup comedian say, "Yesterday afternoon I was walking down the street and turned into a drugstore," this remark is funny because "turned into" can have two incompatible meanings. Here the language itself furnishes its own incongruity. A student once wrote that in high school he had sung in the "archipelago choir." This inadvertent verbal mistake is called a *malapropism*, after Mrs. Malaprop, a character in Sheridan's eighteenth-century play *The Rivals*. If you know about unaccompanied choirs, you expect to see *a capella*, or at least a recognizable misspelling of the phrase. When you see *archipelago*, however, a word that makes sense (if you are speaking about islands) and that looks something like *a capella*, you laugh, or at least smile. Incongruity is the quality common to all these instances of laughter. In the literary creation of such verbal slips, the tone is directed against the speaker, and both readers and author alike share the enjoyment.

3. *Safety and/or good will.* Seeing a person slipping on a banana peel

and hurtling through the air may cause laughter as long as we ourselves are not that person, for our laughter depends on our insulation from danger and pain. In farce, where much physical abuse takes place (such as falling through trapdoors or being hit in the face by cream pies), the abuse never harms the participants. The incongruity of such situations causes laughter, and the fact that no one gets hurt prevents grave or even horrified responses. Good will enters into laughter in romantic comedy or in works where you are drawn into general sympathy with the major figures, such as Smirnov and Mrs. Popov in Chekhov's play *The Bear*. Here the infectiousness of laughter and happiness governs your responses. As the author leads the characters toward the admission of their love, your involvement with them produces happiness, smiles, and even sympathetic laughter.

4. *Unfamiliarity, newness, uniqueness, spontaneity.* Laughter depends on seeing something new or unique, or on experiencing a known thing freshly. Because laughter is prompted by a flash of insight or a sudden revelation, the circumstances promoting laughter are always spontaneous. Perhaps you have had someone explain a joke or funny situation, only to find that the explanation dampened the spontaneity needed for laughter. Although spontaneity is most often a quality of the unfamiliar, it is not lost just because a thing is well known. Indeed, the task of the comic writer is to develop ordinary materials to a point when spontaneity frees the reader to laugh. Thus it is possible to read and re-read *The Bear* and laugh each time because the work leads you to expect one outcome, but then gives you a surprisingly different one. The love between Smirnov and Mrs. Popov is and always will be comic because it is so illogical, unexpected, incongruous, and spontaneous.

IRONY

One of the most human traits is the capacity to have two or more attitudes toward someone or something. We know that people are not perfect, but we love a number of them anyway. Therefore we speak to them not only with love and praise, but also with banter and criticism. (And they, in turn, may choose to inform us about our own imperfections.) On occasions, you may have bought greeting cards that are amusing or even mildly insulting rather than sentimental. If you give such cards, you do so in the expectation that your loved ones will not be affronted, but instead will be amused. As you share smiles and laughs, you also remind your loved ones of your affection for them.

The term **irony** describes such situations and expressions by which a writer conveys a specific idea or attitude by stating something apparently opposite or contradictory. Irony is natural to human beings who are aware of the ambiguities and complexities in life. It is a function of the realization that life does not always measure up to promise, that friends and loved ones may sometimes be angry and bitter toward each other, that the universe contains incomprehensible mysteries, that doubt exists even in the certainty of knowledge and faith, and that human character is built through chagrin, regret, and pain as much as through emulation and praise. In expressing an idea ironically, writers pay the greatest compliment to their readers, for they assume that readers have sufficient skill and understanding to see through the quizzical or ambiguous surface statement into the clarity beneath.

The major types of irony are *verbal, situational,* and *dramatic.* In **verbal irony,** one thing is said and another is meant. For example, one of the American astronauts was once asked how he would feel if all his reentry safety equipment failed as he was coming back to earth. He answered, "A thing like that could ruin your whole day." His words would have been appropriate for day-to-day minor mishaps, but since failed safety equipment would cause his death, his answer was ironic (doubly so since the loss in 1986 of the space shuttle *Challenger*). This form of verbal irony is **understatement.** By contrast, **overstatement,** or **hyperbole,** is deliberate exaggeration for effect, as in "And I will love thee still, my Dear, / Till all the seas go dry" (lines from "A Red, Red Rose," by Robert Burns).

Often verbal irony is ambiguous, having double meaning or **double-entendre.** At the end of Collier's "The Chaser," for example, the old man responds to Austen's "Good-bye" with the French farewell "Au revoir." This phrase, meaning "Until I see you again," is not unusual, and on the surface it seems innocent, but the context makes clear that these words are a dire prediction that Austen will return one day for the untraceable poison. In other words, the old man's goodbye has two meanings, one innocent and the other sinister. Ambiguity of course may be used in relation to any topic. Quite often double entendre is used in statements about sexuality and love, usually for the amusement of listeners or readers.

The term **situational irony,** or **irony of situation,** refers to conditions which are measured against forces that transcend and overpower human capacities. These forces may be psychological, social, political, or environmental. In Margaret Atwood's "Rape Fantasies," for example, the narrator Estelle concludes by stating her inability to understand why men can not be satisfied by human relationships with women rather than rapacious ones. Though "Rape Fantasies" is not a sociological document, Estelle's uneasiness underscores the irony of the political and social conditions that produce rape. The situational irony of traditional marriage is brought out in Kate Chopin's "The Story of an Hour." Because Louise Mallard, the main character, has concluded that her husband's death has released her from the virtual serfdom of her role as wife, her heart fails when she sees her husband, alive, at the bottom of the stairway. The irony is that the doctors, like everyone else, conclude that her death results from the shock of joy, not from the true shock of disappointment.

A special kind of situational irony that develops out of a pessimistic or fatalistic view of life is **cosmic irony,** or **irony of fate.** By the standard of cosmic irony, the universe is indifferent to individuals, who are subject to blind chance, accident, perpetual misfortune, and misery. Even if things temporarily seem to be going well, people's lives inevitably end badly, and their best efforts do not rescue them or make them happy. Such is the irony of fate we find in "The Hammon and the Beans" by Américo Parédes. In the setting of Mexican-American families living in poverty near the border in Texas, the dead little girl, Chonita, is no more than a minor statistic; her life is only an insignificant part of a gigantic pattern of social and political neglect. If we consider her as a human being with great potential for growth, however, we may conclude that she might have matured to adulthood and led a productive, happy life. With her life of poverty and poor education, care, and nutrition, she never has a chance. Her situation, like that of many like her, is cosmically ironic, for the implication of "The Hammon and the Beans" is that human beings are caught in a web of circumstances from which they cannot escape.

Like cosmic irony, **dramatic irony** is a special kind of situational irony; it applies when a character perceives a situation in a limited way while the audience, including other characters, may see it in greater perspective. The character therefore is able to understand things in only one way, while the audience can perceive two ways. Allan Austen in "The Chaser" is locked into such irony; he believes that the only potion he will ever need is the one to win him love, while the old man and the readers know that one day he will return for the poison. The classic example of dramatic irony is found in the play *Oedipus the King* by Sophocles. All his life Oedipus has been driven by fate, which he can never escape. As the play draws to its climax and Oedipus believes that he is about to discover the murderer of his father, the audience knows—as he does not—that he is approaching his own self destruction: As he condemns the murderer, he also condemns himself.

KATE CHOPIN   (1851–1904)

The Story of an Hour   *1894*

Knowing that Mrs. Mallard was afflicted with a heart trouble, great care was taken to break to her as gently as possible the news of her husband's death.

It was her sister Josephine who told her, in broken sentences; veiled hints that revealed in half concealing. Her husband's friend Richards was there, too, near her. It was he who had been in the newspaper office when intelligence of the railroad disaster was received, with Brently Mallard's name leading the list of "killed." He had only taken the time to assure himself of its truth by a second telegram, and had hastened to forestall any less careful, less tender friend in bearing the sad message.

She did not hear the story as many women have heard the same, with a paralyzed inability to accept its significance. She wept at once, with sudden, wild abandonment, in her sister's arms. When the storm of grief had spent itself she went away to her room alone. She would have no one follow her.

There stood, facing the open window, a comfortable, roomy armchair. Into this she sank, pressed down by a physical exhaustion that haunted her body and seemed to reach into her soul.

She could see in the open square before her house the tops of trees that   5
were all aquiver with the new spring life. The delicious breath of rain was in the air. In the street below a peddler was crying his wares. The notes of a distant song which some one was singing reached her faintly, and countless sparrows were twittering in the eaves.

There were patches of blue sky showing here and there through the clouds that had met and piled one above the other in the west facing her window.

She sat with her head thrown back upon the cushion of the chair, quite motionless, except when a sob came up into her throat and shook her, as a child who has cried itself to sleep continues to sob in its dreams.

She was young, with a fair, calm face, whose lines bespoke repression and even a certain strength. But now there was a dull stare in her eyes, whose gaze was fixed away off yonder on one of those patches of blue sky. It was not a glance of reflection, but rather indicated a suspension of intelligent thought.

There was something coming to her and she was waiting for it, fearfully. What was it? She did not know; it was too subtle and elusive to name. But she felt it, creeping out of the sky, reaching toward her through the sounds, the scents, the color that filled the air.

Now her bosom rose and fell tumultuously. She was beginning to recognize   10
this thing that was approaching to possess her, and she was striving to beat it back with her will—as powerless as her two white slender hands would have been.

When she abandoned herself a little whispered word escaped her slightly parted lips. She said it over and over under her breath: "free, free, free!" The vacant stare and the look of terror that had followed it went from her eyes. They stayed keen and bright. Her pulses beat fast, and the coursing blood warmed and relaxed every inch of her body.

She did not stop to ask if it were or were not a monstrous joy that held her. A clear and exalted perception enabled her to dismiss the suggestion as trivial.

She knew that she would weep again when she saw the kind, tender hands folded in death; the face that had never looked save with love upon her, fixed and gray and dead. But she saw beyond that bitter moment a long procession of years to come that would belong to her absolutely. And she opened and spread her arms out to them in welcome.

There would be no one to live for during those coming years; she would live for herself. There would be no powerful will bending hers in that blind persistence with which men and women believe they have a right to impose a private will upon a fellow-creature. A kind intention or a cruel intention made the act seem no less a crime as she looked upon it in that brief moment of illumination. And yet she had loved him—sometimes. Often she had not. What did it matter! What could love, the unsolved mystery, count for in face of this possession of self-assertion which she suddenly recognized as the strongest impulse of her being!   15

"Free! Body and soul free!" she kept whispering.

Josephine was kneeling before the closed door with her lips to the keyhole, imploring for admission. "Louise, open the door! I beg; open the door—you will make yourself ill. What are you doing, Louise? For heaven's sake open the door."

"Go away. I am not making myself ill." No; she was drinking in a very elixir of life through that open window.

Her fancy was running riot along those days ahead of her. Spring days, and summer days, and all sorts of days that would be her own. She breathed a quick prayer that life might be long. It was only yesterday she had thought with a shudder that life might be long.

She arose at length and opened the door to her sister's importunities. There was a feverish triumph in her eyes, and she carried herself unwittingly like a goddess of Victory. She clasped her sister's waist, and together they descended the stairs. Richards stood waiting for them at the bottom.   20

Some one was opening the front door with a latchkey. It was Brently Mallard who entered, a little travel-stained, composedly carrying his grip-sack and umbrella. He had been far from the scene of accident, and did not even know there had been one. He stood amazed at Josephine's piercing cry; at Richards' quick motion to screen him from the view of his wife.

But Richards was too late.

When the doctors came they said she had died of heart disease—of joy that kills.

QUESTIONS

1. What do we learn about Louise Mallard's husband? To what extent has he justified her responses? How are your judgments about him controlled by the context of the story?

2. Analyze the tone of paragraph 5. How does the imagery here (and in the following paragraphs) contradict the grief she should be feeling? How does it seem appropriate for her developing mood? How may this paragraph be interpreted ironically?

3. What is the apparent attitude of the narrator toward the institution of marriage, and what elements of tone make this apparent?

4. What do Louise's sister and Richards have in common? How are your attitudes toward her affected by their understanding of her feelings? How do their attitudes contribute to the irony of the story?

5. Consider the tone of the last paragraph, in which we learn the judgment by the doctors about the cause of Louise's death. What response is invited by the phrasing in this paragraph? What judgment is being made about how men view their importance to women?

6. Describe the development of the plot. What is the conflict, and who or what is the antagonist? Where is the crisis, the climax? How is the conflict resolved?

AMÉRICO PARÉDES (b. 1915)

The Hammon and the Beans   *1963*

Once we lived in one of my grandfather's houses near Fort Jones.° It was just a block from the parade grounds, a big frame house painted a dirty yellow. My mother hated it, especially because of the pigeons that cooed all day about the eaves. They had fleas, she said. But it was a quiet neighborhood at least, too far from the center of town for automobiles and too near for musical, night-roaming drunks.

At this time Jonesville-on-the-Grande was not the thriving little city that it is today. We told off our days by the routine on the post. At six sharp the flag was raised on the parade grounds to the cackling of the bugles, and a field piece thundered out a salute. The sound of the shot bounced away through the morning mist until its echoes worked their way into every corner of town. Jonesville-on-the-Grande woke to the cannon's roar, as if to battle, and the day began.

At eight the whistle from the post laundry sent us children off to school. The whole town stopped for lunch with the noon whistle, and after lunch everybody went back to work when the post laundry said that it was one o'clock, except for those who could afford to be old-fashioned and took the siesta. The post was the town's clock, you might have said, or like some insistent elder person who was always there to tell you it was time.

At six the flag came down, and we went to watch through the high wire fence that divided the post from the town. Sometimes we joined in the ceremony, standing at salute until the sound of the cannon made us jump. That must have been when we had just studied about George Washington in school, or recited "The Song of Marion's Men"° about Marion the Fox and the British cavalry that chased him up and down the broad Santee. But at other times we stuck out our tongues and jeered at the soldiers. Perhaps the night before we had hung at the edges of a group of old men and listened to tales about Aniceto Pizaña and the "border troubles,"° as the local paper still called them when it referred to them gingerly in passing.

Fort Jones: The setting of Fort Jones and Jonesville-on-the-Grande in Texas is fictional. The story takes place in the mid-1920s, one of the most turbulent periods of Mexican history and only a few years after the deaths of two of the greatest heroes of the Mexican revolution— Pancho Villa (1877–1923) and Emiliano Zapata (ca. 1879–1919).

"*Song of Marion's Men*": A poem by William Cullen Bryant (1794–1878) about Colonel Francis Marion (ca. 1732–1795), who was a leader of irregular guerilla forces in South Carolina during the Revolutionary War. Because of his hit-and-run tactics, involving his hiding in the swamps near the "broad Santee" river in South Carolina, Marion was nicknamed the "Swamp Fox."

border troubles: The most serious border incidents occurred in 1916, when Pancho Villa was responsible for deaths of Americans on both sides of the border. He made repeated raids into New Mexico and Texas.

It was because of the border troubles, ten years or so before, that the soldiers   5
had come back to old Fort Jones. But we did not hate them for that; we admired
them even, at least sometimes. But when we were thinking about the border troubles
instead of Marion the Fox we hooted them and the flag they were lowering, which
for the moment was theirs alone, just as we would have jeered an opposing ball
team, in a friendly sort of way. On these occasions even Chonita would join in
the mockery, though she usually ran home at the stroke of six. But whether we
taunted or saluted, the distant men in khaki uniforms went about their motions
without noticing us at all.

The last word from the post came in the night when a distant bugle blew.
At nine it was all right because all the lights were on. But sometimes I heard it at
eleven when everything was dark and still, and it made me feel that I was all
alone in the world. I would even doubt that I was me, and that put me in such a
fright that I felt like yelling out just to make sure I was really there. But next
morning the sun shone and life began all over again. With its whistles and cannon
shots and bugles blowing. And so we lived, we and the post, side by side with the
wire fence in between.

The wandering soldiers whom the bugle called home at night did not wander
in our neighborhood, and none of us ever went into Fort Jones. None except
Chonita. Every evening when the flag came down she would leave off playing
and go down towards what was known as the "lower" gate of the post, the one
that opened not on Main Street but against the poorest part of town. She went
into the grounds and to the mess halls and pressed her nose against the screens
and watched the soldiers eat. They sat at long tables calling to each other through
food-stuffed mouths.

"Hey bud, pass the coffee!"

"Give me the ham!"

"Yeah, give me the beans!"   10

After the soldiers were through the cooks came out and scolded Chonita,
and then they gave her packages with things to eat.

Chonita's mother did our washing, in gratefulness—as my mother put it—
for the use of a vacant lot of my grandfather's which was a couple of blocks down
the street. On the lot was an old one-room shack which had been a shed long
ago, and this Chonita's father had patched up with flattened-out pieces of tin. He
was a laborer. Ever since the end of the border troubles there had been a development
boom in the Valley, and Chonita's father was getting his share of the good times.
Clearing brush and building irrigation ditches he sometimes pulled down as much
as six dollars a week. He drank a good deal of it up, it was true. But corn was
just a few cents a bushel in those days. He was the breadwinner, you might say,
while Chonita furnished the luxuries.

Chonita was a poet too. I had just moved into the neighborhood when a
boy came up to me and said, "Come on! Let's go hear Chonita make a speech."

She was already on top of the alley fence when we got there, a scrawny
little girl of about nine, her bare dirty feet clinging to the fence almost like hands.
A dozen other kids were there below her, waiting. Some were boys I knew at
school; five or six were her younger brothers and sisters.

"Speech! Speech!" they all cried. "Let Chonita make a speech! Talk in English,   15
Chonita!"

They were grinning and nudging each other except for her brothers and sisters, who looked up at her with proud serious faces. She gazed out beyond us all with a grand, distant air and then she spoke.

"Give me the hammon and the beans!" she yelled. "Give me the hammon and the beans!"

She leaped off the fence and everybody cheered and told her how good it was and how she could talk English better than the teachers at the grammar school.

I thought it was a pretty poor joke. Every evening almost, they would make her get up on the fence and yell, "Give me the hammon and the beans!" And everybody would cheer and make her think she was talking English. As for me, I would wait there until she got it over with so we could play at something else. I wondered how long it would be before they got tired of it all. I never did find out because just about that time I got the chills and fever, and when I got up and around Chonita wasn't there anymore.

In later years I thought of her a lot, especially during the thirties when I   20
was growing up. Those years would have been just made for her. Many's the time I have seen her in my mind's eyes, in the picket lines demanding not bread, not cake, but the hammon and the beans. But it didn't work out that way.

One night Doctor Zapata came into our kitchen through the back door. He set his bag on the table and said to my father, who had opened the door for him, "Well, she is dead."

My father flinched. "What was it?" he asked.

The doctor had gone to the window and he stood with his back to us, looking out toward the light of Fort Jones. "Pneumonia, flu, malnutrition, worms, the evil eye," he said without turning around. "What the hell difference does it make?"

"I wish I had known how sick she was," my father said in a very mild tone. "Not that it's really my affair, but I wish I had."

The doctor snorted and shook his head.   25

My mother came in and I asked her who was dead. She told me. It made me feel strange but I did not cry. My mother put her arm around my shoulders. "She is in Heaven now," she said. "She is happy."

I shrugged her arm away and sat down in one of the kitchen chairs.

"They're like animals," the doctor was saying. He turned round suddenly and his eyes glistened in the light. "Do you know what that brute of a father was doing when I left? He was laughing! Drinking and laughing with his friends."

"There's no telling what the poor man feels," my mother said.

My father made a deprecatory gesture. "It wasn't his daughter anyway."   30

"No?" the doctor said. He sounded interested.

"This is the woman's second husband," my father explained. "First one died before the girl was born, shot and hanged from a mesquite limb. He was working too close to the tracks the day the Olmito train was derailed."

"You know what?" the doctor said. "In classical times they did things better. Take Troy, for instance. After they stormed the city they grabbed the babies by the heels and dashed them against the wall. That was more humane."

My father smiled. "You sound very radical. You sound just like your relative down there in Morelos."°

"No relative of mine," the doctor said. "I'm a conservative, the son of a   35
conservative, and you know that I wouldn't be here except for that little detail."

Morelos: the home state of Zapata.

"Habit," my father said. "Pure habit, pure tradition. You're a radical at heart."

"It depends on how you define radicalism," the doctor answered. "People tend to use words too loosely. A dentist could be called a radical, I suppose. He pulls up things by the roots."

My father chuckled.

"Any bandit in Mexico nowadays can give himself a political label," the doctor went on, "and that makes him respectable. He's a leader of the people."

"Take Villa, now—" my father began.   40

"Villa was a different type of man," the doctor broke in.

"I don't see any difference."

The doctor came over to the table and sat down. "Now look at it this way," he began, his finger in front of my father's face. My father threw back his head and laughed.

"You'd better go to bed and rest," my mother told me. "You're not completely well, you know."

So I went to bed, but I didn't go to sleep, not right away. I lay there for a   45
long time while behind my darkened eyelids Emiliano Zapata's cavalry charged down to the broad Santee, where there were grave men with hoary hairs.° I was still awake at eleven when the cold voice of the bugle went gliding in and out of the dark like something that couldn't find its way back to wherever it had been. I thought of Chonita in Heaven, and I saw her in her torn and dirty dress, with a pair of bright wings attached, flying round and round like a butterfly shouting, "Give me the hammon and the beans!"

Then I cried. And whether it was the bugle, or whether it was Chonita or what, to this day I do not know. But cry I did, and I felt much better after that.

Grave men with hoary hairs: Cf. lines 49–52 of Bryant's "Song of Marion's Men:"

> Grave Men there are by broad Santee,
> Grave men with hoary hairs;
> Their hearts are all with Marion,
> For Marion are their prayers.

QUESTIONS

1. How does Parédes establish the setting of the story? What is the significance of the fort? Of the "dirty yellow" paint? Of the vacant lot and the shack?

2. What is the point of view in the story? Who is the narrator? About how old was the narrator when the events related in the story occurred? About how old is the narrator as he or she tells the story? What effect is produced by this difference in age?

3. Is Chonita a round or flat character? Dynamic or static? Individual or representative? To what extent do the author's choices about this character allow her to work as a symbol or representative of a whole ethnic group?

4. What is the tone of the story (some possibilities: joyful, sorrowful, ironic, cynical, resigned, bitter, resentful)? What techniques does Parédes use to control the tone?

5. To what extent does the characterization of Doctor Zapata help to control

the tone? How does the doctor's own attitude toward Chonita's death and the words he uses to announce it help to control the tone?

6. Describe the concern in the story with political, social, and broadly human problems. How does the tale of Chonita's brief life and her death fit into the larger sociopolitical framework of the story?

7. Describe the irony of the situation in which the Mexican-American children learn in school about Washington, the American Revolutionary War, and the guerilla tactics of Marion, but seem to be taught nothing about the political movements represented by Villa and Zapata.

8. Near the end of Bryant's "Song of Marion's Men," the following four lines appear:

And lovely ladies greet our band [i.e., of soldiers]
With kindliest welcoming,
And smiles like those of summer,
And tears like those of spring.

—lines 53–56

Contrast the women of these lines with the narrator's vision of Chonita in heaven. How might this vision affect the narrator's thoughts about the meaning of Chonita's life in subsequent years (he says that he thought about her many times in the 1930's)?

JOHN COLLIER (1901–1980)

The Chaser   *1940*

Alan Austen, as nervous as a kitten, went up certain dark and creaky stairs in the neighborhood of Pell Street, and peered about for a long time on the dim landing before he found the name he wanted written obscurely on one of the doors.

He pushed open this door, as he had been told to do, and found himself in a tiny room, which contained no furniture but a plain kitchen table, a rocking-chair, and an ordinary chair. On one of the dirty buff-coloured walls were a couple of shelves, containing in all perhaps a dozen bottles and jars.

An old man sat in the rocking-chair, reading a newspaper. Alan, without a word, handed him the card he had been given. "Sit down, Mr. Austen," said the old man very politely. "I am glad to make your acquaintance."

"Is it true," asked Alan, "that you have a certain mixture that has—er—quite extraordinary effects?"

"My dear sir," replied the old man, "my stock in trade is not very large—I don't deal in laxatives and teething mixtures—but such as it is, it is varied. I think nothing I sell has effects which could be precisely described as ordinary."

"Well, the fact is . . ." began Alan.

"Here, for example," interrupted the old man, reaching for a bottle from the shelf. "Here is a liquid as colourless as water, almost tasteless, quite imperceptible in coffee, wine, or any other beverage. It is also quite imperceptible to any known method of autopsy."

5

"Do you mean it is a poison?" cried Alan, very much horrified.

"Call it a glove-cleaner if you like," said the old man indifferently. "Maybe it will clean gloves. I have never tried. One might call it a life-cleaner. Lives need cleaning sometimes."

"I want nothing of that sort," said Alan.   10

"Probably it is just as well," said the old man. "Do you know the price of this? For one teaspoonful, which is sufficient, I ask five thousand dollars. Never less. Not a penny less."

"I hope all your mixtures are not as expensive," said Alan apprehensively.

"Oh dear, no," said the old man. "It would be no good charging that sort of price for a love potion, for example. Young people who need a love potion very seldom have five thousand dollars. Otherwise they would not need a love potion."

"I am glad to hear that," said Alan.

"I look at it like this," said the old man. "Please a customer with one article,   15
and he will come back when he needs another. Even if it *is* more costly. He will save up for it, if necessary."

"So," said Alan, "you really do sell love potions?"

"If I did not sell love potions," said the old man, reaching for another bottle, "I should not have mentioned the other matter to you. It is only when one is in a position to oblige that one can afford to be so confidential."

"And these potions," said Alan. "They are not just—just—er—"

"Oh, no," said the old man. "Their effects are permanent, and extended far beyond the mere casual impulse. But they include it. Oh, yes, they include it. Bountifully, insistently. Everlastingly."

"Dear me!" said Alan, attempting a look of scientific detachment. "How very   20
interesting!"

"But consider the spiritual side," said the old man.

"I do, indeed," said Alan.

"For indifference," said the old man, "they substitute devotion. For scorn, adoration. Give one tiny measure of this to the young lady—its flavour is imperceptible in orange juice, soup, or cocktails—and however gay and giddy she is, she will change altogether. She will want nothing but solitude and you."

"I can hardly believe it," said Alan. "She is so fond of parties."

"She will not like them any more," said the old man. "She will be afraid of   25
the pretty girls you may meet."

"She will actually be jealous?" cried Alan in a rapture. "Of me?"

"Yes, she will want to be everything to you."

"She is, already. Only she doesn't care about it."

"She will, when she has taken this. She will care intensely. You will be her sole interest in life."

"Wonderful!" cried Alan.   30

"She will want to know all you do," said the old man. "All that has happened to you during the day. Every word of it. She will want to know what you are thinking about, why you smile suddenly, why you are looking sad."

"That is love!" cried Alan.

"Yes," said the old man. "How carefully she will look after you! She will never allow you to be tired, to sit in a draught, to neglect your food. If you are an hour late, she will be terrified. She will think you are killed, or that some siren has caught you."

"I can hardly imagine Diana like that!" cried Alan, overwhelmed with joy.

"You will not have to use your imagination," said the old man. "And, by   35
the way, since there are always sirens, if by any chance you *should*, later on, slip a little, you need not worry. She will forgive you, in the end. She will be terribly hurt, of course, but she will forgive you—in the end."

"That will not happen," said Alan fervently.

"Of course not," said the old man. "But, if it did, you need not worry. She would never divorce you. Oh, no! And, of course, she will never give you the least, the very least, grounds for—uneasiness."

"And how much," said Alan, "is this wonderful mixture?"

"It is not as dear," said the old man, "as the glove-cleaner, or life-cleaner, as I sometimes call it. No. That is five thousand dollars, never a penny less. One has to be older than you are, to indulge in that sort of thing. One has to save up for it."

"But the love potion?" said Alan.   40

"Oh, that," said the old man, opening the drawer in the kitchen table, and taking out a tiny, rather dirty-looking phial. "That is just a dollar."

"I can't tell you how grateful I am," said Alan, watching him fill it.

"I like to oblige," said the old man. "Then customers come back, later in life, when they are better off, and want more expensive things. Here you are. You will find it very effective."

"Thank you again," said Alan. "Good-bye."

"Au revoir," said the old man.   45

QUESTIONS

1. Summarize the plot of this story. What are the qualities of the poison that the old man tells Austen about? What are the powers of the love potion? What is the connection between the love potion and the "spot remover"?

2. Are the two characters in this story static or dynamic? Round or flat? Representative or individual? To what extent do these choices help focus the story and control the tone?

3. How is the setting of the story described? What is the old man's apartment like? How does this description contribute to the mood of the story and the characterization of the old man?

4. To what extent do the words of the story control the tone and attitude? What specific words help us form an attitude toward Alan Austen? Toward the old man?

5. To what extent is the story ironic? What do we and the old man know that Alan Austen doesn't?

6. How is the title of the story ironic? What is a "chaser"? How are the old man's last words in the story ironic?

7. What point does this story make about love? About youth? About human desire? How can the story be taken as a commentary about the need for

developing love relationships that preserve individuality as well as romantic commitment?

MARGARET ATWOOD   (b. 1939)

Rape Fantasies   1977

The way they're going on about it in the magazines you'd think it was just invented, and not only that but it's something terrific, like a vaccine for cancer. They put it in capital letters on the front cover, and inside they have these questionnaires like the ones they used to have about whether you were a good enough wife or an endomorph or an ectomorph, remember that? with the scoring upside down on page 73, and then these numbered do-it-yourself dealies, you know? RAPE, TEN THINGS TO DO ABOUT IT, like it was ten new hairdos or something. I mean, what's so new about it?

So at work they all have to talk about it because no matter what magazine you open, there it is, staring you right between the eyes, and they're beginning to have it on the television, too. Personally I'd prefer a June Allyson° movie anytime but they don't make them any more and they don't even have them that much on the Late Show. For instance, day before yesterday, that would be Wednesday, thank god it's Friday as they say, we were sitting around in the women's lunch room—the *lunch* room, I mean you'd think you could get some peace and quiet in there—and Chrissy closes up the magazine she's been reading and says, "How about it, girls, do you have rape fantasies?"

The four of us were having our game of bridge the way we always do, and I had a bare twelve points counting the singleton with not that much of a bid in anything. So I said one club, hoping Sondra would remember about the one club convention, because the time before when I used that she thought I really meant clubs and she bid us up to three, and all I had was four little ones with nothing higher than a six, and we went down two and on top of that we were vulnerable. She is not the world's best bridge player. I mean, neither am I but there's a limit.

Darlene passed but the damage was done, Sondra's head went round like it was on ball bearings and she said, "*What* fantasies?"

"Rape fantasies," Chrissy said. She's a receptionist and she looks like one; she's pretty but cool as a cucumber, like she's been painted all over with nail polish, if you know what I mean. Varnished. "It says here all women have rape fantasies."

"For Chrissake, I'm eating an egg sandwich," I said, "and I bid one club and Darlene passed."

"You mean, like some guy jumping you in an alley or something," Sondra said. She was eating her lunch, we all eat our lunches during the game, and she bit into a piece of that celery she always brings and started to chew away on it with this thoughtful expression in her eyes and I knew we might as well pack it in as far as the game was concerned.

"Yeah, sort of like that," Chrissy said. She was blushing a little, you could see it even under her makeup.

June Allyson: Actress (b. 1917) known for her bright smile and scratchy voice. She specialized in "sweet" movies and musical roles, 1943–1959, and still appears in TV commercials.

"I don't think you should go out alone at night," Darlene said, "you put yourself in a position," and I may have been mistaken but she was looking at me. She's the oldest, she's forty-one though you wouldn't know it and neither does she, but I looked it up in the employees' file. I like to guess a person's age and then look it up to see if I'm right. I let myself have an extra pack of cigarettes if I am, though I'm trying to cut down. I figure it's harmless as long as you don't tell. I mean, not everyone has access to that file, it's more or less confidential. But it's all right if I tell you, I don't expect you'll ever meet her, though you never know, it's a small world. Anyway.

"For *heaven's* sake, it's only *Toronto*," Greta said. She worked in Detroit for   10
three years and she never lets you forget it, it's like she thinks she's a war hero or something, we should all admire her just for the fact that she's still walking this earth, though she was really living in Windsor° the whole time, she just worked in Detroit. Which for me doesn't really count. It's where you sleep, right?

"Well, do you?" Chrissy said. She was obviously trying to tell us about hers but she wasn't about to go first, she's cautious, that one.

"I certainly don't," Darlene said, and she wrinkled up her nose, like this, and I had to laugh. "I think it's disgusting." She's divorced, I read that in the file too, she never talks about it. It must've been years ago anyway. She got up and went over to the coffee machine and turned her back on us as though she wasn't going to have anything more to do with it.

"Well," Greta said. I could see it was going to be between her and Chrissy. They're both blondes, I don't mean that in a bitchy way but they do try to outdress each other. Greta would like to get out of Filing, she'd like to be a receptionist too so she could meet more people. You don't meet much of anyone in Filing except other people in Filing. Me, I don't mind it so much, I have outside interests.

"Well," Greta said, "I sometimes think about, you know my apartment? It's got this little balcony, I like to sit out there in the summer and I have a few plants out there. I never bother that much about locking the door to the balcony, it's one of those sliding glass ones, I'm on the eighteenth floor for heaven's sake, I've got a good view of the lake and the CN Tower and all. But I'm sitting around one night in my housecoat, watching TV with my shoes off, you know how you do, and I see this guy's feet, coming down past the window, and the next thing you know he's standing on the balcony, he's let himself down by a rope with a hook on the end of it from the floor above, that's the nineteenth, and before I can even get up off the chesterfield he's inside the apartment. He's all dressed in black with black gloves on"—I knew right away what show she got the black gloves off because I saw the same one—"and then he, well, you know."

"You know what?" Chrissy said, but Greta said, "And afterwards he tells   15
me that he goes all over the outside of the apartment building like that, from one floor to another, with his rope and his hook . . . and then he goes out to the balcony and tosses his rope, and he climbs up it and disappears."

"Just like Tarzan," I said, but nobody laughed.

"Is that all?" Chrissy said. "Don't you ever think about, well, I think about being in the bathtub, with no clothes on . . ."

"So who takes a bath in their clothes?" I said, you have to admit it's stupid

---

Windsor: City south of Detroit, noted as the only place where any portion of Canada is south of the United States.

when you come to think of it, but she just went on, ". . . with lots of bubbles, what I use is Vitabath, it's more expensive but it's so relaxing, and my hair pinned up, and the door opens and this fellow's standing there. . . ."

"How'd he get in?" Greta said.

"Oh, I don't know, through a window or something. Well, I can't very well   20
get out of the bathtub, the bathroom's too small and besides he's blocking the doorway, so I just *lie* there, and he starts to very slowly take his own clothes off, and then he gets into the bathtub with me."

"Don't you scream or anything?" said Darlene. She'd come back with her cup of coffee, she was getting really interested. "I'd scream like bloody murder."

"Who'd hear me?" Chrissy said. "Besides, all the articles say it's better not to resist, that way you don't get hurt."

"Anyway you might get bubbles up your nose," I said, "from the deep breathing," and I swear all four of them looked at me like I was in bad taste, like I'd insulted the Virgin Mary or something. I mean, I don't see what's wrong with a little joke now and then. Life's too short, right?

"Listen," I said, "those aren't *rape* fantasies. I mean, you aren't getting *raped*, it's just some guy you haven't met formally who happens to be more attractive than Derek Cummins"—he's the Assistant Manager, he wears elevator shoes or at any rate they have these thick soles and he has this funny way of talking, we call him Derek Duck—"and you have a good time. Rape is when they've got a knife or something and you don't want to."

"So what about you, Estelle," Chrissy said, she was miffed because I laughed   25
at her fantasy, she thought I was putting her down. Sondra was miffed too, by this time she'd finished her celery and she wanted to tell about hers, but she hadn't got in fast enough.

"All right, let me tell you one," I said "I'm walking down this dark street at night and this fellow comes up and grabs my arm. Now it so happens that I have a plastic lemon in my purse, you know how it always says you should carry a plastic lemon in your purse? I don't really do it, I tried it once but the darn thing leaked all over my chequebook, but in this fantasy I have one, and I say to him, "You're intending to rape me, right?" and he nods, so I open my purse to get the plastic lemon, and I can't find it! My purse is full of all this junk, Kleenex and cigarettes and my change purse and my lipstick and my driver's licence, you know the kind of stuff: so I ask him to hold out his hands, like this, and I pile all this junk into them and down at the bottom there's the plastic lemon, and I can't get the top off. So I hand it to him and he's very obliging, he twists the top off and hands it back to me, and I squirt him in the eye."

I hope you don't think that's too vicious. Come to think of it, it is a bit mean, especially when he was so polite and all.

"*That's* your rape fantasy?" Chrissy says, "I don't believe it."

"She's a card," Darlene says, she and I are the ones that've been here the longest and she never will forget the time I got drunk at the office party and insisted I was going to dance under the table instead of on top of it, I did a sort of Cossack number° but then I hit my head on the bottom of the table—actually

---

Cossack number: A Ukranian folk dance movement performed in a squatting position, with much hand-clapping.

it was a desk—when I went to get up, and I knocked myself out cold. She's decided that's the mark of an original mind and she tells everyone new about it and I'm not sure that's fair. Though I did do it.

"I'm being totally honest," I say. I always am and they know it. There's no   30
point in being anything else, is the way I look at it, and sooner or later the truth will out so you might as well not waste the time, right? "You should hear the one about the Easy-Off Cleaner."

But that was the end of the lunch hour, with one bridge game shot to hell, and the next day we spent most of the time arguing over whether to start a new game or play out the hands we had left over from the day before, so Sondra never did get a chance to tell about her rape fantasy.

It started me thinking though, about my own rape fantasies. Maybe I'm abnormal or something, I mean I have fantasies about handsome strangers coming in through the window too, like Mr. Clean, I wish one would, please god somebody without flat feet and big sweat marks on his shirt, and over five feet five, believe me being tall is a handicap though it's getting better, tall guys are starting to like someone whose nose reaches higher than their belly button. But if you're being totally honest you can't count those as rape fantasies. In a real rape fantasy, what you should feel is this anxiety, like when you think about your apartment building catching on fire and whether you should use the elevator or the stairs or maybe just stick your head under a wet towel, and you try to remember everything you've read about what to do but you can't decide.

For instance, I'm walking along this dark street at night and this short, ugly fellow comes up and grabs my arm, and not only is he ugly, you know, with a sort of puffy nothing face, like those fellows you have to talk to in the bank when your account's overdrawn—of course I don't mean they're all like that—but he's absolutely covered in pimples. So he gets me pinned against the wall, he's short but he's heavy, and he starts to undo himself and the zipper gets stuck. I mean, one of the most significant moments in a girl's life, it's almost like getting married or having a baby or something, and he sticks the zipper.

So I say, kind of disgusted, "Oh for Chrissake," and he starts to cry. He tells me he's never been able to get anything right in his entire life, and this is the last straw, he's going to go jump off a bridge.

"Look," I say, I feel so sorry for him, in my rape fantasies I always end up   35
feeling sorry for the guy, I mean there has to be something *wrong* with them, if it was Clint Eastwood° it'd be different but worse luck it never is. I was the kind of little girl who buried dead robins, know what I mean? It used to drive my mother nuts, she didn't like me touching them, because of the germs I guess. So I say, "Listen, I know how you feel. You really should do something about those pimples, if you got rid of them you'd be quite good looking, honest; then you wouldn't have to go around doing stuff like this. I had them myself once," I say, to comfort him, but in fact I did, and it ends up I give him the name of my old dermatologist, the one I had in high school, that was back in Leamington,° except I used to go to St. Catharine's for the dermatologist. I'm telling you, I was really lonely when

---

Clint Eastwood: born 1930, star of many tough-guy detective and western movies; most famous as "Dirty Harry" (1971).
Leamington: In Ontario on the north shore of Lake Erie, southeast of Windsor.

I first came here; I thought it was going to be such a big adventure and all, but it's a lot harder to meet people in a city. But I guess it's different for a guy.

Or I'm lying in bed with this terrible cold, my face is all swollen up, my eyes are red and my nose is dripping like a leaky tap, and this fellow comes in through the window and *he* has a terrible cold too, it's a new kind of flu that's been going around. So he says, "I'b goig do rabe you"—I hope you don't mind me holding my nose like this but that's the way I imagine it—and he lets out this terrific sneeze, which slows him down a bit, also I'm no object of beauty myself, you'd have to be some kind of pervert to want to rape someone with a cold like mine, it'd be like raping a bottle of LePages mucilage the way my nose is running. He's looking wildly around the room, and I realize it's because he doesn't have a piece of Kleenex! "Id's ride here," I say, and I pass him the Kleenex, god knows why he even bothered to get out of bed, you'd think if you were going to go around climbing in windows you'd wait till you were healthier, right? I mean, that takes a certain amount of energy. So I ask him why doesn't he let me fix him a NeoCitran and scotch, that's what I always take, you still have the cold but you don't feel it, so I do and we end up watching the Late Show together. I mean, they aren't all sex maniacs, the rest of the time they must lead a normal life. I figure they enjoy watching the Late Show just like anybody else.

I do have a scarier one though . . . where the fellow says he's hearing angel voices that're telling him he's got to kill me, you know, you read about things like that all the time in the papers. In this one I'm not in the apartment where I live now, I'm back in my mother's house in Leamington and the fellow's been hiding in the cellar, he grabs my arm when I go downstairs to get a jar of jam and he's got hold of the axe too, out of the garage, that one is really scary. I mean, what do you say to a nut like that?

So I start to shake but after a minute I get control of myself and I say, is he sure the angel voices have got the right person, because I hear the same angel voices and they've been telling me for some time that I'm going to give birth to the reincarnation of St. Anne who in turn has the Virgin Mary and right after that comes Jesus Christ and the end of the world, and he wouldn't want to interfere with that, would he? So he gets confused and listens some more, and then he asks for a sign and I show him my vaccination mark, you can see it's sort of an odd-shaped one, it got infected because I scratched the top off, and that does it, he apologizes and climbs out the coal chute° again, which is how he got in in the first place, and I say to myself there's some advantage in having been brought up a Catholic even though I haven't been to church since they changed the service into English,° it just isn't the same, you might as well be a Protestant. I must write to Mother and tell her to nail up that coal chute, it always has bothered me. Funny, I couldn't tell you at all what this man looks like but I know exactly what kind of shoes he's wearing, because that's the last I see of him, his shoes going up the coal chute, and they're the old-fashioned kind that lace up the ankles, even though he's a young fellow. That's strange, isn't it?

coal chute: Trough for delivering coal from a truck into a basement coal bin. Estelle's remark indicates that the chute was not fastened over the opening to the bin, thus permitting an illegal entry.

into English: In accord with the Second Vatican Council (1962–65), the Latin Mass was replaced by vernacular languages in the late 1960s.

Let me tell you though I really sweat until I see him safely out of there and I go upstairs right away and make myself a cup of tea. I don't think about that one much. My mother always said you shouldn't dwell on unpleasant things and I generally agree with that, I mean, dwelling on them doesn't make them go away. Though not dwelling on them doesn't make them go away either, when you come to think of it.

Sometimes I have these short ones where the fellow grabs my arm but I'm really a Kung-Fu° expert, can you believe it, in real life I'm sure it would just be a conk on the head and that's that, like getting your tonsils out, you'd wake up and it would be all over except for the sore places, and you'd be lucky if your neck wasn't broken or something, I could never even hit the volleyball in gym and a volleyball is fairly large, you know?—and I just go *zap* with my fingers into his eyes and that's it, he falls over, or I flip him against a wall or something. But I could never really stick my fingers in anyone's eyes, could you? It would feel like hot jello and I don't even like cold jello, just thinking about it gives me the creeps. I feel a bit guilty about that one, I mean how would you like walking around knowing someone's been blinded for life because of you?

But maybe it's different for a guy.

The most touching one I have is when the fellow grabs my arm and I say, sad and kind of dignified, "You'd be raping a corpse." That pulls him up short and I explain that I've just found out I have leukaemia and the doctors have only given me a few months to live. That's why I'm out pacing the streets alone at night, I need to think, you know, come to terms with myself. I don't really have leukaemia but in the fantasy I do, I guess I chose that particular disease because a girl in my grade four class died of it, the whole class sent her flowers when she was in the hospital. I didn't understand then that she was going to die and I wanted to have leukaemia too so I could get flowers. Kids are funny, aren't they? Well, it turns out that he has leukaemia himself, and *he* only has a few months to live, that's why he's going around raping people, he's very bitter because he's so young and his life is being taken from him before he's really lived it. So we walk along gently under the street lights, it's spring and sort of misty, and we end up going for coffee, we're happy we've found the only other person in the world who can understand what we're going through, it's almost like fate, and after a while we just sort of look at each other and our hands touch, and he comes back with me and moves into my apartment and we spend our last months together before we die, we just sort of don't wake up in the morning, though I've never decided which one of us gets to die first. If it's him I have to go on and fantasize about the funeral, if it's me I don't have to worry about that, so it just about depends on how tired I am at the time. You may not believe this but sometimes I even start crying. I cry at the end of movies, even the ones that aren't all that sad, so I guess it's the same thing. My mother's like that too.

The funny thing about these fantasies is that the man is always someone I don't know, and the statistics in the magazines, well, most of them anyway, they say it's often someone you do know, at least a little bit, like your boss or something— I mean, it wouldn't be *my* boss, he's over sixty and I'm sure he couldn't rape his way out of a paper bag, poor old thing, but it might be someone like Derek Duck,

40

Kung-Fu: An elaborate self-defense system developed in China, similar to Karate.

in his elevator shoes, perish the thought—or someone you just met, who invites you up for a drink, it's getting so you can hardly be sociable any more, and how are you supposed to meet people if you can't trust them even that basic amount? You can't spend your whole life in the Filing Department or cooped up in your own apartment with all the doors and windows locked and the shades down. I'm not what you would call a drinker but I like to go out now and then for a drink or two in a nice place, even if I am by myself, I'm with Women's Lib on that even though I can't agree with a lot of the other things they say. Like here for instance, the waiters all know me and if anyone, you know, bothers me . . . I don't know why I'm telling you all this, except I think it helps you get to know a person, especially at first, hearing some of the things they think about. At work they call me the office worry wart, but it isn't so much like worrying, it's more like figuring out what you should do in an emergency, like I said before.

Anyway, another thing about it is that there's a lot of conversation, in fact I spend most of my time, in the fantasy that is, wondering what I'm going to say and what he's going to say, I think it would be better if you could get a conversation going. Like, how could a fellow do that to a person he's just had a long conversation with, once you let them know you're human, you have a life too, I don't see how they could go ahead with it, right? I mean, I know it happens but I just don't understand it, that's the part I really don't understand.

QUESTIONS

1. What elements of the various rape fantasies are comic? How is the comedy brought out (e.g., through subject matter, circumstances of description, attitudes and understanding of the characters, comments by the narrator)?

2. What do the various fantasies of the narrator Estelle have in common, and what do they show about her character? How does Atwood control the tone so as to keep Estelle from considering rape as a problem in psychology or criminology?

3. Describe the tone in this story. How does tone affect your perception of Estelle?

4. Consider the tone of the very last paragraph of the story. What is the apparent attitude of Atwood toward the subject? How is it tempered by her attitude toward Estelle?

5. Studies point out that rape is an act of violence rather than sexuality. What do the women around the bridge table do to deflect the seriousness of the potential violence involved?

6. Describe the plot of the story. Who is the protagonist? The antagonist? How is the plot resolved?

WRITING ABOUT TONE

In the prewriting stages of your essay about tone, it is important to note those elements of the work that touch particularly on attitudes or authorial consideration. Thus, for example, you may be studying Collier's "The

Chaser," where it would be necessary to consider whether the story asks too much of the reader: Is the old man's prediction really the horror at the end of the road for all romantic loves? In this respect the story may cause a certain mental squirming. But is this right? Does Collier want the squirming to occur? Perhaps if the question is phrased another way, the tone might be more adequately understood. If Alan Austen is seen to want "overly possessive love" rather than simply "romantic love," the story may seem less disturbing. In seeking answers like this one, you will find that the author has been directing you and guiding your responses; that is, that the author's control over tone is firmly established.

Similar questions apply when you study internal qualities such as style and characterization. Do all the speeches seem right for speaker and situation? Are all descriptions appropriate, all actions believable? If the work is comic, does the writer seem to be involved with the things, characters, situations, language, or objects at which she or he directs laughter? In serious situations, does the work give evidence of pity? Does the writer ask you to lament the human condition? What kind of character is evidenced by the speaker? Is he or she intelligent, friendly, idealistic, realistic? Do any words seem unusual or especially noteworthy, such as dialect, polysyllabic words, foreign words or phrases that the author assumes you know, or especially connotative or emotive words?

Organizing Your Essay

INTRODUCTION. The introduction describes the general situation of the work and the mood or impression that it may leave with you. The central idea should be about the aspect or aspects that you plan to develop in the body, such as that the work leads to cynicism, as in "The Chaser," or the role of comedy in "Rape Fantasies." Or your central idea might be that the diction of the work is designed to portray the life of ordinary people, or to show the pretentiousness of various speakers or characters, or to call upon the reader's ability to visualize experience. Problems connected with interpreting the tone of the work should also be mentioned here. The thesis sentence contains the major aspects to be explored in the body.

BODY. In the body you should examine all aspects bearing on the tone of the work. Some of the things to cover might be these:

1. *Audience, situation, and characters.* Is any person or group directly addressed by the author's voice? What attitude seems to be expressed (love, respect, condescension, confidentiality, confidence, and so on)? What is the basic situation in the work? Do you find irony? If so, what kind is it? What does the irony show about the author's apparent attitudes (optimism or pessimism, for example)? How is the situation controlled to shape your

responses? That is, can actions, situations, or characters be seen as expressions of attitude, or as embodiments of certain favorable or unfavorable ideas or positions? What is the nature of the speaker or persona? Why does the speaker seem to speak exactly as he or she does? How is the speaker's character manipulated to show apparent authorial attitude and to elicit reader response? Does the work promote respect, admiration, dislike, or other feelings about character or situation? How? Through what ways are these feelings made clear?

2. *Descriptions, diction.* Analysis of these is stylistic, but your concern here is to relate style to attitude. Are there any systematic references, such as to colors, sounds, noises, natural scenes, and so on, that collectively reflect an attitude? Do connotative meanings of words control response in any way? Does it seem that special knowledge of any sort is expected of the reader to understand references and words? What is the extent of this knowledge? Do speech or dialect patterns indicate attitudes about speakers or their condition of life? Are speech patterns normal and standard, or slang or substandard? What is the effect of these patterns? Are there unusual or particularly noteworthy expressions? If so, what attitudes do these show? Does the author use verbal irony? To what effect?

3. *Humor.* Is the work funny? How funny, how intense? How is the humor achieved? Does the humor develop out of incongruous situations or language, or both? Is there an underlying basis of attack in the humor, or are the objects of laughter still respected or even loved despite having humor directed against them?

4. *Ideas.* Ideas may be advocated, defended mildly, or attacked. Which do you seem to have in the work you have been studying? How does the author make his or her attitude clear—directly, by statement, or indirectly, through understatement, overstatement, or the language of a character? In what ways does the work assume a common ground of assent between author and reader? That is, are there apparently common assumptions about religious views, political ideas, moral and behavioral standards, and so on? Are these commonly assumed ideas readily acceptable, or is any concession needed by the reader to approach the work? (For example, a major subject of "First Confession" is the proper preparation for a child about to take first confession in the Catholic faith. Not everyone can grant the importance of this action of faith, but even an irreligious reader might find common ground in the psychological situation of the story, or in the desire to learn as much as possible about human beings.)

5. *Unique characteristics of the work.* Each work has unique properties that may contribute to the tone. Thus, Collier's "The Chaser," is developed almost entirely through the dialogue between the old man and Austen. The tone of the story is therefore to be perceived by an awareness of the attitudes of each of the participants, almost as though the story is a drama. A reversal of roles is found in Glaspell's "A Jury of Her Peers" (Chapter 2), in which the focus is on how the two women are better detectives

than the husbands who are searching the farmhouse. Without them, we would have no story; the author invites us to perceive the irony of this fact. In other stories there might be some recurring word or theme that seems special. For example, Mark Twain in "Luck" (Chapter 7) develops a passage centering on the word "blunder," and thereby makes his attitude clear about the boob hero, Scoresby. When you study any story, be alert for such special and unique things to bring out in your essay.

CONCLUSION.   The conclusion may summarize the main points of the essay and from there go on to any concluding thoughts about the tone of the work. Redefinitions, explanations, or afterthoughts might belong here, together with reinforcing ideas in support of earlier points. If there are any personal thoughts, any changes of mind, or any awakening awarenesses, a brief account of these would also be appropriate here as long as you demonstrate that they arise out of your study and writing for the assignment. Finally, you might mention some other major aspect of the work's tone that you have not developed in the body of the essay.

SAMPLE ESSAY

The Situational and Verbal Irony of Collier's "The Chaser"*

[1] John Collier's "The Chaser" is based on the situational irony of the unreal hope of youth as opposed to the extreme disillusion of age and experience. Collier builds the brief story almost entirely in dialogue between a young man, Alan Austen, who is deeply in love and wants to possess his sweetheart entirely, and an unnamed old man who believes in a life free of romantic involvement. The situation reflects disillusionment so completely that the story may in fact be called cynical.° This attitude is made plain by the situation, the old man, and the use of double meaning.□

[2] The situation between the two men establishes the story's dominant tone of cynicism. Austen, the young man full of illusions and unreal expectations about love, has come to the old man to buy a love potion so that his sweetheart, Diana, will love him with slavelike adoration. Collier makes it clear that the old man has seen many young men like Austen in the grips of romantic desire before, and he therefore knows that their possessive love will eventually bore and anger them. He knows, because he has already seen these disillusioned customers return to buy the "chaser," which is a deadly, untraceable poison, so that they could kill the women for whom they previously bought the love potion. Thus Collier creates the ironic situation of the story—the beginning of an inevitable process in which Austen, like other young men before him, are made to appear so unrealistic and self-defeating that their enthusiastic passion will someday change into hate and murderousness.

* See page 311 for this story.
° Central idea.
□ Thesis sentence.

[3]   The sales method used by the old man reveals his cynical understanding of men like Austen. Collier makes clear that the old man knows why Austen has come: Before showing his love potion, the old man describes the untraceable poison, which he calls a "glove cleaner" or "life cleaner." His aim is actually to sell the expensive poison by using the love potion as inexpensive bait. Thus we see the old man's art of manipulation, for even though Austen is at the moment horrified by the poison, the seed has been planted in his mind. He will always know, when his love for Diana changes, that he will have the choice of "cleaning" his life. This unscrupulous sales method effectively corrupts Austen in advance. Such a calculation on the old man's part is grimly cynical.

[4]   Supporting the tone of cynicism in the old man's sales technique is his use of double meaning. For example, his concluding words, "Au revoir" (that is, "until I see you again"), carry an ironic double meaning. On the one hand, the words conventionally mean "goodbye," but on the other, they suggest that the old man expects a future meeting when Austen will return to buy the poison to kill Diana. The old man's acknowledgement of Austen's gratitude shows the same ironic double edge. He says,

> I like to oblige. . . . Then customers come back, later in life, when they are better off, and want more expensive things.

Clearly the "expensive" thing is "the chaser," the undetectable poison. Through such ironic speeches, the old man is politely but cynically telling Austen that his love will not last and that it will eventually bore, irritate, and then torment him to the point where he will want to murder Diana rather than to continue living with her potion-induced possessiveness.

[5]   Before "The Chaser" is dismissed as cynical, however, we should note that Austen's ideas about love must inevitably produce just such cynicism. The old man's descriptions of the total enslavement that Austen has dreamed about would leave no breathing room for either Austen or Diana. This sort of love, because it excludes everything else in life, suffocates rather than pleases. It is normal to wish freedom from such psychological imprisonment, even if the prison is of one's own making. Under these conditions, the cynical tone of "The Chaser" suggests that the desire to be totally possessing and possessed—to "want nothing but solitude" and the loved one—can lead only to disaster for both man and woman. The old man's cynicism and the young man's desire suggest the need for an ideal of love that permits interchange, individuality, and understanding. Even though this better ideal is not described anywhere in the story, it is compatible with Collier's situational irony. Thus, cynical as the story unquestionably is, it does not exclude an idealism of tolerant and more human love.

Commentary on the Essay

This essay presents a way in which you can write about a story of dominating pessimism and cynicism without giving in to the underlying negative situational irony. Therefore the essay shows how understanding tone aids objective literary judgment.

The introductory paragraph indicates that the aspect of tone to be discussed will be an ironic situation—youthful but unrealistic hope in the context of aged cynicism. The thesis sentence indicates that the body of the essay will deal with (1) this situation and how it is related to (2) the sales method of a major character—the old man—and (3) his speeches containing double meaning.

Paragraph 2 establishes the situational irony by describing the desires of Austen and the cynical attitude of the old man. In paragraph 3 the topic is the sinister manipulation of Austen as a result of the old man's skillful and subtle salesmanship. By stressing that the old man plants the seeds of corruption in Austen, this paragraph continues the topic of the tone of cynicism which is the thematic basis of the essay. The subject of paragraph 4, the last in the body of the essay, is Collier's use of double meaning in the speeches of the old man to emphasize the idea that Austen will someday want to kill his wife.

The concluding paragraph is reflective. In view of the cynical tone of the story, this paragraph suggests that a more realistic and optimistic attitude about love is not only possible but necessary—a conclusion that is not stated in the story, but which nevertheless provides a basis for judging the characters.

WRITING TOPICS FOR CHAPTER 8

1. Compare the attitudes toward widowhood as reflected in the tone of these stories: Porter's "The Jilting of Granny Weatherall," Allende's "The Judge's Wife," and Chopin's "The Story of an Hour."

2. Write an essay that compares and contrasts the modes of presentation of Mrs. Mallard in "The Story of an Hour" and Mrs. Wright in "A Jury of Her Peers." How does the presentation control your understanding of their conditions and your attitudes toward them?

3. Consider a short story in which the narrator is the central character (for example, "Rape Fantasies," "A & P," "First Confession," "Everyday Use," "Blue Winds Dancing," "I Stand Here Ironing"). Write an essay showing how the language of the characters establishes your attitudes toward them (that is, your sympathy for them, your interest in their narratives, your feelings toward the other characters and what they do). Be sure to emphasize the relationship between their language and your responses.

4. Assume that you are writing a story involving, say, a student, a supervisor, or a politician. Write a fragment treating your character with dramatic irony; that is, your character thinks he or she knows all the details about a situation, but really does not (e.g., a woman declares her interest in a man without realizing that he is engaged to another woman, or the supervisor expresses distrust in a person who is one of the best workers in the firm). What action, words, and situations do you choose to make your irony clear?

9

Symbolism and Allegory: Keys to Extended Meaning

SYMBOLISM

Symbolism and *allegory* are modes of literary expression that are designed to extend meaning. **Symbolism** is derived from a Greek word meaning "to throw together" (*syn*, together, and *ballein*, to throw). In literature, a symbol pulls or draws together (1) a specific thing with (2) ideas, values, persons, or ways of life, in a direct relationship that otherwise would not be apparent. A symbol might also be regarded as a substitute for the elements being signified, much as the flag stands for the ideals of the nation.

In short stories and other types of literature, a symbol is usually a person, thing, place, action, situation, or even thought. It possesses its own reality and meaning and may function at the normal level of reality within a story. There is often a topical or integral relationship between the symbol and things it stands for, but a symbol may also have no apparent connection and therefore may be considered arbitrary. What is important, however, is that the symbol points beyond itself to greater and more complex meaning. When a symbol is introduced, like a key opening a lock, it signifies a specific combination of attitudes, a sustained constancy of meaning, and the potential for wide-ranging application. A symbol might appear over and over again in the same story, yet it always maintains the same meaning. Thus you might think of a symbol as a constant against a background of variables, like a theme without variations.

To determine whether something in a story is symbolic, we must decide if it consistently refers beyond itself to a significant idea, emotion, or quality. For example, the ancient mythological character Sisyphus may be considered as a symbol because he is consistently linked with specific ideas. According to legend, he is doomed in the underworld to roll a large boulder up a high hill forever. Just as he gets it to the top, it rolls down, and he is fated to roll it up again, and again, and again, because the rock always rolls back as he gets it to the top. His plight may be seen as a symbol of the human condition: A person rarely if ever completes anything. Work must always be done over and over in every generation, and the same problems confront humanity in each age without any final solution. In the light of such infinitely fruitless effort, life seems to have little meaning. Nevertheless there is hope. People who meet frustration like that experienced by Sisyphus remain involved and active in their work and even if they are never more than temporarily successful, they may find meaning in their lives. A writer using Sisyphus as a symbol would want us to understand these ideas as a result of the reference. Symbolism, as you can see, can be a conventionalized shorthand form of communication.

There are other symbols like Sisyphus that are generally or universally recognized, and authors referring to them rely on this common understanding. These types of symbols are sometimes called **cultural** or **universal** symbols. They embody ideas or emotions that the writer and the reader share in common as a result of their social and cultural heritage. When using these symbols, a writer does not have to take the time to invest objects or people with symbolic resonance within the story; she or he can simply assume that the reader knows what the symbol represents. Thus, water, which is the substance in the sacrament of baptism, is acknowledged to be a symbol of life. When water spouts up in a fountain, it may symbolize optimism (as upwelling, bubbling life). A stagnant pool may symbolize life being polluted or diminished. In terms of psychology, water is often understood as a reference to sexuality. Thus, lovers may meet by a quiet lake, a cascading waterfall, a murmuring stream, a wide river, or a stormy sea. The condition of the water in each instance may be interpreted as a symbol of the lovers' romantic relationship. Another generally recognized universal symbol is the serpent, which is often used to represent the Devil, or simply evil. The original symbol is in the Book of Genesis (3:1–7), where Satan in the form of a serpent tempts Eve in the Garden of Eden. Drawing on this story, Hawthorne in "Young Goodman Brown" describes a walking stick that "bore the likeness of a great black snake," in this way instantly evoking the idea of Satanic evil. However, because the stick "might almost be seen to twist and wriggle itself like a living serpent," it may also symbolize human tendencies to see evil where it does not exist.

Objects and descriptions that are not universally recognized as symbols can be developed as symbols only within an individual work. These types of symbols may be termed **private, authorial,** or **contextual** symbols. Unlike universal symbols, these are not derived from common historical, cultural, or religious ground but gain their symbolic meaning within the *context* of the specific work of fiction. For example, the jug of beer carried by Jackie's grandmother in O'Connor's "First Confession" is one of the things that symbolize the grandmother's peasantlike and boorish habits. Similarly, the chrysanthemums tended by Elisa in Steinbeck's "The Chrysanthemums" seem at first nothing more than deeply prized flowers. As the story progresses, however, the flowers gain symbolic significance. The traveling tinsmith's apparent interest in them is the wedge he uses to get a small mending job from Elisa. Her description of the care needed in planting and tending the flowers suggests that they signify her qualities of kindness, love, orderliness, femininity, and, ultimately, her maternal instincts. When, at the end of the story, the flowers are seen dumped at the side of the road, we may conclude that her values have also been dumped and that she has been used and deceived. In short, the chrysanthemums are a major symbol in the story. If you were to encounter references to porter or chrysanthemums in a context other than "First Confession" and "The Chrysanthemums," however, they would not necessarily be symbolic.

In determining whether a particular object or person in a story is a symbol, you need to make decisions based on your judgment of its total significance. If it appears to be of major importance, you can claim it has symbolic value as long as you can show its scope and sustained reference beyond itself. Thus, at the end of Welty's "A Worn Path," Phoenix plans to buy a toy windmill for her sick grandson. The windmill is a small thing, and she will spend all her money for it. It will break soon under constant use, like her life and that of her grandson, but buying it is her attempt to give the boy a little pleasure despite her poverty and the hopelessness of her life. For all these reasons it is justifiable to interpret the windmill as a symbol of her strong character, generous nature, and pathetic existence.

ALLEGORY

Allegory is like symbolism in that both use one thing to refer to something else. The term is derived from the Greek word *allégorein*, which means "to speak so as to imply other than what is said." Allegory, however, tends to be more complex and sustained than symbolism. An allegory is to a symbol as a motion picture is to a still picture; allegory puts symbols into consistent and sustained action. In form, an allegory is a complete and self-sufficient narrative, but it also signifies another series or level of events or conditions of life as expressed in a habit of thought, a philosophy, or a religion. While some works are allegories from beginning to end, many works that are not allegories contain sections or episodes that may be considered allegories.

Allegories and the allegorical method do not exist simply to enable authors to engage in mysterious literary exercises. Rather it was understood at some point in the past that people might more willingly listen to stories instead of moral lessons. Thus, the allegorical method evolved to entertain and instruct at the same time. In addition, the threat of reprisal or censorship sometimes caused authors to express their views indirectly in the form of allegory rather than to write directly. The double meaning that you will find in allegory is hence based in both need and reality.

As you study a work for allegory, you should try to determine how an entire story, or a self-contained episode, may be construed as having an extended, allegorical meaning that points consistently to a system of ideas or events beyond the actual occurrences in the text. The popularity of the film *Star Wars* and its sequels, for example, is attributable at least partly to the fact that it may be taken as an allegory of the conflict between good and evil. Obi Wan Kenobi (intelligence) enlists the aid of Luke Skywalker (heroism, boldness) and instructs him in "the force" (religious faith). Thus armed and guided, Skywalker opposes the strength of Darth Vader (evil) to rescue the Princess Leia (purity and goodness) with the aid of the latest spaceships and weaponry (technology). The story is accompanied by ingenious special effects and almost tactile sound effects and music, and hence as an adventure film it stands by itself. With the clear allegorical overtones, however, it stands for any person's quest for self-fulfillment.

To see how it applies, let us consider that Vader is so strong that he imprisons Skywalker for a time, and Skywalker must exert all his skill and strength to get free and to overcome the evil Vader. In the allegorical application of the episode to people generally, it would not be improper to take the temporary imprisonment to refer to those moments of doubt, discouragement, and depression that often beset people seeking an education, a work goal, the good life, a satisfactory marriage, or whatever.

In one form or another, this allegory has been told over and over again. At one time the substance was the hero who went to far lands to gain the prize of the golden fleece; at another, the knight who braved dangers to overcome the dragon. The allegory, in short, is as old as the capacity of human beings to tell stories. As long as the parallel interpretation is kept close and consistent, as in the *Star Wars* films, an extended allegorical interpretation will have validity.

Fable, Parable, and Myth

There are three narrative forms that are special types of allegory: *fable*, *parable*, and *myth*.

FABLE.   A **fable** is a short story, often featuring animals with human traits, to which writers and editors attach "morals" or explanations. Such stories are often called **beast fables.** Fables are a very old literary form and have found a place in the literature of most societies. Aesop (sixth century B.C.) was supposedly a slave who composed beast fables in ancient Greece. His fable of "The Fox and the Grapes," for example, signifies the tendency to belittle those things we cannot have. Joel Chandler Harris

(1848–1908) was an American writer whose "Uncle Remus" stories are also beast fables. Walt Disney's "Mickey Mouse" and Walt Kelly's "Pogo" are part of the tradition.

PARABLE.   A **parable** is really a short, simple allegory usually used in religious teachings. Parables are often associated with Jesus, who used them to embody religious insights and truth. Parables like those of the Good Samaritan and the Prodigal Son are interpreted to show God's active love, concern, understanding, and forgiveness for human beings.

MYTH.   A **myth** is a story, like the myth of Sisyphus, that is associated with the religion, philosophy, and collective psychology of various groups of cultures. Myths sometimes embody scientific truths for prescientific societies; they codify the social and cultural values of the civilization in which they are composed. Sometimes, unfortunately, the term *mythical* is used to suggest that something is untrue. This minimizing of the word reflects a limited appreciation of the psychological and social truths embedded in myths. The truths in mythology are not found literally in the stories themselves, but rather in our symbolic or allegorical interpretation of them.

ALLUSION IN SYMBOLISM AND ALLEGORY

Universal or cultural symbols and allegories often allude to other works from our western cultural heritage, such as the Bible, Greco-Roman mythology, or classical literature. Sometimes understanding a story may require knowledge of politics and history. Thus, for example, a major character in Hawthorne's "Young Goodman Brown" is Brown's wife, Faith, who stays at home when he leaves to go on his journey. Later, in the forest, when Brown is seeing his vision of sinful human beings, he exclaims, "My Faith is gone." On the primary level of reading, this statement makes perfect sense, because Brown has concluded that his wife has been lost. However, the symbol of his being married to Faith takes on additional meaning when one notes that it is also an allusion to the Biblical book of Ephesians (2:8) and to the Protestant-Calvinist tradition that the virtue faith is a key to salvation:

> For by grace you have been saved through faith; and this is not your own doing, it is the gift of God—

This biblical passage might easily take a volume of explanation, but in brief the allusion makes clear that Brown's loss of faith also indicates his perception that he has been abandoned by God. Here is an instance where a symbol gains its resonance and impact through allusion.

This example brings up the issue of how much background you need for detecting allusions in symbolism and allegory. You can often rely on your own knowledge. Sometimes, however, an allusion may escape you if you do not pursue the point in a dictionary or other reference work. The scope of your college dictionary will surprise you. If you cannot find an entry in your dictionary, however, try one of the major encyclopedias, or ask your reference librarian about standard guides like *The Oxford Companion to English Literature*, *The Oxford Companion to Classical Literature*, and William Rose Benet's *The Reader's Encyclopaedia*. A useful aid in finding Biblical references is *Cruden's Complete Concordance*, which in various editions has been used by scholars and readers for more than two centuries (since 1737). This work lists all words used in the King James translation of the Bible, so that you may easily locate the chapter and verse of any Biblical quotation. If you still have trouble after using sources like these, see your instructor for more help.

AESOP

The Fox and the Grapes (*ca. 6th C.* B.C.)

A hungry Fox coming into a vineyard where there hung delicious clusters of ripe Grapes, his mouth watered to be at them; but they were nailed up to a trellis so high, that with all his springing and leaping he could not reach a single bunch. At last, growing tired and disappointed, "Let who will take them!" says he "they are but green and sour; so I'll e'en let them alone."

QUESTIONS

1. How much do you learn about the characteristics of the fox? How are these characteristics related to the moral or message of the fable?
2. What is the plot of the fable, the principal conflict? What is the resolution of the conflict?
3. In your own words, explain the meaning of the fable. Is the "sour grape" explanation a satisfactory excuse, or is it a rationalization for failure?
4. From your reading of "The Fox and the Grapes," explain the characteristics of the fable as a type of literature.

THE GOSPEL OF ST. LUKE 15:11–32

The Parable of the Prodigal Son (*ca. 80* A.D.)

11 ¶ And he said, A certain man had two sons:
12 And the younger of them said to *his* father, Father, give me the portion of goods that falleth *to me*. And he divided unto them *his* living.°

---

divided . . . his living: one-third of the father's estate; the son had to renounce all further claim.

13 And not many days after the younger son gathered all together, and took his journey into a far country,° and there wasted his substance with riotous living.

14 And when he had spent all, there arose a mighty famine in that land; and he began to be in want.

15 And he went and joined himself to a citizen of that country; and he sent him into his fields to feed swine.°

16 And he would fain have filled his belly with the husks° that the swine did eat: and no man gave unto him.

17 And when he came to himself, he said, How many hired servants of my father's have bread enough and to spare, and I perish with hunger!

18 I will arise and go to my father, and will say unto him, Father, I have sinned against heaven, and before thee,

19 And am no more worthy to be called thy son: make me as one of thy hired servants.

20 And he arose, and came to his father. But when he was yet a great way off, his father saw him, and had compassion, and ran, and fell on his neck, and kissed him.

21 And the son said unto him, Father, I have sinned against heaven, and in thy sight, and am no more worthy to be called thy son.

22 But the father said to his servants, Bring forth the best robe, and put *it* on him; and put a ring on his hand, and shoes on *his* feet:

23 And bring hither the fatted calf,° and kill *it*; and let us eat, and be merry:

24 For this my son was dead, and is alive again; he was lost, and is found. And they began to be merry.

25 Now his elder son was in the field: and as he came and drew nigh to the house, he heard musick and dancing.

26 And he called one of the servants, and asked what these things meant.

27 And he said unto him, Thy brother is come; and thy father hath killed the fatted calf, because he hath received him safe and sound.

28 And he was angry, and would not go in: therefore came his father out, and intreated him.

29 And he answering said to *his* father, Lo, these many years do I serve thee, neither transgressed I at any time thy commandment: and yet thou never gavest me a kid, that I might make merry with my friends:

30 But as soon as this thy son was come, which hath devoured thy living with harlots, thou hast killed for him the fatted calf.

31 And he said unto him, Son, thou art ever with me, and all that I have is thine.

32 It was meet° that we should make merry, and be glad: for this thy brother was dead, and is alive again: and was lost, and is found.

---

far country: countries of the Jewish dispersal, or *diaspora*, in the areas bordering the Mediterranean Sea.

feed swine: In Jewish custom, pigs were unclean.

husks: pods of the carob tree, the eating of which was thought to be penitential.

fatted calf: grain-fed calf.

meet: appropriate.

QUESTIONS

1. Describe the character of the Prodigal Son. If one considers the parable a story, is this character flat or round, representative or individual? Why is it necessary that the character be considered representatively, even though he has individual characteristics?

2. What is the plot of the parable? What is the force of the antagonism against which the Prodigal Son must contend? Considering the moral and religious point of the parable, why is it necessary that the brother be resentful of the brother's return?

3. What is the resolution of the parable? Why is there no "they lived happily ever after" ending?

4. Using verse numbers, analyze the structure of the parable. What determines your division of the parts? Do these parts coincide with the development of the plot? On the basis of your answer, describe the relationship of plot to structure in the parable.

5. What is the point of view of the parable? Is it consistently applied? How does the emphasis shift with verse 22?

6. On the basis of the fact that there are many characteristics here of many of the stories you have read, write a description of the parable as a type of literature.

NATHANIEL HAWTHORNE (1804–1864)

Young Goodman Brown   *1835*

Young Goodman Brown came forth at sunset, into the street of Salem village,° but put his head back, after crossing the threshold, to exchange a parting kiss with his young wife. And Faith, as the wife was aptly named, thrust her own pretty head into the street, letting the wind play with the pink ribbons of her cap, while she called to Goodman Brown.

"Dearest heart," whispered she, softly and rather sadly, when her lips were close to his ear, "prithee, put off your journey until sunrise, and sleep in your own bed to-night. A lone woman is troubled with such dreams and such thoughts, that she's afeared of herself, sometimes. Pray, tarry with me this night, dear husband, of all nights in the year!"

"My love and my Faith," replied young Goodman Brown, "of all nights in the year, this one night must I tarry away from thee. My journey, as thou callest it, forth and back again, must needs be done 'twixt now and sunrise. What, my sweet, pretty wife, dost thou doubt me already, and we but three months married!"

"Then God bless you!" said Faith with the pink ribbons, "and may you find all well, when you come back."

"Amen!" cried Goodman Brown. "Say thy prayers, dear Faith, and go to   5
bed at dusk, and no harm will come to thee."

Salem village: in Massachusetts, about fifteen miles north of Boston.

So they parted; and the young man pursued his way, until, being about to turn the corner by the meeting-house, he looked back and saw the head of Faith still peeping after him, with a melancholy air, in spite of her pink ribbons.

"Poor little Faith!" thought he, for his heart smote him. "What a wretch am I, to leave her on such an errand! She talks of dreams, too. Methought, as she spoke, there was trouble in her face, as if a dream had warned her what work is to be done to-night. But no, no! 't would kill her to think it. Well; she's a blessed angel on earth; and after this one night, I'll cling to her skirts and follow her to Heaven."

With this excellent resolve for the future, Goodman Brown felt himself justified in making more haste on his present evil purpose. He had taken a dreary road, darkened by all the gloomiest trees of the forest, which barely stood aside to let the narrow path creep through, and closed immediately behind. It was all as lonely as could be; and there is this peculiarity in such a solitude, that the traveller knows not who may be concealed by the innumerable trunks and the thick boughs overhead; so that, with lonely footsteps, he may yet be passing through an unseen multitude.

"There may be a devilish Indian behind every tree," said Goodman Brown to himself; and he glanced fearfully behind him, as he added, "What if the devil himself should be at my very elbow!"

His head being turned back, he passed a crook of the road, and looking forward again, beheld the figure of a man, in grave and decent attire, seated at the foot of an old tree. He arose at Goodman Brown's approach, and walked onward, side by side with him.   10

"You are late, Goodman Brown," said he. "The clock of the Old South° was striking, as I came through Boston; and that is full fifteen minutes agone."

"Faith kept me back awhile," replied the young man, with a tremor in his voice, caused by the sudden appearance of his companion, though not wholly unexpected.

It was now deep dusk in the forest, and deepest in that part of it where these two were journeying. As nearly as could be discerned, the second traveller was about fifty years old, apparently in the same rank of life as Goodman Brown, and bearing a considerable resemblance to him, though perhaps more in expression than features. Still, they might have been taken for father and son. And yet, though the elder person was as simply clad as the younger, and as simple in manner too, he had an indescribable air of one who knew the world, and would not have felt abashed at the governor's dinner-table, or in King William's° court, were it possible that his affairs should call him thither. But the only thing about him that could be fixed upon as remarkable, was his staff, which bore the likeness of a great black snake, so curiously wrought, that it might almost be seen to twist and wriggle itself like a living serpent. This, of course, must have been an ocular deception, assisted by the uncertain light.

"Come, Goodman Brown!" cried his fellow-traveller, "this is a dull pace for the beginning of a journey. Take my staff, if you are so soon weary."

"Friend," said the other, exchanging his slow pace for a full stop, "having kept covenant by meeting thee here, it is my purpose now to return whence I came. I have scruples, touching the matter thou wot'st of."   15

Old South: The Old South Church, in Boston, is still there.
King William: William IV, King of England from 1830 to 1837.

"Sayest thou so?" replied he of the serpent, smiling apart. "Let us walk on, nevertheless, reasoning as we go, and if I convince thee not, thou shalt turn back. We are but a little way in the forest, yet."

"Too far, too far!" exclaimed the goodman, unconsciously resuming his walk. "My father never went into the woods on such an errand, nor his father before him. We have been a race of honest men and good Christians, since the days of the martyrs.° And shall I be the first of the name of Brown that ever took this path and kept—"

"Such company, thou wouldst say," observed the elder person, interrupting his pause. "Well said, Goodman Brown! I have been as well acquainted with your family as with ever a one among the Puritans; and that's no trifle to say. I helped your grandfather, the constable, when he lashed the Quaker woman so smartly through the streets of Salem. And it was I that brought your father a pitch-pine knot, kindled at my own hearth, to set fire to an Indian village, in King Philip's war.° They were my good friends, both; and many a pleasant walk have we had along this path, and returned merrily after midnight. I would fain be friends with you, for their sake."

"If it be as thou sayest," replied Goodman Brown, "I marvel they never spoke of these matters. Or, verily, I marvel not, seeing that the least rumor of the sort would have driven them from New England. We are a people of prayer, and good works to boot, and abide no such wickedness."

"Wickedness or not," said the traveller with twisted staff, "I have a very   20
general acquaintance here in New England. The deacons of many a church have drunk the communion wine with me; the selectmen, of divers towns, make me their chairman; and a majority of the Great and General Court are firm supporters of my interest. The governor and I, too—but these are state secrets."

"Can this be so!" cried Goodman Brown, with a stare of amazement at his undisturbed companion. "Howbeit, I have nothing to do with the governor and council; they have their own ways, and are no rule for a simple husbandman like me. But, were I to go on with thee, how should I meet the eye of that good old man, our minister, at Salem village? Oh, his voice would make me tremble, both Sabbath-day and lecture-day!"

Thus far, the elder traveller had listened with due gravity, but now burst into a fit of irrepressible mirth, shaking himself so violently, that his snakelike staff actually seemed to wriggle in sympathy.

"Ha! ha! ha!" shouted he, again and again; then composing himself, "Well, go on, Goodman Brown, go on; but, prithee, don't kill me with laughing!"

"Well, then, to end the matter at once," said Goodman Brown, considerably nettled, "there is my wife, Faith. It would break her dear little heart; and I'd rather break my own!"

"Nay, if that be the case," answered the other, "e'en go thy ways, Goodman   25
Brown. I would not, for twenty old women like the one hobbling before us, that Faith should come to any harm."

As he spoke, he pointed his staff at a female figure on the path, in whom

days of the martyrs: The martyrdoms of Protestants in England during the reign of Queen Mary (1553–1558).

King Philip's War (1675–1676): It resulted in the suppression of Indian tribal life in New England and prepared the way for unlimited settlement of the area by European immigrants. "Philip" was the English name of Chief Metacomet of the Wampanoag Indian Tribe.

Goodman Brown recognized a very pious and exemplary dame, who had taught him his catechism in youth, and was still his moral and spiritual adviser, jointly with the minister and Deacon Gookin.

"A marvel, truly, that Goody° Cloyse should be so far in the wilderness, at nightfall!" said he. "But, with your leave, friend, I shall take a cut through the woods, until we have left this Christian woman behind. Being a stranger to you, she might ask whom I was consorting with, and whither I was going."

"Be it so," said his fellow-traveller. "Betake you to the woods, and let me keep the path."

Accordingly, the young man turned aside, but took care to watch his companion, who advanced softly along the road, until he had come within a staff's length of the old dame. She, meanwhile, was making the best of her way, with singular speed for so aged a woman, and mumbling some indistinct words, a prayer, doubtless, as she went. The traveller put forth his staff, and touched her withered neck with what seemed the serpent's tail.

"The devil!" screamed the pious old lady.   30

"Then Goody Cloyse knows her old friend?" observed the traveller, confronting her, and leaning on his writhing stick.

"Ah, forsooth, and is it your worship, indeed?" cried the good dame. "Yea, truly is it, and in the very image of my old gossip,° Goodman Brown, the grandfather of the silly fellow that now is. But, would your worship believe it? My broomstick hath strangely disappeared, stolen, as I suspect, by that unhanged witch, Goody Cory,° and that, too, when I was all anointed with the juice of smallage and cinquefoil and wolf's-bane—"

"Mingled with fine wheat and the fat of a new-born babe," said the shape of old Goodman Brown.

"Ah, your worship knows the recipe," cried the old lady, cackling aloud. "So, as I was saying, being all ready for the meeting, and no horse to ride on, I made up my mind to foot it; for they tell me there is a nice young man to be taken into communion to-night. But now your good worship will lend me your arm, and we shall be there in a twinkling."

"That can hardly be," answered her friend. "I will not spare you my arm,   35 Goody Cloyse, but here is my staff, if you will.

So saying, he threw it down at her feet, where, perhaps, it assumed life, being one of the rods which its owner had formerly lent to the Egyptian Magi.° Of this fact, however, Goodman Brown could not take cognizance. He had cast up his eyes in astonishment, and looking down again, beheld neither Goody Cloyse nor the serpentine staff, but his fellow-traveller alone, who waited for him as calmly as if nothing had happened.

"That old woman taught me my catechism!" said the young man; and there was a world of meaning in this simple comment.

They continued to walk onward, while the elder traveller exhorted his companion to make good speed and persevere in the path, discoursing so aptly, that his

---

Goody: a shortened form of "goodwife," a respectful name for a married woman of low rank. A "Goody Cloyse" was one of the women sentenced to execution by Hawthorne's great grandfather, Judge John Hawthorne.
    gossip: from "good sib" or "good relative."
    Goody Cory: the name of a woman who was also sent to execution by Judge Hawthorne.
    lent to the Egyptian Magi: See Exodus 7:10–12.

arguments seemed rather to spring up in the bosom of his auditor, than to be suggested by himself. As they went he plucked a branch of maple, to serve for a walking-stick, and began to strip it of the twigs and little boughs, which were wet with evening dew. The moment his fingers touched them, they became strangely withered and dried up, as with a week's sunshine. Thus the pair proceeded, at a good free pace, until suddenly, in a gloomy hollow of the road, Goodman Brown sat himself down on the stump of a tree, and refused to go any farther.

"Friend," said he, stubbornly, "my mind is made up. Not another step will I budge on this errand. What if a wretched old woman do choose to go to the devil, when I thought she was going to Heaven! Is that any reason why I should quit my dear Faith, and go after her?"

"You will think better of this by and by," said his acquaintance, composedly. 40 "Sit here and rest yourself a while; and when you feel like moving again, there is my staff to help you along."

Without more words, he threw his companion the maple stick, and was as speedily out of sight as if he had vanished into the deepening gloom. The young man sat a few moments by the roadside, applauding himself greatly, and thinking with how clear a conscience he should meet the minister, in his morning walk, nor shrink from the eye of good old Deacon Gookin. And what calm sleep would be his, that very night, which was to have been spent so wickedly, but purely and sweetly now, in the arms of Faith! Amidst these pleasant and praiseworthy meditations, Goodman Brown heard the tramp of horses along the road, and deemed it advisable to conceal himself within the verge of the forest, conscious of the guilty purpose that had brought him thither, though now so happily turned from it.

On came the hoof-tramps and the voices of the riders, two grave old voices, conversing soberly as they drew near. These mingled sounds appeared to pass along the road, within a few yards of the young man's hiding-place; but owing, doubtless, to the depth of the gloom, at that particular spot, neither the travellers nor their steeds were visible. Though their figures brushed the small boughs by the wayside, it could not be seen that they intercepted, even for a moment, the faint gleam from the strip of bright sky, athwart which they must have passed. Goodman Brown alternately crouched and stood on tiptoe, pulling aside the branches, and thrusting forth his head as far as he durst, without discerning so much as a shadow. It vexed him the more, because he could have sworn, were such a thing possible, that he recognized the voices of the minister and Deacon Gookin, jogging° along quietly, as they were wont to do, when bound to some ordination or ecclesiastical council. While yet within hearing, one of the riders stopped to pluck a switch.

"Of the two, reverend Sir," said the voice like the deacon's, "I had rather miss an ordination dinner than to-night's meeting. They tell me that some of our community are to be here from Falmouth and beyond, and others from Connecticut and Rhode Island; besides several of the Indian powwows,° who, after their fashion, know almost as much deviltry as the best of us. Moreover, there is a goodly young woman to be taken into communion."

jogging: riding a horse at a slow trot.
powwow: a Narragansett Indian word describing a ritual ceremony of dancing, incantation, and magic.

"Mighty well, Deacon Gookin!" replied the solemn old tones of the minister. "Spur up, or we shall be late. Nothing can be done, you know, until I get on the ground."

The hoofs clattered again, and the voices, talking so strangely in the empty   45
air, passed on through the forest, where no church had ever been gathered, nor solitary Christian prayed. Whither, then, could these holy men be journeying, so deep into the heathen wilderness? Young Goodman Brown caught hold of a tree, for support, being ready to sink down on the ground, faint and over-burthened with the heavy sickness of his heart. He looked up to the sky, doubting whether there really was a Heaven above him. Yet, there was the blue arch, and the stars brightening in it.

"With Heaven above, and Faith below, I will yet stand firm against the devil!" cried Goodman Brown.

While he still gazed upward, into the deep arch of the firmament, and had lifted his hands to pray, a cloud, though no wind was stirring, hurried across the zenith, and hid the brightening stars. The blue sky was still visible, except directly overhead, where this black mass of cloud was sweeping swiftly northward. Aloft in the air, as if from the depths of the cloud, came a confused and doubtful sound of voices. Once, the listener fancied that he could distinguish the accents of town's people of his own, men and women, both pious and ungodly, many of whom he had met at the communion-table, and had seen others rioting at the tavern. The next moment, so indistinct were the sounds, he doubted whether he had heard aught but the murmur of the old forest, whispering without a wind. Then came a stronger swell of those familiar tones, heard daily in the sunshine, at Salem village, but never, until now, from a cloud at night. There was one voice, of a young woman, uttering lamentations, yet with an uncertain sorrow, and entreating for some favor, which, perhaps, it would grieve her to obtain. And all the unseen multitude, both saints and sinners, seemed to encourage her onward.

"Faith!" shouted Goodman Brown, in a voice of agony and desperation; and the echoes of the forest mocked him, crying—"Faith! Faith!" as if bewildered wretches were seeking her, all through the wilderness.

The cry of grief, rage, and terror was yet piercing the night, when the unhappy husband held his breath for a response. There was a scream, drowned immediately in a louder murmur of voices fading into far-off laughter, as the dark cloud swept away, leaving the clear and silent sky above Goodman Brown. But something fluttered lightly down through the air, and caught on the branch of a tree. The young man seized it and beheld a pink ribbon.

"My Faith is gone!" cried he, after one stupefied moment. "There is no   50
good on earth, and sin is but a name. Come, devil! for to thee is this world given."

And maddened with despair, so that he laughed loud and long, did Goodman Brown grasp his staff and set forth again, at such a rate, that he seemed to fly along the forest path, rather than to walk or run. The road grew wilder and drearier, and more faintly traced, and vanished at length, leaving him in the heart of the dark wilderness, still rushing onward, with the instinct that guides mortal man to evil. The whole forest was peopled with frightful sounds; the creaking of the trees, the howling of wild beasts, and the yell of Indians; while, sometimes, the wind tolled like a distant church bell, and sometimes gave a broad roar around the traveller, as if all Nature were laughing him to scorn. But he was himself the chief horror of the scene, and shrank not from its other horrors.

"Ha! ha! ha!" roared Goodman Brown, when the wind laughed at him. "Let us hear which will laugh loudest! Think not to frighten me with your deviltry! Come witch, come wizard, come Indian powwow, come devil himself! and here comes Goodman Brown. You may as well fear him as he fear you!"

In truth, all through the haunted forest, there could be nothing more frightful than the figure of Goodman Brown. On he flew, among the black pines, brandishing his staff with frenzied gestures, now giving vent to an inspiration of horrid blasphemy, and now shouting forth such laughter, as set all the echoes of the forest laughing like demons around him. The fiend in his own shape is less hideous, than when he rages in the breast of man. Thus sped the demoniac on his course, until, quivering among the trees, he saw a red light before him, as when the felled trunks and branches of a clearing have been set on fire, and throw up their lurid blaze against the sky, at the hour of midnight. He paused, in a lull of the tempest that had driven him onward, and heard the swell of what seemed a hymn, rolling solemnly from a distance, with the weight of many voices. He knew the tune. It was a familiar one in the choir of the village meeting-house. The verse died heavily away, and was lengthened by a chorus, not of human voices, but of all the sounds of the benighted wilderness, pealing in awful harmony together. Goodman Brown cried out; and his cry was lost to his own ear, by its unison with the cry of the desert.

In the interval of silence, he stole forward, until the light glared full upon his eyes. At one extremity of an open space, hemmed in by the dark wall of the forest, arose a rock, bearing some rude, natural resemblance either to an altar or a pulpit, and surrounded by four blazing pines, their tops aflame, their stems untouched, like candles at an evening meeting. The mass of foliage, that had overgrown the summit of the rock, was all on fire, blazing high into the night, and fitfully illuminating the whole field. Each pendent twig and leafy festoon was in a blaze. As the red light arose and fell, a numerous congregation alternately shone forth, then disappeared in shadow, and again grew, as it were, out of the darkness, peopling the heart of the solitary woods at once.

"A grave and dark-clad company!" quoth Goodman Brown.

55

In truth, they were such. Among them, quivering to-and-fro, between gloom and splendor, appeared faces that would be seen, next day, at the council-board of the province, and others which, Sabbath after Sabbath, looked devoutly heavenward, and benignantly over the crowded pews, from the holiest pulpits in the land. Some affirm that the lady of the governor was there. At least, there were high dames well known to her, and wives of honored husbands, and widows a great multitude, and ancient maidens, all of excellent repute, and fair young girls, who trembled lest their mothers should espy them. Either the sudden gleams of light, flashing over the obscure field, bedazzled Goodman Brown, or he recognized a score of the church members of Salem village, famous for their especial sanctity. Good old Deacon Gookin had arrived, and waited at the skirts of that venerable saint, his reverend pastor. But, irreverently consorting with these grave, reputable, and pious people, these elders of the church, these chaste dames and dewy virgins, there were men of dissolute lives and women of spotted fame, wretches given over to all mean and filthy vice, and suspected even of horrid crimes. It was strange to see, that the good shrank not from the wicked, nor were the sinners abashed by the saints. Scattered, also, among their pale-faced enemies, were the Indian priests, or powwows, who had often scared their native forest with more hideous incantations than any known to English witchcraft.

"But, where is Faith?" thought Goodman Brown; and, as hope came into his heart, he trembled.

Another verse of the hymn arose, a slow and mournful strain, such as the pious love, but joined to words which expressed all that our nature can conceive of sin, and darkly hinted at far more. Unfathomable to mere mortals is the lore of fiends. Verse after verse was sung, and still the chorus of the desert swelled between, like the deepest tone of a mighty organ. And, with the final peal of that dreadful anthem, there came a sound, as if the roaring wind, the rushing streams, the howling beasts, and every other voice of the unconverted wilderness were mingling and according with the voice of guilty man, in homage to the prince of all. The four blazing pines threw up a loftier flame, and obscurely discovered shapes and visages of horror on the smoke-wreaths, above the impious assembly. At the same moment, the fire on the rock shot redly forth, and formed a glowing arch above its base, where now appeared a figure. With reverence be it spoken, the apparition bore no slight similitude, both in garb and manner, to some grave divine of the New England churches.

"Bring forth the converts!" cried a voice, that echoed through the field and rolled into the forest.

At the word, Goodman Brown stepped forth from the shadow of the trees, and approached the congregation, with whom he felt a loathful brotherhood, by the sympathy of all that was wicked in his heart. He could have well-nigh sworn, that the shape of his own dead father beckoned him to advance, looking downward from a smoke-wreath, while a woman, with dim features of despair, threw out her hand to warn him back. Was it his mother? But he had no power to retreat one step, nor to resist, even in thought, when the minister and good old Deacon Gookin seized his arms, and led him to the blazing rock. Thither came also the slender form of a veiled female, led between Goody Cloyse, that pious teacher of the catechism, and Martha Carrier, who had received the devil's promise to be queen of hell. A rampant hag was she! And there stood the proselytes, beneath the canopy of fire.

"Welcome, my children," said the dark figure, "to the communion of your race! Ye have found, thus young, your nature and your destiny. My children, look behind you!"

They turned; and flashing forth, as it were, in a sheet of flame, the fiend-worshippers were seen; the smile of welcome gleamed darkly on every visage.

"There," resumed the sable form, "are all whom ye have reverenced from youth. Ye deemed them holier than yourselves, and shrank from your own sin, contrasting it with their lives of righteousness and prayerful aspirations heavenward. Yet, here are they all, in my worshipping assembly! This night it shall be granted you to know their secret deeds; how hoary-bearded elders of the church have whispered wanton words to the young maids of their households; how many a woman, eager for widow's weeds, has given her husband a drink at bedtime, and let him sleep his last sleep in her bosom; how beardless youths have made haste to inherit their father's wealth; and how fair damsels—blush not, sweet ones!—

60

have dug little graves in the garden, and bidden me, the sole guest, to an infant's funeral. By the sympathy of your human hearts for sin, ye shall scent out all the places—whether in church, bed-chamber, street, field, or forest—where crime has been committed, and shall exult to behold the whole earth one stain of guilt, one mighty blood-spot. Far more than this! It shall be yours to penetrate, in every bosom, the deep mystery of sin, the fountain of all wicked arts, and which inexhaustibly supplies more evil impulses than human power—than my power, at its utmost!—can make manifest in deeds. And now, my children, look upon each other."

They did so; and, by the blaze of the hell-kindled torches, the wretched man beheld his Faith, and the wife her husband, trembling before that unhallowed altar.

"Lo! there ye stand, my children," said the figure, in a deep and solemn   65
tone, almost sad, with its despairing awfulness, as if his once angelic nature could yet mourn for our miserable race. "Depending upon one another's hearts, ye had still hoped that virtue were not all a dream! Now are ye undeceived!—Evil is the nature of mankind. Evil must be your only happiness. Welcome, again, my children, to the communion of your race!"

"Welcome!" repeated the fiend-worshippers, in one cry of despair and triumph.

And there they stood, the only pair, as it seemed, who were yet hesitating on the verge of wickedness, in this dark world. A basin was hollowed, naturally, in the rock. Did it contain water, reddened by the lurid light? or was it blood? or, perchance, a liquid flame? Herein did the Shape of Evil dip his hand, and prepare to lay the mark of baptism upon their foreheads, that they might be partakers of the mystery of sin, more conscious of the secret guilt of others, both in deed and thought, than they could now be of their own. The husband cast one look at his pale wife, and Faith at him. What polluted wretches would the next glance show them to each other, shuddering alike at what they disclosed and what they saw!

"Faith! Faith!" cried the husband. "Look up to Heaven, and resist the Wicked One!"

Whether Faith obeyed, he knew not. Hardly had he spoken, when he found himself amid calm night and solitude, listening to a roar of the wind, which died heavily away through the forest. He staggered against the rock, and felt it chill and damp, while a hanging twig, that had been all on fire, besprinkled his cheek with the coldest dew.

The next morning, young Goodman Brown came slowly into the street of   70
Salem village staring around him like a bewildered man. The good old minister was taking a walk along the grave-yard, to get an appetite for breakfast and meditate his sermon, and bestowed a blessing, as he passed, on Goodman Brown. He shrank from the venerable saint, as if to avoid an anathema. Old Deacon Gookin was at domestic worship, and the holy words of his prayer were heard through the open window. "What God doth the wizard pray to?" quoth Goodman Brown. Goody Cloyse, that excellent old Christian, stood in the early sunshine, at her own lattice, catechising a little girl, who had brought her a pint of morning's milk. Goodman Brown snatched away the child, as from the grasp of the fiend himself. Turning the corner by the meetinghouse, he spied the head of Faith, with the pink ribbons, gazing anxiously forth, and bursting into such joy at sight of him that she skipt along the street, and almost kissed her husband before the whole village. But

Goodman Brown looked sternly and sadly into her face, and passed on without a greeting.

Had Goodman Brown fallen asleep in the forest, and only dreamed a wild dream of a witch-meeting?

Be it so, if you will. But, alas! it was a dream of evil omen for young Goodman Brown. A stern, a sad, a darkly meditative, a distrustful, if not a desperate man did he become, from the night of that fearful dream. On the Sabbath day, when the congregation were singing a holy psalm, he could not listen, because an anthem of sin rushed loudly upon his ear, and drowned all the blessed strain. When the minister spoke from the pulpit, with power and fervid eloquence, and with his hand on the open Bible, of the sacred truths of our religion, and of saint-like lives and triumphant deaths, and of future bliss or misery unutterable, then did Goodman Brown turn pale, dreading lest the roof should thunder down upon the gray blasphemer and his hearers. Often, awaking suddenly at midnight, he shrank from the bosom of Faith, and at morning or eventide, when the family knelt down at prayer, he scowled, and muttered to himself, and gazed sternly at his wife, and turned away. And when he had lived long, and was borne to his grave, a hoary corpse, followed by Faith, an aged woman, and children and grand-children, a goodly procession, besides neighbors not a few, they carved no hopeful verse upon his tombstone; for his dying hour was gloom.

QUESTIONS

1. Who is the protagonist in the story? Who *seems* to be the antagonist? What, if anything, do you think the antagonist really is?

2. What *seems* to be the central conflict in the story? How is this apparent conflict resolved? How is Goodman Brown's life changed by this resolution? To what extent does this change in Goodman Brown point to another conflict that remains unresolved?

3. Near the end of the story the narrator intrudes to ask the following: "Had Goodman Brown fallen asleep in the forest, and only dreamed a wild dream of a witch-meeting?" What do you think the answer to this question is? If Goodman Brown's visions come out of his own dreams (mind, subconscious), what do they tell us about him?

4. Is Goodman Brown a round or flat character? Individual or representative? To what extent is he designed to serve as a symbolic "everyman" or representative of humankind?

5. Consider Hawthorne's use of symbolism in the story, such as the symbolism of sunset and night, the walking stick, the witches' sabbath, the marriage to Faith, and the vague shadows amid the darkness, together with other symbols that you may find.

6. What details go into the establishment of the two distinct settings in this story? What characterizes Salem? The woods? Why might we be justified in seeing the forest as a symbolic setting?

7. To what extent are the people, objects, and events in Goodman Brown's adventure invested with enough *consistent* symbolic resonance to justify calling his episode in the woods an allegory? Consider Brown's wife, Faith, as an

allegorical figure. What do you make of Brown's statements that "I'll cling to her skirts and follow her to Heaven" (paragraph 7) and "Faith kept me back awhile" (paragraph 12). In this same light, consider the other characters Brown meets in the forest, the sunset, the walk into the forest, and the staff "which bore the likeness of a great black snake."

MARJORIE PICKTHALL   (1883–1922)

The Worker in Sandalwood   *1923*

I like to think of this as a true story, but you who read may please yourselves, siding either with the curé,° who says Hyacinthe dreamed it all, and did the carving himself in his sleep, or with Madame. I am sure that Hyacinthe thinks it true, and so does Madame, but then she has the cabinet, with the little birds and the lilies carved at the corners. Monsieur le curé shrugs his patient shoulders; but then he is tainted with the infidelities of cities, good man, having been three times to Montreal, and once, in an electric car, to Saint Anne. He and Madame still talk it over whenever they meet, though it happened so many years ago, and each leaves the other forever unconvinced. Meanwhile the dust gathers in the infinite fine lines of the little birds' feathers, and softens the lily stamens where Madame's duster may not go; and the wood, ageing, takes on a golden gleam as of immemorial sunsets: that pale red wood, heavy with the scent of the ancient East; the wood that Hyacinthe loved.

It was the only wood of that kind which had ever been seen in Terminaison.° Pierre L'Oreillard brought it into the workshop one morning; a small heavy bundle wrapped in sacking, and then in burlap, and then in fine soft cloths. He laid it on a pile of shavings, and unwrapped it carefully and a dim sweetness filled the dark shed and hung heavily in the thin winter sunbeams.

Pierre L'Oreillard rubbed the wood respectfully with his knobby fingers. "It is sandalwood," he explained to Hyacinthe, pride of knowledge making him expansive; "a most precious wood° that grows in warm countries, thou great goblin. Smell it, *imbécile*. It is sweeter than cedar. It is to make a cabinet for the old Madame at the big house. Thy great hands shall smooth the wood, *nigaud*,° and I—I, Pierre the cabinet-maker, shall render it beautiful." Then he went out, locking the door behind him.

When he was gone, Hyacinthe laid down his plane, blew on his stiff fingers, and shambled slowly over to the wood. He was a great clumsy boy of fourteen, dark-faced, very slow of speech, dull-eyed and uncared for. He was clumsy because it is impossible to move gracefully when you are growing very big and fast on quite insufficient food. He was dull-eyed because all eyes met his unlovingly; uncared for, because none knew the beauty of his soul. But his heavy young hands could

curé: a parish priest.
Terminaison: (literally, the "ending"), a town imagined as a part of French Canada.
a most precious wood: Sandalwood is still rare and precious; it is grown mainly in India and yields to exquisite detail in carving and decoration.
nigaud: simpleton.

carve simple things, like flowers and birds and beasts, to perfection, as the curé
pointed out. Simon has a tobacco-jar, carved with pine-cones and squirrels, and
the curé has a pipe whose bowl is the bloom of a moccasin-flower, that I have
seen. But it is all very long ago. And facts, in these lonely villages, easily become
transfigured, touched upon their gray with a golden gleam.

"Thy hands shall smooth the wood, *nigaud*, and I shall render it beautiful,"   5
said Pierre L'Oreillard, and went off to drink brandy at the Cinq Chateaux.

Hyacinthe knew that the making of the cabinet would fall to him, as most
of the other work did. He also touched the strange sweet wood, and at last laid
his cheek against it, while the fragrance caught his breath. "How it is beautiful,"
said Hyacinthe, and for a moment his eyes glowed and he was happy. Then the
light passed, and with bent head he shuffled back to his bench through a foam of
white shavings curling almost to his knees.

"Madame perhaps will want the cabinet next week, for that is Christmas,"
said Hyacinthe, and fell to work harder than ever, though it was so cold in the
shed that his breath hung like a little silver cloud and the steel stung his hands.
There was a tiny window to his right, through which, when it was clear of frost,
one looked on Terminaison, and that was cheerful and made one whistle. But to
the left, through the chink of the ill-fitting door, there was nothing but the forest
and the road dying away in it, and the trees moving heavily under the snow. Yet,
from there came all Hyacinthe's dumb dreams and slow reluctant fancies, which
he sometimes found himself able to tell—in wood, not in words.

Brandy was good at the Cinq Chateaux, and Pierre L'Oreillard gave Hyacinthe
plenty of directions, but no further help with the cabinet.

"That is to be finished for Madame on the festival, *gros escargot!*"° said he,
cuffing Hyacinthe's ears furiously, "finished, and with a prettiness about the corners,
hearest thou, *ourson?*° I suffer from a delicacy of the constitution and a little feebleness
in the legs on these days, so that I cannot handle the tools. I must leave this
work to thee, *gâcheur*.° See it is done properly, and stand up and touch a hand to
thy cap when I address thee, *orvet*,° great slow-worm."

"Yes, monsieur," said Hyacinthe, wearily.   10

It is hard, when you do all the work, to be cuffed into the bargain, and
fourteen is not very old. He went to work on the cabinet with slow, exquisite
skill, but on the eve of Noel, he was still at work, and the cabinet unfinished. It
meant a thrashing from Pierre if the morrow came and found it still unfinished,
and Pierre's thrashings were cruel. But it was growing into a thing of perfection
under his slow hands, and Hyacinthe would not hurry over it.

"Then work on it all night, and show it to me all completed in the morning,
or thy bones shall mourn thy idleness," said Pierre with a flicker of his little eyes.
And he shut Hyacinthe into the workshop with a smoky lamp, his tools, and the
sandalwood cabinet.

It was nothing unusual. The boy had often been left before to finish a piece
of work overnight while Pierre went off to his brandies. But this was Christmas
Eve, and he was very tired. The cold crept into the shed until the scent of the

gros escargot: big snail.
ourson: bear cub.
gâcheur: bungler, spoiler.
orvet: blind worm, slow worm.

sandalwood could not make him dream himself warm, and the roof cracked sullenly in the forest. There came upon Hyacinthe one of those awful, hopeless despairs that children know. It seemed to be a living presence that caught up his soul and crushed it in black hands. "In all the world, nothing!" said he, staring at the dull flame; "no place, no heart, no love! O kind God, is there a place, a love for me in another world?"

I cannot endure to think of Hyacinthe, poor lad, shut up despairing in the workshop with his loneliness, his cold, and his hunger, on the eve of Christmas. He was but an overgrown, unhappy child, and for unhappy children no aid, at this season, seems too divine for faith. So Madame says, and she is very old and very wise. Hyacinthe even looked at the chisel in his hand, and thought that by a touch of that he might lose it all, all, and be at peace, somewhere not far from God; only it was forbidden. Then came the tears, and great sobs that sickened and deafened him, so that he scarcely heard the gentle rattling of the latch.

At least, I suppose it came then, but it may have been later. The story is all so vague here, so confused with fancies that have spoiled the first simplicity. I think that Hyacinthe must have gone to the door, opening it upon the still woods and the frosty stars, and the lad who stood outside must have said: "I see you are working late, comrade. May I come in?" or something like it. | 15

Hyacinthe brushed his ragged sleeve across his eyes, and opened the door wider with a little nod to the other to enter. Those little lonely villages strung along the great river see strange wayfarers adrift inland from the sea. Hyacinthe said to himself that surely here was such a one.

Afterwards he told the curé that for a moment he had been bewildered. Dully blinking into the stranger's eyes, he lost for a flash the first impression of youth and received one of some incredible age or sadness. But this also passed and he knew that the wanderer's eyes were only quiet, very quiet, like the little pools in the wood where the wild does went to drink. As he turned within the door, smiling at Hyacinthe and shaking some snow from his fur cap, he did not seem more than sixteen or so.

"It is very cold outside," he said. "There is a big oak tree on the edge of the fields that has split in the frost and frightened all the little squirrels asleep there. Next year it will make an even better home for them. And see what I found close by!" He opened his fingers, and showed Hyacinthe a little sparrow lying unruffled in his palm.

"*Pauvrette!*"° said the dull Hyacinthe. "*Pauvrette!* Is it then dead?" He touched it with a gentle forefinger.

"No," answered the strange boy, "it is not dead. We'll put it here among | 20 the shavings, not far from the lamp, and it will be well by morning."°

He smiled at Hyacinthe again, and the shambling lad felt dimly as if the scent of sandalwood had deepened, and the lamp-flame burned clearer. But the stranger's eyes were only quiet, quiet.

"Have you come far?" asked Hyacinthe. "It is a bad season for travelling, and the wolves are out in the woods."

"A long way," said the other; "a long, long way. I heard a child cry. . . ."

Pauvrette: poor little thing.
See Psalms 84:4.

"There is no child here," answered Hyacinthe, shaking his head. "Monsieur L'Oreillard is not fond of children, he says they cost too much money. But if you have come far, you must be cold and hungry, and I have no food or fire. At the Cinq Chateaux you will find both!"

The stranger looked at him again with those quiet eyes, and Hyacinthe fancied   25
his face was familiar. "I will stay here," he said, "you are very late at work and you are unhappy."

"Why, as to that," answered Hyacinthe, rubbing again at his cheeks and ashamed of his tears, "most of us are sad at one time or another, the good God knows. Stay here and welcome if it pleases you, and you may take a share of my bed, though it is no more than a pile of balsam boughs and an old blanket, in the loft. But I must work at this cabinet, for the drawer must be finished and the handles put on and these corners carved, all by the holy morning; or my wages will be paid with a stick."

"You have a hard master," put in the other boy, "if he would pay you with blows upon the feast of Noel."

"He is hard enough," said Hyacinthe; "but once he gave me a dinner of sausages and white wine, and once, in the summer, melons. If my eyes will stay open, I will finish this by morning, but indeed I am sleepy. Stay with me an hour or so, comrade, and talk to me of your wanderings, so that the time may pass more quickly."

"I will tell you of the country where I was a child," answered the stranger. And while Hyacinthe worked, he told—of sunshine and dust; of the shadows   30
of vine-leaves on the flat white walls of a house; of rosy doves on the flat roof; of the flowers that come in the spring, crimson and blue, and the white cyclamen in the shadow of the rocks; of the olive, the myrtle and almond; until Hyacinthe's slow fingers ceased working, and his sleepy eyes blinked wonderingly.

"See what you have done, comrade," he said at last; "you have told of such pretty things that I have done no work for an hour. And now the cabinet will never be finished, and I shall be beaten."

"Let me help you," smiled the other; "I also was bred a carpenter."°

At first Hyacinthe would not, fearing to trust the sweet wood out of his own hands, but at length he allowed the stranger to fit in one of the little drawers, and so deftly was the work done, that Hyacinthe pounded his fists on the bench in admiration. "You have a pretty knack," he cried; "it seemed as if you did but hold the drawer in your hands a moment, and hey! ho! it jumped into its place!"

"Let me fit in the other little drawers, while you go and rest a while," said the wanderer. So Hyacinthe curled up among the shavings, and the stranger fell to work upon the little cabinet of sandalwood.

Here begins what the curé will have it is a dream within a dream. Sweetest   35
of dreams was ever dreamed, if that is so. Sometimes I am forced to think with him, but again I see as clearly as with old Madame's eyes, that have not seen the earthly light for twenty years, and with her and Hyacinthe, I say "Credo."°

. . . *bred a carpenter*: See Matthew 13:55.
Credo: "I believe," the opening words of the *Credo* section of the Catholic Mass ("Credo in unum Deum . . ." ["I believe in one God . . ."].

Hyacinthe said that he lay upon the shavings in the sweetness of the sandal-wood, and was very tired. He thought of the country where the stranger had been a boy; of the flowers on the hills; of the laughing leaves of aspen, and poplar; of the golden flowering anise and the golden sun upon the dusty roads, until he was warm. All the time through these pictures, as through a painted veil, he was aware of that other boy with the quiet eyes, at work upon the cabinet, smoothing, fitting, polishing. "He does better work than I," thought Hyacinthe, but he was not jealous. And again he thought, "It is growing towards morning. In a little while I will get up and help him." But he did not, for the dream of warmth and the smell of the sandalwood held him in a sweet drowse. Also he said that he thought the stranger was singing as he worked, for there seemed to be a sense of some music in the shed, though he could not tell whether it came from the other boy's lips, or from the shabby old tools as he used them, or from the stars. "The stars are much paler," thought Hyacinthe, "and soon it will be morning, and the corners are not carved yet. I must get up and help this kind one in a little moment. Only I am so tired, and the music and the sweetness seem to wrap me and fold me close, so that I may not move."

He lay without moving, and behind the forest there shone a pale glow of some indescribable colour that was neither green nor blue, while in Terminaison the church bells began to ring. "Day will soon be here!" thought Hyacinthe, immov-able in that deep dream of his, "and with day will come Monsieur L'Oreillard and his stick. I must get up and help, for even yet the corners are not carved."

But he did not get up. Instead, he saw the stranger look at him again, smiling as if he loved him, and lay his brown finger lightly upon the four empty corners of the cabinet. And Hyacinthe saw the little squares of reddish wood ripple and heave and break, as little clouds when the wind goes through the sky. And out of them thrust forth little birds, and after them the lilies, for a moment living, but even while Hyacinthe looked, growing hard and reddish-brown and settling back into the sweet wood. Then the stranger smiled again, and laid all the tools neatly in order, and, opening the door quietly, went away into the woods.

Hyacinthe lay still among the shavings for a long time, and then he crept slowly to the door. The sun, not yet risen, set its first beams upon the delicate mist of frost afloat beneath the trees, and so all the world was aflame with spendid gold. Far away down the road a dim figure seemed to move amid the glory, but the flow and the splendour were such that Hyacinthe was blinded. His breath came sharply as the glow beat in great waves on the wretched shed; on the foam of shavings; on the cabinet with the little birds and the lilies carved at the corners.

He was too pure of heart° to feel afraid. But, "Blessed be the Lord," whispered   40
Hyacinthe, clasping his slow hands, "for He hath visited and redeemed His people.° But who will believe?"

Then the sun of Christ's day rose gloriously, and the little sparrow came from his nest among the shavings and shook his wings to the light.°

pure of heart: See Matthew 5:8.
His people: See Luke 1:68.
wings to the light: See Malachi 4:2.

QUESTIONS

1. What point of view is employed in the story? Who or what is the narrator? To what extent does the narrator know a great deal more than we might expect? Why does the narrator repeat several times that the events in the story happened "very long ago"?

2. What sort of person is Hyacinthe? How does he deal with his life? How does he react to Pierre L'Oreillard's treatment? Why does the "strange child" with "quiet eyes" appear to him?

3. Why does the narrator stress the quality of Hyacinthe's work in the first and third paragraphs? Why does the narrator stress the possibility that Hyacinthe dreamed the events of the story? To what extent do these points of emphasis keep the story from becoming too fantastic or sentimentalized?

4. To what extent does the setting work symbolically to establish mood and tone? Consider the time of year, the specific night, the description of the shed in which Hyacinthe works, the forest, and the animals noted throughout.

5. Consider the symbolism associated with the "quiet" stranger: his homeland, his training as a carpenter, the sparrow he revives, the heightening of the lamp-flame, and the warming of the workshop. What do these details suggest? How consistent is this symbolism?

6. Would you consider this story an allegory, a myth, a fable, a parable, or simply symbolic? Explain your answer.

JOHN STEINBECK   (1902–1968)

The Chrysanthemums   1937

The high grey-flannel fog of winter closed off the Salinas Valley° from the sky and from all the rest of the world. On every side it sat like a lid on the mountains and made of the great valley a closed pot. On the broad, level land floor the gang plows bit deep and left the black earth shining like metal where the shares had cut. On the foothill ranches across the Salinas River, the yellow stubble fields seemed to be bathed in pale cold sunshine, but there was no sunshine in the valley now in December. The thick willow scrub along the river flamed with sharp and positive yellow leaves.

It was a time of quiet and of waiting. The air was cold and tender. A light wind blew up from the southwest so that the farmers were mildly hopeful of a good rain before long; but fog and rain do not go together.

Across the river, on Henry Allen's foothill ranch there was little work to be done, for the hay was cut and stored and the orchards were plowed up to receive the rain deeply when it should come. The cattle on the higher slopes were becoming shaggy and rough-coated.

Elisa Allen, working in her flower garden, looked down across the yard and

Salinas Valley: in Monterey County, California, about 50 miles south of San José. Steinbeck was born in Salinas, and his home there is open to the public.

saw Henry, her husband, talking to two men in business suits. The three of them stood by the tractor shed, each man with one foot on the side of the little Fordson.° They smoked cigarettes and studied the machines as they talked.

Elisa watched them for a moment and then went back to her work. She was   5
thirty-five. Her face was lean and strong and her eyes were as clear as water. Her figure looked blocked and heavy in her gardening costume, a man's black hat pulled low down over her eyes, clodhopper shoes, a figured print dress almost completely covered by a big corduroy apron with four big pockets to hold the snips, the trowel and scratcher, the seeds and the knife she worked with. She wore heavy leather gloves to protect her hands while she worked.

She was cutting down the old year's chrysanthemum stalks with a pair of short and powerful scissors. She looked down toward the men by the tractor shed now and then. Her face was eager and mature and handsome; even her work with the scissors was over-eager, over-powerful. The chrysanthemum stems seemed too small and easy for her energy.

She brushed a cloud of hair out of her eyes with the back of her glove, and left a smudge of earth on the cheek in doing it. Behind her stood the neat white farm house with red geraniums close-banked around it as high as the windows. It was a hard-swept looking little house, with hard-polished windows, and a clean mud-mat on the front steps.

Elisa cast another glance toward the tractor shed. The strangers were getting into their Ford coupe. She took off a glove and put her strong fingers down into the forest of new green chrysanthemum sprouts that were growing around the old roots. She spread the leaves and looked down among the close-growing stems. No aphids were there, no sowbugs or snails or cutworms. Her terrier fingers destroyed such pests before they could get started.

Elisa started at the sound of her husband's voice. He had come near quietly, and he leaned over the wire fence that protected her flower garden from cattle and dogs and chickens.

"At it again," he said. "You've got a strong new crop coming."   10

Elisa straightened her back and pulled on the gardening glove again. "Yes. They'll be strong this coming year." In her tone and on her face there was a little smugness.

"You've got a gift with things," Henry observed. "Some of those yellow chrysanthemums you had this year were ten inches across. I wish you'd work out in the orchard and raise some apples that big."

Her eyes sharpened. "Maybe I could do it, too. I've a gift with things, all right. My mother had it. She could stick anything in the ground and make it grow. She said it was having planters' hands that knew how to do it."

"Well, it sure works with flowers," he said.

"Henry, who were those men you were talking to?"   15

"Why, sure, that's what I came to tell you. They were from the Western Meat Company. I sold those thirty head of three-year-old steers. Got nearly my own price, too."

"Good," she said. "Good for you."

Fordson: a tractor manufactured by the Ford Motor Company, with large rear steel lugged wheels.

"And I thought," he continued, "I thought how it's Saturday afternoon, and we might go to Salinas for dinner at a restaurant, and then to a picture show—to celebrate, you see."

"Good," she repeated. "Oh, yes. That will be good."

Henry put on his joking tone. "There's fights tonight. How'd you like to go to the fights?"   20

"Oh, no," she said breathlessly. "No, I wouldn't like fights."

"Just fooling, Elisa. We'll go to a movie. Let's see. It's two now. I'm going to take Scotty and bring down those steers from the hill. It'll take us maybe two hours. We'll go in town about five and have dinner at the Cominos Hotel. Like that?"

"Of course I'll like it. It's good to eat away from home."

"All right, then. I'll go get up a couple of horses."

She said, "I'll have plenty of time to transplant some of these sets, I guess."   25

She heard her husband calling Scotty down by the barn. And a little later she saw the two men ride up the pale yellow hillside in search of the steers.

There was a little square sandy bed kept for rooting the chrysanthemums. With her trowel she turned the soil over and over, and smoothed it and patted it firm. Then she dug ten parallel trenches to receive the sets. Back at the chrysanthemum bed she pulled out the little crisp shoots, trimmed off the leaves of each one with her scissors and laid it on a small orderly pile.

A squeak of wheels and plod of hoofs came from the road. Elisa looked up. The country road ran along the dense bank of willows and cottonwoods that bordered the river, and up this road came a curious vehicle, curiously drawn. It was an old spring-wagon, with a round canvas top on it like the cover of a prairie schooner. It was drawn by an old bay horse and a little grey-and-white burro. A big stubble-bearded man sat between the cover flaps and drove the crawling team. Underneath the wagon, between the hind wheels, a lean and rangy mongrel dog walked sedately. Words were painted on the canvas in clumsy, crooked letters. "Pots, pans, knives, sisors, lawn mores. Fixed." Two rows of articles and the trimphantly definitive "Fixed" below. The black paint had run down in little sharp points beneath each letter.

Elisa, squatting on the ground, watched to see the crazy, loose-jointed wagon pass by. But it didn't pass. It turned into the farm road in front of her house, crooked old wheels skirling and squeaking. The rangy dog darted from between the wheels and ran ahead. Instantly the two ranch shepherds flew out at him. Then all three stopped, and with stiff and quivering tails, with taut straight legs, with ambassadorial dignity, they slowly circled, sniffing daintily. The caravan pulled up to Elisa's wire fence and stopped. Now the newcomer dog, feeling outnumbered, lowered his tail and retired under the wagon with raised hackles and bared teeth.

The man on the wagon seat called out. "That's a bad dog in a fight when he gets started."   30

Elisa laughed. "I see he is. How soon does he generally get started?"

The man caught up her laughter and echoed it heartily. "Sometimes not for weeks and weeks," he said. He climbed stiffly down, over the wheel. The horse and the donkey drooped like unwatered flowers.

Elisa saw that he was a very big man. Although his hair and beard were greying, he did not look old. His worn black suit was wrinkled and spotted with grease. The laughter had disappeared from his face and eyes the moment his laughing voice ceased. His eyes were dark and they were full of the brooding that gets in the eyes of teamsters and of sailors. The calloused hands he rested on the wire fence were cracked, and every crack was a black line. He took off his battered hat.

"I'm off my general road, ma'am," he said. "Does this dirt road cut over across the river to the Los Angeles highway?"

Elisa stood up and shoved the thick scissors in her apron pocket. "Well, 35 yes, it does, but it winds around and then fords the river. I don't think your team could pull through the sand."

He replied with some asperity, "It might surprise you what them beasts can pull through."

"When they get started?" she asked.

He smiled for a second. "Yes. When they get started."

"Well," said Elisa, "I think you'll save time if you go back to the Salinas road and pick up the highway there."

He drew a big finger down the chicken wire and made it sing. "I ain't in 40 any hurry, ma'am. I go from Seattle in San Diego and back every year. Takes all my time. About six months each way. I aim to follow nice weather."

Elisa took off her gloves and stuffed them in the apron pocket with the scissors. She touched the under edge of her man's hat, searching for fugitive hairs. "That sounds like a nice kind of a way to live," she said.

He leaned confidentially over the fence. "Maybe you noticed the writing on my wagon. I mend pots and sharpen knives and scissors. You got any of them things to do?"

"Oh, no," she said quickly. "Nothing like that." Her eyes hardened with resistance.

"Scissors is the worst thing," he explained. "Most people just ruin scissors trying to sharpen 'em, but I know how. I got a special tool. It's a little bobbit kind of thing, and patented. But it sure does the trick."

"No. My scissors are all sharp." 45

"All right, then. Take a pot," he continued earnestly, "a bent pot, or a pot with a hole. I can make it like new so you don't have to buy no new ones. That's a saving for you."

"No," she said shortly. "I tell you I have nothing like that for you to do."

His face fell to an exaggerated sadness. His voice took on a whining undertone. "I ain't had a thing to do today. Maybe I won't have no supper tonight. You see I'm off my regular road. I know folks on the highway clear from Seattle to San Diego. They save their things for me to sharpen up because they know I do it so good and save them money."

"I'm sorry," Elisa said irritably. "I haven't anything for you to do."

His eyes left her face and fell to searching the ground. They roamed about 50 until they came to the chrysanthemum bed where she had been working. "What's them plants, ma'am?"

The irritation and resistance melted from Elisa's face. "Oh, those are chrysanthemums, giant whites and yellows. I raise them every year, bigger than anybody around here."

"Kind of a long-stemmed flower? Looks like a quick puff of colored smoke?" he asked.

"That's it. What a nice way to describe them."

"They smell kind of nasty till you get used to them," he said.

"It's a good bitter smell," she retorted, "not nasty at all." 55

He changed his tone quickly. "I like the smell myself."

"I had ten-inch blooms this year," she said.

The man leaned farther over the fence. "Look. I know a lady down the road a piece, has got the nicest garden you ever seen. Got nearly every kind of flower but no chrysanthemums. Last time I was mending a copper-bottom washtub for her (that's a hard job but I do it good), she said to me, 'If you ever run acrost some nice chrysanthemums I wish you'd try to get me a few seeds.' That's what she told me."

Elisa's eyes grew alert and eager. "She couldn't have known much about chrysanthemums. You can raise them from seed, but it's much easier to root the little sprouts you see there."

"Oh," he said. "I s'pose I can't take none to her, then." 60

"Why yes you can," Elisa cried. "I can put some in damp sand, and you can carry them right along with you. They'll take root in the pot if you keep them damp. And then she can transplant them."

"She'd sure like to have some, ma'am. You say they're nice ones?"

"Beautiful," she said. "Oh, beautiful." Her eyes shone. She tore off the battered hat and shook out her dark pretty hair. "I'll put them in a flower pot, and you can take them right with you. Come into the yard."

While the man came through the picket gate Elisa ran excitedly along the geranium-bordered path to the back of the house. And she returned carrying a big red flower pot. The gloves were forgotten now. She kneeled on the ground by the starting bed and dug up the sandy soil with her fingers and scooped it into the bright new flower pot. Then she picked up the little pile of shoots she had prepared. With her strong fingers she pressed them into the sand and tamped around them with her knuckles. The man stood over her. "I'll tell you what to do," she said. "You remember so you can tell the lady."

"Yes, I'll try to remember." 65

"Well, look. These will take root in about a month. Then she must set them out, about a foot apart in good rich earth like this, see?" She lifted a handful of dark soil for him to look at. "They'll grow fast and tall. Now remember this. In July tell her to cut them down, about eight inches from the ground."

"Before they bloom?" he asked.

"Yes, before they bloom." Her face was tight with eagerness. "They'll grow right up again. About the last of September the buds will start."

She stopped and seemed perplexed. "It's the budding that takes the most care," she said hesitantly. "I don't know how to tell you." She looked deep into his eyes, searchingly. Her mouth opened a little, and she seemed to be listening. "I'll try to tell you," she said. "Did you ever hear of planting hands?"

"Can't say I have, ma'am." 70

"Well, I can only tell you what it feels like. It's when you're picking off the buds you don't want. Everything goes right down into your fingertips. You watch your fingers work. They do it themselves. You can feel how it is. They pick and pick the buds. They never make a mistake. They're with the plant. Do you see? Your fingers and the plant. You can feel that, right up your arm. They know. They never make a mistake. You can feel it. When you're like that you can't do anything wrong. Do you see that? Can you understand that?"

She was kneeling on the ground looking up at him. Her breast swelled passionately.

The man's eyes narrowed. He looked away self-consciously. "Maybe I know," he said. "Sometimes in the night in the wagon there—"

Elisa's voice grew husky. She broke in on him. "I've never lived as you do, but I know what you mean. When the night is dark—why, the stars are sharp-pointed, and there's quiet. Why, you rise up and up! Every pointed star gets driven into your body. It's like that. Hot and sharp and—lovely."

Kneeling there, her hand went out toward his legs in the greasy black trousers. 75
Her hesitant fingers almost touched the cloth. Then her hand dropped to the ground. She crouched low like a fawning dog.

He said, "It's nice, just like you say. Only when you don't have no dinner, it ain't."

She stood up then, very straight, and her face was ashamed. She held the flower pot out to him and placed it gently in his arms. "Here. Put it in your wagon, on the seat, where you can watch it. Maybe I can find something for you to do."

At the back of the house she dug in the can pile and found two old and battered aluminum saucepans. She carried them back and gave them to him. "Here, maybe you can fix these."

His manner changed. He became professional. "Good as new I can fix them." At the back of his wagon he set a little anvil, and out of an oily tool box dug a small machine hammer. Elisa came through the gate to watch him while he pounded out the dents in the kettles. His mouth grew sure and knowing. At a difficult part of the work he sucked his under-lip.

"You sleep right in the wagon?" Elisa asked. 80

Right in the wagon, ma'am. Rain or shine. I'm dry as a cow in there."

"It must be nice," she said. "It must be very nice. I wish women could do such things."

"It ain't the right kind of a life for a woman."

Her upper lip raised a little, showing her teeth. "How do you know? How can you tell?" she said.

"I don't know ma'am," he protested. "Of course I don't know. Now here's 85
your kettles, done. You don't have to buy no new ones."

"How much?"

"Oh, fifty cents'll do. I keep my prices down and my work good. That's why I have all them satisfied customers up and down the highway."

Elisa brought him a fifty-cent piece from the house and dropped it in his hand. "You might be surprised to have a rival some time. I can sharpen scissors, too. And I can beat the dents out of little pots. I could show you what a woman might do."

He put his hammer back in the oily box and shoved the little anvil out of sight. "It would be a lonely life for a woman, ma'am, and a scarey life, too, with animals creeping under the wagon all night." He climbed over the single-tree, steadying himself with a hand on the burro's white rump. He settled himself in the seat, picked up the lines. "Thank you kindly, ma'am," he said. "I'll do like you told me; I'll go back and catch the Salinas road."

"Mind," she called, "if you're long in getting there, keep the sand damp." 90

"Sand, ma'am? . . . Sand? Oh, sure. You mean round the chrysanthemums. Sure I will." He clucked his tongue. The beasts leaned luxuriously into their collars. The mongrel dog took his place between the back wheels. The wagon turned and crawled out the entrance road and back the way it had come, along the river.

Elisa stood in front of her wire fence watching the slow progress of the caravan. Her shoulders were straight, her head thrown back, her eyes half-closed, so that the scene came vaguely into them. Her lips moved silently, forming the words "Good-bye—good-bye." Then she whispered, "That's a bright direction. There's a glowing there." The sound of her whisper startled her. She shook herself free and looked about to see whether anyone had been listening. Only the dogs had heard. They lifted their heads toward her from their sleeping in the dust, and then stretched out their chins and settled asleep again. Elisa turned and ran hurriedly into the house.

In the kitchen she reached behind the stove and felt the water tank. It was full of hot water from the noonday cooking. In the bathroom she tore off her soiled clothes and flung them into the corner. And then she scrubbed herself with a little block of pumice, legs and thighs, loins and chest and arms, until her skin was scratched and red. When she had dried herself she stood in front of a mirror in her bedroom and looked at her body. She tightened her stomach and threw out her chest. She turned and looked over her shoulder at her back.

After a while she began to dress, slowly. She put on her newest under-clothing and her nicest stockings and the dress which was the symbol of her prettiness. She worked carefully on her hair, pencilled her eyebrows and rouged her lips.

Before she was finished she heard the little thunder of hoofs and the shouts   95
of Henry and his helper as they drove the red steers into the corral. She heard the gate bang shut and set herself for Henry's arrival.

His step sounded on the porch. He entered the house calling "Elisa, where are you?"

"In my room, dressing. I'm not ready. There's hot water for your bath. Hurry up. It's getting late."

When she heard him splashing in the tub, Elisa laid his dark suit on the bed, and shirt and socks and tie beside it. She stood his polished shoes on the floor beside the bed. Then she went to the porch and sat primly and stiffly down. She looked toward the river road where the willow-line was still yellow with frosted leaves so that under the high grey fog they seemed a thin band of sunshine. This was the only color in the grey afternoon. She sat unmoving for a long time. Her eyes blinked rarely.

Henry came banging out of the door, shoving his tie inside his vest as he came. Elisa stiffened and her face grew tight. Henry stopped short and looked at her. "Why—why, Elisa. You look so nice!"

"Nice? You think I look nice? What do you mean by 'nice'?"   100

Henry blundered on. "I don't know. I mean you look different, strong and happy."

"I am strong? Yes, strong. What do you mean 'strong'?"

He looked bewildered. "You're playing some kind of a game," he said helplessly. "It's a kind of a play. You look strong enough to break a calf over your knee, happy enough to eat it like watermelon."

For a second she lost her rigidity. "Henry! Don't talk like that. You didn't know what you said." She grew complete again. "I'm strong," she boasted. "I never knew before how strong."

Henry looked down toward the tractor shed, and when he brought his eyes back to her, they were his own again. "I'll get out the car. You can put on your coat while I'm starting." 105

Elisa went into the house. She heard him drive to the gate and idle down his motor, and then she took a long time to put on her hat. She pulled it here and pressed it there. When Henry turned the motor off she slipped into her coat and went out.

The little roadster bounced along on the dirt road by the river, raising the birds and driving the rabbits into the brush. Two cranes flapped heavily over the willow-line and dropped into the river-bed.

Far ahead on the road Elisa saw a dark speck. She knew.

She tried not to look as they passed it, but her eyes would not obey. She whispered to herself sadly. "He might have thrown them off the road. That wouldn't have been much trouble, not very much. But he kept the pot," she explained. "He had to keep the pot. That's why he couldn't get them off the road."

The roadster turned a bend and she saw the caravan ahead. She swung full around toward her husband so she could not see the little covered wagon and the mismatched team as the car passed them. 110

In a moment it was over. The thing was done. She did not look back. She said loudly, to be heard above the motor, "It will be good, tonight, a good dinner."

"Now you're changed again," Henry complained. He took one hand from the wheel and patted her knee. "I ought to take you in to dinner oftener. It would be good for both of us. We get so heavy out on the ranch."

"Henry," she asked, "could we have wine at dinner?"

"Sure we could. Say! That will be fine."

She was silent for a little while; then she said, "Henry, at those prize fights, do the men hurt each other very much?" 115

"Sometimes a little, not often. Why?"

"Well, I've read how they break noses, and blood runs down their chests. I've read how the fighting gloves get heavy and soggy with blood."

He looked around at her. "What's the matter, Elisa? I didn't know you read things like that." He brought the car to a stop, then turned to the right over the Salinas River bridge.

"Do any women ever go to the fights?" she asked.

"Oh, sure, some. What's the matter, Elisa? Do you want to go? I don't think you'd like it, but I'll take you if you really want to go." 120

She relaxed limply in the seat. "Oh, no. No. I don't want to go. I'm sure I don't." Her face was turned away from him. "It will be enough if we can have wine. It will be plenty." She turned up her coat collar so he could not see that she was crying weakly—like an old woman.

QUESTIONS

1. What point of view is used in the story? What are the advantages of using this point of view? What does Steinbeck force us to do by using this point of view?

2. Consider the symbolism of the setting in this story with respect to the Salinas Valley, the time of year, and the description of the Allen house. What do these things tell us about Elisa Allen and her world?

3. To what extent is Steinbeck's description of Elisa in paragraphs 5 and 6 symbolic? What is she wearing? What do her clothes hide or suppress? What does this description tell us about Elisa?

4. What do the chrysanthemums symbolize for Elisa? What do they symbolize *about* her? What role do these flowers play in her life?

5. How does Elisa's character or sense of self change during the episode in which she washes and dresses for dinner? To what extent is this washing-dressing episode symbolic? How would you explain the symbolism here?

6. Consider the symbolic impact of Elisa's seeing the chrysanthemum sprouts on the side of the road. How does this vision affect her? What does it tell us about her values?

WRITING ABOUT SYMBOLISM AND ALLEGORY

In preparing to write about symbolism or allegory, you will need to be alert and to employ all facilities that can aid your understanding. In the light of the introductory discussion in this chapter, test the material to determine parallels that may genuinely establish the presence of symbolism or allegory. It is particularly helpful to make a list showing how qualities of symbols may be lined up with qualities of a character or action. Such a list can help you think more deeply about the effectiveness of symbols. Here is such a list for the symbol of the toy windmill in Welty's "A Worn Path":

QUALITIES IN THE WINDMILL		COMPARABLE QUALITIES IN PHOENIX	
1.	Cheap	1.	Poor, but she gives all she has for the windmill
2.	Breakable	2.	Old, and not far from death
3.	A gift	3.	Generous
4.	Not practical	4.	Needs some relief from reality and practicality
5.	Colorful	5.	Same as 4

An aid for figuring out an allegory or allegorical passage can work well with a diagram of parallel lines. You can place corresponding characters, actions, things, or ideas along these lines as follows (using the film *Star Wars* as the specimen work):

STAR WARS	Luke Skywalker	Obi Wan Kenobi	Darth Vader	Princess Leia	Capture	Escape, and defeat of Vader
ALLEGORICAL APPLICATION TO MORALITY AND FAITH	Forces of good	Education and faith	Forces of evil	Object to be saved, ideals to be rescued and restored	Doubt, spiritual negligence	Restoration of faith
ALLEGORICAL APPLICATION TO PERSONAL AND GENERAL CONCERNS	Individual in pursuit of goals	The means by which goals may be reached	Obstacles to be overcome	Occupation, happiness, goals	Temporary failure, depression, discouragement, disappointment	Success

Lists and schemes like this may have the drawback of being too limiting and can reduce complex ideas to simple black and white statements. If you limit your responses only to your visual aid, you might miss much of the impact and resonance of the story. Nevertheless, the knowledge and understanding you use in developing aids of this kind can be helpful when you formulate the ways in which symbolism and allegory work. Therefore they can help you in putting together coherent materials.

In developing a thesis, you should begin by establishing significant general ideas about the story. "Young Goodman Brown," for example, is about the darkening of the soul of the major character, Brown. As he goes into the woods, he resolves to "stand firm against the devil," and he then looks up "to heaven above." As he looks, a "black mass of cloud" suddenly appears to hide the "brightening stars." These descriptions constitute a direct visual symbol of what is happening to his character. Out of this relationship, you could build a thesis about the relationship of symbolism to character development.

As you plan your central idea, also, it is necessary to justify the assertions you wish to make about symbolism or allegory. In the "Parable of the Prodigal Son," for example, the aim is to demonstrate the extreme lowness to which the son sinks. His job feeding pigs, and his sharing food with them, symbolize the depth of his degradation, for a reference to Jewish religion and custom will establish that pigs and pork are unclean and therefore that the son has reached the nadir of life both spiritually and economically. A discussion of the swine as a symbol should include reference to this cultural and religious attitude. In the same way, the allegorical aspects of "Young Goodman Brown" would need to be established in the observation that people lose their ideals and forsake their principles not because they are evil, but because they misperceive and misunderstand the events and people around them.

Organizing Your Essay

INTRODUCTION.   The introduction should establish the grounds for the discussion of symbolism and allegory in the story. There may be a recurring symbol, for example, or a regular pattern of symbolism. Or there may be actions that have clear allegorical applications. The central idea will refer to the nature of the symbols or allegory, like the symbols of darkness in "Young Goodman Brown" or the symbols of awakening life in "The Worker in Sandalwood." The thesis sentence will determine the topics to be developed in the body. These topics may refer to specific things, like the "walking stick," or to classes, like "regenerative symbols."

BODY.   There are a number of ways in which you might approach the topic of symbolism and allegory. You might wish to use one exclusively, or a combination. The choice is yours. If your choice is symbols and symbolism, you might consider the following:

1. *The meaning of a major symbol.* Here you interpret the symbol and try to show what it stands for both inside and outside the work. A few of the questions you might pursue are these: How do you determine that the symbol is really a symbol? How do you derive from the work a reasonable interpretation of the meaning of the symbol? What is the extent of the meaning? Does the symbol undergo any modification if it reappears in the work? By the same token, does the symbol affect your understanding of other parts of the work? How? Does the author create any ironies by using the symbol? Does the symbol give any special strength to the work?

2. *The meaning and relationship of a number of symbols.* What are the symbols? Do they have any specific connection or common bond? Do they suggest a unified reading or a contradictory one? Do the symbols seem to have general significance, or do they operate only in the context of the work? Do the symbols control the form of the work? How? For example, in "The Worker in Sandalwood" the concluding episode begins in doubt during the night of Christmas Eve and ends in success on the morning of Christmas Day. By contrast, the conclusion of Joyce's "Araby" (Chapter 10) begins in anticipation during the day and ends in disillusionment at night. May these contrasting times be viewed symbolically in relationship to the development of the two stories? Other questions you may consider are whether the symbols fit naturally into the context of the story, or whether they seem to be drawn in artificially. Still another question is whether the writer's use of symbols makes for any unique qualities or excellences.

If you choose to write about allegory, you might address the following:

1. *The application of the allegory.* Does the allegory (fable, parable, myth) refer to anything or anyone specific? Does it refer to an action or particular period of history? Or does the allegory refer to human tendencies or ideas? Does it illustrate, point by point, particular philosophies or religions? If so, what are these? If the original meaning of the allegory seems outdated, how much can be salvaged for people living today?

2. *The consistency of the allegory.* Is the allegory maintained consistently throughout the work, or is it intermittently used and dropped? Explain and detail this use. Would it be correct to call your work *allegorical* rather than *an allegory*? Can you determine how elements in the story have been especially introduced because of the requirements of the allegory (such as, perhaps, the complaints of the brother in "The Prodigal Son," which prompt the speech of the joyful father)? Positively, does the element seem natural, or, negatively, does it in any way seem unnatural or arbitrary?

CONCLUSION. In your conclusion you might summarize your main points, describe your general impressions, try to describe the impact of the images or symbolic methods, indicate your personal responses, or show what might further be done along the lines you have been developing in the body. You might also try to assess the quality of the symbolism or allegory and to make a statement about the appropriateness of the specific details to the applied ideas.

SAMPLE ESSAY

Allegory and Symbolism in Hawthorne's "Young Goodman Brown"*

[1]   It is hard to read beyond the third paragraph of "Young Goodman Brown" without finding allegory and symbolism. The opening seems realistic—Goodman Brown, a young Puritan, leaves his home in colonial Salem to take an overnight trip—but his wife's name, "Faith," suggests a symbolic reading. Before long, Brown's walk into the forest becomes an allegorical trip into evil. The idea that Hawthorne shows by this trip is that rigid belief destroys the best human qualities, such as understanding and love.° He develops this thought in the allegory and in many symbols, particularly the sunset, walking-stick, and the path.□

[2]   The allegory is about how people develop destructive ideas. Most of the story is dreamlike and unreal, and therefore the ideas that Brown gains are unreal. After the weird night he thinks of his wife and neighbors not with love, but with hatred for their sins during the "witch meeting" deep in the dream forest. Because of his own dream vision, he condemns everyone around him, and he lives out his life in unforgiving harshness. The story thus allegorizes the harm of following ideals or systems that deny human love and forgiveness.

[3]   The attack on such dehumanizing belief is found not just in the allegory, but also in Hawthorne's many symbols. The seventh word in the story, *sunset*, may be seen as a symbol. Sunset indicates the end of the day. Coming at the beginning of the story, however, it suggests that Goodman Brown is beginning the long night of his hatred, his spiritual death. For him the night will never end because his final days are shrouded in "gloom" (final word).

[4]   The next symbol, the walking-stick, suggests the ambiguous and arbitrary standard by which Brown judges his neighbors. The stick is carried by the guide who looks like Brown's father. It "might almost be seen to twist and wriggle itself like a living serpent" (paragraph 13). The serpent is a clear symbol for Satan, who tempted Adam and Eve (Genesis 3:1–7). The staff is also still a walking-stick, however, and in this respect it is innocent. Given this double vision, it symbolizes our tendencies to see evil where evil does not really exist. This double meaning helps us understand the statement about "the instinct that guides mortal man to evil" (paragraph 50).

---

* See p. 333 for this story.
° Central idea.
□ Thesis sentence.

[5]   In the same vein, the path through the forest is a major symbol of the destructive mental confusion that overcomes Brown. As he walks, the path before him grows "wilder and drearier, and more faintly traced," and "at length" it vanishes (paragraph 50). This is like the description of the "broad" Biblical way that leads "to Destruction" (Matthew 7:13). As a symbol, the path shows that most human acts are bad, while a small number, like the "narrow" way to life (Matthew 7:14), are good. Goodman Brown's path is at first clear, as though sin is at first unique and unusual. Soon, however, it is so indistinct that he can see only sin wherever he turns. The symbol suggests that, as people follow evil, their moral vision becomes blurred and they cannot choose the right way even if it is in front of them.

[6]   Through Hawthorne's allegory and symbols, then, the story presents the paradox of how noble beliefs can backfire destructively. Goodman Brown dies in gloom because he believes that his wrong vision is real. This form of evil is the hardest to stop, no matter what outward set of beliefs it takes, because wrongdoers who are convinced of their own goodness are beyond reach. Such evil and self-righteousness cause Hawthorne to write that "the fiend in his own shape is less hideous than when he rages in the breast of man" (paragraph 53). Young Goodman Brown thus becomes the central symbol of the story. He is one of those who walk in darkness and have forever barred themselves from the light.

Commentary on the Essay

The introduction justifies the treatment of allegory and symbolism because of the way in which Hawthorne early in the story invites a symbolic reading. The central idea relates Hawthorne's method to the idea that rigid belief destroys the best human qualities. The thesis sentence outlines two major areas of discussion: (1) allegory, and (2) symbolism.

Paragraph 2 considers the allegory as a criticism of rigid Puritan morality. Paragraphs 3, 4, and 5 deal with three major symbols: the sunset, the walking-stick, and the path. The aim of this discussion is to show the meaning and application of these symbols for Hawthorne's attack on rigidity of belief. Throughout these three paragraphs the central idea—the relationship of rigidity to destructiveness—is stressed. Hawthorne's allusions to both the Old and New Testaments are pointed out in paragraphs 4 and 5. The concluding paragraph raises questions that lead to the idea that Brown himself is a symbol of Hawthorne's idea that the primary cause of evil is the inability to separate reality from unreality.

WRITING TOPICS FOR CHAPTER 9

1. Write an essay on the relationship of symbols and character development in "Young Goodman Brown."

2. Compare and contrast the symbolism in "The Chrysanthemums" and "The Worker in Sandalwood." To what degree do the stories rely on contextual

symbols? On universal symbols? On the basis of your comparison, how can a case be made for asserting that realism and fantasy are directly related to the nature of the symbolism employed by the writer?

3. On the basis of "The Parable of the Prodigal Son" and "The Worker in Sandalwood," why do you think that religiously oriented stories rely heavily on symbolism?

4. Write a brief story using a universally recognizable symbol (e.g., the flag [patriotism, love of country], [water regeneration, life], the hydrogen bomb [the end of life on earth]). By arranging situations and dialogue, make clear the issues involving your symbol, and also attempt to resolve the conflict that the symbol might bring out among your characters.

5. Write a brief story in which you develop your own contextual symbol. You might, for example, demonstrate how holding a job brings out strengths of a character that were not at first apparent, or how neglecting to care for the inside or outside of a house indicates a character's decline. The principle is to take something that may at first seem normal and ordinary, and then to make that thing symbolic as your story progresses.

10

Idea or Theme: The Meaning and the Message in Fiction

The word **idea** is connected to actions of seeing and knowing; indeed, the words *view* and *wit* (in the sense of knowledge) are close relatives of *idea*. Originally, the word was applied to mental images that, once seen, could be remembered and therefore known. Because of this mental activity, an idea was considered as a conceptual **form** as opposed to external reality. The word is now commonly understood to refer to a concept, thought, opinion, or belief. Some examples of ideas as recognized by philosophers and historians of ideas are these: *infinity, justice, right and good, necessity, the problem of evil, causation*, and, not unsurprisingly, *idea* itself. Other topics that you may consider as ideas, in addition to these, are *power, honor, maturity, persecution, happiness, pain*, and many more. A full consideration of such ideas requires much knowledge, understanding, and thought. In this respect, ideas involve the interrelation of thinking and knowing.

In stories, ideas are not so much about abstract and speculative definitions as about the human side of things. The ancient Greek philosopher Plato, in his *The Republic*, attempts at great length to define the idea of *justice* in the abstract. By contrast, in "Flying Home," the black American writer Ralph Ellison presents a *story* about justice by showing how a young black Air Force pilot is subject to injustice. In "The Lottery," Shirley Jackson causes the unfortunate winner of the lottery to raise questions of fairness and justice as they have affected her in the drawing.

When an idea is brought out in literary works like these, it is often given the name **theme.** This word refers to something laid down, a postulate, a central or unifying idea. Loosely, the *theme* of a work and its *major idea* or *central idea* may be considered as synonyms.

IDEAS, ASSERTIONS, AND MEANING

When a writer creates a story, he or she usually has a unifying idea or theme in mind, or a point to illustrate (but not always consciously or deliberately). This idea may be discovered and traced by readers. Indeed, in studying for themes and ideas, you will find that an idea pervades a story just as a musical composition is controlled by the key, or as a costume is stitched together by thread. A well-written narrative introduces things only as they have a bearing on the idea; actions, characters, statements, symbols, and dialogue may be judged by how closely they relate to the idea or theme. In Tony Cade Bambara's "Raymond's Run," for example, the details are related to the idea that personal rivalries and personal pride are nothing when compared to the need for respect and cooperation in life. In Lawrence's "The Horse Dealer's Daughter," the incidents are all connected by an idea about the overwhelming importance of love, while *obligation* in the sense of duty is a vital idea in Allende's "The Judge's Wife."

Although an idea may be expressed in a phrase or single word, developing an essay about ideas in a work is difficult unless you formulate the idea in a complete sentence to make a clear **assertion.** Thus, we might find stories with assertions that love is necessary but also irrational, hatred is built on misunderstanding, slavery is worse than death, power destroys youthful dreams, or growth is difficult but exciting.

In other words, assertions that you can formulate in studying ideas in effect embody your understanding of a work's **meaning.** In answering the question, "What does this, or that, *mean?*" the response usually takes the form of an assertion about human nature, conduct, or motivation—that is, the form of an idea. For Eudora Welty's "A Worn Path" we might formulate an idea about the character of Phoenix Jackson as follows: "Phoenix illustrates the idea that human beings who are committed to caring for others may suffer for this commitment." Similarly, it might be argued that Mabel in "The Horse Dealer's Daughter" embodies the idea that, "even if a commitment to the dead is strong, the commitment to life is stronger."

DISTINGUISHING AN IDEA
FROM THE RETELLING OF ACTIONS

As you try to phrase assertions about the ideas in a story, it is important to avoid the trap of simply describing plots or main actions. After reading Lawrence's "The Horse Dealer's Daughter," for example, a reader might conclude that the central idea is "about the love between a man and a woman." In fact, this sentence is an obstacle to understanding Lawrence's ideas, since it directs our minds only toward what happens, and does not provide guidance for seeing the characters and events as they relate to an idea. A better way of considering Lawrence's theme or idea is to assert something like "the love of a man and woman is so positive that it can literally rescue people from death." While this formulation implies an understanding that the two major characters fall in love, it more forcefully directs attention to the meaning of their love. The result of this clearer formulation is that details from the story may be focused upon the main idea and away from a summary of events.

IDEAS AND VALUES

The idea or ideas that an author expresses in literature are closely tied to his or her values, or "value system." Unless an idea is completely abstract, as in the idea of a geometric form, it usually implies a value judgment. In "Flying Home," for example, one of Ellison's dominant ideas is the very basic one that all human beings are equal regardless of race. His values are made clear as he directs disapproval against those who are so locked into their own prejudicial habits that they do not help but rather intimidate an injured fellow human being. It is not possible to analyze Ellison's ideas in the story without considering his value system at the same time.

HOW DO YOU FIND IDEAS?

This question is important, because ideas do not just leap out at you from the page. You have to look. Read the story carefully. Consider the main characters, situations, statements, and actions, and evaluate such variables as mood, setting, and atmosphere. Study your notes and observations carefully. At some point, you will be able to formulate an assertion about an idea in the story. There is no hard and fast rule that all statements about ideas should be the same; people notice different things, and individual formulations vary. In Joyce's "Araby," for example, an initial expression of the story's idea might take any of the following forms: (1) The force of sexual attraction is strong and begins early in life. (2) The attraction leads some individuals to strong idealization of the loved one. (3) Sexual feelings are private and may therefore cause embarrassment and shame. (4) This shame may produce ambiguous feelings even among those who are otherwise loyal to what may have been an ultimate cause of the shame (in this story, the Church). Although any one of these choices could be an idea around which to build a study of "Araby," together with others that might be developed, they all have in common the idealization by the narrator of his friend's sister. If, in studying for ideas, you follow a similar process—making a number of formulations for an idea, and then revising them to arrive at a single idea to develop further—you will deal skillfully with ideas in whatever stories you encounter.

With all these things in mind, you will find many ideas in the stories you read. As you read and think, be alert for the following common methods by which authors convey ideas. You should remember, however, that the classifications are neither exhaustive nor restrictive; rather, they are for convenience and reference. In practice, authors may employ all the following methods (and more) at the same time.

Direct Statements by the Author's Unnamed Speaker

Often the unnamed speaker, who may or may not represent the author's exact views, states ideas directly, by way of **commentary,** to guide us or deepen understanding. These ideas may be successful in helping our reading, but they might also disrupt our understanding of the story. In the second paragraph of "The Necklace," for example, Maupassant's authorial voice states the idea that women without strong family connections must rely on their charm and beauty to get on in the world. This idea might seem sexist or patronizing today, but it is nevertheless an accurate restatement of what Maupassant's speaker says. In considering it as an idea, just as you might consider other ideas expressed directly by any other author's unnamed speaker, you might want to adapt it somewhat in line with your own understanding of the story. Thus, an adequate restatement of the Maupassant idea might be this: " 'The Necklace' shows the idea that women, with no power except their charm and beauty, are helpless against chance or bad luck."

Direct Statements by the Persona

Often the first-person narrators or speakers state their own ideas. (For further explanation, see Chapter 5, on Point of View, pp. 197–198.) It is possible that these may be identical with ideas held by the author or the authorial speaker, for the author may use the speaker as a direct mouthpiece for ideas. But there is a danger in making a direct equation, for the author may not be underwriting the ideas of a speaker, but only examining them. Careful consideration is therefore necessary to determine the extent to which the narrator's ideas correspond with or diverge from those of the author. Sometimes the narrators speak views that are directly opposed to what the author might stand for. Usually these instances are clear. Jonathan Swift, for example, makes his speaker Gulliver of *Gulliver's Travels* (1726) say many things that Swift himself clearly rejects. In addition, the author may cause the persona to make statements indicating a limited understanding of the situation he or she is telling about. Thus the adult

Jackie, in O'Connor's "First Confession," says things that show the immaturity of some of his ideas.

Dramatic Statements Made by Characters

In many works, different characters state ideas that are in conflict. The English story writer and novelist Aldous Huxley, for example, frequently introduces "mouthpiece" characters specifically to state ideas related to the fictional story being developed. Authors may thus present thirteen ways of looking at a blackbird and leave the choice up to you. They may provide you with guides for your interpretations, however. For instance, they may create an admirable character whose ideas may be the ones they admire. The reverse is true for a bad character.

Figurative Language

Authors often use figurative language to express or reinforce their ideas. As an example, here is a comparison from Joyce's "Araby," where the narrator describes his youthful admiration for his friend's sister: "But my body was like a harp and her words and gestures were like fingers running upon the wires." This simile is based on the idea that young, first love is a powerful, irresistible force that may possess a person not only deeply but overwhelmingly. Similar uses of language are common in fiction. In "Young Goodman Brown," Hawthorne's descriptions of Brown's wife Faith, and also of the walking stick of the man in the woods suggest that the protagonist's hold on stability and current love are threatened by his ties to a tainted past. In "A Jury of Her Peers" Susan Glaspell compares the dead husband to "a raw wind that gets to the bone." With this language she conveys the idea of bluntness, cruelty, and indifference that so adequately fits this character.

Characters Who Stand for Ideas

Although characters are busy in the action of their respective works, they may also stand symbolically for ideas or values. Mathilde Loisel in "The Necklace" is an embodiment of the idea that women of the nineteenth-century middle class, without the possibility of a career, were hurt by unrealizable dreams of wealth. With two diverse or opposed characters, the ideas they represent may be compared or contrasted. Mrs. Ryan and the priest in O'Connor's "First Confession," for instance, represent opposing ideas about the way in which religion is to be instilled in the young.

In effect, characters who stand for ideas may assume symbolic status. In Ellison's "Flying Home," the character Todd symbolizes the plight of blacks who experience reversals because they are denied the assistance and support that whites take for granted. In Hawthorne's "Young Goodman Brown," the protagonist Brown symbolizes persons who in becoming zealous in any cause go too far and exclude themselves from both love and normal human company. Seen in this way, the statements and actions of characters like Todd and Brown may be construed independently not only as narrative event and dramatic dialogue, but also as idea.

The Work Itself as It Represents Ideas

One of the most important ways in which authors express ideas is to render them as an inseparable part of the total impression of the work. All the events and characters may add up to an idea that is made forceful by the impact of the work itself. Thus, although an idea may not be directly stated in so many words, it will be clear after you have finished reading. For example, in "Flying Home," Ellison makes objective the idea that racial barriers separate human beings and make them cruel when it would be to everyone's interest (such as winning a war) to unite and be helpful. Even "escape literature," which is ostensibly designed to help readers forget about problems, embodies conflicts between good and evil, love and hate, good spies and bad, earthlings and aliens, and so on. Such stories in fact *do* embody ideas and themes, even though they admittedly do not set out to strike readers with the boldness or originality of their ideas.

JAMES JOYCE   (1882–1941)

Araby   *1914*

North Richmond Street,° being blind,° was a quiet street except at the hour when the Christian Brothers' School set the boys free. An uninhabited house of two storeys stood at the blind end, detached from its neighbours in a square ground. The other houses of the street, conscious of decent lives within them, gazed at one another with brown imperturbable faces.

The former tenant of our house, a priest, had died in the back drawing room. Air, musty from having long been enclosed, hung in all the rooms, and the waste room behind the kitchen was littered with old useless papers. Among these I found a few paper-covered books, the pages of which were curled and damp: *The Abbott*, by Walter Scott, *The Devout Communicant*° and *The Memoirs of Vidocq*.° I liked the last best because its leaves were yellow. The wild garden behind the house contained a central apple-tree and a few straggling bushes under one

---

North Richmond Street: Name of a real street in Dublin on which Joyce lived as a boy.
blind: a dead-end street.
The Devout Communicant: A book of meditations by Pacificus Baker, published 1873.
The Memoirs of Vidocq: Published 1829, the story of François Vidocq, a Parisian chief of detectives.

of which I found the late tenant's rusty bicycle-pump. He had been a very charitable priest; in his will he had left all his money to institutions and the furniture of his house to his sister.

When the short days of winter came dusk fell before we had well eaten our dinners. When we met in the street the houses had grown sombre. The space of sky above us was the colour of ever-changing violet and towards it the lamps of the street lifted their feeble lanterns. The cold air stung us and we played till our bodies glowed. Our shouts echoed in the silent street. The career of our play brought us through the dark muddy lanes behind the houses where we ran the gantlet of the rough tribes from the cottages, to the back doors of the dark dripping gardens where odours arose from the ashpits, to the dark odorous stables where a coachman smoothed and combed the horse or shook music from the buckled harness. When we returned to the street light from the kitchen windows had filled the areas. If my uncle was seen turning the corner we hid in the shadow until we had seen him safely housed. Or if Mangan's sister came out on the doorstep to call her brother in to his tea we watched her from our shadow peer up and down the street. We waited to see whether she would remain or go in and, if she remained, we left our shadow and walked up to Mangan's steps resignedly. She was waiting for us, her figure defined by the light from the half-opened door. Her brother always teased her before he obeyed and I stood by the railings looking at her. Her dress swung as she moved her body and the soft rope of her hair tossed from side to side.

Every morning I lay on the floor in the front parlor watching her door. The blind was pulled down within an inch of the sash so that I could not be seen. When she came out on the doorstep my heart leaped. I ran to the hall, seized my books and followed her. I kept her brown figure always in my eye and, when we came near the point at which our ways diverged, I quickened my pace and passed her. This happened morning after morning. I had never spoken to her, except for a few casual words, and yet her name was like a summons to all my foolish blood.

Her image accompanied me even in places the most hostile to romance. 5 On Saturday evenings when my aunt went marketing I had to go to carry some of the parcels. We walked through the flaring street, jostled by drunken men and bargaining women, amid the curses of labourers, the shrill litanies of shop-boys who stood on guard by the barrels of pigs' cheeks, the nasal chanting of street singers, who sang a *come-all-you* about O'Donovan Rossa,° or a ballad about the troubles in our native land. These noises converged in a single sensation of life for me: I imagined that I bore my chalice safely through the throng of foes. Her name sprang to my lips at moments in strange prayers and praises which I myself did not understand. My eyes were often full of tears (I could not tell why) and at times a flood from my heart seemed to pour itself out into my bosom. I thought little of the future. I did not know whether I would ever speak to her or not or, if I spoke to her, how I could tell her of my confused adoration. But my body was like a harp and her words and gestures were like fingers running upon the wires.

O'Donovan Rossa: A popular ballad about Jeremiah O'Donovan (1831–1915), a leader in the movement to free Ireland from English control.

One evening I went into the back drawing-room in which the priest had died. It was a dark rainy evening and there was no sound in the house. Through one of the broken panes I heard the rain impinge upon the earth, the fine incessant needles of water playing in the sodden beds. Some distant lamp or lighted window gleamed below me. I was thankful that I could see so little. All my senses seemed to desire to veil themselves and, feeling that I was about to slip from them, I pressed the palms of my hands together until they trembled, murmuring: *O love! O love!* many times.

At last she spoke to me. When she addressed the first words to me I was so confused that I did not know what to answer. She asked me was I going to *Araby.*° I forget whether I answered yes or no. It would be a splendid bazaar, she said; she would love to go.

—And why can't you? I asked.

While she spoke she turned a silver bracelet round and round her wrist. She could not go, she said, because there would be a retreat° that week in her convent. Her brother and two other boys were fighting for their caps and I was alone at the railings. She held one of the spikes, bowing her head towards me. The light from the lamp opposite our door caught the white curve of her neck, lit up her hair that rested there and, falling, lit up the hand upon the railing. It fell over one side of her dress and caught the white border of a petticoat, just visible as she stood at ease.

—It's well for you, she said.   10

—If I go, I said, I will bring you something.

What innumerable follies laid waste my waking and sleeping thoughts after that evening! I wished to annihilate the tedious intervening days. I chafed against the work of school. At night in my bedroom and by day in the classroom her image came between me and the page I strove to read. The syllables of the word *Araby* were called to me through the silence in which my soul luxuriated and cast an Eastern enchantment over me. I asked for leave to go to the bazaar on Saturday night. My aunt was surprised and hoped it was not some Freemason° affair. I answered few questions in class. I watched my master's face pass from amiability to sternness; he hoped I was not beginning to idle. I could not call my wandering thoughts together. I had hardly any patience with the serious work of life which, now that it stood between me and my desire, seemed to me child's play, ugly monotonous child's play.

On Saturday morning I reminded my uncle that I wished to go to the bazaar in the evening. He was fussing at the hall-stand, looking for the hatbrush, and answered me curtly:

—Yes, boy, I know.

As he was in the hall I could not go into the front parlour and lie at the   15
window. I left the house in bad humour and walked slowly towards the school. The air was pitilessly raw and already my heart misgave me.

When I came home to dinner my uncle had not yet been home. Still it was

---

Araby: A bazaar advertised as "Araby in Dublin," a "Grand Oriental Fete," was held in Dublin from May 14–19, 1894.

    retreat: a special time of two or more days set aside for concentrated religious instruction, discussion, and prayer.

Freemason: and therefore Protestant.

early. I sat staring at the clock for some time and, when its ticking began to irritate me, I left the room. I mounted the staircase and gained the upper part of the house. The high cold empty gloomy rooms liberated me and I went from room to room singing. From the front window I saw my companions playing below in the street. Their cries reached me weakened and indistinct and, leaning my forehead against the cool glass, I looked over at the dark house where she lived. I may have stood there for an hour, seeing nothing but the brown-clad figure cast by my imagination, touched discreetly by the lamplight at the curved neck, at the hand upon the railing and at the border below the dress.

When I came downstairs again I found Mrs Mercer sitting at the fire. She was an old garrulous woman, a pawnbroker's widow, who collected used stamps for some pious purpose. I had to endure the gossip of the tea-table. The meal was prolonged beyond an hour and still my uncle did not come. Mrs Mercer stood up to go: she was sorry she couldn't wait any longer, but it was after eight o'clock and she did not like to be out late, as the night air was bad for her. When she had gone I began to walk up and down the room, clenching my fists. My aunt said:

—I'm afraid you may put off your bazaar for this night of Our Lord.

At nine o'clock I heard my uncle's latchkey in the halldoor. I heard him talking to himself and heard the hall-stand rocking when it had received the weight of his overcoat. I could interpret these signs. When he was midway through his dinner I asked him to give me the money to go to the bazaar. He had forgotten.

—The people are in bed and after their first sleep now, he said.   20

I did not smile. My aunt said to him energetically:

—Can't you give him the money and let him go? You've kept him late enough as it is.

My uncle said he was very sorry he had forgotten. He said he believed in the old saying: *All work and no play makes Jack a dull boy*. He asked me where I was going and, when I had told him a second time he asked me did I know *The Arab's Farewell to his Steed*.° When I left the kitchen he was about to recite the opening lines of the piece to my aunt.

I held a florin° tightly in my hand as I strode down Buckingham Street towards the station. The sight of the streets thronged with buyers and glaring with gas recalled to me the purpose of my journey. I took my seat in a third-class carriage of a deserted train. After an intolerable delay the train moved out of the station slowly. It crept onward among ruinous houses and over the twinkling river. At Westland Row Station a crowd of people pressed to the carriage doors; but the porters moved them back, saying that it was a special train for the bazaar. I remained alone in the bare carriage. In a few minutes the train drew up beside an improvised wooden platform. I passed out on to the road and saw by the lighted dial of a clock that it was ten minutes to ten. In front of me was a large building which displayed the magical name.

I could not find any sixpenny entrance and, fearing that the bazaar would   25
be closed, I passed in quickly through a turnstile, handing a shilling to a weary-looking man. I found myself in a big hall girdled at half its height by a gallery.

The Arab's Farewell to his Steed: A poem by Caroline Norton (1808–1877).
florin: A two-shilling coin in the 1890s (when the story takes place), worth perhaps ten dollars in today's money.

Nearly all the stalls were closed and the greater part of the hall was in darkness. I recognized a silence like that which pervades a church after a service. I walked into the centre of the bazaar timidly. A few people were gathered about the stalls which were still open. Before a curtain, over which the words *Café Chantant* were written in coloured lamps, two men were counting money on a salver. I listened to the fall of the coins.

Remembering with difficulty why I had come I went over to one of the stalls and examined porcelain vases and flowered tea-sets. At the door of the stall a young lady was talking and laughing with two young gentlemen. I remarked their English accents and listened vaguely to their conversation.

—O, I never said such a thing!

—O, but you did!

—O, but I didn't!

—Didn't she say that?   30

—Yes I heard her.

—O, there's a . . . fib!

Observing me the young lady came over and asked me did I wish to buy anything. The tone in her voice was not encouraging; she seemed to have spoken to me out of a sense of duty. I looked humbly at the great jars that stood like eastern guards at either side of the dark entrance to the stall and murmured:

—No, thank you.

The young lady changed the position of one of the vases and went back to   35
the two young men. They began to talk of the same subject. Once or twice the young lady glanced at me over her shoulder.

I lingered before her stall, though I knew my stay was useless, to make my interest in her wares seem the more real. Then I turned away slowly and walked down the middle of the bazaar. I allowed the two pennies to fall against the sixpence in my pocket. I heard a voice call from one end of the gallery that the light was out. The upper part of the hall was now completely dark.

Gazing up into the darkness I saw myself as a creature driven and derided by vanity; and my eyes burned with anguish and anger.

QUESTIONS

1. Describe what you consider to be the story's major idea about youthful admiration and love (if you wish, you might consider the speaker to be describing a childhood "crush")?

2. How might the bazaar, "Araby," be considered symbolically in the story? What does Araby symbolize for the protagonist before he gets there? What does it come to symbolize at the close of the story? To what extent does this symbol embody the story's central idea?

3. Consider the attitude of the speaker toward his home as indicated in the first paragraph. What does he think of the school and of the houses as they represent the people living in them? Why do you think the speaker uses the word *blind* to describe the dead-end street? What relationship exists between the speaker's pain at the end of the story to the ideas in the first paragraph?

4. Who is the narrator? About how old is he at the time of the events related in the story? About how old when he tells the story? What effect is produced by this difference in age between narrator-as-character and narrator-as-story-teller?

D. H. LAWRENCE (1885–1930)

The Horse Dealer's Daughter   *1922*

"Well, Mabel, and what are you going to do with yourself?" asked Joe, with foolish flippancy. He felt quite safe himself. Without listening for an answer, he turned aside, worked a grain of tobacco to the tip of his tongue, and spat it out. He did not care about anything, since he felt safe himself.

The three brothers and the sister sat round the desolate breakfast table, attempting some sort of desultory consultation. The morning's post had given the final tap to the family fortunes, and all was over. The dreary dining-room itself, with its heavy mahogany furniture, looked as if it were waiting to be done away with.

But the consultation amounted to nothing. There was a strange air of ineffectuality about the three men, as they sprawled at table, smoking and reflecting vaguely on their own condition. The girl was alone, a rather short, sullen-looking young woman of twenty-seven. She did not share the same life as her brothers. She would have been good-looking, save for the impassive fixity of her face, "bulldog," as her brothers called it.

There was a confused tramping of horses' feet outside. The three men all sprawled round in their chairs to watch. Beyond the dark holly-bushes that separated the strip of lawn from the high-road, they could see a cavalcade of shire horses swinging out of their own yard, being taken for exercise. This was the last time. These were the last horses that would go through their hands. The young men watched with critical, callous look. They were all frightened at the collapse of their lives, and the sense of disaster in which they were involved left them no inner freedom.

Yet they were three fine, well-set fellows enough. Joe, the eldest, was a man   5
of thirty-three, broad and handsome in a hot, flushed way. His face was red, he twisted his black moustache over a thick finger, his eyes were shallow and restless. He had a sensual way of uncovering his teeth when he laughed, and his bearing was stupid. Now he watched the horses with a glazed look of helplessness in his eyes, a certain stupor of downfall.

The great draught-horses swung past. They were tied head to tail, four of them, and they heaved along to where a lane branched off from the highroad, planting their great hoofs floutingly in the fine black mud, swinging their great rounded haunches sumptuously, and trotting a few sudden steps as they were led into the lane, round the corner. Every movement showed a massive, slumbrous strength, and a stupidity which held them in subjection. The groom at the head looked back, jerking the leading rope. And the cavalcade moved out of sight up the lane, the tail of the last horse, bobbed up tight and stiff, held out taut from the swinging great haunches as they rocked behind the hedges in a motionlike sleep.

Joe watched with glazed hopeless eyes. The horses were almost like his own body to him. He felt he was done for now. Luckily, he was engaged to a woman as old as himself, and therefore her father, who was steward of a neighbouring estate, would provide him with a job. He would marry and go into harness. His life was over, he would be a subject animal now.

He turned uneasily aside, the retreating steps of the horses echoing in his ears. Then, with foolish restlessness, he reached for the scraps of bacon-rind from the plates, and making a faint whistling sound, flung them to the terrier that lay against the fender. He watched the dog swallow them, and waited till the creature looked into his eyes. Then a faint grin came on his face, and in a high, foolish voice he said:

"You won't get much more bacon, shall you, you little b———?"

The dog faintly and dismally wagged its tail, then lowered its haunches, circled round, and lay down again.   10

There was another helpless silence at the table. Joe sprawled uneasily in his seat, not willing to go till the family conclave was dissolved. Fred Henry, the second brother, was erect, clean-limbed, alert. He had watched the passing of the horses with more *sang-froid.*° If he was an animal, like Joe, he was an animal which controls, not one which is controlled. He was master of any horse, and he carried himself with a well-tempered air of mastery. But he was not master of the situations of life. He pushed his coarse brown moustache upwards, off his lip, and glanced irritably at his sister, who sat impassive and inscrutable.

"You'll go and stop with Lucy for a bit, shan't you?" he asked. The girl did not answer.

"I don't see what else you can do," persisted Fred Henry.

"Go as a skivvy,"° Joe interpolated laconically.

The girl did not move a muscle.   15

"If I was her, I should go in for training for a nurse," said Malcolm, the youngest of them all. He was the baby of the family, a young man of twenty-two, with a fresh, jaunty *museau.*°

But Mabel did not take any notice of him. They had talked at her and round her for so many years, that she hardly heard them at all.

The marble clock on the mantel-piece softly chimed the half-hour, the dog rose uneasily from the hearthrug and looked at the party at the breakfast table. But still they sat on in ineffectual conclave.

"Oh, all right," said Joe suddenly, *à propos* of nothing. "I'll get a move on."

He pushed back his chair, straddled his knees with a downward jerk, to get   20
them free, in horsey fashion, and went to the fire. Still he did not go out of the room; he was curious to know what the others would do or say. He began to charge his pipe, looking down at the dog and saying, in a high, affected voice:

"Going wi' me? Going wi' me are ter? Tha'rt goin' further than tha counts on just now, dost hear?"

---

sang-froid: unconcern (literally, cold blood).
skivvy: British slang for housemaid.
museau: French for nose, snout.

The dog faintly wagged its tail, the man stuck out his jaw and covered his pipe with his hands, and puffed intently, losing himself in the tobacco, looking down all the while at the dog, with an absent brown eye. The dog looked up at him in mournful distrust. Joe stood with his knees stuck out, in real horsey fashion.

"Have you had a letter from Lucy?" Fred Henry asked of his sister.

"Last week," came the neutral reply.

"And what does she say?" 25

There was no answer.

"Does she *ask* you to go and stop there?" persisted Fred Henry.

"She says I can if I like."

"Well, then, you'd better. Tell her you'll come on Monday."

This was received in silence. 30

"That's what you'll do then, is it?" said Fred Henry, in some exasperation.

But she made no answer. There was a silence of futility and irritation in the room. Malcolm grinned fatuously.

"You'll have to make up your mind between now and next Wednesday," said Joe loudly, "or else find yourself lodgings on the kerbstone."

The face of the young woman darkened, but she sat on immutable.

"Here's Jack Fergusson!" exclaimed Malcolm, who was looking aimlessly out 35 of the window.

"Where?" exlaimed Joe, loudly.

"Just gone past."

"Coming in?"

Malcolm craned his neck to see the gate.

"Yes," he said. 40

There was a silence. Mabel sat on like one condemned, at the head of the table. Then a whistle was heard from the kitchen. The dog got up and barked sharply. Joe opened the door and shouted:

"Come on."

After a moment, a young man entered. He was muffled up in overcoat and a purple woollen scarf, and his tweed cap, which he did not remove, was pulled down on his head. He was of medium height, his face was rather long and pale, his eyes looked tired.

"Hello Jack! Well, Jack!" exclaimed Malcolm and Joe. Fred Henry merely said "Jack!"

"What's doing?" asked the newcomer, evidently addressing Fred Henry. 45

"Same. We've got to be out by Wednesday.—Got a cold?"

"I have—got it bad, too."

"Why don't you stop in?"

"*Me* stop in? When I can't stand on my legs, perhaps I shall have a chance." The young man spoke huskily. He had a slight Scotch accent.

"It's a knock-out, isn't it," said Joe boisterously, "if a doctor goes round croaking 50 with a cold. Looks bad for the patients, doesn't it?"

The young doctor looked at him slowly.

"Anything the matter with *you*, then?" he asked, sarcastically.

"Not as I know of. Damn your eyes, I hope not. Why?"

"I though you were very concerned about the patients, wondered if you might be one yourself."

"Damn it, no, I've never been patient to no flaming doctor, and hope I   55
never shall be," returned Joe.

At this point Mabel rose from the table, and they all seemed to become
aware of her existence. She began putting the dishes together. The young doctor
looked at her, but did not address her. He had not greeted her. She went out of
the room with the tray, her face impassive and unchanged.

"When are you off then, all of you?" asked the doctor.

"I'm catching the eleven-forty," replied Malcolm. "Are you goin' down wi'
th' trap,° Joe?"

"Yes, I've told you I'm going down wi' th' trap, haven't I?"

"We'd better be getting her in then. —So long, Jack, if I don't see you before   60
I go," said Malcolm, shaking hands.

He went out, followed by Joe, who seemed to have his tail between his legs.

"Well, this is the devil's own," exclaimed the doctor, when he was left alone
with Fred Henry. "Going before Wednesday, are you?"

"That's the orders," replied the other.

"Where, to Northampton?"

"That's it."   65

"The devil!" exclaimed Fergusson, with quiet chagrin.

And there was silence between the two.

"All settled up, are you?" asked Fergusson.

"About."

There was another pause.   70

"Well, I shall miss yer, Freddy boy," said the young doctor.

"And I shall miss thee, Jack," returned the other.

"Miss you like hell," mused the doctor.

Fred Henry turned aside. There was nothing to say. Mabel came in again,
to finish clearing the table.

"What are *you* going to do then, Miss Pervin?" asked Fergusson. "Going to   75
your sister's, are you?"

Mabel looked at him with her steady, dangerous eyes, that always made
him uncomfortable, unsettling his superficial ease.

"No," she said.

"Well, what in the name of fortune *are* you going to do? Say what you *mean*
to do," cried Fred Henry, with futile intensity.

But she only averted her head, and continued her work. She folded the
white table-cloth, and put on the chenille cloth.

"The sulkiest bitch that ever trod!" muttered her brother.   80

But she finished her task with perfectly impassive face, the young doctor
watching her interestedly all the while. Then she went out.

Fred Henry stared about her, clenching his lips, his blue eyes fixing in sharp
antagonism, as he made a grimace of sour exasperation.

"You could bray her into bits, and that's all you'd get out of her," he said,
in a small, narrowed tone.

The doctor smiled faintly.

"What's she *going* to do then?" he asked.   85

"Strike me if *I* know!" returned the other.

trap: a small wagon.

There was a pause. Then the doctor stirred.

"I'll be seeing you to-night, shall I?" he said to his friend.

"Ay—where's it to be? Are we going over to Jessdale?"

"I don't know. I've got such a cold on me. I'll come round to the Moon   90
and Stars, anyway."

"Let Lizzie and May miss their night for once, eh?"

"That's it—if I feel as I do now."

"All's one—"

The two young men went through the passage and down to the back door together. The house was large, but it was servantless now, and desolate. At the back was a small bricked house-yard, and beyond that a big square, gravelled fine and red, and having stables on two sides. Sloping, dank, winter-dark fields stretched away on the open sides.

But the stables were empty. Joseph Pervin, the father of the family, had   95
been a man of no education, who had become a fairly large horse dealer. The stables had been full of horses, there was a great turmoil and come-and-go of horses and of dealers and grooms. Then the kitchen was full of servants. But of late things had declined. The old man had married a second time, to retrieve his fortunes. Now he was dead and everything was gone to the dogs, there was nothing but debt and threatening.

For months, Mabel had been servantless in the big house, keeping the home together in penury for her ineffectual brothers. She had kept house for ten years. But previously, it was with unstinted means. Then, however brutal and coarse everything was, the sense of money had kept her proud, confident. The men might be foul-mouthed, the women in the kitchen might have bad reputations, her brothers might have illegitimate children. But so long as there was money, the girl felt herself established, and brutally proud, reserved.

No company came to the house, save dealers and coarse men. Mabel had no associates of her own sex, after her sister went away. But she did not mind. She went regularly to church, she attended to her father. And she lived in the memory of her mother, who had died when she was fourteen, and whom she had loved. She had loved her father, too, in a different way, depending upon him, and feeling secure in him, until at the age of fifty-four he married again. And then she had set hard against him. Now he had died and left them all hopelessly in debt.

She had suffered badly during the period of poverty. Nothing, however, could shake the curious sullen, animal pride that dominated each member of the family. Now, for Mabel, the end had come. Still she would not cast about her. She would follow her own way just the same. She would always hold the keys of her own situation. Mindless and persistent, she endured from day to day. Why should she think? Why should she answer anybody? It was enough that this was the end, and there was no way out. She need not pass any more darkly along the main street of the small town, avoiding every eye. She need not demean herself any more, going into the shops and buying the cheapest food. This was at an end. She thought of nobody, not even of herself. Mindless and persistent, she seemed in a sort of ecstasy to be coming nearer to her fulfilment, her own glorification, approaching her dead mother, who was glorified.°

who was glorified: see Romans 8:17,30.

In the afternoon she took a little bag, with shears and sponge and a small scrubbing brush, and went out. It was a grey, wintry day, with saddened, dark-green fields and an atmosphere blackened by the smoke of foundries not far off. She went quickly, darkly along the causeway, heeding nobody, through the town to the churchyard.

There she always felt secure, as if no one could see her, although as a matter of fact she was exposed to the stare of everyone who passed along under the churchyard wall. Nevertheless, once under the shadow of the great looming church, among the graves, she felt immune from the world, reserved within the thick churchyard wall as in another country. 100

Carefully she clipped the grass from the grave, and arranged the pinky-white, small chrysanthemums in the tin cross. When this was done, she took an empty jar from a neighbouring grave, brought water, and carefully, most scrupulously sponged the marble headstone and the coping-stone.

It gave her sincere satisfaction to do this. She felt in immediate contact with the world of her mother. She took minute pains, went through the park in a state bordering on pure happiness, as if in performing this task she came into a subtle, intimate connection with her mother. For the life she followed here in the world was far less real than the world of death she inherited from her mother.

The doctor's house was just by the church. Fergusson, being a mere hired assistant, was slave to the countryside. As he hurried now to attend to the outpatients in the surgery, glancing across the graveyard with his quick eye, he saw the girl at her task at the grave. She seemed so intent and remote, it was like looking into another world. Some mystical element was touched in him. He slowed down as he walked, watching her as if spell-bound.

She lifted her eyes, feeling him looking. Their eyes met. And each looked again at once, each feeling, in some way, found out by the other. He lifted his cap and passed on down the road. There remained distinct in his consciousness, like a vision, the memory of her face, lifted from the tombstone in the churchyard, and looking at him with slow, large, portentous eyes. It *was* portentous, her face. It seemed to mesmerise him. There was a heavy power in her eyes which laid hold of his whole being, as if he had drunk some powerful drug. He had been feeling weak and done before. Now the life came back into him, he felt delivered from his own fretted, daily self.

He finished his duties at the surgery as quickly as might be, hastily filling up the bottles of the waiting people with cheap drugs. Then, in perpetual haste, he set off again to visit several cases in another part of his round, before teatime. At all times he preferred to walk, if he could, but particularly when he was not well. He fancied the motion restored him. 105

The afternoon was falling. It was grey, deadened, and wintry, with a slow, moist, heavy coldness sinking in and deadening all the faculties. But why should he think or notice? He hastily climbed the hill and turned across the dark-green fields, following the black cinder-track. In the distance, across a shallow dip in the country, the small town was clustered like smouldering ash, a tower, a spire, a heap of low, raw, extinct houses. And on the nearest fringe of the town, sloping into the dip, was Oldmeadow, the Pervins' house. He could see the stables and the outbuildings distinctly, as they lay towards him on the slope. Well, he would not go there many more times! Another resource would be lost to him, another place gone: the only company he cared for in the alien, ugly little town he was losing. Nothing but work, drudgery, constant hastening from dwelling to dwelling among the colliers and the iron-workers. It wore him out, but at the same time he had a craving for it. It was a stimulant to him to be in the homes of the working people, moving as it were through the innermost body of their life. His nerves were excited and gratified. He could come so near, into the very lives of the rough, inarticulate, powerfully emotional men and women. He grumbled, he said he hated the hellish hole. But as a matter of fact it excited him, the contact with the rough, strongly-feeling people was a stimulant applied direct to his nerves.

Below Oldmeadow, in the green, shallow, soddened hollow of fields, lay a square, deep pond. Roving across the landscape, the doctor's quick eye detected a figure in black passing through the gate of the field, down towards the pond. He looked again. It would be Mabel Pervin. His mind suddenly became alive and attentive.

Why was she going down there? He pulled up on the path on the slope above, and stood staring. He could just make sure of the small black figure moving in the hollow of the failing day. He seemed to see her in the midst of such obscurity, that he was like a clairvoyant, seeing rather with the mind's eye than with ordinary sight. Yet he could see her positively enough, whilst he kept his eye attentive. He felt, if he looked away from her, in the thick, ugly falling dusk, he would lose her altogether.

He followed her minutely as she moved, direct and intent, like something transmitted rather than stirring in voluntary activity, straight down the field towards the pond. There she stood on the bank for a moment. She never raised her head. Then she waded slowly into the water.

He stood motionless as the small black figure walked slowly and deliberately 110 towards the centre of the pond, very slowly, gradually moving deeper into the motionless water, and still moving forward as the water got up to her breast. Then he could see her no more in the dusk of the dead afternoon.

"There!" he exclaimed. "Would you believe it?"

And he hastened straight down, running over the wet, soddened fields, pushing through the hedges, down into the depression of callous wintry obscurity. It took him several minutes to come to the pond. He stood on the bank, breathing heavily. He could see nothing. His eyes seemed to penetrate the dead water. Yes, perhaps that was the dark shadow of her black clothing beneath the surface of the water.

He slowly ventured into the pond. The bottom was deep, soft clay, he sank in, and the water clasped dead cold round his legs. As he stirred he could smell the cold, rotten clay that fouled up into the water. It was objectionable in his lungs. Still, repelled and yet not heeding, he moved deeper into the pond. The cold water rose over his thighs, over his loins, upon his abdomen. The lower part of his body was all sunk in the hideous cold element. And the bottom was so deeply soft and uncertain, he was afraid of pitching with his mouth underneath. He could not swim, and was afraid.

He crouched a little, spreading his hands under the water and moving them round, trying to feel for her. The dead cold pond swayed upon his chest. He moved again, a little deeper, and again, with his hands underneath, he felt all around under the water. And he touched her clothing. But it evaded his fingers. He made a desperate effort to grasp it.

And so doing he lost his balance and went under, horribly, suffocating in   115
the foul earthy water, struggling madly for a few moments. At last, after what seemed an eternity, he got his footing, rose again into the air and looked around. He gasped, and knew he was in the world. Then he looked at the water. She had risen near him. He grasped her clothing, and drawing her nearer, turned to take his way to land again.

He went very slowly, carefully, absorbed in the slow progress. He rose higher, climbing out of the pond. The water was now only about his legs; he was thankful, full of relief to be out of the clutches of the pond. He lifted her and staggered on to the bank, out of the horror of wet, grey clay.

He laid her down on the bank. She was quite unconscious and running with water. He made the water come from her mouth, he worked to restore her. He did not have to work very long before he could feel the breathing begin again in her; she was breathing naturally. He worked a little longer. He could feel her live beneath his hands; she was coming back. He wiped her face, wrapped her in his overcoat, looked round into the dim, dark-grey world, then lifted her and staggered down the bank and across the fields.

It seemed an unthinkably long way, and his burden so heavy he felt he would never get to the house. But at last he was in the stable-yard, and then in the house-yard. He opened the door and went into the house. In the kitchen he laid her down on the hearthrug, and called. The house was empty. But the fire was burning in the grate.

Then again he kneeled to attend to her. She was breathing regularly, her eyes were wide open and as if conscious, but there seemed something missing in her look. She was conscious in herself, but unconscious of her surroundings.

He ran upstairs, took blankets from a bed, and put them before the fire to   120
warm. Then he removed her saturated, earthy-smelling clothing, rubbed her dry with a towel, and wrapped her naked in the blankets. Then he went into the dining-room, to look for spirits. There was a little whiskey. He drank a gulp himself, and put some into her mouth.

The effect was instantaneous. She looked full into his face, as if she had been seeing him for some time, and yet had only just become conscious of him.

"Dr. Fergusson?" she said.

"What?" he answered.

He was divesting himself of his coat, intending to find some dry clothing upstairs. He could not bear the smell of the dead, clayey water, and he was mortally afraid for his own health.

"What did I do?" she asked.   125

"Walked into the pond," he replied. He had begun to shudder like one sick, and could hardly attend to her. Her eyes remained full on him, he seemed to be going dark in his mind, looking back at her helplessly. The shuddering became quieter in him, his life came back in him, dark and unknowing, but strong again.

"Was I out of my mind?" she asked, while her eyes were fixed on him all the time.

"Maybe, for the moment," he replied. He felt quiet, because his strength had come back. The strange fretful strain had left him.

"Am I out of my mind now?" she asked.

"Are you?" he reflected a moment. "No," he answered truthfully, "I don't   130
see that you are." He turned his face aside. He was afraid, now, because he felt
dazed, and felt dimly that her power was stronger than his, in this issue. And she
continued to look at him fixedly all the time. "Can you tell me where I shall find
some dry things to put on?" he asked.

"Did you dive into the pond for me?" she asked.

"No," he answered. "I walked in. But I went in overhead as well."

There was silence for a moment. He hesitated. He very much wanted to go
upstairs to get into dry clothing. But there was another desire in him. And she
seemed to hold him. His will seemed to have gone to sleep, and left him, standing
there slack before her. But he felt warm inside himself. He did not shudder at
all, though his clothes were sodden on him.

"Why did you?" she asked.

"Because I didn't want you to do such a foolish thing," he said.   135

"It wasn't foolish," she said, still gazing at him as she lay on the floor, with
a sofa cushion under her head. "It was the right thing to do. *I* knew best, then."

"I'll go and shift these wet things," he said. But still he had not the power
to move out of her presence, until she sent him. It was as if she had the life of
his body in her hands, and he could not extricate himself. Or perhaps he did not
want to.

Suddenly she sat up. Then she became aware of her own immediate condition.
She felt the blankets about her, she knew her own limbs. For a moment it seemed
as if her reason were going. She looked round, with wild eye, as if seeking something.
He stood still with fear. She saw her clothing lying scattered.

"Who undressed me?" she asked, her eyes resting full and inevitable on his
face.

"I did," he replied, "to bring you round."   140

For some moments she sat and gazed at him awfully, her lips parted.

"Do you love me then?" she asked.

He only stood and stared at her, fascinated. His soul seemed to melt.

She shuffled forward on her knees, and put her arms round him, round
his legs, as he stood there, pressing her breasts against his knees and thighs, clutching
him with strange, convulsive certainty, pressing his thighs against her, drawing
him to her face, her throat, as she looked up at him with flaring, humble eyes of
transfiguration, triumphant in first possession.

"You love me," she murmured, in strange transport, yearning and triumphant   145
and confident. "You love me. I know you love me, I know."

And she was passionately kissing his knees, through the wet clothing, passionately and indiscriminately kissing his knees, his legs, as if unaware of everything.

He looked down at the tangled wet hair, the wild, bare, animal shoulders.
He was amazed, bewildered, and afraid. He had never thought of loving her. He
had never wanted to love her. When he rescued her and restored her, he was a
doctor, and she was a patient. He had had no single personal thought of her.
Nay, this introduction of the personal element was very distasteful to him, a violation
of his professional honour. It was horrible to have her there embracing his knees.
It was horrible. He revolted from it, violently. And yet—and yet—he had not the
power to break away.

She looked at him again, with the same supplication of powerful love, and that same transcendent, frightening light of triumph. In view of the delicate flame which seemed to come from her face like a light, he was powerless. And yet he had never intended to love her. He had never intended. And something stubborn in him could not give way.

"You love me," she repeated, in a murmur of deep, rhapsodic assurance. "You love me."

Her hands were drawing him, drawing him down to her. He was afraid,   150
even a little horrified. For he had, really, no intention of loving her. Yet her hands were drawing him towards her. He put out his hand quickly to steady himself, and grasped her bare shoulder. A flame seemed to burn the hand that grasped her soft shoulder. He had no intention of loving her: his whole will was against his yielding. It was horrible— And yet wonderful was the touch of her shoulder, beautiful the shining of her face. Was she perhaps mad? He had a horror of yielding to her. Yet something in him ached also.

He had been staring away at the door, away from her. But his hand remained on her shoulder. She had gone suddenly very still. He looked down at her. Her eyes were now wide with fear, with doubt, the light was dying from her face, a shadow of terrible greyness was returning. He could not bear the touch of her eyes' question upon him, and the look of death behind the question.

With an inward groan he gave way, and let his heart yield towards her. A sudden gentle smile came on his face. And her eyes, which never left his face, slowly, slowly filled with tears. He watched the strange water rise in her eyes, like some slow fountain coming up. And his heart seemed to burn and melt away in his breast.

He could not bear to look at her any more. He dropped on his knees and caught her head with his arms and pressed her face against his throat. She was very still. His heart, which seemed to have broken, was burning with a kind of agony in his breast. And he felt her slow, hot tears wetting his throat. But he could not move.

He felt the hot tears wet his neck and the hollows of his neck, and he remained motionless, suspended through one of man's eternities. Only now it had become indispensable to him to have her face pressed close to him; he could never let her go again. He could never let her head go away from the close clutch of his arm. He wanted to remain like that for ever, with his heart hurting him in a pain that was also life to him. Without knowing, he was looking down on her damp, soft brown hair.

Then, as it were suddenly, he smelt the horrid stagnant smell of that water.   155
And at the same moment she drew away from him and looked at him. Her eyes were wistful and unfathomable. He was afraid of them, and he fell to kissing her, not knowing what he was doing. He wanted her eyes not to have that terrible, wistful, unfathomable look.

When she turned her face to him again, a faint delicate flush was glowing, and there was again dawning that terrible shining of joy in her eyes, which really terrified him, and yet which he now wanted to see, because he feared the look of doubt still more.

"You love me?" she said, rather faltering.

"Yes." The word cost him a painful effort. Not because it wasn't true. But because it was too newly true, the *saying* seemed to tear open again his newly-torn heart. And he hardly wanted it to be true, even now.

She lifted her face to him, and he bent forward and kissed her on the mouth gently, with the one kiss that is an eternal pledge. And as he kissed her his heart strained again in his breast. He never intended to love her. But now it was over. He had crossed over the gulf to her, and all that he had left behind had shrivelled and become void.

After the kiss, her eyes again slowly filled with tears. She sat still, away from him, with her face drooped aside, and her hands folded in her lap. The tears fell very slowly. There was complete silence. He too sat there motionless and silent on the hearthrug. The strange pain of his heart that was broken seemed to consume him. That he should love her? That this was love! That he should be ripped open in this way!—Him, a doctor!—How they would all jeer if they knew!—It was agony to him to think they might know. 160

In the curious naked pain of the thought he looked again to her. She was sitting there drooped into a muse. He saw a tear fall, and his heart flared hot. He saw for the first time that one of her shoulders was quite uncovered, one arm bare, he could see one of her small breasts; dimly, because it had become almost dark in the room.

"Why are you crying?" he asked, in an altered voice.

She looked up at him, and behind her tears the consciousness of her situation for the first time brought a dark look of shame to her eyes.

"I'm not crying, really," she said, watching him half frightened.

He reached his hand, and softly closed it on her bare arm. 165

"I love you! I love you!" he said in a soft, low vibrating voice, unlike himself.

She shrank, and dropped her head. The soft, penetrating grip of his hand on her arm distressed her. She looked up at him.

"I want to go," she said. "I want to go and get you some dry things."

"Why?" he said. "I'm all right."

"But I want to go," she said. "And I want you to change your things." 170

He released her arm, and she wrapped herself in the blanket, looking at him rather frightened. And still she did not rise.

"Kiss me," she said wistfully.

He kissed her, but briefly, half in anger.

Then, after a second, she rose nervously, all mixed up in the blanket. He watched her in her confusion, as she tried to extricate herself and wrap herself up so that she could walk. He watched her relentlessly, as she knew.

And as she went, the blanket trailing, and as he saw a glimpse of her feet and her white leg, he tried to remember her as she was when he had wrapped her in the blanket. But then he didn't want to remember, because she had been nothing to him then, and his nature revolted from remembering her as she was when she was nothing to him. 175

A tumbling muffled noise from within the dark house startled him. Then he heard her voice:—"There are clothes." He rose and went to the foot of the stairs, and gathered up the garments she had thrown down. Then he came back to the fire, to rub himself down and dress. He grinned at his own appearance, when he had finished.

The fire was sinking, so he put on coal. The house was now quite dark, save for the light of a street-lamp that shone in faintly from beyond the holly trees. He lit the gas with matches he found on the mantel-piece. Then he emptied the pockets of his own clothes, and threw all his wet things in a heap into the scullery. After which he gathered up her sodden clothes, gently, and put them in a separate heap on the copper-top in the scullery.

It was six o'clock on the clock. His own watch had stopped. He ought to be back to the surgery. He waited, and still she did not come down. So he went to the foot of the stairs and called:

"I shall have to go."   180

Almost immediately he heard her coming down. She had on her best dress of black voile, and her hair was tidy, but still damp. She looked at him—and in spite of herself, smiled.

"I don't like you in those clothes," she said.

"Do I look a sight?" he answered.

They were shy of one another.

"I'll make you some tea," she said.

"No, I must go."   185

"Must you?" And she looked at him again with the wide, strained, doubtful eyes. And again, from the pain of his breast, he knew how he loved her. He went and bent to kiss her, gently, passionately, with his heart's painful kiss.

"And my hair smells so horrible," she murmured in distraction. "And I'm so awful, I'm so awful! Oh, no, I'm too awful." And she broke into bitter, heartbroken sobbing. "You can't want to love me, I'm horrible."

"Don't be silly, don't be silly," he said, trying to comfort her, kissing her, holding her in his arms. "I want you, I want to marry you, we're going to be married, quickly, quickly—to-morrow if I can."

But she only sobbed terribly, and cried.

"I feel awful. I feel awful. I feel I'm horrible to you."   190

"No, I want you, I want you," was all he answered, blindly, with that terrible intonation which frightened her almost more than her horror lest he should *not* want her.

QUESTIONS

1. What idea is Lawrence illustrating by the breakup of the Pervin brothers and sister (following the death of the father) at the story's beginning?

2. Consider the narrator's comparison of Joe Pervin and the draft horses (i.e., work horses). What does this comparison mean with regard specifically to Joe, and generally to people without love?

3. What kind of person is Mabel? How do her brothers treat her? How does she feel about her brothers? What dilemma does she face as the story begins?

4. Fergusson watches Mabel in the churchyard and at the pond. How does she affect him in both instances? How does this effect contribute to Lawrence's ideas about love between individuals?

5. How does the setting of the brackish, muddy pond reinforce action, mood, and idea when Fergusson rescues Mabel?

6. What do Mabel and Fergusson realize about themselves and each other in

the Pervin home as he revives and warms her? What is Mabel's attitude toward this realization? Fergusson's attitude? How do their responses signify their growth as characters?

7. Why does the narrator tell us at the story's end that Fergusson "had no intention of loving" Mabel? What idea about love does this repeated assertion convey?

8. Often, popular stories say little more about people who fall in love beyond the statement or implication that they live happily ever after. In "The Horse Dealer's Daughter," however, there is an extensive exploration of the ambiguous feelings of both Fergusson and Mabel after they realize their love for each other. What does Lawrence mean by exploring these feelings so extensively?

RALPH ELLISON   (b. 1914)

Flying Home°

1944

When Todd came to,° he saw two faces suspended above him in a sun so hot and blinding that he could not tell if they were black or white. He stirred, feeling a pain that burned as though his whole body had been laid open to the sun which glared into his eyes. For a moment an old fear of being touched by white hands seized him. Then the very sharpness of the pain began slowly to clear his head. Sounds came to him dimly. He done come to. Who are they? he thought. Naw he ain't, I coulda sworn he was white. Then he heard clearly:

"You hurt bad?"

Something within him uncoiled. It was a Negro sound.

"He's still out," he heard.

"Give 'im time. . . . Say, son, you hurt bad?"   5

Was he? There was that awful pain. He lay rigid, hearing their breathing and trying to weave a meaning between them and his being stretched painfully upon the ground. He watched them warily, his mind traveling back over a painful distance. Jagged scenes, swiftly unfolding as in a movie trailer, reeled through his mind, and he saw himself piloting a tailspinning plane and landing and falling from the cockpit and trying to stand. Then, as in a great silence, he remembered the sound of crunching bone, and now, looking up into the anxious faces of an old Negro man and a boy from where he lay in the same field, the memory sickened him and he wanted to remember no more.

"How you feel, son?"

Todd hesitated, as though to answer would be to admit an inacceptable weakness. Then, "It's my ankle," he said.

"Which one?"

"The left."   10

"Flying Home" is the title of a song made popular by Glenn Miller in the early 1940s.
When Todd came to: Todd is a military pilot in training in the South during World War II (1941–1945). He is black and has just crashed in a field owned by a white man.

With a sense of remoteness he watched the old man bend and remove his boot, feeling the pressure ease.

"That any better?"

"A lot. Thank you."

He had the sensation of discussing someone else, that his concern was with some far more important thing, which for some reason escaped him.

"You done broke it bad," the old man said. "We have to get you to a doctor."   15

He felt that he had been thrown into a tailspin. He looked at his watch; how long had he been here? He knew there was but one important thing in the world, to get the plane back to the field before his officers were displeased.

"Help me up," he said. "Into the ship."

"But it's broke too bad. . . ."

"Give me your arm!"

"But, son . . ."   20

Clutching the old man's arm he pulled himself up, keeping his left leg clear, thinking, "I'd never make him understand," as the leather-smooth face came parallel with his own.

"Now, let's see."

He pushed the old man back, hearing a bird's insistent shrill. He swayed giddily. Blackness washed over him, like infinity.

"You best sit down."

"No, I'm OK."   25

"But, son. You jus' gonna make it worse. . . ."

It was a fact that everything in him cried out to deny, even against the flaming pain in his ankle. He would have to try again.

"You mess with that ankle they have to cut your foot off," he heard.

Holding his breath, he started up again. It pained so badly that he had to bite his lips to keep from crying out and he allowed them to help him down with a pang of despair.

"It's best you take it easy. We gon' git you a doctor."   30

Of all the luck, he thought. Of all the rotten luck, now I have done it. The fumes of high-octane gasoline clung in the heat, taunting him.

"We kin ride him into town on old Ned," the boy said.

Ned? He turned, seeing the boy point toward an ox team browsing where the buried blade of a plow marked the end of a furrow. Thoughts of himself riding an ox through the town, past streets full of white faces, down the concrete runways of the airfield made swift images of humiliation in his mind. With a pang he remembered his girl's last letter. "Todd," she had written, "I don't need the papers to tell me you had the intelligence to fly. And I have always known you to be as brave as anyone else. The papers annoy me. Don't you be contented to prove over and over again that you're brave or skillful just because you're black, Todd. I think they keep beating that dead horse because they don't want to say why you boys are not yet fighting. I'm really disappointed, Todd. Anyone with brains can learn to fly, but then what? What about using it, and who will you use it for? I wish, dear, you'd write about this. I sometimes think they're playing a trick on us. It's very humiliating. . . ." He wiped cold sweat from his face, thinking, What does she know of humiliation? She's never been down South. Now the humiliation would come. When you must have them judge you, knowing that they never accept your mistakes as your own, but hold it against your whole race—that was humiliation. Yes, and humiliation was when you could never be simply yourself, when you were always a part of this old black ignorant man. Sure, he's all right. Nice and kind and helpful. But he's not you. Well, there's one humiliation I can spare myself.

"No," he said, "I have orders not to leave the ship. . . ."

"Aw," the old man said. Then turning to the boy, "Teddy, then you better   35
hustle down to Mister Graves and get him to come. . . ."

"No, wait!" he protested before he was fully aware. Graves might be white. "Just have him get word to the field, please. They'll take care of the rest."

He saw the boy leave, running.

"How far does he have to go?"

"Might' nigh a mile."

He rested back, looking at the dusty face of his watch. But now they know   40
something has happened, he thought. In the ship there was a perfectly good radio, but it was useless. The old fellow would never operate it. That buzzard knocked me back a hundred years, he thought. Irony danced with him like the gnats circling the old man's head. With all I've learned I'm dependent upon this "peasant's" sense of time and space. His leg throbbed. In the plane, instead of time being measured by the rhythms of pain and a kid's legs, the instruments would have told him at a glance. Twisting upon his elbows he saw where dust had powdered the plane's fuselage, feeling the lump form in his throat that was always there when he thought of flight. It's crouched there, he thought, like the abandoned shell of a locust. I'm naked without it. Not a machine, a suit of clothes you wear. And with a sudden embarrassment and wonder he whispered, "It's the only dignity I have. . . ."

He saw the old man watching, his torn overalls clinging limply to him in the heat. He felt a sharp need to tell the old man what he felt. But that would be meaningless. If I tried to explain why I need to fly back, he'd think I was simply afraid of white officers. But it's more than fear . . . a sense of anguish clung to him like the veil of sweat that hugged his face. He watched the old man, hearing him humming snatches of a tune as he admired the plane. He felt a furtive sense of resentment. Such old men often came to the field to watch the pilots with childish eyes. At first it had made him proud; they had been a meaningful part of a new experience. But soon he realized they did not understand his accomplishments and they came to shame and embarrass him, like the distasteful praise of an idiot. A part of the meaning of flying had gone then, and he had not been able to regain it. If I were a prizefighter I would be more human, he thought. Not a monkey doing tricks, but a man. They were pleased simply that he was a Negro who could fly, and that was not enough. He felt cut off from them by age, by understanding, by sensibility, by technology and by his need to measure himself against the mirror of other men's appreciation. Somehow he felt betrayed, as he had when as a child he grew to discover that his father was dead. Now for him any real appreciation lay with his white officers; and with them he could never be sure. Between ignorant black men and condescending whites, his course of flight seemed mapped by the nature of things away from all needed and natural landmarks. Under some sealed orders, couched in ever more technical and mysterious terms, his path curved swiftly away from both the shame the old man symbolized and the cloudy terrain of white men's regard. Flying blind, he knew but one point of landing and there he would receive his wings. After that the enemy would appreciate his skill and he would assume his deepest meaning, he thought sadly, neither from those who condescended nor from those who praised without understanding, but from the enemy who would recognize his manhood and skill in terms of hate. . . .

He sighed, seeing the oxen making queer, prehistoric shadows against the dry brown earth.

"You just take it easy, son," the old man soothed. "That boy won't take long. Crazy as he is about airplanes."

"I can wait," he said.

"What kinda airplane you call this here'n?"   45

"An Advanced Trainer," he said, seeing the old man smile. His fingers were like gnarled dark wood against the metal as he touched the low-slung wing.

" 'Bout how fast can she fly?"

"Over two hundred an hour."

"Lawd! That's so fast I bet it don't seem like you moving!"

Holding himself rigid, Todd opening his flying suit. The shade had gone   50
and he lay in a ball of fire.

"You mind if I take a look inside? I was always curious to see. . . ."

"Help yourself. Just don't touch anything."

He heard him climb upon the metal wing, grunting. Now the questions would start. Well, so you don't have to think to answer. . . .

He saw the old man looking over into the cockpit, his eyes bright as a child's.

"You must have to know a lot to work all these here things."   55

He was silent, seeing him step down and kneel beside him.

"Son, how come you want to fly way up there in the air?"

Because it's the most meaningful act in the world . . . because it makes me less like you, he thought.

But he said: "Because I like it, I guess. It's as good a way to fight and die as I know."

"Yeah? I guess you right," the old man said. "But how long you think before   60
they gonna let you all fight?"

He tensed. This was the question all Negroes asked, put with the same timid hopefulness and longing that always opened a greater void within him than that he had felt beneath the plane the first time he had flown. He felt light-headed. It came to him suddenly that there was something sinister about the conversation, that he was flying unwillingly into unsafe and uncharted regions. If he could only be insulting and tell this old man who was trying to help him to shut up!

"I bet you one thing. . . ."

"Yes?"

"That you was plenty scared coming down."

He did not answer. Like a dog on a trail the old man seemed to smell out   65
his fears, and he felt anger bubble within him.

"You sho' scared me. When I seen you coming down in that thing with it a-rollin' and a-jumpin' like a pitchin' hoss, I thought sho' you was a goner. I almost had me a stroke!"

He saw the old man grinning. "Ever'thin's been happening round here this morning, come to think of it."

"Like what?" he asked.

"Well, first thing I know, here come two white fellers looking for Mister Rudolph, that's Mister Graves's cousin. That got me worked up right away. . . ."

"Why?"

"Why? 'Cause he done broke outta the crazy house, that's why. He liable to kill somebody," he said. "They oughta have him by now though. Then here you come. First I think it's one of them white boys. Then doggone if you don't fall outta there. Lawd, I'd done heard about you boys but I haven't never seen one o' you-all. Cain't tell you how it felt to see somebody what look like me in a airplane!"

The old man talked on, the sound streaming around Todd's thoughts like air flowing over the fuselage of a flying plane. You were a fool, he thought, remembering how before the spin the sun had blazed bright against the billboard signs beyond the town, and how a boy's blue kite had bloomed beneath him, tugging gently in the wind like a strange, odd-shaped flower. He had once flown such kites himself and tried to find the boy at the end of the invisible cord. But he had been flying too high and too fast. He had climbed steeply away in exultation. Too steeply, he thought. And one of the first rules you learn is that if the angle of thrust is too steep the plane goes into a spin. And then, instead of pulling out of it and going into a dive you let a buzzard panic you. A lousy buzzard!

"Son, what made all that blood on the glass?"

"A buzzard," he said, remembering how the blood and feathers had sprayed back against the hatch. It had been as though he had flown into a storm of blood and blackness.

"Well, I declare! They's lots of 'em around here. They after dead things. Don't eat nothing what's alive."

"A little bit more and he would have made a meal out of me," Todd said grimly.

"They bad luck all right. Teddy's got a name for 'em, calls 'em jimcrows,"° the old man laughed.

"It's a damned good name."

"They the damnedest birds. Once I seen a hoss all stretched out like he was sick, you know. So I hollers, 'Gid up from there, suh!' Just to make sho! An' doggone, son, if I don't see two ole jimcrows come flying right up outa that hoss's insides! yessuh! The sun was shinin' on 'em and they couldn't a been no greasier if they'd been eating barbecue."

Todd thought he would vomit, his stomach quivered.

"You made that up," he said.

"Nawsuh! Saw him just like I see you."

"Well, I'm glad it was you."

"You see lots a funny things down here, son."

"No, I'll let you see them," he said.

---

jimcrows: An insulting name for Negroes. Jim Crow (from an old Negro minstrel song) refers to discriminatory practices against blacks.

70

75

80

85

"By the way, the white folks round here don't like to see you boys up there in the sky. They ever bother you?"

"No."

"Well, they'd like to."

"Someone always wants to bother someone else," Todd said. "How do you know?"

"I just know."   90

"Well," he said defensively, "no one has bothered us."

Blood pounded in his ears as he looked away into space. He tensed, seeing a black spot in the sky, and strained to confirm what he could not clearly see.

"What does that look like to you?" he asked excitedly.

"Just another bad luck, son."

Then he saw the movement of wings with disappointment. It was gliding   95
smoothly down, wings outspread, tail feathers gripping the air, down swiftly—
gone behind the green screen of trees. It was like a bird he had imagined there,
only the sloping branches of the pines remained, sharp against the pale stretch
of sky. He lay barely breathing and stared at the point where it had disappeared,
caught in a spell of loathing and admiration. Why did they make them so disgusting
and yet teach them to fly so well? It's like when I was up in heaven, he heard,
starting.

The old man was chuckling, rubbing his stubbled chin.

"What did you say?"

"Sho', I died and went to heaven . . . maybe by time I tell you about it
they be done come after you."

"I hope so," he said wearily.

"You boys ever sit around and swap lies?"   100

"Not often. Is this going to be one?"

"Well, I ain't so sho', on account of it took place when I was dead."

The old man paused, "That wasn't no lie 'bout the buzzards, though."

"All right," he said.

"Sho' you want to hear 'bout heaven?"   105

"Please," he answered, resting his head upon his arm.

"Well, I went to heaven and right away started to sproutin' me some wings.
Six good ones, they was. Just like them the white angels had. I couldn't hardly
believe it. I was so glad that I went off on some clouds by myself and tried 'em
out. You know, 'cause I didn't want to make a fool outta myself the first thing. . . ."

It's an old tale, Todd thought. Told me years ago. Had forgotten. But at
least it will keep him from talking about buzzards.

He closed his eyes, listening.

". . . First thing I done was to git up on a low cloud and jump off. And   110
doggone, boy, if them wings didn't work! First I tried the right; then I tried the
left; then I tried 'em both together. Then Lawd, I started to move on out among
the folks. I let 'em see me. . . ."

He saw the old man gesturing flight with his arms, his face full of mock
pride as he indicated an imaginary crowd, thinking, It'll be in the newspapers, as
he heard, ". . . so I went and found me some colored angels—somehow I didn't
believe I was an angel till I seen a real black one, ha, yes! Then I was sho'—but
they tole me I better come down 'cause us colored folks had to wear a special kin'

a harness when we flew. That was how come they wasn't flyin'. Oh yes, an' you had to be extra strong for a black man even, to fly with one of them harnesses. . . ."

This is a new turn, Todd thought, what's he driving at?

"So I said to myself, I ain't gonna be bothered with no harness! O naw! 'Cause if God let you sprout wings you oughta have sense enough not to let nobody make you wear something what gits in the way of flyin'. So I starts to flyin'. Heck, son," he chuckled, his eyes twinkling, "you know I had to let eve'ybody know that old Jefferson could fly good as anybody else. And I could too, fly smooth as a bird! I could even loop-the-loop—only I had to make sho' to keep my long white robe down roun' my ankles. . . ."

Todd felt uneasy. He wanted to laugh at the joke, but his body refused, as of an independent will. He felt as he had as a child when after he had chewed a sugar-coated pill which his mother had given him, she had laughed at his efforts to remove the terrible taste.

". . . Well," he heard, "I was doin' all right 'til I got to speeding. Found out I could fan up a right strong breeze, I could fly so fast. I could do all kin'sa stunts too. I started flyin' up to the stars and divin' down and zoomin' roun' the moon. Man, I like to scare the devil outa some ole white angels. I was raisin' hell. Not that I meant any harm, son. But I was just feelin' good. It was so good to know I was free at last. I accidentally knocked the tips offa some stars and they tell me I caused a storm and a coupla lynchings down here in Macon County— though I swear I believe them boys what said that was making up lies on me. . . ." 115

He's mocking me, Todd thought angrily. He thinks it's a joke. Grinning down at me. . . . His throat was dry. He looked at his watch; why the hell didn't they come? Since they had to, why? One day I was flying down one of them heavenly streets. You got yourself into it, Todd thought. Like Jonah in the whale.

"Justa throwin' feathers in everybody's face. An' ole Saint Peter called me in. Said, 'Jefferson, tell me two things, what you doin' flyin' without a harness; an' how come you flyin' so fast?' So I tole him I was flyin' without a harness 'cause it got in my way, but I couldn'ta been flyin' so fast, 'cause I wasn't usin' but one wing. Saint Peter said, 'You wasn't flyin' with but one wing?' 'Yessuh,' I says, scared-like. So he says, 'Well, since you got sucha extra fine pair of wings you can leave off yo' harness awhile. But from now on none of that there one-wing flyin', 'cause you gittin' up too damn much speed!"

And with one mouth full of bad teeth you're making too damned much talk, thought Todd. Why don't I send him after the boy? His body ached from the hard ground and seeking to shift his position he twisted his ankle and hated himself for crying out.

"It gittin' worse?"

"I. . . . I twisted it," he groaned. 120

"Try not to think about it, son. That's what I do."

He bit his lip, fighting pain with counter-pain as the voice resumed its rhythmical droning. Jefferson seemed caught in his own creation.

". . . After all that trouble I just floated roun' heaven in slow motion. But I forgot, like colored folks will do, and got to flyin' with one wing again. This time I was restin' my old broken arm and got to flyin' fast enough to shame the devil. I was comin' so fast, Lawd, I got myself called befo' ole Saint Peter again. He said, 'Jeff, didn't I warn you 'bout that speedin'?' 'Yessuh,' I says, 'but it was an accident.' He looked at me sadlike and shook his head and I knowed I was gone. He said, 'Jeff, you and that speedin' is a danger to the heavenly community. If I was to let you keep on flyin', heaven wouldn't be nothin' but uproar. Jeff, you got to go!' Son, I argued and pleaded with that old white man, but it didn't do a bit of good. They rushed me straight to them pearly gates and gimme a parachute and a map of the state of Alabama. . . ."

Todd heard him laughing so that he could hardly speak, making a screen between them upon which his humiliation glowed like fire.

"Maybe you'd better stop awhile," he said, his voice unreal.   125

"Ain't much more," Jefferson laughed. "When they gimme the parachute ole Saint Peter ask me if I wanted to say a few words before I went. I felt so bad I couldn't hardly look at him, specially with all them white angels standin' around. Then somebody laughed and made me mad. So I tole him, 'Well, you done took my wings. And you puttin' me out. You got charge of things so's I can't do nothin' about it. But you got to admit just this: While I was up here I was the flyinest sonofabitch what ever hit heaven!' "

At the burst of laughter Todd felt such an intense humiliation that only great violence would wash it away. The laughter which shook the old man like a boiling purge set up vibrations of guilt within him which not even the intricate machinery of the plane would have been adequate to transform and he heard himself screaming, "Why do you laugh at me this way?"

He hated himself at that moment, but he had lost control. He saw Jefferson's mouth fall open, "What—?"

"Answer me!"

His blood pounded as though it would surely burst his temples and he tried   130
to reach the old man and fell, screaming, "Can I help it because they won't let us actually fly? Maybe we are a bunch of buzzards feeding on a dead horse, but we can hope to be eagles, can't we? Can't we?"

He fell back, exhausted, his ankle pounding. The saliva was like straw in his mouth. If he had the strength he would strangle this old man. This grinning, gray-headed clown who made him feel as he felt when watched by the white officers at the field. And yet this old man had neither power, prestige, rank nor technique. Nothing that could rid him of this terrible feeling. He watched him, seeing his face struggle to express a turmoil of feeling.

"What you mean, son? What you talkin' 'bout . . . ?"

"Go away. Go tell your tales to the white folks."

"But I didn't mean nothin' like that . . . I . . . I wasn't tryin' to hurt your feelings. . . ."

"Please. Get the hell away from me!"   135

"But I didn't, son. I didn't mean all them things a-tall."

Todd shook as with a chill, searching Jefferson's face for a trace of the mockery he had seen there. But now the face was somber and tired and old. He was confused. He could not be sure that there had ever been laughter there, that Jefferson had ever really laughed in his whole life. He saw Jefferson reach out to touch him and shrank away, wondering if anything except the pain, now causing his vision to waver, was real. Perhaps he had imagined it all.

"Don't let it get you down, son," the voice said pensively.

He heard Jefferson sigh wearily, as though he felt more than he could say. His anger ebbed, leaving only the pain.

"I'm sorry," he mumbled. 140

"You just wore out with pain, was all. . . ."

He saw him through a blur, smiling. And for a second he felt the embarrassed silence of understanding flutter between them.

"What you was doin' flyin' over this section, son? Wasn't you scared they might shoot you for a cow?"

Todd tensed. Was he being laughed at again? But before he could decide, the pain shook him and a part of him was lying calmly behind the screen of pain that had fallen between them, recalling the first time he had ever seen a plane. It was as though an endless series of hangars had been shaken ajar in the air base of his memory and from each, like a young wasp emerging from its cell, arose the memory of a plane.

The first time I ever saw a plane I was very small and planes were new in 145 the world. I was four-and-a-half and the only plane that I had ever seen was a model suspended from the ceiling of the automobile exhibit at the State Fair. But I did not know that it was only a model. I did not know how large a real plane was, nor how expensive. To me it was a fascinating toy, complete in itself, which my mother said could only be owned by rich little white boys. I stood rigid with admiration, my head straining backwards as I watched the gray little plane describing arcs above the gleaming tops of the automobiles. And I vowed that, rich or poor, someday I would own such a toy. My mother had to drag me out of the exhibit and not even the merry-go-round, the Ferris wheel, or the racing horse could hold my attention for the rest of the Fair. I was too busy imitating the tiny drone of the plane with my lips, and imitating with my hands the motion, swift and circling, that it made in flight.

After that I no longer used the pieces of lumber that lay about our back yard to construct wagons and autos . . . now it was used for airplanes. I built biplanes, using pieces of board for wings, a small box for the fuselage, another piece of wood for the rudder. The trip to the Fair had brought something new into my small world. I asked my mother repeatedly when the Fair would come back again. I'd lie in the grass and watch the sky, and each fighting bird became a soaring plane. I would have been good a year just to have seen a plane again. I became a nuisance to everyone with my questions about airplanes. But planes were new to the old folks, too, and there was little that they could tell me. Only my uncle knew some of the answers. And better still, he could carve propellers from pieces of wood that would whirl rapidly in the wind, wobbling noisily upon oiled nails.

I wanted a plane more than I'd wanted anything; more than I wanted the red wagon with rubber tires, more than the train that ran on a track with its train of cars. I asked my mother over and over again:

"Mamma?"

"What do you want, boy?" she'd say.

"Mamma, will you get mad if I ask you?" I'd say. 150

"What do you want now? I ain't got time to be answering a lot of fool questions. What you want?"

"Mamma, when you gonna get me one . . ?" I'd ask.

"Get you one what?" she'd say.

"You know, Mamma; what I been asking you. . . ."

"Boy," she'd say, "if you don't want a spanking you better come on an' tell   155
me what you talking about so I can get on with my work."

"Aw, Mamma, you know. . . ."

"What I just tell you?" she'd say.

"I mean when you gonna buy me a airplane."

"Airplane! Boy, is you crazy? How many times I have to tell you to stop
that foolishness. I done told you them things cost too much. I bet I'm gon'
wham the living daylight out of you if you don't quit worrying me 'bout them
things!"

But this did not stop me, and a few days later I'd try all over again.   160

Then one day a strange thing happened. It was spring and for some reason
I had been hot and irritable all morning. It was a beautiful spring. I could feel it
as I played barefoot in the backyard. Blossoms hung from the thorny black locust
trees like clusters of fragrant white grapes. Butterflies flickered in the sunlight
above the short new dew-wet grass. I had gone in the house for bread and butter
and coming out I heard a steady unfamiliar drone. It was unlike anything I had
ever heard before. I tried to place the sound. It was no use. It was a sensation
like that I had when searching for my father's watch, heard ticking unseen in a
room. It made me feel as though I had forgotten to perform some task that my
mother had ordered. . . . then I located it, overhead. In the sky, flying quite low
and about a hundred yards off was a plane! It came so slowly that it seemed
barely to move. My mouth hung wide; my bread and butter fell into the dirt. I
wanted to jump up and down and cheer. And when the idea struck I trembled
with excitement: "Some little white boy's plane's done flew away and all I got to
do is stretch out my hands and it'll be mine!" It was a little plane like that at the
Fair, flying no higher than the eaves of our roof. Seeing it come steadily forward
I felt the world grow warm with promise. I opened the screen and climbed over
it and clung there, waiting. I would catch the plane as it came over and swing
down fast and run into the house before anyone could see me. Then no one
could come to claim the plane. It droned nearer. Then when it hung like a silver
cross in the blue directly above me I stretched out my hand and grabbed. It was
like sticking my finger through a soap bubble. The plane flew on, as though I
had simply blown my breath after it. I grabbed again, frantically, trying to catch
the tail. My fingers clutched the air and disappointment surged tight and hard in
my throat. Giving one last desperate grasp, I strained forward. My fingers ripped
from the screen. I was falling. The ground burst hard against me. I drummed
the earth with my heels and when my breath returned, I lay there bawling.

My mother rushed through the door.

"What's the matter, chile! What on earth is wrong with you?"

"It's gone! It's gone!"

"What gone?"   165

"The airplane. . . ."

"Airplane?"

"Yessum, jus' like the one at the Fair. . . . I . . . . I tried to stop it an' it kep'
right on going. . . ."

"When, boy?"

"Just now," I cried, through my tears.   170

"Where it go, boy, what way?"

"Yonder, there . . ."

She scanned the sky, her arms akimbo and her checkered apron flapping in the wind as I pointed to the fading plane. Finally she looked down at me, slowly shaking her head.

"It's gone! It's gone!" I cried.

"Boy, is you a fool?" she said. "Don't you see that there's a real airplane   175
'stead of one of them toy ones?"

"Real. . . ?" I forgot to cry. "Real?"

"Yass, real. Don't you know that thing you reaching for is bigger'n a auto? You here trying to reach for it and I bet it's flying 'bout two hundred miles higher'n this roof." She was disgusted with me. "You come on in this house before somebody else sees what a fool you done turned out to be. You must think these here lil ole arms of you'n is mighty long. . . ."

I was carried into the house and undressed for bed and the doctor was called. I cried bitterly, as much from the disappointment of finding the plane so far beyond my reach as from the pain.

When the doctor came I heard my mother telling him about the plane and asking if anything was wrong with my mind. He explained that I had had a fever for several hours. But I was kept in bed for a week and I constantly saw the plane in my sleep, flying just beyond my fingertips, sailing so slowly that it seemed barely to move. And each time I'd reach out to grab it I'd miss and through each dream I'd hear my grandma warning:

> Young man, young man,
> Yo' arms too short
> To box with God. . . .

"Hey, son!"   180

At first he did not know where he was and looked at the old man pointing, with blurred eyes.

"Ain't that one of you-all's airplanes comin' after you?"

As his vision cleared he saw a small black shape above a distant field, soaring through waves of heat. But he could not be sure and with the pain he feared that somehow a horrible recurring fantasy of being split in twain by the whirling blades of a propeller had come true.

"You think he sees us?" he heard.

"See? I hope so."   185

"He's comin' like a bat outa hell!"

Straining, he heard the faint sound of a motor and hoped it would soon be over.

"How you feelin'?"

"Like a nightmare," he said.

"Hey, he's done curved back the other way!"   190

"Maybe he saw us," he said. "Maybe he's gone to send out the ambulance and ground crew." And, he thought with despair, maybe he didn't even see us.

"Where did you send the boy?"

"Down to Mister Graves," Jefferson said. "Man what owns this land."

"Do you think he phoned?"

Jefferson looked at him quickly.   195

"Aw sho'. Dabney Graves is got a bad name on accounta them killings but he'll call though. . . ."

"What killings?"

"Them five fellers . . . ain't you heard?" he asked with surprise.

"No."

"Everybody knows 'bout Dabney Graves, especially the colored. He done   200
killed enough of us."

Todd had the sensation of being caught in a white neighborhood after dark.

"What did they do?" he asked.

"Thought they was men," Jefferson said, "An' some he owed money, like he do me. . . ."

"But why do you stay here?"

"You black, son."   205

"I know, but . . ."

"You have to come by the white folks, too."

He turned away from Jefferson's eyes, at once consoled and accused. And I'll have to come by them soon, he thought with despair. Closing his eyes, he heard Jefferson's voice as the sun burned blood-red upon his lips.

"I got nowhere to go," Jefferson said, "an' they'd come after me if I did. But Dabney Graves is a funny fellow. He's all the time makin' jokes. He can be means as hell, then he's liable to turn right around and back the colored against the white folks. I seen him do it. But me, I hates him for that more'n anything else. 'Cause just as soon as he gits tired helpin' a man he don't care what happens to him. He just leaves him stone cold. And then the other white folks is double hard on anybody he done helped. For him it's just a joke. He don't give a hilla beans for nobody—but hisself. . . ."

Todd listened to the thread of detachment in the old man's voice. It was   210
as though he held his words arm's length before him to avoid their destructive meaning.

"He'd just as soon do you a favor and then turn right around and have you strung up. Me, I stays outa his way 'cause down here that's what you gotta do."

If my ankle would only ease for a while, he thought. The closer I spin toward the earth the blacker I become, flashed through his mind. Sweat ran into his eyes and he was sure that he would never see the plane if his head continued whirling. He tried to see Jefferson, what it was that Jefferson held in his hand. It was a little black man, another Jefferson! A little black Jefferson that shook with fits of belly-laughter while the other Jefferson looked on with detachment. Then Jefferson looked up from the thing in his hand and turned to speak, but Todd was far away, searching the sky for a plane in a hot dry land on a day and age he had long forgotten. He was going mysteriously with his mother through empty streets where black faces peered from behind drawn shades and someone was rapping at a window and he was looking back to see a hand and a frightened face frantically beckoning from a cracked door and his mother was looking down the empty perspective of the street and shaking her head and hurrying him along and at first it was only a flash he saw and a motor was droning as through the sun-glare he saw it gleaming silver as it circled and he was seeing a burst like a puff of white smoke and hearing his mother yell, Come along, boy, I got no time for them fool airplanes, I got no time, and he saw it a second time, the plane flying high, and the burst appeared suddenly and fell slowly, billowing out and sparkling like fireworks and he was watching and being hurried along as the air filled with a flurry of white pinwheeling cards that caught in the wind and scattered over the rooftops and into the gutters and a woman was running and snatching a card and reading it and screaming and he darted into the shower, grabbing as in winter he grabbed for snowflakes and bounding away at his mother's, Come on here, boy! Come on, I say! and he was watching as she took the card away, seeing her face grow puzzled and turning taut as her voice quavered, "Niggers Stay From the Polls," and died to a moan of terror as he saw the eyeless sockets of a white hood staring at him from the card and above he saw the plane spiraling gracefully, agleam in the sun like a fiery sword. And seeing it soar he was caught, transfixed between a terrible horror and a horrible fascination.

The sun was not so high now, and Jefferson was calling and gradually he saw three figures moving across the curving roll of the field.

"Look like some doctors, all dressed in white," said Jefferson.

They're coming at last, Todd thought. And he felt such a release of tension within him that he thought he would faint. But no sooner did he close his eyes than he was seized and he was struggling with three white men who were forcing his arms into some kind of coat. It was too much for him, his arms were pinned to his sides and as the pain blazed in his eyes, he realized that it was a straitjacket. What filthy joke was this?   215

"That oughta hold him, Mister Graves," he heard.

His total energies seemed focused in his eyes as he searched their faces. That was Graves: the other two wore hospital uniforms. He was poised between two poles of fear and hate as he heard the one called Graves saying, "He looks kinda purty in that there suit, boys. I'm glad you dropped by."

"This boy ain't crazy, Mister Graves," one of the others said. "He needs a doctor, not us. Don't see how you led us way out here anyway. It might be a joke to you, but your cousin Rudolph liable to kill somebody. White folks or niggers, don't make no difference. . . ."

Todd saw the man turn red with anger. Graves looked down upon him, chuckling.

"This nigguh belongs in a straitjacket, too, boys. I knowed that the minit   220
Jeff's kid said something 'bout a nigguh flyer. You all know you cain't let the nigguh git up that high without his going crazy. The nigguh brain ain't built right for high altitudes. . . ."

Todd watched the drawling red face, feeling that all the unnamed horror and obscenities that he had ever imagined stood materialized before him.

"Let's git outta here," one of the attendants said.

Todd saw the other reach toward him, realizing for the first time that he lay upon a stretcher as he yelled.

"Don't put your hands on me!"

They drew back, surprised.   225

"What's that you say, nigguh?" asked Graves.

He did not answer and thought that Graves's foot was aimed at his head. It landed on his chest and he could hardly breathe. He coughed helplessly, seeing Graves's lips stretch taut over his yellow teeth, and tried to shift his head. It was as though a half-dead fly was dragging slowly across his face and a bomb seemed to burst within him. Blasts of hot, hysterical laughter tore from his chest, causing his eyes to pop and he felt that the veins in his neck would surely burst. And then a part of him stood behind it all, watching the surprise in Graves's red face and his own hysteria. He thought he would never stop, he would laugh himself to death. It rang in his ears like Jefferson's laughter and he looked for him, centering his eyes desperately upon his face, as though somehow he had become his sole salvation in an insane world of outrage and humiliation. It brought a certain relief. He was suddenly aware that although his body was still contorted it was an echo that no longer rang in his ears. He heard Jefferson's voice with gratitude.

"Mister Graves, the Army done tole him not to leave his airplane."

"Nigguh, Army or no, you gittin' off my land! That airplane can stay 'cause it was paid for by taxpayers' money. But you gittin' off. An' dead or alive, it don't make no difference to me."

Todd was beyond it now, lost in a world of anguish.   230

"Jeff," Graves said, "you and Teddy come and grab holt. I want you to take this here black eagle over to that nigguh airfield and leave him."

Jefferson and the boy approached him silently. He looked away, realizing and doubting at once that only they could release him from his overpowering sense of isolation.

They bent for the stretcher. One of the attendants moved toward Teddy.

"Think you can manage it, boy?"

"I think I can, suh," Teddy said.   235

"Well, you better go behind then, and let yo' pa go ahead so's to keep that leg elevated."

He saw the white men walking ahead as Jefferson and the boy carried him along in silence. Then they were pausing and he felt a hand wiping his face; then he was moving again. And it was as though he had been lifted out of his isolation, back into the world of men. A new current of communication flowed between the man and boy and himself. They moved him gently. Far away he heard a mockingbird liquidly calling. He raised his eyes, seeing a buzzard poised unmoving in space. For a moment the whole afternoon seemed suspended and he waited for the horror to seize him again. Then like a song within his head he heard the boy's soft humming and saw the dark bird glide into the sun and glow like a bird of flaming gold.

QUESTIONS

1. What is the point of view in "Flying Home"? What advantage does this point of view give the author? Whose thoughts are accessible to us?

2. Who is the protagonist in the story? Who or what is the antagonist? What is the central conflict?

3. What is the climax of the story? To what extent is the central conflict resolved?

Do you think the protagonist is completely victorious, completely defeated, or something in between? What sorts of ideas does the climax suggest?

4. What do flying and airplanes symbolize for Todd? How is this symbolism developed in the long digression in which Todd remembers his childhood feelings about airplanes (paragraphs 146 through 179)? What ideas do these symbols embody?

5. To what extent are animals and setting used symbolically to express ideas? Consider especially the dust, the sun, mule, oxen, and the buzzard. Why does Ellison (through Jefferson) carefully point out that buzzards are called "jimcrows"?

6. How would you describe Jefferson and the black boy? Are they round or flat characters? Static or dynamic? Individual or representative? How do they help establish the ideas of the story?

7. To what extent can Jefferson's story about his experiences in heaven be considered an allegory of the plight of blacks in twentieth-century America? What ideas about life can be derived from this episode?

8. The story contains two long digressions—Jefferson's story about heaven and Todd's childhood memories. How effectively are these worked into the story? How do they advance the story's message or meaning?

9. How is the symbolism of flying associated with Todd modified and even undercut by the crash, the image of the soaring buzzard, and Jefferson's story about heaven? What ideas emerge from the interaction of all these symbols and episodes?

10. What do we learn about Dabney Graves? What type of character is he (round or flat, static or dynamic, individual or representative)? How do his presence and behavior clarify the story's message?

11. To what extent is the straitjacket put on Todd at the end of the story symbolic? What ideas are expressed with this object?

WRITING ABOUT MEANING IN FICTION

As you take notes and sketch your plan of attack, you should explore all the methods of studying for ideas as described at the beginning of this chapter, and use as many as you think will best give you useful information. It may be that you rely most heavily on the direct statements of the authorial voice, or on a combination of these and your interpretation of characters and actions. Or you might focus exclusively on a persona or speaker and use his or her ideas as a means of determining those of the author, as nearly as they can be established.

In your prewriting and early drafts, as in your final essay, you should make clear the sources of your details, and also distinguish the sources from your own commentary. The patterns to establish are like these:

> In "The Horse Dealer's Daughter," Lawrence's anonymous narrator describes the reservations that Mabel and Dr. Fergusson have about their new-found

love. This description illustrates his idea that love not only creates the excitement of anticipated joy, but also brings out resistance to the possibility of being as controlled as a draught animal in harness. [Here the first sentence refers to a statement by the author's unnamed persona. The second sentence interprets this statement.]

Near the end of "A Jury of her Peers," the county attorney draws attention to the "strange way" in which Mr. Wright was strangled. Because either of the women present would have known, upon seeing the rope used in the murder, that the knot was a type used in quilting (a familiar occupation of small-town women) this language vividly shows Glaspell's idea about the separation of men and women and the divergence of their interests and knowledge. [Here the source of the detail in the first sentence is a dramatic statement by a character in the story. The second sentence is interpretive.]

The speaker in "Araby" states that the boys from the Christian Brothers School are like inmates just released from prison when school lets out for the day. This comparison, coming as it does right at the beginning, establishes a slightly comic tone that emphasizes the childish, rather embarrassed confession that the speaker goes on to make in the story. [Here the first sentence locates the source as the first-person narrator, while the second is interpretive.]

In "First Confession," the priest's thoughtful, good-humored treatment of Jackie, as contrasted with the harsh, punishing treatment by the others, shows the idea that religious incentive is best implanted by kindness and understanding, not by fear. [Here the idea, expressed as a single sentence, is derived from a consideration of the work as a whole].

Recognizing sources in this way keeps the lines of your conclusions clear. Thereby you will help your reader in verifying and following your arguments.

In developing and writing your essay, you can help yourself by answering questions like these: What is the best wording of the idea that you can make? What has the author done with the idea? How can the actions be related to the idea as you have stated it? Might any characters be measured according to whether they do or do not live up to the idea? What values does the idea seem to suggest? Does the author seem to be proposing a particular cause? Is this cause personal, social, economic, political, scientific, ethical, esthetic, or religious? Can the idea be shown to affect the organization of the work? How? Does imagery or symbolism develop or illustrate the idea?

Organizing Your Essay

INTRODUCTION.   In your introduction you might state any special circumstances in the work that affect ideas generally or your idea specifically.

Your statement of the idea will serve as the central idea for your essay. Your thesis sentence should indicate the particular parts or aspects of the story that you will examine.

BODY. The exact form of your essay will be controlled by your goals, which are (1) to define the idea, and (2) to show its importance in the work. Each story will invite its own approach, but here are a number of areas and strategies that might be helpful in the development of the body of your essay:

1. *The form of the work as a plan, scheme, or logical format.* Example: "The idea makes for a two-part work, the first showing religion as punishment and the second showing religion as kindness and reward."
2. *A speech or speeches.* Example: "The priest's conversation and responses to Jackie show in operation the idea that kindness and understanding are the best means to encourage religious commitment."
3. *A character or characters.* Example: "Todd is an embodiment of the idea that black Americans can achieve success and recognition only through their own efforts, and then only against many obstacles."
4. *An action or actions.* Example: "Dr. Fergusson's saving Mabel from drowning indicates the story's idea that love is an outgoing, physical force that almost literally rescues human lives."
5. *Shades or variations of the idea.* Example: "The idea of punishment as a corrective is brought out through the simplicity of the father's 'flaking' of Jackie, the spitefulness of Nora, and the sadistic threats of pain and cosmic intimidation by Mrs. Ryan."
6. *A combination of these together with any other aspect relevant to the work.* Example: "The idea in 'Araby' that devotion is complex and contradictory is shown in the narrator's romantic mission as a carrier of parcels, his outcries to love in the backroom of his house, and his self-reproach and shame at the story's end." [Here the idea is to be traced as action, speech, and character in the story.]

CONCLUSION. You might wish to begin your conclusion with a summary of ideas as appropriate to what you have written in the body of the essay. You might also add your own thoughts, such as your evaluation of the validity or force of the idea. If you are convinced, you might wish to say that the author has expressed the idea forcefully and convincingly, or else to show possible application of the idea to current conditions. If you are not convinced, it is never enough just to say that you disagree; you should try to show the reasons for your disagreement, or to demonstrate the shortcomings or limitations of the idea. If you wish to mention an idea related to the one you have discussed, you might introduce that here, being sure to stress the connections.

SAMPLE ESSAY

The Idea in D. H. Lawrence's "The Horse Dealer's Daughter"*
That Human Destiny Is to Love

[1]
There are many ideas in "The Horse Dealer's Daughter" about the love between men and women. The story suggests that love is a part of the uncontrollable and emotional side of human life, and that love cannot exist without a physical basis. It also suggests that love transforms life into something new, that love gives security, that only love gives meaning to life, and that love is not only something to live for but something to be feared. The one idea that takes in all these is that loving is an essential part of human nature and that it is human destiny to love.° This idea controls the form of Lawrence's story, and the characters are judged on the standard of how they live up to it. The idea is embodied negatively in characters who are without love, and positively in characters who find love.□

[2]
In the first part of the story, loveless characters are negative and incomplete. Their lack of love causes them to be sullen, argumentative, and even cruel. Their lives are similar to those of the draught horses on the Pervin farm, who move with "a massive, slumbrous strength, and a stupidity which [holds] . . . them in subjection" (paragraph 6). The idea is brought across with force, for the story implies that time is running out on people in this condition, and unless they find love they are doomed to misery. And the love they find must be real, for the underlying theme is that anything short of that is an evasion and will hasten their doom. Joe, the eldest of the Pervin brothers, is the major example of what can happen without love, for even though he is planning to marry, he is doing so without love. His motives are destroying him; as the narrator says, Joe's "life was over, he would be a subject animal" like the horses (paragraph 7).

[3]
The thought that life is impossible without love is exemplified most fully in Mabel Pervin. She is alone among the males in the Pervin family, and the character for whom the story is named. Just as the death of the father is breaking up the family, so is it forcing her to drastic action. She assumes that the loss of first her mother and now her father has deprived her of all love. Therefore, her attempted suicide symbolically demonstrates the futility of the loveless, purposeless life.

[4]
Rather than ending Mabel's life, however, the pond really begins it, for it is the occasion of her finding love. Dr. Fergusson, who rescues her, is her destiny. He has been introduced as a person leading a life of quiet desperation. His common cold, which is mentioned when he first appears in the Pervin home, may be seen as an indication of the sickness of the soul without love. When he leaves the house his route is aimless and without any eagerly sought

---

* See p. 373 for this story.
° Central idea.
□ Thesis sentence.

goal, and his seeing Mabel go into the water is not deliberate but accidental. When he acts heroically, therefore, he saves not only Mabel, but himself too. The rescue thus suggests the idea that once love is attained, it restores life.

[5]

But love is also complex, and it creates new problems once it has been found. It brings out new and strange emotions, and it upsets the habits and attitudes of a lifetime. Indeed, there is a strong element of fear in love; it changes life so completely that no one can ever be the same after experiencing it. We see this kind of fearful change in Doctor Fergusson. The narrator tells us that the doctor "had no intention of loving" Mable, but that destiny drives him into this state. The final paragraph of the story indicates the mixture of desire and terror that love and change can produce:

"No, I want you, I want you," was all he answered, blindly, with that terrible intonation which frightened her almost more than the horror lest he should *not* want her (paragraph 191).

Thus, the story suggests that the human destiny that drives people toward love is both joyful and fearful at the same time.

[6]

This realistic presentation of human emotions raises Lawrence's treatment of his idea above the popular or romantic conception of love. Love creates problems as great as those it solves, but it also builds a platform of emotional strength from which these new problems can be attacked. This strength can be achieved only when men and women know love, because only then are they living life as it was designed. The problems facing them then are the real ones that men and women should face, since such problems are a natural result of destiny. By contrast, men and women without love, like those at the beginning of the story, have never reached fulfillment. Consequently, they face problems that are irrelevant to life as it should be lived. The entire story of Mabel and Jack is an illustration of the idea that it is the destiny of men and women to love.

Commentary on the Essay

The introductory paragraph first illustrates the many formulations of the ideas about love that the story suggests, and then produces a comprehensive statement of the theme which is made the central idea of the essay. This assertion is developed as it applies (1) to characters without love and (2) to those who find it. In the body of the essay, paragraphs 2 and 3 emphasize the emptiness of the lives of characters without love. The relationship of these two paragraphs to the main idea is that if the characters are not living in accord with human destiny, they are cut off from life. Thus Joe is dismissed in the story as a "subject animal," and Mable, his sister, attempts suicide. These details are brought out in support of the essay's central idea. Paragraphs 4 and 5 treat the positive aspects of the main idea, focusing on the renewing effect of love on both Mabel and Dr. Fergusson, but also on the complexity of their emotional response to their new love. The last paragraph evaluates the idea or theme of the story and concludes that it is realistic and well balanced.

WRITING TOPICS FOR CHAPTER 10

1. The pilot in "Flying Home" experiences great danger. What does he learn about himself and about his relationship with the men who help him through this experience? What ideas do you think Ellison is trying to assert by this relationship?

2. Choose a story (not from this chapter) and write an essay summing up its main theme. Indicate what you find in the story that makes this theme clear. Do you agree with all the points the author is making? Be sure to support your reasons for agreeing or disagreeing.

3. On the basis of ideas, write an essay criticizing a story in this anthology which you disliked or to which you were indifferent. You might consult Appendix A, on evaluation, for ideas about how to proceed and also the likes and dislikes section of Chapter 1. Explain your response in terms of your own beliefs and ideas, and be sure that your criticism is based on a sound analysis of the story.

4. Compare two stories with similar themes (examples: "Lady with Lapdog" and "The Season of Divorce"; "The Chrysanthemums" and "The Jilting of Granny Weatherall"; "A Worn Path" and "Death"; "A Good Man Is Hard to Find" and "The Lottery"; etc.). For help in developing your essay, consult Appendix B on the technique of comparison-contrast.

5. Select an idea that particularly interests you, and write a story showing how characters may or may not live up to the idea. If you have difficulty getting started, you might use one of these possible ideas:
   a. Interest and enthusiasm are difficult to maintain for a long period of time.
   b. People always seem to want more than they have or need.
   c. The concerns of an adult are different from those of a child.
   d. Justice is difficult to achieve, because it depends on the attempt to determine truth from falsehood.
   e. Work and activity make life meaningful and positive.
   f. It is awkward to confront another person about a wrong or a grievance.

11

Additional Stories

ISABEL ALLENDE (b. 1942)

The Judge's Wife 1987

Translated from the Spanish by Nick Caistor

Nicolas Vidal always knew he would lose his head over a woman. So it was foretold on the day of his birth, and later confirmed by the Turkish woman in the corner store the one time he allowed her to read his fortune in the coffee grounds. Little did he imagine though that it would be on account of Casilda, Judge Hidalgo's wife. It was on her wedding day that he first glimpsed her. He was not impressed, preferring his women dark-haired and brazen. This ethereal slip of a girl in her wedding gown, eyes filled with wonder, and fingers obviously unskilled in the art of rousing a man to pleasure, seemed to him almost ugly. Mindful of his destiny, he had always been wary of any emotional contact with women, hardening his heart and restricting himself to the briefest of encounters whenever the demands of manhood needed satisfying. Casilda however appeared so insubstantial, so distant, that he cast aside all precaution and, when the fateful moment arrived, forgot the prediction that usually weighed in all his decisions. From the roof of the bank, where he was crouching with two of his men, Nicolas Vidal peered down at this young lady from the capital. She had a dozen equally pale and dainty relatives with her, who spent the whole of the ceremony fanning themselves with an air of utter bewilderment, then departed straight away, never to return. Along with everyone else in the town, Vidal was convinced the young bride would not withstand the climate, and that within a few months the old women would be dressing her up again, this time for her funeral. Even if she did survive the heat, and the dust that filtered in through every pore to lodge itself in the soul, she would be bound to succumb to the fussy habits of her confirmed bachelor of a husband. Judge Hidalgo was twice her age, and had slept alone for so many years he didn't have the slightest notion of how to go about pleasing a woman. The severity and stubbornness with which he executed the law even at the expense of justice had made him feared throughout the province. He refused to apply any common sense in the exercise of his profession, and was equally harsh in his condemnation of the theft of a chicken and of a premeditated murder. He dressed formally in black, and, despite the all-pervading dust in this god-forsaken town, his boots always shone with beeswax. A man such as he was never meant to be a husband, and yet not only did the gloomy wedding-day prophecies remain unfulfilled, but Casilda emerged happy and smiling from three pregnancies in rapid succession. Every Sunday at noon she would go to mass with her husband, cool and collected beneath her Spanish mantilla, seemingly untouched by our pitiless summer, as wan and frail-looking as on the day of her arrival: a perfect example of delicacy and refinement. Her loudest words were a soft-spoken greeting; her most expressive gesture was a graceful nod of the head. She was such an airy, diaphanous creature that a moment's carelessness might mean she disappeared altogether. So slight an impression did she make that the changes noticeable in the Judge were all the more remarkable. Though outwardly he remained the same—he still dressed as black as a crow and was as stiff-necked and brusque as ever—his judgments in court altered dramatically. To general amazement, he found the youngster who robbed the Turkish shop-keeper innocent, on the grounds that she had been selling him short for years, and the money he had taken could therefore be seen as compensation. He also refused to punish an adulterous wife, arguing that since her husband himself kept a mistress he did not have the moral authority to demand fidelity. Word in the town had it that the Judge was transformed the minute he crossed the threshold at home: that he flung off his gloomy apparel, rollicked with his children, chuckled as he sat Casilda on his lap. Though no one ever succeeded in confirming these rumours, his wife got the credit for his new-found kindness, and her reputation grew accordingly. None of this was of the slightest interest to Nicolas Vidal, who as a wanted man was sure there would be no mercy shown him the day he was brought in chains before the Judge. He paid no heed to the talk about Doña Casilda, and the rare occasions he glimpsed her from afar only confirmed his first impression of her as a lifeless ghost.

Born thirty years earlier in a windowless room in the town's only brothel, Vidal was the son of Juana the Forlorn and an unknown father. The world had no place for him. His mother knew it, and so tried to wrench him from her womb with sprigs of parsley, candle butts, douches of ashes and other violent purgatives, but the child clung to life. Once, years later, Juana was looking at her mysterious son and realized that, while all her infallible methods of aborting may have failed to dislodge him, they had nevertheless tempered his soul to the hardness of iron. As soon as he came into the world, he was lifted in the air by the midwife who examined him by the light of an oil-lamp. She saw he had four nipples.

"Poor creature: he'll lose his head over a woman," she predicted, drawing on her wealth of experience.

Her words rested on the boy like a deformity. Perhaps a woman's love would have made his existence less wretched. To atone for all her attempts to kill him before his birth, his mother chose him a beautiful first name, and an imposing family name picked at random. But the lofty name of Nicolas Vidal was no protection against the fateful cast of his destiny. His face was scarred from knife fights before he reached his teens, so it came as no surprise to decent folk that he ended up a bandit. By the age of twenty, he had become the leader of a band of desperadoes. The habit of violence toughened his sinews. The solitude he was condemned to for fear of falling prey to a woman lent his face a sad expression. As soon as they saw him, everyone in the town knew from his eyes, clouded by tears he would never allow to fall, that he was the son of Juana the Forlorn. Whenever there was an outcry after a crime had been committed in the region, the police set out with dogs to track him down, but after scouring the hills they invariably returned empty-handed. In all honesty they preferred it that way, because they could never have fought him. His gang gained such a fearsome reputation that the surrounding villages and estates paid to keep them away. This money would have been plenty for his men, but Nicolas Vidal kept them constantly on horseback in a whirlwind of death and destruction so they would not lose their taste for battle. Nobody dared take them on. More than once, Judge Hidalgo had asked the government to send troops to reinforce the police, but after several useless forays the soldiers returned to their barracks and Nicolas Vidal's gang to their exploits. On one occasion only did Vidal come close to falling into the hands of justice, and then he was saved by his hardened heart.

Weary of seeing the laws flouted, Judge Hidalgo resolved to forget his scruples 5
and set a trap for the outlaw. He realized that to defend justice he was committing an injustice, but chose the lesser of two evils. The only bait he could find was Juana the Forlorn, as she was Vidal's sole known relative. He had her dragged from the brothel where by now, since no clients were willing to pay for her exhausted charms, she scrubbed floors and cleaned out the lavatories. He put her in a specially made cage which was set up in the middle of the Plaza de Armas, with only a jug of water to meet her needs.

"As soon as the water's finished, she'll start to squawk. Then her son will come running, and I'll be waiting for him with the soldiers," Judge Hidalgo said.

News of this torture, unheard of since the days of slavery, reached Nicolas Vidal's ears shortly before his mother drank the last of the water. His men watched as he received the report in silence, without so much as a flicker of emotion on his blank lone wolf's face, or a pause in the sharpening of his dagger blade on a leather strap. Though for many years he had had no contact with Juana, and retained few happy childhood memories, this was a question of honour. No man can accept such an insult, his gang reasoned as they got guns and horses ready to rush into the ambush and, if need be, lay down their lives. Their chief showed no sign of being in a hurry. As the hours went by tension mounted in the camp. The perspiring, impatient men stared at each other, not daring to speak. Fretful, they caressed the butts of their revolvers and their horses' manes, or busied themselves coiling their lassoos. Night fell. Nicholas Vidal was the only one in the camp who slept. At dawn, opinions were divided. Some of the men reckoned he was even more heartless than they had ever imagined, while others maintained their leader was planning a spectacular ruse to free his mother. The one thing that never crossed any of their minds was that his courage might have failed him, for he had always proved he had more than enough to spare. By noon, they could bear the suspense no longer, and went to ask him what he planned to do.

"I'm not going to fall into his trap like an idiot," he said.
"What about your mother?"
"We'll see who's got more balls, the Judge or me," Nicolas Vidal coolly replied.

By the third day, Juana the Forlorn's cries for water had ceased. She lay curled on the cage floor, with wildly staring eyes and swollen lips, moaning softly whenever she regained consciousness, and the rest of the time dreaming she was in Hell. Four armed guards stood watch to make sure nobody brought her water. Her groans penetrated the entire town, filtering through closed shutters or being carried by the wind through the cracks in doors. They got stuck in corners, where dogs worried at them, and passed them on in their howls to the newly-born, so that whoever heard them was driven to distraction. The Judge couldn't prevent a steady stream of people filing through the square to show their sympathy for the old woman, and was powerless to stop the prostitutes going on a sympathy strike just as the miners' fortnight holiday was beginning. That Saturday, the streets were thronged with lusty workmen desperate to unload their savings, who now found nothing in town apart from the spectacle of the cage and this universal wailing carried mouth to mouth down from the river to the coast road. The priest headed a group of Catholic ladies to plead with Judge Hidalgo for Christian mercy and to beg him to spare the poor old innocent woman such a frightful death, but the man of the law bolted his door and refused to listen to them. It was then that they decided to turn to Doña Casilda.

The Judge's wife received them in her shady living-room. She listened to their pleas looking, as she always did, bashfully down at the floor. Her husband had not been home for three days, having locked himself in his office to wait for Nicolas Vidal to fall into his trap. Without so much as looking out of the window, she was aware of what was going on, for Juana's long-drawn-out agony had forced its way even into the vast rooms of her residence. Doña Casilda waited until her visitors had left, dressed her children in their Sunday best, tied a black ribbon round their arms as a token of mourning, then strode out with them in the direction of the square. She carried a food hamper and a bottle of fresh water for Juana the Forlorn. When the guards spotted her turning the corner, they realized what she was up to, but they had strict orders, and barred her way with their rifles. When, watched now by a small crowd, she persisted, they grabbed her by the arms. Her children began to cry.

Judge Hidalgo sat in his office overlooking the square. He was the only person in the town who had not stuffed wax in his ears, because his mind was intent on the ambush and he was straining to catch the sound of horses' hoofs, which would be the signal for action. For three long days and nights he put up with Juana's groans and the insults of the townspeople gathered outside the court-room, but when he heard his own children start to wail he knew he had reached the bounds of his endurance. Vanquished, he walked out of the office with his three days' beard, his eyes bloodshot from keeping watch, and the weight of a thousand years on his back. He crossed the street, turned into the square and came face to face with his wife. They gazed at each other sadly. In seven years, this was the first time she had gone against him, and she had chosen to do so in front of the whole town. Easing the hamper and the bottle from Casilda's grasp, Judge Hidalgo himself opened the cage to release the prisoner.

"Didn't I tell you he wouldn't have the balls?" laughed Nicolas Vidal when the news reached him.

His laughter turned sour the next day, when he heard that Juana the Forlorn had hanged herself from the chandelier in the brothel where she had spent her life, overwhelmed by the shame of her only son leaving her to fester in a cage in the middle of the Plaza de Armas.

"That Judge's hour has come," said Vidal.

He planned to take the judge by surprise, put him to a horrible death, then dump him in the accursed cage for all to see. The Turkish storekeeper sent him word that the Hidalgo family had left that same night for a seaside resort to rid themselves of the bitter taste of defeat.

The Judge learned he was being pursued when he stopped to rest at a wayside inn. There was little protection for him there until an army patrol could arrive, but he had a few hours' start, and his motor car could outrun the gang's horses. He calculated he could make it to the next town and summon help there. He ordered his wife and children into the car, put his foot down on the accelerator and sped off along the road. He ought to have arrived with time to spare, but it had been ordained that Nicolas Vidal was that day to meet the woman who would lead him to his doom.

Overburdened by the sleepless nights, the townspeople's hostility, the blow to his pride and the stress of this race to save his family, Judge Hidalgo's heart gave a massive jolt, then split like a pomegranate. The car ran out of control, turned several somersaults and finally came to a halt in the ditch. It took Doña Casilda some minutes to work out what had happened. Her husband's advancing years had often led her to think about what it would be like to be left a widow, yet she had never imagined he would leave her at the mercy of her enemies. She wasted little time dwelling on her situation, knowing she must act at once to get her children to safety. When she gazed around her, she almost burst into tears. There was no sign of life in the vast plain baked by a scorching sun, only barren cliffs beneath an unbounded sky bleached colourless by the fierce light. A second look revealed the dark shadow of a passage or cave on a distant slope, so she ran towards it with two children in her arms and the third clutching her skirts.

One by one she carried her children up the cliff. The cave was a natural one, typical of many in the region. She peered inside to be certain it wasn't the den of some wild animal, sat her children against its back wall, then, dry-eyed, kissed them goodbye.

"The troops will come to find you a few hours from now. Until then, don't for any reason whatsoever come out of here, even if you hear me screaming—do you understand?"

Their mother gave them one final glance as the terrified children clung to each other, then clambered back down to the road. She reached the car, closed her husband's eyes, smoothed back her hair and settled down to wait. She had no idea how many men were in Nicolas Vidal's gang, but prayed there were a lot of them so it would take them all the more time to have their way with her. She gathered strength pondering on how long it would take her to die if she determined to do it as slowly as possible. She willed herself to be desirable, luscious, to create more work for them and thus gain time for her children.

Casilda did not have long to wait. She soon saw a cloud of dust on the horizon and heard the gallop of horses' hoofs. She clenched her teeth. Then, to her astonishment, she saw there was only one rider, who stopped a few yards from her, gun at the ready. By the scar on his face she recognized Nicolas Vidal, who had set out all alone in pursuit of Judge Hidalgo, as this was a private matter between the two men. The Judge's wife understood she was going to have to endure something far worse than a slow death.

A single glance at her husband was enough to convince Vidal that the Judge was safely out of his reach in the peaceful sleep of death. But there was his wife, a shimmering presence in the plain's glare. He leaped from his horse and strode over to her. She did not flinch or lower her gaze, and to his amazement he realized that for the first time in his life another person was facing him without fear. For several seconds that stretched to eternity, they sized each other up, trying to gauge the other's strength, and their own powers of resistance. It gradually dawned on both of them that they were up against a formidable opponent. He lowered his gun. She smiled.

Casilda won each moment of the ensuing hours. To all the wiles of seduction   25
known since the beginning of time she added new ones born of necessity to bring this man to the heights of rapture. Not only did she work on his body like an artist, stimulating his every fibre to pleasure, but she brought all the delicacy of her spirit into play on her side. Both knew their lives were at stake, and this added a new and terrifying dimension to their meeting. Nicolas Vidal had fled from love since birth, and knew nothing of intimacy, tenderness, secret laughter, the riot of the senses, the joy of shared passion. Each minute brought the detachment of troops and the noose that much nearer, but he gladly accepted this in return for her prodigious gifts. Casilda was a passive, demure, timid woman who had been married to an austere old man in front of whom she had never even dared appear naked. Not once during that unforgettable afternoon did she forget that her aim was to win time for her children, and yet at some point, marvelling at her own possibilities, she gave herself completely, and felt something akin to gratitude towards him. That was why, when she heard the soldiers in the distance, she begged him to flee to the hills. Instead, Nicolas Vidal chose to fold her in a last embrace, thus fulfilling the prophecy that had sealed his fate from the start.

TONI CADE BAMBARA   (b. 1939)

Raymond's Run   1970

I don't have much work to do around the house like some girls. My mother does that. And I don't have to earn my pocket money by hustling; George runs errands for the big boys and sells Christmas cards. And anything else that's got to get done, my father does. All I have to do in life is mind my brother Raymond, which is enough.

Sometimes I slip and say my little brother Raymond. But as any fool can see he's much bigger and he's older too. But a lot of people call him my little brother cause he needs looking after cause he's not quite right. And a lot of smart mouths got lots to say about that too, especially when George was minding him. But now, if anybody has anything to say to Raymond, anything to say about his big head, they have to come by me. And I don't play the dozens° or believe in standing around with somebody in my face doing a lot of talking. I much rather just knock you down and take my chances even if I am a little girl with skinny arms and a squeaky voice, which is how I got the name Squeaky. And if things get too rough, I run. And as anybody can tell you, I'm the fastest thing on two feet.

There is no track meet that I don't win the first-place medal. I used to win the twenty-yard dash when I was a little kid in kindergarten. Nowadays, it's the fifty-yard dash. And tomorrow I'm subject to run the quarter-meter relay all by myself and come in first, second, and third. The big kids call me Mercury° cause I'm the swiftest thing in the neighborhood. Everybody knows that—except two people who know better, my father and me. He can beat me to Amsterdam Avenue° with me having a two-fire-hydrant head start and him running with his hands in his pockets and whistling. But that's private information. Cause can you imagine some thirty-five-year-old man stuffing himself into PAL shorts to race little kids?° So as far as everyone's concerned, I'm the fastest and that goes for Gretchen, too, who has put out the tale that she is going to win the first-place medal this year. Ridiculous. In the second place, she's got short legs. In the third place, she's got freckles. In the first place, no one can beat me and that's all there is to it.

I'm standing on the corner admiring the weather and about to take a stroll down Broadway so I can practice my breathing exercises, and I've got Raymond walking on the inside close to the buildings, cause he's subject to fits of fantasy and starts thinking he's a circus performer and that the curb is a tightrope strung high in the air. And sometimes after a rain he likes to step down off his tightrope right into the gutter and slosh around getting his shoes and cuffs wet. Then I get hit when I get home. Or sometimes if you don't watch him he'll dash across traffic to the island in the middle of Broadway and give the pigeons a fit. Then I have to go behind him apologizing to all the old people sitting around trying to get some sun and getting all upset with the pigeons fluttering around them, scattering their newspapers and upsetting the wax paper lunches in their laps. So I keep Raymond on the inside of me, and he plays like he's driving a stagecoach which is O.K. by me so long as he doesn't run me over or interrupt my breathing exercises, which I have to do on account of I'm serious about my running, and I don't care who knows it.

Now some people like to act like things come easy to them, won't let on   5 that they practice. Not me. I'll high-prance down 34th Street like a rodeo pony to keep my knees strong even if it does get my mother uptight so that she walks ahead like she's not with me, don't know me, is all by herself on a shopping trip,

---

the dozens: A children's game in which the participants chant insults at each other.

Mercury: Ancient Roman god of travel, portrayed with winged sandals to show his speed.

Amsterdam Avenue: All the street references, except for 34th Street (paragraph 5), are to places in Harlem.

PAL . . . little kids: A reference to children's racing events sponsored by the Police Athletic League.

and I am somebody else's crazy child. Now you take Cynthia Procter for instance. She's just the opposite. If there's a test tomorrow, she'll say something like, "Oh, I guess I'll play handball this afternoon and watch television tonight," just to let you know she ain't thinking about the test. Or like last week when she won the spelling bee for the millionth time, "A good thing you got 'receive,' Squeaky, cause I would have got it wrong. I completely forgot about the spelling bee." And she'll clutch the lace on her blouse like it was a narrow escape. Oh, brother. But of course when I pass her house on my early morning trots around the block, she is practicing the scales on the piano over and over and over and over. Then in music class she always lets herself get bumped around so she falls accidently on purpose onto the piano stool and is so surprised to find herself sitting there that she decides just for fun to try out the ole keys. And what do you know—Chopin's waltzes just spring out of her fingertips and she's the most surprised thing in the world. A regular prodigy. I could kill people like that. I stay up all night studying the words for the spelling bee. And you can see me any time of day practicing running. I never walk if I can trot, and shame on Raymond if he can't keep up. But of course he does, cause if he hangs back someone's liable to walk up to him and get smart, or take his allowance from him, or ask him where he got that great big pumpkin head. People are so stupid sometimes.

So I'm strolling down Broadway breathing out and breathing in on counts of seven, which is my lucky number, and here comes Gretchen and her sidekicks: Mary Louise, who used to be a friend of mine when she first moved to Harlem from Baltimore and got beat up by everybody till I took up for her on account of her mother and my mother used to sing in the same choir when they were young girls, but people ain't grateful, so now she hangs out with the new girl Gretchen and talks about me like a dog; and Rosie, who is as fat as I am skinny and has a big mouth where Raymond is concerned and is too stupid to know that there is not a big deal of difference between herself and Raymond and that she can't afford to throw stones. So they are steady coming up Broadway and I see right away that it's going to be one of those Dodge City scenes° cause the street ain't that big and they're close to the buildings just as we are. First I think I'll step into the candy store and look over the new comics and let them pass. But that's chicken and I've got a reputation to consider. So then I think I'll just walk straight on through them or even over them if necessary. But as they get to me, they slow down. I'm ready to fight, cause like I said I don't feature a whole lot of chitchat, I much prefer to just knock you down right from the jump and save everybody a lotta precious time.

"You signing up for the May Day races?" smiles Mary Louise, only it's not a smile at all. A dumb question like that doesn't deserve an answer. Besides, there's just me and Gretchen standing there really, so no use wasting my breath talking to shadows.

"I don't think you're going to win this time," says Rosie, trying to signify with her hands on her hips all salty, completely forgetting that I have whupped her behind many times for less salt than that.

Dodge City scenes: The location of "Gunsmoke," a popular TV Western serial, was Dodge City. The opening of the show focused on the protagonist and another man in a showdown gunfight.

"I always win cause I'm the best," I say straight at Gretchen who is, as far as I'm concerned, the only one talking in this ventriloquist-dummy routine. Gretchen smiles, but it's not a smile, and I'm thinking that girls never really smile at each other because they don't know how and don't want to know how and there's probably no one to teach us how, cause grownup girls don't know either. Then they all look at Raymond who has just brought his mule team to a standstill. And they're about to see what trouble they can get into through him.

"What grade you in now, Raymond?"   10

"You got anything to say to my brother, you say it to me, Mary Louise Williams of Raggedy Town, Baltimore."

"What are you, his mother?" sasses Rosie.

"That's right, Fatso. And the next word out of anybody and I'll be *their* mother too." So they just stand there and Gretchen shifts from one leg to the other and so do they. Then Gretchen puts her hands on her hips and is about to say something with her freckle-face self but doesn't. Then she walks around me looking me up and down but keeps walking up Broadway, and her sidekicks follow her. So me and Raymond smile at each other and he says, "Giddyap" to his team and I continue with my breathing exercises, strolling down Broadway toward the ice man on 145th with not a care in the world cause I am Miss Quicksilver herself.

I take my time getting to the park on May Day because the track meet is the last thing on the program. The biggest thing on the program is the Maypole dancing, which I can do without, thank you, even if my mother thinks it's a shame I don't take part and act like a girl for a change. You'd think my mother'd be grateful not to have to make me a white organdy dress with a big satin sash and buy me new white baby-doll shoes that can't be taken out of the box till the big day. You'd think she'd be glad her daughter ain't out there prancing around a Maypole getting the new clothes all dirty and sweaty and trying to act like a fairy or a flower or whatever you're supposed to be when you should be trying to be yourself, whatever that is, which is, as far as I am concerned, a poor black girl who really can't afford to buy shoes and a new dress you only wear once a lifetime cause it won't fit next year.

I was once a strawberry in a Hansel and Gretel pageant when I was in nursery   15
school and didn't have no better sense than to dance on tiptoe with my arms in a circle over my head doing umbrella steps and being a perfect fool just so my mother and father could come dressed up and clap. You'd think they'd know better than to encourage that kind of nonsense. I am not a strawberry. I do not dance on my toes. I run. That is what I am all about. So I always come late to the May Day program, just in time to get my number pinned on and lay in the grass till they announce the fifty-yard dash.

I put Raymond in the little swings, which is a tight squeeze this year and will be impossible next year. Then I look around for Mr. Pearson, who pins the numbers on. I'm really looking for Gretchen if you want to know the truth, but she's not around. The park is jam-packed. Parents in hats and corsages and breast-pocket handkerchiefs peeking up. Kids in white dresses and light blue suits. The parkees unfolding chairs and chasing the rowdy kids from Lenox as if they had no right to be there. The big guys with their caps on backwards, leaning against the fence swirling the basketballs on the tips of their fingers, waiting for all these crazy people to clear out the park so they can play. Most of the kids in my class are carrying bass drums and glockenspiels and flutes. You'd think they'd put in a few bongos or something for real like that.

Then here comes Mr. Pearson with his clipboard and his cards and pencils and whistles and safety pins and fifty million other things he's always dropping all over the place with his clumsy self. He sticks out in a crowd because he's on stilts. We used to call him Jack and the Beanstalk to get him mad. But I'm the only one that can outrun him and get away, and I'm too grown for that silliness now.

"Well, Squeaky," he says, checking my name off the list and handing me number seven and two pins. And I'm thinking he's got no right to call me Squeaky, if I can't call him Beanstalk.

"Hazel Elizabeth Deborah Parker," I correct him and tell him to write it down on his board.

"Well, Hazel Elizabeth Deborah Parker, going to give someone else a break this year?" I squint at him real hard to see if he is seriously thinking I should lose the race on purpose just to give someone else a break. "Only six girls running this time," he continues, shaking his head sadly like it's my fault all of New York didn't turn out in sneakers. "That new girl should give you a run for your money." He looks around the park for Gretchen like a periscope in a submarine movie. "Wouldn't it be a nice gesture if you were . . . to ahhh . . ."

I give him such a look he couldn't finish putting that idea into words. Grownups got a lot of nerve sometimes. I pin number seven to myself and stomp away, I'm so burnt. And I go straight for the track and stretch out on the grass while the band winds up with "Oh, the Monkey Wrapped His Tail Around the Flagpole,"° which my teacher calls by some other name. The man on the loudspeaker is calling everyone over to the track and I'm on my back looking at the sky, trying to pretend I'm in the country, but I can't, because even grass in the city feels hard as sidewalk, and there's just no pretending you are anywhere but in a "concrete jungle" as my grandfather says.

The twenty-yard dash takes all of two minutes cause most of the little kids don't know no better than to run off the track or run the wrong way or run smack into the fence and fall down and cry. One little kid, though, has got the good sense to run straight for the white ribbon up ahead so he wins. Then the second-graders line up for the thirty-yard dash and I don't even bother to turn my head to watch cause Raphael Perez always wins. He wins before he even begins by psyching the runners, telling them they're going to trip on their shoelaces and fall on their faces or lose their shorts or something, which he doesn't really have to do since he is very fast, almost as fast as I am. After that is the forty-yard dash which I use to run when I was in first grade. Raymond is hollering from the swings cause he knows I'm about to do my thing cause the man on the loudspeaker has just announced the fifty-yard dash, although he might just as well be giving a recipe for angel food cake cause you can hardly make out what he's saying for the static. I get up and slip off my sweat pants and then I see Gretchen standing at the starting line, kicking her legs out like a pro. Then as I get into place I see that ole Raymond is on line on the other side of the fence, bending down with

Oh . . . Flagpole: The first line of obscene lyrics to Sousa's "Washington Post" march.

his fingers on the ground just like he knew what he was doing. I was going to yell at him but then I didn't. It burns up your energy to holler.

Every time, just before I take off in a race, I always feel like I'm in a dream, the kind of dream you have when you're sick with fever and feel all hot and weightless. I dream I'm flying over a sandy beach in the early morning sun, kissing the leaves of the trees as I fly by. And there's always the smell of apples, just like in the country when I was little and used to think I was a choo-choo train, running through the fields of corn and chugging up the hill to the orchard. And all the time I'm dreaming this, I get lighter and lighter until I'm flying over the beach again, getting blown through the sky like a feather that weighs nothing at all. But once I spread my fingers in the dirt and crouch over the Get on Your Mark, the dream goes and I am solid again and am telling myself, Squeaky you must win, you must win, you are the fastest thing in the world, you can even beat your father up Amsterdam if you really try. And then I feel my weight coming back just behind my knees then down to my feet then into the earth and the pistol shot explodes in my blood and I am off and weightless again, flying past the other runners, my arms pumping up and down and the whole world is quiet except for the crunch as I zoom over the gravel in the track. I glance to my left and there is no one. To the right, a blurred Gretchen, who's got her chin jutting out as if it would win the race all by itself. And on the other side of the fence is Raymond with his arms down to his side and the palms tucked up behind him, running in his very own style, and it's the first time I ever saw that and I almost stop to watch my brother Raymond on his first run. But the white ribbon is bouncing toward me and I tear past it, racing into the distance till my feet with a mind of their own start digging up footfuls of dirt and brake me short. Then all the kids standing on the side pile on me, banging me on the back and slapping my head with their May Day programs, for I have won again and everybody on 151st Street can walk tall for another year.

"In first place . . ." the man on the loudspeaker is clear as a bell now, but then he pauses and the loudspeaker starts to whine. Then static. And I lean down to catch my breath and here comes Gretchen walking back, for she's overshot the finish line too, huffing and puffing with her hands on her hips taking it slow, breathing in steady time like a real pro and I sort of like her a little for the first time. "In first place . . ." and then three or four voices get all mixed up on the loudspeaker and I dig my sneaker into the grass and stare at Gretchen who's staring back, we both wondering just who did win. I can hear old Beanstalk arguing with the man on the loudspeaker and then a few others running their mouths about what the stopwatches say. Then I hear Raymond yanking at the fence to call me and I wave to shush him, but he keeps rattling the fence like a gorilla in a cage like in them gorilla movies, but then like a dancer or something he starts climbing up nice and easy but very fast. And it occurs to me, watching how smoothly he climbs hand over hand and remembering how he looked running with his arms down to his side and with the wind pulling his mouth back and his teeth showing and all, it occurred to me that Raymond would make a very fine runner. Doesn't he always keep up with me on my trots? And he surely knows how to breathe in counts of seven cause he's always doing it at the dinner table, which drives my brother George up the wall. And I'm smiling to beat the band cause if I've lost this race, or if me and Gretchen tied, or even if I've won, I can always retire as a runner and begin a whole new career as a coach with Raymond as my champion. After all, with a little more study I can beat Cynthia and her phony self at the spelling bee. And if I bugged my mother, I could get piano lessons and become a star. And I have a big rep as the baddest thing around. And I've got a roomful of ribbons and medals and awards. But what has Raymond got to call his own?

So I stand there with my new plans, laughing out loud by this time as Raymond   25
jumps down from the fence and runs over with his teeth showing and his arms down to the side, which no one before him has quite mastered as a running style. And by the time he comes over I'm jumping up and down so glad to see him— my brother Raymond, a great runner in the family tradition. But of course everyone thinks I'm jumping up and down because the men on the loudspeaker have finally gotten themselves together and compared notes and are announcing "In first place— Miss Hazel Elizabeth Deborah Parker." (Dig that.) "In second place—Miss Gretchen P. Lewis." And I look at Gretchen wondering what the "P" stands for. And I smile. Cause she's good, no doubt about it. Maybe she'd like to help me coach Raymond; she obviously is serious about running, as any fool can see. And she nods to congratulate me and then she smiles. And I smile. We stand there with this big smile of respect between us. It's about as real a smile as girls can do for each other, considering we don't practice real smiling every day, you know, cause maybe we too busy being flowers or fairies or strawberries instead of something honest and worthy of respect . . . you know . . . like being people.

JOHN CHEEVER   (1912–1982)

The Season of Divorce   *1973*

My wife has brown hair, dark eyes, and a gentle disposition. Because of her gentle disposition, I sometimes think that she spoils the children. She can't refuse them anything. They always get around her. Ethel and I have been married for ten years. We both come from Morristown, New Jersey, and I can't even remember when I first met her. Our marriage has always seemed happy and resourceful to me. We live in a walk-up in the East Fifties. Our son, Carl, who is six, goes to a good private school, and our daughter, who is four, won't go to school until next year. We often find fault with the way we were educated, but we seem to be struggling to raise our children along the same lines, and when the time comes, I suppose they'll go to the same school and colleges that we went to.

Ethel graduated from a women's college in the East, and then went for a year to the University of Grenoble. She worked for a year in New York after returning from France, and then we were married. She once hung her diploma above the kitchen sink, but it was a short-lived joke and I don't know where the diploma is now. Ethel is cheerful and adaptable, as well as gentle, and we both come from that enormous stratum of the middle class that is distinguished by its ability to recall better times. Lost money is so much a part of our lives that I am sometimes reminded of expatriates, of a group who have adapted themselves energetically to some alien soil but who are reminded, now and then, of the escarpments of their native coast. Because our lives are confined by my modest salary, the surface of Ethel's life is easy to describe.

She gets up at seven and turns the radio on. After she is dressed, she rouses the children and cooks the breakfast. Our son has to be walked to the school bus at eight o'clock. When Ethel returns from this trip, Carol's hair has to be braided. I leave the house at eight-thirty, but I know that every move that Ethel makes for the rest of the day will be determined by the housework, the cooking, the shopping, and the demands of the children. I know that on Tuesdays and Thursdays she will be at the A & P between eleven and noon, that on every clear afternoon she will be on a certain bench in a playground from three until five, that she cleans the house on Mondays, Wednesdays, and Fridays, and polishes the silver when it rains. When I return at six, she is usually cleaning the vegetables or making some other preparation for dinner. Then when the children have been fed and bathed, when the dinner is ready, when the table in the living room is set with food and china, she stands in the middle of the room as if she has lost or forgotten something, and this moment of reflection is so deep that she will not hear me if I speak to her, or the children if they call. Then it is over. She lights the four white candles in their silver sticks, and we sit down to a supper of corned-beef hash or some other modest fare.

We go out once or twice a week and entertain about once a month. Because of practical considerations, most of the people we see live in our neighborhood. We often go around the corner to the parties given by a generous couple named Newsome. The Newsomes' parties are large and confusing, and the arbitrary impulses of friendship are given a free play.

We became attached at the Newsomes' one evening, for reasons that I've never understood, to a couple named Dr. and Mrs. Trencher. I think that Mrs. Trencher was the aggressor in this friendship, and after our first meeting she telephoned Ethel three or four times. We went to their house for dinner, and they came to our house, and sometimes in the evening when Dr. Trencher was walking their old dachshund, he would come up for a short visit. He seemed like a pleasant man to have around. I've heard other doctors say that he's a good physician. The Trenchers are about thirty; at least he is. She is older.

I'd say that Mrs. Trencher is a plain woman, but her plainness is difficult to specify. She is small, she has a good figure and regular features, and I suppose that the impression of plainness arises from some inner modesty, some needlessly narrow view of her chances. Dr. Trencher doesn't smoke or drink, and I don't know whether there's any connection or not, but the coloring in his slender face is fresh—his cheeks are pink, and his blue eyes are clear and strong. He has the singular optimism of a well-adjusted physician—the feeling that death is a chance misfortune and that the physical world is merely a field for conquest. In the same way that his wife seems plain, he seems young.

The Trenchers live in a comfortable and unpretentious private house in our neighborhood. The house is old-fashioned; its living rooms are large, its halls are gloomy, and the Trenchers don't seem to generate enough human warmth to animate the place, so that you sometimes take away from them, at the end of an evening, an impression of many empty rooms. Mrs. Trencher is noticeably attached

5

to her possessions—her clothes, her jewels, and the ornaments she's bought for the house—and to Fräulein, the old dachshund. She feeds Fräulein scraps from the table, furtively, as if she has been forbidden to do this, and after dinner Fräulein lies beside her on the sofa. With the play of green light from a television set on her drawn features and her thin hands stroking Fräulein, Mrs. Trencher looked to me one evening like a good-hearted and miserable soul.

Mrs. Trencher began to call Ethel in the mornings for a talk or to ask her for lunch or a matinee. Ethel can't go out in the day and she claims to dislike long telephone conversations. She complained that Mrs. Trencher was a tireless and aggressive gossip. Then late one afternoon Dr. Trencher appeared at the playground where Ethel takes our two children. He was walking by, and he saw her and sat with her until it was time to take the children home. He came again a few days later, and then his visits with Ethel in the playground, she told me, became a regular thing. Ethel thought that perhaps he didn't have many patients and that with nothing to do he was happy to talk with anyone. Then, when we were washing dishes one night, Ethel said thoughtfully that Trencher's attitude toward her seemed strange. "He stares at me," she said. "He sighs and stares at me." I know what my wife looks like in the playground. She wears an old tweed coat, overshoes, and Army gloves, and a scarf is tied under her chin. The playground is a fenced and paved lot between a slum and the river. The picture of the well-dressed, pink-cheeked doctor losing his heart to Ethel in this environment was hard to take seriously. She didn't mention him then for several days, and I guessed that he had stopped his visits. Ethel's birthday came at the end of the month, and I forgot about it, but when I came home that evening, there were a lot of roses in the living room. They were a birthday present from Trencher, she told me. I was cross at myself for having forgotten her birthday, and Trencher's roses made me angry. I asked her if she'd seen him recently.

"Oh, yes," she said, "he still comes to the playground nearly every afternoon. I haven't told you, have I? He's made his declaration. He loves me. He can't live without me. He'd walk through fire to hear the notes of my voice." She laughed. "That's what he said."

"When did he say this?"   10

"At the playground. And walking home. Yesterday."

"How long has he known?"

"That's the funny part about it," she said. "He knew before he met me at the Newsomes' that night. He saw me waiting for a crosstown bus about three weeks before that. He just saw me and he said that he knew then, the minute he saw me. Of course, he's crazy."

I was tired that night and worried about taxes and bills, and I could think of Trencher's declaration only as a comical mistake. I felt that he was a captive of financial and sentimental commitments, like every other man I know, and that he was no more free to fall in love with a strange woman he saw on a street corner than he was to take a walking trip through French Guiana or to recommence his life in Chicago under an assumed name. His declaration, the scene in the playground, seemed to me to be like those chance meetings that are a part of the life of any large city. A blind man asks you to help him across the street, and as you are about to leave him, he seizes your arm and regales you with a passionate account of his cruel and ungrateful children; or the elevator man who is taking you up to a party turns to you suddenly and says that his grandson has infantile paralysis. The city is full of accidental revelation, half-heard cries for help, and strangers who will tell you everything at the first suspicion of sympathy, and Trencher seemed to me like the blind man or the elevator operator. His declaration had no more bearing on the business of our lives than these interruptions.

Mrs. Trencher's telephone conversations had stopped, and we had stopped   15
visiting the Trenchers, but sometimes I would see him in the morning on the crosstown bus when I was late going to work. He seemed understandably embarrassed whenever he saw me, but the bus was always crowded at that time of day, and it was no effort to avoid one another. Also, at about that time I made a mistake in business and lost several thousand dollars for the firm I work for. There was not much chance of my losing my job, but the possibility was always at the back of my mind, and under this and under the continuous urgency of making more money the memory of the eccentric doctor was buried. Three weeks passed without Ethel's mentioning him, and then one evening, when I was reading, I noticed Ethel standing at the window looking down into the street.

"He's really there," she said.

"Who?"

"Trencher. Come here and see."

I went to the window. There were only three people on the sidewalk across the street. It was dark and it would have been difficult to recognize anyone, but because one of them, walking toward the corner, had a dachshund on a leash, it could have been Trencher.

"Well, what about it?" I said. "He's just walking the dog."   20

"But he wasn't walking the dog when I first looked out of the window. He was just standing there, staring up at this building. That's what he says he does. He says that he comes over here and stares up at our lighted windows."

"When did he say this?"

"At the playground."

"I thought you went to another playground."

"Oh, I do, I do, but he followed me. He's crazy, darling. I know he's crazy,   25
but I feel so sorry for him. He says that he spends night after night looking up at our windows. He says that he sees me everywhere—the back of my head, my eyebrows—that he hears my voice. He says that he's never compromised in his life and that he isn't going to compromise about this. I feel so sorry for him, darling. I can't help but feel sorry for him."

For the first time then, the situation seemed serious to me, for in his helplessness I knew that he might have touched an inestimable and wayward passion that Ethel shares with some other women—an inability to refuse any cry for help, to refuse any voice that sounds pitiable. It is not a reasonable passion, and I would almost rather have had her desire him than pity him. When we were getting ready for bed that night, the telephone rang, and when I picked it up and said hello, no one answered. Fifteen minutes later, the telephone rang again, and when there was no answer this time, I began to shout and swear at Trencher, but he didn't reply—there wasn't even the click of a closed circuit—and I felt like a fool. Because I felt like a fool, I accused Ethel of having led him on, of having encouraged him, but these accusations didn't affect her, and when I finished them, I felt worse, because I knew that she was innocent, and that she had to go out on the street to buy groceries and air the children, and that there was no force of law that could keep Trencher from waiting for her there, or from staring up at our lights.

We went to the Newsomes' one night the next week, and while we were taking off our coats, I heard Trencher's voice. He left a few minutes after we arrived, but his manner—the sad glance he gave Ethel, the way he sidestepped me, the sorrowful way that he refused the Newsomes when they asked him to stay longer, and the gallant attentions he showed his miserable wife—made me angry. Then I happened to notice Ethel and saw that her color was high, that her eyes were bright, and that while she was praising Mrs. Newsome's new shoes, her mind was not on what she was saying. When we came home that night, the baby-sitter told us crossly that neither of the children had slept. Ethel took their temperatures. Carol was all right, but the boy had a fever of a hundred and four. Neither of us got much sleep that night, and in the morning Ethel called me at the office to say that Carl had bronchitis. Three days later, his sister came down with it.

For the next two weeks, the sick children took up most of our time. They had to be given medicine at eleven in the evening and again at three in the morning, and we lost a lot of sleep. It was impossible to ventilate or clean the house, and when I came in, after walking through the cold from the bus stop, it stank of cough syrups and tobacco, fruit cores and sickbeds. There were blankets and pillows, ashtrays, and medicine glasses everywhere. We divided the work of sickness reasonably and took turns at getting up in the night, but I often fell asleep at my desk during the day, and after dinner Ethel would fall asleep in a chair in the living room. Fatigue seems to differ for adults and children only in that adults recognize it and so are not overwhelmed, and when we were tired, we were unreasonable, cross, and the victims of transcendent depressions. One evening after the worst of the sickness was over, I came home and found some roses in the living room. Ethel said that Trencher had brought them. She hadn't let him in. She had closed the door in his face. I took the roses and threw them out. We didn't quarrel. The children went to sleep at nine, and a few minutes after nine I went to bed. Sometime later, something woke me.

A light was burning in the hall. I got up. The children's room and the living room were dark. I found Ethel in the kitchen sitting at the table, drinking coffee.

"I've made some fresh coffee," she said. "Carol felt croupy again, so I steamed   30
her. They're both asleep now."

"How long have you been up?"

"Since half past twelve," she said. "What time is it?"

"Two."

I poured myself a cup of coffee and sat down. She got up from the table and rinsed her cup and looked at herself in a mirror that hangs over the sink. It was a windy night. A dog was wailing somewhere in an apartment below ours, and a loose radio antenna was brushing against the kitchen window.

"It sounds like a branch," she said.   35

In the bare kitchen light, meant for peeling potatoes and washing dishes, she looked very tired.

"Will the children be able to go out tomorrow?"

"Oh, I hope so," she said. "Do you realize that I haven't been out of this apartment in over two weeks?" She spoke bitterly and this startled me.

"It hasn't been quite two weeks."

"It's been over two weeks," she said.   40

"Well, let's figure it out," I said. "The children were taken sick on a Saturday night. That was the fourth. Today is the—"

"Stop it, stop it," she said. "I know how long it's been. I haven't had my shoes on in two weeks."

"You make it sound pretty bad."

"It is. I haven't had on a decent dress or fixed my hair."

"It could be worse."   45

"My mother's cooks had a better life."

"I doubt that."

"My mother's cooks had a better life," she said loudly.

"You'll wake the children."

"My mother's cooks had a better life. They had pleasant rooms. No one   50
could come into the kitchen without their permission." She knocked the coffee grounds into the garbage and began to wash the pot.

"How long was Trencher here this afternoon?"

"A minute. I've told you."

"I don't believe it. He was in here."

"He was not. I didn't let him in. I didn't let him in because I looked so badly. I didn't want to discourage him."

"Why not?"   55

"I don't know. He may be a fool. He may be insane but the things he's told me have made me feel marvelously, he's made me feel marvelously."

"Do you want to go?"

"Go? Where would I go?" She reached for the purse that is kept in the kitchen to pay for groceries and counted out of it two dollars and thirty-five cents. "Ossining? Montclair?"

"I mean with Trencher."

"I don't know, I don't know," she said, "but who can say that I shouldn't?   60
What harm would it do? What good would it do? Who knows. I love the children but that isn't enough, that isn't nearly enough. I wouldn't hurt them, but would I hurt them so much if I left you? Is divorce so dreadful and of all the things that hold a marriage together how many of them are good?" She sat down at the table.

"In Grenoble," she said, "I wrote a long paper on Charles Stuart in French. A professor at the University of Chicago wrote me a letter. I couldn't read a French newspaper without a dictionary today, I don't have the time to follow any newspaper, and I am ashamed of my incompetence, ashamed of the way I look. Oh, I guess I love you, I do love the children, but I love myself, I love my life, it has some value and some promise for me and Trencher's roses make me feel that I'm losing this, that I'm losing my self-respect. Do you know what I mean, do you understand what I mean?"

"He's crazy," I said.

"Do you know what I mean? Do you understand what I mean?"

"No," I said. "No."

Carl woke up then and called for his mother. I told Ethel to go to bed. I   6.
turned out the kitchen light and went into the children's room.

The children felt better the next day, and since it was Sunday, I took them
for a walk. The afternoon sun was clement and pure, and only the colored shadows
made me remember that it was midwinter, that the cruise ships were returning,
and that in another week jonquils would be twenty-five cents a bunch. Walking
down Lexington Avenue, we heard the drone bass of a church organ sound from
the sky, and we and the others on the sidewalk looked up in piety and bewilderment,
like a devout and stupid congregation, and saw a formation of heavy bombers
heading for the sea. As it got late, it got cold and clear and still, and on the
stillness the waste from the smokestacks along the East River seemed to articulate,
as legibly as the Pepsi-Cola plane, whole words and sentences. Halcyon. Disaster.
They were hard to make out. It seemed the ebb of the year—an evil day for
gastritis, sinus, and respiratory disease—and remembering other winters, the markings of the light convinced me that it was the season of divorce. It was a long
afternoon, and I brought the children in before dark.

I think that the seriousness of the day affected the children, and when they
returned to the house, they were quiet. The seriousness of it kept coming to
me with the feeling that this change, like a phenomenon of speed, was affecting
our watches as well as our hearts. I tried to remember the willingness with
which Ethel had followed my regiment during the war, from West Virginia to the
Carolinas and Oklahoma, and the day coaches and rooms she had lived in, and
the street in San Francisco where I said goodbye to her before I left the country, but I could not put any of this into words, and neither of us found anything to say. Sometime after dark, the children were bathed and put to bed, and
we sat down to our supper. At about nine o'clock, the doorbell rang, and when
I answered it and recognized Trencher's voice on the speaking tube, I asked him
to come up.

He seemed distraught and exhilarated when he appeared. He stumbled on
the edge of the carpet. "I know that I'm not welcome here," he said in a hard
voice, as if I were deaf. "I know that you don't like me here. I respect your feelings.
This is your home. I respect a man's feelings about his home. I don't usually go
to a man's home unless he asks me. I respect your home. I respect your marriage.
I respect your children. I think everything ought to be aboveboard. I've come
here to tell you that I love your wife."

"Get out," I said.

"You've got to listen to me," he said. "I love your wife. I can't live without   70
her. I've tried and I can't. I've even thought of going away—of moving to the
West Coast—but I know that it wouldn't make any difference. I want to marry
her. I'm not romantic. I'm matter-of-fact. I'm very matter-of-fact. I know that
you have two children and that you don't have much money. I know that there
are problems of custody and property and things like that to be settled. I'm not
romantic. I'm hardheaded. I've talked this all over with Mrs. Trencher, and she's
agreed to give me a divorce. I'm not underhanded. Your wife can tell you that. I
realize all the practical aspects that have to be considered—custody, property, and
so forth. I have plenty of money. I can give Ethel everything she needs, but there
are the children. You'll have to decide about them between yourselves. I have a

check here. It's made out to Ethel. I want her to take it and go to Nevada. I'm a practical man and I realize that nothing can be decided until she gets her divorce."

"Get out of here!" I said. "Get the hell out of here!"

He started for the door. There was a potted geranium on the mantelpiece, and I threw this across the room at him. It got him in the small of the back and nearly knocked him down. The pot broke on the floor. Ethel screamed. Trencher was still on his way out. Following him, I picked up a candlestick and aimed it at his head, but it missed and bounced off the wall. "Get the hell out of here!" I yelled, and he slammed the door. I went back into the living room. Ethel was pale but she wasn't crying. There was a loud rapping on the radiator, a signal from the people upstairs for decorum and silence—urgent and expressive, like the communications that prisoners send to one another through the plumbing in a penitentiary. Then everything was still.

We went to bed, and I woke sometime during the night. I couldn't see the clock on the dresser, so I don't know what time it was. There was no sound from the children's room. The neighborhood was perfectly still. There were no lighted windows anywhere. Then I knew that Ethel had wakened me. She was lying on her side of the bed. She was crying.

"Why are you crying?" I asked.

"Why am I crying?" she said. "Why am I crying?" And to hear my voice and to speak set her off again, and she began to sob cruelly. She sat up and slipped her arms into the sleeves of a wrapper and felt along the table for a package of cigarettes. I saw her wet face when she lighted a cigarette. I heard her moving around in the dark.

"Why do you cry?"

"Why do I cry? Why do I cry?" she asked impatiently. "I cry because I saw an old woman cuffing a little boy on Third Avenue. She was drunk. I can't get it out of my mind." She pulled the quilt off the foot of our bed and wandered with it toward the door. "I cry because my father died when I was twelve and because my mother married a man I detested or thought that I detested. I cry because I had to wear an ugly dress—a hand-me-down dress—to a party twenty years ago, and I didn't have a good time. I cry because of some unkindness that I can't remember. I cry because I'm tired—because I'm tired and I can't sleep." I heard her arrange herself on the sofa and then everything was quiet.

I like to think that the Trenchers have gone away, but I still see Trencher now and then on a crosstown bus when I'm late going to work. I've also seen his wife, going into the neighborhood lending library with Fräulein. She looks old. I'm not good at judging ages, but I wouldn't be surprised to find that Mrs. Trencher is fifteen years older than her husband. Now when I come home in the evenings, Ethel is still sitting on the stool by the sink cleaning vegetables. I go with her into the children's room. The light there is bright. The children have built something out of an orange crate, something preposterous and ascendant, and their sweetness, their compulsion to build, the brightness of the light are reflected perfectly and increased in Ethel's face. Then she feeds them, bathes them, and sets the table, and stands for a moment in the middle of the room, trying to make some connection between the evening and the day. Then it is over. She lights the four candles, and we sit down to our supper.

ANTON CHEKHOV (1860–1904)

Lady with Lapdog   *1899*

Translated by David Magarshack.

I

The appearance on the front of a new arrival—a lady with a lapdog—became the topic of general conversation. Dmitry Dmitrich Gurov, who had been a fortnight in Yalta and got used to its ways, was also interested in new arrivals. One day, sitting on the terrace of Vernet's restaurant, he saw a young woman walking along the promenade; she was fair, not very tall, and wore a toque; behind her trotted a white pomeranian.

Later he came across her in the park and in the square several times a day. She was always alone, always wearing the same toque, followed by the white pomeranian. No one knew who she was, and she became known simply as the lady with the lapdog.

"If she's here without her husband and without any friends," thought Gurov, "it wouldn't be a bad idea to strike up an acquaintance with her."

He was not yet forty, but he had a twelve-year-old daughter and two schoolboy sons. He had been married off when he was still in his second year at the university, and his wife seemed to him now to be almost twice his age. She was a tall, black-browed woman, erect, dignified, austere, and, as she liked to describe herself, a "thinking person." She was a great reader, preferred the new "advanced" spelling, called her husband by the more formal "Dimitry" and not the familiar "Dmitry"; and though he secretly considered her not particularly intelligent, narrow-minded, and inelegant, he was afraid of her and disliked being at home. He had been unfaithful to her for a long time, he was often unfaithful to her, and that was why, perhaps, he almost always spoke ill of women, and when men discussed women in his presence, he described them as *the lower breed*.

He could not help feeling that he had had enough bitter experience to have   5
the right to call them as he pleased, but all the same without *the lower breed* he could not have existed a couple of days. He was bored and ill at ease among men, with whom he was reticent and cold, but when he was among women he felt at ease, he knew what to talk about with them and how to behave, even when he was silent in their company he experienced no feeling of constraint. There was something attractive, something elusive in his appearance, in his character and his whole person that women found interesting and irresistible; he was aware of it, and was himself drawn to them by some irresistible force.

Long and indeed bitter experience had taught him that every new affair, which at first relieved the monotony of life so pleasantly and appeared to be such a charming and light adventure, among decent people and especially among Muscovites, who are so irresolute and so hard to rouse, inevitably developed into an extremely complicated problem and finally the whole situation became rather cumbersome. But at every new meeting with an attractive woman he forgot all about this experience, he wanted to enjoy life so badly and it all seemed so simple and amusing.

And so one afternoon, while he was having dinner at a restaurant in the park, the woman in the toque walked in unhurriedly and took a seat at the table next to him. The way she looked, walked and dressed, wore her hair, told him that she was of good social standing, that she was married, that she was in Yalta for the first time, that she was alone and bored. . . . There was a great deal of exaggeration in the stories about the laxity of morals among the Yalta visitors, and he dismissed them with contempt, for he knew that such stories were mostly made up by people who would gladly have sinned themselves if they had had any idea how to go about it; but when the woman sat down at the table three yards away from him he remembered these stories of easy conquests and excursions to the mountains and the tempting thought of a quiet and fleeting affair, an affair with a strange woman whose very name he did not know, suddenly took possession of him.

He tried to attract the attention of the dog by calling softly to it, and when the pomeranian came up to him he shook a finger at it. The pomeranian growled. Gurov again shook a finger at it.

The woman looked up at him and immediately lowered her eyes.

"He doesn't bite," she said and blushed.

"May I give him a bone?" he asked, and when she nodded, he said amiably: "Have you been long in Yalta?"

"About five days."

"And I am just finishing my second week here."

They said nothing for the next few minutes.

"Time flies," she said without looking at him, "and yet it's so boring here."   15

"That's what one usually hears people saying here. A man may be living in Belev and Zhizdra or some other God-forsaken hole and he isn't bored, but the moment he comes here all you hear from him is "Oh, it's so boring! Oh, the dust!" You'd think he'd come from Granada!"

She laughed. Then both went on eating in silence, like complete strangers; but after dinner they strolled off together, and they embarked on the light playful conversation of free and contented people who do not care where they go or what they talk about. They walked, and talked about the strange light that fell on the sea; the water was of such a soft and warm lilac, and the moon threw a shaft of gold across it. They talked about how close it was after a hot day. Gurov told her that he lived in Moscow, that he was a graduate in philology but worked in a bank, that he had at one time thought of singing in a private opera company but had given up the idea, that he owned two houses in Moscow. . . . From her he learnt that she had grown up in Petersburg, but had got married in the town of S——, where she had been living for the past two years, that she would stay another month in Yalta, and that her husband, who also needed a rest, might join her. She was quite unable to tell him what her husband's job was, whether he served in the offices of the provincial governor or the rural council, and she found this rather amusing herself. Gurov also found out that her name and patronymic were Anna Sergeyevna.

Later, in his hotel room, he thought about her and felt sure that he would meet her again the next day. It had to be. As he went to bed he remembered that she had only recently left her boarding school, that she had been a schoolgirl like his own daughter; he recalled how much diffidence and angularity there was in her laughter and her conversation with a stranger—it was probably the first time in her life she had found herself alone, in a situation when men followed her, looked at her, and spoke to her with only one secret intention, an intention she could hardly fail to guess. He remembered her slender, weak neck, her beautiful grey eyes.

"There's something pathetic about her, all the same," he thought as he fell asleep.

II

A week had passed since their first meeting. It was a holiday. It was close indoors, while in the streets a strong wind raised clouds of dust and tore off people's hats. All day long one felt thirsty, and Gurov kept going to the terrace of the restaurant, offering Anna Sergeyevna fruit drinks and ices. There was nowhere to go.

In the evening, when the wind had dropped a little, they went to the pier to watch the arrival of the steamer. There were a great many people taking a walk on the landing pier; some were meeting friends, they had bunches of flowers in their hands. It was there that two peculiarities of the Yalta smart set at once arrested attention: the middle-aged women dressed as if they were still young girls and there was a great number of generals.

Because of the rough sea the steamer arrived late, after the sun had set, and she had to swing backwards and forwards several times before getting alongside the pier. Anna Sergeyevna looked at the steamer and the passengers through her lorgnette, as though trying to make out some friends, and when she turned to Gurov her eyes were sparkling. She talked a lot, asked many abrupt questions, and immediately forgot what it was she had wanted to know; then she lost her lorgnette in the crowd of people.

The smartly dressed crowd dispersed; soon they were all gone, the wind had dropped completely, but Gurov and Anna were still standing there as though waiting to see if someone else would come off the boat. Anna Sergeyevna was no longer talking. She was smelling her flowers without looking at Gurov.

"It's a nice evening," he said. "Where shall we go now? Shall we go for a drive?"

She made no answer.

Then he looked keenly at her and suddenly put his arms round her and kissed her on the mouth. He felt the fragrance and dampness of the flowers and immediately looked around him fearfully: had anyone seen them?

"Let's go to your room," he said softly.

And both walked off quickly.

It was very close in her hotel room, which was full of the smell of the scents she had bought in a Japanese shop. Looking at her now, Gurov thought: "Life is full of strange encounters!" From his past he preserved the memory of carefree, good-natured women, whom love had made gay and who were grateful to him for the happiness he gave them, however short-lived; and of women like his wife, who made love without sincerity, with unnecessary talk, affectedly, hysterically, with such an expression, as though it were not love or passion, but something much more significant; and of two or three very beautiful, frigid women, whose faces suddenly lit up with a predatory expression, an obstinate desire to take, to snatch from life more than it could give; these were women no longer in their first youth, capricious, unreasoning, despotic, unintelligent women, and when Gurov

20

25

lost interest in them, their beauty merely aroused hatred in him and the lace trimmings on their négligés looked to him then like the scales of a snake. But here there was still the same diffidence and angularity of inexperienced youth—an awkward feeling; and there was also the impression of embarrassment, as if someone had just knocked at the door. Anna Sergeyevna, this lady with the lapdog, apparently regarded what had happened in a peculiar sort of way, very seriously, as though she had become a fallen woman—so it seemed to him, and he found it odd and disconcerting. Her features lengthened and drooped, and her long hair hung mournfully on either side of her face; she sank into thought in a despondent pose, like a woman taken in adultery in an old painting.

"It's wrong," she said. "You'll be the first not to respect me now."

There was a water-melon on the table. Gurov cut himself a slice and began to eat it slowly. At least half an hour passed in silence.

Anna Sergeyevna was very touching; there was an air of a pure, decent, naïve woman about her, a woman who had very little experience of life; the solitary candle burning on the table scarcely lighted up her face, but it was obvious that she was unhappy.

"But, darling, why should I stop respecting you?" Gurov asked. "You don't know yourself what you're saying."

"May God forgive me," she said, and her eyes filled with tears. "It's terrible."

"You seem to wish to justify yourself."

"How can I justify myself? I am a bad, despicable creature. I despise myself and have no thought of justifying myself. I haven't deceived my husband, I've deceived myself. And not only now. I've been deceiving myself for a long time. My husband is, I'm sure, a good and honest man, but, you see, he is a flunkey. I don't know what he does at his office, all I know is that he is a flunkey. I was only twenty when I married him, I was eaten up by curiosity, I wanted something better. There surely must be a different kind of life, I said to myself. I wanted to live. To live, to live! I was burning with curiosity. I don't think you know what I am talking about, but I swear I could no longer control myself, something was happening to me, I could not be held back, I told my husband I was ill, and I came here. . . . Here too I was going about as though in a daze, as though I was mad, and now I've become a vulgar worthless woman whom everyone has a right to despise."

Gurov could not help feeling bored as he listened to her; he was irritated by her naïve tone of voice and her repentance, which was so unexpected and so out of place; but for the tears in her eyes, he might have thought that she was joking or play-acting.

"I don't understand," he said gently, "what it is you want."

She buried her face on his chest and clung close to him.

"Please, please believe me," she said. "I love a pure, honest life. I hate immorality. I don't know myself what I am doing. The common people say "the devil led her astray," I too can now say about myself that the devil has led me astray."

"There, there . . ." he murmured.

He gazed into her staring, frightened eyes, kissed her, spoke gently and affectionately to her, and gradually she calmed down and her cheerfulness returned; both of them were soon laughing.

Later, when they went out, there was not a soul on the promenade, the town with its cypresses looked quite dead, but the sea was still roaring and dashing itself against the shore; a single launch tossed on the waves, its lamp flickering sleepily.

They hailed a cab and drove to Oreanda.   45

"I've just found out your surname, downstairs in the lobby," said Gurov. "Von Diederitz. Is your husband a German?"

"No. I believe his grandfather was German. He is of the Orthodox faith himself."

In Oreanda they sat on a bench not far from the church, looked down on the sea, and were silent. Yalta could scarcely be seen through the morning mist. White clouds lay motionless on the mountain tops. Not a leaf stirred on the trees, the cicadas chirped, and the monotonous, hollow roar of the sea, coming up from below, spoke of rest, of eternal sleep awaiting us all. The sea had roared like that down below when there was no Yalta or Oreanda, it was roaring now, and it would go on roaring as indifferently and hollowly when we were here no more. And in this constancy, in this complete indifference to the life and death of each one of us, there is perhaps hidden the guarantee of our eternal salvation, the never-ceasing movement of life on earth, the never-ceasing movement towards perfection. Sitting beside a young woman who looked so beautiful at the break of day, soothed and enchanted by the sight of all that fairy-land scenery—the sea, the mountains, the clouds, the wide sky—Gurov reflected that, when you came to think of it, everything in the world was really beautiful, everything but our own thoughts and actions when we lose sight of the higher aims of existence and our dignity as human beings.

Someone walked up to them, a watchman probably, looked at them, and went away. And there seemed to be something mysterious and also beautiful in this fact, too. They could see the Theodosia boat coming towards the pier, lit up by the sunrise, and with no lights.

"There's dew on the grass," said Anna Sergeyevna, breaking the silence.   50

"Yes. Time to go home."

They went back to town.

After that they met on the front every day at twelve o'clock, had lunch and dinner together, went for walks, admired the sea. She complained of sleeping badly and of her heart beating uneasily, asked the same questions, alternately worried by feelings of jealousy and by fear that he did not respect her sufficiently. And again and again in the park or in the square, when there was no one in sight, he would draw her to him and kiss her passionately. The complete idleness, these kisses in broad daylight, always having to look round for fear of someone watching them, the heat, the smell of the sea, and the constant looming into sight of idle, well-dressed, and well-fed people seemed to have made a new man of him; he told Anna Sergeyevna that she was beautiful, that she was desirable, made passionate love to her, never left her side, while she was often lost in thought and kept asking him to admit that he did not really respect her, that he was not in the least in love with her and only saw in her a vulgar woman. Almost every night they drove out of town, to Oreanda or to the waterfall; the excursion was always a success, and every time their impressions were invariably grand and beautiful.

They kept expecting her husband to arrive. But a letter came from him in which he wrote that he was having trouble with his eyes and implored his wife to return home as soon as possible. Anna Sergeyevna lost no time in getting ready for her journey home.

"It's a good thing I'm going," she said to Gurov. "It's fate." 55

She took a carriage to the railway station, and he saw her off. The drive took a whole day. When she got into the express train, after the second bell, she said:

"Let me have another look at you. . . . One last look. So."

She did not cry, but looked sad, just as if she were ill, and her face quivered.

"I'll be thinking of you, remembering you," she said. "Good-bye. You're staying, aren't you? Don't think badly of me. We are parting for ever. Yes, it must be so, for we should never have met. Well, good-bye. . . ."

The train moved rapidly out of the station; its lights soon disappeared, and 60 a minute later it could not even be heard, just as though everything had conspired to put a quick end to this sweet trance, this madness. And standing alone on the platform gazing into the dark distance, Gurov listened to the churping of the grasshoppers and the humming of the telegraph wires with a feeling as though he had just woken up. He told himself that this had been just one more affair in his life, just one more adventure, and that it too was over, leaving nothing but a memory. He was moved and sad, and felt a little penitent that the young woman, whom he would never see again, had not been happy with him; he had been amiable and affectionate with her, but all the same in his behaviour to her, in the tone of his voice and in his caresses, there was a suspicion of light irony, the somewhat coarse arrogance of the successful male, who was, moreover, almost twice her age. All the time she called him good, wonderful, high-minded; evidently she must have taken him to be quite different from what he really was, which meant that he had involuntarily deceived her.

At the railway station there was already a whiff of autumn in the air; the evening was chilly.

"Time I went north, too," thought Gurov, as he walked off the platform. "High time!"

III

At home in Moscow everything was already like winter: the stoves were heated, and it was still dark in the morning when the children were getting ready to go to school and having breakfast, so that the nurse had to light the lamp for a short time. The frosts had set in. When the first snow falls and the first day one goes out for a ride in a sleigh, one is glad to see the white ground, the white roofs, the air is so soft and wonderful to breathe, and one remembers the days of one's youth. The old lime trees and birches, white with rime, have such a benignant look, they are nearer to one's heart than cypresses and palms, and beside them one no longer wants to think of mountains and the sea.

Gurov had been born and bred in Moscow, and he returned to Moscow on a fine frosty day; and when he put on his fur coat and warm gloves and took a walk down Petrovka Street, and when on Saturday evening he heard the church bells ringing, his recent holiday trip and the places he had visited lost their charm for him. Gradually he became immersed in Moscow life, eagerly reading three newspapers a day and declaring that he never read Moscow papers on principle. Once more, he could not resist the attraction of restaurants, clubs, banquets, and anniversary celebrations, and once more he felt flattered that well-known lawyers and actors came to see him and that in the Medical Club he played cards with a professor as his partner. Once again he was capable of eating a whole portion of the Moscow speciality of sour cabbage and meat served in a frying-pan. . . .

Another month and, he thought, nothing but a memory would remain of   65
Anna Sergeyevna; he would remember her as through a haze and only occasionally dream of her with a wistful smile, as he did of the others before her. But over a month passed, winter was at its height, and he remembered her as clearly as though he had only parted from her the day before. His memories haunted him more and more persistently. Every time the voices of his children doing their homework reached him in his study in the stillness of the evening, every time he heard a popular song or some music in a restaurant, every time the wind howled in the chimney—it all came back to him: their walks on the pier, early morning with the mist on the mountains, the Theodosia boat, and the kisses. He kept pacing the room for hours remembering it all and smiling, and then his memories turned into daydreams and the past mingled in his imagination with what was going to happen. He did not dream of Anna Sergeyevna, she accompanied him everywhere like his shadow and followed him wherever he went. Closing his eyes, he saw her as clearly as if she were before him, and she seemed to him lovelier, younger, and tenderer than she had been; and he thought that he too was much better than he had been in Yalta. In the evenings she gazed at him from the bookcase, from the fireplace, from the corner—he heard her breathing, the sweet rustle of her dress. In the street he followed women with his eyes, looking for anyone who resembled her. . . .

He was beginning to be overcome by an overwhelming desire to share his memories with someone. But at home it was impossible to talk of his love, and outside his home there was no one he could talk to. Not the tenants who lived in his house, and certainly not his colleagues in the bank. And what was he to tell them? Had he been in love then? Had there been anything beautiful, poetic, edifying, or even anything interesting about his relations with Anna Sergeyevna? So he had to talk in general terms about love and women, and no one guessed what he was driving at, and his wife merely raised her black eyebrows and said:

"Really, Dimitry, the role of a coxcomb doesn't suit you at all!"

One evening, as he left the Medical Club with his partner, a civil servant, he could not restrain himself, and said:

"If you knew what a fascinating woman I met in Yalta!"

The civil servant got into his sleigh and was about to be driven off, but   70
suddenly he turned round and called out:

"I say!"

"Yes?"

"You were quite right: the sturgeon *was* a bit off."

These words, so ordinary in themselves, for some reason hurt Gurov's feelings: they seemed to him humiliating and indecent. What savage manners! What faces! What stupid nights! What uninteresting, wasted days! Crazy gambling at cards, gluttony, drunkenness, endless talk about one and the same thing. Business that was of no use to anyone and talk about one and the same thing absorbed the greater part of one's time and energy, and what was left in the end was a sort of dock-tailed, barren life, a sort of nonsensical existence, and it was impossible to escape from it, just as though you were in a lunatic asylum or a convict chaingang! Gurov lay awake all night, fretting and fuming, and had a splitting headache the whole of the next day. The following nights too he slept badly, sitting up in bed thinking, or walking up and down his room. He was tired of his children, tired of the bank, he did not feel like going out anywhere or talking about anything.

In December, during the Christmas holidays, he packed his things, told his wife that he was going to Petersburg to get a job for a young man he knew, and set off for the town of S——. Why? He had no very clear idea himself. He wanted to see Anna Sergeyevna, to talk to her, to arrange a meeting, if possible.

He arrived in S—— in the morning and took the best room in a hotel, with a fitted carpet of military grey cloth and an inkstand grey with dust on the table, surmounted by a horseman with raised hand and no head. The hall porter supplied him with all the necessary information: Von Diederitz lived in a house of his own in Old Potter's Street, not far from the hotel. He lived well, was rich, kept his own carriage horses, the whole town knew him. The hall-porter pronounced the name: Dridiritz.

Gurov took a leisurely walk down Old Potter's Street and found the house. In front of it was a long grey fence studded with upturned nails.

"A fence like that would make anyone wish to run away," thought Gurov, scanning the windows and the fence.

As it was a holiday, he thought, her husband was probably at home. It did not matter either way, though, for he could not very well embarrass her by calling at the house. If he were to send in a note it might fall into the hands of the husband and ruin everything. The best thing was to rely on chance. And he kept walking up and down the street and along the fence, waiting for his chance. He watched a beggar enter the gate and the dogs attack him; then, an hour later, he heard the faint indistinct sounds of a piano. That must have been Anna Sergeyevna playing. Suddenly the front door opened and an old woman came out, followed by the familiar white pomeranian. Gurov was about to call to the dog, but his heart began to beat violently and in his excitement he could not remember its name.

He went on walking up and down the street, hating the grey fence more and more, and he was already saying to himself that Anna Sergeyevna had forgotten him and had perhaps been having a good time with someone else, which was indeed quite natural for a young woman who had to look at that damned fence from morning till night. He went back to his hotel room and sat on the sofa for a long time, not knowing what to do, then he had dinner and after dinner a long sleep.

"How stupid and disturbing it all is," he thought, waking up and staring at the dark windows: it was already evening. "Well, I've had a good sleep, so what now? What am I going to do tonight?"

He sat on a bed covered by a cheap grey blanket looking exactly like a hospital blanket, and taunted himself in vexation:

"A *lady* with a lapdog! Some adventure, I must say! Serves you right!"

At the railway station that morning he had noticed a poster announcing in huge letters the first performance of *The Geisha Girl* at the local theatre. He recalled it now, and decided to go to the theatre.

"Quite possibly she goes to first nights," he thought.

The theatre was full. As in all provincial theatres, there was a mist over the chandeliers and the people in the gallery kept up a noisy and excited conversation; in the first row of the stalls stood the local dandies with their hands crossed behind their backs; here, too, in the front seat of the Governor's box, sat the Governor's daughter, wearing a feather boa, while the Governor himself hid modestly behind the portière so that only his hands were visible; the curtain stirred, the orchestra took a long time tuning up. Gurov scanned the audience eagerly as they filed in and occupied their seats.

Anna Sergeyevna came in too. She took her seat in the third row, and when Gurov glanced at her his heart missed a beat and he realized clearly that there was no one in the world nearer and dearer or more important to him than that little woman with the stupid lorgnette in her hand, who was in no way remarkable. That woman lost in a provincial crowd now filled his whole life, was his misfortune, his joy, and the only happiness that he wished for himself. Listening to the bad orchestra and the wretched violins played by second-rate musicians, he thought how beautiful she was. He thought and dreamed.

A very tall, round-shouldered young man with small whiskers had come in with Anna Sergeyevna and sat down beside her; he nodded at every step he took and seemed to be continually bowing to someone. This was probably her husband, whom in a fit of bitterness at Yalta she had called a flunkey. And indeed there was something of a lackey's obsequiousness in his lank figure, his whiskers, and the little bald spot on the top of his head. He smiled sweetly, and the gleaming insignia of some scientific society which he wore in his buttonhole looked like the number on a waiter's coat.

In the first interval the husband went out to smoke and she was left in her seat. Gurov, who also had a seat in the stalls, went up to her and said in a trembling voice and with a forced smile: 90

"Good evening!"

She looked up at him and turned pale, then looked at him again in panic, unable to believe her eyes, clenching her fan and lorgnette in her hand and apparently trying hard not to fall into a dead faint. Both were silent. She sat and he stood, frightened by her embarrassment and not daring to sit down beside her. The violinists and the flautist began tuning their instruments, and they suddenly felt terrified, as though they were being watched from all the boxes. But a moment later she got up and walked rapidly towards one of the exits; he followed her, and both of them walked aimlessly along corridors and up and down stairs. Figures in all sorts of uniforms—lawyers, teachers, civil servants, all wearing badges—flashed by them; ladies, fur coats hanging on pegs, the cold draught bringing with it the odour of cigarette-ends. Gurov, whose heart was beating violently, thought:

"Oh, Lord, what are all these people, that orchestra, doing here?"

At that moment, he suddenly remembered how after seeing Anna Sergeyevna off he had told himself that evening at the station that all was over and that they would never meet again. But how far they still were from the end!

She stopped on a dark, narrow staircase with a notice over it: "To the Upper 95 Circle."

"How you frightened me!" she said, breathing heavily, still looking pale and stunned. "Oh, dear, how you frightened me! I'm scarcely alive. Why did you come? Why?"

"But, please, try to understand, Anna," he murmured hurriedly. "I beg you, please, try to understand. . . ."

She looked at him with fear, entreaty, love, looked at him intently, so as to fix his features firmly in her mind.

"I've suffered so much," she went on, without listening to him. "I've been thinking of you all the time. The thought of you kept me alive. And yet I tried so hard to forget you—why, oh, why did you come?"

On the landing above two schoolboys were smoking and looking down, but Gurov did not care. He drew Anna Sergeyevna towards him and began kissing her face, her lips, her hands.

"What are you doing? What are you doing?" she said in horror, pushing him away. "We've both gone mad. You must go back tonight, this minute. I implore you, by all that's sacred . . . Somebody's coming!"

Somebody was coming up the stairs.

"You must go back," continued Anna Sergeyevna in a whisper. "Do you hear? I'll come to you in Moscow. I've never been happy, I'm unhappy now, and I shall never be happy, never! So please don't make me suffer still more. I swear I'll come to you in Moscow. But now we must part. Oh, my sweet, my darling, we must part!"

She pressed his hand and went quickly down the stairs, looking back at him all the time, and he could see from the expression in her eyes that she really was unhappy. Gurov stood listening for a short time, and when all was quiet he went to look for his coat and left the theatre.

IV

Anna Sergeyevna began going to Moscow to see him. Every two or three months she left the town of S——, telling her husband that she was going to consult a Moscow gynaecologist, and her husband believed and did not believe her. In Moscow she stayed at the Slav Bazaar and immediately sent a porter in a red cap to inform Gurov of her arrival. Gurov went to her hotel, and no one in Moscow knew about it.

One winter morning he went to her hotel as usual (the porter had called with his message at his house the evening before, but he had not been in). He had his daughter with him, and he was glad of the opportunity of taking her to school, which was on the way to the hotel. Snow was falling in thick wet flakes.

"It's three degrees above zero," Gurov was saying to his daughter, "and yet it's snowing. But then, you see, it's only warm on the earth's surface, in the upper layers of the atmosphere the temperature's quite different."

"Why isn't there any thunder in winter, Daddy?"

He explained that, too. As he was speaking, he kept thinking that he was going to meet his mistress and not a living soul knew about it. He led a double life: one for all who were interested to see, full of conventional truth and conventional deception, exactly like the lives of his friends and acquaintances; and another which went on in secret. And by a kind of strange concatenation of circumstances, possibly quite by accident, everything that was important, interesting, essential, everything about which he was sincere and did not deceive himself, everything that made up the quintessence of his life, went on in secret, while everything that was a lie, everything that was merely the husk in which he hid himself to conceal the truth, like his work at the bank, for instance, his discussions at the club, his ideas of the lower breed, his going to anniversary functions with his wife—all that happened in the sight of all. He judged others by himself, did not believe what he saw, and was always of the opinion that every man's real and most interesting life went on in secret, under cover of night. The personal, private life of an individual was kept a secret, and perhaps that was partly the reason why civilized man was so anxious that his personal secrets should be respected.

Having seen his daughter off to her school, Gurov went to the Slav Bazaar. He took off his fur coat in the cloakroom, went upstairs, and knocked softly on the door. Anna Sergeyevna, wearing the grey dress he liked most, tired out by her journey and by the suspense of waiting for him, had been expecting him since the evening before; she was pale, looked at him without smiling, but was in his arms the moment he went into the room. Their kiss was long and lingering, as if they had not seen each other for two years. [110]

"Well," he asked, "how are you getting on there? Anything new?"

"Wait, I'll tell you in a moment. . . . I can't . . ."

She could not speak because she was crying. She turned away from him and pressed her handkerchief to her eyes.

"Well, let her have her cry," he thought, sitting down in an armchair. "I'll wait."

Then he rang the bell and ordered tea; while he was having his tea, she was still standing there with her face to the window. She wept because she could not control her emotions, because she was bitterly conscious of the fact that their life was so sad: they could only meet in secret, they had to hide from people, like thieves! Was not their life ruined?" [115]

"Please stop crying!" he said.

It was quite clear to him that their love would not come to an end for a long time, if ever. Anna Sergeyevna was getting attached to him more and more strongly, she worshipped him, and it would have been absurd to tell her that all this would have to come to an end one day. She would not have believed it, anyway.

He went up to her and took her by the shoulders, wishing to be nice to her, to make her smile; and at that moment he caught sight of himself in the looking glass.

His hair was already beginning to turn grey. It struck him as strange that he should have aged so much, that he should have lost his good looks in the last few years. The shoulders on which his hands lay were warm and quivering. He felt so sorry for this life, still so warm and beautiful, but probably soon to fade and wilt like his own. Why did she love him so? To women he always seemed different from what he was, and they loved in him not himself, but the man their imagination conjured up and whom they had eagerly been looking for all their lives; and when they discovered their mistake they still loved him. And not one of them had ever been happy with him. Time had passed, he had met women, made love to them, parted from them, but not once had he been in love; there had been everything between them, but no love.

It was only now, when his hair was beginning to turn grey, that he had fallen in love properly, in good earnest—for the first time in his life. [120]

He and Anna Sergeyevna loved each other as people do who are very dear and near, as man and wife or close friends love each other; they could not help feeling that fate itself had intended them for one another, and they were unable to understand why he should have a wife and she a husband; they were like two migrating birds, male and female, who had been caught and forced to live in separate cages. They had forgiven each other what they had been ashamed of in the past, and forgave each other everything in their present, and felt that this love of theirs had changed them both.

Before, when he felt depressed, he had comforted himself by all sorts of arguments that happened to occur to him on the spur of the moment, but now he had more serious things to think of, he felt profound compassion, he longed to be sincere, tender. . . .

"Don't cry, my sweet," he said. "That'll do, you've had your cry. . . . Let's talk now, let's think of something."

Then they had a long talk. They tried to think how they could get rid of the necessity of hiding, telling lies, living in different towns, not seeing one another for so long. How were they to free themselves from their intolerable chains?

"How? How?" he asked himself, clutching at his head. "How?"   125

And it seemed to them that in only a few more minutes a solution would be found and a new, beautiful life would begin; but both of them knew very well that the end was still a long, long way away and that the most complicated and difficult part was only just beginning.

JOSEPH CONRAD   (1857–1924)

Youth   *1902*

This could have occurred nowhere but in England, where men and sea interpenetrate, so to speak—the sea entering into the life of most men, and the men knowing something or everything about the sea, in the way of amusement, of travel, or of breadwinning.

We were sitting round a mahogany table that reflected the bottle, the claret glasses, and our faces as we leaned on our elbows. There was a director of companies, an accountant, a lawyer, Marlow, and myself. The director had been a *Conway*° boy, the accountant had served four years at sea, the lawyer—a fine crusted Tory, High Churchman, the best of old fellows, the soul of honor—had been chief officer in the P. & O.° service in the good old days when mailboats were square-rigged at least on two masts, and used to come down the China Sea before a fair monsoon with stun'sails set alow and aloft. We all began life in the merchant service. Between the five of us there was the strong bond of the sea, and also the fellowship of the craft, which no amount of enthusiasm for yachting, cruising, and so on can give, since one is only the amusement of life and the other is life itself.

Marlow (at least I think that is how he spelt his name) told the story, or rather the chronicle, of a voyage:

"Yes, I have seen a little of the Eastern seas; but what I remember best is

Conway: The Merchant Navy Cadet School in Angelsey, a training academy for naval officers.

P & O: The Pacific and Orient Line, still in existence.

my first voyage there. You fellows know there are those voyages that seem ordered for the illustration of life, that might stand for a symbol of existence. You fight, work, sweat, nearly kill yourself, sometimes do kill yourself, trying to accomplish something—and you can't. Not from any fault of yours. You simply can do nothing, neither great nor little—not a thing in the world—not even marry an old maid, or get a wretched 600-ton cargo of coal to its port of destination.

"It was altogether a memorable affair. It was my first voyage to the East,   5
and my first voyage as second mate; it was also my skipper's first command. You'll admit it was time. He was sixty if a day; a little man, with a broad, not very straight back, with bowed shoulders and one leg more bandy than the other, he had that queer twisted-about appearance you see so often in men who work in the fields. He had a nutcracker face—chin and nose trying to come together over a sunken mouth—and it was framed in iron-gray fluffy hair, that looked like a chinstrap of cotton-wool sprinkled with coaldust. And he had blue eyes in that old face of his, which were amazingly like a boy's, with that candid expression some quite common men preserve to the end of their days by a rare internal gift of simplicity of heart and rectitude of soul. What induced him to accept me was a wonder. I had come out of a crack Australian clipper, where I had been third officer, and he seemed to have a prejudice against crack clippers as aristocratic and high-toned. He said to me, 'You know, in this ship you will have to work.' I said I had to work in every ship I had ever been in. 'Ah, but this is different, and you gentlemen out of them big ships; . . . but there! I dare say you will do. Join tomorrow.'

"I joined tomorrow. It was twenty-two years ago; and I was just twenty. How time passes! It was one of the happiest days of my life. Fancy! Second mate for the first time—a really responsible officer! I wouldn't have thrown up my new billet for a fortune. The mate looked me over carefully. He was also an old chap, but of another stamp. He had a Roman nose, a snow-white, long beard, and his name was Mahon, but he insisted that it should be pronounced Mann. He was well connected; yet there was something wrong with his luck, and he had never got on.

"As to the captain, he had been for years in coasters, then in the Mediterranean, and last in the West Indian trade. He had never been round the Capes. He could just write a kind of sketchy hand, and didn't care for writing at all. Both were thorough good seamen of course, and between those two old chaps I felt like a small boy between two grandfathers.

"The ship also was old. Her name was the *Judea*. Queer name, isn't it? She belonged to a man Wilmer, Wilcox—some name like that; but he has been bankrupt and dead these twenty years or more, and his name don't matter. She had been laid up in Shadwell basin for ever so long. You may imagine her state. She was all rust, dust, grime—soot aloft, dirt on deck. To me it was like coming out of a palace into a ruined cottage. She was about 400 tons, had a primitive windlass, wooden latches to the doors, not a bit of brass about her, and a big square stern. There was on it, below her name in big letters, a lot of scrollwork, with the gilt off, and some sort of coat of arms, with the motto 'Do or Die' underneath. I remember it took my fancy immensely. There was a touch of romance in it, something that made me love the old thing—something that appealed to my youth!

"We left London in ballast—sand ballast—to load a cargo of coal in a northern port of Bangkok. Bangkok! I thrilled. I had been six years at sea, but had only seen Melbourne and Sydney, very good places, charming places in their way— but Bangkok!

"We worked out of the Thames under canvas,° with a North Sea pilot on 10 board. His name was Jermyn, and he dodged all day long about the gallery drying his handkerchief before the stove. Apparently he never slept. He was a dismal man, with a perpetual tear sparkling at the end of his nose, who either had been in trouble, or was in trouble, or expected to be in trouble—couldn't be happy unless something went wrong. He mistrusted my youth, my common sense, and my seamanship, and made a point of showing it in a hundred little ways. I dare say he was right. It seems to me I knew very little then, and I know not much more now; but I cherish a hate for that Jermyn to this day.

"We were a week working up as far as Yarmouth Roads, and then we got into a gale—the famous October gale of twenty-two years ago. It was wind, lightning, sleet, snow, and a terrific sea. We were flying light, and you may imagine how bad it was when I tell you we had smashed bulwarks and a flooded deck. On the second night she shifted her ballast into the lee bow, and by that time we had been blown off somewhere on the Dogger Bank. There was nothing for it but go below with shovels and try to right her, and there we were in that vast hold, gloomy like a cavern, the tallow dips stuck and flickering on the beams, the gale howling above, the ship tossing about like mad on her side; there we all were, Jermyn, the captain, everyone, hardly able to keep our feet, engaged on that grave-digger's work, and trying to toss shovelfuls of wet sand up to windward. At every tumble of the ship you could see vaguely in the dim light men falling down with a great flourish of shovels. One of the ship's boys (we had two), impressed by the weirdness of the scene, wept as if his heart would break. We could hear him blubbering somewhere in the shadows.

"On the third day the gale died out, and by and by a north-country tug picked us up. We took sixteen days in all to get from London to the Tyne! When we got into dock we had lost our turn for loading, and they hauled us off to a pier where we remained for a month. Mrs. Beard (the captain's name was Beard) came from Colchester to see the old man. She lived on board. The crew of runners had left, and there remained only the officers, one boy and the steward, a mulatto who answered to the name of Abraham. Mrs. Beard was an old woman, with a face all wrinkled and ruddy like a winter apple, and the figure of a young girl. She caught sight of me once, sewing on a button, and insisted on having my shirts to repair. This was something different from the captains' wives I had known on board crack clippers. When I brought her the shirts, she said: 'And the socks? They want mending, I am sure, and John's—Captain Beard's—things are all in order now. I would be glad of something to do.' Bless the old woman. She overhauled my outfit for me, and meantime I read for the first time *Sartor Resartus* and Burnaby's *Ride to Khiva*. I didn't understand much of the first then; but I remembered I preferred the soldier to the philosopher at the time; a preference which life has only confirmed. One was a man, and the other was either more—or less. However,

---

under canvas: The *Judea* is powered totally by sail, as contrasted with the *Somerville* (paragraph 69) which is a steamer. The story is presumably taking place at a time of transition from sail to steam.

they are both dead and Mrs. Beard is dead, and youth, strength, genius, thoughts, achievements, simple hearts—all dies. . . . No matter.

"They loaded us at last. We shipped a crew. Eight able seamen and two boys. We hauled off one evening to the buoys at the dock gates, ready to go out, and with a fair prospect of beginning the voyage next day. Mrs. Beard was to start for home by a late train. When the ship was fast we went to tea. We sat rather silent through the meal—Mahon, the old couple, and I. I finished first, and slipped away for a smoke, my cabin being in a deckhouse just against the poop. It was high water, blowing fresh with a drizzle; the double dock gates were opened, and the steam colliers were going in and out in the darkness with their lights burning bright, a great plashing of propellers, rattling of winches, and a lot of hailing on the pierheads. I watched the procession of headlights gliding high and of green lights gliding low in the night, when suddenly a red gleam flashed at me, vanished, came into view again, and remained. The fore end of a steamer loomed up close. I shouted down the cabin, 'Come up, quick!' and then heard a startled voice saying afar in the dark, 'Stop her, sir.' A bell jingled. Another voice cried warningly, 'We are going right into that bark, sir.' The answer to this was a gruff 'All right,' and the next thing was a heavy crash as the steamer struck a glancing blow with the bluff of her bow about our forerigging. There was a moment of confusion, yelling, and running about. Steam roared. Then somebody was heard saying, 'All clear, sir.' . . . 'Are you all right?' asked the gruff voice. I had jumped forward to see the damage, and hailed back, 'I think so.' 'Easy astern,' said the gruff voice. A bell jingled. 'What steamer is that?' screamed Mahon. By that time she was no more to us than a bulky shadow maneuvering a little way off. They shouted at us some name—a woman's name, Miranda or Melissa—or some such thing. 'This means another month in this beastly hole,' said Mahon to me, as we peered with lamps about the splintered bulwarks and broken braces. 'But where's the captain?'

'We had not heard or seen anything of him all that time. We went aft to look. A doleful voice arose hailing somewhere in the middle of the dock, '*Judea* ahoy!' . . . How the devil did he get there? . . . 'Hallo!' we shouted. 'I am adrift in our boat without oars,' he cried. A belated water-man offered his services, and Mahon struck a bargain with him for a half crown to tow our skipper alongside; but it was Mrs. Beard that came up the ladder first. They had been floating about the dock in that mizzly cold rain for nearly an hour. I was never so surprised in my life.

"It appears that when he heard my shout 'Come up' he understood at once   15
what was the matter, caught up his wife, ran on deck, and across, and down into our boat, which was fast to the ladder. Not bad for a sixty-year-old. Just imagine that old fellow saving heroically in his arms that old woman—the woman of his life. He set her down on a thwart, and was ready to climb back on board when the painter came adrift somehow, and away they went together. Of course in the confusion we did not hear him shouting. He looked abashed. She said cheerfully, 'I suppose it does not matter my losing the train now?' 'No, Jenny—you go below and get warm.' he growled. Then to us: 'A sailor has no business with a wife—I say. There I was, out of the ship. Well, no harm done this time. Let's go and look at what that fool of a steamer smashed.'

"It wasn't much, but it delayed us three weeks. At the end of that time, the captain being engaged with his agents, I carried Mrs. Beard's bag to the railway station and put her all comfy into a third-class carriage. She lowered the window to say, 'You are a good young man. If you see John—Captain Beard—without his muffler at night, just remind him from me to keep his throat well wrapped up.' 'Certainly, Mrs. Beard,' I said. 'You are a good young man; I noticed how attentive you are to John—to Captain——' The train pulled out suddenly; I took my cap off to the old woman: I never saw her again. . . . Pass the bottle.

"We went to sea next day. When we made that start for Bangkok we had been already three months out of London. We had expected to be a fortnight or so—at the outside.

"It was January, and the weather was beautiful—the beautiful sunny winter weather that has more charm than in the summertime, because it is unexpected, and crisp, and you know it won't, it can't, last long. It's like a windfall, like a godsend, like an unexpected piece of luck.

"It lasted all down the North Sea, all down Channel; and it lasted till we were three hundred miles or so to the westward of the Lizards; then the wind went round to the sou'west and began to pipe up. In two days it blew a gale. The *Judea*, hove to, wallowed on the Atlantic like an old candle-box. It blew day after day: it blew with spite, without interval, without mercy, without rest. The world has nothing but an immensity of great foaming waves rushing at us, under a sky low enough to touch with the hand and dirty like a smoked ceiling. In the stormy space surrounding us there was as much flying spray as air. Day after day and night after night there was nothing round the ship but the howl of the wind, the tumult of the sea, the noise of water pouring over her deck. There was no rest for her and no rest for us. She tossed, she pitched, she stood on her head, she sat on her tail, she rolled, she groaned, and we had to hold on while on deck and cling to our bunks when below, in a constant effort of body and worry of mind.

"One night Mahon spoke through the small window of my berth. It opened right into my very bed, and I was lying there sleepless, in my boots, feeling as though I had not slept for years, and could not if I tried. He said excitedly:

" 'You got the sounding rod in here, Marlow? I can't get the pumps to suck. By God! It's no child's play.'

"I gave him the sounding rod and lay down again, trying to think of various things—but I thought only of the pumps. When I came on deck they were still at it, and my watch relieved at the pumps. By the light of the lantern brought on deck to examine the sounding rod I caught a glimpse of their weary, serious faces. We pumped all the four hours. We pumped all night, all day, all the week—watch and watch. She was working herself loose, and leaked badly—not enough to drown us at once, but enough to kill us with the work at the pumps. And while we pumped the ship was going from us piecemeal: the bulwarks went, the stanchions were torn out, the ventilators smashed, the cabin door burst in. There was not a dry spot in the ship. She was being gutted bit by bit. The longboat changed, as if by magic, into matchwood where she stood in her gripes. I had lashed her myself, and was rather proud of my handiwork, which had withstood so long the malice of the sea. And we pumped. And there was no break in the weather. The sea was white like a sheet of foam, like a caldron of boiling milk; there was not a break in the clouds, no—not the size of a man's hand—no, not for so much as ten seconds. There was for us no sky, there were for us no stars,

20

no sun, no universe—nothing but angry clouds and an infuriated sea. We pumped watch and watch, for dear life; and it seemed to last for months, for years, for all eternity, as though we had been dead and gone to a hell for sailors. We forgot the day of the week, the name of the month, what year it was, and whether we had ever been ashore. The sails blew away, she lay broadside on under a weather cloth, the ocean poured over her, and we did not care. We turned those handles, and had the eyes of idiots. As soon as we had crawled on deck I used to take a round turn with a rope about the men, the pumps, and the mainmast, and we turned, we turned incessantly, with the water to our waists, to our necks, over our heads. It was all one. We had forgotten how it felt to be dry.

"And there was somewhere in me the thought: By Jove! This is the deuce of an adventure—something you read about; and it is my first voyage as second mate—and I am only twenty—and here I am lasting it out as well as any of these men, and keeping my chaps up to the mark. I was pleased. I would not have given up the experience for worlds. I had moments of exultation. Whenever the old dismantled craft pitched heavily with her counter high in the air, she seemed to me to throw up, like an appeal, like a defiance, like a cry to the clouds without mercy, the words written on her stern: '*Judea*, London. Do or Die.'

"O youth! The strength of it, the faith of it, the imagination of it! To me she was not an old rattletrap carting about the world a lot of coal for a freight—to me she was the endeavor, the test, the trial of life. I think of her with pleasure, with affection, with regret—as you would think of someone dead you have loved. I shall never forget her. . . . Pass the bottle.

"One night when tied to the mast, as I explained, we were pumping on, deafened with the wind, and without spirit enough in us to wish ourselves dead, a heavy sea crashed aboard and swept clean over us. As soon as I got my breath I shouted, as in duty bound, 'Keep on, boys!' when suddenly I felt something hard floating on deck strike the calf of my leg. I made a grab at it and missed. It was so dark we could not see each other's faces within a foot—you understand.

"After that thump the ship kept quiet for a while, and the thing, whatever it was, struck my leg again. This time I caught it—and it was a saucepan. At first, being stupid with fatigue and thinking of nothing but the pumps, I did not understand what I had in my hand. Suddenly it dawned upon me, and I shouted, 'Boys, the house on deck is gone. Leave this, and let's look for the cook.'

"There was a deckhouse forward, which contained the galley, the cook's berth, and the quarters of the crew. As we had expected for days to see it swept away, the hands had been ordered to sleep in the cabin—the only safe place in the ship. The steward, Abraham, however, persisted in clinging to his berth, stupidly, like a mule—from sheer fright I believe, like an animal that won't leave a stable falling in an earthquake. So we went to look for him. It was chancing death, since once out of our lashings we were as exposed as if on a raft. But we went. The house was shattered as if a shell had exploded inside. Most of it had gone overboard—stove, men's quarters, and their property, all was gone; but two posts, holding a portion of the bulkhead to which Abraham's bunk was attached, remained as if by a miracle. We groped in the ruins and came upon this, and there he was, sitting in his bunk, surrounded by foam and wreckage, jabbering cheerfully to himself. He was out of his mind; completely and forever mad, with this sudden shock coming upon the fag-end of his endurance. We snatched him up, lugged

25

him aft, and pitched him headfirst down the cabin companion. You understand there was no time to carry him down with infinite precautions and wait to see how he got on. Those below would pick him up at the bottom of the stairs all right. We were in a hurry to go back to the pumps. That business could not wait. A bad leak is an inhuman thing.

"One would think that the sole purpose of that fiendish gale had been to make a lunatic of that poor devil of a mulatto. It eased before morning, and next day the sky cleared, and as the sea went down the leak took up. When it came to bending a fresh set of sails the crew demanded to put back—and really there was nothing else to do. Boats gone, decks swept clean, cabin gutted, men without a stitch but what they stood in, stores spoiled, ship strained. We put her head for home, and—would you believe it? The wind came east right in our teeth. It blew fresh, it blew continuously. We had to beat up every inch of the way, but she did not leak so badly, the water keeping comparatively smooth. Two hours' pumping in every four is no joke—but it kept her afloat as far as Falmouth.

"The good people there live on casualties of the sea, and no doubt were glad to see us. A hungry crowd of shipwrights sharpened their chisels at the sight of that carcass of a ship. And, by Jove! they had pretty pickings off us before they were done. I fancy the owner was already in a tight place. There were delays. Then it was decided to take part of the cargo out and calk her topsides. This was done, the repairs finished, cargo reshipped; a new crew came on board, and we went out—for Bangkok. At the end of a week we were back again. The crew said they weren't going to Bangkok—a hundred and fifty days' passage—in a something hooker that wanted pumping eight hours out of the twenty-four; and the nautical papers inserted again the little paragraph: '*Judea.* Bark. Tyne to Bangkok; coals; put back to Falmouth leaky and with crew refusing duty.'

"There were more delays—more tinkering. The owner came down for a day, and said she was as right as a little fiddle. Poor old Captain Beard looked like the ghost of a Geordie skipper—through the worry and humiliation of it. Remember he was sixty, and it was his first command. Mahon said it was a foolish business, and would end badly. I loved the ship more than ever, and wanted awfully to get to Bangkok. To Bangkok! Magic name, blessed name. Mesopotamia wasn't a patch on it. Remember I was twenty, and it was my first second-mate's billet, and the East was waiting for me.

"We went out and anchored in the outer roads with a fresh crew—the third. She leaked worse than ever. It was as if those confounded shipwrights had actually made a hole in her: This time we did not even go outside. The crew simply refused to man the windlass.

"They towed us back to the inner harbor, and we became a fixture, a feature, an institution of the place. People pointed us out to visitors as 'That 'ere bark that's going to Bangkok—has been here six months—put back three times.' On holidays the small boys pulling about in boats would hail, '*Judea*, ahoy!' and if a head showed above the rail shouted, 'Where you bound to?—Bangkok?' and jeered. We were only three on board. The poor old skipper mooned in the cabin. Mahon undertook the cooking, and unexpectedly developed all a Frenchman's genius for preparing nice little messes. I looked languidly after the rigging. We became citizens of Falmouth. Every shopkeeper knew us. At the barber's or tobacconist's they asked familiarly, 'Do you think you will ever get to Bangkok?' Meantime the owner,

30

the underwriters, and the charters squabbled amongst themselves in London, and our pay went on. . . . Pass the bottle.

"It was horrid. Morally it was worse than pumping for life. It seemed as though we had been forgotten by the world, belonged to nobody, would get nowhere, it seemed that, as if bewitched, we would have to live for ever and ever in that inner harbor, a derision and a byword to generations of longshore loafers and dishonest boatmen. I obtained three months' pay and a five days' leave, and made a rush for London. It took me a day to get there and pretty well another to come back—but three months' pay went all the same. I don't know what I did with it. I went to a music hall, I believe, lunched, dined, and supped in a swell place in Regent Street, and was back on time, with nothing but a complete set of Byron's works and a new railway rug to show for three months' work. The boatman who pulled me off to the ship said: 'Hallo! I thought you had left the old thing. *She* will never get to Bangkok.' 'That's all *you* know about it,' I said, scornfully—but I didn't like that prophecy at all.

"Suddenly a man, some kind of agent to somebody, appeared with full powers. He had grog-blossoms all over his face, an indomitable energy, and was a jolly soul. We leaped into life again. A hulk came alongside, took our cargo, and then we went into dry dock to get our copper stripped. No wonder she leaked. The poor thing, strained beyond endurance by the gale, had, as if in disgust, spat out all the oakum of her lower seams. She was recalked, new-coppered, and made as tight as a bottle. We went back to the hulk and reshipped our cargo.

"Then, on a fine moonlight night, all the rats left the ship.   35

"We had been infested with them. They had destroyed our sails, consumed more stores than the crew, affably shared our beds and our dangers, and now, when the ship was made seaworthy, concluded to clear out. I called Mahon to enjoy the spectacle. Rat after rat appeared on our rail, took a last look over his shoulder, and leaped with a hollow thud into the empty hulk. We tried to count them, but soon lost the tale. Mahon said: 'Well, well! don't talk to me about the intelligence of rats. They ought to have left before, when we had that narrow squeak from foundering. There you have the proof how silly is the superstition about them. They leave a good ship for an old rotten hulk, where there is nothing to eat, too, the fools! . . . I don't believe they know what is safe or what is good for them, any more than you or I.'

"And after some more talk we agreed that the wisdom of rats had been grossly overrated, being in fact no greater than that of men.

The story of the ship was known, by this, all up the Channel from Land's End to the Forelands, and we could get no crew on the south coast. They sent us one all complete from Liverpool, and we left once more—for Bangkok.

"We had fair breezes, smooth water right into the tropics, and the old *Judea* lumbered along in the sunshine. When she went eight knots everything cracked aloft, and we tied our caps to our heads; but mostly she strolled on at the rate of three miles an hour. What could you expect? She was tired—that old ship. Her youth was where mine is—where yours is—you fellows who listen to this yarn; and what friend would throw your years and your weariness in your face? We didn't grumble at her. To us aft, at least, it seemed as though we had been born in her, reared in her, had lived in her for ages, had never known any other ship.

I would just as soon have abused the old village church at home for not being a cathedral.

"And for me there was also my youth to make me patient. There was all the East before me, and all life, and the thought that I had been tried in that ship and had come out pretty well. And I thought of men of old who, centuries ago, went that road in ships that sailed no better, to the land of palms, and spices, and yellow sands, and of brown nations ruled by kings more cruel than Nero the Roman, and more splendid than Solomon the Jew. The old bark lumbered on, heavy with her age and the burden of her cargo, while I lived the life of youth in ignorance and hope. She lumbered on through an interminable procession of days; and the fresh gilding flashed back at the setting sun, seemed to cry out over the darkening sea the words painted on her stern, '*Judea*, London, Do or Die.'

"Then we entered the Indian Ocean and steered northerly for Java Head. The winds were light. Weeks slipped by. She crawled on, do or die, and people at home began to think of posting us as overdue.

"One Saturday evening, I being off duty, the men asked me to give them an extra bucket of water or so—for washing clothes. As I did not wish to screw on the fresh-water pump so late, I went forward whistling, and with a key in my hand to unlock the forepeak scuttle, intending to serve the water out of a spare tank we kept there.

"The smell down below was as unexpected as it was frightful. One would have thought hundreds of paraffin lamps had been flaring and smoking in that hole for days. I was glad to get out. The man with me coughed and said, 'Funny smell, sir.' I answered negligently, 'It's good for the health, they say,' and walked aft.

"The first thing I did was to put my head down the square of the midship ventilator. As I lifted the lid a visible breath, something like a thin fog, a puff of faint haze, rose from the opening. The ascending air was hot, and had a heavy, sooty, paraffiny smell. I gave one sniff, and put down the lid gently. It was no use choking myself. The cargo was on fire.

"Next day she began to smoke in earnest. You see it was to be expected, for though the coal was of a safe kind, that cargo had been so handled, so broken up with handling, that it looked more like smithy coal than anything else. Then it had been wetted—more than once. It rained all the time we were taking it back from the hulk, and now with this long passage it got heated, and there was another case of spontaneous combustion.

"The captain called us into the cabin. He had a chart spread on the table, and looked unhappy. He said, "The coast of West Australia is near, but I mean to proceed to our destination. It is the hurricane month, too; but we will just keep her head for Bangkok, and fight the fire. No more putting back anywhere, if we all get roasted. We will try first to stifle this 'ere damned combustion by want of air.'

"We tried. We battened down everything, and still she smoked. The smoke kept coming out through imperceptible crevices; it forced itself through bulkheads and covers; it oozed here and there and everywhere in slender threads, in an invisible film, in an incomprehensible manner. It made its way into the cabin, into the forecastle; it poisoned the sheltered places on the deck; it could be sniffed as high as the mainyard. It was clear that if the smoke came out the air came in. This was disheartening. This combustion refused to be stifled.

"We resolved to try water, and took the hatches off. Enormous volumes of smoke, whitish, yellowish, thick, greasy, misty, choking, ascended as high as the trucks. All hands cleared out aft. Then the poisonous cloud blew away, and we went back to work in a smoke that was no thicker now than that of an ordinary factory chimney.

"We rigged the force pump, got the hose along, and by and by it burst. Well, it was as old as the ship—a prehistoric hose, and past repair. Then we pumped with the feeble head pump, drew water with buckets, and in this way managed in time to pour lots of Indian Ocean into the main hatch. The bright stream flashed in sunshine, fell into a layer of white crawling smoke, and vanished on the black surface of coal. Steam ascended mingling with the smoke. We poured salt water as into a barrel without a bottom. It was our fate to pump in that ship, to pump out of her, to pump into her; and after keeping water out of her to save ourselves from being drowned, we frantically poured water into her to save ourselves from being burnt.

"And she crawled on, do or die, in the serene weather. The sky was a miracle   50
of purity, a miracle of azure. The sea was polished, was blue, was pellucid, was sparkling like a precious stone, extending on all sides, all round to the horizon—as if the whole terrestrial globe had been one jewel, one colossal sapphire, a single gem fashioned into a planet. And on the luster of the great calm waters the *Judea* glided imperceptibly, enveloped in languid and unclean vapors, in a lazy cloud that drifted to leeward, light and slow; a pestiferous cloud defiling the splendor of sea and sky.

"All this time of course we saw no fire. The cargo smoldered at the bottom somewhere. Once Mahon, as we were working side by side, said to me with a queer smile: 'Now, if she only would spring a tidy leak—like that time when we first left the Channel—it would put a stopper on this fire. Wouldn't it?' I remarked irrelevantly, 'Do you remember the rats?'

"We fought the fire and sailed the ship too as carefully as though nothing had been the matter. The steward cooked and attended on us. Of the other twelve men, eight worked while four rested. Everyone took his turn, captain included. There was equality, and if not exactly fraternity, then a deal of good feeling. Sometimes a man, as he dashed a bucketful of water down the hatchway, would yell out, 'Hurrah for Bangkok!' and the rest laughed. But generally we were taciturn and serious—and thirsty. Oh! how thirsty! And we had to be careful with the water. Strict allowance. The ship smoked, the sun blazed. . . . Pass the bottle.

"We tried everything. We even made an attempt to dig down to the fire. No good, of course. No man could remain more than a minute below. Mahon, who went first, fainted there, and the man who went to fetch him out did likewise. We lugged them out on deck. Then I leaped down to show how easily it could be done. They had learned wisdom by that time, and contented themselves by fishing for me with a chainhook tied to a broom handle, I believe. I did not offer to go and fetch up my shovel, which was left down below.

"Things began to look bad. We put the longboat into the water. The second boat was ready to swing out. We had also another, a fourteen-foot thing, on davits aft, where it was quite safe.

"Then, behold, the smoke suddenly decreased. We redoubled our efforts to 55 flood the bottom of the ship. In two days there was no smoke at all. Everybody was on the broad grin. This was on a Friday. On Saturday no work, but sailing the ship of course, was done. The men washed their clothes and their faces for the first time in a fortnight, and had a special dinner given them. They spoke of spontaneous combustion with contempt, and implied *they* were the boys to put out combustions. Somehow we all felt as though we each had inherited a large fortune. But a beastly smell of burning hung about the ship. Captain Beard had hollow eyes and sunken cheeks. I had never noticed so much before how twisted and bowed he was. He and Mahon prowled soberly about hatches and ventilators, sniffing. It struck me suddenly poor Mahon was a very, very old chap. As to me, I was pleased and proud as though I had helped to win a great naval battle. O youth!

"The night was fine. In the morning a homewardbound ship passed us hull down—the first we had seen for months; but we were nearing the land at last, Java Head being about 190 miles off, and nearly due north.

"Next day it was my watch on deck from eight to twelve. At breakfast the captain observed, 'It's wonderful how that smell hangs about the cabin.' About ten, the mate being on the poop, I stepped down on the main deck for a moment. The carpenter's bench stood abaft the mainmast: I leaned against it sucking at my pipe, and the carpenter, a young chap, came to talk to me. He remarked, 'I think we have done very well, haven't we?' and then I perceived with annoyance the fool was trying to tilt the bench. I said curtly, 'Don't, Chips,' and immediately became aware of a queer sensation, of an absurd delusion—I seemed somehow to be in the air. I heard all around me like a pent-up breath released—as if a thousand giants simultaneously had said Phoo!—and felt a dull concussion which made my ribs ache suddenly. No doubt about it—I was in the air, and my body was describing a short parabola. But short as it was, I had the time to think several thoughts in, as far as I can remember, the following order: 'This can't be the carpenter—What is it?—Some accident—Submarine volcano?—Coals, gas!—By Jove! We are being blown up—Everybody's dead—I am falling into the afterhatch—I see fire in it.'

"The coaldust suspended in the air of the hold had glowed dull-red at the moment of the explosion. In the twinkling of an eye, in an infinitesimal fraction of a second since the first tilt of the bench, I was sprawling full length on the cargo. I picked myself up and scrambled out. It was quick like a rebound. The deck was a wilderness of smashed timber, lying crosswise like trees in a wood after a hurricane; an immense curtain of solid rags waved gently before me—it was the mainsail blown·to strips. I thought: the masts will be toppling over directly; and to get out of the way bolted on all fours towards the poop ladder. The first person I saw was Mahon, with eyes like saucers, his mouth open, and the long white hair standing straight on end round his head like a silver halo. He was just about to go down when the sight of the main deck stirring, heaving up, and changing into splinters before his eyes, petrified him on the top step. I stared at him in unbelief, and he stared at me with a queer kind of shocked curiosity. I did not know that I had no hair, no eyebrows, no eyelashes, that my young mustache was burnt off, that my face was black, one cheek laid open, my nose cut, and my chin bleeding. I had lost my cap, one of my slippers, and my shirt was torn to rags. Of all this I was not aware. I was amazed to see the ship still afloat, the poop deck whole—and, most of all, to see anybody alive. Also the peace of the sky and the serenity of the sea were distinctly surprising. I suppose I expected to see them convulsed with horror. . . . Pass the bottle.

"There was a voice hailing the ship from somewhere—in the air, in the sky—I couldn't tell. Presently, I saw the captain—and he was mad. He asked me eagerly, 'Where's the cabin table?' and to hear such a question was a frightful shock. I had just been blown up, you understand, and vibrated with that experience— I wasn't quite sure whether I was alive. Mahon began to stamp with both feet and yelled at him. 'Good God! don't you see the deck's blown out of her?' I found my voice, and stammered out as if conscious of some gross neglect of duty, 'I don't know where the cabin table is.' It was like an absurd dream.

"Do you know what he wanted next? Well, he wanted to trim the yards. Very placidly, and as if lost in thought, he insisted on having the foreyard squared. 'I don't know if there's anybody alive,' said Mahon, almost tearfully. 'Surely,' he said, gently, 'there will be enough left to square the foreyard.' 60

"The old chap, it seems, was in his own berth winding up the chronometers when the shock sent him spinning. Immediately it occurred to him—as he said afterwards—that the ship had struck something, and ran out into the cabin. There, he saw, the cabin table had vanished somewhere. The deck being blown up, it had fallen down into the lazarette of course. Where we had our breakfast that morning he saw only a great hole in the floor. This appeared to him so awfully mysterious, and impressed him so immensely, that what he saw and heard after he got on deck were mere trifles in comparison. And, mark, he noticed directly the wheel deserted and his bark off her course—and his only thought was to get that miserable, stripped, undecked, smoldering shell of a ship back again with her head pointing at her port of destination. Bangkok! That's what he was after. I tell you this quiet, bowed, bandy-legged, almost deformed little man was immense in the singleness of his idea and in his placid ignorance of our agitation. He motioned us forward with a commanding gesture, and went to take the wheel himself.

"Yes; that was the first thing we did—trim the yards of that wreck! No one was killed, or even disabled, but everyone was more or less hurt. You should have seen them! Some were in rags, with black faces, like coal heavers, like sweeps, and had bullet heads that seemed closely cropped, but were in fact singed to the skin. Others, of the watch below, awakened by being shot out from their collapsing bunks, shivered incessantly, and kept on groaning even as we went about our work. But they all worked. That crew of Liverpool hard cases had in them the right stuff. It's my experience they always have. It is the sea that gives it—the vastness, the loneliness surrounding their dark stolid souls. Ah! Well! We stumbled, we crept, we fell, we barked our shins on the wreckage, we hauled. The masts stood, but we did not know how much they might be charred down below. It was nearly calm, but a long swell ran from the west and made her roll. They might go at any moment. We looked at them with apprehension. One could not foresee which way they would fall.

"Then we retreated aft and looked about us. The deck was a tangle of planks on edge, of planks on end, of splinters, of ruined woodwork. The masts rose from that chaos like big trees above a matted undergrowth. The interstices of that mass of wreckage were full of something whitish, sluggish, stirring—of something that was like a greasy fog. The smoke of the invisible fire was coming up again, was trailing, like a poisonous thick mist in some valley choked with dead wood. Already lazy wisps were beginning to curl upwards amongst the mass of splinters. Here and there a piece of timber stuck upright, resembled a post. Half of a fife rail had been shot through the foresail, and the sky made a patch of glorious blue in the ignobly soiled canvas. A portion of several boards holding together had fallen across the rail, and one end protruded overboard, like a gangway leading upon nothing, like a gangway leading over the deep sea, leading to death—as if inviting us to walk the plank at once and be done with our ridiculous troubles. And still the air, the sky—a ghost, something invisible was hailing the ship.

"Someone had the sense to look over, and there was the helmsman, who had impulsively jumped overboard, anxious to come back. He yelled and swam lustily like a merman, keeping up with the ship. We threw him a rope, and presently he stood amongst us streaming with water and very crestfallen. The captain had surrendered the wheel, and apart, elbow on rail and chin in hand, gazed at the sea wistfully. We asked ourselves. What next? I thought, Now, this is something like. This is great. I wonder what will happen. O youth!

"Suddenly Mahon sighted a steamer far astern. Captain Beard said, 'We may do something with her yet.' We hoisted two flags, which said in the international language of the sea, 'On fire. Want immediate assistance.' The streamer grew bigger rapidly, and by and by spoke with two flags on her foremast, 'I am coming to your assistance.' 65

"In half an hour she was abreast, to windward, within hail, and rolling slightly, with her engines stopped. We lost our composure, and yelled all together with excitement, 'We've been blown up.' A man in a white helmet, on the bridge, cried, 'Yes! All right! all right!' and he nodded his head, and smiled, and made soothing motions with his hand as though at a lot of frightened children. One of the boats dropped in the water, and walked towards us upon the sea with her long oars. Four Calashes pulled a swinging stroke. This was my first sight of Malay seamen. I've known them since, but what struck me then was their unconcern: they came alongside, and even the bowman standing up and holding to our main chains with the boathook did not deign to lift his head for a glance. I thought people who had been blown up deserved more attention.

"A little man, dry like a chip and agile like a monkey, clambered up. It was the mate of the steamer. He gave one look, and cried, 'O boys—you had better quit!'

"We were silent. He talked apart with the captain for a time—seemed to argue with him. Then they went away together to the steamer.

"When our skipper came back we learned that the steamer was the *Somerville*, Captain Nash, from West Australia to Singapore via Batavia with mails, and that the agreement was she should tow us to Anjer or Batavia, if possible, where we could extinguish the fire by scuttling, and then proceed on our voyage—to Bangkok! The old man seemed excited. 'We will do it yet,' he said to Mahon, fiercely. He shook his fist at the sky. Nobody else said a word.

"At noon the steamer began to tow. She went ahead slim and high, and what was left of the *Judea* followed at the end of seventy fathoms of towrope— 70 followed her swiftly like a cloud of smoke with mastheads protruding above. We went aloft to furl the sails. We coughed on the yards, and were careful about the bunts. Do you see the lot of us there, putting a neat furl on the sails of that ship doomed to arrive nowhere? There was not a man who didn't think that at any moment the masts would topple over. From aloft we could not see the ship for smoke, and they worked carefully, passing the gaskets with even turns. 'Harbor furl—aloft there!' cried Mahon from below.

"You understand this? I don't think one of those chaps expected to get down in the usual way. When we did I heard them saying to each other, 'Well, I thought we would come down overboard, in a lump—sticks and all—blame me if I didn't.' 'That's what I was thinking to myself,' would answer wearily another battered and bandaged scarecrow. And, mind, these were men without the drilled-in habit of obedience. To an onlooker they would be a lot of profane scallywags without a redeeming point. What made them do it—what made them obey me when I, thinking consciously how fine it was, made them drop the bunt of the foresail twice to try and do it better? What? They had no professional reputation—no examples, no praise. It wasn't a sense of duty; they all knew well enough how to shirk, and laze, and dodge—when they had a mind to it—and mostly they had. Was it the two pounds ten a month that sent them there? They didn't think their pay half good enough. No; it was something in them, something inborn and subtle and everlasting. I don't say positively that the crew of a French or German merchant-man wouldn't have done it, but I doubt whether it would have been done in the same way. There was a completeness in it, something solid like a principle, and masterful like an instinct—a disclosure of something secret—of that hidden something, that gift of good or evil that makes racial difference, that shapes the fate of nations.

"It was that night at ten that, for the first time we had been fighting it, we saw the fire. The speed of the towing had fanned the smoldering destruction. A blue gleam appeared forward, shining below the wreck of the deck. It wavered in patches, it seemed to stir and creep like the light of a glowworm. I saw it first, and told Mahon. 'Then the game's up,' he said. 'We had better stop this towing, or she will burst out suddenly fore and aft before we can clear out.' We set up a yell; rang bells to attract their attention; they towed on. At last Mahon and I had to crawl forward and cut the rope with an axe. There was no time to cast off the lashings. Red tongues could be seen licking the wilderness of splinters under our feet as we made our way back to the poop.

"Of course they very soon found out in the steamer that the rope was gone. She gave a loud blast of her whistle, her lights were seen sweeping in a wide circle, she came up ranging close alongside, and stopped. We were all in a tight group on the poop looking at her. Every man had saved a little bundle or a bag. Suddenly a conical flame with a twisted top shot up forward and threw upon the black sea circle of light, with the two vessels side by side and heaving gently in its center. Captain Beard had been sitting on the gratings still and mute for hours, but now he rose slowly and advanced in front of us, to the mizzen-shrouds. Captain Nash hailed: 'Come along! Look sharp. I have mailbags on board. I will take you and your boats to Singapore.'

" 'Thank you! No! said our skipper. 'We must see the last of the ship.'

" 'I can't stand by any longer,' shouted the other. 'Mails—you know.'

" 'Ay! ay! We are all right.'

75

" 'Very well! I'll report you in Singapore. . . . Good-by!'

"He waved his hand. Our men dropped their bundles quietly. The steamer moved ahead, and passing out of the circle of light, vanished at once from our sight, dazzled by the fire which burned fiercely. And then I knew that I would see the East first as commander of a small boat. I thought it fine; and the fidelity to the old ship was fine. We should see the last of her. Oh, the glamor of youth! Oh, the fire of it, more dazzling than the flames of the burning ship, throwing a magic light on the wide earth, leaping audaciously to the sky, presently to be quenched by time, more cruel, more pitiless, more bitter than the sea—and like the flames of the burning ship surrounded by an impenetrable night.

"The old man warned us in his gentle and inflexible way that it was part of our duty to save for the underwriters as much as we could of the ship's gear. Accordingly we went to work aft, while she blazed forward to give us plenty of light. We lugged out a lot of rubbish. What didn't we save? An old barometer fixed with an absurd quantity of screws nearly cost me my life: a sudden rush of smoke came upon me, and I just got away in time. There were various stores, bolts of canvas, coils of rope; the poop looked like a marine bazaar, and the boats were lumbered to the gunwales. One would have thought the old man wanted to take as much as he could of his first command with him. He was very, very quiet, but off his balance evidently. Would you believe it? He wanted to take a length of old stream-cable and a kedge anchor with him in the longboat. We said, 'Ay, ay, sir,' deferentially, and on the quiet let the things slip overboard. The heavy medicine chest went that way, two bags of green coffee, tins of paint—fancy, paint!— a whole lot of things. Then I was ordered with two hands into the boats to make a stowage and get them ready against the time it would be proper for us to leave the ship.

"We put everything straight, stepped the longboat's mast for our skipper, who was to take charge of her, and I was not sorry to sit down for a moment. My face felt raw, every limb ached as if broken, I was aware of all my ribs, and would have sworn to a twist in the backbone. The boats, fast astern, lay in a deep shadow, and all around I could see the circle of the sea lighted by the fire. A gigantic flame arose forward straight and clear. It flared fierce, with noises like the whirr of wings, with rumbles as of thunder. There were cracks, detonations, and from the cone of flame the sparks flew upwards, as man is born to trouble, to leaky ships, and to ships that burn. 80

"What bothered me was that the ship, lying broadside to the swell and to such wind as there was—a mere breath—the boats would not keep astern where they were safe, but persisted, in a pigheaded way boats have, in getting under the counter and then swinging alongside. They were knocking about dangerously and coming near the flame, while the ship rolled on them, and, of course, there was always the danger of the masts going over the side at any moment. I and my two boatkeepers kept them off as best we could, with oars and boathooks; but to be constantly at it became exasperating, since there was no reason why we should not leave at once. We could not see those on board, nor could we imagine what caused the delay. The boatkeepers were swearing feebly, and I had not only my share of the work but also had to keep at it two men who showed a constant inclination to lay themselves down and let things slide.

"At last I hailed, 'On deck there,' and someone looked over. 'We're ready here,' I said. The head disappeared, and very soon popped up again. 'The captain says, All right, sir, and to keep the boats well clear of the ship.'

"Half an hour passed. Suddenly there was a frightful racket, rattle, clanking of chain, hiss of water, and millions of sparks flew up into the shivering column of smoke that stood leaning slightly above the ship. The catheads had burned away, and the two red-hot anchors had gone to the bottom, tearing out after them two hundred fathom of red-hot chain. The ship trembled, the mass of flame swayed as if ready to collapse, and the fore-topgallant mast fell. It darted down like an arrow of fire, shot under, and instantly leaping up within an oar's length of the boats, floated quietly, very black on the luminous sea. I hailed the deck again. After some time a man in an unexpectedly cheerful but also muffled tone, as though he had been trying to speak with his mouth shut, informed me, 'Coming directly, sir,' and vanished. For a long time I heard nothing but the whirr and roar of the fire. There were also whistling sounds. The boats jumped, tugged at the painters, ran at each other playfully, knocked their sides together, or, do what we would, swung in a bunch against the ship's side. I couldn't stand it any longer, and swarming up a rope, clambered aboard over the stern.

"It was as bright as day. Coming up like this, the sheet of fire facing me was a terrifying sight, and the heat seemed hardly bearable at first. On a settee cushion dragged out of the cabin Captain Beard, his legs drawn up and one arm under his head, slept with the light playing on him. Do you know what the rest were busy about? They were sitting on deck right aft, round an open case, eating bread and cheese and drinking bottled stout.

"On the background of flames twisting in fierce tongues above their heads 85 they seemed at home like salamanders, and looked like a band of desperate pirates. The fire sparkled in the whites of their eyes, gleamed on patches of white skin seen through the torn shirts. Each had the marks of a battle about him—bandaged heads, tied-up arms, a strip of dirty rag round a knee—and each man had a bottle between his legs and a chunk of cheese in his hand. Mahon got up. With his handsome and disreputable head, his hooked profile, his long white beard, and with an uncorked bottle in his hand, he resembled one of those reckless sea robbers of old making merry amidst violence and disaster. 'The last meal on board,' he explained solemnly. 'We had nothing to eat all day, and it was no use leaving all this.' He flourished the bottle and indicated the sleeping skipper. 'He said he couldn't swallow anything, so I got him to lie down,' he went on; and as I stared, 'I don't know whether your are aware, young fellow, the man had no sleep to speak of for days—and there will be dam' little sleep in the boats.' 'There will be no boats by and by if you fool about much longer,' I said, indignantly. I walked up to the skipper and shook him by the shoulder. At last he opened his eyes, but did not move. 'Time to leave her, sir,' I said quietly.

'He got up painfully, looked at the flames, at the sea sparkling round the ship, and black, black as ink farther away; he looked at the stars shining dim through a thin veil of smoke in a sky black, black as Erebus.

" 'Youngest first,' he said.

"And the ordinary seaman, wiping his mouth with the back of his hand, got up, clambered over the taffrail, and vanished. Others followed. One, on the point of going over, stopped short to drain his bottle, and with a great swing of his arm flung it at the fire. 'Take this!' he cried.

"The skipper lingered disconsolately, and we left him to commune alone for a while with his first command. Then I went up again and brought him away at last. It was time. The ironwork on the poop was hot to the touch.

"Then the painter of the longboat was cut, and the three boats, tied together, drifted clear of the ship. It was just sixteen hours after the explosion when we abandoned her. Mahon had charge of the second boat, and I had the smallest— the fourteen-foot thing. The longboat would have taken the lot of us; but the skipper said we must save as much property as we could—for the underwriters— and so I got my first command. I had two men with me, a bag of biscuits, a few tins of meat, and a breaker of water. I was ordered to keep close to the longboat, that in case of bad weather we might be taken into her.

"And do you know what I thought? I thought I would part company as soon as I could. I wanted to have my first command all to myself. I wasn't going to sail in a squadron if there were a chance for independent cruising. I would make land by myself. I would beat the other boats. Youth! All youth! The silly, charming, beautiful youth.

"But we did not make a start at once. We must see the last of the ship. And so the boats drifted about that night, heaving and setting on the swell. The men dozed, waked, sighed, groaned. I looked at the burning ship.

"Between the darkness of earth and heaven she was burning fiercely upon a disc of purple sea shot by the blood-red play of gleams; upon a disc of water glittering and sinister. A high, clear flame, an immense and lonely flame, ascended from the ocean, and from its summit the black smoke poured continuously at the sky. She burned furiously; mournful and imposing like a funeral pile kindled in the night, surrounded by the sea, watched over by the stars. A magnificent death had come like a grace, like a gift, like a reward to that old ship at the end of her laborious days. The surrender of her weary ghost to the keeping of stars and sea was stirring like the sight of a glorious triumph. The masts fell just before daybreak, and for a moment there was a burst and turmoil of sparks that seemed to fill with flying fire the night patient and watchful, the vast night lying silent upon the sea. At daylight she was only a charred shell, floating still under a cloud of smoke and bearing a glowing mass of coal within.

"Then the oars were got out, and the boats forming in a line moved round her remains as if in procession—the longboat leading. As we pulled across her stern a slim dart of fire shot out viciously at us, and suddenly she went down, head first, in a great hiss of steam. The unconsumed stern was the last to sink; but the paint had gone, had cracked, had peeled off, and there were no letters, there was no word, no stubborn device that was like her soul, to flash at the rising sun her creed and her name.

"We made our way north. A breeze sprang up, and about noon all the boats came together for the last time. I had no mast or sail in mine, but I made a mast out of a spare oar and hoisted a boat-awning for a sail, with a boathook for a yard. She was certainly over-masted, but I had the satisfaction of knowing that with the wind aft I could beat the other two. I had to wait for them. Then we all had a look at the captain's chart, and, after a sociable meal of hard bread and water, got our last instructions. These were simple: steer north, and keep together as much as possible. 'Be careful with that jury-rig, Marlow,' said the captain: and Mahon, as I sailed proudly past his boat, wrinkled his curved nose and hailed,

90

95

'You will sail that ship of yours under water, if you don't look out, young fellow.' He was a malicious old man—and may the deep sea where he sleeps now rock him gently, rock him tenderly to the end of time!

"Before sunset a thick rain-squall passed over the two boats, which were far astern, and that was the last I saw of them for a time. Next day I sat steering my cockleshell—my first command—with nothing but water and sky round me. I did sight in the afternoon the upper sails of a ship far away, but said nothing, and my men did not notice her. You see I was afraid she might be homeward bound, and I had no mind to turn back from the portals of the East. I was steering for Java—another blessed name—like Bangkok, you know. I steered many days.

"I need not tell you what it is to be knocking about in an open boat. I remember nights and days of calm, when we pulled, we pulled, and the boat seemed to stand still, as if bewitched within the circle of the sea horizon. I remember the heat, the deluge of rain-squalls that kept up baling for dear life (but filled our water cask), and I remember sixteen hours on end with a mouth dry as a cinder and a steering oar over the stern to keep my first command head on to a breaking sea. I did not know how good a man I was till then. I remember the drawn faces, the dejected figures of my two men, and I remember my youth and the feeling that will never come back any more—the feeling that I could last forever, outlast the sea, the earth, and all men; the deceitful feeling that lures us on to joys, to perils, to love, to vain effort—to death; the triumphant conviction of strength, the heat of life in the handful of dust, the glow in the heart that with every year grows dim, grows cold, grows small, and expires—and expires, too soon, too soon—before life itself.

"And this is how I see the East. I have seen its secret places and have looked into its very soul; but now I see it always from a small boat, a high outline of mountains, blue and afar in the morning; like faint mist at noon; a jagged wall of purple at sunset. I have the feel of the oar in my hand, the vision of a scorching blue sea in my eyes. And I see a bay, a wide bay, smooth as glass and polished like ice, shimmering in the dark. A red light burns far off upon the gloom of the land, and the night is soft and warm. We drag at the oars with aching arms, and suddenly a puff of wind, a puff faint and tepid and laden with strange odors of blossoms, of aromatic wood, comes out of the still night—the first sigh of the East on my face. That I can never forget. It was impalpable and enslaving, like a charm, like a whispered promise of mysterious delight.

"We had been pulling this finishing spell for eleven hours. Two pulled, and he whose turn it was to rest sat at the tiller. We had made out the red light in that bay and steered for it, guessing it must mark some small coasting port. We passed two vessels, outlandish and high-sterned, sleeping at anchor, and, approaching the light, now very dim, ran the boat's nose against the end of a jutting wharf. We were blind with fatigue. My men dropped the oars and fell off the thwarts as if dead. I made fast to a pile. A current rippled softly. The scented obscurity of the shore was grouped into vast masses, a density of colossal clumps of vegetation, probably—mute and fantastic shapes. And at their foot the semicircle of a beach gleamed faintly, like an illusion. There was not a light, not a stir, not a sound. The mysterious East faced me, perfumed like a flower, silent like death, dark like a grave.

"And I sat weary beyond expression, exulting like a conqueror, sleepless   100
and entranced as if before a profound, a fateful enigma.

"A splashing of oars, a measured dip reverberating on the level of water,
intensified by the silence of the shore into loud claps, made me jump up. A boat,
a European boat, was coming in. I invoked the name of the dead; I hailed; '*Judea
ahoy!*' A thin shout answered.

"It was the captain. I had beaten the flagship by three hours, and I was
glad to hear the old man's voice again, tremulous and tired. 'Is it you, Marlow?'
'Mind the end of that jetty, sir,' I cried.

"He approached cautiously, and brought up with the deep-sea lead line which
we had saved—for the underwriters. I eased my painter and fell alongside. He
sat, a broken figure at the stern, wet with dew, his hands clasped in his lap. His
men were asleep already. 'I had a terrible time of it,' he murmured. 'Mahon is
behind—not very far.' We conversed in whispers, in low whispers, as if afraid to
wake up the land. Guns, thunder, earthquakes would not have awakened the men
just then.

"Looking round as we talked, I saw away at sea a bright light traveling in
the night. 'There's a steamer passing the bay,' I said. She was not passing, she
was entering, and she even came close and anchored. 'I wish,' said the old man,
'you would find out whether she is English. Perhaps they could give us a passage
somewhere.' He seemed nervously anxious. So by dint of punching and kicking I
started one of my men into a state of somnambulism, and giving him an oar,
took another and pulled towards the lights of the steamer.

"There was a murmur of voices in her, metallic hollow clangs of the engine   105
room, footsteps on the deck. Her ports shone, round like dilated eyes. Shapes
moved about, and there was a shadowy man high up on the bridge. He heard
my oars.

"And then, before I could open my lips, the East spoke to me, but it was in
a Western voice. A torrent of words was poured into the enigmatical, the fateful
silence; outlandish, angry words, mixed with words and even whole sentences of
good English, less strange but even more surprising. The voice swore and cursed
violently; it riddled the solemn peace of the bay by a volley of abuse. It began by
calling me Pig, and from that went crescendo into unmentionable adjectives—in
English. The man up there raged aloud in two languages, and with a sincerity in
his fury that almost convinced me I had, in some way, sinned against the harmony
of the universe. I could hardly see him, but began to think he would work himself
into a fit.

"Suddenly he ceased, and I could hear him snorting and blowing like a
porpoise. I said:

" 'What steamer is this, pray?'

" 'Eh? What's this? And who are you?'

" 'Castaway crew of an English bark burnt at sea. We came here tonight. I   110
am the second mate. The captain is in the longboat, and wishes to know if you
would give us a passage somewhere.'

" 'Oh, my goodness! I say. . . . This is the *Celestial* from Singapore on her
return trip. I'll arrange with your captain in the morning, . . . and, . . . I say,
. . . did you hear me just now?'

" 'I should think the whole bay heard you.'

"'I thought you were a shoreboat. Now, look here—this infernal lazy scoundrel of a caretaker has gone to sleep again—curse him. The light is out, and I nearly ran foul of the end of this damned jetty. This is the third time he plays me this trick. Now, I ask you, can anybody stand this kind of thing? It's enough to drive a man out of his mind. I'll report him. . . . I'll get the Assistant Resident to give him the sack, by—! See—there's no light. It's out, isn't it? I take you to witness the light's out. There should be a light, you know. A red light on the—'

"'There was a light,' I said, mildly.

"'But it's out, man! What's the use of talking like this? You can see for yourself it's out—don't you? If you had to take a valuable steamer along this Godforsaken coast you would want a light, too. I'll kick him from end to end of his miserable wharf. You'll see if I don't. I will—'   115

"'So I may tell my captain you'll take us?' I broke in.

"'Yes, I'll take you. Good night,' he said, brusquely.

"I pulled back, made fast again to the jetty, and then went to sleep at last. I had faced the silence of the East. I had heard some of its language. But when I opened my eyes again the silence was as complete as though it had never been broken. I was lying in a flood of light, and the sky had never looked so far, so high, before. I opened my eyes and lay without moving.

"And then I saw the men of the East—they were looking at me. The whole length of the jetty was full of people. I saw brown, bronze, yellow faces, the black eyes, the glitter, the color of an Eastern crowd. And all these beings stared without a murmur, without a sigh, without a movement. They stared down at the boats, at the sleeping men who at night had come to them from the sea. Nothing moved. The fronds of palms stood still against the sky. Not a branch stirred along the shore, and the brown roofs of hidden houses peeped through the green foliage, through the big leaves that hung shining and still like leaves forged of heavy metal. This was the East of the ancient navigators, so old, so mysterious, resplendent and somber, living and unchanged, full of danger and promise. And these were the men. I sat up suddenly. A wave of movement passed through the crowd from end to end, passed along the heads, swayed the bodies, ran along the jetty like a ripple on the water, like a breath of wind on a field—and all was still again. I see it now—the wide sweep of the bay, the glittering sands, the wealth of green infinite and varied, the sea blue like the sea of a dream, the crowd of attentive faces, the blaze of vivid color—the water reflecting it all, the curve of the shore, the jetty, the high-sterned outlandish craft floating still, and the three boats with the tired men from the West sleeping, unconscious of the land and the people and of the violence of sunshine. They slept thrown across the thwarts, curled on bottomboards, in the careless attitudes of death. The head of the old skipper, leaning back in the stern of the longboat, had fallen on his breast, and he looked as though he would never wake. Farther out old Mahon's face was upturned to the sky, with the long white beard spread out on his breast, as though he had been shot where he sat at the tiller; and a man, all in a heap in the bows of the boat, slept with both arms embracing the stemhead and with his cheek laid on the gunwale. The East looked at them without a sound.

"I have known its fascination since; I have seen the mysterious shores, the   120
still water, the lands of brown nations, where a stealthy Nemesis lies in wait, pursues, overtakes so many of the conquering race, who are proud of their wisdom, of

their knowledge, of their strength. But for me all the East is contained in that vision of my youth. It is all in that moment when I opened my young eyes on it. I came upon it from a tussle with the sea—and I was young—and I saw it looking at me. And this is all that is left of it! Only a moment; a moment of strength, of romance, of glamor—of youth! . . . A flick of sunshine upon a strange shore, the time to remember, the time for a sigh, and—good-by!—Night—Good-by . . . !"

He drank.

"Ah! The good old time—the good old time. Youth and the sea. Glamor and the sea! The good, strong sea, the salt, bitter sea, that could whisper to you and roar at you and knock your breath out of you."

He drank again.

"By all that's wonderful it is the sea, I believe, the sea itself—or is it youth alone? Who can tell? But you here—you all had something out of life: money, love—whatever one gets on shore—and, tell me, wasn't that the best time, that time when we were young at sea, young and had nothing, on the sea that gives nothing except hard knocks—and sometimes a chance to feel your strength—that only—that you all regret?"

And we all nodded at him: the man of finance, the man of accounts, the   125
man of law, we all nodded at him over the polished table that like a still sheet of brown water reflected our faces, lined, wrinkled; our faces marked by toil, by deceptions, by success, by love; our weary eyes looking still, looking always, looking anxiously for something out of life, that while it is expected is already gone—has passed unseen, in a sigh, in a flash—together with the youth, with the strength, with the romance of illusions.

GABRIEL GARCÍA MÁRQUEZ   (b. 1928)

A Very Old Man with Enormous Wings   *1971*

Translated by Gregory Rabassa

A TALE FOR CHILDREN

On the third day of rain they had killed so many crabs inside the house that Pelayo had to cross his drenched courtyard and throw them into the sea, because the newborn child had a temperature all night and they thought it was due to the stench. The world had been sad since Tuesday. Sea and sky were a single ash-gray thing and the sands of the beach, which on March nights glimmered like powdered light, had become a stew of mud and rotten shellfish. The light was so weak at noon that when Pelayo was coming back to the house after throwing away the crabs, it was hard for him to see what it was that was moving and groaning in the rear of the courtyard. He had to go very close to see that it was an old man, a very old man, lying face down in the mud, who, in spite of his tremendous efforts, couldn't get up, impeded by his enormous wings.

Frightened by that nightmare, Pelayo ran to get Elisenda, his wife, who was putting compresses on the sick child, and he took her to the rear of the courtyard.

They both looked at the fallen body with mute stupor. He was dressed like a ragpicker. There were only a few faded hairs left on his bald skull and very few teeth in his mouth, and his pitiful condition of a drenched great-grandfather had taken away any sense of grandeur he might have had. His huge buzzard wings, dirty and half-plucked, were forever entangled in the mud. They looked at him so long and so closely that Pelayo and Elisenda very soon overcame their surprise and in the end found him familiar. Then they dared speak to him, and he answered in an incomprehensible dialect with a strong sailor's voice. That was how they skipped over the inconvenience of the wings and quite intelligently concluded that he was a lonely castaway from some foreign ship wrecked by the storm. And yet, they called in a neighbor woman who knew everything about life and death to see him, and all she needed was one look to show them their mistake.

"He's an angel," she told them. "He must have been coming for the child, but the poor fellow is so old that the rain knocked him down."

On the following day everyone knew that a flesh-and-blood angel was held captive in Pelayo's house. Against the judgment of the wise neighbor woman, for whom angels in those times were the fugitive survivors of a celestial conspiracy, they did not have the heart to club him to death. Pelayo watched over him all afternoon from the kitchen, armed with his bailiff's club, and before going to bed he dragged him out of the mud and locked him up with the hens in the wire chicken coop. In the middle of the night, when the rain stopped, Pelayo and Elisenda were still killing crabs. A short time afterward the child woke up without a fever and with a desire to eat. Then they felt magnanimous and decided to put the angel on a raft with fresh water and provisions for three days and leave him to his fate on the high seas. But when they went out into the courtyard with the first light of dawn, they found the whole neighborhood in front of the chicken coop having fun with the angel, without the slightest reverence, tossing him things to eat through the openings in the wire as if he weren't a supernatural creature but a circus animal.

Father Gonzaga arrived before seven o'clock, alarmed at the strange news. By that time onlookers less frivolous than those at dawn had already arrived and they were making all kinds of conjectures concerning the captive's future. The simplest among them thought that he should be named mayor of the world. Others of sterner mind felt that he should be promoted to the rank of five-star general in order to win all wars. Some visionaries hoped that he could be put to stud in order to implant on earth a race of winged wise men who could take charge of the universe. But Father Gonzaga, before becoming a priest, had been a robust woodcutter. Standing by the wire, he reviewed his catechism in an instant and asked them to open the door so that he could take a close look at that pitiful man who looked more like a huge decrepit hen among the fascinated chickens. He was lying in a corner drying his open wings in the sunlight among the fruit peels and breakfast leftovers that the early risers had thrown him. Alien to the impertinences of the world, he only lifted his antiquarian eyes and murmured something in his dialect when Father Gonzaga went into the chicken coop and said good morning to him in Latin. The parish priest had his first suspicion of an imposter when he saw that he did not understand the language of God or know how to greet His ministers. Then he noticed that seen close up he was much too human: he had an unbearable smell of the outdoors, the back side of his wings was strewn with parasites and his main feathers had been mistreated by terrestrial winds, and nothing about him measured up to the proud dignity of angels. Then he came out of the chicken coop and in a brief sermon warned the curious against the risks of being ingenuous. He reminded them that the devil had the bad habit of making use of carnival tricks in order to confuse the unwary.° He argued that if wings were not the essential element in determining the difference between a hawk and an airplane, they were even less so in the recognition of angels. Nevertheless, he promised to write a letter to his bishop so that the latter would write to his primate so that the latter would write to the Supreme Pontiff° in order to get the final verdict from the highest courts.

His prudence fell on sterile hearts. The news of the captive angel spread with such rapidity that after a few hours the courtyard had the bustle of a marketplace and they had to call in troops with fixed bayonets to disperse the mob that was about to knock the house down. Elisenda, her spine all twisted from sweeping up so much marketplace trash, then got the idea of fencing in the yard and charging five cents admission to see the angel.

The curious came from far away. A traveling carnival arrived with a flying acrobat who buzzed over the crowd several times, but no one paid any attention to him because his wings were not those of an angel but, rather, those of a sidereal bat. The most unfortunate invalids on earth came in search of health: a poor woman who since childhood had been counting her heartbeats and had run out of numbers; a Portuguese man who couldn't sleep because the noise of the stars disturbed him; a sleepwalker who got up at night to undo the things he had done while awake; and many others with less serious ailments. In the midst of that shipwreck disorder that made the earth tremble, Pelayo and Elisenda were happy with fatigue, for in less than a week they had crammed their rooms with money and the line of pilgrims waiting their turn to enter still reached beyond the horizon.

The angel was the only one who took no part in his own act. He spent his time trying to get comfortable in his borrowed nest, befuddled by the hellish heat of the oil lamps and sacramental candles that had been placed along the wire. At first they tried to make him eat some mothballs, which, according to the wisdom of the wise neighbor woman, were the food prescribed for angels. But he turned them down, just as he turned down the papal lunches that the penitents brought him, and they never found out whether it was because he was an angel or because he was an old man that in the end he ate nothing but eggplant mush. His only supernatural virtue seemed to be patience. Especially during the first days, when the hens pecked at him, searching for the stellar parasites that proliferated in his wings, and the cripples pulled out feathers to touch their defective parts with, and even the most merciful threw stones at him, trying to get him to rise so they could see him standing. The only time they succeeded in arousing him was when they burned his side with an iron for branding steers, for he had been motionless for so many hours that they thought he was dead. He awoke with a start, ranting in his hermetic language and with tears in his eyes, and he flapped his wings a

---

He . . . the unwary: See *Hamlet*, act 2 scene 2, lines 573–578, for a further explanation of this power of the devil.
Supreme Pontiff: the Pope in Rome.

couple of times, which brought on a whirlwind of chicken dung and lunar dust and a gale of panic that did not seem to be of this world. Although many thought that his reaction had been one not of rage but of pain, from then on they were careful not to annoy him, because the majority understood that his passivity was not that of a hero taking his ease but that of a cataclysm in repose.

Father Gonzaga held back the crowd's frivolity with formulas of maidservant inspiration while awaiting the arrival of a final judgment on the nature of the captive. But the mail from Rome showed no sense of urgency. They spent their time finding out if the prisoner had a navel, if his dialect had any connection with Aramaic, how many times he could fit on the head of a pin, or whether he wasn't just a Norwegian with wings. Those meager letters might have come and gone until the end of time if a providential event had not put an end to the priest's tribulations.

It so happened that during those days, among so many other carnival attrac-   10
tions, there arrived in town the traveling show of the woman who had been changed into a spider for having disobeyed her parents. The admission to see her was not only less than the admission to see the angel, but people were permitted to ask her all manner of questions about her absurd state and to examine her up and down so that no one would ever doubt the truth of her horror. She was a frightful tarantula the size of a ram and with the head of a sad maiden. What was most heart-rending, however, was not her outlandish shape but the sincere affliction with which she recounted the details of her misfortune. While still practically a child she had sneaked out of her parents' house to go to a dance, and while she was coming back through the woods after having danced all night without permission, a fearful thunderclap rent the sky in two and through the crack came the lightning bolt of brimstone that changed her into a spider. Her only nourishment came from the meatballs that charitable souls chose to toss into her mouth. A spectacle like that, full of so much human truth and with such a fearful lesson, was bound to defeat without even trying that of a haughty angel who scarcely deigned to look at mortals. Besides, the few miracles attributed to the angel showed a certain mental disorder, like the blind man who didn't recover his sight but grew three new teeth, or the paralytic who didn't get to walk but almost won the lottery, and the leper whose sores sprouted sunflowers. Those consolation miracles, which were more like mocking fun, had already ruined the angel's reputation when the woman who had been changed into a spider finally crushed him completely. That was how Father Gonzaga was cured forever of his insomnia and Pelayo's courtyard went back to being as empty as during the time it had rained for three days and crabs walked through the bedrooms.

The owners of the house had no reason to lament. With the money they saved they built a two-story mansion with balconies and gardens and high netting so that crabs wouldn't get in during the winter, and with iron bars on the windows so that angels wouldn't get in. Pelayo also set up a rabbit warren close to town and gave up his job as bailiff for good, and Elisenda bought some satin pumps with high heels and many dresses of iridescent silk, the kind worn on Sunday by the most desirable women in those times. The chicken coop was the only thing that didn't receive any attention. If they washed it down with creolin° and burned

---

creolin: a creosote-based disinfectant.

tears of myrrh° inside it every so often, it was not in homage to the angel but to drive away the dungheap stench that still hung everywhere like a ghost and was turning the new house into an old one. At first, when the child learned to walk, they were careful that he not get too close to the chicken coop. But then they began to lose their fears and got used to the smell, and before the child got his second teeth he'd gone inside the chicken coop to play, where the wires were falling apart. The angel was no less standoffish with him than with other mortals, but he tolerated the most ingenious infamies with the patience of a dog who had no illusions. They both came down with chicken pox at the same time. The doctor who took care of the child couldn't resist the temptation to listen to the angel's heart, and he found so much whistling in the heart and so many sounds in his kidneys that it seemed impossible for him to be alive. What surprised him most, however, was the logic of his wings. They seemed so natural on that completely human organism that he couldn't understand why other men didn't have them too.

When the child began school it had been some time since the sun and rain had caused the collapse of the chicken coop. The angel went dragging himself about here and there like a stray dying man. They would drive him out of the bedroom with a broom and a moment later find him in the kitchen. He seemed to be in so many places at the same time that they grew to think that he'd been duplicated, that he was reproducing himself all through the house, and the exasperated and unhinged Elisenda shouted that it was awful living in that hell full of angels. He could scarcely eat and his antiquarian eyes had also become so foggy that he went about bumping into posts. All he had left were the bare cannulae° of his last feathers. Pelayo threw a blanket over him and extended him the charity of letting him sleep in the shed, and only then did they notice that he had a temperature at night, and was delirious with the tongue twisters of an old Norwegian. That was one of the few times they became alarmed, for they thought he was going to die and not even the wise neighbor woman had been able to tell them what to do with dead angels.

And yet he not only survived his worst winter, but seemed improved with the first sunny days. He remained motionless for several days in the farthest corner of the courtyard, where no one would see him, and at the beginning of December some large, stiff feathers began to grow on his wings, the feathers of a scarecrow, which looked more like another misfortune of decrepitude. But he must have known the reason for those changes, for he was quite careful that no one should notice them, that no one should hear the sea chanteys that he sometimes sang under the stars. One morning Elisenda was cutting some bunches of onions for lunch when a wind that seemed to come from the high seas blew into the kitchen. Then she went to the window and caught the angel in his first attempts at flight. They were so clumsy that his fingernails opened a furrow in the vegetable patch and he was on the point of knocking the shed down with the ungainly flapping that slipped on the light and couldn't get a grip on the air. But he did manage to gain altitude. Elisenda let out a sigh of relief, for herself and for him, when she saw him pass over the last houses, holding himself up in some way with the risky

myrrh: a fragrant plant resin used in making incense and perfume.
cannulae: the hollow central stems of feathers.

flapping of a senile vulture. She kept watching him even when she was through cutting the onions and she kept on watching until it was no longer possible for her to see him, because then he was no longer an annoyance in her life but an imaginary dot on the horizon of the sea.

LANGSTON HUGHES 1902–1967

Slave on the Block   *1938*

They were people who went in for Negroes—Michael and Anne—the Carraways. But not in the social-service, philanthropic sort of way, no. They saw no use in helping a race that was already too charming and naive and lovely for words. Leave them unspoiled and just enjoy them, Michael and Anne felt. So they went in for the Art of Negroes—the dancing that had such jungle life about it, the songs that were so simple and fervent, the poetry that was so direct, so real. They never tried to influence that art, they only bought it and raved over it, and copied it. For they were artists, too.

In their collection they owned some Covarrubias originals. Of course Covarrubias wasn't a Negro, but how he caught the darky spirit! They owned all the Robeson records and all the Bessie Smith. And they had a manuscript of Countee Cullen's. They saw all the plays with or about Negroes, read all the books, and adored the Hall Johnson Singers. They had met Doctor DuBois, and longed to meet Carl Van Vechten. Of course they knew Harlem like their own backyard, that is, all the speakeasies and night clubs and dance halls, from the Cotton Club and the ritzy joints where Negroes couldn't go themselves, down to places like the Hot Dime, where white folks couldn't get in—unless they knew the man. (And tipped heavily.)

They were acquainted with lots of Negroes, too—but somehow the Negroes didn't seem to like them very much. Maybe the Carraways gushed over them too soon. Or maybe they looked a little like poor white folks, although they were really quite well off. Or maybe they tried too hard to make friends, dark friends, and the dark friends suspected something. Or perhaps their house in the Village was too far from Harlem, or too hard to find, being back in one of those queer and expensive little side streets that had once been alleys before the art invasion came. Anyway, occasionally, a furtive Negro might accept their invitation for tea, or cocktails; and sometimes a lesser Harlem celebrity or two would decorate their rather slow parties; but one seldom came back for more. As much as they loved Negroes, Negroes didn't seem to love Michael and Anne.

But they were blessed with a wonderful colored cook and maid—until she took sick and died in her room in their basement. And then the most marvellous ebony boy walked into their life, a boy as black as all the Negroes they'd ever known put together.

"He *is* the jungle," said Anne when she saw him.   5

"He's 'I Couldn't Hear Nobody Pray,'" said Michael.

For Anne thought in terms of pictures: she was a painter. And Michael thought in terms of music: he was a composer for the piano. And they had a most wonderful idea of painting pictures and composing music that went together, and then having a joint "concert-exhibition" as they would call it. Her pictures and his music. The Carraways, a sonata and a picture, a fugue and a picture. It would be lovely, and such a novelty, people would have to like it. And many of their things would be Negro. Anne had painted their maid six times. And Michael had composed several themes based on the spirituals, and on Louis Armstrong's jazz. Now here was this ebony boy. The essence in the flesh.

They had nearly missed the boy. He had come, when they were out, to gather up the things the cook had left, and take them to her sister in Jersey. It seems that he was the late cook's nephew. The new colored maid had let him in and given him the two suitcases of poor dear Emma's belongings, and he was on his way to the Subway. That is, he was in the hall, going out just as the Carraways, Michael and Anne, stepped in. They could hardly see the boy, it being dark in the hall, and he being dark, too.

"Hello," they said. "Is this Emma's nephew?"

"Yes'm," said the maid. "Yes'm."   10

"Well, come in," said Anne, "and let us see you. We loved your aunt so much. She was the best cook we ever had."

"You don't know where I could get a job, do you?" said the boy. This took Michael and Anne back a bit, but they rallied at once. So charming and naive to ask right away for what he wanted.

Anne burst out, "You know, I think I'd like to paint you."

Michael said, "Oh, I say now, that would be lovely! He's so utterly Negro."

The boy grinned.   15

Anne said, "Could you come back tomorrow?"

And the boy said, "Yes, indeed. I sure could."

The upshot of it was that they hired him. They hired him to look after the garden, which was just about as big as Michael's grand piano—only a little square behind the house. You know those Village gardens. Anne sometimes painted it. And occasionally they set the table there for four on a spring evening. Nothing grew in the garden really, practically nothing. But the boy said he could plant things. And they had to have some excuse to hire him.

The boy's name was Luther. He had come from the South to his relatives in Jersey, and had had only one job since he got there, shining shoes for a Greek in Elizabeth. But the Greek fired him because the boy wouldn't give half his tips over to the proprietor.

"I never heard of a job where I had to pay the boss, instead of the boss   20
paying me," said Luther. "Not till I got here."

"And then what did you do?" said Anne.

"Nothing. Been looking for a job for the last four months."

"Poor boy," said Michael; "poor, dear boy."

"Yes," said Anne. "You must be hungry." And they called the cook to give him something to eat.

Luther dug around in the garden a little bit that first day, went out and   25
bought some seeds, came back and ate some more. They made a place for him to sleep in the basement by the furnace. And the next day Anne started to paint him, after she'd bought the right colors.

"He'll be good company for Mattie," they said. "She claims she's afraid to stay alone at night when we're out, so she leaves." They suspected, though, that Mattie just liked to get up to Harlem. And they thought right. Mattie was not as settled as she looked. Once out, with the Savoy open until three in the morning, why come home? That was the way Mattie felt.

In fact, what happened was that Mattie showed Luther where the best and cheapest hot spots in Harlem were located. Luther hadn't even set foot in Harlem before, living twenty-eight miles away, as he did, in Jersey, and being a kind of quiet boy. But the second night he was there Mattie said, "Come on, let's go. Working for white folks all day, I'm tired. They needn't think I was made to answer telephones all night." So out they went.

Anne noticed that most mornings Luther would doze almost as soon as she sat him down to pose, so she eventually decided to paint Luther asleep. "The Sleeping Negro," she would call it. Dear, natural childlike people, they would sleep anywhere they wanted to. Anyway, asleep, he kept still and held the pose.

And he *was* an adorable Negro. Not tall, but with a splendid body. And a slow and lively smile that lighted up his black, black face, for his teeth were very white, and his eyes, too. Most effective in oil and canvas. Better even than Emma had been. Anne could stare at him at leisure when he was asleep. One day she decided to paint him nude, or at least half nude. A slave picture, that's what she would do. The market at New Orleans for a background. And call it "The Boy on the Block."

So one morning when Luther settled down in his sleeping pose, Anne said, "No," she had finished that picture. She wanted to paint him now representing to the full the soul and sorrow of his people. She wanted to paint him as a slave about to be sold. And since slaves in warm climates had no clothes, would he please take off his shirt. 30

Luther smiled a sort of embarrassed smile and took off his shirt.

"Your undershirt, too," said Anne. But it turned out that he had on a union suit, so he had to go out and change altogether. He came back and mounted the box that Anne said would serve just then for a slave block, and she began to sketch. Before luncheon Michael came in, and went into rhapsodies over Luther on the box without a shirt, about to be sold into slavery. He said he must put him into music right now. And he went to the piano and began to play something that sounded like Deep River in the jaws of a dog, but Michael said it was a modern slave plaint, 1850 in terms of 1933. Vieux Carré° remembered on 135th Street, Slavery in the Cotton Club.

Anne said, "It's too marvellous!" And they painted and played till dark, with rest periods in between for Luther. Then they all knocked off for dinner. Anne and Michael went out later to one of Lew Leslie's new shows. And Luther and Mattie said, "Thank God!" and got dressed up for Harlem.

Funny, they didn't like the Carraways. They treated them nice and paid them well. "But they're too strange," said Mattie, "they makes me nervous."

"They is mighty funny," Luther agreed. 35

They didn't understand the vagaries of white folks, neither Luther nor Mattie, and they didn't want to be bothered trying.

Vieux Carré: the old quarter of New Orleans.

"I does my work," said Mattie. "After that I don't want to be painted, or asked to sing songs, nor nothing like that."

The Carraways often asked Luther to sing, and he sang. He knew a lot of southern worksongs and reels, and spirituals and ballads.

> *"Dear Ma, I'm in hard luck*:
> *Three days since I et*,
> *And the stamp on this letter's*
> *Gwine to put me in debt."*

The Carraways allowed him to neglect the garden altogether. About all Luther did was pose and sing. And he got tired of that.

Indeed, both Luther and Mattie became a bit difficult to handle as time   40
went on. The Carraways blamed it on Mattie. She had got hold of Luther. She was just simply spoiling a nice simple young boy. She was old enough to know better. Mattie was in love with Luther.

As least, he slept with her. The Carraways discovered this one night about one o'clock when they went to wake Luther up (the first time they'd ever done such a thing) and ask him if he wouldn't sing his own marvellous version of John Henry for a man who had just come from Saint Louis and was sailing for Paris tomorrow. But Luther wasn't in his own bed by the furnace. There was a light in Mattie's room, so Michael knocked softly. Mattie said, "Who's that?" And Michael poked his head in, and here were Luther and Mattie in bed together!

Of course, Anne condoned them. "It's so simple and natural for Negroes to make love." But Mattie, after all, was forty if she was a day. And Luther was only a kid. Besides Anne thought that Luther had been ever so much nicer when he first came than he was now. But from so many nights at the Savoy, he had become a marvellous dancer, and he was teaching Anne the Lindy Hop to Cab Calloway's records. Besides, her picture of "The Boy on the Block" wasn't anywhere near done. And he did take pretty good care of the furnace. So they kept him. At least, Anne kept him, although Michael said he was getting a little bored with the same Negro always in the way.

For Luther had grown a bit familiar lately. He smoked up all their cigarettes, drank their wine, told jokes on them to their friends, and sometimes even came upstairs singing and walking about the house when the Carraways had guests in who didn't share their enthusiasm for Negroes, natural or otherwise.

Luther and Mattie together were a pair. They quite frankly lived with one another now. Well, let that go. Anne and Michael prided themselves on being different; artists, you know, and liberal-minded people—maybe a little scatter-brained, but then (secretly, they felt) that came from genius. They were not ordinary people, bothering about the liberties of others. Certainly, the last thing they would do would be to interfere with the delightful simplicity of Negroes.

But Mattie must be giving Luther money and buying him clothes. He was   45
really dressing awfully well. And on her Thursday afternoons off she would come back loaded down with packages. As far as the Carraways could tell, they were all for Luther.

And sometimes there were quarrels drifting up from the basement. And often, all too often, Mattie had moods. Then Luther would have moods. And it was pretty awful having two dark and glowering people around the house. Anne couldn't paint and Michael couldn't play.

One day, when she hadn't seen Luther for three days, Anne called downstairs and asked him if he wouldn't please come up and take off his shirt and get on the box. The picture was almost done. Luther came dragging his feet upstairs and humming:

> *"Before I'd be a slave*
> *I'd be buried in ma grave*
> *And go home to my Jesus*
> *And be free."*

And that afternoon he let the furnace go almost out.

That was the state of things when Michael's mother (whom Anne had never liked) arrived from Kansas City to pay them a visit. At once neither Mattie nor Luther liked her either. She was a mannish old lady, big and tall, and inclined to be bossy. Mattie, however, did spruce up her service, cooked delicious things, and treated Mrs. Carraway with a great deal more respect than she did Anne.

"I never play with servants," Mrs. Carraway had said to Michael, and Mattie must have heard her.

But Luther, he was worse than ever. Not that he did anything wrong, Anne thought, but the way he did things! For instance, he didn't need to sing now all the time, especially since Mrs. Carraway had said she didn't like singing. And certainly not songs like "You Rascal, You."

But all things end! With the Carraways and Luther it happened like this: One forenoon, quite without a shirt (for he expected to pose) Luther came sauntering through the library to change the flowers in the vase. He carried red roses. Mrs Carraway was reading her morning scripture from the Health and Life.

"Oh, good morning," said Luther. "How long are you gonna stay in this house?"

"I never liked familiar Negroes," said Mrs. Carraway, over her nose glasses.

"Huh!" said Luther. "That's too bad! I never liked poor white folks."

Mrs. Carraway screamed, a short, loud, dignified scream. Michael came running in bathrobe and pyjamas. Mrs. Carraway grew tall. There was a scene. Luther talked. Michael talked. Anne appeared.

"Never, never, never," said Mrs. Carraway, "have I suffered such impudence from servants—and a nigger servant—in my own son's house."

"Mother, Mother, Mother," said Michael. "Be calm. I'll discharge him." He turned on the nonchalant Luther. "Go!" he said, pointing toward the door. "Go, go!

"Michael," Anne cried, "I haven't finished 'The Slave on the Block.'" Her husband looked nonplussed. For a moment he breathed deeply.

"Either he goes or I go," said Mrs. Carraway, firm as a rock.

"He goes," said Michael with strength from his mother.

"Oh!" cried Anne. She looked at Luther. His black arms were full of roses he had brought to put in the vases. He had on no shirt. "Oh!" His body was ebony.

"Don't worry 'bout me!' said Luther. "I'll go."

"Yes, we'll go," boomed Mattie from the doorway, who had come up from below, fat and belligerent. "We've stood enough foolery from you white folks! Yes, we'll go. Come on, Luther."

What could she mean, "stood enough"? What had they done to them. Anne and Michael wondered. They had tried to be kind. "Oh!"

"Sneaking around knocking on our door at night," Mattie went on. "Yes,   65 we'll go. Pay us! Pay us! Pay us!" So she remembered the time they had come for Luther at night. That was it.

"I'll pay you," said Michael. He followed Mattie out.

Anne looked at her black boy.

"Goody-bye," Luther said. "You fix the vases."

He handed her his armful of roses, glanced impudently at old Mrs. Carraway and grinned—grinned that wide, beautiful, white-toothed grin that made Anne say when she first saw him, "He looks like the jungle." Grinned, and disappeared in the dark hall, with no shirt on his back.

"Oh," Anne moaned distressfully, "my 'Boy on the Block'!"   70

"Huh!" snorted Mrs. Carraway.

FRANZ KAFKA (1883–1924)

A Hunger Artist   *1924*

Translated by Willa and Edwin Muir

During these last decades the interest in professional fasting has markedly diminished. It used to pay very well to stage such great performances under one's own management, but today that is quite impossible. We live in a different world now. At one time the whole town took a lively interest in the hunger artist; from day to day of his fast the excitement mounted; everybody wanted to see him at least once a day; there were people who bought season tickets for the last few days and sat from morning till night in front of his small barred cage; even in the nighttime there were visiting hours, when the whole effect was heightened by torch flares; on fine days the cage was set out in the open air, and then it was the children's special treat to see the hunger artist; for their elders he was often just a joke that happened to be in fashion, but the children stood openmouthed, holding each other's hands for greater security, marveling at him as he sat there pallid in black tights, with his ribs sticking out so prominently, not even on a seat but down among straw on the ground, sometimes giving a courteous nod, answering questions with a constrained smile, or perhaps stretching an arm through the bars so that one might feel how thin it was, and then again withdrawing deep into himself, paying no attention to anyone or anything, not even to the all-important striking of the clock that was the only piece of furniture in his cage, but merely staring into vacancy with half-shut eyes, now and then taking a sip from a tiny glass of water to moisten his lips.

Besides casual onlookers there were also relays of permanent watchers selected by the public, usually butchers, strangely enough, and it was their task to watch the hunger artist day and night, three of them at a time, in case he should have some secret recourse to nourishment. This was nothing but a formality, instituted to reassure the masses, for the initiates knew well enough that during his fast the artist would never in any circumstances, not even under forcible compulsion, swallow the smallest morsel of food; the honor of his profession forbade it. Not every watcher, of course, was capable of understanding this, there were often groups of night watchers who were very lax in carrying out their duties and deliberately huddled together in a retired corner to play cards with great absorption, obviously intending to give the hunger artist the chance of a little refreshment, which they supposed he could draw from some private hoard. Nothing annoyed the artist more than such watchers; they made him miserable; they made his fast seem unendurable; sometimes he mastered his feebleness sufficiently to sing during their watch for as long as he could keep going, to show them how unjust their suspicions were. But that was of little use; they only wondered at his cleverness in being able to fill his mouth even while singing. Much more to his taste were the watchers who sat close up to the bars, who were not content with the dim night lighting of the hall but focused him in the full glare of the electric pocket torch given them by the impresario. The harsh light did not trouble him at all, in any case he could never sleep properly, and he could always drowse a little, whatever the light, at any hour, even when the hall was thronged with noisy onlookers. He was quite happy at the prospect of spending a sleepless night with such watchers; he was ready to exchange jokes with them, to tell them stories out of his nomadic life, anything at all to keep them awake and demonstrate to them again that he had no eatables in his cage and that he was fasting as not one of them could fast. But his happiest moment was when the morning came and an enormous breakfast was brought them, at his expense, on which they flung themselves with the keen appetite of healthy men after a weary night of wakefulness. Of course there were people who argued that this breakfast was an unfair attempt to bribe the watchers, but that was going rather too far, and when they were invited to take on night's vigil without a breakfast, merely for the sake of the cause, they made themselves scarce, although they stuck stubbornly to their suspicions.

Such suspicions, anyhow, were a necessary accompaniment to the profession of fasting. No one could possibly watch the hunger artist continuously, day and night, and so no one could produce first-hand evidence that the fast had really been rigorous and continuous; only the artist himself could know that, he was therefore bound to be the sole completely satisfied spectator of his own fast. Yet for other reasons he was never satisfied; it was not perhaps mere fasting that had brought him to such skeleton thinness that many people had regretfully to keep away from his exhibitions, because the sight of him was too much for them, perhaps it was dissatisfaction with himself that had worn him down. For he alone knew, what no other initiate knew, how easy it was to fast. It was the easiest thing in the world. He made no secret of this, yet people did not believe him, at the best they set him down as modest; most of them, however, thought he was out for publicity or else was some kind of cheat who found it easy to fast because he had discovered a way of making it easy, and then had the impudence to admit the fact, more or less. He had to put up with all that, and in the course of time had got used to it, but his inner dissatisfaction always rankled, and never yet, after any term of fasting—this must be granted to his credit—had he left the cage of his own free will. The longest period of fasting was fixed by his impresario at forty days, beyond that term he was not allowed to go, not even in great cities, and there was good reason for it, too. Experience had proved that for about forty days the interest of the public could be stimulated by a steadily increasing pressure of advertisement, but after that the town began to lose interest, sympathetic support began notably to fall off; there were of course local variations as between one town and another or one country and another, but as a general rule forty days marked the limit. So on the fortieth day the flower-bedecked cage was opened, enthusiastic spectators filled the hall, a military band played, two doctors entered the cage to measure the results of the fast, which were announced through a megaphone, and finally two young ladies appeared, blissful at having been selected for the honor, to help the hunger artist down the few steps leading to a small table on which was spread a carefully chosen invalid repast. And at this very moment the artist always turned stubborn. True, he would entrust his bony arms to the outstretched helping hands of the ladies bending over him, but stand up he would not. Why stop fasting at this particular moment, after forty days of it? He had held out for a long time, an illimitably long time; why stop now, when he was in his best fasting form, or rather, not yet quite in his best fasting form? Why should he be cheated of the fame he would get for fasting longer, for being not only the record hunger artist of all time, which presumably he was already, but for beating his own record by a performance beyond human imagination, since he felt that there were no limits to his capacity for fasting? His public pretended to admire him so much, why should it have so little patience with him; if he could endure fasting longer, why shouldn't the public endure it? Besides, he was tired, he was comfortable sitting in the straw, and now he was supposed to lift himself to his full height and go down to a meal the very thought of which gave him a nausea that only the presence of the ladies kept him from betraying, and even that with an effort. And he looked up into the eyes of the ladies who were apparently so friendly and in reality so cruel, and shook his head, which felt too heavy on its strengthless neck. But then there happened yet again what always happened. The impresario came forward, without a word—for the band made speech impossible— lifted his arms in the air above the artist, as if inviting Heaven to look down upon its creature here in the straw, this suffering martyr, which indeed he was, although in quite another sense; grasped him around the emaciated waist, with exaggerated caution, so that the frail condition he was in might be appreciated; and committed him to the care of the blenching ladies, not without secretly giving him a shaking so that his legs and body tottered and swayed. The artist now submitted completely; his head lolled on his breast as if it had landed there by chance; his body was hollowed out; his legs in a spasm of self-preservation clung close to each other at the knees, yet scraped on the ground as if it were not really solid ground, as if they were only trying to find solid ground; and the whole weight of his body, a featherweight after all, relapsed onto one of the ladies, who, looking around for help and panting a little—this post of honor was not at all what she had expected it to be—first stretched her neck as far as she could to keep her face at least free from contact with the artist, then finding this impossible, and her more fortunate companion not coming to her aid but merely holding extended in her own trembling hand the little bunch of knucklebones that was the artist's, to the great delight of the spectators burst into tears and had to be replaced by an attendant who had long been stationed in readiness. Then came the food, a little of which the impresario managed to get between the artist's lips, while he sat in a kind of half-fainting trance, to the accompaniment of cheerful patter designed to distract the public's attention from the artist's condition; after that, a toast was drunk to the public, supposedly prompted by a whisper from the artist in the impresario's ear; the band confirmed it with a mighty flourish, the spectators melted away, and no one had any cause to be dissatisfied with the proceedings, no one except the hunger artist himself, he only, as always.

So he lived for many years, with small regular intervals of recuperation, in visible glory, honored by the world, yet in spite of that troubled in spirit, and all the more troubled because no one would take his trouble seriously. What comfort could he possibly need? What more could he possibly wish for? And if some good-natured person, feeling sorry for him, tried to console him by pointing out that his melancholy was probably caused by fasting, it could happen, especially when he had been fasting for some time, that he reacted with an outburst of fury and to the general alarm began to shake the bars of his cage like a wild animal. Yet the impresario had a way of punishing these outbreaks which he rather enjoyed putting into operation. He would apologize publicly for the artist's behavior, which was only to be excused, he admitted, because of the irritability caused by fasting; a condition hardly to be understood by well-fed people; then by natural transition he went on to mention the artist's equally incomprehensible boast that he could fast for much longer than he was doing; he praised the high ambition, the good will, the great self-denial undoubtedly implicit in such a statement; and then quite simply countered it by bringing out photographs, which were also on sale to the public, showing the artist on the fortieth day of a fast lying in bed almost dead from exhaustion. This perversion of the truth, familiar to the artist though it was, always unnerved him afresh and proved too much for him. What was a consequence of the premature ending of his fast was here presented as the cause of it! To fight against this lack of understanding, against a whole world of nonunderstanding, was impossible. Time and again in good faith he stood by the bars listening to the impresario, but as soon as the photographs appeared he always let go and sank with a groan back onto his straw, and the reassured public could once more come close and gaze at him.

A few years later when the witnesses of such scenes called them to mind, they often failed to understand themselves at all. For meanwhile the aforementioned change in public interest had set in; it seemed to happen almost overnight; there may have been profound causes for it, but who was going to bother about that; at any rate the pampered hunger artist suddenly found himself deserted one fine day by the amusement-seekers, who went streaming past him to other more-favored attractions. For the last time the impresario hurried him over half Europe to discover whether the old interest might still survive here and there; all in vain; everywhere, as if by secret agreement, a positive revulsion from professional fasting was in evidence. Of course it could not really have sprung up so suddenly as all that, and many premonitory symptoms which had not been sufficiently remarked or suppressed during the rush and glitter of success now came retrospectively to mind, but it was now too late to take any countermeasures. Fasting would surely come into fashion again at some future date, yet that was no comfort for those living in the present. What, then, was the hunger artist to do? He had been applauded

5

by thousands in his time and could hardly come down to showing himself in a street booth at village fairs, and as for adopting another profession, he was not only too old for that but too fanatically devoted to fasting. So he took leave of the impresario, his partner in an unparalleled career, and hired himself to a large circus; in order to spare his own feelings he avoided reading the conditions of his contract.

A large circus with its enormous traffic in replacing and recruiting men, animals, and aparatus can always find a use for people at any time, even for a hunger artist, provided of course that he does not ask too much, and in this particular case anyhow it was not only the artist who was taken on but his famous and long-known name as well; indeed considering the peculiar nature of his performance, which was not impaired by advancing age, it could not be objected that here was an artist past his prime, no longer at the height of his professional skill, seeking a refuge in some quiet corner of a circus; on the contrary, the hunger artist averred that he could fast as well as ever, which was entirely credible, he even alleged that if he were allowed to fast as he liked, and this was at once promised him without more ado, he could astound the world by establishing a record never yet achieved, a statement that certainly provoked a smile among the other professionals, since it left out of account the change in public opinion, which the hunger artist in his zeal conveniently forgot.

He had not, however, actually lost his sense of the real situation and took it as a matter of course that he and his cage should be stationed, not in the middle of the ring as a main attraction, but outside, near the animal cages, on a site that was after all easily accessible. Large and gaily painted placards made a frame for the cage and announced what was to be seen inside it. When the public came thronging out in the intervals to see the animals, they could hardly avoid passing the hunger artist's cage and stopping there for a moment, perhaps they might even have stayed longer had not those pressing behind them in the narrow gangway, who did not understand why they should be held up on their way toward the excitements of the menagerie, made it impossible for anyone to stand gazing quietly for any length of time. And that was the reason why the hunger artist, who had of course been looking forward to these visiting hours as the main achievement of his life, began instead to shrink from them. At first he could hardly wait for the intervals; it was exhilarating to watch the crowds come streaming his way, until only too soon—not even the most obstinate self-deception, clung to almost consciously, could hold out against the fact—the conviction was borne in upon him that these people, most of them, to judge from their actions, again and again, without exception, were all on their way to the menagerie. And the first sight of them from the distance remained the best. For when they reached his cage he was at once deafened by the storm of shouting and abuse that arose from the two contending factions, which renewed themselves continuously, of those who wanted to stop and stare at him—he soon began to dislike them more than the others—not out of real interest but only out of obstinate self-assertiveness, and those who wanted to go straight on to the animals. When the first great rush was past, the stragglers came along, and these, whom nothing could have prevented from stopping to look at him as long as they had breath, raced past with long strides, hardly even glancing at him, in their haste to get to the menagerie in time. And all too rarely did it happen that he had a stroke of luck, when some father of a family fetched up before him with his children, pointed a finger at the hunger artist, and explained at length what the phenomenon meant, telling stories of earlier years when he himself had watched similar but much more thrilling performances, and the children, still rather uncomprehending, since neither inside nor outside school had they been sufficiently prepared for this lesson—what did they care about fasting?—yet showed by the brightness of their intent eyes that new and better times might be coming. Perhaps, said the hunger artist to himself many a time, things would be a little better if his cage were set not quite so near the menagerie. That made it too easy for people to make their choice, to say nothing of what he suffered from the stench of the menagerie, the animals' restlessness by night, the carrying past of raw lumps of flesh for the beasts of prey, the roaring at feeding times, which depressed him continually. But he did not dare to lodge a complaint with the management; after all, he had the animals to thank for the troops of people who passed his cage, among whom there might always be one here and there to take an interest in him, and who could tell where they might schedule him if he called attention to his existence and thereby to the fact that, strictly speaking, he was only an impediment on the way to the menagerie.

A small impediment, to be sure, one that grew steadily less. People grew familiar with the strange idea that they could be expected, in times like these, to take an interest in a hunger artist, and with this familiarity the verdict went out against him. He might fast as much as he could, and he did so; but nothing could save him now, people passed him by. Just try to explain to anyone the art of fasting! Anyone who has no feeling for it cannot be made to understand it. The fine placards grew dirty and illegible, they were torn down; the little notice board telling the number of fast days achieved, which at first was changed carefully every day, had long stayed at the same figure, for after the first few weeks even this small task seemed pointless to the staff; and so the artist simply fasted on and on, as he had once dreamed of doing, and it was no trouble to him, just as he had always foretold, but no one counted the days, no one, not even the artist himself, knew what records he was already breaking, and his heart grew heavy. And when once in a while some leisurely passer-by stopped, made merry over the old figure on the board, and spoke of swindling, that was in its way the stupidest lie ever invented by indifference and inborn malice, since it was not the hunger artist who was cheating, he was working honestly, but the world was cheating him of his reward.

Many more days went by, however, and that too came to an end. An overseer's eye fell on the cage one day and he asked the attendants why this perfectly good cage should be left standing there unused with dirty straw inside it; nobody knew, until one man, helped out by the notice board, remembered about the hunger artist. They poked into the straw with sticks and found him in it. "Are you still fasting?" asked the overseer, "when on earth do you mean to stop?" "Forgive me, everybody," whispered the hunger artist; only the overseer, who had his ear to the bars, understood him. "Of course," said the overseer, and tapped his forehead with a finger to let the attendants know what state the man was in, "we forgive you." "I always wanted you to admire my fasting," said the hunger artist. "We do admire it," said the overseer, affably. "But you shouldn't admire it," said the hunger artist. "Well then we don't admire it," said the overseer, "but why shouldn't we admire it?" "Because I have to fast, I can't help it," said the hunger artist. "What a fellow you are," said the overseer, "and why can't you help it?" "Because," said the hunger artist, lifting his head a little and speaking, with his lips pursed, as if for a kiss, right into the overseer's ear, so that no syllable might be lost, "because I couldn't find the food I liked. If I had found it, believe me, I should have made no fuss and stuffed myself like you or anyone else." These were his last words, but in his dimming eyes remained the firm though no longer proud persuasion that he was still continuing to fast.

"Well, clear this out now!" said the overseer, and they buried the hunger   10
artist, straw and all. Into the cage they put a young panther. Even the most insensitive felt it refreshing to see this wild creature leaping around the cage that had so long been dreary. The panther was all right. The food he liked was brought him without hesitation by the attendants; he seemed not even to miss his freedom; his noble body, furnished almost to the bursting point with all that it needed, seemed to carry freedom around with it too; somewhere in his jaws it seemed to lurk; and the joy of life streamed with such ardent passion from his throat that for the onlookers it was not easy to stand the shock of it. But they braced themselves, crowded around the cage, and did not want ever to move away.

DORIS LESSING (b. 1919)

The Old Chief Mshlanga   *1951*

They were good, the years of ranging the bush over her father's farm which, like every white farm, was largely unused, broken only occasionally by small patches of cultivation. In between, nothing but trees, the long sparse grass, thorn and cactus and gully, grass and outcrop and thorn. And a jutting piece of rock which had been thrust up from the warm soil of Africa unimaginable eras of time ago, washed into hollows and whorls by sun and wind that had travelled so many thousands of miles of space and bush, would hold the weight of a small girl whose eyes were sightless for anything but a pale willowed river, a pale gleaming castle—a small girl singing: "Out flew the web and floated wide, the mirror cracked from side to side . . ."

Pushing her way through the green aisles of the mealie° stalks, the leaves arching like cathedrals veined with sunlight far overhead, with the packed red earth underfoot, a fine lace of red starred witchweed would summon up a black bent figure croaking premonitions: the Northern witch, bred of cold Northern forests, would stand before her among the mealie fields, and it was the mealie fields that faded and fled, leaving her among the gnarled roots of an oak, snow falling thick and soft and white, the woodcutter's fire glowing red welcome through crowding tree trunks.

A white child, opening its eyes curiously on a sun-suffused landscape, a gaunt and violent landscape, might be supposed to accept it as her own, to take the msasa trees and the thorn trees as familiars, to feel her blood running free and responsive to the swing of the seasons.

---

mealie: A word for corn in Southern Africa.

This child could not see a msasa tree, or the thorn, for what they were. Her books held tales of alien fairies, her rivers ran slow and peaceful, and she knew the shape of the leaves of an ash or an oak, the names of the little creatures that lived in English streams, when the words "the veld"° meant strangeness, though she could remember nothing else.

Because of this, for many years, it was the veld that seemed unreal; the sun   5
was a foreign sun, and the wind spoke a strange language.

The black people on the farm were as remote as the trees and the rocks. They were an amorphous black mass, mingling and thinning and massing like tadpoles, faceless, who existed merely to serve, to say "Yes, Baas,"° take their money and go. They changed season by season, moving from one farm to the next, according to their outlandish needs, which one did not have to understand, coming from perhaps hundreds of miles North or East, passing on after a few months—where? Perhaps even as far away as the fabled gold mines of Johannesburg, where the pay was so much better than the few shillings of month and the double handful of mealie meal twice a day which they earned in that part of Africa.

The child was taught to take them for granted: the servants in the house would come running a hundred yards to pick up a book if she dropped it. She was called "Nkosikaas"—Chieftainess, even by the black children her own age.

Later, when the farm grew too small to hold her curiosity, she carried a gun in the crook of her arm and wandered miles a day, from vlei° to vlei, from *kopje* to *kopje*,° accompanied by two dogs: the dogs and the gun were an armour against fear. Because of them she never felt fear.

If a native came into sight along the kaffir° paths half a mile away, the dogs would flush him up a tree as if he were a bird. If he expostulated (in his uncouth language which was by itself ridiculous) that was cheek. If one was in a good mood, it could be a matter for laughter. Otherwise one passed on, hardly glancing at the angry man in the tree.

On the rare occasions when white children met together they could amuse   10
themselves by hailing a passing native in order to make a buffoon of him; they could set the dogs on him and watch him run; they could tease a small black child as if he were a puppy—save that they would not throw stones and sticks at a dog without a sense of guilt.

Later still, certain questions presented themselves in the child's mind; and because the answers were not easy to accept, they were silenced by an even greater arrogance of manner.

It was even impossible to think of the black people who worked about the house as friends, for if she talked to one of them, her mother would come running anxiously: "Come away; you mustn't talk to natives."

It was this instilled consciousness of danger, of something unpleasant, that made it easy to laugh out loud, crudely, if a servant made a mistake in his English of if he failed to understand an order—there is a certain kind of laughter that is fear, afraid of itself.

veld: Also *veldt*, a vast, open grass-covered area used for grazing.
Baas: boss.
vlei: A slough or pond (valley).
kopje: A small hill covered with vegetation and rocks. Usually pronounced "copy."
kaffir: A pejorative word for the various Bantu peoples and their languages.

One evening, when I was about fourteen, I was walking down the side of a mealie field that had been newly ploughed, so that the great red clods showed fresh and tumbling to the vlei beyond, like a choppy red sea; it was that hushed and listening hour, when the birds send long sad calls from tree to tree, and all the colours of earth and sky and leaf are deep and golden. I had my rifle in the curve of my arm, and the dogs were at my heels.

In front of me, perhaps a couple of hundred yards away, a group of three Africans came into sight around the side of a big antheap. I whistled the dogs close in to my skirts and let the gun swing in my hand, and advanced, waiting for them to move aside, off the path, in respect for my passing. But they came on steadily, and the dogs looked up at me for the command to chase. I was angry. It was "cheek" for a native not to stand off a path, the moment he caught sight of you.

In front walked an old man, stooping his weight on to a stick, his hair grizzled white, a dark red blanket slung over his shoulders like a cloak. Behind him came two young men, carrying bundles of pots, assegais, hatchets.

The group was not a usual one. They were not natives seeking work. These had an air of dignity, of quietly following their own purpose. It was the dignity that checked my tongue. I walked quietly on, talking softly to the growling dogs, till I was ten paces away. Then the old man stopped, drawing his blanket close.

"Morning, Nkosikaas," he said, using the customary greeting for any time of the day.

"Good morning," I said. "Where are you going?" My voice was a little truculent.

The old man spoke in his own language, then one of the young men stepped forward politely and said in careful English: "My Chief travels to see his brothers beyond the river."

A Chief! I thought, understanding the pride that made the old man stand before me like an equal—more than an equal, for he showed courtesy, and I showed none.

The old man spoke again, wearing dignity like an inherited garment, still standing ten paces off, flanked by his entourage, not looking at me (that would have been rude) but directing his eyes somewhere over my head at the trees.

"You are the little Nkosikaas from the farm of Baas Jordan?"

"That's right," I said.

"Perhaps your father does not remember," said the interpreter for the old man, "but there was an affair with some goats. I remember seeing you when you were . . ." The young man held his hand at knee level and smiled.

We all smiled.

"What is your name?" I asked.

"This is Chief Mshlanga," said the young man.

"I will tell my father that I met you," I said.

The old man said: "My greetings to your father, little Nkosikaas."

"Good morning," I said politely, finding the politeness difficult, from lack of use.

"Morning, little Nkosikaas," said the old man, and stood aside to let me pass.

I went by, my gun hanging awkwardly, the dogs sniffing and growling, cheated of their favorite game of chasing natives like animals.

Not long afterwards I read in an old explorer's book the phrase: "Chief Mshlanga's country." It went like this: "Our destination was Chief Mshlanga's country, to the north of the river; and it was our desire to ask his permission to prospect for gold in his territory."

The phrase "ask his permission" was so extraordinary to a white child, brought   35
up to consider all natives as things to use, that it revived those questions, which could not be suppressed: they fermented slowly in my mind.

On another occasion one of those old prospectors who still move over Africa looking for neglected reefs, with their hammers and tents, and pans for sifting gold from crushed rock, came to the farm and, in talking of the old days, used that phrase again: "This was the Old Chief's country," he said. "It stretched from those mountains over there way back to the river, hundreds of miles of country." That was his name for our district: "The Old Chief's Country"; he did not use our name for it—a new phrase which held no implication of usurped ownership.

As I read more books about the time when this part of Africa was opened up, not much more than fifty years before, I found Old Chief Mshlanga had been a famous man, known to all the explorers and prospectors. But then he had been young; or maybe it was his father or uncle they spoke of—I never found out.

During that year I met him several times in the part of the farm that was traversed by natives moving over the country. I learned that the path up the side of the big red field where the birds sang was the recognized highway for migrants. Perhaps I even haunted it in the hope of meeting him: being greeted by him, the exchange of courtesies, seemed to answer the questions that troubled me.

Soon I carried a gun in a different spirit; I used it for shooting food and not to give me confidence. And now the dogs learned better manners. When I saw a native approaching, we offered and took greetings; and slowly that other landscape in my mind faded, and my feet struck directly on the African soil, and I saw the shapes of tree and hill clearly, and the black people moved back, as it were, out of my life: it was as if I stood aside to watch a slow intimate dance of landscape and men, a very old dance, whose steps I could not learn.

But I thought: this is my heritage, too; I was bred here; it is my country as   40
well as the black man's country; and there is plenty of room for all of us, without elbowing each other off the pavements and roads.

It seemed it was only necessary to let free that respect I felt when I was talking with old Chief Mshlanga, to let both black and white people meet gently, with tolerance for each other's differences: it seemed quite easy.

Then, one day, something new happened. Working in our house as servants were always three natives: cook, houseboy, garden boy. They used to change as the farm natives changed: staying for a few months, then moving on to a new job, or back home to their kraals.° They were thought of as "good" or "bad" natives; which meant: how did they behave as servants? Were they lazy, efficient, obedient, or disrespectful? If the family felt good-humoured, the phrase was: "What can you expect from raw black savages?" If we were angry, we said: "These damned niggers, we would be much better off without them."

kraals: Fenced-in native villages.

This was not at all like our farm compound, a dirty and neglected place, a temporary home for migrants who had no roots in it.

And now I did not know what to do next. I called a small black boy, who was sitting on a lot playing a stringed gourd, quite naked except for the strings of blue beads round his neck, and said: "Tell the Chief I am here." The child stuck his thumb in his mouth and stared shyly back at me.

For minutes I shifted my feet on the edge of what seemed a deserted village, till at last the child scuttled off, and then some women came. They were draped in bright cloths, with brass glinting in their ears and on their arms. They also stared, silently; then turned to chatter among themselves.

I said again: "Can I see Chief Mshlanga?" I saw they caught the name; 65 they did not understand what I wanted. I did not understand myself.

At last I walked through them and came past the huts and saw a clearing under a big shady tree, where a dozen old men sat cross-legged on the ground, talking. Chief Mshlanga was leaning back against the tree, holding a gourd in his hand, from which he had been drinking. When he saw me, not a muscle of his face moved, and I could see he was not pleased: perhaps he was afflicted with my own shyness, due to being unable to find the right forms of courtesy for the occasion. To meet me, on our own farm, was one thing; but I should not have come here. What had I expected? I could not join them socially: the thing was unheard of. Bad enough that I, a white girl, should be walking the veld alone as a white man might: and in this part of the bush where only Government officials had the right to move.

Again I stood, smiling foolishly, while behind me stood the groups of brightly clad, chattering women, their faces alert with curiosity and interest, and in front of me sat the old men, with old lined faces, their eyes guarded, aloof. It was a village of ancients and children and women. Even the two young men who kneeled beside the Chief were not those I had seen with him previously: the young men were all away working on the white men's farms and mines, and the Chief must depend on relatives who were temporarily on holiday for his attendants.

"The small white Nkosikaas is far from home," remarked the old man at last.

"Yes," I agreed, "it is far." I wanted to say: "I have come to pay you a friendly visit, Chief Mshlanga." I could not say it. I might now be feeling an urgent helpless desire to get to know these men and women as people, to be accepted by them as a friend, but the truth was I had set out in a spirit of curiosity: I had wanted to see the village that one day our cook, the reserved and obedient young man who got drunk on Sundays, would one day rule over.

"The child of Nkosi Jordan is welcome," said Chief Mshlanga. 70

"Thank you," I said, and could think of nothing more to say. There was a silence, while the flies rose and began to buzz around my head; and the wind shook a little in the thick green tree that spread its branches over the old men.

"Good morning," I said at last. "I have to return now to my home."

"Morning, little Nkosikaas," said Chief Mshlanga.

I walked away from the indifferent village, over the rise past the staring amber-eyed goats, down through the tall stately trees into the great rich green valley where the river meandered and the pigeons cooed tales of plenty and the woodpecker tapped softly.

The fear was gone; the loneliness had set into stiff-necked stoicism; there 75 was now a queer hostility in the landscape, a cold, hard, sullen indomitability that walked with me, as strong as a wall, as intangible as smoke; it seemed to say to me: you walk here as a destroyer. I went slowly homewards, with an empty heart: I had learned that if one cannot call a country to heel like a dog, neither can one dismiss the past with a smile in an easy gush of feeling, saying: I could not help it, I am also a victim.

I only saw Chief Mshlanga once again.

One night my father's big red land was trampled down by small sharp hooves, and it was discovered that the culprits were goats from Chief Mshlanga's kraal. This had happened once before, years ago.

My father confiscated all the goats. Then he sent a message to the old Chief that if he wanted them he would have to pay for the damage.

He arrived at our house at the time of sunset one evening, looking very old and bent now, walking stiffly under his regally draped blanket, leaning on a big stick. My father sat himself down in his big chair below the steps of the house; the old man squatted carefully on the ground before him, flanked by his two young men.

The palaver was long and painful, because of the bad English of the young   80
man who interpreted, and because my father could not speak dialect, but only kitchen kaffir.

From my father's point of view, at least two hundred pounds' worth of damage had been done to the crop. He knew he could not get the money from the old man. He felt he was entitled to keep the goats. As for the old Chief, he kept repeating angrily: "Twenty goats! My people cannot lose twenty goats! We are not rich; like the Nkosi Jordan, to lose twenty goats at once."

My father did not think of himself as rich, but rather as very poor. He spoke quickly and angrily in return, saying that the damage done meant a great deal to him, and that he was entitled to the goats.

At last it grew so heated that the cook, the Chief's son, was called from the kitchen to be interpreter, and now my father spoke fluently in English, and our cook translated rapidly so that the old man could understand how very angry my father was. The young man spoke without emotion, in a mechanical way, his eyes lowered, but showing how he felt his position by a hostile uncomfortable set of the shoulders.

It was now in the late sunset, the sky a welter of colours, the birds singing their last songs, and the cattle, lowing peacefully, moving past us towards their sheds for the night. It was the hour when Africa is most beautiful; and here was this pathetic, ugly scene, doing no one any good.

At last my father stated finally: "I'm not going to argue about it. I am keeping   85
the goats."

The old Chief flashed back in his own language: "That means that my people will go hungry when the dry season comes."

"Go to the police, then," said my father, and looked triumphant.

There was, of course, no more to be said.

The old man sat silent, his head bent, his hands dangling helplessly over his withered knees. Then he rose, the young men helping him, and he stood facing my father. He spoke once again, very stiffly; and turned away and went home to his village.

"What did he say?" asked my father of the young man, who laughed uncom-   90
fortably and would not meet his eyes.

"What did he say?" insisted my father.

Our cook stood straight and silent, his brows knotted together. Then he spoke. "My father says: All this land, this land you call yours, is his land, and belongs to our people."

Having made this statement, he walked off into the bush after his father, and we did not see him again.

Our next cook was a migrant from Nyasaland, with no expectations of greatness.

Next time the policeman came on his rounds he was told this story. He   95
remarked: "That kraal has no right to be there; it should have been moved long ago. I don't know why no one has done anything about it. I'll have a chat with the Native Commissioner next week. I'm going over for tennis on Sunday, anyway."

Some time later we heard that Chief Mshlanga and his people had been moved two hundred miles east, to a proper Native Reserve; the Government land was going to be opened up for white settlement soon.

I went to see the village again, about a year afterwards. There was nothing there. Mounds of red mud, where the huts had been, had long swathes of rotting thatch over them, veined with the red galleries of the white ants. The pumpkin vines rioted everywhere, over the bushes, up the lower branches of trees so that the great golden balls rolled underfoot and dangled overhead: it was a festival of pumpkins. The bushes were crowding up, the new grass sprang vivid green.

The settler lucky enough to be allotted the lush warm valley (if he chose to cultivate this particular section) would find, suddenly, in the middle of a mealie field, the plants were growing fifteen feet tall, the weight of the cobs dragging at the stalks, and wonder what unsuspected vein of richness he had struck.

FLANNERY O'CONNOR   (1925–1964)

A Good Man Is Hard to Find   *1953*

The grandmother didn't want to go to Florida. She wanted to visit some of her connections in east Tennessee and she was seizing at every chance to change Bailey's mind. Bailey was the son she lived with, her only son. He was sitting on the edge of his chair at the table, bent over the orange sports section of the *Journal*. "Now look here, Bailey," she said, "see here, read this," and she stood with one hand on her thin hip and the other rattling the newspaper at his bald head. "Here this fellow that calls himself The Misfit is aloose from the Federal Pen and headed toward Florida and you read here what it says he did to these people. Just you read it. I wouldn't take my children in any direction with a criminal like that aloose in it. I couldn't answer to my conscience if I did."

Bailey didn't look up from his reading so she wheeled around then and faced the children's mother, a young woman in slacks, whose face was as broad and innocent as a cabbage and was tied round with a green head-kerchief that had two points on the top like rabbit's ears. She was sitting on the sofa, feeding the baby his apricots out of a jar. "The children have been to Florida before," the old lady said. "You all ought to take them somewhere else for a change so they would see different parts of the world and be broad. They never have been to east Tennessee."

The children's mother didn't seem to hear her but the eight-year-old boy, John Wesley, a stocky child with glasses, said, "If you don't want to go to Florida, why dontcha stay at home?" He and the little girl, June Star, were reading the funny papers on the floor.

"She wouldn't stay at home to be queen for a day," June Star said without raising her yellow head.

"Yes and what would you do if this fellow, The Misfit, caught you?" the   5
grandmother asked.

"I'd smack his face," John Wesley said.

"She wouldn't stay at home for a million bucks," June Star said. "Afraid she'd miss something. She has to go everywhere we go."

"All right, Miss," the grandmother said. "Just remember that the next time you want me to curl your hair."

June Star said her hair was naturally curly.

The next morning the grandmother was the first one in the car, ready to   10
go. She had her big black valise that looked like the head of a hippopotamus in one corner, and underneath it she was hiding a basket with Pitty Sing, the cat, in it. She didn't intend for the cat to be left alone in the house for three days because he would miss her too much and she was afraid he might brush against one of the gas burners and accidentally asphyxiate himself. Her son, Bailey, didn't like to arrive at a motel with a cat.

She sat in the middle of the back seat with John Wesley and June Star on either side of her. Bailey and the children's mother and the baby sat in the front and they left Atlanta at eight forty-five with the mileage on the car at 55890. The grandmother wrote this down because she thought it would be interesting to say how many miles they had been when they got back. It took them twenty minutes to reach the outskirts of the city.

The old lady settled herself comfortably, removing her white cotten gloves and putting them up with her purse on the shelf in front of the back window. The children's mother still had on slacks and still had her head tied up in a green kerchief, but the grandmother had on a navy blue straw sailor hat with a bunch of white violets on the brim and a navy blue dress with a small white dot in the print. Her collar and cuffs were white organdy trimmed with lace and at her neckline she had pinned a purple spray of cloth violets containing a sachet. In case of an accident, anyone seeing her dead on the highway would know at once that she was a lady.

She said she thought it was going to be a good day for driving, neither too hot nor too cold, and she cautioned Bailey that the speed limit was fifty-five miles an hour and that the patrolmen hid themselves behind billboards and small clumps of trees and sped out after you before you had a chance to slow down. She pointed out interesting details of the scenery: Stone Mountain; the blue granite that in some places came up to both sides of the highway; the brilliant red clay banks slightly streaked with purple; and the various crops that made rows of green lacework on the ground. The trees were full of silver-white sunlight and the meanest of them sparkled. The children were reading comic magazines and their mother had gone back to sleep.

"Let's go through Georgia fast so we won't have to look at it much," John Wesley said.

"If I were a little boy," said the grandmother, "I wouldn't talk about my native state that way. Tennessee has the mountains and Georgia has the hills."

"Tennessee is just a hillbilly dumping ground," John Wesley said, "and Georgia is a lousy state too."

"You said it," June Star said.

"In my time," said the grandmother, folding her thin veined fingers, "children were more respectful of their native states and their parents and everything else. People did right then. Oh look at the cute little pickaninny!" she said and pointed to a Negro child standing in the door of a shack. "Wouldn't that make a picture, now?" she asked and they all turned and looked at the little Negro out of the back window. He waved.

"He didn't have any britches on," June said.

"He probably didn't have any," the grandmother explained. "Little niggers in the country don't have things like we do. If I could paint, I'd paint that picture," she said.

The children exchanged comic books.

The grandmother offered to hold the baby and the children's mother passed him over the front seat to her. She set him on her knee and bounced him and told him about the things they were passing. She rolled her eyes and screwed up her mouth and stuck her leathery thin face into his smooth bland one. Occasionally he gave her a faraway smile. They passed a large cotton field with five or six graves fenced in the middle of it, like a small island. "Look at the graveyard!" the grandmother said, pointing it out. "That was the old family burying ground. That belonged to the plantation."

"Where's the plantation?" John Wesley asked.

"Gone With the Wind," said the grandmother. "Ha. Ha."

When the children finished all the comic books they had brought, they opened the lunch and ate it. The grandmother ate a peanut butter sandwich and an olive and would not let the children throw the box and the paper napkins out the window. When there was nothing else to do they played a game by choosing a cloud and making the other two guess what shape it suggested. John Wesley took one the shape of a cow and June Star guessed a cow and John Wesley said, no, an automobile, and June Star said he didn't play fair, and they began to slap each other over the grandmother.

The grandmother said she would tell them a story if they would keep quiet. When she told a story, she rolled her eyes and waved her head and was very dramatic. She said once when she was a maiden lady she had been courted by a Mr. Edgar Atkins Teagarden from Jasper, Georgia. She said he was a very good-looking man and a gentleman and that he brought her a watermelon every Saturday afternoon with his initials cut in it, E. A. T. Well, one Saturday, she said, Mr. Teagarden brought the watermelon and there was nobody at home and he left it on the front porch and returned in his buggy to Jasper, but she never got the

15

20

25

watermelon, she said, because a nigger boy ate it when he saw the initials, E. A. T.! This story tickled John Wesley's funny bone and he giggled and giggled but June Star didn't think it was any good. She said she wouldn't marry a man that just brought her a watermelon on Saturday. The grandmother said she would have done well to marry Mr. Teagarden because he was a gentleman and had bought Coca-Cola stock when it first came out and that he had died only a few years ago, a very wealthy man.

They stopped at The Tower for barbecued sandwiches. The Tower was a part stucco and part wood filling station and dance hall set in a clearing outside of Timothy. A fat man named Red Sammy Butts ran it and there were signs stuck here and there on the building and for miles up and down the highway saying, TRY RED SAMMY'S FAMOUS BARBECUE. NONE LIKE FAMOUS RED SAMMY'S! RED SAM! THE FAT BOY WITH THE HAPPY LAUGH. A VETERAN! SAMMY'S YOUR MAN!

Red Sammy was lying on the bare ground outside The Tower with his head under a truck while a gray monkey about a foot high, chained to a small chinaberry tree, chattered nearby. The monkey sprang back into the tree and got on the highest limb as soon as he saw the children jump out of the car and run toward him.

Inside, The Tower was a long dark room with a counter at one end and tables at the other and dancing space in the middle. They all sat down at a broad table next to the nickelodeon and Red Sam's wife, a tall burnt-brown woman with hair and eyes lighter than her skin, came and took their order. The children's mother put a dime in the machine and played "The Tennessee Waltz," and the grandmother said the tune always made her want to dance. She asked Bailey if he would like to dance but he only glared at her. He didn't have a naturally sunny disposition like she did and trips made him nervous. The grandmother's brown eyes were very bright. She swayed her head from side to side and pretended she was dancing in her chair. June Star said play something she could tap to so the children's mother put in another dime and played a fast number and June Star stepped out onto the dance floor and did her tap routine.

"Ain't she cute?" Red Sam's wife said, leaning over the counter. "Would you like to come be my little girl?"   30

"No I certainly wouldn't," June Star said. "I wouldn't live in a broken-down place like this for a million bucks!" and she ran back to the table.

"Ain't she cute?" the woman repeated, stretching her mouth politely.

"Aren't you ashamed?" hissed her grandmother.

Red Sam came in and told his wife to quit lounging on the counter and hurry with these people's order. His khaki trousers reached just to his hip bones and his stomach hung over them like a sack of meal swaying under his shirt. He came over and sat down at a table nearby and let out a combination sigh and yodel. "You can't win," he said. "You can't win," and he wiped his sweating red face with a gray handkerchief. "These days you don't know who to trust," he said. "Ain't that the truth?"

"People are certainly not nice like they used to be," said the grandmother.   35

"Two fellers come in here last week," Red Sammy said, "driving a Chrysler. It was a old beat-up car but it was a good one and these boys looked all right to me. Said they worked at the mill and you know I let them fellers charge the gas they bought? Now why did I do that?"

"Because you're a good man!" the grandmother said at once.

"Yes'm, I suppose so," Red Sam said as if he were struck with the answer.

His wife brought the orders, carrying the five plates all at once without a tray, two in each hand and one balanced on her arm. "It isn't a soul in this green world of God's that you can trust," she said. "And I don't count anybody out of that, not nobody," she repeated, looking at Red Sammy.

"Did you read about that criminal, The Misfit, that's escaped?" asked the grandmother.   40

"I wouldn't be a bit surprised if he didn't attack this place right here," said the woman. "If he hears about it being here, I wouldn't be none surprised to see him. If he hears it's two cent in the cash register, I wouldn't be a tall surprised if he . . ."

"That'll do," Red Sam said. "Go bring these people their Co'Colas," and the woman went off to get the rest of the order.

"A good man is hard to find," Red Sammy said. "Everything is getting terrible. I remember the day you could go off and leave your screen door unlatched. Not no more."

He and the grandmother discussed better times. The old lady said that in her opinion Europe was entirely to blame for the way things were now. She said the way Europe acted you would think we were made of money and Red Sam said it was no use talking about it, she was exactly right. The children ran outside into the white sunlight and looked at the monkey in the lacy chinaberry tree. He was busy catching fleas on himself and biting each one carefully between his teeth as if it were a delicacy.

They drove off again into the hot afternoon. The grandmother took cat naps and woke up every few minutes with her own snoring. Outside of Toombsboro she woke up and recalled an old plantation that she had visited in this neighborhood once when she was a young lady. She said the house had six white columns across the front and that there was an avenue of oaks leading up to it and two little wooden trellis arbors on either side in front where you sat down with your suitor after a stroll in the garden. She recalled exactly which road to turn off to get to it. She knew that Bailey would not be willing to lose any time looking at an old house, but the more she talked about it, the more she wanted to see it once again and find out if the little twin arbors were still standing. "There was a secret panel in this house," she said craftily, not telling the truth but wishing that she were, "and the story went that all the family silver was hidden in it when Sherman° came through but it was never found . . ."   45

"Hey!" John Wesley said, "Let's go see it! We'll find it! We'll poke all the woodwork and find it! Who lives there? Where do you turn off at? Hey Pop, can't we turn off there?"

"We never have seen a house with a secret panel!" June Star shrieked. "Let's go to the house with the secret panel! Hey, Pop, can't we go see the house with the secret panel!"

"It's not far from here, I know," the grandmother said. "It wouldn't take over twenty minutes."

Sherman: William Tecumseh Sherman (1820–1891), Union general during the Civil War.

Bailey was looking straight ahead. His jaw was as rigid as a horseshoe. "No." he said.

The children began to yell and scream that they wanted to see the house 50
with the secret panel. John Wesley kicked the back of the front seat and June
Star hung over her mother's shoulder and whined desperately into her ear that
they never had any fun even on their vacation, and that they could never do
what THEY wanted to do. The baby began to scream and John Wesley kicked the
back of the seat so hard that his father could feel the blows in his kidney.

"All right!" he shouted, and drew the car to a stop at the side of the road.
"Will you all shut up? Will you all just shut up for one second? If you don't shut
up, we won't go anywhere."

"It would be very educational for them," the grandmother murmured.

"All right," Bailey said, "but get this: this is the only time we're going to
stop for anything like this. This is the one and only time."

"The dirt road that you have to turn down is about a mile back," the grandmother directed. "I marked it when we passed."

"A dirt road," Bailey groaned. 55

After they had turned around and were headed toward the dirt road, the
grandmother recalled other points about the house, the beautiful glass over the
front doorway and the candle-lamp in the hall. John Wesley said that the secret
panel was probably in the fireplace.

"You can't go inside this house," Bailey said. "You don't know who lives
there."

"While you all talk to the people in front, I'll run around behind and get in
a window," John Wesley suggested.

"We'll all stay in the car," his mother said.

They turned onto the dirt road and the car raced roughly along in a swirl 60
of pink dust. The grandmother recalled the times when there were no paved
roads and thirty miles was a day's journey. The dirt road was hilly and there
were sudden washes in it and sharp curves on dangerous embankments. All at
once they would be on a hill, looking down over the blue tops of trees for miles
around, then the next minute, they would be in a red depression with the dust-
coated trees looking down on them.

"This place had better turn up in a minute," Bailey said, "or I'm going to
turn around."

The road looked as if no one had traveled on it in months.

"It's not much farther," the grandmother said and just as she said it, a horrible
thought came to her. The thought was so embarrassing that she turned red in
the face and her eyes dilated and her feet jumped up, upsetting her valise in the
corner. The instant the valise moved, the newspaper top she had over the basket
under it rose with a snarl and Pitty Sing, the cat, sprang onto Bailey's shoulder.

The children were thrown to the floor and their mother, clutching the baby,
was thrown out the door onto the ground, the old lady was thrown into the front
seat. The car turned over once and landed right-side-up in a gulch on the side of
the road. Bailey remained in the driver's seat with the cat—gray-striped with a
broad white face and an orange nose—clinging to his neck like a caterpillar.

As soon as the children saw they could move their arms and legs, they scram- 65
bled out of the car, shouting, "We've had an ACCIDENT!" The grandmother was

curled up under the dashboard, hoping she was injured so that Bailey's wrath would not come down on her all at once. The horrible thought she had had before the accident was that the house she had remembered so vividly was not in Georgia but in Tennessee.

Bailey removed the cat from his neck with both hands and flung it out the window against the side of a pine tree. Then he got out of the car and started looking for the children's mother. She was sitting against the side of the red gutted ditch, holding the screaming baby, but she only had a cut down her face and a broken shoulder. "We've had an ACCIDENT!" the children screamed in a frenzy of delight.

"But nobody's killed," June Star said with disappointment as the grandmother limped out of the car, her hat still pinned to her head but the broken front brim standing up at a jaunty angle and the violet spray hanging off the side. They all sat down in the ditch, except the children, to recover from the shock. They were all shaking.

"Maybe a car will come along," said the children's mother hoarsely.

"I believe I have injured an organ," said the grandmother, pressing her side, but no one answered her. Bailey's teeth were clattering. He had on a yellow sport shirt with bright blue parrots designed in it and his face was as yellow as the shirt. The grandmother decided that she would not mention that the house was in Tennessee.

The road was about ten feet above and they could see only the tops of the trees on the other side of it. Behind the ditch they were sitting in there were more woods, tall and dark and deep. In a few minutes they saw a car some distance away on top of a hill, coming slowly as if the occupants were watching them. The grandmother stood up and waved both arms dramatically to attract their attention. The car continued to come on slowly, disappeared around a bend and appeared again, moving even slower, on top of the hill they had gone over. It was a big black battered hearse-like automobile. There were three men in it. 70

It came to a stop just over them and for some minutes, the driver looked down with a steady expressionless gaze to where they were sitting, and didn't speak. Then he turned his head and muttered something to the other two and they got out. One was a fat boy in black trousers and a red sweat shirt with a silver stallion embossed on the front of it. He moved around on the right side of them and stood staring, his mouth partly open in a kind of loose grin. The other had on khaki pants and a blue striped coat and a gray hat pulled down very low, hiding most of his face. He came around slowly on the left side. Neither spoke.

The driver got out of the car and stood by the side of it, looking down at them. He was an older man than the other two. His hair was just beginning to gray and he wore silver-rimmed spectacles that gave him a scholarly look. He had a long creased face and didn't have on any shirt or undershirt. He had on blue jeans that were too tight for him and was holding a black hat and a gun. The two boys also had guns.

"We've had an ACCIDENT!" the children screamed.

The grandmother had the peculiar feeling that the bespectacled man was someone she knew. His face was as familiar to her as if she had known him all her life but she could not recall who he was. He moved away from the car and began to come down the embankment, placing his feet carefully so that he wouldn't slip. He had on tan and white shoes and no socks, and his ankles were red and thin. "Good afternoon," he said. "I see you all had a little spill."

"We turned over twice!" said the grandmother.   75

"Oncet," he corrected. "We seen it happen. Try their car and see will it run, Hiram," he said quietly to the boy with the gray hat.

"What you got that gun for?" John Wesley asked, "Whatcha gonna do with that gun?"

"Lady," the man said to the children's mother, "would you mind calling them children to sit down by you? Children make me nervous. I want all you all to set down right together there where you're at."

"What are you telling us what to do for?" June Star asked.

Behind them the line of woods gaped like a dark open mouth. "Come here,"   80
said their mother.

"Look here now," Bailey began suddenly, "we're in a predicament! We're in . . ."

The grandmother shrieked. She scrambled to her feet and stood staring. "You're The Misfit!" she said. "I recognized you at once."

"Yes'm," the man said, smiling slightly as if he were pleased in spite of himself to be known, "but it would have been better for all of you, lady, if you hadn't reckernized me."

Bailey turned his head sharply and said something to his mother that shocked even the children. The old lady began to cry and The Misfit reddened.

"Lady," he said, "don't you get upset: Sometimes a man says things he don't   85
mean. I don't reckon he meant to talk to you thataway."

"You wouldn't shoot a lady, would you?" the grandmother said and removed a clean handkerchief from her cuff and began to slap at her eyes with it.

The Misfit pointed the toe of his shoe into the ground and made a little hole and then covered it up again. "I would hate to have to," he said.

"Listen," the grandmother almost screamed, "I know you're a good man. You don't look a bit like you have common blood. I know you must come from nice people!"

"Yes mam," he said, "finest people in the world." When he smiled he showed a row of strong white teeth. "God never made a finer woman than my mother and my daddy's heart was pure gold," he said. The boy with the red sweat shirt had come around behind them and was standing with his gun at his hip. The Misfit squatted down on the ground. "Watch them children, Bobby Lee," he said. "You know they make me nervous." He looked at the six of them huddled together in front of him and he seemed to be embarrassed as if he couldn't think of anything to say. "Ain't a cloud in the sky," he remarked, looking up at it. "Don't see no sun but don't see no cloud neither."

"Yes, it's a beautiful day," said the grandmother. "Listen," she said, "you   90
shouldn't call yourself The Misfit because I know you're a good man at heart. I can just look at you and tell."

"Hush!" Bailey yelled. "Hush! Everybody shut up and let me handle this!" He was squatting in the position of a runner about to sprint forward but he didn't move.

"I pre-chate that, lady," The Misfit said and drew a little circle in the ground with the butt of his gun.

"It'll take a half a hour to fix this here car," Hiram called, looking over the raised hood of it.

"Well, first you and Bobby Lee get him and that little boy to step over yonder with you," The Misfit said, pointing to Bailey and John Wesley. "The boys want to ask you something," he said to Bailey. "Would you mind stepping back in them woods there with them?"

"Listen," Bailey began, "we're in a terrible predicament. Nobody realizes   95
what this is," and his voice cracked. His eyes were as blue and intense as the parrots in his shirt and he remained perfectly still.

The grandmother reached up to adjust her hat brim as if she were going to the woods with him but it came off in her hand. She stood staring at it and after a second she let it fall to the ground. Hiram pulled Bailey up by the arm as if he were assisting an old man. John Wesley caught hold of his father's hand and Bobby Lee followed. They went off toward the woods and just as they reached the dark edge, Bailey turned and supporting himself against a gray naked pine trunk, he shouted, "I'll be back in a minute, Mamma, wait on me!"

"Come back this instant!" his mother shrilled but they all disappeared into the woods.

"Bailey Boy!" the grandmother called in a tragic voice but she found she was looking at The Misfit squatting on the ground in front of her. "I just know you're a good man," she said desperately. "You're not a bit common!"

"Nome, I ain't a good man," The Misfit said after a second as if he had considered her statement carefully, "but I ain't the worst in the world neither. My daddy said I was different breed of dog from my brothers and sisters. 'You know,' Daddy said, 'it's some that can live their whole life out without asking about it and it's others has to know why it is, and this boy is one of the latters. He's going to be into everything!'" He put on his black hat and looked up suddenly and then away deep into the woods as if he were embarrassed again. "I'm sorry I don't have on a shirt before you ladies," he said, hunching his shoulders slightly. "We buried our clothes that we had on when we escaped and we're just making do until we can get better. We borrowed these from some folks we met," he explained.

"That's perfectly all right," the grandmother said. "Maybe Bailey has an   100
extra shirt in his suitcase."

"I'll look and see terrectly," the Misfit said.

"Where are they taking him?" the children's mother screamed.

"Daddy was a card himself," the Misfit said. "You couldn't put anything over on him. He never got in trouble with the Authorities though. Just had the knack of handling them."

"You could be honest too if you'd only try," said the grandmother. "Think how wonderful it would be to settle down and live a comfortable life and not have to think about somebody chasing you all the time."

The Misfit kept scratching in the ground with the butt of his gun as if he   105
were thinking about it. "Yes'm, somebody is always after you," he murmured.

The grandmother noticed how thin his shoulder blades were just behind his hat because she was standing up looking down on him. "Do you ever pray?" she asked.

He shook his head. All she saw was the black hat wiggle between his shoulder blades. "Nome," he said.

There was a pistol shot from the woods, followed closely by another. Then silence. The old lady's head jerked around. She could hear the wind move through the tree tops like a long satisfied insuck of breath. "Bailey Boy!" she called.

"I was a gospel singer for a while," The Misfit said. "I been most everything. Been in the arm service, both land and sea, at home and abroad, been twict married, been an undertaker, been with the railroads, plowed Mother Earth, been in a tornado, seen a man burnt alive oncet," and he looked up at the children's mother and the little girl who were sitting close together, their faces white and their eyes glassy; "I even seen a woman flogged," he said.

"Pray, pray," the grandmother began, "pray, pray . . ."   110

"I never was a bad boy that I remember of," The Misfit said in an almost dreamy voice, "but somewheres along the line I done something wrong and got sent to the penitentiary. I was buried alive," and he looked up and held her attention to him by a steady stare.

"That's when you should have started to pray," she said. "What did you do to get sent to the penitentiary that first time?"

"Turn to the right, it was a wall," The Misfit said, looking up again at the cloudless sky. "Turn to the left, it was a wall. Look up it was a ceiling, look down it was a floor. I forgot what I done, lady. I set there and set there, trying to remember what it was I done and I ain't recalled it to this day. Oncet in a while, I would think it was coming to me, but it never come."

"Maybe they put you in by mistake," the old lady said vaguely.

"Nome," he said. "It wasn't no mistake. They had the papers on me."   115

"You must have stolen something," she said.

The Misfit sneered slightly. "Nobody had nothing I wanted," he said. "It was a head-doctor at the penitentiary said what I had done was kill my daddy but I know that for a lie. My daddy died in nineteen ought nineteen of the epidemic flu and I never had a thing to do with it. He was buried in the Mount Hopewell Baptist churchyard and you can go there and see for yourself."

"If you would pray," the old lady said, "Jesus would help you."

"That's right," The Misfit said.

"Well then, why don't you pray?" she asked trembling with delight suddenly.   120

"I don't want no hep," he said. "I'm doing all right by myself."

Bobby Lee and Hiram came ambling back from the woods. Bobby Lee was dragging a yellow shirt with bright blue parrots in it.

"Throw me that shirt, Bobby Lee," The Misfit said. The shirt came flying at him and landed on his shoulder and he put it on. The grandmother couldn't name what the shirt reminded her of. "No, lady," The Misfit said while he was buttoning it up. "I found out the crime don't matter. You can do one thing or you can do another, kill a man or take a tire off his car, because sooner or later you're going to forget what it was you done and just be punished for it."

The children's mother had begun to make heaving noises as if she couldn't get her breath. "Lady," he asked, "would you and that little girl like to step off yonder with Bobby Lee and Hiram and join your husband?"

"Yes, thank you," the mother said faintly. Her left arm dangled helplessly   125
and she was holding the baby, who had gone to sleep, in the other. "Hep that lady up, Hiram," The Misfit said as she struggled to climb out of the ditch, "and Bobby Lee, you hold onto that little girl's hand."

"I don't want to hold hands with him," June Star said. "He reminds me of a pig."

The fat boy blushed and laughed and caught her by the arm and pulled her off into the woods after Hiram and her mother.

Alone with The Misfit, the grandmother found that she had lost her voice. There was not a cloud in the sky nor any sun. There was nothing around her but woods. She wanted to tell him that he must pray. She opened and closed her mouth several times before anything came out. Finally she found herself saying, "Jesus, Jesus," meaning Jesus will help you, but the way she was saying it, it sounded as if she might be cursing.

"Yes'm," The Misfit said as if he agreed. "Jesus thown everything off balance. It was the same case with Him as with me except He hadn't committed any crime and they could prove I had committed one because they had the papers on me. Of course," he said, "they never shown me any papers. That's why I sign myself now. I said long ago, you get you a signature and sign everything you do and keep a copy of it. Then you'll know what you done and you can hold up the crime to the punishment and see do they match and in the end you'll have something to prove you ain't been treated right. I call myself The Misfit," he said, "because I can't make what all I done wrong fit what all I gone through in punishment."

There was a piercing scream from the woods, followed closely by a pistol report. "Does it seem right to you, lady, that one is punished a heap and another ain't punished at all?"   130

"Jesus!" the old lady cried. "You've got good blood! I know you wouldn't shoot a lady! I know you come from nice people! Pray! Jesus, you ought not to shoot a lady: I'll give you all the money I've got!"

"Lady," The Misfit said, looking beyond her far into the woods, "there never was a body that give the undertaker a tip."

There were two more pistol reports and the grandmother raised her head like a parched old turkey hen crying for water and called, "Bailey Boy, Bailey Boy!" as if her heart would break.

"Jesus was the only One that ever raised the dead," The Misfit continued, "and He shouldn't have done it. He thrown everything off balance. If He did what He said, then it's nothing for you to do but thow away everything and follow Him, and if He didn't, then it's nothing for you to do but enjoy the few minutes you got left the best way you can—by killing somebody or burning down his house or doing some other meanness to him. No pleasure but meanness," he said and his voice had become almost a snarl.

"Maybe He didn't raise the dead," the old lady mumbled, not knowing what   135
she was saying and feeling so dizzy that she sank down in the ditch with her legs twisted under her.

"I wasn't there so I can't say He didn't," The Misfit said, "I wisht I had of been there," he said, hitting the ground with his fist. "It ain't right I wasn't there because if I had of been there I would of known. Listen lady," he said in a high voice, "if I had of been there I would of known and I wouldn't be like I am now." His voice seemed about to crack and the grandmother's head cleared for an instant. She saw the man's face twisted close to her own as if he were going to cry and she murmured, "Why you're one of my babies. You're one of my own children!" She reached out and touched him on the shoulder. The Misfit sprang back as if a snake had bitten him and shot her three times through the chest. Then he put his gun down on the ground and took off his glasses and began to clean them.

Hiram and Bobby Lee returned from the woods and stood over the ditch, looking down at the grandmother who half-sat and half lay in a puddle of blood with her legs crossed under her like a child's and her face smiling up at the cloudless sky.

Without his glasses, The Misfit's eyes were red-rimmed and pale and defenseless-looking. "Take her off and thow her where you thown the others," he said, picking up the cat that was rubbing itself against his leg.

"She was a talker, wasn't she?" Bobby Lee said, sliding down the ditch with a yodel.

"She would of been a good woman," The Misfit said, "if it had been somebody there to shoot her every minute of her life."   140

"Some fun!" Bobby Lee said.

"Shut up, Bobby Lee," The Misfit said. "It's no real pleasure in life."

FRANK O'CONNOR   (1903–1966)

First Confession   1951

All the trouble began when my grandfather died and my grandmother—my father's mother—came to live with us. Relations in the one house are a strain at the best of times, but, to make matters worse, my grandmother was a real old country-woman and quite unsuited to the life in town. She had a fat, wrinkled old face, and, to Mother's great indignation, went round the house in bare feet—the boots had her crippled, she said. For dinner she had a jug of porter° and a pot of potatoes with—sometimes—a bit of salt fish, and she poured out the potatoes on the table and ate them slowly, with great relish, using her fingers by way of a fork.

Now, girls are supposed to be fastidious, but I was the one who suffered most from this. Nora, my sister, just sucked up to the old woman for the penny she got every Friday out of the old-age pension, a thing I could not do. I was too honest, that was my trouble; and when I was playing with Bill Connell, the sergeant-major's son, and saw my grandmother steering up the path with the jug of porter sticking out from beneath her shawl I was mortified. I made excuses not to let him come into the house, because I could never be sure what she would be up to when we went in.

When Mother was at work and my grandmother made the dinner I wouldn't touch it. Nora once tried to make me, but I hid under the table from her and took the bread-knife with me for protection. Nora let on to be very indignant (she wasn't, of course, but she knew Mother saw through her, so she sided with Gran) and came after me. I lashed out at her with the bread-knife, and after that she left me alone. I stayed there till Mother came in from work and made my dinner, but when Father came in later Nora said in a shocked voice: "Oh, Dadda,

porter: a dark-brown beer.

do you know what Jackie did at dinnertime?" Then, of course, it all came out; Father gave me a flaking; Mother interfered, and for days after that he didn't speak to me and Mother barely spoke to Nora. And all because of that old woman! God knows, I was heart-scalded.

Then, to crown my misfortune, I had to make my first confession and communion. It was an old woman called Ryan who prepared us for these. She was about the one age with Gran; she was well-to-do, lived in a big house on Montenotte, wore a black cloak and bonnet, and came every day to school at three o'clock when we should have been going home, and talked to us of hell. She may have mentioned the other place as well, but that could only have been by accident, for hell had the first place in her heart.

She lit a candle, took out a new half-crown, and offered it to the first boy   5
who would hold one finger—only one finger!—in the flame for five minutes by the school clock. Being always very ambitious I was tempted to volunteer, but I thought it might look greedy. Then she asked were we afraid of holding one finger—only one finger!—in a little candle flame for five minutes and not afraid of burning all over in roasting hot furnaces for all eternity. "All eternity! Just think of that! A whole lifetime goes by and it's nothing, not even a drop in the ocean of your sufferings." The woman was really interesting about hell, but my attention was all fixed on the half-crown. At the end of the lesson she put it back in her purse. It was a great disappointment; a religious woman like that, you wouldn't think she'd bother about a thing like a half-crown.

Another day she said she knew a priest who woke one night to find a fellow he didn't recognize leaning over the end of his bed. The priest was a bit frightened— naturally enough—but he asked the fellow what he wanted, and the fellow said in a deep, husky voice that he wanted to go to confession. The priest said it was an awkward time and wouldn't it do in the morning, but the fellow said that last time he went to confession, there was one sin he kept back, being ashamed to mention it, and now it was always on his mind. Then the priest knew it was a bad case, because the fellow was after making a bad confession and committing a mortal sin. He got up to dress, and just then the cock crew in the yard outside, and—lo and behold!—when the priest looked round there was no sign of the fellow, only a smell of burning timber, and when the priest looked at his bed didn't he see the print of two hands burned in it? That was because the fellow had made a bad confession. This story made a shocking impression on me.

But the worst of all was when she showed us how to examine our conscience. Did we take the name of the Lord, our God, in vain? Did we honour our father and our mother? (I asked her did this include grandmothers and she said it did.) Did we love our neighbours as ourselves? Did we covet our neighbour's goods? (I thought of the way I felt about the penny that Nora got every Friday.) I decided that, between one thing and another, I must have broken the whole ten commandments, all on account of that old woman, and so far as I could see, so long as she remained in the house I had no hope of ever doing anything else.

I was scared to death of confession. The day the whole class went I let on to have a toothache, hoping my absence wouldn't be noticed; but at three o'clock, just as I was feeling safe, along comes a chap with a message from Mrs. Ryan that I was to go to confession myself on Saturday and be at the chapel for communion with the rest. To make it worse, Mother couldn't come with me and sent Nora instead.

Now, that girl had ways of tormenting me that Mother never knew of. She held my hand as we went down the hill, smiling sadly and saying how sorry she was for me, as if she were bringing me to the hospital for an operation.

"Oh, God help us!" she moaned. "Isn't it a terrible pity you weren't a good   10
boy? Oh, Jackie, my heart bleeds for you! How will you ever think of all your sins? Don't forget you have to tell him about the time you kicked Gran on the shin."

"Lemme go!" I said, trying to drag myself free of her. "I don't want to go to confession at all."

"But sure, you'll have to go to confession, Jackie," she replied in the same regretful tone. "Sure, if you didn't, the parish priest would be up to the house, looking for you. 'Tisn't, God knows, that I'm not sorry for you. Do you remember the time you tried to kill me with the bread-knife under the table? And the language you used to me? I don't know what he'll do with you at all, Jackie. He might have to send you up to the bishop."

I remember thinking bitterly that she didn't know the half of what I had to tell—if I told it. I knew I couldn't tell it, and understood perfectly why the fellow in Mrs. Ryan's story made a bad confession; it seemed to me a great shame that people wouldn't stop criticizing him. I remember that steep hill down to the church, and the sunlit hillsides beyond the valley of the river, which I saw in the gaps between the houses like Adam's last glimpse of Paradise.°

Then, when she had manœuvered me down the long flight of steps to the chapel yard, Nora suddenly changed her tone. She became the raging malicious devil she really was.

"There you are!" she said with a yelp of triumph, hurling me through the   15
church door. "And I hope he'll give you the penitential psalms, you dirty little caffler."

I knew then I was lost, given up to eternal justice. The door with the coloured-glass panels swung shut behind me, the sunlight went out and gave place to deep shadow, and the wind whistled outside so that the silence within seemed to crackle like ice under my feet. Nora sat in front of me by the confession box. There were a couple of old women ahead of her, and then a miserable-looking poor devil came and wedged me in at the other side, so that I couldn't escape even if I had the courage. He joined his hands and rolled his eyes in the direction of the roof, muttering aspirations in an anguished tone, and I wondered had he a grandmother too. Only a grandmother could account for a fellow behaving in that heartbroken way, but he was better off than I, for he at least could go and confess his sins; while I would make a bad confession and then die in the night and be continually coming back and burning people's furniture.

Nora's turn came, and I heard the sound of something slamming, and then her voice as if butter wouldn't melt in her mouth, and then another slam, and out she came. God, the hypocrisy of women! Her eyes were lowered, her head was bowed, and her hands were joined very low down on her stomach, and she walked up the aisle to the side altar looking like a saint. You never saw such an exhibition of devotion, and I remembered the devilish malice with which she had tormented me all the way from our door, and wondered were all religious people

---

Adam's last glimpse of Paradise: Genesis 3:23–24.

like that, really. It was my turn now. With the fear of damnation in my soul I went in, and the confessional door closed of itself behind me.

It was pitch-dark and I couldn't see priest or anything else. Then I really began to be frightened. In the darkness it was a matter between God and me, and He had all the odds. He knew what my intentions were before I even started; I had no chance. All I had ever been told about confession got mixed up in my mind, and I knelt to one wall and said: "Bless me, father, for I have sinned; this is my first confession." I waited for a few minutes, but nothing happened, so I tried it on the other wall. Nothing happened there either. He had me spotted all right.

It must have been then that I noticed the shelf at about one height with my head. It was really a place for grown-up people to rest their elbows, but in my distracted state I thought it was probably the place you were supposed to kneel. Of course, it was on the high side and not very deep, but I was always good at climbing and managed to get up all right. Staying up was the trouble. There was room only for my knees, and nothing you could get a grip on but a sort of wooden moulding, a bit above it. I held on to the moulding and repeated the words a little louder, and this time something happened all right. A slide was slammed back; a little light entered the box, and a man's voice said: "Who's there?"

"'Tis me, father," I said for fear he mightn't see me and go away again. I couldn't see him at all. The place the voice came from was under the moulding, about level with my knees, so I took a good grip of the moulding and swung myself down till I saw the astonished face of a young priest looking up at me. He had to put his head on one side to see me, and I had to put mine on one side to see him, so we were more or less talking to one another upside-down. It struck me as a queer way of hearing confessions, but I didn't feel it my place to criticize. 20

"Bless me, father, for I have sinned; this is my first confession," I rattled off all in one breath, and swung myself down the least shade more to make it easier for him.

"What are you doing up there?" he shouted in an angry voice, and the strain the politeness was putting on my hold of the moulding, and the shock of being addressed in such an uncivil tone, were too much for me. I lost my grip, tumbled, and hit the door an unmerciful wallop before I found myself flat on my back in the middle of the aisle. The people who had been waiting stood up with their mouths open. The priest opened the door of the middle box and came out, pushing his biretta back from his forehead; he looked something terrible. Then Nora came scampering down the aisle.

"Oh, you dirty little caffler!" she said. "I might have known you'd do it. I might have known you'd disgrace me. I can't leave you out of my sight for one minute."

Before I could even get to my feet to defend myself she bent down and gave me a clip across the ear. This reminded me that I was so stunned I had even forgotten to cry, so that people might think I wasn't hurt at all, when in fact I was probably maimed for life. I gave a roar out of me.

"What's all this about?" the priest hissed, getting angrier than ever and pushing 25 Nora off me. "How dare you hit the child like that, you little vixen?"

"But I can't do my penance with him, father," Nora cried, cocking an outraged eye up to him.

"Well, go and do it, or I'll give you some more to do," he said, giving me a hand up. "Was it coming to confession you were, my poor man?" he asked me.

"'Twas, father," said I with a sob.

"Oh," he said respectfully, "a big hefty fellow like you must have terrible sins. Is this your first?"

"'Tis, father," said I.

30

"Worse and worse," he said gloomily. "The crimes of a lifetime. I don't know will I get rid of you at all today. You'd better wait now till I'm finished with these old ones. You can see by the looks of them they haven't much to tell."

"I will, father," I said with something approaching joy.

The relief of it was really enormous. Nora stuck out her tongue at me from behind his back, but I couldn't even be bothered retorting. I knew from the very moment that man opened his mouth that he was intelligent above the ordinary. When I had time to think, I saw how right I was. It only stood to reason that a fellow confessing after seven years would have more to tell than people that went every week. The crimes of a lifetime, exactly as he said. It was only what he expected, and the rest was the cackle of old women and girls with their talk of hell, the bishop, and the penitential psalms. That was all they knew. I started to make my examination of conscience, and barring the one bad business of my grandmother it didn't seem so bad.

The next time, the priest steered me into the confession box himself and left the shutter back the way I could see him get in and sit down at the further side of the grille from me.

"Well, now," he said, "what do they call you?"

35

"Jackie, father," said I.

"And what's a-trouble to you, Jackie?"

"Father," I said, feeling I might as well get it over while I had him in good humour, "I had it all arranged to kill my grandmother."

He seemed a bit shaken by that, all right, because he said nothing for quite a while.

"My goodness," he said at last, "that'd be a shocking thing to do. What put that into your head?"

40

"Father," I said, feeling very sorry for myself, "she's an awful woman."

"Is she?" he asked. "What way is she awful?"

"She takes porter, father," I said, knowing well from the way Mother talked of it that this was a mortal sin, and hoping it would make the priest take a more favourable view of my case.

"Oh, my!" he said, and I could see he was impressed.

"And snuff, father," said I.

45

"That's a bad case, sure enough, Jackie," he said.

"And she goes round in her bare feet, father," I went on in a rush of self-pity, "and she knows I don't like her, and she gives pennies to Nora and none to me, and my da sides with her and flakes me, and one night I was so heartscalded I made up my mind I'd have to kill her."

"And what would you do with the body?" he asked with great interest.

"I was thinking I could chop that up and carry it away in a barrow I have," I said.

"Begor, Jackie," he said, "do you know you're a terrible child?"

50

"I know, father," I said, for I was just thinking the same thing myself. "I tried to kill Nora too with a bread-knife under the table, only I missed her."

"Is that the little girl that was beating you just now?" he asked.

"'Tis, father."

"Someone will go for her with a bread-knife one day, and he won't miss her," he said rather cryptically. "You must have great courage. Between ourselves, there's a lot of people I'd like to do the same to but I'd never have the nerve. Hanging is an awful death."

"Is it, father?" I asked with the deepest interest—I was always very keen on hanging. "Did you ever see a fellow hanged?" 55

"Dozens of them," he said solemnly. "And they all died roaring."

"Jay!" I said.

"Oh, a horrible death!" he said with great satisfaction. "Lots of fellows I saw killed their grandmothers too, but they all said ' 'twas never worth it."

He had me there for a full ten minutes talking, and then walked out the chapel yard with me. I was genuinely sorry to part with him, because he was the most entertaining character I'd ever met in the religious line. Outside, after the shadow of the church, the sunlight was like the roaring of waves on a beach; it dazzled me; and when the frozen silence melted and I heard the screech of trams on the road my heart soared. I knew now I wouldn't die in the night and come back, leaving marks on my mother's furniture. It would be a great worry to her, and the poor soul had enough.

Nora was sitting on the railing, waiting for me, and she put on a very sour 60 puss when she saw the priest with me. She was made jealous because a priest had never come out of the church with her.

"Well," she asked coldly, after he left me, "what did he give you?"

"Three Hail Marys," I said.

"Three Hail Marys," she repeated incredulously. "You mustn't have told him anything."

"I told him everything," I said confidently.

"About Gran and all?" 65

"About Gran and all."

(All she wanted was to be able to go home and say I'd made a bad confession.)

"Did you tell him you went for me with the bread-knife?" she asked with a frown.

"I did to be sure."

"And he only gave you three Hail Marys?" 70

"That's all."

She slowly got down from the railing with a baffled air. Clearly, this was beyond her. As we mounted the steps back to the main road she looked at me suspiciously.

"What are you sucking?" she asked.

"Bullseyes."

"Was it the priest gave them to you?" 75

" 'Twas."

"Lord God," she wailed bitterly, "some people have all the luck! ' 'Tis no advantage to anybody trying to be good. I might just as well be a sinner like you."

TILLIE OLSEN   (b. 1913)

I Stand Here Ironing   *1953–1954*

I stand here ironing, and what you asked me moves tormented back and forth with the iron.

"I wish you would manage the time to come in and talk with me about your daughter. I'm sure you can help me understand her. She's a youngster who needs help and whom I'm deeply interested in helping."

"Who needs help." . . . . Even if I came, what good would it do? You think because I am her mother I have a key, or that in some way you could use me as a key? She has lived for nineteen years. There is all that life that has happened outside of me, beyond me.

And when is there time to remember, to sift, to weigh, to estimate, to total? I will start and there will be an interruption and I will have to gather it all together again. Or I will become engulfed with all I did or did not do, with what should have been and what cannot be helped.

She was a beautiful baby. The first and only one of our five that was beautiful   5
at birth. You do not guess how new and uneasy her tenancy in her now-loveliness. You did not know her all those years she was thought homely, or see her poring over her baby pictures, making me tell her over and over how beautiful she had been—and would be, I would tell her—and was now, to the seeing eye. But the seeing eyes were few or nonexistent. Including mine.

I nursed her. They feel that's important nowadays. I nursed all the children, but with her, with all the fierce rigidity of first motherhood, I did like the books then said. Though her cries battered me to trembling and my breasts ached with swollenness, I waited till the clock decreed.

Why do I put that first? I do not even know if it matters, or if it explains anything.

She was a beautiful baby. She blew shining bubbles of sound. She loved motion, loved light, loved color and music and textures. She would lie on the floor in her blue overalls patting the surface so hard in ecstasy her hands and feet would blur. She was a miracle to me, but when she was eight months old I had to leave her daytimes with the woman downstairs to whom she was no miracle at all, for I worked or looked for work and for Emily's father, who "could no longer endure" (he wrote in his good-bye note) "sharing want with us."

I was nineteen. It was the pre-relief, pre-WPA world of the depression. I would start running as soon as I got off the streetcar, running up the stairs, the place smelling sour, and awake or asleep to startle awake, when she saw me she would break into a clogged weeping that could not be comforted, a weeping I can hear yet.

After a while I found a job hashing at night so I could be with her days,   10
and it was better. But it came to where I had to bring her to his family and leave her.

It took a long time to raise the money for her fare back. Then she got chicken pox and I had to wait longer. When she finally came, I hardly knew her, walking quick and nervous like her father, looking like her father, thin, and dressed in a shoddy red that yellowed her skin and glared at the pockmarks. All the baby loveliness gone.

She was two. Old enough for nursery school they said, and I did not know then what I know now—the fatigue of the long day, and the lacerations of group life in the kinds of nurseries that are only parking places for children.

Except that it would have made no difference if I had known. It was the only place there was. It was the only way we could be together, the only way I could hold a job.

And even without knowing, I knew. I knew the teacher that was evil because all these years it has curdled into my memory, the little boy hunched in the corner, her rasp, "why aren't you outside, because Alvin hits you? that's no reason, go out, scaredy." I knew Emily hated it even if she did not clutch and implore "don't go Mommy" like the other chidren, mornings.

She always had a reason why we should stay home. Momma, you look sick.   15
Momma, I feel sick. Momma, the teachers aren't there today, they're sick. Momma, we can't go, there was a fire there last night. Momma, it's a holiday today, no school, they told me.

But never a direct protest, never rebellion. I think of our others in their three-, four-year-oldness—the explosions, the tempers, the denunciations, the de-mands—and I feel suddenly ill. I put the iron down. What in me demanded that goodness in her? And what was the cost, the cost to her of such goodness?

The old man living in the back once said in his gentle way: "You should smile at Emily more when you look at her." What *was* in my face when I looked at her? I loved her. There were all the acts of love.

It was only with the others I remembered what he said, and it was the face of joy, and not of care or tightness or worry I turned to them—too late for Emily. She does not smile easily, let alone almost always as her brothers and sisters do. Her face is closed and sombre, but when she wants, how fluid. You must have seen it in her pantomimes, you spoke of her rare gift for comedy on the stage that rouses a laughter out of the audience so dear they applaud and applaud and do not want to let her go.

Where does it come from, that comedy? There was none of it in her when she came back to me that second time, after I had had to send her away again. She had a new daddy now to learn to love, and I think perhaps it was a better time.

Except when we left her alone nights, telling ourselves she was old enough.   20
"Can't you go some other time, Mommy, like tomorrow?" she would ask. "Will it be just a little while you'll be gone? Do you promise?"

The time we came back, the front door open, the clock on the floor in the hall. She rigid awake. "It wasn't just a little while. I didn't cry. Three times I called you, just three times, and then I ran downstairs to open the door so you could come faster. The clock talked loud. I threw it away, it scared me what it talked."

She said the clock talked loud again that night I went to the hospital to have Susan. She was delirious with the fever that comes before red measles, but she was fully conscious all the week I was gone and the week after we were home when she could not come near the new baby or me.

She did not get well. She stayed skeleton thin, not wanting to eat, and night after night she had nightmares. She would call for me, and I would rouse from exhaustion to sleepily call back: "You're all right, darling, go to sleep, it's just a dream," and if she still called, in a sterner voice, "now go to sleep, Emily, there's nothing to hurt you." Twice, only twice, when I had to get up for Susan anyhow, I went in to sit with her.

Now when it is too late (as if she would let me hold and comfort her like I   25
do the others) I get up and go to her at once at her moan or restless stirring. "Are you awake, Emily? Can I get you something?" And the answer is always the same: "No, I'm all right, go back to sleep, Mother."

They persuaded me at the clinic to send her away to a convalescent home in the country where "she can have the kind of food and care you can't manage for her, and you'll be free to concentrate on the new baby." They still send children to that place. I see pictures on the society page of sleek young women planning affairs to raise money for it, or dancing at the affairs, or decorating Easter eggs or filling Christmas stockings for the children.

They never have a picture of the children so I do not know if the girls still wear those gigantic red bows and the ravaged looks on the every other Sunday when parents can come to visit "unless otherwise notified"—as we were notified the first six weeks.

Oh it is a handsome place, green lawns and tall trees and fluted flower beds. High up on the balconies of each cottage the children stand, the girls in their red bows and white dresses, the boys in white suits and giant red ties. The parents stand below shrieking up to be heard and the children shriek down to be heard, and between them the invisible wall "Not To Be Contaminated by Parental Germs or Physical Affection."

There was a tiny girl who always stood hand in hand with Emily. Her parents never came. One visit she was gone. "They moved her to Rose Cottage" Emily shouted in explanation. "They don't like you to love anybody here."

She wrote once a week, the labored writing of a seven-year-old. "I am fine.   30
How is the baby. If I write my leter nicly I will have a star. Love." There never was a star. We wrote every other day, letters she could never hold or keep but only hear read—once. "We simply do not have room for children to keep any personal possessions," they patiently explained when we pieced one Sunday's shriek-ing together to plead how much it would mean to Emily, who loved so to keep things, to be allowed to keep her letters and cards.

Each visit she looked frailer. "She isn't eating," they told us.

(They had runny eggs for breakfast or mush with lumps, Emily said later, I'd hold it in my mouth and not swallow. Nothing ever tasted good, just when they had chicken.)

It took us eight months to get her released home, and only the fact that she gained back so little of her seven lost pounds convinced the social worker.

I used to try to hold and love her after she came back, but her body would stay stiff, and after a while she'd push away. She ate little. Food sickened her, and I think much of life too. Oh she had physical lightness and brightness, twinkling by on skates, bouncing like a ball up and down up and down over the jump rope, skimming over the hill; but these were momentary.

She fretted about her appearance, thin and dark and foreign-looking at a   35
time when every little girl was supposed to look or thought she should look a

chubby blonde replica of Shirley Temple. The doorbell sometimes rang for her, but no one seemed to come and play in the house or be a best friend. Maybe because we moved so much.

There was a boy she loved painfully through two school semesters. Months later she told me how she had taken pennies from my purse to buy him candy. "Licorice was his favorite and I brought him some every day, but he still liked Jennifer better'n me. Why, Mommy?" The kind of question for which there is no answer.

School was a worry to her. She was not glib or quick in a world where glibness and quickness were easily confused with ability to learn. To her overworked and exasperated teachers she was an overconscientious "slow learner" who kept trying to catch up and was absent entirely too often.

I let her be absent, though sometimes the illness was imaginary. How different from my now-strictness about attendance with the others. I wasn't working. We had a new baby, I was home anyhow. Sometimes, after Susan grew old enough, I would keep her home from school, too, to have them all together.

Mostly Emily had asthma, and her breathing, harsh and labored, would fill the house with a curiously tranquil sound. I would bring the two old dresser mirrors and her boxes of collections to her bed. She would select beads and single earrings, bottle tops and shells, dried flowers and pebbles, old postcards and scraps, all sorts of oddments; then she and Susan would play Kingdom, setting up landscapes and furniture, peopling them with action.

Those were the only times of peaceful companionship between her and Susan. 40
I have edged away from it, that poisonous feeling between them, that terrible balancing of hurts and needs I had to do between the two, and did so badly, those earlier years.

Oh there are conflicts between the others too, each one human, needing, demanding, hurting, taking—but only between Emily and Susan, no, Emily toward Susan that corroding resentment. It seems so obvious on the surface, yet it is not obvious. Susan, the second child, Susan, golden- and curly-haired and chubby, quick and articulate and assured, everything in appearance and manner Emily was not; Susan, not able to resist Emily's precious things, losing or sometimes clumsily breaking them; Susan telling jokes and riddles to company for applause while Emily sat silent (to say to me later: that was *my* riddle, Mother, I told it to Susan); Susan, who for all the five years' difference in age was just a year behind Emily in developing physically.

I am glad for that slow physical development that widened the difference between her and her contemporaries, though she suffered over it. She was too vulnerable for that terrible world of youthful competition, of preening and parading, of constant measuring of yourself against every other, of envy, "If I had that copper hair," "If I had that skin. . . ." She tormented herself enough about not looking like the others, there was enough of the unsureness, the having to be conscious of words before you speak, the constant caring—what are they thinking of me? without having it all magnified by the merciless physical drives.

Ronnie is calling. He is wet and I change him. It is rare there is such a cry now. That time of motherhood is almost behind me when the ear is not one's own but must always be racked and listening for the child cry, the child call. We sit for a while and I hold him, looking out over the city spread in charcoal with its soft aisles of light. *"Shoogily,"* he breathes and curls closer. I carry him back to bed, asleep. *Shoogily.* A funny word, a family word, inherited from Emily, invented by her to say: *comfort.*

In this and other ways she leaves her seal, I say aloud. And startle at my saying it. What do I mean? What did I start to gather together, to try and make coherent? I was at the terrible, growing years. War years. I do not remember them well. I was working, there were four smaller ones now, there was not time for her. She had to help be a mother, a housekeeper, and shopper. She had to set her seal. Mornings of crisis and near hysteria trying to get lunches packed, hair combed, coats and shoes found, everyone to school or Child Care on time, the baby ready for transportation. And always the paper scribbled on by a smaller one, the book looked at by Susan then mislaid, the homework not done. Running out to that huge school where she was one, she was lost, she was a drop; suffering over the unpreparedness, stammering and unsure in her classes.

There was so little time left at night after the kids were bedded down. She would struggle over books, always eating (it was in those years she developed her enormous appetite that is legendary in our family) and I would be ironing, or preparing food for the next day, or writing V-mail to Bill, or tending the baby. Sometimes, to make me laugh, or out of her despair, she would imitate happenings or types at school.   45

I think I said once: "Why don't you do something like this in the school amateur show?" One morning she phoned me at work, hardly understandable through the weeping: "Mother, I did it. I won, I won; they gave me first prize; they clapped and clapped and wouldn't let me go."

Now suddenly she was Somebody, and as imprisoned in her difference as she had been in anonymity.

She began to be asked to perform at other high schools, even in colleges, then at city and statewide affairs. The first one we went to, I only recognized her that first moment when thin, shy, she almost drowned herself into the curtains. Then: Was this Emily? The control, the command, the convulsing and deadly clowning, the spell, then the roaring, stamping audience, unwilling to let this rare and precious laughter out of their lives.

Afterwards: You ought to do something about her with a gift like that—but without money or knowing how, what does one do? We have left it all to her, and the gift has as often eddied inside, clogged and clotted, as been used and growing.

She is coming. She runs up the stairs two at a time with her light graceful   50
step, and I know she is happy tonight. Whatever it was that occasioned your call did not happen today.

"Aren't you ever going to finish the ironing, Mother? Whistler painted his mother in a rocker. I'd have to paint mine standing over an ironing board." This is one of her communicative nights and she tells me everything and nothing as she fixes herself a plate of food out of the icebox.

She is so lovely. Why did you want me to come in at all? Why were you concerned? She will find her way.

She starts up the stairs to bed. "Don't get me up with the rest in the morning." "But I thought you were having midterms." "Oh, those," she comes back in, kisses me, and says quite lightly, "in a couple of years when we'll all be atom-dead they won't matter a bit."

She has said it before. She *believes* it. But because I have been dredging the past, and all that compounds a human being is so heavy and meaningful in me, I cannot endure it tonight.

I will never total it all. I will never come in to say: She was a child seldom   55
smiled at. Her father left me before she was a year old. I had to work her first six years when there was work, or I sent her home and to his relatives. There were years she had care she hated. She was dark and thin and foreign-looking in a world where the prestige went to blondeness and curly hair and dimples, she was slow where glibness was prized. She was a child of anxious, not proud, love. We were poor and could not afford for her the soil of easy growth. I was a young mother, I was a distracted mother. There were the other children pushing up, demanding. Her younger sister seemed all that she was not. There were years she did not want me to touch her. She kept too much in herself, her life was such she had to keep too much in herself. My wisdom came too late. She has much to her and probably little will come of it. She is a chld of her age, of depression, of war, of fear.

Let her be. So all that is in her will not bloom—but in how many does it? There is still enough left to live by. Only help her to know—help make it so there is cause for her to know—that she is more than this dress on the ironing board, helpless before the iron.

GRACE PALEY (b. 1922)

Goodbye and Good Luck 1959

I was popular in certain circles, says Aunt Rose. I wasn't no thinner then, only more stationary in the flesh. In time to come, Lillie, don't be surprised—change is a fact of God. From this no one is excused. Only a person like your mama stands on one foot, she don't notice how big her behind is getting and sings in the canary's ear for thirty years. Who's listening? Papa's in the shop. You and Seymour, thinking about yourself. So she waits in a spotless kitchen for a kind word and thinks—poor Rosie. . . .

Poor Rosie! If there was more life in my little sister, she would know my heart is a regular college of feelings and there is such information between my corset and me that her whole married life is a kindergarten.

Nowadays you could find me any time in a hotel, uptown or downtown. Who needs an apartment to live like a maid with a dustrag in the hand, sneezing? I'm in very good with the bus boys, it's more interesting than home, all kinds of people, everybody with a reason.

And my reason, Lillie, is a long time ago I said to the forelady, "Missus, if I can't sit by the window, I can't sit." "If you can't sit, girlie," she says politely, "go stand on the street corner." And that's how I got unemployed in novelty wear.

For my next job I answered an ad which said: "Refined young lady, medium   5

salary, cultural organization." I went by trolley to the address, the Russian Art
Theater of Second Avenue where they played only the best Yiddish plays. They
needed a ticket seller, someone like me, who likes the public but is very sharp on
crooks. The man who interviewed me was the manager, a certain type.

Immediately he said: "Rosie Lieber, you surely got a build on you!"

"It takes all kinds, Mr. Krimberg."

"Don't misunderstand me, little girl," he said. "I appreciate, I appreciate. A
young lady lacking fore and aft, her blood is so busy warming the toes and the
finger tips, it don't have time to circulate where it's most required."

Everybody likes kindness. I said to him: "Only don't be fresh, Mr. Krimberg,
and we'll make a good bargain."

We did: Nine dollars a week, a glass of tea every night, a free ticket once a   10
week for Mama, and I could go watch rehearsals any time I want.

My first nine dollars was in the grocer's hands ready to move on already,
when Krimberg said to me, "Rosie, here's a great gentleman, a member of this
remarkable theater, wants to meet you, impressed no doubt by your big brown
eyes"

And who was it, Lillie? Listen to me, before my very eyes was Volodya Vlashkin,
called by the people of those days the Valentino of Second Avenue. I took one
look, and I said to myself: Where did a Jewish boy grow up so big? "Just outside
Kiev," he told me.

How? "My mama nursed me till I was six. I was the only boy in the village
to have such health."

"My goodness, Vlashkin, six years old! She must have had shredded wheat
there, not breasts, poor woman."

"My mother was beautiful," he said. "She had eyes like stars."   15

He had such a way of expressing himself, it brought tears.

To Krimberg, Vlashkin said after this introduction: "Who is responsible for
hiding this wonderful young person in a cage?"

"That is where the ticket seller sells."

"So, David, go in there and sell tickets for a half hour. I have something in
mind in regards to the future of this girl and this company. Go, David, be a good
boy. And you, Miss Lieber, please, I suggest Feinberg's for a glass of tea. The
rehearsals are long. I enjoy a quiet interlude with a friendly person."

So he took me there, Feinberg's, then around the corner, a place so full of   20
Hungarians, it was deafening. In the back room was a table of honor for him.
On the tablecloth embroidered by the lady of the house was "Here Vlashkin Eats."
We finished one glass of tea in quietness, out of thirst, when I finally made up
my mind what to say.

"Mr. Vlashkin, I saw you a couple weeks ago, even before I started working
here, in *The Sea Gull*. Believe me, if I was that girl, I wouldn't look even for a
minute on the young bourgeois fellow. He could fall out of the play altogether.
How Chekhov could put him in the same play as you, I can't understand."

"You liked me?" he asked, taking my hand and kindly patting it. "Well,
well, young people still like me . . . so, and you like the theater too? Good. And
you, Rose, you know you have such a nice hand, so warm to the touch, such a
fine skin, tell me, why do you wear a scarf around your neck? You only hide
your young, young throat. These are not olden times, my child, to live in shame."

"Who's ashamed?" I said, taking off the kerchief, but my hand right away went to the kerchief's place, because the truth is, it really was olden times, and I was still of a nature to melt with shame.

"Have some more tea, my dear."

"No, thank you, I am a samovar already."   25

"Dorfmann!" he hollered like a king. "Bring this child a seltzer with fresh ice!"

In weeks to follow I had the privilege to know him better and better as a person—also the opportunity to see him in his profession. The time was autumn; the theater full of coming and going. Rehearsing without end. After *The Sea Gull* flopped *The Salesman from Istanbul* played, a great success.

Here the ladies went crazy. On the opening night, in the middle of the first scene, one missus—a widow or her husband worked too long hours—began to clap and sing out, "Oi, oi, Vlashkin." Soon there was such a tumult, the actors had to stop acting. Vlashkin stepped forward. Only not Vlashkin to the eyes . . . a younger man with pitch-black hair, lively on restless feet, his mouth clever. A half a century later at the end of the play he came out again, a gray philosopher, a student of life from only reading books, his hands as smooth as silk. . . . I cried to think who I was—nothing—and such a man could look at me with interest.

Then I got a small raise, due to he kindly put in a good word for me, and also for fifty cents a night I was given the pleasure together with cousins, in-laws, and plain stage-struck kids to be part of a crowd scene and to see like he saw every single night the hundreds of pale faces waiting for his feelings to make them laugh or bend down their heads in sorrow.

The sad day came, I kissed my mama goodbye. Vlashkin helped me to get   30
a reasonable room near the theater to be more free. Also my outstanding friend would have a place to recline away from the noise of the dressing rooms. She cried and she cried. "This is a different way of living, Mama," I said. "Besides I am driven by love."

"You! You, a nothing, a rotten hole in a piece of cheese, are you telling me what is life?" she screamed.

Very insulted, I went away from her. But I am good-natured—you know fat people are like that—kind, and I thought to myself, poor Mama . . . it is true she got more of an idea of life than me. She married who she didn't like, a sick man, his spirit already swallowed up by God. He never washed. He had an unhappy smell. His teeth fell out, his hair disappeared, he got smaller, shriveled up little by little, till goodbye and good luck he was gone and only came to Mama's mind when she went to the mailbox under the stairs to get the electric bill. In memory of him and out of respect for mankind, I decided to live for love.

Don't laugh, you ignorant girl.

Do you think it was easy for me? I had to give Mama a little something. Ruthie was saving up together with your papa for linens, a couple knives and forks. In the morning I had to do piecework if I wanted to keep by myself. So I made flowers. Before lunch time every day a whole garden grew on my table.

This was my independence, Lillie dear, blooming, but it didn't have no roots   35
and its face was paper.

Meanwhile Krimberg went after me too. No doubt observing the success of Vlashkin, he thought, "Aha, open sesame. . ." Others in the company similar.

After me in those years were the following: Krimberg I mentioned. Carl Zimmer, played innocent young fellows with a wig. Charlie Peel, a Christian who fell in the soup by accident, a creator of beautiful sets. "Color is his middle name," says Vlashkin, always to the point.

I put this in to show you your fat old aunt was not crazy out of loneliness. In those noisy years I had friends among interesting people who admired me for reasons of youth and that I was a first-class listener.

The actresses—Raisele, Marya, Esther Leopold—were only interested in to-morrow. After them was the rich men, producers, the whole garment center; their past is a pincushion, future the eye of a needle.

Finally the day came, I no longer could keep my tact in my mouth. I said: "Vlashkin, I hear by carrier pigeon you have a wife, children, the whole combination."

"True, I don't tell stories. I make no pretense."   40

"That isn't the question. What is this lady like? It hurts me to ask, but tell me, Vlashkin . . . a man's life is something I don't clearly see."

"Little girl, I have told you a hundred times, this small room is the convent of my troubled spirit. Here I come to your innocent shelter to refresh myself in the midst of an agonized life."

"Ach, Vlashkin, serious, serious, who is this lady?"

"Rosie, she is a fine woman of the middle classes, a good mother to my children, three in number, girls all, a good cook, in her youth handsome, now no longer young. You see, could I be more frank? I entrust you, dear, with my soul."

It was some few months later at the New Year's ball of the Russian Artists   45
Club, I met Mrs. Vlashkin, a woman with black hair in a low bun, straight and too proud. She sat at a small table speaking in a deep voice to whoever stopped a moment to converse. Her Yiddish was perfect, each word cut like a special jewel. I looked at her. She noticed me like she notices everybody, cold like Christmas morning. Then she got tired. Vlashkin called a taxi and I never saw her again. Poor woman, she did not know I was on the same stage with her. The poison I was to her role, she did not know.

Later on that night in front of my door I said to Vlashkin, "No more. This isn't for me. I am sick from it all. I am no home breaker."

"Girlie," he said, "don't be foolish."

"No, no, goodbye, good luck," I said. "I am sincere."

So I went and stayed with Mama for a week's vacation and cleaned up all the closets and scrubbed the walls till the paint came off. She was very grateful, all the same her hard life made her say, "Now we see the end. If you live like a bum, you are finally a lunatic."

After this few days I came back to my life. When we met, me and Vlashkin,   50
we said only hello and goodbye, and then for a few sad years, with the head we nodded as if to say, "Yes, yes, I know who you are."

Meanwhile in the field was a whole new strategy. Your mama and your grandmama brought around—boys. Your own father had a brother, you never even seen him. Ruben. A serious fellow, his idealism was his hat and his coat, "Rosie, I offer you a big new free happy unusual life." How? "With me, we will raise up the sands of Palestine to make a nation. That is the land of tomorrow for us Jews." "Ha-ha, Ruben, I'll go tomorrow then." "Rosie!" says Ruben. "We need strong women like you, mothers and farmers." "You don't fool me, Ruben, what you need is dray horses. But for that you need more money." "I don't like your attitude, Rose." "In that case, go and multiply. Goodbye."

Another fellow: Yonkel Gurstein, a regular sport, dressed to kill, with such an excitable nature. In those days—it looks to me like yesterday—the youngest girls wore undergarments like Battle Creek, Michigan. To him it was a matter of seconds. Where did he practice, a Jewish boy? Nowadays I suppose it is easier, Lillie? My goodness, I ain't asking you nothing—touchy, touchy. . . .

Well, by now you must know yourself, honey, whatever you do, life don't stop. It only sits a minute and dreams a dream.

While I was saying to all these silly youngsters "no, no, no," Vlashkin went to Europe and toured a few seasons . . . Moscow, Prague, London, even Berlin— already a pessimistic place. When he came back he wrote a book, you could get from the library even today, *The Jewish Actor Abroad*. If someday you're interested enough in my lonesome years, you could read it. You could absorb a flavor of the man from the book. No, no, I am not mentioned. After all, who am I?

When the book came out I stopped him in the street to say congratulations. But I am not a liar, so I pointed out, too, the egotism of many parts—even the critics said something along such lines. 55

"Talk is cheap," Vlashkin answered me. "But who are the critics? Tell me, do they create? Not to mention," he continues, "there is a line in Shakespeare in one of the plays from the great history of England. It says, 'Self-loving is not so vile a sin, my liege, as self-neglecting.'° This idea also appears in modern times in the moralistic followers of Freud. . . . Rosie, are you listening? You asked a question. By the way, you look very well. How come no wedding ring?"

I walked away from this conversation in tears. But this talking in the street opened the happy road up for more discussions. In regard to many things. . . . For instance, the management—very narrow-minded—wouldn't give him any more certain young men's parts. Fools. What youngest man knew enough about life to be as young as him?

"Rosie, Rosie," he said to me one day, "I see by the clock on your rosy, rosy face you must be thirty."

"The hands are slow, Vlashkin. On a week before Thursday I was thirty-four."

"Is that so? Rosie, I worry about you. It has been on my mind to talk to 60 you. You are losing your time. Do you understand it? A woman should not lose her time."

"Oi, Vlashkin, if you are my friend, what is time?"

For this he had no answer, only looked at me surprised. We went instead, full of interest but not with our former speed, up to my new place on Ninety-fourth Street. The same pictures on the wall, all of Vlashkin, only now everything painted red and black, which was stylish, and new upholstery.

A few years ago there was a book by another member of that fine company, an actress, the one that learned English very good and went uptown—Marya Kavkaz, in which she says certain things regarding Vlashkin. Such as, he was her lover for

self-loving . . . self-neglecting: Henry V, 2.4. 74–75.

eleven years, she's not ashamed to write this down. Without respect for him, his wife and children, or even others who also may have feelings in the matter.

Now, Lillie, don't be surprised. This is called a fact of life. An actor's soul must be like a diamond. The more faces it got the more shining is his name. Honey, you will no doubt love and marry one man and have a couple kids and be happy forever till you die tired. More than that, a person like us don't have to know. But a great artist like Volodya Vlashkin . . . in order to make a job on the stage, he's got to practice. I understand it now, to him life is like a rehearsal.

Myself, when I saw him in *The Father-in-law*—an older man in love with a   65
darling young girl, his son's wife, played by Raisele Maisel—I cried. What he said to this girl, how he whispered such sweetness, how all his hot feelings were on his face . . . Lillie, all this experience he had with me. The very words were the same. You can imagine how proud I was.

So the story creeps to an end.

I noticed it first on my mother's face, the rotten handwriting of time, scribbled up and down her cheeks, across her forehead back and forth—a child could read—it said, old, old, old. But it troubled my heart most to see these realities scratched on Vlashkin's wonderful expression.

First the company fell apart. The theater ended. Esther Leopold died from being very aged. Krimberg had a heart attack. Marya went to Broadway. Also Raisele changed her name to Roslyn and was a big comical hit in the movies. Vlashkin himself, no place to go, retired. It said in the paper, "an actor without peer, he will write his memoirs and spend his last years in the bosom of his family among his thriving grandchildren, the apple of his wife's doting eye."

This is journalism.

We made for him a great dinner of honor. At this dinner I said to him, for   70
the last time, I thought, "Goodbye, dear friend, topic of my life, now we part." And to myself I said further: Finished. This is your lonesome bed. A lady what they call fat and fifty. You made it personally. From this lonesome bed you will finally fall to a bed not so lonesome, only crowded with a million bones.

And now comes? Lillie, guess.

Last week, washing my underwear in the basin, I get a buzz on the phone. "Excuse me, is this the Rose Lieber formerly connected with the Russian Art Theater?"

"It is."

"Well, well, how do you do, Rose? This is Vlashkin."

"Vlashkin! Volodya Vlashkin?"   75

"In fact. How are you, Rose?"

"Living, Vlashkin, thank you."

"You are all right? Really, Rose? Your health is good? You are working?"

"My health, considering the weight it must carry, is first-class. I am back for some years now where I started, in novelty wear."

"Very interesting."   80

"Listen, Vlashkin, tell me the truth, what's on your mind?"

"My mind? Rosie, I am looking up an old friend, an old warmhearted companion of more joyful days. My circumstances, by the way, are changed. I am retired, as you know. Also I am a free man."

"What? What do you mean?"

"Mrs. Vlashkin is divorcing me."

"What come over her? Did you start drinking or something from melancholy?" 85

"She is divorcing me for adultery."

"But, Vlashkin, you should excuse me, don't be insulted, but you got maybe seventeen, eighteen years on me, and even me, all this nonsense—this daydreams and nightmares—is mostly for the pleasure of conversation alone."

"I pointed all this out to her. My dear, I said, my time is past, my blood is as dry as my bones. The truth is, Rose, she isn't accustomed to have a man around all day, reading out loud from the papers the interesting events of our time, waiting for breakfast, waiting for lunch. So all day she gets madder and madder. By nighttime a furious old lady gives me my supper. She has information from the last fifty years to pepper my soup. Surely there was a Judas in that theater, saying every day, 'Vlashkin, Vlashkin, Vlashkin . . .' and while my heart was circulating with his smiles he was on the wire passing the dope to my wife."

"Such a foolish end, Volodya, to such a lively story. What is your plans?"

"First, could I ask you for dinner and the theater—uptown, of course? After 90
this . . . we are old friends. I have money to burn. What your heart desires. Others are like grass, the north wind of time has cut out their heart. Of you, Rosie, I recreate only kindness. What a woman should be to a man, you were to me. Do you think, Rosie, a couple of old pals like us could have a few good times among the material things of this world?"

My answer, Lillie, in a minute was altogether. "Yes, yes, come up," I said. "Ask the room by the switchboard, let us talk."

So he came that night and every night in the week, we talked of his long life. Even at the end of time, a fascinating man. And like men are, too, till time's end, trying to get away in one piece.

"Listen, Rosie," he explains the other day. "I was married to my wife, do you realize, nearly half a century. What good was it? Look at the bitterness. The more I think of it, the more I think we would be fools to marry."

"Volodya Vlashkin," I told him straight, "when I was young I warmed your cold back many a night, no questions asked. You admit it, I didn't make no demands. I was softhearted. I didn't want to be called Rosie Lieber, a breaker up of homes. But now, Vlashkin, you are a free man. How could you ask me to go with you on trains to stay in strange hotels, among Americans, not your wife? Be ashamed."

So now, darling Lillie, tell this story to your mama from your young mouth. 95
She don't listen to a word from me. She only screams, "I'll faint, I'll faint," Tell her after all I'll have a husband, which, as everybody knows, a woman should have at least one before the end of the story.

My goodness, I am already late. Give me a kiss. After all, I watched you grow from a plain seed. So give me a couple wishes on my wedding day. A long and happy life. Many years of love. Hug Mama, tell her from Aunt Rose, goodbye and good luck.

LESLIE MARMON SILKO   (b. 1948)

Lullaby   *1981*

The sun had gone down but the snow in the wind gave off its own light. It came in thick tufts like new wool—washed before the weaver spins it. Ayah reached out for it like her own babies had, and she smiled when she remembered how she had laughed at them. She was an old woman now, and her life had become memories. She sat down with her back against the wide cottonwood tree, feeling the rough bark on her back bones; she faced east and listened to the wind and snow sing a high-pitched Yeibechei song. Out of the wind she felt warmer, and she could watch the wide fluffy snow fill in her tracks, steadily, until the direction she had come from was gone. By the light of the snow she could see the dark outline of the big arroyo° a few feet away. She was sitting on the edge of Cebolleta Creek, where in the springtime the thin cows would graze on grass already chewed flat to the ground. In the wide deep creek bed where only a trickle of water flowed in the summer, the skinny cows would wander, looking for new grass along winding paths splashed with manure.

Ayah pulled the old Army blanket over her head like a shawl. Jimmie's blanket—the one he had sent to her. That was a long time ago and the green wool was faded, and it was unraveling on the edges. She did not want to think about Jimmie. So she thought about the weaving and the way her mother had done it. On the tall wooden loom set into the sand under a tamarack tree for shade. She could see it clearly. She had been only a little girl when her grandma gave her the wooden combs to pull the twigs and burrs from the raw, freshly washed wool. And while she combed the wool, her grandma sat beside her, spinning a silvery strand of yarn around the smooth cedar spindle. Her mother worked at the loom with yarns dyed bright yellow and red and gold. She watched them dye the yarn in boiling black pots full of beeweed petals, juniper berries, and sage. The blankets her mother made were soft and woven so tight that rain rolled off them like birds' feathers. Ayah remembered sleeping warm on cold windy nights, wrapped in her mother's blankets on the hogan's° sandy floor.

The snow drifted now, with the northwest wind hurling it in gusts. It drifted up around her black overshoes—old ones with little metal buckles. She smiled at the snow which was trying to cover her little by little. She could remember when they had no black rubber overshoes; only the high buckskin leggings that they wrapped over their elkhide moccasins. If the snow was dry or frozen, a person could walk all day and not get wet; and in the evenings the beams of the ceiling would hang with lengths of pale buckskin leggings, drying out slowly.

She felt peaceful remembering. She didn't feel cold any more. Jimmie's blanket seemed warmer than it had ever been. And she could remember the morning he was born. She could remember whispering to her mother, who was sleeping on the other side of the hogan, to tell her it was time now. She did not want to wake the others. The second time she called to her, her mother stood up and pulled on her shoes; she knew. They walked to the old stone hogan together, Ayah walking

arroyo: A narrow ravine or stream bed.
hogan: Navajo Indian dwelling made of earth and timbers.

a step behind her mother. She waited alone, learning the rhythms of the pains while her mother went to call the old woman to help them. The morning was already warm even before dawn and Ayah smelled the bee flowers blooming and the young willow growing at the springs. She could remember that so clearly, but his birth merged into the births of the other children and to her it became all the same birth. They named him for the summer morning and in English they called him Jimmie.

It wasn't like Jimmie died. He just never came back, and one day a dark   5
blue sedan with white writing on its doors pulled up in front of the boxcar shack where the rancher let the Indians live. A man in a khaki uniform trimmed in gold gave them a yellow piece of paper and told them that Jimmie was dead. He said the Army would try to get the body back and then it would be shipped to them; but it wasn't likely because the helicopter had burned after it crashed. All of this was told to Chato because he could understand English. She stood inside the doorway holding the baby while Chato listened. Chato spoke English like a white man and he spoke Spanish too. He was taller than the white man and he stood straighter too. Chato didn't explain why; he just told the military man they could keep the body if they found it. The white man looked bewildered; he nodded his head and he left. Then Chato looked at her and shook his head, and then he told her, "Jimmie isn't coming home anymore," and when he spoke, he used the words to speak of the dead. She didn't cry then, but she hurt inside with anger. And she mourned him as the years passed, when a horse fell with Chato and broke his leg, and the white rancher told them he wouldn't pay Chato until he could work again. She mourned Jimmie because he would have worked for his father then; he would have saddled the big bag horse and ridden the fence lines each day, with wire cutters and heavy gloves, fixing the breaks in the barbed wire and putting the stray cattle back inside again.

She mourned him after the white doctors came to take Danny and Ella away. She was at the shack alone that day they came. It was back in the days before they hired Navajo women to go with them as interpreters. She recognized one of the doctors. She had seen him at the children's clinic at Cañoncito about a month ago. They were wearing khaki uniforms and they waved papers at her and a black ball-point pen, trying to make her understand their English words. She was frightened by the way they looked at the children, like the lizard watches the fly. Danny was swinging on the tire swing on the elm tree behind the rancher's house, and Ella was toddling around the front door, dragging the broomstick horse Chato made for her. Ayah could see they wanted her to sign the papers, and Chato had taught her to sign her name. It was something she was proud of. She only wanted them to go, and to take their eyes away from her children.

She took the pen from the man without looking at his face and she signed the papers in three different places he pointed to. She stared at the ground by their feet and waited for them to leave. But they stood there and began to point and gesture at the children. Danny stopped swinging. Ayah could see his fear. She moved suddenly and grabbed Ella into her arms; the child squirmed, trying to get back to her toys. Ayah ran with the baby toward Danny; she screamed for him to run and then she grabbed him around his chest and carried him too. She ran south into the foothills of juniper trees and black lava rock. Behind her she heard the doctors running, but they had been taken by surprise, and as the hills became steeper and the cholla cactus were thicker, they stopped. When she reached the top of the hill, she stopped to listen in case they were circling around her. But in a few minutes she heard a car engine start and they drove away. The children had been too surprised to cry while she ran with them. Danny was shaking and Ella's little fingers were gripping Ayah's blouse.

She stayed up in the hills for the rest of the day, sitting on a black lava boulder in the sunshine where she could see for miles all around her. The sky was light blue and cloudless, and it was warm for late April. The sun warmth relaxed her and took the fear and anger away. She lay back on the rock and watched the sky. It seemed to her that she could walk into the sky, stepping through clouds endlessly. Danny played with little pebbles and stones, pretending they were birds eggs and then little rabbits. Ella sat at her feet and dropped fistfuls of dirt into the breeze, watching the dust and particles of sand intently. Ayah watched a hawk soar high above them, dark wings gliding; hunting or only watching, she did not know. The hawk was patient and he circled all afternoon before he disappeared around the high volcanic peak the Mexicans called Guadalupe.

Late in the afternoon, Ayah looked down at the gray boxcar shack with the paint all peeled from the wood; the stove pipe on the roof was rusted and crooked. The fire she had built that morning in the oil drum stove had burned out. Ella was asleep in her lap now and Danny sat close to her, complaining that he was hungry; he asked when they would go to the house. "We will stay up here until your father comes," she told him, "because those white men were chasing us." The boy remembered then and he nodded at her silently.

If Jimmie had been there he could have read those papers and explained   10
to her what they said. Ayah would have known then, never to sign them. The doctors came back the next day and they brought a BIA° policeman with them. They told Chato they had her signature and that was all they needed. Except for the kids. She listened to Chato sullenly; she hated him when he told her it was the old woman who died in the winter, spitting blood; it was her old grandma who had given the children this disease. "They don't spit blood," she said coldly. "The whites lie." She held Ella and Danny close to her, ready to run to the hills again. "I want a medicine man first," she said to Chato, not looking at him. He shook his head. "It's too late now. The policeman is with them. You signed the paper." His voice was gentle.

It was worse than if they had died: to lose the children and to know that somewhere, in a place called Colorado, in a place full of sick and dying strangers, her children were without her. There had been babies that died soon after they were born, and one that died before he could walk. She had carried them herself, up to the boulders and great pieces of the cliff that long ago crashed down from Long Mesa; she laid them in the crevices of sandstone and buried them in fine brown sand with round quartz pebbles that washed down the hills in the rain. She had endured it because they had been with her. But she could not bear this pain. She did not sleep for a long time after they took her children. She stayed on the hill where they had fled the first time, and she slept rolled up in the blanket Jimmie had sent her. She carried the pain in her belly and it was fed by everything she saw: the blue sky of their last day together and the dust and pebbles they

BIA: Bureau of Indian Affairs.

played with; the swing in the elm tree and broomstick horse choked life from her. The pain filled her stomach and there was no room for food or for her lungs to fill with air. The air and the food would have been theirs.

She hated Chato, not because he let the policeman and doctors put the screaming children in the government car, but because he had taught her to sign her name. Because it was like the old ones always told her about learning their language or any of their ways: it endangered you. She slept alone on the hill until the middle of November when the first snows came. Then she made a bed for herself where the children had slept. She did not lie down beside Chato again until many years later, when he was sick and shivering and only her body could keep him warm. The illness came after the white rancher told Chato he was too old to work for him anymore, and Chato and his old woman should be out of the shack by the next afternoon because the rancher had hired new people to work there. That had satisfied her. To see how the white man repaid Chato's years of loyalty and work. All of Chato's fine-sounding English talk didn't change things.

It snowed steadily and the luminous light from the snow gradually diminished into the darkness. Somewhere in Cebolleta a dog barked and other village dogs joined with it. Ayah looked in the direction she had come, from the bar where Chato was buying the wine. Sometimes he told her to go on ahead and wait; and then he never came. And when she finally went back looking for him, she would find him passed out at the bottom of the wooden steps to Azzie's Bar. All the wine would be gone and most of the money too, from the pale blue check that came to them once a month in a government envelope. It was then that she would look at his face and his hands, scarred by ropes and the barbed wire for all those years, and she would think, this man is a stranger; for forty years she had smiled at him and cooked his food, but he remained a stranger. She stood up again, with the snow almost to her knees, and she walked back to find Chato.

It was hard to walk in the deep snow and she felt the air burn in her lungs. She stopped a short distance from the bar to rest and readjust the blanket. But this time he wasn't waiting for her on the bottom step with his old Stetson hat° pulled down and his shoulders hunched up in his long wool overcoat.

She was careful not to slip on the wooden steps. When she pushed the door 15 open, warm air and cigarette smoke hit her face. She looked around slowly and deliberately, in every corner, in every dark place that the old man might find to sleep. The bar owner didn't like Indians in there, especially Navajos, but he let Chato come in because he could talk Spanish like he was one of them. The men at the bar stared at her, and the bartender saw that she left the door open wide. Snowflakes were flying inside like moths and melting into a puddle on the oiled wood floor. He motioned to her to close the door, but she did not see him. She held herself straight and walked across the room slowly, searching the room with every step. The snow in her hair melted and she could feel it on her forehead. At the far corner of the room, she saw red flames at the mica window of the old stove door; she looked behind the stove just to make sure. The bar got quiet

Stetson hat: A high, broad-brimmed hat worn by Western cowboys.

except for the Spanish polka music playing on the jukebox. She stood by the stove and shook the snow from her blanket and held it near the stove to dry. The wet wool smell reminded her of new-born goats in early March, brought inside to warm near the fire. she felt calm.

In past years they would have told her to get out. But her hair was white now and her face was wrinkled. They looked at her like she was a spider crawling slowly across the room. They were afraid; she could feel the fear. She looked at their faces steadily. They reminded her of the first time the white people brought her children back to her that winter. Danny had been shy and hid behind the thin white woman who brought them. And the baby had not known her until Ayah took her into her arms, and then Ella had nuzzled close to her as she had when she was nursing. The blonde woman was nervous and kept looking at a dainty gold watch on her wrist. She sat on the bench near the small window and watched the dark snow clouds gather around the mountains; she was worrying about the unpaved road. She was frightened by what she saw inside too: the strips of venison drying on a rope across the ceiling and the children jabbering excitedly in a language she did not know. So they stayed for only a few hours. Ayah watched the government car disappear down the road and she knew they were already being weaned from these lava hills and from this sky. The last time they came was in early June, and Ella stared at her the way the men in the bar were now staring. Ayah did not try to pick her up; she smiled at her instead and spoke cheerfully to Danny. When he tried to answer her, he could not seem to remember and he spoke English words with the Navajo. But he gave her a scrap of paper that he had found somewhere and carried in his pocket; it was folded in half, and he shyly looked up at her and said it was a bird. She asked Chato if they were home for good this time. He spoke to the white woman and she shook her head. "How much longer?" he asked, and she said she didn't know; but Chato saw how she stared at the boxcar shack. Ayah turned away then. She did not say good-bye.

She felt satisfied that the men in the bar feared her. Maybe it was her face and the way she held her mouth with teeth clenched tight, like there was nothing anyone could do to her now. She walked north down the road, searching for the old man. She did this because she had the blanket, and there would be no place for him except with her and the blanket in the old adobe barn near the arroyo. They always slept there when they came to Cebolleta. If the money and the wine were gone, she would be relieved because then they could go home again; back to the old hogan with a dirt roof and rock walls where she herself had been born. And the next day the old man could go back to the few sheep they still had, to follow along behind them, guiding them, into dry sandy arroyos where sparse grass grew. She knew he did not like walking behind old ewes when for so many years he rode big quarter horses and worked with cattle. But she wasn't sorry for him; he should have known all along what would happen.

There had not been enough rain for their garden in five years; and that was when Chato finally hitched a ride into the town and brought back brown boxes of rice and sugar and big tin cans of welfare peaches. After that, at the first of the month they went to Cebolleta to ask the postmaster for the check;

and then Chato would go to the bar and cash it. They did this as they planted the garden every May, not because anything would survive the summer dust, but because it was time to do this. The journey passed the days that smelled silent and dry like the caves above the canyon with yellow painted buffaloes on their walls.

He was walking along the pavement when she found him. He did not stop or turn around when he heard her behind him. She walked beside him and she noticed how slowly he moved now. He smelled strong of woodsmoke and urine. Lately he had been forgetting. Sometimes he called her by his sister's name and she had been gone for a long time. Once she had found him wandering on the road to the white man's ranch, and she asked him why he was going that way; he laughed at her and said, "You know they can't run that ranch without me," and he walked on determined, limping on the leg that had been crushed many years before. Now he looked at her curiously, as if for the first time, but he kept shuffling along, moving slowly along the side of the highway. His gray hair had grown long and spread out on the shoulders of the long overcoat. He wore the old felt hat pulled down over his ears. His boots were worn out at the toes and he had stuffed pieces of an old red shirt in the holes. The rags made his feet look like little animals up to their ears in snow. She laughed at his feet, the snow muffled the sound of her laugh. He stopped and looked at her again. The wind had quit blowing and the snow was falling straight down; the southeast sky was beginning to clear and Ayah could see a star.

"Let's rest awhile," she said to him. They walked away from the road and   20
up the slope to the giant boulders that had tumbled down from the red sandrock mesa throughout the centuries of rainstorms and earth tremors. In a place where the boulders shut out the wind, they sat down with their backs against the rock. She offered half of the blanket to him and they sat wrapped together.

The storm passed swiftly. The clouds moved east. They were massive and full, crowding together across the sky. She watched them with the feeling of horses— steely blue-gray horses startled across the sky. The powerful haunches pushed into the distances and the tail hairs streamed white mist behind them. The sky cleared. Ayah saw that there was nothing between her and the stars. The light was crystalline. There was no shimmer, no distortion through earth haze. She breathed the clarity of the night sky; she smelled the purity of the half moon and the stars. He was lying on his side with his knees pulled up near his belly for warmth. His eyes were closed now, and in the light from the stars and the moon, he looked young again.

She could see it descend out of the night sky: an icy stillness from the edge of the thin moon. She recognized the freezing. It came gradually, sinking snowflake by snowflake until the crust was heavy and deep. It had the strength of the stars in Orion, and its journey was endless. Ayah knew that with the wine he would sleep. He would not feel it. She tucked the blanket around him, remembering how it was when Ella had been with her; and she felt the rush so big inside her heart for the babies. And she sang the only song she knew to sing for babies. She could not remember if she had ever sung it to her children, but she knew that her grandmother had sung it and her mother had sung it:

The earth is your mother,
      she holds you.
The sky is your father,
      he protects you.
Sleep,
sleep.
Rainbow is your sister,
      she loves you.
The winds are your brothers,
      they sing to you.
Sleep,
sleep.
We are together always
We are together always
There never was a time
when this
was not so.

POETRY

12

Meeting Poetry: Simple Theme and Form

Poetry and **poem** describe a wide variety of spoken and written forms, styles, and patterns, and also a wide variety of subjects. Because of this variety, it is not possible to make a single, comprehensive definition. The origin is the Greek word *poiema*; that is, "something made or fashioned [in words]"—a meaning that applies to both poetry and poems. Naturally, a **poet** is a person who does the making or fashioning. Rather than seek brief definitions that limit more than they explain, we believe the best way to understand poetry is to read it, learn it, experience it, and enjoy it. As your understanding deepens you will develop your own ideas, and, let us hope, your own definitions.

Let us begin right away with a poem based in the life of students and teachers alike:

BILLY COLLINS   (b. 1941)

Schoolsville   1985

Glancing over my shoulder at the past,
I realize the number of students I have taught
is enough to populate a small town.

I can see it nestled in a paper landscape,
chalk dust flurrying down in winter,   5
nights dark as a blackboard.

The population ages but never graduates.
On hot afternoons they sweat the final in the park
and when it's cold they shiver around stoves

reading disorganized essays out loud.   10
A bell rings on the hour and everybody zigzags
in the streets with their books.

I forgot all their last names first and their
first names last in alphabetical order.
But the boy who always had his hand up   15
is an alderman and owns the haberdashery.
The girl who signed her papers in lipstick
leans against the drugstore, smoking,
brushing her hair like a machine.

Their grades are sewn into their clothes   20
like references to Hawthorne.   [*i.e., The Scarlet Letter*]
The A's stroll along with other A's.
The D's honk whenever they pass another D.

All the creative writing students recline
on the courthouse lawn and play the lute.   25
Wherever they go, they form a big circle.

Needless to say, I am the mayor.
I live in the white colonial at Maple and Main.
I rarely leave the house. The car deflates
in the driveway. Vines twirl around the porchswing.   30

Once in a while a student knocks on the door
with a term paper fifteen years late
or a question about Yeats or double-spacing.
And sometimes one will appear in a window pane
to watch me lecturing the wall paper,   35
quizzing the chandelier, reprimanding the air.

QUESTIONS

1. What are the circumstances in this poem? Why is the poem entitled "Schools-ville"? Is this title appropriate?

2. Describe the profession, current situation, and characteristics of the speaker. What attitudes do you find in the poem about the speaker, and about the speaker's past students?

3. What recognizable situations from school experiences do you find here? Are the details of these situations appropriate to the poem? To what degree are the situations exaggerated? What things being described are funny? What things in the poem indicate a sense of tolerance and affection?

4. Compare the details of this poem with those in Theodore Roethke's "Dolor" (p. 594). Though the specific details of the two poems differ, what similarities do you find in the choice and appropriateness of detail? What differences do you note in your impressions of the two poems?

The Collins poem shows us much about poetry. The topic material is drawn from life—the life we have all experienced in various schools or colleges. The references are introduced to make assertions about life, not to tell a story, although many poems may indeed tell stories. The connecting element in the poem is therefore the fanciful and comic but also affectionate views the speaker expresses about the sameness and also the changes that characterize school life. The detail in the poem is sharply observed and recorded, such as the chalk dust flurrying down like snow, the girl who signs her name in lipstick, and the students forming a circle when they meet. The poem is arranged in lines, but does not follow measured rhythmical patterns, nor does it rhyme. The most important thing about it is that, as it engages us and amuses us, it also rings of truth. Once we have read and followed the poem, we will not forget it, and it will echo in our minds as time passes. Like all good poetry, in short, this poem is alive, and if we read it sensitively it will become a part of us.

THE NATURE OF POETRY

"Schoolsville" is unique; it is at once serious and original, and it is also amusing. There is no other poem like it. Indeed, all good poems are unique in their own ways, and because this is so we cannot formulate a single definition of poetry to account for all poems. Nevertheless, we can offer a number of descriptive statements about poetry that may be helpful. To begin with, poems are imaginative works expressed in words that are used with the utmost compression, force, and economy. Unlike prose, which is expansive and exhaustive, most poems are brief but also comprehensive, offering us high points of thought, feeling, reflection, and resolution. Poems may take just about any shape that permits coherence and development, from a line of a single word to lines of twenty, thirty, or more words, and these lines may be organized into any number of repeating or nonrepeating patterns. Some poems may make us think, give us new and unexpected insights, and generally instruct us, while other poems may arouse our emotions, surprise us, amuse us, and inspire us. Ideally, reading and understanding poetry should prompt us to reexamine, reinforce, and reshape our ideas, our attitudes, our feelings, and our lives.

POETRY IN THE ENGLISH LANGUAGE

Today, most nations with their own languages have their own literatures, including poetry, with their own unique characteristics and histories. In this anthology we are concerned with poetry in our own language by American, English, and Canadian poets.

The earliest poems in English date back to late in the period of Old English (A.D. 450–1150). Many of these early English poems reflect the influence of Christianity. Indeed, the most famous poem, the epic *Beowulf*, was probably interpreted as a Christian allegory even though it concerns the secular themes of adventure, courage, and war. Ever since the Middle English period (A.D. 1150–1500), poets have written about many other subjects, even though religious themes have also maintained their importance. Today, we may find poetry on virtually all topics.

In short, poetry is alive and flourishing. People read it aloud in front of audiences, friends, and families, and also silently in the privacy of their rooms. Set to music and sung aloud, poetry can be exceedingly powerful. Francis Scott Key's "The Star-Spangled Banner," for example, which he wrote about events in a battle in the War of 1812, has become our national anthem. More recently, musical groups like The Beatles and U-2, along with the solo singer Bruce Springsteen, have gained great popularity by expressing ideas that masses of people have taken to heart. Ever since the 1960s, people devoted to civil rights have been strengthened and unified by the simple lyrics of "We Shall Overcome," not only in the United States but throughout the world. The strength and vitality of poetry could be similarly documented time and time again.

HOW POETRY WORKS

With poetry, as with any other form of literature, the more effort we put into understanding, the greater will be our reward. Poems are often about subjects that we have never experienced directly ourselves; we never met the poet, never had his or her exact experiences, and never thought about things in exactly the same way. To recapture the experience of the poem, we need to understand the language, ideas, attitudes, and frames of reference that will make the poem come alive. Consider the following poem by an American poet:

RANDALL JARRELL   (1914–1965)

The Death of the Ball Turret Gunner   *1945*

From my mother's sleep I fell into the State
And I hunched in its belly till my wet fur froze.
Six miles from earth, loosed from its dream of life,
I woke to black flak and the nightmare fighters.
When I died they washed me out of the turret with a hose.   5

To understand and appreciate this poem, we need to know a number of things: The topic is the violent death of a gunner on a World War II bomber, imagined as being told by the dead gunner himself. The poet, Jarrell, tells us in a note that "a ball turret was a Plexiglas sphere set into the belly of a B-17 or B-24 [both large, four-engine, high-altitude, precision-bombing aircraft] and inhabited by two .50-calibre machine guns and one man, a short small man. When this gunner tracked with his machine guns a fighter attacking his bomber from below, he revolved with the turret; hunched upside-down in his little sphere, he looked like a fetus in the womb. The fighters which attacked him were armed with cannon firing exploding shells. The hose was a steam hose." We add that *Flak* (an acronym from the German word for anti-aircraft gun, *FLiegerAbwehrKanone*) describes the high-altitude explosions of anti-aircraft shells fired from the ground.

This explanation helps us understand and experience Jarrell's poem. It does not make us smile, like Collins's "Schoolsville," but instead it dramatizes the grisly reality of aerial warfare in World War II. The opening comparison draws a parallel between an infant in the womb and the gunner in his little sphere. Thus the "wet fur" of line 2 refers specifically to the fur collar of a flight jacket, and it also suggests the hair of an unborn or newly born infant or animal. Expanding on this comparison, the poem suggests that the gunner is typical of young men who fight in war and die before they become adults. The gunner's death is particularly horrible. His identity is reduced to insignificance by the image of his mangled and shapeless remains being washed "out of the turret with a hose." Although there is no explicitly stated message or moral, we may easily conclude that Jarrell is saying that war is mindless, brutal, indifferent, and wasteful.

HOW TO READ A POEM

Carefully, thoughtfully, and sympathetically. These words sum up the best approach to reading poetry. The economy and compression of poetry mean that every part of the poem must carry some of the impact and meaning, and thus every part repays careful attention. There should be an interaction between the poem and you, the reader. You cannot sit back and expect the poem (or the poet) to do all the work. The poem contributes its language, imagery, rhythms, ideas, and all the other aspects that make it poetry, but you, the reader, will need to open your mind to the poem's impact.

No single technique for reading poetry can guarantee a valuable and enjoyable experience, but we can suggest general approaches that will help you read, absorb, and appreciate poems. In Chapter 1, we suggest a number of steps that you might take with any work of literature (pp. 11–13). These are also applicable for studying poetry. In addition, read each poem more than once, keeping a number of objectives in mind. These are:

1. *Read straight through to get a general sense of what the poem is about.* In this first reading, do not stop to puzzle out difficult passages or obscure words; just read through from beginning to end.

2. *Develop an understanding of the basic meaning and organization of the poem.* As you read and reread the poem, study the following:

a. THE TITLE. The title usually supplies important information. The title "Death of the Ball Turret Gunner" tells about the subject and the circumstances of the poem, while the title of Robert Frost's "Stopping by Woods on a Snowy Evening" tells us about the poem's setting and situation.

b. THE SPEAKER. The poem is usually a dramatic construction, with a speaker who may be "inside," as a person directly involved in the action (like the gunner in "The Death of the Ball Turret Gunner"), or "outside," as in "Sir Patrick Spens," in which the speaker is an observer uninvolved in the action, much like a third-person speaker in prose fiction (see Chapter 5, pp. 199–200).

c. THE MEANING OF FAMILIAR AND UNFAMILIAR WORDS. Some poems are written in a style that is immediately clear to you, but with other poems you will need to look up unfamiliar words (and sometimes even familiar words) and references. You therefore will need help from dictionaries, encyclopedias, reference works on mythology, and so on. Take as much time as you need for looking things up, for when you are finished you should have developed a fairly clear grasp of the poem's content. If you are unable to locate a reference, or if you continue having difficulty even after using your sources, be sure to ask your instructor.

d. THE SETTING AND SITUATION OF THE POEM. Some poems establish their settings and circumstances vividly. "Stopping by Woods on a Snowy Evening," for example, describes a scene in which the speaker stops his horse-drawn sleigh by a woods in the evening, during a snowfall, so that he may watch the snow pile up amid the trees. Although many poems do not establish setting and situation so clearly or so quickly, you should always try to figure out as much as you can about the *where* and *when* of a given poem.

e. THE SUBJECT AND THEME OF THE POEM. The subject indicates the general or specific topic, while the theme refers to the idea or ideas that the poem explores. Jarrell's poem announces its subject in the title. The theme, however, concerns the destructiveness of war and the senseless brutality of death in battle, the poignancy of the loss of young lives, the stupidity of state-directed hostilities, the callousness and indifference of the living toward the dead, and the suddenness with which war forces young people to face cruelty and horror.

f. THE BASIC FORM AND DEVELOPMENT OF THE POEM. Some poems, like "Sir Patrick Spens," are narratives; others, like "Death of the Ball Turret Gunner," are personal statements; still others may be speeches to another person. The poems may be in a sonnet form, or may develop in two-line sequences (couplets). They may contain stanzas, each of which is unified by a particular action or thought. Try to determine the form and to trace the way in which the poem unfolds, part by part.

3. *Read the poem aloud, sounding each word clearly.* This reading will give you the chance to hear the music of the poem, and to assess the contributions that rhythm, rhyme, and sound make to the total effect. If you read "Death of the Ball Turret Gunner" aloud, for example, you will notice the impact of rhyming *froze* with *hose* and the suggestion of the percussive sounds of cannon fire in the repeated and rhyming *l, a,* and *k* sounds of *black flak* (for further discussion of sounds in poetry, see Chapter 18).

4. *Prepare a PARAPHRASE of the poem, and make an EXPLICATION of the ideas and themes that you have discovered there.* A **paraphrase** is a restatement of the poem in your own words. Paraphrasing helps you crystallize your understanding. An **explication,** either of brief passages or of the entire poem, goes beyond paraphrase to consider the significance of anything and everything in the poem. In an explication, you may bring out the knowledge and ideas you have gained in your reading and study. Paraphrasing and explication are discussed in detail later on in this chapter.

STUDYING POETRY

Let us now look at a poem in some detail. We have already noted that poems may tell stories. As an example, the following poem was composed orally as a song sometime during the late Middle Ages or early Renaissance, when ordinary people got much of their information about the outside world from strolling balladeers who sang the news to them. It tells a story which is probably true, or which is at least based on a real event.

ANONYMOUS

Sir Patrick Spens   *Fifteenth century*

The king sits in Dumferline town,
 Drinking the blood-red wine:
"O where will I get a good sailor
 To sail this ship of mine?"

Up and spoke an eldern° knight,   *old, elderly*   5
 Sat at the king's right knee:
"Sir Patrick Spens is the best sailor
 That sails upon the sea."

The king has written a braid° letter   *large*
 And signed it wi'° his hand,   *with*   10
And sent it to Sir Patrick Spens,
 Was walking on the sand.

The first line that Sir Patrick read,
  A loud laugh laughèd he;
The next line that Sir Patrick read,   15
  A tear blinded his eye.

"O who is this has done this deed,
  This ill deed done to me,
To send me out this time o' the year,
  To sail upon the sea?"   20

"Make haste, make haste, my merry men all,
  Our good ship sails the morn."
"O say not so, my master dear,
  For I fear a deadly storm.

Late late yestere'en° I saw the new moon   *last evening*   25
  Wi' the old moon in her arm,
And I fear, I fear, my dear master,
  That we will come to harm."

O our Scots nobles were right loath
  To wet their cork-heeled shoon,°   *shoes*   30
But long ere a'° the play were played   *all*
  Their hats they swam aboon.°   *above*

O long, long may their ladies sit,
  Wi' their fans into their hand,
Or e'er they see Sir Patrick Spens   35
  Come sailing to the land.

O long, long may the ladies stand,
  Wi' their gold combs in their hair,
Waiting for their own dear lords,
  For they'll see them no more.   40

Half o'er, half o'er to Aberdour
  It's fifty fathom deep,
And there lies good Sir Patrick Spens,
  Wi' the Scots lords at his feet.

"Sir Patrick Spens" is a type of poem called a **narrative ballad.** A narrative tells a story, and the term *ballad* defines the poem's shape or form. The first two stanzas set up the general situation: The king needs a sailor to undertake a vital mission, and an old knight—one of the king's close advisers—suggests the appointment of Sir Patrick Spens. We know that this knight is a powerful adviser since he sits "at the king's right knee."

The rest of the poem focuses on the feelings and eventual deaths of Sir Patrick and his men. The third stanza provides a transition from the king to Sir Patrick. The king writes a letter ordering Sir Patrick to sea, and Sir Patrick reads it. On reading the first line, Sir Patrick laughs—maybe because the king begins by flattering him, or maybe because Sir Patrick at first believes that an order to go to sea at an obvious time of danger is nothing more than a grim joke. But when he reads the next line and realizes that the order is real, he foresees disaster. He weeps at the prospect of danger, and wonders who (among the king's advisers) is responsible for sending him seaward "this time o' the year." Our sense of impending calamity is increased when we learn that Sir Patrick's crew is also frightened (lines 23–28).

The actual shipwreck, which is described in stanza 8, is presented with ironic understatement. There is no description of the storm or of the crew's panic, nor does the speaker describe the masts splitting or the ship sinking under the waves. Although these horrors are omitted, the floating hats are grim evidence of destruction and death. The remainder of the poem continues in this vein of understatement. In stanzas 9 and 10 the focus shifts back to the land, and to the ladies who will wait a "long, long" time (forever) for Sir Patrick and his men to return. The poem ends with a vision of Sir Patrick and the "Scots lords" lying "fifty fathom deep."

On first reflection, "Sir Patrick Spens" tells a sad tale without complications. The subject seems to be no more than the unfortunate drowning of Sir Patrick and his crew of sailors and Scots noblemen, and one might therefore claim that the poem does not have a clear theme. Even the understated irony of the floating hats and the waiting ladies is reasonably straightforward and unambiguous. However, you might consider what the poem suggests about the conflict between individual judgment and obedience to authority. Sir Patrick knows the risks when he sets sail, yet he still obeys the king's command. There are contradictory and conflicting forces at work here. In addition, there is a suggestion in lines 5 and 32 of political infighting. The "eldern knight" is in effect responsible for the consignment of the ship to the bottom; and the "play" being "played" suggests that a political game is taking place over and beyond the grim game of the men caught in the deadly storm (if Sir Patrick knows the danger, would not the knight also know it, and would this knight not also know the consequences of choosing Sir Patrick?). These political motives are not spelled out, but are implied. Thus the poem is not only a sad tale, but is also a poignant dramatization of how power operates, of how a loyal person responds to a tragic dilemma, and of the pitiful consequences of that response.

In reading poetry, then, let the individual poem be your guide. Get all the words, try to understand dramatic situations, follow the emotional cues provided for you by the poet, and try to develop explanations for everything that is happening. If you find implications in the poem that you believe are important (as with the discussion in the previous paragraph about the political overtones of "Sir Patrick Spens") be sure to support your observations carefully. Resist the temptation to "uncover" unusual or far-fetched elements in the poem (as a student once did by claiming that Frost's "Stopping by Woods on a Snowy Evening" is a celebration of Santa Claus, stopping on Christmas eve for a brief rest before carrying out his mission to deliver presents throughout the world). Draw only those conclusions that the poem itself will support. As long as you follow the poem, and are able to show that your observations are firmly based, your reading of poetry will be an experience that is both exciting and rewarding.

POEMS FOR STUDY

WILLIAM SHAKESPEARE   (1564–1616)

Sonnet 55:
Not Marble, Nor the Gilded Monuments   *1609*

Not marble, nor the gilded monuments
Of princes, shall outlive this powerful rhyme;
But you shall shine more bright in these contents
Than unswept stone, besmeared with sluttish time.
When wasteful war shall statues overturn,   5
And broils root out the work of masonry,
Nor° Mars his° sword nor war's quick fire shall burn   *Neither; Mars's*
The living record of your memory.
'Gainst death and all-oblivious enmity
Shall you pace forth; your praise shall still find room
Even in the eyes of all posterity   10
That wear this world out to the ending doom.°   *Judgment day*
So, till the judgment that yourself arise,
You live in this, and dwell in lovers' eyes.

QUESTIONS

1. Who (or what) is the speaker of this poem?
2. To whom is the poem spoken?
3. What powers of destruction are mentioned in the poem?
4. What does the speaker claim will survive all these forces of destruction?
5. What exactly is "the living record of your memory" mentioned in line 8?
6. What is the subject of the poem? What is the theme?

EMILY DICKINSON (1830–1886)

Because I Could Not Stop for Death   *1890 (c. 1863)*

Because I could not stop for Death –
He kindly stopped for me –
The Carriage held but just Ourselves –
And Immortality.

We slowly drove – He knew no haste   5
And I had put away
My labor and my leisure too,
For His Civility –

We passed the School, where Children strove
At Recess – in the Ring –   10
We passed the Fields of Gazing Grain –
We passed the Setting Sun –

Or rather – He passed Us –
The Dews drew quivering and chill –
For only Gossamer,° my Gown –   *thin fabric*   15
My Tippet° – only Tulle° –   *cape, scarf; thin silk*

We paused before a House that seemed
A Swelling of the Ground –
The Roof was scarcely visible –
The Cornice – in the Ground –   20

Since then – 'tis Centuries – and yet
Feels shorter than the Day
I first surmised the Horses' Heads
Were toward Eternity –

QUESTIONS

1. How is the speaker characterized? Why couldn't she stop for death?

2. How is death characterized in the poem? How is this characterization unconventional?

3. What do the passengers in the carriage pass on their journey? What do these things suggest?

4. What event is suggested by the fact that the sun passes the speaker in line 13?

5. What is the carriage (line 3)? What is the house (line 17)?

6. Where is the speaker in the present time? From what perspective is the poem spoken?

A. E. HOUSMAN (1859–1936)

Loveliest of Trees, the Cherry Now   *1896*

Loveliest of trees, the cherry now
Is hung with bloom along the bough,
And stands about the woodland ride°   *path*
Wearing white for Eastertide.

Now, of my threescore years and ten,   5
Twenty will not come again,
And take from seventy springs a score,
It only leaves me fifty more.

And since to look at things in bloom
Fifty springs are little room,   10
About the woodland I will go
To see the cherry hung with snow.

QUESTIONS

1. In what season or time of year is the poem set?
2. How old is the speaker? How can you tell? Why does he assume he will live
   seventy years ("threescore years and ten")?
3. How would you describe the speaker's perception or sense of time? What is
   the effect of the words *only* (line 8) and *little* (line 10)?
4. What ideas about time, beauty, and life does this poem explore? What does
   it suggest about the way we should live?

THOMAS HARDY (1840–1928)

The Man He Killed   *1902*

"Had he and I but met
    By some old ancient inn,
We should have sat us down to wet
    Right many a nipperkin!°   *half-pint cup*

"But ranged as infantry,   5
    And staring face to face,
I shot at him as he at me,
    And killed him in his place.

"I shot him dead because –
  Because he was my foe.   10
Just so: my foe of course he was;
  That's clear enough; although

"He thought he'd 'list,° perhaps,   *enlist*
  Off-hand like – just as I –
Was out of work – had sold his traps° –   *possessions* 15
  No other reason why.

"Yes; quaint and curious war is!
  You shoot a fellow down
You'd treat if met where any bar is,
  Or help to half-a-crown."°   20

THE MAN HE KILLED.   20 *half a crown*: today about 40 cents, but at the time, the
equivalent of $10 or $20.

QUESTIONS

1. Who and what is the speaker? What do you learn about him?
2. What situation and event is the speaker recalling and relating?
3. What can you deduce about the speaker from his language and choice of
    words?
4. What is the effect produced by repeating the word *because* in lines 9 and 10
    and using the word *although* in line 12?
5. What is the speaker's attitude toward his "foe" and toward what he has done?
6. What point, if any, does this poem make about war? What are the similarities
    between this poem and Jarrell's "The Death of the Ball Turret Gunner"?
    The differences?

ROBERT FROST   (1874–1963)

Stopping By Woods on a Snowy Evening   *1923*

Whose woods these are I think I know.
His house is in the village though;
He will not see me stopping here
To watch his woods fill up with snow.

My little horse must think it queer   5
To stop without a farmhouse near
Between the woods and frozen lake
The darkest evening of the year.

He gives his harness bells a shake
To ask if there is some mistake. 10
The only other sound's the sweep
Of easy wind and downy flake.

The woods are lovely, dark and deep,
But I have promises to keep,
And miles to go before I sleep, 15
And miles to go before I sleep.

QUESTIONS

1. What do we learn about the speaker of this poem? Where is he? What is he doing?

2. What is the setting of this poem? What is the weather like? What time is it?

3. Why do you suppose that the speaker wants to watch the "woods fill up with snow"?

4. What evidence do we find in the poem to conclude that the speaker is embarrassed or self-conscious about stopping? Consider the words *though* in line 2 and *must* in line 5.

5. The last stanza offers two alternative attitudes and courses of action. What are they? Which does the speaker choose?

6. To what extent does the sound of this poem contribute to its impact? Note especially the *s* words in line 11 and the *w* sounds in line 12.

7. How does Frost use the sound of his rhyme words to hold the poem together and link one stanza to the next? How and why is the pattern of rhyme sounds different in the last stanza?

JAMES WRIGHT (1927–1980)

Two Hangovers *1963*

NUMBER ONE
I slouch in bed.
Beyond the streaked trees of my window,
All groves are bare.
Locusts and poplars change to unmarried women 5
Sorting slate from anthracite
Between railroad ties:
The yellow-bearded winter of the depression
Is still alive somewhere, an old man
Counting his collection of bottle caps 10

In a tarpaper shack under the cold trees
Of my grave.

I still feel half drunk,
And all those old women beyond my window
Are hunching toward the graveyard.   15

Drunk, mumbling Hungarian,
The sun staggers in,
And his big stupid face pitches
Into the stove.
For two hours I have been dreaming   20
Of green butterflies searching for diamonds
In coal seams;
And children chasing each other for a game
Through the hills of fresh graves.
But the sun has come home drunk from the sea,   25
And a sparrow outside
Sings of the Hanna Coal Co. and the dead moon.
The filaments of cold light bulbs tremble
In music like delicate birds.
Ah, turn it off.   30

NUMBER TWO: I TRY TO WAKEN AND GREET THE WORLD ONCE AGAIN
In a pine tree,
A few yards away from my window sill,
A brilliant blue jay is springing up and down, up and down,
On a branch.   35
I laugh, as I see him abandon himself
To entire delight, for he knows as well as I do
That the branch will not break.

QUESTIONS

1. What do we learn about the speaker in hangover "Number One"? What is his physical condition? Where is he? What is he trying to do?
2. How does the speaker's condition affect the way he views the trees outside his window? The world? His own life?
3. Who or what is drunk and "mumbling Hungarian" in line 16?
4. Do you think the sun really "staggers in" and falls "into the stove"? What does the sun stand for in "Number One"?
5. Find all the images of death and desolation that you can in "Number One." Why do you suppose these images are so dominant?
6. Why is hangover "Number Two" so much shorter than "Number One"?
7. How does the speaker's mood, attitude, perspective, or tone of voice change from hangover "Number One" to hangover "Number Two"? How do you account for this shift?

PARAPHRASING POETRY

To paraphrase a poem, you rewrite it as prose in your own words. The length of your paraphrase is determined partly by the length of the poem and partly by the amount of detail you include. When you deal with lyrics, sonnets, and other short poems, you may include all the details, and thus your paraphrase may be as long as the work, or even longer. Paraphrases of long poems, however, are usually much shorter than the originals because some details must be summarized briefly while others may be cut out entirely.

Paraphrasing is especially useful in the study of poetry. It fixes both the general shape and the details of a poem in your mind, and also reveals the poetic devices at work. A comparison of the original poem with the paraphrase highlights the techniques and the language that make the poem effective.

In preparing to write a paraphrase, try to be accurate. In your own words, write a version of the poem's actions, statements, and ideas. To help yourself to use only your own words, read through the poem several times; then, put the poem out of sight and write your paraphrase. Next, go back to the poem and check whether you have been accurate and have used only your own words. Paraphrasing also requires that you make careful decisions about detail. If your poem is short, you will probably want to include almost everything. With longer poems, however, you will need to decide which details to include completely, which to include briefly, and which to eliminate entirely. Above all, remain faithful to the poem, but avoid drawing conclusions and making unnecessary explanations. It would be wrong in a paraphrase of Jarrell's "The Death of the Ball Turret Gunner," for example, to begin by asserting that "this poem makes a forceful argument against the brutal and wasteful deaths caused by war." While this assertion might be a good wording of the poem's theme, it does not reflect the *actual content* of the poem.

Organizing Your Paraphrase

In paraphrasing a poem, your task is to rewrite the work in your own words with as little distortion as possible. Your organization should reflect the form or development of the poem. Paraphrase material in the order in which it occurs. When dealing with short poems, organize your paraphrase to reflect the poem's development line by line or stanza by stanza. In paraphrasing Shakespeare's "Not Marble, Nor the Gilded Monuments," for example, you would want to follow the natural subdivisions of the sonnet and deal in sequence with each quatrain and then with the couplet. With longer poems, look for natural divisions like groups of related stanzas, verse paragraphs, or other units suggested by the work. In every situation, the shape of the poem should determine the structure of your paraphrase.

SAMPLE ESSAY

A Paraphrase of Thomas Hardy's "The Man He Killed"*

[1] If the man I killed had met me in an inn, we would have sat down together and had many drinks. But because we belonged to armies of warring footsoldiers lined up on a battlefield, we shot at each other, and my shot killed him.

[2] The reason I killed him, I think, was that he and I were enemies—just that. But as I think of it, I realize that he had enlisted, just the way I did. Perhaps he did it on a whim, or perhaps he had lost his job and sold everything he owned. There was no other reason to enlist.

[3] Being at war is certainly unusual and strange. You are forced to kill a man for whom you would buy a drink, or whom you would help out with half a crown in a time of need.

Commentary on the Essay

Because Hardy's poem is short, the paraphrase attempts to include all its details. The organization closely follows the poem's development. Paragraph 1, for example, restates the contents of the first two stanzas. Paragraph 2 restates stanzas three and four. Finally, the last paragraph paraphrases the last stanza. This stanza is given its own paragraph because it contains the reflections made by the poem's "I" speaker; it concludes the paraphrase just as the last stanza concludes the poem.

Notice that the sample essay does not abstract details from the poem, such as "The dead man might have become a dependable and important friend in peacetime" for stanza 5; neither does it extend details, such as "We would have gotten acquainted, had drinks together, told many stories, and done quite a bit of laughing" for stanza 1 (even though both stanzas suggest these details). Although the poem is a dramatization of strong anti-war sentiments, it would be out of place to use a sentence such as "By his very directness, the narrator brings out the senselessness and brutality of warfare," which discusses these feelings. What is needed is a short restatement of the poem to demonstrate the essay writer's understanding of what the poem actually contains, and no more.

* See p. 528 for this poem.

WRITING AN EXPLICATION OF POETRY

Explication, which means to explain and interpret, gives you an opportunity to show your understanding of a poem, for an explication goes beyond the assimilation required for a paraphrase. A complete explication requires that a poem be examined and explained word by word and line by line— a technique that is also, obviously, exhaustive. Thus, a full explication of a poem like "The Man He Killed" might take twenty or thirty pages (yes, pages). Many sentences would be needed, for example, to consider questions like these: Why does the speaker hesitate in stanza three, when he tries to explain why he killed his "foe"? What sort of ideas of war's justification that he may have heard from others is he unable to reproduce in his own words? After he explains that the other man was his foe, why does he go on to repeat the phrase? How do his hesitation and his subsequent insistence show his true feelings? Does he himself really understand his true feelings? Because of the obvious need to keep essays within limits, therefore, such detailed explication should be limited to a few lines of poetry or to a stanza. The goal is to demonstrate your ability to understand the poem, not your capacity to write about it forever.

The more manageable technique to use is the **general explication,** which devotes attention to the meaning of individual parts in relationship to the entire work, as in the discussion of "Sir Patrick Spens" earlier. You might therefore think of a general explication as your explanation, or as your "reading," of the poem. Literally, everything in the poem could be the subject of your essay. Because your reading is a general one, however, and because you are not expected to go into exhaustive detail, you will need to be selective. Therefore you should prepare to write about things like the general content, the main idea, difficult or unusual words or expressions, and noteworthy elements of style, character, humor, and the like.

Organizing the Essay

In a general explication essay, you demonstrate your ability (a) to follow the essential details of the poem (the same as in paraphrase), (b) to understand the issues and the meaning the poem reveals, (c) to explain some of the relationships of content to technique, and (d) to note and discuss especially important or unique aspects of the poem.

INTRODUCTION. As with any introduction, use your central idea to express a general view of the poem, which your essay will bear out. The discussion of "Sir Patrick Spens" above suggests some possible central ideas, namely that (1) the poem highlights a conflict between self-preservation and obedience to authority, and (2) innocent people may be caught in political infighting. In the following sample essay on Hardy's "The Man

He Killed," the central idea is that the poem shows the senselessness of war. Once you have indicated your central idea, your thesis sentence should indicate the topics you will include in the body.

BODY.   The first thing to include in the body is a brief explanation of what the poem contains, not an exact paraphrase, but your own organizing elements. Hence, if the speaker of the poem is "inside" the poem as a first-person involved "I," you do not need to reproduce this voice yourself, as we did with the sample essay paraphrasing "The Man He Killed." Instead, *describe* the poem in your own words, with whatever brief introductory phrases you find necessary, as in the second paragraph of the following sample essay.

Next, go on to explicate the poem in relationship to your central idea. You choose the order of discussion, depending on your topics. You should, however, keep stressing your central idea with each new topic. Thus, you may wish to follow your description by discussing what you consider to be the poem's meaning, or even by presenting two or more possible interpretations. You might also wish to bring in various techniques as they are significant in the poem. For example, in "Sir Patrick Spens" a noteworthy aspect of technique is the use of unintroduced quotations (i.e., quotations appearing without any "he said" or "quoth he" phrases) as the ballad writer's means of dramatizing the commands and responses of Sir Patrick and his doomed crew. You might also wish to introduce special topics, like the crewman who explains that bad luck is about to follow the phenomenon of the new moon having "the old moon in her arm" (line 26). Such a reference to superstition in the poem might include the explanation of the crewman's assumptions, the relationship of his uneasiness to the remainder of the poem, and also how the ballad writer attains narrative brevity. In short, the body is the place for discussing those aspects of meaning and technique that bear upon the interpretation you wish to assert.

CONCLUSION.   To reinforce the thematic structure of your essay, stress again your major idea in the conclusion. Especially in a general explication, there will be parts of the poem that you will not have discussed. In the conclusion, you might therefore mention what might be gained from an exhaustive discussion of various parts of the poem (do not, however, begin to exhaust any subject in the conclusion of an essay). The last stanza of Hardy's "The Man He Killed," for example, contains the words "quaint and curious" in reference to war. These words are unusual, particularly because the speaker might have chosen "hateful," "senseless," "destructive," or other similarly descriptive words. Why did Hardy have his speaker make such a choice? With brief attention to such a problem, you may conclude.

SAMPLE ESSAY

An Explication of Hardy's "The Man He Killed"*

[1] "The Man He Killed" exposes the senselessness of war.° It does this through a silent contrast between the needs of ordinary people, as represented by a young man—the speaker—who has killed an enemy soldier in battle, and the anti-human and unnatural deaths of war. Of major note in this contrast are the circumstances described by the speaker, his language, his similarity with the dead man, and his typical concerns and wishes.°

[2] The speaker begins by contrasting the circumstances of warfare with those of peace. He does not identify himself, but his speech reveals that he is an ordinary sort—a person, one of "the people"—who enjoys drinking in a bar and who prefers friendship and helpfulness to violence. If he and the man he killed had met in an inn, he says, they would have had many drinks together, but because they met on a battlefield they shot at each other, and he killed the other man. The speaker tries to justify the killing, but can produce no stronger reason than that the dead man was his "foe." Once he states this reason, he again thinks of the similarities between himself and the dead man, and then concludes that warfare is "quaint and curious" (line 17) because one is forced to kill a person he would have befriended if they had met during a time of peace.

[3] To make the irony of warfare clear, the poem uses easy, colloquial language to bring out the speaker's ordinary qualities. His manner of speech is conversational, as in "We should have sat us down" (line 3), and " 'list" (for "enlist," line 13), and his use of "you" in the last stanza. Also, his choice of words is common and informal for the time when the poem was written, as in "nipperkin," "traps," and "fellow" (lines 4, 15, and 18). This language is important, because it establishes that the speaker is an ordinary man who has been thrust into an unnatural role because of war.

[4] As another means of stressing the grim stupidity of war, the poem makes clear that the two men—the live soldier who killed and the dead soldier who was killed—were so alike that they could have been brothers or even twins. They had similar ways of life, similar economic troubles, similar wishes to help other people, and similar motives in doing things like enlisting in the army. Symbolically, at least, the "man he killed" is the speaker himself, and hence warfare forces not only homicide, but suicide. The poem thus raises the question of why two people who are almost identical should be shoved into opposing battle lines in order to try killing each other. This question is rhetorical, for the obvious answer is that there is no good reason at all.

Because the speaker (and also, very likely, the dead man) is shown as a person embodying the virtues of friendliness and helpfulness, Hardy's poem is a strong disapproval of war. Clearly, political reasons for violence as policy are irrelevant to the characters and concerns of the men who fight.

* See p. 528 for this poem.
° Central idea.
° Thesis sentence.

They, like the speaker, would prefer to follow their own needs rather than distant and nameless political leaders. The failure of complex but irrelevant political explanations is brought out most clearly in the third stanza, in which the speaker tries to give a reason for shooting the other man. Hardy's use of punctuation—the dashes—stresses the fact that the speaker has no ideological commitment to the cause he served when killing. Thus the speaker stops at the word "because—" and gropes for a good reason (line 9). Not being subtle or articulate, he can say only "Because he was my foe./Just so: my foe of course he was;/ That's clear enough" (lines 10–12). These short bursts of language indicate that he cannot explain things to himself or to anyone else except in the most obvious and trite terms, and in apparent embarrassment he inserts "of course" as an expected way of emphasizing hostility even though he felt no hostility toward the man he killed.

[5]

A reading thus shows the power of Hardy's dramatic argument in the poem. Hardy does not establish closely detailed reasons against war as a policy, but rather dramatizes the idea that all political arguments are unimportant in view of the central and glaring brutality of war—the killing of human beings by human beings. Hardy's speaker does not seem able to express deep feelings; rather he is confused and perplexed because he is an average sort whose idea of life is to live and let live, and enjoy a drink in a bar with friends. But it is this very commonness that stresses the point that everyone is victimized by war—both those who die and those who are forced to kill. Once the poem is finished, the thoughtful reader reflects that it is a powerful argument for peace and reconciliation.

[6]

Commentary on the Essay

This explication begins by stating a central idea about "The Man He Killed," and then indicates the topics to follow that will develop the idea. Although nowhere does the speaker state that war is senseless, the essay takes the position that the poem embodies this idea. A more detailed examination of the themes of the poem might develop the idea by contrasting the ways in which individuals are caught up in social and political forces that send them to war, or the contrast between individuality and the state. In this essay, however, the simple statement of the idea is sufficient.

Paragraph 2 describes the major details of the poem, with guiding words like "the speaker begins," "he says," and "he again thinks." Thus the paragraph goes over the poem, like a paraphrase, but explains how things occur, as is appropriate for an explication. Paragraph 3 is devoted to the speaker's words and idioms, with the idea that his conversational manner is part of the poem's contrasting method of argument. If the essay were to be a more detailed stylistic analysis, this topic could be more fully developed as an aspect of Hardy's implied arguments against war.

Paragraph 4 is an extension of paragraph 3 inasmuch as it points out the similarities of the speaker and the man he killed. If the situation were reversed, in other words, the dead man might say exactly the same things about the present speaker. It is this affinity that underlies the idea that war is not only senseless, but also suicidal. Paragraph 5 treats the style of the poem's fourth stanza. In this context, the treatment is brief. A fuller treatment for a more detailed explication, by contrast, is suggested above (p. 534). The last paragraph goes over the main idea of the essay, and concludes with a brief tribute to the poem as an argument.

The entire essay, therefore, represents a reading and explanation of the high points of the poem. It stresses a particular interpretation, and briefly shows how various aspects of the poem bear it out.

WRITING TOPICS FOR CHAPTER 12

1. Skim the titles of poems listed in the Table of Contents. Judging by the topics of these poems, describe and discuss the possible range of subject matter for poetry. What topics seem most suitable? Do any topics seem to be ruled out? What additional subject matter would you suggest?

2. How accurate is the proposition that poetry is a particularly compressed form of expression? To support your position, you might refer to poems such as "The Man He Killed" and "Stopping by Woods on a Snowy Evening."

3. Write two poems about the future and your own future plans. In one, begin with the assumption that the world is a stable place and will go on forever. In the other, assume the news that a large asteroid is out of orbit and is hurtling toward earth at great speed, and that a collision, expected in two months, will bring untold destruction, and perhaps even the end of life on earth. After composing your poems, write a brief explanation of how and why they differ in terms of language, references, attitudes toward friends, family, country, religion, and so on.

13

Character and Setting: Who, When, Where, and What

Poets, like other writers, bring their works alive through the interactions of fictional characters who experience love and hatred, pleasure and pain, and all the conditions and situations that life offers. As in fiction, characters in poetry are created and defined by what they say, what they do, how they react with other characters, and what other characters say about them. Because poetry may be developed in many ways other than narrative, however, our concern with character in poems is to see character in relation to someone or something else. The interactions of speakers with listeners or with the reader, the inner conflicts of a speaker discussing the state of his or her spirit, and the issues of love, hate, admiration, emulation, idea, action, and so on that are brought out in the experiences that people have with each other and with the society.

In addition, we may also look to setting as a major means of measuring character (see Chapter 6: "Setting: Place and Objects in Fiction"). Poetic protagonists, like those in stories, are necessarily influenced by the things around them and by the times in which they live. Poems therefore abound with references to events and situations, and also to objects such as beaches, forests, battlefields, graveyards, teaspoons, museums, paintings, and so on. However, while in fiction we consider setting in a number of different ways, in poetry we focus on the influences that object, place, and time have upon character. The time that people have had in a relationship, their relative wealth or poverty, their social and economic circumstances—all have a bearing on what they are like. Later in this chapter we will take a closer look at the relationship of poetic setting to character.

Let us turn now to a discussion of character in poetry. In this anthology we are concerned with three specific character types: the speaker, the listener, and the participant or subject.

CHARACTER IN POETRY

The Speaker or Persona

The most significant of the three character types in poetry is the *speaker*, also called the *persona* (plural *personae*, from the Latin word meaning "mask"). In prose fiction we use "speaker" and "persona" for this character too, but we usually prefer the word *narrator* because of the obvious role of storyteller. Sometimes in poetry the speaker's role is so clearly indicated that the speaker may be taken as a distinct dramatic character, with individual characteristics and a well-imagined and detailed life and background. In Emily Dickinson's "Because I Could Not Stop for Death," for example (p. 527), the speaker states that she has been dead for hundreds of years and is now looking back from eternity to the moment of her death. Her calm acceptance of death as a friendly and supportive ally invites us to interpret death as being different from the more common view involving anguish, pain, and bereavement.

Alternatively, certain poetic speakers act as the embodiment of a particular position or stance which the poet selects for purposes of putting a case or advancing an argument. The poet is thus the undeniable speaker, but the voice we hear may be considered a brief dramatization of an aspect of the poet's personality or need. John Donne in his Holy Sonnets adopts such a stance—the position of a suppliant or penitent praying for divine forgiveness and favor. In these sonnets it is clear that Donne is not just creating a separate dramatic character in deep religious anguish, but that his speaker's hopes and fears are largely his own.

One of the first things to decide in reading a poem is whether the speaker is *inside* or *outside* the poem. What is the **point of view** used by the poet (see Chapter 5, pp. 194–96). The speaker is *inside* the poem if the point of view is first person. Here is such a poem, written by an unknown poet:

Western Wind, When Will Thou Blow?   *Fifteenth century?*

Western wind, when will thou blow?
The small rain down can rain?
Christ, if my love were in my arms,
And I in my bed again.

In this poem the "my" and "I" pronouns indicate that the speaker is *inside* the poem speaking in the first person, wishing for warm spring rains and the renewal of life and love that is signaled by spring.

The speaker is *outside* the poem, however, if the third person is used. In such poems, the speaker is usually not involved with the action; he or she simply describes what is happening to others, as with this anonymous Scots ballad that is likely based on a real-life occurrence:

Bonny George Campbell   *Late sixteenth century*

High upon Highlands
   And low upon Tay,°
Bonny George Campbell
   Rode out on a day.

But toom° came his saddle,   *empty*   5
   All bloody to see,
Oh, home came his good horse,
   But never came he.

Down came his old mother,
   Greeting full sair°   *weeping full sore*   10
And down came his bonny wife,
   Wringing her hair.

Saddled, and bridled,
   And booted rode he;
And home came his good horse,   15
   But never came he.

"My meadow lies green,
   And my corn is unshorn,°   *grain is not harvested*
My barn is to build°   *yet to be built*
   And my babe is unborn."   20

Saddled, and bridled,
   And booted rode he;
Toom home came the saddle,
   But never came he.

BONNY GEORGE CAMPBELL.   2 *Tay*: Loch Tay, a lake in Perth County, Scotland, about sixty miles north of Glasgow.

QUESTIONS

   1. Who are the three characters in this ballad? How fully are they described? What can you deduce about their social status, way of life, and feelings?

2. What has happened to Bonny George Campbell? Why are you left to infer the precise nature of this event?
3. Why are there quotation marks around the fifth stanza? Who is the speaker here? What effect has the absence of George Campbell had upon this speaker?
4. What is the effect of repetition in this poem? How does it shape your responses?

In this ballad the speaker is not involved in the action and dramatically limits his or her perspective to the people left behind, who loved Campbell. They do not learn his precise fate beyond what they learn from the bloody saddle, nor do we, because the speaker does not assume an omniscient stance to tell us. However, the speaker does describe the effects of the loss upon Campbell's mother and wife, even quoting the wife's lamentation because Campbell's death has deprived her of husband, breadwinner, and father of her unborn child. By avoiding entering the poem as an "I," the speaker maintains objectivity and lets the details speak for themselves. No intrusion is necessary, and the result is great poignancy.

Poets have used all sorts of speakers to voice their poems. This anthology contains poems spoken by kings and dukes, husbands and wives, lovers and killers, shepherds, secretaries, civil servants, children, beggars, and almost every other kind of person you can imagine. In addition, you will meet speakers who are gods, historical figures, mythological heroes and heroines, corpses, and ghosts. The speaker in a poem does not even have to be human; animals can be the speakers, or clouds, buildings, whirlwinds, computers, or whatever the imagination may decide.

It's not enough to identify who the speaker is. We must also find out what the speaker does and any other facts we can find in the poem. One place to begin is by considering the poem's title. Take, for example, Marlowe's "The Passionate Shepherd to His Love" (p. 546). This title tells us that the speaker herds sheep for a living, that he has a lady love, and that he is filled with desire. In addition to the title of the poem, we should also look at the speaker's own words, for intentionally or unintentionally, they provide autobiographical information. In "Loveliest of Trees" by A. E. Housman (p. 528), the speaker reveals that he is twenty years old, that he doesn't think his remaining fifty years (the biblical life expectancy) will give him enough time to experience and observe life fully, that he enjoys the flowering of spring, that he knows enough of Church rituals to recognize that the whiteness of cherry blossoms coincides with the liturgical color of white for Easter, and that he is a meditative person. All this is quite a bit of information from so short a poem.

If we look with the same care at every poem we encounter, we will discover many other details about speakers. Grammatical forms, for example, together with choice of words, may define the speaker's social class or educational level. Similarly, the selection of topics may indicate the speaker's knowledge or the lack of it, self-esteem, stance in relation to others, emotional state, personal or philosophical interests, and much more.

The Listener

The second type of character we encounter in poetry is the listener—a person who may be involved with the poem in a number of ways and is therefore addressed as *thou/thy/thee/thine* and *you/your/yours*. Of course if the poem is a dialogue, like Hardy's "The Workbox," the characters are both listeners and speakers. When, however, the listener is silent and passive, such a listener may sometimes be imagined as present, and the poem should be considered a one-way conversation. We will see such examples in this chapter in "The Passionate Shepherd to His Love" by Christopher Marlowe and "The Nymph's Reply to the Shepherd" by Sir Walter Raleigh. The passive listener is not always present, but may instead be the intended recipient of the poem. In this case the speaker is like the writer of a letter while the listener is the "addressee." Such a listener is the *thou/thee/thine* in Ben Jonson's well-known "Drink to Me, Only, with Thine Eyes," in which the speaker is addressing his lady love, who has just spurned him by returning his gift of a "rosy wreath":

BEN JONSON   (1573–1637)

Drink to Me, Only, with Thine Eyes   *1616*

Drink to me, only, with thine eyes,	
And I will pledge° with mine;	*drink a toast*
Or leave a kiss but in the cup,	
And I'll not look for wine.	
The thirst that from the soul doth rise	5
Doth ask a drink divine:	
But might I of Jove's nectar° sup	
I would not change° for thine.	*exchange it [i.e., nectar]*
I sent thee, late, a rosy wreath,	
Not so much honoring thee,	10
As giving it a hope, that there	
It could not withered be.	
But thou thereon did'st only breathe,	
And sent'st it back to me:	
Since when° it grows, and smells, I swear,	*that time, then* 15
Not of itself, but thee.	

DRINK TO ME, ONLY, WITH THINE EYES.   7 *Jove's nectar*: Jove, or Jupiter, was the principal Roman god; nectar was the drink of the gods; a mortal drinking it would attain immortality.

QUESTIONS

1. Who is the speaker? What do you learn about him, his knowledge, his concern for his lady love, his capacity for expression, his ability to develop a thought or comparison? What level of education does he show?
2. Before writing the poem, what has the speaker sent to the object of his affections? What did she do, and why is he still writing to her?
3. Do you think the speaker might be trying to "top" his lady's form of rejection? Does he show interest in pleasing her by his compliments, or does he seem more interested in showing his own ingenuity? Why do you make either of these choices?

Although an imagined listener, like Jonson's ladyfriend, does not participate in the poem, something that person has done has prompted the speaker to begin writing. At least part of the interaction we may therefore consider should concern the listener's possible responses.

A related but distinct type of situation involving a listener is the **dramatic monologue,** in which the speaker talks directly to a present listener who reacts to what the speaker says and who therefore directly affects the course of the poem. Browning's "My Last Duchess" is such a poem. In it the speaker, the Duke, addresses as "you" the listener who has apparently been given the task of arranging financial terms with the Duke about the dowry to be awarded him by the "Count" upon his forthcoming marriage to the Count's daughter.

Ultimately, of course, we as readers are the listeners to all poems, and it is important to determine how the poet establishes this relationship. Sometimes the poet addresses us directly in our role as readers, as in this brief dedicatory poem that Ben Jonson uses to begin his book of epigrams published in 1616:

To the Reader   1616

Pray thee, take care, that tak'st my book in hand,
To read it well: that is, to understand.

Here, we readers are part of a large audience, but the poet speaks to us singly and individually (we are the single "thee . . . that tak'st") as a real member of a group of listeners. Although we are invited to take action (to read well and understand), we are separated from the poem by space and time, and are therefore clearly "outside" the poem.

Only rarely do poets address us directly, as Jonson does. For this reason it is important to determine what is meant when a poet uses the "you" pronoun. Often the "you" may refer to the speaker himself or herself, and not to listeners or to us as readers. The speaker of Hardy's "The

Man He Killed," for example, uses such a conversational *you* as a reference to himself and to people generally (p. 528). Similarly, Richard Hugo's "Degrees of Gray in Philipsburg" (p. 564) begins "You might come here Sunday on a whim." The *you* in this poem is neither the reader nor an internal listener. Rather it is an oblique or indirect way for the speaker to talk about himself. Most of the time, in other words, we are not so much listeners as spectators. In poems like Hardy's "The Workbox" and Browning's "My Last Duchess," we are almost literally an audience, whereas in a poem like Housman's "Loveliest of Trees," we are outside listeners, eavesdropping as the speaker meditates on time, death, and beauty. Most poems will put us, as readers, into situations more or less like the latter one.

The Participant or Subject

Poets also create characters who are either participants or subjects, not speakers or listeners. Thus we are concerned in poetry with appearances, actions, responses, expressions, and speeches—and how we learn about them. As in prose fiction, the speaker is usually a reliable observer whose accuracy about characters is not to be questioned. The speaker of "Sir Patrick Spens" (p. 523), is such a reliable guide, for he or she is straightforward and objective in describing the actions of the king, the adviser, Sir Patrick, the crew, the Scots lords, and the ladies who wait in vain for the ship to return. We may take as true what the poem tells us about these characters. In some poems, however, we should be alert for subjectivity and distortion in the speaker's descriptions of others—also as in prose fiction. In "My Last Duchess," the speaker talks at length about his dead wife, the Duchess, who is one of the three central characters of the poem even though she is no longer "on stage." The poem soon makes clear that we cannot accept the accuracy of the Duke's descriptions of her. We must therefore use our judgment to distinguish her true character from his distortions and lies.

SETTING AND CHARACTER IN POETRY

The people in poetry, like all people, do not exist in a vacuum. They are a product of the time, place, thought, social conventions, and general circumstances of their lives. Let us consider love poetry as an example of the connections that can be made between character and setting. When making arguments in favor of love, the speaking lover might develop assumptions about the condition of the natural and economic world as a part of his or her argument. Thus, the speaker of "The Passionate Shepherd to His Love" speaks of time to be spent in open nature with his lady love, listening to the "madrigals" of birds and sharing the sights of "valleys, groves, hills, and fields." Here his use of setting as an Arcadian dream world is designed as a power of attraction to complement his own. By contrast, the speaker of Hardy's "The Walk" talks about nature at a time when his beloved is infirm, and can no longer share the view of the "hilltop tree / By the gated ways" that the two enjoyed when the world was young and beautiful for them both. The differences between the ages and expectations of the speakers of these two poems indicates the importance of settings involving time and health in the relationships rendered by the poets.

Setting is of course not confined to romantic relationships, but may be used to enhance political, philosophical, and religious thoughts, as in Gray's "Elegy Written in a Country Churchyard." Here the early evening hour, bringing the end of day "in darkness," causes the speaker to think of the "rude forefathers of the hamlet" sleeping in their churchyard graves. This fact prompts him to compare human aims and pretentions with the ultimate fact of death, and he draws conclusions about the human potential, both for good and also for ill, that has been cut off by death. The interaction here is a complex one, involving the constant interweaving of character and history with the natural and cultural descriptions and images. A poem similarly connecting character and setting is Wordsworth's "Lines Composed . . . Above Tintern Abbey." This poem, based on the relationship of the past, present, and future of the speaker to the natural scenes he describes, is a model of the fusion in poetry of setting and character.

It is no exaggeration to say that setting interacts with character in many ways. In Browning's "My Last Duchess," the Duke's art collection forms a setting that exposes his greed, lust for power, and cruelty. Blake's "London" introduces the vision of streets and walls, together with the sounds of cries, sighs, and curses, to evoke a response of repulsion and rejection. As the representation of a philosophical judgment, the setting of Arnold's "Dover Beach" demonstrates the changeability and impermanence of life. The speaker tries to establish a commitment to fidelity in a human relationship as something permanent amid surroundings of change, dissolution, and brutality. To a greater or lesser degree, each poem we encounter will offer similar connections of setting and character.

POEMS FOR STUDY

CHRISTOPHER MARLOWE   (1564–1593)

The Passionate Shepherd to His Love   *1599*

Come live with me and be my love,
And we will all the pleasures prove°   test
That valleys, groves, hills, and fields,
Woods, or steepy mountain yields.

And we will sit upon the rocks,   5
Seeing the shepherds feed their flocks,
By shallow rivers to whose falls
Melodious birds sing madrigals.

And I will make thee beds of roses
And a thousand fragrant posies,   10
A cap of flowers, and a kirtle°   *long dress*
Embroidered all with leaves of myrtle;

A gown made of the finest wool
Which from our pretty lambs we pull;
Fair lined slippers for the cold,   15
With buckles of the purest gold;

A belt of straw and ivy buds,
With coral clasps and amber studs;
And if these pleasures may thee move,
Come live with me, and be my love.   20

The shepherds' swains° shall dance and sing   *lovers*
For thy delight each May morning:
If these delights thy mind may move,
Then live with me and be my love.

QUESTIONS

1. Who is the speaker? What do you learn about the speaker? Describe the speaker's character.
2. Who is the listener? What relationship is established between the speaker and the listener?
3. What specific gifts, and what sort of world, does the speaker offer the listener?
4. What is unrealistic about the conditions of life that the speaker describes? From what is both presented and not presented, how can you determine the speaker's degree of awareness of this unreality?

SIR WALTER RALEIGH   (1552–1618)

The Nymph's Reply to the Shepherd   *1600*

If all the world and love were young,
And truth in every shepherd's tongue,
These pretty pleasures might me move
To live with thee and be thy love.

Time drives the flocks from field to fold°   *fenced field*   5
When rivers rage and rocks grow cold,

And Philomel° becometh dumb;   *the nightingale*
The rest complains of cares to come.

The flowers do fade, and wanton fields
To wayward winter reckoning yields;   10
A honey tongue, a heart of gall,
Is fancy's spring, but sorrow's fall.

Thy gowns, thy shoes, thy beds of roses,
Thy cap, thy kirtle,° and thy posies°   *long dress; flowers and poems*
Soon break, soon wither, soon forgotten—   15
In folly ripe, in reason rotten.

Thy belt of straw and ivy buds,
Thy coral clasps and amber studs,
All these in me no means can move
To come to thee and be thy love.   20

But could youth last and love still° breed,   *always*
Had joys no date nor age no need,
Then these delights my mind might move
To live with thee and be thy love.

QUESTIONS

1. Who is the speaker? What do we learn about the speaker? Who is the listener?

2. How does the form of this poem (rhythm, rhyme pattern, stanza form) relate
    to Marlowe's poem?

3. How are the ideas of love and the world in this poem different from those
    in Marlowe's poem?

4. To what extent is this poem a parody (an imitation that makes fun) of Marlowe's
    poem? To what extent is it a refutation of Marlowe's poem?

5. Determine the steps of the speaker's logical argument in this poem.

THOMAS GRAY   (1716–1771)

Elegy Written in a Country Churchyard   *1751*

The curfew tolls the knell of parting day,
    The lowing herd wind slowly o'er the lea,
The ploughman homeward plods his weary way,
    And leaves the world to darkness and to me.

Now fades the glimm'ring landscape on the sight,   5
    And all the air a solemn stillness holds,

Save where the beetle wheels his droning flight,
  And drowsy tinklings lull the distant folds;

Save that from yonder ivy-mantled tower
  The moping owl does to the moon complain   10
Of such as wand'ring near her secret bower
  Molest her ancient solitary reign.

Beneath those rugged elms, that yew-tree's shade,
  Where heaves the turf in many a mold'ring heap,
Each in his narrow cell forever laid,   15
  The rude forefathers of the hamlet sleep.

The breezy call of incense-breathing morn,
  The swallow twitt'ring from the straw-built shed,
The cock's shrill clarion, or the echoing horn,°   *hunting horn*
  No more shall rouse them from their lowly bed.   20

For them no more the blazing hearth shall burn,
  Or busy housewife ply her evening care;
No children run to lisp their sire's return,
  Or climb his knees the envied kiss to share.

Oft did the harvest to their sickle yield,   25
  Their furrow oft the stubborn glebe° has broke;   *church land*
How jocund did they drive their team afield!
  How bowed the woods beneath their sturdy stroke!

Let not Ambition mock their useful toil
  Their homely joys, and destiny obscure;   30
Nor Grandeur hear with a disdainful smile
  The short and simple annals of the poor.

The boast of heraldry, the pomp of power,
  And all that beauty, all that wealth e'er gave,
Awaits alike th'inevitable hour.   35
  The paths of glory lead but to the grave.

Nor you, ye proud, impute to these the fault,
  If mem'ry o'er their tomb no trophies raise,
Where through the long-drawn aisle and fretted vault
  The pealing anthem swells the note of praise.   40

Can storied urn or animated bust
  Back to its mansion call the fleeting breath?
Can Honor's voice provoke the silent dust,
  Or Flatt'ry soothe the dull cold ear of death?

Perhaps in this neglected spot is laid   45
  Some heart once pregnant with celestial fire;
Hands that the rod of empire might have swayed,
  Or waked to ecstasy the living lyre.

But Knowledge to their eyes her ample page
   Rich with the spoils of time did ne'er unroll;   50
Chill Penury repressed their noble rage,
   And froze the genial current of the soul.

Full many a gem of purest ray serene,
   The dark unfathomed caves of ocean bear;
Full many a flower is born to blush unseen,   55
   And waste its sweetness on the desert air.

Some village Hampden,° that with dauntless breast
   The little tyrant of his fields withstood;
Some mute inglorious Milton here may rest,
   Some Cromwell guiltless of his country's blood.   60

Th'applause of list'ning senates to command,
   The threats of pain and ruin to despise,
To scatter plenty o'er a smiling land,
   And read their hist'ry in a nation's eyes

Their lot forbade: nor circumscribed alone   65
   Their growing virtues, but their crimes confined;
Forbade to wade through slaughter to a throne,
   And shut the gates of mercy on mankind,

The struggling pangs of conscious truth to hide,
   To quench the blushes of ingenuous shame,   70
Or heap the shrine of luxury and pride
   With incense kindled at the Muse's flame.

Far from the madding°crowd's ignoble strife,   *raving*
   Their sober wishes never learned to stray;
Along the cool sequestered vale of life   75
   They kept the noiseless tenor of their way.

Yet ev'n these bones from insult to protect
   Some frail memorial still erected nigh,
With uncouth rhymes and shapeless sculpture decked,
   Implores the passing tribute of a sigh.   80

Their names, their years, spelt by th'unlettered Muse,
   The place of fame and elegy supply;
And many a holy text around she strews,
   That teach the rustic moralist to die.

ELEGY WRITTEN IN A COUNTRY CHURCHYARD.   57 *Hampden*: John Hampden
(1594–1643), English statesman who defended the rights of the people against King Charles
I and who died in the English Civil War of 1642–1646.

For who to dumb forgetfulness a prey,   85
    This pleasing anxious being e'er resigned,
Left the warm precincts of the cheerful day,
    Nor cast one longing ling'ring look behind?

On some fond breast the parting soul relies,
    Some pious drops the closing eye requires;   90
Ev'n from the tomb the voice of Nature cries,
    Ev'n in our ashes live their wonted fires.

For thee, who mindful of th'unhonored dead
    Dost in these lines their artless tale relate;
If chance, by lonely contemplation led,   95
    Some kindred spirit shall inquire thy fate,

Haply some hoary-headed swain may say,
    "Oft have we seen him at the peep of dawn
Brushing with hasty steps the dews away
    To meet the sun upon the upland lawn.   100

"There, at the foot of yonder nodding beech
    That wreathes its old fantastic roots so high,
His listless length at noontide would he stretch
    And pore upon the brook that babbles by.

"Hard by yon wood, now smiling as in scorn,   105
    Mutt'ring his wayward fancies he would rove,
Now drooping, woeful wan, like one forlorn,
    Or crazed with care, or crossed in hopeless love.

"One morn I missed him on the 'customed hill,
    Along the heath and near his fav'rite tree;   110
Another came; nor yet beside the rill,
    Nor up the lawn, nor at the wood was he;

"The next with dirges due in sad array
    Slow through the church-way path we saw him borne.
Approach and read (for thou canst read) the lay,   115
    Graved on the stone beneath yon aged thorn."

The Epitaph
Here rests his head upon the lap of earth
    A youth to fortune and to fame unknown;
Fair Science frowned not on his humble birth,
    And Melancholy marked him for her own.   120

Large was his bounty, and his soul sincere,
    Heav'n did a recompense as largely send:
He gave to mis'ry all he had, a tear:
    He gain'd from Heav'n ('twas all he wished) a friend.

No farther seek his merits to disclose,   125
   Or draw his frailties from their dread abode,
(There they alike in trembling hope repose)
   The bosom of his Father and his God.

QUESTIONS

1. What time of day is described as the time of the speaker's meditation? What
   is happening in nature and the world as the poem opens?
2. Why does it seem natural to shift from the close of day to the "forefathers
   of the hamlet" sleeping in their graves?
3. What kinds of people are buried in the church graveyard? What different
   talents might they have realized and fulfilled if they had not died? On balance,
   has the world been a loser because of these premature deaths?
4. Who is the "thee" of line 93? What sort of life does he lead? What happens
   to him?
5. Describe Gray's use of sights and sounds in the poem. How do these descriptions complement the sober mood that Gray evokes?

WILLIAM BLAKE   (1757–1827)

London   *1794*

I wander thro' each charter'd° street,
Near where the charter'd Thames does flow,
And mark in every face I meet
Marks of weakness, marks of woe.

In every cry of every Man,   5
In every Infant's cry of fear,
In every voice, in every ban,°   *public pronouncement*
The mind-forg'd manacles I hear.

How the Chimney-sweeper's cry
Every blackning Church appalls;°   10
And the hapless Soldier's sigh
Runs in blood down Palace walls.

But most thro' midnight streets I hear
How the youthful Harlot's curse
Blasts the new-born Infant's tear,   15
And blights with plagues the Marriage hearse.

LONDON.   1 *charter'd*: privileged, licensed, authorized.   10 *appalls*: weakens, makes
pale; shocks.

QUESTIONS

1. What does London represent to the speaker? How does the speaker's observation of the persons who live there contribute to the poem's ideas about the oppressed state of humanity?

2. What sounds does the speaker mention specifically as a part of the London scene? What would these sounds be like? Characterize the meaning of these sounds in relation to the poem's main idea.

3. Why are the words *charter'd* and *mark* repeated in the first stanza? Explain the speaker's choice of the words *blast* and *blights* in stanza 4.

4. Because of the tension in the poem between civilized, ordered, regulated activity (as represented in the chartering of the street and the river) and free human impulses, explain how the poem might be considered revolutionary.

5. The poem is part of a collection entitled *Songs of Experience*, which Blake published in 1794. Explain the appropriateness of his including the poem in a collection so named.

WILLIAM WORDSWORTH (1770–1850)

Lines Composed a Few Miles Above Tintern Abbey on Revisiting the Banks of the Wye During a Tour, June 13, 1798°   1798

Five years have past; five summers, with the length
Of five long winters! and again I hear
These waters, rolling from their mountain-springs
With a soft inland murmur.—Once again
Do I behold these steep and lofty cliffs,   5
That on a wild secluded scene impress
Thoughts of more deep seclusion, and connect
The landscape with the quiet of the sky.
The day is come when I again repose
Here, under this dark sycamore, and view   10
These plots of cottage-ground, these orchard-tufts,
Which at this season, with their unripe fruits,
Are clad in one green hue, and lose themselves
'Mid groves and copses. Once again I see
These hedge-rows, hardly hedge-rows, little lines   15
Of sportive wood run wild; these pastoral farms,
Green to the very door; and wreaths of smoke
Sent up, in silence, from among the trees!
With some uncertain notice, as might seem

LINES COMPOSED ABOVE TINTERN ABBEY.   Wordsworth first visited the valley of the Wye in southwest England in August 1793 at age 23. On this second visit he was accompanied by his sister Dorothy (the "friend" in line 115).

Of vagrant dwellers in the houseless woods,   20
Or of some Hermit's cave, where by his fire
The Hermit sits alone.
                              These beauteous forms,
Through a long absence, have not been to me
As is a landscape to a blind man's eye:
But oft, in lonely rooms, and 'mid the din   25
Of towns and cities, I have owed to them
In hours of weariness, sensations sweet,
Felt in the blood, and felt along the heart;
And passing even into my purer mind,
With tranquil restoration:—feelings too   30
Of unremembered pleasure: such, perhaps,
As have no slight or trivial influence
On that best portion of a good man's life,
His little, nameless, unremembered acts
Of kindness and of love. Nor less, I trust,   35
To them I may have owed another gift,
Of aspect more sublime; that blessed mood,
In which the burden of the mystery,
In which the heavy and the weary weight
Of all this unintelligible world,   40
Is lightened:—that serene and blessed mood,
In which the affections gently lead us on,—
Until, the breath of this corporeal frame
And even the motion of our human blood
Almost suspended, we are laid asleep   45
In body, and become a living soul:
While with an eye made quiet by the power
Of harmony, and the deep power of joy,
We see into the life of things.
                                    If this
Be but a vain belief, yet, oh!—how oft—   50
In darkness and amid the many shapes
Of joyless daylight; when the fretful stir
Unprofitable, and the fever of the world,
Have hung upon the beatings of my heart—
How oft, in spirit, have I turned to thee,   55
O sylvan Wye! thou wanderer thro' the woods,
How often has my spirit turned to thee!
   And now, with gleams of half extinguished thought,
With many recognitions dim and faint,
And somewhat of a sad perplexity,   60
The picture of the mind revives again:
While here I stand, not only with the sense
Of present pleasure, but with pleasing thoughts
That in this moment there is life and food
For future years. And so I dare to hope,   65

Though changed, no doubt, from what I was when first
I came among these hills; when like a roe
I bounded o'er the mountains, by the sides
Of the deep rivers, and the lonely streams,
Wherever nature led: more like a man   70
Flying from something that he dreads, than one
Who sought the thing he loved. For nature then
(The coarser pleasures of my boyish days,
And their glad animal movements all gone by)
To me was all in all.—I cannot paint   75
What then I was. The sounding cataract
Haunted me like a passion: the tall rock,
The mountain, and the deep and gloomy wood,
Their colours and their forms, were then to me
An appetite; a feeling and a love,   80
That had no need of a remoter charm,
By thought supplied, nor any interest
Unborrowed from the eye.—That time is past,
And all its aching joys are now no more,
And all its dizzy raptures. Not for this   85
Faint I, nor mourn nor murmur; other gifts
Have followed; for such loss, I would believe,
Abundant recompense. For I have learned
To look on nature, not as in the hour
Of thoughtless youth; but hearing oftentimes   90
The still, sad music of humanity,
Nor harsh nor grating, though of ample power
To chasten and subdue. And I have felt
A presence that disturbs me with the joy
Of elevated thoughts; a sense sublime   95
Of something far more deeply interfused,
Whose dwelling is the light of setting suns,
And the round ocean, and the living air,
And the blue sky, and in the mind of man;
A motion and a spirit, that impels   100
All thinking things, all objects of all thought,
And rolls through all things. Therefore am I still
A lover of the meadows and the woods,
And mountains; and of all that we behold
From this green earth; of all the mighty world   105
Of eye, and ear,—both what they half create,
And what perceive; well pleased to recognize
In nature and the language of the sense,
The anchor of my purest thoughts, the nurse,
The guide, the guardian of my heart, and soul   110
Of all my mortal being.
             Nor perchance,
If I were not thus taught, should I the more

Suffer my genial spirits to decay:
For thou art with me here upon the banks
Of this fair river; thou my dearest Friend,
My dear, dear Friend; and in thy voice I catch   115
The language of my former heart, and read
My former pleasures in the shooting lights
Of thy wild eyes. Oh! yet a little while
May I behold in thee what I was once,   120
My dear, dear Sister! and this prayer I make,
Knowing that Nature never did betray
The heart that loved her; 'tis her privilege,
Through all the years of this our life, to lead
From joy to joy: for she can so inform   125
The mind that is within us, so impress
With quietness and beauty, and so feed
With lofty thoughts, that neither evil tongues,
Rash judgments, nor the sneers of selfish men,
Nor greetings where no kindness is, nor all   130
The dreary intercourse of daily life,
Shall e'er prevail against us, or disturb
Our cheerful faith that all which we behold
Is full of blessings. Therefore let the moon
Shine on thee in thy solitary walk;   135
And let the misty mountain-winds be free
To blow against thee: and, in after years,
When these wild ecstasies shall be matured
Into a sober pleasure; when thy mind
Shall be a mansion for all lovely forms,   140
Thy memory be as a dwelling-place
For all sweet sounds and harmonies; oh! then,
If solitude, or fear, or pain, or grief,
Should be thy portion, with what healing thoughts
Of tender joy wilt thou remember me,   145
And these my exhortations! Nor, perchance—
If I should be where I no more can hear
Thy voice, nor catch from thy wild eyes these gleams
Of past existence—wilt thou then forget
That on the banks of this delightful stream   150
We stood together; and that I, so long
A worshipper of Nature, hither came
Unwearied in that service: rather say
With warmer love—oh! with far deeper zeal
Of holier love. Nor wilt thou then forget,   155
That after many wanderings, many years
Of absence, these steep woods and lofty cliffs,
And this green pastoral landscape, were to me
More dear, both for themselves and for thy sake!

QUESTIONS

1. What is the scene at the beginning of the poem? How much time has elapsed since the speaker viewed the scene he is revisiting?

2. Is the scene specific or general? What has it meant to the speaker during the previous five years? Where was he when he remembered the scenes?

3. To the speaker, what is the relationship between remembered scenes and the development of moral behavior?

4. What effect does the speaker consider that this present experience will have on him in future years?

5. Study lines 93–111. How successful is the speaker in making concrete his ideas about the moral forces he perceives along with his vision of the natural scenes?

6. Whom does the speaker address beginning with line 111?

7. What is the power that the speaker attributes to Nature? Characterize the "cheerful faith" described in lines 133–134.

8. Is the setting in this poem purely descriptive, or is it more clearly the basis of the speaker's philosophic discourse?

ROBERT BROWNING (1812–1889)

My Last Duchess°   *1842*

FERRARA

That's my last Duchess painted on the wall,
Looking as if she were alive. I call
That piece a wonder, now: Frà Pandolf's° hands
Worked busily a day, and there she stands.
Will't please you sit and look at her? I said   5
"Frà Pandolf" by design, for never read
Strangers like you that pictured countenance,
The depth and passion of its earnest glance,
But to myself they turned (since none puts by
The curtain I have drawn for you, but I)   10
And seemed as they would ask me, if they durst,°   *dared*
How such a glance came there; so, not the first
Are you to turn and ask thus. Sir, 'twas not
Her husband's presence only, called that spot
Of joy into the Duchess' cheek: perhaps   15
Frà Pandolf chanced to say "Her mantle laps
Over my lady's wrist too much," or "Paint

MY LAST DUCHESS.   The poem is based on incidents in the life of Alfonso II., Duke of Ferrara, whose first wife died in 1561. Some claimed she was poisoned. The Duke negotiated his second marriage to the daughter of the Count of Tyrol through an agent.   3 *Frà Pandolf*: an imaginary painter who is also a monk.

Must never hope to reproduce the faint
Half-flush that dies along her throat": such stuff
Was courtesy, she thought, and cause enough   20
For calling up that spot of joy. She had
A heart—how shall I say?—too soon made glad,
Too easily impressed; she liked whate'er
She looked on, and her looks went everywhere.
Sir, 'twas all one! My favor at her breast,   25
The dropping of the daylight in the West,
The bough of cherries some officious fool
Broke in the orchard for her, the white mule
She rode with round the terrace—all and each
Would draw from her alike the approving speech,   30
Or blush, at least. She thanked men—good! but thanked
Somehow—I know not how—as if she ranked
My gift of a nine-hundred-years-old name
With anybody's gift. Who'd stoop to blame
This sort of trifling? Even had you skill   35
In speech—(which I have not)—to make your will
Quite clear to such an one, and say, "Just this
Or that in you disgusts me; here you miss,
Or there exceed the mark"—and if she let
Herself be lessoned so, nor plainly set   40
Her wits to yours, forsooth, and made excuse
—E'en then would be some stooping; and I choose
Never to stoop. Oh sir, she smiled, no doubt,
Whene'er I passed her; but who passed without
Much the same smile? This grew; I gave commands;   45
Then all smiles stopped together. There she stands
As if alive. Will't please you rise? We'll meet
The company below, then. I repeat,
The Count your master's known munificence
Is ample warrant that no just pretense   50
Of mine for dowry will be disallowed;
Though his fair daughter's self, as I avowed
At starting, is my object. Nay, we'll go
Together down, sir. Notice Neptune,° though,
Taming a sea horse, thought a rarity,   55
Which Claus of Innsbruck° cast in bronze for me!

54 *Neptune*: Roman god of the sea.   56 *Claus of Innsbruck*: an imaginary sculptor.

QUESTIONS

   1. Who is the speaker of the poem? The listener?
   2. What are the setting and situation? Where are the characters? What are
       they looking at?

3. What third character is described? Who describes her? What was she like?
4. How is your final opinion of this third character different from the speaker's?
    How can you account for the difference?
5. What kind of person do you finally decide the speaker is? Why?

MATTHEW ARNOLD   (1822–1888)

Dover Beach   *1867 (1849)*

The sea is calm tonight.
The tide is full, the moon lies fair
Upon the straits—on the French coast the light
Gleams and is gone; the cliffs of England stand,
Glimmering and vast, out in the tranquil bay.   5
Come to the window, sweet is the night air!
Only, from the long line of spray
Where the sea meets the moon-blanched land,
Listen! you hear the grating roar
Of pebbles which the waves draw back, and fling,   10
At their return, up the high strand,
Begin, and cease, and then again begin,
With tremulous cadence slow, and bring
The eternal note of sadness in.

Sophocles long ago   15
Heard it on the Aegean, and it brought
Into his mind the turbid ebb and flow
Of human misery; we
Find also in the sound a thought,
Hearing it by this distant northern sea.   20

The Sea of Faith
Was once, too, at the full, and round earth's shore
Lay like the folds of a bright girdle furled.
But now I only hear
Its melancholy, long, withdrawing roar,   25
Retreating, to the breath
Of the night wind, down the vast edges drear
And naked shingles° of the world.   *beaches*

Ah, love, let us be true
To one another! for the world, which seems   30
To lie before us like a land of dreams,
So various, so beautiful, so new,
Hath really neither joy, nor love, nor light,
Nor certitude, nor peace, nor help for pain;
And we are here as on a darkling plain   35

Swept with confused alarms of struggle and flight,
Where ignorant armies clash by night.

QUESTIONS

1. Who is the speaker? To whom is the poem spoken?
2. What is the setting (place, time, location)? What specific words, details, and phrases in the first fourteen lines establish the setting?
3. Where are the speaker and listener? What can they see? Hear?
4. What sort of movement may be topographically traced in the first six lines of the poem, so that the scene finally focuses on the speaker and the listener?
5. What do the sounds of lines 9–14 evoke in the speaker's mind?
6. What is the effect of the speaker's comparison of the English Channel with the Aegean Sea, and of the effect of the Aegean surf on the thought of Sophocles?
7. What kind of faith remains in light of the loss of absolute religious faith? Defend the assertion that the faith is the speaker's commitment to personal fidelity rather than love.

CHRISTINA ROSSETTI (1830–1894)

A Christmas Carol   *1872*

In the bleak mid-winter
  Frosty wind made moan,
Earth stood hard as iron,
  Water like a stone;
Snow had fallen, snow on snow,   5
  Snow on snow,
In the bleak mid-winter
  Long ago.

Our God, Heaven cannot hold Him   10
  Nor earth sustain;
Heaven and earth shall flee away
  When He comes to reign:
In the bleak mid-winter
  A stable-place sufficed°   *see Luke 2:7*
The Lord God Almighty   15
  Jesus Christ.

Enough for Him whom cherubim
  Worship night and day,
A breastful of milk
  And a mangerful of hay;   20

Enough for Him whom angels
  Fall down before,
The ox and ass and camel
  Which adore.

Angels and archangels   25
  May have gathered there,
Cherubim and seraphim
  Throng'd the air,
But only His mother
  In her maiden bliss   30
Worshipped the Beloved
  With a kiss.

What can I give Him,
  Poor as I am?
If I were a shepherd°   *see Luke 2:8–20* 35
  I would bring a lamb,
If I were a wise man°   *see Matthew 2:1–12*
  I would do my part,—
Yet what I can I give Him,
  Give my heart.   40

QUESTIONS

1. What is the place and time visualized by the speaker for the events of the poem? Why do you think that the poet stressed the bitterness and bleakness of the winter setting?

2. What is the location where the "Lord God almighty" "comes to reign"? Why does the speaker stress the simplicity of the birthplace? From what sources is the setting derived?

3. How does the fourth stanza, with its stress both on the angelic scene and the presence of the mother, prepare you for the speaker's description of her own condition in stanza 5?

4. What gifts does the speaker consider giving? How are these objects part of the setting traditionally associated with the appearance of Jesus? Which is the only gift the speaker can choose? How does this choice reveal the nature of her character?

THOMAS HARDY (1840–1928)

The Walk   *1913*

You did not walk with me
Of late to the hilltop tree
  By the gated ways,
  As in earlier days;

You were weak and lame,   5
   So you never came,
And I went alone, and I did not mind,
Not thinking of you as left behind.

I walked up there today
Just in the former way;   10
   Surveyed around
   The familiar ground
   By myself again:
   What difference, then?
Only that underlying sense   15
Of the look of a room on returning thence.

QUESTIONS

1. What relationship does the speaker have to the person being addressed?
2. Why did the speaker's companion not walk to the hilltop tree? Does the speaker admit to being in solitude even though the most recent walk was done alone? How does his conclusion reveal his character?
3. What does the poem seem to be saying about the effects of age upon companionship?
4. Consider the final two lines. What impression do they convey about the location where the couple used to walk?

THOMAS HARDY (1840–1928)

Channel Firing   *1914*

That night your great guns, unawares,
Shook all our coffins° as we lay,
And broke the chancel window-squares,
We thought it was the Judgment Day

And sat upright. While drearisome   5
Arose the howl of wakened hounds:
The mouse let fall the altar-crumb,
The worms drew back into the mounds,

The glebe° cow drooled. Till God called, "No;
It's gunnery practice out at sea   10

CHANNEL FIRING.   2. *coffins*: It has been common practice in England for hundreds of years to bury people in the floors or basement of churches.   9 *glebe*: a parcel of land adjoining and belonging to a church. Cows were grazed there to keep the grass short.

Just as before you went below;
The world is as it used to be:

"All nations striving strong to make
Red war yet redder. Mad as hatters
They do no more for Christés sake   15
Than you who are helpless in such matters.

"That this is not the judgment hour
For some of them's a blessed thing,
For if it were they'd have to scour
Hell's floor for so much threatening. . . .   20

"Ha, ha. It will be warmer when
I blow the trumpet (if indeed
I ever do; for you are men,
And rest eternal sorely need)."

So down we lay again. "I wonder,   25
Will the world ever saner be,"
Said one, "than when He sent us under
In our indifferent century!"

And many a skeleton shook his head.
"Instead of preaching forty year,"   30
My neighbor Parson Thirdly said,
"I wish I had stuck to pipes and beer."

Again the guns disturbed the hour,
Roaring their readiness to avenge,
As far inland as Stourton Tower.°   35
And Camelot,° and starlit Stonehenge.°

35 *Stourton Tower*: tower commemorating King Alfred the Great's defeat of the Danes in
879 A.D.   36 *Camelot*: legendary seat of King Arthur's court.   *Stonehenge*: group of
standing stones on Salisbury Plain, probably built as a place of worship before 1000 B.C.

QUESTIONS

1. Who or what is the speaker in this poem? What is the setting? The situation?
2. To whom does the *your* in line 1 refer? The *our* in line 2?
3. What has awakened the speaker and his companions? What mistake have
   they made?
4. Beyond the primary speaker, what three other voices are heard in the poem?
   How are their character traits revealed?
5. What is the effect of the references to Stourton Tower, Camelot, and Stonehenge in the last two lines?
6. What ideas about war and the nature of humanity does this poem explore?

C. DAY LEWIS   (1904–1972)

Song   1935

Come, live with me and be my love,
And we will all the pleasures prove
Of peace and plenty, bed and board,
That chance employment may afford.

I'll handle dainties on the docks
And thou shalt read of summer frocks: 5
At evening by the sour canals
We'll hope to hear some madrigals.

Care on thy maiden brow shall put
A wreath of wrinkles, and thy foot
Be shod with pain: not silken dress   10
But toil shall tire thy loveliness.

Hunger shall make thy modest zone
And cheat fond death of all but bone—
If these delights thy mind may move,
Then live with me and be my love.   15

QUESTIONS

1. What is the connection or relationship between this poem and Marlowe's "Passionate Shepherd to His Love"?
2. To what other poems in this chapter is this poem related? How?
3. Who is the speaker in this poem? The listener?
4. What sort of life does the speaker offer the listener?
5. What is the effect of words like *chance employment* (line 4), *read* (line 6), and *hope* (line 8)?
6. How is the world of this poem different from the world in Marlowe's poem?

RICHARD HUGO   (1923–1982)

Degrees of Gray in Philipsburg   1973

You might come here Sunday on a whim.
Say your life broke down. The last good kiss
you had was years ago. You walk these streets
laid out by the insane, past hotels
that didn't last, bars that did, the tortured try   5
of local drivers to accelerate their lives.
Only churches are kept up. The jail

turned 70 this year. The only prisoner
is always in, not knowing what he's done.

The principal supporting business now 10
is rage. Hatred of the various grays
the mountain sends, hatred of the mill,
The Silver Bill repeal, the best liked girls
who leave each year for Butte. One good
restaurant and bars can't wipe the boredom out. 15
The 1907 boom, eight going silver mines,
a dance floor built on springs—
all memory resolves itself in gaze,
in panoramic green you know the cattle eat
or two stacks high above the town, 20
two dead kilns, the huge mill in collapse
for fifty years that won't fall finally down.

Isn't this your life? That ancient kiss
still burning out your eyes? Isn't this defeat
so accurate, the church bell simply seems 25
a pure announcement: ring and no one comes?
Don't empty houses ring? Are magnesium
and scorn sufficient to support a town,
not just Philipsburg, but towns
of towering blondes, good jazz and booze 30
the world will never let you have
until the town you came from dies inside?

Say no to yourself. The old man, twenty
when the jail was built, still laughs
although his lips collapse. Someday soon, 35
he says, I'll go to sleep and not wake up.
You tell him no. You're talking to yourself.
The car that brought you here still runs.
The money you buy lunch with,
no matter where it's mined, is silver 40
and the girl who serves your food
is slender and her red hair lights the wall.

QUESTIONS

1. How does the speaker characterize Philipsburg? What was the past like there? Why has so much changed? Who is the "you" addressed in line 1?
2. What is life like in the town now? What is the principal supporting business?
3. What does the speaker think should characterize a living, as opposed to a dead, town? What does his thought tell you about his character?
4. How does the fading of life in Philipsburg suggest that life generally is going to fade along with it?

5. How can this poem be seen as a philosophic reflection on the ability of human beings to endure and adjust even though new circumstances change previous ways of life?

JAMES MERRILL   (b. 1926)

Laboratory Poem   *1958*

Charles used to watch Naomi, taking heart
And a steel saw, open up turtles, live.
While she swore they felt nothing, he would gag
At blood, at the blind twitching, even after
The murky dawn of entrails cleared, revealing   5
Contours he knew, egg-yellows like lamps paling.

Well then. She carried off the beating heart
To the kymograph° and rigged it there, a rag
In fitful wind, now made to strain, now stopped
By her solutions tonic or malign°   10
Alternately in which it would be steeped.
What the heart bore, she noted on a chart,

For work did not stop only with the heart.
He thought of certain human hearts, their climb
Through violence into exquisite disciplines   15
Of which, as it now appeared, they all expired.
Soon she would fetch another and start over,
Easy in the presence of her lover.

LABORATORY POEM.   8 *kymograph*: an instrument that measures pulsations or variations of pressure and records them on a revolving scroll of paper.   10 *tonic or malign*: healthful or poisonous, virtuous or evil.

QUESTIONS

1. What can you determine about the speaker here? Is he *inside* or *outside* the poem? Engaged in the action or detached?
2. Who are the two characters in the poem? What are they like? What is their relationship? What are they doing?
3. Which character's thoughts does the speaker relate? What are they? What conclusions does this character come to about science? Love? Human endeavor?
4. What is the setting of the poem? The situation? The event described? What aspects of human existence does the poem explore?

JAMES WRIGHT   (1927–1980)

A Blessing   *1963*

Just off the highway to Rochester, Minnesota,
Twilight bounds softly forth on the grass.
And the eyes of those two Indian ponies
Darken with kindness.
They have come gladly out of the willows   5
To welcome my friend and me.
We step over the barbed wire into the pasture
Where they have been grazing all day, alone.
They ripple tensely, they can hardly contain their happiness
That we have come.   10
They bow shyly as wet swans. They love each other.
There is no loneliness like theirs.
At home once more,
They begin munching the young tufts of spring in the darkness.
I would like to hold the slenderer one in my arms.   15
For she has walked over to me
And nuzzled my left hand.
She is black and white,
Her mane falls wild on her forehead,
And the light breeze moves me to caress her long ear   20
That is delicate as the skin over a girl's wrist.
Suddenly I realize
That if I stepped out of my body I would break
Into blossom.

QUESTIONS

1. What has happened just before the poem opens? Account for the poet's
    use of the present tense in his descriptions.
2. Is the setting here portrayed as specific or general? What happens as the
    poem progresses?
3. What realization overtakes the speaker? How does this realization constitute
    a "blessing," and what does it show about his character?
4. To what degree is it necessary for the poet to include all the detail of the
    first 21 lines before the realization of the last three?

MAURA STANTON   (b. 1946)

The Conjurer   *1975*

In a mayonnaise jar I keep the tiny
people I shrank with my magic; I didn't
know they'd hold each other's hands & cry

so sharply when I said, no, the spell's
irreversible, do you eat grass or breadcrumbs?   5
Two are lovers who claim the air's bad
down there, & bite my fingers when I offer
a ride. They don't understand me.
I keep the jar by a window, washing
soot off the glass walls periodically . . .   10
When I gave them a flower, some ants
in the stamen attacked viciously,
gnawing the man-in-the-fur-cap's leg
completely off, while the others squealed
at the punched lid for his rescue: 15
I thumbed the ant dead, but were they grateful?
Lately they've begun to irritate me,
refusing raw meat, demanding more privacy
as if they were parrots who need cage covers
for daytime sleep. The awkward lovers   20
break apart at my shadow, nonchalant . . .
They're weaving something out of grass,
a blanket maybe, growing thin to save
their stalks, eating only breadcrumbs.
Don't they see? I could dump them   25
out into a real garden, let them tunnel
through the weeds to an anthill.
One night I dreamed those lovers crawled
inside my left ear with candles,
trying to find my brain in a fog.   30
They moved deep among the stalactites
searching for the magic spell they thought
I'd lost in sleep. I knew better.
Still, I woke with something resurrected
in my memory, maybe only a trick,   35
yes, a trick, I'll tell them to close
their eyes I've something for them.

QUESTIONS

1. Who is the speaker?
2. What is the speaker's attitude toward the other characters in the poem?
3. Who are the other characters in the poem? What is their attitude toward the speaker?
4. How does the speaker treat these other characters? What does he or she treat them as?
5. What "trick" do you think the speaker has in mind for these other characters?
6. What is your final assessment of the speaker? Describe the speaker's character.

WRITING ABOUT CHARACTER IN POETRY

Writing about character involves many of the same considerations we discussed in prose fiction. You might therefore review Chapter 4, pages 143–148. However, there are some important differences between the two writing tasks. One of these is the way you find out about characters. In prose fiction you can usually judge a character from the details the narrator provides about the character's actions, thoughts, appearance, opinions, and the like. In poetry, however, the speaker is less likely to present fully detailed information. Consequently, many conclusions about characters in poems must be inferred from the suggestions and hints the speaker gives us along with the details.

Another difference between writing about character in fiction and poetry concerns the types of characters. In fiction you have a broad range of options for writing: You may choose to write about the protagonist, the antagonist, the narrator, or any of the incidental characters. By contrast, in poetry you are usually limited to the speaker or to one of the characters described by the speaker, although you may sometimes be able to discuss the listener, too. In writing about Browning's "My Last Duchess," for example, you could focus on either the Duke or the Duchess, for you learn enough from the poem to write about either.

In planning and prewriting, find out as much as you can about the characters and their relationship to their situations; that is, to the action, emotion, ideas, setting, and other characters in the poem. In examining a speaker, for example, you may want to consider the following: Who is the speaker? What is he or she doing? What has already occurred? What autobiographical information does he or she reveal? What information about others? What judgments and opinions does the speaker express? How knowledgeable is the speaker? What do the speaker's choice of words reveal about his or her education and social standing? Does the language give us an idea about his or her philosophy of life? What tone of voice is suggested in the speaker's presentation? How deeply involved is the speaker with the action or thought of the poem and with the other characters?

When you prepare to write about characters other than the speaker, you need to rely on the speaker's descriptions of action, appearance, emotions, responses, and ideas. You should try to find answers to some of the following questions: How does the character respond to the natural and artificial surroundings? What is he or she trying to achieve? How is the character affected by others and how do others respond to him or her? What degree of control does the character exert, and what does this effort reveal? How does the character speak and behave, and what do you learn from these words and actions? Usually you may rely on the views expressed by the speaker, but be wary of a distorted or slanted presentation, as with the Duke-speaker in Browning's "My Last Duchess." When you perceive an obvious bias, be sure to take it into consideration when interpreting the speaker's views.

Organizing the Essay

INTRODUCTION.   The introduction should state the central idea. This is usually a general and accurate statement about the character you are discussing. If you are writing about the Duke in "My Last Duchess," for example, your central idea might be that he is arrogant, cruel, greedy, and power-mad. In writing about Sir Patrick Spens, your central idea might be concerned with the qualities of Sir Patrick brought out by his responses to the King's command and by his acceptance of sacrifice required by the King's service.

When you write about a single character, the central idea will usually provide a focused conclusion about personality or status. If the topic is a set of characters, the central idea should express some relationship or commonality among them. Thus the characters in "Bonny George Campbell" are designed to respond with grief to Campbell's sudden and unexpected death, and the characters in "London" to illustrate the withering effects that discriminatory law and religion produce in human beings. Your thesis sentence should contain the major points you will develop in the body.

BODY.   You might wish to organize your essay according to one of the following approaches:

1. *Character as revealed by action.* Often the speaker describes himself or herself as a major character or major mover in the action of the poem. What does the action reveal about the character? In Stanton's "The Conjurer," the speaker reveals that she has miniaturized a number of people, and is keeping them in a bottle. What does this action show? In Gray's "Elegy Written in a Country Churchyard" we may conclude that the speaker is entering the churchyard at the close of day, and that his meditation among the tombstones is brought about by the quiet and solemnity of his surroundings. This beginning action causes him to think of a number of other actions involving his judgments about life, glory, fame, fortune, and religious dedication. What do his speculations and conclusions reveal about his character? In a parallel way, the speaker of Wordsworth's "Tintern Abbey" has returned to a scene visited five years before. His thoughts on the occasion deal with his actions as a child and an adult, and prompt him to connect the natural sights he sees to the general relationship of Nature with the development of his own identity as a human being and also with his future actions. In the light of this spectrum of action, what conclusions might we make about his character?

2. *Character as revealed by interaction.* Poems that are based in a clearly

defined dramatic situation will yield best to this sort of treatment. "My Last Duchess" is a fine example, as are Hardy's "Channel Firing," and Jonson's "Drink to Me, Only, with Thine Eyes." In Hardy's "The Walk," the speaker talks directly to a presumably infirm listener who has not been able to go on the walk that the two had shared in times of mutual good health. What do the speaker's descriptions and expressed attitudes toward the listener tell us about his character? What do you learn about relationships from this and other poems? How have these relationships affected the characters involved?

3. *Character as revealed by circumstance / setting.* The essay based on the interrelationship of character and setting presupposes that conditions of time, place, object, money, family, culture, and history influence character and motivation, and also that individual and collective traits are developed as people try to control and alter the world around them. For instance, the speaker of Wright's "A Blessing" describes a moment of looking at the world around him, and at the end of the poem he feels as though he is about to "break / Into blossom." What leads to the interaction enabling him to reach this happy conclusion? How do the things and animals that he sees produce this effect? Why does he feel safe rather than frightened in the pasture? Why does he believe in the benevolence of the two ponies, and, in turn, why do the ponies treat him with affection? What aspects of character enable him to step over the barbed wire without fear, and to believe that the experience is really a "blessing"? Would such an experience have been possible at a more suspicious, less civilized time, when people stepping uninvited onto property might have been considered intruders? In short, how has setting in the very broadest sense entered into the character of the speaker?

In dealing with the interrelationship of character and external situation, you might be able to organize the body of your essay by relying on certain aspects of the setting. Thus you might select the details about time in past, present, and future, as Wordsworth does in "Tintern Abbey." Similarly, details about the roaring surf and the dim lights in Arnold's "Dover Beach" would provide the thematic ties for an essay you might write about the speaker's sense of alienation, loss, and dedication. As you can see, aspects of setting can serve not only as topics to shed light on character but also as shaping and guiding influences for your essay.

Whatever strategy you choose, remember that your organization will finally be determined by the poem you are writing about. Each poem will suggest its own avenues of exploration, leading to your own shaping of your essay. Your goal, as always, is to support your central idea logically and coherently.

CONCLUSION.   The conclusion of the essay should be as firm and assertive as the introduction. Here you might summarize your major points about the character or characters, or you might also tie your conclusions into an assessment of the poem as a whole. Thus, you might briefly discuss the connection between character and character, character and environment, character and death, character and greed, character and love, and so on, and deal with these topics generally as you bring your essay to a close.

SAMPLE ESSAY

The Character of the Duke in Browning's "My Last Duchess"*

[1]   In this dramatic monologue, Browning skillfully develops the character of his speaker, who holds the high position of Duke of Ferrara (in Italy) during the days of aristocratic absolutism. Because the Duke is at the top of the aristocracy, he also has the power to exert absolute control, whether for good or for bad. Browning's Duke is more than bad—he is totally evil.° Browning does not make a direct accusation of evil, but he does not need to. The Duke reveals his evil nature as he carries on his one-way conversation with the listener, who is apparently an envoy of a less powerful aristocrat, the Count, whose daughter the Duke is going to marry. The Duke's evil character is brought out by his indulgence in power, his intimidation of others, his manipulation of his dead wife, the Duchess, and his general contempt for other people.°

[2]   The Duke's indulgence in power, the basis of his evil, is apparent in his use of indirect speech. On the surface, Browning makes him seem intelligent, civilized, gracious, and friendly. The Duke begins his monologue by pointing out to his listener the beauty of a painting of his "last Duchess," but his entire speech—comprising the entire poem—reveals the depth of his self-indulgence. Although his description of how he treated the Duchess is indirect, it is threatening enough to show us that he delights in his own evil. When he says "I gave commands; / Then all smiles stopped together" (lines 45–46), he is actually bragging about his power and about how he had the Duchess killed. He is coldly horrible, the more so because Browning makes clear that he covers over his absolute evil with quiet words and a love of good art.

Another of the Duke's horrible qualities is the way he intimidates people. Although at first it seems that he is doing no more than discussing his dead wife and the life he had with her, it is clear at the poem's end that all the time he has been intimidating both his listener and also the listener's master, the Count. The last nine lines (lines 48–56) indicate that his monologue should have been a dialogue, in which he should have negotiated the terms for money and property that he is to receive as dowry from the Count. The fact

* See p. 557 for this poem.
° Central idea.
□ Thesis sentence.

that he has talked only about how he got rid of his "last Duchess" shows his arrogance and disregard for the good will of the Count. Thus, there is no mention of dowry until lines 48–53, when the Duke states that he will make a "just pretense" for a dowry which of course the Count will honor. It seems clear that the "just pretense" will in fact be a demand for most of the Count's money and land. In addition, the Duke's commands: "Will't please you rise? We'll meet / The company below then," (lines 47–48) indicate that the negotiation that never began is now over, and that the envoy is totally in his power. This is intimidation, and the character who intimidates by describing one of his own death sentences (by having his wife killed), is totally ruthless and inhuman—evil.

[3]

In addition to the Duke's ruthless intimidation, the evil characteristic of manipulation and control is brought out in his description of his treatment of the Duchess. If we look through his words at what the Duchess was really like, we may conclude that she was even-tempered and pleasant to all. In fact, it would be hard to say that she was anything but perfect. But the Duke, rather than indicating pleasure with her, states that she was ungrateful to him by not being submissive. So he complains that the smile she gave to others was the same as the smile she gave to him. In other words, he complains because she did not defer to him, as he felt was his due.

[4]

> O sir, she smiled, no doubt,
> Whene'er I passed her; but who passed without
> Much the same smile?   (lines 43–45)

These lines show that the Duke is a manipulator of the worst sort and that the poor Duchess was in an impossible situation under his power. No matter how good she was, there is no way she could have pleased such a man. He would have manipulated her into an unfavorable position, in his eyes, that would have justified his giving the "commands" to remove her.

Perhaps the worst of the Duke's traits is the contempt he shows for people by thinking of them not as human beings but rather as things. Most notable is the way he thinks of the Duchess; he calls her painting a "piece" (line 3) to hang on a wall, looking "as if she were alive" (line 2). And he speaks about the bronze statue of Neptune "taming a sea horse" (line 55) as being equal to her. (It is worth noting that the subject of this statue is domination). This same contempt for people is shown in his claim that his interest in the Count's daughter is the "fair daughter's self" (line 52), while the rest of the poem makes clear that he looks on the new bride as no more than the means to the additional wealth and power he will gain from the dowry. Oddly, also, he seems to think of himself less as a person than as a "nine-hundred-years-old name" (line 33), and it is this intangible thing that he prizes above his own humanity. In other words, he views even his own humanity with contempt.

[5]

Browning's Duke, then, is a monster, a person with absolute power but without the kindness and understanding to use it for anyone but himself. His complaints about the dead Duchess are meaningless, for they are no more than pretexts for his cruel self-indulgence. He is at the top of the aristo-

cratic power structure, and is able to do what he wants without fear of reprisal. People must defer to him and obey him, but only because he makes everyone afraid. His intimidation, his manipulation, his lust for power—all govern him,
[6]   and leave him unable to look at human beings as anything more than pawns in his self-indulgent game for control over everything he sees. He is an example of the old saying that absolute power corrupts absolutely, and his character is therefore a frightening portrait of evil.

Commentary on the Essay

This essay focuses on the character of Browning's Duke. Because the Duke is the speaker, the essay is based partially on details presented by him, but is also partially based on interpretations of detail. The principal subject matter for the essay is the interaction the Duke has with the subject of the poem—the "last Duchess"—in addition to his interaction with the listener, who is a representative of an inferior aristocrat, and whom he therefore treats with contempt. Elements of setting are also introduced to illuminate the Duke's character: his works of art, the absolute power of his aristocratic position, the prestige of his name and title, and the wealth that he possesses and may accumulate as a result of his power. The essay thus demonstrates how character may be analyzed with reference (a) to interactions among people, and also (b) to responses of people to their environment.

The central idea of the essay is that the Duke, the character being analyzed, is evil. This point is made in the first paragraph, with sufficient accompanying detail to explain that the Duke's position enables him to exercise absolute power. Paragraph 2 shows that indulgence in power is one of the Duke's primary evil traits, while paragraphs 3, 4, and 5 bring out traits of intimidation, manipulation, and contempt. The final paragraph, 6, contains the summary, but it also asserts that the Duke's justifications for doing away with his wife are meaningless in the light of his greed and desire for power.

As the essay develops, transitions are effected by phrases such as "another," "in addition," "perhaps the worst," "this same," and "then." The assertions in the essay are supported by references to specific details from the poem, quotations from the poem (with line numbers noted), and interpretations of details.

WRITING TOPICS FOR CHAPTER 13

1. Write an essay comparing the speakers of the various "Passionate Shepherd" poems (by Marlowe, Raleigh, and Lewis). How are the speakers alike and how are they different? How do their words and references indicate their characters to you? How do the speakers influence your judgment of the poems in which they appear?

2. Write an essay discussing the relationships between location, thought, and character as asserted in the poems by Blake, Arnold, and Wordsworth. What importance do place and time have upon the opportunity for life and the development of character? How do responses to time, historical period, and place influence ideas about how to live?

3. Write a short biographical or autobiographical poem, showing how certain places and experiences have shaped current qualities of character and/or certain decisions about life, friends, and goals.

14

Words: The Building Blocks of Poetry

Poems are constructed of words. Words create the rhythm, rhyme, meter, and stanza form. They define the speaker, the other characters, the setting, and the situation. They also carry the ideas and the emotions of the poem. For this reason, each poet seeks the perfect and indispensable word, the word that looks right, sounds right, and conveys all the compressed meanings, overtones, and emotions that the poem requires.

We can see evidence of this quest for the perfect word in the numerous revisions that poems go through as poets shape them. When a poet's manuscripts survive, we can actually look at some of the various stages of specific poems. William Butler Yeats's notebooks contain six complete or fragmentary revisions of "Leda and the Swan," all different from the version finally published in 1924. Here is the first line of each version:

(1st)   Now can the swooping Godhead have his will
(2nd)   The trembl godhead is half hovering still
(3rd)   The swooping godhead is half hovering still
(4th)   A rush upon great wings and hovering still
(5th)   A swoop upon great wings and hovering still
(6th)   A rush, a sudden wheel and hovering still
(1924) A sudden blow: the great wings beating still

As we move through this sequence of revisions, we can almost feel the poet striving to find the absolutely right combination of words. Note, for example, the way "have his will" becomes "hovering still" and finally "beating still." Each revision is more active, more immediate, and more violent.

WORDS AND MEANING

All systems of communication are based on signs that have acquired conventional and accepted meanings. In any natural language, words are the signifiers for thoughts, things, or actions. Life, and poetry, would be a great deal simpler (and less interesting) if there were an exact one-to-one correspondence between words and the ideas they are supposed to signify. We find an approximation of this close correspondence in artificial language systems such as chemical equations and computer languages that convey exact meanings. Such correspondence, however, is not characteristic of English or any other natural language. Instead, words have the independent (and wonderful) habit of moving around and acquiring a vast array of different meanings.

Most of us recognize the slippery nature of words at some level, even if we have not devoted much time to thinking about language. Much of our humor is built on the ambiguities of words and phrases. When the comedian says, "Take my wife, please," the joke works because *take* has two entirely different meanings, both of which come into play. In reading poetry, we must recognize this ambiguity and understand that poets exploit the shifty nature of words and language; they rejoice in the movement of words.

DENOTATION AND CONNOTATION

Because individual words are much more important in poetry than in any other form of literature, we will consider denotation and connotation in more detail here than we did in our previous discussion (see Chapter 7, p. 266). **Denotation** refers to the standard dictionary meaning of a word; it indicates conventional correspondences between a sign (the word) and an idea. We might expect that denotation would be fairly straightforward. However, most English words have multiple denotations. The word *house*, for example, can refer to a home, a chamber of congress, a theater, an audience, a fraternity, and a brothel. Although context often makes the denotation of *house* more specific, the six different meanings give this simple word some built-in ambiguity. The situation becomes far more complicated with a word like *fall*, which has over fifty different definitions or denotations. As a verb, *fall* means descend, hang down, succumb to temptation, be overthrown, killed, and chopped down. As a noun, the word denotes a descent, a season of the year, a slope, the state of sin, a capture, and even a hairpiece, among other things. In prose, a writer will usually try to limit the denotative value of *fall* to one of these meanings. Poets, however, frequently try to hold on to as many useful and appropriate denotations as possible.

We can see an example of the poet's use of multiple denotation in the couplet that ends Shakespeare's Sonnet 115:

> No want of conscience hold it that I call
> Her "love" for whose dear love I rise and fall.

Shakespeare employs the multiple denotations of such words as *want* (lack), *hold*, *love*, and *rise* here. For the sake of our example, let us focus on *dear* and *fall*. *Dear* means beloved, but it also means costly or expensive. *Fall* means to drop, droop, die, succumb to sin or temptation, and be overthrown. The context does not exclude *any* of these denotations. As a result, the couplet says a great deal with very few words. *Dear* means that the speaker cherishes both his beloved and his emotions, but it also means that both are costly (or even exhausting) in terms of effort, emotion, and cash. A paraphrase of the couplet, though much less elegant than the original, gives us a chance to display the full range of *dear* and *fall*: "I don't consider it a failure or lack of conscience that I call that woman my "love" for whose beloved, expensive, and exhausting love I rise and am overthrown, drop, droop, descend, succumb to temptation, sink into sin, and die.

Denotation can also present us with problems because of the way words gain new meanings and lose old ones over long periods of time. Language changes slowly, but the shift can be quite dramatic over several centuries. In reading poems written before the nineteenth century, we occasionally encounter words that have changed meaning so completely that a modern dictionary is not much help. Consider, for example, the word *vegetable* in Andrew Marvell's "To His Coy Mistress." The speaker asserts that "My vegetable love should grow / Vaster than empires and more slow." Our first impulse may be to imagine a giant and passionate cabbage. When we turn to a modern dictionary, we discover that "vegetable" is an adjective that means "plantlike," but "plantlike love" does not get us much beyond "vegetable love." A reference to the *Oxford English Dictionary*, (*OED*), however, tells us that "vegetable" was used as an adjective in the seventeenth century to mean "living or growing like a plant." Thus, we find out that "vegetable love" can be an emotion that grows slowly and steadily larger.

Connotation refers to the emotional, psychological, or social overtones that words carry in addition to their denotations. We can see connotation at work in the synonyms *childish* and *childlike*. According to the dictionary, these two adjectives both denote the state of being like a child. Nevertheless, the two words connote or imply very different sets of characteristics. *Childish* suggests a person who is bratty, stubborn, immature, silly, and petulant. *Childlike*, on the other hand, describes a person who is innocent, charming, and unaffected. These very different descriptions are based entirely on the connotations of the two words; the denotations make little distinction.

We encounter the manipulation of connotation all the time, even though we may be unaware of it. Advertising depends to a large extent on the skillful management of connotation. This manipulation may be as simple as calling a "used" car "previously owned" to avoid the **negative connotations** of the word *used*. On the other hand, it may be as sophisticated as the current use of the words *lite* or *light* to describe specific foods and drinks. In all these products, the word *lite* means dietetic, low-calorie, or even weak. The distinction—and the selling point—is found in connotation. Imagine how difficult it would be to sell a drink called "dietetic beer" or "weak beer." *Light* and *lite*, however, carry none of the negative connotations of *weak* or *dietetic*. Instead, *lite* suggests a product that is pleasant, sparkling, bright, and healthy. "Weak beer" would grow dusty on the shelves; "lite beer" sells very well indeed.

Denotation and connotation are important factors in any consideration of language and literature, but they become especially significant in poetry. Poets often work a single word as hard as they can; they strive to make the word carry as many appropriate and effective denotations and connotations as possible. To put it another way, poets often try to use *packed* or *loaded* words that will carry a broad range of meaning and association. In reading poems, one of our jobs is to "unpack" these loaded words and to enjoy the play of language. With this in mind, take a look at the following poem by Robert Graves.

ROBERT GRAVES   (1895–1985)

The Naked and the Nude   *1957*

For me, the naked and the nude
(By lexicographers° construed
As synonyms that should express
The same deficiency of dress
Or shelter) stand as wide apart   5
As love from lies, or truth from art.

Lovers without reproach will gaze
On bodies naked and ablaze;
The Hippocratic° eye will see
In nakedness, anatomy;   10
And naked shines the Goddess when
She mounts her lion among men.

THE NAKED AND THE NUDE.   2 *lexicographers*: people who write dictionaries.
9 *Hippocratic*: medical; the adjective derives from Hippocrates, an ancient Greek considered the father of medicine.

The nude are bold, the nude are sly
To hold each treasonable eye.
While draping by a showman's trick   15
Their dishabille° in rhetoric,
They grin a mock-religious grin
Of scorn at those of naked skin.

The naked, therefore, who compete
Against the nude may know defeat;   20
Yet when they both together tread
The briary pastures of the dead,
By Gorgons° with long whips pursued,
How naked go the sometime nude!

16 *dishabille*: being carelessly or partly dressed.   23 *Gorgons*: hideous mythological female
monsters who had snakes for hair.

QUESTIONS

1. What does the speaker tell us about the denotations of *naked* and *nude* in
   the first stanza? About the connotations?
2. What examples of "the naked" does the second stanza provide? What do
   the examples have in common?
3. How are "the nude" described in the third stanza? What are the connotations
   of words like *sly*, *draping*, *dishabille*, *rhetoric*, and *grin*?
4. What attitude do "the nude" have toward "the naked"? What does the speaker
   suggest about this attitude?
5. Where will both "the naked" and "the nude" go after death? Which will be
   punished more severely? How is *naked* used in a new way in the last line?
6. What is suggested by the fact that *naked* is derived from the Old English
   word *nacod* while *nude* is derived from the Latin *nudus*?

"The Naked and the Nude" explores the connotative distinctions between two words that share a common denotation. The title tells us that
the poem will consider "the naked and the nude" and that we are dealing
with both words and people. If the speaker were simply considering the
words, she or he would say "naked" and "nude" instead of "*the* naked
and *the* nude." The speaker's use of *the* signifies a double focus on human
conditions and values as well as language.

The denotations of *naked* and *nude* are identical. The dictionary defines
naked as nude or without clothing, and *nude* as without clothing or naked.
Lines 1–5 of the poem express this commonality. The speaker observes
that "lexicographers" consider naked and nude to be "synonyms" that
"should express / The same deficiency of dress" (lines 2–4). Although these

lines establish the common denotation of *naked* and *nude*, they also question this commonality through the utilization of elevated and complex words. By using terms like *lexicographers, construed, express,* and *deficiency* instead of simpler and more common words, the poem implies that the connection between "the naked" and "the nude" is artificial.

The first stanza also explores the connotative distinction between "the naked" and "the nude." The speaker asserts that "for me" the words and the people "stand as wide apart / As love from lies, or truth from art" (lines 5–6). Thus, the speaker announces the poem's thesis: There is a vast difference between the naked and the nude. The sentence structure of this assertion also begins the process of attaching connotations to the words and people under consideration. The syntax offers three parallel compound phrases:

The naked	and	the nude
As love	from	lies
or truth	from	art

As this arrangement suggests, the effect of this sentence structure is to link the naked with "love" and "truth," and the nude with "lies" and "art." The first stanza thus begins to clarify the connotative distinction between the naked and the nude. The naked are linked with passion (love) and honesty (truth), but the nude are associated with dishonesty (lies) and faking (art, more specifically, *artifice*).

In the second stanza the speaker focuses on "the naked" and provides three examples that expand the web of connotations: lovers (lines 7–8), physicians (9–10), and the Goddess (11–12). The lovers are naked and "gaze" on "bodies naked and ablaze" without shame or "reproach." Graves continues to exploit connotative overtones here; he uses *gaze* instead of *look* because the word implies intensity and rapture. The physician ("The Hippocratic eye"), like the lovers, looks on nakedness and the naked without shame; she or he is consumed with the passion of the quest for knowledge and the truth of "anatomy." Finally, the Goddess is naked when "She mounts her lion among men." Like lovers and physicians, she exists beyond shame or guilt; the word *shines* suggests both passion and truth. In all three examples, nakedness and the naked are without shame, trickery, temptation, or deceit; they are linked with honesty, passion, truth, and love.

The connotative flavor of the poem changes in the third stanza, when the speaker begins to consider "the nude." They are described as "bold" and "sly," words with negative connotations that suggest dishonesty. *Bold* implies a pushy and defiant attitude while *sly* hints at cunning and shiftiness. This sense of dishonesty is amplified by the speaker's reference to "each treasonable eye" (line 14). The word *treasonable* suggests that the nude are associated with treachery and shame; it condemns both the nude and those who look at nudity. In addition, the phrase reminds us of "the Hippocratic eye" and might, through the association of sound, imply "hypocritical eye."

The dishonest trickery of the nude is conveyed in their ability to drape "by a showman's trick / Their dishabille in rhetoric" (lines 15–16). These lines imply that the nude can be dressed and undressed at the same time. By using loaded words like *draping, showman's trick, dishabille*, and *rhetoric*, the speaker asserts that this ambiguity is intentional. *Draping* (instead of dressing or clothing) connotes contrived carelessness and fakery. When it is combined with *showman's trick*, we get a sense of a now-you-see-it-now-you-don't staginess. *Dishabille* means being partly or carelessly dressed; it thus reinforces the connotations of *draping*. *Rhetoric* denotatively refers to the study of the effective use of language. It returns our attention to the key words in the poem. But *rhetoric* has also come to connote the dishonest or deceptive use of language to prove a dubious case or to defend a questionable position with dazzling verbal trickery. The term thus points in two directions—toward the lexical meanings of words and toward contrived deceptions.

In the last stanza the speaker admits that "the nude" will almost always triumph over "the naked" in this world, but goes on to point out that the nude will "tread the briary pastures of the dead" and be pursued by "Gorgons with long whips" (lines 21–23). Here, the speaker imagines the thorny fields of Hades, the underworld of classical mythology. In Hades, the naked and the nude will be "together" just as the words are "together" for "lexicographers." In the last line, however, Graves inverts the terms, claiming that "the sometime nude" will be "naked" in the underworld. In this context, *naked* takes on another meaning; it implies that the nude will be completely at the mercy of the pursuing Gorgons, and will thus be punished for seductive and deceptive trickery. The nakedness of "the nude" in this last line may also suggest that trickery and artifice disappear in the face of the reality of existence.

DICTION

English is one of the richest languages in the world; we can usually find half a dozen words that mean pretty much the same thing. Given this wealth of vocabulary, poets are inevitably blessed with choices among words. **Diction** refers to the specific words and types of words selected by a writer to produce a desired effect. We discuss diction at some length in Chapter 7 (pp. 262–264); you might review this material. Again, however, word choice is so important in poetry that the subject deserves reexamination.

Types of Words: Specific or General and Concrete or Abstract

The distinctions among these types of words are centrally important to poetry because the choices can determine the impact and immediacy in a poem. **Specific** words refer to objects or conditions that can easily be seen or imagined, while **general** words signify broad classes of persons or things. Similarly, **concrete** words describe conditions or qualities that are exact and vivid, while **abstract** words refer to circumstances that are difficult to envision. These distinctions become clear when we consider the difference between Housman's "three score years and ten" or "Cherry . . . hung with bloom" and Richard Eberhart's "infinite spaces" or "eternal truth." The terms and images that Housman uses in "Loveliest of Trees" (p. 528) are specific and concrete; they evoke an exact and focused sense of time and object. Eberhart's terms, in "The Fury of Aerial Bombardment" (p. 595), are general and abstract; it is hard to envision "infinite spaces" or "eternal truth" with any vivid clarity or exactness.

As these examples indicate, poets can employ all four types of words to good effect. The choice is often determined by the subject and the emotional response the poet wants to evoke in the reader. Poems written in predominantly general and abstract terms are detached and cerebral; they often deal in an impersonal manner with universal questions or emotions. Poems written in concrete and specific terms, on the other hand, are usually more immediate, familiar, and compelling. For the most part, poets employ a mixture of these types of diction. Theodore Roethke's "Dolor" (p. 594), for example, uses a large number of specific and concrete words to define a series of more abstract emotional states.

Levels of Diction

Like other writers, poets have recourse to three levels of diction: high or formal, middle or neutral, and low or informal. **Formal diction** is elevated and elaborate; it requires the proper words in the proper order and avoids idioms, colloquialisms, contractions, or slang. Beyond such correctness, formal language is often characterized by complex words and a lofty tone. Robert Graves uses formal diction in "The Naked and the Nude" when the speaker asserts that the terms are "By lexicographers construed / As synonyms that should express / The same deficiency of dress." These Latinate words heighten the diction and tone. We find "lexicographers" instead of *writers of dictionaries*, "construed" (from the Latin *construere*) instead of *thought*, "express" (from the Latin *expressus*) instead of *say* or *show*, and deficiency (from the Latin *deficientia*) instead of *lack*.

Middle or **neutral diction** maintains the correct language and word order of formal diction but avoids the elaborate words and elevated tone.

Emily Dickinson's "Because I Could Not Stop for Death" (p. 527) is almost entirely in neutral diction.

Informal or **low diction** is the plain language of everyday use; it is relaxed, colloquial, and conversational. Poems using informal diction often include common and simple words, slang, idiomatic expressions, and contractions. We can see informal diction in Thomas Hardy's "The Man He Killed" (p. 528), where the poet uses words and phrases like "many a nipperkin," "He thought he'd 'list," and "off-hand like." In general, formal diction uses words from French, Latin, and Greek, whereas informal diction utilizes words from historical English.

In the 1700s, many writers believed that only formal diction was appropriate to poetry. These writers developed rules about the subjects and styles that were suitable; common life and colloquial language were almost always excluded. These rules of **poetic decorum** (appropriateness, suitability) made it necessary to use elevated language rather than common words and phrases. For example, an eighteenth-century poet might refer to "finny prey" for fish (Pope), "lowing herd" for cattle (Gray), or "reddening Phoebus lifts his golden fires" for "the sun is rising" (Gray). Alexander Pope, one of the greatest English poets of that century, maintained these rules of decorum and made fun of them at the same time in his mock-epic poem *The Rape of the Lock*, and more fully in a mock-critical work entitled *The Art of Sinking in Poetry*. In *The Rape of the Lock*, for example, he refers to a scissors as a "glittering forfex," and in describing a social scene he makes the following couplet for the pouring of coffee:

> From silver spouts the grateful liquors glide,
> While China's earth receives the smoking tide.

The comic mode here is that the elaborate phrases "China's earth" for "cups" and "smoking tide" for "coffee" create a verbal anticlimax that causes amusement. Since the eighteenth century, poets have had the option to choose formal, middle, informal, or any combination of levels of language in their poetry.

Special Types of Diction

In addition to the three levels of diction already described, poets and writers may use four special types of words and phrases: *idiom, dialect, slang,* and *jargon*.

An **idiom** is a word, phrase, or pattern of expression that is acceptable and correct for certain needs. Many idioms have become standard in our language and we therefore hardly notice them. Thus, for example, we speak about being "*in* love," and walking "*alongside* a road," and so on. The proper use of such prepositions, along with the phrases which they govern, is one element characterizing standard English. Sometimes idioms, along with words, have passed out of use. Thus, Shakespeare writes that "In me thou seest the glowing of such fire / That on the ashes of *his* youth doth lie." Here the possessive *his* was one of the forms Shakespeare used where today we use *its* exclusively. Poets may select idiomatic expressions to create special qualities in their poems. For example, Paul Zimmer, in "The Day Zimmer Lost Religion," wryly uses the phrase "ready for him now," an idiom from the boxing world describing a fighter in top condition. Linda Pastan uses "gives me an A" and "I'm dropping out," both phrases from school life, to create comic effects in "Marks." E. E. Cummings was fond of using idioms for satiric effect, as in "she being Brand/ -new" and "next to of course god america i." Popular idioms enable poets to achieve levels of colloquial and substandard diction, depending on their purposes, but we must note again that standard language is also dependent on the proper and correct use of standard idioms.

Dialect refers to the words and pronunciation of a particular region or group. We can recognize certain common dialects such as Brooklynese, American Black English, Yiddish English, Texan, Southern, and Scottish English. Dialect is concerned with whether we refer to a *pail* (general American) or a *bucket* (Southern), or sit on a *sofa* (Eastern) or a *davenport* (Midwestern), and drink *soda* (Eastern), *pop* (Midwestern), or *tonic* (Bostonian), or use all the standard verb forms. The anonymous "Bonny George Campbell," Sanchez's "right on: white america," and Brooks's "We Real Cool" illustrate the use of dialect in poems.

Slang refers to very informal and sub-standard vocabulary. It is made up of spontaneous words and phrases which may exist for a time and then vanish. For a brief period recently, for example, the word "bad" was used as a slang form for "good." Slang has a way of persisting, however, as may be seen in the many phrases that Americans have developed to describe dying, such as "kick the bucket," "croak," "be wasted," "be disappeared," and "be offed." A non-native speaker of English would have difficulty understanding that a person who "kicked the bucket" or was "offed" had actually died. Even when a slang expression becomes widely accepted, it usually goes no farther than colloquial or conversational levels. If it is introduced into a standard context it will mar and jar, as in Larkin's "Next, Please" (p. 847), where the speaker describes the female statue at the bow of a ship as "a figurehead with golden tits." Because the poem is designed to expose the fatuousness of unreal hopes, the slang word creates a jarring, clashing, deflating effect that is complementary to this intention.

Jargon refers to words and phrases developed by a particular group to fit their own needs. Without some kind of initiation, people not in the group cannot understand the special language. Usually such groups are specific professions or trades. For example, lawyers, plumbers, astronauts, doctors, and football players all have terms and phrases that are particular to their trades. Jargon becomes interesting and problematic when it moves into the mainstream of English or is used in literature to create specific effects. Two poems in this chapter that illustrate the poet's use of jargon for effect are Henry Reed's "Naming of Parts" and Richard Eberhart's "The Fury of Aerial Bombardment." In both cases the poets use military jargon to create tone, setting, and contrast.

SYNTAX

Syntax is a general term that refers to word order and sentence structure. The normal word order in English sentences is firmly fixed in a subject–verb–object sequence. At the simplest level, we tend to say "John (subject) threw (verb) the ball (object)." This rigid order is necessary to convey meaning; when we change English word order, we usually change the meaning as well. "Dog bites man," for instance, is obviously very different from "Man bites dog."

Word order in English is so rigidly established that any shift or adjustment is likely to have a significant impact on the meaning of a sentence. When poets employ irregular word order, they usually do so to achieve a specific effect. Sometimes normal word order is altered in poetry to meet the demands of meter or the rhyme scheme. In other instances, however, the word order may be shifted out of the ordinary to create emphasis, to heighten the connection between two words, or to pick up on specific implications or traditions.

Clear examples of the alteration of word order for effect are the first sentences of John Milton's *Paradise Lost* and Alexander Pope's *The Rape of the Lock*. Both poems are in the epic tradition and both imitate many aspects of Vergil's *Aeneid*; Milton's is an epic, while Pope's is a mock epic (an **epic** is usually a long narrative poem that features heroic characters and highly elevated diction). Vergil (70–19 B.C.) was a Roman poet who modeled his national epic on Homer's *Iliad* and *Odyssey*. The *Aeneid* begins, *"Arma virumque cano,"* which translates literally as "Of arms and the man I sing." The word order here is typical of Latin, in which the verb is usually placed at the end of a phrase or sentence. In normal English word order, we would translate this opening as "I sing of arms and the man." Milton's *Paradise Lost* begins as follows:

Of man's first disobedience, and the fruit
Of that forbidden tree whose mortal taste
Brought death into the world, and all our woe,
With loss of Eden, till one greater Man
Restore us, and regain the blissful seat,
Sing, Heavenly Muse . . .

Pope begins *The Rape of the Lock* in a similar manner:

What dire offense from amorous causes springs,
What mighty contests rise from trivial things,
I sing.

In both cases the word order is shifted so that the sentence reflects Latin syntax; as in the beginning of the *Aeneid*, the verb is moved from its normal position in English to the end of the phrase. Both Milton and Pope readjust the normal word order to emphasize the epic quality of their poems and the affinity of their work to the *Aeneid*. Similarly, both use the verb *sing* to echo Vergil's *cano* (I sing).

Many other adjustments to word order create specific effects. One of these is the placement of adjectives. Normally, adjectives are placed immediately before the nouns they modify; we speak, for example, of sunny days and bloody war. If we were to reverse the sequence, and refer to days sunny or war bloody, the word order would strike us as peculiar. Nevertheless, this sort of reversal is employed frequently in poetry to good advantage. Early in *Paradise Lost*, for example, Milton speaks of the time when Satan rebelled against God and "Raised impious war in Heaven and battle proud." The word order is unusual in two respects. In the first place, we would normally find both "impious war" and "battle proud" before the modifying prepositional phrase "in Heaven." Second, we expect the adjective *proud* to be before *battle*. Instead of writing, "Raised impious war and proud battle in Heaven," Milton readjusted the normal word order twice in order to place the word *proud* at the end of the line. The altered word order partly serves metrical demands, but it also stresses the word *proud*. This emphasis is consistent with the overall focus of *Paradise Lost* on human and Satanic pride.

These examples illustrate a general technique. There are hundreds, perhaps thousands, of ways that word order can be shifted for impact. It is impossible to describe or illustrate all of them here. As a general rule, however, you should pay careful attention to any variation in normal word order. Most variations have a purpose; your task is to figure out the effect that is produced by such adjustments.

One major area of syntax that becomes important in understanding poetry is sentence structure. We discuss this subject in Chapter 7 (pp. 267–268), but two specific aspects merit a closer look in connection with poetry. One of these is **repetition.** Repeating the same phrase or structure several times in a poem usually adds emphasis and sharpens focus. In William Blake's "The Lamb," for example, the same question is repeated four times with slight variation in the first stanza:

Little Lamb, who made thee?
Dost thou know who made thee?
        · · ·
Little Lamb who made thee?
Dost thou know who made thee?

This repetition has two primary effects. Initially, it tends to make the poem sound simple and childlike. At the same time, however, the repetitive structure focuses our attention on the central concern of the poem: the nature of the creator.

Another aspect of sentence structure that has a significant effect on poetry is **parallelism,** a rhetorical figure in which the same grammatical forms are repeated in the same order (see pp. 268–269). This technique is closely related to repetition; indeed, repetition may be called parallelism carried to an extreme. The effect of parallelism on poetry is twofold. It produces balanced lines that mirror each other form for form, and it allows the poet to link dissimilar concepts in parallel grammatical constructs. We have already examined an interesting example of parallelism in our discussion of the first stanza of Robert Graves's "The Naked and the Nude." Graves uses three parallel phrases—"the naked and the nude," "As love from lies," and "or truth from art"—that repeat the same pattern of noun–conjunction/preposition–noun. The parallel syntax thus associates "the naked" with "love" and "truth" and "the nude" with "lies" and "art."

POEMS FOR STUDY

BEN JONSON   (1572–1632)

On My First Son°   *1616 (1603?)*

Farewell, thou child of my right hand,° and joy;
My sin was too much hope of thee, loved boy;
Seven years thou wert lent to me, and I thee pay,
Exacted by thy fate, on the just day.
Oh, could I lose all father, now! For why   5
Will man lament the state he should envy?
To have so soon scaped° world's, and flesh's rage,   *escaped*
And, if no other misery, yet age?
Rest in soft peace, and, asked, say here doth lie

ON MY FIRST SON.   Jonson's eldest son, also named Benjamin, died on his seventh birthday in 1603.   1 *child of my right hand:* a literal translation of the Hebrew name Benjamin (*ben* means "son of" and *jamin* means "right hand").

Ben Jonson his° best piece of poetry,   *Jonson's*   10
For whose sake, henceforth, all his vows be such,
As what he loves may never like too much.

QUESTIONS

1. What special language is evoked by the phrase "child of my right hand"?
2. What metaphor is developed in lines 3–4? How do words like *lent, pay, exacted*, and *just* advance this comparison? Explain the irregular word order in line 3.
3. What does the speaker mean by "all father" (line 5)? What point does he make about his sadness and his son's present state in lines 5–8?
4. What kind of special diction is reflected in "Rest in soft peace" and "here doth lie" (line 9)? Where are such phrases normally found? Why are they here?
5. To whom does "Ben Jonson" (line 10) refer? How is the name used two ways?
6. The speaker calls his son "his best piece of poetry" (line 10). Look up the derivation of the word *poet* and explain this assertion.

JOHN DONNE (1572–1631)

Holy Sonnet 14: Batter My Heart, Three-Personed God   *1633*

Batter my heart, three-personed God; for You
As yet but knock, breathe, shine, and seek to mend;
That I may rise and stand, o'erthrow me, and bend
Your force to break, blow, burn and make me new.
I, like an usurped° town, to another due,   *stolen*   5
Labor to admit You, but Oh, to no end;
Reason, Your viceroy in me, me should defend,
But is captived, and proves weak or untrue.
Yet dearly I love You, and would be loved fain,°   *gladly*
But am betrothed unto Your enemy.   10
Divorce me, untie or break that knot again;
Take me to You, imprison me, for I,
Except You enthrall me, never shall be free,
Nor ever° chaste, except you ravish me.   *never*

QUESTIONS

1. What kind of God is suggested by the words *batter, knock, overthrow*, and *break*? What does "three-personed God" mean?
2. With which person of God might the verbs *knock* and *break* be associated? The verbs *breathe* and *blow*? The verbs *shine* and *burn*? What pun lurks behind this last pair of verbs?

3. To what does the speaker compare himself in lines 5–8? To what does he compare his "Reason"? Who is the usurper?

4. What is the effect of the altered word order at the ends of lines 7 and 9?

5. To what does the speaker compare himself in lines 9–14? Who is "your enemy"? What is the metaphorical relationship between the speaker and this enemy?

6. Explain the words *enthrall* (line 13) and *ravish* (line 14) to resolve the apparent paradox or contradiction in the last two lines.

WILLIAM BLAKE   (1757–1827)

The Lamb   *1789*

> Little Lamb, who made thee?
>   Dost thou know who made thee?
> Gave thee life & bid thee feed,
> By the stream & o'er the mead;
> Gave thee clothing of delight,   5
> Softest clothing wooly bright;
> Gave thee such a tender voice,
> Making all the vales rejoice!
>   Little Lamb who made thee?
>   Dost thou know who made thee?   10
>
> Little Lamb I'll tell thee,
>   Little Lamb I'll tell thee!
> He is callèd by thy name,
> For he calls himself a Lamb:
> He is meek & he is mild,   15
> He became a little child:
> I a child & thou a lamb,
> We are callèd by his name.
>   Little Lamb God bless thee.
>   Little Lamb God bless thee.   20

QUESTIONS

1. Who or what is the speaker in this poem? The listener? How are they related?

2. What central question does the poem ask and then answer?

3. What is the effect of repetition in the poem?

4. How would you characterize the diction in this poem? High, middle, or low? Abstract or concrete? How is it consistent with the speaker?

5. What are the connotations of *softest, bright, tender, meek,* and *mild*? What do these words imply about the Creator?

6. Describe the characteristics of the Creator imagined in this poem. Compare the image presented here with the image of God in Donne's "Batter My Heart, Three-Personed God." What differences do you find?

LEWIS CARROLL (1832–1898)

Jabberwocky°   *1871*

'Twas brillig, and the slithy toves
  Did gyre and gimble in the wabe;
All mimsy were the borogoves,
  And the mome raths outgrabe.

"Beware the Jabberwock, my son!   5
  The jaws that bite, the claws that catch!
Beware the Jubjub bird, and shun
  The frumious Bandersnatch!"

He took his vorpal sword in hand;
  Long time the manxome foe he sought—   10
So rested he by the Tumtum tree,
  And stood awhile in thought.

And, as in uffish thought he stood,
  The Jabberwock, with eyes of flame,
Came whiffling through the tulgey wood,   15
  And burbled as it came!

One, two! One, two! And through and through
  The vorpal blade went snicker-snack!
He left it dead, and with its head
  He went galumphing back.   20

"And hast thou slain the Jabberwock?
  Come to my arms, my beamish boy!
O frabjous day! Callooh! Callay!"
  He chortled in his joy.

'Twas brillig, and the slithy toves   25
  Did gyre and gimble in the wabe;
All mimsy were the borogoves,
  And the mome raths outgrabe.

JABBERWOCKY. The poem, which appears in the first chapter of *Through the Looking Glass*, is full of nonsense words that Carroll made up with the sound (rather than the sense) in mind. Alice admits that the poem makes some sense even though she does not know the words: "It seems very pretty . . . but it's rather hard to understand! . . . Somehow it seems to fill my head with ideas—only I don't exactly know what they are!"

QUESTIONS

1. Summarize in your own words the story that this poem tells.

2. Humpty Dumpty begins to explain or explicate this poem for Alice in chapter
   6 of *Through the Looking Glass*. He explains that " 'brillig' means four o'clock
   in the afternoon—the time when you begin *broiling* things for dinner." He
   also explains that " 'slithy' means 'lithe' and 'slimy.' 'Lithe' is the same as
   'active.' You see it's like a portmanteau—there are two meanings packed
   into one word." Go through the poem and list all the portmanteau words
   you can find. Then unpack the words; try to determine what combinations
   of words are packed into these portmanteau words. *Brillig*, for example,
   might be seen as a combination of *broiling*, *brilliant*, and *light*.

EDWIN ARLINGTON ROBINSON   (1869–1935)

Richard Cory   *1897*

Whenever Richard Cory went down town,
We people on the pavement looked at him:
He was a gentleman from sole to crown,
Clean favored, and imperially slim.

And he was always quietly arrayed,   5
And he was always human when he talked;
But still he fluttered pulses when he said,
'Good-morning,' and he glittered when he walked.

And he was rich—yes, richer than a king—
And admirably schooled in every grace: 10
In fine, we thought that he was everything
To make us wish that we were in his place.

So on we worked, and waited for the light,
And went without the meat, and cursed the bread;
And Richard Cory, one calm summer night,   15
Went home and put a bullet through his head.

QUESTIONS

1. What can you surmise about the speaker of this poem? What is his or her
   status?

2. What is the effect of using *down town*, *pavement*, *meat*, and *bread* in connection
   with the people who admire Richard Cory?

3. What are the connotations and implications of the name *Richard Cory?* Of the word *gentleman?*
4. Why does the poet use "sole to crown" instead of "head to toe" and "imperially slim" instead of "very thin" to describe Cory?
5. What effect does repetition produce in this poem? Consider especially the six lines that begin with "And."
6. What positive characteristics does Richard Cory possess (at least from the perspective of the speaker) besides wealth?
7. What ideas about the human condition does this poem explore?

WALLACE STEVENS   (1879–1955)

Disillusionment of Ten O'Clock   *1923*

The houses are haunted
By white night-gowns.
None are green,
Or purple with green rings,
Or green with yellow rings,   5
Or yellow with blue rings.
None of them are strange,
With socks of lace
And beaded ceintures.°   *belts*
People are not going   10
To dream of baboons and periwinkles.
Only, here and there, an old sailor,
Drunk and asleep in his boots,
Catches tigers
In red weather.   15

QUESTIONS

1. Is the "Ten O'Clock" here morning or night? How can you tell?
2. What do "haunted" and "white night-gowns" suggest about the people who live in the houses? What do the negative images in lines 3–9 suggest?
3. To whom are these people contrasted in lines 12–15?
4. What are the connotations of "socks with lace" and "beaded ceintures"? With which character in the poem would you associate these things?
5. What is the effect of using words and images like *baboons, periwinkles, tigers,* and *red weather* in lines 11–15? Who will dream of these things?
6. What do the people in "white night-gowns" lack that the "old sailor" has?
7. Unpack the term *disillusionment* and explore its relation to the point that this poem makes about dreams, images, and imagination.

THEODORE ROETHKE   (1907–1963)

Dolor   1943

I have known the inexorable sadness of pencils,
Neat in their boxes, dolor of pad and paper-weight,
All the misery of manila folders and mucilage,
Desolation in immaculate public places,
Lonely reception room, lavatory, switchboard,   5
The unalterable pathos of basin and pitcher,
Ritual of multigraph, paper-clip, comma,
Endless duplication of lives and objects.
And I have seen dust from the walls of institutions,
Finer than flour, alive, more dangerous than silica,   10
Sift, almost invisible, through long afternoons of tedium,
Dropping a fine film on nails and delicate eyebrows,
Glazing the pale hair, the duplicate grey standard faces.

QUESTIONS

1. What does *dolor* mean? Locate all the words in the poem related to "dolor."
    What do they have in common? Are they concrete or abstract? Specific or
    general? Latinate or common?
2. How are specific and concrete words used in this poem to define concepts
    and conditions that are presented in general and abstract terms?
3. What are the institutions, conditions, and places that the speaker associates
    with "dolor"? What do these institutions and places have in common?
4. What point does this poem make about the public world and about the
    details of day-to-day existence?

HENRY REED   (b. 1914)

Naming of Parts   1946

To-day we have naming of parts. Yesterday,
We had daily cleaning. And to-morrow morning,
We shall have what to do after firing. But to-day,
To-day we have naming of parts. Japonica
Glistens like coral in all of the neighboring gardens,   5
      And to-day we have naming of parts.

This is the lower sling swivel. And this
Is the upper sling swivel, whose use you will see,
When you are given your slings. And this is the piling swivel,
Which in your case you have not got. The branches   10

Hold in the gardens their silent, eloquent gestures,
    Which in our case we have not got.

This is the safety-catch, which is always released
With an easy flick of the thumb. And please do not let me
See anyone using his finger. You can do it quite easy   15
If you have any strength in your thumb. The blossoms
Are fragile and motionless, never letting anyone see
    Any of them using their finger.

And this you can see is the bolt. The purpose of this
Is to open the breech, as you see. We can slide it   20
Rapidly backwards and forwards: we call this
Easing the spring. And rapidly backwards and forwards
The early bees are assaulting and fumbling the flowers:
    They call it easing the Spring.

They call it easing the Spring: it is perfectly easy   25
If you have any strength in your thumb: like the bolt,
And the breech, and the cocking-piece, and the point of balance,
Which in our case we have not got; and the almond-blossom
Silent in all of the gardens and the bees going backwards and forwards,
    For to-day we have naming of parts.   30

QUESTIONS

1. There may be two speakers in this poem, or one speaker repeating the words
   of another and adding his own thoughts. In any event, what two voices do
   you hear?
2. What is the setting? The situation? How do these affect the speaker?
3. What two completely different sets of "parts" are named in this poem? How
   are the two sets related to each other?
4. How and why is jargon used in the poem? With what set of "parts" is the
   jargon initially associated? How does this change?
5. How are phrases like "easing the spring" (lines 22, 24, 25) and "point of
   balance" (27) used with more than one meaning? What is the effect of repetition?
6. What ideas about war, the military, and nature does this poem explore?

RICHARD EBERHART   (b. 1904)

The Fury of Aerial Bombardment   1947

You would think the fury of aerial bombardment
Would rouse God to relent; the infinite spaces
Are still silent. He looks on shock-pried faces.
History, even, does not know what is meant.

You would feel that after so many centuries   5
God would give man to repent; yet he can kill
As Cain could, but with multitudinous will,
No farther advanced than in his ancient furies.

Was man made stupid to see his own stupidity?
Is God by definition indifferent, beyond us all?   10
Is the eternal truth man's fighting soul
Wherein the Beast ravens in its own avidity?

Of Van Wettering I speak, and Averill,
Names on a list, whose faces I do not recall
But they are gone to early death, who late in school   15
Distinguished the belt feed lever from the belt holding pawl.

QUESTIONS

1. Who or what is the speaker in this poem? What does the last stanza tell you about him? (Eberhart was a gunnery instructor during World War II.)

2. To whom does the "you" in lines 1 and 5 refer?

3. What type and level of diction predominate in lines 1–12? What observations about God are made in these lines? Compare the image of God presented here with the one found in Donne's "Batter My Heart, Three-Personed God," and Blake's "The Lamb." What similarities or differences do you find?

4. How does the level and type of diction change in the last stanza? What is the effect of these changes? How is jargon used here?

5. What ideas about humanity and war does this poem explore? Compare this poem with Thomas Hardy's "Channel Firing" (p. 562). How are the ideas in the poems similar?

WRITING ABOUT DICTION AND SYNTAX IN POETRY

In setting out to write an essay on a poem's diction or syntax, you will usually be looking for a connection between one of these elements and another element of poetry, such as character, setting, or ideas. Consequently, you cannot begin to develop your own ideas about the impact of language until you have a clear general understanding of the poem you have chosen to consider.

First note down as much as you can about the speaker, the listener, the other characters, the setting and situation, the subject, and the ideas of the poem. You may use little of this material in your essay, but it will help shape your response to questions of diction and syntax. Moreover, you will find that the diction and syntax contribute to the development and impact of these other elements. Thus, you are likely to end up writing about word choice or language in connection with some other crucial element of poetry.

Once you understand the general meaning and impact, move back through the poem and examine it word by word and sentence by sentence. Look for any consistent patterns of diction or syntax that relate to the elements you have already considered. If you were planning to write about diction in Frost's "Stopping By Woods on a Snowy Evening" (p. 529), for example, you might isolate the following words and phrases connected with setting and situation: "woods," "fill up with snow," "without a farm-house," "between the woods and frozen lake," "sound's the sweep," "easy wind," "downy flake," "lovely," "dark," and "deep." Some of these are quite straightforward, but others lend themselves to further investigation and explanation. You might consider the implications of "fill up," "without a farmhouse near," and "between the woods and frozen lake"; these phrases all suggest more than they say. In addition, you might deal with the connotative values of words like *woods, darkest, sweep, easy, downy,* and *deep.* A careful analysis of the diction employed here will lead you to a series of connected discoveries about Frost's language. These discoveries, in turn, can produce the raw materials for an essay about the link between diction and setting in "Stopping by Woods."

As you develop your ideas, look for any effective and consistent patterns of word choice, connotation, repetition, or the like that help create and reinforce the conclusions you have already reached about the poem. You might ask yourself the following questions:

1. Does the poem contain many loaded or connotative words in connection with any single element like setting, speaker, or theme?
2. Does the poem contain a large number of general and abstract or specific and concrete words? What is the effect of these choices?
3. Is the level of diction in the poem elevated, neutral, or informal, and how does this level affect your perception of the speaker, subject, and the like?
4. Does the poem contain examples of special diction such as jargon? If so, how do these help shape your response to the poem as a whole?
5. Can you find instances of abnormal English word order in the poem, and if so, what is the effect of these alterations?
6. Has the poet used any striking patterns of sentence structure such as parallelism or repetition? If so, what is the effect?

These questions isolate places to begin an exploration of diction or syntax with an eye to writing an effective essay. Eventually, you should focus your efforts on a single aspect of word choice or language. Once you deal with these six questions, however, the most fruitful area of investigation should be clear.

When you have narrowed your examination down to one or two specific areas of diction or syntax, list relevant words, phrases, and sentences, and investigate the full range of meaning and effect produced by the examples. At this point, begin to look for examples that work in similar ways or produce similar effects. Doing this will allow you to group related examples together as you organize your notes. Eventually, you will want to reorganize your initial list of instances and explanations so that related examples are grouped together in units that will become paragraphs when you write the essay.

Finally, you will be ready to formulate a tentative central idea and arrange your examples in the most effective way to support this thesis. The central idea will naturally emerge from your investigation of the specific group or groups of examples of diction or syntax that prove to be most fruitful and interesting. Since diction and syntax contribute to the general impact and meaning of the poem, your thesis and examples will almost always relate to conclusions you have reached about the poem through other avenues of exploration.

Organizing Your Essay

INTRODUCTION.   The introduction should begin by making a general observation about theme, character, speaker, or other key elements in the poem under consideration. The central idea of the essay—a focused statement about the effects of word choice or language—should relate to this general point. If you are writing an essay about "The Naked and the Nude," for example, your central idea might assert that Graves employs words with multiple denotations and connotations to emphasize the moral and lexical distinctions between "the naked" and "the nude." Such a formulation makes a clear connection between diction and meaning. The introduction should also suggest the ways in which the central idea will be supported in the body.

BODY.   The body of the essay normally provides evidence, in an orderly and convincing manner, to support the assertion about diction or syntax made in the introduction. There are many different ways that such material can be organized. If you choose to deal with only one aspect of diction, such as connotative words or jargon, you might treat these in the order in which they appear in the poem. When you deal with two or three different aspects of diction and syntax, however, you can group related examples together regardless of where they occur. Thus, you might treat examples of multiple denotation, then connotation, and finally jargon in a series of paragraphs. In this instance, the organization of the essay is controlled by the types of material under consideration rather than by the order in which the words occur in the poem.

Alternatively, you might deal with the impact of diction or syntax on a series of other elements, such as character, setting, *and* situation. In such a paper you would focus on a single type of lexical or syntactic device as it relates to these different elements in sequence. Thus, you might discuss the link between connotation and character, then setting, and finally situation in sequential paragraphs. Whatever organization you select initially, keep in mind that each poem will finally suggest its own avenues of exploration and strategies of organization.

CONCLUSION.   The conclusion should bring the essay to a strong and assertive close. Here, you can summarize the conclusions you have reached about the impact of diction or syntax in the poem. You can also consider the larger implications of your ideas in connection with the thoughts and emotions conveyed by the poem and evoked in your reading.

SAMPLE ESSAY

Diction and Character in Edwin Arlington Robinson's "Richard Cory"*

[1]
In "Richard Cory," Edwin Arlington Robinson makes a general observation about the human condition; namely, that nothing can ensure happiness. Robinson explores this idea by focusing on a central character—Richard Cory—who seems to have everything: wealth, status, dignity, taste, respect, and humanity. Cory's suicide at the end of the poem, however, reveals that these things cannot be equated with happiness. Robinson sets us up for the surprising reversal in the last two lines—the suicide—by creating a gulf between Cory and the people of the town who admire and envy him. This distinction is produced, at least in part, through Robinson's use of loaded words that demean the general populace and elevate the central character.° The speaker and his or her fellow workers have words associated with them that connote their common lot, while Richard Cory is described in terms that imply nobility and privilege.□

[2]
For the most part, the poem focuses on Richard Cory. This character is seen, however, from the perspective of the townspeople, who wished "that we were in his place" (line 12). Robinson skillfully employs words in connection with these common folk to suggest their low status and impoverished way of life. In the first line of the poem, for example, the speaker places himself or herself and these other people "down town." The phrase denotes the central business district of a city. Nevertheless, it also carries all the denotations and connotations of the word *down*. The term thus implies that Cory's journey to town is a descent or a lowering "down" and that the people exist continually in this "down" condition. We find a similar instance of loaded diction in the term *pavement* (line 2). Robinson employs *pavement* instead of *sidewalk* to create a stronger sense of inferiority for the speaker and the common people.

* See p. 592 for this poem.
° Central idea.
□ Thesis sentence.

Pavement can mean sidewalk, but it can also mean street or roadbed. The net effect of the term *pavement* here is to place "we people" even lower than Richard Cory—literally on the street.

[3] In contrast to these few examples of diction that suggest the negative status of the people, the poem overflows with terms that connote Richard Cory's elevated status. Many of these words and phrases also carry the suggestion of nobility or royalty. These implications begin with the title of the poem and the name "Richard Cory." *Richard* contains the word *rich*, thus implying wealth and privileged status through sound. It is also the name of a number of English kings, including Richard the Lion Hearted ("Richard Coeur de Lion"). The name *Cory* is equally connotative. On first reading, it reminds us of the word *core*, the central or innermost part of anything. The name thus points toward Cory's singular position and significance in the town and in the poem. Through sound, *Cory* also suggests both the French word *cour* (court) and the English word *court*. The name "Richard Cory" thus begins a process of association through sound and implication that links the central character of this poem with images of kingship and the court.

[4] We find similarly loaded words throughout the first stanza of the poem. The speaker describes Richard Cory as "a gentleman from sole to crown" (line 3). *Gentleman* denotes a civilized and well-mannered individual, but it also means "highborn" or "noble" in older usage. The phrase "from sole to crown" means "from head to toe," but it connotes a great deal more than that. *Sole* means both "the bottom of a shoe or foot" and "alone" or "singular"; thus, the word suggests Cory's isolation and separation from the common folk. The word is also a pun and a homonym on *soul*, implying that Cory's gentility is inward as well as external. The final touch is the word *crown*. In context, the term denotes the top of the head, but its aristocratic and royal connotations are self-evident.

[5] The speaker also describes Cory as "clean favored" and "imperially slim" (line 4). "Clean favored," instead of the more common *good looking*, connotes crisp and untouched features; it again suggests that Cory is set apart and isolated. More to the point, the term *favored* also means "preferred," "elevated," "honored," and "privileged." "Imperially slim," instead of *thin*, is equally connotative of wealth and status. While both terms denote the same physical condition, *slim* connotes elegance, wealth, and choice, while *thin* suggests poverty, disease, and necessity. The adverb *imperially*, like *crown*, makes an explicit connection between Cory and emperors.

[6] Although instances of this type of diction taper off after the first stanza, Robinson employs enough similar terms in the rest of the poem to sustain the connotative link between Richard Cory and royalty. In the second stanza, for example, we find "quietly arrayed" and "glittered." Both carry elevated and imperial connotations. *Arrayed* means "dressed," but it is not a verb we associate with commonplace clothing. Rather, it implies elegant finery. "Quietly arrayed" means dressed with taste and modesty, but *quietly* also suggests solitude and introversion. *Glittered* works against *quietly*; it connotes richness of dress and manner, suggesting that the man himself is golden. In the third stanza, the deliberate cliché "richer than a king" again clearly links Richard Cory to royalty. The speaker also notes that Cory was "schooled in every

grace" (line 10). The phrase means that Cory was trained in manners and social niceties, but *grace* also connotes privilege and nobility, because it is the formal title used when addressing a monarch or member of the nobility (as in "Your Grace").

[7]
In conclusion, we can see that Robinson uses loaded words and connotation to lower the common folk and elevate the central character in "Richard Cory." The words linked with the speaker and the other townspeople have demeaning and negative implications. At the same time, the poet uses a series of words and phrases that connote royalty and privilege in connection with Cory. This careful manipulation of diction widens the gulf between Richard Cory and the speaker. It also heightens our sense that Cory is possessed of aristocratic looks, manners, taste, and breeding. The network of associations between Cory and royalty built through this skillful diction shapes our image of the central figure and thus makes the ending of the poem that much more shocking. The diction reinforces the poem's message that wealth, looks, breeding, and status cannot ensure happiness.

Commentary on the Essay

This essay deals with the ways in which Robinson uses loaded and connotative words to define and differentiate the townspeople and the central character in "Richard Cory." The opening paragraph makes a general assertion about the theme of the poem, connects character to this assertion, and argues that Robinson manipulates diction to achieve specific effects in connection with character. The central idea and the thesis sentence both assert that the poet employs diction to demean the common people (and the speaker of the poem) and to elevate Richard Cory.

The body of the essay deals with several instances of word choice and diction in five paragraphs. The organization illustrates a modified version of the first strategy discussed above. The examples of connotative words are arranged to reflect partly the characters they define and partly the order in which they appear in the poem. Thus, paragraph 2 discusses the common people and the speaker in connection with two loaded words: *down town* and *pavement*.

The next four paragraphs (3–6) focus on Richard Cory and words or phrases that suggest royalty and privilege. The examples of diction examined here are taken up in the order in which they appear in the poem. Thus, paragraph 3 considers Cory's name, and the fourth explores the connotative effects of *gentleman* and "sole to crown." Paragraphs 5 and 6 continue this process, examining instances of diction that sustain the association between Richard Cory and nobility. Taken together, the four paragraphs devoted to this central character illustrate Robinson's consistent manipulation of diction to enoble and isolate Cory.

The conclusion of the essay summarizes the observations about word choice and connotation made in the body. It also ties these observations back into a general consideration of character and theme. The conclusion asserts that Robinson's management of diction contributes to the isolation of Richard Cory from the other characters in the poem and that it adds to the impact of Cory's suicide in the last two lines. In this way, the words and phrases examined in the essay are linked to the poem's exploration of ideas about the human condition.

WRITING TOPICS FOR CHAPTER 14

1. Using the poems of Reed and Eberhart in this chapter, Jarrell (p. 520), and Owen (p. 659), study the words that these poets use to indicate the weapons and actions of warfare. Write an essay which considers these questions. How are the poets similar? How are they different? What details do they select commonly, and separately? How do their word choices assist them in making their various points about war as action, tragedy, and horror?

2. Write an essay in which you consider the sound qualities of the invented words in "Jabberwocky." Some obvious choices are "brillig," "frumious," "vorpal," and "manxome," but you are free to choose any or all of them. What is the relationship between the sound and apparent meaning of these words? What effect do the surrounding normal words and normal word order have upon the special words? How does Carroll succeed in creating a narrative "structure" even though the key words are, on the surface, nonsense?

3. Write a short poem describing a violent crime and commenting on it. Then, assume that you are the "perpetrator" of the crime, and write another poem on the same topic. Even though you describe the same details, how do your words differ, and why have you made these different choices? Explain the other different word choices you have made, with perhaps a discussion of words that you considered using but rejected.

15

Imagery: The Poem's Link to the Senses

In literature, **imagery** refers to words that trigger your imagination to recall and recombine **images**—to fuse together old and new memories or mental pictures of sights, sounds, tastes, smells, and sensations of touch. When particular words or descriptions cause you to form mental images, you put together selected memories and apply them to your understanding of what you are reading or hearing. (When you go just a step beyond, to write a poem or develop a new way to do a particular task, you are also using your imagination.) Through the deliberate use of imagery, therefore, poets tap your selected experiences in order to make their works lively and stimulating.

For example, the word "lake" may cause you to imagine or visualize a particular lake that you remember vividly. You may think of a distant view of calm waters reflecting blue sky, a nearby view of rippling waves stirred up by a wind, a close-up view from a boat looking at the lake bottom, or an overhead view of a sandy and sunlit shoreline. Similarly, the words "rose," "apple," "hot dog," "malted milk," and "pizza" all cause you to visualize these things and in addition may bring to your memory their smells and tastes. Active and pictorial words such as "row," "swim," and "dive" cause you to imagine someone performing these actions. Words like these, which poets use to make your imagination work, are images.

OUR RESPONSES AND THE POET'S USE OF DETAIL

In studying imagery, we need to determine how the writer brings the world alive so that we may reconstruct in our imaginations something like the set of pictures and impressions presented in the work. We must read the writer's words, but then let them simmer and percolate in our minds to develop what he or she intended. To get our imaginations stirring, we might follow Coleridge in this description from "Kubla Khan" (lines 37–41):

> A damsel with a dulcimer
> In a vision once I saw:
> It was an Abyssinian maid,
> And on her dulcimer she played,
> Singing of Mount Abora.

We do not read about the color of the damsel's clothing, or anything else about her appearance except that she is playing a stringed instrument, a dulcimer, and that she is singing a song about a mountain in a foreign, remote land. But Coleridge's reference is enough. From it we can imagine a magically distant, exotic, vivid picture of a woman singing and the loveliness of song. The image lives.

IMAGERY OF THE SENSES

IMAGES OF SIGHT.   Sight is the most significant of our senses, for sight is the key to our remembrance or recollection of other impressions. As might be expected, therefore, the most frequent imagery in literature is to things we can visualize either exactly or approximately—**visual images.** John Masefield, in his poem "Cargoes" (the subject of the sample essay at the end of this chapter), asks us to recreate mental pictures or images of ocean-going merchant vessels from three periods of human history.

JOHN MASEFIELD   (1878–1967)

Cargoes   *1902*

Quinquereme° of Nineveh° from distant Ophir,°
Rowing home to haven in sunny Palestine,
With a cargo of ivory,
And apes and peacocks,
Sandalwood, cedarwood, and sweet white wine.   5

CARGOES.   1 *quinquereme*: one of the largest types of ancient ships, having five tiers of oars.   *Nineveh*: capital of ancient Assyria, an "exceeding great city" (Jonah 3:3).   *Ophir*: a seaport, probably in Africa, from which cargoes like those described by Masefield were brought to King Solomon. See I Kings 9:11, 10:11, 10:22, and 2 Chronicles 9:2. Masefield echoes some of these verses in his first stanza.

Stately Spanish galleon coming from the Isthmus,°
Dipping through the Tropics by the palm-green shores,
With a cargo of diamonds,
Emeralds, amethysts,
Topazes, and cinnamon, and gold moidores.°   10

Dirty British coaster with a salt-caked smoke-stack,
Butting through the Channel in the mad March days,
With a cargo of Tyne coal,°
Road-rails, pig-lead,
Firewood, iron-ware, and cheap tin trays.   15

6 *Isthmus*: of Panama.   10 *moidores*: former coin of Brazil and Portugal.   13 *Tyne coal*:
Newcastle-upon-Tyne, in northern England, famous for its coal.

QUESTIONS

1. Consider the images that you find in each of the stanzas as they picture
   life during three periods of history: Ancient Israel at the time of Solomon,
   sixteenth-century Spain, and modern England. What do these images tell
   you about Masefield's interpretation of modern commercial life?

2. Consider the nature and type of the images in the poem. That is, do they
   refer mainly to things that you might see, or hear? What is the range of
   the imagery?

3. There are no complete sentences in this poem. Why do you think Masefield
   uses only the verbals (*rowing*, *dipping*, *butting*) that begin the second line of
   each stanza rather than finite verbs?

4. Let us suppose that the rowing of the Quinquereme of Nineveh was done
   by slaves and that the cargo of the Spanish galleons was seized by force
   from natives of Central America. Might these unpleasant suppositions disturb
   the romanticized impressions that Masefield intends for stanzas 1 and 2?

Masefield's images in "Cargoes" are vivid as they stand and need no
more detailed amplification. In order to reconstruct them imaginatively,
for example, we do not need ever to have seen "distant Ophir" (scholars
are uncertain about where it was anyway), or to have seen or handled
"pig-lead." We have seen enough in our lives both firsthand and in pictures
to *imagine* places and objects like these, and hence Masefield is successful
in implanting his visual images into our minds.

IMAGES OF SOUND.   Obviously, poets create images derived from the
other senses. **Auditory images,** or references to sound, are frequent. For
auditory images in a poem, let us consider Wilfred Owen's "Anthem for
Doomed Youth."

WILFRED OWEN (1893–1918)

Anthem for Doomed Youth   *1920*

What passing-bells for these who die as cattle?
Only the monstrous anger of the guns.
Only the stuttering rifles' rapid rattle
Can patter out their hasty orisons.°   *prayers*
No mockeries for them from prayers or bells,   5
Nor any voice of mourning save the choirs—
The shrill, demented choirs of wailing shells;
And bugles calling for them from sad shires.

What candles may be held to speed them all?
Not in the hands of boys, but in their eyes   10
Shall shine the holy glimmers of good-byes.
The pallor of girls' brows shall be their pall;
Their flowers the tenderness of patient minds,
And each slow dusk a drawing-down of blinds.

QUESTIONS

1. What is the predominant type of imagery in the first eight lines? How does
   the imagery change in the last six lines?

2. Describe the contrast throughout the poem of the sorts of images usually
   associated with death as observed in religious funerals and death as experienced on the battlefield. What is the effect of this contrast on your ability
   to experience and understand this poem?

3. Consider the following phrases as images: "holy glimmers of good-byes";
   "pallor of girls' brows"; "patient minds"; "drawing-down of blinds." Who
   are the people who are being considered in these images? What is their
   relationship to the doomed youth?

In asking what "passing-bells" may be tolled for "these who die as
cattle," Owen's speaker is referring to the traditional ringing of a parish
church bell to announce to the community the death ("passing") of a parish-
ioner. Such a ceremonial ringing suggests a period of peace and order, a
time when respect for the dead may be properly observed. But the poem
then points out that the only sound for those who have fallen in battle is
the "rapid rattle" of "stuttering" rifles—in other words, not the solemn,
dignified sounds of peace, but the horrifying noises of war. Owen's auditory
images evoke corresponding sounds in our imaginations, and help us experience the poem and hate the uncivilized depravity of war.

IMAGES OF SMELL, TASTE, AND TOUCH.   In addition to sight and sound,
you will find images derived from the other senses as well. An **olfactory**

image refers to smell, a **gustatory image** to taste, and a **tactile image** to touch. Love poetry, for example, often includes observations about the fragrance of flowers. As a twist on this common olfactory imagery, Shakespeare's speaker in Sonnet 130, "My Mistress' Eyes," candidly says that the breath of his woman friend is less pleasant than the scent of roses (see p. 612, lines 7–8).

Images derived from and referring to taste—gustatory images—are also common, though less frequent than those referring to sight and sound. In line 5 of Masefield's "Cargoes," for example, there is a reference to "sweet white wine," and in line 10 to "cinnamon." Although the poem refers to these things as cargoes, the words themselves inevitably register in our minds as gustatory images because they appeal to our sense of taste.

Tactile images of touch and texture are not as common in poems because touch is internally felt and is therefore subjective and difficult to render. In the short poem "Heat" (p. 618), H.D. refers to heat as an enclosing, stifling perception of feeling. Interestingly, however, she uses visual and kinetic images to render the tactile sensation of oppressive heat. In love poetry one might expect many tactile images. However, poets usually describe yearning and hope rather than fulfillment, because tactile images of love verge on the sensual and erotic (and sometimes on the pornographic) rather than on the strictly sensuous.

IMAGES OF MOTION AND ACTIVITY

The frames of reference of imagery may also take in virtually every sort of activity in which living beings may engage. Motion and action are common in poetry. Imagery referring to activities is termed *kinetic* if general motion is described, or *kinesthetic* if the imagery applies to human or animal activity. Masefield's reference to the British coaster butting through the channel is a kinetic image. Amy Lowell's reference to the speaker's walking in the garden after hearing about her fiancé's death is kinesthetic. Both types may be seen at the conclusion of "The Fish" by Elizabeth Bishop.

ELIZABETH BISHOP   (1911–1979)

The Fish   *1946*

I caught a tremendous fish
and held him beside the boat
half out of water, with my hook
fast in a corner of his mouth.
He didn't fight.   5

He hadn't fought at all.
He hung a grunting weight,
battered and venerable
and homely. Here and there
his brown skin hung in strips   10
like ancient wallpaper,
and its pattern of darker brown
was like wallpaper:
shapes like full-blown roses
stained and lost through age.   15
He was speckled with barnacles,
fine rosettes of lime,
and infested
with tiny white sea-lice,
and underneath two or three   20
rags of green weed hung down.
While his gills were breathing in
the terrible oxygen
—the frightening gills,
fresh and crisp with blood,   25
that can cut so badly—
I thought of the coarse white flesh
packed in like feathers,
the big bones and the little bones,
the dramatic reds and blacks   30
of his shiny entrails,
and the pink swim-bladder
like a big peony.
I looked into his eyes
which were far larger than mine   35
but shallower, and yellowed,
the irises backed and packed
with tarnished tinfoil
seen through the lenses
of old scratched isinglass.   40
They shifted a little, but not
to return my stare.
—It was more like the tipping
of an object toward the light.
I admired his sullen face,   45
the mechanism of his jaw,
and then I saw
that from his lower lip
—if you could call it a lip—
grim, wet, and weaponlike,   50
hung five old pieces of fish-line,
or four and a wire leader
with the swivel still attached,

with all their five big hooks
grown firmly in his mouth.
A green line, frayed at the end   55
where he broke it, two heavier lines,
and a fine black thread
still crimped from the stain and snap
when it broke and he got away.   60
Like medals with their ribbons
frayed and wavering,
a five-haired beard of wisdom
trailing from his aching jaw.
I stared and stared   65
and victory filled up
the little rented boat,
from the pool of bilge
where oil had spread a rainbow
around the rusted engine   70
to the bailer rusted orange,
the sun-cracked thwarts,
the oarlocks on their strings,
the gunnels—until everything
was rainbow, rainbow, rainbow!   75
And I let the fish go.

QUESTIONS

1. What are the images of actions in the poem? Are they ordinary or are they unusual?

2. What sort of impression does the fish make upon the speaker? Is the fish beautiful? Ugly? Why is the fish described in such detail?

3. What do the "five old pieces of fish-line" indicate about the previous existence of the fish?

4. How is the rainbow being formed around the engine of the boat? What does this rainbow suggest to the speaker?

5. Does the letting go of the fish seem abrupt, or is there a connection between the previous images of the fish and the release?

6. To what degree does it seem to be a matter of right for the fish to be free? Does the speaker seem to have a right to keep the fish? Why does the speaker finally let the fish go?

The kinetic images at the end of "The Fish" are those of victory filling the boat (difficult to visualize) and the oil spreading to make a rainbow (easier to visualize). The kinesthetic images are readily imagined—the speaker's staring, observing, and letting the fish go—yet they are vivid and real. The final gesture is the necesssary outcome of the observed contrast between the deteriorating artifacts of human beings and the natural world of the fish, and it is a vivid expression of the right of the natural world to exist without the intervention and pollution of human civilization. Bishop's kinetic and kinesthetic imagery, in short, is designed to objectivize the need for freedom not only for human beings but for all creatures.

The range of objects or activities that poets employ as imagery is both vast and unpredictable. Indeed, an important quality about imagery is its very unpredictability. At a first reading of "The Pulley," by George Herbert, for example, you might be hard put to explain the connection between the title and the poem itself. Here is the poem:

GEORGE HERBERT   (1593–1633)

The Pulley   *1633*

> When God at first made man,
> Having a glass of blessings standing by,
>   "Let us," said he, "pour on him all we can.
> Let the world's riches, which dispersed lie,
>   Contract into a span."°   5
>
>   So strength first made a way;
> Then beauty flowed, then wisdom, honor, pleasure.
>   When almost all was out, God made a stay,
> Perceiving that, alone of all his treasure,
>   Rest° in the bottom lay.   10
>
>   "For if I should," said he,
> "Bestow this jewel also on my creature.
>   He would adore my gifts instead of me.
> And rest in Nature, not the God of Nature;
>   So both should losers be.   15
>
>   "Yet let him keep the rest,
> But keep them with repining restlessness.
>   Let him be rich and weary, that at least,
> If goodness lead him not, yet weariness
>   May toss him to my breast."   20

THE PULLEY.   5 *span*: that is, within the control of human beings.   10 *rest*: (1) repose, security; (2) all that remains.

QUESTIONS

1. Describe the dramatic scene of the poem. Who is doing what?
2. What are the particular "blessings" that God confers on humanity, according to the speaker? Why should these be considered as blessings?

3. What remaining blessing does God withhold from all the treasures that have been bestowed on human beings? What is God's rationale, according to Herbert, for withholding it?

4. How might restlessness be manifested in human behavior? How adequate are the following words as synonyms for what Herbert seems to mean by restlessness: *dissatisfaction, anxiety, aimlessness, uncertainty, unhappiness, rootlessness, alienation?*

5. To what extent is it true or possible, as Herbert suggests, that "repining restlessness" might be the means that leads human beings to become religious?

6. Consider the image of the pulley as the means, or device, by which God has arranged that people will become worshipful.

The connection between title and poem becomes clear if we recall that pulleys, because they increase mechanical advantage, may enable large and heavily resistant objects to be moved easily by only a small force. Herbert's image of the pulley makes the human race such a resistant object. People, according to Herbert's speaker, have been blessed with so much that they can easily neglect God. But God nevertheless has mechanical advantage because human beings are never satisfied with all their blessings. God's hold is human restlessness and dissatisfaction, and God uses these conditions to pull human beings away from their worldly preoccupations toward faith and adoration. Using this mechanical image, Herbert makes the unpredictable relevant. Indeed, once we have finished "The Pulley," the image somehow seems no longer unusual or unpredictable at all, because it so aptly illustrates the connection between human behavior and divine power. Herbert, in other words, has chosen and developed his image in a masterly way.

The areas from which kinetic and kinesthetic imagery may be derived are almost too varied to describe. Occupations, trades, professions, businesses, recreational activities—all these might furnish images. One poet introduces references from gardening, another from money and banking, another from modern real-estate developments, another from life within jungles. The freshness, newness, and surprise of literature result from the many and varied areas from which poets draw their images.

IMAGERY, COMPLETENESS, AND TRUTH

Poets do not create imagery just to present a series of pictures or other sensory impressions. Their aim is to help you see the world in a new way, to widen your understanding, to transfer their own ideas by the *authenticating* effects of the vision and perceptions underlying them. Strong, vivid images are thus a means by which literature renders truth. It would be difficult to give assent to Masefield's views about modern commercial life if his image of the "Dirty British coaster with a salt-caked smoke-stack" did not ring true. It does.

Comparable imagery used for a different purpose may be seen in Shakespeare's Sonnet 130, "My Mistress' Eyes." Here Shakespeare's speaker expressly denies the overly romanticized compliments that men give women, stressing instead that his woman friend lives in the everyday world. By this emphasis, Shakespeare gains assent to the view that everyday life is superior to dream life, if for no other reason than that it provides a basis for a relationship between people. As you read poems and find images in them, try to determine their aptness, consistency, and reliability, for the life of literature generally and poetry specifically is only as durable as the authenticity of their imagery.

POEMS FOR STUDY

WILLIAM SHAKESPEARE (1564–1616)

Sonnet 130: My Mistress' Eyes Are Nothing Like the Sun   *1609*

My mistress'° eyes are nothing like the sun;	*woman friend*	
Coral is far more red than her lips' red;		
If snow be white, why then her breasts are dun;		
If hairs be wires, black wires grow on her head.		
I have seen roses damasked,° red and white,	*set in an elaborate bouquet*	5
But no such roses see I in her cheeks;		
And in some perfumes is there more delight		
Than in the breath that from my mistress reeks.		
I love to hear her speak, yet well I know		
That music hath a far more pleasing sound;		10
I grant I never saw a goddess go;		
My mistress, when she walks, treads on the ground.		
And yet, by heaven, I think my love as rare		
As any she belied with false compare.		

QUESTIONS

1. To what does the speaker negatively compare his mistress's eyes? Lips? Breasts? Hair? Cheeks? Breath? Voice? Walk? What kinds of images are created in these negative comparisons?

2. What conventional images and comparisons does this poem ridicule? What sort of poem is Shakespeare mocking by using the negative images in lines 1–12?

3. Do the images seem insulting? In the light of the last two lines, do you think the speaker intends the images as insults? If not as insults, how should they be taken?

4. Are most of the images in the poem auditory, olfactory, visual, or kinesthetic? Explain your answer.

5. What point does this poem make about love poetry? About human relationships? How does the imagery contribute to the development of both points?

RICHARD CRASHAW (1613–1649)

On Our Crucified Lord, Naked and Bloody   1646

Th' have° left Thee naked,° Lord, O that they had;   *they have*
This garment too I would they had denied.
Thee with Thyself they have too richly clad,
Opening the purple° wardrobe of Thy side.°
  O never could be found garments too good   5
  For Thee to wear, but these, of Thine own blood.

ON OUR CRUCIFIED LORD, NAKED AND BLOODY. 1 *naked*: See Mark 15:24.
3–4 *Thee . . . side*: John 20:34. 4 *purple*: Mark 15:17.

QUESTIONS

1. Describe the two aspects of the imagery of clothing in this poem. How might the blood of Christ be considered as a garment?

2. Explain the contradiction and irony in the poem. Why does clothing made by human beings seem unworthy of being draped upon the crucified Lord?

3. What is meant by "this garment" in line 2? What is the relationship between this phrase and "Thee with Thyself" in line 3?

4. Does the emphasis on the blood of Christ in this poem seem appropriate or inappropriate for a devotional poem?

WILLIAM BLAKE (1757–1827)

The Tyger°   1794

Tyger! Tyger! burning bright
In the forests of the night,
What immortal hand or eye
Could frame thy fearful symmetry?

In what distant deeps or skies   5
Burnt the fire of thine eyes?
On what wings dare he aspire?
What the hand, dare seize the fire?

THE TYGER The title refers not only to a tiger, but to any large, wild, ferocious cat.

And what shoulder, & what art,
Could twist the sinews of thy heart?   10
And when thy heart began to beat,
What dread hand? & what dread feet?

What the hammer? what the chain?
In what furnace was thy brain?
What the anvil? what dread grasp   15
Dare its deadly terrors clasp?

When the stars threw down their spears,
And water'd heaven with their tears,
Did he smile his work to see?
Did he who made the Lamb make thee?   20

Tyger! Tyger! burning bright
In the forests of the night,
What immortal hand or eye
Dare frame thy fearful symmetry?

QUESTIONS

1. What do the associations of the image of "burning" suggest? Why is the burning being done in the forests of the night rather than the day? What does the image of night suggest?
2. What is meant by "immortal hand or eye"?
3. Describe the kinesthetic images of lines 4–20. What ideas is Blake's speaker representing by these images? What sorts of actions are mentioned? What possible attributes does the speaker suggest may belong to the blacksmith-type initiator of these actions?
4. Line 20 is a question about the kinesthetic image of a creator. What is implied in the question concerning the mixture of good and evil in the world? What answer do you think the poem is suggesting? Why does Blake phrase this line as one of the many questions in the poem, rather than as an assertion?
5. Stanza 6 repeats stanza 1 with only one change of imagery of action. Contrast these stanzas, stressing the difference between *could* in 4 and *dare* in 24.

SAMUEL TAYLOR COLERIDGE   (1772–1834)

Kubla Khan   *1816*

In Xanadu did Kubla Khan
A stately pleasure dome decree:
Where Alph,° the sacred river, ran

KUBLA KHAN.   3 *Alph*: possibly a reference to the river Alpheus in Greece, as described by the ancient writers Virgil and Pausanias.

Through caverns measureless to man
  Down to a sunless sea.   5
So twice five miles of fertile ground
With walls and towers were girdled round:
And there were gardens bright with sinuous rills,
Where blossomed many an incense-bearing tree;
And here were forests ancient as the hills,   10
Enfolding sunny spots of greenery.

But oh! that deep romantic chasm which slanted
Down the green hill athwart a cedarn cover!
A savage place! as holy and enchanted
As e'er beneath a waning moon was haunted   15
By woman wailing for her demon lover!
And from this chasm, with ceaseless turmoil seething,
As if this earth in fast thick pants were breathing,
A mighty fountain momently was forced:
Amid whose swift half-intermitted burst   20
Huge fragments vaulted like rebounding hail,
Or chaffy grain beneath the thresher's flail:
And 'mid these dancing rocks at once and ever
It flung up momently the sacred river.
Five miles meandering with a mazy motion   25
Through wood and dale the sacred river ran,
Then reached the caverns measureless to man,
And sank in tumult to a lifeless ocean:
And 'mid this tumult Kubla heard from far
Ancestral voices prophesying war!   30
  The shadow of the dome of pleasure
  Floated midway on the waves;
  Where was heard the mingled measure
  From the fountain and the caves.
It was a miracle of rare device,   35
A sunny pleasure dome with caves of ice!

  A damsel with a dulcimer
  In a vision once I saw:
  It was an Abyssinian maid,
  And on her dulcimer she played   40
  Singing of Mount Abora.°
Could I revive within me
Her symphony and song,
To such a deep delight 'twould win me,
That with music loud and long,   45
I would build that dome in air,
That sunny dome! those caves of ice!

41 *Mount Abora*: a mountain of Coleridge's imagination. But see John Milton, *Paradise Lost*, IV, lines 268–284.

And all who heard should see them there,
And all should cry, Beware! Beware!
His flashing eyes, his floating hair!   50
Weave a circle round him thrice,
And close your eyes with holy dread,
For he on honeydew hath fed,
And drunk the milk of Paradise.

QUESTIONS

1. What is imagined as the poem's locale?

2. Study the poem's images closely. How many of them might be sketched or visualized? Which ones would be panoramic landscapes? Which might be closeups?

3. Discuss the poem's auditory imagery. What is the effect of images such as "wailing," "fast thick pants," "tumult," "ancestral voices prophesying war," and "mingled measure"?

4. When Coleridge was writing this poem, he was recalling it from a dream. At line 54 he was interrupted, and when he resumed he could write no more. Does the poem seem unfinished? How might an argument be made that the poem is finished?

5. How do lines 35–36 establish the pleasure dome as a place of mysterious oddity? What is the effect of the words *miracle* and *rare*? The effect of combining the images "sunny" with "caves of ice"?

6. Why does the speaker yearn for the power of the singing Abyssinian maid? What kinesthetic images end the poem? What importance do these images possess as part of the speaker's desire to reconstruct the vision of the pleasure dome?

GERARD MANLEY HOPKINS   (1844–1889)

Spring   *1877*

Nothing is so beautiful as Spring—
    When weeds, in wheels, shoot long and lovely and lush;
    Thrush's eggs look little low heavens, and thrush
Through the echoing timber does so rinse and wring
The ear, it strikes like lightnings to hear him sing;   5
    The glassy peartree leaves and blooms, they brush
    The descending blue; that blue is all in a rush
With richness; the racing lambs too have fair their fling.

What is all this juice and all this joy?
    A strain of the earth's sweet being in the beginning   10

In Eden garden.—Have, get, before it cloy,
  Before it cloud, Christ, lord, and sour with sinning,
Innocent mind and Mayday in girl and boy,
  Most, O maid's child, thy choice and worthy the winning.

QUESTIONS

1. What images does the speaker mention as support for his first line, "Nothing is so beautiful as Spring"? Are these images those that you would normally expect? To what degree do they seem to be new or unusual?

2. What images of motion and activity do you find in the poem? Are these mainly static or dynamic? What do these suggest about the speaker's view of spring?

3. What is the relationship between "Eden garden" in line 11 and the scene described in lines 1–8? To what extent can spring and "innocent mind and Mayday" be considered a glimpse of what life might have been like in the Garden of Eden?

4. Christ is mentioned in line 12 and again in line 14 (as "maid's child"). Do these references seal the poem off from readers who are not Christian? Why or why not?

EZRA POUND   (1885–1972)

In a Station of the Metro°   *1916*

The apparition of these faces in the crowd;
Petals on a wet, black bough.

IN A STATION OF THE METRO.   *Metro*: the Paris subway.

QUESTIONS

1. Does the image of the petals on the wet, black bough evoke cheer or sadness? If the petals were "blooming" on a tree in the sunlight in spring, would the image be more pleasant? Explain.

2. What is the meaning of the image suggested by *apparition*? Does it suggest a positive or negative view of human life?

3. This poem contains only two lines. Is it proper to consider it as a poem nevertheless? If it is not to be considered as a poem, how should it be considered?

H. D. (HILDA DOOLITTLE)   (1886–1961)

Heat   *1916*

O wind, rend open the heat,
cut apart the heat,
rend it to tatters.

Fruit cannot drop
through this thick air—   5
fruit cannot fall into heat
that presses up and blunts
the points of pears
and rounds the grapes.

Cut the heat—   10
plough through it,
turning it on either side
of your path.

QUESTIONS

1. What is the meaning of the images of rending and cutting in the first three lines?
2. In lines 4–9, is it literally true that fruit cannot fall? If it is not, what is the meaning of the image that heat may blunt the points of pears and make grapes round?
3. Discuss the image of a plough as a cutter and separator of heat.
4. In the light of the various images in the poem, what impression of heat does the poet succeed in expressing?

WRITING ABOUT IMAGERY

In preparing to write about imagery, you should work with a thoughtfully developed set of notes. With imagery it will be particularly important to be ready to classify references to the various senses to which they belong, such as sight and sound. In determining other classifications, you may be able to find a consistent pattern of references to a particular activity or related set of activities. If accurate classification is not possible, you may be able to make much of your poet's diversity of images.

Organizing Your Essay

INTRODUCTION.   Here you will set out the main points that you plan for the body of your essay; for example, you might assert that the poet refers heavily to images of sight or sound or action, and so on. Your central idea should clearly delineate your objective, and your thesis sentence should contain brief references to the topics of the following paragraphs or groups of paragraphs, depending on the length of your essay.

BODY. There are a number of aspects of imagery that may be developed in the body of your essay. You might choose one of these exclusively, but quite likely your essay may bring in two or more of the following approaches:

1. *The types of images.* Is there a predominance of a particular type of imagery, such as references to sight, or is there a blending? Is there a bunching of types at particular points in the poem? What might be a reason for this bunching? Is there any shifting from type to type as the poem develops? How do the images relate to the content, to the ideas, of the poem? Are they appropriate? Do they assist in making the ideas seem convincing? If there seems to be any inappropriateness, what is the effect upon the total impact of the poem?

2. *The level of images.* Do the images lend themselves to the establishment of any particular mood in the poem? Do they seem cheerful? Melancholy? Exciting? Vivid? Do they seem to be conducive to humor? Or surprise? How does the poet manipulate the images to achieve these effects? Are the images what they at first seem, or may they be taken a different way as the poem progresses? (For example, Shakespeare's references in Sonnet 130 might initially be construed as insults. However, in a total consideration of the sonnet, are they insults or compliments?)

3. *The development of any systems of images.* In effect this is another way of considering the appropriateness of the imagery in a poem. Do all the images adhere consistently to a particular frame of reference, such as the life of a big fish (see Bishop's "The Fish"), or the building of a vast forest and garden (Coleridge's "Kubla Khan"), or the sailing of merchant vessels (Masefield's "Cargoes")? Is there anything unusual or unique about the set of images? Do they provide you with any unexpected or new responses to the situation and ideas of the poem?

4. *The creation of a characteristic mode of images.* Does the poet rely on a particular type of image? If you find such a characteristic line of images, this line may be considered a mode for that poem if not for that poet. It may be hard to determine a modal type on the basis of only one poem, but there are questions to help you determine if there is a mode in the poem you have studied. Does the imagery seem to rely upon shapes, colors, sounds, actions? Is it especially vivid, and if so, how does the poet achieve this vividness? Does the poet present the images completely or sketchily? Is one type of image used rather than another—for example, as images of natural scenery rather than interiors, or loud sounds rather than silence? What kinds of conclusions can you draw about the poem and the author as a result of your answers?

CONCLUSION.   While in the body of the essay you will have been developing a fairly detailed analysis of the types and appropriateness of the poet's images, in your conclusion you might wish to stress any insights you have gained from your study. It would not be proper to introduce entirely new directions here, but you might briefly take up one or more of the conclusions you had reached but did not develop in the body. In short, what have you learned from your study of imagery in the poem about which you have written?

SAMPLE ESSAY

The Images in John Masefield's Poem "Cargoes"*

[1] In the three-stanza poem "Cargoes," John Masefield develops imagery to create a negative impression of modern commercial life.° There is a contrast between the first two stanzas and the third, with the first two evoking the romantic, distant past and the third demonstrating the modern, gritty, grimy present. Masefield's images are thus both positive and lush, on the one hand, and negative and stark, on the other.□

[2] The most evocative and pleasant images in the poem are included in the first stanza. The speaker asks that we imagine a "Quinquereme of Nineveh from distant Ophir," an ocean-going, many-oared vessel loaded with treasure for the biblical King Solomon. The visual impression is colorful, rich, and romantic. The word ivory (line 3) creates an image of riches while "apes and peacocks" bring to the reader's mind strange and colorful images. The speaker adds to the fullness of this scene by referring to sandalwood, cedarwood, and sweet white wine, thus adding images of smell and taste. The "sunny" light of ancient Palestine illuminates the scene, and invites readers to imagine the sun's warming touch. The references to animals and birds also suggest images of the sound these exotic creatures would make. Thus, in this lush first stanza, images derived from all the senses are introduced to create the life and impressions of a glorious past.

[3] Almost equally lush are the images of the second stanza, which completes the first part of the poem. Here the visual imagery evokes the royal splendor of a tall-masted, full-sailed galleon at the height of Spain's commercial power in the sixteenth century. The cargo of the galleon suggests great wealth, with sparkling diamonds and amethysts, and "gold moidores" of Portugal gleaming in colorful chests. Masefield also includes a reference to the pleasant-tasting spice cinnamon.

The negative imagery of the third stanza is in stark contrast to the first two stanzas. Here the poem draws the visual image of a modern "Dirty

---

* See p. 604 for the poem.
° Central idea.
□ Thesis sentence.

British coaster" to focus on the griminess and suffocation of modern civilization. This spray-swept ship is loaded with materials designed to pollute the earth with noise and smoke. The smokestack of the coaster (line 11) and the firewood it is carrying suggest the creation of choking smog. The "Tyne coal" (line 13) and "road-rails" (line 14) suggest the noise and smoke of puffing railroad engines. As if this were not enough, the "pig-lead" (line 14) to be used in

[4] various industrial processes indicates not just more unpleasantness, but also something more poisonous and deadly. In contrast to the lush and stately imagery of the first two stanzas, the images in the third stanza invite the conclusion that people now, when the "Dirty British coaster" butts through the English Channel, are surrounded and endangered by commercial activities that reduce the quality of life under the pretext of making it better.

The poem thus establishes a romantic past and ugly present through images of sight, smell, and sound. The images of motion also complement this view. In stanzas 1 and 2 the quinquereme is "rowing" and the galleon is "dipping." These kinetic images suggest dignity and lightness. By contrast,

[5] the British coaster is "butting," an image denoting bull-like hostility and blind force. These, together with all the other images, focus the poem's negative views of today's consumer-oriented society. Masefield's "Cargoes" is therefore a poem showing that images alone, without any further explanations, may be translated directly into judgment and commentary.

Commentary on the Essay

The introductory paragraph of the essay presents the central idea that Masefield uses his images climactically to lead to his negative view of modern commercialism. The thesis sentence indicates that the topics to be developed are (1) lushness, and (2) starkness.

Paragraphs 2 and 3 form a unit in which the lushness and exoticism of the images in stanzas 1 and 2 of the poem are stressed. All the examples—derived directly from the poem—emphasize the qualities of Masefield's images. The discussion in paragraphs 2 and 3 illustrates that no more than the minimal use of imagination is needed to make adequate sense of the images. Thus, in the real world, the peacocks of stanza 1 would have had feathers containing a number of bright, arresting colors, but these colors are not stressed in this essay beyond a reference to the general colorfulness of these birds. Ivory would unquestionably have been sculpted into various statues and ornaments, but because no mention is made by Masefield to any such shapes, the essay does not try to go beyond Masefield's general reference to "ivory." His images, in short, are considered only as they evoke an impression of lushness and richness. The illustrative value of this discussion is that in interpretation, readers should not go beyond where writers invite them to go, no matter how great the temptation.

Paragraph 4 stresses the contrast of Masefield's images in stanza 3 with those of stanzas 1 and 2. To this end, the paragraph illustrates the need for a high enough degree of imaginative reconstruction to develop an understanding of this contrast. The unpleasantness, annoyance, and even the danger of the cargoes mentioned in stanza 3 are therefore emphasized as the qualities evoked by the images.

The last paragraph demonstrates that the imagery of motion—not stressed in the poem—is in agreement with Masefield's other imagery. This paragraph therefore adds balance to the analysis carried out in paragraphs 2, 3, and 4.

WRITING TOPICS FOR CHAPTER 15

1. In the last six lines of "Anthem for Doomed Youth," the images referring to life in the homes of dead soldiers are particularly effective in the poem's condemnation of war. Write an essay explaining why they are effective. If Owen had chosen more violent images, how might the poem have been different, and would violent images have made the poem more effective?

2. Based on the poems by Crashaw, Blake, Coleridge, H.D., and Hopkins, write an essay discussing the poetic use of images drawn from the natural world. What sorts of references do the poets make? What attitudes do they express about the details they select? What is the relationship between the images and religious views? What judgments about God and nature do the poets show by the selection of their images?

3. Write a poem describing one of these:
    a. Athletes who have just completed an exhausting run.
    b. Children getting out of school for the day.
    c. Your recollection of having been lost as a child.
    d. The antics of your dog, cat, horse, or other pet.
    e. A particularly good meal you had recently.
    f. A good concert, rock or otherwise.

    Then write an analysis of the images you selected for your poem, and try to explain your choices. Are the details the things that stand out in your mind? What do you recall best—sight, smell, sound, action? What is the relationship between your images and the ideas you express in your poem?

16

Rhetorical Figures: A Source of Depth and Range in Poetry

Figurative language refers to expressions that conform to particular patterns and arrangements of thought. These patterns, or **rhetorical figures,** are the tools that help make literary works effective, persuasive, and forceful. Although rhetorical figures, also called **devices,** may be used in any literary work, they are most commonly found in poetry.

The two most important rhetorical figures are *metaphor* and *simile*. Others include *paradox, apostrophe, personification, synecdoche and metonymy, synesthesia, the pun* (or *paronomasia*), and *overstatement and understatement*. All these figures are modes of making comparisons, and they may be carried out through single words, phrases, clauses, and entire structures. Figures enable writers, especially poets, to extend and deepen their subject matter in ways similar to the operation of symbolism (see pp. 62, 326–328). The term *metaphorical* is sometimes broadly applied to most rhetorical figures, including symbols.

METAPHOR AND SIMILE

A **metaphor** (the "carrying out of a change") is the direct verbal equation of something unknown with something known, so that the unknown may be explained and made clear. A metaphor by Shakespeare that has become a favorite is "All the world's a stage, / And all the men and women merely players" (from *As You Like It*, act 2, scene 7), whereby Shakespeare's character Jacques explains aspects of human life (the unknown) by equating them with the life of the theatre (the known). Shakespeare's metaphor does not state that the world is *like* a stage, but that it literally *is* a stage.

While a metaphor thus merges identities, a **simile** (the "showing of similarity or oneness") explains the unknown by showing its **similarity** to the known. A simile is distinguishable from a metaphor because it is introduced by "like" with nouns and "as" (also "as if" and "as though") with clauses. Campion's sentence "Her brows like bended bows do stand," from the poem "Cherry Ripe" (p. 918), points out that the young woman being described is able to put down potential offenders with frowns that are as effective as arrows shot from a bow. Because the simile is introduced by "like," the emphasis of the figure is on the *similarity* of her eyebrows to bows and arrows, not on the *identification* of the two.

IMAGERY, METAPHOR, AND SIMILE

To see the relationship of metaphor and simile to imagery (see also Chapter 15, pp. 603–22), you should remember that imagery requires readers to use their imaginations to remember experiences that are suggested by language in a literary work. The images in the work arise as a function of the topic material. By duplicating the images intellectually and emotionally, through the use of imagination, readers may understand and verify the poet's ideas.

Metaphors and similes go beyond imagery by introducing comparisons that may be unusual, unpredictable, and even surprising. They connect the thing or things unknown and to be communicated—such as qualities of love or the excitement of unexpected discovery—with a new insight that is made objective through the comparison of a simile or the equation of a metaphor. For example, in "A Valediction: Forbidding Mourning," Donne's speaker points out that a trip away from a loved one is not really a separation, but is instead just a thinning out, like the hammering of the malleable element gold. How many people have ever thought that love is like a metal? But is it not true that the comparison emphasizes the permanence of the bond between two lovers, and also that gold itself shows how valuable the bond is? Such a figure extends knowledge and awareness by introducing new perspectives that otherwise would never come to light. First and foremost, then, metaphors and similes are a mode of expression, but more important, they are one of the ways in which great literature leads us to see the world originally and freshly.

For example, to communicate a character's joy and excitement, the sentence "She was happy" is accurate but not interesting or effective. A more vivid way of saying the same thing is to use an image of an action, such as, "She jumped for joy." This image gives us a concrete picture of something that a person might do out of happiness. An even better way of communicating a happy state is the following simile: "She felt as if she had just inherited five million tax-free dollars." Because readers can easily sense the excitement, disbelief, and exhilaration that such an event would bring, they also readily understand the range of the character's happiness.

It is the simile that evokes this perception. No simple description can help a reader comprehend the variety of emotion.

For a poetic example, let us refer to John Keats's sonnet "On First Looking into Chapman's Homer." Keats was inspired to write the poem after reading the translation by Elizabethan writer John Chapman of *The Iliad* and *The Odyssey*, epic poems attributed to the ancient Greek poet Homer. Keats's main idea is that Chapman not only translated Homer's words but also transmitted his greatness. A brief paraphrase of the poem is this:

> I have enjoyed much art and read much European literature, and have been told that Homer is the best writer of all, but not knowing Greek, I could not genuinely appreciate his works until I discovered them in Chapman's translation. To me, this experience was exciting and awe-inspiring.

This paraphrase destroys the poem's sense of exhilaration and discovery. Contrast the second sentence of the paraphrase with the last six lines of the sonnet as Keats writes them.

JOHN KEATS (1795–1821)

On First Looking into Chapman's Homer   *1816*

Much have I travell'd in the realms of gold,
   And many goodly states and kingdoms seen:
   Round many western islands have I been
Which bards in fealty to Apollo° hold.
Oft of one wide expanse had I been told   5
   That deep-brow'd Homer ruled as his demesne;°
   Yet did I never breathe its pure serene°
Till I heard Chapman speak out loud and bold:
Then felt I like some watcher of the skies
   When a new planet swims into his ken;°   10
Or like stout Cortez° when with eagle eyes
   He star'd at the Pacific—and all his men
Look'd at each other with a wild surmise—
   Silent, upon a peak in Darien.

ON FIRST LOOKING INTO CHAPMAN'S HOMER. George Chapman (c. 1560–1634) published his translations of Homer's *Iliad* in 1612 and *Odyssey* in 1614–15.   4 *bards . . . Apollo*: writers who are sworn subjects of Apollo, the Greek god of light, music, poetry, prophecy, and the sun.   6 *demesne*: realm, estate.   7 *serene*:   a clear expanse of air; also grandeur, clarity; rulers were also sometimes called "serene majesty."   10 *ken*: field of sight.   11 *Cortez*: Hernando Cortez (1485–1547), a Spanish general and the conqueror of Mexico. Keats has confused him with Vasco de Balboa (c. 1475–1519), the first European to see the Pacific Ocean (in 1510) from Darien, an old name for the Isthmus of Panama.

QUESTIONS

1. What is being discovered in this poem? To what extent is this process of discovery a universal experience?

2. Explain the metaphor of land and travel that Keats develops in lines 1–6. Be careful to consider the words *realms, states, kingdoms, islands, expanse,* and *demesne.*

3. In what way does Keats use the word "serene" in line 7? How is it possible, except in a metaphorical sense, to "breathe" serene? What do you think Keats intended by this phraseology?

4. How successfully does Keats convey a sense of excitement through the similes in lines 9–10 and 11–14? Create a simile of your own to express a feeling about discovery; how does yours compare with Keats's?

5. Describe the metaphor of *swims* in line 10. What might have been the impact if Keats had used words such as *drifts, floats, flows,* or *wanders?*

If all we had of the poem were our paraphrase, we would probably pay little attention to it, for it carries absolutely no sense of stimulation or discovery. But let us notice the power of the poem, particularly the two powerful similes in the last six lines ("like some watcher" and "like stout Cortez"). We should not just read these similes and pass them by, but should use our imaginations to experience them. In considering them and mulling them over, we might suppose that we actually *are* an astronomer just discovering a new planet, and that we actually *are* the first people to see the Pacific Ocean. As we imagine ourselves in these roles, we should think of our accompanying amazement, wonder, excitement, anticipation, joy, and sense of accomplishment. If we imagine these feelings, then Keats has unlocked experiences that the relatively unpromising title does not suggest. He has given us something new. He has enlarged us.

VEHICLE AND TENOR

To describe the relationship between a writer's ideas and the metaphors and similes chosen to objectify them, two useful terms have been coined by I. A. Richards (in *The Philosophy of Rhetoric*). First is the **tenor,** which is the totality of ideas and attitudes not only of the literary speaker but also of the author. Second is the **vehicle,** or the details that carry the tenor. The vehicle of the simile about the five-million dollars is the description of the inheritance, while the tenor is joy. Similarly, the tenor of the similes in the last six lines of Keats's sonnet is awe and wonder; the vehicle is the reference to astronomical and geographical discovery.

CHARACTERISTICS OF METAPHORICAL LANGUAGE

It would be difficult to find any good piece of writing that does not employ at least some metaphorical language. Such language is most vital, however, in imaginative writing, particularly poetry, where it compresses thought, promotes understanding, and shapes response.

As we have seen in the section on imagery above, images are embodied in words or descriptions denoting sense experience that leads to many associations. A single word naming a flower, say *rose*, evokes a positive response. A person might think of the color of a rose, recall its smell, associate it with the summer sun and pleasant days, and recall the love and respect that a bouquet of roses means as a gift. But the word *rose* is not a metaphor or simile until its associations are used in a comparative or analogical way, as in "A Red, Red Rose" by Robert Burns:

ROBERT BURNS (1759–1796)

A Red, Red Rose   *1796*

O my Luve's like a red, red rose,
   That's newly sprung in June:
O my Luve's like the melodie
   That's sweetly play'd in tune.

As fair art thou, my bonnie lass,   5
   So deep in luve am I;
And I will luve thee still, my Dear,
   Till a'° the seas gang° dry.   *all; go*

Till a' the seas gang dry, my Dear,
   And the rocks melt wi'° the sun: *with*   10
And I will luve thee still, my Dear,
   While the sands o' life shall run.

And fare thee weel, my only Luve!
   And fare thee weel, awhile!
And I will come again, my Luve,   15
   Tho' it were ten thousand mile!

QUESTIONS

1. What sort of person is the speaker? What is the situation he is speaking about?

2. Describe the shift in the person being addressed from stanza 1 to the remaining stanzas. How are the last three stanzas related to the first?
3. In light of the character and background of the speaker, do the two similes that open the poem seem common or unusual? If they are no more than ordinary comparisons, does that fact diminish their value? How and why?
4. Consider the metaphors in lines 9–16 concerning the passage of time and the traveling of great distance. How do the metaphors assist in the comprehension of the speaker's character?

In the first stanza, the speaker is talking about his sweetheart. While a doting lover might go on and on, the poet avoids boring us with a lengthy discourse. For this reason the similes are brief, but also strong. To dwell on the rose, the speaker asks us to bring to our minds all the possible associations that we might have with roses, in addition to those already mentioned. After winter's drabness and leaflessness, springtime's lush growth marks a new beginning, an entirely new and colorful earth as contrasted with the monochrome dullness of winter. Thus the rose suggests love, loveliness, colorfulness, the end of dreariness, and the seasonal fertility of the earth. Once we have expanded upon the simile in this way, we have come close to comprehending the speaker's enthusiasm about his lady.

To see how metaphorical language may be used to compress a writer's thought, consider Shakespeare's Sonnet 30. The opening metaphor equates lawcourt hearings ("sessions") with personal reverie and self-evaluation:

WILLIAM SHAKESPEARE   (1564–1616)

Sonnet 30:
When to the Sessions of Sweet Silent Thought   *1609*

When to the sessions° of sweet silent thought	*court hearings*
I summon up remembrance of things past,	
I sigh the lack of many a thing I sought,	
And with old woes new wail° my dear time's waste:	*lament again*
Then can I drown an eye (un-used to flow)	5
For precious friends hid in death's dateless° night,	*endless*
And weep afresh love's long since cancelled° woe,	*paid in full*
And moan th'expense° of many a vanished sight.	*cost, loss*
Then can I grieve at grievances foregone,	
And heavily from woe to woe tell° o'er	*count* 10
The sad account of fore-bemoanèd moan,	
Which I new pay, as if not paid before.	
But if the while I think on thee (dear friend)	
All losses are restored, and sorrows end.	

QUESTIONS

1. Explain the metaphor of "sessions" and "summon" in lines 1–2. Where are the *sessions* being held? What is a *summons* for remembrance?
2. What metaphor is brought out by the word *cancelled* in line 7? In what sense might a "woe" of love be cancelled? Explain the metaphor of *expense* in line 8.
3. What type of transaction does Shakespeare refer to in the metaphor of lines 9–12? What understanding does the metaphor provide about the sadness and regret that a person feels about past mistakes and sorrows?
4. What role does the speaker assign to the "dear friend" of line 13 in relation to the metaphors of the poem?

The word *sessions* is the legal name for that period of time when judges, juries, lawyers, and witnesses carry out the court's business (i.e., "the court is now in *session;*" think also of "school is now in *session*"). The word *summon* is the legal command for a person to appear before a court, usually to stand as a defendant for an alleged wrongdoing. Through these metaphors, the speaker says that in moments of reflection he (assuming a male speaker) thinks about past sorrows and regrets, and wonders whether he always did the right things. In a way, the speaker asks us to visualize his "sweet silent thought" as though he is sitting as a combination lawyer-judge over his memories, which he has commanded to reappear. The implication of this metaphor is that the total experience of a person is constantly alive and present; that the memory is like an entire society with wrongs, shortcomings, and transgressions; that judgment and reassessment are constant living processes; and that the consciousness of individuals is not an unchanging, solid state, but is instead a series of conflicting or contrasting impulses.

This development of Shakespeare's metaphor may seem at first like a great deal more than Shakespeare intended; indeed, we have used more words in prose than he uses in verse. Once we have understood his language, however, our minds are unlocked, and we may then allow ourselves this kind of expansion as we consider the full ramifications of the comparison.

OTHER RHETORICAL FIGURES

1. PARADOX. A **paradox** is a device in which an apparent contradiction reveals an unexpected truth. The wit of the figure is hence that the contradiction is not a contradiction at all. The second line of Sir Thomas Wyatt's sonnet "I Find No Peace," for example (p. 634), shows two paradoxes. One contrasts fear and hope, the other fire and ice: "I fear and hope; I burn and freeze like ice." These paradoxes reflect the contradictory states that people in love often have. On the one hand they want to love, but on the other they are apprehensive about the changes in their lives that their feelings may bring about. There is also here the lover's concern about unrequited love. The paradox thus brings to life both the satisfaction and uncertainty felt by people who wage the "war" of love and personal commitment.

2. APOSTROPHE.   The **apostrophe** (originally a "turning away") is a dramatic device whereby the speaker addresses a real or imagined listener who is not present. In use, it creates the situation of a virtual public speech, with the readers drawn in as audience. The speaker may thus develop ideas and attitudes that might arise naturally on a public occasion, as in Wordsworth's sonnet "London, 1802," which is addressed to the long dead English poet Milton. In the following sonnet by Keats, "Bright Star," the speaker addresses an inanimate object that is as far removed from earth as any object could be, yet through apostrophe the speaker assumes that it has human understanding and divine power.

JOHN KEATS   (1795–1822)

Bright Star (*1819*)   *1838*

Bright star! would I were steadfast as thou art—
  Not in lone splendor hung aloft the night,
And watching, with eternal lids apart,
  Like Nature's patient, sleepless eremite,°   *hermit*
The moving waters at their priestlike task   5
  Of pure ablution round earth's human shores,
Or gazing on the new soft-fallen mask
  Of snow upon the mountains and the moors;
No—yet still steadfast, still unchangeable,
  Pillowed upon my fair love's ripening breast,   10
To feel forever its soft fall and swell,
  Awake forever in a sweet unrest,
    Still, still to hear her tender-taken breath,
    And so live ever—or else swoon to death.

QUESTIONS

1. With what topic is the speaker concerned in this sonnet? How does he compare himself with the distant star?

2. What qualities does the speaker attribute specifically to the star? What sort of role does he seem to assign to it? In light of this role, and the qualities needed to serve in it, how might the star be compared to a divine and benign presence?

3. In light of the stress made on the words "forever" and "ever" in lines 11–14, how appropriate is the choice of the star as the subject of the apostrophe in the poem?

In this sonnet Keats addresses the star as though it is a person or god, an object of adoration, and the poem is therefore like a petitional prayer. The star is idealized with qualities that the speaker wishes to establish in himself. One quality is steadfastness of position; a second is eternal watchfulness and fidelity. The point of the apostrophe is thus to dramatize the speaker's yearning, and to stress the permanence of space and eternity as contrasted with the impermanence of life on earth. We as readers are witnesses, for we may well imagine the speaker looking at the night sky and connecting its vastness and mystery to our own lives.

3. PERSONIFICATION. Hand-in-hand with apostrophe is the device of **personification,** which is the attribution of human traits to nonhuman or abstract things. Since prehistoric times humans have personified inanimate objects and phenomena. In the belief that spirits inhabited trees, mountains, lakes, and so on, earlier civilizations addressed them as deities. Poets build on personification to explore the relationships between people and their environments, their ideals, or their inner lives. In "Bright Star," as we have just seen, Keats personifies the star addressed by the speaker. Shakespeare, in Sonnet 146, "Poor Soul, the Center of My Sinful Earth" (p. 975), personifies his own soul so that he can deal with earthly versus heavenly concerns. Other examples of personification may be seen in Keats's poems "To Autumn" and "Ode on a Grecian Urn," and Shelley's "Ode to the West Wind."

4. SYNECDOCHE AND METONYMY. These figures are close in purpose and effect. **Synecdoche** (taking one thing out of another) is a device in which a part stands for the whole, or a whole for a part, like the expression "All hands aboard" to signify that a ship's crew should return to ship. **Metonymy** (a transfer of name) refers to the substitution of one thing for another closely identified thing; for example, using "the White House" to signify the policies and activities of the President. The objective of both devices is to express new ideas and insights in a new perspective. Because synecdoche and metonymy extend meaning in this way, they are similar to simile and metaphor.

Synecdoche may be seen in Keats's "To Autumn," where the gourd and hazel shells in lines 7–8 stand for the entire autumnal harvest. In Wordsworth's "London, 1802" (p. 638), the phrase "thy heart" (line 13) is a synecdoche referring to the entire person and mind of Milton. An example of metonymy may be seen in "To Autumn" where "granary floor," the place where grain is stored, is used with the transferred meaning of the harvest stored there. In "Exit, Pursued by a Bear," Ogden Nash metonymically uses brand names, the names of artists, and the names of cities to mean objects, artworks, and places. Thus "Chippendale" is a metonym for a valuable piece of ornate antique furniture, and "Picasso" is a metonym substituting the name of the artist for the work of art. Nash's entire poem is built up with such metonyms, which cumulatively symbolize the cultured civilization that may so disastrously be destroyed by nuclear war.

5. SYNESTHESIA.   A figure that also transfers one thing to another, and therefore resembles synecdoche and metonymy, is **synesthesia,** which is the union of differing sensations or feelings. With this device a poet describes one type of perception or thought with words appropriate to another. An often cited example is in "The Garden," where Andrew Marvel speaks of a "green thought" in reference to thinking that is conducive to life and the nurture of living things. A thought obviously cannot be green —who has ever *seen* a thought, let alone a *green* one?—nevertheless, "green thought" makes vivid sense. Of all poets, Keats is the one who makes most use of synesthesia, as, for example, in the "Ode to a Nightingale" (p. 749), where a plot of ground is "melodious," a draught of wine tastes of "Dance, and Provencal song, and sunburnt mirth," and beaded bubbles of wine "wink" at the brim of a glass.

6. THE PUN, OR PARONOMASIA.   Another transferring figure is the **pun** (which probably originally meant a *point* or a *puncture*), or **paronomasia.** A pun is a word play in which the writer surprisingly reveals that words with different meanings have similar or identical sounds. Because puns can be outrageous, people often groan when they hear them (even while they probably are enjoying them). Also, because puns often seem to play only with sound, they have not always enjoyed critical acclaim, but good puns may always be relished because they work with sounds to *reveal* ideas. John Gay, for example, utilizes clever and complex puns in the following chorus from act 2 of *The Beggar's Opera* (1728):

JOHN GAY   (1685–1732)

Let Us Take the Road   *1728*

Let us take the road.
  Hark! I hear the sound of coaches!
  The hour of attack approaches,
To your arms, brave boys, and load.
    See the ball I hold! [*holding up a bullet*]   5
  Let the chymists toil like asses,
  Our fire their fire surpasses,
    And turns all our lead to gold.

QUESTIONS

1. What sort of traits are shown by the speakers of this poem? What kind of activity are they about to engage in? Why do they not seem frightening, despite what they plan to do?
2. To what profession is the language of the poem appropriate? How is it inappropriate in this context?
3. Describe the puns in the poem. What kind of knowledge is needed to explain them fully? How many puns are there? How are they connected? Why do the puns seem particularly witty and also outrageous?

Here *fire*, *lead*, and *gold* are puns. *Lead* was the "base" or "low" metal that the medieval alchemists ("chymists") tried to transform into *gold*, using the heat from their *fires*. The puns develop because the gang of cutthroats singing the song is about to go out to rob people riding in horse-drawn coaches. Hence their "lead" is in the form of bullets, which will be transformed into the "gold" coins they steal. Their "fire" is not the alchemists' fire, but rather the fire of pistols. Through these puns, Gay's villains charm us by their wit, even though the threatening situation they describe would be frightening in real life.

7. OVERSTATEMENT AND UNDERSTATEMENT. Two devices conferring emphasis are **overstatement** or **hyperbole**, and **understatement. Overstatement,** also called the **overreacher,** is exaggeration for effect. In "London, 1802," for example, Wordsworth declares that England is a "fen of stagnant waters." That is, the country and its people make up collectively a stinking, smelly, polluted marsh, a muddy dump. What Wordsworth establishes by this overstatement is his judgment that England in 1802 needed a writer to unite the people around noble moral and political ideas, just as Milton had once done.

On the other side of the scale, **understatement** is the deliberate underplaying or undervaluing of a thing for purposes of emphasis. One of the most famous poetic understatements is in Andrew Marvell's "To His Coy Mistress" (p. 836):

> The grave's a fine and private place,
> But none, I think, do there embrace.

Here the understatement grimly emphasizes the eternity of death by contrasting the permanent privacy of the grave with the temporary privacy of a trysting place sought by lovers. Another ironic use of understatement is in lines 17–20 of Ogden Nash's "Exit, Pursued by a Bear," where the speaker indicates that the "lion and the lizard" cannot hear "heavenly harmonies." In this figure Nash emphasizes that the people have been killed who once inhabited the rooms where such melodies were played, and therefore he emphasizes the ignorance and horror of war.

POEMS FOR STUDY

SIR THOMAS WYATT   (1503–1542)

I Find No Peace   *1557*

I find no peace, and all my war is done,
  I fear and hope; I burn and freeze like ice;
  I fly above the wind yet can I not arise;
  And naught I have and all the world I season.
That looseth nor locketh holdeth me in prison,°   5
  And holdeth me not, yet can I scape° nowise;   *escape*
  Nor letteth me live nor die at my devise,°   *choice*
  And yet of death it giveth none occasion.
Without eyen° I see, and without tongue I plain;°   *eyes*
  I desire to perish, and yet I ask health;   10
  I love another, and thus I hate myself;
I feed me in sorrow, and laugh in all my pain.
  Likewise displeaseth me both death and life°
  And my delight is causer of this strife.

I FIND NO PEACE.   5 *that . . . prison*: that is, "that which neither lets me go nor contains me holds me in prison." At the time of Wyatt, -*eth* was used for the third person singular present tense.   9 *plain*: express desires about love.   13 *likewise . . . life*: literally, "it is displeasing to me, in the same way, both death and life." That is, "both death and life are equally distasteful to me."

QUESTIONS

1. What situation is the speaker reflecting upon? What metaphors and similes does he use to express his feelings? How successfully do these figures convey his feelings?

2. How many separate paradoxes are in the poem? What is the cumulative effect of so many? What is the general topic of the paradoxes in lines 1–4? In lines 5–8? Why does the speaker in line 11 declare that hating himself is a consequence of loving another? Why is it ironic that his "delight" is the "causer of this strife"?

3. To what extent do you think the paradoxes are an accurate expression of the feelings of a person in love, particularly in light of the fact that in the sixteenth century the completely free and unchaperoned meetings of lovers were not easily arranged?

4. To what extent do the paradoxes help you feel and experience the agonies of the speaker? How do they bring alive the implications about love in the poem?

WILLIAM SHAKESPEARE (1564–1616)

Sonnet 18: Shall I Compare Thee to a Summer's Day?   *1609*

Shall I compare thee to a summer's day?
Thou art more lovely and more temperate:
Rough winds do shake the darling buds of May,
And summer's lease hath all too short a date:
Sometime too hot the eye of heaven° shines,   *the sun*   5
And often is his gold complexion dimmed;
And every fair from fair sometime declines,
By chance, or nature's changing course, untrimmed;
But thy eternal summer shall not fade,
Nor lose possession of that fair thou owest°;   *ownest*   10
Nor shall Death brag thou wander'st in his shade,
When in eternal lines to time thou growest:
  So long as men can breathe, or eyes can see,
  So long lives this, and this gives life to thee.

QUESTIONS

1. What is a possible dramatic situation out of which this poem springs?
2. Is the comparison offered in the first line a common or uncommon one?
3. What are the metaphors in lines 1–8 designed to assert? Why is the speaker emphasizing the brevity of life?
4. What is meant by *temperate* (line 2)? What sense of fragility is brought out by the metaphor of "darling buds of May"?
5. What is the metaphorical meaning of *lease* and *date* in line 4?
6. In lines 5 and 6, what happens to the sun, and why is the comparison appropriate to the person being addressed?
7. How does the topic shift in line 9? What new metaphor is introduced in line 11?
8. What is the relationship of the last two lines to the rest of the sonnet? What is the *this* that gives the life that will last beyond a day in summer? What sort of immortality is it that Shakespeare's speaker is exalting in the sonnet?

JOHN DONNE (1572–1631)

A Valediction: Forbidding Mourning   *1633*

As virtuous men pass mildly away,
  And whisper to their souls to go,
Whilst some of their sad friends do say
  The breath goes now, and some say, No;

So let us melt, and make no noise,   5
   No tear-floods, nor sigh-tempests move,
'Twere profanation° of our joys
   To tell the laiety° our love.

Moving of th'earth° brings harms and fears,   *earthquakes*
   Men reckon what it did and meant;   10
But trepidation° of the spheres,
   Though greater far, is innocent.

Dull sublunary lovers' love
   (Whose soul is sense°) cannot admit
Absence, because it doth remove   15
   Those things which elemented it.

But we by a love so much refined
   That our selves know not what it is,
Inter-assured of the mind,
   Care less, eyes, lips, and hands to miss.   20

Our two souls therefore, which are one,
   Though I must go, endure not yet
A breach, but an expansion,
   Like gold to airy thinness beat.°

If they be two, they are two so   25
   As stiff twin compasses° are two;
Thy soul, the fixt foot, makes no show
   To move, but doth, if th'other do.

And though it in the center sit,
   Yet when the other far doth roam,   30
It leans and harkens after it,
   And grows erect, as that comes home.

Such wilt thou be to me, who must
   Like th'other foot, obliquely run;
Thy firmness draws my circle just,°   35
   And makes me end where I begun.

A VALEDICTION: FORBIDDING MOURNING.   7, 8 *profanation . . . laity*: as though
the lovers are priests of love, whose love is a mystery.   11 *trepidation*: Before Sir Isaac
Newton explained the precession of the equinoxes, it was assumed that the positions of
heavenly bodies should be constant and perfectly circular. The clearly observable irregularities
(caused by the slow wobbling of the earth's axis) were explained by the concept of *trepidation*,
or a trembling or oscillation that occurred in the outermost of the spheres surrounding the
earth.   14 *soul is sense*: lovers whose attraction is totally physical.   24 *gold to airy thinness
beat*: a reference to the malleability of gold.   26 *compasses*: a compass used for drawing
circles.   35 *just*: perfectly round.

QUESTIONS

1. What is the situation envisioned as the occasion for the poem? Who is talking to whom? What is their relationship?

2. What is the intention of the first two stanzas? Do you think the phrases "tear-floods" and "sigh-tempests" might be sufficiently comic to cause a stopping of tears?

3. Describe the effect of the opening simile about men on their death beds.

4. What is the metaphor of stanza 3 (lines 9–12)? In what sense might the "trepidation of the spheres" be less harmful than the parting of the lovers?

5. In lines 13–20 there is a comparison making the love of the speaker and his sweetheart superior to the love of average lovers. What is the basis for the speaker's claim?

6. What is the comparison begun by the word *refined* in line 17 and continued by the simile in line 24?

HENRY KING   (1592–1669)

Sic Vita°   *1657*

Like to the falling of a star,
Or as the flights of eagles are,
Or like the fresh spring's gaudy hue,
Or silver drops of morning dew,
Or like a wind that chafes the flood,   5
Or bubbles which on water stood:
Even such is man, whose borrowed light
Is straight called in, and paid to night.
   The wind blows out, the bubble dies;
   The spring entombed in autumn lies;   10
   The dew dries up, the star is shot;
   The flight is past, and man forgot.

SIC VITA. (Latin): Such is life.

QUESTIONS

1. Consider the following groups of lines as distinct sections of this poem: 1–6; 7–8; 9–12. Explain causes for these divisions.

2. How many similes do you find in lines 1–6? Describe the range of references; that is, from what sources are the similes derived? What do all these similes (and references) have in common?

3. Explain the two metaphors in lines 7–8. (One is brought out by the words *borrowed*, *called in*, and *paid*; the other by *light* and *night*.)

4. Explain the continuation in lines 9–12 of the similes in 1–6. Do you think

that these last four lines are essential, or might the poem have been successfully concluded with line 8? Explain.

5. What point does this poem make about humanity? In what ways do the similes in the poem help explore these ideas and bring them to life?

WILLIAM WORDSWORTH   (1770–1850)

London, 1802   *1807 (1802)*

Milton! thou should'st be living at this hour:
England hath need of thee: she is a fen°   *bog, marsh*
Of stagnant waters: altar, sword, and pen,
Fireside, the heroic wealth of hall and bower,
Have forfeited their ancient English dower°   *widow's inheritance*   5
Of inward happiness. We are selfish men;
Oh! raise us up, return to us again;
And give us manners,° virtue, freedom, power.
Thy soul was like a star, and dwelt apart:
Thou hadst a voice whose sound was like the sea: 10
Pure as the naked heavens, majestic, free,
So didst thou travel on life's common way,
In cheerful godliness; and yet thy heart
The lowliest duties on herself did lay.

LONDON, 1802.   8 *manners*: customs, moral modes of social and political conduct.

QUESTIONS

1. What is the effect of Wordsworth's apostrophe to Milton? What elements of Milton's career as a writer does Wordsworth emphasize?
2. In lines 3 and 4, the device of metonymy is used. What do these details represent, and how does Wordsworth judge the respective institutions represented by the details?
3. Consider the use of overstatement, or hyperbole, from lines 2–6. What effect does Wordsworth achieve by using the device as extensively as he does here?
4. What effect does Wordsworth make through his use of overstatement in his praise of Milton in lines 9–14? What does he mean by the metonymic references to *soul* (line 9) and *heart* (line 13)?

JOHN KEATS   (1795–1821)

To Autumn   *1820 (1819)*

Season of mists and mellow fruitfulness!
   Close bosom-friend of the maturing sun;
Conspiring with him how to load and bless

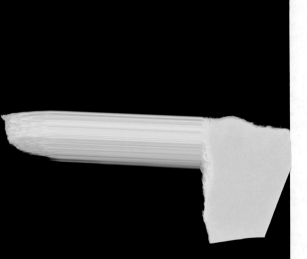

With fruit the vines that round the thatch-eaves run;
To bend with apples the mossed cottage-trees,   5
And fill all fruit with ripeness to the core;
    To swell the gourd, and plump the hazel shells
With a sweet kernel; to set budding more,
And still more, later flowers for the bees,
Until they think warm days will never cease,   10
    For Summer has o'erbrimmed their clammy cells.

Who hath not seen thee oft amid thy store?
    Sometimes whoever seeks abroad may find
Thee sitting careless on a granary floor,
    Thy hair soft-lifted by the winnowing wind,   15
Or on a half-reaped furrow sound asleep,
Drowsed with the fume of poppies, while thy hook
    Spares the next swath and all its twinèd flowers;
And sometimes like a gleaner thou dost keep
    Steady thy laden head across a brook;   20
    Or by a cider-press, with patient look,
Thou watchest the last oozings hours by hours.

Where are the songs of Spring? Ay, where are they?
    Think not of them, thou hast thy music too,—
While barrèd clouds bloom the soft-dying day,   25
    And touch the stubble-plains with rosy hue;
Then in a wailful choir the small gnats mourn
    Among the river sallows, borne aloft
    Or sinking as the light wind lives or dies;
And full-grown lambs loud bleat from hilly bourn;   30
    Hedge-crickets sing; and now with treble soft
The redbreast whistles from a garden-croft;
    And gathering swallows twitter in the skies.

QUESTIONS

1. How is personification used in the first stanza? How does it change in the
   second? What is the effect of such personification?
2. How does Keats structure the poem to accord with his apostrophe to autumn?
   That is, in what ways may the stanzas be distinguished by the type of discourse addressed to the season?
3. Analyze Keats's use of metonymy in stanza 1 and synecdoche in stanza 2.
   What effects does he achieve with these devices for the transference of meaning?
4. How, through the use of images, does Keats develop his idea that autumn
   is a season of "mellow fruitfulness"?

T. S. ELIOT   (1888–1965)

Eyes That Last I Saw in Tears   1924

Eyes that last I saw in tears
Through division
Here in death's dream kingdom
The golden vision reappears
I see the eyes but not the tears   5
This is my affliction

This is my affliction
Eyes I shall not see again
Eyes of decision
Eyes I shall not see unless   10
At the door of death's other kingdom
Where, as in this,
The eyes outlast a little while
A little while outlast the tears
And hold us in derision.   15

QUESTIONS

1. What do *eyes* and *tears* signify as a synecdoche and as a metonymy?
2. What is the cause of the tears (line 2)? What is meant by the eyes outlasting
   the tears (lines 13, 14)? Why should the eyes "hold us in derision"? In line
   9 the eyes are "of decision." What does this synecdoche mean?
3. Explain the paradox of the speaker's declaration in line 5 that he sees the
   eyes but not the tears. Why does he say that this is his "affliction"?
4. Why might the entire poem be considered a paradox? What happened in
   life? What does the speaker look forward to in death?
5. What is the distinction in the poem between "death's dream kingdom" and
   "death's other kingdom."
6. What effect is achieved in the poem by the use of repeated words and phrases?

OGDEN NASH   (1902–1970)

Exit, Pursued by a Bear   1954

Chipmunk chewing the Chippendale,°
Mice on the Meissen° shelf,

EXIT, PURSUED BY A BEAR. The title is a stage direction in Shakespeare's *The Winter's
Tale* (act 3. scene 3, 58). The character is torn apart by the bear. When this poem was first
published, the atomic bomb had existed for nine years, and the hydrogen bomb for two. In
late 1953, Russia, which is sometimes symbolized by a bear, announced that it possessed the
hydrogen bomb.   1 *Chippendale*: ornate furniture made by Thomas Chippendale (1718–
1779).   2 *Meissen*: expensive chinaware made in Meissen, Germany. Also called "Dresden
China."

Pigeon stains on the Aubusson,°
Spider lace on the delf.°

Squirrel climbing the Sheraton,°   5
Skunk on the Duncan Phyfe,°
Silverfish in the Gobelins°
And the calfbound volumes of *Life*.

Pocks on the pink Picasso,
Dust on the four Cézannes,   10
Kit on the keys of the Steinway,
Cat on the Louis Quinze.°

Rings on the Adam° mantel
From a thousand bygone thirsts,
Mold on the Henry Millers°   15
And the Ronald Firbank° firsts.

The lion and the lizard°
No heavenly harmonies hear
From the high-fidelity speaker
Concealed behind the Vermeer.   20

Jamshid° squats in a cavern
Screened by a waterfall,
Catered by Heinz and Campbell,
And awaits the fireball.

---

3 *Aubusson*: carpet imported from France.   4 *delf*: expensive pottery made in Delft, The
Netherlands.   5 *Sheraton*: furniture made by Thomas Sheraton (1751–1806).   6 *Duncan
Phyfe*: furniture made by Duncan Phyfe (1768–1854), a Scotsman who came to America in
1783.   7 *Gobelins*: rare and exquisitely crafted tapestries made by Gobelin of Paris.
12 *Louis Quinze*: furniture made in France during the reign of Louis XV (1710–1774).
13 *Adam*: Robert Adam (1728–1792) was one of the most famous English architects.
15 *Henry Miller*: American author (1891–1980).   16 *Ronald Firbank*: Arthur Ainsley Ronald
Firbank (1886–1926), British author.   17 *The lion and the lizard*: see Edward Fitzgerald's
(1809–1883) version of *The Rubáiyát of Omar Khayyam*, stanza 18, particularly in reference to
Nash's last stanza.   21 *Jamshid*: a reference to the legendary Persian hero Jamshid, who
found a cup containing the elixir of life and lived for 700 years. At one point in the story
Jamshid remained hidden for a hundred years. Note also the reference to Fitzgerald's *Rubáiyát*,
stanza 18.

QUESTIONS

1. In relationship to the serious subject matter of the poem, what is the effect
   of the title? What is the possible pun on the word *bear*?

2. What location is the speaker describing? How is metonymy used to suggest
   the wealth of the collections of household items and art? What sort of lifestyle
   is suggested by the metonymy?

3. Hypothetically, what has occurred so that animals rather than people are
   living with the expensive artifacts? Judging from the evidence of line 14,
   how long has this situation existed?

4. How might the situation presented in the poem be considered as a paradox?
5. What fireball is expected (line 24)?

LANGSTON HUGHES   (1902–1967)

Harlem   *1951*

What happens to a dream deferred?

> Does it dry up
> like a raisin in the sun?
> Or fester like a sore—
> And then run?   5
> Does it stink like rotten meat?
> Or crust and sugar over—
> like a syrupy sweet?
>
> Maybe it just sags
> like a heavy load.   10
>
> Or does it explode?

QUESTIONS

1. In the light of the black experience with the "American Dream," what do you think is meant by the phrase "dream deferred"?
2. Explain the structure of the poem in terms of the speaker's questions and answers. How is the structure here similar to the one in Shakespeare's sonnet, "Shall I Compare Thee to a Summer's Day" (p. 635)?
3. Explain the similes in lines 3, 4, 6, 8, and 10. Why are these apt comparisons? What sorts of human actions are implied in these figures?
4. What is the meaning of the metaphor in line 11? Why do you think Hughes shifted from similes to a metaphor in this line?

ELIZABETH BISHOP   (1911–1979)

Rain Towards Morning   *1947*

The great light cage has broken up in the air,
freeing, I think, about a million birds
whose wild ascending shadows will not be back,
and all the wires come falling down.
No cage, no frightening birds; the rain   5
is brightening now. The face is pale

that tried the puzzle of their prison
and solved it with an unexpected kiss,
whose freckled unsuspected hands alit.

QUESTIONS

1. What sort of personal situation is being described in the poem? How much does the poet allow you to learn about the situation? Do you discover enough to determine the general pattern of what is happening?

2. Describe the poet's use of overstatement in lines 1–4. What effect is achieved? In light of the "kiss" mentioned in line 8, which is more powerful: understatement or overstatement?

3. What is the meaning of the "great light cage" in lines 1–4? What is the "puzzle" of the birds' prison in line 7?

4. How can the "face" of line 6 and the "kiss" in line 8 be explained, through the figure of synecdoche, to have "hands" in line 9? What do these figures suggest about the nature of the experience being described?

5. Explain the paradox of how rain can be brightening (line 6).

SYLVIA PLATH   (1932–1963)

Metaphors   *1960*

I'm a riddle in nine syllables,
An elephant, a ponderous house,
A melon strolling on two tendrils.
O red fruit, ivory, fine timbers!
This loaf's big with its yeasty rising.   5
Money's new-minted in this fat purse.
I'm a means, a stage, a cow in calf.
I've eaten a bag of green apples,
Boarded the train there's no getting off.

QUESTIONS

1. What evidence can you find in the poem that the speaker here is a woman?

2. The speaker calls herself a "riddle in nine syllables." What is the answer to the riddle? Why nine syllables (as opposed to eight or ten)? In what sense is the poem also a riddle? How are the answers to both riddles related?

3. What do all the metaphors in the poem have in common? How effectively does each one convey part of the feelings and experience of the speaker? Do they strike you as commonplace or unusual? Why?

4. Which of the metaphors do you find amusing, shocking, or demeaning? What do these suggest about the speaker's attitude toward herself?

5. What aspect of the speaker's condition is captured in the "bag of green apples" metaphor (line 8)? What two meanings are suggested by the *stage* metaphor (line 7)? Why is the *train* metaphor (line 9) appropriate to the speaker's condition and the results of that condition?

MARGE PIERCY (b. 1934)

A Work of Artifice   *1973*

The bonsai tree
in the attractive pot
could have grown eighty feel tall
on the side of a mountain
till split by lightning.   5
But a gardener
carefully pruned it.
It is nine inches high.
Every day as he
whittles back the branches   10
the gardener croons,
It is your nature
to be small and cozy,
domestic and weak;
how lucky, little tree,   15
to have a pot to grow in.
With living creatures
one must begin very early
to dwarf their growth:
the bound feet,   20
the crippled brain,
the hair in curlers,
the hands you
love to touch.

QUESTIONS

1. What is a bonsai tree? In what ways is it an apt metaphor for women? The tree "could have grown eighty feet tall." What would be the comparable growth and development of a woman?

2. What do you make of the gardener's song (lines 12–16)? If the bonsai tree were able to respond, would it accept the gardener's consolation for its truncated life? What conclusions about women's lives are implied by the metaphor of the tree?

3. How does the poem shift in method and focus at line 17? To what extent do the four images that follow (lines 20–24) embody the lives of women? How are the images metaphorical?

JUDITH MINTY (b. 1937)

Conjoined *1981*

a marriage poem

The onion in my cupboard, a monster, actually
two joined under one transparent skin:
each half-round, then flat and deformed
where it pressed and grew against the other.

An accident, like the two-headed calf rooted   5
in one body, fighting to suck at its mother's teats;
or like those other freaks, Chang and Eng,° twins
joined at the chest by skin and muscle, doomed
to live, even make love, together for sixty years.

Do you feel the skin that binds us   10
together as we move, heavy in this house?
To sever the muscle could free one,
but might kill the other. Ah, but men
don't slice onions in the kitchen, seldom see
what is invisible. We cannot escape each other.   15

CONJOINED.   7 *Chang and Eng*: Born in 1811, the original and most famous Siamese
twins. Although they were never separated, they nevertheless fathered twenty-two children.
They died in 1874.

QUESTIONS

1. What are the two things—the "us" and "we" of lines 10 and 11—that are
    conjoined? Since this is "a marriage poem," might they be the man and the
    woman? Why might they also be considered as the body and soul of the
    speaker; or the desire to be married and subordinated, on the one hand,
    and to be free and in control of destiny, on the other?

2. Explore the metaphor of the onion and the similes of the two-headed calf
    and the Siamese twins. Why do you think the poet introduces the words
    monster, accident, and *freaks* into these figures in lines 1, 5, and 7? In what
    sense do you believe that these words are applicable to the nature and plight
    of women?

3. Explain what is meant by lines 12 and 13. Does the idea here, together
    with the last sentence in line 15, represent a reconciliation, a decision to
    adjust, a reluctant concession, or an angry admission of defeat?

4. Is it true that *all* "men / don't slice onions in the kitchen, seldom see / what
    is invisible"? Explain.

DIANE WAKOSKI   (b. 1937)

Inside Out   *1965*

I walk the purple carpet into your eye,
carrying the silver butter server,
but a trunk rumbles by,
           leaving its black tire prints on my foot,

and old images—   5
          the sound of banging screen doors on hot afternoons
          and a fly buzzing over Kool-Aid spilled on the sink—
flicker, as reflections on the metal surface.

Come in, you said,
inside your paintings, inside the blood factory, inside the   10
old songs that line your hands, inside
eyes that change like a snowflake every second,

inside spinach leaves holding that one piece of gravel,

inside the whiskers of a cat,

inside your old hat, and most of all inside your mouth where you   15
grind the pigments with your teeth, painting
with a broken bottle on the floor, and painting
with an ostrich feather on the moon that rolls out of my mouth.

You cannot let me walk inside you too long
inside the veins where my small feet touch   20
bottom.
You must reach inside and pull me
like a silver bullet°
from your arm.

INSIDE OUT.   23 *silver bullet*: According to legend, silver bullets were used to kill vampires.
The Lone Ranger, of the radio and television series popular in the 1940s and 1950s, always
used silver bullets as a trademark of his pursuit of justice.

QUESTIONS

1. Who is the speaker? Who is the person being addressed? From what the
   speaker says in lines 15–19, what is the profession of the addressee? What
   sort of relationship does the speaker have with him? How close, how intimate,
   are they? What knowledge of domestic details do they have in common?
   How may this knowledge be used in the drawing of conclusions about their
   relationship?

2. What "inside out" details of the listener's anatomy does the speaker mention?
   What do you think is meant by the poem's title?

3. Consider details of the eye and the veins as synecdoche, and the paintings and the old hat as metonymy. In the determination of the poem's characterization of the "you" inside the poem, what do these details stand for?

4. Consider the truck's black tire prints on the speaker's foot (lines 3–4) as an instance of synesthesia, that is, the application of one set of sensuous references to another sense. What might this figure mean? Do the same for the mouth with the ground pigments (lines 15–16), the ostrich feather and the rolling moon (line 18), and the walk inside the veins (lines 19–20).

5. What is meant by lines 19–24? Why, after the establishment of so personal and intimate a relationship, might the speaker express the reservations that are contained here? How might these lines be interpreted as a reflection upon the paradoxical nature of the love relationship generally?

6. Describe the paradox implicit in the speaker's mentioning the red carpet in line 1 and the silver butter server in line 2.

WRITING ABOUT RHETORICAL FIGURES

When you plan to write about metaphors, similes, and other rhetorical figures, you will not know what direction your essay will take. Thus you will need to record your discoveries as you study the work. Determine the use, line by line, of metaphors or similes, if these are the objects of your study, or of other rhetorical figures. Obviously, similes are the easiest figures to recognize because they use the words "like" or "as" or other comparatives. Metaphors may be recognized because they transfer the subject or vehicle to the actual meaning or tenor. If the subject is memory, for example, but the poem speaks of lawcourts, you are looking at a metaphor. Similarly, if the poet is addressing an absent person, or a natural object, or if you find clear double meanings in words, you may have apostrophe, personification, and puns.

Once you have listed all the figures that you can identify, try to formulate answers to questions like these: What figures does the work contain? Where do they occur? Under what circumstances? How extensive are they? Are they signaled by a single word, like "bows" in Campion's "Cherry Ripe," or are they more extensive, as in Shakespeare's "When to the Sessions of Sweet Silent Thought"? Structurally, how are the figures developed? How do they rise out of the situation? How are they related to the major idea? How do they relate to other aspects of the poem? How do they broaden, deepen, or otherwise assist in making the ideas in the poem forceful? How vivid are they? How obvious? How unusual? What kind of effort is needed to understand them in context?

Next, attempt to describe the thoughts that are embodied in the figures: What ideas can you locate and delineate there? What impressions of experience, what attitudes? How extensively do the figures bear the burden of thought and development? Are the figures the major means of development, or are they no more than an embellishment of a more discursive or conversational mode? If you have discovered a number of figures, what relationships can you find among them (such as the judicial and financial connections in Shakespeare's Sonnet 30)? Is one type of figure used in a particular section while another predominates in another? Why? In short, how appropriate and meaningful are the figures in the poem, and how well do they assist you in your understanding and appreciation?

For this essay, two types of compositions are possible. One is a full-scale essay. The other, because some rhetorical figures may occupy only a small part of the poem, is a single paragraph. Let us consider the single paragraph first.

1. *A Paragraph.* For a single paragraph there needs to be only one topic, such as the opening paradox in Eliot's "Eyes That Last I Saw in Tears" (p. 640), or the opening metonym in the same poem. The goal should be to deal with the single figure and its relationship to the main idea of the poem. Thus the figure should be described, and its meaning and implications should be discussed. It is important to begin with a comprehensive topic sentence, such as one that explains the cleverness of the puns in Gay's "Let Us Take the Road" (p. 632), or the use of synesthesia in Keats's "Ode to a Nightingale" (p. 749).

2. *A Full-Length Essay.* Where one particular figure in the poem is pervasive enough to justify a full treatment, you could write a full-length essay about it, usually discussing in detail the poet's use of metaphors and similes. Another type of essay might explore the meaning and effect of two or more figures, with the various parts of the body of the essay being taken up with each of the figures. The unity of this second kind of essay is achieved by the linking of a series of two or three different rhetorical devices to a single idea or emotion conveyed in the poem.

Once you decide what sort of essay to develop, and have a good set of notes, you are ready to develop your essay.

INTRODUCTION.   In determining your central idea you should relate the quality of the figures to the general nature of the work you are studying. If there is any discrepancy between the metaphorical language and the topic material, consider that contrast as a possible central idea, for if such were the case your writer would clearly be developing an ironic perspective. Suppose that the topic of the poem is love, but the figures put you in mind of darkness and cold, what would the writer be saying about the quality of love? You should also try to justify any claims that you make about the figures. For example, one of the similes in Coleridge's "Kubla Khan" compares the sounds of a "mighty fountain" to the breathing of the earth in "fast thick pants." How is this simile to be taken? As a reference to the animality of the earth? As a suggestion that the fountain, and the earth, are dangerous? Or simply as a comparison suggesting immense, forceful noise? How do you explain the answers you select? Your introduction is the place to establish ideas and justifications of this sort. Once you have determined your central idea, you should develop your thesis sentence to guide your reader for the remainder of your essay.

Body.   In discussing rhetorical figures, you may use any and all of the following approaches in any combination you wish.

1. *Interpret the meaning and effect of the figures.* Here you explain how the figures enable you to make an interpretation. In stanza 2 of "A Valediction: Forbidding Mourning," for example, Donne introduces a metaphor equating the condition of love with the structure of the Church:

> 'Twere profanation of our joys
> To tell the laity our love.

Here Donne emphasizes the private, mystical relationship of two lovers, drawing the metaphor from the religious tradition whereby any explanation of religious mysteries is considered a desecration. The idea that Donne is promoting is that love is rare, heaven-sent, private, privileged, and so fragile that it would be hurt if it were made public. This interpretive approach is a direct one, requiring that metaphors, similes, or other figures be explained and expanded, with the introduction of necessary references and allusions to make your expansion fully meaningful.

2. *Analyze the frames of reference, and their appropriateness to the subject matter.* Here you classify and locate the sources and types of the references, and determine the appropriateness of these to the subject matter of the poem. Questions are similar to those you might ask in a study of imagery: Does the poet or speaker in the poem refer extensively to nature, science, warfare, politics, business, reading? For example, in Sonnet 30 Shakespeare expands a metaphor equating personal reverie with courtroom proceedings. Because such proceedings are public and methodical, while self-evaluation is private and relatively unplanned, how appropriate is the metaphor? Does Shakespeare make it seem right as he develops it in the poem? How? In considering any metaphors and similes in the work you analyze, you would need similarly to classify according to sources, and try to determine the appropriateness of this body of figures to the poet's ideas.

3. *Focus on the interests and sensibilities of the poet.* Although similar to the second approach, the emphasis here is on what the poet's choices show about his or her vision and interests. You might begin by listing the figures in the poem and then determining the sources, just as you would do in discussing the sources of images generally. But then you should

raise questions like the following: Does the poet use figures derived from one sense rather than another (i.e., sight, hearing, taste, smell, touch)? Does he or she record color, brightness, shadow, shape, depth, height, number, size, slowness, speed, emptiness, fullness, richness, drabness? Has the poet relied on the associations of figures of sense? Do metaphors and similes referring to green plants and trees, to red roses, or to rich fabrics, for example, suggest that life is full and beautiful, or do references to touch suggest amorous warmth? This approach is designed to help you draw whatever conclusions you can about the poet's—or the speaker's—taste or sensibility as a result of your study.

4. *Examine the effect of one figure on the other figures and ideas of the poem.* The assumption of this approach is that each literary work is unified and organically whole, so that each part is closely related and inseparable from everything else. Usually it is best to pick a figure that occurs at the beginning of the poem and then to determine how this figure influences your perception of the rest of the poem. Your aim here is to consider the relationship of part to parts, and part to whole. The beginning of Donne's "A Valediction: Forbidding Mourning," for example, contains a simile comparing the parting of the speaker and his woman friend to the quiet dying of "virtuous men." What is the effect of this comparison upon the rest of the poem? To help you in approaching such a question, you might substitute a totally different detail, such as, here, the violent death of a condemned criminal, or the slaughter of a domestic animal, rather than the deaths of "virtuous men." Such suppositions, which would clearly be out of place and inappropriate, may help you to understand and then explain the poet's rhetorical figures.

CONCLUSION.   In your conclusion you might summarize your main points, describe your general impressions, try to describe the impact of the figures, indicate your personal responses, or show what might further be done along the lines you have been developing in the body of your essay. If you know other works by the same writer, or other works by other writers with comparable or contrasting figures, you might briefly consider these other works and the light they shed on your present analysis.

FIRST SAMPLE ESSAY: A PARAGRAPH

Wordsworth's Use of Overstatement in "London, 1802"*

Through overstatement, Wordsworth emphasizes his tribute to Milton as a master of idealistic thought. The speaker's claim that England is "a fen/ Of stagnant waters" (lines 2–3) is overstated, just as is the implication that

* See p. 638 for this poem.

people ("we") in England have no "manners, virtue, freedom, [or] power" (line 8). With the overstatement, however, Wordsworth makes the case that the nation's well-being depends on the constant flow of creative thoughts by persons of great ideas. Because Milton was clearly the greatest of these, in the view of Wordsworth's speaker, the overstatement stresses the importance of voices of leadership. Milton is the model, and the overstated need lays the foundation in the real political and moral world for a revival of Milton's ideas. Thus, through overstatement, Wordsworth emphasizes the importance of Milton, and in this way pays tribute to him.

Commentary on the Paragraph

This sample illustrates how a single rhetorical figure may become the basis of a short paragraph. The rhetorical figure you choose to write on does not have to be prominent in the poem. The topic is Wordsworth's use of overstatement in "London, 1802." The detail of overstatement selected from the poem is Wordsworth's assertion about the immoral state of his country in 1802. The goal of the paragraph is not to describe the details of the figure, however, but to show how the figure affects Wordsworth's poetic tribute to Milton. Even in a short writing assignment make sure you support your major point in a direct, clear way.

SECOND SAMPLE ESSAY

A Study of Shakespeare's Metaphors in Sonnet 30*

[1] In this sonnet Shakespeare's speaker stresses the sadness and regret of remembered experience, but he states that a person with these feelings may be cheered by the thought of a friend. His metaphors, cleverly used, create new and fresh ways of seeing personal life in this perspective.° He presents metaphors drawn from the public and business worlds of lawcourts, money, and banking or money-handling.▫

[2] The courtroom metaphor of the first four lines shows that memories of past experience are constantly present and influential. Like a judge commanding defendants to appear in court, the speaker "summon[s]" his memory of "things past" to appear on trial before him. This metaphor suggests that people are their own judges and that their ideals and morals are like laws by which they measure themselves. The speaker finds himself guilty of wasting his time in the past. Removing himself, however, from the strict punishment that a real judge might require, he does not condemn himself for his "dear time's waste," but instead laments it (line 4). The metaphor is thus used to

---

* See p. 628 for this poem.
° Central idea.
▫ Thesis sentence.

indicate that a person's consciousness is made up just as much of self-doubt and reproach as by more positive influences.

[3]   With the closely related reference of money in the next group of four lines, Shakespeare shows that living is a lifelong investment and is valuable for this reason. According to the money metaphor, living requires the spending of emotions and commitment to others. When friends move away and loved ones die, it is as though this expenditure has been lost. Thus, the speaker's dead friends are "precious" because he invested time and love in them, and the "sights" that have "vanished" from his eyes make him "moan" because he went to great "expense" for them (line 8).

[4]   Like the money metaphor, the metaphor of banking or money-handling in the next four lines emphasizes the fact that life's experiences are on deposit in the mind. They are recorded there, and may be withdrawn in moments of "sweet silent thought" just as a depositor may withdraw money. Thus the speaker states that he counts out his woes just as a merchant or banker counts money ("And heavily from woe to woe tell o'er"). Because strong emotions still accompany his memories of mistakes made long ago, he pays again with "new" woe the accounts that he had already paid with old woe in the past. The metaphor suggests that the past is so much a part of the present that a person never finishes paying both the principal and interest of past emotional investments. By means of this combination of figures on banking and the law, the speaker indicates that his memory puts him in double jeopardy, for the thoughts of his losses overwhelm him in the present just as much as they did in the past.

[5]   The legal, financial, and money-handling metaphors combine in the last two lines to show how a healthy present life may overcome past regrets. The "dear friend" being addressed in these lines has the resources (financial) to settle all the emotional judgments that the speaker as a self-judge has made against himself (legal). It is as though the friend is a rich patron who rescues him from emotional bankruptcy (legal and financial) and the possible doom resulting from the potential sentence of emotional misery and depression (legal).

[6]   In these metaphors, therefore, Shakespeare's references are drawn from everyday public and business transactions, but his use of them is creative, unusual, and excellent. In particular, the idea of line 8 ("And moan th'expense of many a vanished sight") stresses that people spend much emotional energy on others. Without such personal commitment, one cannot have precious friends and loved ones. In keeping with this metaphor of money and investment, one could measure life not in months or years, but in the spending of emotion and involvement in personal relationships. Shakespeare, by inviting readers to explore the values brought out by his metaphors, gives new insights into the nature and value of life.

Commentary on the Essay

This essay treats the three metaphorical figures that Shakespeare presents in Sonnet 30. It thus illustrates the second approach (p. 649) by analyzing the frames of reference and their appropriateness. But the aim of the discussion is not only to explore the extent and nature of the comparison between the metaphors and the personal situations spoken about in the sonnet. The goal is also to explain how the metaphors develop Shakespeare's meaning. The essay therefore also illustrates the first approach (p. 649) by interpreting the meaning and effect of the figures.

In addition to providing a brief description of the sonnet, the introduction brings out the central idea and provides the thesis sentence. Paragraph 2 deals with the meaning of Shakespeare's courtroom metaphor. His money metaphor is explained in paragraph 3. Paragraph 4 considers the banking, or money-handling, figure while paragraph 5 shows how Shakespeare's last two lines bring together the three separate metaphors. The conclusion comments generally on the creativity of Shakespeare's metaphors, and it also amplifies on the way in which the money metaphor leads toward an increased understanding and valuation of life.

Throughout the essay, transitions from one topic to the next are brought about by linking words in the topic sentences. In paragraph 3, for example, the words "closely related" and "next group" move the reader from paragraph 2 to the new content. In paragraph 4, the words effecting the transition are "like the money metaphor" and "the next four lines." The opening sentence of paragraph 5 refers collectively to the subjects of paragraphs 2, 3, and 4, thereby focusing them on the new topic of paragraph 5.

THIRD SAMPLE ESSAY

Paradox in Sir Thomas Wyatt's "I Find No Peace"*

[1]
Wyatt's "I Find No Peace" is a sonnet built on paradox. The first-person speaker is describing the effects his love has upon him, and he indicates forcefully that he is caught between commitment, on the one hand, and the desire to be free, on the other. Because of his conflict, he describes his own conditions of amazement, dismay, and also amusement, but he states also that he is reconciled to his contrary states. His situation blends naturally with the rhetorical pattern of paradox.° In the poem, the paradox is extended to the speaker's personal reactions, his attitude toward his beloved, and his general public situation.°

The speaker's personal reactions are most vividly described within the contrary states defined by paradox. Thus the speaker at the beginning declares his satisfaction at having won his "war" because he has apparently convinced his sweetheart to love him. But at the same time he can never really be sure

* See p. 634 for this poem.
° Central idea.
° Thesis sentence.

[2] of her. Hence he also states the paradox that he can "find no peace." Throughout the sonnet the speaker develops these contradictory emotional states. He is at the height of desire, but he cannot find consummation. He therefore speaks ambiguously of his sexual frustration (line 7, where he cannot "live or die at . . . [his] devise," with *die* being a sexual pun), and the frustration in turn continues his uncertainty. Throughout, in almost every line, the speaker stresses other paradoxes that point out his inner anguish.

[3] In the speaker's descriptions of his attitude toward his beloved, the same paradoxes are apparent. He calls her his "delight," for example (line 14), and yet he confesses that he is blind to whatever human faults she might possess ("Without eyen I see," line 9). He would like to pursue his quest further but does not want to offend, and thus he states, "without tongue I plain" (line 9). In short, his sweetheart is also a human being to whom he must grant individuality and freedom. Because of the gap between this recognition and his desire, he paradoxically experiences the joy of love and the pain of uncertainty.

[4] Finally, the speaker claims that his attempts to carry on normally in life are also afflicted with his paradoxical personal condition. In line 12 the speaker explains that he continues to eat and also to laugh; that is, his life has not stopped, and he goes about his affairs. But all the time he is at meals, which should be a joyful time, he is in sorrow, and even when he is laughing, he is also in pain. In this way, the poet develops the paradox in which a person functioning well publicly is personally torn and uncertain.

[5] The poem thus stresses the paradoxical effects of intense love in all major phases of the speaker's life. The human basis of the paradoxes is the difficulty that people have in truly knowing each other, even the ones they love most dearly. In the poem, this inability to know the true mind of the beloved, even though she is "all the world" to the speaker (line 4), creates the uncertainty out of which the paradoxes arise. This state is convincingly real, particularly because of the speaker's intensity of feeling. Wyatt's complete incorporation of paradox into the sonnet therefore dramatizes the conflicting feelings of a person in love. Paradox here is precisely fitted to the subject of the poem.

Commentary on the Essay

This sample illustrates how a pervasive rhetorical figure may be divided for consideration in a full-length essay. The figure chosen is paradox because it is so prominent in "I Find No Peace." For any other poem in which any particular figure is important, the same method might be followed. If the essay were to be based on two or more figures, each one of these might form a separate part or paragraph in the body.

In the introduction to this particular essay, attention is focused on the figure of paradox and its importance in the situation described in the poem. The central idea proposes the argument that idea and figure are blended. The thesis sentence lists three areas of the poem to be explored in the body. Paragraph 2 describes the paradox as developed in the speaker's perception of his own condition as a lover. Because the sonnet is primarily about the speaker rather than about his love, this paragraph is the longest in the body of the essay. Paragraph 3 is concerned with the paradox as it affects the speaker's descriptions of his beloved. His difficulty results from the fact that she is an individual, and hence he cannot control her as much as his love would dictate that he would like to do. Paragraph 4, the shortest of the body, is concerned with the sparse information that the speaker discloses about his public life as it is affected by the paradox of his private turmoil. The conclusion briefly summarizes the main topics of the body, and then it attempts to explain the paradoxes in terms of the difficulty people have in knowing each other. The last sentence is a restatement of the central idea.

WRITING TOPICS FOR CHAPTER 16

1. Study the simile of the "stiff twin compasses" in Donne's "A Valediction: Forbidding Mourning." Using such a compass, or a drawing of one, write an essay which demonstrates the accuracy of Donne's descriptions. What light does the simile shed on the relationship of two lovers? How does it emphasize any or all of these aspects of love: closeness, immediacy, extent, importance, duration, intensity?

2. Consider some of the metaphors and similes in the poems included in this chapter. Write an essay which answers the following questions. How effective are the figures you select? (Examples: the bonsai tree [Piercy], the Siamese twins [Minty], the explosive [Hughes], the summer's day [Shakespeare].) What insights do the figures provide within the contexts of their respective poems? How appropriate are they? Might they be expanded more fully, and if they were, what would be the effect?

3. Consider some of the other rhetorical figures to be found in the poems of the chapter. On the basis of the figures you have selected, write an essay describing the importance of figures in creating emphasis and in extending and deepening the ideas of poetry.

4. Write a poem in which you create a governing metaphor or simile. An example might be: My girl/boy friend is like (a) an opening flower, (b) a difficult book, (c) an insoluble mathematical problem, (d) a bill that cannot be paid, (e) a slow-moving chess game. Another example: Teaching a person how to do a particular job is like (a) shoveling heavy snow, (b) climbing a mountain during a landslide, (c) having someone force you underwater when you are gasping for breath. For the poem you write, describe the relationship between the development/structure of your poem and the comparison you have made.

17

Tone: The Creation of Attitude in Poetry

Tone (also discussed in Chapter 8) is the means by which poets reveal attitudes and feelings. You may remember that the term is borrowed from the phrase *tone of voice* as applied to speech. In the study of tone in poetry, the object is to consider the ways in which poets express and control attitudes. Literally everything in the poem helps convey the tone. The poet's stance toward the material and toward possible readers is one of the most important aspects. In establishing a speaker or an authorial voice, the poet must develop a character to do the speaking in relation to the purpose of the poem: How much self-awareness, how many traits, what kind of background, what kind of relationship to establish between the speaker and the readers? How much knowledge to assume for both the speaker and the readers? What kind of interests and assumptions to attribute to the readers? All these enter into the writing of the poem and therefore influence its tone.

In addition, things like irony, understatement, overstatement, the creation of humor or seriousness, the use of diction and the control of connotation, the images, similes, and metaphors, are a part of tone. The sentences must be just long enough, no shorter and no longer, for the intended effect of the material. If a conversational style is established, overly formal words must be avoided; similarly, slang would not suit a formal style. In a serious poem, the use of jingling or bouncing rhythms might seem frivolous and therefore inappropriate. Any ambiguities should be deliberate and not unintentional. In all these aspects that collectively make up the tone of a poem, the poet's consistency is of primary importance. If anything falls short, the poem sinks and the poet will have failed.

TONE, CHOICE, AND READER RESPONSE

Remember that a major rhetorical objective of poets is to gain reader acceptance, no matter what their topic. They may wish to shape, enrich, stimulate, inform, and, generally affect readers. Thus, poets may begin their poems with not much more than a brief idea, a vague feeling, or a fleeting impression. Then, in the light of their developing design, their own attitudes, and their judgment of possible reader responses, they *choose* what to say, what form in which to present the material, and what words and phrases to use. "Theme for English B" by Langston Hughes (the topic of the sample essay) illustrates almost in outline form the process by which a poet structures reader response in order to gain acceptance. Hughes's speaker lays out those areas of his life in which he and his intended audience, the English teacher, share a common bond of interests. In this way Hughes establishes grounds for acceptance of his ideas of human equality, regardless of color.

In order to balance poetic intention with the full range of reader responses, the poet must have great skill. The poet's control over tone is essential, so that readers may respond with appropriate recognition, understanding, and emotion. In the long run readers might not agree with all the ideas in the poem, but the successful poem will have gained the reader's acceptance because the poet's control over tone will have been right.

Each poem, in short, attempts to evoke total responses, which any interfering lapse of tone might destroy. Such lapses may take the form of an objectionable assumption about the qualities of a person or idea in the poem, a misinterpretation of how readers will take an idea, an uncertain expression, or some ambiguity that will create a misimpression. Let us look at a poem that misses, and misses badly, in its control of tone.

CORNELIUS WHUR   (1782–1853)

The First-Rate Wife   *1837*

This brief effusion I indite,
  And my vast wishes send,
That thou mayst be directed right,
And have ere long within thy sight
  A most *enchanting* friend!   5

The *maiden* should have *lovely face*,
  And be of *genteel mien*;
If not, within thy dwelling place,

There may be vestige of disgrace,
    Not much admired—when seen.   10

Nor will thy dearest be complete
    Without *domestic* care;
If otherwise, howe'er discreet,
Thine eyes will very often meet
    What none desire to share!   15

And further still—thy future *dear*,
    Should have some *mental* ray;
If not, thou mayest drop a tear,
Because no *real sense* is there
    To charm life's dreary day!   20

QUESTIONS

1. What is the situation of the poem? What sort of person is the speaker? Who is the listener? Why does the speaker address the listener? How does the speaker's tone reveal his character? In light of the tone of line 3, what relationship does the speaker establish between himself and the listener?

2. What requirements does the speaker create for the "first-rate wife"? In what ways might the advice be considered helpful? From the tone of the speaker's requirements, what attitude toward women does the speaker expect his listener to share?

3. Consider the tone of these phrases: "vestige of disgrace" (line 9), "what none desire to share" (line 15), and "to charm life's dreary day" (line 20). What does this tone show about the assumptions and attitudes toward marriage held by the speaker?

4. What sorts of requirements does the speaker *not* include about a "first-rate wife"? What do these omissions demonstrate about him?

In "The First-Rate Wife" the speaker is giving advice to a male listener about what traits to look for in a young lady who might make him an excellent wife. In stanza 1 the speaker sets himself up as advice-giver; in stanzas 2, 3, and 4 he asserts that the three basic qualities desired in a woman are beauty, ability to keep house, and intelligence—in that order. From the tone of the speaker's remarks it is clear that he regards the decision to marry as being roughly comparable to the hiring of a house-keeper or the buying of a diverting book. Note the tone of the phrase "some *mental* ray," for example. The word *some* does not mean "a great deal," but in this instance is more like "*at least* some," as though it would be unreasonable to expect anything more of a woman. From the tone of the last three lines it is clear that the speaker's requirement for intelligence does not mean that the woman should be on par with the man intellectually but rather that she should be charming enough to rescue him from dreariness and boredom. Even allowing for the fact that the poem was written in the nineteenth century and represents a traditional masculine view of marriage, the poem's shortsighted attitude may be offensive to the modern reader. Do you wonder why you probably never heard of Cornelius Whur before?

TONE AND THE NEED FOR CONTROL

"The First-Rate Wife" emphasizes the need for the poet to be in control over the entire situation of the poem. The speaker must be aware of his or her situation and should not, like the speaker of "The First-Rate Wife," demonstrate any smugness or insensitivity, unless the poet is deliberately revealing the shortcomings of the speaker by dramatizing them for the reader's amusement, as E. E. Cummings does in the poem "next to of course god" (p. 920). In a poem characterized by well-controlled tone, values should be clear, details should be introduced correctly, and the climax of the poem should come at the right spot. The following poem exhibits such control over tone.

WILFRED OWEN (1893–1918)

Dulce et Decorum Est°   *1920*

Bent double, like old beggars under sacks,
Knock-kneed, coughing like hags, we cursed through sludge,
Till on the haunting flares we turned our backs
And towards our distant rest began to trudge.
Men marched asleep. Many had lost their boots   5
But limped on, blood-shod. All went lame; all blind;
Drunk with fatigue; deaf even to the hoots
Of tired, outstripped Five-Nines° that dropped behind.

Gas!° GAS! Quick boys!—An ecstasy of fumbling,
Fitting the clumsy helmets° just in time;   10
But someone still was yelling out and stumbling
And flound'ring like a man in fire or lime . . .
Dim, through the misty panes and thick green° light,
As under a green sea, I saw him drowning.

DULCE ET DECORUM EST. The Latin title comes from Horace, *Odes*, Book 3, line 13: *"Dulce et decorum est pro patria mori"* ("It is sweet and honorable to die for one's country). See last line of poem.   8 *Five-Nines*: Artillery shells that made a hooting sound just before landing.   9 *Gas*: Poisonous gas was first used as an anti-personnel weapon in 1915 by the Germans.   10 *helmets*: Soldiers carried gas masks as a part of normal battle equipment.   13 *thick green*: The chlorine gas used in gas attacks has a greenish-yellow color.

In all my dreams, before my helpless sight,   15
He plunges at me, guttering, choking, drowning.

If in some smothering dreams you too could pace
Behind the wagon that we flung him in.
And watch the white eyes writhing in his face,
His hanging face, like a devil's sick of sin;   20
If you could hear, at every jolt, the blood
Come gargling from the froth-corrupted lungs,
Obscene as cancer, bitter as the cud
Of vile, incurable sores on innocent tongues.—
My friend, you would not tell with such high zest   25
To children ardent for some desperate glory,
The old Lie: Dulce et decorum est
Pro patria mori.°   *to die for one's country*

QUESTIONS

1. What scene is described in lines 1–8? What expressions does the speaker use to indicate his attitude toward the conditions?
2. What does the title of the poem mean? What attitude or conviction does it embody?
3. What is the tonal relationship between the patriotic fervor of the Latin phrase and the images of the poem? How does this tonal difference create the dominant tone of the poem? What is the dominant tone?
4. Does the speaker really mean "my friend" in line 25? In what tone of voice might this phrase be spoken?

In "Dulce et Decorum Est" the poet is in command of the tone. The speaker is addressing a listener, whom he identifies as "you" and "my friend," who before the poem begins has presumably been talking about the need for young men to die in the service of their country. The reader is not being addressed, but instead is a witness to the scene. The speaker is recounting an incident in which he, as a soldier in World War I, witnessed the painful, agonized death of a comrade in a gas attack. Once he finishes his narrative, the speaker testifies to the grisly horror by claiming that it has dominated his dreams. Then he addresses the listener directly, claiming that if the friend could witness the horror of warfare, he would never again claim that dying, even for one's country, is sweet or appropriate.

The tone never once lapses in the poem. The poet intends the description to evoke a response of horror from the reader. He contrasts the strategic goals of warfare with the up-close grimness and pain of death in battle. The language skillfully emphasizes first the dreariness and fatigue of warfare (with words like *sludge*, *trudge*, *lame*, and *blind*) and second the agony of violent death from gas (embodied in the participles *guttering, choking, drown-*

ing, smothering, and *writhing*). With these details carefully established, the concluding attack against the "glory" of war is difficult to refute, even if warfare is undertaken in preservation of one's country. Although the details about the agonized death clearly create distress or discomfort for a sensitive reader, they are not designed to do that alone but instead are integral to the poem's argument. Ultimately, it is the contrast between the high ideals of the Latin phrase and the realities of death during a gas attack that creates the dominant tone of the poem. The Latin phrase treats war and death in the abstract; the poem brings images of battle and death vividly alive. The resultant tone is that of controlled bitterness and irony.

COMMON GROUNDS OF ASSENT

This is not to say that all those reading "Dulce et Decorum Est" will immediately deny that war is ever necessary. The issues of politics and warfare are far too complex for that. But the poem does show another important aspect of tone, namely, the degree to which the poet judges and tries to control the possible responses of readers through the establishment of a **common ground of assent.** An appeal to a bond of commonly held interests, concerns, and assumptions is essential if a poet is to maintain an effective tone. Wilfred Owen, for example, does not create arguments against the necessity of a just war. Instead, he bases the poem upon realistic details about the death suffered by the speaker's comrade, and he makes the poem appeal to emotions that everyone, pacifist and militarist alike, would agree upon—a sense of horror at the contemplation of violent death. Even assuming a widely divergent audience, in other words, the *tone* of the poem is successful because it is based on commonly acknowledged facts and commonly felt emotions. Faced with a poem like this one, even advocates of warfare would need to defend their ideas on the grounds of *prevention* of just such needless, ugly deaths. Owen has wisely and carefully considered the responses of his readers and has controlled speaker, situation, detail, and argument in order to make the poem acceptable for the broadest possible spectrum of opinion.

TONE AND IRONY

Irony is a mode of indirection, a means of establishing an assertion by the emphasis upon a discrepancy or opposite (see also pp. 302–4). Thus Owen uses the title "Dulce et Decorum Est" to emphasize that death in warfare is not fitting and noble, but rather horrible and painful. The title ironically reminds us of eloquent national holiday speeches at the tombs of unknown soldiers, but as we have seen, it also reminds us of the reality of the agonized death of Owen's soldier. As an aspect of tone, therefore, irony is a powerful way of conveying attitudes, for it draws your attention to at least two ways of seeing the situation being presented, and through such a perspective it enables you not only to understand, but also to feel.

     SITUATIONAL IRONY.   Poetry shares with fiction and drama the various kinds of ironies that poets believe may afflict human life. "The Workbox," by Thomas Hardy, illustrates a skillful manipulation of irony.

THOMAS HARDY   (1840–1928)

The Workbox   1914

"See, here's the workbox, little wife,
   That I made of polished oak."
He was a joiner,° of village life;   *cabinetmaker*
   She came of borough folk.

He holds the present up to her   5
   As with a smile she nears
And answers to the profferer,
   " 'Twill last all my sewing years!"

"I warrant it will. And longer too.
   'Tis a scantling° that I got   10
Off poor John Wayward's coffin, who
   Died of they knew not what.

"The shingled pattern that seems to cease
   Against your box's rim
Continues right on in the piece   15
   That's underground with him.

"And while I worked it made me think
   Of timber's varied doom:
One inch where people eat and drink,
   The next inch in a tomb.   20

"But why do you look so white, my dear,
   And turn aside your face?
You knew not that good lad, I fear,
   Though he came from your native place?"

"How could I know that good young man,   25
   Though he came from my native town,

THE WORKBOX.   4.5 *village, borough*: A village was small and rustic; a borough was
larger and more sophisticated.   10 *scantling*: a small, leftover piece of wood.

When he must have left far earlier than
   I was a woman grown?"

"Ah, no. I should have understood!
   It shocked you that I gave   30
To you one end of a piece of wood
   Whose other is in a grave?"

"Don't, dear, despise my intellect,
   Mere accidental things
Of that sort never have effect   35
   On my imaginings."

Yet still her lips were limp and wan,
   Her face still held aside,
As if she had known not only John,
   But known of what he died.   40

QUESTIONS

1. Who does most of the speaking in this poem? What does the tone of the
    speeches show about the characters of the man and the wife? What does
    the tone indicate about the poet's attitude toward them?
2. In lines 21–40, what does the dialogue indicate about the wife's knowledge
    of John and about her possible earlier relationship with him? Why does the
    wife deny such knowledge? What does the last stanza suggest about her?
    What is the possible insinuation about her in these lines? Why is a mystery
    preserved about the cause of John's death?
3. In lines 17–20, the man describes the "varied doom" of timber. What sort
    of irony is suggested by the symbolism of the wood made into the workbox?
4. In what way is the irony described by the man more complex than he realizes?
5. The narrator, or speaker, of the poem speaks only in lines 3–7 and 37–40.
    How much of the explanation he gives is essential? How much indicates his
    attitude? How might the poem have been more effectively concluded?

"The Workbox" is a little domestic drama of deception and sadness.
The extremely complex details are evidence of **situational irony;** that is,
an awareness that human beings do not control themselves but are rather
controlled by powerful, overwhelming forces—in this case, both death and
earlier feelings and commitments. Beyond this irony evolving out of the
domestic scene, Hardy also emphasizes symbolically the direct connection
that death has with the living. As a result of the husband's gift made of
the same wood with which he has also made a coffin for the dead man,
the wife will live all the rest of her days with the constant reminder of
this man. Her future will be characterized by regret and also by the apparently endless need to deny her true emotions.

DRAMATIC IRONY.   In addition to situational irony, the deception practiced by the wife reveals that the husband is in a situation of **dramatic irony.** The character understands one set of circumstances while the readers understand, in greater perspective, something completely different. In this poem, the husband does not know that the wife is not being truthful or open about her earlier relationship with the dead man. The tone of "The Workbox" suggests that the husband may be suspicious, however. By his emphasis on the piece of wood, he may be trying to draw her out. But he does not actually *know* the true circumstances, and hence he is unsure of his wife's attitude toward him. Because of this mixture of dramatic and situational irony, Hardy has created a poem of great complexity.

VERBAL IRONY.   Poetry may also contain **verbal irony,** that is, ambiguous language. "She being Brand / -new" by E. E. Cummings (p. 669) is filled with double meaning. Using terms of breaking in a new car, the speaker of the poem is actually describing a sexual encounter, and the entire poem is a virtuoso piece of *double-entendre.* Another example of verbal irony may be seen in Theodore Roethke's "My Papa's Waltz" (p. 672), in which the speaker uses the name of this orderly, stately dance to describe his childhood memory of his father's whirling him around the kitchen in wild, boisterous drunkenness.

SATIRE

Satire, of major importance as an aspect of tone, is designed to expose human follies and vices. In method, a satiric poem may be bitter and vituperative in its attack, but quite often it employs humor and irony, on the grounds that anger turns readers away while a comic tone more easily gains agreement. The speaker of a satiric poem either may attack folly and vice *directly*, or may dramatically *embody* the folly or vice, and thus serve as an illustration of the subject of satire. An example of the first type is the following short poem by Alexander Pope, in which the speaker directly attacks a listener who has claimed identity as a poet, but whom the speaker considers as nothing more than a fool. The speaker cleverly uses insult as the tone of attack.

ALEXANDER POPE   (1688–1744)

Epigram from the French   *1732*

Sir, I admit your general rule
That every poet is a fool:

But you yourself may serve to show it,
That every fool is not a poet.

An example of the second type of satiric poem is the following short epigram by the same poet, in which the speaker is an actual embodiment of the subject of attack.

ALEXANDER POPE   (1688–1744)

*Epigram. Engraved on the Collar of a Dog which I gave
to his Royal Highness*   1738 (1737)

I am his Highness' dog at Kew:°   *one of the royal palaces, near London*
Pray tell me sir, whose dog are you?

Here the speaker is the King's dog at the palace at Kew, and the listener an unknown dog. Pope's satire is directed not against canine habits, however, but against human class pretentiousness. The tone of the first line ridicules derived, not earned, status, while the tone of the second line implies an unwillingness to recognize the listener until the question of rank is resolved. Pope, by using the dog as a speaker, reduces such snobbishness to an absurdity. Another satiric poem attacking pretentiousness is "next to of course god" by E. E. Cummings (p. 920), where the speaker voices a set of patriotic platitudes, and in doing so illustrates Cummings's satiric point that such claims are often void of understanding and thought. Satiric tone may thus range widely, sometimes being objective, comic, and distant; sometimes deeply concerned and scornful; and sometimes dramatic, ingenuous, and revelatory. Always, however, the satiric mode confronts and exposes.

READING FOR TONE IN POETRY

In order to understand and describe the tone of any poem, you need to determine the situation, the speaker, the listener, and the assumptions that are expected of you as a reader. What common grounds does the poet establish to help you understand the material? Are there also special concessions you need to make as a reader to further your understanding of the poem? Any such concessions should be reasonable and realistic, such as those for accepting the verbal irony of Cummings's, "she being Brand / -new," or for accepting the description of the horrible death in

"Dulce et Decorum Est." By contrast, in "The First-Rate Wife," the reader must accept the qualification of the pompous speaker to offer marital guidance to his listener—clearly an unacceptable concession.

With regard to expressions and language, it is necessary to determine that denotations and connotations are appropriate. Many words or expressions may at first seem unusual, even though they are obviously the ones intended by the poet. Assuming that the poet controlled word choice carefully, any unusual phrases will require detailed consideration, such as the references in "she being Brand / -new" by Cummings, or the descriptions of the boy dancing with the father in "My Papa's Waltz." The goal in this consideration should be to determine if diction is an appropriate aspect of the tone of the poem.

POEMS FOR STUDY

ANNE BRADSTREET   (1612–1672)

The Author to Her Book   *1678*

Thou ill-formed offspring of my feeble brain,
Who after birth did'st by my side remain,
Till snatched from thence by friends, less wise than true,
Who thee abroad exposed to public view;
Made thee in rags, halting, to the press to trudge,   5
Where errors were not lessened, all may judge.
At thy return my blushing was not small,
My rambling brat° (in print) should mother call;
I cast thee by as one unfit for light,
Thy visage was so irksome in my sight;   10
Yet being mine own, at length affection would
Thy blemishes amend, if so I could:
I washed thy face, but more defects I saw,
And rubbing off a spot, still made a flaw.
I stretched thy joints to make thee even feet,°   *regular poetic meter*   15
Yet still thou run'st more hobbling than is meet;
In better dress to trim thee was my mind,
But nought save homespun cloth, in the house I find.
In this array, 'mongst vulgars may'st thou roam;   20
In criticks hands beware thou dost not come;
And take thy way where yet thou are not known.

THE AUTHOR TO HER BOOK.   8 *brat*: The word here emphasizes the insignificance rather than the unpleasant aspects of a child.

If for thy Father asked, say thou had'st none;
And for thy Mother, she alas is poor,
Which caused her thus to send thee out of door.

25

QUESTIONS

1. What is the tone of the speaker's references to those friends who "exposed" her book to "public view" (that is, circulated it without her consent)? How does this tone indicate her ambiguous feelings about them?
2. How does the speaker excuse the fact that she is issuing her book of poetry on her own initiative? How does the tone produce humor? How does the tone of the concluding metaphor encourage you to smile, or even to laugh?
3. What attitude toward herself does the speaker express? How do you react to this attitude? How do you think you are expected by the poet to react?
4. What is the tone of the extended metaphor of the child in lines 11–18?

ANNE FINCH, COUNTESS OF WINCHELSEA   (1661–1720)

To the Nightingale   *1713*

Exert thy voice, sweet harbinger° of spring!   *forerunner, herald*
   This moment is thy time to sing,
   This moment I attend to praise,
And set my numbers to thy lays.°   *ballads*
   Free as thine shall be my song   5
   As thy music, short or long.
Poets, wild as thee, were born,
   Pleasing best when unconfined,
   When to please is least designed,
Soothing but their cares to rest;   10
   Cares do still their thoughts molest,
   And still the unhappy poet's breast,
Like thine, when best he sings, is placed against a thorn.°

   She begins. Let all be still!
      Muse, thy promise now fulfil!   15
   Sweet, oh sweet! still sweeter yet!
   Can thy words such accents fit,
   Canst thou syllables refine,
   Melt a sense that shall retain
   Still some spirit of the brain,   20

TO THE NIGHTINGALE.   13 *thorn*: a reference to the (untrue) legend that nightingales sing most sweetly only when they are in pain because of thorns.

Till with sounds like these it join?
    'Twill not be! then change thy note,
    Let division shake thy throat.°
Hark! division now she tries,
Yet as far the Muse outflies.   25
    Cease then, prithee, cease thy tune!
    Trifler, wilt thou sing till June?
Till thy business all lies waste,
And the time of building's past?
    Thus we poets that have speech,   30
Unlike what thy forests teach,
    If a fluent vein be shown
    That's transcendent to our own,
Criticize, reform, or preach,
Or censure what we cannot reach.

23 *division*: In music, the rapid singing of many notes.   35

QUESTIONS

1.   What is the tone of the speaker's description of the nightingale? Is the tone consistent or mixed? How do you know?

2.   For what reasons does the speaker admire the song of the bird? Describe the tone of the speaker's description of the bird's song as noted from lines 14–25. Why does the speaker censure the bird in lines 26–29? What attitude toward the speaker does the poet intend by the tone of these lines?

3.   What is the tone of the connection the speaker makes between the song of the nightingale and the works of poets? What ideas does the speaker derive from this connection about the future of poetic creativity?

4.   In lines 11–13 what is the tone of the speaker's metaphor of the thorn? How does the tone reveal the speaker's attitude toward herself?

5.   What is the purpose of lines 30–35? What does the tone of these lines show about the speaker's attitude toward herself? Why does the speaker say "we poets"?

ARTHUR O'SHAUGHNESSY   (1844–1881)

A Love Symphony   *1881*

Along the garden° ways just now   *a green area*
   I heard the flowers speak;
The white rose told me of your brow,
   The red rose of your cheek;
The lily of your bended head,   5
   The bindweed of your hair;

Each looked its loveliest and said
   You were more fair.

I went into the wood anon,°   *later, soon after*
   And heard the wild birds sing   10
How sweet you were; they warbled on,
   Piped, trilled the self-same thing,
Thrush, blackbird, linnet, without pause
   The burden did repeat,
And still began again because   15
   You were more sweet.

And then I went down to the sea,
   And heard it murmuring too,
Part of an ancient mystery,
   All made of me and you.   20
How many a thousand years ago
   I loved, and you were sweet—
Longer I could not stay, and so
   I fled back to your feet.

QUESTIONS

1. What is the "symphony" of love? What is the tone of the speaker's descriptions of the symphony as coming from flowers, birds, and the sea?

2. What is the tone of the phrase "ancient mystery / All made of me and you" (lines 19–20)? Compare this use of the idea of religious mysteriousness and love with the use in John Donne's "The Canonization" (p 864) and Anne Finch's "To Mr. Finch, now Earl of Winchelsea" (p. 782). What common attitudes about love do these three poems contain? What differences?

3. What tone is expressed about the loved one in lines 23–24? In the light of his tone in describing her qualities, what sort of relationship is he celebrating?

E. E. CUMMINGS (1894–1962)

she being Brand / -new   *1926*

she being Brand

-new;and you
know consequently a
little stiff i was
careful of her and(having   5

thoroughly oiled the universal
joint tested my gas felt of
her radiator made sure her springs were O.

K.)i went right to it flooded-the-carburetor cranked her

up,slipped the   10
clutch(and then somehow got into reverse she
kicked what
the hell)next
minute i was back in neutral tried and

again slo-wly;bare,ly nudg.   ing(my   15

lev-er Right-
oh and her gears being in

A 1 shape passed
from low through
second-in-to-high like   20
greasedlightning) just as we turned the corner of Divinity

avenue i touched the accelerator and give

her the juice,good

                      (it
was the first ride and believe i we was   25
happy to see how nice she acted right up to
the last minute coming back down by the Public
Gardens i slammed on
the

internalexpanding   30
&
externalcontracting
brakes Bothatonce and

brought allofher tremB
-ling   35
to a:dead.

stand-
;Still)

QUESTIONS

1. How extensive is the verbal irony, the *double-entendre*, in this poem? This
   poem is considered comic. Do you agree? Why or why not?
2. How do the spacing and alignment affect your reading of the poem? How
   does the unexpected and sometimes absent punctuation—such as in line
   15, "again slo-wly;bare,ly nudg. ing(my"—contribute to the humor?
3. Can this poem in any respect be called off color or bawdy? How might you
   refute such charges in light of the tone the speaker uses to equate a first
   sexual experience with the breaking in of a new car?

LANGSTON HUGHES   (1902–1967)

Theme for English B   *1959*

The instructor said,

   Go home and write
   a page tonight.
   And let that page come out of you—
   Then, it will be true.   5

I wonder if it's that simple?

I am twenty-two, colored, born in Winston-Salem.
I went to school there, then Durham, then here
to this college on the hill above Harlem.°
I am the only colored student in my class.   10
The steps from the hill lead down to Harlem,
through a park, then I cross St. Nicholas,
Eighth Avenue, Seventh, and I come to the Y,
the Harlem Branch Y, where I take the elevator
up to my room, sit down, and write this page: 15

It's not easy to know what is true for you or me
at twenty-two, my age. But I guess I'm what
I feel and see and hear. Harlem, I hear you:
hear you, hear me—we two—you, me talk on this page.
(I hear New York, too.) Me—who?   20

Well, I like to eat, sleep, drink, and be in love.
I like to work, read, learn, and understand life.
I like a pipe for a Christmas present,
or records—Bessie,° bop,° or Bach.°

I guess being colored doesn't make me not like   25
the same things other folks like who are other races.
So will my page be colored that I write?
Being me, it will not be white.
But it will be
a part of you, instructor.   30
You are white—
yet a part of me, as I am a part of you.
That's American.

THEME FOR ENGLISH B.   9 *college* . . . *Harlem*: A reference to Columbia University
in the Columbia Heights section of New York City. The other streets and buildings mentioned
in lines 11–14 refer to specific places in the same vicinity.   24 *Bessie*: Bessie Smith
(c. 1898–1937), American jazz singer, famed as the "Empress of the Blues."   *bop*: a type
of popular music which was in vogue in the 1940s through the 1960s.   *Bach*: Johann
Sebastian Bach (1685–1750), German composer, considered the master of the Baroque style
of music.

Sometimes perhaps you don't want to be a part of me.
Nor do I often want to be a part of you.   35
But we are, that's true!
As I learn from you,
I guess you learn from me—
although you're older—and white—
and somewhat more free.   40

This is my page for English B.

QUESTIONS

1. What is the tone of the speaker's assessment of himself? What does
   the tone indicate about his feelings toward the situation in the class and at
   the Y?
2. What tone is implicit in the fact that the speaker, in response to a theme
   assignment, has composed a poem rather than a prose essay?
3. What is the tone of lines 21–24, where the speaker indicates a number of
   his likes? Why does the poet have him include these details? In what way
   may the characteristics brought out in these lines serve as an argument for
   social and political equality?
4. How does the tone in lines 27–40, particularly lines 34–36, prevent the statements of the speaker from becoming overly assertive or strident?

THEODORE ROETHKE   (1907–1963)

My Papa's Waltz   *1942*

The whiskey on your breath
Could make a small boy dizzy;
But I hung on like death:
Such waltzing was not easy.

We romped until the pans   5
Slid from the kitchen shelf;
My mother's countenance
Could not unfrown itself.

The hand that held my wrist
Was battered on one knuckle;   10
At every step you missed
My right ear scraped a buckle.

You beat time on my head
With a palm caked hard by dirt,
Then waltzed me off to bed   15
Still clinging to your shirt.

QUESTIONS

1. What is the tone of the speaker's opening description of his father? What is the tone of the phrases "like death" and "such waltzing"?
2. What is the "waltz" the speaker describes? What is the tone of his words describing it in lines 5–15?
3. What does the reference to his "mother's countenance" contribute to the tone of the poem? What sort of situation is suggested by the selection of the word "unfrown"?
4. What does the tone of the physical descriptions of the father contribute to your understanding of the speaker's attitude toward his childhood experiences as his father's dancing partner?

WRITING ABOUT TONE IN POETRY

In writing an essay about tone in a poem, a first task is to determine what kinds of attitudes the poem presents. For example, the poet may seem closely involved with the material or relatively distant from it. You may determine that the poet seems amused by the material, but even then it is important to make conclusions about how to take the amusement. Does the poet seem to be involved with the characters, situations, language, or objects at which she or he laughs? Does he or she share delight with the reader? In more serious situations, the poem may give evidence of a degree of pity, or the poet may seem to be lamenting the human condition. It is up to you to determine what attitudes are present in a poem and what you think produces these attitudes. It is reasonable for you to presume that the emotional response you have to a work was intended by the poet. Your job is to discover what specific aspects of the poem caused you to have this response.

In taking notes about what to include in your essay, therefore, you should concentrate on those features of the poem that most prominently produce or emphasize the attitudes. Thus, one avenue of exploration may be about the apparent assumptions that the poet shares with the reader: What are these assumptions? How do you learn, from the poem, what is expected of you as a reader? Are these assumptions valid, or do they require any kind of special effort or concession?

Another approach might be to concentrate on the apparent attitude of the poet toward the speaker of the poem: What sort of person is he or she? Does this person seem to be intelligent or stupid, cowardly or heroic, exceptional or ordinary, idealistic or realistic? What attitudes does the poet intend as a result of these characterizations?

Another avenue of study might be the diction of the poem. In selecting details for study, you'll need to write down both the normal words and any special words, such as dialect, difficult words, foreign words or phrases, or loaded or connotative words, as well as the effect of these. No matter what the topic or topics you finally treat in your essay, it will be necessary throughout your preparation to keep pinpointing the ways in which the poet brings out the attitudes you find in the poem.

Organizing Your Essay

INTRODUCTION.   The introduction describes the general situation of the poem and the mood or impression that the poem gives. The central idea should be about the aspect or aspects that you plan to develop in the body, such as that the diction is designed to portray the life of ordinary people, or to convey the idea that the speaker is pretentious, or to call upon the reader's ability to visualize an experience, or to feel happiness, or revulsion. The thesis sentence will state the major aspects to be explored in the body.

BODY.   There are a number of ways to approach a discussion of tone. One or more of the approaches listed below may supply useful hints as you prepare your essay.

1. *The situation of the poem.* Here the goal is to discuss the situation in the poem and to determine how the poet has controlled the attitudes. Who is talking to whom? What situation has prompted the speech? Is there any interchange (assuming that there are two characters in the poem)? What do the speakers say, and what do they withhold (and how do you know what they are withholding)? Why do they speak as they do? To what degree do their speeches seem controlled specifically by the situation in which they find themselves? What do their speeches show about the poet's attitudes toward them? How do the speeches indicate how the poet has attempted to structure reader response toward the characters and toward the situation?

2. *"Common ground" of poet, listeners, and readers.* Here the goal is to establish the attitudes that the poet assumes in common with the readers or with persons being addressed. What are the common attitudes? How sincerely are they expressed in the poem? To what degree are they special, unusual, or conventional? What kind of relationship do they suggest between the speaker and the listener, or person being addressed? How do you know what these common attitudes are? Are the attitudes easily accepted, or do they demand a concession? What might the concession be? For example, a religious poem like George Herbert's "The Pulley" (p. 610) might ask the reader to assume an overwhelming need for religious devotion. Not everyone can grant such a need, but a reader might find common ground on the basis of psychological or historical interest, or interest based simply on learning the maximum amount possible about

human beings. With such a concession of commonality, the tone of a religious poem may be approached just like that of any other poem.

3. *Diction and reference.* Here the idea is to analyze the language of the poem to determine how word choice is evidence of the poet's attitude toward the subject matter. Are the words and references in normal use, or does the level indicate that the poet assumes special knowledge by the reader? In Ogden Nash's "Exit, Pursued by a Bear," for example (p. 640), the references to art and furniture, together with the title, indicate that Nash assumes that his readers will be highly literate and knowledgeable. In William Butler Yeats's "The Second Coming" (p. 788), the poet introduces special, personal references, such as the gyre, and he assumes that the interested reader will follow these to derive the poet's attitudes of concern and apprehension about the ominous future of human civilization. References such as these indicate the special pact, or bond, that poets make with their intended readers.

4. *Direct appeals to emotion.* In a comic poem the poet's goal may be to evoke laughter or at least to entertain. In a serious poem the goal may be to produce sorrow or elevation. Whatever the emotion, an avenue of analysis is to determine how the poet achieves the desired effect. In "she being Brand / -new," for example, E. E. Cummings relies for the poem's humor on the reader's ability to understand the sexual ambiguity of a description of breaking in a new car. In "Theme for English B," Langston Hughes relies on the reader's sense of involvement in causes of justice so that the poem may effectively make its assertions about human equality. The same capacity for involvement is assumed by Wilfred Owen in "Dulce et Decorum Est," where it is almost impossible not to be deeply moved.

5. *Special characteristics.* Poems, like stories, are individual, separate works of art, each with its own characteristics. Because there is so much that is specific to each poem, any consideration of tone would need to take these specifics into consideration. Anne Bradstreet, for example, in "The Author to Her Book" introduces the metaphor of her work being like an unwanted child that she is sending out into the world. Her apology for the work hence introduces a tone of amused but sincere self-effacement that the reader must consider. Theodore Roethke's "My Papa's Waltz" is a brief narrative in which the speaker's feelings about memories of his childhood participation in his father's boisterous behavior must be inferred from understatement like "waltz." Each poem may thus offer something unique for consideration under a topic of tone.

CONCLUSION.   Just as with any conclusion, you might wish to summarize your main points about the tone of the poem, perhaps emphasizing one of the points as you go over them. In addition, you might feel that you have missed stressing some special aspect that makes the poem forceful, or there might be some particularly weak part of the poem that you wish to emphasize again. If the study of tone has enabled you to draw any conclusions about the way of life mentioned in the poem, or has changed your own perceptions about life or people around you, a brief discussion of these conclusions would be appropriate here. Finally, you might wish to discuss some other major aspect of the tone of the poem that you did not include in the body of your essay. Any or all of these details would be fitting here, so long as your emphasize aspects of the poet's technique as a poet.

SAMPLE ESSAY

The Tone of Confidence in "Theme for English B" by Langston Hughes*

[1]   "Theme for English B" grows from the situational irony of racial differences. The situation is unequal opportunity, seen from the perspective of a college student from the oppressed race. This situation might easily produce bitterness, anger, outrage, or vengefulness. However, the poem contains none of these. It is not angry or indignant; it is not an appeal for revenge or revolution. It is rather a declaration of personal independence and individuality. The tone is one of objectivity, daring, occasional playfulness, but above all, confidence.° These attitudes are made plain in the speaker's situation, the ideas, the poetic form, the diction, and the expressions.□

[2]   Hughes's treatment of the situation is objective, factual, and personal, not emotional or political. The poem contains a number of factual details presented clearly, like these: The speaker is black in an otherwise all-white college English class. He has come from North Carolina, and is now living alone at the Harlem YMCA, away from family and roots. He is also, at 22, an older student. The class is for freshman (English B), yet he is the age of many seniors. All this is evidence of disadvantage, yet the speaker does no more than present the facts objectively, without comment. He is in control, presenting the details straightforwardly, in a tone of total objectivity.

[3]   Hughes's thoughts about equality—the idea underlying the poem—are presented in the same objective, cool manner. The speaker writes to his instructor as an equal, not as an inferior. In describing himself, he does not deal in abstractions, but rather in reality. Thus, he defines himself in language descriptive of everyday abilities, needs, activities, and likes. He is cool and direct here, for his presentation takes the form of a set of inclusive principles emphasizing the sameness and identity of everyone regardless of race or background. The idea is that everyone should put away prejudices and begin

* See p. 671 for this poem.
° Central idea.
□ Thesis sentence.

to treat people as people, not as representatives of any race. By causing the speaker to avoid emotionalism and controversy, Hughes makes counter-arguments difficult, if not impossible. He is so much in control that the facts themselves carry his argument for equality.

[4] The selection of a poetic form demonstrates bravery and confidence. One would normally expect a short prose theme in response to an "assignment" in an English class, but a poem is unexpected and therefore daring and original. It is as though the speaker is showing his mettle and imagination, thereby personally justifying the idea that he is on an equal footing with the instructor. The wit behind the use of the form itself is a basis for equality.

Hughes's diction is in keeping with the tone of confidence and daring. Almost all the words in the poem are short, of no more than one or two syllables. This high proportion of short words reflects a conscious attempt to keep the diction clear and direct. A result is that Hughes avoids any possible ambiguities, as the following section of the poem shows:

[5]
> Well, I like to eat, sleep, drink, and be in love.
> I like to work, read, learn, and understand life.
> I like a pipe for a Christmas present,
> or records—Bessie, bop, or Bach.

With the exception of what it means to "understand life," these words are straightforward, descriptive, and free of emotional overtones. They reflect the speaker's confidence that the time for recognizing human equality has replaced the time for allowing inequality and prejudice to continue.

A number of the speaker's phrases and expressions also show this same confidence. Although most of the material is expressed straightforwardly, one can perceive playfulness and irony, too. Thus, in lines 18–20 there seems to be a deliberate use of confusing language to bring about a verbal merging of the identities of the speaker, the instructor, Harlem, and the greater New York area:

> Harlem, I hear you:
> hear you, hear me—we two—you, me talk on this page.
> (I hear New York, too.) Me—who?

[6] The speaker's confidence is strong enough to allow him to write and keep an expression that seems almost childish. This expression is in the second line of the following excerpt:

> I guess being colored doesn't make me not like
> the same things other folks like who are other races.

There is also whimsicality in the way in which the speaker treats the irony of the black-white situation:

> So will my page be colored that I write?

Underlying this last expression is an awareness that, despite the claim that people are equal and are tied to each other by common humanity, there are also strong differences among individuals. The speaker is confidently asserting grounds for independence as well as equality.

[7]

Thus, an examination of "Theme for English B" reveals vitality and confidence. The poem is a statement of trust and an almost open challenge on the personal level to the unachieved ideal of equality. Hughes is saying that since it is American to have such ideas, there is nothing to do but to live up to them. He makes this point through the almost conscious naiveté of the speaker's simple words and descriptions. Yet the poem is not without irony, particularly at the end, where the speaker mentions that the instructor is "somewhat more free" than he is. "Theme for English B" is complex and engaging. It shows the speaker's confidence through objectivity, daring, and playfulness.

Commentary on the Essay

The central idea in this essay is that the dominant attitude in "Theme for English B" is the speaker's confidence, and that this confidence is shown in the similar but separable attitudes of objectivity, daring, and playfulness. The purpose of the theme is to discuss how Hughes makes plain these and other related attitudes. The tone is studied as it is shown in five separate aspects of the poem.

Paragraph 2 deals with the situational irony of the speaker in relation to a larger set of social and political circumstances, in this case racial discrimination (see approach 1, above). Paragraph 3 considers the idea of equality as Hughes presents it through the speaker's eyes (approach 4). The aim of the paragraph, however, is not to consider equality *as an idea*, but to show how the speaker expresses his attitude toward it. Paragraph 4 contains a discussion of how the selection of the poetic form is a mark of the speaker's assurance (approach 5). Paragraphs 5 and 6 consider the stylistic matters of word choice and expression (approach 2). The attention given to monosyllabic words is justified by the preponderance of such words in the poem.

The concluding paragraph stresses again the attitude of confidence in the poem, and also notes additional attitudes of trust, challenge, ingenuousness, irony, daring, and playfulness.

Because this essay embodies a number of approaches by which tone may be studied in any work (situation, common ground, diction, special characteristics), it is typical of many essays that use a combined, eclectic approach to tone. Paragraph 4 is particularly instructive, for it shows how a topic that might ordinarily be taken for granted, such as the basic form of expression, can be seen as a unique feature of tone.

WRITING TOPICS FOR CHAPTER 17

1. Consider "A Love Symphony," "she being Brand / -new," "The Workbox," and "The First-Rate Wife" as poems about love. What similarities do you find among the poems? That is, do the poets seem to state that love creates joy, satisfaction, distress, embarrassment, trouble? How does the tone of each of the poems make it possible for you to draw your conclusions? What differences do you find in the ways the poets either control or do not control tone?

2. Consider the tone of "My Papa's Waltz." Some readers have concluded that the speaker is expressing fond memories of his childhood experiences with his father. Others believe that the speaker is ambiguous about the father, and that he therefore blocks out remembered pain as he also describes the amusing boisterousness in the kitchen. On the basis of the tone, what conclusions can you draw about the way in which the poem should be interpreted?

3. Write a poem about something that has made you either glad or angry. Try, in your poem, to create the same feelings in your reader, but create these feelings through your rendering of situations and your choices of the right words. (Possible topics: a social injustice, an unfair grade, the landing of a good job, the winning of a game, a rise in the price of gasoline, a good book or movie, and so on.)

18

Prosody: Sound, Rhythm, and Rhyme in Poetry

Prosody refers to the study of sounds and rhythms in poetry. Poets, attuned to language, select words not just for content but also for sound, and arrange words so that important ideas and climaxes of sound coincide. Some people think of rhythm and sound as the *music* of poetry, since it refers to measured sounds much like rhythms and tempos in music. Also like music, poetry requires some regularity of beat, but the tempo and loudness may be freer and less regular, and a reader may linger over certain sounds and words, depending on their position in a line. *Prosody* is the word most often used in reference to sound and rhythm, but other descriptive words are *metrics*, *versification*, and *mechanics of verse*.

THINGS TO CONSIDER IN STUDYING PROSODY

To consider prosody you will need a few basic linguistic facts. Words are made up of individually meaningful sounds (*segmental phonemes*), which here we will call simply **segments.** Thus, in the word *top* there are three segments: *t*, *o*, and *p*. When you hear these three sounds in order, you recognize the sounds as the word "top." It takes three alphabetical letters— *t*, *o*, and *p*—to spell **(graph)** "top," because each letter is identical with a segment. Sometimes it takes more than one letter to spell a segment. In the word *enough*, for example, there are four segments (*e*, *n*, *ŭ*, *f*) but six letters: *e*, *n*, *ou*, and *gh*. The last two segments (*ŭ* and *f*) require two letters each (two letters forming one segment are called a **digraph**). In the word *through* there are three segments but seven letters. To be correctly spelled in this word, the o͞o segment must have four letters (*ough*). Note, however, that in the word *flute* the o͞o segment requires only one letter, *u*.

Individual sounds in combination make up words, and separate words in combination make up lines of poetry. When we study the combined flow of words, we are concerned with **rhythm,** and when we study the effects of various segments in relationship to the rhythms and the content, we are concerned with sound, more specifically *alliteration, assonance,* and *rhyme*.

It is important to emphasize that prosody should never be separated from the content of a poem. Prosody is significant only as it supports and underscores content. Alexander Pope wrote that "the sound [of poetry] must seem an echo to the sense." In short, words count, and not only for their meanings, but also for their sounds and their contributions to a rhythmical flow. Thus, the study of prosody is an attempt to determine how poets have arranged the words of their poems to make sound complement content.

DISTINGUISHING SOUNDS FROM SPELLING

In the study of prosody, it is essential to distinguish between spelling, or **graphics,** and pronunciation, or **phonetics.** Not all English sounds are spelled and pronounced in the same way. Thus the letter *s* has three very different sounds in the words *sweet, sugar,* and *flows*: s, sh and z. On the other hand, the words *shape, ocean, nation, sure,* and *machine* use different letters or combinations of letters (as digraphs) to spell the same *sh* sound.

Vowel sounds also vary in spelling and pronunciation. For example, the *ē* sound (as the alphabet letter) can be spelled *i* in *machine,* *ee* in *speed,* *ea* in *eat, e* in *even,* and *y* in *funny,* yet the vowel sounds in *eat, break,* and *bear* are not the same although they are spelled the same. Remember this: With both consonants and vowel sounds, do not confuse spellings with sounds.

RHYTHM IN POETRY AND PROSE

Rhythm in speech is a combination of vocal speeds, rises and falls, starts and stops, vigor and slackness, and relaxation and tension. Every spoken utterance is rhythmical to some extent, but in ordinary speech and in the reading of prose, rhythm is usually less important than the flow of ideas. Rhythm is more significant in poetry, however, because poetry is so emotionally charged, compact, and intense. So poets habitually devote great attention and skill to the sounds and rhythms of language. Poets invite readers to stop at words, to dwell upon sounds, to slow down at times, and to speed up at others. As language becomes more dramatic and intense, it also becomes more rhythmical. Therefore when you read poetry—and the best way is to read it aloud—you will give great attention to individual words; your units of expression will be shorter than in prose; your voice will go through a wider range of pitch; and you can rely on greater ranges of dramatic intensity.

The unit of rhythm in poetry and prose is the syllable, which consists of a single strand of sound such as *a* in "*a* table," *fine* in "*fine* linen," *sleds* in "new *sleds*," and *flounce* in "the little girls *flounce* into the room." (While "a" is a syllable of only one segment, "flounce" consists of six segments: *f*, *l*, *ow*, *n*, *t*, and *s*). The rhythm of English poetry in the *closed form* (discussed in Chapter 19) is determined by the measured relationship of heavily stressed to less heavily stressed syllables. In pronouncing words and phrases, you give some syllables more force and intensity than others (note the comparative intensities of the syllables as you say, for example, "the bucket," or "the old oaken bucket"). In analyzing prosody, we say that the more intense syllables are given *heavy stress*, while the relatively less intense syllables are given *light stress*. In closed form verse, poets regularize the syllables into patterns called *feet*, which normally consist of one heavily stressed syllable and one or more lightly stressed syllables.

There are various types of metrical feet, each with a definite pattern. A **metrical foot**, the basic building block of poetry, is the pattern of one stressed syllable and one or more lightly stressed syllables in a line. Poets of traditional or closed forms usually fill their lines with a specific number of the same feet, and that number determines the **meter,** or measure of that line. Thus five feet in a line are **pentameter,** four are **tetrameter,** three are **trimeter,** and two are **dimeter.** To these may be added the less common line lengths **hexameter,** a six-foot line, **heptameter** or **the septenary,** seven feet, and **octameter,** eight feet. In terms of **accent** or **beat,** a trimeter line has three beats (or heavy stresses), a pentameter line five beats, and so on.

Frequently, rhetorical needs cause poets to substitute other feet for the regular foot established in the poem. Whether there is substitution or not, however, the number and kind of feet in each line constitute the metrical description of that line. To discover the prevailing metrical system in any poem, you *scan* the poem. The act of scanning is called **scansion.**

Notational System to Indicate Rhythms

In scansion, it is important to use an agreed-upon notational system to record stress or accent. A heavy or primary stress is commonly indicated by an acute accent or prime mark ('). A light stress may be indicated by a short accent mark (˘) or by a tiny circle or degree symbol placed above the syllable (°). To separate one foot from another, a virgule (/) or slash is used. Thus, the following line from Coleridge's "The Rime of the Ancient Mariner" may be schematized in this way:

Wa - ter, / wa - ter, / ev - ery where,

Here the virgules show that the line may be divided into two two-syllable feet and one three-syllable foot.

METRICAL FEET

Equipped with this knowledge, you are ready to scan poems in order to determine their rhythmical patterns. The most important metrical feet may be generally classed as the two-syllable foot, the three syllable foot, and the imperfect (or one-syllable) foot.

The Two-Syllable Foot

1. IAMB.   The iambic foot consists of a light stress followed by a heavy stress:

/ the winds /

The iamb is the most common foot in English poetry because it most nearly reflects natural speech. It is the most versatile of poetic feet, capable of great variation. Even within the same line, iambic feet may vary in intensity, so that they may support or undergrid the shades of meaning designed by the poet. For example, in this line from Wordsworth, each foot is unique:

The winds / that will / be howl- / ing at / all hours.

Such variability, approximating the stresses and rhythms of actual speech, makes the iamb suitable for both serious or light verse, and it therefore assists poets in focusing attention on ideas and emotions. If they use it with skill, it never becomes monotonous, for it does not distract readers by drawing attention to its own rhythm.

2. TROCHEE.   A heavy stress followed by a light stress:

/ flow - er /

Most English words are characteristically trochaic, for example:

water, snowfall, author, willow, morning, early, follow,

singing, something

Because trochaic rhythm has often been called *falling, dying, light,* or *anticli-mactic*, while iambic rhythm is *rising, elevating, serious,* or *climatic*, poets have preferred the iambic foot. They therefore have arranged various placements of two-syllable words, using single-syllable words and a variety of other means, so that the stressed syllable is at the end of the foot, as in Shakespeare's

his bend - / ing sick - / le's com - / pass come /

in which three successive trochaic words are arranged to match the iambic meter.

3. Spondee.   Two successive, equally heavy stresses, as in *men's eyes* in Shakespeare's line:

When, in / dis -grace / with for - / tune and / men's eyes.

The spondee—sometimes called a **hovering accent**—is mainly a substitute foot in English verse, because at a certain point successive spondees would more properly develop as iambs or trochees. For this reason it is virtually impossible, within traditional metrical patterns, for an entire poem to be written in spondees (but see Gwendolyn Brooks's poem "We Real Cool," p. 705). As an occasional substitute foot, however, the spondee creates emphasis. The usual way to indicate the spondaic foot is to link the two syllables together with chevronlike marks ($\bigwedge$).

4. Pyrrhic.   Two unstressed syllables (even though one of them may be in a normally stressed position), as in *on their* in Pope's line:

Now sleep - / ing flocks / on their / soft fleec - / es lie.

The pyrrhic consists of weakly accented words such as prepositions and articles. Like the spondee, it is usually substituted for an iamb or trochee, and therefore a complete poem cannot be in pyrrhics. As a substitute foot, however, the pyrrhic acts as a kind of rhythmic catapult to move the reader swiftly to the next strongly accented syllable, and therefore it undergirds the ideas conveyed by more important words.

The Three-Syllable Foot

1. Anapaest.   Two light stresses followed by a heavy:

by the dawn's / ear - ly light.

2. DACTYL.   A heavy stress followed by two lights (as in the first two feet in this line):

Thís ĭs thĕ / fór - ĕst prí - / mḗ - văl.

The Imperfect Foot

The imperfect foot consists of a single syllable: (´) by itself, or (˘) by itself. This foot is a variant or substitute occurring in a poem in which one of the major feet forms the metrical pattern. The second line of "The Star-Spangled Banner," for example, is anapaestic, but it contains an imperfect foot at the end:

Whăt sŏ próud - / lў wĕ haíled / ăt thĕ twí - / lĭght's lăst gleám - / ĭng.

Uncommon Meters

In many poems you might encounter variants other than those described above. Poets like Browning, Tennyson, Poe, and Swinburne experimented with uncommon meters. Other poets manipulated pauses or *caesurae* (discussed below) to create the effects of uncommon meters. For these reasons, you might need to refer to metrical feet such as the following:

1. AMPHIBRACH.   A light, heavy, light pattern:

Ăh feéd mĕ / ănd fíll mĕ / wĭth pleás - sŭre   (Swinburne).

2. AMPHIMACER OR CRETIC.   A heavy, light, heavy pattern:

Lóve ĭs bést   (Browning).

3. BACCHIUS OR BACCHIC.   A light stress followed by two heavy stresses, as in "Some late lark":

Sŏme láte lárk / sĭng - ĭng   (Henley).

4. DIPODIC MEASURE.   Dipodic measure (literally, "two feet" combining to make one) develops in longer lines when a poet submerges two regular feet under a stronger beat, so that a galloping or rollicking rhythm results. The following line from Browning's "A Toccata of Galuppi's," for example, may be scanned as trochaic heptameter, with the last foot being an amphimacer:

Dĭd yŏung / péo - plĕ / take théir / pléas - ure / whĕn thĕ / séa wăs / wárm

ĭn Máy?

In recitation, however, a stronger beat is superimposed, which makes one foot out of two, resulting in dipodic measure:

Dĭd yŏung péoplĕ / take théir pléasŭre / whĕn thĕ séa / wăs wárm ĭn Máy?

5. ACCENTUAL, STRONG-STRESS, AND "SPRUNG" RHYTHMS.   Accentual or strong-stress lines are historically derived from Old English poetry, in which each line was divided in two, with two major stresses occurring in each half. In the nineteenth century, Gerard Manley Hopkins developed what he called "sprung" rhythm, in which the major stresses are released or "sprung" from the line. The method is too complex to describe, but one characteristic is the juxtaposing of one-syllable stressed words, as in this line from his poem "Pied Beauty." To scan it you must be sure to pause longer at the semicolons than at the commas.

With swíft, slów; swéet, sóur; ădázzle, dím;

Here a number of elements combine to create six major stresses in the line, which contains only nine syllables. Many of Hopkins's lines combine alliteration and strong stresses in this way to create the same effect of heavy emphasis.

A parallel instance of strongly stressed lines may be seen in "We Real Cool" by Gwendolyn Brooks. In this poem the effect is achieved by the exclusive use of monosyllabic stressed words combined with internal rhyme, repetition, and alliteration.

THE CAESURA, OR PAUSE

Whenever we speak, we utter a number of syllables without pause of any sort, and stop only after a definite group of meaningful words is finished. These groups of words, rhythmically, are **cadence groups.** In poetry, the short or heavy pause separating cadence groups is called a **caesura** (plural **caesurae**). For scansion, the caesura may be marked by two diagonal lines or virgules (//) to distinguish it from the single virgule separating feet. Sometimes the caesura coincides with the end of a foot, as in this line by William Blake ("To Mrs. Anna Flaxman"):

With hánds / dĭ - víne // hĕ mov'd / thĕ gén - / tlĕ Sód. /

The caesura, however, may fall within a foot, and there may be more than one in a line, as in this line by Ben Jonson ("Penshurst"):

Thou art / not, / / Pens - / hurst, / / built / to en - / vious show. /

When a caesura ends a line, usually marked by a comma, semicolon, or period, that line is **end-stopped,** as in this line which opens Keats's "Endymion":

Ă thing / of beau - / ty / / is / a joy / for - ev -er. / /

If a line has no punctuation at the end and runs over to the next line, it is called **run-on.** A term also used to indicate run-on lines is **enjambement** (French for "spanning" or "straddling"). The following passage, a continuation of the preceding line from Keats, contains three run-on lines:

> Its loveliness increases; / / it will never
> Pass into nothingness; / / but still will keep
> A bower quiet for us, / / and a sleep
> Full of sweet dreams, / / . . .

SUBSTITUTION PATTERNS

Emphasis by Formal Substitution

Most closed form poems follow a regular pattern that may be formally analyzed according to the regular feet we have been describing here. For interest and emphasis, however (and also perhaps because of the natural rhythms of English speech), poets use **substitution** of variant feet for the regular feet of the poem. For example, the following line is from the "January" Eclogue of Edmund Spenser's *Shepherd's Calendar*. Although the pattern of the poem is iambic pentameter (i.e., five iambs per line), Spenser includes two substitute feet in the following line:

All in / a sun - / shine day, / as did / be - fall. /

In the first foot, *All in* is a trochee, and *shine day* is a spondee. These are formal substitutions; that is, Spenser uses separate, formally structured feet in place of the normal iambic feet. The effect is to move from "All" to "sunshine day" in a rapid, climactic sweep, in keeping with the idea that a springlike day in winter is an indescribable pleasure.

Emphasis by Rhetorical Substitution

The effects provided by formal substitution may also be achieved by the manipulation of the caesura. If the pauses are arranged within feet, they may create the actual *hearing* of trochees, amphibrachs, and other variant feet even though the line may scan regularly in the dominant meter. This variation may be called **rhetorical substitution.** A noteworthy example in an iambic pentameter line is this one from Pope's *Essay on Man*:

His ăc̆ - / tiŏns', / / pás - / siŏns', / / bĕ - / ing's, / / use / and end.

Ordinarily there is one caesura in a line of this type (after the fourth syllable), but in this one Pope has made three, each producing a strong pause. The line is regularly iambic but in reading, the effect is different. Because of the caesurae after the third, fifth, and seventh syllables, the rhythm produces an amphibrach, a trochee, another trochee, and an amphimacer, thus:

His ăc̆ - tiŏns', / / pás - siŏns', / / bĕ - ing's, / / use and end.
    AMPHIBRACH   TROCHEE   TROCHEE   AMPHIMACER

Thus the spoken substitutions produced by the caesurae in this regular line produce the effect of substitution, and therefore tension and interest.

When studying rhythm, then, your main concern in noting substitutions is to determine the formal metrical pattern, and then to analyze the formal and rhetorical variations on this pattern and their principal techniques and effects. Always try to show how these variations have enabled the poet to get points across and to achieve emphasis.

SEGMENTAL POETIC DEVICES

Once you have completed your analysis of rhythms, you may go on to consider the segmental poetic devices in the poem. Usually these devices are used to create emphasis, but sometimes in context they may echo or imitate some of the things being described. The segmental devices most common in poetry are *assonance*, *alliteration*, and *onomatopoeia*.

ASSONANCE.   The repetition of identical *vowel* sounds in different words—for example, the short *ĭ* in "swift Camĭlla skĭms"—is called **assonance.** It is a strong means of emphasis, as in the following line, where the *ŭ* sound connects the two words *lull* and *slumber*, and the short *ĭ* connects *him*, *in*, and *his*:

And more, to lull him in his slumber soft.

In some cases, poets may use assonance elaborately, as in the first line of Pope's *An Essay on Criticism*:

'Tis hard to say, if greater want of skill.

Here the line is framed and balanced with the short *ĭ* in *'Tis*, *if*, and *skill*. The *ä* in *hard* and *want* forms another, internal frame, and the *ā* in *say* and *greater* creates still another frame. Such a balanced use of vowels is unusual, however, for in most lines assonance occurs primarily as a means of highlighting important words, without such elaborate patterning.

ALLITERATION.   Like assonance, **alliteration** is a means of highlighting ideas by the selection of words containing the same *consonant* sound—for example, the repeated *m* in Spenser's "*M*ixed with a *m*ur*m*uring wind," or the *s* sound in Waller's "Your never-failing *s*word made war to *c*ease," which emphasizes the connection between the words "sword" and "cease."

There are two kinds of alliteration. (1) Most commonly, alliteration is regarded as the repetition of identical consonant sounds that *begin* syllables in close patterns—for example, in Pope's lines "*L*aborious, heavy, *b*usy, *b*old, and *b*lind," and "While *p*ensive *p*oets *p*ainful vigils keep." Used judiciously, alliteration gives strength to ideas by emphasizing key words, but too much *c*an *c*ause *c*omic and *c*atastrophic *c*onsequences. (2) Another form of alliteration occurs when a poet repeats identical or similar consonant sounds that do not begin syllables but nevertheless create a pattern—for example, the *z* segment in the line "In the*s*e place*s* free*z*ing bree*z*es easily cau*s*e snee*z*es," or the *b*, *m*, and *p* segments (all of which are made *b*ilabially; that is, with both lips) in "The *m*u*mb*ling and *m*ur*m*uring *b*eggar throws *p*egs and *p*e*bb*les in the *b*u*bb*ling *p*ool." Such patterns, apparently deliberately organized, are hard to overlook.

ONOMATOPOEIA.   **Onomatopoeia** is a blending of consonant and vowel sounds designed to imitate or suggest a situation or action. It is made possible in poetry because many words in English are **echoic** in origin; that is, they are verbal echoes of the actions they describe, such as *buzz*, *bump*, *slap*, *spirit*, and so on. Edgar Allan Poe used such words to create onomatopoeia in "The Bells," where through the combined use of assonance and alliteration he imitates the kinds of bells he celebrates. Thus, wedding bells sound softly with "molten golden notes" (*ō*), while alarm bells "clang and clash and roar" (*kl*). David Wagoner includes imitative words like *tweedledy*, *thump*, and *wheeze* to suggest the sounds of the music produced by the protagonist of his "March for a One-Man Band."

EUPHONY AND CACOPHONY

Words describing smooth or jarring sounds, particularly those resulting from consonants, are euphony and cacophony. **Euphony** ("good sound") refers to words containing consonants that permit an easy and smooth flow of spoken sound. Although there is no rule that some consonants are inherently more pleasant than others, students of poetry often cite sounds like *m*, *n*, *ng*, *l*, *v*, and *z*, and also *w* and *y*, as being especially easy on the ears. The opposite of euphony is **cacophony** ("bad sound"), in which percussive and choppy sounds make for particularly vigorous and noisy pronunciation. The combination of cacophonous words and sounds creates harshness, as in tongue-twisters like "black bug's blood" and "selfish shellfish in a sushi dish." Obviously, unintentional cacophony is a mark of imperfect control. When a poet deliberately creates it for effect, however, as in Tennyson's "The bare black cliff clang'd round him," Pope's "The hoarse, rough verse should like the torrent roar," and Coleridge's "Huge fragments vaulted like rebounding hail, / Or chaffy grain beneath the thresher's flail," cacophony is a mark of poetic skill. Although poets generally aim at easily flowing, euphonious lines, cacophony does have a place, always depending on the poet's intention and subject matter.

RHYME AND ITS FUNCTIONS

Rhyme is the repetition of identical or similar concluding syllables in different words, most often at the ends of lines. Words with the same concluding vowel sounds rhyme; such rhymes are a special kind of assonance. Thus *day* rhymes with *weigh*, *grey*, *bouquet*, and *matinee*. Rhyme may also combine assonance and identical consonant sounds, as in *ache*, *bake*, *break*, and *opaque*, or *turn*, *yearn*, *fern*, and *adjourn*. As these examples illustrate, rhyme is predominantly a function of *sound* rather than spelling; the words do not have to be spelled the same way or look alike to rhyme.

Rhyme is not a universal feature of poetry; thousands of excellent poems have been written without any recourse to rhyming whatsoever. Indeed, many contemporary poets have abandoned rhyme completely in favor of other ways of joining sound and sense because they find rhyme too restrictive or artificial. Nevertheless, rhyme has been an important aspect of poetry for hundreds of years, and it remains a valid and useful poetic technique today.

When rhyme is employed to good effect in poetry, it becomes much more than a simple ornament. Rhyme adds to the sensory impact of poetry by providing a pleasing network of related sounds that echo in the mind. Through rhyme, sound may join with sense in a coherent whole. Rhyme can also contribute significantly to the impression that a given poem makes on our memories. In its simplest form, it jingles in the mind, with rhymes like *bells* and *tells*, but rhyme can also provide emphasis and can reinforce ideas. It is a powerful way of clinching a thought by the physical link of related sounds.

Rhyme is closely connected with the degree to which a given poem moves us or leaves us flat. Wherever rhyme is employed with skill and originality, it leads the mind into fresh, unusual, and even surprising turns of thought. Poets may thus be judged, at least to some extent, on their rhymes. Some rhymers are satisfied with easy rhymes, or *cliché rhymes*, like *trees* and *breeze* (a rhyme criticized by Pope). But good rhymes and good poets go together, in creative cooperation. For example, the seventeenth-century poet John Dryden, who wrote volumes of rhyming couplets, acknowledged that the need to find rhymes inspired ideas that he had not anticipated. In this sense, rhyme has been—and still is—a vital element of poetic creativity.

TYPES OF RHYMES

The effects of rhyme are closely connected with those of rhythm and meter. Rhymes that are produced with one-syllable words—like *moon, June, tune,* and *soon*—or with multisyllabic words in which the accent falls on the last syllable—like *combine, decline, refine, consign* and *repine*—are called **heavy stress rhyme, accented rhyme,** or **rising rhyme.** In general, rising rhyme lends itself to serious effects. The accenting of heavy stress rhyme appears in the opening lines of Robert Frost's "Stopping by Woods on a Snowy Evening" (p. 529);

Whose woods / these are / I think / I *know*
His house / is in / the vil - / lage *though.*

Here, the rhyming sounds are produced by one-syllable words—*know* and *though*—that occur in the final accented positions of the lines (which are iambic tetrameter with initial spondees).

Rhymes using words of two or more syllables in which the accent falls on any syllable other than the last are called **trochaic** or **double rhyme** for rhymes of two syllables and **dactylic** or **triple rhyme** for rhymes of three syllables. Less technically, these types of rhymes are also called **falling** or **dying rhymes;** this is probably because the energy of pronunciation drops away on the light accent or accents following the heavy accent.

In general, double and triple rhymes lend themselves more readily to amusing or light poetry than they do to serious verse. The accents of falling rhyme may be seen in lines 2 and 4 of the first stanza of "Miniver Cheevy" by Edwin Arlington Robinson:

> Miniver Cheevy, child of scorn,
>   Grew lean while he assailed the *seasons*;
> He wept that he was ever born,
>   And he had *reasons*.

In this poem the effect of the double rhyme is humorous and thus helps to make Miniver Cheevy a slightly ridiculous and pathetic figure. Occasionally, however, double rhyme can be used successfully in a serious poem, as in Robert Herrick's "To the Virgins, to Make Much of Time":

> Gather ye rosebuds while ye may,
>   Old time is still *a-flying*;
> And this same flower that smiles today
>   Tomorrow will be *dying*.

A-flying and *dying* (our italics) are both double rhymes; indeed, falling rhymes are utilized in the second and fourth lines of every stanza of this poem. Herrick's use of falling rhymes throughout this poem lightens the tone a bit, but it does not modify the seriousness of the poem's idea at all.

Dactylic or triple rhyme is extremely rare and almost always humorous in effect. It may be seen in these lines from Robert Browning's "The Pied Piper of Hamlin."

> Small feet were *pattering*, wooden shoes *clattering*,
> Little hands clapping and little tongues *chattering*.
> And, like fowls in a farm-yard when barley is *scattering*,

Here, the words that end the lines, *clattering*, *chattering*, and *scattering*, are all instances of triple rhyme. The first line also offers an example of **internal rhyme,** the presence of a rhyming word within a line of verse. In this case, *pattering* rhymes with *clattering* and also maintains the triple rhyme pattern.

VARIANTS IN RHYME

A wide latitude of rhyming forms has traditionally been accepted in English. Perfect rhyming words, where both the vowel and the consonant sounds rhyme, are called **exact rhymes.** Not all rhymes, however, are exact. We often find in poetry words that *almost* rhyme; in most of these instances, the vowel segments are different while the consonants are the same. This type of rhyme is variously called **slant rhyme, near rhyme, half rhyme,** or **off rhyme.** In employing slant rhyme, a poet can pair *bleak* with *broke* or *could* with *solitude*. Emily Dickinson uses slant rhyme extensively in "To Hear an Oriole Sing"; in the second stanza of the poem she rhymes *Bird*, *unheard*, and *Crowd*. *Bird* and *unheard* make up an exact rhyme, but the vowel and consonant shift in *Crowd* produces a slant rhyme.

Another variant that shows up in poetry written in English is **eye rhyme** or **sight rhyme**. In these instances, we find the pairing of words that look alike but do not sound alike. Thus, according to eye rhyme, "I *wind* [a clock]" may be joined to "The North *Wind*" or *bough* may be rhymed with *cough*, *dough*, *enough*, and *tough*. Ben Jonson's "To Celia" begins with a typical eye rhyme:

> Come, my Celia, let us *prove*,
> While we can, the sports of *love*

Prove and *love* look as though they ought to rhyme, but when the lines are read aloud, we realize that they do not. As in all other instances of eye rhyme, the spelling is more important than the sound.

RHYME SCHEMES

A **rhyme scheme** refers to the pattern of rhyming sounds in a given poem. To describe rhyme schemes, alphabetical letters are used to indicate the rhyming sounds. Each repeated letter indicates a rhyme. Therefore, lines ending with *love* and *dove* would be indicated as *a a*. Each new rhyming sound is signified by a new letter. Thus, lines ending with the words *love*, *moon*, *dove*, *June*, *above*, and *croon* would be schematized as *a b a b a b*. To formulate a rhyme scheme or pattern, you should include the meter and the number of feet in each line as well as the letters indicating rhymes. Here is such a formulation:

> Iambic pentameter: *a b a b,   c d c d*

This scheme shows that all the lines in the poem are iambic, with five feet in each. It also indicates that the rhyming lines are 1 and 3, 2 and 4, 5, and 7, 6 and 8. Finally, it signifies that the poem is two stanzas and eight lines in length. Should the number of feet in the lines of a specific poem vary, you can show this fact by using a number in front of each letter:

> Iambic *4a 3b 4a 3b*

This formulation shows that the poem (or stanza) under consideration alternates lines of iambic tetrameter with iambic trimeter; it also signifies that lines 1 and 3 rhyme and 2 and 4 rhyme. The absence of a rhyme sound is indicated by an *x*. Thus, you might find a rhyme scheme formulated like this:

Iambic: *4x 3a 4x 3a*

Again, the stanza under consideration alternates iambic tetrameter with trimeter, and again the stanza is four lines long. This time, however, only lines 2 and 4 rhyme; there is no end rhyme in lines 1 and 3.

POEMS FOR STUDY

WILLIAM SHAKESPEARE   (1564–1616)

Sonnet 73: That Time of Year Thou Mayest in Me Behold   *1609*

That time of year thou mayst in me behold
When yellow leaves, or none, or few, do hang
Upon those boughs which shake against the cold,
Bare ruined choirs,° where late the sweet birds sang.
In me thou see'st the twilight of such day   5
As after sunset fadeth in the west;
Which by and by black night doth take away,
Death's second self,° that seals up all in rest.
In me thou see'st the glowing of such fire,
That on the ashes of his° youth doth lie,   *its*   10
As the death-bed whereon it must expire,
Consumed with that which it was nourished by,°
This thou perceivest, which makes thy love more strong,
To love that well which thou must leave ere long.

SONNET 73.   4 *choirs*: the part of a church just in front of the altar.   8 *Death's . . . self*; that is, night is a mirror image of death inasmuch as it brings the sleep of rest just as death brings the sleep of actual death.   12 *Consumed . . . by*: that is, the ashes of the fuel burned at the fire's height now prevent the fire from continuing, and in fact extinguish it.

QUESTIONS

1. Describe the content of lines 1–4, 5–8, and 9–12. What common link connects these three sections of the poem? How does the concluding couplet relate to the first twelve lines?

2. Analyze the iambic pentameter of the poem. Consider the spondees in lines 2 (*do hang*), 4 (*bare ru-* and *birds sang*), 5 (*such day*), 7 (*black night*), 8 (*death's sec-*), 9 (*such fire*), 10 (*doth lie*), 11 (*death-bed*), 13 (*more strong*), and 14 (*ere*

long). What effect do these substitutions have upon the development and flow of the ideas of the poem?

3. Consider Shakespeare's use of enjambement in lines 1–3 and 5–6. How do these lines seem to conclude as lines even though grammatically they carry over to form sentences?

4. In lines 2, 5, 6, and 9, where does Shakespeare place the caesurae? What relationship is there between the rhythms produced by these caesurae and the content of lines 1–12? In lines 13 and 14, how do the rising stressed caesurae relate to the content?

ROBERT HERRICK (1591–1674)

Upon Julia's Voice   *1648*

So smooth, so sweet, so silv'ry is thy voice,
As, could they hear, the damned would make no noise,
But listen to thee (walking in thy chamber)
Melting melodious words, to lutes of amber.

QUESTIONS

1. Does the poet praise Julia's speaking or singing voice? What effect do the words *silv'ry* and *amber* contribute to the praise? How powerful does the speaker claim that Julia's voice is?

2. What is the "joke" of the poem; that is, why should the damned make no noise if they could hear her? How can the praise of Julia's voice be interpreted as general praise for Julia herself?

3. How and where is alliteration used in the poem? Which of the alliterative sounds, if any, best complement the words praising the sweetness of Julia's voice?

JONATHAN SWIFT (1667–1745)

A Description of the Morning   *1709*

Now hardly here and there a hackney-coach
Appearing, showed the ruddy morn's approach.
Now Betty from her master's bed had flown.
And softly stole to discompose her own.
The slip-shod 'prentice from his master's door   5
Had pared the dirt, and sprinkled round the floor.
Now Moll had whirled her mop with dextrous airs,
Prepared to scrub the entry and the stairs.

The youth with broomy stumps began to trace
The kennel's edge,° where wheels had worn the place.   10
The small-coal man° was heard with cadence deep,   *charcoal seller*
Till drowned in shriller notes of chimney-sweep.
Duns° at his lordship's gate began to meet;   *bill collectors*
And brickdust Moll had screamed through half the street.
The turnkey° now his flock returning sees,   15
Duly let out a-nights to steal for fees.
The watchful bailiffs take their silent stands,
And schoolboys lag° with satchels in their hands.

A DESCRIPTION OF THE MORNING.   10 *kennel's edge*: i.e., the edge of the gutter.
Swift annotated this line "To find old Nails."   15 *turnkey*: an entrepreneur, operating a
jail for profit, who allowed prisoners to go free at night so that they might bring him a
night's booty to pay for the necessities provided them in jail.   18 *schoolboys lag*: cf.
Shakespeare's *As You Like It*, act 2, scene 7, lines 145–147.

QUESTIONS

1. What anti-heroic images of life in London in 1709 are presented in this
    poem? What level of life is described? What attitude does the speaker show
    toward "his lordship," a member of the nobility who nevertheless is clearly
    in debt?
2. Analyze the poem for alliterative patterns. What is their effect in the poem?
3. Make the same kind of analysis for assonance. How many different assonantal
    patterns are there? What is their effect?
4. Iambic rhyming couplets are often called "heroic." How does Swift's choice
    of this form affect the subject matter of the poem?

ALFRED, LORD TENNYSON   (1809–1892)

From *Idylls of the King*: *The Passing of Arthur*   *1869 (1842)*

    But, as he walked, King Arthur panted hard,
Like one that feels a nightmare on his bed   345
When all the house is mute. So sighed the King,
Muttering and murmuring at his ear, "Quick, quick!
I fear it is too late, and I shall die."
But the other swiftly strode from ridge to ridge,
Clothed with his breath, and looking, as he walked,   350
Larger than human on the frozen hills.
He heard the deep behind him, and a cry
Before. His own thought drove him like a goad.
Dry clashed his harness in the icy caves
And barren chasms, and all to left and right   355

The bare black cliff clanged round him, as he based
His feet on juts of slippery crag that rang
Sharp-smitten with the dint of armed heels—
And on a sudden, lo! the level lake,
And the long glories of the winter moon.   360

Then saw they how there hove a dusky barge,
Dark as a funeral scarf from stem to stern,
Beneath them; and descending they were ware°   *aware*
That all the decks were dense with stately forms,
Black-stoled, black-hooded, like a dream—by these   365
Three Queens with crowns of gold: and from them rose
A cry that shivered to the tingling stars,
And, as it were one voice, an agony
Of lamentation, like a wind that shrills
All night in a waste land, where no one comes,   370
Or hath come, since the making of the world.

Then murmured Arthur, "Place me in the barge."
So to the barge they came. There those three Queens
Put forth their hands, and took the King, and wept.
But she, that rose the tallest of them all   375
And fairest, laid his head upon her lap,
And loosed the shattered casque,° and chafed his hands,   *helmet*
And called him by his name, complaining loud,
And dropping bitter tears against a brow
Striped with dark blood: for all his face was white   380
And colorless, and like the withered moon
Smote by the fresh beam of the springing east;
And all his greaves and cuisses° dashed with drops   *pieces of armor*
Of onset;° and the light and lustrous curls—   *blood*
That made his forehead like a rising sun   385
High from the dais-throne—were parched with dust:
Or, clotted into points and hanging loose,
Mixed with the knightly growth that fringed his lips.
So like a shattered column lay the King:
Not like that Arthur who, with lance in rest,   390
From spur to plume a star of tournament,
Shot through the lists at Camelot, and charged
Before the eyes of ladies and of kings.

QUESTIONS

1. What events occur in this passage? How does Tennyson develop the mood
   of depression and loss associated with the dying of Arthur? What is the
   effect of the concluding simile?

2. Analyze the patterns of assonance and alliteration in the passage. What patterns are developed most extensively? What effects are thus achieved?

3. Describe Tennyson's use of onomatopoeia in lines 349–360, 369–371, and 380–383. What segments does he use for the onomatopoeic effect, and how do these segments contribute to this effect?

EDGAR ALLAN POE   (1809–1849)

The Bells   *1849*

I
    Hear the sledges with the bells—
        Silver bells!
What a world of merriment their melody foretells!
How they tinkle, tinkle, tinkle,
    In the icy air of night!   5
While the stars that oversprinkle
All the heavens, seem to twinkle
    With a crystalline delight;
        Keeping time, time, time,
        In a sort of Runic rhyme,   10
To the tintinnabulation that so musically wells
        From the bells, bells, bells, bells,
            Bells, bells, bells—
From the jingling and the tinkling of the bells.

II
    Hear the mellow wedding bells—   15
        Golden bells!
What a world of happiness their harmony foretells!
    Through the balmy air of night
    How they ring out their delight!—
        From the molten-golden notes,   20
        And all in tune,
    What a liquid ditty floats
To the turtle-dove that listens, while she gloats
        On the moon!
        Oh, from out the sounding cells,   25
What a gush of euphony voluminously wells!
        How it swells!
        How it dwells
        On the Future!—how it tells
        Of the rapture that impels   30
    To the swinging and the ringing
        Of the bells, bells, bells—
Of the bells, bells, bells, bells,
        Bells, bells, bells—
To the rhyming and the chiming of the bells!   35

III
　Hear the loud alarum bells—
　　Brazen bells!
What a tale of terror, now, their turbulency tells!
　In the startled ear of night
　How they scream out their affright!　　　　　　　　　　40
　　Too much horrified to speak,
　　They can only shriek, shriek,
　　　Out of tune,
In a clamorous appealing to the mercy of the fire,
In a mad expostulation with the deaf and frantic fire,　　45
　　　Leaping higher, higher, higher,
　　With a desperate desire,
　　And a resolute endeavor
　　Now—now to sit, or never,
By the side of the pale-faced moon.　　　　　　　　　50
　　Oh, the bells, bells, bells!
　　What a tale their terror tells
　　　Of Despair!
　　How they clang, and clash, and roar!
　　What a horror they outpour　　　　　　　　　　　55
On the bosom of the palpitating air!
　Yet the ear, it fully knows,
　　By the twanging
　　And the clanging,
　How the danger ebbs and flows;　　　　　　　　　60
　Yet the ear distinctly tells,
　　In the jangling
　　And the wrangling,
How the danger sinks and swells,
By the sinking or the swelling in the anger of the bells—　65
　　Of the bells,—
Of the bells, bells, bells, bells,
　Bells, bells, bells—
In the clamor and the clangor of the bells!

IV
　Hear the tolling of the bells—　　　　　　　　　　70
　　Iron bells!
What a world of solemn thought their monody compels!
　In the silence of the night,
　How we shiver with affright
At the melancholy menace of their tone!　　　　　　75
　For every sound that floats
　From the rust within their throats
　　　Is a groan.
　　And the people—ah, the people—

They that dwell up in the steeple,   80
    All alone,
And who tolling, tolling, tolling,
    In that muffled monotone,
Feel a glory in so rolling
    On the human heart a stone—   85
They are neither man nor woman—
They are neither brute nor human—
    They are Ghouls:—
And their king it is who tolls:—
And he rolls, rolls, rolls,   80
    Rolls
    A paean from the bells!
And his merry bosom swells
    With the paean of the bells!
And he dances, and he yells;   95
Keeping time, time, time,
In a sort of Runic rhyme,
    To the paean of the bells—
    Of the bells:
Keeping time, time, time,   100
In a sort of Runic rhyme,
    To the throbbing of the bells—
Of the bells, bells, bells—
    To the sobbing of the bells;
Keeping time, time, time,   105
    As he knells, knells, knells.
In a happy Runic rhyme,
    To the rolling of the bells—
    Of the bells, bells, bells:—
    To the tolling of the bells—   110
Of the bells, bells, bells, bells,
    Bells, bells, bells—
To the moaning and the groaning of the bells.

QUESTIONS

1. What kinds of bells does Poe extol in each of the stanzas? What metals and
    images does he associate with each type of bell? How appropriate are these?
    Why do you think the stanzas become progressively longer?
2. What segmental sounds does Poe utilize as imitative of the various bells?
    What differences in vowels are observable between the silver sledge bells,
    for example, and the brass ("brazen") alarum bells? Between the vowels de-
    scribing the iron bells and the golden bells?
3. What is the effect of the repetition of the word *bells* throughout? What onoma-
    topoeic effect is created by these repetitions?
4. Describe the pattern of rhymes in this poem.

EMILY DICKINSON (1830–1886)

To Hear an Oriole Sing   *1891 (c. 1862)*

To hear an Oriole sing
May be a common thing –
Or only a divine.

It is not of the Bird
Who sings the same, unheard,   5
As unto Crowd –

The Fashion of the Ear
Attireth that it hear
In Dun, or fair –

So whether it be Rune,   10
Or whether it be none
Is of within.

The "Tune is in the Tree –"
The Skeptic – showeth me –
"No Sir! In Thee!"   15

QUESTIONS

  1. What can you deduce about the speaker? The listener? Who speaks in line
     13? To whom is line 15 addressed?
  2. What idea about the way people hear things and respond to them does this
     poem explore? What connection do you see between this idea and the old
     saying, "Beauty is in the eye of the beholder"?
  3. Formulate the rhyme scheme of this poem. How does it help subdivide the
     poem into cohesive units of thought? To what extent does it unify the poem?
  4. Locate all the slant rhymes in this poem. What effect do these have on your
     reading and perception? How is the rhyme here like the oriole's song?
  5. To what degree does rhyme reinforce meaning? Note especially the rhyme
     words in the final stanza.

CHRISTINA ROSSETTI (1830–1894)

Echo   *1862*

Come to me in the silence of the night;
  Come in the speaking silence of a dream;
Come with soft rounded cheeks and eyes as bright

As sunlight on a stream;
  Come back in tears,   5
O memory, hope, love of finished years.

O dream how sweet, too sweet, too bitter sweet,
  Whose wakening should have been in Paradise,
Where souls brimful of love abide and meet;
  Where thirsty longing eyes   10
    Watch the slow door
That opening, letting in, lets out no more.

Yet come to me in dreams, that I may live
  My very life again though cold in death;
Come back to me in dreams, that I may give   15
  Pulse for pulse, breath for breath:
    Speak low, lean low,
As long ago, my love, how long ago.

QUESTIONS

1. What can we surmise about the speaker of this poem? To whom or what is
   the poem addressed? What does the speaker want the listener to do?
2. In what ways is present reality contrasted with memory in this poem? In
   what ways is the real world contrasted with dreams? Which does the speaker
   prefer?
3. To what extent does repetition contribute to the fusion of sound and sense
   in this poem? How are alliteration and assonance used?
4. What type of rhyme predominates? To what extent does rhyme advance
   the meaning and impact of the poem? In this regard, consider especially
   night–bright, *sweet–meet*, and *death–breath*. Also consider that rhyme itself is a
   kind of echo.

GERARD MANLEY HOPKINS   (1844–1889)

God's Grandeur   1877

The world is charged with the grandeur of God.
  It will flame out, like shining from shook foil;
  It gathers to a greatness, like the ooze of oil
Crushed. Why do men then now not reck his rod?°
Generations have trod, have trod, have trod;   5
  And all is seared with trade; bleared, smeared with toil;
  And wears man's smudge and shares man's smell: the soil
Is bare now, nor can foot feel, being shod.

---

4 *reck his rod*: God as king holds a scepter, making official laws through scriptures which
people ("men") disobey.

And for all this, nature is never spent;
  There lives the dearest freshness deep down things;   10
And though the last lights off the black West went
  Oh, morning, at the brown brink eastward, springs—
Because the Holy Ghost over the bent
  World broods with warm breast and with ah! bright wings.

QUESTIONS

1. What is the contrast between the assertions in lines 1–4 and 5–8? How do lines 9–14 develop out of this contrast?

2. What manifestations of God does Hopkins describe in the poem? What metaphors does he employ to embody his praise and adoration?

3. Analyze Hopkins's use of alliteration. What alliterative patterns occur? How do these affect meter and emphasis? On the basis of your analysis, describe "sprung rhythm" as used by Hopkins.

4. What instances of assonance, repetitions, and internal rhyme do you find?

FRANCIS THOMPSON   (1859–1907)

To a Snowflake   *1897*

What heart could have thought you?
Past our devisal
(O filigree petal!)
Fashioned so purely,
Fragilely, surely,   5
From what Paradisal
Imagineless metal,
Too costly for cost?
Who hammered you, wrought you
From argentine vapour?—   10
"God was my shaper.
Passing surmisal,
He hammered, He wrought me.
From curled silver vapour,
To lust of His mind:—   15
Thou could'st not have thought me!
So purely, so palely,
Tinily, surely,
Mightily, frailly,
Insculped and embossed,   20
With His hammer of wind,
And His graver of frost."

QUESTIONS

1. This poem takes the shape of questions and answers. Who is speaking, and who responds? What metaphor of creation dominates the poem? How might the poem be considered a religious tribute?

2. The poem is in dimeter (lines consisting of two feet). Why is this short line appropriate to the subject?

3. What is the prevailing metrical pattern? How is this meter appropriate for the subject of a snowflake? Would iambs have been more or less appropriate? What variations on the predominant foot can you find in the poem? Why do you think the poet made the last three lines conclude with stressed syllables?

4. Why are some of the rhymes placed on heavy stressed syllables even though most of the rhymes are linked with falling or trochaic rhythms?

5. Compare this poem with Blake's "The Lamb" (p. 590) and "The Tyger" (p. 613). To which of the two Blake poems is "To a Snowflake" more similar? Why? In what ways is Thompson's poem different from those of Blake?

T. S. ELIOT   (1888–1965)

Macavity: The Mystery Cat   *1939*

Macavity's a Mystery Cat: he's called the Hidden Paw—
For he's the master criminal who can defy the Law.
He's the bafflement of Scotland Yard, the Flying Squad's despair:
For when they reach the scene of the crime—*Macavity's not there!*

  Macavity, Macavity, there's no one like Macavity,   5
He's broken every human law, he breaks the law of gravity.
His powers of levitation would make a fakir stare,
And when you reach the scene of crime—*Macavity's not there!*
You may seek him in the basement, you may look up in the air—
But I tell you once and once again, *Macavity's not there!*   10

  Macavity's a ginger cat, he's very tall and thin;
You would know him if you saw him, for his eyes are sunken in.
His brow is deeply lined with thought, his head is highly domed;
His coat is dusty from neglect, his whiskers are uncombed.
He sways his head from side to side, with movements like a snake;   15
And when you think he's half asleep, he's always wide awake.

  Macavity, Macavity, there's no one like Macavity,
For he's a fiend in feline shape, a monster of depravity.
You may meet him in a by-street, you may see him in the square—
But when a crime's discovered, then *Macavity's not there!*   20

  He's outwardly respectable. (They say he cheats at cards.)
And his footprints are not found in any file of Scotland Yard's.
And when the larder's looted, or the jewel-case is rifled,

Or when the milk is missing, or another Peke's been stifled,°
Or the greenhouse glass is broken, and the trellis past repair—
Ay, there's the wonder of the thing! *Macavity's not there!*   25

    And when the Foreign Office find a Treaty's gone astray,
Or the Admiralty lose some plans and drawings by the way,
There may be a scrap of paper in the hall or on the stair—
But it's useless to investigate—*Macavity's not there!*   30
And when the loss has been disclosed, the Secret Service say:
"It *must* have been Macavity!"—but he's a mile away.
You'll be sure to find him resting, or a-licking of his thumbs,
Or engaging in doing complicated long division sums.

    Macavity, Macavity, there's no one like Macavity,   35
There never was a Cat of such deceitfulness and suavity.
He always has an alibi, and one or two to spare:
At whatever time the deed took place—MACAVITY WASN'T THERE!
And they say that all the Cats whose wicked deeds are widely known
(I might mention Mungojerrie, I might mention Griddlebone)   40
Are nothing more than agents for the Cat who all the time
Just controls their operations: the Napoleon of Crime!

MACAVITY: THE MYSTERY CAT.   24 *Peke's been stifled*: a Pekinese dog (a small animal,
with silky hair) has been found dead.

QUESTIONS

1. What are some of Macavity's major "crimes" as a master criminal and "mystery cat"? What attitude does the speaker express toward Macavity? How, if the "crimes" had been attributed to a human being, would they be grievous wrongs? Since they are attributed to a cat, how do they add to the comic qualities of the poem?

2. What is the basic metrical foot of the poem? How many feet are contained in each of the lines? What is the norm?

3. Once you begin reading and "getting into" the lines, what new kind of pattern emerges? How many major stresses appear in each line? In light of the nature of the poem, how is the dipodic rhythm appropriate?

GWENDOLYN BROOKS   (b. 1917)

We Real Cool   *1959*

The Pool Players.
Seven at the Golden Shovel.

We real cool. We
Left school. We

Lurk late. We
Strike straight. We

Sing sin. We   5
Thin gin. We

Jazz June. We
Die soon.

QUESTIONS

1. What is the major idea of the poem? Who is the speaker? How is the last
    sentence a climax? How is this sentence consistent with the declarations in
    lines 1–7? How is the poet's attitude made clear?
2. Describe the patterning of stresses in the poem. Explain the absence of light
    stresses in view of the shortness of the lines. What method is employed to
    achieve the constant strong stresses?

JAMES EMANUEL   (b. 1921)

The Negro   *1968*

Never saw him.
Never can.
Hypothetical,
Haunting man:

Eyes a-saucer,   5
Yessir bossir,
Dice a-clicking,
Razor flicking.

The-ness froze him
In a dance.   10
A-ness never
Had a chance.

QUESTIONS

1. What attributes of the black man are described in lines 1–4, lines 5 and 6,
    and lines 7 and 8? Are these attributes new or conventional? What attitude
    does the poem convey about the plight of the black?
2. What is the meaning of *The-ness* and *A-ness* in the third stanza?
3. What metrical foot is dominant in the poem? Why do you think the poet
    chose this foot in preference to a foot having a rising rhythm, such as the
    iamb?

EDWIN ARLINGTON ROBINSON (1869–1935)

Miniver Cheevy   *1910*

Miniver Cheevy, child of scorn,
  Grew lean while he assailed the seasons;
He wept that he was ever born,
  And he had reasons.

Miniver loved the days of old   5
  When swords were bright and steeds were prancing;
The vision of a warrior bold
  Would set him dancing.

Miniver sighed for what was not,
  And dreamed, and rested from his labors;   10
He dreamed of Thebes° and Camelot,°
  And Priam's° neighbors.

Miniver mourned the ripe renown
  That made so many a name so fragrant;
He mourned Romance, now on the town,   15
  And Art, a vagrant.

Miniver loved the Medici,°
  Albeit he had never seen one;
He would have sinned incessantly
  Could he have been one.   20

Miniver cursed the commonplace
  And eyed a khaki suit with loathing;
He missed the medieval grace
  Of iron clothing.

Miniver scorned the gold he sought,   25
  But sore annoyed was he without it;
Miniver thought, and thought, and thought,
  And thought about it.

Miniver Cheevy, born too late,
  Scratched his head and kept on thinking;   30
Miniver coughed, and called it fate,
  And kept on drinking.

MINIVER CHEEVY.   11 *Thebes*: a city in Greece prominent in Greek legend and mythology in connection with Cadmus and Oedipus.   *Camelot*: legendary seat of the Round Table and capital of Britain during the reign of King Arthur.   12 *Priam's*: Priam was the king of Troy during the Trojan War.   17 *Medici*: wealthy Italian family that ruled Florence from the fifteenth to the eighteenth century. During the Renaissance, Lorenzo de'Medici was an important patron of the arts.

QUESTIONS

1. Who is the central character in this poem? What is his problem?

2. What is the speaker's attitude toward the central character? How does rhyme help define this attitude?

3. How does diction help shape your poem's image of the central character? Note especially *neighbors* (line 12) and *iron clothing* (line 24)

4. How does repetition reinforce the image of the central character and the speaker's attitude? Consider the beginning of each stanza and lines 27–28.

5. What type of rhyme predominates in lines 2 and 4 of each stanza? How does this reinforce the image of the central character and make sound echo sense?

BARBARA HOWES   (b. 1914)

Death of a Vermont Farm Woman   *1954*

Is it time now to go away?
July is nearly over; hay
Fattens the barn, the herds are strong,
Our old fields prosper; these long
Green evenings will keep death at bay.   5

Last winter lingered; it was May
Before a flowering lilac spray
Barred cold for ever. I was wrong.
        Is it time now?

Six decades vanished in a day!   10
I bore four sons: one lives; they
Were all good men; three dying young
Was hard on us. I have looked long
For these hills to show me where peace lay.
        Is it time now?   15

QUESTIONS

1. Who and what is the speaker? How old is she? What happened in her life? What is she looking for? Waiting for?

2. What is the setting? The season? How do these relate to meaning and impact?

3. What does this poem suggest about the life of "A Vermont Farm Woman"? About the lives of many women?

4. How many different rhyme sounds are used in this poem? What is the effect of using so few?

5. To what extent does rhyme divide the poem into coherent units of thought and tie the whole poem together?

6. Normally, repetition of the same rhyming word is judged to be a flaw in poetry. To what extent is that the case in this poem?

ISABELLA GARDNER   (1915–1981)

At a Summer Hotel   *1979*

I am here with my bountiful womanful child
to be soothed by the sea not roused by these roses roving wild.
My girl is gold in the sun and bold in the dazzling water,
She drowses on the blond sand and in the daisy fields my daughter
dreams. Uneasy in the drafty shade I rock on the veranda   5
reminded of Europa Persephone Miranda.°

AT A SUMMER HOTEL.   6 *Europa Persephone Miranda*: Europa is a princess in Greek
mythology who attracted the attention of Zeus, the king of the gods. He took the form of a
bull and carried her over the sea to Crete. She bore him three sons. Persephone, in Greek
mythology, is the daughter of Zeus and Demeter, the goddess of fertility. She attracted the
attention of Hades, the god of the underworld, who forcibly carried her off and married
her. Miranda is an innocent young woman in Shakespeare's *The Tempest* who was exiled on
an island for twelve years with her father, Prospero. One of his servants—the beastly Caliban—
attempted to rape her.

QUESTIONS

1. What can you surmise about the speaker? Setting? Situation?
2. Who is described in the poem besides the speaker? How is she described? What is she doing? What is her relationship to the speaker?
3. Why is the speaker "uneasy" (line 5)? How do the references to Europa, Persephone, and Miranda help define this uneasiness?
4. To what extent do alliteration and repetition unify the lines and make the sound echo sense? Note especially the *b* and *ful* sounds in line 1, the *s* and *r* sounds in line 2, and the *d* and *dr* sounds in lines 4–5.
5. What is the effect of internal rhyme in this poem?
6. What kind of rhyme (rising or falling, exact or slant) occurs in lines 1–2? To what extent does this rhyme capture a central idea of the poem? What kind of rhyme occurs in lines 3–6? How does this rhyme affect the tone and impact of the poem? To what extent does it capture a central idea of the poem?

DAVID WAGONER   (b. 1926)

March for a One-Man Band   *1983*

He's *a boom a blat* in the uniform
Of an army *tweedledy* band *a toot*

Complete with medals *a honk* cornet
Against *a thump* one side of his lips
And the other stuck with *a sloop a tweet*   5
A whistle *a crash* on top of *a crash*
A helmet *a crash* a cymbal a drum
At his *bumbledy* knee and a *rimshot* flag
A click he stands at attention *a wheeze*
And plays the Irrational Anthem *bang*.   10

QUESTIONS

1. What attitude does the speaker convey about the one-man band? Why is the Anthem "Irrational" rather than "National"?

2. Describe the onomatopoeic effect of the italicized percussive words. What kinds of rhythm are caused by these interjected words? What is the purpose of this rhythm?

3. What possible ambiguity is suggested by the "bang" concluding the last line? How does this ambiguity make the poem seem more than simply an entertaining display of sounds?

4. Compare this poem with Poe's "The Bells" as instances in which the sounds of words are used to focus your attention on real sounds. To what extent does this device work similarly in both poems?

WRITING ABOUT PROSODY

Because studying prosody requires a good deal of specific detail and description, it is best to limit your choice to a short passage or a complete short poem. A sonnet, a stanza from a lyric poem, or an excerpt from a long poem will usually suffice. If you use an excerpt, it should be self-contained, such as an entire speech or short episode or scene (see the example from Tennyson in the first sample essay below).

The analysis of even a short poem can become lengthy, however, because of the need to describe word positions and stresses, and also to determine the various effects. For this reason you do not have to exhaust all aspects of your topic. Try to make your discussion representative of the prosody of the poem or passage you have chosen.

Your first reading in preparation for your essay should be for comprehension. On second and third readings, try to notice sounds, accents, and rhymes by reading the poem aloud. To perceive sounds, one student always reads aloud in an exaggerated way in front of a mirror. Try it yourself. Let yourself go a bit. As you dramatize your reading (maybe even in front of fellow students), you will find that heightened levels of reading also accompany the poet's expression of important ideas. Mark these spots for later analysis, so that you will be able to make good points about the relationship of the poem's prosody to its content.

In planning your essay, it is very important to prepare study sheets, so that your observations will be correct, for if your factual analysis is wrong, some of your writing will also be wrong. Furthermore, your writing task will be made easier by careful preparation. Experience has shown that it is best to type the poem triple-spaced, and make four photocopies or carbons, one for each separate aspect you are going to analyze: (1) rhythm, (2) alliteration, (3) assonance, and (4) rhyme, if any. Of course if you have been assigned just one of these, only one copy will be necessary. Leave spaces between syllables and words for marking out the various feet of the poem. Ultimately, this duplication of the passage, with your scansion and other markings, should be included as the first page (or pages), as in the sample essays.

Carry out your study of the passage in the following way:

1. Number each line of the passage or poem, regardless of length, beginning with *1*, so that you may use these numbers as location references in your essay.

2. For the analysis of rhythm, determine the formal pattern of feet, using the acute accent or prime for heavily stressed syllables (´), and the short symbol for lightly stressed syllables (˘). Use chevrons to mark spondees (/⋀).

3. Indicate the separate feet by a diagonal slash (/). Indicate caesurae and end-of-line pauses by double diagonals (//).

4. Use colored pencils to underline or otherwise mark the formal and rhetorical substitutions that you discover. Because such substitutions may occur throughout the poem, develop a numbering system for each metrical type (e.g., 1 = anapest 3 = spondee, etc., as in the sample worksheet on page 715). Provide a key to your numbers at the bottom of your page.

5. Do the same for alliteration, assonance (also onomatopoeia, if any), and rhyme. It is particularly effective to draw lines to connect the repeating sounds. The use of a separate color for each effect with each separate sound is particularly useful, for the distinctions made by different colors make possible the exact observation needed for this essay. (In the sample worksheets, instead of different colors we have used a variety of solid, wavy, dashed, and dotted lines.)

6. Use your worksheets as a reference for your reader. In writing your essay, however, you will need to make your examples specific by making brief quotations, as in the examples (i.e., words, phrases, and entire lines, with proper marks and accents). Do not rely on line numbers alone.

Once you have analyzed the various effects in the poem under consideration, and you have recorded these on your worksheets and in your notes, you will be ready to formulate a central idea and organization for your essay. The focus of the essay should reflect what you have found to be the most significant features of prosody in relationship to some other element of the poem, such as speaker, tone, or ideas. Thus, in planning an essay about T. S. Eliot's "Macavity," you might argue that the dipodic rhythm augments the amusement of the poem, and makes the "Napoleon of Crime" seem comic.

After forming a tentative idea for your essay, you can gather examples of prosodic evidence that support your central idea. These examples can be grouped into units of related or similar effects that will eventually become paragraphs. Make sure that all examples are relevant to your central idea. If you find the prosodic evidence leading you in new directions, rethink the essay and revise the central idea accordingly.

Organizing Your Essay

Depending on your assignment, you might wish to show the operation of all the component elements of prosody, or you may wish to focus on just one aspect. It would be possible, for example, to devote an entire essay to the discussion of (a) regular meter, (b) one particular variation in meter, such as the anapaest or spondee, (c) the caesura, (d) assonance, (e) alliteration, (f) onomatopoeia, or (g) rhyme. For brevity of illustration, we here treat rhythm and segments together in one essay, and rhyme in a separate essay.

INTRODUCTION.   The introduction should lead as quickly as possible to the central idea. Briefly identify the poem's form and type (for example, that it is a sonnet, a two-stanza lyric, an iambic-pentameter description of a character or action, a dipodic burlesque poem, and so on), and then establish the scope of your essay. You might wish to discuss all aspects of rhythm or sound, or perhaps just one, such as the poet's use of regular meter, a particular substitution, alliteration, or assonance. Your central idea will outline the thought you wish to carry out through your prosodic analysis, such as that regularity of meter is consistent with a happy, firm vision of love or life, or that the use of the spondee emphasizes the solidity of the speaker's wish to love, or that particular sounds emphasize some of the poem's actions. Your thesis sentence should outline the aspects to be treated in the body.

BODY.   Separate guidelines are given below for rhythm, segmental effects, and rhyme.

For Rhythm. You might first establish the formal metrical pattern. What is the dominant metrical foot and line length? Are some lines shorter than the pattern? What relationship do the variable lengths have with the subject matter? If the poem is a lyric, or a sonnet, is the poet successful in placing important words and syllables in stressed positions in order to achieve emphasis? Try to relate line lengths to whatever exposition and development of ideas and whatever rising and falling emotions you find. It is also important to look for either repeating or varying metrical patterns as the subject matter reaches peaks or climaxes. Generally, deal with the relationship between the formal rhythmical pattern and the poet's ideas and attitudes

When noting substitutions, you might analyze the formal variations and the principal effects of these. The aim is to relate substitutions to ideas and emotions emphasized by the poet. If you concentrate on only one substitution, describe any apparent pattern in its use; that is, its locations, recurrences, and effects on meaning.

For caesurae, treat the effectiveness of the poet's control. Can you see any pattern of use? Are the pauses regular, or do they seem randomly placed? Describe any noticeable principles of placement, such as (1) the creation of rhythmical similarities in various parts of the poem, (2) the development of particular rhetorical effects, or (3) the creation of interest through rhythmical variety. Do the caesurae lead to important ideas and attitudes? Are the lines all end-stopped, or do you discover enjambment? How do these rhythmical characteristics aid in the poet's expression of subject matter?

For Segmental Effects. Here you might discuss, collectively or separately, the use and effects of assonance, alliteration, onomatopoeia, and cacophony and euphony. Be sure to establish that the instances you choose have really occurred systematically enough within the poem to be grouped as a pattern. You should illustrate sounds by including relevant words within parentheses. You might wish to make separate paragraphs on alliteration, assonance, and any other seemingly important pattern. Also, because space in an essay is always at a premium, you might wish to concentrate on one noteworthy effect, like a certain pattern of assonance, rather than on everything in the poem. Throughout your discussion, always keep foremost the relationship between content and sound.

Note. To make illustrations clear, underline all sounds to which you are calling attention. If you use an entire word to illustrate a sound, underline only the sound and not the entire word, but put the word within quotation marks (for example, The poet uses a t ["tip," "top," and "terrific"]). When you refer to entire words containing particular segments, however, underline these words (for example, "The poet uses a t in tip, top, and terrific).

For Rhyme. This discussion should include a description of the major features of rhyme, including the scheme and variants, the lengths and rhymes of the rhyming words, and noteworthy segmental characteristics. In discussing the grammatical features of the rhymes, you might note the kinds of words (i.e., verbs, nouns, etc.) used for rhymes: Are they all the same? Does one form predominate? Is there variety? Can you determine the grammatical positions of the rhyming words? How may these characteristics be related to the idea or theme of the poem.

You might also discuss the qualities of the rhyming words. Are the words specific, concrete, or abstract? Are there any striking rhymes? Any surprises? Any rhymes that are clever and witty? Do any rhymes give unique comparisons or contrasts? How?

You might also note any striking or unique rhyming effects. Without becoming overly subtle or farfetched, you can make valid and interesting conclusions. Do any sounds in the rhyming words appear in patterns of assonance or alliteration elsewhere in the poem to an appreciable degree? Do the rhymes enter into any onomatopoeic effects? Broadly, can you detect any aspects of rhyme that are uniquely effective because they are at one with the thought and mood of your poem?

CONCLUSION.   Beyond summarizing your main idea, you might try to develop a short evaluation of the poet's prosodic performance. If we accept the premise that poetry is designed not only to inform, but also to transfer attitudes and to stimulate, to what degree do the prosodic techniques of the poem you have studied contribute to these goals? Without going into excessive detail (and in effect writing another body), what more can you say here? What has been the value of your study to your understanding and appreciating the poem? If you think your analysis has helped you to develop new awareness of the poet's craft, it would be appropriate to state what you have learned.

FIRST SAMPLE ESSAY

A Study of Tennyson's Rhythm and Segments in "The Passing of Arthur," Lines 349–360*

Author's Note. This essay analyzes a passage from "The Passing of Arthur," which is part of Tennyson's long poem *Idylls of the King.* Containing 469 lines, this poem describes the last battle and death of Arthur, legendary king of early Britain. After the fight, in which Arthur has been mortally wounded by the traitor Mordred, only Arthur and his follower Sir Bedivere

* See p. 696 for this poem.

remain alive. Arthur commands Bedivere to throw the royal sword Excalibur into the lake from which Arthur had originally received it. After great hesitation and some false claims, Bedivere does throw the sword into the lake, and a hand rises out of the water to catch it. Bedivere then carries Arthur to the lakeshore, where the dying king is taken aboard a magical funeral barge. In the passage selected for discussion (lines 349–360), Tennyson describes Bedivere carrying Arthur down the hills and cliffs from the battlefield to the lake below.

1. RHYTHMICAL ANALYSIS

But the o- / ther swift- / ly strode / / from ridge / to ridge, / / 1

Clothed with / his breath, / / and look- / ing, / / as / he walk'd, / / 2

Lar-ger / than hu- / man / / on / the fro- / zen hills. / / 3

He heard / the deep / be-hind / him, / / and / a cry 4

Be-fore. / / His own / thought drove / him / / like / a goad. / / 5

Dry clash'd / his har- / ness / / in / the i / cy caves 6

And bar-   ren / chasms, / / and all / to left / and right 7

The bare / black cliff / clang'd round / him, / / as / he based 8

His feet / on juts / of slip- / pe-ry crag / / that rang 9

Sharp- smit- / ten / / with / the / dint / of ar- / med heels— / / 10

And on / a sud- / den, / / lo! / / the lev- / el lake, / / 11

And the / long glor- / ies / / of / the win- / ter moon. / / 12

1 = Anapaest, or effect of anapaest.	4 = Effect of imperfect foot.
2 = Amphibrach, or the effect of amphibrach.	5 = Pyrrhic.
3 = Spondee.	6 = Trochee, or the effect of trochee.

2. ALLITERATION

But the other (s) wiftly (s) trode from ridge to ridge,   1

Clothed with his breath, and looking, as (h) e walked,   2

Larger than (h) uman on the frozen (h) ills.   3

(H) e (h) eard the deep be (h) ind (h) im, and a cry   4

Before. (H) is own thought drove him like a goad.   5

Dry (c) lashed (h) is (h) arness in the icy (c) aves   6

And (b) arren (ch) asms, and all to left and right   7

The (b) are (b) (l) ack (c) (l) iff (c) (l) anged round him, as he (b) ased   8

His feet on juts of s (l) ippery (c) rag that rang   9

Sharp-smitten with the dint of armed heels—   10

And on a sudden, (l) o! the (l) evel (l) ake,   11

And the (l) ong g (l) ories of the winter moon.   12

〰〰〰 = s   ——————— = b

--------- = h   〰〰〰〰 = l as second consonant
                                                             sound in words

············ = k   —·—·—·— = l

3. ASSONANCE

But the other sw (i) ftly str (o) de from r (i) dge to r (i) dge,   1

Cl (o) thed w (i) th h (i) s breath, and looking, as he walked,   2

Larger than human on the fr (o) zen hills.   3

He heard the deep beh (i) nd him, and a cr (y)   4

Before. His (ow) n thought dr (o) ve him l (i) ke a g (oa) d.   5

Dr (y) clashed his harness in the (i) cy caves   6

And barren ch (a) sms, and all to left and r (i) ght   7

The bare bl (a) ck cliff cl (a) nged round him, as he based   8

H (i) s feet on juts of sl (i) ppery cr (a) g that r (a) ng   9

Sh (ar) p-sm (i) tten w (i) th the d (i) nt of (ar) med heels—   10

And on a sudden, lo, the level lake,   11

And the long glories of the winter moon!   12

——————— = ō*   •—·—·—·— = ä

-------- = ī   ∿∿∿∿∿ = ĭ

•••••••• = a

* Pronunciation symbols as in *Webster's New World Dictionary,* 2nd ed.

[1]   This passage describes the ordeal of Sir Bedivere as he carries the dying Arthur from the mountainous heights, where he was wounded, down to the lake, where the king will be sent to his final rest. Tennyson devotes great attention to the ghostly, deserted landscape, emphasizing the bleakness and hostility of the scenes. The passage is unrhymed iambic pentameter— blank verse. But Tennyson's verse is alive; it constantly augments his descriptions and conveys an impression of Bedivere's mood, whether of anguish or relaxation.° The control over prosody enables a true blending of sound and sense, as may be seen in Tennyson's use of rhythm and in his manipulation of segmental devices, including onomatopoeia.□

[2]   Tennyson controls his meter to emphasize Bedivere's exertions and moods. In line 1 the meter is regular, except for an anapaest in the first foot. This regularity may be interpreted as emphasizing the swiftness and surefootedness of Bedivere. But he is about to undergo a severe test, and the rhythm quickly becomes irregular, as though to strain the pentameter verse in illustration of Bedivere's exertions. Tennyson therefore uses variations to highlight key words. For example, he uses the effect of anapaests in a number of lines. In line 2 he emphasizes the chill air and Bedivere's vitality in the following way:

$$\text{Clot}\acute{\text{h}}\text{ed with / h}\breve{\text{i}}\text{s bréath, / /}$$

The image is one of being surrounded by one's own breath that vaporizes on hitting the cold air, and the rhythmical variation—a trochaic substitution in the first foot—enables the voice to build up to the word *breath*, a most effective internal climax.

[3]   Tennyson uses something like the same rhythmical effect in line 3. He emphasizes the *frozen hills* by creating a caesura in the middle of the third foot, and then by making the heavy stress of the third foot fall on the preposition *on*, which with *the* creates in effect the two unstressed syllables of an anapaest including the first, stressed, syllable of *frozen*. The effect is that the voice builds up to the word and thus emphasizes the extreme conditions in which Bedivere is walking:

$$\text{/ / o}\acute{\text{n}}\text{ / the fro - / z}\breve{\text{e}}\text{n hílls. / /}$$

Tennyson uses this effect twelve times in the passage. It is his major means of rhetorical emphasis.

[4]   Perhaps the most effective metrical variation is the spondee, which appears in lines 5, 6, 8, (twice), 10, and 12. These substitutions, occurring mainly in the section in which Sir Bedivere is forcing his way down the frozen hills, permit the lines to ring out, as in:

$$\text{The b}\breve{\text{a}}\text{re / bláck cliff / clang'd round /}$$

and

° Central idea.
□ Thesis sentence.

Dry clash'd / his har - / ness.

The best use of the spondee is in line 5, where the stresses reach a climax on the word *drove*, which suggests the torment Bedivere is feeling:

His own / thought drove / him / / .

[5]   There is other substitution, too, both formal and rhetorical, and the tension these variations create keeps the responsive reader aware of Bedivere's tasks. One type of variation is the appearance of amphibrachic rhythm, which is produced in lines 2, 3, 4, 6, 7, and 11. The effect is achieved by a pattern which complements the rhetorical anapaests. A caesura in the middle of a foot leaves the three preceding syllables as a light, heavy, and light, the rhythmical form of the amphibrach. In line 2, for example, it appears thus:

/ / and look - / ing / /

In line 6 it takes this form:

/ his har - / ness / /

[6]   Still another related variation is that of the apparently imperfect feet in lines 5, 8, 11, and 12. These imperfect feet are produced by a caesura, which isolates the syllable, as *him* is in line 8:

The bare / black cliff / clang'd round / him, / /

In line 11 the syllable (on the word *lo!*) is surrounded by two caesurae, and is therefore thrust into a position of great stress:

And on / a sud - / den / / lo! / / the lev - / el lake

Other, less significant substitutions are the trochees in lines 3 and 7, and the pyrrhic in line 12. All the described variations support the heroic action described in the passage.

[7]   Many of the variations described are produced by Tennyson's handling of his sentence structure, which results in a free placement of the caesurae and in a free use of end-stopping and enjambement. It is interesting that four of the first five lines are end-stopped (two by commas, two by periods). Bedivere is exerting himself during these lines and apparently he is making short tests to gather strength for his ordeal. The ordeal comes during the next four lines, when he makes his precarious descent; none of the lines containing this description is end-stopped. Bedivere is disturbed (being goaded by "his own thought"), but he must keep going, and we may presume that the free sentence structure and the free metrical variation enforce his

difficulty and mental disturbance. But in the last two lines, when he has reached the lake, the lines "relax" with falling caesurae exactly at the fifth syllables.
[7]   In other words, the sentence structure of the last two lines is regular, an effect designed to indicate the return to order and beauty after the previous, rugged chaos.

This rhythmical virtuosity is accompanied by a similarly brilliant control over segmental devices. Alliteration is the most obvious, permitting Tennyson to tie key words and their signifying actions together, as in the s's in "swiftly strode" in line 1, or the b's in "barren," "bare," "black," and"based" in lines 7 and 8. Other notable examples are the aspirated h's in lines 2–6 (he, human,
[8]   hills, heard, behind, him, his, harness); the k's in lines 6–9 (clash'd, caves, chasms, cliff, clang'd, crag); and the l's in lines 11 and 12 (lo, level, lake, long, glories). One might compare these l's with the l's in the more anguished context of lines 8 and 9, where the sounds appear as the second segment in the heavy, ringing words there (black, cliff, clang'd, slippery). The sounds are the same, and the emphasis is similar, but the effects are different.

Assonance is also present throughout the passage. In the first five lines, for example, the ō appears in six words. The first three ō's are in descriptive or metaphoric words (strode, clothed, frozen), while the last three are in words describing the pain and anguish that Bedivere experiences as a result of his efforts in the barren landscape (own, drove, goad). The o therefore ties
[9]   the physical to the psychological. Other patterns of assonance are the ă in lines 7, 8, and 9 (chàsms, clang'd, black, crag, rang), the ä of line 10 (sharp, armed), the ī of lines 4–7 (behind, cry, like, dry, icy, right), and the short ĭ of lines 1 and 2, and 9 and 10 (swiftly, ridge, with, his, slippery, smitten, with, dint). One might remark also that in the last two lines, which describe the level lake and the moon, Tennyson introduces a number of relaxed ō and ōō and similar vowel sounds (ô, u, ō, ô, ô, u, ōō).

The last two lines are, in fact, onomatopoeic, since the liquid l sounds suggest the gentle lapping of waves on a lake shore. There are other examples of onomatopoeia, too. In line 2 Tennyson brings out the detail of Sir Bedivere's walking in the presumably cold air "Clothed with his breath," and in the following
[10]   five lines Tennyson employs many words with the aspirate h (e.g., his harness); in this context, these sounds suggest Sir Bedivere's labored breath as he carries his royal burden. Similarly, the explosive stops b and k, d, and t in lines 6–10 seem to be imitative of the sounds of Sir Bedivere's feet on the "juts of slippery crag."

This short passage is filled with many examples of poetic excellence. The sounds and the rhythms of the words and lines, put into this context
[11]   by Tennyson, actually speak along with the meaning; they emphasize the grandeur of Arthur and his faithful follower, and for one brief moment bring out the magic that Tennyson associated with the fading past.

Commentary on the Essay

This essay presents a full discussion of the prosody of the passage from Tennyson. Paragraphs 2 through 7 discuss the relationship of the rhythm to the content. Note that prosody is not discussed in isolation, but as it serves Tennyson's purpose in describing the action and scenes of the passage. Thus, paragraph 4 refers to the use of the spondee as a means of reinforcing the ideas. In this paragraph there is also a short comparison of alternative ways of saying what Tennyson says so well. While such speculative comparison should not be attempted often, it is effective here in highlighting Tennyson's prosodic excellence.

Paragraphs 8 and 9 present a discussion of the alliteration and assonance of the passage, and paragraph 10 considers onomatopoeia.

SECOND SAMPLE ESSAY

The Rhymes in Christina Rossetti's "Echo"*

	n	
1	*Come* to me in the silence of the *night*;	*5a*
	n	
2	*Come* in the speaking silence of a *dream*;	*5b*
	adj	
3	*Come* with soft rounded cheeks and eyes as *bright*	*5a*
	n	
4	As sunlight on a *stream*;	*3b*
	n	
5	*Come* back in *tears*,	*2c*
	n	
6	O memory, hope, love of finished *years*.	*5c*
	adj	
7	O *dream* how *sweet*, too *sweet*, too bitter *sweet*,	*5d*
	n	
8	Whose wakening should have been in *Paradise*,	*5e*
	v	
9	Where souls brimful of love abide and *meet*;	*5d*
	n	
10	Where thirsty longing *eyes*	*3e*
	n	
11	Watch the slow *door*	*2f*
	adv	
12	That opening, letting in, lets out no *more*.	*5f*
	v	
13	Yet *come* to me in *dreams*, that I may *live*	*5g*

* See p. 701 for this poem.

14   My very life again though cold in *death*;   *5h*

                                              v

15   *Come* back to me in *dreams,* that I may give   *5g*

                                n

16   Pulse for pulse, *breath* for *breath*:   *3h*

                            adv

17   Speak *low,* lean *low*,   *2i*

                            adj

18 As *long ago*, my love, how *long ago*.   *5i*

[1]   In the three-stanza lyric poem "Echo," Christina Rossetti uses rhyme as a way of saying that one might regain in dreams a love that is lost in reality.° As the dream of love is to the real love, so is an echo to an original sound. From this comparison comes the title of the poem and also Rossetti's unique use of rhyme. Aspects of her rhyme are the lyric pattern, the forms and qualities of the rhyming words, and the special use of repetition.□

The rhyme pattern is simple, and, like rhyme generally, it may be thought of as a pattern of echoes. Each stanza contains four lines of alternating rhymes concluded by a couplet, as follows:

Iambic: 5a, 5b, 5a, 3b, 2c, 5c.

[2]   There are nine separate rhymes throughout the poem, three in each stanza. Only two words are used for each rhyme; no rhyme is used twice. Of the eighteen rhyming words, sixteen—almost all—are of one syllable. The remaining two words consist of two and three syllables. With such a great number of single-syllable words, the rhymes are all rising ones, on the accented halves of iambic feet, and the end-of-line emphasis is on simple words.

The grammatical forms and positions of the rhyming words lend support to the inward, introspective subject matter. Although there is variety, more than half the rhyming words are nouns. There are ten in all, and eight are placed as the objects of prepositions. Such enclosure helps the speaker emphasize her yearning to relive her love within dreams. Also, the repeated verb "come" in stanzas one and three is in the form of commands to the absent lover. A careful study shows that most of the verbal energy in the stanzas is in the first parts of the lines, leaving the rhymes to occur in elements modifying the verbs, as in these lines:

[3]

Come to me in the silence of the *night* (1)

° Central idea.
□ Thesis sentence.

> Yet come to me in dreams, that I may *live* (13)
> My very life again though cold in *death*; (14)

Most of the other rhymes are also in such internalized positions. The free rhyming verbs occur in subordinate clauses, and the nouns that are not the objects of prepositions are the subject (10) and object (11) of the same subordinate clause.

[4] The qualities of the rhyming words are also consistent with the poem's emphasis on the speaker's internal life. Most of the words are impressionistic. Even the concrete words—*stream, tears*, eyes, *door*, and *breath*—reflect the speaker's mental condition rather than describe reality. In this regard, the rhyming words of 1 and 3 are effective. These are *night* and *bright*, which contrast the bleakness of the speaker's condition, on the one hand, with the vitality of her inner life, on the other. Another effective contrast is in 14 and 16, where *death* and *breath* are rhymed. This rhyme may be taken to illustrate the sad fact that even though the speaker's love is past, it can yet live in present memory just as an echo continues to sound.

[5] It is in emphasizing how memory echoes experience that Rossetti creates the special use of rhyming words. There is an ingenious but not obtrusive repetition of a number of words—echoes. The major echoing word is of course the verb *come*, which appears six times at the beginnings of lines in stanzas 1 and 3. But rhyming words, stressing as they do the ends of lines, are also repeated systematically. The most notable is *dream*, the rhyming word in 2. Rossetti repeats the word in 7 and uses the plural in 13 and 15. In 7 the rhyming word *sweet* is the third use of the word, a climax of "how *sweet*, too *sweet*, too bitter *sweet*." Concluding the poem, Rossetti repeats *breath* (16), *low* (17), and the phrase *long ago* (18). This special use of repetition justifies the title "Echo," and it also stresses the major idea that it is only in one's memory that past experience has reality, even if dreams are no more than echoes.

[6] Thus rhyme is not just ornamental in "Echo," but integral. The skill of Rossetti here is the same as in her half-serious, half-mocking poem "Eve," even though the two poems are totally different. In "Eve," she uses very plain rhyming words together with comically intended double rhymes. In "Echo," her subject might be called fanciful and maybe even morbid, but the easiness of the rhyming words, like the diction of the poem generally, keeps the focus on regret and yearning rather than self-indulgence. As in all rhyming poems, Rossetti's rhymes emphasize the conclusions of her lines. The rhymes go beyond this effect, however, because of the internal repetition— echoes—of the rhyming words. "Echo" is a poem in which rhyme is inseparable from meaning.

Commentary on the Essay

Throughout the essay, illustrative words are italicized, and numbers are used to indicate the lines from which the illustrations are drawn. The introductory paragraph asserts that rhyme is important in Rossetti's poem. It also attempts to explain the title, "Echo." The thesis sentence indicates the four topics to be developed in the body.

Paragraph 2 deals with the mechanical, mathematical aspects of the poem's rhyme. The high number of monosyllabic rhyming words is used to explain the rising, heavy-stress rhyme.

The third paragraph treats the grammar of the rhymes. For example, an analysis and count reveal that there are ten rhyming nouns and three rhyming verbs. The verb of command "come" is mentioned to show that most of the rhyming words exist within groups modifying this word, and three lines from the poem illustrate this fact. The grammatical analysis is related to the internalized nature of the subject of the poem.

Paragraph 4 emphasizes the impressionistic nature of the rhyming words and also points out two instances in which rhymes stress the contrast between real life and the speaker's introspective life.

Paragraph 5 deals with repetitions within the poem of five rhyming words. This repetition is seen as a pattern of echoes, in keeping with the title of the poem.

In the concluding paragraph, the rhymes in "Echo" are compared briefly with those in "Eve," another poem by Christina Rossetti. The conclusion is that Rossetti is a skilled rhymer because she uses rhyme appropriately in both poems. At the end of the essay the central idea is reiterated.

WRITING TOPICS FOR CHAPTER 18

1. For Shakespeare's Sonnet 73, analyze the ways in which Shakespeare creates his iambics. That is, what is the relationship of lightly accented syllables to the heavily accented ones? Where does Shakespeare use articles (*the*), pronouns (*thou, his*), prepositions (*upon, against, of*), relative clause markers (*which, that*) and adverb clause markers (*as, when*) in relation to syllables of heavy stress? Determine the number and placement of one-syllable words and two-syllable words in the sonnet. On the basis of this study, how would you characterize Shakespeare's control of the iambic foot?

2. Compare the sounds used in Poe's "The Bells" with those of Wagoner's "March for a One-Man Band." What effects are achieved by each poet? What is the relationship in each poem between sound and content? Which poem do you prefer on the basis of sound? Why?

3. The poems "Barbara Allen," "Miniver Cheevy," and "At a Summer Hotel" all utilize falling, or trochaic, rhyme. What is the effect of this rhyming pattern in the three poems? How do the poems achieve seriousness, despite the fact that trochaic rhyme is often used generally to complement humorous and light verse?

4. Try writing a limerick. If you are at a loss for a topic, use one of the following lines to begin:

There once was a man in a rowboat.

Two happy friends tried to study.

Once you have finished, use the same topic and detail for a poem in iambics. Describe the differences and challenges you encounter because of the differences between the rollicking form of the limerick and the more steady pace of the iambics. How do you handle the different demands of the form? What can you say about the iambic foot as a result of this experience?

19

Form: The Shape of the Poem

When we speak about poems, we are likely to identify some as *ballads*, *sonnets*, *limericks*, *lyrics*, or the like. These are the names of specific, traditional forms of poetry. **Form** is the shape or the general pattern of a poem; it indicates the poem's *structure* or *design*. Visually, form is the way a poem looks on the printed page. To a large extent, form is a matter of variables that we have already discussed: meter, line length, and rhyme scheme. When these elements work together, they produce a specific poetic form.

MAJOR POETIC FORMS

The two major subdivisions of poetic form are closed and open. The terms refer to structure and technique rather than to content or ideas. **Closed-form** poetry is written in specific and often traditional patterns of lines produced through rhyme, meter, line length, and line groupings. **Stanzas** are groups of two lines or more, that are grouped together visually in a poem. The *ballad*, *sonnet*, *limerick*, and *lyric* are examples of traditional closed forms that have been used for hundreds of years and are recognizable because of their structure. (We will say more about these forms shortly.) A poem written in a closed form need not conform strictly to a traditional shape; it may use traditional devices in an original way to produce a new pattern. In any event, closed forms are characterized by a clear structure based on rhyme, meter, line length, and stanzas or units of verse.

Open form, on the other hand, identifies a poem that avoids traditional patterns of organization and does not rely on meter, rhyme, line length, or stanzas to produce order. An open-form poem often presents radical variations in line length, no rhyme scheme, and no distinct stanzas at all.

Open-form poetry is not necessarily disorganized or chaotic, however. The poet has merely sought new ways to arrange words and lines, new ways to express thoughts and feelings, and new ways to order the experience of poetry.

CLOSED-FORM POETRY: THE BUILDING BLOCKS

Although closed-form poetry depends on the poet's use of traditional techniques such as meter, rhyme, and line groupings, the basic building block is the line of verse. Various numbers of lines may be grouped together through rhyme to form stanzas or sections of poems. These stanzas or sections may, in turn, be assembled to create traditional forms.

The most common and popular one-line pattern in English poetry is **blank verse,** or unrhymed iambic pentameter (see p. 682). In a poem or play written in blank verse, each line comprises a poetic unit. Since rhyme is not employed in blank verse, the form is defined by the meter (iambic) and the line length (five feet per line). Blank verse has been used by poets and playwrights since the sixteenth century. William Shakespeare, for example, wrote most of his plays in blank verse, and John Milton used the form in his epic, *Paradise Lost.* We can see an example of blank verse in these lines from Shakespeare's *Hamlet,* where the prince is telling his mother that his mourning is real and not an outward show:

Seems, madam? nay it is, I know not "seems."
'Tis not alone my inky cloak good mother,
Nor customary suits of solemn black,
Nor windy suspiration of forced breath,
No, nor the fruitful river in the eye,°   *tears*
Nor the dejected havior° of the visage,°   *appearance; face*
Together with all forms, moods, shapes of grief,
That can denote me truly; these indeed seem,
For they are actions that a man might play,
But I have that within which passes show,
These but the trappings and the suits of woe.   *(Act 1, scene 2, lines 76–86)*

While the verse offers no rhyme scheme (except in the final pair of lines), each line is written in iambic pentameter. Blank verse is one of the most flexible closed forms of poetry since its requirements are only metric.

The basic two-line building block of poetic form is called a **couplet.** The two lines can be any length and any meter, but they must rhyme. In addition, they are usually the same length. Couplets may be made up of extremely short lines; in fact, two single words like "Flee/Me" or "Night/Flight" can comprise a couplet. However, the most common meters and line lengths for couplets are iambic tetrameter (four heavy stresses per line) and iambic pentameter (five stresses). Hamlet's speech on mourning (see above) ends with a couplet in iambic pentameter. The first two lines of Robert Frost's "Stopping by Woods on a Snowy Evening" form an iambic tetrameter couplet:

> Whose woods these are I think I know,
> His house is in the village though.

Couplets are used as components of all sorts of poems. Many sonnets end with a couplet, and many four-line stanzas contain couplets. In other words, couplets can be employed to build larger units or forms of poetry. Couplets can also be used throughout a poem. For instance, Alexander Pope wrote both "An Essay on Criticism" and "The Rape of the Lock" entirely in couplets. In such a case, the pairs of lines that make up each couplet (and stanza) are usually printed together without any break or white space between them.

Couplets have been employed in English poetry since the fourteenth century. They came into widest use in the seventeenth and eighteenth centuries during the careers of John Dryden and Alexander Pope, when poets made extensive use of the **closed** or **heroic couplet,** two rhymed lines of iambic pentameter that are *end-stopped* (see p. 687). The heroic couplet usually expresses a complete idea. It also enables writers to use rhetorical strategies such as parallelism and antithesis. Look, for example, at these lines from Pope's "The Rape of the Lock," a mock-epic poem that tells the story of a stolen lock of hair:

> Here Britain's statesmen oft the fall foredoom
> Of foreign tyrants and of nymphs at home;
> Here thou, great Anna! whom three realms obey,
> Doest sometimes counsel take—and sometimes tea.

These lines describe Hampton Court, a royal palace and residence of Queen Anne (reigned 1702–1714). Notice that the first heroic couplet allows Pope to link "Britain's statesmen" with two very different events: the fall of nations and the seduction of young women. Similarly, the second heroic couplet allows for the outrageous linking of royal meetings of state (*counsel*) and tea time (in the early eighteenth century, *tea* was pronounced "tay"). The heroic couplets here facilitate placing opposite ideas and events in amusing and ironic parallels.

The three-line stanza is called a **tercet** or **triplet.** Tercets may be written in any line length or meter, but the length of the three lines must be uniform and they often contain a single rhyme sound (*a a a, b b b,* and so on). The following poem is written in iambic tetrameter triplets.

ALFRED, LORD TENNYSON (1809–1892)

The Eagle   *1851*

He clasps the crag with crooked hands;
Close to the sun in lonely lands,
Ring'd with the azure world, he stands.

The wrinkled sea beneath him crawls;
He watches from his mountain walls,   5
And like a thunderbolt he falls.

The lines are even and the same rhyme sound is repeated three times in
each stanza. In the first triplet we are viewing the eagle; he passively "clasps"
and "stands" in splendid isolation. In the second, however, our perspective
shifts and we both look at the eagle and see through his eyes. Here, the
verbs become more active: the sea "crawls" and the eagle "falls." While
the two tercets and the shift in perspective seem to divide the poem in
half, alliteration pulls it back together. This is especially true of the "*k*"
sound in *clasps, crag, crooked, close,* and *crawls,* and the "*w*" sound in *with,
world, watches,* and *walls.*

An exception to the triple rhyme of the tercet is **terza rima,** a three-
line stanza form in which each stanza interlocks with the next through
rhyme. Thus, the rhyme pattern in terza rima is *a b a, b c b, c d c,* and so
on. You can see an example of terza rima in Shelley's "Ode to the West
Wind" (p. 751). Still another exception to the *a a a* pattern of the tercet
is found in a traditional verse form called the **villanelle,** in which every
triplet in the poem is rhymed *a b a* (for an example, see Dylan Thomas's
"Do Not Go Gentle Into That Good Night," p. 754). As these two forms
illustrate, the tercet, like the couplet, is very adaptable. No single definition
or illustration can adequately encompass the variability of these traditional
stanza patterns.

The most adaptable and popular building block in English and American poetry is the four-line **quatrain.** This stanza has been popular for
hundreds of years and has lent itself to a great many variations. Like
couplets and triplets, quatrains may be written in any line length and
meter; even the line lengths *within* a quatrain may vary. The determining
factor is always the rhyme scheme, and even that can vary significantly,
given the demands of the form and the desires of the poet. Quatrains
may be rhymed *a a a a,* but they can also be rhymed *a b a b, a b b a, a a b
a,* or even *a b c b.* All these variations are determined, at least in part, by
the larger patterns or forms that quatrains are used to build. Quatrains
are basic components of many traditional closed forms, including ballads
and sonnets.

COMMON TYPES OF CLOSED-FORM POETRY

Over the centuries English and American poetry has evolved or appropriated hundreds of traditional closed forms, all of them determined by some combination of meter, rhyme scheme, line length, and stanza form. Most of them involve some combination of the basic building blocks of poetic form: the couplet, tercet, and quatrain. While it is impossible to provide a complete catalog of all the traditional forms here, we will introduce you to the most common ones.

The Italian, or Petrarchan Sonnet

The sonnet is one of the most durable and popular traditional forms in poetry. All sonnets are fourteen lines long. Initially, they were an Italian poetic form (*sonnetto* means "little song") popularized by Francesco Petrarch (1304–1374), who wrote long collections or *cycles* of sonnets to an idealized mistress named Laura. The form and style of Petrarch's sonnets were adapted to English poetry in the early sixteenth century and have been used ever since. The **Italian** or **Petrarchan sonnet** is written in iambic pentameter and is composed of two quatrains and two tercets. The first eight lines are called the **octave** (indicating an eight-line unit of thought) and the last six are called the **sestet.** The rhyme scheme of the octave is usually fixed in an *a b b a, a b b a* pattern. The sestet offers a number of different rhyming possibilities, including *c d c, c d c* and *c d e, c d e.* An Italian sonnet rarely ends with a couplet. In terms of structure and meaning, the octave of the Italian sonnet usually presents a conflict or dilemma, and the sestet offers some sort of resolution. As a result, there is often a clear shift or turn in thought from the octave to the sestet. John Milton's "When I Consider How My Light Is Spent" (p. 743) is an example of an Italian sonnet.

The English, or Shakespearean Sonnet

The **English,** or **Shakespearean sonnet,** named after its most famous practitioner, is written in iambic pentameter and has the following rhyme scheme: *a b a b, c d c d, e f e f, g g.* The development of the English sonnet from the Italian sonnet in sixteenth-century England represents a major shift in the composition and organization of ideas in a poem. The Shakespearean sonnet, as is indicated by its rhyme scheme, is composed of three quatrains and a couplet. As a result, the pattern of thought shifts from the octave–sestet organization in the Italian sonnet to a four-part argument on a single thought or emotion. Each quatrain usually contains a separate development of the sonnet's central idea, with the couplet providing a conclusion, climax, and resolution. Shakespeare's Sonnet 116, "Let

Me Not to the Marriage of True Minds" (p. 736), is an example of the English sonnet.

The Ballad

The **ballad,** which has its origins in folk literature, is one of the oldest traditional closed forms in English poetry; it has been used continuously from the Middle Ages to the present. Ballads are composed of a long series of quatrains in which lines of iambic tetrameter alternate with iambic trimeter. Normally, only the second and fourth lines of each stanza contain rhyming words, and so the rhyme scheme is *a b c b, d e f e*, and so on. Ballads are often narrative in development, telling a complete story, as in the anonymous "Sir Patrick Spens" (p. 523) and "Barbara Allan" (p. 901).

Common Measure or Hymnal Stanza

Common measure is probably derived from the ballad stanza. It shares with the ballad the alternation of four-beat and three-beat iambic lines but adds a second rhyme to each quatrain: *a b a b, c d c d*, and so on. As with the ballad, the basic building block of common measure is the quatrain. The measure is most commonly used in hymns, so it is sometimes called **hymnal stanza.** Many of Emily Dickinson's poems, including "Because I Could Not Stop for Death" (p. 527), are written in common measure.

The Song or Lyric

The **lyric** is a free stanzaic form that was originally designed to be sung to a repeated melody. The structure and rhyme scheme of the first stanza are therefore duplicated in all subsequent stanzas. Like the ballad, it is one of the oldest traditional closed forms in poetry. The individual stanzas of a lyric may be built from any combination of single lines, couplets, triplets, and quatrains; the line lengths may shift, and a great deal of metrical variation is common. There is theoretically no limit to the number of stanzas in a lyric, although there are usually no more than five or six. We can find a great deal of variation in the structure. A. E. Housman's "Loveliest of Trees" (p. 528), for example, is a lyric made up of three quatrains containing two couplets each; it is written in iambic tetrameter and rhymes *a a b b*. The second and third stanzas repeat the same pattern. Christina Rossetti's "Echo" (p. 701) is also a lyric, but its structure is very different from that of Housman's poem. Here, the structural formulation of each stanza is iambic: *5a 5b 5a 3b 2c 5c*. Lyrics can have very complex and ingenious stanzaic structures. John Donne's "The Canonization" (p. 864), for instance, contains five stanzas that reflect the following pattern:

Iambic: *5a 4b 5b 5a 4c 4c 4c 4a 3a.* The nine-line stanza contains three different rhymes and three different line lengths; nevertheless, the same complicated pattern is repeated in each of the five stanzas.

The Ode

The **ode** is a stanzaic form far more complex than the lyric, with varying line lengths and intricate rhyme schemes. Some odes have repeating patterns that are duplicated in each stanza, while others offer no duplication and introduce a new structure in each stanza. Although some odes were designed to be set to music, most do not fit repeating melodies. There is no set form for the ode; poets have developed their own structures according to their needs. John Keats's great odes were particularly congenial to his ideas, as in the "Ode to a Nightingale" (p. 749), which consists of ten stanzas in iambic pentameter with the repeating form *a b a b c d e 3c d e.* By contrast, each of the ten stanzas in William Wordsworth's "Ode: Intimations of Immortality" (p. 840) introduces a totally new pattern.

Haiku

The haiku originated in Japan where it has been a favored poetic form for hundreds of years. In original form, haiku imposed strict rules on the writer: The poem must be only three lines long and have a total of 17 syllables in a pattern of 5, 7, and 5 syllables per line. The traditional subject matter was nature and the seasons. Today English-language poets have treated many different subjects in haiku, and have also taken liberties with the syllabic count. Because of the rigid pattern, haiku poetry must aim for objectivity, simplicity, and clarity, and should be judged by these standards. The following anonymous haiku illustrates some of these qualities.

Spun in high, dark clouds

Spun in high, dark clouds,
Snow forms vast webs of white flakes
And drifts lightly down.

In the tradition of haiku, the subject of this poem is derived from nature. The major metaphor equates gathering snow with the webs of spiders or silkworms. To supply a degree of tension, the lines contrast "high" with "down," and "dark" with "white." Because of the enforced brevity of the haiku form, the diction is simple and, except for the word *forms,* is of English derivation (*form* is a word derived from French). In addition, the words are mainly monosyllabic, and the poem therefore crowds sixteen words unto the 17-syllable form. Most English haiku will contain a similar preponderance of one-syllable words.

Some Other Closed-Form Types

Many other closed forms have enjoyed long popularity. One of these, the **epigram,** is a short and witty poem that usually makes a humorous or satiric point. Epigrams are usually two to four lines long and written in couplets. The form was developed by the Roman poet Martial (A.D. 40–102) and has remained popular to the present. Humorous **epitaphs,** lines composed to mark the death of someone, can also be epigrams. The following epitaph-epigram was written to commemorate John Hewet and Sara Drew, who were killed by lightning on July 31, 1718, while helping bring in the harvest; it is followed by a selection of epigrams.

ALEXANDER POPE   (1688–1744)

Epitaph on the Stanton-Harcourt Lovers   1718

Here lie two poor Lovers, who had the mishap,
Though very chaste people, to die of a Clap.

SAMUEL TAYLOR COLERIDGE   (1772–1834)

What Is an Epigram   1802

What is an epigram? a dwarfish whole,
Its body brevity, and wit its soul.

E. E. CUMMINGS   (1894–1962)

A Politician   1944

a politician is an arse upon
which everyone has sat except a man.

J. V. CUNNINGHAM   (b. 1911)

Epitaph for Someone or Other   1950

Naked I came, naked I leave the scene,
And naked was my pastime in between.

19/Form: The Shape of the Poem

QUESTIONS

1. What do these four epigrams have in common? To what extent do they share a common tone and form?

2. Consider the relationship between epigrams and the couplets that close English sonnets or the heroic couplets of the eighteenth century. Look at the concluding couplets of Shakespeare's sonnets in this text (use the index) and look at Alexander Pope's couplets in the extract from "The Rape of the Lock" (p. 728). To what extent do these couplets have effects similar to those produced by epigrams?

Another popular closed-form type is the **limerick.** Like the epigram, the limerick is usually humorous, the humor often being reinforced by double or falling rhymes (see pp. 691–92). In addition, contemporary limericks are often bawdy or worse. We do not know who invented the limerick as a form, but it was popularized by Edward Lear (1812–1888), an English artist and humorist. Limericks are always five lines long and the meter is basically anapestic (˘ ˘ ´). The structure of most limericks may thus be described as anapestic: *3a 3a 2b 2b 3a.* Here are a few limericks for your enjoyment.

A diner while dining at Crewe,
Found a rather large mouse in his stew.
    Said the waiter, "Don't shout
    and wave it about,
Or the rest will be wanting one too."

There was a young lady from Trent
Who said that she knew what it meant
    When men asked her to dine:
    Private room, lots of wine.
She knew—O she knew!—but she went.

Humorous closed forms continue to be devised by enterprising writers. Although none has become as popular as the limerick, they illustrate both the pleasures and the agonies of working within closed forms. The **clerihew,** invented in the late nineteenth century by Edmund Clerihew Bentley (1875–1956), is clearly related to the epigram. Clerihews are usually composed of two couplets and focus on a well-known person, who is named in the first line. Here are two clerihews, both written by Bentley and published in 1937.

George the Third
Ought never to have occurred.
One can only wonder
At so grotesque a blunder.

Alfred, Lord Tennyson
Lived upon venison:
Not cheap, I fear,
Because venison's deer.

QUESTIONS

1. What do these clerihews have in common? To what extent do they share a common tone and structure?
2. Write several clerihews about contemporary figures and share them with your class. Try to maintain the tone and style of Bentley's work.

As a final illustration of humorous closed form, we offer the **double dactyl,** devised in the 1960s by Anthony Hecht and John Hollander. The form is related to that of the epigram, limerick, and clerihew, and the rules that govern this form are fairly complex; they dictate the meter, line length, and specific content of lines 1, 2, and 6 or 7. Here are two examples.

ANTHONY HECHT   (b. 1923)

Nominalism   *1967*

Higgledy-piggledy
Juliet Capulet
Cherished the tenderest
Thoughts of a rose:

"What's in a name?" said she,   5
Etymologically,
"Save that all Montagues
Stink in God's nose."

ARTHUR W. MONKS

Twilight's Last Gleaming   *1967*

Higgledy-piggledy
President Jefferson
Gave up the ghost on the
Fourth of July.

So did John Adams, which   5
Shows that such patriots

Propagandistically
Knew how to die.

QUESTIONS

1. How many lines long is a double dactyl? How many stanzas?
2. What form must line 1 take? What requirement governs line 2? Line 6 or 7?
3. What is the dominant meter? How does it change in lines 4 and 8?
4. What rhyming requirements does the form impose?
5. Try to write a few double dactyls, maintaining the tone and spirit of the examples. You will probably have the most trouble with line 2, 6, or 7, but keep at it.

CLOSED FORM AND MEANING

Although traditional closed forms are thought by many contemporary poets to be excessively restrictive, these forms provide a general framework within which a poet can create feeling and express ideas. Closed forms provide a ready-made structure; the poet's challenge is to take this structure and breathe new life into it by arranging images, emotions, and ideas to create something vital and effective. A skillful poet uses the demands of a closed form to his or her own ends. With this in mind, let us look at the way a specific closed form may be employed to shape thoughts and emotions.

WILLIAM SHAKESPEARE   (1564–1616)

Sonnet 116: Let Me Not to the Marriage of True Minds   1609

Let me not to the marriage of true minds
Admit impediments.° Love is not love
Which alters when it alteration finds,
Or bends with the remover to remove:
Oh, no! it is an ever-fixéd mark,   5
That looks on tempests and is never shaken;
It is the star to every wandering bark,
Whose worth's unknown, although his height° be taken.   *altitude*

SONNET 116.   2 *impediments*: a reference to "The Order of Solemnization of Matrimony" in the Anglican *Book of Common Prayer*: "I require that if either of you know any impediment why ye may not be lawfully joined together in Matrimony, ye do now confess it."

Love's not Time's fool,° though rosy lips and cheeks   *slave*
Within his° bending sickle's compass come;   *Time's*   10
Love alters not with his brief hours and weeks,
But bears it out even to the edge of doom.°   *The Last Judgment*
If this be error and upon me proved,
I never writ, nor no man ever loved.

QUESTIONS

1. What is the meter of this poem? The rhyme scheme? The closed form?
2. What point does the speaker make about love in the first quatrain?
3. With what is love metaphorically compared in the second quatrain? What
    qualities does the speaker assert that love has?
4. What opposes love in the third quatrain? What idea about love is explored
    here?
5. How does the couplet clinch the ideas and emotions of the poem?
6. To what extent is the argument of this poem organized by its closed form?

We recognize almost immediately that this poem is a Shakespearean
sonnet; it is written in iambic pentameter and is composed of three quatrains
and a concluding couplet, rhyming *a b a b, c d c d, e f e f, g g.* The general
topic is love, specifically the love or "marriage of true minds." The sonnet
puts forward the idea that love, when based on the union of true minds
or spirits, is unaffected by time and change. The sonnet form provides
shape and organization for the poem's argument; each quatrain advances
a different restatement of the poem's central thought. The final couplet
offers a summation of the argument and clinches the central idea through
rhyme.

The first quatrain advances the *thesis* of the sonnet: true and permanent
love is based on the "marriage of true minds." This kind of love will not
"admit impediments"; nothing will stand in its way. In addition, it will
not change even though the lovers might change ("alteration") or be separated ("remove"). The rhetorical strategy here is negation; the speaker
tells us what true love is *not.* This strategy is indicated by the phrases
"Let me not" and "Love is not." The allusion to the Anglican marriage
ceremony in the term *impediments* makes the tone of this quatrain public
and ceremonial, as though the lines were being spoken during a wedding
or a formal social occasion.

In lines 5–8 the speaker illustrates the permanence of true love by
comparing it to "an ever-fixéd mark" and "the star." The metaphor here
is nautical and navigational; love is compared to an unchanging beacon
and to a fixed star guiding sailors. The "ever-fixéd mark" is unaffected
by changes and turbulence in the world; it "looks on tempests and is never
shaken" (line 6). Similarly, the star is fixed and permanent; although its

"worth" or inner nature might be unknown, its "height" or altitude is known and always dependable in navigation. This quatrain reverses the rhetorical strategy of the first; it tells us what true love *is* rather than what it is not.

The third quatrain returns to the negative strategy of the first, and the speaker asserts that love is "not Time's fool." Time metaphorically becomes a reaper whose sickle eventually cuts down all living things. The speaker admits that time can destroy the physical beauty of the lovers, the "rosy lips and cheeks." Nevertheless, love itself is not subject to the power ("compass") of time; "Love alters not with his [Time's] brief hours and weeks" (line 11). To the contrary, real love will last until the very brink ("the edge") of the Last Judgment.

In the concluding couplet the speaker returns to the public and formal tone of the first quatrain. He invites rebuttal to his assertions about love in the conditional phrasing of line 13—"If this be error, and upon me proved"—and he offers two proofs that his ideas are valid. One of these is the poem itself; the speaker claims that if he is not correct, then "I never writ." Since the poem proves that the speaker wrote, its presence supports the speaker's assertions about love. For the second proof the speaker claims that if he is wrong then "no man ever loved." Because men have obviously loved, the speaker's argument must be valid. In both proofs we must be willing to accept the speaker's conditions in order to validate his conclusions. The couplet thus brings the sonnet neatly to a close. The final two lines and the two rhyming words—*proved* and *loved*—clinch the central idea introduced in the first quatrain.

OPEN-FORM POETRY

As we noted earlier, poets who write in open rather than closed forms avoid the ready-made patterns of traditional structures such as the ballad or sonnet. Similarly, they do not use such traditional devices as rhyme schemes or regular meters to organize their poems. Instead, they look for other ways of organizing letters, words, lines, and sentences into cohesive and effective poetic statements. In many respects, open forms have come to dominate modern and contemporary poetry. As we shall see, however, writing open-form verse is no easier than writing closed forms; it is a different process and concerns itself with different variables.

Open-form poetry was once termed **free verse** (from the French *vers libre*) to signify its freedom from regular metrical rules and its dependence on the rhythms of spoken language. That term is not really appropriate, however. While open-form poetry is indeed liberated from the rigid demands of meter, rhyme, and stanza, there is nothing *free* about the poems; they reflect different types of patterns.

OPEN FORM AND MEANING

Poets who write in open forms must develop a new set of organizing principles for each poem. They give up the shaping power of traditional devices
such as meter, rhyme, and stanza; in exchange, they gain the freedom to
create a new kind of fusion between form and content based on such
devices as rhythm and cadence, line lengths and breaks, pauses, and the
groupings of words and phrases. Poets working in open forms can also
isolate specific words or phrases in a single line and employ the white
spaces within and without a poem for emphasis. They may even write
poems that look exactly like prose and are printed in paragraphs instead
of stanzas or lines. These **prose poems** rely on the cadences of language
and the progression of images to convey the poetic experience. As a general
rule, we should remember that most open-form poetry is neither disorganized nor formless. On the contrary, each poem simultaneously seeks and
speaks its own principles of structure.

   We can see an early instance of open-form poetry in Walt Whitman's
"Reconciliation." It was written as part of *Drum Taps*, a collection of 53
poems concerned with the poet's reaction to Civil War battles in Virginia.

WALT WHITMAN   (1819–1892)

Reconciliation   *1865, 1881*

Word over all, beautiful as the sky,
Beautiful that war and all its deeds of carnage must in time be utterly lost,
That the hands of the sisters Death and Night incessantly softly wash again, and
   ever again, this soil'd world;
For my enemy is dead, a man divine as myself is dead,
I look where he lies white-faced and still in the coffin—I draw near,   5
Bend down and touch lightly with my lips the white face in the coffin.

QUESTIONS

   1. How do individual lines, varying line lengths, punctuation, pauses, and ca-
      dences create rhythm and organize the images and ideas in this poem?
   2. To what extent does alliteration, assonance, and the repetition of words unify
      the poem and reinforce its content?
   3. What is the "word" referred to in line 1? What does the speaker find "beautiful"
      about this "word" and the passage of time?
   4. What instances of personification can you find? What do these personified
      figures do? What does the speaker do in lines 5–6? Why does he do this?

Whitman's "Reconciliation" is an example of open-form poetry; the poem has no dominant meter, rhyme scheme, or stanza pattern. Instead, the poet uses the individual lines and varying line lengths to organize and emphasize the ideas, images, and emotions. He also employs repetition and alliteration to hold each line together, link it to the next, and reinforce meaning. In addition, the punctuation, caesurae (the pause separating cadence groups), and cadences create a strong rhythm when the poem is read aloud.

Line 1 introduces the "word over all" that is "beautiful as the sky." The word may be "peace," "reconciliation," God's word, or even the words of the poem. In any event, the "word" leads to peace and reconciliation in the poem. This image and idea are emphasized by the shortness of this line and its division, by punctuation, into two coequal cadences.

The idea of the "word" is linked through the repetition of *beautiful* and *all* with the idea that war and its carnage "must in time be utterly lost" (line 2). This idea, in turn, is linked through the repetition of *that* to the image of the two personified figures, Death and Night, who "wash" war and carnage out of "this soil'd world" (line 3). In this line, unity and emphasis are created through the repetition of *again* and the alliteration on the "*ly*" sound of *incessantly* and *softly*, the "*s*" sound in *hands, sisters, incessantly, softly,* and *soil'd,* and the "*d*" sound in *hands, Death, soil'd,* and *World.* The punctuation and pauses of the line break it up into units of sound and thought that create a remarkable internal rhythm: "That the hands // of the sisters // Death // and Night // incessantly softly wash // again, // and ever again, // this soil'd world."

To this point, each line has introduced a new idea and a new image, but repetition provides continuity. In addition, the first three lines are held together by the alliteration on the "*w*" sound in *word, war, wash,* and *world.* These "*w*" sounds, combined with the "*s*" sounds in line 3, create a soft and whispering tone that underscores the pathos and desolation of the scene.

In line 4 we become aware of two characters, a more immediate situation, and a symbol of the carnage of war—the corpse of the speaker's enemy. Again, the line is unified and its ideas emphasized through repetition of the words *is dead* and the "*ĕ*" sound in *enemy, dead,* and *myself.* The second part of the line, which is broken into three cadences by caesurae, establishes the common humanity and divinity of the speaker and his enemy.

This commonality and the central idea of reconciliation are reasserted in lines 5–6, when the speaker approaches the coffin, bends down, and kisses the face of his enemy. Again, the images and actions are contained within separate natural cadences of speech that create a rhythm—"I look where he lies // white-faced and still // in the coffin— // I draw near." Similarly, repetition stresses the key ideas and unifies the lines. Here the pattern of repetition includes the *I, white-faced,* and *coffin,* and alliteration on the sound "*l*" in *look, lies, still, lightly,* and *lips.*

VISUAL POETRY AND CONCRETE POETRY

In **visual poetry,** much of the impact comes from the appearance of the poem as a shape on the page. Some visual poetry seeks to strike a balance between the pleasures of seeing and those of hearing the poem; other visual poetry, however, abandons sound completely and invests all its impact in our perception of the visual image or picture. In any event, all visual poetry must sacrifice the pleasures of hearing the poem to some extent since the impact of the form depends on *seeing* it.

Visual poetry is not a recent development; the Chinese have been producing it for thousands of years, and there are surviving examples from ancient Greece. Even in the English tradition, visual poetry dates back to the seventeenth century when ingenious writers created poems in the shapes of squares, circles, triangles, stars, and the like. This type of poetry, called **shaped verse,** was usually more ingenious than significant; there was rarely an organic connection between the shape and the sense of the poem. Exceptional poets, however, produced shaped verse in which the visual image and the meaning strikingly echoed each other.

Although picture poems have existed for many years, they experienced a revival after World War II when visual poetry burst back onto the literary landscape with the birth of a new movement called **concrete poetry.** Poets who work in this tradition focus their attention almost completely on the medium from which the poem is created. In the case of printed work, this means that the writers pay far more attention to the visual arrangement of letters, words, lines, and white spaces than they do to ideas or emotions. Concrete poetry represents a fusion of writing with painting or graphic design, and the emphasis is on the side of the visual arts. The concrete poet is interested in the poem mostly as an object or an image rather than as an expression. For these poets, structure becomes both the means and the end of creation.

FORM AND MEANING IN VISUAL POETRY

In reading visual and concrete poetry, you should seek whatever correspondence may exist between the image and the words. In your consideration, include the shape of the poem, the connotations of this shape, the varying line lengths, the placement of individual words and phrases, and the use of white spaces. We can see a superb example of seventeenth-century visual poetry in George Herbert's "Easter Wings," a poem that offers two different pictures that are both relevant to the content.

This poem is an admission of sin and a prayer for redemption. It compares humanity's fall from grace ("wealth and store") in Eden to the spiritual state of the speaker, who seeks salvation through Christ's sacrifice.

When viewed sideways, the poem resembles a pair of angel's wings. This image is thus linked with the title of the poem and connotes Christ's rising, salvation, and divine grace.

The correspondence between shape and meaning goes even farther. Herbert employs typography to echo the content of each line. Thus, in discussing the spiritual history of humanity, the original "wealth and store" of Eden are described in a line having the broadest (fullest) width. But as the fall from grace is described, the lines get progressively shorter (thinner), until humanity's fallen state is reached in the narrowest, "most poor" line (line 5). This same typographical pattern is repeated in lines 11–15, to describe the sinful state that has left the speaker spiritually "most thin." In the second half of each stanza, this typographical pattern is reversed and the lines gradually expand, echoing the speaker's prayers for grace and salvation. Thus, the fullness of lines 10 and 20 reflects the original states of grace, described in lines 1 and 11, and the glorious wealth of redemption.

GEORGE HERBERT   (1593–1633)

Easter Wings   *1633*

Lord, who createdst man in wealth and store,°   *abundance*
  Though foolishly he lost the same,
    Decaying more and more
      Till he became
        Most poor: 5
        With thee
        O let me rise
      As larks, harmoniously,
    And sing this day thy victories:
Then shall the fall further the flight in me.   10

My tender age in sorrow did begin:
  And still with sicknesses and shame
    Thou didst so punish sin,
      That I became
        Most thin.   15
        With thee
        Let me combine,
      And feel this day thy victory;
    For, if I imp° my wing on thine,
Affliction shall advance the flight in me.   20

EASTER WINGS.   19 *imp*: to repair a falcon's wing or tail by grafting on a feather.

QUESTIONS

1. What does the poem look like when viewed sideways? When viewed straight on? How do these two images echo and emphasize the poem's content?
2. How does the typographical arrangement of the lines of this poem echo the sense? As a starting point, consider lines 5 and 15. How are typography, shape, and meaning fused in these lines?
3. What do lines 1–5 tell you about humanity's spiritual history? What do lines 11–15 tell you about the speaker's spiritual state? How are these parallel?
4. Who or what is the speaker? The listener? What does the speaker want? What is the connection between this desire and the title of the poem?

POEMS FOR STUDY

JOHN MILTON   (1608–1674)

When I Consider How My Light Is Spent°   *1655*

When I consider how my light is spent   a
   Ere half my days, in this dark world and wide,   b
   And that one talent° which is death to hide,   b
   Lodged with me useless, though my soul more bent   a
To serve therewith my Maker, and present   a   5
   My true account, lest he returning chide;   b
   "Doth God exact day-labor, light denied?"   b
I fondly° ask; but Patience to prevent°   a   *foolishly; forestall*
That murmur, soon replies, "God doth not need   c
   Either man's work or his own gifts; who best   d   10
   Bear his mild yoke, they serve him best. His state e
Is kingly. Thousands at his bidding speed   c
   And post o'er land and ocean without rest; d
   They also serve who only stand and wait." e

WHEN I CONSIDER HOW MY LIGHT IS SPENT. Milton began to go blind in the late 1640s and was completely blind by 1651.   3 *talent:* both a skill and a reference to the talents discussed in the parable in Matthew 25: 14–30.

QUESTIONS

1. What is the meter of this poem? The rhyme scheme? The closed form?
2. To what extent do the two major divisions of this form organize the poem's ideas?
3. What problem is raised in the octave? What are the speaker's complaints? Who is the speaker in the sestet? How are the conflicts raised in the octave resolved?

4. Explore the word *talent* and relate its various meanings to the poem as a whole. To understand the term fully, you should refer to the parable in Matthew and see what the term represents there.

PERCY BYSSHE SHELLEY   (1792–1822)

Ozymandias   *1818*

I met a traveller from an antique land,
Who said—"Two vast and trunkless legs of stone
Stand in the desert. . . . Near them, on the sand,
Half sunk, a shattered visage lies, whose frown,
And wrinkled lip, and sneer of cold command,   5
Tell that its sculptor well those passions read
Which yet survive, stamped on these lifeless things,
The hand that mocked them, and the heart that fed;
And on the pedestal, these words appear;
'My name is Ozymandias, King of Kings,   10
Look on my Works, ye Mighty, and despair!'
Nothing beside remains. Round the decay
Of that colossal Wreck, boundless and bare
The lone and level sands stretch far away."

QUESTIONS

1. What is the meter of this poem? The rhyme scheme? What traditional closed form is modified here? How do the modifications affect the poem?

2. To what extent are content and meaning shaped by the closed form? What is described in the octave? In the sestet?

3. Characterize Ozymandias (Ramses II, Pharoah of Egypt, who died in 1225 B.C.) from the way he is portrayed in this poem.

4. Into how many pieces is the statue of Ozymandias shattered? What is the effect of distributing these fragments throughout the poem? Whose "hand" and "heart" are mentioned in line 8?

5. What point does this poem make about power? Time? Art?

CLAUDE McKAY   (1890–1948)

In Bondage   *1953*

I would be wandering in distant fields
Where man, and bird, and beast, lives leisurely,
And the old earth is kind, and ever yields

Her goodly gifts to all her children free;
Where life is fairer, lighter, less demanding,   5
And boys and girls have time and space for play
Before they come to years of understanding—
Somewhere I would be singing, far away.
For life is greater than the thousand wars
Men wage for it in their insatiate lust,   10
And will remain like the eternal stars,
When all that shines to-day is drift and dust.

But I am bound with you in your mean graves,
O black men, simple slaves of ruthless slaves.

QUESTIONS

1. What is the meter of this poem? The rhyme scheme? The form? To what
    extent does the form organize the speaker's thoughts?
2. Lines 1–8 present a conditional (rather than actual) situation that the speaker
    desires. What word signals this conditional nature? What is the speaker's
    wish?
3. What point does the speaker make about life in lines 9–12?
4. To what extent does the couplet undermine the rest of the poem? What
    single word conveys this reversal? How effectively do the rhymes in the couplet
    clinch the poem's meaning? What is the speaker telling us about the lives
    of black people?

JOHN DRYDEN   (1631–1700)

To the Memory of Mr. Oldham   *1684*

Farewell, too little and too lately known,
Whom I began to think and call my own:
For sure our souls were near allied, and thine
Cast in the same poetic mold with mine.
One common note on either lyre did strike,   5
And knaves and fools we both abhorred alike.
To the same goal did both our studies drive;
The last set out the soonest did arrive.
Thus Nisus° fell upon the slipp'ry place,
While his young friend performed and won the race.   10
O early ripe! to thy abundant store

TO THE MEMORY OF MR. OLDHAM. John Oldham (1653–1683) was a young poet whom
Dryden admired.   9 *Nisus:* a character in Vergil's *Aeneid* who slipped in a pool of blood
while running a race, thus allowing his best friend to win.

What could advancing age have added more?
It might (what nature never gives the young)
Have taught the numbers of thy native tongue.
But satire needs not those, and wit will shine   15
Through the harsh cadence of a rugged line;
A noble error, and but seldom made,
When poets are by too much force betrayed.
Thy gen'rous fruits, though gathered ere their prime,
Still showed a quickness; and maturing time   20
But mellows what we write to the dull sweets of rhyme.
Once more, hail and farewell;° farewell, thou young.
But ah too short, Marcellus° of our tongue;
Thy brows with ivy and with laurels° bound;
But fate and gloomy night encompass thee around.   25

22 *hail and farewell*: an echo of the Latin phrase "ave atque vale" spoken by gladiators about
to fight   23 *Marcellus*: a Roman general who was adopted by the Emperor Augustus as
his successor but died at the age of twenty.   24 *laurels*: a plant sacred to Apollo, the
Greek god of poetry; the traditional prize given to poets is a wreath of laurel.

QUESTIONS

1. What is the meter of this poem? The rhyme scheme? The closed form?
    How does the form control the poem's pace or tempo? Why is this tempo
    appropriate?

2. What does the speaker reveal about himself in lines 1–10? About Oldham?
    About his relationship with Oldham? What did the two have in common?

3. What point does the speaker make about Oldham's death in lines 11–25?
    How might his death have been an advantage?

4. What is the effect of Dryden's frequent classical allusions? Which pairs of
    rhyming words most effectively clinch ideas?

JEAN TOOMER   (1894–1967)

Reapers   *1923*

Black reapers with the sound of steel on stones
Are sharpening scythes. I see them place the hones
In their hip-pockets as a thing that's done,
And start their silent swinging, one by one.
Black horses drive a mower through the weeds,   5
And there, a field rat, startled, squealing bleeds,
His belly close to ground. I see the blade,
Blood-stained, continue cutting weeds and shade.

QUESTIONS

1. What is the meter of this poem? The rhyme scheme? The form? How does Toomer use the same form as Dryden (in "Mr. Oldham") in a different way?
2. What are the central images of this poem? How do they relate to each other? How does the image of the bleeding field rat and the "blood-stained" blade heighten the emotional impact?
3. How does alliteration unify this poem and make sound echo sense? Note especially the "*s*" and "*b*" sounds, and the phrase *silent swinging*.
4. What feeling is created by this poem? What does the poem tell us about the lives of black reapers?

GEORGE HERBERT (1593–1633)

Virtue   *1633*

Sweet day, so cool, so calm, so bright,
The bridal of the earth and sky:
The dew shall weep thy fall tonight;
    For thou must die.

Sweet rose, whose hue, angry° and brave,°   *red; splendid*   5
Bids the rash gazer wipe his eye:
Thy root is ever in its grave,
    And thou must die.

Sweet spring, full of sweet days and roses,
A box where sweets° compacted lie: *perfumes*   10
My music shows ye have your closes,°
    And all must die.

Only a sweet and virtuous soul,
Like seasoned timber, never gives;
But though the whole world turn to coal,°   15
    Then chiefly lives.

VIRTUE.   11 *closes*: the musical term for the concluding cadences in songs.   15 *coal*: reduced to ash at the Last Judgment.

QUESTIONS

1. What is the rhyme scheme of this poem? The meter? The form?
2. What point does the speaker make about the "day" in lines 1–4? The "rose" in lines 5–8? The "spring" in lines 9–12? The "soul" in lines 13–16?

3. How does the poet draw the images of the first two stanzas into the third? What do the day, rose, and spring have in common? How is the "virtuous soul" different?
4. To what extent do the rhyme scheme and stanzaic structure of this poem shape and reinforce the poem's theme?

ROBERT FROST   (1874–1963)

Desert Places   *1936*

Snow falling and night falling fast, oh, fast
In a field I looked into going past,
And the ground almost covered smooth in snow,
But a few weeds and stubble showing last.

The woods around it have it—it is theirs.   5
All animals are smothered in their lairs.
I am too absent-spirited to count;
The loneliness includes me unawares.

And lonely as it is that loneliness
Will be more lonely ere it will be less—   10
A blanker whiteness of benighted snow
With no expression, nothing to express.

They cannot scare me with their empty spaces
Between stars—on stars where no human race is.
I have it in me so much nearer home   15
To scare myself with my own desert places.

QUESTIONS

1. What is the meter? The rhyme scheme? The form?
2. What setting and situation are established in lines 1–4? What does the snow affect here? What does it affect in lines 5–8? In lines 9–12?
3. What different kinds of "desert places" is this poem about? Which kind is the most important? Most frightening?
4. How does the type of rhyme (rising or falling) change in the last stanza? To what extent does this change affect the tone and impact of the poem?
5. How does the stanzaic pattern of this poem organize the progression of the speaker's thoughts, feelings, and conclusions?

JOHN KEATS   (1795–1821)

Ode to a Nightingale   *1819*

1

My heart aches, and a drowsy numbness pains
  My sense, as though of hemlock° I had drunk,   *a poisonous herb*
Or emptied some dull opiate to the drains
  One minute past, and Lethe-wards° had sunk:
'Tis not through envy of thy happy lot,   5
  But being too happy in thine happiness,—
    That thou, light-winged Dryad° of the trees,
      In some melodious plot
  Of beechen green, and shadows numberless,
  Singest of summer in full-throated ease.   10

2

O, for a draught of vintage! that hath been
Cool'd a long age in the deep-delved earth,
Tasting of Flora° and the country green,
Dance, and Provençal song, and sunburnt mirth!
O for a beaker full of the warm South,   15
  Full of the true, the blushful Hippocrene,°
    With beaded bubbles winking at the brim,
      And purple-stained mouth;
  That I might drink, and leave the world unseen,
  And with thee fade away into the forest dim: 20

3

Fade far away, dissolve, and quite forget
  What thou among the leaves hast never known,
The weariness, the fever, and the fret
  Here, where men sit and hear each other groan;
Where palsy shakes a few, sad, last gray hairs,   25
  Where youth grows pale, and spectre-thin, and dies;
    Where but to think is to be full of sorrow
      And leaden-eyed despairs,
  Where Beauty cannot keep her lustrous eyes,
  Or new Love pine at them beyond to-morrow.   30

ODE TO A NIGHTINGALE.   4 *Lethe-wards*: toward the river of forgetfulness in Hades,
the underworld of Greek mythology.   7 *Dryad*: in Greek mythology, a semidivine tree
spirit.   13 *Flora*: the Roman goddess of flowers.   16 *Hippocrene*: the fountain of the
Muses on Mt. Helicon in Greek mythology; the phrase thus refers to both the waters of
poetic inspiration and a cup of wine.

4

Away! away! for I will fly to thee,
    Not charioted by Bacchus° and his pards,°   *leopards*
But on the viewless wings of Poesy,°   *poetry*
    Though the dull brain perplexes and regards:
Already with thee! tender is the night,   35
    And haply the Queen-Moon is on her throne,
        Cluster'd around by all her starry Fays;°   *fairies*
            But here there is no light,
    Save what from heaven is with the breezes blown
    Through verdurous glooms and winding mossy ways.   40

5

I cannot see what flowers are at my feet,
    Nor what soft incense hangs upon the boughs,
But, in embalmed° darkness, guess each sweet   *fragrant*
    Wherewith the seasonable month endows
The grass, the thicket, and the fruit-tree wild;   45
    White hawthorn, and the pastoral eglantine;°   *honeysuckle*
        Fast fading violets cover'd up in leaves;
            And mid-May's eldest child,
    The coming musk-rose, full of dewy wine,
        The murmurous haunt of flies on summer eves.   50

6

Darkling° I listen; and, for many a time   *in the dark*
    I have been half in love with easeful Death,
Call'd him soft names in many a mused rhyme,
    To take into the air my quiet breath;
Now more than ever seems it rich to die,   55
    To cease upon the midnight with no pain,
        While thou art pouring forth thy soul abroad
            In such an ecstasy!
    Still wouldst thou sing, and I have ears in vain—
        To thy high requiem become a sod.   60

7

Thou wast not born for death, immortal Bird!
    No hungry generations tread thee down;
The voice I hear this passing night was heard
    In ancient days by emperor and clown:
Perhaps the self-same song that found a path   65
    Through the sad heart of Ruth,° when, sick for home,
        She stood in tears amid the alien corn;°   *wheat*
            The same that oft-times hath
    Charm'd magic casements, opening on the foam
        Of perilous seas, in faery lands forlorn.   70

32 *Bacchus*: the Greek god of wine.   66 *Ruth*: the widow of Boaz in the biblical Book of
Ruth.

8

Forlorn! the very word is like a bell
  To toll me back from thee to my sole self!
Adieu! the fancy° cannot cheat so well   *imagination*
  As she is fam'd to do, deceiving elf.
Adieu! adieu! thy plaintive anthem fades   75
  Past the near meadows, over the still stream,
    Up the hill-side; and now 'tis buried deep
      In the next valley-glades:
  Was it a vision, or a waking dream?
    Fled is that music:—Do I wake or sleep?   80

QUESTIONS

1. Formulate the structure (meter of each line and rhyme scheme) of the first
    stanza, and then see if it is repeated in the second and third. What traditional
    form is employed here?

2. What is the speaker's mental and emotional state in stanza 1? What similes
    are employed to describe this condition?

3. What does the speaker want in stanza 2? Whom does he want to join? Why?
    From what aspects of the world (stanza 3) does he want to escape?

4. How do the speaker's mood and perspective change in stanza 4? How does
    he achieve this transition? What characterizes the world that the speaker
    enters in stanza 5? What senses are employed to describe this world?

5. In the sixth stanza the speaker comes up with another way of achieving a
    visionary state. What is it? Why will it not work?

6. What does the speaker establish about the nightingale's song in the seventh
    stanza? What does the song come to symbolize?

PERCY BYSSHE SHELLEY   (1792–1822)

Ode to the West Wind   *1820*

I

O wild West Wind, thou breath° of Autumn's being,
Thou, from whose unseen presence the leaves dead
Are driven, like ghosts from an enchanter fleeing,

Yellow, and black, and pale, and hectic° red,
Pestilence-stricken multitudes: O Thou,   5
Who chariotest to their dark wintry bed

ODE TO THE WEST WIND.   4 *hectic*: a tubercular fever that produces flushed
cheeks.

The winged seeds, where they lie cold and low,
Each like a corpse within its grave, until
Thine azure sister of the Spring° shall blow

Her clarion o'er the dreaming earth, and fill   10
(Driving sweet buds like flocks to feed in air)
With living hues and odours plain and hill:

Wild Spirit, which art moving everywhere;
Destroyer and Preserver; hear, O hear!

                                        II
Thou on whose stream, 'mid the steep sky's commotion,   15
Loose clouds like Earth's decaying leaves are shed,
Shook from the tangled boughs of Heaven and Ocean,

Angels of rain and lightning: there are spread
On the blue surface of thine aery surge,
Like the bright hair uplifted from the head   20

Of some fierce Maenad,° even from the dim verge
Of the horizon to the zenith's height,
The locks of the approaching storm. Thou Dirge

Of the dying year, to which this closing night
Will be the dome of a vast sepulchre,   25
Vaulted with all thy congregated might

Of vapours,° from whose solid atmosphere   *clouds*
Black rain and fire and hail will burst: O hear!

                                        III
Thou who didst waken from his summer dreams
The blue Mediterranean, where he lay,   30
Lulled by the coil of his crystalline streams,

Beside a pumice isle in Baiae's bay,°
And saw in sleep old palaces and towers
Quivering within the wave's intenser day,

All overgrown with azure moss and flowers   35
So sweet, the sense faints picturing them! Thou
For whose path the Atlantic's level powers

Cleave themselves into chasms, while far below
The sea-blooms and the oozy woods which wear
The sapless foliage of the ocean, know   40

Thy voice, and suddenly grow grey with fear,
And tremble and despoil themselves: O hear!

9 *Spring*: the wind that will blow in the spring.   21 *Maenad*: a frenzied female worshipper
of Dionysus, the god of wine and fertility in Greek mythology.   32 *Baiae's bay*: a bay of
the Mediterranean Sea west of Naples, famous for the elaborate villas built on the shore by
Roman emperors.

IV

If I were a dead leaf thou mightest bear;
If I were a swift cloud to fly with thee;
A wave to pant beneath thy power, and share   45

The impulse of thy strength, only less free
Than thou, O Uncontrollable! If even
I were as in my boyhood, and could be

The comrade of thy wanderings over Heaven,
As then, when to outstrip thy skiey speed   50
Scarce seemed a vision; I would ne'er have striven

As thus with thee in prayer in my sore need,
Oh! lift me as a wave, a leaf, a cloud!
I fall upon thorns of life! I bleed!

A heavy weight of hours has chained and bowed   55
One too like thee: tameless, and swift, and proud.

V

Make me thy lyre,° even as the forest is:
What if my leaves are falling like its own!
The tumult of thy mighty harmonies

Will take from both a deep, autumnal tone,   60
Sweet though in sadness. Be thou, Spirit fierce,
My spirit! Be thou me, impetuous one!

Drive my dead thoughts over the universe
Like withered leaves to quicken a new birth!
And, by the incantation of this verse,   65

Scatter, as from an unextinguished hearth
Ashes and sparks, my words among mankind!
Be through my lips to unawakened Earth

The trumpet of a prophecy! O Wind,
If Winter comes, can Spring be far behind?   70

57 *lyre*: an Aeolian harp, a musical device which is sounded by the wind blowing across strings.

QUESTIONS

1. Formulate the structure (meter of each line and rhyme scheme) of the first stanza, and then see if it is repeated throughout the poem. What two traditional closed forms are combined in this poem?

2. How many times (and where) is the *e* rhyme of the first stanza repeated as a rhyme sound throughout the poem? What is the effect of this repetition?

3. What aspect of the natural world does the wind affect in the first section of the poem? The second section? The third?

4. What does the speaker assert (in section 4) that time has done to him? What does he want from the West Wind? What does he want to become?

5. To what extent are the thoughts and feelings of the speaker organized by the five sections of this poem? What is the logical progression from section to section?

6. What does the West Wind symbolize? Compare this poem to Keats's "Ode to a Nightingale." How are the nightingale's song and the West Wind related to each other as symbols?

DYLAN THOMAS   (1914–1953)

Do Not Go Gentle Into That Good Night   *1951*

Do not go gentle into that good night,
Old age should burn and rave at close of day;
Rage, rage against the dying of the light.

Though wise men at their end know dark is right,
Because their words had forked no lightning they   5
Do not go gentle into that good night.

Good men, the last wave by, crying how bright
Their frail deeds might have danced in a green bay,
Rage, rage against the dying of the light.

Wild men who caught and sang the sun in flight,   10
And learn, too late, they grieved it on its way,
Do not go gentle into that good night.

Grave men, near death, who see with blinding sight
Blind eyes could blaze like meteors and be gay,
Rage, rage against the dying of the light.   15

And you, my father, there on the sad height,
Curse, bless, me now with your fierce tears, I pray.
Do not go gentle into that good night.
Rage, rage against the dying of the light.

QUESTIONS

1. This poem is written in a traditional closed form called the **villanelle,** which was developed in France during the Middle Ages. A villanelle must be 19 lines long. There are additional rules governing the length and structure of stanzas, the rhyme scheme, and the repetition of complete lines. Try to formu-

late these rules. To look at another example, see Roethke's "The Waking"
(p. 968).

2. What can you surmise about the speaker here? The listener? The situation?

3. What four different kinds of men does the speaker discuss in lines 4–15? What do they have in common?

4. What puns and connotative words can you find in this poem? Consider the *good* of "good night" and the word *grave* (line 13).

5. What does the speaker want the listener to do? What is the poem's theme?

DUDLEY RANDALL (b. 1914)

Ballad of Birmingham   *1966*

(On the bombing of a church in Birmingham, Alabama, 1963)

"Mother dear, may I go downtown
Instead of out to play,
And march the streets of Birmingham
In a Freedom March today?"

"No, baby, no, you may not go,   5
For the dogs are fierce and wild,
And clubs and hoses, guns and jails
Aren't good for a little child."

"But, mother, I won't be alone.
Other children will go with me,   10
And march the streets of Birmingham
To make our country free."

"No, baby, no, you may not go,
For I fear those guns will fire.
But you may go to church instead   15
And sing in the children's choir."

She has combed and brushed her night-dark hair,
And bathed rose petal sweet,
And drawn white gloves on her small brown hands,
And white shoes on her feet.   20

The mother smiled to know her child
Was in the sacred place,
But that smile was the last smile
To come upon her face.

BALLAD OF BIRMINGHAM. Four black children were killed when the 16th Street Baptist Church in Birmingham, Alabama, was bombed in 1963. A man was finally indicted for the murders in 1977 and convicted in 1982.

For when she heard the explosion,   25
Her eyes grew wet and wild.
She raced through the streets of Birmingham
Calling for her child.

She clawed through bits of glass and brick,
Then lifted out a shoe   30
"Oh, here's the shoe my baby wore,
But, baby, where are you?"

QUESTIONS

1. Formulate the structure (meter, rhyme scheme, stanza form) of this poem. What traditional closed form is employed here?
2. Who is the speaker in stanzas 1 and 3? In stanzas 2 and 4? How are quotation and repetition employed to create tension?
3. What ironies do you find in the mother's assumptions? In the poem as a whole? In the society pictured in the poem?
4. Compare this poem to "Sir Patrick Spens" (p. 523) and to "Barbara Allan" (p. 901). How are the structures of all three alike? What devices do you find in all three? To what extent do all three deal with the same type of subject matter?

WALT WHITMAN   (1819–1892)

When I Heard the Learn'd Astronomer   1865

When I heard the learn'd astronomer,
When the proofs, the figures, were ranged in columns before me,
When I was shown the charts and diagrams, to add, divide, and measure them,
When I sitting heard the astronomer where he lectured with much applause in
    the lecture-room,
How soon unaccountable I became tired and sick,   5
Till rising and gliding out I wander'd off by myself,
In the mystical moist night-air, and from time to time,
Look'd up in perfect silence at the stars.

QUESTIONS

1. Is the form of this poem closed or open? Explain why.
2. How does Whitman use line lengths, phrases, and punctuation to create rhythm?
3. What are the effects produced by lists, repetitions, and alliteration?

E. E. CUMMINGS (1894–1962)

Buffalo Bill's Defunct°   1923

Buffalo Bill's
defunct
          who used to
          ride a watersmooth-silver
                              stallion   5
and break onetwothreefourfive pigeonsjustlikethat
                                        Jesus

he was a handsome man
                    and what i want to know is
how do you like your blueeyed boy   10
Mister Death

BUFFALO BILL'S DEFUNCT.   The poem has no title; it is usually referred to as "Portrait" or by its first two lines. Buffalo Bill (William F. Cody, 1846–1917) was an American plainsman, hunter, army scout, sharpshooter, and showman whose Wild West show began touring the world in 1883; he became a symbol of the Wild West.

QUESTIONS

1. What is the effect of devoting a whole line to *Buffalo Bill's* (line 1), *defunct* (line 2), *stallion* (line 5), *Jesus* (line 7), and *Mister Death* (line 11)? How does this technique reflect and emphasize the content of the poem?

2. How does the typographical arrangement of line 6 contribute to the fusion of sound and sense? What other examples of this technique are found in the poem?

3. Explain the denotations and connotations of *defunct*. What would be lost (or gained) by using the term *dead* or *deceased* instead?

4. To what extent is this poem a "portrait" of Buffalo Bill? What do we learn about him? Is the portrait respectful, mocking, or something in between?

WILLIAM CARLOS WILLIAMS (1883–1963)

The Dance   1944

In Breughel's° great picture, The Kermess,
the dancers go round, they go round and
around, the squeal and the blare and the
tweedle of bagpipes, a bugle and fiddles

THE DANCE.   1 *Breughel's*: Peter Breughel (c. 1525–1569), a Flemish painter who often portrayed a world of robust and joyful peasants. *The Kermess* shows peasants dancing in celebration of a feast day (see color plate 1).

tipping their bellies (round as the thick-   5
sided glasses whose wash they impound)
their hips and their bellies off balance
to turn them. Kicking and rolling about
the Fair Grounds, swinging their butts, those
shanks must be sound to bear up under such   10
rollicking measures, prance as they dance
in Breughel's great picture, The Kermess.

QUESTIONS

1. What effect is produced by repeating the first line of the poem as the last
    line?

2. How do repetition, alliteration, assonance, onomatopoeia, and internal rhyme
    affect the tempo, feeling, and meaning of the poem? How do the numerous
    participles (like *tipping*, *kicking*, *rolling*) make sound echo sense?

3. What words are capitalized? What effect is produced by omitting the capital
    letters at the beginning of each line? How does this typographical choice
    reinforce the sound and the sense of the poem?

4. Most of the lines of this poem are run-on rather than end-stopped, and
    many of them end with fairly weak words such as *and*, *the*, *about*, and *such*.
    What effect is produced through these techniques?

5. How successful is Williams in making the words and sentence rhythms of
    his poem echo the visual rhythms in Breughel's painting? Why is this open
    form more appropriate to the images of the poem than any closed form
    could be?

ALLEN GINSBERG   (b. 1926)

A Supermarket in California   1955

What thoughts I have of you tonight, Walt Whitman,° for
I walked down the sidestreets under the trees with a headache
self-conscious looking at the full moon.
    In my hungry fatigue, and shopping for images, I went   5
into the neon fruit supermarket, dreaming of your enumerations!°
What   peaches   and   what   penumbras!   Whole   families

A SUPERMARKET IN CALIFORNIA.   1 *Walt Whitman*: American poet (1819–1892) who
experimented with open forms and significantly influenced the development of twentieth-
century poetry in Europe and the Americas.   6 *enumerations*: many of Whitman's poems
contain long lists.

shopping at night! Aisles full of husbands! Wives in the avocados, babies in the tomatoes!—and you, Garcia Lorca,° what were you doing down by the watermelons?   10

I saw you, Walt Whitman, childless, lonely old grubber, poking among the meats in the refrigerator and eyeing the grocery boys.

I heard you asking questions of each: Who killed the pork chops? What price bananas? Are you my Angel?   15

I wandered in and out of the brilliant stacks of cans following you, and followed in my imagination by the store detective.

We strode down the open corridors together in our solitary fancy tasting artichokes, possessing every frozen delicacy, and   20
never passing the cashier.

Where are we going, Walt Whitman? The doors close in an hour. Which way does your beard point tonight?

(I touch your book and dream of our odyssey in the supermarket and feel absurd.)   25

Will we walk all night through solitary streets? The trees add shade to shade, lights out in the houses, we'll both be lonely.

Will we stroll dreaming of the lost America of love past blue automobiles in driveways, home to our silent cottage?   30

Ah, dear father, graybeard, lonely old courage-teacher, what America did you have when Charon° quit poling his ferry and you got out on a smoking bank and stood watching the boat disappear on the black waters of Lethe?°

---

9 *Garcia Lorca*: Spanish surrealist poet and playwright (1896–1936) whose late poetry became progressively more like prose.   32 *Charon*: boatman in Greek mythology who ferried the souls of the dead across the river Styx into Hades, the underworld.   34 *Lethe*: the river of forgetfulness in Hades. The dead drank from this river and forgot their former lives.

QUESTIONS

1. Where is the speaker? What is he doing? What is his problem? His condition?

2. What effect is produced by placing Whitman and Lorca in the market?

3. To what extent do we find Whitman-like enumerations in this work? What is the effect of such enumerations?

4. Why is this a poem? What poetic devices are employed here? To what extent might it make more sense to consider this prose rather than poetry?

NIKKI GIOVANNI   (b. 1943)

Nikki-Rosa   *1968*

childhood remembrances are always a drag
if you're Black
you always remember things like living in Woodlawn°
with no inside toilet
and if you become famous or something   5
they never talk about how happy you were to have your mother
all to yourself and
how good the water felt when you got your bath from one of those
big tubs that folk in chicago barbecue in
and somehow when you talk about home   10
it never gets across how much you
understood their feelings
as the whole family attended meetings about Hollydale
and even though you remember
your biographers never understand   15
your father's pain as he sells his stock
and another dream goes
and though you're poor it isn't poverty that
concerns you
and though they fought a lot   20
it isn't your father's drinking that makes any difference
but only that everybody is together and you
and your sister have happy birthdays and very good christmasses
and I really hope no white person ever has cause to write about me
because they never understand Black love is Black wealth and they'll   25
probably talk about my hard childhood and never understand that
all the while I was quite happy

NIKKI-ROSA.   3 *Woodlawn*: a predominantly black suburb of Cincinnati, Ohio.

QUESTIONS

1. To what extent do individual lines, caesurae, and cadences create a rhythm
   and reinforce the sense of this poem?
2. What points does the speaker make about childhood in general, the childhoods
   of blacks, and his or her own childhood? What images of childhood are
   evoked?
3. What is the speaker's attitude toward himself or herself? What expectations
   does the speaker seem to have?
4. What ideas about the ways in which whites understand or misunderstand
   blacks does this poem explore?

MAY SWENSON (b. 1919)

Women   *1968*

<pre>
Women   Or they
  should be   should be
    pedestals   little horses
      moving   those wooden
        pedestals   sweet   5
          moving   oldfashioned
          to the   painted
        motions   rocking
          of men   horses

        the gladdest things in the toyroom   10

          The   feelingly
          pegs   and then
          of their   unfeelingly
          ears   To be
          so familiar   joyfully   15
          and dear   ridden
        to the trusting rockingly
      fists   ridden until
  To be chafed   the restored

egos dismount and the legs stride away   20

Immobile   willing
  sweetlipped   to be set
    sturdy   into motion
      and smiling   Women
        women   should be   25
          should always   pedestals
            be waiting   to men
</pre>

QUESTIONS

1. Is this poem an instance of closed form, open form, or visual poetry? In what different ways or sequences can it be read? How do the different sequences change the meaning?

2. How well does the image of the poem reinforce its meaning? Would the effect be different if the columns of words were straight instead of undulating?

3. How does the typography affect rhythm and emphasize meaning? Note especially isolated words, the arrangements of lines 10 and 20, and capitalization.

4. To what extent do repetition and alliteration help to organize the poem and underscore its sense. Note especially the "*w*," "*m*," "*f*," "*r*," and "*s*" sounds.

5. What does this poem *say* that women should be? Does it mean what it says?

How are men characterized? What is the speaker's attitude toward men? In what ways might this poem be ironic?

MARY ELLEN SOLT   (b. 1920)

Forsythia   *1966*

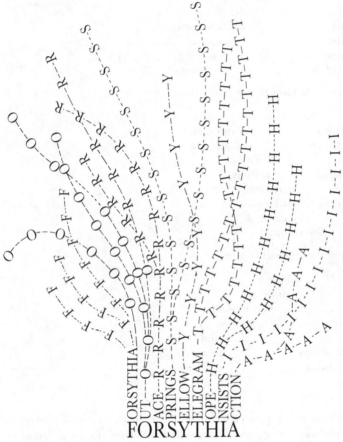

QUESTIONS

1. Is this a poem or is it rather what is called in art a "wordwork"? What does this work tell you about forsythia?

2. When this work was originally published, it was printed over a square of yellow. What additional visual effect might have been produced by this field of yellow?

3. What is the significance of the dots and dashes placed between each letter of "FORSYTHIA"? What is the link between this device and the word "TELE-GRAM"?

4. What meaning or emotion, if any, does this work convey beyond its visual image? Is this a poem, an object of graphic art, or both?

EDWIN MORGAN (b. 1920)

The Computer's First Christmas Card   1968

```
jollymerry
hollyberry
jollyberry
merryholly
happyjolly                                                    5
jollyjelly
jellybelly
bellymerry
hollyheppy
jollyMolly                                                    10
marryJerry
merryHarry
hoppyBarry
heppyJarry
boppyheppy                                                    15
berryjorry
jorryjolly
moppyjelly
Mollymerry
Jerryjolly                                                    20
bellyboppy
jorryhoppy
hollymoppy
Barrymerry
Jarryhappy                                                    25
happyboppy
boppyjolly
jollymerry
merrymerry
merrymerry                                                    30
merryChris
ammerryasa
Chrismerry
asMERRYCHR
YSANTHEMUM                                                    35
```

QUESTIONS

1. To what extent is the effect of this work visual? What aspects or devices link it to a computer?
2. The writer (or computer) has generated some interesting word variations

and images. To what extent can you find logic in the movement from line
to line?

3. How successful is this work in conveying ideas or images of Christmas? How
far away from Christmas does "the computer" wander? What do you make
of the fact that the work ends "asMERRYCHR / YSANTHEMUM"?

4. Why might you consider this a poem?

JOHN HOLLANDER   (b. 1929)

Swan and Shadow   *1969*

```
                          Dusk
                        Above the
                     water hang the
                          loud
                          flies                                        5
                          Here
                          O so
                          gray
                          then
                     What              A pale signal will appear       10
                     When            Soon before its shadow fades
                     Where           Here in this pool of opened eye
                     In us       No Upon us As at the very edges
                         of where we take shape in the dark air
                           this object bares its image awakening       15
                           ripples of recognition that will
                              brush darkness up into light
even after this bird this hour both drift by atop the perfect sad instant now
                           already passing out of sight
                         toward yet-untroubled reflection              20
                         this image bears its object darkening
                     into memorial shades Scattered bits of
                     light        No of water Or something across
                     water            Breaking up No Being regathered
                     soon               Yet by then a swan will have    25
                     gone                   Yes out of mind into what
                          vast
                          pale
                          hush
                          of a                                         30
                          place
                          past
                     sudden dark as
                        if a swan
                          sang                                         35
```

QUESTIONS

1. How effectively and consistently does the shape image reinforce the meaning?
2. What specific words, phrases, and lines are emphasized by the typographical arrangement? To what extent does this effect give added impact to the poem?
3. What are the verbal images of the poem? How well does the structure echo these?
4. Do you find John Hollander's experiment with shaped verse as successful as George Herbert's in "Easter Wings" (p. 742)? If so, demonstrate how it succeeds. If not, explain why.

WRITING ABOUT FORM IN POETRY

Your aim in writing an essay about form in poetry is to demonstrate a relationship between structure and content. The form or shape of a poem should not be discussed in isolation; such an essay would simply produce a detailed description. Instead, structural analysis should always be tied into an evaluation of some aspect of the poem's content. As with essays about meter, sound, and rhyme, composition follows a double process of discovery in which both the sense and the form of the poem are investigated.

Your first task, of course, is to find an appropriate poem. If the choice is left up to you, you will have to decide at the outset whether you want to work with a closed form or an open form. In either event, you should select a poem that is short enough so that you can deal with the entire form and several structural components.

The next step in the prewriting process is a detailed investigation of the poem's sense. Consider the various elements that contribute to the poem's impact and effectiveness: the speaker, listener, setting, situation, diction, imagery, rhetorical devices, and the like. Once you understand these aspects of the poem, it will be easier to find the connection between form and content.

When you have completed a general consideration of the poem's impact and meaning, you will be ready to focus on the connection between form and content. At this point, it will be helpful if you prepare a worksheet much like the one employed when writing about meter (p. 715), sound (p. 716), or rhyme (p. 721). In this case the worksheet will highlight structural elements. For closed forms, these will include the rhyme scheme, meter, line lengths, and stanzaic pattern. They may also include significant words and phrases that link specific stanzas together. The worksheet for an open-form poem should indicate variables such as the rhythm and phrases, pauses or enjambements, significant words that are isolated or emphasized through typography, and patterns of repeated sounds, words, phrases, or images.

As you begin to consider the relationship between form and content, you will inevitably examine all the components of structure. In dealing with a closed form, you might want to consider the following questions:

1. What is the predominant meter? Line length? Rhyme scheme? To what extent do these establish and/or reinforce the form?

2. What is the form of each stanza or unit of the poem? What basic building blocks make up the stanza or the poem? How many stanzas or divisions does the poem contain? Is the pattern that is established in the first stanza or unit repeated in each subsequent unit?

3. Does the poem exemplify a traditional closed form such as the ballad or sonnet? If so, what is it? Does the poem sustain the form, or does it introduce variations? If there are variations, what is their effect?

4. How effectively does the structure create or reinforce the poem's internal logic? Can you find and explain a logical progression from unit to unit?

5. To what extent does the form organize the images of the poem? Are key images developed *within* single units or stanzas? Do images recur in several units? How does the structure help create a meaningful progression of images?

6. To what extent does the form help to create an organized pattern for the ideas or emotions of the poem? How does the structure emphasize these?

In dealing with open-form poetry, the questions you should ask are slightly different, but the concerns remain the same. With open forms you might explore the following areas:

1. What does the poem look like on the page? How does its general shape reflect its meaning?

2. How does the poet use variable line lengths, white spaces, punctuation, capitalization, and the like to shape the poem? To what extent do these variables contribute to the poem's sense?

3. What rhythms are built into the poem through language or typography? How are these cadences relevant to the poem's content?

4. Can you find a logical progression of ideas, images, and/or emotions? If so, how is this logic created and how does it contribute to the poem's impact?

5. How extensively are specific words or phrases isolated or grouped and thus emphasized through form or typography? What is the effect of such emphasis? To what extent is this technique one of the organizing principles of the poem?

6. What repeated patterns of words or sounds can you find in the poem? To what degree do these repetitions create order or structure? How do they underscore the sense of the poem?

In dealing with all these questions, you are seeking the most significant areas of interaction between form and content. Not every poem may provide meaningful answers to all the questions, but investigation of these topics will provide a great deal of information and will supply the raw materials for your essay.

At this stage in prewriting, you can begin to organize your information and formulate a tentative central idea for the essay. This idea should be as clearly focused and limited as possible. Since you cannot hope to deal with every aspect of form in a single essay, concentrate on the most important and effective ways that form shapes or reflects content.

In developing a central idea, it is not enough simply to assert that form organizes and underscores meaning; you should try to explain *how* this occurs. If you are planning an essay on Shakespeare's Sonnet 116, "Let Me Not to the Marriage of True Minds," for example, you might argue that form controls meaning. Such an assertion, while perhaps true, is not an adequate central idea. A better initial formulation might be stated as follows: "The sonnet form organizes the speaker's thoughts into a four-part argument in which each quatrain examines a different aspect of love's permanence, and the couplet provides a conclusion."

Sometimes the formation of a central idea can involve a two-step connection between form and content. In planning an essay on William Carlos Williams's "The Dance," for instance, you might decide that meaning is most effectively reinforced and echoed through rhythm. Hence, you would focus on the ways in which form creates rhythm and your central idea would link form to rhythm and meaning.

As with many other essays about literature, formulating an adequate thesis is half the battle. Once you have managed this, you can organize your data into logical and cohesive units that will become paragraphs. At the same time, you can begin to select examples and aspects of the poem to support your central idea. Here, as in any other essay, you should make sure that all your evidence is clearly relevant to the original thesis. If you find that your examples are leading you away from your central idea, you should rethink the essay and revise to reflect this new direction.

Organizing Your Essay

INTRODUCTION. The introduction may contain some general remarks about the poem, but it should focus on the connection between form and substance. It should include the thesis of the essay—a statement about the ways in which structure and content interact—and a brief survey of the specific topics that will be discussed in the body.

BODY. The body of the essay is devoted to supporting and proving the assertion made in the introduction. As a general rule, the topics covered in the body should be taken up in subsequent paragraphs in the same order in which they are mentioned in the first paragraph. The organization of these supporting paragraphs will reflect the discoveries about the linkage between form and content that you made while planning the essay. You will also want to provide a paragraph that describes the structure of the poem fairly early in the essay. In dealing with closed forms, this paragraph will detail such standard features as the traditional form, meter, rhyme scheme, stanzaic structure, and number of stanzas. With open-form poetry, the paragraph should focus on the most striking and significant features of the verse.

CONCLUSION.   The conclusion of your essay might contain any additional observations about shape or structure that seem relevant. It should also include a summation of your argument. Here, as in all other essays about literature, you should make sure that you reach an actual conclusion rather than simply a stopping point.

SAMPLE ESSAY

Structure and Meaning in George Herbert's "Virtue"*

[1]
George Herbert's poem, "Virtue," considers the difference between those things of the world that will inevitably die and the immortality of the "virtuous soul." Every component of structure works harmoniously in this poem to organize the images in a logical progression and to underscore the difference between things that "must die" and that one thing that "chiefly lives."° The organization of the stanzas of the poem creates a structural and visual distinction between the "sweet" soul and the rest of creation through the skillful use of line groupings, rhyme scheme, and repeated words.□

[2]
"Virtue" is a seventeenth-century lyric of four quatrains containing three lines of iambic tetrameter and a final line of iambic dimeter. This shift from four to two beats gives the concluding line of each quatrain great impact. Each stanza also follows the same basic *a b a b* rhyme scheme. Since some rhyme sounds and words are repeated throughout the first three stanzas, however, the structure of the poem may be formulated as *4a 4b 4a 2b, 4c 4b 4c 2b, 4d 4b 4d 2b, 4e 4f 4e 2f.*

The stanzaic structure of this lyric provides a pattern of organization for the images of the poem and simultaneously underscores the logic of the ideas. The first stanza focuses on the image of the "Sweet day"; it compares the day to "The bridal of the earth and sky" (line 2) and asserts that the day inevitably "must die." Similarly, the second stanza focuses exclusively on the image of the "Sweet rose" and asserts that it too "must die." The third stanza shifts to the image of the "Sweet spring." Here the poet combines the images of the first two stanzas into the third by noting that the "Sweet

---

* See p. 747 for this poem.
° Central idea.
□ Thesis sentence.

spring" is "full of sweet days and roses" (line 9). The stanza concludes that "all must die." In this way, the third stanza becomes the climax of both the images used to this point and the idea of universal mortality. The last stanza introduces a totally new image—"a sweet and virtuous soul"—and an assertion which is the opposite of the ideas expressed in the previous three. Although

[3]   the day, the rose, and the spring "must die," the soul "never gives" and "chiefly lives" even though "the whole world turn to coal" (line 15). This separate stanza presents the logical conclusion of the argument and the key image of the poem—the "virtuous soul." The pattern of organization of the lyric form allows this key image of the one thing that lives to be separated structurally from the images of things that die.

This structural organization of images and ideas is repeated and reinforced by several other techniques that help establish the poem's overall form. The rhyme scheme, for example, contributes significantly to the linkage among the first three stanzas and the isolation of the fourth. The first three

[4]   all repeat the *b* rhyme at the ends of the second and fourth lines, rhyming *a b a b, c b c b,* and *d b d b.* In the fourth stanza, however, the *b* rhyme is replaced by an *f* rhyme. The rhyme scheme thus produces effects parallel to the grouping of images and the logic of the ideas. The final stanza is separated and isolated from the rest of the poem by the deletion of the *b* rhyme and the introduction of the *f* rhyme.

Also, the repetition of key words and phrases further emphasizes both the connection of the images and ideas of the first three stanzas and their isolation from the last. Each of the first three stanzas begins with *sweet* and ends with *must die.* This repetition of *must die* drives home the idea that death is universal. In the last stanza, however, this pattern of repetition is

[5]   abandoned. The initial *sweet* that characterized the first three stanzas is replaced by *Only* (line 13). Similarly, *must die* is replaced with *chiefly lives.* Both substitutions create a striking separation between this final stanza and the three previous stanzas. More important, the shift in the verbal pattern emphasizes the conceptual transition from death to the immortality of the "virtuous soul."

We have seen that the lyric form of Herbert's "Virtue" provides an organizational pattern for the poem's images and ideas. At the same time, the pattern of stanzas and the rhyme scheme allow the poet to draw a

[6]   vivid structural distinction between the corruptible world and the immortal soul. Form in this poem is not arbitrary or incidental; it becomes another way of asserting the singularity of the key image, the "sweet and virtuous soul."

Commentary on the Essay

This essay considers the relationship between form and meaning in Herbert's "Virtue." The introductory paragraph begins by stating the focus of the poem itself: the distinction between the "virtuous soul" and everything else. It goes on, in the second sentence, to assert a specific connection between form and meaning. Finally, the third sentence lists a series of ways in which form organizes and reinforces the substance of the poem.

Paragraph 2 is purely descriptive; it identifies the traditional closed form exemplified by "Virtue," notes some of the significant structural features of the poem, and closes with a schematic formulation of the entire lyric. While this paragraph does not advance the argument of the essay, it does provide a summary of information that will be useful later in the paper.

The last sentence of the opening paragraph speaks of line groupings (or stanzas), rhyme schemes, and repeated words and phrases as the structural elements that shape the poem and underscore meaning. The body of the essay (paragraphs 3, 4, and 5) takes up these subjects in exactly the same order. The focus of paragraph 3 is on the organization of both images and ideas from stanza to stanza. Here, the essay demonstrates that the image of the "virtuous soul" and the idea of immortality are isolated and emphasized through the stanzaic pattern.

Paragraph 4 begins with a transitional sentence that repeats part of the essay's central idea and, at the same time, connects it to paragraph 3. In this way, paragraph 4 is closely tied to both paragraphs 1 and 3. The main topic here, the rhyme scheme of "Virtue," is introduced in the second sentence, which asserts that it also reinforces the division between mortality and immortality.

Paragraph 5 takes up the last structural element mentioned in the introduction—the repetition of key words and phrases. This paragraph is linked with the first because its topic is noted there. Transition between the previous paragraph and this one is established with the first phrase of the opening sentence: "In a similar manner." The paragraph goes on to illustrate that repeated words and phrases underscore the central division between the mortality of the world and the immortality of the "virtuous soul."

The conclusion provides an overview and summation of the essay's argument. In addition, it concludes that form in "Virtue" is neither arbitrary nor incidental, but rather an integral part of the poem's meaning.

WRITING TOPICS FOR CHAPTER 19

1. Consider the form of Whitman's "When I Heard the Learn'd Astronomer." Describe the way in which the topic material changes as the poem progresses. Why are the earlier lines comparatively free and unstructured, while the very last line is perfectly regular iambic pentameter?

2. Describe the use of the ode form as exemplified by Shelley's "Ode to the West Wind" and Keats's "Ode to a Nightingale." What patterns of regularity do you find? What differences do you find in the form and content of the poems?

3. How do Cummings, Thomas, Randall, and Dryden use totally different forms to consider the subject of death (in "Buffalo Bill's defunct," "Do not Go Gentle," "Ballad of Birmingham," and "To the Memory of Mr. Oldham")? What differences in form and treatment do you find? What similarities do you find, despite these differences?

4. Write a "visual" poem, and explain the principles on which you develop your lines. Some possible topics (just to get you started):

   A "boom-box," a duck, a beer bottle, a sweater, a snowshovel, a skunk.

   After creating your poem, write a short essay that considers these questions: How serious does the visual form enable your poem to become? What are the strengths and limitations of the visual form, according to the experience you have acquired in writing such a poem?

5. Write a haiku. Be sure to fit your poem to the 5–7–5 pattern of syllables. What challenges and problems do you encounter when writing in this form? Once you have completed your haiku (which, to be traditional, should be on a topic concerned with nature), try to cut the number of syllables to 4–5–4. Explain how you establish the first haiku pattern, and also explain how you go about cutting the total number of syllables. Be sure to consider the kinds and lengths of your words.

20

Symbolism and Allusion: Windows to a Wide Expanse of Meaning

Symbolism refers to the use of symbols in literary works. A **symbol** is something that has meaning in and of itself but also stands for something else, like the flag for the country or the school song for the school. Symbols occur in stories as well as in poems, but poetry relies more heavily on symbolism than does fiction, for it is more concise and involves more forms than fiction, which relies on a narrative structure.

In a broad sense, almost all words can be thought of as symbols, for they stand for various objects without actually being those objects. When we say *horse*, for example, or *tree*, these words are not horses or trees, but only symbols for these things; they direct our minds to things in the real world that we have seen and can therefore imagine easily when we read or hear the words. In literature, however, symbolism implies a special relationship that extends beyond our ordinary understanding of words, descriptions, and arguments. We will explore that relationship in this chapter.

SYMBOLISM AS A WINDOW TO GREATER MEANING

Symbolism goes beyond the close referral of word to thing; it is more like a window through which one can get a glimpse at the extensive world outside. Poetry, remember, is a compact form that may be structured in many more ways than fiction. Symbolism is a shorthand way of referring to extensive ideas or attitudes that otherwise would be impossible in the relatively brief format of poetry. Thus William Butler Yeats, who believed that the city of Constantinople, or Byzantium, represented a high point of human civilization, used the city as a symbol of the highest state of human achievement in peace, politics, and particularly art and literature.

His poem "Sailing to Byzantium" (p. 1001) does not expand upon the full meaning and interpretation of this idea, for it would take a long history and a detailed analysis of Byzantine art and literature to do that. The poem, does, however, take Byzantium and its excellence as a base of meaning from which Yeats develops his own worries about what he thought was the declining state of civilization during the twentieth century. The use of symbols, in other words, becomes a means by which poets assume a common extensive knowledge and are therefore freed to consider their thoughts and attitudes resulting from this knowledge.

HOW DOES SYMBOLISM OPERATE?

The effect of symbolism is thus to expand meaning beyond the normal connotation of words. For example, at the time of William Blake (1757–1827) the word *tiger*, had the general meaning of a large, wild cat in addition to the specific animal we call tiger. Its obvious connotation linked it with wildness, predation, and fierceness. As a symbol in the poem "The Tyger," however, Blake uses the tiger as a stand-in for the negativism and evil in the world—the sum total of savage, wild forces which prompt human beings to evil actions. Thus the tiger as a symbol is more meaningful than either the denotation or the connotation of the word would indicate.

In poetry, some symbols possess a ready-made, clearly agreed-upon meaning. These are the kinds of symbols described in Chapter 9 as **general, cultural,** or **universal symbols.** Many such symbols, like the tiger, are drawn directly from the world of nature. Springtime and morning are ready-made symbols signifying beginnings, growth, hope, optimism, and love. A reference to spring is normal and appropriate in a love poem. If the topic were death, however, the symbol of spring would still be appropriate as the basis of ironic observations about the untimeliness with which death claims its victims.

Cultural symbols are drawn from history and custom. Because the Judeo-Christian tradition has been so pervasive a force in Western culture for 3,000 years, many religious symbols have been taken up by poets. References to the lamb, Eden, bondage, shepherds, exile, temple, blood, water, bread, the cross, and wine—all Jewish and/or Christian symbols—appear over and over again in poetry of the English language. Sometimes these symbols occur in purely devotional poems; at other times they may be contrasted with symbols of warfare and corruption to show how far removed people have become from their moral and religious obligations.

Symbols that are not widely or universally recognized are termed **private, authorial,** or **contextual symbols** (these are also discussed in Chapter 9). Some of these have a natural relationship with the things being symbolized. Snow, for example, is cold and white, and when it falls it covers everything. A poet can thus exploit this particular quality and make snow a symbol. At the beginning of the extensive poem "The Waste Land," T. S. Eliot uses the symbol of snow ironically to symbolize a retreat from life, an intellectual and moral hibernation. Another poem utilizing snow as a symbol linking the living and the dead both literally and figuratively is "Snow," by Virginia Scott:

VIRGINIA SCOTT   (b. 1938)

Snow   1977

A doe stands at the roadside,
spirit of those who have lived here
and passed known through our memory.
The doe stands at the edge of the icy road,
then darts back into the woods.   5

Snow falling,
mother-spirit hovering,
white on the drops in the road and fields,
light from the windows
of the old house   10
brightening the snow.

Presences: mother,
grandmother,
here in their place
at the foot of *ben lomond*,°   15
green trees black in the hemlock night.

The doe stands at the edge of the icy road,
then darts back into the woods.

Golden Grove, New Brunswick, Canada
January 5, 1977

SNOW.   15 *ben lomond*: a small mountain in Golden Grove, not far from Saint John,
New Brunswick. The Scots name reflects that the area, not far from the Maine border, was
settled by Scots immigrants.

QUESTIONS

1. What visual images are described in the poem? What actions? Colors? Textures?
2. How is snow described in the poem? How and where is it seen? As a symbol, what does it signify in relationship to the doe, the memory of persons, the

mother-spirit, the old house, the light, the presences, the mountains, and the trees?

3. Explain the structural purpose for which the doe is mentioned three times in the poem, with lines 17 and 18 repeating 4 and 5. As a symbol, what might the doe signify?

4. What are the relationships described in the poem between memory of the past and existence in the present?

This poem describes a real circumstance at a real place at a real time; the poet has even provided an actual location and date, just as we do in a letter. The snow was real snow, falling at a time in the evening when lights had been put on in the nearby house. This detail by itself would be sufficient as a realistic image. But as Scott develops the poem, the snow symbolizes the link between the speaker's memory of the past and perception of the present. The reality of the moment is suffused with the memory of the people—"mother,/grandmother"—who "lived here." The poet is meditating on the idea that individuals, though they may often be alone like the speaker, are never alone as long as the memory of the past is a vivid part of their consciousness. The past and present are in effect connected just as the snow covers the scene. At the conclusion of the poem, the symbolic doe darting into the woods suggests a linking of the present with the future. The poem is dealing with difficult questions of identity. Because it is also quite brief, the idea of connection and continuity would be difficult to achieve without the suggestive symbols of the snow and the deer. Both symbols in this poem—the snow and the doe—are private and contextual; they are established and developed within the poem. By this means the poet has converted a very private and meditative moment into a symbolic one.

Similarly, seemingly ordinary materials may become symbolic if the poet emphasizes them or repeats details about them. John Keats in "La Belle Dame Sans Merci" (p. 785), for example, repeats the image of the sedge, or grass, being withered around the lake. What might seem like no more than an appropriate detail therefore becomes symbolic of loss and bewilderment felt by people when the persons they love seem to be unreal, faithless, and destructive rather than genuine, loyal, and supportive.

THE INTRODUCTION OF SYMBOLS

SINGLE WORDS.   Poets may introduce symbols into their poems in many ways. With general or universal symbols, a single word is sufficient, like references to the lamb, shepherd, cross, or to summer and winter, or to drought and flood, morning and night, heat and shade, or storm and calm. The nightingale may be taken as an example of how a single word may become instantly symbolic. Because the bird has such a beautiful song, it frequently symbolizes natural, unspoiled beauty as contrasted with the contrived attempts by human beings to create beauty. Keats refers to the bird in this way in his "Ode to a Nightingale," where he compares the virtually eternal beauty of this singer with his own mortality.

Anne Finch, in "To the Nightingale" (p. 667), makes a similar comparison between the human poet and the nightingale, drawing attention to the legend that the "unhappy poet's breast,/Like thine, when best he sings, is plac'd against a thorn." Here the symbol emphasizes the claim that poetic expression originates in the deep pain and feeling of poets. By contrast, T. S. Eliot uses the less idealistic aspects of the bird in "Sweeney Among the Nightingales." Here Eliot refers to the bird's song not as a symbol of beauty, but rather as a backdrop for the horror of the murder of the ancient king Agamemnon. The only contribution the nightingales make as a symbol is their droppings—a staining, dirtying commentary on human affairs. Despite Eliot's usage, however, poets usually emphasize the lovelier aspects of the bird in their symbols.

ACTIONS.   Not only words but also actions may be presented as symbols. In Virginia Scott's "Snow," as we have just observed, the doe darting into the darkening woods symbolizes both the renewal and the mystery of life. In Thomas Hardy's "In Time of 'The Breaking of Nations' " (p. 787), the action of the man plowing a field symbolizes the continued life and vitality of the folk, the people, despite political and military changes that are constantly raging in the world.

SETTING.   Sometimes a setting or natural scene may be symbolic. For example, Randall Jarrell's brief poem "The Death of the Ball Turret Gunner" (p. 520), equates the ball turret of a World War II high-altitude bomber with a mother's womb, symbolically indicating that war and brutal death are the human lot from the very beginning of life. Similarly, the "elfin grot" (grotto) of the "lady in the meads" in Keats's "La Belle Dame Sans Merci" is an unreal and magical womblike location symbolizing both the allure and the disappointment that sometimes characterize sexual attraction.

CHARACTERS.   The many characters or people in poetry may also reach symbolic status if the poet designs them to represent ideas or values. In E. E. Cummings's "In Just-," for example, the balloon man is such a figure. Although the balloon man is not extensively visualized, Cummings includes enough detail about him to indicate that he symbolizes the basic and primitive vitality, joy, and sexuality with which children are literally called out of childhood. The fairy child of "La Belle Dame Sans Merci" is a symbol of the mystery of love. The figures in Hardy's "In Time of 'The Breaking of Nations'" are symbolic of the poet's faith in the power of unimportant people to endure even though "Dynasties pass."

SITUATIONS.   In addition, situations, circumstances, or conditions may be symbolic. The condition of Jarrell's ball turret gunner, exposed and helpless six miles in the air, may be understood as a symbol of the condition of all people in the age of fear and anxiety produced by the threat of global wars and technologically expert destructiveness. The speaker of Anne Finch's "To Mr. F., Now Earl of W." symbolizes human confrontation with the emotion of a love so strong that it transcends human capacity for expression and hence must remain unexpressed and private.

QUALITIES OF SYMBOLS

Just as symbols may be expressed in these various ways, the meanings of symbols may be placed on a continuum of qualities from good to bad, high to low, favorable to unfavorable. For example, Cummings's old balloon man of "In Just-" is on the positive end, symbolizing the irresistible and joyfull call of growth and sexuality. Outright horror is suggested by the symbol of the rough beast slouching toward Bethlehem in Yeats's "The Second Coming" (p. 788). This symbol is not like Jesus, who was born in Bethlehem, but ironically is a horrible force of anger, suppression, and brutality that in Yeats's judgment was becoming dominant in twentieth-century politics, even long before the development of nuclear warfare.

ALLUSION IN POETRY

Just as symbolism enriches meaning, so does *allusion*. **Allusion,** which is also discussed in Chapter 9, refers to the inclusion, in a work, of unacknowledged quotations from other works and of references to historical events and any aspect of human culture—art, music, literature, and so on. It is a means of recognizing both the literary tradition and broader cultural environment of which the poet is a part. In addition it assumes a common bond of knowledge between the poet and the reader. On the one hand, allusion compliments the heritage of the past, and on the other it salutes the reader who is able to recognize it and find meaning in it.

Allusions may be no more than a single word, provided the word is unusual enough or associative enough to bear the weight of the reference. Virginia Scott's "Snow," for example, speaks of "green trees black in the hemlock night." *Hemlock* refers to a type of evergreen tree in the woods observed by the speaker, but hemlock was also the poison drunk by Socrates when he was executed by the ancient Athenians. Just about any literary reference to hemlock calls to mind the death of Socrates and also the idea that death is oblivion and the common end of all life. At the beginning of "Ode to a Nightingale" (p. 749), Keats's speaker describes a numbness that might come "As though of hemlock . . . [he] had drunk." Here the allusion is placed in the context of a wish to be connected and united to the universal spirit not of oblivion but of creative power.

Allusions may also consist of extensive phrases, descriptions, or situations. These allusions add their own interest and power before the poet moves on to other ideas. Line 6 of Scott's "Snow," for example, is simply "Snow falling." This phrase is descriptive and accurate, but it also is a direct quotation from the first line of Robert Frost's poem "Desert Places" (p. 748). The context is of course different. Frost's line introduces the topic of the speaker's fear of bleakness, unconcern, coldness—his "desert places"—whereas in "Snow" Scott is referring to the continuity of the past and the present. There are bleakness and isolation in Scott's scene, but her old house also throws light on the snow, and the dead are fondly remembered because their spirit and memory are as alive as the doe who darts back into the woods. By making the allusion, Scott actually emphasizes the difference between her idea and Frost's.

THE SOURCES OF ALLUSIONS.   Allusions may be drawn from just about any area of life, history, and art. Sometimes symbols are allusions as well as symbols. In "The Second Coming" Yeats's "lion body and the head of a man" is a descriptive allusion to the sphinx, which was an ancient mythical monster that destroyed those who could not solve its riddle. As Yeats uses the description, he is referring to the monstrous aspects of the sphinx as a means of focusing on both the horror and mystery, the brutality and coldness that often infest human political institutions. As works become well known and popular, they become a source of allusions. One of Robert Frost's most famous lines, for example, is the conclusion of "Stopping by Woods on a Snowy Evening": "And miles to go before I sleep." This line is so often quoted that it has become a metaphor for having a task to complete before one may rest or relax in recreational activities. Isabella Gardner alludes to the line in her poem "Collage of Echoes," a poem that is deliberately built out of allusions. Interestingly enough, Frost's line itself echoes a line in Keats's sonnet "Keen Fitful Gusts," where Keats says "The stars are very cold about the sky,/And I have many miles on foot to fare." Any allusion to the line in Frost is therefore also an indirect allusion to Keats's lines.

ALLUSIONS AND THE ORIGINAL CONTEXT.   If an allusion is made to a literary work, it carries with it the entire context of the work from which it is drawn. Perhaps the richest storehouses of such ready-made stories and quotations are the King James version of the Bible and the plays of Shakespeare. In "Ode to a Nightingale" Keats alludes to the biblical story of Ruth, who, he says, was "sick with tears amid the alien corn." This allusion is particularly rich, because Ruth became the mother of Jesse; it was from the line of Jesse that King David was born, and it was from the house of David that Jesus was born. Thus Keats's nightingale is not only a symbol of natural beauty, but through this biblical allusion it becomes symbolic of regeneration and redemption, much in keeping with Keats's assertion that the bird was not born for death. In Yeats's "The Second Coming" the reference to the "blood-dimmed tide" suggests the soliloquy in the second act of Shakespeare's *Macbeth*, when Macbeth, after murdering Duncan, asks if there is enough water in Neptune's ocean to wash the blood from his hands. His immediate, guilt-ridden response is that Duncan's blood will instead stain the ocean, turning the green of the water to red. This image of crime being so bloody that it can stain the water of the ocean is the allusion of Yeats's "blood-dimmed tide," for Yeats's authorial speaker is just as concerned about the global implications of evil as is Shakespeare's Macbeth.

Allusions are therefore an important means by which poets broaden the context and deepen the meaning of their poems. The issues raised by a poet in a specific poem, in other words, not only are important there, but are linked through allusion to issues raised earlier by other thinkers or brought out by previous events, places, or persons. With connections made through allusions, poets attempt to make the significance and applicability of their own ideas plain. The situations in their works are not isolated, but are general problems for many times and places. Allusion is hence not literary "theft," but rather a means of literary enrichment.

STUDYING FOR SYMBOL AND ALLUSION

As you study poetry for its symbols and allusions, it is important to realize that these devices do not come ready marked with special notice and fanfare. A decision to call a feature of a poem symbolic is based on qualities within the poem: Perhaps a major item of importance is introduced at a climactic part of the poem, or a description has something noteworthy or unusual about it, such as the connection between "stony sleep" and the "rough beast" in Yeats's "The Second Coming." When such a connection occurs, the element may no longer be taken just literally, but may be read as a symbol.

Even after you have found a hint such as this, however, you may have to expend considerable effort to learn its symbolism. Thus the "rough beast" raises questions about what Yeats meant. In the context of the poem the phrase might refer to the person or persons hinted at in traditional interpretations of the New Testament as the "anti-Christ." In a secular frame of reference, the associations of blankness and pitilessness suggest that some aspect of brutality and suppression is being suggested. Still further, however, if the twentieth century were not a period in which millions of people have been persecuted and exterminated in military and secret police operations, even these associations might make the "rough beast" quizzical but not necessarily symbolic. But because of the rightness of the application together with the traditional biblical associations, the "rough beast" clearly should be construed as a symbol.

As you can see, the interpretation of a symbol requires that you be able to identify and objectivize the person, thing, situation, or action in question. To the degree that the element can be seen as general and representative—characteristic of the condition of a large number of human beings—it assumes the nature of a symbol, for it then stands for a universal element. As a rule, the more ideas you can associate specifically with the element, the more likely it is to be a symbol.

With regard to allusions in poetry, there is less possible ambiguity but also greater difficulty, depending on your background and education. There is a vast body of written tradition and history to which a poet may allude at any time. Not all of this tradition is readily available to all readers. Explanatory footnotes, of course, are an obvious help, for they give information about the allusion. However, an allusion, though it refers only briefly to a source, place, person, or event, may ask readers to call to mind the entire situation in the original. Theoretically, the reader might be required to study the original sources of all allusions, and such an extensive task would be too great for most readers of poetry.

In one respect, then, identification of an allusion is quite simple. Either a word, situation, or phrase is an allusion or it is not, and hence the matter is easily settled once an original reference can be located. The problem comes in determining how the allusion affects the context of the poem you are reading. Thus we have determined that Virginia Scott alludes to Robert Frost's "Desert Places" by using the phrase "Snow falling" in the poem "Snow." Once this allusion is identified, its purpose must still be established. Thus the allusion might mean that the situation in "Snow" is the same as in Frost's poem, namely that the authorial speaker is making observations about interior blankness—Frost's "desert places." On the other hand, the poet may be using the allusion in a new sense—for example, Frost uses the falling snow to symbolize a coldness of spirit whereas Scott uses it, more warmly, to connect the natural scene to the memory of family. In other words, once the presence of an allusion is established, the business of reading and understanding must still continue.

POEMS FOR STUDY

GEORGE HERBERT (1593–1633)

The Collar°   *1633*

I struck the board, and cry'd, "No more;
    I will abroad!
What? shall I ever sigh and pine?
My lines and life are free; free as the road,
  Loose as the wind, as large as store,
    Shall I be still in suit?°   5
  Have I no harvest but a thorn°
  To let me blood, and not restore
What I have lost with cordial fruit?
    Sure there was wine   10
Before my sighs did dry it: there was corn
  Before my tears did drown it.
Is the year only lost to me?
  Have I no bays° to crown it?
No flowers, no garlands gay? all blasted?   15
    All wasted?
  Not so, my heart: but there is fruit,
    And thou hast hands.
Recover all thy sigh-blown age
On double pleasures: leave thy cold dispute   20
Of what is fit, and not; forsake thy cage,
    Thy rope of sands,
Which petty thoughts have made, and made to thee
  Good cable, to enforce and draw,
    And be thy law,   25
While thou didst wink and wouldst not see.
    Away; take heed:
    I will abroad.
Call in thy death's head there: tie up thy fears.
    He that forbears   30
  To suit° and serve his need,
    Deserves his load."

                       follow

THE COLLAR.   *collar*: (1) the collar worn by a member of the clergy; (2) the collar of the harness of a draught animal such as a horse; (3) a restraint placed on prisoners; (4) a pun on *choler* (yellow bile), a bodily substance that was thought to cause quick rages.   6 *in suit*: waiting upon a person of power to gain favor or position.   7 *thorn*: see Mark 15:17. 14 *bays*: laurel crowns to signify victory and honor.

But as I rav'd and grew more fierce and wild
> At every word,
Me thought I heard one calling, "Child:"   35
> And I replied, *"My Lord."*

QUESTIONS

1. What situation does the speaker describe at the opening of the poem? Why is he angry or impatient? Who is speaking to whom? Against what role in life is the speaker complaining?

2. In light of the many possible meanings of *collar* (see note), explain the title as a symbol in the poem.

3. Explain the symbolism of the thorn (line 7), blood (line 8), wine (line 10), bays (line 14), flowers and garlands (line 15), cage (line 21), rope of sands (line 22), death's head (line 29), and the dialogue in lines 35 and 36.

4. What arguments does the speaker make against his vocation as a member of the clergy? What argument is proposed in favor of his role? Which argument is more compelling, according to the speaker?

5. Consider the allusions to the thorn (line 7), wine (line 10), and the New Testament concept that God is like a parent to human beings (lines 35 and 36). How do these allusions assist in developing the arguments made by the speaker in the poem?

ANNE FINCH, COUNTESS OF WINCHELSEA   (1661–1720)

To Mr. F[inch], Now Earl of W[inchelsea]   *1689*

Who going abroad, had desired Ardelia° to write some verses upon whatever subject she thought fit, against his return in the evening.

No sooner, Flavio,° were you gone,
But your injunction thought upon,
> Ardelia took the pen;
Designing to perform the task
Her Flavio did so kindly ask,   5
> Ere he returned again.

TO MR. F., NOW EARL OF W.   *Ardelia*: the name Anne Finch used in her personal poems in reference to herself, so that she could use the third person to refer to her feelings and attitudes. The name suggests warmth and devotion (ardency).   1 *Flavio*: the name that she assigned to Mr. Finch, her husband. The name *Flavio* was common in ancient Rome. Cnaeus Flavianus, a Roman of the fourth century B.C., was particularly known for his justice and leadership.

Unto Parnassus° straight she sent,
And bid the messenger, that went
  Unto the Muses' court,°
Assure them she their aid did need,
And begg'd they'd use their utmost speed,   10
  Because the time was short.

The hasty summons was allow'd:
And being well-bred they rose and bow'd,
  And said they'd post away:
That well they did Ardelia know,   15
And that no female's voice below
  They sooner would obey.

That many of that rhyming train°   *poets*
On like occasions sought in vain   20
  Their industry t' excite:
But for Ardelia all they'd leave.
Thus flatt'ring can the Muse deceive
  And wheedle us to write.

Yet since there was such haste requir'd,   25
To know the subject 'twas desired
  On which they must infuse,°   *give judgment*
That they might temper words and rules,
And with their counsel carry tools
  As country doctors use.   30

Wherefore to cut off all delays,
'Twas soon replied, a husband's praise
  (Tho' in these looser times)
Ardelia gladly would rehearse
A husband's who indulged her verse,   35
  And now requir'd her rhymes.

"A husband!" echo'd all around:
And to Parnassus sure that sound
  Had never yet been sent.
Amazement in each face was read,   40
In haste th' affrighted sisters fled,
  And into council went.

Erato° cried, "since Grizel's° days,
Since Troy-town pleas'd, and Chevy Chase,°

---

7 *Parnassus*: Mount Parnassus was the home of the nine muses and was also sacred to Apollo, the God of Poetry, Music, and Dance. 9 *Muses' court*: the court of the muses, who governed art, music, literature, and the sciences. 43 *Erato*: the muse of lyrical love poetry. *Grizel*: Griselda, in Chaucer's "Clerk's Tale," was known for her patient and forgiving love for her husband, Walter. 44 *Troy-town, Chevy Chase*: Ancient Troy ("Troy-town") was besieged by the Greeks. Hector, the most famous Trojan hero, was deeply loved by his wife, Andromache. In the late medieval ballad of Chevy Chase, the Douglases and Percies made war against each other and were mourned by their wives (Child Ballads A57; B55–56).

No such design was known;" 45
And 'twas their business to take care
It reach'd not to the public ear,
    Or got about the town.

Nor came where evening beaux° were met,   *dandies*
O'er billet-doux° and chocolate,   *love letters* 50
    Lest it destroyed the house:
For in that place who could dispense
(That wore his clothes with common sense)
    With mention of a spouse?

'Twas put unto the vote at last, 55
And in the negative it passed,
    None to her aid should move;
Yet since Ardelia was a friend,
Excuses 'twas agreed to send
    Which plausible might prove: 60

That Pegasus° of late had been
So often rid thro' thick and thin
    With neither fear nor wit,
In panegyric° been so spurr'd,   *poems of praise*
He could not from the stall be stirr'd, 65
    Nor would endure a bit.

Melpomene° had given a bond
By the new house° alone to stand
    And write alone of war and strife;
Thalia,° she had taken fees 70
And stipends from the patentees,
    And durst not for her life.

Urania° only liked the choice;
Yet not to thwart the public voice,
    She whispering did impart: 75
"They need no foreign aid invoke,
No help to draw a moving stroke,
    Who dictate from the heart."

"Enough!" the pleas'd Ardelia cried:
And slighting ev'ry Muse beside, 80
    Consulting now her breast.
Perceived that ev'ry tender thought
Which from abroad she vainly sought
    Did there in silence rest:

61 *Pegasus*: the famous winged horse of Greek mythology.   67 *Melpomene*: the muse of
tragedy.   68 *new house*: There were two authorized or "patent" theaters in London in
1689. The "new house" was the Drury Lane Theater, built in 1673. "Patentees" (line 71)
were the managers; a dramatist who contracted to write plays for them could not do the
same for someone else without breaking the contract. The allusion may be to the well-publicized
breach of contract by the poet laureate John Dryden in 1682.   70 *Thalia*: the muse of
pastoral poetry and also of comedy.   73 *Urania*: The muse of astronomers; hence the
muse closest to heaven.

And should unmov'd that post maintain,   85
Till in his quick return again,
  Met in some neighb'ring grove,
(Where vice nor vanity appear)
Her Flavio them alone might hear
  In all the sounds of love.   90

For since the world does so despise
Hymen's° endearments and its ties,
  They should mysterious be:
Till we that pleasure too possess
(Which makes their fancied happiness)   95
  Of stolen secrecy.

92 *Hymen*: the Greek god of marriage

QUESTIONS

  1. What situation prompts the speaker to write the poem? What imaginary
      journey does Ardelia make, and for what reason? Whom does she meet,
      and what happens? What traits does Ardelia show? How does she feel about
      Flavio?

  2. Describe the structure and development of the narrative of Ardelia's mission
      to the muses. At what point does the narrative change to describe Ardelia's
      analysis of her love for Flavio?

  3. Why is the response of the muses comic? Upon what usual assessment of
      married love is the muses' response based (see lines 91, 92)? Why do the
      muses think Ardelia's request is unusual?

  4. Describe the poet's symbolic use of allusions in lines 43 and 44. What are
      these symbols introduced to represent? What do the beaux symbolize (line
      49)? How may the situation between Ardelia and Flavio be seen as symbolic
      of the privacy of marital love?

JOHN KEATS   (1795–1821)

La Belle Dame Sans Merci: A Ballad   *1820 (1819)*

                    1
O what can ail thee, knight at arms,
  Alone and palely loitering?
The sedge has wither'd from the lake,
  And no birds sing.

LA BELLE DAME SANS MERCI: French for "The beautiful lady without pity" (that is,
"The heartless woman"). "La Belle Dame Sans Merci" is the title of a medieval poem by
Alain Chartier; Keats's poem bears no other relationship to the medieval poem, which was
thought at the time to have been by Chaucer.

2

O what can ail thee, knight at arms,   5
   So haggard and so woe-begone?
The squirrel's granary is full,
    And the harvest's done.

3

I see a lily on thy brow
   With anguish moist and fever dew,   10
And on thy cheeks a fading rose
    Fast withereth too.

4

I met a lady in the meads,°   *meadows*
   Full beautiful, a fairy's child;
Her hair was long, her foot was light,   15
    And her eyes were wild.

5

I made a garland for her head,
   And bracelets too, and fragrant zone;°   *belt*
She look'd at me as she did love,
    And made sweet moan.   20

6

I set her on my pacing steed,
   And nothing else saw all day long,
For sidelong would she bend, and sing
    A fairy's song.

7

She found me roots of relish° sweet,   *magical potion*   25
   And honey wild, and manna° dew,   *see Exodus 16:14–36*
And sure in language strange she said—
   I love thee true.

8

She took me to her elfin grot,°   *grotto*
   And there she wept, and sigh'd full sore,   30
And there I shut her wild wild eyes
    With kisses four.

9

And there she lullèd me asleep,
   And there I dream'd—Ah! woe betide!
The latest° dream I ever dream'd   *last*   35
    On the cold hill's side.

10

I saw pale kings, and princes too,
   Pale warriors, death pale were they all;
They cried—"La belle dame sans merci
    Hath thee in thrall!"°   *slavery*   40

11

I saw their starv'd lips in the gloam
   With horrid warning gapèd wide,

And I awoke and found me here
   On the cold hill's side.
12
And this is why I sojourn here,
   Alone and palely loitering,   45
Though the sedge is wither'd from the lake,
   And no birds sing.

QUESTIONS

1. How is the poem developed? Who is the speaker of stanzas 1–3? Who speaks after that?

2. What is the structure of the story of the poem? What is the source of information on which the knight concludes that he has been put into thrall?

3. In light of the dreamlike content of the poem, how can the knight's experience be viewed as symbolic? What is being symbolized?

4. Consider *relish* (line 25), *honey* (line 26), and *manna* (line 26) as symbols. Are they realistic or mythical? What does the allusion represented by manna signify? What is symbolized by the "pale kings, and princes too" and "Pale warriors"?

5. Consider the aspects of setting as described in the poem as symbols of the knight's state of mind.

THOMAS HARDY (1840–1928)

In Time of "The Breaking of Nations"   *1916 (1915)*

Only a man harrowing clods
   In a slow silent walk,
With an old horse that stumbles and nods
   Half asleep as they stalk.

Only thin smoke without flame   5
   From the heaps of couch grass:°   *quack grass*
Yet this will go onward the same
   Though Dynasties pass.

Yonder a maid and her wight°
   Come whispering by;   *fellow*
War's annals will fade into night   10
   Ere their story die.

IN TIME OF "THE BREAKING OF NATIONS." See Jeremiah 51:20, "with you I break nations in pieces."

QUESTIONS

1. What does Hardy symbolize by the man and the horse, the smoke, and the couple? How realistic and vivid are these symbols? Are they universal or contextual? As images, to what senses do they refer (for example, sight, sound, and so on)?

2. How does Hardy in stanzas 2 and 3 show that the phrase "breaking of nations" is to be taken symbolically? What meaning is gained by the biblical allusion of this phrase?

3. Contrast the structure of stanza 1 with that of stanzas 2 and 3. How does the form of stanzas 2 and 3 enable Hardy to emphasize the main idea in the poem?

4. How does the speaker show his evaluation of the importance of the life of the common people as opposed to the business of warfare and international politics? You might wish to consider that at the time (1915), World War I was raging in Europe.

WILLIAM BUTLER YEATS   (1865–1939)

The Second Coming°   *1920 (1919)*

Turning and turning in the widening gyre°
The falcon cannot hear the falconer;

THE SECOND COMING. The phrase "second coming" has been traditionally used to refer to expectations of the return of Jesus for the salvation of believers, as described in the New Testament. The prophecies foretold that Christ's return would be preceded by famine, epidemics, wars between nations, and general civil disturbance. Yeats believed that human history could be measured in cycles of approximately 2,000 years (see line 19, "twenty centuries"). According to this system, the birth of Jesus ended the Greco-Roman cycle and in 1919, when Yeats wrote "The Second Coming," it appeared to him that the Christian period was ending and a new era was about to take its place. The New Testament expectation was that Jesus would reappear. Yeats, by contrast, holds that the disruptions of the twentieth century were preceding a takeover by the forces of evil.   1 *gyre*: a radiating spiral, cone, or vortex. Yeats used the intersecting of two of these shapes as a visual symbol of his cyclic theory. As one gyre spiraled and widened out, to become dissipated, one period of history would end; at the same time a new gyre, closer to the center, would begin and spiral in a reverse direction to the starting point of the old gyre. A drawing of this plan looks like this:

The falcon of line 2 is at the broadest, centrifugal point of one gyre, symbolically illustrating the end of a cycle. The "indignant desert birds" of line 17 "reel" in a tighter circle, symbolizing the beginning of the new age in the new gyre.

Things fall apart; the center cannot hold;
Mere anarchy is loosed upon the world,
The blood-dimmed tide° is loosed, and everywhere   5
The ceremony of innocence is drowned;
The best lack all conviction, while the worst
Are full of passionate intensity.

Surely some revelation is at hand;
Surely the Second Coming is at hand.   10
The Second Coming! Hardly are those words out
When a vast image out of *Spiritus Mundi*°
Troubles my sight; somewhere in sands of the desert
A shape with lion body and the head of a man,°
A gaze blank and pitiless as the sun,   15
Is moving its slow thighs, while all about it
Reel shadows of the indignant desert birds.
The darkness drops again; but now I know
That twenty centuries of stony sleep
Were vexed to nightmare by a rocking cradle,   20
And what rough beast, its hour come round at last,
Slouches towards Bethlehem to be born?

5 *blood-dimmed tide*: quotation from Shakespeare's *Macbeth*, act 2, scene 2, lines 60–63.
12 *Spiritus Mundi*: literally, the spirit of the world, a collective human consciousness that
furnished writers and thinkers with a common fund of images and symbols. Yeats referred
to this collective repository as "a great memory passing on from generation to generation."
14 *lion body and the head of a man*: i.e., the Sphinx, which in ancient Egypt symbolized the
pharaoh as a spirit of the sun. Because of this pre-Christian origin, the reincarnation of a
sphinx could therefore represent qualities associated in New Testament books like Revelation
(11, 13, 17), Mark (13:14–20) and 2 Thessalonians (2:1–12) with a monstrous, superhuman,
satanic figure. For a picture of the Sphinx, see color plate 4.

QUESTIONS

1. Consider the following as symbols: the gyre, the falcon, the "blood-dimmed
   tide," the ceremony of innocence, the "worst" who are "full of passionate
   intensity." What ideas and values do these symbolize in the poem?

2. Why does Yeats capitalize the phrase "Second Coming"? To what does this
   phrase refer? Explain the irony of Yeats's use of the phrase in this poem.

3. Consider the structure of the poem. What does the space after line 8 do by
   way of dividing the poem into parts?

4. Contrast the symbols of the falcon of line 2 and the desert birds of line
   17. Considering that these are realistically presented, how does the realism
   contribute to their identity as symbols?

5. What attributes are symbolized by the sphinx being revealed as a "rough
   beast"? What is the significance of the beast's going "to Bethlehem to be
   born"?

ROBINSON JEFFERS (1887–1962)

The Purse-Seine   *1937*

1

Our sardine fishermen work at night in the dark of the moon; daylight or moonlight
They could not tell where to spread the net, unable to see the phosphorescence
    of the shoals of fish.
They work northward from Monterey, coasting Santa Cruz; off New Year's Point
    or off Pigeon Point
The look-out man will see some lakes of milk-color light on the seas's night-purple;
    he points, and the helmsman
Turns the dark prow, the motorboat circles the gleaming shoal and drifts out   5
    her seine-net. They close the circle
And purse the bottom of the net, then with great labor haul it in.

2

                                        I cannot tell you
How beautiful the scene is, and a little terrible, then, when the crowded fish
Know they are caught, and wildly beat from one wall to the other of their closing
    destiny the phosphorescent
Water to a pool of flame, each beautiful slender body sheeted with flame, like a   10
    live rocket
A comet's tail wake of clear yellow flame; while outside the narrowing
Floats and cordage of the net great sea-lions come up to watch, sighing in the
    dark; the vast walls of night
Stand erect to the stars.

3

                    Lately I was looking from a night mountain-top
On a wide city, the colored splendor, galaxies of light: how could I help but recall   15
    the seine-net
Gathering the luminous fish? I cannot tell you how beautiful the city appeared,
    and a little terrible.
I thought, We have geared the machines and locked all together into
    interdependence; we have built the great cities; now
There is no escape. We have gathered vast populations incapable of free survival,
    insulated
From the strong earth, each person in himself helpless, on all dependent. The
    circle is closed, and the net
Is being hauled in. They hardly feel the cords drawing, yet they shine already.   20
    The inevitable mass-disasters
Will not come in our time nor in our children's, but we and our children
Must watch the net draw narrower, government take all powers—or revolution,
    and the new government
Take more than all, add to kept bodies kept souls—or anarchy, the mass-disasters.

4

                  These things are Progress;
Do you marvel our verse is troubled or frowning, while it keeps its reason? Or it   25
    lets go, lets the mood flow

In the manner of the recent young men into mere hysteria, splintered gleams,
  crackled laughter. But they are quite wrong.
There is no reason for amazement: surely one always knew that cultures decay,
  and life's end is death.

QUESTIONS

1. Describe how the purse-seine is used to haul in the sardines. What is the speaker's reaction to the scene as described in stanza 2?

2. How does the speaker explain in stanza 3 that the purse-seine is to be understood as a symbol? What does it symbolize? What do the sardines symbolize? Of what is the poet speaking?

3. Compare the ideas of Jeffers in this poem with those of Yeats in "The Second Coming." In contrast with Yeats's cyclical scheme, are the ideas of Jeffers more or less methodical?

4. Why is the word *Progress* capitalized in line 24? What is usually meant by progress? How does Jeffers indicate that he is using the word and the idea ironically?

5. Is the statement at the end to be taken as recognition of a fact or as a resigned acceptance of that fact? In the light of the poem's major symbol, does the poem offer any solution to the problem? What is it that the speaker fears?

6. How may the sea lions of line 12, and their sighs, be construed as a symbol? Might the "you" of line 25 be responding to the poem in the way the sea lions respond to the capture of the sardines?

T. S. ELIOT (1888–1965)

Sweeney Among the Nightingales°

1918

ὤμοι, πέπληγμαι καιρίαν πληγὴν ἔσω.

Apeneck Sweeney spreads his knees
Letting his arms hang down to laugh,
The zebra stripes along his jaw
Swelling to maculate° giraffe.   *dirty, stained*

SWEENEY AMONG THE NIGHTINGALES. Eliot wrote two other works featuring Sweeney. These are "Sweeney Erect" (a poem) and *Sweeney Agonistes* (a drama). The character represents the grosser aspects of modern human beings. In the play, Sweeney says "Birth, and copulation, and death, / That's all, that's all, that's all." Sweeney is also the name of a hero of Irish legend and folklore.   The Greek epigraph below the title is from Aeschylus, *Agamemnon*, line 1348, and may be translated "Alas I am struck with a mortal blow within." This is the off-stage cry of Agamemnon when he is being murdered.

The circles of the stormy moon   5
Slide westward toward the River Plate,°
Death and the Raven° drift above
And Sweeney guards the hornéd gate.°

Gloomy Orion° and the Dog°   10
Are veiled; and hushed the shrunken seas;
The person in the Spanish cape
Tries to sit on Sweeney's knees

Slips and pulls the tablecloth
Overturns a coffee-cup,   15
Reorganized upon the floor
She yawns and draws a stocking up;

The silent man in mocha brown°   *Sweeney*
Sprawls at the window sill and gapes;
The waiter brings in oranges   20
Bananas figs and hothouse grapes;

The silent vertebrate in brown°   *Sweeney*
Contracts and concentrates, withdraws;
Rachel *née* Rabinovitch
Tears at the grapes with murderous paws;

She and the lady in the cape   25
Are suspect, thought to be in league;
Therefore the man with heavy eyes
Declines the gambit, shows fatigue,

Leaves the room and reappears
Outside the window, leaning in,   30
Branches of wistaria
Circumscribe a golden grin;

The host with someone indistinct°
Converses at the door apart,
The nightingales are singing near   35
The Convent of the Sacred Heart,

---

6 *River Plate*: The River Plate, or Rio de la Plata, is the large estuary extending from the
Atlantic Ocean to Buenos Aires. It separates Argentina and Uruguay.   7 *Raven*: a bird
of ill omen; also the constellation Corvus.   8 *hornéd gate*: One of the two gates of the
underworld, according to Virgil, *Aeneid*, book 6:1192–1193. The usual guardian of the gates
was the three-headed dog, Cerberus.   9 *Orion*: a mythological Greek giant and hunter.
Because of a misunderstanding, he was killed by Artemis, the Goddess of the Moon and of
the Hunt. Orion is also one of the most prominent winter constellations.   *Dog*: Orion's
dog. The "dog star," Sirius, is in the constellation Canis Major, east of Orion, and it is the
brightest star in the sky.   33 *someone indistinct*: a murderer, corresponding to Aegisthus,
the murderer of Agamemnon.

And sang within the bloody° wood
When Agamemnon cried aloud,
And let their liquid siftings fall
To stain the stiff dishonored shroud.

40

37 *bloody:* A pun: (1) covered with blood, (2) a vulgar word in British slang.

QUESTIONS

1. What does Sweeney represent as a symbol? Why does the poet use as the epigraph the passage from Aeschylus in which Agamemnon cries out in the pain of death? Why do you think the speaker describes Sweeney as "apeneck" (line 1) and as a "vertebrate in brown (line 21)"?

2. Why do you think Eliot included references to the constellations in the first part of the poem? Consider also the geography in the poem (i.e., South America, Greece, the Greek mythological underworld) in addition to the constellations. What is the effect of this broad set of references upon the symbolic meaning of the central incidents involving Agamemnon and Sweeney?

3. In stanza 2, how might the reference to the moon, westward, the raven, and hornéd gate be considered as symbols? What do these symbols represent?

4. Why does the speaker describe "Rachel *née* Rabinovitch" as being like an animal (with "murderous paws"). Knowing that Sweeney is the name of a hero of Irish folklore, what do you make of Eliot's selection of that name for his anti-hero?

5. What are the host and the "indistinct" man conferring about? What is going to happen to Sweeney?

6. What do nightingales usually symbolize? What do they represent here? How may this use of the nightingales be considered as ironic?

7. Consider the setting of the poem as a symbol of the circumstances of life in the twentieth century. What comforts and advantages of modern life are included? To what extent does the poem suggest that these improvements in the quality of life have had any effect upon human nature and greed?

E. E. CUMMINGS   (1894–1962)

In Just-   *1923*

in Just-
spring   when the world is mud-
luscious the little
lame balloonman

whistles   far   and wee

5

and eddieandbill come
running from marbles and
piracies and it's
spring

when the world is puddle-wonderful   10

the queer
old balloonman whistles
far   and   wee
and bettyandisbel come dancing

from hop-scotch and jump-rope and   15

it's
spring
and
     the
          goat-footed°   20

balloonMan   whistles
far
and
wee

IN JUST-,   20 *goat-footed*: The mythological Greek god Pan, a free-spirited and lascivious
god who presided over fields, forests, and herds, was portrayed with the body of a man and
the legs of a goat.

QUESTIONS

1. Consider and explain the following as symbols: spring, mud-luscious, marbles, puddle-wonderful, hop-scotch. What does the whistle of the balloonman symbolize?

2. In what way is the balloonman symbolic?

3. Besides the balloonman, there are four other characters in the poem. Who are they? Why does Cummings run their names together? What impulses do these characters represent symbolically?

4. Why do you think the poem ends as it does? How is the final *wee* different from the word as it appears in lines 5 and 13?

5. Read the poem aloud. Taking into account the spacing and alignment, how does the physical arrangement on the page influence your reading and perception of the lines?

ISABELLA GARDNER   (1915–1981)

Collage of Echoes   *1979*

I have no promises to keep
Nor miles to go before I sleep,°
For miles of years I have made promises
and (mostly) kept them.
      It's time I slept.   5
Now I lay me down to sleep°
With no promises to keep.
      My sleeves are ravelled°
      I have travelled.°

COLLAGE OF ECHOES.   2 *miles to go before I sleep*: see Robert Frost, "Stopping by Woods on a Snowy Evening" (p. 529), lines 13–16.   6 *Now I lay me down to sleep*: from the child's prayer: Now I lay me down to sleep; / I pray the Lord my soul to keep. / If I should die before I wake, / I pray the Lord my soul to take.   8 *My sleeves are ravelled*: see *Macbeth*, act 2, scene 2, line 37: "Sleep that knits up the ravelled sleeve of care."   9 *I have travelled*: see Keats, "On First Looking into Chapman's Homer" (p. 625), line 1.

QUESTIONS

1. Given the allusions in the poem, what do you conclude about the speaker's judgment of the reader's knowledge of literature?

2. What is the effect of the echoes? Consider the contexts of the sources being echoed. How reliant is "Collage of Echoes" upon these contexts? How do the echoes assist in enabling enjoyment and appreciation of the poem? Has the speaker truly incorporated them into the poem?

3. In relation to the speaker's character as demonstrated in the poem, consider the phrases "(mostly) kept them," "With no promises to keep," and "My sleeves are ravelled." What do they show about the speaker's self-assessment? In what way might these phrases be considered comic?

CAROL MUSKE   (b. 1945)

Real Estate   *1981*

You think you earned this space on earth,
but look at the gold face of the teen-age
pharaoh,° smug as a Shriner, in his box

REAL ESTATE.   3 *teen-age pharaoh*: Tutankhamen, the Egyptian "boy king" of the fourteenth century B.C. The discovery of his tomb in 1922, when hundreds of precious household objects were found with the sarcophagus, showed the lavishness of Egyptian royal burials. The mummy of King Tut was covered with a mask of gold and colored metals.

with no diploma, a plot flashy enough
for Manhattan.° Early death, then what.   5
a task dragging a sofa into the grave,
a couple of floor lamps, the alarm set

for another century. Someday we'll heed
the testament of that paid escort watching
himself in all the ballroom mirrors: slide   10

with each slide of the old trombone,
be good to the bald, press up against
the ugly duck-like.° Time is never old,

never lies. What a past you'd have
if you'd only admit to it: the real estate   15
your family dabbled in for generations,
the vacant lots° developed like the clan

overbite—through years of sudden
foreclosure. Who knows what it costs?
First you stand for the national anthem,   20

then you start waltzing around without
strings, reminding yourself of yourself,
expecting to live in that big city
against daddy's admonition: buy land°

get some roots down under those spike   25
heels, let the river bow and scrape as
it enters the big front door of your property.

5 *Manhattan*: In 1981 a large number of treasures from Tutankhamen's tomb were displayed
at the Metropolitan Museum of Art in Manhattan.   13 *ugly duck-like*: "The Ugly Duckling"
is a children's story by Hans Christian Andersen.   17 *vacant lots*: see T. S. Eliot, "Preludes,"
concluding lines.   24 *buy land*: see Robert Frost's poem "Build Soil" (1932).

QUESTIONS

1. Who is speaking? Who is being addressed? What sort of person is the speaker?
    What does she think of old age? Of sex? What advice does she offer as a
    security against advancing age?

2. What does "the teen-age pharaoh" symbolize? Why does the poet mention
    a modern set of objects that might be found in a comparable tomb of a
    person of the twentieth century? What might these things symbolize? How
    do the things contrast?

3. What does the "paid escort" (line 9) symbolize? What does the "old trombone"
    symbolize? What does the choice of these symbolize about the traditional
    role of women with regard to men? What attitude is conveyed by this choice?

4. Consider the ambiguity of lines 25–27. What might "roots" and "property" signify as the means of causing the "river" to "bow and scrape"? Why is it difficult to understand these lines without resorting to symbolic explanations?

5. Consider the allusion in line 24 to Robert Frost's "Build Soil" (1932). Frost delivered his poem at Columbia University just before the party conventions of 1932. The United States was in its worst economic depression. Frost spoke about agriculture, world politics and the need for developing the nation's resources. In comparison, what does Muske achieve by the allusion?

WRITING ABOUT SYMBOLISM AND ALLUSION IN POETRY

As you read the poem on which you will be writing, take notes and make all the observations you can about the presence of symbols and/or allusions. Footnotes will help you establish basic information, but you still will need to explain meanings and give interpretations in your own words. Use a dictionary to build up your understanding of words or phrases that seem to be worthy of further study. For allusions, you might wish to go to the original source to determine the situation referred to. Try to determine the ways in which your poem is similar to, or different from, the original work or source, and then try to determine the purpose served by the allusion.

In the perception of symbols, call on whatever personal experience you have had with symbols. Perhaps dinner time has been especially important in your family—a time when everyone gets together and chats over events of the day. If you are currently living away from home, you might miss the symbolic significance of this gathering time. Try to determine if a similar process of association might enable you to conclude that elements in the poem you are considering may be taken as symbols. Look for noteworthy or highlighted things; try to determine whether they are general or universal, particular or contextual. If you think that an element is symbolic, write a brief paragraph describing why you think it is. Determine how many symbols there are in the poem, and try to describe their nature. Consider a question like whether the poem would work in the same way if the element were not symbolic. Once you have set up a pattern of study in this way, you can begin developing and drafting your essay.

Organizing Your Essay

INTRODUCTION.   Your introduction might begin with a brief description of the poem and of the symbols or allusions in it. A symbol might be central to the poem, or an allusion might be made at a particularly important point at the climax. Your central idea should briefly state the theme of the essay, such as that the symbolism is visual and particular, or that it is not particularized and also general; the nature of the symbol may make it applicable to political or personal topic material; allusions may emphasize the differences between the poem and the source or sources of the allusions; symbols or allusions may make the poem seem optimistic, or pessimistic, and so on. The thesis sentence connects the central idea to the various points about symbols or allusions to be explored in the body of the essay.

BODY.   Some possible approaches for the body of the essay, which may be combined as need arises, are described below.

1. *The meaning of symbols or allusions.* This approach is the most natural one to take. If you have discovered a symbol or allusion, the intent is to explain the meaning as best you can. In effect, you are writing about the ideas of the poem as they are carried primarily by the devices you are exploring. What is the major idea of the poem? How do you know that this interpretation is valid? How far can the symbol or allusion be extended? To what degree do the materials in the rest of the poem serve as evidence for the ideas? If you have determined that there are many symbols or allusions in the poem, which of these, if any, predominate? What do they mean? Do the ideas of one relate to those of another? How?

2. *The importance of symbols or allusions to the form of the poem.* Here the goal should be to determine how symbolism or allusion is related to poetic structure. Where does the symbol occur in the poem? If it is early, how do the following parts relate to the ideas of the symbol? What logical or chronological function does the symbol serve in the development of the poem? Is the symbol repeated? What effect does the repetition produce? If the symbol is introduced later in the poem, is it anticipated earlier? Can it be described in any way as being climactic? What might the structure of the poem have been like if the symbolism had not been used? (Answering this question can give an idea of how the symbol has influenced the structure of the poem.) In addition, for an allusion, it would be important to compare the contexts of both the poem and the source to determine how the poet has used the allusion for an illuminating, reinforcing, or contrasting effect.

3. *The relationship between the literal and the symbolic.* The object here is to describe the literal nature of the symbols and then to determine their appropriateness in the context of the poem. If the symbol emerges as a part of a narrative, what is its literal function? If the symbol is a person, object of some sort, or setting, what physical aspects are described? Are colors included? Shapes? Sizes? Sounds? In the light of this actual description, how applicable is the symbol to the ideas it crystallizes? How appropriate is the literal condition to the symbolic? The answers to

these and similar questions should lead not so much to a detailed account of the meaning of the symbols, but rather to an analysis of enough of the meaning to explain the appropriateness of the relationship.

4. *Implications and resonances of symbols and allusions.* We have used the term *resonance* elsewhere in this book to refer to the complex of suggestions and associations that are brought out by a particular aspect of literature. The term is rather vague, but in a major respect it is at the very heart of literary experience. Here, particularly, it could be a fruitful direction to take for an essay. Ideas to explore would be about the chain of thinking that is brought out through symbols or allusions. In a way, you would be following a process of thought similar to the poet's, except that you are free to move in your own direction as long as you base your discussion on the symbols and allusions in the poem under consideration. If the poet is speaking in general terms about the end of an era, for example, as in "The Second Coming" and "The Purse-Seine," then you could include your own thoughts about the observations. It is difficult to summon the knowledge and authority to contradict the work of a poet, but if you are able to point out shortcomings in the thought of the symbols or allusions, you should go right ahead.

CONCLUSION. Your conclusion might contain a summary of the main points in the body of your essay. If the poem is particularly rich in symbols or allusions, you might also consider briefly some of these elements that you did not consider fully in the body and try to tie these together with those you have already discussed. It would also be appropriate to introduce any personal responses you developed as a result of your study.

SAMPLE ESSAY

Symbol and Allusion in Yeats's "The Second Coming"*

[1] "The Second Coming" is a prophetical poem that lays out reasons for being scared about the future. The poet uses symbolism and allusion from ancient history and literature as well as his own visual scheme designed to explain the rise and fall of civilizations. These symbols and allusions are arranged to explain both the disruption of our present but old culture, and also the installation of a fearsome new one.° To make the explanation clear, Yeats uses the symbols of the gyre and the sphinx-like creature, and he alludes to New Testament prophecy.□

Yeats's first symbol, the gyre, or rather two gyres interconnecting, ap-

---

* See p. 788 for this poem.
° Central idea.
□ Thesis sentence.

pears throughout the poem, for it indicates the cyclical nature of political changes. The top of the gyre symbolizes our present era, while the falcon rotating introduces the idea that "the center cannot hold." The desert birds, hovering around the "lion body and the head of a man," show a tighter circle in a second gyre symbolizing the new civilization establishing itself. Thus [2] the widening symbolic gyre in line 1 is interpenetrating with the narrowing gyre pointing at the "rough beast." This blending and intersecting show that new things blend into old things, while separating from them at the same time. The order of the past is breaking up, while the future order is about to take the shape of the past not at its best, but rather at its worst.

Embodying this horror-to-be, the second major symbol is the sphinx-like creature moving its slow thighs in the sands of the desert. The attributes of the creature—a monster, really—are blankness and pitilessness. Yeats describes it as a "rough beast," with "indignant desert birds," perhaps vultures, [3] flying in circles above it. This description of the symbol emphasizes the brutal nature of the new age. Yeats wrote the poem in 1919, right after the conclusion of World War I, which had seen particularly senseless trench warfare. The disruption of life caused by this war was a disturbing indicator of what the future would hold.

The possible emergence of brutality causes the poem's major allusion, to the "second coming" to be ironic. Yeats makes the allusion in the title, and also in lines 10 and 11 of the poem. The allusion is to the usual understanding of the New Testament prophecies about the return of Christ to rescue and save true believers. In the Bible, war and rumors of war are claimed as being the signs indicating that the return, or "second coming," is near. The [4] twist, however, is that Yeats is suggesting in the allusion that after the breakup of the present age, the new age will be marked not by Christ but by the rough beast. Because Yeats describes the beast as a sphinx, his model is the kind of despotism known in ancient Egypt, when power was held absolutely by the pharaoh and when few people were granted any freedom or civil rights.

"The Second Coming" is therefore a poem rich in symbols that are both traditional and also personal with Yeats, but there are additional symbols and allusions. The most easily visualized of these is the falcon out of control, flying higher and higher and farther away from the falconer to symbolize the anarchy that Yeats mentions in line 4 as being "loosed" in the world. An [5] example of a symbol being used ironically is that of Bethlehem, the town where Jesus, the "Prince of Peace," was born. In "The Second Coming," Yeats asserts that the new birth in Bethlehem will not lead to peace, but instead will bring about a future age of repression and brutality. The poem thus offers a rich but also disturbing fabric of symbol and allusion.

Commentary on the Essay

This essay combines the topics of symbolism and allusion, and illustrates how each may be handled. The introduction briefly characterizes the poem and asserts that the arguments are made through the use of symbols and allusions. The central idea is about the replacement of the old by the new, and the thesis sentence lists two major symbols and one allusion to be discussed in the body. Paragraph 2 describes the shape of the symbol, thus illustrating method 2 as described above, and also explains it, illustrating method 1. Paragraph 3 considers the "rough beast" as a symbol of emerging brutality. Paragraph 4 treats the title's allusion to New Testament prophetic tradition, showing how Yeats makes his point by reversing the outcome that tradition had predicted. The concluding paragraph summarizes and characterizes the body briefly and proceeds to illustrate the richness of "The Second Coming" with brief reference to additional symbols and other allusions.

WRITING TOPICS FOR CHAPTER 20

1. Analyze the ways in which Keats, Herbert, and Jeffers use symbols to convey the fact and idea of capture and thralldom ("La Belle Dame sans Merci," "The Collar," "The Purse-Seine"). What major symbols do the three poets use? How appropriate is each symbol in its respective poem? How do the poets use the symbols to focus upon the problems they present in their poems?

2. Describe the differences in the ways in which Anne Finch, E. E. Cummings, T. S. Eliot, and W. B. Yeats use allusions in "To Mr. Finch," "In Just-," "Sweeney among the Nightingales," and "The Second Coming." How possible is it to understand these poems without an explanation of the poetic allusions? How much explanation is actually necessary? To what extent does the allusiveness make the poems difficult? Challenging? Interesting? Enriching?

3. Write a poem in which you develop a major symbol, as Jeffers does in "The Purse-Seine" and Yeats does in "The Second Coming." Some symbols you might think about selecting are these:

   Atomic waste, or nuclear weapons.
   Foreign-made cars.
   A superstar athlete.
   A computer.
   A dog staring out a window as children leave for school.

   Now, write an essay describing the process of your creation: How do you begin? How much detail do you think is necessary? How many conclusions do you need to draw about your symbol? When do you think you have said enough?

4. Write a poem in which you make your own allusions to things you know, such as the Bible, school, a book, a movie character, or a recent artistic or political event. What assumptions do you make about your reader when you use an allusion? How do you make the allusion (i.e., by a quotation, a name, a title, an indirect reference)? How does your allusion deepen your meaning? How does the use of your allusion increase your own powers of expression?

21

Myth: Systems of Symbolic Allusion in Poetry

THE NATURE OF MYTHOLOGY

The term *myth* is derived from the Greek word *mythos*, which means story, narrative, or plot. Myths are thus stories that illustrate or define the religion, philosophy, culture, collective psychology, or history of a specific group or civilization. In addition, myths often explain particular features of a people's environment—like an especially high mountain in Greece or the seemingly endless winters in Northern Europe—and they frequently embody explanations of scientific facts for prescientific societies. The stories organize and formalize a civilization's social and cultural values. When these stories combine to form a system of belief and religious or historical doctrine, they become a **mythology** or a *mythos*. Thus, **myth** may briefly be defined as a system of belief sometimes (but not always) based on supernatural figures or "gods" who control the physical universe, who shape (or at least know) the destinies of human beings, and who influence the flow of history.

When poets employ mythology in their verse, they are actually using a special kind of symbolism and allusion. We have already defined a **symbol** (in Chapters 9 and 20) as a person, place, action, thing, situation, or thought that possesses its own meaning but also points beyond itself to a greater and more complex meaning. Also in Chapter 20 we define **allusion** as a direct or indirect reference to any significant moment, event, character, action, or phrase from history or literature. Both these devices produce **resonance,** an emotional and intellectual reverberation and amplification of the ideas or images evoked. Poets who retell myths or employ mythic material combine these two techniques to pull a vast body of meaning and resonance into their poems.

Two considerations should modify our assumptions about myths and systems of mythology. On the one hand, myths can reflect truth symbolically even if the stories themselves are impossible; the truths of mythology are not found in the actual stories but rather in what they suggest about humanity. On the other hand, the term *myth* or *mythos* has come to refer to any organized system of narratives—true or false—that accounts for the origins and beliefs of a specific group. In this sense, the Old Testament embodies the mythos of the Jews just as Homer's *Iliad* and *Odyssey* represent the mythic histories of the Trojans and the Greeks. Thus, we can refer to the Islamic mythos, the Christian mythos, or the Jewish mythos without implying any sense of evaluation; the term simply refers to a system of belief.

Almost every culture has generated its own mythic system or absorbed the mythology of another people and adapted it to its own ends. The Romans, for example, swallowed up the whole body of Greek mythology and fused it with their own stories and values; most Roman myths and mythic figures parallel those in Greek mythology. Moreover, mythic systems have been produced in both primitive and sophisticated civilizations.

Why myths exist or why they have been generated by so many civilizations throughout the ages is difficult to tell. In fact, there are too many rather than too few explanations. We may begin by assuming that myths satisfy a basic human need to explain, organize, and humanize events or conditions that would otherwise remain mysterious and frightening. Thus, various cultures have produced myths that account for such natural phenomena as thunder and lightning, summer and winter, the ebb and flow of the sea, earthquakes and volcanoes. Most societies have also created myths that address the basic elements of human existence: birth, death, sexuality, and the existence of the world.

Since myths address common human fears and events, it is not surprising to find various cultures separated by vast amounts of time and space producing parallel myths that relate to similar phenomena. Most cultures, for example, have stories that account for the creation of the world. The details of the myths may be quite different, but the patterns are often similar and the aim in every case remains the desire to explain the existence of the universe. Similarly, most civilizations have produced myths that deal with the coming of summer, the return of the earth's fertility, and humanity's redemption from the death and sterility of winter. These myths often involve the sacrifice of a god-hero or goddess-heroine to ensure the coming of spring and renewed vitality. In *The Golden Bough*, a massive collection and analysis of mythic stories, Sir James Frazer (1854–1941) compares a series of myths that account for the end of winter and the renewal of the earth through the death and subsequent rebirth or return of a god or goddess. Among such sacrificed and reborn gods are Thammuz (Babylonia), Attis (Phrygia), Osiris (Egypt), and Adonis, Dionysus, and Persephone (Greece). Again, the specific myths take many different forms, but they reflect the same mysteries, fears, and hopes.

Scholars and anthropologists like Frazer were among the first to notice the interrelationships among myths produced by diverse cultures. The Swiss psychoanalyst Carl Gustav Jung (1875–1961) offered one explanation for this duplication. Jung noticed that specific images, characters, and events drawn from literature, mythology, and religion recurred in the dreams of his patients. He termed these recurrent images *archetypes* (from the Greek word meaning "model" or "first mold") and theorized the existence of a universal or collective unconscious mind shared by all humanity. Even if we dismiss Jung's theories completely, the fact remains that specific types of mythic figures and events such as dragons, centaurs, sacrifices, and heroic quests recur throughout various mythologies and resonate in our literature and our minds.

MYTHOLOGY AND LITERATURE

Many people believe that literature actually started as mythology; the very first stories and poems probably retold myths. In any event, we are concerned here with the opposite process—the absorption of mythology into poetry. When Greek or Roman poets like Homer or Ovid recounted mythic stories in their verse, the result was a combination of literature and religion that served the double purpose of teaching and entertaining. Their poetry offered both a religious and an esthetic experience to their listeners. This remarkable combination of literature and religious doctrine occurred whether or not the poet believed the myths he was retelling. When an English poet in the sixteenth or seventeenth century includes Greek mythology in his or her verse, however, the effect is quite different. The poem no longer reinforces the dominant mythos of the society. Instead, it draws upon the body of mythology referred to in the work to symbolize universal truths or patterns of thought.

For thousands of years poets and other writers have found mythology to be an attractive and useful source of symbols, images, patterns, and ideas. To this day, mythology remains a significant storehouse of poetic symbol and allusion. In the English language we find poems that use mythology in virtually every age and generation since the earliest Anglo-Saxon poems and legends. The poet's impulse to retell and rework myth is as alive today as it was in the Renaissance or the Victorian age; indeed, most of the poems in this chapter are from the twentieth century.

Most poets who incorporate mythological material into their verse turn to long-standing and well-established systems of myth, particularly Greco-Roman, Norse-Teutonic, and Judeo-Christian mythology. We might term these systems of mythology **public** or **universal,** since they are part of most people's common knowledge. Like public symbols, they exist outside the mind and the work of specific writers; they make up a common reservoir of material that all writers are free to employ. Thus, John Milton draws extensively on the Judeo-Christian mythos in his epic poem *Paradise Lost*, and T. S. Eliot alludes to the Buddhist mythos and pagan myths of fertility and rebirth in *The Waste Land*.

Some poets—like William Blake (1757–1827) and William Butler Yeats (1865–1939)—go beyond the allusive and symbolic use of public mythologies and invent their own mythic systems. Blake, for example, created a private system of mythology based on various semidivine figures called the Four Zoas. Similarly, Yeats invented a private mythos based on 2,000-year-long cycles or gyres of history and the phases of the moon (see p. 788). Poets who resort to such private mythic systems risk making their poetry inaccessible to many readers. Fortunately, much of their work is often meaningful and effective without any knowledge of their private mythologies.

STRATEGIES FOR DEALING WITH MYTHOLOGY IN POETRY

When a poet incorporates a mythic story or figure into a poem, he or she expects the readers to recognize the mythic allusion and the symbolic resonance produced in the work. If a poet mentions Ulysses (the Latin name for Homer's Odysseus), for example, the reader is expected to recall the stories associated with this mythic Greek hero, his role in the Trojan War, and the adventures he endured in his ten-year efforts to return home from Troy. Most of this material is recounted in Homer's *Iliad* and *Odyssey*. Thus, when we read Tennyson's "Ulysses" (p. 808), we are expected to understand the dissatisfaction and the desires of this character in Tennyson's poem.

In the past, British and American poets could assume that their readers had a solid knowledge of classical literature and mythology. Today, however, poets can no longer make that assumption. So if modern poets wish to use mythological allusions in their poems, they must either confine themselves to instantly recognizable figures, or else they must expect their readers to keep an encyclopedia of mythology handy when they read a poem.

When dealing with a poem that employs mythic material, make every effort to identify the mythological allusion and to understand its implications or overtones. In some cases, poets (or editors) help with this process by providing brief explanatory notes that identify the events or figures alluded to in the poem. In *The Waste Land*, for example, T. S. Eliot wrote his own notes to explain some of the more obscure mythic allusions. Even in these cases, however, the notes rarely give enough information to help you understand fully the implications and symbolic power of the mythic allusion.

You may, therefore, need to leave the poem and find out as much as you can about the mythic elements in the work. A good place to start is a dictionary or general encyclopedia, which often provide brief identifications of mythic figures and a key to further reading. Eventually you will want access to more detailed information about the mythic allusions. Any appropriate anthology of myths will help in this respect. Thus, if you find allusions to Paul Bunyan and Johnny Appleseed, you would want to look in a collection of American folk tales. References to Odin, Thor, the Valkyries, or Asgard should lead you to a collection of Norse-Teutonic mythology. The most frequent mythic allusions in Western poetry are to Greco-Roman mythology. To learn more about these figures and events, you may turn to any anthology of Greek and Roman mythology. Two well-known books that retell these stories are Thomas Bulfinch's *The Age of Fable* and Edith Hamilton's *Mythology*.

STUDYING MYTHOLOGY IN POETRY

We are now ready to look at a poem that depends to a great extent on the resonance of its mythic allusions. The poem is by William Butler Yeats (1865–1939), but it does not refer extensively to his private mythic system. Rather, it draws on the well-known body of Greco-Roman mythology.

WILLIAM BUTLER YEATS   (1865–1939)

Leda and the Swan   1924 *(1923)*

A sudden blow: the great wings beating still
Above the staggering girl, her thighs caressed
By the dark webs, her nape caught in his bill,
He holds her helpless breast upon his breast.

How can those terrified vague fingers push   5
The feathered glory from her loosening thighs?
And how can body, laid in that white rush,
But feel the strange heart beating where it lies?

A shudder in the loins engenders there
The broken wall, the burning roof and tower   10
And Agamemnon dead.
                    Being so caught up,
So mastered by the brute blood of the air,
Did she put on his knowledge with his power
Before the indifferent beak could let her drop?   15

QUESTIONS

1. What does the title tell you? What mythic event is recounted in the poem? Who was Leda? The swan? Who were Leda's children? What mythological and historical events are alluded to in lines 10 and 11?

2. What is the meter of the poem? The rhyme scheme? The form? Do you find significant irregularities in any of these? If so, what is their effect? To what extent are the events recounted in the poem organized by the structure?

3. How is Leda described? What words suggest her helplessness? How is the swan described? What phrases suggest his power, mystery, and divinity?

4. What question is raised in the last two lines? To what extent does the poem provide an answer to this question?

Yeats's poem focuses on a specific mythic event—the rape of Leda by Zeus—and the mythological and historical consequences of that event. The poem is thus very rich in mythic allusion and symbolism. The two central characters—Leda and the swan—are identified only in the title. The title consequently becomes an important key to understanding and experiencing the poem. The poem is an Italian sonnet (see p. 730) and follows an octave-sestet organization. It is composed of two quatrains (*a b a b, c d c d*) and two triplets (*e f g, e f g*).

At a basic level, the sonnet retells the mythological story of Zeus's rape of Leda, a Spartan queen. In the attack, the king of the gods took the form of a massive white swan. According to one version of the myth, the children born from this rape were Helen of Troy and Clytemnestra. The later rape of Helen by Paris was the central cause of the Trojan War (from which the ancient Greeks dated their civilization). Thus, the "broken wall, the burning roof and tower" (line 10) refers to the destruction of Troy. Clytemnestra married Agamemnon, the king of Mycenae and leader of the Greek forces at Troy. Because Agamemnon had sacrificed their daughter as a part of the war effort, Clytemnestra vowed revenge and murdered him when he returned home from the Trojan War (line 11).

Yeats's first quatrain (lines 1–4) details the violence of Zeus's attack on Leda, while the second quatrain (lines 5–8) presents the consummation of the rape. Leda's subjugation is expressed in words and phrases like "blow" (line 1), "helpless" (line 4), "terrified vague fingers" (line 5) and "loosening thighs" (line 6). The first half of the sestet (lines 9–11) presents both the climax of the rape and the consequences of it. Helen and Clytemnestra, however, are not named, but instead are replaced by the events they were to cause.

The final three-and-a-half lines raise the central issues of the sonnet. These questions are by no means limited to the person of Leda, even though they are specifically asked about her. While Leda seemingly took on some of Zeus's divine power (through the process of childbearing), the poem asks whether she also "put on" some of his divine knowledge.

Literally, the question is whether Leda understood the historical consequences of the divine violence while it was occurring—whether she acquired
Zeus's foreknowledge of the fall of Troy, the murder of Agamemnon,
and, by extension, all subsequent events in history.

If all the poem did, however, were to raise questions about the ancient
myth, it would have little interest for modern readers. It is rather to concerns
of today's world that the poem should direct our attention. If we make
the safe assumption that the answer to the question about Leda is negative,
we may also assume from the poem that human beings (at any time) do
not have preknowledge about anything, but have only their own culture
and experience as the basis of knowledge and control. If divine beings
exist, they have no more than an intermittent interest in human affairs
and quickly become "indifferent" (line 14) and uninvolved, leaving us to
our own devices. As an extension of the myth, therefore, violence seems
implicit in creation, and we will be assisted by no divine knowledge to
stop it. The myth suggests that the burden of civilization is on human
beings themselves, and that if knowledge is ever to be combined with
power for constructive goals, that blending must be a human achievement.

Yeats thus employs mythic material in this sonnet to assert the difficulty
of historical processes and to raise vital questions about the nature of existence, knowledge, and power. The historical process is embodied in the
rape, the children born out of it, and their troubles. As the virtual originator
of the process, Leda herself may be seen as the mythical focal point of
circumstances and questions that have extended from the distant past to
the present, and that will likely extend into the future. Thus, myth is not
so much a part of the dead past as it is of the living present, for while
the specifics have changed, the troubles are constant.

POEMS FOR STUDY

ALFRED, LORD TENNYSON   (1809–1892)

Ulysses   *1842 (1833)*

It little profits that an idle king,
By this still hearth, among these barren crags,
Matched with an aged wife, I mete and dole
Unequal laws° unto a savage race,   *rewards and punishments*
That hoard, and sleep, and feed, and know not me.   5

I cannot rest from travel; I will drink
Life to the lees.° All times I have enjoyed   *dregs*
Greatly, have suffered greatly, both with those

That loved me, and alone; on shore, and when
Through scudding drifts the rainy Hyades° 10
Vexed the dim sea. I am become a name;
For always roaming with a hungry heart
Much have I seen and known—cities of men
And manners, climates, councils, governments,
Myself not least, but honored of them all— 15
And drunk delight of battle with my peers,
Far on the ringing plains of windy Troy.
I am a part of all that I have met;
Yet all experience is an arch wherethrough
Gleams that untraveled world whose margin fades 20
Forever and forever when I move.
How dull it is to pause, to make an end,
To rust unburnished, not to shine in use!
As though to breathe were life! Life piled on life
Were all too little, and of one to me 25
Little remains; but every hour is saved
From that eternal silence, something more,
A bringer of new things; and vile it were
For some three suns to store and hoard myself,
And this gray spirit yearning in desire 30
To follow knowledge like a sinking star,
Beyond the utmost bound of human thought.

    This is my son, mine own Telemachus,
To whom I leave the scepter and the isle—°
Well-loved of me, discerning to fulfill 35
This labor, by slow prudence to make mild
A rugged people, and through soft degrees
Subdue them to the useful and the good.
Most blameless is he, centered in the sphere
Of common duties, decent not to fail 40
In offices of tenderness, and pay
Meet adoration to my household gods,
When I am gone. He works his work, I mine.

    There lies the port; the vessel puffs her sail;
There gloom the dark, broad seas. My mariners, 45
Souls that have toiled, and wrought, and thought with me—
That ever with a frolic welcome took
The thunder and the sunshine, and opposed
Free hearts, free foreheads—you and I are old;
Old age hath yet his honor and his toil. 50
Death closes all; but something ere the end,
Some work of noble note, may yet be done,

ULYSSES.   10 *Hyades*: nymphs who were placed among the stars by Zeus, the king of the gods. The name means "rain," and the rising of the stars was thought to precede a storm.   34 *isle*: Ithaca, the island realm ruled by Odysseus.

Not unbecoming men that strove with Gods.
The lights begin to twinkle from the rocks;
The long day wanes; the slow moon climbs; the deep   55
Moans round with many voices. Come, my friends,
'Tis not too late to seek a newer world.
Push off, and sitting well in order smite
The sounding furrows; for my purpose holds
To sail beyond the sunset, and the baths   60
Of all the western stars, until I die.
It may be that the gulfs will wash us down;
It may be we shall touch the Happy Isles,°
And see the great Achilles,° whom we knew.

Though much is taken, much abides; and though   65
We are not now that strength which in old days
Moved earth and heaven, that which we are, we are—
One equal temper of heroic hearts,
Made weak by time and fate, but strong in will   70
To strive, to seek, to find, and not to yield.

63 *Happy Isles*: the Elysian Fields, dwelling place of mortals who have been made immortal
by the gods.   64 *Achilles*: Greek hero of the Trojan War who killed Hector and was, in
turn, killed by Paris.

QUESTIONS

  1. What information does the title convey? Who was Ulysses (or Odysseus)?
      What role did he play in the Trojan War? What happened to him on the
      way home from Troy? How much time has passed between his return home
      and the present of the poem?

  2. Who is the speaker of the poem? To whom is he speaking? What is his
      attitude toward his life in Ithaca and his wife? What key phrases and adjectives
      in lines 1–5 establish this attitude?

  3. How have Ulysses's past experiences affected his present character and desires?
      What is his attitude toward life? What does he want to do?

  4. Who is Telemachus? What is the speaker's attitude toward him? How are
      the speaker and Telemachus different?

  5. What aspects of Ulysses are emphasized in this poem? to what extent does
      he become symbolic? What does he symbolize?

DOROTHY PARKER   (1893–1967)

Penelope   *1936*

In the pathway of the sun,
  In the footsteps of the breeze,
Where the world and sky are one,

He shall ride the silver seas,
   He shall cut the glittering wave.   5
I shall sit at home, and rock;
Rise, to heed a neighbor's knock;
Brew my tea, and snip my thread;
Bleach the linen for my bed.
   They will call him brave.   10

QUESTIONS

1. What information does the title of this poem give you? Who was Penelope? Who is the speaker of the poem?

2. Who is "he" referred to in lines 1–5? How is he described? What things will he do? Who are "they" referred to in line 10?

3. How does the speaker describe her life? How is her life different from that of the male figure described in lines 1–5?

4. On what aspects of Penelope's life does this poem focus? To what extent does Penelope become a symbol? What does she symbolize? How does our knowledge of the myth deepen our response to this symbolism?

5. What ideas about the lives of men and women and about the preconceived notions of society in the 1930s does this poem explore? Are these ideas still valid?

W. S. MERWIN (b. 1927)

Odysseus   *1960*

Always the setting forth was the same,
Same sea, same dangers waiting for him
As though he had got nowhere but older.
Behind him on the receding shore
The identical reproaches, and somewhere   5
Out before him, the unravelling patience
He was wedded to. There were the islands
Each with its woman and twining welcome
To be navigated, and one to call "home."
The knowledge of all that he betrayed   10
Grew till it was the same whether he stayed
Or went. Therefore he went. And what wonder
If sometimes he could not remember
Which was the one who wished on his departure
Perils that he could never sail through,   15
And which, improbable, remote, and true,
Was the one he kept sailing home to?

QUESTIONS

1. What aspects of the Odysseus myth are evoked in this poem? What point does the poem make about Odysseus's experiences?

2. What mythic figures are alluded to in the phrase "identical reproaches"? The phrase "the one who wished on his departure / Perils that he could never sail through"? The phrases "unravelling patience" and "the one he kept sailing home to"?

3. What ideas about life and experience does this poem explore? To what extent does Odysseus become symbolic of a specific kind of life and attitude toward life? How does our knowledge of Odysseus contribute to the impact and meaning of the poem?

4. Compare the image of Penelope in this poem with the one in Dorothy Parker's "Penelope." How is the same mythic material used toward different ends in these poems?

5. Compare the image of Odysseus in this poem with the one in Alfred, Lord Tennyson's "Ulysses." What are the similarities and/or differences? Explain how and why the same mythic figure can be used to convey such different ideas.

MARGARET ATWOOD   (b. 1939)

Siren Song   *1974*

This is the one song everyone
would like to learn: the song
that is irresistible:

the song that forces men   5
to leap overboard in squadrons
even though they see the beached skulls

the song nobody knows
because anyone who has heard it
is dead, and the others can't remember.

Shall I tell you the secret   10
and if I do, will you get me
out of this bird suit?

I don't enjoy it here
squatting on this island
looking picturesque and mythical   15

with these two feathery maniacs,
I don't enjoy singing
this trio, fatal and valuable.

I will tell the secret to you,
to you, only to you.
Come closer. This song   20

is a cry for help: Help me!
Only you, only you can,
you are unique

at last. Alas   25
it is a boring song
but it works every time.

QUESTIONS

1. What does the title tell you? Who were the sirens in Greek mythology? What
    was their song? What effect did their song have on men?
2. Who is the speaker in this poem? What is the effect of her colloquial diction?
    What does she tell you about her song?
3. Who is the "you" referred to in lines 10–24? What does the speaker offer
    to tell this person? What is the speaker's "secret"? What does the speaker
    say about her life? What happens to the "you" at the close of the poem?
    What "works every time"?
4. To what extent does your knowledge about the sirens help you to understand
    this poem? What does the siren in the poem symbolize? What does the listener
    symbolize?
5. What point does this poem make about women? About men? About gullibility,
    ego, and manipulation?

OLGA BROUMAS (b. 1949)

Circe   *1977*

The Charm

   The fire bites, the fire bites. Bites
   to the little death. Bites

   till she comes to nothing. Bites
   on her own sweet tongue. She goes on. Biting.   5

The Anticipation

   They tell me a woman waits, motionless
   till she's wooed. I wait

   spiderlike, effortless as they weave
   even my web for me, tying the cord in knots   10

with their courting hands.   Such power
over them.   And the spell

their own.   Who could release them?   Who
would untie the cord

with a cloven hoof?   15

The Bite

What I wear in the morning pleases
me: green shirt, skirt of wine.   I am wrapped

in myself as the smell of night
wraps round my sleep when I sleep   20

outside. By the time
I get to the corner

bar, corner store, corner construction
site, I become divine.   I turn

men into swine.   Leave   25
them behind me whistling, grunting, wild.

QUESTIONS

1. Who was Circe in mythology? What powers did she have? What could she
    do to men?
2. Who or what is the speaker in this poem? What is the connection between
    the speaker and Circe? Why is the poem entitled "Circe"?
3. What do Circe and the speaker symbolize in the poem? What is the source
    of Circe's power in the myth and the poem? What does this power symbolize?
4. What is the "fire" (lines 1–5)? Who are "they" (lines 6–15)? What is the
    effect of "spiderlike" (line 9) and "courting hands" (line 11)? What is "the
    spell" (line 12)? What is the significance of "a cloven hoof" (line 15)?
5. What is the speaker's attitude toward herself in lines 16–26? What happens
    to her in these lines? What happens to the men she encounters?
6. How does knowledge of Circe help you understand this poem? What symbolic
    resonances are drawn from the myth into the poem? What does the poem
    suggest about women? Men? Sexuality?

MURIEL RUKEYSER   (b. 1913)

Myth   *1978*

Long afterward, Oedipus, old and blinded, walked the
roads.   He smelled a familiar smell.   It was

the Sphinx.°   Oedipus said, "I want to ask one question.
Why didn't I recognize my mother?"   "You gave the
wrong answer," said the Sphinx.   "But that was what   5
made everything possible," said Oedipus.   "No," she said.
"When I asked, What walks on four legs in the morning,
two at noon, and three in the evening, you answered,
Man.   You didn't say anything about woman."
"When you say Man," said Oedipus, "you include women   10
too. Everyone knows that."   She said, "That's what
you think."

MYTH.   3 *Sphinx*: For the best-known representation of the Sphinx, see color plate 4.

QUESTIONS

1. Who was Oedipus? The Sphinx? What was wrong with Oedipus's answer to
    the Riddle of the Sphinx?

2. What elements and techniques in this work allow you to consider it a poem?

3. What explorations of diction occur in this work? Consider the words *myth*
    and *man*. What are the two myths and meanings of *myth* embodied in the
    title?

4. To what extent does the colloquial language in this poem undercut or revitalize
    the mythic material?

5. What point does this poem make about men? Women? Men's attitudes toward
    women? How does our knowledge of the Oedipus myth help clarify these
    aspects of the poem?

POEMS ABOUT ICARUS

The next five poems, written between 1933 and 1963, all draw on the
same mythic material—the story of the death of Icarus—to create symbolic
resonance, meaning, and impact. According to Greek myth, Icarus was
the son of Daedalus, an inventor and craftsman who was employed by
Minos, the king of Crete, to design and build a labyrinth in which the
king wanted to imprison the Minotaur, a monster that was half man and
half bull. With Daedalus's help, Theseus killed the Minotaur and freed
Athens from its annual tribute of sacrificial youths. As punishment for
helping Theseus, Minos imprisoned Daedalus and Icarus in a tower. He
also posted guards permanently on all roads and at the seaport to prevent
escape. Daedalus realized that he and Icarus could escape only by air, so
he fashioned two pairs of wings made of feathers and wax. As father and
son were about to fly away from Crete and imprisonment, Daedalus warned

Icarus not to fly too near the sun, because the heat would melt the wax and destroy the wings. In the glory of flight, however, Icarus forgot his father's warnings and began to soar higher and higher toward the sun. Icarus continued to mount upward, despite his father's passionate cries, until the wax melted and the wings fell apart; he plunged into the sea and drowned.

Although all the following poems feature Icarus as the central mythic figure, the focus and the symbolic resonance is different in each. Each poet went to the common storehouse of Greek mythology, selected the story and the figure of Icarus, and shaped these materials according to his or her own poetic goals. These goals are different in each poem. Thus, Icarus is used in various ways to illustrate and symbolize ideas about pride, daring, suffering, creativity, idealism, society, and the tedium of daily life. Each of the "Icarus" poems offers its own meaning, impact, and poetic experience. Taken together, however, the group of poems illustrates the way myth can be used for very different effects in various poetic contexts. As you study these poems, try to answer the following questions.

1. What is Icarus's symbolic meaning or value in the myth? What qualities or characteristics does Icarus represent in mythology?
2. On what aspects of the Icarus myth does each poet focus? Some possibilities include character, action, motivation, emotion, death, suffering, or the implications of the action.
3. To what extent does the allusion to Icarus contribute symbolic resonance and meaning to each poem? In what ways is the poetic effect of the mythic allusion different in each?
4. How do such poetic elements as diction, meter, rhyme, tone, and form help to reshape the myth and the figure of Icarus in each poem?
5. What themes or ideas are explored in each poem? Explain the connection between the Icarus myth and the meaning in each poem.

STEPHEN SPENDER   (1909–1986)

Icarus   1933

He will watch the hawk with an indifferent eye
  Or pitifully;
Nor on those eagles that so feared him, now
  Will strain his brow;
Weapons men use, stone, sling and strong-thewed bow   5
  He will not know.

This aristocrat, superb of all instinct,
  With death close linked

Had paced the enormous cloud, almost had won
   War on the sun;   10
Till now, like Icarus mid-ocean-drowned,
   Hands, wings, are found.

W. H. AUDEN   (1907–1973)

Musée des Beaux Arts°   *1940*

About suffering they were never wrong,
The Old Masters: how well they understood
Its human position; how it takes place
While someone else is eating or opening a window or just walking dully along;
How, when the aged are reverently, passionately waiting   5
For the miraculous birth, there always must be
Children who did not specially want it to happen, skating
On a pond at the edge of the wood:
They never forgot
That even the dreadful martyrdom must run its course   10
Anyhow in a corner, some untidy spot
Where the dogs go on with their doggy life and the torturer's horse
Scratches its innocent behind on a tree.
In Brueghel's° *Icarus*, for instance: how everything turns away
Quite leisurely from the disaster; the ploughman may   15
Have heard the splash, the forsaken cry,
But for him it was not an important failure; the sun shone
As it had to on the white legs disappearing into the green
Water; and the expensive delicate ship that must have seen
Something amazing, a boy falling out of the sky,   20
Had somewhere to get to and sailed calmly on.

MUSÉE DES BEAUX ARTS: "Museum of Fine Arts."   14 *Brueghel*: Pieter Brueghel or
Breughel (ca. 1525–1569) was a Flemish painter whose subjects included the Nativity ("the
miraculous birth"), the Crucifixion ("the dreadful martyrdom"), and the fall of Icarus. See
pp. 757 and 818 for two other poems based on the work of Brueghel.

ANNE SEXTON   (1928–1974)

To a Friend Whose Work Has Come to Triumph°   *1962*

Consider Icarus, pasting those sticky wings on,
testing that strange little tug at his shoulder blade,

TO A FRIEND WHOSE WORK HAS COME TO TRIUMPH. The title alludes to and
reverses the title of a poem by William Butler Yeats, "To a Friend Whose Work Has Come
to Nothing" (1914).

and think of that first flawless moment over the lawn
of the labyrinth. Think of the difference it made!
There below are the trees, as awkward as camels;   5
and here are the shocked starlings pumping past
and think of innocent Icarus who is doing quite well:
larger than a sail, over the fog and the blast
of the plushy ocean, he goes. Admire his wings!
Feel the fire at his neck and see how casually   10
he glances up and is caught, wondrously tunneling
into that hot eye. Who cares that he fell back to the sea?
See him acclaiming the sun and come plunging down
while his sensible daddy goes straight into town.

WILLIAM CARLOS WILLIAMS (1883–1963)

Landscape with the Fall of Icarus   *1962*

According to Brueghel°
when Icarus fell
it was spring

a farmer was ploughing
his field   5
the whole pageantry

of the year was
awake tingling
near

the edge of the sea   10
concerned
with itself

sweating in the sun
that melted
the wings' wax   15

unsignificantly
off the coast
there was

a splash quite unnoticed
this was   20
Icarus drowning

LANDSCAPE WITH THE FALL OF ICARUS.   1 *Brueghel*: See the note for line 14 in
Auden's "Musée des Beaux Arts," p. 817. See color plate 2 for the Brueghel painting *Landscape
with the Fall of Icarus.*

EDWARD FIELD   (b. 1924)

Icarus   *1963*

Only the feathers floating around the hat
Showed that anything more spectacular had occurred
Than the usual drowning. The police preferred to ignore
The confusing aspects of the case,
And the witnesses ran off to a gang war.   5
So the report filed and forgotten in the archives read simply
"Drowned," but it was wrong: Icarus
Had swum away, coming at last to the city
Where he rented a house and tended the garden.

"That nice Mr. Hicks" the neighbors called him,   10
Never dreaming that the gray, respectable suit
Concealed arms that had controlled huge wings
Nor that those sad, defeated eyes had once
Compelled the sun. And had he told them
They would have answered with a shocked, uncomprehending stare.   15
No, he could not disturb their neat front yards;
Yet all his books insisted that this was a horrible mistake:
What was he doing aging in a suburb?
Can the genius of the hero fall
To the middling stature of the merely talented?   20

And nightly Icarus probes his wound
And daily in his workshop, curtains carefully drawn,
Constructs small wings and tries to fly
To the lighting fixture on the ceiling:
Fails every time and hates himself for trying.   25

He had thought himself a hero, had acted heroically,
And dreamt of his fall, the tragic fall of the hero;
But now rides commuter trains,
Serves on various committees,
And wishes he had drowned.   30

WRITING ABOUT MYTH IN POETRY

An essay on myth in poetry will normally connect the mythic material in
a poem to some other consideration, such as speaker, tone, or meaning.
This suggests a two-part exploration of the poem, one concerned with its
general sense, and the other concerned with the ways in which myth shapes
and controls that sense.

    When planning an essay on the mythic elements in a poem, you
should first go through the process of discovery and investigation described

earlier in this chapter. If you can select the poem, choose one that is short enough to be handled well in a brief essay and yet offers a wealth of mythic allusion with which you are somewhat familiar. Always read the poem carefully several times, note any allusions to myth, and try to find out as much as possible.

Once you have both a general understanding of the poem and specific information about the mythic content, you can work back through the poem to develop the raw materials for your essay; you can begin to think about a central idea and supporting evidence. At this point, you should be considering the mythological content of the poem and its effect on other elements, including speaker, character, action, setting, situation, imagery, form, and meaning.

As you reexamine the poem in the light of its references to myth, you will be dealing with a number of variables. In general, you are looking for the ways in which myth enriches the poem and focuses its meaning. Thus, you should seek the most significant area of interaction between myth and poem. The following questions should help:

1. To what extent does the title help identify the mythic content of the poem and thus provide a key for understanding?

2. Who is the speaker in this poem? The central figure or figures? Is the speaker also the central figure, or is there a distinction?

3. Is either the speaker or the central character drawn from mythology? If so, what qualities and characteristics of the mythic figure are evoked by the speaker or character in the poem? To what extent does our understanding of the relevant myth help us explain the speaker and/or the characters in the poem?

4. If the characters are drawn from mythology, how are they symbolic in the *myth* (apart from the poem)? What aspects of this symbolism are carried into the poem? How does the poem maintain, undercut, increase, or change the symbolism?

5. Does the poem retell a myth? In other words, how much of the poem's action, setting, and situation are borrowed from mythology? What is the significance of the action in the myth? To what extent is this material symbolic? How does the poet reshape the action and its significance to his or her own ends?

6. Beyond character and action, what mythic images occur in the poem? How do these affect the poem's meaning and impact?

7. How do the various formal elements of poetry such as diction, rhyme, meter, and form reshape the mythic material and the impact or meaning of the myth? Do specific words and phrases, for instance, undercut or reinforce the ideas and implications that we find in the myth itself? Does the rhyme (if any) lead us to deal with the mythic content seriously or humorously? Does the tone of the poem support or undercut the implications of the myth?

8. How does the mythic content help create and clarify what the poem is about?

Not every poem will provide meaningful answers to all these questions. Nor is this list exhaustive; you will often find other subjects worthy of examination. Nevertheless, the answers to these sorts of questions will yield a great deal of information about the role of myth in the poem. In addition, these data will usually point toward the specific area in which the myth and the poem interact most profoundly. This area will become the subject of the essay.

As with most other essays, developing a tentative focus or central idea is the most difficult part of prewriting. Whatever discoveries you have made about the poem and its mythic elements will be most helpful in this respect. If, for example, you find that the poem retells a myth in order to make a point about history or society, your central idea will reflect that connection. Similarly, if the poem employs a speaker or character from mythology to convey ideas about war or heroism, your essay will focus on the linkage among myth, character, and those ideas.

When you formulate a tentative central idea, draft it as a complete sentence that conveys the full scope of your own ideas about the poem. It is not enough merely to assert that a given poem contains a great deal of mythic material. If you are writing an essay about Yeats's "Leda and the Swan," for example, you might be tempted to form a central idea that argues that "William Butler Yeats's 'Leda and the Swan' retells the myth of Leda's rape by Zeus and the consequences of that event." That sentence does not tell the reader anything about the *way* myth works in the poem. Nor does it provide a basis for moving beyond simple summary and paraphrase. A more effective formulation of a central idea might read as follows: "In Yeats's 'Leda and the Swan,' the myth of Leda's rape by Zeus and the consequences of that rape are employed to illustrate the historical process and to question the connection between knowledge and power." This sentence points to a specific connection between mythological content and the poem's effect, and it gives a clear direction to the essay.

Once you have formed a tentative focus and central idea, reorganize your data in support of the thesis. At this point, you can begin to shape your insights and conclusions into tentative paragraphs. You may have to rethink or refocus the central idea of the essay several times. Do not let such revising bother you; it is quite normal and, in fact, helpful. Indeed, rethinking and revision should occur at virtually every stage of both the prewriting and the writing processes.

Organizing Your Essay

INTRODUCTION. The introduction should name the poet and the poem and make whatever general points you wish about the poem. For instance, you might want to provide relevant information about the poem's form or any special circumstances of composition. More important, the introduction should state the essay's central idea and the way that idea will be supported in the body. Thus, the introduction should identify the important mythic aspects of the poem, link them with other relevant poetic elements, and make an assertion about the effect of this connection.

BODY.   The body of the essay will prove the central idea stated in the introduction with supporting details drawn from the poem. Because this central idea will normally assert a connection between the mythic material and another poetic element—speaker, character, action, image, meaning, or the like—you will have to deal with both the myth and the poem, continually discussing the relationship between the two. At some point early in the essay, you might want to summarize briefly the relevant parts of the myth under consideration. For the most part, however, the essay should focus on the poem (and the mythic material within the poem) rather than on the myth itself.

Various strategies can be employed to organize the body of the essay. You might decide to echo the organization of the poem, and shape the central paragraphs so as to reflect the line-by-line or stanza-by-stanza logic of the poem (as in the discussion of "Leda and the Swan" on p. 807). Alternatively, you might choose an organization based on a series of different mythic elements or figures. If a poem alludes to Odysseus, his wife Penelope, and his son Telemachus, for instance, you might devote a paragraph or two to the way each figure shapes the impact and meaning of the poem. As a third option, you might use the relevant elements of poetry as the focal points of organization. Thus, if you argue that diction, rhyme, and tone shape the mythological material in a poem to produce significant effects, you would deal with each element in turn.

CONCLUSION.   The conclusion should bring the essay to a convincing and assertive close rather than a mere stopping point. To do this, you can summarize the major points that were asserted in the introduction and supported in the body. At the same time, you can draw the reader's attention to the significance of your observations and to any further implications that might arise from the unique fusion of myth and the poetry under consideration.

SAMPLE ESSAY

Myth and Meaning in Dorothy Parker's "Penelope"*

Dorothy Parker's short lyric poem "Penelope" uses mythic allusion and symbolism to make a point about men and women and the way society per-

* See p. 810 for this poem.

ceives them. The mythic figure who speaks the poem and becomes one of its central symbols is Penelope. This speaker, and thus the poem, suggests that women must endure tedium and suffering in silence, and that society consistently misjudges and undervalues women's lives.° Through diction, tone, and mythic resonance, the speaker describes the active and heroic life of Odysseus, her own passive existence, and society's mistaken evaluation of both.□

[1]

[2]   The key to the poem's mythic resonance is the title, "Penelope." This is the only place where the mythological speaker of the poem is named. The title alludes to the wife of Odysseus, who waited at home in Ithaca for twenty years while her husband fought in the Trojan War and struggled against Poseidon, the god of the sea, to return home. Penelope's story is found in Homer's *Odyssey*, where we learn that her ten-year wait for Odysseus's return after the end of the Trojan War was anything but peaceful or pleasant. Her palace was filled with boorish suitors who assumed that Odysseus was dead and demanded that the queen of Ithaca choose a new husband. Only Penelope and Telemachus, her son, clung to the hope that Odysseus was still alive. Penelope kept the arrogant suitors at bay by promising to marry one of them after she finished weaving a shroud for Odysseus's father. In order to delay this eventuality, she worked at the loom each day and unraveled the work each night. Thus, she lived a domestic but stressful life for ten years in which she bravely resisted both despair and the demands of the suitors.

[3]   Although the title refers directly to Penelope, the poem itself draws on mythic material that relates to both Penelope and Odysseus. Lines 1–5 evoke our memory of Odysseus; his wanderings and adventures are alluded to in phrases like "He shall ride the silver seas" (line 4) and "He shall cut the glittering wave" (line 5). Odysseus is never mentioned by name, and none of his specific adventures is cited. Nevertheless, the poem's title naturally leads to the assumption that the "he" in these lines is Odysseus. At the same time, however, the absence of any specific identification allows us to see this male figure as a symbol for all men who leave home and pursue an active life of adventure. The adjectives and verbs used in these lines make this active life seem attractive and exciting. Such phrases as "the pathway of the sun" (line 1) and "the footsteps of the breeze" (line 2) add a sense of romance and mystery to the active life of the male. The adjectives *silver* and *glittering* connote splendor and glory. Verbs such as *ride* and *cut* reinforce the active and violent nature of the male's existence. We also find, however, a subtle undercutting of this heroic male figure in the same lines. Many of these phrases, like "ride the silver seas," are clichés. The speaker's use of such clichés suggests that this image of the active hero is both trite and, to some extent, inaccurate.

Just as "he" in lines 1–5 refers to both Odysseus and a symbolic representative of all men, so the speaker of the poem is both Penelope and an embodiment of all women. This symbolic speaker contrasts her own life to

----

° Central idea.
□ Thesis sentence.

[4] the active life of Odysseus and mankind in lines 6–9. Here we find no adjectives at all; the woman's existence is thus rendered drab and tedious. In addition, the verbs represent passive and domestic activities: *sit, rock, rise, brew, snip,* and *bleach.* These last two verbs are especially effective. The phrase "snip my thread" (line 8) is the only allusion to Penelope's unhappy existence in Ithaca; it refers to her daring deception of the suitors through weaving and unraveling the shroud. At the same time, *snip* is contrasted with the verb *cut* used earlier in the poem. While the words are synonyms, they carry very different connotations; *cut* implies grand and violent action while *snip* suggests careful and delicate activity. *Bleach* is equally connotative; although it refers directly to "the linen for my bed," it implies that the speaker's life is faded and colorless.

[5] The final line of the poem crystallizes its message and clarifies the speaker's attitude toward the different roles that men and women play. Here, the speaker asserts that "They will call him brave." *They* refers to society, to the world at large, and to generations of readers who have admired Odysseus in Homer's *Iliad* and *Odyssey.* The speaker assures us that he—both Odysseus in particular and the active male in general—will be admired by society. The meter of the line places a great deal of stress on the word *him,* thus emphasizing the speaker's ironic tone and her realization that society will always ignore or dismiss the quiet bravery of women. In myth and in life, the woman's role often demands more courage and conviction than the man's. Certainly Penelope's desperate existence for ten years in Ithaca, besieged in her own home by arrogant suitors who ignored her wishes, testifies to the strength and bravery of women. Nevertheless, Penelope, speaking for all women in all nations and all ages, ironically observes that "they will call *him* brave."

[6] This poem thus employs mythic figures and events to examine the roles traditionally played by men and women, and society's distorted perception of those roles. Odysseus, as a symbol for all men, is presented as both a heroic and a trite figure; the words that describe his life carry implications of mystery, adventure, and splendor, yet they are often clichés. Penelope, as a symbol for all women, describes her own life as tedious, drab, and passive. She hints, however, at the courage and desperation that often lurk behind domestic routine. Our knowledge of Penelope's courageous survival in Ithaca during her husband's absence adds significantly to the impact of these implications. Finally, the mythic figures and symbols in this poem illustrate the degree to which society admires the active male and ignores the strength and courage of women.

Commentary on the Essay

The sample essay deals with the connection between mythic characters and meaning in Dorothy Parker's "Penelope." The introduction identifies the poem as a lyric and Penelope as the central mythic figure. Most important, it states the central idea of the essay and presents the ways that idea will be supported in the body. Thus, the introduction asserts that two mythic characters, redefined by diction and tone, are employed symbolically in the poem to make a point about the lives of women and men and the way society values those lives.

The body of the essay is organized along the lines of the first strategy mentioned on page 822; it follows the organization of the poem itself. Thus, paragraph 2 focuses on the title, paragraph 3 on lines 1–5, paragraph 4 on lines 6–9, and paragraph 5 on the last line of the poem. Each of the paragraphs also advances a specific aspect of the essay's central idea. In paragraph 2 Penelope is identified and the relevant mythic material is summarized. The title and its mythic resonance are used, in turn, to introduce Odysseus and the symbol of the heroic male in paragraph 3. Here, the point is made that Parker's diction undercuts the active male while it also seems to be glorifying him. The paragraph thus asserts that Odysseus is employed in the poem symbolically to represent the ideal *and* the cliché of the active and heroic male.

The first sentence of paragraph 4 provides transition from the discussion of Odysseus and heroic males to that of Penelope and the perceived passiveness of women. Again, the essay explores the way diction and mythic allusion in the poem demonstrate that women's lives can be domestic and desperate at the same time. Paragraph 5 looks at the poem's final line in relation to the contrasted lives of heroic men and passive women. Here, the essay takes up tone and meter to reveal the speaker's attitude toward these contrasting lives and society's misperception of them.

The conclusion basically summarizes the major points of the essay. Thus, the first sentence repeats the subject of the poem. The next three summarize the essay's observations about Odysseus and Penelope. Finally, the last two sentences of the conclusion reconnect the poem to the myth and repeat the poem's central point about society's mistaken evaluation of bravery in women and men.

WRITING TOPICS FOR CHAPTER 21

1. In the poems "Ulysses," "Penelope," "Odysseus," "Siren Song," and "Circe," the poets evoke the same myth but for different purposes. What are these purposes? What views do you find about adventure, domesticity, and sexuality? What attitudes toward figures in the myth (Odysseus, Penelope, the Siren, Circe) do the poets bring out? How does word choice, selection of detail, and point of view influence the conclusions presented by each poet?

2. The myth of Icarus is used by Spender, Auden, Sexton, Williams, and Field. Basing your conclusions on two or more of their poems, what similarities and differences can you describe? How do the poets present the myth? How do they use the myth to create unusual or surprising endings, and to comment on contemporary but also permanent attitudes about life and the sufferings of others?

3. What point does Muriel Rukuyser's "Myth" make about both men and women and their attitudes toward each other? How does our knowledge of the Oedipus

myth (see Sophocles' play *Oedipus the King* in the Drama section) help clarify these aspects of the poem? In what respects is the poem particularly contemporary?

4. Select a myth from among the many that are a part of our tradition (e.g., Oedipus, Odysseus, Antigone, Sisyphus, the fight between God and Satan, the Children of Israel as the chosen people, Robin Hood, Paul Bunyan, Davy Crockett, the Lone Ranger; the log cabin, the American West, the homesteaders, etc.). Write a poem based on the myth, and attempt to present your own view about the importance, timeliness, intelligence, and truth of the myth. What kinds of detail do you select? How do you present the figures of the myth? How do you make your own attitudes apparent by your arrangement of detail and your word choice (see, for example, how Broumas and Rukuyser present their figures).

22

Theme: The Ideas and the Meaning in Poetry

Usually, the words *theme* and *meaning* convey a general sense of ideas, or the specific sense of a major or central idea. In this chapter we use these senses, but in addition we take into account all the expressive skills and devices that poets use to make their poems come alive. In this comprehensive sense, **theme** and **meaning** refer to the total impact and effect of a poem upon readers, from initial understanding, to interpretation, and finally to comprehension and assimilation.

To determine the total effect of poems, we begin with the basic things we have been working with throughout this book. The first of these is **subject.** Subjects are often general, and may include such broad categories as love, death, war, art, youth, age, work, and nature. Thomas Hardy's "Channel Firing" (p. 562) and Wilfred Owen's "Dulce et Decorum Est" (p. 659), for example, share the same subject—war.

But the subject of a poem is only the beginning of our comprehension, for subjects alone are static. To move us, poems must take us somewhere. Along with the subject, therefore, we also consider both the primary and secondary ideas in a poem—that is, theme and meaning. We have seen that a poem's theme or main idea is a specific "point" that a poem makes about the subject. In prose, points are made directly and openly; for example, the Declaration of Independence asserts that human beings have the unalienable rights of life, liberty, and the pursuit of happiness. In poetry, however, points are made dramatically and indirectly. Indeed, there are some who assert that poetry is self-sufficient, and that it may be read and felt without any major reference to ideas or points. Even if we grant that many poems may have no *overt* intention to express ideas (poems are not newspaper articles, or sermons), it is nevertheless true that most poems are based in views about their subjects that we may consider as a major aspect of their total meaning.

Thus, Hardy's "Channel Firing" and Owen's "Dulce et Decorum Est" are both powerful and dramatic poems which affect us deeply. They share the common subject of war, and they also share a common thread of hostility toward war as a human institution. But in addition, both poems may be read as strong statements of ideas. Hardy's poem asserts that war is perpetually linked with human beings, as a virtual condition of life, and that despite the perversity of war it will likely continue to threaten all the positive and noble achievements that humanity has created. Owen's poem, dealing with a destructive gas attack in war, asserts that war is obscene and that ideas about war's nobility are unreal and untrue. Both poems, in short, contain clear ideas.

Moreover, no matter what the subject, poems achieve much of their impact through the strength of their ideas. For example, Andrew Marvell's "To His Coy Mistress" and Robert Herrick's "To the Virgins, to Make Much of Time" both concern the subject of love within the context of passing time. But while Herrick's poem argues that the pressure of eventual death should lead people toward delight in marriage, Marvell's poem asserts that this same pressure should lead toward the full but desperate pursuit of pleasures through the "iron gates of life." These ideas, like those of Hardy and Owen, are not frivolous expressions of idle poetic moments, but are deeply felt ideas that people should know, think about, and apply or not apply, as they wish, to their own lives. The same depth of impact and strength of idea are to be found in most good poems, and it is this richness and breadth that makes poetry both challenging and effective.

STRATEGIES FOR DEALING WITH MEANING

So that we may comprehend the total meaning of a poem, we need to consider its ideas together with its intellectual and emotional impact. In effect, meaning involves us in a transfer of experience from the poet's mind to our own. It is no exaggeration to claim that the structure and development of a poem also produces a corresponding development of thoughts, reactions, considerations, and emotions in readers. To get at meaning, then, is to get at all the ways in which poetry brings these effects about.

We have noted that the theme of a poem is established partly by *what* the poem says and partly by the *way* the poem says it. An initial understanding of meaning can be gained by a close, sentence-by-sentence reading, but for most poems our initial reading is affected by many of the poet's devices beyond straightforward statement. As often as not, the poem's theme is implied as well as stated, and many elements shape the message and meaning. These include speaker, character, setting and situation, action, diction, sound, imagery, metaphor and simile, tone, meter, rhyme, form, symbol, allusion, and others.

SPEAKER. The identity and circumstances of the speaker can significantly affect a poem's meaning. It is essential for us to understand, for example, that the speaker of Hardy's "Channel Firing" is a corpse who has been wakened in his grave by the noise of "great guns" at sea, and that the speaker in Sharon Olds's "35/10" is a mother brushing her daughter's hair. The attitudes and ironies so essential to the meanings of these poems would not be clear if we did not know who these speakers are and what they are doing at the "time" of the poems. Similarly, it is important to determine whether a speaker is trustworthy. In Browning's "My Last Duchess," for example, the speaker presents himself as a friendly and intelligent man of integrity, but his words betray him as intimidating, cold, cruel, and heartless. In short, each poem produces its own unique speaker, whose circumstances have a vital bearing on the content and meaning of the poem.

CHARACTER, SETTING, ACTION. The characters, settings, and actions in a poem do much to shape the meaning. A poem that is set in a graveyard and that refers to gunnery practice at sea (Hardy's "Channel Firing") conveys a different meaning from one that tells about a walk through the woodland in spring (Housman's "Loveliest of Trees") or that tells about a mother brushing her daughter's hair at bedtime (Olds's "35/10"). Even if all three poems deal with the common subject of death, their radically different contexts and actions produce a new perspective, a different emotional response, a new experience, and a different meaning.

DICTION. The words of a poem—denotation, connotation, diction, and syntax—all shape the poem's total meaning and emotional impact. In Robert Herrick's "To the Virgins, to Make Much of Time," for example, the speaker advises virgins to gather "rosebuds," which could easily be interpreted as an invitation to promiscuous sexuality. However, the poem concludes on the advice to "go marry," and thereby it places the urgency of sex in a context of socially and religiously approved behavior. By contrast, in Ben Jonson's "To Celia," the speaker urges "sports of love" and "love's fruit," but provides no additional context. Thus "To Celia" primarily advises seduction, while "To the Virgins" provides happy but mature advice about life, even though both poems similarly belong to the "seize the day," or "carpe diem" tradition of love poetry.

IMAGERY AND RHETORICAL FIGURES. Imagery, metaphor, simile, and other devices of language make abstract ideas and situations concrete and immediate. We have stressed how Keats creates a sense of excitement through his simile of the "watcher of the skies" in "On First Looking into Chapman's Homer" (p. 625). Beyond such uses, a poet may use imagery and metaphorical language to reinforce or to negate what appears to be the speaker's major thrust. In Owen's "Dulce et Decorum Est," for example, soldiers are described as "Bent double, like old beggars under sacks." The simile is consistent with the rest of the poem; it defines the speaker's dislike of the drudgery and difficulty of war, and it shapes the poem's ultimate point that war is unrelievedly demeaning and horrible. In contrast, the first part of Dorothy Parker's "Penelope" (p. 810) contains clichéd images that undercut the heroic ideal; the poem thereby emphasizes the negative truth that heroes, while pursuing their goals, may also be self-centered and neglectful.

TONE.   The tone of a poem has a significant effect on theme. Most often, it reinforces a poem's total meaning. In Arthur O'Shaughnessy's "A Love Symphony," for example (p. 668), the speaker's admiration for the listener is clear, unambiguous, and unreserved, as is indicated by phrases like "You were more sweet." Tone may sometimes create ambiguity, however, or it may even work against the stated purpose of the speaker. As we just noted in "Penelope" Parker ironically condemns the hero Odysseus through clichés about heroism; in addition, the irony of the final line forces us to recognize that Penelope has been thrust into an unfair position by the absence of her husband. Through irony, therefore, the poem points out that Penelope, and not Odysseus, is the hero. Irony is also present in Marvell's "To His Coy Mistress," in which the *carpe diem* mode is colored by the speaker's many details about death and eternity. In short, although the speaker's ostensible purpose is persuasion and seduction, the tone makes the poem not happy and loving but instead serious and philosophical.

RHYTHM, METER, AND SOUND.   Elements such as rhythm, alliteration, assonance, and onomatopoeia rarely shape meaning independently of other elements. Rather, they usually reinforce the ideas and emotions created through the other aspects of the poem. Such elements can, however, refine and focus meaning significantly. Rhythm and meter may throw particularly important words into strong positions of emphasis, and therefore they may shape our perception of the importance of particular ideas. Similarly, meaning can be refined through the skillful use of alliteration, assonance, and the repetition of identical or similar sounds. In Pope's line, "The sound must seem an echo to the sense," for example, the alliteration of the *s* sound connects the key words "sound," "seem," and "sense." The words are important in themselves, but they are made more emphatic, in the context, by Pope's linking them by sound.

RHYME, STRUCTURE, AND FORM.   Rhyme may be employed to clinch ideas, regulate the tone, and thus shape meaning. The falling or double rhymes in Herrick's "To the Virgins" lighten the tone and thus modify the poem's message. Structure can be equally important in shaping meaning. Form too can provide a method for ordering and shaping a poem's theme and meaning. The coherent units or stanzas of a closed form often reflect specific steps in the poem's expression of meaning. Such is the case in Spenser's *Amoretti* 75, "One Day I Wrote Her Name upon the Strand." In this poem the formal divisions of the sonnet reflect a logical pattern that moves from an action to a reaction and finally to an explanation.

SYMBOL AND ALLUSION.   Poets employ symbol and allusion as a kind of shorthand to convey very complex ideas and a great deal of information as quickly and economically as possible. In "To the Virgins," for example, two symbols—rosebuds and flowers—point beyond themselves to human sexuality, marriage and families, and full engagement with life. The symbols thus carry much of the poem's impact and message. Allusion can be equally important. In "To His Coy Mistress" we find geographic and biblical allusions that are crucial in shaping the meaning of the first part of the poem's argument.

These eight areas may seem like a large number of variables to consider in working toward an understanding of a poem's central idea and total meaning; at first, the process may seem quite difficult. Keep in mind, however, that all eight are seldom equally relevant to a given poem. As you study more poetry, you will learn how to focus your attention on two or three significant aspects of a poem and to give others only secondary consideration. Eventually, you will be able to evaluate the impact of most of these elements on meaning rather quickly. Indeed, experienced readers of poetry do much of this step-by-step analysis almost unconsciously and simultaneously as they read a poem.

STUDYING MESSAGE AND MEANING IN POETRY

Let us now turn to a specific poem and see how we might arrive at an understanding of its theme and meaning. The poem, "Ars Poetica," which means "the art of poetry," should help us understand the nature of meaning in poetry, since it is "about" that very thing.

ARCHIBALD MacLEISH   (1892–1982)

Ars Poetica   *1926*

A poem should be palpable and mute
As a globed fruit,

832 22/Theme: The Ideas and the Meaning in Poetry

Dumb
As old medallions to the thumb,

Silent as the sleeve-worn stone   5
Of casement ledges where the moss has grown—

A poem should be wordless
As the flight of birds.

                    *   *   *

A poem should be motionless in time
As the moon climbs,   10

Leaving, as the moon releases
Twig by twig the night-entangled trees,

Leaving, as the moon behind the winter leaves,
Memory by memory the mind—

A poem should be motionless in time   15
As the moon climbs.

                    *   *   *

A poem should be equal to:
Not true.

For all the history of grief
An empty doorway and a maple leaf.   20

For love
The leaning grasses and two lights above the sea—

A poem should not mean
But be.

QUESTIONS

1. What is the subject of this poem? To what extent does the title help define
   the subject? Why did the poet call it "Ars Poetica" instead of "The Art of
   Poetry"?

2. What does the first section (lines 1–8) assert that a poem should be? How
   are similes employed to make this assertion clearer and more concrete?

3. How can a poem be "mute" (line 1), "dumb" (line 3), "silent" (line 5), and
   "wordless" (line 7)? Since a poem (and this poem) must be made of words,
   how can this paradox be resolved?

4. What does the second section (lines 9–16) assert about a poem? How are
   symbolism and simile used to clarify this assertion? How can something be
   "motionless" and "climb" at the same time? What is the effect of repetition
   in this section?

5. What does the third section (lines 17–24) assert about a poem? What symbolizes "all the history of grief" here? What symbolizes "love"? Why are these two examples of symbolism included in the poem?

6. What does this poem finally assert about poetry? To what extent does "Ars Poetica" embody and illustrate its own ideas and total meaning?

The subject of "Ars Poetica" is the art of poetry and the nature of poems. The elevated diction of the Latin title connotes philosophical seriousness and great scholarship. Indeed, the title is borrowed from a treatise on poetry written by the Roman poet Horace (65–8 B.C.). The title is partly ironic. Although the poem treats the nature of poetry quite seriously, it is certainly not a scholarly essay.

"Ars Poetica" represents an attempt to define and describe poetry. It does so in two ways: it *tells* us and it *shows* us what a poem should be. The poem's central idea is found in the third section, where the speaker asserts that "A poem should be equal to: / Not true" and that "A poem should not mean / But be." In other words, a poem should embody an experience that is parallel to reality rather than simply convey a specific idea or truth. Does this mean that a poem should have no theme? Not really, although this may appear to be the point of "Ars Poetica" at first. Rather, the poem asserts that the total experience of a poem is more important and valuable than any single stated idea it might relate.

The first section of "Ars Poetica" tells us that a poem should be "mute" (line 1), "dumb" (line 3), "silent" (line 5), and "wordless" (line 7). This appears to be a paradox; poems are obviously made of words. The poem goes on, however, in this section to show us exactly what "wordless" means. Thus, each two-line stanza contains a simile that makes both the meaning and the experience of wordless or silent existence clear. The four comparisons—to "globed fruit," "old medallions," "sleeve-worn stone," and "the flights of birds"—present images of silence that we can recreate and experience in our minds.

A closer look at one of these similes shows how it evokes the state of "wordless" silence with words. Lines 5 and 6 assert that a poem should be "Silent as the sleeve-worn stone / Of casement ledges where the moss has grown." The image begins as a cliché: "as quiet or as still as a stone." But the poet breathes new life into the cliché by particularizing the stone. The stone is "sleeve-worn," worn down by the friction of many people's arms over hundreds of years. It is also the stone of a "casement ledge" or windowsill where the moss has grown." This focusing of the image of the stone expands our sense of silence by adding overtones of elapsed time, slow erosion, and quiet natural growth. The image embodies not only the feeling and the idea of silence, but also a state of being that we can experience. This brings us back to perhaps the most important word in the first section of the poem: *palpable* (line 1), which means easily seen, heard, perceived, or felt. This section of the poem suggests that a poem cannot simply be words; it must be a process that unites reader and text in an emotional, sensual, and intellectual experience.

The second section of the poem (lines 9–16) also defines an aspect of poetry and begins with what appears to be a paradox: "A poem should be motionless in time / As the moon climbs." How can something be "motion-less" and "climb" (or move) at the same time? The answer lies in the way we experience the moon and poetry. The moon becomes both the central image and symbol here. The moon appears to be motionless; yet over the course of an entire night it does move, rising in the east, crossing the heavens, and setting in the west. "Motionless," like "wordless," has more to do with the way we perceive and experience things than it does with actuality. The image thus emphasizes the parallel between poetry and our experience of time, motion, and the moon.

Here, as in the first section, the poem offers two similes that clarify the way we experience motionless movement in time and in poetry. The two middle stanzas compare the effect of moonlight on the landscape to the effect of poetry on the reader; just as moonlight "releases" the shadows of the trees "twig by twig," so the poem should leave the mind "memory by memory," evoking timeless responses and experiences in us. This process of timeless and motionless experience in poetry is also illustrated in the structure of this middle section. The lines that open the section also close it. Thus, the beginning and the end are identical; we end up where we started. MacLeish employs repetition to make concrete the experience of motionless and timeless processes in poetry.

The poem offers two more sets of symbols as examples of the way poetry creates experience. The first example suggests that "all the history of grief" may be symbolized by "An empty doorway and a maple leaf" (lines 19–20). The second symbolizes "love" by "The leaning grasses and two lights above the sea" (line 22). The "empty doorway" suggests that someone is gone, missing, dead; "doorway" presupposes presence and movement, but "empty" conveys absence. In a like manner, the "maple leaf" implies seasonal change and death. The symbols create experiences parallel to grief and love. More important, however, they illustrate the importance of symbolism as a vehicle for meaning.

These symbols embody a key concept for poetry: provide the concrete detail to evoke the experience of the abstract whole. This is one of the processes of poetry; this is the way imagery, simile, and symbol work in the poem and in the reader. "Ars Poetica" is not "mute." It asserts that poems should create a "palpable" experience that parallels (but is not the same as) life. And as this poem illustrates, that experience is created through imagery, comparison, and symbolism. The poem also makes it clear that the experience is more important than either the words that create it or the words evoked in the reader by it. In that sense, a poem is "mute" and

Plate 1 Pieter Brueghel (the Elder), *La Kermesse.*
Vienna Kunsthistorisches Museum. Art Resource

Plate 2 Pieter Brueghel (the Elder), *Landscape with the "Fall of Icarus."* Scala/Art Resource

Plate 3 Greek vase. Lekythos, black-figured, showing a wedding procession, dancers, and musicians. The Metropolitan Museum of Art, Walter C. Baker Gift Fund, 1956

Plate 4 The great sphynx at Cheops, Egypt. SEF/Art Resource

Plate 5 Pablo Picasso, *Guernica*. Prado Museum, Madrid

Plate 6   Fernand Léger, *The City.*
Philadelphia Museum of Art, The A. E. Gallatin Collection

"wordless"; its existence and value derive from the experience it offers us.

POEMS FOR STUDY

BEN JONSON   (1572–1632)

To Celia   *1606*

Come my Celia, let us prove,°   try
While we may, the sports of love;
Time will not be ours forever;
He at length our good will sever.
Spend not then his gifts in vain.   5
Suns that set may rise again;
But if once we lose this light,
'Tis with us perpetual night.
Why should we defer our joys?
Fame° and rumor are but toys.   reputation   10
Cannot we delude the eyes
Of a few poor household spies,
Or his° easier ears beguile,   Celia's husband
So removed by our wile?
'Tis no sin love's fruit to steal;   15
But the sweet theft to reveal,
To be taken, to be seen,
These have crimes accounted been.

TO CELIA. The poem is from Jonson's play *Volpone*; it is spoken by Volpone (the name means "the fox") to Celia, a married woman whom he is trying to seduce.

QUESTIONS

1. What is the speaker like? What is his attitude toward time? Love? Celia?
2. What is personified in lines 3–5? What power does this force have?
3. This type of poem (and the specific argument in lines 1–8) is called *carpe diem* (Latin for "seize the day"). How is the idea of "seizing the day" relevant to the first eight lines of this poem?
4. How does the speaker's argument change in the last ten lines (9–18)? What does he claim that he and Celia can do? What assertions does he (and the poem) make about time, love, reputation, and crime?
5. How consistent is the speaker's argument? How convincing? How moral?
6. What is the tone of the poem? How is it created? How does it affect the total meaning of the poem?

ANDREW MARVELL   (1621–1678)

To His Coy Mistress   *1681*

Had we but world enough, and time,
This coyness, lady, were no crime.
We would sit down, and think which way
To walk, and pass our long love's day.
Thou by the Indian Ganges'° side   5
Shouldst rubies find; I by the tide
Of Humber° would complain. I would
Love you ten years before the flood°,   *Noah's flood*
And you should, if you please, refuse
Till the conversion of the Jews.°   10
My vegetable love should grow
Vaster than empires and more slow;
An hundred years should go to praise
Thine eyes, and on thy forehead gaze;
Two hundred to adore each breast,   15
But thirty thousand to the rest;
An age at least to every part,
And the last age should show your heart.
For, lady, you deserve this state,
Nor would I love at lower rate.   20
    But at my back I always hear
Time's wingéd chariot hurrying near;
And yonder all before us lie
Deserts of vast eternity.
Thy beauty shall no more be found,   25
Nor, in thy marble vault, shall sound
My echoing song; then worms shall try
That long-preserved virginity,
And your quaint honor turn to dust,
And into ashes all my lust: 30
The grave's a fine and private place,
But none, I think, do there embrace.
    Now therefore, while the youthful hue
Sits on thy skin like morning dew,
And while thy willing soul transpires   35
At every pore with instant fires,
Now let us sport us while we may,
And now, like amorous birds of prey,
Rather at once our time devour

TO HIS COY MISTRESS.   5 *Ganges*: a large river that runs across most of India.
7 *Humber*: a small river that runs through the north of England to the North Sea.
10 *Jews*: traditionally, this conversion is supposed to occur just before the Last Judgment.

Than languish in his slow-chapped° power.   *slow-jawed*   40
Let us roll all our strength and all
Our sweetness up into one ball,
And tear our pleasures with rough strife
Thorough° the iron gates of life: *through*
Thus, though we cannot make our sun   45
Stand still, yet we will make him run.

QUESTIONS

1. What can we deduce about the speaker in this poem? The listener? What does the title tell us? What does the speaker want?

2. In lines 1 through 20 the speaker sets up a hypothetical situation and the first part of a pseudo-logical proof: If *A* then *B*. What specific words indicate the logic of this section? What hypothetical situation is established?

3. How do geographic and biblical allusions affect our sense of time and place?

4. In lines 21 through 32 the speaker presents the second step of his argument; he refutes the hypothetical condition set up in the first twenty lines. What specific word indicates that this is a refutation? How does the speaker refute the first part of his argument? How does imagery help create and reinforce meaning here?

5. The last part of the poem (lines 33–46) presents the speaker's "logical" conclusion. What words indicate that this is a conclusion? What is the conclusion?

ROBERT HERRICK   (1591–1674)

To the Virgins, to Make Much of Time   *1648*

Gather ye rosebuds while ye may,
   Old time is still a-flying;
And this same flower that smiles today
   Tomorrow will be dying.

The glorious lamp of heaven, the sun,   5
   The higher he's a-getting,
The sooner will his race be run,
   And nearer he's to setting.

That age is best which is the first,
   When youth and blood are warmer;   10
But being spent, the worse, and worst
   Times still succeed the former.

Then be not coy, but use your time,
   And, while ye may, go marry;

For, having lost but once your prime,   15
   You may forever tarry.

QUESTIONS

1. What does the title of this poem tell us? What can we deduce about the speaker? To whom is the poem addressed?
2. What point does this poem make about time? Life? Love?
3. How does symbolism help shape the message and meaning of the poem? Consider especially "rosebuds," "flower," and "the sun."
4. How do rhyme and tone help create and focus the meaning of this poem?
5. Compare this poem to Jonson's "To Celia" and Marvell's "To His Coy Mistress." How well does this poem express the central idea of the *carpe diem* tradition? How are the tone and message of this poem similar to and different from those in the poems by Jonson and Marvell?

EDMUND SPENSER   (1552–1599)

Amoretti 75: One Day I Wrote Her Name upon the Strand   *1595*

One day I wrote her name upon the strand,°   beach
But came the waves and washèd it away:
Again I wrote it with a second hand,
But came the tide and made my pains his prey.
"Vain man," said she, "that doest in vain assay,   5
A mortal thing so to immortalize,
For I myself shall like to this decay,
And eek° my name be wiped out likewise."   also, indeed
"Not so," quod° I, "let baser things devise,   said
To die in dust, but you shall live by fame: 10
My verse your virtues rare shall eternize,
And in the heavens write your glorious name.
Where whenas death shall all the world subdue,
Our love shall live, and later life renew."

QUESTIONS

1. What action is described in the first quatrain of this sonnet? What point does the speaker's mistress make about this action in the second quatrain?
2. How does the speaker deal with his mistress's objections in the third quatrain and the couplet? What point does he make about her "fame" or reputation?
3. What is the subject of this poem? What is its theme?
4. To what extent do rhyme, meter, and form contribute to the formation of this poem's meaning?

MARIANNE MOORE   (1887–1982)

Poetry   *1921*

I, too, dislike it: there are things that are important beyond all this fiddle.
  Reading it, however, with a perfect contempt for it, one discovers in
  it after all, a place for the genuine.
     Hands that can grasp, eyes
     that can dilate, hair that can rise   5
       if it must, these things are important not because a

high-sounding interpretation can be put upon them but because they are
  useful. When they become so derivative as to become unintelligible,
  the same thing may be said for all of us, that we
     do not admire what   10
     we cannot understand: the bat
       holding on upside down or in quest of something to

eat, elephants pushing, a wild horse taking a roll, a tireless wolf under
  a tree, the immovable critic twitching his skin like a horse that feels a
       flea, the base-
     ball fan, the statistician—   15
      nor is it valid
       to discriminate against 'business documents and

school-books';° all these phenomena are important. One must make a distinction
  however: when dragged into prominence by half poets, the result is not poetry,
  nor till the poets among us can be   20
     'literalists of
     the imagination'° —above
      insolence and triviality and can present

for inspection, 'imaginary gardens with real toads in them', shall we have
  it. In the meantime, if you demand on the one hand,   25
  the raw material of poetry in
     all its rawness and
     that which is on the other hand
      genuine, you are interested in poetry.

POETRY. In the last edition of her *Collected Poems*, Moore deleted everything in this
poem following "genuine" in line 3.   17–18 *"business . . . school-books"*: the phrase is quoted
from the Russian novelist, Leo Tolstoy (1828–1910). Moore's original note cites a passage
in Tolstoy's *Diaries* (1917) in which he discusses the difference between prose and poetry:
"Where the boundary between prose and poetry lies, I shall never be able to understand.
. . . . Poetry is verse: prose is not verse. Or else poetry is everything with the exception of
business documents and school books" (p. 96).   21–22 *literalists of the imagination*:
Moore's original note refers to W. B. Yeats's discussion of William Blake in *Ideas of Good
and Evil* (1903), where Yeats observes that Blake was "a too literal realist of imagination"
(p. 182).

QUESTIONS

1. What can we surmise about the speaker in this poem? To whom is the poem addressed? What does the speaker assume about the listener?
2. What is the tone of this poem? How do words like *fiddle* (line 1) and *perfect contempt* (line 2) affect the tone? How does tone affect the meaning?
3. What is the subject of this poem? The theme?
4. How does the speaker modify his or her initial assertion about poetry? What can poetry provide? What is its value? How should we experience it?
5. What does the speaker say about poems "we cannot understand" (line 11)? How does imagery clarify the speaker's assertion about incomprehensible things?
6. What does the speaker assert that poets must be and must do before we shall have "it" (line 25)? What is "it"?
7. To what extent does this poem provide the experience it asserts is necessary to have poetry?

WILLIAM WORDSWORTH   (1770–1850)

Ode: Intimations of Immortality
from Recollections of Early Childhood°   *1807 (1802–1804)*

The Child is father of the Man;
And I could wish my days to be
Bound each to each by natural piety.

1

There was a time when meadow, grove, and stream,
The earth, and every common sight,
        To me did seem
        Appareled in celestial light,
The glory and the freshness of a dream.   5
It is not now as it hath been of yore—
        Turn whereso'er I may,
            By night or day,
The things which I have seen I now can see no more.

2

        The Rainbow comes and goes,   10
        And lovely is the Rose,
        The Moon doth with delight
Look round her when the heavens are bare,

ODE: INTIMATIONS OF IMMORTALITY. The ideas in this poem are based, in part, on the Platonic theory of the preexistence of the soul before birth and the Neoplatonic theory that the glory of the unborn soul is gradually lost as it is immersed in the physical matter of the body and the world.

Waters on a starry night
  Are beautiful and fair;   15
The sunshine is a glorious birth;
But yet I know, where'er I go,
That there hath passed away a glory from the earth.

3

Now while the birds thus sing a joyous song,
  And while the young lambs bound
    As to the tabor's° sound,   *small drum*   20
To me alone there came a thought of grief:
A timely utterance gave that thought relief,
  And I again am strong:
The cataracts blow their trumpets from the steep;   25
No more shall grief of mine the season wrong;
I hear the Echoes through the mountains throng,
The Winds come to me from the fields of sleep,
  And all the earth is gay;
    Land and sea   30
  Give themselves up to jollity,
    And with the heart of May
Doth every Beast keep holiday—
    Thou Child of Joy,
Shout round me, let me hear thy shouts, thou happy   35
  Shepherd-boy!

4

Ye blessed Creatures, I have heard the call
  Ye to each other make; I see
The heavens laugh with you in your jubilee;
  My heart is at your festival,   40
    My head hath its coronal,°   *wreath of flowers*
The fullness of your bliss, I feel—I feel it all.
    Oh, evil day! if I were sullen
    While Earth herself is adorning,
      This sweet May morning,   45
    And the Children are culling
      On every side,
    In a thousand valleys far and wide,
    Fresh flowers; while the sun shines warm,
And the Babe leaps up on his Mother's arm—   50
  I hear, I hear, with joy I hear!
  —But there's a Tree, of many, one,
A single Field which I have looked upon,
Both of them speak of something that is gone:
      The Pansy at my feet   55
      Doth the same tale repeat:
Whither is fled the visionary gleam?
Where is it now, the glory and the dream?

5

Our birth is but a sleep and a forgetting:
The Soul that rises with us, our life's Star,°   *sun*   60
    Hath had elsewhere its setting,
      And cometh from afar:
    Not in entire forgetfulness,
    And not in utter nakedness,
But trailing clouds of glory do we come   65
      From God, who is our home:
Heaven lies about us in our infancy!
Shades of the prison-house° begin to close   *i.e., the world*
    Upon the growing Boy
      But he   70
Beholds the light, and whence it flows,
    He sees it in his joy;
The Youth, who daily farther from the east°   *from birth and God*
    Must travel, still is Nature's Priest,
    And by the vision splendid   75
    Is on his way attended;
At length the Man perceives it die away,
And fade into the light of common day.

6

Earth fills her lap with pleasures of her own;
Yearnings she hath in her own natural kind,   80
And, even with something of a Mother's mind,
    And no unworthy aim,
    The homely° Nurse doth all she can   *simple, friendly*
To make her foster child, her Inmate Man,
    Forget the glories he hath known,   85
And that imperial palace whence he came.

7

Behold the Child among his newborn blisses,
A six-years' Darling of a pygmy size!
See, where 'mid work of his own hand he lies,
Fretted by sallies of his mother's kisses,   90
With light upon him from his father's eyes!
See, at his feet, some little plan or chart,
Some fragment from his dream of human life,
Shaped by himself with newly-learned art;
    A wedding or a festival,   95
    A mourning or a funeral;
      And this hath now his heart,
    And unto this he frames his song;
      Then will he fit his tongue
To dialogues of business, love, or strife;   100
    But it will not be long
    Ere this be thrown aside,
    And with new joy and pride

The little Actor cons another part;
Filling from time to time his "humorous° stage"   *moody, changing*   105
With all the Persons, down to palsied Age,
That Life brings with her in her equipage;
    As if his whole vocation
    Were endless imitation.

8

Thou, whose exterior semblance doth belie
    Thy Soul's immensity;   110
Thou best Philosopher, who yet dost keep
Thy heritage, thou Eye among the blind,
That, deaf and silent, read'st the eternal deep,
Haunted forever by the eternal mind—   115
    Mighty Prophet! Seer blest!
    On whom those truths do rest,
Which we are toiling all our lives to find,
In darkness lost, the darkness of the grave;
Thou, over whom thy Immortality   120
Broods like the Day, a Master o'er a Slave,
A Presence which is not to be put by;
Thou little Child, yet glorious in the might
Of heaven-born freedom on thy being's height,
Why with such earnest pains dost thou provoke   125
The years to bring the inevitable yoke,
Thus blindly with thy blessedness at strife?
Full soon thy Soul shall have her earthly freight,
And custom lie upon thee with a weight,
Heavy as frost, and deep almost as life!   130

9

    O joy! that in our embers
    Is something that doth live,
    That nature yet remembers
    What was so fugitive!
The thought of our past years in me doth breed   135
Perpetual benediction: not indeed
For that which is most worthy to be blest;
Delight and liberty, the simple creed
Of Childhood, whether busy or at rest,
With new-fledged hope still fluttering in his breast—   140
    Not for these I raise
    The song of thanks and praise;
    But for those obstinate questionings
    Of sense and outward things,
    Fallings from us, vanishings;   145
    Blank misgivings of a Creature
Moving about in worlds not realized,°   *seeming real*
High instincts before which our mortal Nature
Did tremble like a guilty Thing surprised;

But for those first affections,   150
     Those shadowy recollections,
  Which, be they what they may,
Are yet the fountain light of all our day,
Are yet a master light of all our seeing;
     Uphold us, cherish, and have power to make   155
Our noisy years seem moments in the being
Of the eternal Silence: truths that wake,
          To perish never;
Which neither listlessness, nor mad endeavor,
          Nor Man nor Boy,   160
Nor all that is at enmity with joy,
Can utterly abolish or destroy!
     Hence in a season of calm weather
     Though inland far we be,
Our Souls have sight of that immortal sea   165
     Which brought us hither,
     Can in a moment travel thither,
And see the Children sport upon the shore,
And hear the mighty waters rolling evermore.

10

Then sing, ye Birds, sing, sing a joyous song!   170
     And let the young Lambs bound
     As to the tabor's sound!
We in thought will join your throng,
  Ye that pipe and ye that play,
  Ye that through your hearts today   175
     Feel the gladness of the May!
What though the radiance which was once so bright
Be now forever taken from my sight,
     Though nothing can bring back the hour
Of splendor in the grass, of glory in the flower;   180
     We will grieve not, rather find
     Strength in what remains behind;
     In the primal sympathy
     Which having been must ever be;
     In the soothing thoughts that spring   185
     Out of human suffering;
     In the faith that looks through death,
In years that bring the philosophic mind.

11

And O, ye Fountains, Meadows, Hills, and Groves,
Forebode not any severing of our loves!   190
Yet in my heart of hearts I feel your might;
I only have relinquished one delight
To live beneath your more habitual sway.
I love the Brooks which down their channels fret,
Even more than when I tripped lightly as they;   195

The innocent brightness of a newborn Day
   Is lovely yet;
The clouds that gather round the setting sun
Do take a sober coloring from an eye
That hath kept watch o'er man's mortality;   200
Another race hath been, and other palms are won.
Thanks to the human heart by which we live,
Thanks to its tenderness, its joys, and fears,
To me the meanest flower that blows can give
Thoughts that do often lie too deep for tears.   205

QUESTIONS

1. In the first four stanzas of the ode the speaker realizes he has lost something. What did he once have? What has he lost? How do images drawn from nature show the speaker and us that he (rather than the world) has changed?

2. This first section (stanzas 1 through 4) ends with two questions. What are they? How do they relate to the speaker's changed perception of nature? How does the loss noted here relate to poetry and to the imagination?

3. In stanzas 5 and 6 the speaker provides one answer to his own questions by discussing the soul. What does he assert about the soul? What does the soul bring with it from its source? What happens to the soul as a person grows older?

4. How are stanzas 7 and 8 related to 5 and 6? What does the child in stanzas 7 and 8 exemplify? What warning does the speaker give the child?

5. In the last three stanzas the speaker offers an alternative answer to the problem of maturity and the loss of the "visionary gleam." What is this answer? What replaces the "gleam"?

6. To what extent can we experience the speaker's initial grief and ultimate consolation through the images and structure of the ode?

JOHN KEATS (1795–1821)

Ode on a Grecian Urn   *1820 (1819)*

1

Thou still unravish'd bride of quietness,
  Thou foster-child of silence and slow time,
Sylvan historian, who canst thus express
A flowery tale more sweetly than our rhyme:

ODE ON A GRECIAN URN. The imaginary Grecian urn to which the poem is addressed combines design motifs from many different existing urns. This imaginary one is decorated with a border of leaves and trees, men (or gods) chasing women, a young musician sitting under a tree, lovers, and a priest and congregation leading a heifer to sacrifice. (For a picture of an ancient Greek vase, see color plate 3.)

Each big approach, leaning with brasswork prinked,
Each rope distinct,

Flagged, and the figurehead with golden tits
Arching our way, it never anchors; it's
No sooner present than it turns to past.   15
Right to the last

We think each one will heave to and unload
All good into our lives, all we are owed
For waiting so devoutly and so long.
But we are wrong: 20

Only one ship is seeking us, a black-
Sailed unfamiliar, towing at her back
A huge and birdless silence. In her wake
No waters breed or break.

QUESTIONS

1. What is the subject of the poem? The theme? What point does it make about time, expectation, human nature, and the way we live our lives?

2. Why does the speaker use the pronouns *we* and *us* throughout the poem; what do the speaker and listener(s) have in common?

3. What cliché does the extended metaphor that begins in the second stanza ironically revitalize and reverse? How does this metaphor make the total meaning of the poem clearer and more palpable?

4. How do elements such as meter, rhyme, and diction help create meaning? Consider, for example, the metrical variation in the fourth line of each stanza, rhyming pairs such as *waste-haste* and *wake-break*, or words such as *bluff* and *armada*.

5. Compare this poem to the three *carpe diem* poems in this chapter. To what extent is "Next, Please" a *carpe diem* poem?

DONALD JUSTICE   (b. 1925)

On the Death of Friends in Childhood   *1960*

We shall not ever meet them bearded in heaven,
Nor sunning themselves among the bald of hell;
If anywhere, in the deserted schoolyard at twilight,
Forming a ring, perhaps, or joining hands
In games whose very names we have forgotten,   5
Come, memory, let us seek them there in the shadows.

QUESTIONS

1. What is the subject of this poem: the living, or the dead? How accurate is the title as a guide to subject and theme?
2. What point (if any) does this poem make about death? Time? Memory? The living?
3. How do imagery, diction, rhetoric and tone contribute to the total meaning of this poem? Consider phrases like "bearded in heaven" and "sunning themselves among the bald of hell." What is personified in the last line?
4. To what extent do you think the age of the reader controls her or his (your) response to this poem?

LINDA PASTAN (b. 1932)

Ethics   *1980*

In ethics class so many years ago
our teacher asked this question every fall:
if there were a fire in a museum
which would you save, a Rembrandt painting
or an old woman who hadn't many   5
years left anyhow? Restless on hard chairs
caring little for pictures or old age
we'd opt one year for life, the next for art
and always half-heartedly. Sometimes
the woman borrowed my grandmother's face   10
leaving her usual kitchen to wander
some drafty, half-imagined museum.
One year, feeling clever, I replied
why not let the woman decide herself?
Linda, the teacher would report, eschews   15
the burdens of responsibility.
This fall in a real museum I stand
before a real Rembrandt, old woman,
or nearly so, myself. The colors
within this frame are darker than autumn,   20
darker even than winter—the browns of earth,
though earth's most radiant elements burn
through the canvas. I know now that woman
and painting and season are almost one
and all beyond saving by children.   25

QUESTIONS

1. What can we surmise about the speaker in this poem? How does this knowledge contribute to our understanding of theme?

2. What are the two settings, situations, and actions presented here? How are they related? How much time has passed between them? How does the contrast between them help create meaning?

3. What question was asked "every fall" in the ethics class? What were the speaker's and her classmates' attitudes toward "pictures" and "old age" (line 7) in the past?

4. How has the passage of time changed the speaker's attitudes? What does she now realize about "woman / and painting and season" (lines 23–24)? About children?

5. What is the subject of this poem? The theme? What point does it make about art, life, time, and values?

SHARON OLDS (b. 1942)

35/10   *1984*

Brushing out my daughter's dark
silken hair before the mirror
I see the grey gleaming on my head,
the silver-haired servant behind her. Why is it
just as we begin to go   5
they begin to arrive, the fold in my neck
clarifying as the fine bones of her
hips sharpen? As my skin shows
its dry pitting, she opens like a small
pale flower on the tip of a cactus;   10
as my last chances to bear a child
are falling through my body, the duds among them,
her full purse of eggs, round and
firm as hard-boiled yolks, is about
to snap its clasp. I brush her tangled   15
fragrant hair at bedtime. It's an old
story—the oldest we have on our planet—
the story of replacement.

QUESTIONS

1. What is the speaker in this poem? What is she doing? What is the setting?

2. How does the speaker contrast her own state of being to her daughter's stage of life? How are images, metaphors, and similes used to clarify this contrast? How does this contrast help convey the poem's meaning?

3. What point does this poem make about life and nature? To what extent does the last sentence clarify (or overclarify) the poem's theme?

4. Does this poem create a palpable experience? Do you identify more fully

with the speaker or the daughter? To what extent does the age of the reader control his or her (your) experience of this poem?

WRITING ABOUT THEME AND MEANING IN POETRY

When you set out to write an essay about the meaning of a poem, you will be dealing with three related topics: (1) what the poem says, (2) the way the poem says it, and (3) the experience the poem creates. The prewriting process for such an essay includes a period of reading and studying, developing your initial ideas about the poem, testing those ideas against the poem itself, formulating a tentative thesis for the essay, and organizing your observations about the poem into coherent units.

Once the poem is chosen or assigned, you should move through the process of study and discovery about theme and meaning outlined earlier in this chapter. At the beginning of your study, you should deal with three basic questions: (1) What is the poem's subject? (2) What is the poem's theme? (3) What aspects of the poem contribute most significantly to the creation of meaning? In other words, you will deal with *what* the theme is and *how* it is created. The answers to these questions will almost always become parts of the finished essay. More important, they will help you considerably in the planning stage to formulate a tentative central idea and to organize your support for this idea.

The *what* and *how* of a poem are finally inseparable; the way a poem tells us and shows us what it means are parts of its total meaning. Your essay will connect the poem's theme and meaning to some other poetic elements, such as speaker, imagery, metaphor, symbol, or tone. In the prewriting stage it is essential to consider the relationship between meaning and all the other elements of poetry. The following questions may be helpful in planning the focus and finding the information necessary for such an essay:

1. What does the title of the poem tell you about subject and meaning?
2. What can you discover about the speaker? How does the speaker shape and communicate theme?
3. How do the other characters in the poem (if any) affect theme and meaning?
4. What impact do setting, situation, and action have on theme?
5. How does diction affect theme? How are multiple denotations and connotations employed? To what extent are special types of diction or word order used?
6. How do imagery, metaphor, simile, and other rhetorical devices help determine the impact and theme of the poem? To what extent do they particularize the ideas and events of the poem to create a palpable experience?
7. What is the poem's tone? What effect does tone have on theme?

8. What role do rhythm, meter, sound, and rhyme play (if any) in shaping and emphasizing the theme and total meaning of the poem?

9. How does the form of the poem help shape its theme and your response?

10. How are symbol, allusion, or myth used to create the poem's theme and impact?

You will find poems for which all these questions are relevant; some poets employ every element and device in the poetic repertoire to create meaning and impact. Other poems will offer useful information in only a few of these areas. Whatever you discover about the poem at hand, you cannot deal with all these variables in one paper; your essay would be too unwieldy and fragmented. Look for those few elements that have the most profound impact on the poem's theme and on your ability to experience the poetic moment. These will become the secondary focuses of the essay.

Once you have a full set of notes about the poem, you can formulate a tentative central idea and a thesis sentence. Most of the time, this "working" idea will restate what you consider to be the poem's theme. Be careful, however, to distinguish between subject and theme. In planning to write about Larkin's "Next, Please," for example, you might write the following: " 'Next, Please' makes a clear assertion about human habits of expectation." This sentence describes the poem's *subject*, and might even be a good beginning sentence for your essay. It is not, however, a good central idea because it tells the reader nothing about the poem's theme or meaning. A better central idea might be, " 'Next, Please' exposes the futility of those who hope for a better future while ignoring the things they have in the present." This sentence summarizes the theme of the poem and makes a strong statement on which to build an effective paper.

Forming a tentative central idea is half the battle; now you can focus on the relationship between this idea and the ways in which the poem creates meaning. Use the information gained from answering the ten questions listed above. Look for the links between the meaning and the methods of the poem, and plan your organization. Thus, if you find that a poem's theme is established through symbol and allusion, your plan should express this connection by relating meaning to these elements. Such a plan might be: (1) theme, (2) theme and symbol, and (3) theme and allusion. Or it might be that the poet's meaning is made plain through a dominant image or metaphor pervading the poem. You might then plan to develop the idea part by part, and show how the metaphor develops it, or you might want to stress the metaphor itself as it grows and develops as a support for the poem's idea, as in the sample essay.

Organize your observations about the poem into coherent units that support the central idea and that will become paragraphs in the body of your essay. At this stage, however, reexamine the poem and your notes to make sure that everything is hanging together. As with other essays, this final stage of prewriting affords another opportunity to revise and fine-tune your central idea and tentative organization. Such revision, as we have noted, is a crucial and valuable part of both the prewriting and writing processes.

Organizing Your Essay

INTRODUCTION. As with most other essays discussed in this text, we recommend a traditional three-part organization that includes an introduction, a supporting body, and a conclusion. In the introduction, make any general points about the poem that seem relevant to the essay. If the poem under consideration was written by a British soldier in 1917, for example, you might want to establish its context in World War I. In any event, the introduction should make four specific statements: (1) announce the author and title of the poem, (2) state what you consider to be the poem's subject, (3) establish the central idea of the essay and what you think is the theme of the poem, and (4) briefly enumerate the ways in which the body of the essay will support the assertion made in the introduction. In other words, the first paragraph should tell your reader what the essay is going to prove about the poem and how it is going to do it. The introduction thus becomes a plan for *writing* and *reading* the whole essay.

BODY. In general, your organization will depend on your observations about the poem. As you organize and develop your paragraphs, keep in mind the following structural patterns. They will be useful for almost all the poems you encounter: (1) The poem of your choice may convey meaning through *direct statement*. In such a case you might organize your essay to reflect the line-by-line or sentence-by-sentence structure of the poem itself. (2) You might find that the *logic* of the speaker's argument most effectively creates meaning. To follow such a pattern of logic, for example, would be useful in an essay about the meaning of Andrew Marvell's "To His Coy Mistress." (3) The poet's use of a *single element*, such as a metaphor or simile, or a set of consistent references (such as discoverers, bankers, or darkness), might bring out the poem's meaning. Your organization might reflect the ways the element works and develops in the poem. (4) Finally, it might be that a number of *different poetic elements* (such as rhythm, rhyme, metaphor, level of language, imagery, and so on) work together to shape theme and impact. The structure of an essay dealing with such elements can be based on a sequential discussion of each element as it contributes to meaning.

In short, each poem offers its own particular method and mode of rendering experience that can be used in the controlling and shaping of an essay. The four structural patterns noted above can be modified and combined. To accommodate the specific poem you are considering, you should always be prepared to adjust whatever plan you choose.

Since the thesis statement in the introduction provides a brief outline for the body, you should prepare a general structure before you begin to write. As you draft the body, however, you may find that some subjects or elements are less or more important than you had originally thought. When this happens, you can rethink the shape of your essay, and revise the introduction accordingly.

CONCLUSION.   In the conclusion, you have the opportunity to pull all the strands of the essay back together and to reaffirm the connection between the poem's method and meaning. This can often be done through a summary of the major points in the essay. The conclusion is also the place where you can consider additional aspects of the poem's theme and impact. The ideas and experiences created when you read a poem often point beyond themselves to other ideas or implications. Similarly, you might want to consider the extent to which your own circumstances (such as age, sex, race, or religion) help determine the meaning and impact that the poem has for you. However you conclude the essay, make sure that the end is as strong and assertive as the beginning.

SAMPLE ESSAY

Metaphor and Meaning in Philip Larkin's "Next, Please"*

[1]
Philip Larkin's "Next, Please" exposes the futility of those who hope for a better future while ignoring the things they have in the present. The idea is borne out in the poem's assertions that the fulfillment of our expectations is slow and rare but that disappointment and death are certain.° This theme is conveyed through the single extended metaphor of an "armada of promises" that begins in the second stanza and runs throughout the rest of the poem; within the metaphor, diction and meter reinforce the meaning of the poem and the moment of human experience that it creates.□

[2]
The poem announces its subject and begins to develop its theme through the title and the direct statements of the first stanza. The title refers to the human desire to move on, and look ahead. It suggests that we are never satisfied with what we have, but always expect happiness just around the corner. These implications are brought into focus in the first stanza, where the speaker notes that we are "Always too eager for the future" and that "we / Pick up bad habits of expectancy" (lines 1–2). Our habitual focus on the promise of the future is captured in the speaker's observation that "every

* See p. 847 for this poem.
° Central idea.
□ Thesis sentence.

day / *Till then* we say" (lines 3–4). By using the pronouns *we* and *us* here and throughout, the speaker states that all of us, including himself, habitually indulge in such wishful thinking.

To this point, the speaker has isolated a specific human characteristic—our belief that better things will happen. Beginning in the second stanza, however, the poem asserts that these "bad habits of expectancy" leave us disappointed. The poem makes this point through an extended metaphor

[3] that is based on a hidden cliché: "someday my ship will come in." The cliché expresses the belief that we will get everything we want or deserve "someday" in the future. Larkin's metaphor, however, shows us that the cliché is wrong; it draws out the cliché into a dramatic experience to suggest that our hopes for the future inevitably lead to failure and death.

The extended metaphor creates meaning by placing us in a dramatic situation that we can experience. We are "Watching from a bluff" as the "tiny, clear, / Sparkling armada of promises draw near" (lines 5–6). Our ship has become an entire fleet. Even at this early point, however, the diction begins to undercut the cliché and our habit of expectation. We are watching

[4] from a *bluff* rather than a cliff; a *bluff* is a hill, but it is also an attempt to mislead or deceive through false confidence. The word thus suggests that our hopes for the future stand on self-deception and false confidence. *Armada* is similarly loaded. For British and American readers, the term evokes the memory of a specific Spanish fleet that sailed against England in 1588 and was destroyed by sea battles and storms. Overtones of failure and destruction are thus built into the metaphor.

The metaphor makes the poem's meaning vivid and immediate through a wealth of detail. We notice that the "armada of promises" moves very slowly: "How slow they are! And how much time they waste, / Refusing to make haste" (lines 7–8). As the metaphor is extended, more and more details are brought to our attention; we see progressively more of each ship as the speaker

[5] mentions the shining "brasswork," "Each rope distinct," the flag, and "the figurehead with golden tits / Arching our way" (lines 11–14). Through such details, the metaphor suggests that the fleet draws ever closer. Even as we experience this approach, however, the failure of such promise is also estab-lished: "Yet still they leave us holding wretched stalks / Of disappointment" (lines 9–10). This image—within the metaphor—leaves us standing on the "bluff" holding wilted flowers and hopes.

This disappointment is brought into explicit focus as the "armada" meta-phor continues in the fourth stanza. We see that the fleet "never anchors"; "it's / No sooner present than it turns to past" (lines 14–15). Most of these words carry double meanings. *It*, for example, refers to both the ships and

[6] time. *Turns to* indicates both a change of course and the inevitable transforma-tion of the present into the past. Similarly, *present* and *past* signify both the physical status of the ships and the movement of time. The metaphor thus conveys the experience of disappointment both in terms of the "armada of promises" and the time we waste waiting for future reward.

The last two stanzas of "Next, Please" conclude the armada metaphor and expand on the theme of inevitable disappointment. The fifth stanza summa-rizes the development of the metaphor and so the entire poem; the speaker

observes that we always expect one of these ships to "heave to" and to deliver "All good into our lives" (line 18). The last line of the stanza, however, completely undercuts all hope. Here, we sense the impact of a metrical technique
that Larkin has employed throughout. The poem is mostly in iambic pentameter, but the fourth line of each stanza is cut short to two or three feet. This
metrical falling-off creates a sound parallel to the feeling of disappointment;
like the "armada" and the future, each stanza fails to deliver what we expect.

[7]   The force of this device strikes us at the close of the fifth stanza, when the
final two-beat line bleakly tells us, "But we are wrong" (line 20). The metaphor
and the falling meter make it clear that our ship will never "heave to" and
deliver. There is, however, "one ship" that "is seeking us" (line 21). It is not
a ship full of good things; instead, it is a "black- / Sailed unfamiliar" ship
"towing at her back / A huge and birdless silence" (lines 22–23). This is the
only ship that will come in for us if we passively await the future—the ship of
death.

"Next, Please" thus tells us that a life spent in passive expectation
and hope for the future will offer only disappointment and death. The poem
lets us experience this meaning through an extended metaphor in which an
"armada of promises" approaches and then leaves without yielding anything
but disappointment. The meaning of the poem becomes our movement through
[8]   the metaphor, and our experience of the metaphor is disappointment and a
vision of death. At the same time, the poem implies that we should stop
living lives of false expectation. Instead, we should live in and for the present,
making the most of what we have. To this extent, "Next, Please" may be
considered a *carpe diem* poem; it suggests that we should "seize" today
rather than hope for tomorrow.

Commentary on the Essay

The essay illustrates the need to combine and adjust abstract strategies
of organization when you are dealing with a specific poem; it combines a
focus on a specific poetic element (metaphor) with secondary interest in
two other elements (diction and meter). The essay thus represents a modification and combination of the third and fourth organizational plans noted
earlier (p. 853). Basically, however, it traces the development of theme
and meaning through the progressive stages of a dominant and central
metaphor.

The introduction conveys a great deal of information and lays out a
plan for the entire essay. The first sentence announces author, title, and
subject. The second briefly explains how the poem establishes its subject;
this material is expanded in the second paragraph. The third sentence
contains both the central idea of the essay and a summary of the poem's
theme. The fourth sentence makes the connection between *what* the poem
says and *how* it says it. The paragraph thus promises that the essay will
deal with the way metaphor, diction, and meter combine to create meaning.

Paragraph 2 deals primarily with the subject of the poem; it grows directly out of the first two sentences of the introduction. This discussion is essential because it provides the foundation for the essay's subsequent treatment of theme and meaning.

Paragraphs 3 through 7 develop out of the last two sentences of the introduction; they treat the connection between metaphor and meaning, and they take up the secondary subjects of diction and meter. Paragraph 3 provides transition from subject to theme, introduces the dominant metaphor, and explains the hidden cliché on which the metaphor is based. Paragraph 4 examines the way that the "armada" metaphor begins to create a palpable experience and how diction immediately begins to undercut the promise of the future. The first sentence of this paragraph links it both to the introduction and to the previous paragraph through its reference to metaphor and meaning.

Paragraph 5 sustains the focus on the link between metaphor and meaning through attention to the details that the speaker mentions in the second, third, and fourth stanzas of the poem. Again, the first sentence connects this paragraph to both the introduction and the previous paragraph. Similarly, the concluding sentence leads into paragraph 6, which takes up the next stage of the extended metaphor and the articulation of disappointment. This focus on the end of the metaphor and on the experience of disappointment is continued in paragraph 7, which explores the poem's assertion that if we wait passively, only death will arrive. Here, the essay also deals with the impact of meter on meaning.

The concluding paragraph begins by repeating the poem's theme; it thus links the end of the essay to the introduction. The next two sentences similarly reiterate the connection between this theme and the extended metaphor that makes it palpable; they summarize the material in paragraphs 3 through 7. Finally, the conclusion considers the implications of the poem's meaning, offers a second and implied theme for the poem, and connects "Next, Please" to a longstanding poetic tradition.

WRITING TOPICS FOR CHAPTER 22

1. Compare two or all of the following poems: Jonson's "To Celia," Herrick's "To the Virgins, to Make Much of Time" (and also "Corinna's Going A-Maying," in Chapter 24), and Marvell's "To His Coy Mistress" as *carpe diem* poems. How well does each poem express the central idea of the *carpe diem* tradition? How are the tone and ideas of the poems similar, and how are they different? To what degree is it accurate to say that these poems are not about seduction but rather about life and values?

2. On the basis of ideas about age, change, and the loss of time and life, compare Pastan's "Ethics," Olds's "35/10," Wordsworth's "Immortality" ode, and Justice's "On the Death of Friends in Childhood." How do the ideas of the poems merge, even though they are about different subjects? Which of the poems do you prefer? Why?

3. Keats's line "Beauty is truth, truth beauty" from his "Ode on a Grecian Urn" has generated considerable discussion. What do you think it means? How does the material in the poem support Keats's idea? Would the idea be tenable if it had come early in the poem rather than late? Why?

4. Write your own poem in which you stress a particular idea. You might write about a friend or acquaintance who has: endured an illness, performed an important service, admitted a mistake or failure, or succeeded in a task. Other possible topics are: a social, religious, or political issue; or some aspect of education, work, or community life. When you finish, explain how you go about making the situation clear to your reader, and how you use the situation to bring out your ideas. Do not neglect the title as one of the means of expressing ideas.

23

Poetic Careers: The Work of Three Poets

We have looked at poetry in terms of its elements and effects. Let us now consider a collection of poems by three individual poets: John Donne (1572–1631), Emily Dickinson (1830–1886), and Robert Frost (1874–1963). Donne, one of the most important English poets of the seventeenth century, developed what we call the metaphysical or philosophical style. Emily Dickinson and Robert Frost are both American poets and New Englanders; Dickinson is considered a significant formative influence on American poetry, and Frost represents one of the dominant poetic voices of twentieth-century America. While the poems included here cannot present full pictures of poetic careers, they do provide an opportunity to read and consider a body of works by individual poets. We have chosen poems that illustrate the central concerns and major characteristics of each poet's work. Thus, the material provides an opportunity to look for common themes and techniques or for sudden shifts of concern within a poet's career.

JOHN DONNE (1572–1631)

Traditionally, scholars have argued that John Donne had two poetic careers, one as a love poet and satirist in his youth and another as a religious poet after he became an Anglican priest in 1615. Such a clear division cannot be maintained, however, since Donne wrote a great deal of religious verse before 1615 and very little poetry at all after that year. Donne's poetry does fall into two broad categories, love poetry and religious verse, but his style remains constant.

Donne was born to a Roman Catholic family in a newly Protestant land; religion thus had a significant impact on his life even before he took holy orders. Although he attended both Oxford and Cambridge universities between 1584 and 1590, his Catholicism barred him from receiving degrees. In 1591 Donne moved to London and enrolled at the law school at Lincoln's Inn, where he studied science, philosophy, law, languages, and literature. All these subjects (and more) were worked into his poetry. During these years Donne had a reputation as a wit and a ladies' man; he wrote many love poems and satires, and circulated them among his friends (very little of his poetry was published until 1633).

In 1593 Donne converted to Anglicanism (the official state religion in England) and began to rise in aristocratic circles. He became private secretary to Sir Thomas Egerton (an important court official) in 1598, and was on the verge of a brilliant career when he eloped (in 1601) with Egerton's sixteen-year-old niece, Anne More. This destroyed his chances for advancement; the girl's father had Donne dismissed from court, had him jailed, and barred his further employment. Donne spent the next fourteen years writing poetry, eking out a meager living at various jobs, and desperately seeking royal employment. King James I (reigned 1603–1625) was sympathetic, but he refused to help Donne, believing that Donne's proper place was as a priest in the Anglican Church.

Donne finally gave in to this inevitability; in 1615 he took holy orders and began a meteoric rise in the church. In 1621 he was appointed dean of St. Paul's Cathedral in London, the most fashionable church in seventeenth-century England. He became a famous preacher—over 130 of his sermons were published—and the noble and wealthy flocked to his services. Donne remained a powerful speaker and poet up to his death in May 1631; he previewed his own funeral sermon before the king on February 25, 1631, and supposedly wrote his last poem eight days before his death.

Donne's poetry is commonly termed *metaphysical*, a word used to describe poetry that is highly intellectual and characterized by complexity, subtlety and elaborate imagery. The label was made by the poet-critic John Dryden (1631–1700), who asserted in *A Discourse Concerning the Origin and Progress of Satire* (1693) that Donne's love poetry "affects the metaphysics" and "perplexes the minds of the fair sex with nice [i.e., careful] speculations of philosophy." Although Dryden originally used the word to disparage Donne's work, it has come to signify both the style of his verse and a "school" of poetry.

POETIC CHARACTERISTICS.   In *poetic style*, Donne's poetry represents a radical departure from earlier Elizabethan verse. He rebelled against the smooth rhythms, flowery language, and conventional imagery of the sixteenth century. His poems are characterized by abrupt beginnings, dramatic shifts in tone, irregular rhythms, puns, paradoxes, and rigorous logic. Their major characteristic, however, is the *metaphysical conceit*. A **conceit** is an elaborate metaphor, and a **metaphysical conceit** is an extended comparison that links two unrelated fields or subjects in a surprising and revealing conjunction of ideas. Above all else, Donne's poems illustrate *wit*, the ability to advance a complex or even outrageous argument through subtle logic, unusual analogy, and diverse allusion.

In terms of *diction and language*, Donne's verse is equally unconventional. The poems include a great deal of harsh language and numerous terms borrowed from various fields of learning, including alchemy, law, theology, philosophy, and geography. The characteristic *poetic forms* for both the love poetry and the religious verse include the lyric and the sonnet. The stanzaic structure of Donne's lyrics is quite inventive, with varying line lengths and complex rhyme schemes.

POETIC SUBJECTS. Donne's love poetry, written mostly between 1590 and 1615, established the metaphysical style. These poems are ingenious, and overflow with images and allusions. Taken as a group, they suggest that passion is both wonderful and dangerous and that love is a mystery much like religion. They also imply that lovers can and should be self-sufficient and separate from the public world.

The religious verse maintains the characteristics of the love poetry but shifts the ground from human passion to divine love. In the Holy Sonnets, for instance, Donne uses a traditional poetic form normally associated with love poetry and considers human sin and divine grace. In these poems Donne often employs the techniques of religious meditation, focusing at first on a specific time or event and then considering the meaning of that event in connection with his own spiritual state. In "At the Round Earth's Imagined Corners," for example, Donne begins with a vivid meditation on the moment of the Last Judgment. The Hymns, like the Holy Sonnets, maintain the metaphysical style and deal with spiritual matters. The "Hymn to God the Father," for instance, plays repeatedly with a pun on Donne's name. Similarly, the "Hymn to God My God, In My Sickness," (not included here) supposedly written eight days before Donne died in May 1631, is full of puns, paradoxes, convoluted logic, and metaphysical conceits.

BIBLIOGRAPHIC SOURCES. Donne's poetry received little attention during his lifetime. Although an awareness of Donne's work was growing in the late 1800s, two events in the twentieth century dramatically rekindled interest in his poetry. One was the publication of Sir Herbert Grierson's complete edition of *The Poems of John Donne* (1912) and the other was T. S. Eliot's spirited defense of Donne and metaphysical poetry (see, for example, Eliot's essay, "The Metaphysical Poets," published in 1921 and reprinted in 1960 in his *Selected Essays*). Although Donne's verse may have seemed unpoetic and overly complex to earlier generations, it appeals with great strength to the sensibilities of the contemporary world. More recent editions of Donne's work include Helen Gardner's edition of *The Divine Poems* (1952) and of *The Elegies and the Songs and Sonnets* (1965). Significant critical discussions of Donne's work may be found in Cleanth Brooks, *The Well-Wrought Urn* (1932), Helen White, *The Metaphysical Poets* (1936), J. B. Leishman, *The Monarch of Wit* (1951), Louis L. Martz, *The Poetry of Meditation* (1954), Richard E. Hughes, *The Progress of the Soul* (1968), and John Carey, *John Donne: Life, Mind and Art* (1981). Additional poems by Donne may be found in this text by reference to the index.

The Good Morrow   *1633*

I wonder, by my troth, what thou and I
Did, till we loved! Were we not weaned till then,
But sucked on country pleasures, childishly?
Or snorted we in the seven sleepers' den?°
T'was so; But this, all pleasures fancies be.   5
If ever any beauty I did see,
Which I desired, and got, t'was but a dream of thee.

And now good morrow to our waking souls,
Which watch not one another out of fear;
For love all love of other sights controls,   10
And makes one little room an everywhere.
Let sea-discoverers to new worlds have gone,
Let maps to other,° worlds on worlds have shown,
Let us possess one world; each hath one, and is one.

My face in thine eye, thine in mine appears,°   15
And true plain hearts do in the faces rest;
Where can we find two better hemispheres
Without sharp North, without declining West?
Whatever dies was not mixed equally;°
If our two loves be one, or thou and I   20
Love so alike that none do slacken, none can die.

THE GOOD MORROW.   4 *seven sleepers' den*: a reference to the miracle of the seven Christian youths who took shelter in a cave to avoid religious persecution by the Emperor Decius (ca. A.D. 250) and were sealed inside. The young men supposedly slept for about 185 years and emerged in perfect health during the reign of Theodosius II (ca. A.D. 435). 13 *other*: others, that is, other discoverers.   15 *My face . . . appears*: each face is reflected in the pupils of the other lover's eyes.   19 *Whatever . . . equally*: Scholastic philosophy argues that elements that are either perfectly balanced or united will never change or decay; hence, such a mixture cannot die.

Song   *1633*

Go and catch a falling star,
  Get with child a mandrake root,°
Tell me where all past years are,
  Or who cleft the Devil's foot,
Teach me to hear mermaids singing,   5
  Or to keep off envy's stinging,
      And find
      What wind
Serves to advance an honest mind.

If thou beest born to strange sights,   10
  Things invisible to see,
Ride ten thousand days and nights,
  Till age snow white hairs on thee,
Thou, when thou return'st, wilt tell me
All strange wonders that befell thee,   15
      And swear
      Nowhere
Lives a woman true, and fair.

If thou findst one, let me know,
  Such a pilgrimage were sweet;   20
Yet do not, I would not go,
  Though at next door we might meet;
Though she were true when you met her,
And last till you write your letter,
      Yet she   25
      Will be
False, ere I come, to two, or three.

SONG.   2 *mandrake root*: the mandrake, or mandragora, is a European narcotic herb once considered an aphrodisiac. The fleshy, forked root was thought to resemble the human form. To impregnate such a root, of course, is impossible.

The Sun Rising   *1633*

    Busy old fool, unruly sun,
      Why dost thou thus,
Through windows and through curtains call on us?
Must to thy motions lovers' seasons run?
      Saucy pedantic wretch, go chide   5
      Late school boys and sour prentices,°   *apprentices*
    To tell court huntsmen that the King will ride,
    Call country ants to harvest offices;°   *duties*

Love, all alike, no season knows nor clime,
Nor hours, days, months, which are the rags of time.   10

    Thy beams, so reverend and strong
    Why shouldst thou think?
I could eclipse and cloud them with a wink,
But that I would not lose her sight so long;
    If her eyes have not blinded thine,   15
    Look, and tomorrow late, tell me,
    Whether both the Indias of spice and mine°
Be where thou leftst them, or lie here with me.
Ask for those kings whom thou saw'st yesterday,
And thou shalt hear, All here in one bed lay.   20

    She is all states, and all princes, I,
    Nothing else is.
Princes do but play us; compared to this,
All honor's mimic, all wealth alchemy.°   *counterfeit*
    Thou, sun, art half as happy as we,   25
    In that the world's contracted thus;
    Thine age asks ease, and since thy duties be
To warm the world, that's done in warming us.
Shine here to us, and thou art everywhere;
This bed thy center° is, these walls, thy sphere.   30

THE SUN RISING.   17 *Indias of spice and mine*: the India of "spice" is East India or the
East Indies; the India of "mine" or gold is the West Indies.   30 *center*: the central point
of the sun's orbit.

The Canonization   *1633*

For God's sake hold your tongue,° and let me love,
    Or chide my palsy, or my gout,
My five gray hairs, or ruined fortune, flout,
    With wealth your state, your mind with arts improve,
        Take you a course,° get you a place,°   5
        Observe His Honor, or His Grace,
Or the King's real, or his stamped face°
        Contemplate,—what you will, approve,°   *test, try*
        So you will let me love.

Alas, alas, who's injured by my love?   10
    What merchant's ships have my sighs drowned?
Who says my tears have overflowed his ground?

THE CANONIZATION.   1 *your tongue*: "your" refers to either the public world in general
or a specific but unheard critic who attacks the speaker's love.   5 *course*: a course of action.
place: office or position, probably at court.   7 *stamped face*: the king's portrait on coins.

When did my colds a forward spring remove?
  When did the heats which my veins fill
  Add one more to the plaguy bill?°   15
Soldiers find wars, and lawyers find out still
  Litigious men, which quarrels move,
  Though she and I do love.

Call us what you will, we are made such by love;
  Call her one, me another fly,   20
We're tapers too, and at our own cost die,°
  And we in us find the eagle and the dove.°
    The phoenix riddle° hath more wit
    By us,—we two being one, are it.
So, to one neutral thing both sexes fit.   25
  We die and rise the same, and prove
  Mysterious by this love.

We can die by it, if not live by love,
  And if unfit for tombs and hearse
Our legend be, it will be fit for verse;   30
  And if no piece of chronicle we prove,
    We'll build in sonnets pretty rooms;
    As well a well-wrought urn becomes°   *befits, suits*
The greatest ashes, as half-acre tombs,
  And by these hymns, all shall approve°   35
  Us canonized for love:

And thus invoke us: "You whom reverend love
  Made one another's hermitage;
You, to whom love was peace, that now is rage;
  Who did the whole world's soul contract, and drove   40
    Into the glasses of your eyes
    (So made such mirrors, and such spies,
That they did all to you epitomize)
  Countries, towns, courts: Beg from above
  A pattern of your love!"°   45

---

15 *plaguy bill*: a weekly list of people who have died from the plague.   20–21 *fly . . . die*: both flies and candles are symbols of the brevity of life. Since the word *die* was a common euphemism in the seventeenth century for sexual orgasm, the line suggests that each sex act shortens the lovers' lives.   22 *eagle and the dove*: proverbial symbols of male strength and female mildness.   23 *phoenix riddle*: the riddle of the phoenix's perpetuation; the phoenix is a mythological Arabian bird—only one exists at a time—that lives for a thousand years and then burns itself to ashes on a funeral pyre. A new phoenix then miraculously rises from the ashes of the old. The phoenix thus symbolizes immortality, death, and resurrection, and the rekindling of sexual desire.   35 *hymns . . . approve*: the hymns refer to the speaker's poetry and this poem in particular. The idea is that succeeding generations will confirm ("approve") the sainthood of the lovers in a new religion of love because of this poem.   37–45 *"You . . . love"*: these lines are spoken by lovers in succeeding generations who are praying to the lover-saints that the speaker and his beloved have become. Hence, *You* (line 37) refers to the speaker and his mistress.

A Fever   1633

Oh do not die, for I shall hate
  All women so, when thou art gone,
That thee I shall not celebrate,°   *mourn*
  When I remember, thou wast one.

But yet thou canst not die, I know;   5
  To leave this world behind, is death;
But when thou from this world wilt go,
  The whole world vapours° with thy breath.   *evaporates*

Or if, when thou, the world's soul, goest,
  It stay, 'tis but thy carcase then;   10
The fairest woman, but thy ghost,
  But corrupt worms, the worthiest men.

O wrangling schools,° that search what fire
  Shall burn this world, had none the wit
Unto this knowledge to aspire,   15
  That this her fever might be it?

And yet she cannot waste by this,
  Nor long bear this torturing wrong,
For much corruption needful is,
  To fuel such a fever long.°   *for long*   20

These burning fits but meteors be,
  Whose matter in thee is soon spent:
Thy beauty, and all parts which are thee,
  Are unchangeable firmament.°

Yet 'twas of my mind, seizing thee,   25
  Though it in thee cannot persever:°   *persist*
For I had rather owner be
  Of thee one hour, than all else ever.

A FEVER.   13 *wrangling schools*: competing sects of pagan and Christian philosophy that
debated what sort of fire would ultimately destroy the world.   24 *firmament*: the vault of
heaven and the stars.

The Flea   1633

Mark° but this flea, and mark in this,   *note, look at*
How little that which thou deniest me is;
It sucked me first, and now sucks thee,
And in this flea our two bloods mingled be;
Thou know'st that this cannot be said°   *called*   5

A sin, nor shame, nor loss of maidenhead,
  Yet this enjoys before it woo,°   *marry*
  And pampered swells with one blood made of two,°
  And this, alas, is more than we would do.

Oh stay, three lives in one flea spare,   10
Where we almost, yea more than married, are.
This flea is you and I, and this
Our marriage bed and marriage temple is;
Though parents grudge, and you,° w'are met,
And cloister'd in these living walls of jet,   15
  Though use° make you apt to kill me   *custom*
  Let not to that, self-murder added be,
  And sacrilege, three sins in killing three.

Cruel and sudden, hast thou since
Purpled thy nail, in blood of innocence?°   20
Wherein could this flea guilty be,
Except in that drop which it sucked from thee?
Yet thou triumph'st, and say'st that thou
Find'st not thy self nor me the weaker now;
  'Tis true, then learn how false fears be;   25
  Just so much honor, when thou yield'st to me,
  Will waste, as this flea's death took life from thee.

THE FLEA.   8 *two*: the flea has bitten both the speaker and the lady and thus mingles their blood; the image also suggests pregnancy.   14 *you*: you [the lady] also "grudge" or resent the idea of premarital sex.   20 *innocence*: a possible allusion to Herod's slaughter of the innocents (Matthew 2:16).

Holy Sonnet 6: This Is My Play's Last Scene   *1633*

This is my play's last scene; here heavens appoint
My pilgrimage's last mile; and my race
Idly, yet quickly run, hath this last pace,
My span's last inch, my minute's last point,
And gluttonous Death will instantly unjoint   5
My body, and soul, and I shall sleep a space,
But my ever-waking part° shall see that face,   *the soul*
Whose fear already shakes my every joint.
Then, as my soul, t'heaven her first seat, takes flight,
And earth-borne body, in the earth shall dwell,   10
So, fall my sins, that all may have their right,
To where they are bred, and would press me, to hell.
Impute me righteous, thus purged of evil,
For thus I leave the world, the flesh, and devil.

Holy Sonnet 7: At the Round Earth's Imagined Corners   *1633*

At the round earth's imagined corners, blow
Your trumpets, angels,° and arise, arise
From death, you numberless infinities
Of souls, and to your scattered bodies go,
All whom the flood did, and fire shall o'erthrow,   5
All whom war, dearth, age, agues, tyrannies,
Despair, law, chance, hath slain, and you whose eyes
Shall behold God, and never taste death's woe.°
But let them sleep, Lord, and me mourn a space,
For, if above all these, my sins abound,   10
'Tis late to ask abundance of Thy grace,
When we are there. Here on this lowly ground,
Teach me how to repent; for that's as good
As if Thou hadst sealed my pardon with Thy blood.

AT THE ROUND EARTH'S IMAGINED CORNERS.   1–2 *At . . . angels*: the lines
combine the image of the angels or winds drawn at the four corners of old maps with an
allusion to the four angels mentioned in Revelations 7:1.   7–8 *you whose eyes . . . woe*: a
reference to those people who are still living on the day of the Last Judgment and thus
move directly from life to judgment without experiencing death.

Holy Sonnet 10: Death Be Not Proud   *1633*

Death, be not proud, though some have called thee
Mighty and dreadful, for thou art not so;
For those whom thou think'st thou dost overthrow
Die not, poor Death, nor yet canst thou kill me.
From rest and sleep, which but thy pictures° be,   *images*   5
Much pleasure; then from thee much more must flow,
And soonest our best men with thee do go,
Rest of their bones, and soul's delivery.
Thou art slave to fate, chance, kings, and desperate men,
And dost with poison, war, and sickness dwell,   10
And poppy° or charms can make us sleep as well   *opium*
And better than thy stroke; why swell'st° thou then?   *puff up with pride*
One short sleep past, we wake eternally°   *on Judgment Day*
And death shall be no more; Death, thou shalt die.

A Hymn to God the Father   *1633 (1623?)*

Wilt Thou forgive that sin where I begun,
    Which is my sin, though it were done before?
Wilt Thou forgive those sins through which I run,
    And do them still, though still I do deplore?

When Thou hast done, Thou hast not done,   5
  For I have more.

Wilt Thou forgive that sin by which I won
  Others to sin and made my sin their door?
Wilt Thou forgive that sin which I did shun
  A year or two, but wallowed in a score?   10
    When Thou hast done, Thou hast not done,
      For I have more.

I have a sin of fear, that when I have spun
  My last thread, I shall perish on the shore;
Swear by Thy self, that at my death Thy sun   15
  Shall shine as it shines now and heretofore;
    And, having done that, Thou hast done,
      I have no more.

EMILY DICKINSON (1830–1886)

Emily Dickinson lived in the small, religious, and tradition-bound community of Amherst, Massachusetts. Her life was shaped by a combination of public submission and poetic rebellion against authority. Although she spent three years at school—two at Amherst Academy and one at South Hadley Seminary for Women (now Mount Holyoke College)—she was largely self-taught and her life was restricted to Amherst and her family home. After 1862 she became progressively more reclusive and shut off from the world at large.

Although Dickinson never married or had a real love affair, nevertheless much of her poetry is concerned with love and the psychology of human relationships. This choice of subject may have resulted from her relationships with three men around whom she built an emotional life in her poetry. The first of these was Benjamin Newton, a young law student whom she met in 1848 and who began to direct and encourage her reading. This guidance was cut short when Newton married and moved away; he died of tuberculosis in 1856. Scholars have assumed that Newton is one of the two persons referred to in Dickinson's "I Never Lost as Much But Twice," written about 1858.

The second man who influenced Emily Dickinson's life and career was the Reverend Charles Wadsworth, a minister whom she met on a visit to Philadelphia in 1855. Because Wadsworth was married, a romantic involvement never occurred. But her poetry was most prolific during this period, and focuses directly on love, marriage, and relationships. "I Cannot Live with You" (ca. 1862), for example, seems to deal with Dickinson's internalized relationship with Wadsworth. The relationship ended in 1862, when Wadsworth accepted a ministry in San Francisco.

After Wadsworth left, Dickinson became even more reclusive. In 1862 she began to correspond with Thomas Wentworth Higginson, a literary critic who had written an article encouraging young writers. Dickinson wrote to him, enclosing some of her poetry and asking if her verses were "alive" and ready for publication. She may have viewed Higginson initially as another mentor, but she soon discovered that his literary judgments were conventional and traditional. Ironically, Higginson became one of the first editors of her work after her death in 1886.

We can never know the exact connection between the events in Dickinson's life and the poems she wrote. She began writing poetry in her early twenties; her earliest efforts were occasional poems and valentines. She did not begin writing in earnest until around 1858, and between 1858 and 1861 she wrote about 300 poems. At this point she seems to have experienced a burst of creative energy; she wrote 366 poems in 1862, 141 in 1863, 174 in 1864, and about 80 in 1865. After 1865 she wrote about 20 poems a year until her death. In all there are 1,775 poems from her pen. Since she produced about one-third of her total poetic work in the three years between 1862 and 1864, we can only surmise that this prodigious output was connected in some way with the loss of Reverend Wadsworth. It was, no doubt, also connected with her growth as a poet and her increasing skepticism about the values of her family and community.

Poetic characteristics.   Dickinson's *poetic style* might best be described as metaphysical. Her poetry is simple and passionate and at the same time economical and concentrated. We see in her verse, as in John Donne's, a highly elliptical style that produces both concentration of language and the rapid movement of thoughts and images. In terms of *language and diction*, Dickinson's verse is full of grammatical irregularities and eccentricities of punctuation. The most obvious of these is her frequent abandonment of conventional punctuation in favor of the dash. She even developed a special length of dash that helps to control the rhythm and pauses in her poetry.

The *poetic forms* that Emily Dickinson most frequently used are common measure and ballad stanza (see p. 731). She may have gained her interest in these forms from the Protestant hymnal, the major poetic text of her youth. Within these quatrain forms, Dickinson achieves remarkable flexibility and variation through the skillful use of metrical substitution and an abundance of slant rhyme. Although these irregularities in rhyme and meter clearly annoyed Dickinson's first editors, they have since been recognized as important and effective elements of her poetry.

Poetic subjects.   For *poetic subjects*, Emily Dickinson turned to her immediate world of village and garden and to her inner life of emotion and skepticism. The characteristic subjects of her poetry include love, nature, faith, death, and immortality. Beyond these, however, her poems also chart her inner growth, the world that she created for herself in her own mind, and a broad range of psychological insights. Her ideas are witty, unconventional, and rebellious.

Of Dickinson's 1,775 poems, only seven were published during her lifetime, anonymously and in rather obscure periodicals. She may have rejected further publication because of editors' tendencies to "adjust" her verse or because of Higginson's discouraging advice. In any event, she stopped publishing early on and wrote mostly for herself. After Dickinson's death, her sister Lavinia was amazed to find boxes of small, handwritten and bound pamphlets of verse that contained about twenty poems each. Lavinia recognized the significance of her sister's work and eventually turned some of the poems over to Mabel L. Todd and Higginson for editing and publication. They produced three volumes of Dickinson's work (published in 1890, 1891, and 1896), each containing about 100 poems. In these editions, the editors made Dickinson's poetry conform to accepted standards; they eliminated slant rhymes, smoothed out the meter, revised those metaphors that struck them as outrageous, and regularized the punctuation.

BIBLIOGRAPHIC SOURCES.   The well-intended but destructive adjustments to Dickinson's poetry remained intact until 1955, when the Harvard University Press published Thomas H. Johnson's three-volume edition of her poems. Johnson went back to the manuscripts to establish the original text of each poem (with variants), and his edition is definitive. Important critical and biographical studies include Charles R. Anderson, *Emily Dickinson's Poetry* (1960); Albert Gelpi, *Emily Dickinson: The Mind of the Poet* (1965); Ruth Miller, *The Poetry of Emily Dickinson* (1968); Richard B. Sewall, *The Life of Emily Dickinson* (1974); and Robert Weisbuch, *Emily Dickinson's Poetry* (1975). Since the mid-1970s Dickinson has also been reevaluated from the perspective of feminist criticism. Three significant books in this vein are Antonina Clarke Mossberg, *Emily Dickinson: When a Writer Is a Daughter* (1982); Susan Juhasz, *The Undiscovered Continent: Emily Dickinson and the Space of the Mind* (1983); and *Feminist Critics Read Emily Dickinson* (1983), a collection of essays edited by Juhasz. One of the hour-long programs in the PBS "Voices and Visions" series (1987) features her work. Additional poems by Emily Dickinson may be found in this text by reference to the index.

I Never Lost as Much But Twice   1890 *(ca. 1858)*

I never lost as much but twice,
And that was in the sod.
Twice have I stood a beggar
Before the door of God!

Angels – twice descending   5
Reimbursed my store –
Burglar! Banker – Father!
I am poor once more!

Success Is Counted Sweetest   1878, 1890 (ca. 1859)

Success is counted sweetest
By those who ne'er succeed.
To comprehend a nectar
Requires sorest need.

Not one of all the purple Host   5
Who took the Flag today
Can tell the definition
So clear of Victory

As he defeated – dying –
On whose forbidden ear   10
The distant strains of triumph
Burst agonized and clear!

"Faith" Is a Fine Invention   1891 (ca. 1860)

"Faith" is a fine invention
When Gentlemen can *see* –
But *Microscopes* are prudent
In an Emergency.

I Taste a Liquor Never Brewed   1861, 1891 (ca. 1860)

I taste a liquor never brewed –
From Tankards scooped in Pearl –
Not all the Frankfort Berries°   *grapes*
Yield such an Alcohol!

Inebriate of Air – am I –
And Debauchee of Dew –   5
Reeling – thro endless summer days –
From inns of Molten Blue –

When "Landlords" turn the drunken Bee
Out of the Foxglove's door –
When Butterflies – renounce their "drams" –   10
I shall but drink the more!

Till Seraphs swing their snowy Hats –
And Saints – to windows run –
To see the little Tippler
From Manzanilla° come!   15

I TASTE A LIQUOR NEVER BREWED   16 *Manzanilla*: a pale sherry from Spain.
Dickinson may also have been thinking of Manzanillo, a Cuban city often associated with
rum.

Safe in Their Alabaster Chambers   *1862, 1890 (1861)*

Safe in their Alabaster Chambers –
Untouched by Morning –
And untouched by Noon –
Lie the meek members of the Resurrection –
Rafter of Satin – and Roof of Stone!   5

Grand go the Years – in the Crescent – above them –
Worlds scoop their Arcs –
And Firmaments – row –
Diadems – drop – and Doges° – surrender –
Soundless as dots – on a Disc of Snow –   10

SAFE IN THEIR ALABASTER CHAMBERS.   9 *Doges*: Renaissance rulers of the Italian
city-states of Venice and Genoa.

Wild Nights – Wild Nights!   *1890 (ca. 1861)*

Wild Nights – Wild Nights!
Were I with thee
Wild Nights should be
Our luxury!

Futile – the Winds –   5
To a Heart in port –
Done with the Compass –
Done with the Chart!

Rowing in Eden –
Ah, the Sea!   10
Might I but moor – Tonight –
In Thee!

There's a Certain Slant of Light   *1890 (ca. 1861)*

There's a certain Slant of light,
Winter Afternoons –

That oppresses, like the Heft
Of Cathedral Tunes –

Heavenly Hurt, it gives us –   5
We can find no scar,
But internal difference,
Where the Meanings, are –

None may teach it – Any –
'Tis the Seal Despair –   10
An imperial affliction
Sent us of the Air –

When it comes, the Landscape listens –
Shadows – hold their breath –
When it goes, 'tis like the Distance   15
On the look of Death –

The Soul Selects Her Own Society   1890 (ca. 1862)

The Soul selects her own Society –
Then – shuts the Door –
To her divine Majority –
Present no more –

Unmoved – she notes the Chariots – pausing –   5
At her low Gate –
Unmoved – an Emperor be kneeling
Upon her Mat –

I've known her – from an ample nation –
Choose One –   10
Then – close the Valves of her attention –
Like Stone –

Some Keep the Sabbath Going to Church   1864 (ca. 1862)

Some keep the Sabbath going to Church –
I keep it, staying at Home –
With a Bobolink for a Chorister –
And an Orchard, for a Dome –

Some keep the Sabbath in Surplice –   5
I just wear my Wings –
And instead of tolling the Bell, for Church,
Our little Sexton – sings.

God preaches, a noted Clergyman –
And the sermon is never long,   10

So instead of getting to Heaven, at last —
I'm going, all along.

After Great Pain, a Formal Feeling Comes

1929 (*ca. 1862*)

After great pain, a formal feeling comes —
The Nerves sit ceremonious, like Tombs —
The stiff Heart questions was it He, that bore,
And Yesterday, or Centuries before?

The Feet, mechanical, go round —   5
Of Ground, or Air, or Ought° —   *anything, nothing*
A Wooden way
Regardless grown,
A Quartz contentment, like a stone —

This is the Hour of Lead —   10
Remembered, if outlived,
As Freezing persons, recollect the Snow —
First — Chill — then Stupor — then the letting go —

Much Madness Is Divinest Sense

1890 (*ca. 1862*)

Much Madness is divinest Sense —
To a discerning Eye —
Much Sense — the starkest Madness —
'Tis the Majority
In this, as All, prevail —   5
Assent — and you are sane —
Demur — you're straightway dangerous —
And handled with a Chain —

I Heard a Fly Buzz — When I Died

1896 (*ca. 1862*)

I heard a Fly buzz — when I died —
The Stillness in the Room
Was like the Stillness in the Air —
Between the Heaves of Storm —

The Eyes around — had wrung them dry —   5
And Breaths were gathering firm
For that last Onset — when the King
Be witnessed — in the Room —

I willed my Keepsakes — Signed away
What portion of me be   10

Assignable – and then it was
There interposed a Fly –

With Blue – uncertain stumbling Buzz –
Between the light – and me –
And then the Windows failed – and then   15
I could not see to see –

I Like to See It Lap the Miles   1891 (ca. 1862)

I like to see it lap the Miles –
And lick the Valleys up –
And stop to feed itself at Tanks –
And then – prodigious step

Around a Pile of Mountains –   5
And supercilious peer
In Shanties – by the sides of Roads –
And then a Quarry pare

To fit its sides
And crawl between
Complaining all the while   10
In horrid – hooting stanza –
Then chase itself down Hill –

And neigh like Boanerges° –
Then – prompter than a Star
Stop – docile and omnipotent   15
At it's own stable door –

I LIKE TO SEE IT LAP THE MILES.   14 *Boanerges*: a surname meaning "the sons of
thunder" that appears in Mark 3:17.

I Cannot Live with You   1890 (ca. 1862)

I cannot live with You –
It would be Life –
And Life is over there –
Behind the Shelf

The Sexton keeps the Key to –   5
Putting up
Our Life – His Porcelain –
Like a Cup –

Discarded of the Housewife –
Quaint – or Broke –   10

A newer Sevres° pleases –
Old Ones crack –

a fine French porcelain

I could not die – with You –
For One must wait
To shut the Other's Gaze down –
You – could not –

15

And I – Could I stand by
And see You – freeze –
Without my Right of Frost –
Death's privilege?

20

Nor could I rise – with You –
Because Your Face
Would put out Jesus' –
That New Grace

Glow plain – and foreign
On my homesick Eye –
Except that You than He
Shone closer by –

25

They'd judge Us – How –
For You – served Heaven – You know,
Or sought to –
I could not –

30

Because You saturated Sight –
And I had no more Eyes
For sordid excellence
As Paradise

35

And were You lost, I would be –
Though My Name
Rang loudest
On the Heavenly fame –

40

And were You – saved –
And I – condemned to be
Where You were not –
That self – were Hell to Me –

So We must meet apart –
You there – I – here –
With just the Door ajar
That Oceans are – and Prayer –
And that White Sustenance –
Despair –

45

50

One Need Not Be a Chamber — To Be Haunted   1891 (ca. 1863)

One need not be a Chamber — to be Haunted —
One need not be a House —
The Brain has Corridors — surpassing
Material Place —

Far safer, of a Midnight Meeting   5
External Ghost
Than its interior Confronting —
That Cooler Host.

Far safer, through an Abbey gallop,
The Stones a'chase —   10
Than Unarmed, one's a'self encounter —
In lonesome Place —

Ourself behind ourself, concealed —
Should startle most —
Assassin hid in our Apartment   15
Be Horror's least.

The Body — borrows a Revolver —
He bolts the Door —
O'erlooking a superior spectre —
Or More —   20

The Bustle in a House   1890 (ca. 1866)

The Bustle in a House
The Morning after Death
Is solemnest of industries
Enacted upon Earth —

The Sweeping up the Heart   5
And putting Love away
We shall not want to use again
Until Eternity.

My Triumph Lasted Till the Drums   1935 (ca. 1872)

My Triumph lasted till the Drums
Had left the Dead alone
And then I dropped my Victory
And chastened stole along
To where the finished Faces   5
Conclusion turned on me

And then I hated Glory
And wished myself were They.

What is to be is best descried
When it has also been –   10
Could Prospect taste of Retrospect
The tyrannies of Men
Were Tenderer – diviner
The Transitive toward.
A Bayonet's contrition   15
Is nothing to the Dead.

The Heart Is the Capital of the Mind   *1929 (ca. 1876)*

The Heart is the Capital of the Mind –
The Mind is a single State –
The Heart and the Mind together make
A single Continent –

One – is the Population –   5
Numerous enough –
This ecstatic Nation
Seek – it is Yourself.

My Life Closed Twice Before Its Close   *1896*

My life closed twice before its close;
It yet remains to see
If Immortality unveil
A third event to me,

So huge, so hopeless to conceive   5
As these that twice befel.
Parting is all we know of heaven,
And all we need of hell.

ROBERT FROST (1874–1963)

When Robert Frost's first book of poems, *A Boy's Will*, was published in
England in 1913, he was virtually unknown in the United States. At the
time Ezra Pound wrote, "it is a sinister thing that so American . . . a
talent . . . should have to be exported before it can find due encouragement
and recognition." Time, of course, brought Frost all the encouragement
and recognition he could want. He eventually received over twenty honorary
degrees and four Pulitzer Prizes. Indeed, he came as close as possible to
becoming America's official poet—a sort of poet laureate—when he read

"The Gift Outright" at the inauguration of President John F. Kennedy in 1961. In his own lifetime Robert Frost became one of the most visible and admired American poets. His poetry continues to earn him that recognition to this day.

Frost, who presented himself as the quintessential New Englander in person and in his poetry, was actually born in San Francisco on March 26, 1874. His father had moved the family west so that he could write for the *San Francisco Bulletin*; when the father died of tuberculosis in 1885, Frost's mother brought the family back to Lawrence, Massachusetts. Frost attended Lawrence High School, studied classics, began writing poetry, and graduated in 1892 as co-valedictorian with Eleanor White, the woman he married in 1895. After high school, Frost attended Dartmouth College for seven weeks and then turned to newspaper work and schoolteaching; he continued to write poetry, little of which was published. He returned to college after his marriage, attending classes at Harvard from 1897 to 1899, but he left again without a degree. His prospects were bleak.

In 1900 Frost's grandfather gave him a farm in Derry, New Hampshire, and for the next twelve years he worked the farm, wrote poetry, and taught English at Pinkerton Academy. The life was hard and the poetry mostly ignored. In 1912 Frost decided to sell the farm and devote himself to writing. He moved to England, where he met a number of emerging and established poets, including Ezra Pound and William Butler Yeats. His first two books of poetry were published in England and received very favorable reviews. These books, *A Boy's Will* (1913) and *North of Boston* (1914), were published in the United States in 1915, and Frost finally began to receive recognition at home.

That same year Frost and his family returned to the United States and took up residence on a farm near Franconia, New Hampshire. More books of poetry and greater acclaim followed quickly. In 1916 Frost published *Mountain Interval*, a book containing "The Road Not Taken," "Birches," and "Out, Out—." He also gave a poetry reading at Harvard and became poet-in-residence at Amherst College, a relationship that would continue sporadically for much of his life. He also began to develop his public persona as the wry and philosophical country poet. Later, it became more difficult to separate this public mask from what Randall Jarrell calls "The Other Frost," the often agonized and troubled man who wrote the poems.

More books of poetry and more recognition followed throughout Frost's life. In 1923 he published *Selected Poems* and *New Hampshire*. The latter book, for which Frost won a Pulitzer Prize, contains some of his best-known work: "Stopping by Woods on a Snowy Evening," "Fire and Ice," and "Nothing Gold Can Stay." These were followed by *West-Running Brook* (1928), *Collected Poems* (1930), *A Further Range* (1936), *A Witness Tree* (1942), *Steeple Bush* (1947), *Complete Poems* (1949), *Aforesaid* (1954), and *In the Clearing* (1962).

POETIC CHARACTERISTICS.   Robert Frost's *poetic style* remained fairly consistent throughout his career; we do not see significant development or change in his work. We can find in his poems a clear sense of the land, of history, and of human nature. The poetry seems, at first, to be simple, lucid, straightforward, and descriptive. Further reading, however, reveals the subtleties of wit, humor, and irony that often underlie Frost's meditations on common events or objects.

Frost's *language and diction* are conversational; his words are plain and his phrases simple and direct. More often than not, he uses and refines the natural speech patterns and rhythms of New England, polishing the language that people actually speak to a compact and terse poetic texture.

In terms of *poetic structure*, Frost's poems often move from an event or an object through a metaphor to an idea in a smooth, uninterrupted flow. Within this pattern, Frost usually describes a complete event rather than a single vision. The heart of the process is the image or metaphor. Frost's metaphors are sparse and careful; they are brought sharply into focus and skillfully interwoven with the whole poem. Frost himself saw the metaphor as the beginning of the process. In *Education by Poetry* (1931) he wrote that "poetry begins in trivial metaphors, pretty metaphors, 'grace' metaphors, and goes on to the profoundest thinking that we have. Poetry provides the one permissible way of saying one thing and meaning another."

Frost's poems also reflect traditional *poetic forms* and meters. The poet once asserted that writing "free verse" was like playing tennis without a net. Consequently, we find conventional rhyme schemes and clear iambic meters in much of his work. Similarly, we find such closed forms as couplets, terza rima, quatrains, and blank verse.

POETIC SUBJECTS.   Frost's *poetic subjects* are generally common and rural events, objects, and characters: digging gardens, mending walls, cutting wood; snow, trees, insects, spring, and fall; children, parents, husbands and wives. Often, the poems move from these objects, events, or characters to philosophical generalizations about life and death, survival and responsibility, nature and humanity, that are so simple and right as to verge on the obvious.

BIBLIOGRAPHIC SOURCES.   The standard edition of Frost's work is *The Poetry of Robert Frost* (1969), edited by Edward Connery Lathem. The standard biography was written in three volumes by Lawrence Thompson: *Robert Frost: The Early Years* (1966), *The Years of Triumph* (1970), and *The Later Years* (1977). The last volume was completed after Thompson's death by R. H. Winnick. Recent and useful criticism of the poetry includes Reginald Cook, *The Dimensions of Robert Frost* (1958) and his *Robert Frost: A Living Voice* (1975), Ruben Brower, *The Poetry of Robert Frost* (1963), J. F. Lynan, *The Pastoral Art of Robert Frost* (1964), Philip L. Gerber, *Robert Frost*

(1966), and John C. Kemp, *Robert Frost and New England* (1979). One of the hour-long programs in the PBS "Voices and Visions" series (1987) features his work. Additional poems by Frost may be found in this book by reference to the index.

The Tuft of Flowers   1906

I went to turn the grass once after one
Who mowed it in the dew before the sun.

The dew was gone that made his blade so keen
Before I came to view the leveled scene.

I looked for him behind an isle of trees;   5
I listened for his whetstone on the breeze.

But he had gone his way, the grass all mown,
And I must be, as he had been,—alone,

'As all must be,' I said within my heart,
'Whether they work together or apart.'   10

But as I said it, swift there passed me by
On noiseless wing a bewildered butterfly,

Seeking with memories grown dim o'er night
Some resting flower of yesterday's delight.

And once I marked his flight go round and round,   15
As where some flower lay withering on the ground.

And then he flew as far as eye could see,
And then on tremulous wing came back to me.

I thought of questions that have no reply,
And would have turned to toss the grass to dry;   20

But he turned first, and led my eye to look
At a tall tuft of flowers beside a brook,

A leaping tongue of bloom the scythe had spared
Beside a reedy brook the scythe had bared.

The mower in the dew had loved them thus,   25
By leaving them to flourish, not for us,

Nor yet to draw one thought of ours to him,
But from sheer morning gladness at the brim.

The butterfly and I had lit upon,
Nevertheless, a message from the dawn,   30

That made me hear the wakening birds around,
And hear his long scythe whispering to the ground,

And feel a spirit kindred to my own;
So that henceforth I worked no more alone;

But glad with him, I worked as with his aid,   35
And weary, sought at noon with him the shade;

And dreaming, as it were, held brotherly speech
With one whose thought I had not hoped to reach.

'Men work together,' I told him from the heart,
'Whether they work together or apart.'   40

Mending Wall   *1914*

Something there is that doesn't love a wall,
That sends the frozen-ground-swell under it,
And spills the upper boulders in the sun;
And makes gaps even two can pass abreast.
The work of hunters is another thing: 5
I have come after them and made repair
Where they have left not one stone on a stone,
But they would have the rabbit out of hiding,
To please the yelping dogs. The gaps I mean,
No one has seen them made or heard them made,   10
But at spring mending-time we find them there.
I let my neighbor know beyond the hill;
And on a day we meet to walk the line
And set the wall between us once again.
We keep the wall between us as we go.   15
To each the boulders that have fallen to each.
And some are loaves and some so nearly balls
We have to use a spell to make them balance:
'Stay where you are until our backs are turned!'
We wear our fingers rough with handling them.   20
Oh, just another kind of outdoor game,
One on a side. It comes to little more:
There where it is we do not need the wall:
He is all pine and I am apple orchard.
My apple trees will never get across   25
And eat the cones under his pines, I tell him.
He only says, 'Good fences make good neighbors.'
Spring is the mischief in me, and I wonder
If I could put a notion in his head:
'*Why* do they make good neighbors? Isn't it   30
Where there are cows? But here there are no cows.
Before I built a wall I'd ask to know

What I was walling in or walling out,
And to whom I was like to give offense.
Something there is that doesn't love a wall,   35
That wants it down.' I could say 'Elves' to him,
But it's not elves exactly, and I'd rather
He said it for himself. I see him there
Bringing a stone grasped firmly by the top
In each hand, like an old-stone savage armed.   40
He moves in darkness as it seems to me,
Not of woods only and the shade of trees.
He will not go behind his father's saying,
And he likes having thought of it so well
He says again, 'Good fences make good neighbors.'   45

Birches   *1915*

When I see birches bend to left and right
Across the lines of straighter darker trees,
I like to think some boy's been swinging them.
But swinging doesn't bend them down to stay
As ice-storms do. Often you must have seen them   5
Loaded with ice a sunny winter morning
After a rain. They click upon themselves
As the breeze rises, and turn many-colored
As the stir cracks and crazes their enamel.
Soon the sun's warmth makes them shed crystal shells   10
Shattering and avalanching on the snow-crust—
Such heaps of broken glass to sweep away
You'd think the inner dome of heaven had fallen.
They are dragged to the withered bracken by the load,
And they seem not to break; though once they are bowed   15
So low for long, they never right themselves:
You may see their trunks arching in the woods
Years afterwards, trailing their leaves on the ground
Like girls on hands and knees that throw their hair
Before them over their heads to dry in the sun.   20
But I was going to say when Truth broke in
With all her matter-of-fact about the ice-storm
I should prefer to have some boy bend them
As he went out and in to fetch the cows—
Some boy too far from town to learn baseball,   25
Whose only play was what he found himself,
Summer or winter, and could play alone.
One by one he subdued his father's trees
By riding them down over and over again
Until he took the stiffness out of them,   30

And not one but hung limp, not one was left
For him to conquer. He learned all there was
To learn about not launching out too soon
And so not carrying the tree away
Clear to the ground. He always kept his poise   35
To the top branches, climbing carefully
With the same pains you use to fill a cup
Up to the brim, and even above the brim.
Then he flung outward, feet first, with a swish,
Kicking his way down through the air to the ground.   40
So was I once myself a swinger of birches.
And so I dream of going back to be.
It's when I'm weary of considerations,
And life is too much like a pathless wood
Where your face burns and tickles with the cobwebs   45
Broken across it, and one eye is weeping
From a twig's having lashed across it open.
I'd like to get away from earth awhile
And then come back to it and begin over.
May no fate willfully misunderstand me   50
And half grant what I wish and snatch me away
Not to return. Earth's the right place for love:
I don't know where it's likely to go better.
I'd like to go by climbing a birch tree,
And climb black branches up a snow-white trunk   55
Toward Heaven, till the tree could bear no more,
But dipped its top and set me down again.
That would be good both going and coming back.
One could do worse than be a swinger of birches.

The Road Not Taken   *1915*

Two roads diverged in a yellow wood,
And sorry I could not travel both
And be one traveler, long I stood
And looked down one as far as I could
To where it bent in the undergrowth;   5

Then took the other, as just as fair,
And having perhaps the better claim,
Because it was grassy and wanted wear;
Though as for that the passing there
Had worn them really about the same,   10
And both that morning equally lay
In leaves no step had trodden black.

Oh, I kept the first for another day!
Yet knowing how way leads on to way,
I doubted if I should ever come back.   15

I shall be telling this with a sigh
Somewhere ages and ages hence:
Two roads diverged in a wood, and I—
I took the one less traveled by,
And that has made all the difference.   20

'Out, Out—'   *1916*

The buzz saw snarled and rattled in the yard
And made dust and dropped stove-length sticks of wood,
Sweet-scented stuff when the breeze drew across it.
And from there those that lifted eyes could count
Five mountain ranges one behind the other   5
Under the sunset far into Vermont.
And the saw snarled and rattled, snarled and rattled,
As it ran light, or had to bear a load.
And nothing happened: day was all but done.
Call it a day, I wish they might have said   10
To please the boy by giving him the half hour
That a boy counts so much when saved from work.
His sister stood beside them in her apron
To tell them 'Supper.' At the word, the saw,
As if to prove saws knew what supper meant,   15
Leaped out at the boy's hand, or seemed to leap—
He must have given the hand. However it was,
Neither refused the meeting. But the hand!
The boy's first outcry was rueful laugh,
As he swung toward them holding up the hand   20
Half in appeal, but half as if to keep
The life from spilling. Then the boy saw all—
Since he was old enough to know, big boy
Doing a man's work, though a child at heart—
He saw all spoiled. 'Don't let him cut my hand off—   25
The doctor, when he comes. Don't let him, sister!'
So. But the hand was gone already.
The doctor put him in the dark of ether.
He lay and puffed his lips out with his breath.
And then—the watcher at his pulse took fright.   30
No one believed. They listened at his heart.
Little—less—nothing!—and that ended it.
No more to build on there. And they, since they
Were not the one dead, turned to their affairs.

Fire and Ice

1920

Some say the world will end in fire,
Some say in ice.
From what I've tasted of desire
I hold with those who favor fire.
But if it had to perish twice,   5
I think I know enough of hate
To say that for destruction ice
Is also great
And would suffice.

Nothing Gold Can Stay

1923

Nature's first green is gold,
Her hardest hue to hold.
Her early leaf's a flower;
But only so an hour.
Then leaf subsides to leaf.   5
So Eden sank to grief,
So dawn goes down to day.
Nothing gold can stay.

Misgiving

1923

All crying, 'We will go with you, O Wind!'
The foliage follow him, leaf and stem;
But a sleep oppresses them as they go,
And they end by bidding him stay with them.

Since ever they flung abroad in spring   5
The leaves had promised themselves this flight,
Who now would fain seek sheltering wall,
Or thicket, or hollow place for the night.

And now they answer his summoning blast
With an ever vaguer and vaguer stir,   10
Or at utmost a little reluctant whirl
That drops them no further than where they were.

I only hope that when I am free
As they are free to go in quest
Of the knowledge beyond the bounds of life   15
It may not seem better to me to rest.

Acquainted with the Night   1928

I have been one acquainted with the night.
I have walked out in rain—and back in rain.
I have outwalked the furthest city light.

I have looked down the saddest city lane.
I have passed by the watchman on his beat   5
And dropped my eyes, unwilling to explain.

I have stood still and stopped the sound of feet
When far away an interrupted cry
Came over houses from another street,

But not to call me back or say good-by;   10
And further still at an unearthly height,
One luminary clock against the sky

Proclaimed the time was neither wrong nor right.
I have been one acquainted with the night.

Design   1936

I found a dimpled spider, fat and white,
On a white heal-all,° holding up a moth
Like a white piece of rigid satin cloth—
Assorted characters of death and blight
Mixed ready to begin the morning right,   5
Like the ingredients of a witches' broth—
A snow-drop spider, a flower like a froth,
And dead wings carried like a paper kite.

What had that flower to do with being white,
The wayside blue and innocent heal-all?   10
What brought the kindred spider to that height,
Then steered the white moth thither in the night?
What but design of darkness to appall?—
If design govern in a thing so small.

DESIGN.   2 *heal-all*: a flower, usually blue, thought to have healing powers.

A Considerable Speck   1942

(Microscopic)

A speck that would have been beneath my sight
On any but a paper sheet so white
Set off across what I had written there.

And I had idly poised my pen in air
To stop it with a period of ink   5
When something strange about it made me think.
This was no dust speck by my breathing blown,
But unmistakably a living mite
With inclinations it could call its own.
It paused as with suspicion of my pen,   10
And then came racing wildly on again
To where my manuscript was not yet dry;
Then paused again and either drank or smelt—
With loathing, for again it turned to fly.
Plainly with an intelligence I dealt.   15
It seemed too tiny to have room for feet,
Yet must have had a set of them complete
To express how much it didn't want to die.
It ran with terror and with cunning crept.
It faltered: I could see it hesitate;   20
Then in the middle of the open sheet
Cower down in desperation to accept
Whatever I accorded it of fate.
I have none of the tenderer-than-thou
Collectivistic regimenting love   25
With which the modern world is being swept
But this poor microscopic item now!
Since it was nothing I knew evil of
I let it lie there till I hope it slept.
I have a mind myself and recognize   30
Mind when I meet with it in any guise.
No one can know how glad I am to find
On any sheet the least display of mind.

WRITING ABOUT A POET'S WORK

It is difficult to write an effective essay on a poet's entire career based on a small selection of the poet's verse. It is both possible and reasonable, however, to write about a limited number of poems by a single author. There are three potential approaches to this type of essay: biographical, developmental, and comparative.

The *biographical essay* is perhaps the least productive; it seeks to relate poems to specific events or stages in a poet's life. Thus, you might attempt an essay that connects specific events in Emily Dickinson's life with specific poems; this type of essay requires extensive biographical research.

The *developmental essay* traces the growth of a single image, concept, or technique throughout a poet's career. Such an essay presupposes both development and the ability to look at a poet's work in the order in which it was written. An essay of this type might focus, for example, on Frost's use of snow imagery or Dickinson's employment of slant rhyme. In either case, the object would be to discover, assert, and prove through examples that development occurred over the poet's creative life.

The *comparative essay* is perhaps the easiest to formulate and the most common, since it neither assumes development nor requires biographical research (see Appendix B for an additional discussion of comparison as a strategy). Like the developmental essay, the comparative essay focuses on a specific element, image, idea, or technique in a poet's work; however, the object is to assert *continuity* or *commonality* rather than development and to use each work to clarify the others. Thus, such an essay will usually argue that a poet uses the same devices or addresses the same concerns in a similar way in a number of his or her poems to establish related ideas or emotions. Such an essay might deal with snow imagery in three of Robert Frost's poems, biblical allusions in four of Donne's poems, or the subject of death in four of Dickinson's poems.

Almost any essay dealing with a number of poems by the same author will inevitably focus on a specific element of the poems rather than attempt a wholesale treatment. The potential subjects for this type of essay include virtually every aspect of poetry. Thus, you might choose to work with speaker, setting and situation, diction, imagery, tone, rhythm, rhyme and form, symbol, allusion, or theme. The choice, of course, is never completely arbitrary; you should look for an element or technique that strikes you as especially significant and effective.

Prewriting strategies for either a developmental or comparative essay include selecting a poet, an approach, and a focus. These choices are not always easy, but some investigation of the works at hand will usually help you narrow the options considerably. As you plan the essay, you should remember that your aim is to discover development or commonality. With this in mind, you might consider the following questions in connection with a given poet.

1. Are the speakers in the poems similar or related to each other? Does the speaker remain constant throughout the poems, develop gradually, or change radically from poem to poem? To what extent do the speakers share a common tone or attitude? Do tone and attitude remain constant, or do they change?

2. Do the poems have common or similar settings or situations? Are these established vividly and quickly, or left undeveloped? To what extent do setting and situation produce similar effects in a number of poems by the same author?

3. Can you find common threads of diction, imagery, metaphor, simile, symbol, or allusion in a number of poems by the same author? Are these common devices always used the same way and to the same effect, or do the method and impact change?

4. Does the poet's use of the elements of form—rhythm, rhyme, meter, stanza—remain constant or develop? Does form consistently reinforce meaning? Does the connection between form and content remain constant or become less or more effective?

5. Does the poet deal with the same subject or convey similar ideas in a significant number of poems? To what extent do the poet's attitudes toward this subject and treatment of the idea remain constant or change? To what extent can you see logical connection or development among the poems in question?

These questions obviously cover a broad range of topics. In actual practice, however, the poems at hand will usually direct you to specific areas of consideration rather quickly. As you answer the questions that seem relevant to the poems, the focus of the essay should begin to emerge.

Once you have chosen a poet, isolated an area of interest, and selected a series of poems for examination, you can begin to shape a tentative central idea for the essay. As usual, this is probably the most difficult step in the prewriting process. Discovering an area of commonality or development is only half the battle; you must go on to assert a central fact about this common thread. It is not enough, for example, to argue in an essay that "we find the idea of death in three of Emily Dickinson's poems" or that "snow imagery recurs in a number of Robert Frost's poems." Rather, you must link the common thread to an assertion about its effect, impact, or significance. Thus, you might formulate a tentative thesis that argues that "death is presented in a number of Emily Dickinson's poems as the natural and welcome end to a life of toil" or that "the common image of snow in many of Robert Frost's poems grows progressively more grim and ironic throughout his career." Notice that both these formulations identify an area of commonality *and* make an assertion about that area. The first thesis would produce a comparative essay, the second a developmental one.

Having formulated a tentative central idea, go back through the poet's work and reexamine those poems that offer support and illustration. Look for aspects of specific poems that will eventually form the body of the essay. During this stage you may find it necessary to revise or refocus the thesis several times to solidify the connection between the essay's central idea and the supporting details.

Organizing Your Essay

INTRODUCTION. The introductory paragraph should indicate, at least indirectly, the type of approach that will be taken in the essay. After reading the first paragraph, a reader should be able to tell if the essay is biographical, developmental, or comparative. More often than not, this information is conveyed through the formulation of the central idea. The introduction will also specify the area or element of the poet's work about which you are writing. This information too is usually incorporated into the statement of the central idea. The thesis or central idea of the essay should assert a specific point about the subject or element under consideration in the poet's work. Finally, the introduction should specify which poems will be examined to support the central idea of the essay.

BODY.   The organization of the body of the essay is determined almost completely by the strategy outlined in the introduction. A biographical essay would probably be organized around crucial events in the poet's life and key poems that reflect those events. A developmental essay would naturally consider a number of the author's poems in chronological order, based on approximate or exact dates of composition. A comparative essay, on the other hand, might take up one poem at a time in almost any order.

As with other essays, the main thrust of the body is to support and prove the assertion made in the introduction. To do this with conviction, you should normally plan to work with no more than three to five poems. Thus, one effective strategy for organizing the body of the essay is to deal with one poem at a time, stanza by stanza or unit by unit, focusing on the aspect under consideration. Be especially careful to provide clear transitions between your treatments of each poem and to tie each separate discussion back into the central idea and the introductory paragraph so that your essay does not break down into three or four disjointed discussions. In addition, discussions of poems later in the essay should be connected to earlier ones through comparison or contrast.

CONCLUSION.   The conclusion should pull together all the strands of your argument and provide an overview. This can be done by summarizing the main points and observations. At the same time, you might use the conclusion to relate your argument to a broader consideration of the poet's work. Thus, an essay on the speaker in three of Frost's poems might conclude with a sentence or two that connects this narrative voice with the dominant tones or moods of Frost's poetry.

SAMPLE ESSAY

Images of Expanding and Contracting Space in John Donne's Love Poetry*

[1]   John Donne's love poetry has extended images and metaphors that emphasize the mystery and the power of love. Images that expand or contract space recur in much of this poetry; they help to create a private and separate

---

* See "The Good Morrow" (p. 862), "The Sun Rising" (p. 863), and "The Flea" (p. 866).

world for the lovers and to demonstrate the power of love.° We can see this skillful and effective use of spatial imagery in "The Good Morrow," "The Sun Rising," and "The Flea."□

"The Good Morrow," a three-stanza lyric spoken by a lover to his mistress, contains spatial images that illustrate both the expansion and the contraction of space to create a private world of love. The central image in this poem is the world or the globe; this image is skillfully manipulated to demonstrate the power of love. The speaker introduces the image in the second stanza when he asserts "For love all love of other sights controls, / And makes one little room an everywhere" (lines 10–11). This image suggests that love is powerful enough to expand "one little room" into an entire world that contains everything the lovers might desire. In the rest of the stanza, the image of the world becomes even more explicit:

[2]

Let sea-discoverers to new worlds have gone,
Let maps to other, worlds on worlds have shown,
Let us possess one world; each hath one, and is one. (lines 12–14)

The movement of the spatial imagery here is complex but consistent. These lines make a clear distinction between the public world of "sea-discoverers" or "maps" and the private world of the lovers. The speaker asserts that the lovers should "possess" their own world; each lover is a world and "hath" the other lover-world. More to the point, the movement here is inward and progressively contracting, from the actual globe to maps and finally to the lovers as little worlds.

This contraction of the world and space—the movement inward—is continued in the third stanza with the image of reflected faces: "My face in thine eye, thine in mine appears, / And true plain hearts do in the faces rest" (lines 15–16). At first, this image of reflected faces and hearts seems to depart from the spatial imagery of the second stanza. The connection, however, is established when we realize that eyes are spheres or globes, and that the reflection occurs on the outward half or "hemisphere" of the eyes. This witty

[3]

contraction of worlds to eyes is brought home in the next two lines: "Where can we find two better hemispheres / Without sharp North, without declining West?" (lines 17–18). Here, the image finally contracts to a single world or globe, and the lovers become that world. Thus, the poem simultaneously contracts global space to the physical presence of the lovers and expands their "little room" into a total cosmos.

We find a similar manipulation of spatial imagery in "The Sun Rising," another three-stanza lyric spoken by a lover. This time, however, the poem is addressed to the sun, which has awakened the lover and his mistress. In stanza 1 the speaker establishes the distinction between the lovers and the outside world—the "school boys," "sour prentices," "huntsmen," and "country ants." The second stanza returns to images of expanding and contracting

---

° Central idea.
□ Thesis sentence.

space that define love as self-sufficient and all-encompassing. Here the speaker tells the sun:

> Look, and tomorrow late, tell me,
> Whether both the Indias of spice and mine
> Be where thou leftst them, or lie here with me.

[4]
> Ask for those kings whom thou saw'st yesterday,
> And thou shalt hear, All here in one bed lay. (lines 16–20)

In this instance, the image contracts space, pulling most of the world into the bed and into the lovers themselves. The lady becomes both the East Indies of spices and the West Indies of gold. Similarly, the speaker becomes all the kings of the earth.

This imagery of spatial contraction becomes far more vivid in the last stanza of "The Sun Rising," when the speaker asserts that "She is all states, and all princes, I, / Nothing else is" (lines 21–22). The woman thus becomes the world and the speaker the ruler of "all states." The spatial contraction, pulling "all states" into bed with the speaker, underscores the irrelevance of the world at large and the importance of the lovers as a self-contained world. The speaker goes on, in lines 25 and 26, to argue that the sun should be happy "that the world's contracted thus" since warming it will be that much easier. And in the concluding two lines, the lovers and their bed become

[5] not only the world but also the center of the solar system: "Shine here to us, and thou art everywhere; / This bed thy center is, these walls, thy sphere" (lines 29–30). The movement of the image in this poem, as in "The Good Morrow," is thus both contracting and expanding. The outer world—the Indies, all kings, all states, all princes—is pulled into the room, the bed, and the physical being of the lovers. At the same time, the bed and the lovers expand to become a world unto themselves and the center of the solar system; the walls of their room become the outer limits of the sun's orbit. In this way, the spatial imagery creates a tone of comic outrageousness that helps define the power of love.

Although "The Flea" is a very different type of poem than either "The Good Morrow" or "The Sun Rising," similar images of spatial manipulation emphasize the singularity and power of love. Unlike the other two lyrics, "The Flea" is a song of seduction spoken by an eager lover to an unwilling lady. Again, however, space expands and contracts to create a private (and in

[6] this case amusing) world for the lovers. Reduced to its basic logic, the poem asserts that the loss of virginity is no more significant than a flea bite. The master image of the poem is the flea and the blood of the eager lover and resistant lady that has been "mingled" in the flea. Indeed, the first stanza is given over to the image of the flea biting each lover and swelling "with one blood made of two" (line 8).

The speaker does not begin to manipulate spatial imagery until the second stanza of "The Flea," where images of expanding and contracting space become both amusing and bizarre. Working from the premise established in the first stanza, that the flea contains both the speaker's and the lady's blood, the flea suddenly becomes all three beings: "Oh stay, three lives in one flea spare, / Where we almost, yea more than married, are" (lines 10–11). In terms of the dramatic situation, the lady is about to kill the flea; the speaker argues that they are married within the flea since their bloods are "mingled." This sets up one of Donne's most outrageous spatial images:

This flea is you and I, and this
Our marriage bed and marriage temple is;
Though parents grudge, and you, w'are met,
[7]   And cloister'd in these living walls of jet. (lines 12–15)

This manipulation of space and place is obviously witty and bizarre, but it is also consistent with the images of expanding and contracting space that occur in "The Good Morrow" and "The Sun Rising." Here the lovers contract or the flea expands until it has become both a "marriage bed and marriage temple." At the end of the passage we see that the image and the outrageous logic create the lovers' private world; they are "met / And cloister'd" within the black sides of the flea.

[8]   In each of these poems, images of space are thus manipulated to demonstrate the power of love and the private world of the lovers. In all three instances, extended metaphors establish the power of love (or desire) to contract the whole world into one bed or to expand a little room (or even a little flea) into an everywhere. Such imagery is consistent with the attitude toward love expressed throughout Donne's songs and sonnets; love and passion are private, powerful, and mysterious. Images of expanding and contracting space are simply one of the many techniques that Donne employs to emphasize and describe the miracle of love.

Commentary on the Essay

The sample is a comparative essay that deals with a common thread of imagery that runs through a number of Donne's poems. The introduction establishes the blueprint for the entire essay. The first sentence announces the focus—images and metaphors—and makes a generalization about Donne's love poetry. The second sentence establishes the central idea of the essay: images of expanding and contracting space demonstrate both the private world of lovers and the power of love. At the same time, the formulation of this sentence makes it clear that the essay is comparative rather than developmental or biographical; the statement makes no claims for development and avoids any reference to the poet's life. Finally, the last sentence of the introduction specifies the poems that will be discussed to support the central idea in the body of the essay.

The body—paragraphs 2 through 7—takes up the three poems mentioned at the close of the introduction in the order in which they are noted. Thus, paragraphs 2 and 3 deal with "The Good Morrow," 4 and 5 with "The Sun Rising," and 6 and 7 with "The Flea." Each of these two-paragraph units is organized the same way. In each, the topic sentence (the first sentence in paragraphs 2, 4, and 6) names the poem, makes a general observation about the poem, and restates part of the central idea of the essay. Thus, each separate discussion is tied back into the introduction. In addition, the topic sentences in paragraphs 4 and 6 establish transition from poem to poem (and discussion to discussion) by using transitional words like *similar, another,* and *although.* In this way, each discussion is linked to the previous one. One additional linking device is employed in each discussion; at some point in each, the poem under discussion is directly compared with the poem or poems previously discussed. All these strategies help to unify the essay.

Within the body of this essay two paragraphs are devoted to each poem. This need not always be the case; in many instances you can make the necessary point using one paragraph for each poem. Here, however, there is too much material to cover each poem in a single paragraph. Thus, each two-paragraph unit is organized to follow the structure of the poem itself; the first paragraph deals with material in earlier stanzas, and the second with examples in later stanzas. The second paragraph in each unit also begins with a topic sentence that connects the material to the central idea and provides transition from the previous paragraph. In this way, each paragraph in the essay returns to the "straight line" of the central idea.

The conclusion (paragraph 8) restates the central idea of the essay and summarizes the major point illustrated with each poem. In addition, it relates these observations about spatial imagery to the broader context of Donne's love poetry. Thus, the essay ends as it began, with a general assertion about Donne's songs and sonnets.

WRITING TOPICS FOR CHAPTER 23

On John Donne

1. Themes and ideas in Donne's religious poems.
2. Donne's use of metaphor and simile.
3. Donne's use of specific and general words in two or three poems.

On Emily Dickinson

4. Dickinson's characteristic brevity in her poems.
5. Dickinson's use of personal but not totally disclosed subject matter.
6. Dickinson's ideas about (a) death, or (b) religion, or (c) personal pain.
7. Dickinson's humor and irony.

On Robert Frost

8. Frost's use of topics based on recollections and reflections of personal experience.
9. Frost's characteristic pattern of structure, moving from specific to general, in three poems.
10. Frost's use of images drawn from everyday rural life.

24

Additional Poems

LEONARD ADAMÉ   (b. 1947)

My Grandmother Would Rock Quietly and Hum   *1973*

in her house
she would rock quietly and hum
until her swelled hands
calmed

in summer   5
she wore thick stockings
sweaters
and grey braids

(when "el cheque" came
we went to Payless°   *a grocery store*   10
and I laughed greedily
when given a quarter)

mornings,
sunlight barely lit
the kitchen   15
and where
there were shadows
it was not cold

she quietly rolled
flour tortillas—   20
the "papas"°   *potatoes*
cracking in hot lard
would wake me

she had lost her teeth
and when we ate   25
she had bread
soaked in "café"

always her eyes
were clear
and she could see   30
as I cannot yet see—
through her eyes
she gave me herself

she would sit
and talk   35
of her girlhood—
of things strange to me:
    México
    epidemics
    relatives shot   40
    her father's hopes
    of this country—
how they sank
with cement dust
to his insides   45

now
when I go
to the old house
the worn spots
by the stove   50
echo of her shuffling
and
México
still hangs in her
fading   55
calendar pictures

A. R. Ammons (b. 1926)

Dunes   *1964*

Taking root in windy sand
  is not an easy
way
to go about
  finding a place to stay.   5

A ditchbank or wood's-edge
  has firmer ground.

In a loose world though
  something can be started—
a root touch water,
  a tip break sand—   10

Mounds from that can rise
  on held mounds,
a gesture of building, keeping,
  a trapping   15
into shape.

Firm ground is not available ground.

MAYA ANGELOU   (b. 1928)

My Arkansas   *1978*

There is a deep brooding
in Arkansas.
Old crimes like moss pend
from poplar trees.
The sullen earth   5
is much too
red for comfort.

Sunrise seems to hesitate
and in that second
lose its   10
incandescent aim, and
dusk no more shadows
than the noon.
The past is brighter yet.

Old hates and   15
ante-bellum° lace, are rent
but not discarded.
Today is yet to come
in Arkansas.
It writhes. It writhes in awful   20
waves of brooding.

MY ARKANSAS.   16 *ante-bellum*: before the U.S. Civil War (1861–1865).

ANONYMOUS

Barbara Allan   *Sixteenth century*

It was in and about the Martinmas° time,   *November 11*
  When the green leaves were a-fallin',
That Sir John Graeme in the West Country
  Fell in love with Barbara Allan.

He sent his man down through the town   5
  To the place where she was dwellin':
"O haste and come to my master dear,
  Gin° ye be Barbara Allan."   *if*

O slowly, slowly rose she up,
  To the place where he was lyin',   10
And when she drew the curtain by:
  "Young man, I think you're dyin'."

"O it's I'm sick, and very, very sick,
  And 'tis all for Barbara Allan."
"O the better for me ye shall never be,   15
  Though your heart's blood were a-spillin'."

"O dinna ye mind,° young man," said she,   *don't you recall*
  "When ye the cups were fillin',
That ye made the healths° go round and round,   *toasts*
  And slighted Barbara Allan?"   20

He turned his face unto the wall,
  And death with him was dealin':
"Adieu, adieu,° my dear friends all,   *farewell*
  And be kind to Barbara Allan."

And slowly, slowly, rose she up,   25
  And slowly, slowly left him;
And sighing said she could not stay,
  Since death of life had reft° him.   *bereft, taken from*

She had not gone a mile but twa,°   *two*
  When she heard the dead-bell knellin',   30
And every jow° that the dead-bell ga'ed°   *stroke; made*
  It cried, "Woe to Barbara Allan!"

"O mother, mother, make my bed,
  O make it soft and narrow:
Since my love died for me today,   35
  I'll die for him tomorrow."

ANONYMOUS

Edward   *Sixteenth century*

"Why does your brand° so drip wi' blood,   sword
    Edward, Edward?
Why does your brand so drip wi' blood?
    And why so sad gang° ye, O?"   go
"O, I have killed my hawk so good,   5
    Mother, mother,
O, I have killed my hawk so good,
    And I had no more but he, O."

"Your hawk's blood was never so red,
    Edward, Edward,   10
Your hawk's blood was never so red,
    My dear son I tell thee, O."
"O, I have killed my red-roan steed,
    Mother, mother,
O, I have killed my red-roan steed,   15
    That erst° was so fair and free, O."   once

"Your steed was old, and ye have got more,
    Edward, Edward,
Your steed was old, and ye have got more:
    Some other dule° ye dree°, O,"   sorrow, suffer 20
"O, I have killed my father dear,
    Mother, mother,
O, I have killed my father dear,
    Alas and woe is me, O!"

"And whatten° penance will ye dree for that,   what sort of   25
    Edward, Edward?
And whatten penance will ye dree for that?
    My dear son, now tell me, O."
"I'll set my feet in yonder boat,
    Mother, mother,   30
I'll set my feet in yonder boat,
    And I'll fare over the sea, O."

"And what will ye do wi' your towers and your hall,
    Edward, Edward?
And what will ye do wi' your towers and your hall,   35
    That were so fair to see, O?"
"I'll let them stand till they down fall,
    Mother, mother,
I'll let them stand till they down fall,
For here never more maun° I be, O."   must   40

"And what will ye leave to your bairns° and your wife,   *children*
  Edward, Edward?
And what will ye leave to your bairns and your wife,
 When ye gang over the sea, O?"
"The world's room let them beg through life,   45
  Mother, mother
The world's room, let them beg through life,
 For them never more will I see, O."

"And what will ye leave to your own mother dear,
  Edward, Edward?   50
And what will ye leave to your own mother dear,
 My dear son, now tell me, O?"
"The curse of hell from me shall ye bear,
  Mother, mother,
The curse of hell from me shall ye bear,   55
 Such counsels ye gave to me, O."

ANONYMOUS

Lord Randal   *Sixteenth century*

"Oh, where have you been, Lord Randal, my son?
Oh, where have you been, my handsome young man?"
"Oh, I've been to the wildwood; mother, make my bed soon,
I'm weary of hunting and I fain° would lie down."   *gladly*

"And whom did you meet there, Lord Randal, my son?   5
And whom did you meet there, my handsome young man?"
"Oh, I met with my true love; mother, make my bed soon,
I'm weary of hunting and I fain would lie down."

"What got you for supper, Lord Randal, my son?
What got you for supper, my handsome young man?"   10
"I got eels boiled in broth; mother, make my bed soon,
I'm weary of hunting and I fain would lie down."

"And who got your leavings, Lord Randal, my son?
And who got your leavings, my handsome young man?"
"I gave them to my dogs; mother, make my bed soon,   15
I'm weary of hunting and I fain would lie down."

"And what did your dogs do, Lord Randal, my son?
And what did your dogs do, my handsome young man?"
"Oh, they stretched out and died; mother, make my bed soon,
I'm weary of hunting and I fain would lie down."   20

"Oh, I fear you are poisoned, Lord Randal, my son,
Oh, I fear you are poisoned, my handsome young man."
"Oh, yes, I am poisoned; mother, make my bed soon,
For I'm sick at my heart and I fain would lie down."

"What will you leave your mother, Lord Randal, my son?   25
What will you leave your mother, my handsome young man?"
"My house and my lands; mother, make my bed soon,
For I'm sick at my heart and I fain would lie down."

"What will you leave your sister, Lord Randal, my son?
What will you leave your sister, my handsome young man?"   30
"My gold and my silver; mother, make my bed soon,
For I'm sick at my heart and I fain would lie down."

"What will you leave your brother, Lord Randal, my son?
What will you leave your brother, my handsome young man?"
"My horse and my saddle; mother, make my bed soon,   35
For I'm sick at my heart and I fain would lie down."

"What will you leave your true-love, Lord Randal, my son?
What will you leave your true-love, my handsome young man?"
"A halter to hang her; mother, make my bed soon,
For I'm sick at my heart and I want to lie down."   40

ANONYMOUS

The Three Ravens   *Sixteenth century*

There were three ravens sat on a tree,
  Down a down, hay down, hay down,
There were three ravens sat on a tree,
  With a down,
There were three ravens sat on a tree,   5
They were as black as they might be,
  With a down, derry, derry, derry, down, down.°

The one of them said to his mate,
"Where shall we our breakfast take?"

"Down in yonder green field   10
There lies a knight slain under his shield.

"His hounds they lie down at his feet,
So well they can their master keep.

"His hawks they fly so eagerly,°   *fiercely*
There's no fowl° dare him come nigh."   *bird*   15

THE THREE RAVENS.   7 *down*: In singing this ballad, the first line of each stanza is
repeated three times and the refrain is repeated as in stanza 1.

| Down there comes a fallow° doe, | *light brown* |
| As great with young as she might go,° | *walk* |

She lifted up his bloody head,
And kissed his wounds that were so red.

| She got him up upon her back, | 20 |
| And carried him to earthen lake.° | *pit* |

She buried him before the prime,°	*morning prayer service*
She was dead herself ere evensong time.°	
God send every gentleman	
Such hawks, such hounds, and such a lemman.°	*mistress* 25

23 *evensong time*: the time for the evening prayer service.

W. H. AUDEN   (1907–1973)

The Unknown Citizen   *1940*

(*To JS/07/M/378*
This Marble Monument
Is Erected by the State

He was found by the Bureau of Statistics to be
One against whom there was no official complaint,
And all the reports on his conduct agree
That, in the modern sense of an old-fashioned word, he was a saint,
For in everything he did he served the Greater Community.   5

Except for the War till the day he retired	
He worked in a factory and never got fired,	
But satisfied his employers, Fudge Motors Inc.	
Yet he wasn't a scab° or odd in his views.	*strikebreaker*
For his Union reports that he paid his dues,	10
(Our report on his Union shows it was sound)	
That he was popular with his mates° and liked a drink.	*co-workers*

The Press are convinced that he bought a paper every day
And that his reactions to advertisements were normal in every way.   15
Policies taken out in his name prove that he was fully insured,
And his Health-card shows he was once in hospital but left it cured.
Both Producers Research and High-Grade Living declare
He was fully sensible to the advantages of the Instalment Plan
And had everything necessary to the Modern Man,   20
A phonograph, a radio, a car and a frigidaire.
Our researchers into Public Opinion are content
That he held the proper opinions for the time of year;

When there was peace, he was for peace; when there was war, he went.
He was married and added five children to the population,   25
Which our Eugenist says was the right number for a parent of his generation,
And our teachers report that he never interfered with their education.
Was he free? Was he happy? The question is absurd:
Had anything been wrong, we should certainly have heard.

MARGARET AVISON   (b. 1918)

Tennis   *1960*

Service is joy, to see or swing. Allow
All tumult to subside. Then tensest winds
Buffet, brace, viol and sweeping bow.
Courts are for love and volley. No one minds
The cruel ellipse of service and return,   5
Dancing white galliardes° at tape or net
Till point, on the wire's tip, or the long burn-
ing arc to nethercourt marks game and set.
Purpose apart, perched like an umpire, dozes,
Dreams golden balls whirring through indigo.   10
Clay blurs the whitewash but day still encloses
The albinos, bounded in their flick and flow.
Playing in musicked gravity, the pair
Score liquid Euclids° in foolscaps of air.

TENNIS.   6 *galliarde*: a lively French dance.   14 *Euclids*: Euclid (ca. B.C. 300) was a
Greek mathematician and geometrician; the term thus suggests geometric shapes.

IMAMU AMIRI BARAKA (LEROI JONES)   (b. 1934)

Ka 'Ba   *1969*

A closed window looks down
on a dirty courtyard, and black people
call across or scream across or walk across
defying physics in the stream of their will

Our world is full of sound   5
Our world is more lovely than anyone's
tho we suffer, and kill each other
and sometimes fail to walk the air

We are beautiful people
with african imaginations   10
full of masks and dances and swelling chants

with african eyes, and noses, and arms,
though we sprawl in grey chains in a place
full of winters, when what we want is sun.

We have been captured,   15
brothers. And we labor
to make our getaway, into
the ancient image, into a new

correspondence with ourselves
and our black family. We need magic   20
now we need the spells, to raise up
return, destroy, and create. What will be

the sacred words?

APHRA BEHN   (1640–1689)

Love Armed   *1665*

Love in Fantastic Triumph sat,
Whilst Bleeding Hearts around him flowed,
For whom Fresh pains he did Create,
And strange Tyrannic power he showed;
From thy Bright Eyes he took his fire,   5
Which round about, in sport he hurled;
But 'twas from mine he took desire,
Enough to undo the Amorous World

From me he took his sighs and tears,
From thee his Pride and Cruelty;   10
From me his Languishments and Fears,
And every Killing Dart from thee;
Thus thou and I, the God° have armed.   *Cupid, god of love*
And set him up a Deity;
But my poor Heart alone is harmed,   15
Whilst thine the Victor is, and free.

MARVIN BELL   (b. 1937)

Things We Dreamt We Died for   *1969*

Flags of all sorts.
The literary life.
Each time we dreamt we'd done
the gentlemanly thing,
covering our causes   5

in closets full of bones
to remove ourselves forever
from dearest possibilities,
the old weapons re-injured us,
the old armies conscripted us,   10
and we gave in to getting even,
a little less like us
if a lot less like others.
Many, thus, gained fame
in the way of great plunderers,   15
retiring to the university
to cultivate grand plunder-gardens
in the service of literature,
the young and no more wars.
Their continuing tributes   20
make them our greatest saviours,
whose many fortunes are followed
by the many who have not one.

EARLE BIRNEY   (b. 1904)

Can. Lit.°   *1962*

(or *them able leave her ever*)

since we'd always sky about
when we had eagles they flew out
leaving no shadow bigger than wren's
to trouble even our broodiest hens
too busy bridging loneliness   5
to be alone
we hacked in railway ties
what Emily° etched in bone

we French & English never lost
our civil war
endure it still
a bloody civil bore

the wounded sirened off
no Whitman° wanted
it's only by our lack of ghosts   15
we're haunted

CAN. LIT. The title is an abbreviation for "Canadian Literature."   8 *Emily*: Emily Dickinson
(1830–1886), American poet (see pp. 869–79).   14 *Whitman*: Walt Whitman (1819–1892),
American poet.

WILLIAM BLAKE   (1757–1827)

The Sick Rose   *1794*

O Rose thou art sick.
The invisible worm
That flies in the night,
In the howling storm:

Has found out thy bed   5
Of crimson joy:
And his dark secret love
Does thy life destroy.

WILLIAM BLAKE   (1757–1827)

Ah Sun-flower   *1794*

Ah Sun-flower! weary of time,
Who counts the steps of the Sun,
Seeking after that sweet golden clime
Where the traveller's journey is done;

Where the Youth pined away with desire,   5
And the pale Virgin shrouded in snow,
Arise from their graves and aspire,
Where my Sun-flower wishes to go.

ROBERT BLY   (b. 1926)

Snowfall in the Afternoon   *1962*

1.
The grass is half-covered with snow.
It was the sort of snowfall that starts in late afternoon.
And now the little houses of the grass are growing dark.

2.
If I reached my hands down, near the earth,
I could take handfuls of darkness!   5
A darkness was always there, which we never noticed.

3.
As the snow grows heavier, the cornstalks fade further away,
And the barn moves nearer to the house.
The barn moves all alone in the growing storm.

4.
The barn is full of corn, and moving toward us now,   10
Like a hulk blown toward us in a storm at sea;
All the sailors on deck have been blind for many years.

LOUISE BOGAN (1879–1970)

Women   *1923*

Women have no wilderness in them,
They are provident instead,
Content in the tight hot cell of their hearts
To eat dusty bread.

They do not see cattle cropping red winter grass,   5
They do not hear
Snow water going down under culverts
Shallow and clear.

They wait, when they should turn to journeys,
They stiffen, when they should bend.   10
They use against themselves that benevolence
To which no man is friend.

They cannot think of so many crops to a field
Or of clean wood cleft by an axe.
Their love is an eager meaninglessness   15
Too tense, or too lax.

They hear in every whisper that speaks to them
A shout and a cry.
As like as not, when they take life over their door-sills
They should let it go by.   20

ARNA BONTEMPS (1902–1973)

A Black Man Talks of Reaping   *1940*

I have sown beside all waters in my day.
I planted deep, within my heart the fear
that wind or fowl would take the grain away.
I planted safe against this stark, lean year.

I scattered seed enough to plant the land   5
in rows from Canada to Mexico
but for my reaping only what the hand
can hold at once is all that I can show.

Yet what I sowed and what the orchard yields
my brother's sons are gathering stalk and root;
small wonder then my children glean in fields
they have not sown, and feed on bitter fruit.

10

ANNE BRADSTREET (1612–1672)

To My Dear and Loving Husband

1678

If ever two were one, then surely we.
If ever man were loved by wife, then thee;
If ever wife was happy in a man,
Compare with me ye women if you can.
I prize thy love more than whole mines of gold,
Or all the riches that the East doth hold.
My love is such that rivers cannot quench,
Nor ought but love from thee give recompense.
Thy love is such I can no way repay;
The heavens reward thee manifold, I pray.
Then while we live, in love let's so persever,
That when we live no more we may live ever.

5

10

ROBERT BRIDGES · (1844–1930)

Nightingales

1893

Beautiful must be the mountains whence ye come,
And bright in the fruitful valleys the streams, wherefrom
     Ye learn your song:
Where are those starry woods? O might I wander there,
  Among the flowers, which in that heavenly air
     Bloom the year long!

5

Nay, barren are those mountains and spent the streams:
Our song is the voice of desire, that haunts our dreams,
     A throe of the heart,
Whose pining visions dim, forbidden hopes profound,
  No dying cadence nor long sigh can sound,
     For all our art.

10

Alone, aloud in the raptured ear of men
We pour our dark nocturnal secret; and then,
     As night is withdrawn
From these sweet-springing meads° and bursting boughs of May.   *meadows*
  Dream, while the innumerable choir of day
     Welcome the dawn.

15

GWENDOLYN BROOKS   (b. 1917)

Primer for Blacks   *1980*

Blackness
is a title,
is a preoccupation,
is a commitment Blacks
are to comprehend—   5
and in which you are
to perceive your Glory.

The conscious shout
of all that is white is
"It's Great to be white."   10
The conscious shout
of the slack in Black is
"It's Great to be white."
Thus all that is white
has white strength and yours.   15

The word Black
has geographic power,
pulls everybody in:
Blacks here—
Blacks there—   20
Blacks wherever they may be.
And remember, you Blacks, what they told you—
remember your Education:
"one Drop—one Drop
maketh a brand new Black."   25
    Oh mighty Drop.
——And because they have given us kindly
so many more of our people

Blackness
stretches over the land.   30
Blackness—
the Black of it,
the rust-red of it,
the milk and cream of it,
the tan and yellow-tan of it,   35
the deep-brown middle-brown high-brown of it,
the "olive" and ochre of it—
Blackness
marches on.

The huge, the pungent object of our prime out-ride   40
is to Comprehend,

to salute and to Love the fact that we are Black,
which *is* our "ultimate Reality,"
which is the lone ground
from which our meaningful metamorphosis,   45
from which our prosperous staccato,
group of individual, can rise.

Self-shriveled Blacks.
Begin with gaunt and marvelous concession:
YOU are our costume and our fundamental bone.   50

  All of you—
    you COLORED ones,
    you NEGRO ones,
those of you who proudly cry
    "I'm half INDian"—   55
    those of you who proudly screech
    "I'VE got the blood of George WASHington in
      MY veins"—

ALL of you—
    you proper Blacks,   60
you half-Blacks,
you wish-I-weren't Blacks,
Niggeroes and Niggerenes.

You.

ELIZABETH BARRETT BROWNING (1806–1861)

Number 43: Sonnets from the Portuguese   *1850*

How do I love thee? Let me count the ways.
I love thee to the depth and breadth and height
My soul can reach, when feeling out of sight
For the ends of Being and ideal Grace.
I love thee to the level of every day's   5
Most quiet need, by sun and candlelight.
I love thee freely, as men strive for Right;
I love thee purely, as they turn from Praise.
I love thee with the passion put to use
In my old griefs, and with my childhood's faith.   10
I love thee with a love I seemed to lose
With my lost saints,—I love thee with the breath,
Smiles, tears, of all my life!—and, if God choose,
I shall but love thee better after death.

ROBERT BROWNING   (1812–1889)

Soliloquy of the Spanish Cloister   *1842*

1

Gr-r-r—there go, my heart's abhorrence!
    Water your damned flowerpots, do!
If hate killed men, Brother Lawrence,
    God's blood, would not mine kill you!
What? your myrtle bush wants trimming?   5
    Oh, that rose has prior claims—
Needs its leaden vase filled brimming?
    Hell dry you up with its flames!

2

At the meal we sit together:
    Salve tibi!° I must hear   *Hail to thee!*   10
Wise talk of the kind of weather,
    Sort of season, time of year:
Not a plenteous cork crop: scarcely
    Dare we hope oak-galls, I doubt:
What's the Latin name for "parsley"?   15
    What's the Greek name for Swine's Snout?

3

Whew! We'll have our platter burnished,
    Laid with care on our own shelf!
With a fire-new spoon we're furnished,
    And a goblet for ourself,   20
Rinsed like something sacrificial
    Ere 'tis fit to touch our chaps°   *jaws*
Marked with L. for our initial!
    (He-he! There his lily snaps!)

4

Saint, forsooth! While brown Dolores   25
    Squats outside the Convent bank
With Sanchicha, telling stories,
    Steeping tresses in the tank,
Blue-black, lustrous, thick like horsehairs,
    —Can't I see his dead eye glow,   30
Bright as 'twere a Barbary corsair's?°   *pirate's*
    (That is, if he'd let it show!)

5

When he finishes refection,°   *dinner*
    Knife and fork he never lays
Cross-wise, to my recollection,   35
    As do I, in Jesu's praise.
I the Trinity illustrate,
    Drinking watered orange-pulp—

In three sips the Arian° frustrate;   Anti-Trinitarian (a heretic)
   While he drains his at one gulp.   40

          6
Oh, those melons? If he's able
   We're to have a feast! so nice!
One goes to the Abbot's table,
   All of us get each a slice.
How go on your flowers? None double?   45
   Not one fruit-sort can you spy?
Strange!—And I, too, at such trouble,
Keep them close-nipped on the sly!

          7
There's a great text in Galatians,°   perhaps 5:19–21 or 3:10
   Once you trip on it, entails   50
Twenty-nine distinct damnations,
   One sure, if another fails:
If I trip him just a-dying,
   Sure of heaven as sure can be,
Spin him round and send him flying   55
   Off to hell, a Manichee?°   heretic

          8
Or, my scrofulous° French novel   pornographic
   On gray paper with blunt type!
Simply glance at it, you grovel
   Hand and foot in Belial's° gripe: the Devil   60
If I double down its pages
   At the woeful sixteenth print,
When he gathers his greengages,
   Ope a sieve and slip it in't?

          9
Or, there's Satan!—one might venture   65
   Pledge one's soul to him, yet leave
Such a flaw in the indenture°   contract
   As he'd miss till, past retrieve,
Blasted lay that rose-acacia
   We're so proud of! *Hy, Zy, Hine . . .*   70
'St, there's Vespers! *Plena gratiâ*°   full of grace
   Ave, Virgo!° Gr-r-r—you swine!   Hail Virgin!

ROBERT BURNS   (1759–1796)

To a Mouse   *1786*

ON TURNING HER UP IN HER NEST WITH
THE PLOW, NOVEMBER, 1785

Wee, sleekit,° cow'rin', tim'rous beastie,   sleek
O, what a panic's in thy breastie!

Thou need na start awa sae hasty,
    Wi' bickering brattle!°   *scamper*
I wad be laith° to rin an' chase thee   *loath* 5
    Wi' murd'ring pattle!°   *plowstaff*

I'm truly sorry man's dominion
Has broken Nature's social union,
An' justifies that ill opinion
    Which makes thee startle   10
At me, thy poor, earth-born companion,
    An' fellow mortal!

I doubt na, whiles,° but thou may thieve;   *sometimes*
What then? poor beastie, thou maun° live!   *must*
A daimen-icker° in a thrave°   15
    'S a sma' request:
I'll get a blessin' wi' the lave,°   *remainder*
    And never miss 't!

Thy wee-bit housie, too, in ruin!
Its silly° wa's the win's are strewin'!   *feeble* 20
An' naething, now, to big° a new ane,   *build*
    O' foggage° green!   *moss*
An' bleak December's winds ensuin',
    Baith snell° an' keen!   *bitter*

Thou saw the fields laid bare and waste,   25
An' weary winter comin' fast,
An' cozie here, beneath the blast,
    Thou thought to dwell,
Till crash! the cruel coulter° passed   *cutter-blade*
    Out-through thy cell.   30

That wee-bit heap o'leaves an' stibble°   *stubble*
Has cost thee money a weary nibble!
Now thou's turned out, for a' thy trouble,
    But° house or hald,°   *Without; hold*
To thole° the winter's sleety dribble,   *endure* 35
    An' cranreuch° cauld!   *hoarfrost*

But Mousie, thou art no thy lane,°   *not alone*
In proving foresight may be vain:
The best-laid schemes o' mice an' men
    Gang aft a-gley,°   *go often awry* 40
An' lea'e us nought but grief an' pain,
    For promised joy.

TO A MOUSE.   15 *daimen-icker*: an occasional ear of corn.   *thrave*: a unit of measure
for unthreshed grain, equal to twenty-four sheaves.

Still thou art blest compared wi' me!
The present only toucheth thee:
But och! I backward cast my e'e
      On prospects drear!
An' forward though I canna see,
      I guess an' fear!

45

GEORGE GORDON, LORD BYRON   (1788–1824)

The Destruction of Sennacherib°

1815

The Assyrian came down like the wolf on the fold,
And his cohorts were gleaming in purple and gold;
And the sheen of their spears was like stars on the sea,
When the blue wave rolls nightly on deep Galilee.

Like the leaves of the forest when summer is green,
That host with their banners at sunset were seen:
Like the leaves of the forest when autumn hath blown,
That host on the morrow lay withered and strown.

For the Angel of Death spread his wings on the blast,
And breathed in the face of the foe as he passed;
And the eyes of the sleepers waxed deadly and chill,
And their hearts but once heaved—and for ever grew still!

And there lay the steed with his nostril all wide,
But through it there rolled not the breath of his pride;
And the foam of his gasping lay white on the turf,
And cold as the spray of the rock-beating surf.

And there lay the rider distorted and pale,
With the dew on his brow, and the rust on his mail;
And the tents were all silent, the banners alone,
The lances unlifted, the trumpet unblown.

And the widows of Ashur° are loud in their wail,
And the idols are broke in the temple of Baal;°
And the might of the Gentile, unsmote by the sword,
Hath melted like snow in the glance of the Lord!

5
10
15
20

THE DESTRUCTION OF SENNACHERIB. Sennacherib was king of the ancient Near
Eastern empire of Assyria from 705 to 681 B.C. He laid siege to Jerusalem in about 702
B.C., even though King Hezekiah had already rendered tribute to Assyria. According to 2
Kings 19:35–36, a miracle occurred to save the besieged Hebrews: "the angel of the Lord
went out and smote . . . [185,000 Assyrian soldiers]; and when they [the Hebrews] arose
early in the morning, behold, they [the Assyrians] were all dead corpses."   21 *Ashur*: the
land of the Assyrians.   22 *Baal*: a god who supposedly controlled weather and storms.

THOMAS CAMPION   (1567–1620)

Cherry Ripe   *1617*

There is a garden in her face,
Where roses and white lilies grow;
A heavenly paradise is that place,
Wherein all pleasant fruits do flow.
There cherries grow, which none may buy   5
Till "Cherry ripe" themselves do cry.

Those cherries fairly do enclose
Of orient pearl a double row;
Which when her lovely laughter shows,
They look like rosebuds filled with snow.   10
Yet them nor peer nor prince can buy
Till "Cherry ripe" themselves do cry.

Her eyes like angels watch them still;
Her brows like bended bows do stand,
Threatening with piercing frowns to kill   15
All that attempt, with eye or hand,
Those sacred cherries to come nigh
Till "Cherry ripe" themselves do cry.

LUCILLE CLIFTON   (b. 1936)

My Mama Moved Among the Days   *1969*

My Mama moved among the days
like a dreamwalker in a field;
seemed like what she touched was hers
seemed like what touched her couldn't hold,
she got us almost through the high grass   5
then seemed like she turned around and ran
right back in
right back on in

STEPHEN CRANE   (1871–1900)

Do Not Weep, Maiden, for War Is Kind   *1896, 1899 (1895)*

Do not weep, maiden, for war is kind.
Because your lover threw wild hands toward the sky
And the affrighted steed ran on alone,

Do not weep.
War is kind.   5

    Hoarse, booming drums of the regiment
    Little souls who thirst for fight,
    These men were born to drill and die
    The unexplained glory flies above them
    Great is the battle-god, great, and his kingdom—   10
    A field where a thousand corpses lie.

Do not weep, babe, for war is kind.
Because your father tumbled in the yellow trenches,
Raged at his breast, gulped and died,
Do not weep.   15
War is kind.

    Swift, blazing flag of the regiment
    Eagle with crest of red and gold,
    These men were born to drill and die
    Point for them the virtue of slaughter   20
    Make plain to them the excellence of killing
    And a field where a thousand corpses lie.

Mother whose head hung humble as a button
On the bright splendid shroud of your son,
Do not weep.   25
War is kind.

ISABELLA VALANCY CRAWFORD   (1850–1887)

From *Gisli, the Chieftain*: The Song of the Arrow   *1884*

What know I,
As I bite the blue veins of the throbbing sky;
To the quarry's breast,
Hot from the sides of the sleek smooth nest?

What know I   5
Of the will of the tense bow from which I fly!
What the need or jest,
That feathers my flight to its bloody rest.

What know I
Of the will of the bow that speeds me on high?   10
What doth the shrill bow
Of the hand on its singing soul-string know?

Flame—swift speed I—
And the dove and the eagle shriek out and die;
Whence comes my sharp zest   15
For the heart of the quarry? the Gods know best.
Deep pierc'd the red gaze of the eagle
The breast of a cygnet° below him;   *young swan*
Beneath his dun wing from the eastward
Shrill-chaunted the long shaft of Gisli!   20
Beneath his dun wing from the westward
Shook a shaft that laugh'd in its biting—
Met in the fierce breast of the eagle
The arrows of Gisli and Brynhild!

COUNTEE CULLEN   (1903–1946)

Yet Do I Marvel   1925

I doubt not God is good, well-meaning, kind,
And did He stoop to quibble could tell why
The little buried mole continues blind,
Why flesh that mirrors Him must some day die.
Make plain the reason tortured Tantalus°   5
Is baited by the fickle fruit, declare
If merely brute caprice dooms Sisyphus°
To struggle up a never-ending stair.
Inscrutable His ways are, and immune
To catechism by a mind too strewn   10
With petty cares to slightly understand
What awful brain compels His awful hand.
Yet do I marvel at this curious thing:
To make a poet black, and bid him sing!

YET DO I MARVEL.   5 *Tantalus*: a figure in Greek mythology condemned to eternal
hunger and thirst. He stood in Hades chin deep in water with a fruit-laden branch just
above his head, but could never eat or drink.   7 *Sisyphus*: a figure in Greek mythology
condemned to eternally useless labor. He was fated to roll a huge boulder up a hill in
Hades, but each time he neared the top, the stone slipped and he had to begin anew. See
also pp. 326–27.

E. E. CUMMINGS   (1894–1962)

next to of course god america i   1926

"next to of course god america i
love you land of the pilgrims' and so forth oh
say can you see by the dawn's early my

country 'tis of centuries come and go
and are no more what of it we should worry   5
in every language even deafanddumb
thy sons acclaim your glorious name by gorry
by jingo by gee by gosh by gum
why talk of beauty what could be more beaut-
iful than these heroic happy dead   10
who rushed like lions to the roaring slaughter
they did not stop to think they died instead
then shall the voice of liberty be mute?"

He spoke. And drank rapidly a glass of water

E. E. CUMMINGS   (1894–1962)

if there are any heavens   *1931*

if there are any heavens my mother will(all by herself)have
one.   It will not be a pansy heaven nor
a fragile heaven of lilies-of-the-valley but
it will be a heaven of blackred roses

my father will be(deep like a rose   5
tall like a rose)

standing near my

swaying over her
(silent)
with eyes which are really petals and see   10

nothing with the face of a poet really which
is a flower and not a face with
hands
which whisper
This is my beloved my   15

                    (suddenly in sunlight

he will bow,

& the whole garden will bow)

JAMES DICKEY   (b. 1923)

The Lifeguard   *1962*

In a stable of boats I lie still,
From all sleeping children hidden.
The leap of a fish from its shadow

Makes the whole lake instantly tremble.
With my foot on the water, I feel   5
The moon outside

Take on the utmost of its power.
I rise and go out through the boats.
I set my broad sole upon silver,
On the skin of the sky, on the moonlight,   10
Stepping outward from earth onto water
In quest of the miracle

This village of children believed
That I could perform as I dived
For one who had sunk from my sight.   15
I saw his cropped haircut go under.
I leapt, and my steep body flashed
Once, in the sun.

Dark drew all the light from my eyes.
Like a man who explores his death   20
By the pull of his slow-moving shoulders,
I hung head down in the cold,
Wide-eyed, contained, and alone
Among the weeds,

And my fingertips turned into stone   25
From clutching immovable blackness.
Time after time I leapt upward
Exploding in breath, and fell back
From the change in the children's faces
At my defeat.   30

Beneath them I swam to the boathouse
With only my life in my arms
To wait for the lake to shine back
At the risen moon with such power
That my steps on the light of the ripples   35
Might be sustained.

Beneath me is nothing but brightness
Like the ghost of a snowfield in summer.
As I moved toward the center of the lake,
Which is also the center of the moon,   40
I am thinking of how I may be
The saviour of one

Who has already died in my care.
The dark trees fade from around me.
The moon's dust hovers together.   45
I call softly out, and the child's
Voice answers through blinding water.
Patiently, slowly,

He rises, dilating to break
The surface of stone with his forehead.   50
He is one I do not remember
Having ever seen in his life.
The ground I stand on is trembling
Upon his smile.

I wash the black mud from my hands.   55
On a light given off by the grave
I kneel in the quick of the moon
At the heart of a distant forest
And hold in my arms a child
Of water, water, water.   60

H. D. (HILDA DOOLITTLE)   (1886–1961)

Pear Tree   *1916*

Silver dust
lifted from the earth,
higher than my arms reach,
you have mounted,
O silver,   5
higher than my arms reach
you front us with great mass;

no flower ever opened
so staunch a white leaf,
no flower ever parted silver   10
from such rare silver;

O white pear,
your flower-tufts
thick on the branch
bring summer and ripe fruits   15
in their purple hearts.

RITA DOVE   (b. 1952)

Ö°   *1980*

Shape the lips to an *o*, say *a*.
That's *island*.

One word of Swedish has changed the whole neighborhood.
When I look up, the yellow house on the corner
is a galleon stranded in flowers. Around it   5

Ö: the Swedish word for "island," pronounced as explained in lines 1 and 2.

the wind. Even the high roar of a leaf-mulcher
could be the horn-blast from a ship
as it skirts the misted shoals.

We don't need much more to keep things going.   10
Families complete themselves
and refuse to budge from the present,
the present extends its glass forehead to sea
(backyard breezes, scattered cardinals)

and if, one evening, the house on the corner
took off over the marshland,   15
neither I nor my neighbor
would be amazed. Sometimes

a word is found so right it trembles
at the slightest explanation.
You start out with one thing, end   20
up with another, and nothing's
like it used to be, not even the future.

MICHAEL DRAYTON   (1563–1631)

Since There's No Help   *1619*

Since there's no help, come let us kiss and part;
Nay, I have done, you get no more of me,
And I am glad, yea glad with all my heart
That thus so cleanly I myself can free;
Shake hands forever, cancel all our vows,   5
And when we meet at any time again,
Be it not seen in either of our brows
That we one jot of former love retain.
Now at the last gasp of love's latest breath,
When, his pulse failing, passion speechless lies,   10
When faith is kneeling by his bed of death,
And innocence is closing up his eyes;
Now if thou wouldst, when all have given him over,
From death to life thou mightst him yet recover.

PAUL LAURENCE DUNBAR   (1872–1906)

Sympathy   *1895*

I know what the caged bird feels, alas!
When the sun is bright on the upland slopes;

When the wind stirs soft through the springing grass
And the river flows like a stream of glass;
When the first bird sings and the first bud opes,   5
And the faint perfume from its chalice steals—
I know what the caged bird feels!

I know why the caged bird beats his wing
Till its blood is red on the cruel bars;
For he must fly back to his perch and cling   10
When he fain would be on the bough a-swing;
And a pain still throbs in the old, old scars
And they pulse again with a keener sting—
I know why he beats his wing!

I know why the caged bird sings, ah me,   15
When his wing is bruised and his bosom sore,
When he beats his bars and would be free;
It is not a carol of joy or glee,
But a prayer that he sends from his heart's deep core,
But a plea, that upward to Heaven he flings—   20
I know why the caged bird sings!

RICHARD EBERHART   (b. 1904)

The Groundhog   *1936*

In June, amid the golden fields,
I saw a groundhog lying dead.
Dead lay he; my senses shook,
And mind outshot our naked frailty.
There lowly in the vigorous summer   5
His form began its senseless change,
And made my senses waver dim
Seeing nature ferocious in him.
Inspecting close his maggots' might
And seething cauldron of his being,   10
Half with loathing, half with a strange love,
I poked him with an angry stick.
The fever arose, became a flame
And Vigour circumscribed the skies,
Immense energy in the sun,   15
And through my frame a sunless trembling.
My stick had done nor good nor harm.
Then stood I silent in the day
Watching the object, as before;
And kept my reverence for knowledge   20
Trying for control, to be still,

To quell the passion of the blood;
Until I had bent down on my knees
Praying for joy in the sight of decay.
And so I left; and I returned   25
In Autumn strict of eye, to see
The sap gone out of the groundhog,
But the bony sodden hulk remained.
But the year had lost its meaning,
And in intellectual chains   30
I lost both love and loathing,
Mured up in the wall of wisdom.
Another summer took the fields again
Massive and burning, full of life,
But when I chanced upon the spot   35
There was only a little hair left,
And bones bleaching in the sunlight
Beautiful as architecture;
I watched them like a geometer,
And cut a walking stick from a birch.   40
It has been three years, now.
There is no sign of the groundhog.
I stood there in the whirling summer,
My hand capped a withered heart,
And thought of China and of Greece,   45
Of Alexander° in his tent;
Of Montaigne° in his tower,
Of Saint Theresa° in her wild lament.

THE GROUNDHOG.   46 *Alexander*: Alexander the Great (B.C. 356–323), king of
Macedonia and conquerer of virtually the entire civilized world.   47 *Montaigne*: Michel
de Montaigne (1553–1592), French essayist and commentator on human nature and society.
48 *Saint Theresa*: Theresa de Avila (1515–1582), Spanish religious mystic, writer, and founder
of a religious order.

T. S. ELIOT   (1888–1965)

The Love Song of J. Alfred Prufrock°   1915 (1910–11)

S'io credesse che mia risposta fosse
A persona che mai tornasse al mondo,
Questa fiamma staria senza piu scosse.

THE LOVE SONG OF J. ALFRED PRUFROCK. The poem is a monologue spoken by
Prufrock; the name is invented but suggests a businessman.   EPIGRAPH: The Italian epigraph
is quoted from Dante's *Inferno* (Canto 27, lines 61–66) and is spoken by a man who relates
his evil deeds to Dante because he assumes that Dante will never return to the world: "If I
believed that my response were made to a person who would ever revisit the world, this
flame would stand motionless. But since none has ever returned from this depth alive, if I
hear the truth, I answer you without fear of infamy."

Ma perciocche giammai di questo fondo
Non torno vivo alcun, s'i'odo il vero,
Senza tema d'infamia ti rispondo.°

Let us go then, you and I,
When the evening is spread out against the sky
Like a patient etherized upon a table;
Let us go, through certain half-deserted streets,
The muttering retreats   5
Of restless nights in one-night cheap hotels
And sawdust restaurants with oyster shells;
Streets that follow like a tedious argument
Of insidious intent
To lead you to an overwhelming question . . .   10
Oh, do not ask, "What is it?"
Let us go and make our visit.

In the room the women come and go
Talking of Michelangelo.°

The yellow fog that rubs its back upon the windowpanes,   15
The yellow smoke that rubs its muzzle on the windowpanes
Licked its tongue into the corners of the evening,
Lingered upon the pools that stand in drains,
Let fall upon its back the soot that falls from chimneys,
Slipped by the terrace, made a sudden leap,   20
And seeing that it was a soft October night,
Curled once about the house, and fell asleep.

And indeed there will be time
For the yellow smoke that slides along the street,
Rubbing its back upon the windowpanes;   25
There will be time, there will be time°
To prepare a face to meet the faces that you meet;
There will be time to murder and create,
And time for all the works and days° of hands
That lift and drop a question on your plate;   30
Time for you and time for me,
And time yet for a hundred indecisions,
And for a hundred visions and revisions,
Before the taking of a toast and tea.

In the room the women come and go   35
Talking of Michelangelo.

---

14 *Michelangelo*: one of the greatest Italian Renaissance artists and sculptors (1475–1564).
The name suggests that the women are cultured, or at least pretending to be so.   26 *time*:
a possible allusion to Andrew Marvell's "To His Coy Mistress" (p. 836).   29 *works and
days*: the title of a poem about farming by the Greek poet Hesiod. Here the phrase ironically
refers to social gestures.

And indeed there will be time
To wonder, "Do I dare?" and, "Do I dare?"
Time to turn back and descend the stair,
With a bald spot in the middle of my hair— 40
(They will say: "How his hair is growing thin!")
My morning coat, my collar mounting firmly to the chin,
My necktie rich and modest, but asserted by a simple pin—
(They will say: "But how his arms and legs are thin!")
Do I dare 45
Disturb the universe?
In a minute there is time
For decisions and revisions which a minute will reverse.

For I have known them all already, known them all—
Have known the evenings, mornings, afternoons, 50
I have measured out my life with coffee spoons;
I know the voices dying with a dying fall°
Beneath the music from a farther room.
    So how should I presume?

And I have known the eyes already, known them all— 55
The eyes that fix you in a formulated phrase,
And when I am formulated, sprawling on a pin,
When I am pinned and wriggling on the wall,
Then how should I begin
To spit out all the butt-ends of my days and ways? 60
And how should I presume?

And I have known the arms already, known them all—
Arms that are braceleted and white and bare
(But in the lamplight, downed with light brown hair!)
Is it perfume from a dress 65
That makes me so digress?
Arms that lie along a table, or wrap about a shawl.
    And should I then presume?
    And how should I begin?

Shall I say, I have gone at dusk through narrow streets 70
And watched the smoke that rises from the pipes
Of lonely men in shirt-sleeves, leaning out of windows? . . .

I should have been a pair of ragged claws
Scuttling across the floors of silent seas.

And the afternoon, the evening, sleeps so peacefully! 75
Smoothed by long fingers,
Asleep . . . tired . . . or it malingers,°

---

52 *dying fall*: an allusion to a speech by Orsino in Shakespeare's *Twelfth Night* (act I, scene 1, line 4).   77 *malingers*: pretends to be ill.

Stretched on the floor, here beside you and me.
Should I, after tea and cakes and ices,
Have the strength to force the moment to its crisis?   80
But though I have wept and fasted, wept and prayed,
Though I have seen my head (grown slightly bald) brought in upon a platter,°
I am no prophet—and here's no great matter;
I have seen the moment of my greatness flicker,
And I have seen the eternal Footman hold my coat, and snicker,   85
And in short, I was afraid.

And would it have been worth it, after all,
After the cups, the marmalade, the tea,
Among the porcelain, among some talk of you and me,
Would it have been worth while,   90
To have bitten off the matter with a smile,
To have squeezed the universe into a ball°
To roll it toward some overwhelming question,
To say: "I am Lazarus,° come from the dead,
Come back to tell you all, I shall tell you all"—   95
If one, setting a pillow by her head.
    Should say: "That is not what I meant at all.
    That is not it, at all."

And would it have been worth it, after all,
Would it have been worth while,   100
After the sunsets and the dooryards and the sprinkled streets,
After the novels, after the teacups, after the skirts that trail along the floor—
And this, and so much more?—
It is impossible to say just what I mean!
But as if a magic lantern threw the nerves in patterns on a screen: 105
Would it have been worth while
If one, setting a pillow or throwing off a shawl,
And turning toward the window, should say:
    "That is not it at all,
    That is not what I meant, at all."   110

No! I am not Prince Hamlet,° nor was meant to be;
Am an attendant lord, one that will do
To swell a progress,° start a scene or two,
Advise the prince; no doubt, an easy tool,
Deferential, glad to be of use,   115
Politic, cautious, and meticulous;
Full of high sentence,° but a bit obtuse;

82 *platter*: as was the head of John the Baptist; see Mark 6:17–28 and Matthew 14:3–11.
92 *ball*: another allusion to Marvell's "Coy Mistress."   94 *Lazarus*: See John 11:1–44.
111 *Prince Hamlet*: the hero of Shakespeare's play *Hamlet*.   *113 swell a progress*: enlarge
a royal procession.   117 *sentence*: ideals, opinions, sentiment.

At times, indeed, almost ridiculous—
Almost, at times, the Fool.

I grow old . . . I grow old . . .   120
I shall wear the bottoms of my trousers rolled.°

Shall I part my hair behind? Do I dare to eat a peach?
I shall wear white flannel trousers, and walk upon the beach.
I have heard the mermaids singing, each to each.

I do not think that they will sing to me.   125

I have seen them riding seaward on the waves
Combing the white hair of the waves blown back
When the wind blows the water white and black.

We have lingered in the chambers of the sea
By sea-girls wreathed with seaweed red and brown   130
Till human voices wake us, and we drown.

121 *rolled*: a possible reference to cuffs, which were becoming fashionable in 1910.

JOHN ENGELS (b. 1931)

Naming the Animals   *1981*

Since spring I've seen two deer,
one lashed to a fender. The other fed
in a clearing on the back slope
of Bean Hill, his big rack° still   *antlers*
in velvet. The shot buck bled,   5

its tongue frozen
to the rusty hood.
But the other, in its simpler stance,
felt merely the delicate itch
of antler skin.   10

And three does, mildly alert,
cocked ears toward where I watched from
in the hemlocks. I saw, of course,
five deer; but I
count only what by plain necessity of death   15

or feeding is oblivious to me,
does not watch back.

MARI EVANS

I Am a Black Woman   *1970*

I am a black woman
the music of my song
some sweet arpeggio of tears
is written in a minor key
and I   5
can be heard humming in the night
Can be heard
    humming
in the night

I saw my mate leap screaming to the sea   10
and I/with these hands/cupped the lifebreath
from my issue in the canebrake
I lost Nat's° swinging body in a rain of tears

and heard my son scream all the way from Anzio°
for Peace he never knew. . . . I   15
learned Da Nang° and Pork Chop Hill°
in anguish
Now my nostrils know the gas
and these trigger tire/d fingers
seek the softness in my warrior's beard   20

I
am a black woman
tall as a cypress
strong
beyond all definition still   25
defying place
and time
and circumstance
    assailed
        impervious   30
            indestructible

Look
    on me and be
renewed

I AM A BLACK WOMAN.   13 *Nat's swinging body*: Nat Turner was hanged in 1831 for
leading a slave revolt in Southampton, Virginia.   14 *Anzio*: seacoast town in Italy, the
scene of fierce fighting between the Allies and the Germans in 1944 during World War II.
16 *Da Nang*: major American military base in South Vietnam, frequently attacked during
the Vietnam War.   *Pork Chop Hill*: site of a bloody battle between U.N. and Communist
forces during the Korean War (1950–1953).

JOHN FANDEL   (b. 1925)

Indians   *1959*

Margaret mentioned Indians,
And I began to think about Indians—

Indians once living
Where now we are living—

About Indians. Oh, I know   5
About Indians. Oh, I know

What I have heard. Not much,
When I think how much

I wonder about them,
When a mere mention of them,   10

Indians, starts me. I
Think of their wigwams. I

Think of canoes. I think
Of quick arrows. I think

Of things Indian. And still   15
I think of their bright, still

Summers, when these hills
And meadows on these hills

Shone in the morning
Suns before this morning.   20

CAROLYN FORCHÉ   (b. 1950)

Because One Is Always Forgotten

IN MEMORIAM, JOSÉ RUDOLFO VIERA
1939–1981: EL SALVADOR

When Viera was buried we knew it had come to an end,
his coffin rocking into the ground like a boat or a cradle.

I could take my heart, he said, and give it to a *campesino*°   *peasant*
and he would cut it up and give it back:

you can't eat heart in those four dark   5
chambers where a man can be kept years.

A boy soldier in the bone-hot sun works his knife
to peel the face from a dead man

and hang it from the branch of a tree
flowering with such faces.   10

The heart is the toughest part of the body.
Tenderness is in the hands.

NIKKI GIOVANNI   (b. 1943)

Woman   *1978*

she wanted to be a blade
of grass amid the fields
but he wouldn't agree
to be the dandelion

she wanted to be a robin singing   5
through the leaves
but he refused to be
her tree

she spun herself into a web
and   looking for a place to rest   10
turned to him
but he stood straight
declining to be her corner

she tried to be a book
but he wouldn't read   15
she turned herself into a bulb
but he wouldn't let her grow

she decided to become
a woman
and though he still refused
to be a man
she decided it was all
right

MARILYN HACKER   (b. 1942)

Sonnet Ending with a Film Subtitle

For Judith Landry

Life has its nauseating ironies:
The good die young, as often has been shown;
Chaste spouses catch Venereal Disease;
And feminists sit by the telephone.
Last night was rather bleak, tonight is starker.   5

I may stare at the wall till half-past-one.
My friends are all convinced Dorothy Parker
Lives, but is not well, in Marylebone.°   *a district in London*
I wish that I could imitate my betters
And fortify my rhetoric with guns.   10
Some day we women all will break our fetters
And raise our daughters to be Lesbians.
(I wonder if the bastard kept my letters?)
Here follow untranslatable French puns.

DANIEL HALPERN   (b. 1945)

Snapshot of Hue   *1982*

For Robert Stone

They are riding bicycles on the other side
of the Perfume River.

A few months ago the bridges were down
and there was no one on the streets.

There were the telling piles on corners,   5
debris that contained a little of everything.

There was nothing not under cover—
even the sky remained impenetrable

day after day. And if you were seen
on the riverbank you were knocked down.   10

It is clear today. The litter in the streets
has been swept away. It couldn't have been

that bad, one of us said, the river barely moving,
the bicycles barely moving, the sun posted above.

FRANCES E. W. HARPER   (1825–1911)

She's Free!   *1854*

How say that by law we may torture and chase
A woman whose crime is the hue of her face?—
With her step on the ice, and her arm on her child,
The danger was fearful, the pathway was wild. . . .
But she's free! yes, free from the land where the slave,   5
From the hand of oppression, must rest in the grave;

Where bondage and blood, where scourges and chains,
Have placed on our banner indelible stains. . . .

The bloodhounds have miss'd the scent of her way,
The hunter is rifled and foiled of his prey,   10
The cursing of men and clanking of chains
Make sounds of strange discord on Liberty's plains. . . .
Oh! poverty, danger and death she can brave,
For the child of her love is no longer a slave.

MICHAEL S. HARPER (b. 1938)

Called   *1975*

Digging the grave
through black dirt,
gravel and rocks
that will hold her down,   5
we speak of her heat
which has driven her out
over the highway
in her first year.

A fly glides from her mouth
as we take her four legs,   10
and the great white neck
muddled at the lakeside
bends gracefully into the arc
of her tongue, colorless, now,
and we set her in the bed   15
of earth and rock
which will hold her as the sun
sets over her shoulders.

You had spoken of her brother,
100 lbs or more,   20
and her slight frame
from the diet of chain
she had broken;
on her back
as the spade cools her brow   25
with black dirt, rocks,
sand, white tongue,
what pups does she hold
that are seeds unspayed
in her broken body;   30
what does her brother say

to the seed gone out over
the prairie, on the hunt
of the unreturned:
and what do we say   35
to the master of the dog dead,
heat, highway, this bed
on the shoulder
of the road west
where her brother called, calls.   40

ROBERT HAYDEN   (b. 1913)

Those Winter Sundays   *1962*

Sundays too my father got up early
and put his clothes on in the blueblack cold,
then with cracked hands that ached
from labor in the weekday weather made
banked fires blaze. No one ever thanked him.   5

I'd wake and hear the cold splintering, breaking,
When the rooms were warm, he'd call,
and slowly I would rise and dress,
fearing the chronic angers of that house,

Speaking indifferently to him,   10
who had driven out the cold
and polished my good shoes as well.
What did I know, what did I know
of love's austere and lonely offices?

SEAMUS HEANEY   (b. 1939)

Valediction   *1966*

Lady with the frilled blouse
And simple tartan skirt,
Since you have left the house
Its emptiness has hurt
All thought. In your presence   5
Time rode easy, anchored
On a smile; but absence
Rocked love's balance, unmoored
The days. They buck and bound
Across the calendar   10

Pitched from the quiet sound
Of your flower-tender
Voice. Need breaks on my strand;
You've gone, I am at sea.
Until you resume command   15
Self is in mutiny.

GEORGE HERBERT   (1593–1633)

Love (III)°   *1633*

Love bade me welcome: yet my soul drew back,
    Guilty of dust and sin.
But quick-eyed Love, observing me grow slack
    From my first entrance in,
Drew nearer to me, sweetly questioning   5
    If I lacked° anything.

"A guest," I answered, "worthy to be here":
    Love said, "You shall be he."
"I, the unkind, ungrateful? Ah, my dear,
    I cannot look on thee."   10
Love took my hand, and smiling did reply,
    "Who made the eyes but I?"

"Truth, Lord; but I have marred them; let my shame
    Go where it doth deserve."
"And know you not," says Love, "who bore the blame?"   15
    "My dear, then I will serve."
"You must sit down," says Love, "and taste my meat."
    So I did sit and eat.

LOVE (III). cf. I John 4:8: "He that loveth not knoweth not God; for God is love."   6 *lacked*: wanted; the phrase is a standard question asked by innkeepers. 17 *and taste my meat*: Job 12:11: "Doth not the ear try words? and the mouth taste his meat?" 17–18 *You must sit down . . . eat*: Luke 13:37: "Blessed are those servants, whom the Lord when he cometh shall find watching: verily I say unto you, that he shall gird himself, and make them to sit down to meat, and will come forth and serve them."

ROBERT HERRICK   (1591–1674)

Corinna's Going A-Maying   *1648*

Get up! get up for shame! the blooming morn
Upon her wings presents the god unshorn°   *Apollo, god of the sun*
   See how Aurora° throws her fair   *Roman goddess of dawn*

Fresh-quilted colors through the air:
Get up, sweet slug-a-bed, and see   5
The dew bespangling herb and tree.
Each flower has wept and bowed toward the cast
Above an hour since, yet you not dressed;
    Nay, not so much as out of bed?
    When all the birds have matins° said,   *morning prayers*   10
    And sung their thankful hymns, 'tis sin,
    Nay, profanation to keep in,
Whenas a thousand virgins on this day
Spring, sooner than the lark, to fetch in May.°   *May Day*

Rise, and put on your foliage, and be seen   15
To come forth, like the springtime, fresh and green,
    And sweet as Flora.° Take no care   *Roman goddess of flowers*
    For jewels for your gown or hair;
    Fear not; the leaves will strew
    Gems in abundance upon you;   20
Besides, the childhood of the days has kept,
Against you come, some orient° pearls unwept;   *eastern*
    Come and receive them while the light
    Hangs on the dew-locks of the night,
    And Titan° on the eastern hill   *the sun*   25
    Retires himself, or else stands still
Till you come forth. Wash, dress, be brief in praying:
Few beads° are best when once we go a-Maying.   *prayers, rosaries*

Come, my Corinna, come; and, coming, mark°   *note*
How each field turns° a street, each street a park   *turns into*   30
    Made green and trimmed with trees: see how
    Devotion gives each house a bough
    Or branch: each porch, each door ere this,
    An ark, a tabernacle is,
Made up of whitethorn neatly interwove,   35
As if here were those cooler shades of love.
    Can such delights be in the street
    And open fields, and we not see 't?
    Come, we'll abroad; and let's obey
    The proclamation made for May,   40
And sin no more, as we have done, by staying;
But, my Corinna, come, let's go a-Maying.

There's not a budding boy or girl this day
But is got up and gone to bring in May;
    A deal° of youth, ere this, is come   *great many*   45
    Back, and with whitethorn laden home.,
    Some have dispatched their cakes and cream
    Before that we have left to dream;

And some have wept, and wooed, and plighted troth,
And chose their priest, ere we can cast off sloth.   50
  Many a green-gown° has been given,   *green with grass stains*
  Many a kiss, both odd and even;
  Many a glance, too, has been sent
  From out the eye, love's firmament;
Many a jest told of the keys betraying   55
This night, and locks picked; yet we're not a-Maying.

Come, let us go while we are in our prime,
And take the harmless folly of the time.
  We shall grow old apace, and die
  Before we know our liberty.   60
  Our life is short, and our days run
  As fast away as does the sun;
And, as a vapor or a drop of rain
Once lost, can ne'er be found again;
  So when or you or I are made
  A fable, song, or fluting shade,   65
  All love; all liking, all delight
  Lies drowned with us in endless night.
Then while time serves, and we are but decaying,
Come, my Corinna, come, let's go a-Maying.   70

ROBERTA HILL   (b. 1947)

Dream of Rebirth   *1970*

We stand on the edge of wounds, hugging canned meat,
waiting for owls to come grind
nightsmell in our ears. Over fields,
darkness has been rumbling. Crows gather.
Our luxuries are hatred. Grief. Worn-out hands   5
carry the pale remains of forgotten murders.
If I could only lull or change this slow hunger,
this midnight swollen four hundred years.

Groping within us are cries yet unheard.
We are born with cobwebs in our mouths   10
bleeding with prophecies.
Yet within this interior, a spirit kindles
moonlight glittering deep into the sea.
These seeds take root in the hush
of dusk. Songs, a thin echo, heal the salted marsh,   15
and yield visions untrembling in our grip.

GERARD MANLEY HOPKINS   (1844–1889)

The Windhover°   *1918 (1877)*

To Christ Our Lord

I caught this morning morning's minion,° king-   *darling*
   dom of daylight's dauphin,° dapple-dawn-drawn Falcon, in his riding
   Of the rolling level underneath his steady air, and striding
High there, how he rung upon the rein of a wimpling wing
In his ecstasy! then off, off forth on swing,   5
   As a skate's heel sweeps smooth on a bow-bend: the hurl and gliding
   Rebuffed the big wind. My heart in hiding
Stirred for a bird,—the achieve of, the mastery of the thing!

Brute beauty and valour and act, oh, air, pride, plume, here
   Buckle!° AND the fire that breaks from thee then, a billion   *join*   10
Times told lovelier, more dangerous. O my chevalier!°   *knight*

   No wonder of it: shéer plód makes plough down sillion°
Shine, and blue-bleak embers, ah my dear,
   Fall, gall themselves, and gash gold-vermilion.

THE WINDHOVER: The title refers to a kestrel or falcon that glides or hovers in the
wind.   2 *dauphin*: prince, heir to the throne of France.   12 *sillion*: the ridge of earth
between two plowed furrows in a field.

GERARD MANLEY HOPKINS   (1844–1889)

Pied Beauty   *(1918) 1877*

Glory be to God for dappled things—
   For skies of couple-colour as a brinded cow;
      For rose-moles all in stipple upon trout that swim;
Fresh-firecoal chestnut-falls;° finches' wings;
   Landscape plotted and pieced°—fold,° fallow,° and plough;   5
      And áll trádes, their gear and tackle and trim.

All things counter,° original, spare,° strange;
   Whatever is fickle, freckled (who knows how?)
      With swift, slow; sweet, sour; adazzle, dim;
He fathers-forth whose beauty is past change: 10
         Praise him.

PIED BEAUTY.   4 *Chestnut-falls*: the meat of a roasted chestnut.   5 *pieced*: divided into
fields of different colors, depending on the crops or use.   *fold*: an enclosed field for animals.
fallow: a plowed but unplanted field.   7 *counter*: opposed, as in contrasting patterns.
spare: rare.

LANGSTON HUGHES (1902–1967)

Negro   *1958*

I am a Negro:
    Black as the night is black,
    Black like the depths of my Africa.

I've been a slave:
    Caesar told me to keep his door-steps clean.   5
    I brushed the boots of Washington.

I've been a worker:
    Under my hand the pyramids arose.
    I made mortar for the Woolworth Building.

I've been a singer: 10
    All the way from Africa to Georgia
    I carried my sorrow songs.
    I made ragtime.

I've been a victim:
    The Belgians cut off my hands in the Congo.   15
    They lynch me still in Mississippi.

I am a Negro:
    Black as the night is black,
    Black like the depths of my Africa.

ROBINSON JEFFERS (1887–1962)

The Answer   *1937*

Then what is the answer?—Not to be deluded by dreams.
To know that great civilizations have broken down into violence, and their tyrants
    come, many times before.

When open violence appears, to avoid it with honor or choose the least ugly faction;
    these evils are essential.
To keep one's own integrity, be merciful and uncorrupted and not wish for evil;
    and not be duped
By dreams of universal justice or happiness. These dreams will not be fulfilled.   5
To know this, and know that however ugly the parts appear the whole remains
    beautiful. A severed hand
Is an ugly thing, and man dissevered from the earth and stars and his history
    . . . for contemplation or in fact . . .

Often appears atrociously ugly. Integrity is wholeness, the greatest beauty is
Organic wholeness, the wholeness of life and things, the divine beauty of the
    universe. Love that, not man

Apart from that, or else you will share man's pitiful confusions, or drown in despair   10
   when his days darken.

CAROLYN KIZER   (b. 1925)

Night Sounds

imitated from the Chinese

The moonlight on my bed keeps me awake;
Living alone now, aware of the voices of evening,
A child weeping at nightmares, the faint love-cries of a woman,
Everything tinged by terror or nostalgia.

No heavy, impassive back to nudge with one foot   5
While coaxing, "Wake up and hold me,"
When the moon's creamy beauty is transformed
Into a map of impersonal desolation.

But, restless in this mock dawn of moonlight
That so chills the spirit, I alter our history: 10
You were never able to lie quite peacefully at my side,
Not the night through. Always withholding something.

Awake before morning, restless and uneasy,
Trying not to disturb me, you would leave my bed
While I lay there rigidly, feigning sleep.   15
Still—the night was nearly over, the light not as cold
As a full cup of moonlight.

And there were the lovely times when, to the skies' cold *No*
You cried to me, *Yes*! Impaled me with affirmation.
Now when I call out in fear, not in love, there is no answer.   20
Nothing speaks in the dark but the distant voices,
A child with the moon on his face, a dog's hollow cadence.

ETHERIDGE KNIGHT   (b. 1933)

Haiku°   *1968*

            1
Eastern guard tower
glints in sunset; convicts rest
like lizards on rocks.

HAIKU. The haiku is a Japanese lyric verse form consisting of three lines that total seventeen
syllables, divided 5–7–5. See discussion on p. 732.

2

The piano man
is sting at 3 am
his songs drop like plum.

3

Morning sun slants cell.
Drunks stagger like cripple flies
On Jailhouse floor.

4

To write a blues song
is to regiment riots
and pluck gems from graves.   10

5

A bare pecan tree
slips a pencil shadow down
a moonlit snow slope.   15

6

The falling snow flakes
Can not blunt the hard aches nor
Match the steel stillness.

7

Under moon shadows
A tall boy flashes knife and
Slices star bright ice.   20

8

In the August grass
Struck by the last rays of sun
The cracked teacup screams.

9

Making jazz swing in
Seventeen syllables AIN'T   25
No square poet's job.

MAXINE KUMIN   (b. 1925)

Woodchucks   *1972*

Gassing the woodchucks didn't turn out right.
The knockout bomb from the Feed and Grain Exchange
was featured as merciful, quick at the bone
and the case we had against them was airtight,
both exits shoehorned shut with puddingstone,   5
but they had a sub-sub-basement out of range.

Next morning they turned up again, no worse
for the cyanide than we for our cigarettes
and state-store Scotch, all of us up to scratch.
They brought down the marigolds as a matter of course   10
and then took over the vegetable patch
nipping the broccoli shoots, beheading the carrots.

The food from our mouths, I said, righteously thrilling
to the feel of the .22, the bullet's neat noses.   15
I, a lapsed pacifist fallen from grace
puffed with Darwinian pieties° for killing,
now drew a bead on the littlest woodchuck's face.
He died down in the everbearing roses.

Ten minutes later I dropped the mother. She
flipflopped in the air and fell, her needle teeth   20
still hooked in a leaf of early Swiss chard.
Another baby next. O one-two-three
the murderer inside me rose up hard,
the hawkeye killer came on stage forthwith.

There's one chuck left. Old wily fellow, he keeps   25
me cocked and ready day after day after day.
All night I hunt his humped-up form. I dream
I sight along the barrel in my sleep.
If only they'd all consented to die unseen
gassed underground the quiet Nazi way.°   30

WOODCHUCKS.   16 *Darwinian pieties*: Charles Darwin (1809–1892) was a British
naturalist who formulated the theory of evolution; the piety is "survival of the fittest."
30 *gassed . . . way*: a reference to the extermination of 11 million people in gas chambers
by the Germans before and during World War II.

PHILIP LARKIN   (b. 1922)

Church Going   *1955*

Once I am sure there's nothing going on
I step inside, letting the door thud shut.
Another church: matting, seats, and stone,
And little books; sprawlings of flowers, cut
For Sunday, brownish now; some brass and stuff   5
Up at the holy end; the small neat organ;
And a tense, musty, unignorable silence,
Brewed God knows how long. Hatless, I take off
My cycle-clips in awkward reverence,

Move forward, run my hand around the font.   10
From where I stand, the roof looks almost new—

Cleaned, or restored? Someone would know: I don't.
Mounting the lectern, I peruse a few
Hectoring° large-scale verses, and pronounce   *intimidating*
'Here endeth' much more loudly than I'd meant.   15
The echoes snigger briefly. Back at the door
I sign the book, donate an Irish sixpence,
Reflect the place was not worth stopping for.

Yet stop I did: in fact I often do,
And always end much at a loss like this,   20
Wondering what to look for; wondering, too,
When churches fall completely out of use
What we shall turn them into, if we shall keep
A few cathedrals chronically on show,
Their parchment, plate and pyx° in locked cases,   25
And let the rest rent-free to rain and sheep.
Shall we avoid them as unlucky places?

Or, after dark, will dubious women come
To make their children touch a particular stone;
Pick simples° for a cancer; or on some   *medicinal herbs*   30
Advised night see walking a dead one?
Power of some sort or other will go on
In games, in riddles, seemingly at random;
But superstition, like belief, must die,
And what remains when disbelief has gone?   35
Grass, weedy pavement, brambles, buttress, sky,

A shape less recognisable each week,
A purpose more obscure. I wonder who
Will be the last, the very last, to seek
This place for what it was; one of the crew   40
That tap and jot and know what rood-lofts were?
Some ruin-bibber, randy for antique,
Or Christmas-addict, counting on a whiff
Of gown-and-bands and organ-pipes and myrrh?
Or will he be my representative,   45

Bored, uninformed, knowing the ghostly silt
Dispersed, yet tending to this cross of ground
Through suburb scrub because it held unsplit
So long and equably what since is found
Only in separation—marriage, and birth,   50
And death, and thoughts of these—for whom was built
This special shell? For, though I've no idea
What this accoutred frowsty barn is worth,
It pleases me to stand in silence here;

CHURCH GOING.   25 *pyx*: the box or vessel in an Anglican Church in which communion
wafers are kept.

A serious house on serious earth it is,   55
In whose blent air all our compulsions meet,
Are recognised, and robed as destinies.
And that much never can be obsolete,
Since someone will forever be surprising
A hunger in himself to be more serious,   60
And gravitating with it to this ground,
Which, he once heard, was proper to grow wise in,
If only that so many dead lie round.

IRVING LAYTON   (b. 1912)

Rhine Boat Trip°   1977

The castles on the Rhine
are all haunted
by the ghosts of Jewish mothers
looking for their ghostly children

And the clusters of grapes   5
in the sloping vineyards
are myriads of blinded eyes
staring at the blind sun

The tireless Lorelei°
can never comb from their hair   10
the crimson beards
of murdered rabbis

However sweetly they sing
one hears only
the low wailing of cattle-cars°   15
moving invisibly across the land

RHINE BOAT TRIP: The title refers to the Rhine River, which flows through Germany.
9 *Lorelei*: legendary seductive nymphs who lived in the cliffs overlooking the Rhine, and
whose singing lured sailors to shipwreck.   15 *cattle-cars*: railroad cars designed to transport
cattle but used by the Nazis to transport Jews from the cities of Europe to extermination
camps.

DON L. LEE   (b. 1942)

Change Is Not Always Progress (for Africa & Africans)   1970

Africa.

don't let them
steal

your face   or
take your circles
and make them squares.

don't let them
steel
your body   as to put
100 stories of concrete on you   10

so that you
          arrogantly
scrape
the

sky.   15

RICHARD LOVELACE (1618–1657)

To Lucasta, Going to the Wars   *1649*

Tell me not, Sweet, I am unkind
That from the nunnery
Of thy chaste breast and quiet mind,
To war and arms I fly.

True, a new mistress now I chase,   5
The first foe in the field;
And with a stronger faith embrace
A sword, a horse, a shield.

Yet this inconstancy is such
As you too shall adore;   10
I could not love thee, Dear, so much,
Loved I not honor more.

AMY LOWELL (1874–1925)

Patterns   *1916*

I walk down the garden paths,
And all the daffodils
Are blowing, and the bright blue squills.
I walk down the patterned garden-paths
In my stiff, brocaded gown.   5
With my powdered hair and jewelled fan,
I too am a rare
Pattern. As I wander down
The garden paths.

My dress is richly figured,   10
And the train
Makes a pink and silver stain
On the gravel, and the thrift
Of the borders.
Just a plate of current fashion   15
Tripping by in high-heeled, ribboned shoes.
Not a softness anywhere about me,
Only whalebone° and brocade.
And I sink on a seat in the shade
Of a lime tree. For my passion   20
Wars against the stiff brocade.
The daffodils and squills
Flutter in the breeze
As they please.
And I weep;   25
For the lime-tree is in blossom
And one small flower has dropped upon my bosom.

And the plashing of waterdrops
In the marble fountain
Comes down the garden-paths.   30
The dripping never stops.
Underneath my stiffened gown
Is the softness of a woman bathing in a marble basin,
A basin in the midst of hedges grown
So thick, she cannot see her lover hiding,   35
But she guesses he is near,
And the sliding of the water
Seems the stroking of a dear
Hand upon her.
What is Summer in a fine brocaded gown!   40
I should like to see it lying in a heap upon the ground.
All the pink and silver crumpled up on the ground.

I would be the pink and silver as I ran along the paths,
And he would stumble after,
Bewildered by my laughter.   45
I should see the sun flashing from his sword-hilt and buckles on his shoes.
I would choose
To lead him in a maze along the patterned paths,
A bright and laughing maze for my heavy-booted lover.
Till he caught me in the shade,   50
And the buttons of his waistcoat bruised my body as he clasped me,
Aching, melting, unafraid.
With the shadows of the leaves and the sundrops,

PATTERNS.   18 *whalebone*: Bones from whales were used to make extremely rigid corsets
for women.

And the plopping of the waterdrops,
All about us in the open afternoon—   55
I am very like to swoon
With the weight of this brocade,
For the sun sifts through the shade.

Underneath the fallen blossom
In my bosom,   60
Is a letter I have hid.
It was brought to me this morning by a rider from the Duke.
Madam, we regret to inform you that Lord Hartwell
Died in action Thursday se'nnight.°
As I read it in the white, morning sunlight,   65
The letters squirmed like snakes.
"Any answer, Madam," said my footman.
"No," I told him.
"See that the messenger takes some refreshment.

No, no answer."   70
And I walked into the garden,
Up and down the patterned paths,
In my stiff, correct brocade.
The blue and yellow flowers stood up proudly in the sun,
Each one.   75
I stood upright too,
Held rigid to the pattern
By the stiffness of my gown.
Up and down I walked.
Up and down.   80

In a month he would have been my husband.
In a month, here, underneath this lime,
We would have broken the pattern;
He for me, and I for him,
He as Colonel, I as Lady,   85
On this shady seat.
He had a whim
That sunlight carried blessing.
And I answered, "It shall be as you have said."
Now he is dead.   90

In Summer and in Winter I shall walk
Up and down
The patterned garden-paths
In my stiff, brocaded gown.
The squills and daffodils   95
Will give peace to pillared roses, and to asters, and to snow.
I shall go

64 *se'nnight*: seven nights, hence a week ago.

Up and down,
In my gown.
Gorgeously arrayed,   100
Boned and stayed.
And the softness of my body will be guarded from embrace
By each button, hook, and lace.
For the man who should loose me is dead,
Fighting with the Duke in Flanders,°   105
In a pattern called a war.
Christ! What are patterns for?

105 *Flanders*: A place of frequent warfare in Belgium. The speaker's clothing (lines 5,6)
suggests the time of the Duke of Marlborough's Flanders campaigns of 1702–10. The Battle
of Waterloo (1815) was also fought nearby under the Duke of Wellington. During World
War I, fierce fighting against the Germans occurred in Flanders in 1914 and 1915, with
great loss of life.

ROBERT LOWELL   (1917–1977)

For the Union Dead°   *1960*

"Relinquunt omnia servare rem publicam."°

The old South Boston Aquarium stands
in a Sahara of snow now. Its broken windows are boarded.
The bronze weathervane cod has lost half its scales.
The airy tanks are dry.

Once my nose crawled like a snail on the glass;   5
my hand tingled
to burst the bubbles
drifting from noses of the cowed, compliant fish.

My hand draws back. I often sigh still
for the dark downward and vegetating kingdom   10
of the fish and reptile. One morning last March,
I pressed against the new barbed and galvanized

fence on the Boston Common. Behind their cage,
yellow dinosaur steamshovels were grunting
as they cropped up tons of mush and grass   15
to gouge their underworld garage.

FOR THE UNION DEAD: The poem was first published in 1959 with the title, "Colonel
Shaw and the Massachusetts 54th." Robert Gould Shaw (1837–1863) was the commander
of the first regiment of blacks formed in the Union to fight in the Civil War. He was killed
leading an attack at Fort Wagner in South Carolina. The "Civil War relief" in bronze described
in the poem was sculpted by Augustus Saint-Gaudens (1848–1907), dedicated in 1897, and
stands on the Boston Common (a central park or green) across from the Massachusetts
State House.   EPIGRAPH: The Latin epigraph inscribed on the sculpture means, "They
give up everything to serve the republic."

Parking spaces luxuriate like civic
sandpiles in the heart of Boston.
A girdle of orange, Puritan-pumpkin colored girders
braces the tingling Statehouse,   20

shaking over the excavations, as it faces Colonel Shaw
and his bell-cheeked Negro infantry
on St. Gaudens' shaking Civil War relief,
propped by a plank splint against the garage's earthquake.

Two months after marching through Boston,   25
half the regiment was dead;
at the dedication,
William James° could almost hear the bronze Negroes breathe.

Their monument sticks like a fishbone
in the city's throat.   30
Its Colonel is as lean
as a compass-needle.

He has an angry wrenlike vigilance,
a greyhound's gentle tautness;
he seems to wince at pleasure,   35
and suffocate for privacy.

He is out of bounds now. He rejoices in man's lovely,
peculiar power to choose life and die—
when he leads his black soldiers to death,
he cannot bend his back.   40

On a thousand small town New England greens,
the old white churches hold their air
of sparse, sincere rebellion; frayed flags
quilt the graveyards of the Grand Army of the Republic.°

The stone statues of the abstract Union Soldier   45
grow slimmer and younger each year—
wasp-waisted, they doze over muskets
and muse through their sideburns . . .

Shaw's father wanted no monument
except the ditch,   50
where his son's body was thrown
and lost with his "niggers."
The ditch is nearer.
There are no statues for the last war° here;

28 *William James*: American philosopher and psychologist (1842–1910) who taught at Harvard.
44 *Grand Army of the Republic*: an organization, founded in 1866, of men who served in the
Union Army and Navy.   54 *last war*: World War II.

on Boylston Street,° a commercial photograph   55
shows Hiroshima° boiling

over a Mosler Safe, the "Rock of Ages"
that survived the blast. Space is nearer.
Where I crouch to my television set,
the drained faces of Negro school-children rise like balloons.   60

Colonel Shaw
is riding on his bubble,
he waits
for the blessèd break.

The Aquarium is gone. Everywhere,   65
giant finned cars nose forward like fish;
a savage servility
slides by on grease.

55 *Boylston Street*: a street in Boston.   56 *Hiroshima*: Japanese city on which the United
States dropped the first atomic bomb during World War II on August 6, 1945.

CYNTHIA MACDONALD

The Lobster   *1980*

This lobster flown in from Maine to Houston
Lies in a wooden box on cracked ice.
Its green not the green of deep water,
But of decay. Its stalk eyes, which should be
Grains of black caviar, are beads of phlegm.   5
Through the cracks in its shell, the meat
Shines like oil on water or mother-of-pearl.

I see exactly what it is, yet must wrap it up
In my finest linen handkerchief—the one with
The border and initials pulled by Filipino nuns—   10
And take it home to keep in my bureau drawer;
So that its smell invades my private places,
And lobster mold begins to form on the edges of fabrics.

I throw open the doors and jalousies, hoping to
Dilute the crustacean air, and you walk in. I had not   15
Expected to see you again: we had decided.
We inventory everything and redecide: you will stay.
The lobster, smooth and green as deep water, is
Crawling over the blue silk scarf when we
Open the drawer. We cook it for dinner,   20
In water laved with peppercorns and fennel, and spread
A sheet on the table, anticipating the complete repast.

CLAUDE McKAY   (1890–1948)

The White City   *1922*

I will not toy with it nor bend an inch.
Deep in the secret chambers of my heart
I muse my life-long hate, and without flinch
I bear it nobly as I live my part.
My being would be a skeleton, a shell,   5
If this dark Passion that fills my every mood,
And makes my heaven in the white world's hell,
Did not forever feed me vital blood.
I see the mighty city through a mist—
The strident trains that speed the goaded mass,   10
The poles and spires and towers vapor-kissed,
The fortressed port through which the great ships pass,
The tides, the wharves, the dens I contemplate,
Are sweet like wanton loves because I hate.

EDNA ST. VINCENT MILLAY   (1892–1950)

What Lips My Lips Have Kissed, and Where, and Why   *1923*

What lips my lips have kissed, and where, and why,
I have forgotten, and what arms have lain
Under my head till morning; but the rain
Is full of ghosts tonight, that tap and sigh
Upon the glass and listen for reply,   5
And in my heart there stirs a quiet pain
For unremembered lads that not again
Will turn to me at midnight with a cry.
Thus in the winter stands the lonely tree,
Nor knows what birds have vanished one by one,   10
Yet knows it boughs more silent than before:
I cannot say what loves have come and gone,
I only know that summer sang in me
A little while, that in me sings no more.

VASSAR MILLER   (b. 1924)

Loneliness   *1963*

So deep is this silence
that the insects, the birds,
the talk of the neighbors in the distance,
the whir of the traffic, the music

are only its voices   5
and do not contradict it.

So deep is this crying
that the silence, the hush,
the quiet, the stillness, the not speaking,
the never hearing a word   10
are only the surge
of its innumerable waters.

This silence, this crying,
O my God, is my country
with Yours the sole footstep besides my own.   15
Save me amid its landscapes
so terrible, strange
I am almost in love with them!

JOHN MILTON   (1608–1674)

O Nightingale!   *1630*

O Nightingale, that on yon bloomy Spray
    Warbl'st at eve, when all the Woods are still,
    Thou with fresh hope the Lover's heart dost fill,
    While the jolly hours lead on propitious *May*
Thy liquid notes that close the eye of Day,   5
    First heard before the shallow Cuckoo's bill,
    Portend success in love; O, if *Jove's* will
    Have linkt that amorous power to thy soft lay,
Now timely sing, ere the rude Bird of Hate
    Foretell my hopeless doom in some Grove nigh: 10
    As thou from year to year hast sung too late
For my relief; yet hadst no reason why.
    Whether the Muse, or Love call thee his mate,
    Both them I serve, and of their train am I.

OGDEN NASH   (1902–1971)

Very Like a Whale°   *1934*

One thing that literature would be greatly the better for
Would be a more restricted employment by authors of simile and metaphor.
Authors of all races, be they Greeks, Romans, Teutons or Celts,

VERY LIKE A WHALE: See *Hamlet*, act 3, scene 2, line 358.

Can't seem just to say that anything is the thing it is but have to go out of their
 way to say that it is like something else.
What does it mean when we are told   5
That the Assyrian came down like a wolf on the fold?
In the first place, George Gordon Byron had had enough experience
To know that it probably wasn't just one Assyrian, it was a lot of Assyrians.
However, as too many arguments are apt to induce apoplexy and thus hinder
 longevity.
We'll let it pass as one Assyrian for the sake of brevity.   10
Now then, this particular Assyrian, the one whose cohorts were gleaming in purple
 and gold,
Just what does the poet mean when he says he came down like a wolf on the
 fold?
In heaven and earth more than is dreamed of in our philosophy there are a great
 many things,
But I don't imagine that among them there is a wolf with purple and gold cohorts
 or purple and gold anythings.
No, no, Lord Byron, before I'll believe that this Assyrian was actually like a wolf   15
 I must have some kind of proof;
Did he run on all fours and did he have a hairy tail and a big red mouth and big
 white teeth and did he say Woof woof woof?
Frankly I think it very unlikely, and all you were entitled to say, at the very most,
Was that the Assyrian cohorts came down like a lot of Assyrian cohorts about to
 destroy the Hebrew host.
But that wasn't fancy enough for Lord Byron, oh dear me no, he had to invent a
 lot of figures of speech and then interpolate them.
With the result that whenever you mention Old Testament soldiers to people they   20
 say Oh yes, they're the ones that a lot of wolves dressed up in gold and purple
 ate them.
That's the kind of thing that's being done all the time by poets, from Homer to
 Tennyson;
They're always comparing ladies to lilies° and veal to venison.
How about the man who wrote,
Her little feet stole in and out like mice beneath her petticoat?°
Wouldn't anybody but a poet think twice   25
Before stating that his girl's feet were mice?
Then they always say things like that after a winter storm
The snow is a white blanket. Oh it is, is it, all right then, you sleep under a six-
 inch blanket of snow and I'll sleep under a half-inch blanket of unpoetical blanket
 material and we'll see which one keeps warm.
And after that maybe you'll begin to comprehend dimly
What I meant by too much metaphor and simile.   30

7 *George Gordon Byron*: See Byron, "The Destruction of Sennacherib," (p. 917), which Nash
is parodying in this poem.   22 *lades to lilies*: See Campion, "Cherry Ripe," stanza 1, and
also Burns, "A Red, Red Rose."   24 *little feet . . . petticoat*: In Sir John Suckling, "A Ballad
upon a Wedding" (1641), the following lines appear: "Her feet beneath her petticoat / Like
little mice stole in and out." Also in a poem by Robert Herrick complimenting the feet of
Susanna Southwell (1648), he wrote: "Her pretty feet / Like snails did creep."

THOMAS NASHE   (1567–1601)

A Litany in Time of Plague°   1600

Adieu, farewell, earth's bliss;
This world uncertain is;
Fond are life's lustful joys;
Death proves them all but toys;
None from his darts can fly;   5
I am sick, I must die.
   Lord, have mercy on us!

Rich men, trust not in wealth,
Gold cannot buy you health;
Physic himself must fade.   10
All things to end are made,
The plague full swift goes by;
I am sick, I must die.
   Lord, have mercy on us!

Beauty is but a flower   15
Which wrinkles will devour;
Brightness falls from the air;
Queens have died young and fair;
Dust hath closed Helen's° eye.
I am sick, I must die.   20
   Lord, have mercy on us!

Strength stoops unto the grave,
Worms feed on Hector° brave;
Swords may not fight with fate,
Earth still holds ope her gate.   25
"Come, come!" the bells do cry.
I am sick, I must die.
   Lord, have mercy on us.

Wit with his wantonness
Tasteth death's bitterness;   30
Hell's executioner
Hath no ears for to hear
What vain art can reply.
I am sick, I must die.
   Lord, have mercy on us.   35

A LITANY IN TIME OF PLAGUE: A litany is a ceremonial prayer with repeated invocations
to God. The plague is the Black Death, a form of bubonic plague that swept Europe repeatedly
in the Middle Ages and the Renaissance, killing tens of thousands. It was called "black"
because victims turned cyanotic from lack of oxygen before dying.   19 *Helen*: Helen of
Troy, considered to have been one of the most beautiful women in history.   23 *Hector*:
in Homer's *Iliad*, the greatest Trojan Hero and leader of the Trojan forces, killed by Achilles.

Haste, therefore, each degree,°   *social class*
To welcome destiny;
Heaven is our heritage,
Earth but a player's stage;
Mount we unto the sky.   40
I am sick, I must die.
    Lord, have mercy on us.

NAOMI SHIHAB NYE   (b. 1952)

Where Children Live   *1982*

Homes where children live exude a pleasant rumpledness,
like a bed made by a child, or a yard littered with balloons.

To be a child again one would need to shed details
till the heart found itself dressed in the coat with a hood.
Now the heart has taken on gloves and mufflers,   5
the heart never goes outside to find something to "do."
And the house takes on a new face, dignified.
No lost shoes blooming under bushes.
No chipped trucks in the drive.
Grown-ups like swings, leafy plants, slow-motion back and forth.   10
While the yard of a child is strewn with the corpses
of bottle-rockets and whistles,
anything whizzing and spectacular, brilliantly short-lived.

Trees in children's yards speak in clearer tongues.
Ants have more hope. Squirrels dance as well as hide.   15
The fence has a reason to be there, so children can go in and out.
Even when the children are at school, the yards glow
with the leftovers of their affection,
the roots of the tiniest grasses curl toward one another
like secret smiles.   20

FRANK O'HARA   (1926–1966)

Poem   *1952*

The eager note on my door said "Call me,
call when you get in!" so I quickly threw
a few tangerines into my overnight bag,
straightened my eyelids and shoulders, and

headed straight for the door. It was autumn   5
by the time I got around the corner, oh all

unwilling to be either pertinent or bemused, but
the leaves were brighter than grass on the sidewalk!

Funny, I thought, that the lights are on this late
and the hall door open; still up at this hour, a   10
champion jai-alai player like himself? Oh fie!
for shame! What a host, so zealous! And he was

there in the hall, flat on a sheet of blood that
ran down the stairs. I did appreciate it. There are few
hosts who so thoroughly prepare to greet a guest   15
only casually invited, and that several months ago.

SIMON ORTIZ   (b. 1941)

A Story of How a Wall Stands   *1976*

At Açu,° there is a wall almost 400 years old which
supports hundreds of tons of dirt and bones—it's a
graveyard built on a steep incline—and it looks like
it's about to fall down the incline but will not for a long time.

My father, who works with stone,
says, "That's just the part you see,
the stones which seem to be
just packed in on the outside,"
and with his hands put the stone and mud   5
in place. "Underneath
what looks like loose stone,
there is stone woven together.
He ties one hand over the other,
fitting like the bones of his hands   10
and fingers. "That's what is
holding it together."

"It is built that carefully,"
he says, "the mud mixed
to a certain texture," patiently   15
"with the fingers," worked
in the palm of his hand. "So that
placed between the stones, they hold
together for a long, long time."

He tells me those things,   20
the story of them worked

Açu: town in northeast Brazil.

with his fingers, in the palm
of his hands, working the stone
and the mud until they become
the wall that stands a long, long time.   25

AMÉRICO PARÉDES   (b. 1915)

Guitarreros   *1964*

Black against twisted black
The old mesquite
Rears up against the stars
Branch bridle hanging,
While the bull comes down from the mountain   5
Driven along by your fingers,
Twenty nimble stallions prancing up and down the *redil°* of   *the "web" of music*
    the guitars.
One leaning on the trunk, one facing—
Now the song:
Not cleanly flanked, not pacing,   10
But in a stubborn yielding that unshapes
And shapes itself again;
Hard-mouthed, zigzagged, thrusting,
Thrown, not sung,
One to the other.   15
The old man listens in his cloud
Of white tobacco smoke.
"It was so," he says,
"In the old days it was so."

DOROTHY PARKER   (1893–1967)

Résumé   *1936*

Razors pain you;
Rivers are damp;
Acids stain you;
And drugs cause cramp.
Guns aren't lawful;   5
Nooses give;
Gases smells awful;
You might as well live.

LINDA PASTAN   (b. 1932)

Marks   *1978*

My husband gives me an A
for last night's supper,
an incomplete for my ironing,
a B plus in bed.
My son says I am average,   5
an average mother, but if
I put my mind to it
I could improve.
My daughter believes
in Pass/Fail and tells me   10
I pass. Wait 'til they learn
I'm dropping out.

KATHERINE PHILLIPS   (1631–1664)

To My Excellent Lucasia, on Our Friendship   *1667*

I did not live until this time
    Crown'd my felicity,
When I could say without a crime,
    I am not thine, but Thee.

This carcase breath'd, and walkt, and slept,   5
    So that the World believ'd
There was a soul the motions kept;
    But they were all deceiv'd.

For as a watch by art is wound
    To motion, such was mine;   10
But never had Orinda° found
    A soul till she found thine;

Which now inspires, cures and supplies,
    And guides my darkened breast:
For thou art all that I can prize,   15
    My Joy, my Life, my Rest.

No bridegroom's nor crown-conqueror's mirth
    To mine compar'd can be:
They have but pieces of this Earth,
    I've all the World in thee.   20

TO MY EXCELLENT LUCASIA.   11 *Orinda*: name of the woman speaking the poem;
Phillips habitually used this name to refer to herself in poetry.

Then let our flames still light and shine,
   And no false fear control,
As innocent as our design,
   Immortal as our soul.

MARGE PIERCY   (b. 1934)

The Secretary Chant

1973

My hips are a desk.
From my ears hang
chains of paper clips.
Rubber bands form my hair.
My breasts are wells of mimeograph ink.   5
My feet bear casters.
Buzz. Click.
My head is a badly organized file.
My head is a switchboard
where crossed lines crackle.
Press my fingers   10
and in my eyes appear
credit and debit.
Zing. Tinkle.
My navel is a reject button.
From my mouth issue canceled reams.   15
Swollen, heavy, rectangular
I am about to be delivered
of a baby
Xerox machine.   20
File me under W
because I wonce
was
a woman.

SYLVIA PLATH   (1932–1962)

Last Words

1971 (1961)

I do not want a plain box, I want a sarcophagus
With tigery stripes, and a face on it
Round as the moon, to stare up.
I want to be looking at them when they° come

LAST WORDS.   4 *they*: possibly archeologists exploring the speaker's tomb or stone coffin ("sarcophagus").

Picking among the dumb minerals, the roots,   5
I see them already—the pale, star-distance faces.
Now they are nothing, they are not even babies.
I imagine them without fathers or mothers, like the first gods.
They will wonder if I was important.
I should sugar and preserve my days like fruit!   10
My mirror is clouding over—
A few more breaths, and it will reflect nothing at all.
The flowers and the faces whiten to a sheet.

I do not trust the spirit. It escapes like steam
In dreams, through mouth-hole or eye-hole. I can't stop it.   15
One day it won't come back. Things aren't like that.
They stay, their little particular lusters
Warmed by much handling. They almost purr.
When the soles of my feet grow cold,
The blue eye of my turquoise will comfort me.   20
Let me have my copper cooking pots, let my rouge pots
Bloom about me like night flowers, with a good smell.
They will roll me up in bandages, they will store my heart
Under my feet in a neat parcel.°
I shall hardly know myself. It will be dark,   25
And the shine of these small things sweeter than the face of Ishtar.°

19–24 *When . . . parcel*: The objects and procedures here refer to the household goods
normally entombed with a body in ancient Egypt and to the preparations of a mummy.
27 *Ishtar*: Babylonian goddess of fertility, love, and war.

SYLVIA PLATH   (1932–1962)

Mirror   *1965 (1961)*

I am silver and exact. I have no preconceptions.
Whatever I see I swallow immediately
Just as it is, unmisted by love or dislike.
I am not cruel, only truthful—
The eye of a little god, four-cornered.   5
Most of the time I meditate on the opposite wall.
It is pink, with speckles. I have looked at it so long
I think it is a part of my heart. But it flickers.
Faces and darkness separate us over and over.

Now I am a lake. A woman bends over me,   10
Searching my reaches for what she really is.
Then she turns to those liars, the candles or the moon.
I see her back, and reflect it faithfully.

She rewards me with tears and an agitation of hands.
I am important to her. She comes and goes.   15
Each morning it is her face that replaces the darkness.
In me she has drowned a young girl, and in me an old woma
Rises toward her day after day, like a terrible fish.

EZRA POUND (1885–1972)

The River-Merchant's Wife: A Letter°   *1926 (1915)*

While my hair was still cut straight across my forehead
I played about the front gate, pulling flowers.
You came by on bamboo stilts, playing horse,
You walked about my seat, playing with blue plums.
And we went on living in the village of Chokan:°   5
Two small people, without dislike or suspicion.

At fourteen I married My Lord you.
I never laughed, being bashful.
Lowering my head, I looked at the wall.
Called to, a thousand times, I never looked back.   10

At fifteen I stopped scowling,
I desired my dust to be mingled with yours
Forever and forever ·and forever.
Why should I climb the look out?

At sixteen you departed,   15
You went into far Ku-tō-en,° by the river of swirling eddies,
And you have been gone five months.
The monkeys make sorrowful noise overhead.

You dragged your feet when you went out.
By the gate now, the moss is grown, the different mosses,   20
Too deep to clear them away!
The leaves fall early this autumn, in wind.
The paired butterflies are already yellow with August

Over the grass in the West garden;
They hurt me, I grow older.   25
If you are coming down through the narrows of the river Kiang,
Please let me know beforehand,
And I will come out to meet you
        As far as Chō-fū-Sa.°

THE RIVER-MERCHANT'S WIFE: A LETTER. Freely translated from the Chinese of
Li Po (701–762).   5 *Chokan*: a suburb of Nanking, China.   16 *Ku-tō-en*: an island
several hundred miles up the Kiang River from Nanking.   29 *Chō-fū-um-Sa*: a beach near
Ku-tō-en.

E. J. PRATT   (1882–1964)

The Shark   *1923*

He seemed to know the harbour,
So leisurely he swam;
His tin,
Like a piece of sheet-iron,
Three-cornered,   5
And with knife-edge,
Stirred not a bubble
As it moved
With its base-line on the water.

His body was tubular   10
And tapered
And smoke-blue,
And as he passed the wharf
He turned,
And snapped at a flat-fish   15
That was dead and floating.
And I saw the flash of a white throat,
And a double row of white teeth,
And eyes of metallic grey,
Hard and narrow and slit.   20

Then out of the harbour,
With that three-cornered fin
Shearing without a bubble the water
Lithely,
Leisurely,   25
He swam—
That strange fish,
Tubular, tapered, smoke-blue,
Part vulture, part wolf,
Part neither—for his blood was cold.   30

THOMAS RABBITT   (b. 1943)

Gargoyle   *1981*

He looks down to watch the river twist
Like a dead vein into the suburbs.
From his height it is all flat, stone-grey
And ugly. He knows he himself is hideous,
Sterile, the artist's pleasantry set up   5
To scare off devils. He knows nothing.

He is stunning in his pure impossibility.
Enough cherry trees blossom along the river.
Enough paired lovers gaze through the pink air.
Drab birds, disguised as money, sing prettily   10
And the sun blinds itself in the water.
He hears laughter. He knows nothing.
When the lovers glance up, they take him in.
Their looks are incidental, monumental, sweeping.

JOHN CROWE RANSOM (1888–1974)

Bells for John Whiteside's Daughter   *1924*

There was such speed in her little body,
And such lightness in her footfall,
It is no wonder her brown study
Astonishes us all.

Her wars were bruited in our high window.   5
We looked among orchard trees and beyond
Where she took arms against her shadow,
Or harried unto the pond.

The lazy geese, like a snow cloud
Dripping their snow on the green grass,   10
Tricking and stopping, sleepy and proud,
Who cried in goose, Alas,

For the tireless heart within the little
Lady with rod that made them rise
From their noon apple-dreams and scuttle   15
Goose-fashion under the skies!

But now go the bells, and we are ready,
In one house we are sternly stopped
To say we are vexed at her brown study,
Lying so primly propped.   20

ADRIENNE RICH (b. 1929)

Diving into the Wreck   *1972*

First having read the book of myths,
and loaded the camera,
and checked the edge of the knife-blade,

I put on
the body-armor of black rubber
the absurd flippers
the grave and awkward mask.
I am having to do this
not like Cousteau with his
assiduous team
aboard the sun-flooded schooner
but here alone.

There is a ladder.
The ladder is always there
hanging innocently
close to the side of the schooner.
We know what it is for,
we who have used it.
otherwise
it is a piece of maritime floss
some sundry equipment.

I go down.
Rung after rung and still
the oxygen immerses me
the blue light
the clear atoms
of our human air.
I go down.
My flippers cripple me,
I crawl like an insect down the ladder
and there is no one
to tell me when the ocean
will begin.

First the air is blue and then
it is bluer and then green and then
black I am blacking out and yet
my mask is powerful
it pumps my blood with power
the sea is another story
the sea is not a question of power
I have to learn alone
to turn my body without force
in the deep element.

And now: it is easy to forget
what I came for
among so many who have always
lived here
swaying their crenellated fans

between the reefs
and besides   50
you breathe differently down here.

I came to explore the wreck.
The words are purposes.
The words are maps.
I came to see the damage that was done   55
and the treasures that prevail.
I stroke the beam of my lamp
slowly along the flank
of something more permanent
than fish or weed   60

the thing I came for:
the wreck and not the story of the wreck
the thing itself and not the myth
the drowned face always staring
toward the sun   65
the evidence of damage
worn by salt and sway into this threadbare beauty
the ribs of the disaster
curving their assertion
among the tentative haunters.   70

This is the place.
And I am here, the mermaid whose dark hair
streams black, the merman in his armored body.
We circle silently
about the wreck   75
we dive into the hold.
I am she; I am he

whose drowned face sleeps with open eyes
whose breasts still bear the stress
whose silver, copper, vermeil cargo lies   80
obscurely inside barrels
half-wedged and left to rot
we are the half-destroyed instruments
that once held to a course
the water-eaten log   85
the fouled compass

We are, I am, you are
by cowardice or courage
the one who find our way
back to this scene   90
carrying a knife, a camera
a book of myths

in which
our names do not appear.

THEODORE ROETHKE   (1908–1963)

I Knew a Woman   *1958*

I knew a woman, lovely in her bones,
When small birds sighed, she would sigh back at them;
Ah, when she moved, she moved more ways than one:
The shapes a bright container can contain!
Of her choice virtues only gods should speak,   5
Or English poets who grew up on Greek
(I'd have them sing in chorus, cheek to cheek).

How well her wishes went! She stroked my chin,
She taught me Turn, and Counter-turn, and Stand;
She taught me Touch, that undulant white skin;   10
I nibbled meekly from her proffered hand;
She was the sickle; I, poor I, the rake,
Coming behind her for her pretty sake
(But what prodigious mowing we did make).

Love likes a gander, and adores a goose: 15
Her full lips pursed, the errant note to seize;
She played it quick, she played it light and loose;
My eyes, they dazzled at her flowing knees;
Her several parts could keep a pure repose,
Or one hip quiver with a mobile nose   20
(She moved in circles, and those circles moved).

Let seed be grass, and grass turn into hay:
I'm martyr to a motion not my own;
What's freedom for? To know eternity.
I swear she cast a shadow white as stone.   25
But who would count eternity in days?
These old bones live to learn her wanton ways:
(I measure time by how a body sways).

THEODORE ROETHKE   (1908–1963)

The Waking   *1953*

I wake to sleep, and take my waking slow.
I feel my fate in what I cannot fear.
I learn by going where I have to go.

We think by feeling. What is there to know?
I hear my being dance from ear to ear.   5
I wake to sleep, and take my waking slow.

Of those so close beside me, which are you?
God bless the Ground! I shall walk softly there,
And learn by going where I have to go.

Light takes the Tree; but who can tell us how?   10
The lowly worm climbs up a winding stair;
I wake to sleep, and take my waking slow.

Great Nature has another thing to do
To you and me; so take the lively air,
And, lovely, learn by going where to go.   15

This shaking keeps me steady. I should know.
What falls away is always. And is near.
I wake to sleep, and take my waking slow.
I learn by going where I have to go.

LUIS OMAR SALINAS   (b. 1937)

In a Farmhouse   *1973*

Fifteen miles
out of Robstown
with the Texas sun
fading in the distance
I sit in the bedroom
profoundly,   5
animated by the day's work
in the cottonfields.

I made two dollars and
thirty cents today
I am eight years old   10
and I wonder
how the rest of the Mestizos°
do not go hungry
and if one were to die   15
of hunger
what an odd way
to leave for heaven.

IN A FARMHOUSE.   13 *Mestizos*: persons of mixed Spanish and Amerindian ancestry.

SONIA SANCHEZ   (b. 1934)

right on: white america   *1970*

this country might have
been a pio
  neer land
once.
    but.   there ain't   5
no mo
    indians   blowing
custer's° mind
      with a different
image of america.   10
                this country
might have
        needed shoot/
outs/ daily/
      once.   15
         but. there ain't
no mo real/ white/   allamerican
             bad/guys.
just.
    u & me.   20
        blk/ and un/armed.
this country might have
been a pion
      eer land.   once.
                    and it still is.   25
check out
    the falling
gun/shells   on our blk/tomorrows.

RIGHT ON: WHITE AMERICA.   8 *custer's*: General George Armstrong Custer (1839–
1876) was killed in his "last stand" at the Little Bighorn in Montana during a battle with
Sioux Indians.

CARL SANDBURG   (1878–1967)

Chicago   *1916*

    Hog Butcher for the World,
    Tool Maker, Stacker of Wheat,
    Player with Railroads and the Nation's Freight Handler;
    Stormy, husky, brawling,
    City of the Big Shoulders: 5

They tell me you are wicked and I believe them, for I have seen your painted
    women under the gas lamps luring the farm boys.

And they tell me you are crooked and I answer: Yes, it is true I have seen the
    gunman kill and go free to kill again.
And they tell me you are brutal and my reply is: On the faces of women and
    children I have seen the marks of wanton hunger.
And having answered so I turn once more to those who sneer at this my city,
    and I give them back the sneer and say to them:
Come and show me another city with lifted head singing so proud to be alive
    and coarse and strong and cunning.   10
Flinging magnetic curses amid the toil of piling job on job, here is a tall bold
    slugger set vivid against the little soft cities;
Fierce as a dog with tongue lapping for action, cunning as a savage pitted against
    the wilderness,
        Bareheaded,
        Shoveling,
        Wrecking,   15
        Planning,
        Building, breaking, rebuilding,
Under the smoke, dust all over his mouth, laughing with white teeth,
Under the terrible burden of destiny laughing as a young man laughs,
Laughing even as an ignorant fighter laughs who has never lost a battle,   20
Bragging and laughing that under his wrist is the pulse, and under his ribs the
    heart of the people,
        Laughing!
Laughing the stormy, husky, brawling laughter of Youth, half-naked, sweating,
    proud to be Hog Butcher, Tool Maker, Stacker of Wheat, Player with Railroads
    and Freight Handler to the Nation.

SIEGFRIED SASSOON (1886–1967)

Dreamers   *1918*

Soldiers are citizens of death's grey land,
    Drawing no dividend from time's to-morrows.
In the great hour of destiny they stand,
    Each with his feuds, and jealousies, and sorrows.

    Soldiers are sworn to action; they must win   5
    Some flaming, fatal climax with their lives.
Soldiers are dreamers; when the guns begin
    They think of firelit homes, clean beds, and wives.

I see them in foul dug-outs, gnawed by rats,
    And in the ruined trenches, lashed with rain,   10
Dreaming of things they did with balls and bats,
    And mocked by hopeless longing to regain
Bank-holidays,° and picture shows, and spats,
    And going to the office in the train.

DREAMERS.   13 *Bank-holidays*: legal holidays in Great Britain.

ALAN SEEGER   (1888–1916)

I Have a Rendezvous with Death   *1916*

I have a rendezvous with Death
At some disputed barricade,
When Spring comes back with rustling shade
And apple blossoms fill the air—
I have a rendezvous with Death   5
When Spring brings back blue days and fair.

It may be he shall take my hand
And lead me into his dark land
And close my eyes and quench my breath—
It may be I shall pass him still.   10
I have a rendezvous with Death
On some scarred slope of battered hill,
When Spring comes round again this year
And the first meadow flowers appear.

God knows 'twere better to be deep   15
Pillowed in silk and scented down,
Where Love throbs out in blissful sleep,
Pulse nigh to pulse and breath to breath,
Where hushed awakenings are dear. . . .
But I've a rendezvous with Death   20
At midnight in some flaming town,
When Spring trips north again this year,
And I to my pledged word am true,
I shall not fail that rendezvous.

ANNE SEXTON   (1928–1974)

Three Green Windows   *1966 (1962)*

Half awake in my Sunday nap
I see three green windows
in three different lights—
one west, one south, one east.
I have forgotten that old friends are dying.   5
I have forgotten that I grow middle-aged.
At each window such rustlings!
The trees persist, yeasty and sensuous,
as thick as saints.
I see three wet gargoyles covered with birds.   10
Their skins shine in the sun like leather.

I'm on my bed as light as a sponge.
Soon it will be summer.
She is my mother.
She will tell me a story and keep me asleep   15
against her plump and fruity skin.
I see leaves—
leaves that are washed and innocent,
leaves that never knew a cellar,
born in their own green blood   20
like the hands of mermaids.

I do not think of the rusty wagon on the walk.
I pay no attention to the red squirrels
that leap like machines beside the house.
I do not remember the real trunks of the trees   25
that stand beneath the windows
as bulky as artichokes.
I turn like a giant,
secretly watching, secretly knowing,
secretly naming each elegant sea.   30

I have misplaced the Van Allen belt,°
the sewers and the drainage,
the urban renewal and the suburban centers.
I have forgotten the names of the literary critics.
I know what I know.   35
I am the child I was,
living the life that was mine.
I am young and half asleep.
It is a time of water, a time of trees.

THREE GREEN WINDOWS.   31 *Van Allen belt*: radiation belt around the earth, named
after its discoverer.

WILLIAM SHAKESPEARE (1564–1616)

Fear No More the Heat o' the Sun°   *1623 (ca. 1609)*

Fear no more the heat o' the sun,
  Nor the furious winter's rages;
Thou thy worldly task hast done,

FEAR NO MORE THE HEAT O' THE SUN. A dirge or lament sung over the supposedly
dead body of Imogen in act 4 of Shakespeare's *Cymbeline*.

Home art gone, and ta'en° thy wages: *taken*
Golden lads and girls all must,   5
As° chimney-sweepers, come to dust.   *like*

Fear no more the frown o' the great;
  Thou art past the tyrant's stroke;
Care no more to clothe and eat;
  To thee the reed is as the oak: 10
The scepter, learning, physic, must
All follow this, and come to dust.

Fear no more the lightning flash,
  Nor the all-dreaded thunder stone;°
Fear not slander, censure rash;   15
  Thou hast finished joy and moan:°   *sadness*
All lovers young, all lovers must
Consign to thee, and come to dust.

No exorciser harm thee!
Nor no witchcraft charm thee!   20
Ghost unlaid forbear thee!
Nothing ill come near thee!
Quiet consummation have;
And renownéd be thy grave!

14 *thunder stone*: The sound of thunder was believed to be caused by stones falling from the sky.

WILLIAM SHAKESPEARE   (1564–1616)

Sonnet 29: When in Disgrace with Fortune and Men's Eyes   1609

When, in disgrace with fortune and men's eyes,
I all alone beweep my outcast state,
And trouble deaf heaven with my bootless° cries,   *futile, useless*
And look upon myself, and curse my fate,
Wishing me like to one more rich in hope,   5
Featured like him, like him with friends possessed,
Desiring this man's art and that man's scope,
With what I most enjoy contented least;
Yet in these thoughts myself almost despising,
Haply I think on thee—and then my state,   10
Like to the lark at break of day arising
From sullen earth, sings hymns at heaven's gate;
For thy sweet love remembered such wealth brings
That then I scorn to change my state with kings.

WILLIAM SHAKESPEARE (1564–1616)

Sonnet 146: Poor Soul, The Center of My Sinful Earth   *1609*

Poor soul, the center of my sinful earth,
Thrall° to these rebel powers that thee array,°   *captive*
Why dost thou pine within and suffer dearth,
Painting thy outward walls so costly gay?
Why so large cost, having so short a lease,   5
Dost thou upon thy fading mansion speed?
Shall worms, inheritors of this excess,
Eat up thy charge? Is this thy body's end?
Then, soul, live thou upon thy servant's loss,°
And let that pine to aggravate thy store;°   10
Buy terms° divine in selling hours of dross°   *periods; refuse*
Within be fed, without be rich no more:
So shalt thou feed on Death, that feeds on men,
And Death once dead, there's no more dying then.

POOR SOUL.   2 *array*: surround or dress out, as in a military formation.   9 *thy servant's loss*: the loss of the body.   10 *let . . . store*: let the body ("that") dwindle ("pine") to increase ("aggravate") the riches ("store") of the soul.

KARL SHAPIRO (b. 1913)

Auto Wreck   *1941*

Its quick soft silver bell beating, beating,
And down the dark one ruby flare
Pulsing out red light like an artery,
The ambulance at top speed floating down
Past beacons and illuminated clocks   5
Wings in a heavy curve, dips down,
And brakes speed, entering the crowd.
The doors leap open, emptying light;
Stretchers are laid out, the mangled lifted
And stowed into the little hospital.   10
Then the bell, breaking the hush, tolls once,
And the ambulance with its terrible cargo
Rocking, slightly rocking, moves away,
As the doors, an afterthought, are closed.

We are deranged, walking among the cops   15
Who sweep glass and are large and composed.
One is still making notes under the light.
One with a bucket douches ponds of blood
Into the street and gutter.
One hangs lanterns on the wrecks that cling,   20
Empty husks of locusts, to iron poles.

Our throats were tight as tourniquets,
Our feet were bound with splints, but now,
Like convalescents intimate and gauche,
We speak through sickly smiles and warn   25
With the stubborn saw of common sense,
The grim joke and the banal resolution.
The traffic moves around with care,
But we remain, touching a wound
That opens to our richest horror.   30
Already old, the question Who shall die?
Becomes unspoken Who is innocent?
For death in war is done by hands;
Suicide has cause and stillbirth, logic;
And cancer, simple as a flower, blooms.   35
But this invites the occult mind,
Cancels our physics with a sneer,
And spatters all we knew of denouement
Across the expedient and wicked stones.

SIR PHILIP SIDNEY   (1554–1586)

Astrophil and Stella, Number 71   *1591*

Who will in fairest book of Nature know,
How Virtue may best lodged in beauty be,
Let him but learn of Love to read in thee,
Stella, those fair lines, which true goodness show.
There shall he find all vices' overthrow,   5
Not by rude force, but sweetest sovereignty
Of reason, from whose light those night birds fly;
That inward sun in thine eyes shineth so.
And not content to be Perfection's heir
Thyself, dost strive all minds that way to move,   10
Who mark in thee what is in thee most fair.
So while thy beauty draws the heart to love,
As fast thy Virtue bends that love to good:
"But ah," desire still cries, "give me some food."

JON SILKIN   (b. 1930)

Worm   *1971*

Look out, they say, for yourself.
The worm doesn't. It is blind
As a sloe; its death by cutting,

Bitter. Its oozed length is ringed,
With parts swollen. Cold and blind   5
It is graspable, and writhes
In your hot hand; a small snake, unvenomous.
Its seeds furred and moist
It sexes by lying beside another,
In its eking conjunction of seed   10
Wriggling and worm-like.
Its ganglia are in its head,
And if this is severed
It must grow backwards.
It is lowly, useful, pink. It breaks   15
Tons of soil, gorging the humus
Its whole length; its shit a fine cast
Coiled in heaps, a burial mound, or like a shell
Made by a dead snail.
It has a life, which is virtuous   20
As a farmer's, making his own food.
Passionless as a hoe, sometimes, persistent.
Does not want to kill a thing.

LESLIE MARMON SILKO   (b. 1948)

Where Mountain Lion Lay Down with Deer   *1974*

I climb the black rock mountain
   stepping from day to day
                           silently.
I smell the wind for my ancestors
   pale blue leaves
      crushed wild mountain smell.   5
Returning
   up the gray stone cliff
   where I descended
                     a thousand years ago.   10

Returning to faded black stone
   where mountain lion lay down with deer.
It is better to stay up here
                     watching wind's reflection
                     in tall yellow flowers.   15
The old ones who remember me are gone
         the old songs are all forgotten
and the story of my birth.
How I danced in snow-frost moonlight
         distant stars to the end of the Earth,   20

How I swam away
              in freezing mountain water
              narrow mossy canyon tumbling down
                      out of the mountain
                           out of the deep canyon stone   25
        down
            the memory
                    spilling out
                    into the world.

DAVE SMITH   (b. 1942)

Bluejays   *1981*

She tries to call them down,
quicknesses of air.
They bitch and scorn,
they roost away from her.

It isn't that she's brutal.   5
She's just a girl. Worse,
her touch is total.
Her play is dangerous.

Darkly they spit each at each,
from tops of pine and spruce.   10
Her words are shy and sweet,
but it's no use.

Ragged, blue, shrill,
they dart around like boys.
They fear the beautiful   15
but do not fly away.

STEVIE SMITH   (1902–1971)

Not Waving But Drowning   *1957*

Nobody heard him, the dead man,
But still he lay moaning:
I was much further out than you thought
And not waving but drowning.

Poor chap, he always loved larking   5
And now he's dead

It must have been too cold for him his heart gave way,
They said.

Oh, no no no, it was too cold always
(Still the dead one lay moaning)
I was much too far out all my life
And not waving but drowning.

W. D. SNODGRASS   (b. 1926)

Lobsters in the Window   *1963*

First, you think they are dead.
Then you are almost sure
One is beginning to stir.
Out of the crushed ice, slow
As the hands of a schoolroom clock,
He lifts his one great claw
And holds it over his head;
Now, he is trying to walk.

But like a run-down toy;
Like the backward crabs we boys
Splashed after in the creek,
Trapped in jars or a net,
And then took home to keep.
Overgrown, retarded, weak,
He is fumbling yet
From the deep chill of his sleep

As if, in a glacial thaw,
Some ancient thing might wake
Sore and cold and stiff
Struggling to raise one claw
Like a defiant fist;
Yet wavering, as if
Starting to swell and ache
With that thick peg in the wrist.

I should wave back, I guess.
But still in his permanent clench
He's fallen back with the mass
Heaped in their common trench
Who stir, but do not look out
Through the rainstreaming glass.
Hear what the newsboys shout,
Or see the raincoats pass.

CATHY SONG   (b. 1955)

Lost Sister   *1983*

1

In China,
even the peasants
named their first daughters
Jade—°
the stone that in the far fields   5
could moisten the dry season,
could make men move mountains
for the healing green of the inner hills
glistening like slices of winter melon.

And the daughters were grateful: 10
they never left home.
To move freely was a luxury
stolen from them at birth.
Instead, they gathered patience,
learning to walk in shoes   15
the size of teacups,°
without breaking—
the arc of their movements
as dormant as the rooted willow,
as redundant as the farmyard hens.   20
But they traveled far
in surviving,
learning to stretch the family rice,
to quiet the demons,
the noisy stomachs.   25

2

There is a sister
across the ocean,
who relinquished her name,
diluting jade green
with the blue of the Pacific.   30
Rising with a tide of locusts,
she swarmed with others

LOST SISTER.   4 *Jade*: Both the mineral and the name are considered signs of good
fortune and health in China   16 *teacups*: Traditionally, girls' feet were bound at the age
of seven in China because minuscule feet were considered beautiful and aristocratic. The
binding inhibited the natural growth of the feet and made it painful and difficult to walk.

to inundate another shore.
In America,
there are many roads   35
and women can stride along with men.

But in another wilderness,
the possibilities,
the loneliness,
can strangulate like jungle vines.
The meager provisions and sentiments   40
of once belonging—
fermented roots, Mah-Jongg° tiles and firecrackers—
set but a flimsy household
in a forest of nightless cities.
A giant snake rattles above,   40
spewing black clouds into your kitchen.
Dough-faced landlords
slip in and out of your keyholes,
making claims you don't understand,
tapping into your communication systems   50
of laundry lines and restaurant chains.

You find you need China:
your one fragile identification,
a jade link
handcuffed to your wrist.   55
You remember your mother
who walked for centuries,
footless—
and like her.
you have left no footprints,   60
but only because
there is an ocean in between,
the unremitting space of your rebellion.

43 *Mah-Jongg*: a Chinese game played with 144 dominolike tiles marked in suits, counters,
and dice.

ANNE SPENCER   (1882–1975)

At the Carnival   *1922*

Gay little Girl-of-the-Diving-Tank,
I desire a name for you,
Nice, as a right glove fits;
For you—who amid the malodorous

Mechanics of this unlovely thing,   5
Are darling of spirit and form.
I know you—a glance, and what you are
Sits-by-the-fire in my heart.
My Limousine-Lady knows you, or
Why does the slant-envy of her eyes mark   10
Your straight air and radiant inclusive smile?
Guilt pins a fig-leaf; Innocence is its own adorning.
The bull-necked man knows you—this first time
His itching flesh sees from divine and vibrant health,
And thinks not of his avocation.   15
I came incuriously—
Set on no diversion save that my mind
Might safely nurse its brood of misdeeds
In the presence of a blind crowd.
The color of life was gray.   20
Everywhere the setting seemed right
For my mood!
Here the sausage and garlic booth
Sent unholy incense skyward;
There a quivering female-thing   25
Gestured assignations, and lied
To call it dancing;
There, too, were games of chance
With chances for none;
But oh! the Girl-of-the-Tank, at last!   30
Gleaming Girl, how intimately pure and free
The gaze you send the crowd,
As though you know the dearth of beauty
In its sordid life.
We need you—my Limousine-Lady,   35
The bull-necked man, and I.
Seeing you here brave and water-clean,
Leaven for the heavy ones of earth,
I am swift to feel that what makes
The plodder glad is good; and   40
Whatever is good is God.
The wonder is that you are here;
I have seen the queer in queer places,
But never before a heaven-fed
Naiad of the Carnival-Tank!   45
Little Diver, Destiny for you,
Like as for me, is shod in silence;
Years may seep into your soul
The bacilli of the usual and the expedient;
I implore Neptune to claim his child to-day!   50

EDMUND SPENSER   (1552–1599)

Amoretti 54: Of This World's Theater in Which We Stay   1595

Of this world's theater in which we stay,
My love like the spectator idly sits,
Beholding me that all the pageants° play,   roles
Disguising diversly my troubled wits.
Sometimes I joy when glad occasion fits,   5
And mask in mirth like to a comedy:
Soon after when my joy to sorrow flits,
I wail and make my woes a tragedy.
Yet she, beholding me with constant eye,
Delights not in my mirth nor rues° my smart: regrets   10
But when I laugh, she mocks, and when I cry
She laughs and hardens evermore her heart.
What then can move her? if not mirth nor moan,
She is no woman, but a senseless stone.

AMORETTI 54. *Amoretti* means "little loves" or "little love songs."

WILLIAM STAFFORD   (b. 1914)

Traveling Through the Dark   1960

Traveling through the dark I found a deer
dead on the edge of the Wilson River road.
It is usually best to roll them into the canyon:
that road is narrow; to swerve might make more dead.

By glow of the tail-light I stumbled back of the car   5
and stood by the heap, a doe, a recent killing;
she had stiffened already, almost cold.
I dragged her off; she was large in the belly.

My fingers touching her side brought me the reason—
her side was warm; her fawn lay there waiting,   10
alive, still, never to be born.
Beside that mountain road I hesitated.

The car aimed ahead its lowered parking lights;
under the hood purred the steady engine.
I stood in the glare of the warm exhaust turning red;   15
around our group I could hear the wilderness listen.

I thought hard for us all—my only swerving—,
then pushed her over the edge into the river.

GERALD STERN   (b. 1925)

Burying an Animal on the Way to New York   *1977*

Don't flinch when you come across a dead animal lying on the road;
you are being shown the secret of life.
Drive slowly over the brown flesh;
you are helping to bury it.
If you are the last mourner there will be no caress   5
at all from the crushed limbs
and you will have to slide over the dark spot imagining
the first suffering all by yourself
Shreds of spirit and little ghost fragments will be spread out
for two miles above the white highway.   10
Slow down with your radio off and your window open
to hear the twittering as you go by.

WALLACE STEVENS   (1879–1955)

The Emperor of Ice-Cream   *1923*

Call the roller of big cigars,
The muscular one, and bid him whip
In kitchen cups concupiscent curds.
Let the wenches dawdle in such dress
As they are used to wear, and let the boys   5
Bring flowers in last month's newspapers.
Let be be finale° of seem.
The only emperor is the emperor of ice-cream.
Take from the dresser of deal,°
Lacking the three glass knobs, that sheet   10
On which she embroidered fantails° once
And spread it so as to cover her face.
If her horny feet protrude, they come
To show how cold she is, and dumb.
Let the lamp affix its beam.   15
The only emperor is the emperor of ice-cream.

THE EMPEROR OF ICE-CREAM.   7 *finale*: the grand conclusion.   9 *deal*: unfinished
pine or fir used to make cheap furniture.   11 *fantails*: fantail pigeons.

MARK STRAND   (b. 1934)

The Remains   *1969*

I empty myself of the names of others.
I empty my pockets, I empty my shoes and leave them beside
the road. At night I turn back the clocks; I open the family
album and look at myself as a boy.

What good does it do? The hours have done their job.   5
I say my own name. I say goodbye.
The words follow each other downwind.
I love my wife but send her away.

My parents rise out of their thrones
into the milky rooms of clouds. How can I sing?   10
Time tells me what I am. I change and I am the same.
I empty myself of my life and my life remains.

JAMES TATE   (b. 1943)

The Blue Booby   *1969*

The blue booby lives
on the bare rocks
of Galápagos°
and fears nothing.
It is a simple life: 5
they live on fish,
and there are few predators.
Also, the males do not
make fools of themselves
chasing after the young   10
ladies. Rather,
they gather the blue
objects of the world
and construct from them

a nest—an occasional   15
Gaulois° package,
a string of beads,
a piece of cloth from
a sailor's suit. This

THE BLUE BOOBY.   3 *Galápagos*: islands in the Pacific Ocean on the Equator about
600 miles west of Ecuador where many unique species of animals live.   16 *Gaulois*: a
brand of French cigarettes with a blue package.

replaces the need for   20
dazzling plumage;
in fact, in the past
fifty million years
the male has grown
considerably duller,   25
nor can he sing well.
The female, though,

asks little of him—
the blue satisfies her
completely, has   30
a magical effect
on her. When she returns
from her day of
gossip and shopping,
she sees he has found her   35
a new shred of blue foil:
for this she rewards him
with her dark body,
the stars turn slowly
in the blue foil beside them   40
like the eyes of a mild savior.

EDWARD TAYLOR   (1645–1729)

Upon a Spider Catching a Fly   *1939 (ca. 1685)*

Thou sorrow, venom Elfe:°   *elf*
  Is this thy play,
To spin a web out of thyselfe
  To Catch a Fly?
    For why?   5

I saw a pettish° wasp   *ill-humored*
  Fall foule therein.
Whom yet they whorle pins° did not clasp   *spiders' legs*
  Lest he should fling
    His sting.   10

But as affraid, remote
  Didst stand hereat
And with thy little fingers stroke
  And gently tap
    His back.   15

Thus gently him didst treate
  Lest he should pet,

And in a froppish,° waspish heate *fretful*
  Should greatly fret
    Thy net. 20

Whereas the silly Fly,
  Caught by its leg
Thou by the throate tookst hastily,
  And 'hinde the head
    Bite Dead. 25

This goes to pot, that not
  Nature doth call.°
Strive not above what strength hath got
  Lest in the brawle
    Thou fall. 30

This Frey° seems thus to us. *fray, battle*
  Hells Spider gets
His intrails spun to whip Cords thus
  And wove to nets
    And sets. 35

To tangle Adams race
  In's stratigems
To their Destructions, spoil'd, made base
  By venom things
    Damn'd Sins. 40

But mighty, Gracious Lord
  Communicate
Thy Grace to breake the Cord, afford
  Us Glorys Gate
    And State. 45

We'l Nightingaile sing like
  When pearcht on high
In Glories Cage, thy glory, bright,
  [Yea,] thankfully,
    For joy. 50

UPON A SPIDER CATCHING A FLY.   26–27 *This . . . call*: that is, he who does not act according to natural reason goes to ruin ("pot").

ALFRED, LORD TENNYSON (1809–1892)

Tithonus *1860*

  The woods decay, the woods decay and fall,
The vapors weep their burthen to the ground,

Man comes and tills the field and lies beneath,
And after many a summer dies the swan.
Me only cruel immortality   5
Consumes; I wither slowly in thine arms,
Here at the quiet limit of the world,
A white-haired shadow roaming like a dream
The ever-silent spaces of the East,
Far-folded mists, and gleaming halls of morn.   10
   Alas! for this gray shadow, once a man—
So glorious in his beauty and thy choice,
Who madest him thy chosen, that he seemed
To his great heart none other than a God!
I asked thee, "Give me immortality."   15
Then didst thou grant mine asking with a smile,
Like wealthy men who care not how they give.
But thy strong Hours indignant worked their wills,
And beat me down and marred and wasted me,
And though they could not end me, left me maimed   20
To dwell in presence of immortal youth,
Immortal age beside immortal youth,
And all I was in ashes. Can thy love,
Thy beauty, make amends, though even now,
Close over us, the silver star, thy guide,   25
Shines in those tremulous eyes that fill with tears
To hear me? Let me go; take back thy gift.
Why should a man desire in any way
To vary from the kindly race of men,
Or pass beyond the goal of ordinance   30
Where all should pause, as is most meet for all?
   A soft air fans the cloud apart; there comes
A glimpse of that dark world where I was born.
Once more the old mysterious glimmer steals
From thy pure brows, and from thy shoulders pure,   35
And bosom beating with a heart renewed.
Thy cheek begins to redden through the gloom,
Thy sweet eyes brighten slowly close to mine,
Ere yet they blind the stars, and the wild team
Which love thee, yearning for thy yoke, arise,   40
And shake the darkness from their loosened manes,
And beat the twilight into flakes of fire.
   Lo! ever thus thou growest beautiful
In silence, then before thine answer given
Departest, and thy tears are on my cheek.   45
   Why wilt thou ever scare me with thy tears,
And make me tremble lest a saying learnt,
In days far-off, on that dark earth, be true?
"The Gods themselves cannot recall their gifts."
   Ay me! ay me! with what another heart   50

In days far-off, and with what other eyes
I used to watch—if I be he that watched—
The lucid outline forming round thee; saw
The dim curls kindle into sunny rings;
Changed with thy mystic change, and felt my blood   55
Glow with the glow that slowly crimsoned all
Thy presence and thy portals, while I lay,
Mouth, forehead, eyelids, growing dewy-warm
With kisses balmier than half-opening buds
Of April, and could hear the lips that kissed   60
Whispering I knew not what of wild and sweet,
Like that strange song I heard Apollo sing,
While Ilion like a mist rose into towers.
    Yet hold me not forever in thine East;
How can my nature longer mix with thine?   65
Coldly thy rose shadows bathe me, cold
Are all thy lights, and cold my wrinkled feet
Upon thy glimmering thresholds, when the steam
Floats up from those dim fields about the homes
Of happy men that have the power to die,   70
And grassy barrows of the happier dead.
Release me, and restore me to the ground.
Thou seest all things, thou wilt see my grave;
Thou wilt renew thy beauty morn by morn,
I earth in earth forget these empty courts,   75
And thee returning on thy silver wheels.

DYLAN THOMAS   (1914–1953)

A Refusal to Mourn the Death, by Fire, of a Child in London   *1946*

Never until the mankind making
Bird beast and flower
Fathering and all humbling darkness
Tells with silence the last light breaking
And the still hour   5
Is come of the sea tumbling in harness

And I must enter again the round
Zion of the water bead
And the synagogue of the ear of corn
Shall I let pray the shadow of a sound   10
Or sow my salt seed
In the least valley of sackcloth to mourn

The majesty and burning of the child's death.
I shall not murder

The mankind of her going with a grave truth   15
Nor blaspheme down the stations of the breath
With any further
Elegy of innocence and youth.

Deep with the first dead lies London's daughter,
Robed in the long friends,   20
The grains beyond age, the dark veins of her mother,
Secret by the unmourning water
Of the riding Thames.°
After the first death, there is no other.

A REFUSAL TO MOURN.   23 *Thames*: the River Thames, which flows through London.

CHASE TWICHELL   (b. 1950)

Blurry Cow   1983

Two cows stand transfixed
by a trough of floating leaves,
facing as if into the camera,
black and white. One stamps
at the hot sting of a deerfly.   5

Seen from the window of a train,
the hoof lifts forever
over hay crosshatched by speed,
and the scales of the haunches
balance. The rest is lost: 10
the head a sudden slur of light,
the dog loping along the tracks
toward a farm yard
where a woman wavers
in her mirage of laundry.   15
A blurry cow, of all things,
strays into the mind's eye,
the afterimage
of this day on earth.

MONA VAN DUYN   (b. 1921)

Advice to a God   1971

Before you leave her, the woman who thought you lavish,
whose body you led to parade without a blush
the touching vulgarity of the *nouveau-riche*,

whose every register your sexual coin
crammed full, whose ignorant bush mistook for sunshine   5
the cold, brazen battering of your rain,

rising, so little spent, strange millionaire
who feels in his loins' pocket clouds of power
gathering again for shower upon golden shower,

say to her, since she loves you, "Those as unworldly   10
as you are fated, and I can afford, to be
may find in Love's bed the perfect economy,

but, in all of his other places, a populace
living in fear of his management, his excess
of stingy might and extravagant helplessness.   15

Turn from him, Danae. I am greater by far,
whose flower reseeds without love for another flower,
whose seas part without loneliness, whose air

brightens or darkens heartlessly. By chance
I have come to you, and a progeny of events,   20
all that the mind of man calls consequence,

will follow my coming, slaughter and marriage, intrigue,
enchantment, definition of beauty, hag
and hero, a teeming, throwaway catalogue

of the tiniest, riskiest portion of my investment.   25
Yet pity your great landlord, for if I lent
so much as an ear to you, one loving tenant,

your bankrupt scream as I leave might tempt me to see
all creation in the ungainly, ungodly
throes of your individuality."   30

TINO VILLANUEVA   (b. 1941)

Day-Long Day   *1972*

> Again the drag of pisca,° pisca . . . pisca . . .
> Daydreams border on sun-fed hallucinations,
> eyes and hands automatically discriminate
> whiteness of cotton from field of vision.
> Pisca, pisca.
>   "Un Hijo del Sol,"°
>   Genaro Gonzales°

Third-generation timetable.
Sweat day-long dripping into open space;

DAY-LONG DAY.   EPIGRAPH: *pisca*: picking cotton.   *Un Hijo del Sol*: A Son of the Sun.
Genaro Gonzales: Hispanic author, born 1949.

sun blocks out the sky, suffocates the only breeze.
From el amo desgraciado,° a sentence:

"I wanna a bale a day, and the boy here   5
don't hafta go to school."
*   *   *
In time-binding motion—
a family of sinews and backs,
row-trapped,
zigzagging through summer-long rows   10
of cotton: Lubbock by way of Wharton.°
"Está como si escupieran fuego,"° a mother moans
in sweat-patched jeans,
stooping
with unbending dreams.   15
"Estudia para que no seas burro como nosotros,"°
our elders warn, their gloves and cuffs
leaf-stained by seasons.
*   *   *
Bronzed and blurry-eyed by
the blast of degrees,   20
we blend into earth's rotation.
And sweltering toward Saturday, the
day-long day is sunstruck by 6:00 P.M.
One last chug-a-lug from a water jug
old as granddad.   25
Day-long sweat dripping into open space:
Wharton by way of Lubbock.

4 *el amo desgraciado*: the despicable boss.   11 *Lubbock . . . Wharton*: cities on opposite sides
of Texas.   12 *Está . . . fuego*: "It's as if they are spewing fire."   16 *Estudia . . . nosotros*:
"Study so that you will not be a burro like us."

DIANE WAKOSKI   (b. 1937)

The Ring   *1977*

I carry it on my keychain, which itself
is a big brass ring
large enough for my wrist,
holding keys for safe-deposit box,
friends' apartments,   5
my house, office and faithless car.

I would like to wear it,
the only ornament on my plain body,

but it is a relic,
the husband gone to other wives,   10
and it could never be a symbol of sharing,
but like the gold it's made of, stands for possession, power,
the security of a throne.

So, on my keyring,
dull from resting in my dark purse,   15
it hangs, reminding me of failures, of beauty I once had,
of more ancient searches for an enchanted ring.

I understand, now, what that enchantment is, though.
It is being loved.
Or, conversely, loving so much that you feel loved.   20
And the ring hangs there
with my keys,
reminding of failure.

This vain head full of roses,
crystal,   25
bleeding lips,
a voice doomed to listen, forever,
to itself.

ALICE WALKER   (b. 1944)

Revolutionary Petunias   *1972*

Sammy Lou of Rue
sent to his reward
the exact creature who
murdered her husband,
using a cultivator's hoe   5
with verve and skill;
and laughed fit to kill
in disbelief
at the angry, militant
pictures of herself   10
the Sonneteers quickly drew:
not any of them people that
she knew.
A backwoods woman
her house was papered with   15
funeral home calendars and
faces appropriate for a Mississippi
Sunday School. She raised a George,

a Martha, a Jackie and a Kennedy. Also
a John Wesley Junior.°   20
"Always respect the word of God,"
she said on her way to she didn't
know where, except it would be by
electric chair, and she continued
"Don't yall forgit to *water*   25
my purple petunias."

REVOLUTIONARY PETUNIAS.   18–20 *George. . . Junior*: The children are named after
George and Martha Washington, Jackie and John Fitzgerald Kennedy (1917–1963, thirty-
fifth president of the U.S.), and John Wesley (1703–1791), English evangelical preacher
who founded Methodism.

MARGARET WALKER   (b. 1915)

Iowa Farmer   *1942*

I talked to a farmer one day in Iowa.
We looked out far over acres of wheat.
He spoke with pride and yet not boastfully;
he had no need to fumble for his words.
He knew his land and there was love for home   5
within the soft serene eyes of his son.
His ugly house was clean against the storm;
there was no hunger deep within the heart
nor burning riveted within the bone,
but here they ate a satisfying bread.   10
Yet in the Middle West where wheat was plentiful;
where grain grew golden under sunny skies
and cattle fattened through the summer heat
I could remember more familiar sights.

EDMUND WALLER   (1606–1687)

Go, Lovely Rose   *1645*

  Go, lovely rose!
Tell her that wastes her time and me
  That now she knows,
When I resemble° her to thee,   *compare*
How sweet and fair she seems to be.   5

Tell her that's young,
And shuns to have her graces spied,
　That hadst thou sprung
In deserts, where no men abide,
Thou must have uncommended died.　　　　　　　　　10

　Small is the worth
Of beauty from the light retired;
　Bid her come forth,
Suffer herself to be desired,
And not blush so to be admired.　　　　　　　　　15

　Then die! that she
The common fate of all things rare
　May read in thee;
How small a part of time they share
That are so wondrous sweet and fair.　　　　　　　20

ROBERT PENN WARREN　(b. 1905)

Heart of Autumn　　　　　　　　　　　　　　*1978*

Wind finds the northwest gap, fall comes.
Today, under gray cloud-scud and over gray
Wind-flicker of forest, in perfect formation, wild geese
Head for a land of warm water, the *boom*, the lead pellet.

Some crumple in air, fall. Some stagger, recover control,　　5
Then take the last glide for a far glint of water. None
Knows what has happened. Now, today, watching
How tirelessly *V* upon *V* arrows the season's logic,

Do I know my own story? At least, they know
When the hour comes for the great wing-beat. Sky-strider,　　10
Star-strider—they rise, and the imperial utterance,
Which cries out for distance, quivers in the wheeling sky.

That much they know, and in their nature know
The path of pathlessness, with all the joy
Of destiny fulfilling its own name.　　　　　　　15
I have known time and distance, but not why I am here.

Path of logic, path of folly, all
The same—and I stand, my face lifted now skyward,

Hearing the high beat, my arms outstretched in the tingling
Process of transformation, and soon tough legs,   20

With folded feet, trail in the sounding vacuum of passage,
And my heart is impacted with a fierce impulse
To unwordable utterance—
Toward sunset, at a great height.

BRUCE WEIGL (b. 1949)

Song of Napalm

For My Wife

After the storm, after the rain stopped pounding,
We stood in the doorway watching horses
Walk off lazily across the pasture's hill.
We stared through the black screen,
Our vision altered by the distance   5
So I thought I saw a mist
Kicked up around their hooves when they faded
Like cut-out horses
Away from us.
The grass was never more blue in that light, more   10
Scarlet; beyond the pasture
Trees scraped their voices in the wind, branches
Criss-crossed the sky like barbed-wire
But you said they were only branches.

Okay. The storm stopped pounding.   15
I am trying to say this straight: for once
I was sane enough to pause and breathe
Outside my wild plans and after the hard rain
I turned my back on the old curses, I believed
They swung finally away from me . . .   20

But still the branches are wire
And thunder is the pounding mortar,
Still I close my eyes and see the girl
Running from her village, napalm
Stuck to her dress like jelly,   25
Her hands reaching for the no one
Who waits in waves of heat before her.

So I can keep on living,
So I can stay here beside you,
I try to imagine she runs down the road and wings   30
Beat inside her until she rises
Above the stinking jungle and her pain
Eases, and your pain, and mine.

But the lie swings back again.
The lie works only as long as it takes to speak   35
And the girl runs only so far
As the napalm allows
Until her burning tendons and crackling
Muscles draw her up
Into that final position   40
Burning bodies so perfectly assume. Nothing
Can change that; she is burned behind my eyes
And not your good love and not the rain-swept air
And not the jungle green
Pasture unfolding before us can deny it.   45

PHYLLIS WHEATLEY   (1754–1784)

On Being Brought from Africa to America   *1773*

'Twas mercy brought me from my *Pagan* land,
Taught my benighted soul to understand
That there's a God, that there's a *Saviour* too:
Once I redemption neither sought nor knew.
Some view our sable race with scornful eye,   5
"Their colour is a diabolic die."
Remember, *Christians*, *Negroes*, black as *Cain*,
May be refin'd, and join th' angelic train.

RICHARD WILBUR   (b. 1921)

Ballade for the Duke of Orleans   *1961*

> *who offered a prize at Blois, circa 1457, for*
> *the best ballade employing the line "Je*
> *meurs de soif auprès de la fontaine."°*

Flailed from the heart of water in a bow,
He took the falling fly; my line went taut;
Foam was in uproar where he drove below;
In spangling air I fought him and was fought.
Then, wearied to the shallows, he was caught,   5
Gasped in the net, lay still and stony-eyed.
It was no feeling iris I had sought.
I die of thirst, here at the fountain-side.

BALLADE. The refrain line in French means "I am dying of thirst
beside the fountain."

Down in the harbor's flow and counter-flow
I left my ships with hopes and heroes fraught.   10
Ten times more golden than the sun could show,
Calypso° gave the darkness I besought.
Oh, but her fleecy touch was dearly bought:
All spent, I wakened by my only bride,
Beside whom every vision is but nought,   15
And die of thirst, here at the fountain-side.

Where does that Plenty dwell, I'd like to know,
Which fathered poor Desire, as Plato taught?
Out on the real and endless waters go
Conquistador and stubborn Argonaut.   20
Where Buddha bathed, the golden bowl he brought
Gilded the stream, but stalled its living tide.
The sunlight withers as the verse is wrought.
I die of thirst, here at the fountain-side.

ENVOI

Duke, keep your coin. All men are born distraught,   25
And will not for the world be satisfied.
Whether we live in fact, or but in thought,
We die of thirst, here at the fountain-side.

12 *Calypso*: Sea nymph in Homer's *Odyssey* with whom Odysseus lives for seven years.

RICHARD WILBUR   (b. 1921)

The Sirens   *1950*

I never knew the road
From which the whole earth didn't call away,
With wild birds rounding the hill crowns,
Haling out of the heart an old dismay,
Or the shore somewhere pounding its slow code,   5
Or low-lighted towns
Seeming to tell me, stay.

Lands I have never seen
And shall not see, loves I will not forget,
All I have missed, or slighted, or foregone   10
Call to me now. And weaken me. And yet
I would not walk a road without a scene.
I listen going on,
The richer for regret.

WILLIAM CARLOS WILLIAMS   (1883–1963)

The Red Wheelbarrow   *1923*

so much depends
upon

a red wheel
barrow

glazed with rain   5
water

beside the white
chickens.

WILLIAM WORDSWORTH   (1770–1850)

1798

Lines Written in Early Spring

I heard a thousand blended notes,
While in a grove I sate reclined,
In that sweet mood when pleasant thoughts
Bring sad thoughts to the mind.

To her fair works did Nature link   5
The human soul that through me ran;
And much it grieved my heart to think
What man has made of man.

Through primrose tufts, in that green bower,
The periwinkle° trailed its wreaths;   10
And 'tis my faith that every flower
Enjoys the air it breathes.

The birds around me hopped and played,
Their thoughts I cannot measure—
But the least motion which they made,   15
It seemed a thrill of pleasure.

The budding twigs spread out their fan,
To catch the breezy air;
And I must think, do all I can,
That there was pleasure there.   20

It this belief from heaven be sent,
If such be Nature's holy plan,
Have I not reason to lament
What man has made of man?

LINES WRITTEN IN EARLY SPRING.   10 *periwinkle*: a trailing evergreen plant with
blue or white flowers.

WILLIAM WORDSWORTH   (1770–1850)

The Solitary Reaper   1807

Behold her, single in the field,
Yon solitary Highland Lass!
Reaping and singing by herself;
Stop here, or gently pass!

Alone she cuts and binds the grain,   5
And sings a melancholy strain;
O listen! for the Vale profound
Is overflowing with the sound.

No Nightingale did ever chaunt
More welcome notes to weary bands   10
Of travelers in some shady haunt,
Among Arabian sands;
A voice so thrilling ne'er was heard
In springtime from the Cuckoo bird,
Breaking the silence of the seas   15
Among the farthest Hebrides.°

Will no one tell me what she sings?°
Perhaps the plaintive numbers flow
For old, unhappy, far-off things,
And battles long ago;   20
Or is it some more humble lay,
Familiar matter of today?
Some natural sorrow, loss, or pain,
That has been, and may be again?

Whate'er the theme, the Maiden sang   25
As if her song could have no ending;
I saw her singing at her work,
And o'er the sickle bending—
I listened, motionless and still;
And, as I mounted up the hill,   30
The music in my heart I bore,
Long after it was heard no more.

THE SOLITARY REAPER.   16 *Hebrides*: a group of islands belonging to and off the
west coast of Scotland.   17 *Will . . . sings*: the speaker does not understand Scots Gaelic,
the language in which the woman sings.

WILLIAM BUTLER YEATS (1865–1939)

Sailing to Byzantium°   *1927*

1

That is no country for old men. The young
In one another's arms, birds in the trees
—Those dying generations—at their song,
The salmon-falls, the mackerel-crowded seas,
Fish, flesh, or fowl, commend all summer long   5
Whatever is begotten, born, and dies.
Caught in that sensual music all neglect
Monuments of unaging intellect.

2

An aged man is but a paltry thing.
A tattered coat upon a stick, unless   10
Soul clap its hands and sing, and louder sing
For every tatter in its mortal dress,
Nor is there singing school but studying
Monuments of its own magnificence;
And therefore I have sailed the seas and come   15
To the holy city of Byzantium.

3

O sages standing in God's holy fire
As in the gold mosaic of a wall,
Come from the holy fire, perne in a gyre,°
And be the singing-masters of my soul.   20
Consume my heart away; sick with desire
And fastened to a dying animal
It knows not what it is; and gather me
Into the artifice of eternity.

4

Once out of nature I shall never take   25
My bodily form from any natural thing,
But such a form as Grecian goldsmiths make
Of hammered gold and gold enameling
To keep a drowsy Emperor awake;
Or set upon a golden bough to sing   30
To lords and ladies of Byzantium
Of what is past, or passing, or to come.

SAILING TO BYZANTIUM. In Yeats's private mythology, Byzantium (called Constantinople
in Roman times and Istanbul today) symbolizes art, artifice, sophistication, and eternity as
opposed to the natural world and physicality.   19 *perne in a gyre*: turn of spin about in a
spiral motion. See also p. 788*n*.

PAUL ZIMMER   (b. 1934)

The Day Zimmer Lost Religion   *1973*

The first Sunday I missed Mass on purpose
I waited all day for Christ to climb down
Like a wiry flyweight° from the cross and
Club me on my irreverent teeth, to wade into
My blasphemous gut and drop me like a   5
Red hot thurible,° the devil roaring in
Reserved seats until he got the hiccups.

It was a long cold way from the old days
When cassocked and surpliced° I mumbled Latin
At the old priest and rang his obscure bell.   10
A long way from the dirty wind that blew
The soot like venial sins across the schoolyard
Where God reigned as a threatening,
One-eyed triangle high in the fleecy sky.

The first Sunday I missed Mass on purpose   15
I waited all day for Christ to climb down
Like the playground bully, the cuts and mice
Upon his face agleam, and pound me
Till my irreligious tongue hung out.
But of course He never came, knowing that   20
I was grown up and ready for Him now.

THE DAY ZIMMER LOST RELIGION.   3 *flyweight*: a boxer weighing less than 112
pounds.   6 *thurible*: a censer, container in which incense is burned.   9 *cassocked and
surpliced*: wearing the traditional garb of an altar boy during Mass.

DRAMA

25

The Elements of Drama

The word *drama* is derived from the Greek word *dran*, which means "to do" or "to act." In many ways, this "doing" or "acting" is the definitive quality of drama. Although "drama" is often used as a synonym for "play," the word *drama* can also refer to a group of plays (Elizabethan drama) or to all plays collectively. While plays share many things in common with prose fiction and poetry, the single most important difference is that they are designed to be presented by actors on a stage before an audience.

THE HISTORY AND NATURE OF DRAMA

Drama evolved in humanity's past from the rites of primitive cultures. Primitive communities would often act out their deepest fears, strongest desires, or greatest achievements in a religious ritual. A successful hunt, for instance, might have been followed by a rite of thanksgiving in which the hunt was symbolically reenacted. Similarly, in the dead of winter people might have acted out the coming of spring and the regeneration of the earth because they needed to reassure themselves that such a rebirth would occur. By the fifth century B.C. in Greece, drama had evolved from a religious ritual to an art form. The plays of the classical Greek dramatists maintained much of the ritual flavor of primitive drama, often retelling ancient myths and being performed at religious festivals. Nevertheless, the Greek playwrights shaped drama into its modern form with large casts of characters and divisions of the action into separate scenes.

Classical Greece also provided the first drama critic, the philosopher Aristotle (384–322 B.C.). In *The Poetics* he defines drama or acting as *mimesis*, or the *imitation* of human actions. Drama is thus a *mimetic* art in which actors mimic the actions and emotions of people in order to communicate to an audience. Aristotle also provided the first extensive theoretical discussions of the nature and structure of drama and of the differences between comedy and tragedy.

Drama maintained its connection with religion and ritual through much of its history. In the Middle Ages drama was reborn in the churches of England and other Western European countries as part of the Catholic mass. This medieval drama was explicitly linked to Christianity, especially in the **mystery plays,** which dramatized events related in the Bible, and in the **morality plays,** which demonstrated the way to live a Christian life. To this day, a dramatic performance maintains some sense of communal ritual involving both the actors and the audience.

PLAY TEXTS AND PRODUCTIONS

What separates drama from prose fiction and poetry is the acting or *staging* of the play. People who write plays are called *dramatists* or *playwrights* (not "playwrites"; the term combines *play* with the word *wright*, a worker or builder). The text of a play consists of dialogue, monologue, and stage directions. **Dialogue** is conversation among two or more characters. A **monologue** is spoken by a single character who is usually alone on stage. **Stage directions,** the playwright's instructions to the actors and director, are distinguished from the dialogue of the play.

The performance of a play brings immediacy and excitement to the text of a work. In production, the text is fleshed out with all the techniques available to the modern theater. The actors bring the characters and the dialogue to life; they strut or cringe, scream or whimper, embrace or murder. They give their bodies to the characters, providing gestures and voices, facial expressions, intonations, and **blocking** (stage movement and stage groupings). The actors also provide **stage business**—gestures or movements that keep the production active and dynamic. In the modern theater, these aspects of movement and position on-stage are controlled by the *director*, the person who plans the production and *directs* the actors during rehearsals to move, speak, and act in ways that are consistent with his or her vision of the play.

Most modern plays are performed either on a **proscenium stage** (like a room with one wall missing so that the audience may look in on the action) or on a **thrust stage** (an acting area that projects into the audience). On whatever kind of stage, the modern theater is likely to provide **scenery** and **properties** (or **props**), which help to put the action in a specific place and underscore the ideas that the writer or director is trying to convey. **Sets** (the scenery) may be changed many times during a production, or a single set may be used throughout.

The text of a play is also brought to life by **costumes** that help the spectators identify and understand the characters. These may be used realistically (a salesman dressed as a salesman) or symbolically (an evil queen dressed entirely in black).

The modern theater also relies heavily on **lighting** to create effects. Lights were not used in the theater until the seventeenth century; up to that time, plays were performed in daylight. In the seventeenth century, people began to build enclosed theaters that required artificial lighting. Lighting can emphasize different parts of the stage or isolate specific characters. In plays like Tennessee Williams's *The Glass Menagerie* and Arthur Miller's *Death of a Salesman*, lighting is even used to indicate changes in time or place.

In addition, the theater, from its beginnings in ancient Greece, has been enlivened by dancing, music, and sound effects.

The audience too plays a significant role in the theater. The reactions of spectators to the on-stage action provide feedback to the actors, and thus continually alter the pace and timing of a production. Similarly, the audience, sitting together in a darkened auditorium, offers a communal response to the events taking place on stage. Thus, drama *in the theater* is the most immediate and accessible of the literary arts; there is no narrator, as in prose fiction, and no speaker, as in poetry, imposed between us and the stage action.

This clear difference between the text of a play and its production might lead you to ask why we bother to read plays. There are, of course, many answers. Reading a play can be as exciting and rewarding as reading a novel, a short story, or a poem. In reading, we have the chance to imagine settings, costumes, and action with a degree of scope and vividness that the stage rarely duplicates. We also read plays to familiarize ourselves with important literature. Plays are not simply maps to production; they are a significant and valuable part of our literary heritage. Dramas like Sophocles' *Oedipus Rex* and Shakespeare's *Hamlet* have become cultural touchstones and the springboards for other works of literature, art, cinema, and television. Finally, we read plays in order to have the time to study and understand them. Only through reading do we have the opportunity to look at the parts that make up the whole and see how they fit together to create a moving and meaningful experience.

TYPES OF DRAMA

Aristotle divided all drama into tragedy and comedy. **Tragedy** recounts the fall of an individual; it begins in prosperity and ends in adversity. **Comedy** describes the regeneration or reformation of a group of people or a society; it begins in adversity and resolves in prosperity. Although tragedy is normally considered sad and comedy happy, notice that the brief definitions given here have more to do with patterns of action than with our emotional responses to plays. For a much fuller definition of tragedy and comedy, see pp. 1064 and 1320.

Pure forms of tragedy and comedy have rarely been written since the classical period; most British and American plays offer some mixture of the two forms. For example, Shakespeare's tragedies include witty and humorous scenes, and his comedies often deal with serious and threatening problems. In most plays written before the twentieth century, however, one pattern or the other predominates. When the patterns and emotions are truly mixed, the play is called a **tragicomedy,** a term first used by the Roman playwright Plautus around 186 B.C. Today the term encompasses a broad range of plays that offer a mixture of tragic and comic effects. In many ways, tragicomedy is the dominant form of twentieth-century drama.

Other forms of drama that have evolved from tragedy and comedy include farce, melodrama, and social drama. **Farce** is a form of comedy crammed full of humorous actions and dialogue, with rapid shifts in action and emotion. Chekhov's *The Bear* is a good example of farce. **Melodrama** is a debased form of tragedy with a happy ending. The adversities in melodrama all grow out of plot rather than character—the mortgage is due, the family business is failing, the daughter has been kidnapped by the villain. The hero always arrives just in time to pay the mortgage, save the business, and rescue the heroine.

Social dramas, sometimes called *problem plays*, evolved in the nineteenth century and dominated the stage through the early part of the twentieth century. This type of drama explores social problems and the individual's place in society; the plays can be tragic, comic, or mixed. Examples of social drama are Susan Glaspell's *Trifles*, Arthur Miller's *Death of a Salesman*, and Henrik Ibsen's *A Doll's House*.

One further distinction will be helpful in your exploration of drama. **Full-length plays** are dramas that usually contain three or five separate acts (as in *A Doll's House* or *Hamlet*) or a long series of separate scenes (as in *Oedipus* and *The Glass Menagerie*). Such plays, designed for a full performance of about three or more hours in the theater, provide for complete and in-depth development of character, conflict, and idea. Full-length plays containing separate acts, like *Hamlet* and *Death of a Salesman*, are also subdivided. Sometimes these subdivisions, or **scenes,** are not noted in the text, but often they are given formal scene numbers. Characteristic of scenes are a coherent action, a unified setting, and a fixed group of characters.

Shorter dramas do not permit extensive development and subdivision because they are by definition more limited and confined. **One-act plays,** like *Before Breakfast* and *The Bear*, flow smoothly from episode to episode without a break, or they may shift as the scene changes, as in *The Happy Journey to Trenton and Camden*. On the other hand, somewhat longer short plays, like *Love Is the Doctor* and *Am I Blue*, may contain formal scene and act divisions. If you consider parallels with fiction, the full-length play is analogous to the novel, while the one-act play is like the short story. The short play is appropriate for brief performances; sometimes an evening at the theater is made up of two or three one-acters. In addition, the one-act play may be used for studio and classroom performance, or, for that matter, for adaptation as hour- or half-hour performances for film or television.

Given all these terms and types, you should keep in mind that classification is not the goal of reading or seeing plays. It is less important to identify *Am I Blue* as a comedy or *Before Breakfast* as a melodramatic tragedy than it is to feel and understand the experiences and ideas that each play offers us.

THE BASIC ELEMENTS OF DRAMATIC LITERATURE

In the following sections we will consider the basic elements of dramatic literature: *plot, character, point of view, setting, language, tone, symbolism,* and *theme* or *meaning.* Poetic drama, such as Sophocles' *Oedipus the King* and Shakespeare's *Hamlet* and *A Midsummer Night's Dream,* add elements that characterize poetry, such as *meter* and *rhyme.* All these elements have remained relatively constant throughout the history of drama. In *The Poetics,* Aristotle identifies six components of drama: plot, character, language, spectacle, thought, and song. Modern drama cannot be judged exclusively on the basis of Aristotle's six aspects, but his list illustrates the continuity of dramatic elements and techniques.

Plot, Action, and Conflict

Plot, in drama as in fiction, is an ordered chain of physical, emotional, or intellectual events that ties the action together. It is a planned sequence of interrelated actions that begins in a state of imbalance, grows out of conflict, reaches a peak of complication, and resolves into some new situation. It is, of course, easy to oversimplify the idea of plot in a play. Dramatic plots are often more complicated than a single movement toward a single solution or resolution. Some plays have **double plots**—two different but related lines of action going on at the same time. Other plays offer both a **main plot** and a **subplot** that comments, either directly or indirectly, on the main plot. In *A Midsummer Night's Dream* four separate plots are woven together to form a single story.

The mainspring of plot in a play is **conflict,** which can be physical, psychological, social, or all three. It can involve a character's struggle against another person, against the environment, or against himself or herself. Most commonly, the conflict in a play is some combination of these general types. In Edward Albee's *The Sandbox*, for example, Grandma is in conflict with her family, society, and death. Similarly, the hero in *Hamlet* is in conflict with himself, his enemies, and his society all at the same time. Conflict in drama can be more explicit than it is in prose fiction because we actually see the clash of wills and characters on stage or on the page.

In most plays we may trace a five-stage *plot structure*—exposition, complication, crisis or climax, catastrophe, and resolution—that allows the action to unfold in reasonable order. The German critic Gustav Freytag in the nineteenth century noted that this structure follows the pattern of a pyramid, in which the rising action (exposition and complication) leads up to the point of crisis or climax and is followed by the falling action (the catastrophe and resolution).

The Freytag Pyramid of Plot Structure

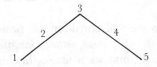

1. Exposition or Introduction
2. Complication and Development
3. Climax or Crisis
4. Falling Action, Catastrophe
5. Resolution or Dénouement

In the first of these stages, the **exposition,** the audience receives essential background information; we are introduced to the characters, the situations, and the conflicts. In *Oedipus the King* this material is conveyed in the prologue. Other playwrights might have several characters discuss the people in the play and the crucial events that occurred before the beginning of the staged action. In *Hamlet*, for example, the conversations of Barnardo, Marcellus, and Horatio provide critical information. Other plays distribute the information throughout the entire action, as, for example, in *Oedipus*.

In the second stage, the **complication,** the conflicts grow heated and the plot becomes more involved. Complication leads into the **crisis** or **climax** (from the Greek word for "ladder"), the turning point of the play. In this third stage the hero or heroine often faces a crucial decision or chooses a course of action that determines the outcome of the play. At this point the complications become so tightly knotted that the play can be resolved in only one direction.

The pyramid begins its downward slope in stage four, the catastrophe. The **catastrophe** (not to be confused with our modern use of the term to mean "disaster") is that single moment of revelation when all the pieces fall into place. It is often caused by the discovery of certain information or event that has been unknown to most of the characters up to that instant. During the final stage, the **resolution,** conflicts are resolved, lives are straightened out or ended, and loose ends are tied up.

Most plays do not perfectly follow this five-stage structure. The pattern is merely a model to explain plot; for most plays it does not provide a perfect road map. Be prepared for plays that offer little exposition, have no dénouement, or modify the general pattern in some other significant and useful way.

Character

A **character** in a play is a person created by a playwright to carry the action, language, ideas, and emotions of the play. Many of the types of characters that populate prose fiction are also found in drama (see pp. 145–47). In drama as in fiction, for instance, we find both **round characters** and **flat characters.** The round characters are fully developed and usually undergo some change in the course of the play; good examples include Shakespeare's Prince Hamlet and Nora in Ibsen's *A Doll's House.* Flat characters, on the other hand, tend to be undeveloped and unchanging. Characters in drama can also be considered either **static**—that is, fixed and unchanging—or **dynamic**—that is, growing and developing. Flat characters are usually static; round characters are often dynamic.

Because drama depends on conflict as fully as does prose fiction, we also find protagonists and antagonists in plays. (The Greek word for conflict or contest was *agon*, from which we derive the word *agony* and both of these terms.) The **protagonist** is usually the character we identify with and cheer on. In full-length plays, the protagonists tend to be round characters. The **antagonist** opposes the protagonist and is often the villain of the piece. In O'Neill's *Before Breakfast*, for example, Alfred Rowland is the protagonist and his wife the antagonist; their relationship forms the central conflict of the play.

There are also characters who serve to set off or highlight aspects of the protagonist, and others who stand on the sidelines and comment on the action rather than getting deeply involved. The first of these types, called a **foil,** is a character whose behavior and attitudes contrast in some way to the protagonist's. In *Hamlet*, for instance, both Laertes and Fortinbras are foils to the prince. The second type of character, called a **choric figure,** has its historical roots in the choruses of Greek tragedy and is usually played by a single character, often a friend or confidant of the protagonist, such as Horatio in *Hamlet*. This type of character is termed a *raisonneur* (from the French word meaning "reasoner") since he or she remains distant from the action and provides reasoned commentary.

Dramatic characters may be realistic, nonrealistic, symbolic, and stereotyped or stock. **Realistic characters** are normally accurate imitations of individualized men and women; they are provided with backgrounds, personalities, desires, motivations, and thoughts. **Nonrealistic characters** are usually stripped of such individualizing touches; they are often undeveloped and symbolic. All the characters in *The Sandbox* are nonrealistic. **Symbolic characters** represent an idea, a way of life, moral values, or some other abstraction. The two women in *Tea Party* thus symbolize the agonized loneliness of old age, while Dr. Fillpocket in *Love Is the Doctor* symbolizes cynicism, greed, charlatanism, and the misuse of responsibility.

Stereotyped, or **stock, characters** have been used in drama and other types of literature throughout the ages. The four general types of stock characters in classical drama are the bumpkin, the braggart, the trickster, and the victim. Other stereotyped characters that survive from classical or Renaissance drama include the stubborn father, the shrewish wife, the lusty youth, and the prodigal son. Modern drama continues to employ these stereotypes, but it has also invented many of its own: the hardboiled detective, the loner cowboy, the honest policeman, the whore with a heart of gold. Playwrights use stereotyped characters so that audiences will instantly understand the nature and the limits of the character. Stock characters thus become a shortcut in characterization for dramatists and in comprehension for spectators and readers.

The major difference between characters in prose fiction or poetry and characters in drama is found in the way they are unfolded. Playwrights do not have the fiction writer's freedom to tell us directly about a character. We learn about characters in plays by paying attention to their words and actions, by listening to what other characters say about them, and by watching what other characters do to them. Finally, however, we arrive at our own judgment or understanding of characters; the playwright will almost never do this for us.

Point of View and Perspective

Point of view in drama is strikingly different from the comparable element in prose fiction or poetry. Since plays almost never have narrators, there is no way to create a perspective that is specifically first-person-protagonist or third-person-omniscient. Instead, playwrights usually employ the **dramatic point of view** in which we receive only the information communicated by the characters. The key to the dramatic point of view is that the playwright gives us the objective raw materials—the action and the words—but does not overtly guide us toward any conclusions. Naturally, we draw conclusions from the details presented in the play.

Within these limits playwrights do have techniques to lead an audience to see from a specific character's perspective. In O'Neill's *Before Breakfast*, the entire play is a monologue spoken by Mrs. Rowland. Another commonly used device is the **soliloquy** in which the hero or villain reveals his or her thoughts directly to the audience. Soliloquies were common techniques for revealing the thoughts and emotions of characters in sixteenth- and seventeenth-century plays. In the twentieth century they have again become an important element in experimental and nonrealistic drama. Another device, called an **aside,** allows a character to address brief remarks to the audience, the reader, or another character which the other characters on stage are unable to hear.

Setting, Sets, and Scenery

Setting in drama serves to place the action in a specific time and place and to help create the appropriate mood. In the text of a play, the setting is described in words, usually in the opening stage direction. In a production, however, the setting is brought to life through lighting, props, and scenery. Like characters, setting (or **set**) may be realistic or nonrealistic. The setting for *Trifles*, for example, is a highly realistic rendering of a Nebraska farm kitchen, complete with stove, sink, and unwashed dishes. In Wilder's *The Happy Journey to Trenton and Camden*, however, the setting is nonrealistic: four chairs and a low platform represent an apartment, an automobile, and a house. Realistic settings require extensive scenery and stage furniture; the idea is to create as real an environment as possible. Nonrealistic settings are symbolic or representational; they are often produced by *unit sets*—a single series of platforms, stairs, and playing areas that serve for all the scenery and the settings of the play.

The setting, usually the first thing we see on stage, helps to establish a specific time and place and conditions our expectations. A set depicting a medieval torture chamber would raise entirely different expectations in our minds than would a set that looked like a basketball court. Even if the plays staged in such different settings were about the same matters, the physical environment could have a profound effect on our reactions.

Playwrights also use settings to convey information about the characters and the world of the play. The shabby apartment in New York City's Greenwich Village in O'Neill's *Before Breakfast* implies conditions and values quite different from those suggested by the comfortable and tastefully decorated living room in Ibsen's *A Doll's House*.

Most one-act plays make do with a single setting and with action that is relatively short. Many of the plays in this anthology, for example, limit their action to a single time and place. That time may be as short as the ten or so minutes required for a performance of *Tea Party*, for example, or it may be visualized as happening in an hour (*Am I Blue*), an afternoon (*Love Is the Doctor*), or an entire day (*The Sandbox*). The underlying theory of time and place here is that the illusion of reality is enhanced if the time of the play is arranged to coincide with the length of the show.

Many full-length plays also confine the action to a single setting and a limited time, as with Sophocles' *Oedipus the King*, which is performed in a single setting, presumably lasting less than a day, before the royal palace in the city of Thebes in ancient Greece. Other longer plays may extend time while keeping to the same place, as in *A Doll's House*, in which the several days of action all take place in only one room of the Helmers' home. Some full-length plays change settings frequently just as they stretch out time. *Hamlet* takes place in a number of different locations, including battlements, a throne room, bed chambers, and a graveyard (all these scene changes put great strain on a production committed to absolute realism in scene design).

Diction, Imagery, Style, and Language

Words give plays their emotional impact and meaning. Characters tell us what they think, hope, fear, and desire; their dialogue can reflect the details of day-to-day living or their deepest thoughts about death and salvation. Most of what we learn about characters, relationships, and conflict in drama is conveyed through language. The language must be appropriate for the play in which it is spoken; it must fit the time, the place, and the characters. It would be as wrong for Hamlet to speak in modern American slang as it would for Willie Loman in Miller's *Death of a Salesman* to speak in Elizabethan blank verse. This sense of appropriateness is called **decorum.**

The words and rhetorical devices spoken in a play delineate character, emotion, and theme, much as they do in prose fiction and poetry. Dramatists can employ words that have wide-ranging connotations (or associations) or that acquire many layers of meaning. Such is the case with the words *trifle* and *knot* in Glaspell's play *Trifles*. Similarly, playwrights can have their characters speak in similes or metaphors that contribute significantly to the impact and meaning of the play. Again in *Trifles*, one of the characters compares another to a bird, and the simile becomes the key to one of the central symbols in the play.

Dramatists also employ accents, dialects, idiom, jargon, or clichés to define character. Both Ma in *The Happy Journey to Trenton and Camden* and most of the characters in *The Glass Menagerie* speak in regional dialects and use slang expressions that help us place them in a specific time and place. Similarly, characters in *The Sandbox* speak in clichés that define the characters' values and help us understand them. In short, playwrights have access to every stylistic and rhetorical device of language in their creation of character, conflict, emotion, and ideas.

Tone and Atmosphere

Tone in drama, as in other literature, signifies the way moods and attitudes are created and conveyed. Tone in plays may be conveyed directly to the spectator through voice or through the stage action that accompanies dialogue, such as abrupt or furtive movement, shrugging, or shaking the head. Even silence can be an effective device for creating tone and mood.

Whereas voice and movement establish tone on the stage, we have no such exacting guides while reading a play. Sometimes a playwright indicates the tone of specific lines through stage directions. In *The Sandbox*, for instance, Albee prefaces many speeches with directions such as *whining*, *vaguely*, *impatiently*, and *mocking*. These are cues to tone that help both actors in performance and readers while studying the play. When such directions are lacking, however, diction, tempo, imagery, and context all become clues to the tone of specific speeches and whole plays.

Tone may create an atmosphere or mood that dominates a play. In the opening scene of *Hamlet*, for instance, Shakespeare uses tempo, diction, and tone to build the dominant mood; it is dark, close to midnight, and Francisco carries a torch:

> BARNARDO.   Who's there?
> FRANCISCO.   Nay, answer me. Stand and unfold yourself.
> BARNARDO.   Long live the king!
> FRANCISCO.   Barnardo?
> BARNARDO.   He.

Notice the short lines, the questions, and the choppy and rapid exchange. The tone of the dialogue is anxious and questioning. The exchange thus suggests nervousness, tension, and insecurity. These, in turn, hint that all is not well in Denmark.

In dealing with tone, be careful to distinguish between the tone of an individual character and the playwright's tone that shapes our total response to the play. Specific characters may be sincere, sarcastic, joyful, or resigned, but the entire drama may reflect only one or even none of these tones. In *Trifles*, for instance, the tones of some speeches are noted as *resentful*, *apologetic*, or *mild*. The play as a whole, however, is predominantly bitter and ironic.

One of the most common methods employed by playwrights to control the tone of a play is **dramatic irony.** This type of situational (as opposed to verbal) irony may be created in any circumstance where the audience knows more than the characters in a play or when one or two characters know more than most of the others in the play. In *Trifles*, one of the characters mockingly dismisses a woman's behavior by noting that "women are used to worrying about such trifles." The line acquires vast dramatic irony as we watch the women in the play achieve understanding through careful attention to "trifles" that the men ignore. Such dramatic irony, when used consistently, creates an ironic tone for the entire work. This is exactly the situation in *Oedipus the King*, where the audience always knows more than the protagonist, and almost every line is ironic.

Symbolism and Allegory

As in fiction and poetry, dramatic **symbols** represent meaning or significance beyond the intrinsic identity of the symbol itself. Symbols in drama can be persons, settings, objects, actions, situations, or statements. Playwrights have access to both universal and private symbols. **Universal symbols**—such as crosses, flags, snakes, flowers—are generally understood by the audience or reader regardless of the context in which they appear. In Act 5 of *Hamlet*, for example, we recognize Yorick's skull as a symbol of death. **Private symbols** develop their impact only within the context of a specific play or even a particular scene. We often don't realize that such objects or actions are symbolic when they first occur; they acquire symbolic meaning through context and continued action. *The Sandbox*, for instance, opens with a "large child's sandbox with a toy pail and shovel" on stage. Initially, this object has no symbolic meaning for us. As the play goes on, however, we realize that the sandbox represents the beach, a refuse pile, the childishness we habitually associate with old age, and the grave.

When a play may be found to offer consistent and sustained symbols that refer to general human experiences, that play may be considered an **allegory,** and may be read allegorically. Keller's *Tea Party* dramatizes the preparations that two elderly women make for a young newspaperboy who avoids their party; as an allegory, the play deals with the pathos of the old, who live out their lives with lost memories and hopeless expectations. A more cheerful allegorical reading may be applied to Chekhov's *The Bear*, which allegorizes the triumph of love, desire, and life over disappointment, renunciation, and death.

Subject and Theme

Playwrights often write plays with specific ideas about the human condition in mind. The aspects of humanity a playwright explores constitute the **subject** of a play. Plays may thus be *about* love, religion, hatred, war, ambition, death, envy, or anything else that is part of the human condition. The ideas that the play dramatizes about its subject make up the play's **theme** or meaning. Thus, a play might explore the idea that love will always find a way or that marriage can be destructive, that pride always leads to disaster, or that grief can be conquered through strength and a commitment to life. Theme is the end result of all the other elements of drama; it is one of the things we are left to think about after we have read a play or seen a production.

Since theme is created and conveyed through all the other elements of drama, it is often somewhat difficult to isolate and identify. Even short plays have rather complex themes. *The Happy Journey to Trenton and Camden*, for example, explores a number of diverse themes: families need a strong central figure to hold them together; religion and optimism can help overcome the griefs of life. Full-length plays may contain even more thematic strands. *A Doll's House* deals with ideas about individual development, marriage, sexism, and society. Some plays may even explore multiple themes that seem to contradict each other, thus complicating analysis still further. *Oedipus the King*, for example, suggests that human beings cannot escape the destiny preordained for them by the gods or the fates or fortune. At the same time, however, it also explores the idea that fate is a product of personality and the choices one makes in life.

Playwrights rarely make explicitly thematic statements. Their characters, because they are involved in the action, *enact* the meaning but do not explain it to us. Two types of drama, however, are exceptions to this rule. **Didactic plays** are designed primarily to teach a specific lesson; **propaganda plays** are written primarily to convince and persuade. In both cases, the theme may be repeatedly and blatantly stated by the characters. In most plays, however, meaning is elusive and unspoken. As a result, we must pay careful attention to the words, actions, and attitudes of the characters in order to understand themes. Frequently, the protagonist and his or her conflicts embody much of the meaning. Hamlet's attempts to prove that his uncle is guilty of murder, and his extended soliloquies of self-accusation bring forward one of the central ideas in the play: that revenge in a Christian society is perhaps questionable and irreligious, and definitely extra-legal or illegal. Similarly, Nora's conflicts with Krogstad and with Helmar in *A Doll's House* dramatize the stereotyped roles of women in society and the failure of communication in marriage.

HOW TO READ A PLAY

Reading or studying a play is a quite different process from reading prose fiction or watching a performance in the theater. Poems, novels, and short stories are complete in and of themselves; they embody the full impact of their meaning and experience. Plays, in contrast, can only suggest their full impact; when we read them, we are missing the elements of live performance. Nevertheless, we enjoy the power of the language and feel the hopes and fears of the characters; we sympathize with the heroine and loathe the villain. We learn about ourselves and about humanity by watching the ways characters deal with the great and small pleasures and pains of living. In short, we experience and enjoy plays through reading exactly the way we do other types of literature.

Reading a play, as opposed to watching a performance, carries both advantages and disadvantages. The major disadvantage is that you lack the immediacy of live theater; you do not hear the whispers of the murderer and the ranting of the madman or see the strutting of the soldier and the furtive glances of the conspirators. You do not have the splendor of the ballroom or the shock of the empty stage, the spotlight that rivets the audience's attention on a single defiant gesture, the blare of trumpets, or the pathos of the beggar's rags. All these may be described in stage directions, but the words only signify the things themselves.

The major advantages to reading are time and freedom; you have the time to consider each element and event in the play at length and the freedom to stage the play in your imagination. In the theater, the action rushes by at whatever pace the director chooses; there is no opportunity to turn back to an interesting scene or to reconsider a confusing speech. In addition, a performance always represents someone else's interpretation of a play; the director or the actors have already made choices that cut off some avenues of exploration and emphasize others. Reading a play lets you avoid these problems. You read at whatever tempo you choose; you turn back and reread a particular speech or scene until you are comfortable with your own reactions to it. Also you have the freedom to explore whatever implications or ideas strike you as interesting; no one else has limited the scope of your considerations.

Try to use the advantages of reading and study to compensate for the disadvantages. You have the time and freedom to read carefully, reflect deeply, and follow your thoughts wherever they might lead. Stage the play as fully as you can in the theater of your mind. Become the director, the set designer, the lighting technician, the costume designer, and all the actors. Build whatever mental sets you like, dress your actors as you see fit, and move the characters across the stage of your mind as you would have them move. Rely on your experiences in watching theatrical productions, movies, and television to enhance your reading.

Plays cannot be experienced passively; they demand careful attention from audiences and readers alike. You should develop the habit of reading plays (and most other literature) several times. Each rereading will usually reveal new aspects of the work and new directions for exploration. You can also reread specific parts of a play that are initially unclear or confusing.

Finally, keep in mind that all drama is based, at least in part, on the dramatic (stage) conventions of its own age and theatrical environment. A **dramatic convention** is a traditional or customary method of presentation (often unrealistic) that is accepted by audiences or readers and allows a playwright to limit and simplify material. Most dramatic conventions reflect either the physical conditions of the theater or the prejudices of society in a given age. Many of these conventions are explained in the introductions to specific plays, which provide information about drama in a given period. The chorus in Greek tragedy, for instance, is made up of fifteen men who chant their speeches in unison. While this is not realistic, it is a conventional device of Greek tragedy that allows the playwright to express the reactions of the common people. The soliloquy is a similarly unrealistic convention of the Elizabethan stage; it permits the characters to reveal thoughts and feelings directly to the audience. Such a convention may strike you as an odd disruption of the action, but it reflects both the intimacy of the Elizabethan theaters and the audience's willingness to accept such a break in the flow of the play. Ultimately, we must be willing to accept dramatic conventions on their own terms, just as we do the conventions of film and television.

BETTY KELLER, *TEA PARTY*

A native of British Columbia, Betty Keller brought a wide variety of experiences to her work for the theater, including such unlikely jobs as adjusting insurance claims, farming, assisting a photographer, and serving as a prison matron. She served as a director in many theatrical workshops, and for four years was a principal director with Playhouse Holiday in Vancouver. She taught drama and theater at the Windsor Secondary School in North Vancouver until 1974, the year she published the collection of short plays and sketches from which *Tea Party* is selected. More recently she has published a biography of the Canadian naturalist and writer Ernest Thompson Seton.

Brief as *Tea Party* is, it illustrates the power of drama to depict character and situation, and to convey emotion. The main characters are two lonely elderly sisters who have outlived their friends and relatives and have no one except the people who occasionally come to their house to perform various services, such as delivering the paper and reading the meters. The sketch presents their plight deftly and succinctly, touching with great tenderness on the pathos of their loneliness.

Tea Party is too short to present difficult choices for the characters, and hence they hardly get the opportunity to go through the responses and changes that are found in full-length plays. Both Alma and Hester are individualized, however, as they carry on a minor controversy about names and dates from their long vanished past. Beyond this, in Alma's last speech, which ends the sketch, one might find a hint of the awareness and recognition that we expect of round, developed dramatic characters. Even though the paperboy is not a speaking part, his unkindness to the sisters is clearly shown, and in this way Keller dramatizes the poignant situation of persons whom life has passed by. It is difficult to find a play that conveys so much of life and feeling in so short a span of time and action.

BETTY KELLER   (b. 1935?)

Tea Party   1974

CHARACTERS

Alma Evans: *seventy-five years old, small and spare framed. Her clothing is simple but not outdated, her grey hair cut short and neat. She walks with the aid of a cane, although she would not be classed as a cripple.*

Hester Evans: *seventy-nine years old. There is little to distinguish her physically from her sister, except perhaps a face a little more pinched and pain-worn. She sits in a wheelchair; but although her legs may be crippled, her mind certainly is not.*

The Boy: *in his early teens, seen only fleetingly.*

SCENE.   *The sitting room of the Evans sisters' home. The door to the street is on the rear wall Upstage Left,° a large window faces the street Upstage Center. On the right wall is the door to the kitchen; on the left, a door to the remainder of the house. Downstage Left is an easy chair, Upstage Right a sofa, Downstage Right a tea trolley. The room is crowded with the knickknacks gathered by its inhabitants in three-quarters of a century of living.*

[*At rise,* ALMA *is positioning* HESTER'S *wheelchair Upstage Left.* ALMA'S *cane is on* HESTER'S *lap.*]

HESTER.   That's it.

[ALMA *takes her cane from* HESTER. *They both survey the room.*]

ALMA.   I think I'll sit on the sofa . . . at the far end.

HESTER.   Yes. That will be cosy. Then he can sit on this end between us.

[ALMA *sits on the Downstage Right end of the sofa. They both study the effect.*]

ALMA: But then he's too close to the door, Hester!

[HESTER *nods, absorbed in the problem.*]

ALMA.   [*moving to the Upstage Left end of sofa.*] Then I'd better sit here.   5

HESTER.   But now he's too far away from me, Alma.

[ALMA *stands; both of them study the room again.*]

ALMA.   But if I push the tea trolley in front of you, he'll have to come to you, won't he?

HESTER.   Oh, all right, Alma. You're sure it's today?

ALMA.   [*pushing the tea trolley laden with cups and napkins, etc. to* HESTER.] The first Thursday of the month.

HESTER.   You haven't forgotten the chocolate biscuits?°   10

Upstage Left: To visualize stage locations, assume that the stage directions are described from the viewpoint of an actor facing the audience. Thus "Right" is actually to the left of the audience, and "Left" is right. "Downstage" refers to the front of the stage, while "Upstage" is the back. The terms *down* and *up* were established at a time when stages were tilted toward the audience, so that spectators at floor level could have as complete a view as possible of the entire stage.   10 *chocolate biscuits*: chocolate cookies.

ALMA.   No dear, they're on the plate. I'll bring them in with the tea. [*Goes to the window, peering up the street to the Right.*]

HESTER.   And cocoa?

ALMA.   I remembered.

HESTER.   You didn't remember for Charlie's visit.

ALMA.   Charlie drinks tea, Hester. I didn't make cocoa for him because he   15
drinks tea.

HESTER.   Oh. He didn't stay last time anyway.

ALMA.   It was a busy day. . . .

HESTER.   Rushing in and out like that. I was going to tell him about father and the *Bainbridge* . . . and he didn't stay.

ALMA.   What about the *Bainbridge?*

HESTER.   Her maiden voyage out of Liverpool . . . when father was gone   20
three months and we thought he'd gone down with her.

ALMA.   That wasn't the *Bainbridge.*

HESTER.   Yes, it was. It was the *Bainbridge.* I remember standing on the dock in the snow when she finally came in. That was the year I'd begun first form, and I could spell out the letters on her side.

ALMA.   It was her sister ship, the *Heddingham.*

HESTER.   The *Bainbridge.* You were too young to remember. Let's see, the year was . . .

ALMA.   Mother often told the story. It was the *Heddingham* and her engine   25
broke down off Cape Wrath beyond the Hebrides.

HESTER.   It was 1902 and you were just four years old.

ALMA.   The *Heddingham,* and she limped into port on January the fifth.

HESTER.   January the fourth just after nine in the morning, and we stood in the snow and watched the *Bainbridge* nudge the pier, and I cried and the tears froze on my cheeks.

ALMA.   The *Heddingham.*

HESTER.   Alma, mother didn't cry, you know. I don't think she ever cried.   30
My memory of names and places is sharp so that I don't confuse them as some others I could mention, but sometimes I can't remember things like how people reacted. But I remember that day. There were tears frozen on my cheeks but mother didn't cry.

ALMA.   [*nodding.*] She said he didn't offer a word of explanation. Just marched home beside her.

HESTER.   [*smiling.*] He never did say much. . . . Is he coming yet?

ALMA.   No, can't be much longer though. Almost half past four.

HESTER.   Perhaps you'd better bring in the tea. Then it will seem natural.

ALMA.   Yes dear, I know. [*Exits out door Upstage Right.*) Everything's ready.   35

HESTER.   What will you talk about?

ALMA.   [*re-entering with the teapot*] I thought perhaps . . . [*carefully putting down the teapot.*] . . . perhaps brother George!

HESTER.   And the torpedo? No, Alma, he's not old enough for that story!

ALMA.   He's old enough to know about courage. I thought I'd show him the medal, too. [*She goes to the window, peers both ways worriedly, then carries on towards the kitchen.*]

HESTER.   Not yet? He's late to-night. You're sure it's today?   40

ALMA.   He'll come. It's the first Thursday. [*Exit.*]

HESTER.   You have his money?

ALMA.   [*returning with the plate of biscuits.*) I've got a twenty dollar bill, Hester.

HESTER.   Alma!

ALMA.   Well, we haven't used that one on him. It was Dennis, the last one,   45
who always had change. We could get two visits this way, Hester.

HESTER.   Maybe Dennis warned him to carry change for a twenty.

ALMA.   It seemed worth a try. [*Goes to the window again.*] Are you going to
tell him about the *Heddingham*?

HESTER.   The *Bainbridge*. Maybe . . . or maybe I'll tell him about the day
the Great War ended. Remember, Alma, all the noise, the paper streamers . . .

ALMA.   And father sitting silent in his chair.

HESTER.   It wasn't the same for him with George gone. Is he coming yet?   50

ALMA.   No dear, maybe he's stopped to talk somewhere. [*looking to the right.*]
. . . No . . . no, there he is, on the Davis' porch now!

HESTER.   I'll pour then. You get the cocoa, Alma.

ALMA.   [*going out.*] It's all ready, I just have to add hot water.

HESTER.   Don't forget the marshmallows!

ALMA.   [*reappearing*) Oh, Hester, what if he comes in and just sits down   55
closest to the door? He'll never stay!

HESTER.   You'll have to prod him along. For goodness sakes, Alma, get his
cocoa!

[*ALMA disappears.*]

HESTER.   He must be nearly here. He doesn't go to the Leschynskis, and
the Blackburns don't get home till after six.

ALMA.   [*returning with the cocoa.*] Here we are! Just in . . .

[*The BOY passes the window. There is a slapping sound as the newspaper lands on the
porch.*]

[*ALMA and HESTER look at the door and wait, hoping to hear a knock, but they both know
the truth. Finally, ALMA goes to the door, opens it and looks down at the newspaper.*]

ALMA.   He's gone on by.

HESTER.   You must have had the day wrong.   60

ALMA.   No, he collected at the Davis'.

HESTER.   [*after a long pause.*] He couldn't have forgotten us.

ALMA.   [*still holding the cocoa, she turns from the door.*] He's collecting at the
Kerighan's now. [*She closes the door and stands forlornly.*]

HESTER.   Well, don't stand there with that cocoa! You look silly. [*ALMA brings
the cocoa to the tea trolley.*] Here's your tea. [*ALMA takes the cup, sits on the Upstage
Left end of the sofa. There is a long silence.*]

HESTER.   I think I'll save that story for the meter man.   65

ALMA.   The *Heddingham*?

HESTER: The *Bainbridge*.

ALMA.   [*after a pause.*] They don't read the meters for two more weeks.

SLOW BLACKOUT

QUESTIONS

1. What is the major conflict in this play? The minor conflict?
2. Why do the two sisters discuss their seating arrangements in preparation for the visit of the paperboy to collect money for papers? How do we learn that they have made these arrangements a number of times before?
3. What does Alma's planned use of the twenty dollar bill show about her character? What does the discussion about the bill and the previous paperboy, together with the discussion about the present paperboy, indicate about the women's self-awareness of what they are doing to have company for tea?
4. For your understanding of the characters of the two sisters, what is achieved by their controversy about the names *Bainbridge* and *Heddingham*? What does Hester's correction of Alma's date indicate about her character? Even if we assume that Hester is right on these details, why does it not follow that Alma is growing forgetful or senile?
5. What do you conclude about the character of the paperboy, and also about his previous experiences at the Evans' house, because of his delivering the paper without collecting?

GENERAL QUESTIONS

1. Consider the description of the setting of *Tea Party*. How does this description aid your visualization of the action, of the tasks each of the women performs in their household? Based on the setting, what conclusions can you draw about the relationship of objects and spatial arrangements to the action and development of a play?
2. Consider the women particularly with regard to their age. In the light of their health and their isolation, how does *Tea Party* present the circumstances of the aged? How can the play be construed as a sociological/political argument, with the elderly as the focus?

ANTON CHEKHOV, *THE BEAR*

Chekhov was born in Southern Russia in 1860, the son of a merchant and grandson of a serf. He entered medical school in Moscow in 1879, graduating in 1884. While at school, he helped support the family by writing scores of stories, jokes, and other potboilers under a variety of pen names, one of which was "The Doctor Without Patients." *The Bear* belongs to the end of this early period, ten years before Chekhov's association with the Moscow Arts Theatre at the end of the century (see p. 1434).

Chekhov minimized this play, referring to it as a "joke" and as a "vaudeville." Nevertheless, this little one-act piece became an immediate hit and was widely appreciated. Three months after its first performance in 1888 he was so pleased with its earnings that he likened *The Bear* to a "milk cow" because it supplied him with money day in and day out.

The Bear is a farce, a dramatic form designed preeminently to make people laugh, and it therefore contains extravagant language and boisterous and sudden action. But there is also an underlying seriousness that sustains the humor. Both Smirnov and Mrs. Popov have been failures; they could easily sink into lives of depression and futility, and both are on a very fine wire as the play begins. Chekhov makes clear that Mrs. Popov is filled with resentment at her unfaithful late husband, and also that she is chafing under her self-imposed resolution to lead a life of mourning and self-denial in his memory. Smirnov is having difficulty with creditors, and admits that his relationships with the many women he has known have ended unhappily. He is therefore both cynical and angry.

The climax of the play is the improbable and preposterous challenge that Smirnov offers to Mrs. Popov, resolved by the equally sudden and preposterous outcome. Though improbable, the actions are not impossible because they are a manifestation of the true internal needs of the major participants. Even Chekhov's friend Tolstoy, who criticized some of Chekhov's late plays, found *The Bear* irresistible. He laughed heartily at the farcical and romantic outcome, thereby joining the laughter of the generations since his time.

ANTON CHEKHOV   (1860–1904)

The Bear: A Joke in One Act   1900

CAST OF CHARACTERS

> Mrs. Popov. *A widow of seven months, Mrs. Popov is small and pretty, with dimples. She is a landowner. At the start of the play, she is pining away in memory of her dead husband.*
>
> Grigory Stepanovich Smirnov. *Easily angered and loud, Smirnov is older. He is a landowner, too, and a gentleman farmer of some substance.*
>
> Luka. *Luka is Mrs. Popov's footman (a servant whose main tasks were to wait table and attend the carriages, in addition to general duties). He is old enough to feel secure in telling Mrs. Popov what he thinks.*
>
> Gardener, Coachman, Workmen, *who enter at the end.*

The drawing room of MRS. POPOV's *country home.*

[MRS. POPOV, *in deep mourning, does not remove her eyes from a photograph.*]

LUKA.   It isn't right, madam . . . you're only destroying yourself. . . . The chambermaid and the cook have gone off berry picking; every living being is rejoicing; even the cat knows how to be content, walking around the yard catching birds, and you sit in your room all day as if it were a convent, and you don't take pleasure in anything. Yes, really! Almost a year has passed since you've gone out of the house!

MRS. POPOV.   And I shall never go out. . . . What for? My life is already ended. *He* lies in his grave; I have buried myself in these four walls . . . we are both dead.

LUKA.   There you go again! Your husband is dead, that's as it was meant to be, it's the will of God, may he rest in peace. . . . You've done your mourning and that will do. You can't go on weeping and mourning forever. My wife died when her time came, too. . . . Well? I grieved, I wept for a month, and that was enough for her; the old lady wasn't worth a second more. [*Sighs.*] You've forgotten all your neighbors. You don't go anywhere or accept any calls. We live, so to speak, like spiders. We never see the light. The mice have eaten my uniform. It isn't as if there weren't any nice neighbors—the district is full of them . . . there's a regiment stationed at Riblov, such officers—they're like candy—you'll never get your fill of them! And in the barracks, never a Friday goes by without a dance; and, if you please, the military band plays music every day. . . . Yes, madam, my dear lady: you're young, beautiful, in the full bloom of youth—if only you took a little pleasure in life . . . beauty doesn't last forever, you know! In ten years' time, you'll be wanting to wave your fanny in front of the officers—and it will be too late.

MRS. POPOV.   [*determined.*] I must ask you never to talk to me like that! You know that when Mr. Popov died, life lost all its salt for me. It may seem to you that I am alive, but that's only conjecture! I vowed to wear mourning to my grave and not to see the light of day. . . . Do you hear me? May his departed spirit see how much I love him. . . . Yes, I know, it's no mystery to you that he was often mean to me, cruel . . . and even unfaithful, but I shall remain true to the grave and show him I know how to love. There, beyond the grave, he will see me as I was before his death. . . .

LUKA.   Instead of talking like that, you should be taking a walk in the garden or have Toby or Giant harnessed and go visit some of the neighbors . . . 5

MRS. POPOV.   Ai! [*She weeps.*]

LUKA.   Madam! Dear lady! What's the matter with you! Christ be with you!

MRS. POPOV.   Oh, how he loved Toby! He always used to ride on him to visit the Korchagins or the Vlasovs. How wonderfully he rode! How graceful he was when he pulled at the reins with all his strength! Do you remember? Toby, Toby! Tell them to give him an extra bag of oats today.

LUKA.   Yes, madam.

[*Sound of loud ringing.*]

MRS. POPOV.   [*shudders.*] Who's that? Tell them I'm not at home! 10

LUKA.   Of course, madam. [*He exits.*]

MRS. POPOV.   [*alone. Looks at the photograph.*] You will see, Nicholas, how much I can love and forgive . . . my love will die only when I do, when my poor heart stops beating. [*Laughing through her tears.*] Have you no shame? I'm a good girl, a virtuous little wife. I've locked myself in and I'll be true to you to the grave, and you . . . aren't you ashamed, you chubby cheeks? You deceived me, you made scenes, for weeks on end you left me alone . . .

LUKA.   [*enters, alarmed.*] Madam, somebody is asking for you. He wants to see you. . . .

MRS. POPOV.   But didn't you tell them that since the death of my husband, I don't see anybody?

LUKA. I did, but he didn't want to listen; he spoke about some very important   15
business.

MRS. POPOV. I am *not at home!*

LUKA. That's what I told him . . . but . . . the devil . . . he cursed and
pushed past me right into the room . . . he's in the dining room right now.

MRS. POPOV. [*losing her temper.*] Very well, let him come in . . . such manners!
[*LUKA goes out.*] How difficult these people are! What does he want from me?
Why should he disturb my peace? [*Sighs.*] But it's obvious I'll have to go live in a
convent. . . . [*Thoughtfully.*] Yes, a convent. . . .

SMIRNOV. [*to LUKA.*] You idiot, you talk too much. . . . Ass! [*Sees MRS. POPOV
and changes to dignified speech.*] Madam, may I introduce myself: retired lieutenant
of the artillery and landowner, Grigory Stepanovich Smirnov! I feel the necessity
of troubling you about a highly important matter. . . .

MRS. POPOV. [*refusing her hand.*] What do you want?   20

SMIRNOV. Your late husband, who I had the pleasure of knowing, has
remained in my debt for two twelve-hundred-ruble notes. Since I must pay the
interest at the agricultural bank tomorrow, I have come to ask you, madam, to
pay me the money today.

MRS. POPOV. One thousand two hundred. . . . And why was my husband
in debt to you?

SMIRNOV. He used to buy oats from me.

MRS. POPOV. [*sighing, to LUKA.*] So, Luka, don't you forget to tell them to
give Toby an extra bag of oats.

[*LUKA goes out.*]

[*To SMIRNOV.*] If Nikolai, my husband, was in debt to you, then it goes without
saying that I'll pay; but please excuse me today. I haven't any spare cash. The
day after tomorrow, my steward will be back from town and I will give him
instructions to pay you what is owed; until then I cannot comply with your wishes.
. . . Besides, today is the anniversary—exactly seven months ago my husband
died, and I'm in such a mood that I'm not quite disposed to occupy myself with
money matters.

SMIRNOV. And I'm in such a mood that if I don't pay the interest tomorrow,   25
I'll be owing so much that my troubles will drown me. They'll take away my estate!

MRS. POPOV. You'll receive your money the day after tomorrow.

SMIRNOV. I don't want the money the day after tomorrow. I want it today.

MRS. POPOV. You must excuse me. I can't pay you today.

SMIRNOV. And I can't wait until after tomorrow.

MRS. POPOV. What can I do, if I don't have it now?   30

SMIRNOV. You mean to say you can't pay?

MRS. POPOV. I can't pay. . . .

SMIRNOV. Hm! Is that your last word?

MRS. POPOV. That is my last word.

SMIRNOV. Positively the last?   35

MRS. POPOV. Positively.

SMIRNOV. Thank you very much. We'll make a note of that. [*Shrugs his
shoulders.*] And people want me to be calm and collected! Just now, on the way
here, I met a tax officer and he asked me: why are you always so angry, Grigory
Stepanovich? Goodness' sake, how can I be anything but angry? I need money

desperately . . . I rode out yesterday early in the morning, at daybreak, and went to see all my debtors; and if only one of them had paid his debt . . . I was dog-tired, spent the night God knows where—a Jewish tavern beside a barrel of vodka. . . . Finally I got here, fifty miles from home, hoping to be paid, and you treat me to a "mood." How can I help being angry?

MRS. POPOV. It seems to me that I clearly said: My steward will return from the country and then you will be paid.

SMIRNOV. I didn't come to your steward, but to you! What the hell, if you'll pardon the expression, would I do with your steward?

Mrs. Popov. Excuse me, my dear sir, I am not accustomed to such profane expressions nor to such a tone. I'm not listening to you any more. [*Goes out quickly.*] 40

SMIRNOV. [*alone.*] Well, how do you like that? "A mood." . . . "Husband died seven months ago"! Must I pay the interest or mustn't I? I ask you: Must I pay, or must I not? So, your husband's dead, and you're in a mood and all that finicky stuff . . . and your steward's away somewhere; may he drop dead. What do you want me to do? Do you think I can fly away from my creditors in a balloon or something? Or should I run and bash my head against the wall? I go to Gruzdev—and he's not at home; Yaroshevich is hiding, with Kuritsin it's a quarrel to the death and I almost throw him out the window; Mazutov has diarrhea, and this one is in a "mood." Not one of these swine wants to pay me! And all because I'm too nice to them. I'm a sniveling idiot, I'm spineless, I'm an old lady! I'm too delicate with them! So, just you wait! You'll find out what I'm like! I won't let you play around with me, you devils! I'll stay and stick it out until she pays. Rrr! . . . How furious I am today, how furious! I'm shaking inside from rage and I can hardly catch my breath. . . . Damn it! My God, I even feel sick! [*He shouts.*] Hey, you!

LUKA. [*enters.*] What do you want?

SMIRNOV. Give me some beer or some water! [*LUKA exits.*] What logic is there in this! A man needs money desperately, it's like a noose around his neck—and she won't pay because, you see, she's not disposed to occupy herself with money matters! . . . That's the logic of a woman! That's why I never did like and do not like to talk to women. I'd rather sit on a keg of gunpowder than talk to a woman. Brr! . . . I even have goose pimples, this broad has put me in such a rage! All I have to do is see one of those spoiled bitches from a distance, and I get so angry it gives me a cramp in the leg. I just want to shout for help.

LUKA. [*entering with water.*] Madam is sick and won't see anyone.

SMIRNOV. Get out! [*LUKA goes.*] Sick and won't see anyone! No need to see 45 me . . . I'll stay and sit here until you give me the money. You can stay sick for a week, and I'll stay for a week . . . if you're sick for a year, I'll stay a year. . . . I'll get my own back, dear lady! You can't impress me with your widow's weeds and your dimpled cheeks . . . we know all about those dimples! [*Shouts through the window.*] Semyon, unharness the horses! We're not going away quite yet! I'm staying here! Tell them in the stable to give the horses some oats! You brute, you let the horse on the left side get all tangled up in the reins again! [*Teasing.*] "Never mind" . . . I'll give you a never mind! [*Goes away from the window.*] Shit! The heat is unbearable and nobody pays up. I slept badly last night and on top of everything else this broad in mourning is "in a mood" . . . my head aches . . . [*Drinks, and grimaces.*] Shit! This is water! What I need is a drink! [*Shouts.*] Hey, you!

LUKA. [*enters.*] What is it?

SMIRNOV.   Give me a glass of vodka. [*LUKA goes out.*] Oaf! [*Sits down and examines himself.*] Nobody would say I was looking well! Dusty all over, boots dirty, unwashed, unkept, straw on my waistcoat. . . . The dear lady probably took me for a robber. [*Yawns.*] It's not very polite to present myself in a drawing room looking like this; oh well, who cares? . . . I'm not here as a visitor but as a creditor, and there's no official costume for creditors. . . .

LUKA.   [*enters with vodka.*] You're taking liberties, my good man. . . .

SMIRNOV.   [*angrily.*] What?

LUKA.   I . . . nothing . . . I only . . .   50

SMIRNOV.   Who are you talking to? Shut up!

LUKA.   [*aside.*] The devil sent this leech. An ill wind brought him. . . . [*LUKA goes out.*]

SMIRNOV.   Oh how furious I am! I'm so mad I could crush the whole world into a powder! I even feel faint! [*Shouts.*] Hey, you!

MRS. POPOV [*enters, eyes downcast*].   My dear sir, in my solitude, I have long ago grown unaccustomed to the masculine voice and I cannot bear shouting. I must request you not to disturb my peace and quiet!

SMIRNOV.   Pay me my money and I'll go.   55

MRS. POPOV.   I told you in plain language: I haven't any spare cash now; wait until the day after tomorrow.

SMIRNOV.   And I also told you respectfully, in plain language: I don't need the money the day after tomorrow, but today. If you don't pay me today, then tomorrow I'll have to hang myself.

MRS. POPOV.   But what can I do if I don't have the money? You're so strange!

SMIRNOV.   Then you won't pay me now? No?

MRS. POPOV.   I can't. . . .   60

SMIRNOV.   In that case, I can stay here and wait until you pay. . . . [*Sits down.*] You'll pay the day after tomorrow? Excellent! In that case I'll stay here until the day after tomorrow. I'll sit here all that time . . . [*Jumps up.*] I ask you: Have I got to pay the interest tomorrow, or not? Or do you think I'm joking?

MRS. POPOV.   My dear sir, I ask you not to shout! This isn't a stable!

SMIRNOV.   I wasn't asking you about a stable but about this: Do I have to pay the interest tomorrow or not?

MRS. POPOV.   You don't know how to behave in the company of a lady!

SMIRNOV.   No, I don't know how to behave in the company of a lady!   65

MRS. POPOV.   No, you don't! You are an ill-bred, rude man! Respectable people don't talk to a woman like that!

SMIRNOV.   Ach, it's astonishing! How would you like me to talk to you? In French, perhaps? [*Lisps in anger.*] *Madame, je vous prie*° . . . how happy I am that you're not paying me the money. . . . Ah, pardon, I've made you uneasy! Such lovely weather we're having today! And you look so becoming in your mourning dress. [*Bows and scrapes.*]

MRS. POPOV.   That's rude and not very clever!

SMIRNOV.   [*teasing.*] Rude and not very clever! I don't know how to behave in the company of ladies. Madam, in my time I've seen far more women than you've seen sparrows. Three times I've fought duels over women; I've jilted twelve women, nine have jilted me! Yes! There was a time when I played the fool; I

Madame, je vous prie: I beg you, Madam.

became sentimental over women, used honeyed words, fawned on them, bowed and scraped. . . . I loved, suffered, sighed at the moon; I became limp, melted, shivered . . . I loved passionately, madly, every which way, devil take me, I chattered away like a magpie about the emancipation of women, ran through half my fortune as a result of my tender feelings; but now, if you will excuse me, I'm on to your ways! I've had enough! Dark eyes, passionate eyes, ruby lips, dimpled cheeks; the moon, whispers, bated breath—for all that I wouldn't give a good goddamn. Present company excepted, of course, but all women, young and old alike, are affected clowns, gossips, hateful, consummate liars to the marrow of their bones, vain, trivial, ruthless, outrageously illogical, and as far as this is concerned [*taps on his forehead.*], well, excuse my frankness, any sparrow could give pointers to a philosopher in petticoats! Look at one of those romantic creatures: muslin, ethereal demigoddess, a thousand raptures, and you look into her soul—a common crocodile! [*Grips the back of a chair; the chair cracks and breaks.*] But the most revolting part of it all is that this crocodile imagines that she has, above everything, her own privilege, a monopoly on tender feelings. The hell with it—you can hang me upside down by that nail if a woman is capable of loving anything besides a lapdog. All she can do when she's in love is slobber! While the man suffers and sacrifices, all her love is expressed in playing with her skirt and trying to lead him around firmly by the nose. You have the misfortune of being a woman, you know yourself what the nature of a woman is like. Tell me honestly; Have you ever in your life seen a woman who is sincere, faithful, and constant? You never have! Only old and ugly ladies are faithful and constant! You're more liable to meet a horned cat or a white woodcock than a faithful woman!

MRS. POPOV.   Pardon me, but in your opinion, who is faithful and constant   70
in love? The man?

SMIRNOV.   Yes, the man!

MRS. POPOV.   The man! [*Malicious laugh.*] Men are faithful and constant in love! That's news! [*Heatedly.*] What right have you to say that? Men are faithful and constant! For that matter, as far as I know, of all the men I have known and now know, my late husband was the best. . . . I loved him passionately, with all my being, as only a young intellectual woman can love; I gave him my youth, my happiness, my life, my fortune; he was my life's breath; I worshipped him as if I were a heathen, and . . . and, what good did it do—this best of men himself deceived me shamelessly at every step of the way. After his death, I found his desk full of love letters; and when he was alive—it's terrible to remember—he used to leave me alone for weeks at a time, and before my eyes he flirted with other women and deceived me. He squandered my money, made a mockery of my feelings . . . and, in spite of all that, I loved him and was true to him . . . and besides, now that he is dead, I am still faithful and constant. I have shut myself up in these four walls forever and I won't remove these widow's weeds until my dying day. . . .

SMIRNOV.   [*laughs contemptuously.*] Widow's weeds! . . . I don't know what you take me for! As if I didn't know why you wear that black outfit and bury yourself in these four walls! Well, well! It's no secret, so romantic! When some fool of a poet passes by this country house, he'll look up at your window and think: "Here lives the mysterious Tamara, who, for the love of her husband, buried herself in these four walls." We know these tricks!

MRS. POPOV.   [*flaring.*] What? How dare you say that to me?

SMIRNOV.   You may have buried yourself alive, but you haven't forgotten   75
to powder yourself!

MRS. POPOV.   How dare you use such expressions with me?

SMIRNOV.   Please don't shout. I'm not your steward! You must allow me to
call a spade a spade. I'm not a woman and I'm used to saying what's on my
mind! Don't you shout at me!

MRS. POPOV.   I'm not shouting, you are! Please leave me in peace!

SMIRNOV.   Pay me my money and I'll go.

MRS. POPOV.   I won't give you any money!   80

SMIRNOV.   Yes, you will.

MRS. POPOV.   To spite you, I won't pay you anything. You can leave me in
peace!

SMIRNOV.   I don't have the pleasure of being either your husband or your
fiancé, so please don't make scenes! [*Sits down.*] I don't like it.

MRS. POPOV.   [*choking with rage.*] You're sitting down?

SMIRNOV.   Yes, I am.   85

MRS. POPOV.   I ask you to get out!

SMIRNOV.   Give me my money . . . [*Aside.*] Oh, I'm so furious! Furious!

MRS. POPOV.   I don't want to talk to impudent people! Get out of here!
[*Pause.*] You're not going? No?

SMIRNOV.   No.

MRS. POPOV.   No?   90

SMIRNOV.   No!

MRS. POPOV.   We'll see about that. [*Rings.*].

[*LUKA enters.*]

Luka, show the gentleman out!

LUKA.   [*goes up to SMIRNOV.*] Sir, will you please leave, as you have been
asked. You mustn't . . .

SMIRNOV.   [*jumping up.*] Shut up! Who do you think you're talking to? I'll   95
make mincemeat out of you!

LUKA.   [*his hand to his heart.*] Oh my God! Saints above! [*Falls into chair.*]
Oh, I feel ill! I feel ill! I can't catch my breath!

MRS. POPOV.   Where's Dasha? Dasha! [*She shouts.*] Dasha! Pelagea! Dasha!
[*She rings.*]

LUKA.   Oh! They've all gone berry picking . . . there's nobody at home
. . . I'm ill! Water!

MRS. POPOV.   Will you please get out!

SMIRNOV.   Will you please be more polite?   100

MRS. POPOV.   [*clenches her fist and stamps her feet.*] You're nothing but a crude
bear! A brute! A monster!

SMIRNOV.   What? What did you say?

MRS. POPOV.   I said that you were a bear, a monster!

SMIRNOV.   [*advancing toward her.*] Excuse me, but what right do you have to
insult me?

MRS. POPOV.   Yes, I am insulting you . . . so what? Do you think I'm afraid   105
of you?

SMIRNOV.   And do you think just because you're one of those romantic creations, that you have the right to insult me with impunity? Yes? I challenge you!

LUKA. Lord in Heaven! Saints above! . . . Water!

SMIRNOV. Pistols!

MRS. POPOV. Do you think just because you have big fists and you can bellow like a bull, that I'm afraid of you? You're such a bully!

SMIRNOV. I challenge you! I'm not going to let anybody insult me, and I 110 don't care if you are a woman, a delicate creature!

MRS. POPOV. [*trying to get a word in edgewise.*] Bear! Bear! Bear!

SMIRNOV. It's about time we got rid of the prejudice that only men must pay for their insults! Devil take it, if women want to be equal, they should behave as equals! Let's fight!

MRS. POPOV. You want to fight! By all means!

SMIRNOV. This minute!

MRS. POPOV. This minute! My husband had some pistols . . . I'll go and 115 get them right away. [*Goes out hurriedly and then returns.*] What pleasure I'll have putting a bullet through that thick head of yours! The hell with you! [*She goes out.*]

SMIRNOV. I'll shoot her down like a chicken! I'm not a little boy or a sentimental puppy. I don't care if she is delicate and fragile.

LUKA. Kind sir! Holy father! [*Kneels.*] Have pity on a poor old man and go away from here! You've frightened her to death and now you're going to shoot her?

SMIRNOV. [*not listening to him.*] If she fights, then it means she believes in equality of rights and emancipation of women. Here the sexes are equal! I'll shoot her like a chicken! But what a woman! [*Imitates her.*] "The hell with you! . . . I'll put a bullet through that thick head of yours! . . ." What a woman! How she blushed, her eyes shone . . . she accepted my challenge! To tell the truth, it was the first time in my life I've seen a woman like that. . . .

LUKA. Dear sir, please go away! I'll pray to God on your behalf as long as I live!

SMIRNOV. That's a woman for you! A woman like that I can understand! 120 A real woman! Not a sour-faced nincompoop but fiery, gunpowder! Fireworks! I'm even sorry to have to kill her!

LUKA. [*weeps.*] Dear sir . . . go away!

SMIRNOV. I positively like her! Positively! Even though she has dimpled cheeks, I like her! I'm almost ready to forget about the debt. . . . My fury has diminished. Wonderful woman!

MRS. POPOV. [*enters with pistols.*] Here they are, the pistols. Before we fight, you must show me how to fire. . . . I've never had a pistol in my hands before . . .

LUKA. Oh dear Lord, for pity's sake. . . . I'll go and find the gardener and the coachman. . . . What did we do to deserve such trouble? [*Exit.*]

SMIRNOV. [*examining the pistols.*] You see, there are several sorts of pistols 125 . . . there are special dueling pistols, the Mortimer with primers. Then there are Smith and Wesson revolvers, triple action with extractors . . . excellent pistols! . . . they cost a minimum of ninety rubles a pair. . . . You must hold the revolver like this . . . [*Aside.*] What eyes, what eyes! A woman to set you on fire!

MRS. POPOV. Like this?

SMIRNOV. Yes, like this . . . then you cock the pistol . . . take aim . . . put your head back a little . . . stretch your arm out all the way . . . that's right . . . then with this finger press on this little piece of goods . . . and that's all there is to do . . . but the most important thing is not to get excited and aim without hurrying . . . try to keep your arm from shaking.

MRS. POPOV. Good . . . it's not comfortable to shoot indoors. Let's go into the garden.

SMIRNOV. Let's go. But I'm giving you advance notice that I'm going to fire into the air.

MRS. POPOV. That's the last straw! Why?   130

SMIRNOV. Why? . . . Why . . . because it's my business, that's why.

MRS. POPOV. Are you afraid? Yes? Aahhh! No, sir. You're not going to get out of it that easily! Be so good as to follow me! I will not rest until I've put a hole through your forehead . . . that forehead I hate so much! Are you afraid?

SMIRNOV. Yes, I'm afraid.

MRS. POPOV. You're lying! Why don't you want to fight?

SMIRNOV. Because . . . because you . . . because I like you.   135

MRS. POPOV. [*laughs angrily.*] He likes me! He dares say that he likes me! [*Points to the door.*] Out!

SMIRNOV. [*loads the revolver in silence, takes cap and goes; at the door, stops for half a minute while they look at each other in silence; then he approaches MRS. POPOV hesitantly.*] Listen. . . . Are you still angry? I'm extremely irritated, but, do you understand me, how can I express it . . . the fact is, that, you see, strictly speaking . . . [*He shouts.*] Is it my fault, really, for liking you? [*Grabs the back of a chair, which cracks and breaks.*] Why the hell do you have such fragile furniture! I like you! Do you understand? I . . . I'm almost in love with you!

MRS. POPOV. Get away from me—I hate you!

SMIRNOV. God, what a woman! I've never in my life seen anything like her! I'm lost! I'm done for! I'm caught like a mouse in a trap!

MRS. POPOV. Stand back or I'll shoot!   140

SMIRNOV. Shoot! You could never understand what happiness it would be to die under the gaze of those wonderful eyes, to be shot by a revolver which was held by those little velvet hands. . . . I've gone out of my mind! Think about it and decide right away, because if I leave here, then we'll never see each other again! Decide . . . I'm a nobleman, a respectable gentleman, of good family. I have an income of ten thousand a year. . . . I can put a bullet through a coin tossed in the air . . . I have some fine horses. . . . Will you be my wife?

MRS. POPOV. [*indignantly brandishes her revolver.*] Let's fight! I challenge you!

SMIRNOV. I'm out of my mind . . . I don't understand anything . . . [*Shouts.*] Hey, you, water!

MRS. POPOV. [*shouts.*] Let's fight!

SMIRNOV. I've gone out of my mind. I'm in love like a boy, like an idiot!   145 [*He grabs her hand, she screams with pain.*] I love you! [*Kneels.*] I love you as I've never loved before! I've jilted twelve women, nine women have jilted me, but I've never loved one of them as I love you. . . . I'm weak, I'm a limp rag. . . . I'm on my knees like a fool, offering you my hand. . . . Shame, shame! I haven't been in love for five years, I vowed I wouldn't; and suddenly I'm in love, like a fish out of water. I'm offering my hand in marriage. Yes or no? You don't want to? You don't need to! [*Gets up and quickly goes to the door.*]

MRS. POPOV. Wait!

SMIRNOV. [*stops.*] Well?

MRS. POPOV. Nothing . . . you can go . . . go away . . . wait. . . . No, get out, get out! I hate you! But—don't go! Oh, if you only knew how furious I am, how angry! [*Throws revolver on table.*] My fingers are swollen from that nasty thing. . . . [*Tears her handkerchief furiously.*] What are you waiting for? Get out!

SMIRNOV. Farewell!

MRS. POPOV. Yes, yes, go away! [*Shouts.*] Where are you going? Stop. . . .   150
Oh, go away! Oh, how furious I am! Don't come near me! Don't come near me!

SMIRNOV. [*approaching her.*] How angry I am with myself! I'm in love like a student. I've been on my knees. . . . It gives me the shivers. [*Rudely.*] I love you! A lot of good it will do me to fall in love with you! Tomorrow I've got to pay the interest, begin the mowing of the hay. [*Puts his arm around her waist.*] I'll never forgive myself for this. . . .

MRS. POPOV. Get away from me! Get your hands away! I . . . hate you! I . . . challenge you!

[*Prolonged kiss. LUKA enters with an ax, the GARDENER with a rake, the COACHMAN with a pitchfork, and WORKMEN with cudgels.*]

LUKA. [*catches sight of the pair kissing.*] Lord in heaven! [*Pause.*]

MRS. POPOV. [*lowering her eyes.*] Luka, tell them in the stable not to give Toby any oats today.

CURTAIN

QUESTIONS

1. What is the situation at the opening of *The Bear*.? How long has Mrs. Popov been in mourning? What are your reactions to her situation and her attitudes?

2. Why has Smirnov come to the house? What is he like, and how do you draw conclusions about him? What does he say about women, and why does he present these conclusions?

3. What kind of life did Mrs. Popov have with her late husband? What did she learn about him after his death? How has this knowledge affected her? To what degree is she concealing some of her feelings about her husband?

4. Of what importance is Luka? What is he like as a character? How do his responses highlight both the action and also the emotions developing between Smirnov and Mrs. Popov?

5. What leads Mrs. Popov to call Smirnov a bear, a brute, a monster? What is his immediate response?

6. What is the significance of Toby? To what extent does he symbolize the shifting of Mrs. Popov's emotions in the course of the play?

7. What are the major and minor conflicts in the play?

GENERAL QUESTIONS

1. Where in the play were you moved to laughter? Analyze those moments and try to determine the circumstances and causes of laughter.
2. On the basis of action and business in the play, what conclusions can you draw about the nature of farce as a dramatic form? You might consider such things as the breaking chairs, the many exclamations and shouts, the sudden anger, the improbable challenge to a duel, the sudden shift of feelings, the unlikely attitude of Smirnov toward being shot, the occasions of laughter, etc.
3. Even though Smirnov and Mrs. Popov have declared their intentions to remain unmarried, they fall in love by the play's end. How does Chekhov's presentation of their characters make their reversal of feelings seem normal and logical, although sudden, unexpected, and surprising?
4. What are the major ideas or themes in *The Bear*? You might consider topics such as the strength of allegiances that the living make to the dead, the difficulty of keeping resolutions, the nature and power of strong emotions, the need for observing expected and conventional behaviors, etc.

SUSAN GLASPELL, *TRIFLES*

Susan Glaspell, a playwright and fiction writer, grew up in Iowa and moved to the Northeast in her thirties. She helped found the Provincetown Players in Massachusetts in 1914 and wrote most of her plays for that company. Much of her work—both plays and short stories—is strongly feminist; it deals with the roles that women play (or are forced to play) in society and with the relationships between men and women. She wrote or co-authored over ten plays for the Provincetown Players, including *Women's Honor* (1918), *Bernice* (1919), *The Inheritors* (1921), and *The Verge* (1921). After 1922, however, she gave up the theater and turned almost exclusively to fiction. The one exception was *Alison's House* (1930), a play loosely based on the life and family of Emily Dickinson, for which Glaspell won a Pulitzer Prize.

Trifles (1916) is Glaspell's best-known play; she wrote it in ten days for the Provincetown Players, and it was produced by them in 1916, during the same season that they staged their first play by Eugene O'Neill. Glaspell was inspired by a murder trial she covered while working as a reporter for a Des Moines newspaper. A year later she rewrote the play as a short story entitled "A Jury of Her Peers," which appears in Chapter 2 of this anthology.

Although *Trifles* concerns a murder investigation, the play is not a murder mystery; the audience and the characters know who did the killing almost as soon as the play begins. The action of the play is concerned with discovering a motive. In terms of theme, the play explores the reasons that such a murder might occur and the differing abilities of men and women to understand those reasons. The men and women in the play seek the motive for this murder in entirely different ways and arrive at radically different conclusions. The men—the County Attorney and the Sheriff—look for obvious signs of violent rage. The women—Mrs. Hale and Mrs. Peters—draw their conclusions on the evidence of "trifles" they find in the kitchen of the house. Finally, the women must decide what to do with this evidence and how to judge the killer. Their decisions embody, at least in part, the themes of the play in regard to women's roles in society and in regard to marriage. The play dramatizes with eloquence and impact the mistaken attitudes that men often have toward women and the prison that marriage can become.

SUSAN GLASPELL (1882–1948)

Trifles   *1916*

CAST OF CHARACTERS

> George Henderson, *county attorney*
> Henry Peters, *sheriff*
> Lewis Hale, *a neighboring farmer*
> Mrs. Peters
> Mrs. Hale

SCENE. *The kitchen in the now abandoned farmhouse of JOHN WRIGHT, a gloomy kitchen, and left without having been put in order—unwashed pans under the sink, a loaf of bread outside the bread-box, a dish-towel on the table—other signs of incompleted work. At the rear the outer door opens and the SHERIFF comes in followed by the COUNTY ATTORNEY and HALE. The SHERIFF and HALE are men in middle life, the COUNTY ATTORNEY is a young man; all are much bundled up and go at once to the stove. They are followed by the two women—the SHERIFF's wife first; she is a slight wiry woman, a thin nervous face. MRS. HALE is larger and would ordinarily be called more comfortable looking, but she is disturbed now and looks fearfully about as she enters. The women have come in slowly, and stand close together near the door.*

COUNTY ATTORNEY. [*Rubbing his hands.*] This feels good. Come up to the fire, ladies.

MRS. PETERS. [*After taking a step forward.*] I'm not—cold.

SHERIFF. [*Unbuttoning his overcoat and stepping away from the stove as if to mark the beginning of official business.*] Now, Mr. Hale, before we move things about, you explain to Mr. Henderson just what you saw when you came here yesterday morning.

COUNTY ATTORNEY. By the way, has anything been moved? Are things just as you left them yesterday?

SHERIFF. [*Looking about.*] It's just the same. When it dropped below zero last night I thought I'd better send Frank out this morning to make a fire for   5 us—no use getting pneumonia with a big case on, but I told him not to touch anything except the stove—and you know Frank.

COUNTY ATTORNEY.   Somebody should have been left here yesterday.

SHERIFF.   Oh—yesterday. When I had to send Frank to Morris Center for that man who went crazy—I want you to know I had my hands full yesterday. I knew you could get back from Omaha by today and as long as I went over everything here myself—

COUNTY ATTORNEY.   Well, Mr. Hale, tell just what happened when you came here yesterday morning.

HALE.   Harry and I had started to town with a load of potatoes. We came along the road from my place and as I got here I said, "I'm going to see if I can't get John Wright to go in with me on a party telephone." I spoke to Wright about it once before and he put me off, saying folks talked too much anyway, and all he asked was peace and quiet—I guess you know about how much he talked himself; but I thought maybe if I went to the house and talked about it before his wife, though I said to Harry that I didn't know as what his wife wanted made much difference to John—

COUNTY ATTORNEY.   Let's talk about that later, Mr. Hale. I do want to talk   10
about that, but tell now just what happened when you got to the house.

HALE.   I didn't hear or see anything; I knocked at the door, and still it was all quiet inside. I knew they must be up, it was past eight o'clock. So I knocked again, and I thought I heard somebody say, "Come in." I wasn't sure, I'm not sure yet, but I opened the door—this door [*Indicating the door by which the two women are still standing.*] and there in that rocker—[*Pointing to it.*] sat Mrs. Wright.

[*They all look at the rocker.*]

COUNTY ATTORNEY.   What—was she doing?

HALE.   She was rockin' back and forth. She had her apron in her hand and was kind of—pleating it.

COUNTY ATTORNEY.   And how did she—look?

HALE.   Well, she looked queer.   15

COUNTY ATTORNEY.   How do you mean—queer?

HALE.   Well, as if she didn't know what she was going to do next. And kind of done up.

COUNTY ATTORNEY.   How did she seem to feel about your coming?

HALE.   Why, I don't think she minded—one way or other. She didn't pay much attention. I said, "How do, Mrs. Wright, it's cold, ain't it?" And she said, "Is it?"—and went on kind of pleating at her apron. Well, I was surprised; she didn't ask me to come up to the stove, or to set down, but just sat there, not even looking at me, so I said, "I want to see John." And then she—laughed. I guess you would call it a laugh. I thought of Harry and the team outside, so I said a little sharp: "Can't I see John?" "No," she says, kind o' dull like. "Ain't he home?" says I. "Yes," says she, "he's home." "Then why can't I see him?" I asked her, out of patience. " 'Cause he's dead," says she. "*Dead?*" says I. She just nodded her head, not getting a bit excited, but rockin' back and forth. "Why—where is he?" says I, not knowing what to say. She just pointed upstairs—like that. [*himself pointing to the room above.*] I got up, with the idea of going up there. I walked from there to here—then I says, "Why, what did he die of?" "He died of a rope round his neck," says she, and just went on pleatin' at her apron. Well, I went out and called Harry. I thought I might—need help. We went upstairs and there he was lyin'—

COUNTY ATTORNEY.   I think I'd rather have you go into that upstairs, where   20
you can point it all out. Just go on now with the rest of the story.

HALE.   Well, my first thought was to get that rope off. It looked . . . [*Stops, his face twitches.*] . . . but Harry, he went up to him, and he said, "No, he's dead all right, and we'd better not touch anything." So we went back downstairs. She was still sitting that same way. "Has anybody been notified?" I asked. "No," says she, unconcerned. "Who did this, Mrs. Wright?" said Harry. He said it businesslike— and she stopped pleatin' of her apron. "I don't know," she says. "You don't *know?*" says Harry. "No," says she. "Weren't you sleepin' in the bed with him?" says Harry. "Yes," says she, "but I was on the inside." "Somebody slipped a rope round his neck and strangled him and you didn't wake up?" says Harry. "I didn't wake up," she said after him. We must 'a looked as if we didn't see how that could be, for after a minute she said, "I sleep sound." Harry was going to ask her more questions but I said maybe we ought to let her tell her story first to the coroner, or the sheriff, so Harry went fast as he could to Rivers' place, where there's a telephone.

COUNTY ATTORNEY.   And what did Mrs. Wright do when she knew that you had gone for the coroner?

HALE.   She moved from that chair to this one over here [*Pointing to a small chair in the corner.*] and just sat there with her hands held together and looking down. I got a feeling that I ought to make some conversation, so I said I had come in to see if John wanted to put in a telephone, and at that she started to laugh, and then she stopped and looked at me—scared. [*The* COUNTY ATTORNEY, *who has had his notebook out, makes a note.*] I dunno, maybe it wasn't scared. I wouldn't like to say it was. Soon Harry got back, and then Dr. Lloyd came, and you, Mr. Peters, and so I guess that's all I know that you don't.

COUNTY ATTORNEY.   [*Looking around.*] I guess we'll go upstairs first—and then out to the barn and around there. [*To the* SHERIFF.] You're convinced that there was nothing important here—nothing that would point to any motive.

SHERIFF.   Nothing here but kitchen things.   25

[*The* COUNTY ATTORNEY, *after again looking around the kitchen, opens the door of a cupboard closet. He gets up on a chair and looks on a shelf. Pulls his hand away, sticky.*]

COUNTY ATTORNEY.   Here's a nice mess.

[*The women draw nearer.*]

MRS. PETERS.   [*To the other woman.*] Oh, her fruit; it did freeze. [*To the* LAWYER.] She worried about that when it turned so cold. She said the fire'd go out and her jars would break.

SHERIFF.   Well, can you beat the women! Held for murder and worryin' about her preserves.

COUNTY ATTORNEY.   I guess before we're through she may have something more serious than preserves to worry about.

HALE.   Well, women are used to worrying over trifles.   30

[*The two women move a little closer together.*]

above. In a low voice.] Mr. Peters says it looks bad for her. Mr. Henderson is awful sarcastic in a speech and he'll make fun of her sayin' she didn't wake up.

MRS. HALE.   Well, I guess John Wright didn't wake when they was slipping that rope under his neck.

MRS. PETERS.   No, it's strange. It must have been done awful crafty and   65
still. They say it was such a—funny way to kill a man, rigging it all up like that.

MRS. HALE.   That's just what Mr. Hale said. There was a gun in the house. He says that's what he can't understand.

MRS. PETERS.   Mr. Henderson said coming out that what was needed for the case was a motive; something to show anger, or—sudden feeling.

MRS. HALE.   [*Who is standing by the table.*] Well, I don't see any signs of anger around here. [*She puts her hand on the dish towel which lies on the table, stands looking down at table, one half of which is clean, the other half messy.*] It's wiped to here. [*Makes a move as if to finish work, then turns and looks at loaf of bread outside the breadbox. Drops towel. In that voice of coming back to familiar things.*] Wonder how they are finding things upstairs. I hope she had it a little more red-up° up there. You know, it seems kind of *sneaking.* Locking her up in town and then coming out here and trying to get her own house to turn against her!

MRS. PETERS.   But Mrs. Hale, the law is the law.

MRS. HALE.   I s'pose 'tis. [*Unbuttoning her coat.*] Better loosen up your things,   70
Mrs. Peters. You won't feel them when you go out.

[*MRS. PETERS takes off her fur tippet,° goes to hang it on hook at back of room, stands looking at the under part of the small corner table.*]

MRS. PETERS.   She was piecing a quilt.

[*She brings the large sewing basket and they look at the bright pieces.*]

MRS. HALE.   It's log cabin pattern. Pretty, isn't it? I wonder if she was goin' to quilt it or just knot it?

[*Footsteps have been heard coming down the stairs. The SHERIFF enters followed by HALE and the COUNTY ATTORNEY.*]

SHERIFF.   They wonder if she was going to quilt it or just knot it!

[*The men laugh; the women look abashed.*]

COUNTY ATTORNEY.   [*Rubbing his hands over the stove.*] Frank's fire didn't do much up there, did it? Well, let's go out to the barn and get that cleared up.

[*The men go outside.*]

MRS. HALE.   [*Resentfully.*] I don't know as there's anything so strange, our   75
takin' up our time with little things while we're waiting for them to get the evidence. [*She sits down at the big table smoothing out a block with decision.*] I don't see as it's anything to laugh about.

MRS. PETERS.   [*Apologetically.*] Of course they've got awful important things on their minds.

---

red-up: neat, arranged in order.
tippet: scarflike garment of fur or wool for the neck and shoulders.

[*Pulls up a chair and joins* MRS. HALE *at the table.*]

MRS. HALE. [*Examining another block.*] Mrs. Peters, look at this one. Here, this is the one she was working on, and look at the sewing! All the rest of it has been so nice and even. And look at this! It's all over the place! Why, it looks as if she didn't know what she was about!

[*After she has said this they look at each other, then start to glance back at the door. After an instant* MRS. HALE *has pulled at a knot and ripped the sewing.*

MRS. PETERS. Oh, what are you doing, Mrs. Hale?

MRS. HALE. [*Mildly.*] Just pulling out a stitch or two that's not sewed very good. [*Threading a needle.*] Bad sewing always made me fidgety.

MRS. PETERS. [*Nervously.*] I don't think we ought to touch things. 80

MRS. HALE. I'll just finish up this end. [*Suddenly stopping and leaning forward.*] Mrs. Peters?

MRS. PETERS. Yes, Mrs. Hale?

MRS. HALE. What do you suppose she was so nervous about?

MRS. PETERS. Oh—I don't know. I don't know as she was nervous. I sometimes sew awful queer when I'm just tired. [*MRS. HALE starts to say something, looks at MRS. PETERS, then goes on sewing.*] Well I must get these things wrapped up. They may be through sooner than we think. [*Putting apron and other things together.*] I wonder where I can find a piece of paper, and string.

MRS. HALE. In that cupboard, maybe. 85

MRS. PETERS. [*Looking in cupboard.*] Why, here's a bird-cage. [*Holds it up.*] Did she have a bird, Mrs. Hale?

MRS. HALE. Why, I don't know whether she did or not—I've not been here for so long. There was a man around last year selling canaries cheap, but I don't know as she took one; maybe she did. She used to sing real pretty herself.

MRS. PETERS. [*Glancing around.*] Seems funny to think of a bird here. But she must have had one, or why would she have a cage? I wonder what happened to it.

MRS. HALE. I s'pose maybe the cat got it.

MRS. PETERS. No, she didn't have a cat. She's got that feeling some people '90 have about cats—being afraid of them. My cat got in her room and she was real upset and asked me to take it out.

MRS. HALE. My sister Bessie was like that. Queer, ain't it?

MRS. PETERS. [*Examining the cage.*] Why, look at this door. It's broke. One hinge is pulled apart.

MRS. HALE. [*Looking too.*] Looks as if someone must have been rough with it.

MRS. PETERS. Why, yes.

[*She brings the cage forward and puts it on the table.*]

MRS. HALE. I wish if they're going to find any evidence they'd be about it. 95 I don't like this place.

MRS. PETERS. But I'm awful glad you came with me, Mrs. Hale. It would be lonesome for me sitting here alone.

MRS. HALE. It would, wouldn't it? [*Dropping her sewing.*] But I tell you what

I do wish, Mrs. Peters. I wish I had come over sometimes when *she* was here. I—
[*Looking around the room.*]—wish I had.

MRS. PETERS.   But of course you were awful busy, Mrs. Hale—your house
and your children.   .

MRS. HALE.   I could've come. I stayed away because it weren't cheerful—
and that's why I ought to have come. I—I've never liked this place. Maybe because
it's down in a hollow and you don't see the road. I dunno what it is, but it's a
lonesome place and always was. I wish I had come over to see Minnie Foster
sometimes. I can see now—

[*Shakes her head.*]

MRS. PETERS.   Well, you mustn't reproach yourself, Mrs. Hale. Somehow   100
we just don't see how it is with other folks until—something comes up.

MRS. HALE.   Not having children makes less work—but it makes a quiet
house, and Wright out to work all day, and no company when he did come in.
Did you know John Wright, Mrs. Peters?

MRS. PETERS.   Not to know him; I've seen him in town. They say he was a
good man.

MRS. HALE.   Yes—good; he didn't drink, and kept his word as well as most,
I guess, and paid his debts. But he was a hard man, Mrs. Peters. Just to pass the
time of day with him—[*Shivers.*] Like a raw wind that gets to the bone. [*Pauses,
her eye falling on the cage.*] I should think she would 'a wanted a bird. But what do
you suppose went with it?

MRS. PETERS.   I don't know, unless it got sick and died.

[*She reaches over and swings the broken door, swings it again, both women watch it.*]

MRS. HALE.   You weren't raised round here, were you? [*MRS. PETERS shakes*   105
her head.*] You didn't know—her?

MRS. PETERS.   Not till they brought her yesterday.

MRS. HALE.   She—come to think of it, she was kind of like a bird herself—
real sweet and pretty, but kind of timid and—fluttery. How—she—did—change.
[*Silence; then as if struck by a happy thought and relieved to get back to everyday things.*]
Tell you what, Mrs. Peters, why don't you take the quilt in with you? It might
take up her mind.

MRS. PETERS.   Why, I think that's a real nice idea, Mrs. Hale. There couldn't
possibly be any objection to it, could there? Now, just what would I take? I wonder
if her patches are in here—and her things.

[*They look in the sewing basket.*]

MRS. HALE.   Here's some red. I expect this has got sewing things in it. [*Brings
out a fancy box.*] What a pretty box. Looks like something somebody would give
you. Maybe her scissors are in here. [*Opens box. Suddenly puts her hand to her nose.*]
Why—[*MRS. PETERS bends nearer, then turns her face away.*] There's something wrapped
up in this piece of silk.

MRS. PETERS.   Why, this isn't her scissors.   110

MRS. HALE.   [*Lifting the silk.*] Oh, Mrs. Peters—its—

[*MRS. PETERS bends closer.*]

MRS. PETERS.   It's the bird.

MRS. HALE.   [*Jumping up.*] But, Mrs. Peters—look at it! Its neck! Look at its neck! It's all—other side *to*.

MRS. PETERS.   Somebody—wrung—its—neck.

[*Their eyes meet. A look of growing comprehension, of horror. Steps are heard outside. MRS. HALE slips box under quilt pieces, and sinks into her chair. Enter SHERIFF and COUNTY ATTORNEY. MRS. PETERS rises.*]

COUNTY ATTORNEY   [*As one turning from serious things to little pleasantries.*] Well,   115
ladies, have you decided whether she was going to quilt it or knot it?

MRS. PETERS.   We think she was going to—knot it.

COUNTY ATTORNEY.   Well, that's interesting, I'm sure. [*Seeing the bird-cage.*] Has the bird flown?

MRS. HALE.   [*Putting more quilt pieces over the box.*] We think the—cat got it.

COUNTY ATTORNEY.   [*Preoccupied.*] Is there a cat?

[*MRS. HALE glances in a quick covert way at MRS. PETERS.*]

MRS. PETERS.   Well, not *now*. They're superstitious, you know. They leave.   120

COUNTY ATTORNEY.   [*To SHERIFF PETERS, continuing an interrupted conversation.*] No sign at all of anyone having come from the outside. Their own rope. Now let's go up again and go over it piece by piece. [*They start upstairs.*] It would have to have been someone who knew just the—

[*MRS. PETERS sits down. The two women sit there not looking at one another, but as if peering into something and at the same time holding back. When they talk now it is in the manner of feeling their way over strange ground, as if afraid of what they are saying, but as if they cannot help saying it.*]

MRS. HALE.   She liked the bird. She was going to bury it in that pretty box.

MRS. PETERS.   [*In a whisper.*] When I was a girl—my kitten—there was a boy took a hatchet, and before my eyes—and before I could get there—[*Covers her face an instant.*] If they hadn't held me back I would have—[*Catches herself, looks upstairs where steps are heard, falters weakly*]—hurt him.

MRS. HALE.   [*With a slow look around her.*] I wonder how it would seem never to have had any children around. [*Pause.*] No, Wright wouldn't like the bird—a thing that sang. She used to sing. He killed that, too.

MRS. PETERS.   [*Moving uneasily.*] We don't know who killed the bird.   125

MRS. HALE.   I knew John Wright.

MRS. PETERS.   It was an awful thing was done in this house that night, Mrs. Hale. Killing a man while he slept, slipping a rope around his neck that choked the life out of him.

MRS. HALE.   His neck. Choked the life out of him.

[*Her hand goes out and rests on the bird-cage.*]

MRS. PETERS.   [*With rising voice.*] We don't know who killed him. We don't know.

MRS. HALE.   [*Her own feeling not interrupted.*] If there'd been years and years   130 of nothing, then a bird to sing to you, it would be awful—still, after the bird was still.

MRS. PETERS.   [*Something within her speaking.*] I know what stillness is. When we homesteaded in Dakota, and my first baby died—after he was two years old, and me with no other then—

MRS. HALE.   [*Moving.*] How soon do you suppose they'll be through, looking for the evidence?

MRS. PETERS.   I know what stillness is. [*Pulling herself back.*] The law has got to punish crime, Mrs. Hale.

MRS. HALE.   [*Not as if answering that.*] I wish you'd seen Minnie Foster when she wore a white dress with blue ribbons and stood up there in the choir and sang. [*A look around the room.*] Oh, I *wish* I'd come over here once in a while! That was a crime! That was a crime! Who's going to punish that?

MRS. PETERS.   [*Looking upstairs.*] We mustn't—take on.   135

MRS. HALE.   I might have known she needed help! I know how things can be—for women. I tell you, it's queer, Mrs. Peters. We live close together and we live far apart. We all go through the same things—it's all just a different kind of the same thing. [*Brushes her eyes, noticing the bottle of fruit, reaches out for it.*] If I was you I wouldn't tell her her fruit was gone. Tell her it *ain't*. Tell her it's all right. Take this in to prove it to her. She—she may never know whether it was broke or not.

MRS. PETERS.   [*Takes the bottle, looks about for something to wrap it in; takes petticoat from the clothes brought from the other room, very nervously begins winding this around the bottle. In a false voice.*] My, it's a good thing the men couldn't hear us. Wouldn't they just laugh! Getting all stirred up over a little thing like a—dead canary. As if that could have anything to do with—with—wouldn't they *laugh*!

[*The men are heard coming down stairs.*]

MRS. HALE.   [*Under her breath.*] Maybe they would—maybe they wouldn't.

COUNTY ATTORNEY.   No, Peters, it's all perfectly clear except a reason for doing it. But you know juries when it comes to women. If there was some definite thing. Something to show—something to make a story about—a thing that would connect up with this strange way of doing it—

[*The women's eyes meet for an instant. Enter HALE from outer door.*]

HALE.   Well, I've got the team around. Pretty cold out there.   140

COUNTY ATTORNEY.   I'm going to stay here a while by myself. [*To the SHERIFF.*] You can send Frank out for me, can't you? I want to go over everything. I'm not satisfied that we can't do better.

SHERIFF.   Do you want to see what Mrs. Peters is going to take in?

[*The COUNTY ATTORNEY goes to the table, picks up the apron, laughs.*]

COUNTY ATTORNEY.   Oh, I guess they're not very dangerous things the ladies have picked out. [*Moves a few things about, disturbing the quilt pieces which cover the box. Steps back.*] No, Mrs. Peters doesn't need supervising. For that matter, a sheriff's wife is married to the law. Ever think of it that way, Mrs. Peters?

MRS. PETERS.   Not—just that way.

SHERIFF.   [*Chuckling.*] Married to the law. [*Moves toward the other room.*] I   145 just want you to come in here a minute, George. We ought to take a look at these windows.

COUNTY ATTORNEY. [*Scoffingly.*] Oh, windows!

SHERIFF. We'll be right out, Mr. Hale.

[*HALE goes outside. The SHERIFF follows the COUNTY ATTORNEY into the other room. Then MRS. HALE rises, hands tight together, looking intensely at MRS. PETERS, whose eyes make a slow turn, finally meeting MRS. HALE'S. A moment MRS. HALE holds her, then her own eyes point the way to where the box is concealed. Suddenly MRS. PETERS throws back quilt pieces and tries to put the box in the bag she is wearing. It is too big. She opens box, starts to take bird out, cannot touch it, goes to pieces, stands there helpless. Sound of a knob turning in the other room. MRS. HALE snatches the box and puts it in the pocket of her big coat. Enter COUNTY ATTORNEY and SHERIFF.*]

COUNTY ATTORNEY. [*Facetiously.*] Well, Henry, at least we found out that she was not going to quilt it. She was going to—what is it you call it, ladies?

MRS. HALE. [*Her hand against her pocket.*] We call it—knot it, Mr. Henderson.

CURTAIN

QUESTIONS

1. How does the setting described in the first stage direction alert you that something has gone wrong at the Wright farm?

2. How does the first entrance of the characters begin to establish a distinction between the men and women in the play?

3. What does Mr. Hale report to the County Attorney in his extended narrative? How observant is he? How accurate?

4. What is needed to make a strong case against Mrs. Wright? What does the Sheriff determine about the kitchen? What do his conclusions show you about the men?

5. What is suggested by the different reactions of the men and women to the freezing of the preserves?

6. What conclusions do the women draw about the bad sewing in the quilt? What does Mrs. Hale do about it? At this point, what conclusions might she be drawing about the murder?

7. Of what importance are Mrs. Hale's descriptions (a) of Minnie Foster (Mrs. Wright) as a young woman and (b) of the Wrights' marriage?

8. What do the women deduce from the broken birdcage and the dead bird? How are these symbolic, and what do they symbolize?

9. Assuming that Minnie Wright is the murderer of her husband, how did she do it? What hints in the play enable you to solve the crime? What information do the women have, not possessed by the men, that permits them to make the right inferences about the crime and the method of strangulation?

10. What is the crisis of the play and where does it occur?

11. What does Mrs. Hale do with the "trifles" of evidence? Why? How is her

reaction to the evidence different from that of Mrs. Peters? What conflict develops between these women? How is it resolved?

12. Why does Mrs. Hale feel guilt about her relationship with Minnie Wright? To what degree does her guilt shape her decisions and actions?

GENERAL QUESTIONS

1. To what does the title of this play refer? Where is the word "trifles" used in the play? To what extent is the word ironic? How does this irony help shape the play's meaning?

2. Are the characters round or flat? Individualized or representative? Static or dynamic? Why do you think Glaspell makes these choices in characterization? How do they contribute to your understanding of the play's themes?

3. What are the men like? How observant are they? What is their attitude toward their jobs? Toward their own importance? Toward the women and "kitchen things"?

4. What is Mrs. Hale like? How observant is she? What is her attitude toward the men and their work, and toward herself?

5. Some critics have argued that Minnie Wright is the most important character in the play, even though she never appears on stage. Do you agree with this assertion? Why do you think Glaspell did not want her to appear as a speaking character?

6. Who or what are the protagonist and the antagonist? What is the central conflict? How and when is it resolved? How does the resolution help establish the play's themes?

7. How is symbolism employed to establish and underscore the play's meaning? Consider especially the birdcage, the dead bird, and the repeated assertion that Mrs. Wright was going to "knot" (tie) rather than "quilt" (sew) the quilt.

EUGENE O'NEILL, *BEFORE BREAKFAST*

Eugene O'Neill is one of America's greatest playwrights and tragedians. He wrote over forty plays, won three Pulitzer Prizes, and received a Nobel Prize for literature in 1936. The son of a well-known actor, in his youth he traveled about the world as a seaman, studied briefly at Princeton and Harvard, and began writing plays in 1912. The first of his plays to be produced, *Bound East for Cardiff*, was acted by the Provincetown Players at Wharf Theater in Provincetown, Massachusetts, in 1916. O'Neill maintained a close connection with this company for several years, providing them with ten one-act plays between 1916 and 1920. His later (and longer) works include *The Emperor Jones* (1920), *Anna Christie* (1921), *Desire Under the Elms* (1924), *Strange Interlude* (1928), *Mourning Becomes Electra* (1931), and *The Iceman Cometh* (1946). O'Neill also wrote an autobiographical play called *A Long Day's Journey Into Night* (1936), which was suppressed at his request until after his death. When it was finally staged on Broadway in 1956, it won O'Neill a third Pulitzer Prize in drama.

Before Breakfast, though one of O'Neill's earliest plays, shows his characteristic control of conflict, character, setting, and point of view. The play was first staged in December 1916 by the Provincetown Players at the Playwright's Theater in New York City's Greenwich Village. There is very little action in the play, and yet it is full of conflict. The plot is simple and straightforward—a wife spends twenty minutes in the morning haranguing her husband. Mr. and Mrs. Rowland are the only characters in the play. The conflict between them is longstanding and bitter, and it is resolved in the play's catastrophe.

Above all else, *Before Breakfast* illustrates O'Neill's skillful employment of dramatic point of view and setting. By giving Mrs. Rowland virtually every word spoken in the play, O'Neill forces the audience to see everything, at least initially, from her perspective. Her vision of her husband and her marriage is radically distorted by her own pettiness and selfishness. Finally, the audience (and the reader) must decide exactly how valid or truthful her perspective is; we must evaluate the characters from our own perspective. Setting is equally important in *Before Breakfast*. O'Neill uses the single stage setting, described at length in the opening stage direction, to show the audience (or tell the reader) a great deal about the characters and their lives. The Rowlands's flat (apartment) in Greenwich Village, a part of New York City that was a traditional gathering place for artists, writers, and actors, instantly defines their status, their relationship, and their way of life. The implications of the setting are confirmed throughout the rest of the play.

EUGENE O'NEILL   (1888–1953)

Before Breakfast   *1916*

CHARACTERS

Mrs. Rowland, *The Wife*
Mr. Alfred Rowland, *The Husband*

SCENE. *A small room serving both as kitchen and dining room in a flat on Christopher Street, New York City. In the rear, to the right, a door leading to the outer hallway. On the left of the doorway, a sink, and a two-burner gas stove. Over the stove, and extending to the left wall, a wooden closet for dishes, etc. On the left, two windows looking out on a fire escape where several potted plants are dying of neglect. Before the windows, a table covered with oilcloth. Two cane-bottomed chairs are placed by the table. Another stands against the wall to the right of door in rear. In the right wall, rear, a doorway leading*

into a bedroom. Farther forward, different articles of a man's and a woman's clothing are hung on pegs. A clothes line is strung from the left corner, rear, to the right wall, forward.
It is about eight-thirty in the morning of a fine, sunshiny day in the early fall.

Mrs. Rowland enters from the bedroom, yawning, her hands still busy putting the finishing touches on a slovenly toilet by sticking hairpins into her hair which is bunched up in a drab-colored mass on top of her round head. She is of medium height and inclined to a shapeless stoutness, accentuated by her formless blue dress, shabby and worn. Her face is characterless, with small regular features and eyes of a nondescript blue. There is a pinched expression about her eyes and nose and her weak, spiteful mouth. She is in her early twenties but looks much older.

She comes to the middle of the room and yawns, stretching her arms to their full length. Her drowsy eyes stare about the room with the irritated look of one to whom a long sleep has not been a long rest. She goes wearily to the clothes hanging on the right and takes an apron from a hook. She ties it about her waist, giving vent to an exasperated "damn" when the knot fails to obey her clumsy fingers. Finally gets it tied and goes slowly to the gas stove and lights one burner. She fills the coffee pot at the sink and sets it over the flame. Then slumps down into a chair by the table and puts a hand over her forehead as if she were suffering from headache. Suddenly her face brightens as though she had remembered something, and she casts a quick glance at the dish closet; then looks sharply at the bedroom door and listens intently for a moment or so.

MRS. ROWLAND. *[In a low voice.]* Alfred! Alfred! *[There is no answer from the next room and she continues suspiciously in a louder tone.]* You needn't pretend you're asleep. *[There is no reply to this from the bedroom, and, reassured, she gets up from her chair and tiptoes cautiously to the dish closet. She slowly opens one door, taking great care to make no noise, and slides out, from their hiding place behind the dishes, a bottle of Gordon gin and a glass. In doing so she disturbs the top dish, which rattles a little. At this sound she starts guiltily and looks with sulky defiance at the doorway to the next room.]*
[Her voice trembling.] Alfred!

[After a pause, during which she listens for any sound, she takes the glass and pours out a large drink and gulps it down; then hastily returns the bottle and glass to their hiding place. She closes the closet door with the same care as she had opened it, and, heaving a great sigh of relief, sinks down into her chair again. The large dose of alcohol she has taken has an almost immediate effect. Her features become more animated, she seems to gather energy, and she looks at the bedroom door with a hard, vindictive smile on her lips. Her eyes glance quickly about the room and are fixed on a man's coat and vest which hang from a hook at right. She moves stealthily over to the open doorway and stands there, out of sight of anyone inside, listening for any movement.]

[Calling in a half-whisper.] Alfred!

[Again there is no reply. With a swift movement she takes the coat and vest from the hook and returns with them to her chair. She sits down and takes the various articles out of each pocket but quickly puts them back again. At last, in the inside pocket of the vest, she finds a letter.]

[Looking at the handwriting—slowly to herself.] Hmm! I knew it.

[She opens the letter and reads it. At first her expression is one of hatred and rage, but as she goes on to the end it changes to one of triumphant malignity. She remains in deep thought for a moment, staring before her, the letter in her hands, a cruel smile on her lips.

Then she puts the letter back in the pocket of the vest, and still careful not to awaken the sleeper, hangs the clothes up again on the same hook, and goes to the bedroom door and looks in.]

[*In a loud, shrill voice.*] Alfred! [*Still louder.*] Alfred! [*There is a muffled, yawning groan from the next room.*] Don't you think it's about time you got up? Do you want to stay in bed all day? [*Turning around and coming back to her chair.*] Not that I've got any doubts about your being lazy enough to stay in bed forever. [*She sits down and looks out of the window, irritably.*] Goodness knows what time it is. We haven't even got any way of telling the time since you pawned your watch like a fool. The last valuable thing we had, and you knew it. It's been nothing but pawn, pawn, pawn, with you—anything to put off getting a job, anything to get out of going to work like a man. [*She taps the floor with her foot nervously, biting her lips.*]

[*After a short pause.*] Alfred! Get up, do you hear me? I want to make that   5
bed before I go out. I'm sick of having this place in a continual muss on your account. [*With a certain vindictive satisfaction.*] Not that we'll be here long unless you manage to get some money some place. Heaven knows I do my part—and more—going out to sew every day while you play the gentleman and loaf around bar rooms with that good-for-nothing lot of artists from the Square.°

[*A short pause during which she plays nervously with a cup and saucer on the table.*]

And where are you going to get money, I'd like to know? The rent's due this week and you know what the landlord is. He won't let us stay a minute over our time. You say you *can't* get a job. That's a lie and you know it. You never even look for one. All you do is moon around all day writing silly poetry and stories that no one will buy—and no wonder they won't. I notice I can always get a position, such as it is; and it's only that which keeps us from starving to death.

[*Gets up and goes over to the stove—looks into the coffee pot to see if the water is boiling; then comes back and sits down again.*]

You'll have to get money to-day some place. I can't do it all, and I won't do it all. You've got to come to your senses. You've got to beg, borrow, or steal it somewhere. [*With a contemptuous laugh.*] But where, I'd like to know? You're too proud to beg, and you've borrowed the limit, and you haven't the nerve to steal.

[*After a pause—getting up angrily.*] Aren't you up yet, for heaven's sake? It's just like you to go to sleep again, or pretend to. [*She goes to the bedroom door and looks in.*] Oh, you are up. Well, it's about time. You needn't look at me like that. Your airs don't fool me a bit any more. I know you too well—better than you think I do—you and your goings-on. [*Turning away from the door—meaningly.*] I know a lot of things, my dear. Never mind what I know, now. I'll tell you before I go, you needn't worry. [*She comes to the middle of the room and stands there, frowning.*]

[*Irritably.*] Hmm! I suppose I might as well get breakfast ready—not that there's anything much to get. [*Questioningly.*] Unless you have some money? [*She pauses for an answer from the next room which does not come.*] Foolish question! [*She gives a short, hard laugh*] I ought to know you better than that by this time. When you left here in such a huff last night I knew what would happen. You can't be trusted for a second. A nice condition you came home in! The fight we had was

Square: Washington Square, at the center of Greenwich Village.

only an excuse for you to make a beast of yourself. What was the use pawning your watch if all you wanted with the money was to waste it in buying drink?

[*Goes over to the dish closet and takes out plates, cups, etc., while she is talking.*]

Hurry up! It don't take long to get breakfast these days, thanks to you. All   10
we got this morning is bread and butter and coffee; and you wouldn't even have that if it wasn't for me sewing my fingers off. [*She slams the loaf of bread on the table with a bang.*]

The bread's stale. I hope you'll like it. *You* don't deserve any better, but I don't see why *I* should suffer.

[*Going over to the stove.*] The coffee'll be ready in a minute, and you needn't expect me to wait for you.

[*Suddenly with great anger.*] What on earth are you doing all this time? [*She goes over to the door and looks in.*] Well, you're *almost* dressed at any rate. I expected to find you back in bed. That'd be just like you. How awful you look this morning! For heaven's sake, shave! You're disgusting! You look like a tramp. No wonder no one will give you a job. I don't blame them—when you don't even look half-way decent. [*She goes to the stove.*] There's plenty of hot water right here. You've got no excuse. [*Gets a bowl and pours some of the water from the coffee pot into it.*] Here.

[*He reaches his hand into the room for it. It is a sensitive hand with slender fingers. It trembles and some of the water spills on the floor.*]

[*Tauntingly*] Look at your hand tremble! You'd better give up drinking. You can't stand it. It's just your kind that get the D.T.'s. *That would be* the last straw! [*Looking down at the floor.*] Look at the mess you've made of this floor—cigarette butts and ashes all over the place. Why can't you put them on a plate? No, you wouldn't be considerate enough to do that. You never think of me. You don't have to sweep the room and that's all you care about.

[*Takes the broom and commences to sweep viciously, raising a cloud of dust. From the inner room comes the sound of a razor being stropped.*]°

[*Sweeping.*] Hurry up! It must be nearly time for me to go. If I'm late I'm   15
liable to lose my position, and then I couldn't support you any longer. [*As an afterthought she adds sarcastically.*] And then you'd have to go to work or something dreadful like that. [*Sweeping under the table.*] What I want to know is whether you're going to look for a job to-day or not. You know your family won't help us any more. They've had enough of you, too. [*After a moment's silent sweeping.*] I'm about sick of all this life. I've a good notion to go home, if I wasn't too proud to let them know what a failure you've been—you, the millionaire Rowland's only son, the Harvard graduate, the poet, the catch of the town—Huh! [*With bitterness.*] There wouldn't be many of them now envy my catch if they knew the truth. What has our marriage been, I'd like to know? Even before your *millionaire* father died owing every one in the world money, you certainly never wasted any of your time on your wife. I suppose you thought I'd ought to be glad you were *honorable* enough to marry me—after getting me into trouble. You were ashamed

---

stropped: Alfred is sharpening a straight razor, the kind barbers still use, with a very sharp five-inch steel blade that is hinged to a handle.

of me with your fine friends because my father's only a grocer, that's what you were. At least he's honest, which is more than any one could say about yours. [*She is sweeping steadily toward the door. Leans on her broom for a moment.*]

You hoped every one'd think you'd been forced to marry me, and pity you, didn't you? You didn't hesitate much about telling me you loved me, and making me believe your lies, before it happened, did you? You made me think you didn't want your father to buy me off as he tried to do. I know better now. I haven't lived with you all this time for nothing. [*Somberly.*] It's lucky the poor thing was born dead, after all. What a father you'd have been!

[*Is silent, brooding moodily for a moment—then she continues with a sort of savage joy.*]

But I'm not the only one who's got you to thank for being unhappy. There's one other, at least, and *she* can't hope to marry you now. [*She puts her head into the next room.*] How about Helen? [*She starts back from the doorway, half frightened.*]

Don't look at me that way! Yes, I read her letter. What about it? I got a right to. I'm your wife. And I know all there is to know, so don't lie. You needn't stare at me so. You can't bully me with your superior airs any longer. Only for me you'd be going without breakfast this very morning. [*She sets the broom back in the corner—whiningly.*] You never did have any gratitude for what I've done. [*She comes to the stove and puts the coffee into the pot.*] The coffee's ready. I'm not going to wait for you. [*She sits down in her chair again.*]

[*After a pause—puts her hand to her head—fretfully.*] My head aches so this morning. It's a shame I've got to go to work in a stuffy room all day in my condition. And I wouldn't if you were half a man. By rights I ought to be lying on my back instead of you. You know how sick I've been this last year; and yet you object when I take a little something to keep up my spirits. You even didn't want me to take that tonic I got at the drug store. [*With a hard laugh.*] I know you'd be glad to have me dead and out of your way; then you'd be free to run after all these silly girls that think you're such a wonderful, misunderstood person—this Helen and the others. [*There is a sharp exclamation of pain from the next room.*]

[*With satisfaction.*] There! I knew you'd cut yourself. It'll be a lesson to you. 20
You know you oughtn't to be running around nights drinking with your nerves in such an awful shape. [*She goes to the door and looks in.*]

What makes you so pale? What are you staring at yourself in the mirror that way for? For goodness sake, wipe that blood off your face! [*With a shudder.*] It's horrible. [*In relieved tones.*] There, that's better. I never could stand the sight of blood. [*She shrinks back from the door a little.*] You better give up trying and go to a barber shop. Your hand shakes dreadfully. Why do you stare at me like that? [*She turns away from the door.*] Are you still mad at me about that letter? [*Defiantly.*] Well, I had a right to read it. I'm your wife. [*She comes to the chair and sits down again. After a pause.*]

I knew all the time you were running around with someone. Your lame excuses about spending the time at the library didn't fool me. Who is this Helen, anyway? One of those artists? Or does she write poetry, too? Her letter sounds that way. I'll bet she told you your things were the best ever, and you believed her, like a fool. Is she young and pretty? I was young and pretty, too, when you fooled me with your fine, poetic talk; but life with you would soon wear anyone down. What I've been through!

[*Goes over and takes the coffee off the stove.*] Breakfast is ready. [*With a contemptuous *glance.*] Breakfast! [*Pours out a cup of coffee for herself and puts the pot on the table.*] Your coffee'll be cold. What are you doing—still shaving, for heaven's sake? You'd better give it up. One of these mornings you'll give yourself a serious cut. [*She cuts off bread and butters it. During the following speeches she eats and sips her coffee.*]

I'll have to run as soon as I've finished eating. One of us has got to work. [*Angrily.*] Are you going to look for a job to-day or aren't you? I should think some of your fine friends would help you, if they really think you're so much. But I guess they just like to hear you talk. [*Sits in silence for a moment.*]

I'm sorry for this Helen, whoever she is. Haven't you got any feelings for other people? What will her family say? I see she mentions them in her letter. What is she going to do—have the child—or go to one of those doctors? That's a nice thing, I must say. Where can she get the money? Is she rich? [*She waits for some answer to this volley of questions.*]

Hmm! You won't tell me anything about her, will you? Much I care. Come to think of it, I'm not so sorry for her after all. She knew what she was doing. She isn't any schoolgirl, like I was, from the looks of her letter. Does she know you're married? Of course, she must. All your friends know about your unhappy marriage. I know they pity you, but they don't know my side of it. They'd talk different if they did.

[*Too busy eating to go on for a second or so.*]

This Helen must be a fine one, if she knew you were married. What does she expect, then? That I'll divorce you and let her marry you? Does she think I'm crazy enough for that—after all you've made me go through? I guess not! And you can't get a divorce from me and you know it. No one can say *I've* ever done anything wrong. [*Drinks the last of her cup of coffee.*]

She deserves to suffer, that's all I can say. I'll tell you what I think; I think your Helen is no better than a common street-walker, that's what I think. [*There is a stifled groan of pain from the next room.*]

Did you cut yourself again? Serves you right. [*Gets up and takes off her apron.*] Well, I've got to run along. [*Peevishly*] This is a fine life for me to be leading! I won't stand for your loafing any longer. [*Something catches her ear and she pauses and listens intently.*] There! You've overturned the water all over everything. Don't say you haven't. I can hear it dripping on the floor. [*A vague expression of fear comes over her face.*] Alfred! Why don't you answer me?

[*She moves slowly toward the room. There is the noise of a chair being overturned and something crashes heavily to the floor. She stands, trembling with fright.*]

Alfred! Alfred! Answer me! What is it you knocked over? Are you still drunk? [*Unable to stand the tension a second longer she rushes to the door of the bedroom.*] Alfred!

[*She stands in the doorway looking down at the floor of the inner room, transfixed with horror. Then she shrieks wildly and runs to the other door, unlocks it and frenziedly pulls it open, and runs shrieking madly into the outer hallway.*]

[*The curtain falls.*]

QUESTIONS

1. What does the setting tell you about the Rowlands?

2. What image of Mrs. Rowland is presented in the opening stage direction? How are adjectives employed to shape your initial response to her? To what extent does the rest of the play sustain or alter this initial image?

3. How do Mrs. Rowland's initial stage actions further define her character? What adjectives and adverbs are used to direct your response to her?

4. How does Mrs. Rowland treat Alfred? What tone does she use in speaking to him? What does she complain about? What does she accuse Alfred of being and doing?

5. What happened during Mrs. Rowland's premarital affair with Alfred? Why do you suppose she didn't let Alfred's father "buy her off"? Why did she marry Alfred?

6. What is Mrs. Rowland's attitude toward Helen? How does she treat her husband's feelings for Helen? What does this suggest about the Rowlands' marriage?

7. Where is the crisis of the play? Which character comes to a crisis? What actions and descriptions indicate that the character and play have reached a crisis?

8. Mrs. Rowland precipitates the catastrophe of this play with her discussion of Alfred's affair with Helen. What do we learn about Helen? What pushes Alfred over the edge? What is the catastrophe?

GENERAL QUESTIONS

1. How does the setting of this play begin to define the characters, their relationship, and their life? What details of setting are especially significant in this respect?

2. Is Mrs. Rowland a flat or round character? Static or dynamic? Individualized or stereotyped? Why does she have no first name? What is the effect of these choices?

3. Why is Alfred Rowland kept off stage (except for his hand) and given no dialogue? How does this affect the play?

4. Alfred Rowland is presented from his wife's point of view. How accurate is this portrait? Is Alfred the man that his wife describes?

5. Why does O'Neill present the history of Alfred's family and his relationship with Mrs. Rowland out of chronological order? What is the effect of such a method of presentation? Try to reconstruct this history in chronological order, beginning with Alfred's graduation from Harvard.

6. Does this play make a point about marriage, or is it simply a study in character and perspective?

WRITING ABOUT THE ELEMENTS OF DRAMA

Although some aspects of drama, such as lighting and stage movement, are singularly theatrical, drama shares a number of elements with prose fiction and poetry. The planning and the writing processes you use in drama are very similar to those you employ for essays on fiction or poetry. Thus, in the following discussion we refer to pages earlier in the text that discuss strategies for writing about specific elements.

As you begin to plan an essay on drama, select a play and an appropriate element or series of elements. Some plays work better than others in dealing with specific elements. It would be inappropriate, for example, to attempt an essay about setting in *The Happy Journey to Trenton and Camden* (p. 1503), because this play offers few details about environment, time, or place. Be certain to choose elements that are clearly defined and have a profound effect on your reading of the play.

Once you select the play, choose a focus for your essay. This focus, which is your central idea, asserts something about a single element or about the relationship among elements in the play. For example, you might argue that a given character is flat, static, nonrealistic, and symbolic of good or evil. Or, to prove relationship among elements, you might want to claim that the meaning of a play is shaped and emphasized through setting and symbolism. In either event, the following considerations will help you determine a focus, gather the raw materials, and form a thesis for your essay.

1. *Plot, action, conflict* (see pp. 1009–11 and 135–42). In planning an essay on plot or structure, you are concerned with demonstrating some significant feature about the way events or conflicts unfold in the play. In addition, you can link this concern to other dramatic elements, such as tone or theme. In general, this topic breaks down into three areas—conflict, plot, and structure. For conflict, determine what the conflicts are, which one is central, and how it is resolved. What kind of conflict is it? Does it suggest any universal patterns of human behavior? For plot, determine the extent to which you can find separate stages of development. What is the climax? The catastrophe? How are they anticipated or foreshadowed? In examining plot structures and patterns, determine if the play has a subplot or second plot. If so, how is it related to the main plot? Is a significant pattern of action repeated? If so, what is the effect? To what extent do these parallel or repetitive patterns relate to theme and meaning? How do they control your emotional response to the play?

2. *Character* (see pp. 1011–12 and 189–93). When you write about character in drama, focus on a significant figure and try to formulate a central idea that expresses key facts about his or her role in the play. You might eventually deal with a character's personality, function, or the connection between the character and the play's meaning. Consider the

nature and the role of the character. Is he or she round or flat? Static or dynamic? Individualized or stereotyped? Realistic or nonrealistic? Is the protagonist (antagonist) a choric, or incidental, character? Symbolic in any way? Other sources of information include the ways a character is presented and defined. How is the character described in the stage directions? By other characters? By himself or herself? What does he or she say? Do? Think? What is the character's attitude toward the environment? The action? Other characters? Himself or herself? To what extent does he or she articulate key ideas in the play?

3. *Point of view and perspective* (see pp. 1012–13 and 222–27). Because most playwrights employ the dramatic point of view, this will rarely be a fruitful area for writing. In some cases, however, the play may be presented from a single character's perspective. When you deal with this technique, consider how such a perspective affects the play's structure and meaning. Why is this point of view useful or striking? What does it suggest about characters? Theme? To what extent does your reaction to the play correspond with or diverge from this perspective?

Even in plays written in the dramatic point of view, the playwright can allow characters to reveal their own point of view and impose a perspective by speaking directly to the audience (see *soliloquy*, p. 1019). In dealing with this device, consider which character delivers most of this direct address. Do you sympathize with him or her? What information is conveyed? What tone does the character use in speaking to the audience? How does such direct address help to shape your response to the play? An essay on dramatic perspective will inevitably also focus on character and meaning.

4. *Setting, sets, and props* (see pp. 1013–14 and 256–61). Normally, you will not write about setting and properties in isolation; such an essay would simply produce a detailed description of the setting(s) and objects in a play. Instead, a discussion of setting in drama should be linked to another element, such as character, mood, or meaning. Thus, such an essay will demonstrate the ways in which setting(s) and objects help to establish the time, place, characters, lifestyle, values, or ideas of a play.

When you are dealing with a single setting, you should pay close attention to the opening stage direction and any subsequent directions and dialogue that describe the environment or objects. In plays with multiple settings you will normally want to select one or two for examination. Ask yourself if the setting is realistic or nonrealistic, and to what extent it may be symbolic. What details and objects are specified? What do these tell you about the time, place, characters, way of life, and values? To what extent do they contribute to the tone, atmosphere, impact, and meaning of the play?

5. *Diction, imagery, style* (see pp. 1014, 618–22, and 293–98). As with setting, you will normally consider the devices of language in a play in order to make a point about another element, such as tone, character,

or meaning. Investigate the level of diction and types of dialect, jargon, slang, or clichés used by the characters. To what extent do these techniques define the characters and support or undercut their ideas? What connotative words or phrases do you find repeated in the play or spoken at a significant moment? What striking or consistent threads of imagery, metaphor, or simile do you find? What impact do these have on character, tone, or meaning? How do all these aspects of language shape your reaction to the play?

6. *Tone and atmosphere* (see pp. 1014–15 and 320–25). When you plan an essay on tone or atmosphere, you will usually deal with *how* the tone is established and *what* impact it has on the play's total meaning. In looking for raw materials, seek those devices the playwright employs to convey the tones of individual characters and to convey his or her own tone throughout. Look for clues in stage directions, diction, imagery, rhetorical devices, tempo, and context. How does tone articulate its meaning—directly, or indirectly through irony? Also evaluate the degree to which you (as reader or spectator) know more than most characters.

7. *Symbol and allegory* (see pp. 1016, 356–62 and 797–801). When you write about symbol and allegory you seek a connection between the symbolic or allegorical features and the themes or meaning of a play. You will write about *what* the symbols are and *how* they contribute to the play's ideas and impact. As you collect data for such an essay, you must first find the characters, objects, settings, situations, actions, words or phrases, and/or costumes that seem to be symbolic. Ask yourself what they symbolize? Are they universal or contextual? Are they instantly symbolic or do they accumulate symbolic meaning? Is the symbolism extensive and consistent enough to form an allegorical system? If so, what are the two levels of meaning addressed by the allegory? To what extent does the symbolism or allegory shape the play's meaning and your response?

8. *Theme* (see pp. 1016–17, 399–404, and 851–58). An essay on theme in drama should discuss *what* the play means and *how* this meaning is most strikingly communicated. Your essay will thus link theme with various other aspects of the play such as character, conflict, action, setting, language, or symbolism. What key ideas does the play explore and what aspects of the play convey these ideas most emphatically? As you gather the information, all the questions and areas of concern noted above should be helpful. In dealing with each topic and question, isolate the elements and devices that have the most profound impact on meaning. These will become the topics you discuss in connection with ideas.

Organizing Your Essay

Your reexamination of the play and the relevant elements, keeping all these questions and topics in mind, will produce enough information for you to frame a tentative central idea and plan of organization for the essay. The central idea states your conclusions about the elements in question. The observations that led you to such conclusions will become the supporting details that will form the body of the essay.

Your ideas may shift or expand significantly during the prewriting and writing process. New directions of investigation and new conclusions will probably develop. The way to deal with these new insights and directions is through constant revision in every phase of planning and writing.

INTRODUCTION.   On the whole, the organization used for essays about prose fiction and poetry are equally valid for writing about plays. The basic pattern includes an introduction, a body, and a conclusion. Your introductory paragraph should state the central idea, clearly establishing the point or points that you plan to make about the play. Begin with a focused thesis statement that holds true for all the separate items you are evaluating. The introduction should also include a thesis sentence that lays out the plan of the essay by enumerating the topics you will consider.

BODY.   The body of your essay should support the central idea with examples and details which you discuss point by point. Here, you can make careful and well chosen use of quotations to help illustrate your assertions. When you use quotations, always explain in your own words exactly how they advance your argument.

The body should be organized in the most logical and convincing manner. A broad array of strategies is available. If you are writing about the theme of loneliness and frustration in Keller's *Tea Party*, for example, you might select a number of objects or occurrences as the launching point for your discussion. Some of these might be the tea trolley and the sofa, or the bringing in of the cocoa and the paperboy's rapid movement past the window. Should you be discussing the specific crimes and guilt of Claudius in *Hamlet*, you might choose (1) the testimony of the Ghost to Hamlet, (2) Claudius's reaction to the players scene, (3) his speech as he is praying, and (4) his poisoning of the cup, to show how these actions convincingly establish his villainy. For such essays, you might devote separate paragraphs to each element, or you might use two or more paragraphs for each element as you expand on your ideas.

Similar strategies might be listed for every possible type of essay on drama. In dealing with character in Glaspell's *Trifles*, for example, you might claim that a number of symbolic props help establish and reinforce the character of Minnie Wright or the ideas about marriage conveyed in the play. You might then use separate paragraphs to discuss these related symbols, such as Minnie's clothes, her dead canary, and her unfinished quilt (see the first sample essay, below). Similarly, in writing about language in plays like Chekhov's *The Bear* or Albee's *The Sandbox*, you would need to establish how the particular play connects qualities of speech to revelations about topics such as character and idea. Thus, in *The Sandbox*, much use is made of clichés, repetition, and connotative words, all of which have a relationship to the traits of the characters. In *The Bear*, Smirnov's constant use of exclamations, shouts, and profanity establish his irascibility, at least until closely before the play's end. The possibilities are virtually endless. Each play and topic will offer a variety of effective methods; any organization that is logical, clear, and convincing will help you produce a strong essay.

CONCLUSION.   The conclusion should reinforce what you have advanced as your central idea in the introduction and body. At the same time, the conclusion should relate the topics with the meaning or impact of the play as a whole. Thus, your conclusion should relate the points you make about aspects such as tone, character, plot, or language to the overall meaning of the play.

SAMPLE ESSAY

The Character of Minnie Wright in Glaspell's *Trifles**

[1]
    Minnie Wright is the main character of Glaspell's *Trifles*. We learn about her, however, not from seeing and hearing her, for she does not appear or speak in the play, but only from secondhand evidence and observation. The speaking characters tell much about her, and their evidence is augmented by the condition of her kitchen, which she had left when she was arrested the day before the action of the play. Lewis Hale, the neighboring farmer, tells about her behavior on the morning after she used a rope to strangle her husband, John, in his sleep. Martha Hale, Hale's wife, tells about Minnie's young womanhood and about how she became alienated from her nearest neighbors because of John's stinginess and unfriendliness. The many objects in the kitchen indicate the emotional upset she was in before the murder. From this information we get a full portrait of how Minnie has changed from passivity to destructive assertiveness.° Her change in character is brought out by a consideration of her clothing, her dead canary, and her unfinished patchwork quilt.▫

    The clothes that Minnie has worn in the past and in the present indicate her character as a person of charm who was withered under neglect and contempt. Martha Hale mentions Minnie's attractive and colorful dresses as a young woman, even recalling a white dress with blue ribbon. This recollection prompts Mrs. Hale to observe that Minnie, when young, had been personable and attractive, though also somewhat shy ("sweet and pretty, but kind of timid

---

* See p. 1035 for this play.
° Central idea.
▫ Thesis sentence.

and—fluttery"). Mrs. Hale also remarks that Minnie had changed, and changed for the worse, during her thirty years of marriage with John Wright, whom Mrs. Hale describes as having been like a "raw wind that gets to the bone."

[2] As more evidence for Minnie's acceptance of her drab life on the farm, Mrs. Peters, the sheriff's wife, says that Minnie asked for no more than an apron and a shawl as extra clothing for her period of arrest in the sheriff's home. These modest and uncolorful garments, as contrasted with the colorful garb of her youth, suggest her habitual suppression of spirit.

The dead canary in Minnie's sewing box, however, indicates not only her love of music, but also the change brought about by inner rage against her husband. For twenty-nine years of marriage Minnie had endured her cheerless farm home, the contempt of her husband, her life of solitude, a general lack of pretty things, and the recognition that she could not share the social

[3] life of the local farm woman as an equal. But her purchase of the canary the year before indicates both the continuance and the reemergence of her love of song, just as it also suggests at least a degree of self-assertion. That her husband wrung the bird's neck may thus be seen as the cause of her change or development, from the acquiescing, self-effacing wife to a person angry enough to kill.

Like her love of song, her unfinished quilt indicates her capacity for creativity. In thirty years on the farm, never having had children, she had no better chance to be creative than to do needlework, such as the quilt that she had recently been piecing together in her kitchen. Both Mrs. Hale and

[4] Mrs. Peters remark about the beauty of her log-cabin design, and a stage direction draws attention to the "bright pieces" in the sewing basket. The inference is that even though Minnie's life had been bleak, she had been able on at least a minor level to indulge her characteristic love of color and form—and also of warmth, granted the purpose of a quilt.

Ironically, the quilt may also be taken to show the creativity in the murder of her husband. Both Mrs. Hale and Mrs. Peters interpret the breakdown of her stitching on the quilt as signs of distress about the dead canary and also of her nervousness in planning revenge. Further, even though nowhere in the play is it said that John is strangled with a quilting knot, there is no other conclusion that one can draw. Both Mrs. Hale and Mrs. Peters agree that Minnie probably intended to knot the quilt rather than sew it in a quilt stitch, and Glaspell pointedly causes the men to learn about this probability also. In other words, Minnie's habitual outlet for creativity in needlework enables her

[5] to perform the murder in the only way she can—by quietly slipping a quilting knot around John's neck without waking him up, and then by quickly drawing this slip-proof knot tight. Even though her plan for the murder is deliberate, however (Mrs. Peters reports that the arrangement of the rope was "crafty"), she is by no means cold or remorseless. Her apparent fear and helplessness after the crime demonstrate that planning an elaborate scheme of evasion of guilt, beyond simple denial, is not in her character. In addition, she is probably not so devilish that she plans or even perceives the irony of the method she uses to kill her husband—by tightening the rope around his neck and thus killing him just as he killed the bird by wringing its neck. The irony, however, is certainly intended by Glaspell.

It is important to emphasize again that Minnie does not appear in the play, and that the few short speeches she makes in response to Hale are only quoted. Readers, and viewers, can learn about her only from the words of others and from things seen or described. Nevertheless, the picture that Glaspell draws is fully realized, round, and poignant. For the greater part of her adult life, Minnie has been representative of women whose capacities for growth and expression have been stunted by the grind of life and the cruelty and insensitivity of others. For her part, she has been patient and accepting of the dreary home with her husband that is so different from the high expectations of her youth. Amid such depressing surroundings, Minnie has suppressed whatever grudges she might have developed, just as she has suppressed her prettiness, colorfulness, and creativity. But the killing of the canary is the last straw. It causes Minnie to change and to destroy her husband in an assertive and also systematic rejection of her subservient role. She is a woman who is slow to anger and who continues her concern about household matters even when in jail, but whose patience finally reaches the breaking point.

Commentary on the Essay

The opening paragraph of this essay begins by stressing how the readers learn about Minnie, the character being analyzed. The purpose is to establish the unusual fact that Minnie never appears in the play, and that therefore all conclusions about her are inferential, based on the words of others and the conclusions they reach from evidence of her actions. The central idea stresses Minnie's change from passivity to assertiveness; thus, she may be considered a round character. The thesis sentence describes an organization stemming from particular objects closely associated with Minnie. Other organizations could also have been chosen, such as the qualities of acquiescence, fortitude, and potential for anger, or the change in Minnie from subservience to vengefulness, or the reported actions of Minnie's singing, knotting quilts, and sitting in the kitchen on the morning after the murder.

In the body of the essay, paragraph 2 considers what Minnie's clothing, both past and present, shows about the suppression of her youthful potential for colorfulness. Paragraph 3 deals with the effect of the dead canary as a breaking point of Minnie's long acceptance of her acquiescent role. Paragraphs 4 and 5 consider the relationship of her unfinished quilt to her capacity for creativity, and also to the actual creativity she shows in the way in which she murders her husband. The last paragraph, 6, summarizes much of the essay, and it also considers how Minnie, though a round character, has a number of flat qualities because she is typical and representative of many other women in her position.

SAMPLE ESSAY

The Idea of the Strength of Love in Chekhov's *The Bear**

[1] In the one-act farce *The Bear*, Anton Chekhov shows a man and woman who have never met before falling suddenly in love. With such an unlikely main action, ideas may seem unimportant, but one can nevertheless find a number of ideas in the play. Some of these are that responsibility to life is stronger than that to death, that people may find justification for even the most contradictory actions, that love makes people do and say unusual and foolish things, and that lifelong commitments may be made with no more than minimal thought. One of the play's major ideas is that love and desire are powerful enough to overcome even the strongest obstacles.° This idea is shown as the force of love conquers commitment to the dead, renunciation of womankind, unfamiliarity, and anger.°

[2] Commitment to her dead husband is the obstacle to love shown in Mrs. Popov. She states that she has made a vow never to see daylight because of her mourning, and she spends her time staring at her husband's picture and comforting herself with her faithfulness. Her devotion to the dead is so intense that she claims at the start that she is already in her grave. In her, Chekhov has created a strong obstacle to love so that he might illustrate his idea that love conquers all. By the play's end, Mrs. Popov's embracing Smirnov is a visual example of the idea.

[3] Renunciation of women is the obstacle for Smirnov. He tells Mrs. Popov that his experience with women has made him bitter and that he no longer gives "a good goddamn" about them. His disillusioned words seem to make him an impossible candidate for love. But, in keeping with Chekhov's idea, Smirnov is the one who is soon confessing to the audience that he has fallen in love suddenly and uncontrollably. For him, the idea about the force of love operates so strongly that he would even claim happiness at being shot by "those little velvet hands."

[4] As if these personal causes were not enough to prevent love permanently, a major obstacle is that the two people are strangers. Not only have they never met, they have never even heard of each other. According to the main idea, however, this unfamiliarity is not insurmountable. Chekhov is dramatizing the power of love, and shows that it is strong enough to overcome lack of familiarity or friendship. Indeed, that Smirnov and Mrs. Popov are total strangers may be almost irrelevant to the idea about love's strength as shown in the play.

Anger and the threat of violence, however, make the greatest obstacles. The two characters become so irritated about Smirnov's demand for payment

---

* See p. 1024 for this play.
° Central idea.
° Thesis sentence.

[5] that, as a climax of their heated words, Smirnov challenges Mrs. Popov to a duel! Along with their own personal barriers against loving, it would seem that the threat of their shooting at each other, even if poor Luka could forestall it, would cause the beginning of lifelong hatred between the two. And yet love knocks down all these obstacles, in line with Chekhov's idea that love's power is irresistible.

[6] The idea, of course, is not new or surprising. It is the subject and substance of many popular songs, stories, and other plays and movies. What is surprising about Chekhov's use of the idea is that love in *The Bear* wins out suddenly against such unlikely conditions. These conditions bring up an interesting and closely related idea: Chekhov is suggesting that intense feelings, even irritation, anger, and professed hatred, may lead to love. In the speeches of Smirnov and Mrs. Popov, one can see hurt, disappointment, regret, frustration, annoyance, anger, and rage. Yet at the high point of these negative feelings, the characters fall in love. Could Chekhov be saying that it is a mixture of such feelings that brings out love? Though *The Bear* is a farce, and a good one, Chekhov's use of the idea of love's power is based in an accurate judgment about human beings.

Commentary on the Essay

This essay is derived from the dialogue, situations, soliloquies, and actions of the two major characters in Chekhov's play. Throughout, these sources are mentioned as the authority for the conclusions.

The introduction notes that the play is a farce but that it nevertheless contains a number of ideas. The major idea to be developed is stated as the capacity of love to reach fulfillment in unlikely or even impossible conditions. In the thesis sentence, these conditions are identified as obstacles to be found in (1) Mrs. Popov, (2) Smirnov, (3) their being strangers, and (4) their anger.

As the operative aspects of Chekhov's idea, paragraphs 2 through 5 detail the nature of the obstacles to be overcome by love. The obstacle discussed in paragraph 2, Mrs. Popov's commitment to her husband's memory, is "strong." The one in paragraph 3, Smirnov's dislike of women as a result of his previous experiences, seems to become "impossible." The one in paragraph 4, their being total strangers is claimed as a "major" obstacle to be overcome. In paragraph 5, the obstacle of anger is detailed as seeming likely to produce not love but "lifelong hatred."

The concluding paragraph indicates that the distinguishing mark of Chekhov's use of this comparatively common idea is surprise. The related idea developed in paragraph 6 is that love, being a strong emotion, may stem easily out of the other strong emotions exhibited by the two characters. Once this last thought is established, the essay is concluded with a tribute to Chekhov's serious use of the major idea.

WRITING TOPICS FOR CHAPTER 25

1. *Tea Party* might be considered a sentimental work, on the grounds that the two elderly characters are presented mainly to evoke sympathy and anguish, not to resemble the life of real persons. Write an essay defending the play against this judgment. As you write your defense, make references to Keller's characterizations and her development of character.

2. *The Bear* is one of Chekhov's most popular plays. Read another Chekhov play (for example, *The Cherry Orchard, The Seagull, Three Sisters, Uncle Vanya*) and compare it to *The Bear* (characters with characters, dialogue with dialogue, situations with situations, and so on). In light of your comparison, write an essay in which you explain and justify the continued popularity of *The Bear*.

3. *Before Breakfast* is set in an apartment in Greenwich Village in lower Manhattan around 1916. It was performed in Greenwich Village in December, 1916. Write an essay that deals with the following questions:

   a. What do you make of this convergence of dramatic and production setting?
   b. What could O'Neill assume about his original audience's reaction to the setting?

4. Write an essay which consider the following questions. Is Glaspell's *Trifles* about crime? Rural life? Marriage? The roles of rural and frontier women? The way men regarded women in 1916, when the play was written? The way men regard women even today? The way in which anger that is bottled up must eventually explode? Write an essay detailing your response, using specific details from the play as evidence in your argument. To what degree is the situation in the play realistic? If it were to be presented as a play about a similar rural murder in the 1980's, would the women have the same freedom to explore the kitchen?

5. Read the story "A Jury of Her Peers" (Chapter 2, pp. 68–83), which Susan Glaspell wrote a year after her play *Trifles*. Write an essay describing the differences you find between the story and the play (for example, the openings of the two works, the various descriptions of how the women react to their discoveries in the kitchen, the amounts of detail used in the play and in the story). Based on your findings, describe some of the characteristics of drama as opposed to fiction.

6. On the basis of the plays included in this chapter, plan and write an essay dealing with the characteristics of the dramatic form. You might wish to consider topics like the use of dialogue, monologue, speech directed at the audience rather than to other characters, action, vocal ranges, staging, comparative lengths of plays, pauses in speech, stage directions, laughter, seriousness, and the means by which the dramatists get you interested in their characters and situations.

26

Tragedy

THE ORIGIN AND NATURE OF TRAGEDY

"A tragedy is a sad story." "A tragedy is a story that ends in death." "A tragedy is the story of the fall of an individual." Everyone has preconceived notions about what constitutes tragedy in literature. Common to most definitions is the element that something bad—usually fatal—happens to the main character.

The idea that the protagonist in tragedy has to suffer and die originated in the belief in the redeeming power of sacrifice. Tragedy, like drama in general, evolved from prehistoric rites celebrating the end of winter and the return of spring, restoring fertility to the earth. In these ancient rites, the ritual sacrifice of a god or hero would be reenacted to ensure the fruitfulness of the land and to redeem the community from the barrenness of winter. Thus while the god/hero suffered a symbolic death, the community was restored and revitalized.

At some point in prehistory these rituals came to include narrative choral songs in which the mythological story of the god/hero was retold. The shift from the narrative to the dramatic mode occurred when one of the members of the chorus took the role of the god/hero and began to speak the words of this central figure. Aristotle (384–322 B.C.), one of the most perceptive and important critics of the ancient Greek world, states that this momentous shift toward tragedy as we know it occurred when the first actor was separated from the chorus by the Greek writer Thespis (in 534 B.C.). The actor assumed the central role, and the chorus became a group of soldiers, citizens, worshippers, or the like.

This shift in thinking whereby the actor becomes impersonator made dialogue and drama possible, for the god/hero could now interact with the chorus. According to Aristotle, a second actor was added by Aeschylus

(525–456 B.C.) and a third by Sophocles (ca. 496–406 B.C.). These actors could play as many different parts as the playwright wished, but the number of players was limited (in the plays of Sophocles) to a chorus and three actors.

By the time of Aristotle in the fourth century B.C., tragedy as a form had developed its own characteristics and customs. Aristotle, who attended many tragedies in the Great Theater of Dionysus in Athens, analyzed and described these characteristics in his critical work *The Poetics*. In chapter 6 he states that tragedy is "an imitation of an action that is serious, complete, and of a certain magnitude; in language embellished with each kind of artistic ornament; . . . in the form of a drama, not of narrative; through pity and fear effecting the proper purgation of these emotions."[1] Bear in mind that Aristotle is not establishing "rules" for writing tragedies, but is rather offering a structural description of the tragedies he has seen—a description that is comprehensive and perceptive. It is interesting to note that most of the examples he cites throughout *The Poetics* are from Sophocles' *Oedipus the King*, the first play in this chapter.

An analysis of the separate parts of Aristotle's definition of tragedy will help you to be a successful reader and critic of tragedies. Let us begin our dissection with Aristotle's assertion that a tragedy is "serious, complete, and of a certain magnitude." "Serious" indicates that the subject matter must be elevated, that the characters must be royal and aristocratic rather than common—in other words, that the characters must be important and worth considering, embodying all the qualities of human nature. By "complete" Aristotle means that the story must have a beginning, a middle, and an end that make a logical, causal, and artistic whole. The playwright need not dramatize *everything* about the story, but rather is free to present no more than *one* of the most significant aspects, for the "magnitude" of the plot suggests that the play must be of "a length which can be easily embraced by memory (Chapter 7)." Thus, the actual *story* of Oedipus covers the protagonist's whole life, but the *play* itself dramatizes only part of the last day of his reign as king of Thebes (Sophocles' other plays about Oedipus concern later episodes of this mythical life).

The tragedy must be "in the form of a drama" rather than a narrative. The plot must be acted out rather than told. By "action," Aristotle means the complete process of working out a single motivation from its beginning in activity to its conclusion in the perception (or recognition) of a truth. Thus, in *Oedipus*, the action develops from the hero's wish, as King of Thebes, to save this royal city from the plague, and to do it by expelling the former king's murderer. (Oedipus, we all know, is that murderer, but he learns this fact only in the course of the play.) Similarly, in *Hamlet* the

---

[1] S. H. Butcher, *Aristotle's Theory of Poetry and Fine Art*, 4th ed. (London: Macmillan, 1932). All quotations are from this edition.

action grows out of Hamlet's resolution to purify Denmark by avenging the murder of his father. In the course of dramatizing the complete working out of an original motive, the action of a tragedy moves from purpose (or activity), through emotion (or *pathos*), and finally to perception. Aristotle uses the term "plot" to describe this whole process.

Perhaps the most interesting part of Aristotle's description of tragedy is his assertion that tragic drama arouses fear and pity in the spectators and leads to a **purgation (catharsis)** of these emotions. Here, Aristotle addresses himself to the reasons we enjoy tragedy. The pity and fear that the play evokes in us allow us to experience these emotions vicariously in an extreme form. At the end of the tragedy, these emotions have been washed out of (purged from) our psyche, and we are refreshed.

The purgation of fear and pity may also be explained more fully with reference to the Freytag pyramid (see p. 1010). Looking at the pyramid, we see that fear and anxiety are touched most heavily during the tension and uncertainty (stages one and two), leading up to the climax, and pity and regret are the major emotions after the climax during the "falling action" (stage four). In other words, just as the tragedy has a clearly perceivable form and organization, it produces a similar patterning of emotions in us, the spectators or readers.

Aristotle narrows his description of tragedy still further in other chapters of *The Poetics*. He asserts, for example, that the misfortunes of the hero are brought about not by "vice" or "depravity," but rather by some "error" or "frailty" (Chapter 13). The Greek term for error or frailty is **hamartia,** which is sometimes translated as "tragic flaw." The idea behind hamartia is that disaster is brought about because of mistakes that any human being might make, regardless of social station. We, as an audience of normally imperfect human beings, can readily identify with the hero or heroine, and sympathize with his or her predicament. If the disaster were brought about by evil or viciousness, instead of feeling pity we would be happy to see a villian destroyed. On the other hand, if the protagonist were a pure soul, without fault, victimized entirely by circumstances, then we would be indignant at the fall of an innocent person, but would be unable to involve ourselves completely with the character. Thus the tragic hero is a character the audience easily identifies with: neither evil nor saintly but somewhere in between, possessing virtues and faults, a character who makes crucial mistakes that begin the process of the tragic fall.

This is not to say that concepts and philosophies about fate, fortune, the gods, and circumstances do not also play a role in the misfortunes of the hero. The Greeks believed that the gods intervened in the affairs of human beings, including tragic heroes, for their own purposes, which ordinary mortals do not understand. Similarly, Shakespeare causes Hamlet to speak about the "divinity that shapes our ends," as though external rather than internal forces control the outcomes of life. In *Death of a Salesman*, Arthur Miller introduces the power of economics in the life of the hero, and suggests that misfortune results from social class and economic forces, over which few of us have any control.

The issue of whether external or internal forces bring about the ups and downs of life is closely related to the problem of free will as opposed to destiny, a question that has perenially occupied philosophers. In tragedy, the question leads to what is often called the "tragic dilemma;" that is, a situation in which the protagonist faces two equally difficult or unacceptable choices. The assumption is that in tragedy, choices must be made, even though choice always leads to disaster. Thus Oedipus must either ignore the problems of Thebes and thereby be a bad king, or take the kingly lead in discovering and eliminating the cause of these problems (himself). Hamlet must either become a murderous avenger, contrary to his own good nature, or avoid the entire situation and retreat into ineffectiveness or suicide. Once the protagonist makes the choice, the destructive result is inevitable. It may seem, therefore, that divinity, fate, or destiny is operating even though the protagonist has apparently exercised free will in making a decision.

To complete the tragic sequence of events, Aristotle introduces two additional elements—the reversal of action and the growth of understanding or self-knowledge. He calls the **reversal** of action or intention the **peripeteia:** that instant when there is "a change by which the action veers around to its opposite" (Chapter 11). In the best tragedies, according to Aristotle, the reversal occurs simultaneously with understanding, a moment that he calls the **"recognition" (anagnorisis).** Indeed, this element is the most important of all, because it is an affirmative signal in the midst of negative events. The protagonist realizes his or her own place in the universal scheme of things, acknowledging the errors that have led to tragedy and accepting the degree to which he or she is responsible for what has happened. In effect, the tragic hero, even though not responsible for the disintegrating state of affairs, nevertheless shoulders the responsibility and accepts the consequences, no matter how catastrophic they are to himself or herself. Without this affirmation, we would have works that might be described as sad, pathetic, or despairing. With the affirmation, however, we have tragedy—the dramatic form that illustrates the heights that human beings can reach even in the lowest depths of adversity.

To this point, we have described tragedy largely with reference to Aristotle and *The Poetics*. This description is not limited to Greek tragedy. You will also learn that not all tragedy is "Aristotelian" in structure, nor is Aristotle's analysis totally descriptive of all later tragedies. Every age has redefined and refashioned tragedy to its own ends and images. In England during the Renaissance, for example, Shakespeare and his contemporaries wrote tragedies with reference to history rather than myth, and to medieval rather than Aristotelian traditions. Similarly, the eighteenth century saw the growth of the middle-class tragic protagonist and **domestic tragedy**. In the twentieth century, tragedy has been reformulated once again to include both working-class protagonists and anti-heroes. Thus Arthur Miller names his hero "Loman" (that is, "low man"), as if to emphasize the distance that modern human beings have traveled from the days of kings and princes. Modern tragedians have loosened the structure of tragic plots, lowered the level of language, and also have stressed the mechanistic nature of the universe and the hopelessness and inevitability of misfortune. Nevertheless, in the end, modern and ancient tragedies meet on common ground, with both asserting that this dramatic form must lead to some learning process, to some growth of recognition and understanding, to some degree of affirmativeness.

LANGUAGE AND TONE IN TRAGEDY

Just as character and action are important, so also are language and tone. Greek tragedy was always written in verse. As a result, Aristotle asserts in *The Poetics* that lofty diction and poetic ornaments are necessary to tragedies. This description is true, for the most part, until the late eighteenth century, on the assumption that just as tragic protagonists are important and elevated, so also is the language that they speak. Roman tragedy is poetic. English Renaissance and Restoration tragedy is written mostly in blank verse and heroic couplets. This does not mean that all tragedy before the nineteenth century is written completely in verse, for Shakespeare and most of his contemporaries mixed verse and prose in their plays. *Hamlet*, for example, shifts between blank verse and prose, depending on the characters and the circumstances. The Elizabethan playwrights also included characters from all social classes in their tragedies, thus making colloquial diction appropriate in many instances—the graveyard scene in *Hamlet* (act 5, scene 1) is a good example. In the twentieth century, tragedy has become a great deal less explicitly poetic and elevated. The shift to the common man or woman as the tragic protagonist has led to a concurrent shift from poetry to colloquial and conversational dialogue. The characters in Miller's *Death of a Salesman*, for example, speak idiomatic American English of the 1940s.

The tone of tragedy is frequently ironic. There are a number of reasons for this tendency. One of the most important is dramatic irony (Chapter 25, p. 1015). As readers or spectators, we almost always know more than the tragic protagonist. We know, for instance, that Oedipus killed his father and that Claudius murdered his brother long before the tragic heroes in either play learn these things. Thus, we see the ironic futility of many actions and statements and also ironies linked to character. For example, a tragic protagonist's greatest strength may also be one of his or her greatest weaknesses. We can see this in Oedipus's determination to unmask a murderer and save his country at all costs. It is similarly ironic that the best characters in tragedy—the most sensitive, intelligent, or honest—are the ones who suffer the most and often die. Perhaps the most effective twist of irony in tragedy is the irony of *anagnorisis*, or recognition. Increased self-knowledge and understanding must occur, but they never come until the protagonist has passed the point of no return; recognition is thus both necessary and ironically useless in averting disaster.

THE THEATER OF SOPHOCLES

In Athens, during Sophocles' lifetime (ca. 496–406 B.C.), plays were performed in the Great Theater of Dionysus during the festival of Dionysus (the god of fertility and wine) in late March or early April. The importance of plays in this festival indicates the continuing relationship between drama and religion. A typical Dionysian festival (a **Dionysia**) lasted five or six days and was an occasion for dramatic productions and an annual theatrical competition. Three tragedians (writers of tragedy) and three to five comedic playwrights were chosen to compete. Each of the comedic writers supplied one play; each of the tragedians was responsible for three related tragedies (a **trilogy**) and one **satyr play,** a short comic interlude perhaps based on the themes of the writer's tragedies.

The congregation (and audience) for the festival was enormous; all citizens of Athens and all visitors normally attended. The first two or three days were devoted to religious processions and poetry contests. The last three days were given over to the playwrights' competition. On each of these days (the festival began at dawn), the spectators watched three tragedies, a satyr play, and a comedy or two. At the end of the festival, prizes were awarded to the playwrights judged to be the best in tragedy and in comedy.

The Great Theater of Dionysus, in which Sophocles' plays were first performed, was a vast semicircular open-air amphitheater built into the side of a hill and seating twenty thousand spectators (see illustration, p. 1070). The central circle, called the **orchestra,** was the area where the chorus sang its lyrical interludes (odes) and performed dances. Tiers of seats were cut into the hills surrounding most of the orchestra. Originally, the spectators simply sat on the ground overlooking the orchestra. Later, wooden seats and then stone seats were installed. Behind the orchestra a small building called the **skene** (in Latin, the *scaena,* from which we get the word "scene") was used as a dressing room and a place for actors to await their cues. The skene was merely a tent at first and later, a wooden

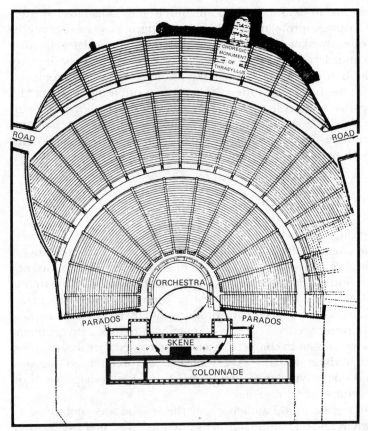

Diagram of the Great Theater of Dionysus as remodeled in the fourth century B.C.
The superimposed circle shows the original location of the *orchestra* before the *skene*
was constructed. (From R. C. Flickinger, *The Greek Theater and Its Drama* (Chicago:
University of Chicago Press, 1918), p. 64.)

building. Eventually it became a permanent building built of stone, its
front facing the audience and decorated with paintings. A sort of crane
installed on top enabled the actors playing gods to be lowered from the
"heavens" or raised up from the "earth." This piece of staging machinery,
often used by inept playwrights to end their plays quickly with the appearance of a god, led to the Latin term ***deus ex machina*** ("god from the
machine"), which is now used to describe an extraordinary and illogical
event that solves all the problems in a work. The skene had three doors
used for entrances and exits: one in the center and one each on the left
and the right. Eventually, a **colonnade** (a row of columns) was built behind
the skene at the Great Theater to provide a permanent backdrop that
suggested a palace or a temple. Some theater historians argue that a raised

wooden stage (called the **proskenion** or, in Latin, the **proscenium)** was constructed in front of the skene to separate the actors from the chorus and make them more clearly visible to the audience.

Plays were performed in this theater in broad daylight without any scenery or artificial lighting and with a minimum of props. To establish a specific time or place for the stage action, the playwright had a character mention the location or time of day in the dialogue. The plays of Sophocles were usually performed by a chorus of fifteen men (including the **choragos,** or choral leader) and three male actors. All parts, including women's roles, were played by men. The three actors could play as many different characters as the playwright required simply by withdrawing into the skene, changing masks, and reentering as a new character. Thus, in a play like *Oedipus the King* a single actor would most likely play both a prophet and a messenger. Mute (silent) characters, like Oedipus's daughters, were not considered roles and thus did not count in the total number of actors.

The chorus entered and exited the orchestra along aisles on each side of the skene called the **parados.** The actors could enter the playing area either from the skene or by way of the parados and could perform in the orchestra, on the wooden stage behind the orchestra, or even on the roof of the skene. The chorus was restricted to the orchestra and always stood between the audience and the actors. This placing of the chorus helped to emphasize its double role as participants in the action and reactors to the action. The chorus thus played an important role in the play and at the same time served as a guide for audience reaction to the drama.

The actors in classical Greek theater performed in stylized masks (called **personae** in Latin, from which we derive the word "person") that helped the audience identify mythic or stock characters. These masks had built-in megaphones that helped to amplify the actors' voices. The actors also wore thick-soled shoes, called **cothurni** or **buskins,** that elevated their height and stylized their appearance. The Athenian audience accepted the stylization (or **conventions**) of their drama as we accept the conventions of grand opera, Westerns, or situation comedies.

Plays written during the age of Sophocles are usually divided into five distinct sections: *prologue, parados, episodia, stasimon, and exodos.* The **prologue** is the part of the play that occurs before the first choral ode; it contains a great deal of exposition. The **parados** is also the name of the first lyrical ode the chorus chants after entering the orchestra for the first time; it presents the initial problems and attitudes of the chorus. The middle part of the play is made up of numerous **episodia** (episodes) and **stasima** (choric odes, the singular is **stasimon**). Each episode begins after a choral ode and ends with another. The episodes are often debates between the tragic protagonist and another character; the stasima are choral reactions to these debates. The **exodos** (exit) is the scene that follows the last choral ode of the play; it contains both the resolution of the drama and the departure (*exodos*) of the actors.

SOPHOCLES, *OEDIPUS THE KING*

When Sophocles dramatized the story of Oedipus, the myth was already hundreds of years old. Most of the Athenians who thronged to the Great Theater of Dionysus around 430 B.C. to watch Sophocles' new play would have known the story of the man who was destined to murder his father and marry his mother. They were familiar with many details of Oedipus's history: the prophecy delivered before his birth; his exposure as an infant on Mount Cithaeron; his upbringing in Corinth as the adopted son of Merope and Polybus; the murder of Laius at the place where three roads meet; his defeat of the Sphinx; his marriage to Jocasta; and his twenty-year reign as king of Thebes. In choosing to dramatize a very well-known story, Sophocles was consistent with the playwriting practices of his age; these, in fact, continued throughout the entire classical period. The dramatists in England during the age of Shakespeare, like the classical Greek tragedians, put no value on originality or timeliness. Rather, they sought new ways to dramatize old and valued tales that remained relevant for the individual and the state.

This practice of dramatizing popular myths and stories had a profound effect on the ultimate shape and impact of plays like *Oedipus the King*. Let us consider what Sophocles lost and what he gained by dramatizing a sequence of events already known to the entire audience. For one thing, he lost the opportunity to change the basic shape of the story or to alter any of the significant details of Oedipus's life. Thus Sophocles gave up any possibility of creating suspense about the resolution or of adding a surprise ending. At the same time, however, much could be gained by working with a well-known myth. Sophocles could assume, for example, that his audience would be completely familiar with the characters in the Oedipus story, so he could focus on nuances of phrasing and characterization and on conflict and meaning. Most important, Sophocles could use his audience's knowledge of the story to create dramatic irony. Early in *Oedipus the King*, for example, when Oedipus curses the murderer of Laius: "may he wear out his life unblest and evil" (line 253), the audience knows that the curse will fall on him, but Oedipus does not know this. The play is full of this kind of dramatic irony. Indeed, *Oedipus* is like a murder mystery in which the reader knows who did it right from the beginning. The pleasure and the agony are produced as we watch Oedipus the detective move step by step through a process of discovery that will ultimately lead to the guilty person—himself.

The mythic material that Sophocles worked with in shaping *Oedipus the King* details the story of Oedipus from the oracle delivered before the tragic hero's birth to his ultimate expulsion from Thebes and his old age. In forming a play from this body of material, Sophocles had to create a unified plot that limited the action to a single motivation and a single process of fall from prosperity to adversity. Sophocles did this by dramatizing only the final hours of Oedipus's reign as king of Thebes. These last hours take us from Apollo's prophecy that Thebes will be saved from the plague only through the expulsion of the murderer of Laius to Oedipus's discovery that he is that murderer. The remainder of Oedipus's story is told through conversations and debates; characters discuss at great length events that happened years before the "present time" of the dramatized day. By choosing to dramatize only part of the last day of Oedipus's reign as king of Thebes, Sophocles was able to produce a highly cohesive play that maintains the traditional **unities of place, time, and action.** The entire play occurs in the courtyard in front of the royal palace of Thebes, and the elapsed time within the play covers only part of a single day. Unity of action is achieved by focusing on a single story and a single motivation: the need to save Thebes from the plague by expelling the murderer of Laius.

Oedipus the King conforms in most respects to Aristotle's description of tragedy. Two aspects of this description are especially noteworthy in *Oedipus*: the reversal (or *peripeteia*) and the recognition (or *anagnorisis*). The play is full of reversals of action or intention. The messenger from Corinth, for example, thinks that he is releasing Oedipus from fear when he tells the king that Merope and Polybus are not his real parents; in fact, the result of this revelation is exactly the opposite of what the messenger intended. In some ways, the entire play is built on the idea of *peripeteia*. Oedipus vows to save the city by rooting out the murderer of Laius and ultimately discovers that he is that murderer. Obviously, the intention and the action have been completely reversed. The recognition of truth in *Oedipus* is tightly bound up with this central reversal. The *peripeteia* of Oedipus's action and intention occurs simultaneously with his own recognition of his errors, sins, guilt, and destiny.

At the end of *Oedipus the King* we are left with a puzzle. We must decide if Oedipus's tragic fall is produced by external forces beyond his control or by aspects of his character that led to errors in judgment and action. The play seems to offer support for both interpretations. On the one hand, Oedipus's crimes and destiny were prophesied before his birth by the oracle of Apollo. Does this mean that he was destined to murder his father and marry his mother, or does it mean that the gods simply knew the future? The distinction here is between predestination and foreknowledge. On the other hand, Oedipus's rage, his overweening pride (hubris), and his compulsive need to know the truth seem to drive him inexorably toward destruction. Finally the choice is ours; Sophocles has left us the central problem of the play to ponder on our own.

SOPHOCLES (ca. 496–406 B.C.)

Oedipus the King   *ca. 430 B.C.*

Translated by Thomas Gould

CHARACTERS

Oedipus,° *The King of Thebes*
Priest of Zeus, *Leader of the Suppliants*
Creon, *Oedipus's Brother-in-law*
Chorus, *a Group of Theban Elders*
Choragos, *Spokesman of the Chorus*
Tiresias, *a blind Seer or Prophet*
Jocasta, *The Queen of Thebes*
Messenger, *from Corinth, once a Shepherd*
Herdsman, *once a Servant of Laius*
Second Messenger, *a Servant of Oedipus*

MUTES

Suppliants, *Thebans seeking Oedipus's help*
Attendants, *for the Royal Family*
Servants, *to lead Tiresias and Oedipus*
Antigone, *Daughter of Oedipus and Jocasta*
Ismene, *Daughter of Oedipus and Jocasta*

[*The action takes place during the day in front of the royal palace in Thebes. There are two altars (left and right) on the Proscenium and several steps leading down to the Orchestra. As the play opens, Thebans of various ages who have come to beg Oedipus for help are sitting on these steps and in part of the Orchestra. These suppliants are holding branches of laurel or olive which have strips of wool° wrapped around them. Oedipus enters from the palace (the central door of the Skene).*]

PROLOGUE

OEDIPUS. My children, ancient Cadmus'° newest care,
    why have you hurried to those seats, your boughs
    wound with the emblems of the suppliant?
    The city is weighed down with fragrant smoke,
    with hymns to the Healer° and the cries of mourners.   5
    I thought it wrong, my sons, to hear your words
    through emissaries, and have come out myself,

Oedipus: The name means "swollen foot." It refers to the mutilation of Oedipus's feet done by his father, Laius, before the infant was sent to Mount Cithaeron to be put to death by exposure.   Stage direction *wool*: Branches wrapped with wool are traditional symbols of prayer or supplication.   1 *Cadmus*: Oedipus's great great grandfather (although he does not know this) and the founder of Thebes.   5 *Healer*: Apollo, god of prophecy, light, healing, justice, purification, and destruction.

I, Oedipus, a name that all men know.

[*Oedipus addresses the* Priest.]

Old man—for it is fitting that you speak
for all—what is your mood as you entreat me,   10
fear or trust? You may be confident
that I'll do anything. How hard of heart
if an appeal like this did not rouse my pity!
Priest.   You, Oedipus, who hold the power here,
you see our several ages, we who sit   15
before your altars—some not strong enough
to take long flight, some heavy in old age,
the priests, as I of Zeus,° and from our youths
a chosen band. The rest sit with their windings
in the markets, at the twin shrines of Pallas,°   20
and the prophetic embers of Ismēnos.°
Our city, as you see yourself, is tossed
too much, and can no longer lift its head
above the troughs of billows red with death.
It dies in the fruitful flowers of the soil,   25
it dies in its pastured herds, and in its women's
barren pangs. And the fire-bearing god°
has swooped upon the city, hateful plague,
and he has left the house of Cadmus empty.
Black Hades° is made rich with moans and weeping.   30
Not judging you an equal of the gods,
do I and the children sit here at your hearth,
but as the first of men, in troubled times
and in encounters with divinities.
You came to Cadmus' city and unbound   35
the tax we had to pay to the harsh singer,°
did it without a helpful word from us,
with no instruction; with a god's assistance

18 *Zeus: father and king of the gods.*   20 *Pallas*: Athena, goddess of wisdom, arts, crafts, and war.   21 *Ismēnos*: a reference to the temple of Apollo near the river Ismēnos in Thebes. Prophecies were made here by "reading" the ashes of the altar fires.   27 *fire-bearing god*: contagious fever viewed as a god.   30 *Black Hades*: refers to both the underworld where the spirits of the dead go and the god of the underworld.   36 *harsh singer*: the Sphinx, a monster with a woman's head, a lion's body, and wings. The "tax" that Oedipus freed Thebes from was the destruction of all the young men who failed to solve the Sphinx's riddle and were subsequently devoured. The Sphinx always asked the same riddle: "What goes on four legs in the morning, two legs at noon, and three legs in the evening, and yet is weakest when supported by the largest number of feet?" Oedipus discovered the correct answer—man, who crawls in infancy, walks in his prime, and uses a stick in old age—and thus ended the Sphinx's reign of terror. The Sphinx destroyed herself when Oedipus answered the riddle. Oedipus's reward for freeing Thebes of the Sphinx was the throne and the hand of the recently widowed Jocasta. (For a picture of the sphinx built in ancient Egypt, see color plate 4.)

you raised up our life, so we believe.
Again now Oedipus, our greatest power,   40
we plead with you, as suppliants, all of us,
to find us strength, whether from a god's response,
or learned in some way from another man.
I know that the experienced among men
give counsels that will prosper best of all.   45
Noblest of men, lift up our land again!
Think also of yourself; since now the land
calls you its Savior for your zeal of old,
oh let us never look back at your rule
as men helped up only to fall again!   50
Do not stumble! Put our land on firm feet!
The bird of omen was auspicious then,
when you brought that luck; be that same man again!
The power is yours; if you will rule our country,
rule over men, not in an empty land.   55
A towered city or a ship is nothing
if desolate and no man lives within.
OEDIPUS.   Pitiable children, oh I know, I know
the yearnings that have brought you. Yes, I know
that you are sick. And yet, though you are sick,   60
there is not one of you so sick as I.
For your affliction comes to each alone,
for him and no one else, but my soul mourns
for me and for you, too, and for the city.
You do not waken me as from a sleep,   65
for I have wept, bitterly and long,
tried many paths in the wanderings of thought,
and the single cure I found by careful search
I've acted on: I sent Menoeceus' son,
Creon, brother of my wife, to the Pythian   70
halls of Phoebus,° so that I might learn
what I must do or say to save this city.
Already, when I think what day this is,
I wonder anxiously what he is doing.
Too long, more than is right, he's been away.   75
But when he comes, then I shall be a traitor
if I do not do all that the god reveals.
PRIEST.   Welcome words! But look, those men have signaled
that it is Creon who is now approaching!
OEDIPUS.   Lord Apollo! May he bring Savior Luck,   80
a Luck as brilliant as his eyes are now!
PRIEST.   His news is happy, it appears. He comes,
forehead crowned with thickly berried laurel.°
OEDIPUS.   We'll know, for he is near enough to hear us.

70–71 *Pythian . . . Phoebus*: The temple of Phoebus Apollo's oracle or prophet at Delphi.
83 *laurel*: Creon is wearing a garland of laurel leaves, sacred to Apollo.

[*Enter CREON along one of the Parados.*]

    Lord, brother in marriage, son of Menoeceus!   85
    What is the god's pronouncement that you bring?
CREON.   It's good. For even troubles, if they chance
    to turn out well, I always count as lucky.
OEDIPUS.   But what was the response? You seem to say
    I'm not to fear—but not to take heart either.   90
CREON.   If you will hear me with these men present,
    I'm ready to report—or go inside.

[*CREON moves up the steps toward the palace.*]

OEDIPUS.   Speak out to all! The grief that burdens me
    concerns these men more than it does my life.
CREON.   Then I shall tell you what I heard from the god.   95
    The task Lord Phoebus sets for us is clear:
    drive out pollution sheltered in our land,
    and do not shelter what is incurable.
OEDIPUS.   What is our trouble? How shall we cleanse ourselves?
CREON.   We must banish or murder to free ourselves   100
    from a murder that blows storms through the city.
OEDIPUS.   What man's bad luck does he accuse in this?
CREON.   My Lord, a king named Laius ruled our land
    before you came to steer the city straight.
OEDIPUS.   I know. So I was told—I never saw him.   105
CREON.   Since he was murdered, you must raise your hand
    against the men who killed him with their hands.
OEDIPUS.   Where are they now? And how can we ever find
    the track of ancient guilt now hard to read?
CREON.   In our own land, he said. What we pursue,   110
    that can be caught; but not what we neglect.
OEDIPUS.   Was Laius home, or in the countryside—
    or was he murdered in some foreign land?
CREON.   He left to see a sacred rite, he said;
    He left, but never came home from his journey.   115
OEDIPUS.   Did none of his party see it and report—
    someone we might profitably question?
CREON.   They were all killed but one, who fled in fear,
    and he could tell us only one clear fact.
OEDIPUS.   What fact? One thing could lead us on to more   120
    if we could get a small start on our hope.
CREON.   He said that bandits chanced on them and killed him—
    with the force of many hands, not one alone.
OEDIPUS.   How could a bandit dare so great an act—
    unless this was a plot paid off from here!   125
CREON.   We thought of that, but when Laius was killed,
    we had no one to help us in our troubles.
OEDIPUS.   It was your very kingship that was killed!
    What kind of trouble blocked you from a search?
CREON.   The subtle-singing Sphinx asked us to turn   130

from the obscure to what lay at our feet.
OEDIPUS.   Then I shall begin again and make it plain.
It was quite worthy of Phoebus, and worthy of you,
to turn our thoughts back to the murdered man,
and right that you should see me join the battle   135
for justice to our land and to the god.
Not on behalf of any distant kinships,
it's for myself I will dispel this stain.
Whoever murdered him may also wish
to punish me—and with the selfsame hand.   140
In helping him I also serve myself.
Now quickly, children: up from the altar steps,
and raise the branches of the suppliant!
Let someone go and summon Cadmus' people:
say I'll do anything.

[*Exit an* ATTENDANT *along one of the Parados.*]

Our luck will prosper   145
if the god is with us, or we have already fallen.
PRIEST.   Rise, my children; that for which we came,
he has himself proclaimed he will accomplish.
May Phoebus, who announced this, also come
as Savior and reliever from the plague.   150

[*Exit* OEDIPUS *and* CREON *into the Palace. The* PRIEST *and the* SUPPLIANTS *exit left and right along the Parados. After a brief pause, the* CHORUS *(including the* CHORAGOS*) enters the Orchestra from the Parados.*]

PARADOS

Strophe 1°

CHORUS.   Voice from Zeus,° sweetly spoken, what are you
that have arrived from golden
Pytho° to our shining
Thebes? I am on the rack, terror
shakes my soul.   155
Delian Healer,° summoned by "iē!"
I await in holy dread what obligation, something new
or something back once more with the revolving years,
you'll bring about for me.

151,162 *Strophe, Antistrophe*: probably refer to the direction in which the Chorus danced while reciting specific stanzas. Strophe may have indicated dance steps to stage left, antistrophe to stage right.   151 *Voice from Zeus*: a reference to Apollo's prophecy. Zeus taught Apollo how to prophesy.   153 *Pytho*: Delphi.   156 *Delian Healer*: Apollo.

Oh tell me, child of golden Hope,   160
    deathless Response!

Antistrophe 1°

I appeal to you first, daughter of Zeus,
    deathless Athena,
    and to your sister who protects this land,
Artemis,° whose famous throne is the whole circle   165
    of the marketplace,
and Phoebus, who shoots from afar: iō!
Three-fold defenders against death, appear!
If ever in the past, to stop blind ruin
    sent against the city,
you banished utterly the fires of suffering,   170
    come now again!

Strophe 2

Ah! Ah! Unnumbered are the miseries
I bear. The plague claims all
our comrades. Nor has thought found yet a spear   175
by which a man shall be protected. What our glorious
earth gives birth to does not grow. Without a birth
from cries of labor
    do the women rise.
One person after another   180
    you may see, like flying birds,
faster than indomitable fire, sped
to the shore of the god that is the sunset.°

Antistrophe 2

And with their deaths unnumbered dies the city.
Her children lie unpitied on the ground,   185
spreading death, unmourned.
Meanwhile young wives, and gray-haired mothers with them,
on the shores of the altars, from this side and that,
suppliants from mournful trouble,
    cry out their grief.
A hymn to the Healer shines,   190
    the flute a mourner's voice.
Against which, golden goddess, daughter of Zeus,
    send lovely Strength.

---

165 *Artemis*: goddess of virginity, childbirth, and hunting.   183 *god . . . sunset*: Hades,
god of the underworld.

Strophe 3

Cause raging Ares°—who,   195
    armed now with no shield of bronze,
burns me, coming on amid loud cries—
to turn his back and run from my land,
with a fair wind behind, to the great
    hall of Amphitritē,°   200
or to the anchorage that welcomes no one,
Thrace's troubled sea!
If night lets something get away at last,
    it comes by day.
Fire-bearing god   205
    you who dispense the might of lightning,
Zeus! Father! Destroy him with your thunderbolt!

[*Enter* OEDIPUS *from the palace.*]

Antistrophe 3

Lycēan Lord!° From your looped
    bowstring, twisted gold,
I wish indomitable missiles might be scattered   210
and stand forward, our protectors; also fire-bearing
radiance of Artemis, with which
    she darts across the Lycian mountains.
I call the god whose head is bound in gold,
with whom this country shares its name,   215
Bacchus,° wine-flushed, summoned by "euoi!,"
    Maenads' comrade,
to approach ablaze
    with gleaming . . . . . .
pine, opposed to that god-hated god.   220

Episode 1

OEDIPUS.   I hear your prayer. Submit to what I say
and to the labors that the plague demands
and you'll get help and a relief from evils.
I'll make the proclamation, though a stranger
to the report and to the deed. Alone,   225
had I no key, I would soon lose the track.
Since it was only later that I joined you,
to all the sons of Cadmus I say this:
whoever has clear knowledge of the man

---

195 *Ares*: god of war and destruction.   200 *Amphitritē*: the Atlantic Ocean.
208 *Lycēan Lord*: Apollo.   216 *Bacchus*: Dionysus, god of fertility and wine.

who murdered Laius, son of Labdacus,   230
I command him to reveal it all to me—
nor fear if, to remove the charge, he must
accuse himself: his fate will not be cruel—
he will depart unstumbling into exile.
But if you know another, or a stranger,   235
to be the one whose hand is guilty, speak:
I shall reward you and remember you.
But if you keep your peace because of fear,
and shield yourself or kin from my command,
hear you what I shall do in that event: 240
I charge all in this land where I have throne
and power, shut out that man—no matter who—
both from your shelter and all spoken words,
nor in your prayers or sacrifices make
him partner, nor allot him lustral° water.   245
All men shall drive him from their homes: for he
is the pollution that the god-sent Pythian
response has only now revealed to me.
In this way I ally myself in war
with the divinity and the deceased.°   250
And this curse, too, against the one who did it,
whether alone in secrecy, or with others:
may he wear out his life unblest and evil!
I pray this, too: if he is at my hearth
and in my home, and I have knowledge of him,   255
may the curse pronounced on others come to me.
All this I lay to you to execute,
for my sake, for the god's, and for this land
now ruined, barren, abandoned by the gods.
Even if no god had driven you to it,   260
you ought not to have left this stain uncleansed,
the murdered man a nobleman, a king!
You should have looked! But now, since, as it happens,
It's I who have the power that he had once,
and have his bed, and a wife who shares our seed,   265
and common bond had we had common children
(had not his hope of offspring had bad luck—
but as it happened, luck lunged at his head);
because of this, as if for my own father,
I'll fight for him, I'll leave no means untried,   270
to catch the one who did it with his hand,
for the son of Labdacus, of Polydōrus,
of Cadmus before him, and of Agēnor.°
This prayer against all those who disobey:

---

245 *lustral*: purifying.   250 *the deceased*: Laius   272–273. *Son . . . Agēnor*: refers to Laius
by citing his genealogy.

the gods send out no harvest from their soil,   275
nor children from their wives. Oh, let them die
victims of this plague, or of something worse.
Yet for the rest of us, people of Cadmus,
we the obedient, may Justice, our ally,
and all the gods, be always on our side!   280
CHORAGOS.   I speak because I feel the grip of your curse:
the killer is not I. Nor can I point
to him. The one who set us to this search,
Phoebus, should also name the guilty man.
OEDIPUS.   Quite right, but to compel unwilling gods—   285
no man has ever had that kind of power.
CHORAGOS.   May I suggest to you a second way?
OEDIPUS.   A second or a third—pass over nothing!
CHORAGOS.   I know of no one who sees more of what
Lord Phoebus sees than Lord Tiresias.   290
My Lord, one might learn brilliantly from him.
OEDIPUS.   Nor is this something I have been slow to do.
At Creon's word I sent an escort—twice now!
I am astonished that he has not come.
CHORAGOS.   The old account is useless. It told us nothing.   295
OEDIPUS.   But tell it to me. I'll scrutinize all stories.
CHORAGOS.   He is said to have been killed by travelers.
OEDIPUS.   I have heard, but the one who did it no one sees.
CHORAGOS.   If there is any fear in him at all,
he won't stay here once he has heard that curse.   300
OEDIPUS.   He won't fear words: he had no fear when he did it.

[*Enter* TIRESIAS *from the right, led by a* SERVANT *and two of Oedipus's* ATTENDANTS.]

CHORAGOS.   Look there! There is the man who will convict him!
It's the god's prophet they are leading here,
one gifted with the truth as no one else.
OEDIPUS.   Tiresias, master of all omens—   305
public and secret, in the sky and on the earth—
your mind, if not your eyes, sees how the city
lives with a plague, against which Thebes can find
no Saviour or protector, Lord, but you.
For Phoebus, as the attendants surely told you,   310
returned this answer to us: liberation
from the disease would never come unless
we learned without a doubt who murdered Laius—
put them to death, or sent them into exile.
Do not begrudge us what you may learn from birds   315
or any other prophet's path you know!
Care for yourself, the city, care for me,
care for the whole pollution of the dead!
We're in your hands. To do all that he can
to help another is man's noblest labor.   320

TIRESIAS.   How terrible to understand and get
no profit from the knowledge! I knew this,
but I forgot, or I had never come.
OEDIPUS.   What's this? You've come with very little zeal.
TIRESIAS.   Let me go home! If you will listen to me,   325
You will endure your troubles better—and I mine.
OEDIPUS.   A strange request, not very kind to the land
that cared for you—to hold back this oracle!
TIRESIAS.   I see your understanding comes to you
inopportunely. So that won't happen to me . . .   330
OEDIPUS.   Oh, by the gods, if you understand about this,
don't turn away! We're on our knees to you.
TIRESIAS.   None of you understands! I'll never bring
my grief to light—I will not speak of yours.
OEDIPUS.   You know and won't declare it! Is your purpose   335
to betray us and to destroy this land!
TIRESIAS.   I will grieve neither of us. Stop this futile
cross-examination. I'll tell you nothing!
OEDIPUS.   Nothing? You vile traitor! You could provoke
a stone to anger! You still refuse to tell?   340
Can nothing soften you, nothing convince you?
TIRESIAS.   You blamed anger in me—you haven't seen.
Can nothing soften you, nothing convince you?
OEDIPUS.   Who wouldn't fill with anger, listening
to words like yours which now disgrace this city?   345
TIRESIAS.   It will come, even if my silence hides it.
OEDIPUS.   If it will come, then why won't you declare it?
TIRESIAS.   I'd rather say no more. Now if you wish,
respond to that with all your fiercest anger!
OEDIPUS.   Now I am angry enough to come right out   350
with this conjecture: you, I think, helped plot
the deed; you did it—even if your hand,
cannot have struck the blow. If you could see,
I should have said the deed was yours alone.
TIRESIAS.   Is that right! Then I charge you to abide   355
by the decree you have announced: from this day
say no word to either these or me,
for you are the vile polluter of this land!
OEDIPUS.   Aren't you appalled to let a charge like that
come bounding forth? How will you get away?   360
TIRESIAS.   You cannot catch me. I have the strength of truth.
OEDIPUS.   Who taught you this? Not your prophetic craft!
TIRESIAS.   You did. You made me say it. I didn't want to.
OEDIPUS.   Say what? Repeat it so I'll understand.
TIRESIAS.   I made no sense? Or are you trying me?   365
OEDIPUS.   No sense I understood. Say it again!
TIRESIAS.   I say you are the murderer you seek.
OEDIPUS.   Again that horror! You'll wish you hadn't said that.

TIRESIAS.   Shall I say more, and raise your anger higher?
OEDIPUS.   Anything you like! Your words are powerless.   370
TIRESIAS.   You live, unknowing, with those nearest to you
 in the greatest shame. You do not see the evil.
OEDIPUS.   You won't go on like that and never pay!
TIRESIAS.   I can if there is any strength in truth.
OEDIPUS.   In truth, but not in you! You have no strength,   375
 blind in your ears, your reason, and your eyes.
TIRESIAS.   Unhappy man! Those jeers you hurl at me
 before long all these men will hurl at you.
OEDIPUS.   You are the child of endless night; it's not
 for me or anyone who sees to hurt you.   380
TIRESIAS.   It's not my fate to be struck down by you.
 Apollo is enough. That's his concern.
OEDIPUS.   Are these inventions Creon's or your own?
TIRESIAS.   No, your affliction is yourself, not Creon.
OEDIPUS.   Oh success!—in wealth, kingship, artistry,   385
 in any life that wins much admiration—
 the envious ill will stored up for you!
 to get at my command, a gift I did not
 seek, which the city put into my hands,
 my loyal Creon, colleague from the start,   390
 longs to sneak up in secret and dethrone me.
 So he's suborned this fortuneteller—schemer!
 deceitful beggar-priest!—who has good eyes
 for gains alone, though in his craft he's blind.
 Where were your prophet's powers ever proved?   395
 Why, when the dog who chanted verse° was here,
 did you not speak and liberate this city?
 Her riddle wasn't for a man chancing by
 to interpret; prophetic art was needed,
 but you had none, it seems—learned from birds   400
 or from a god. I came along, yes I,
 Oedipus the ignorant, and stopped her—
 by using thought, not augury from birds.
 And it is I whom you now wish to banish,
 so you'll be close to the Creontian throne.   405
 You—and the plot's concocter—will drive out
 pollution to your grief: you look quite old
 or you would be the victim of that plot!
CHORAGOS.   It seems to us that this man's words were said
 in anger, Oedipus, and yours as well.   410
 Insight, not angry words, is what we need,
 the best solution to the god's response.
TIRESIAS.   You are the king, and yet I am your equal
 in my right to speak. In that I too am Lord.

396 *dog . . . verse*: The Sphinx.

for I belong to Loxias,° not you.   415
I am not Creon's man. He's nothing to me.
Hear this, since you have thrown my blindness at me:
Your eyes can't see the evil to which you've come,
nor where you live, nor who is in your house.
Do you know your parents? Not knowing, you are   420
their enemy, in the underworld and here.
A mother's and a father's double-lashing
terrible-footed curse will soon drive you out.
Now you can see, then you will stare into darkness.
What place will not be harbor to your cry,   425
or what Cithaeron° not reverberate
when you have heard the bride-song in your palace
to which you sailed? Fair wind to evil harbor!
Nor do you see how many other woes
will level you to yourself and to your children.   430
So, at my message, and at Creon, too,
splatter muck! There will never be a man
ground into wretchedness as you will be.
OEDIPUS. Am I to listen to such things from him!
May you be damned! Get out of here at once!   435
Go! Leave my palace! Turn around and go!

[*TIRESIAS begins to move away from OEDIPUS.*]

TIRESIAS. I wouldn't have come had you not sent for me.
OEDIPUS. I did not know you'd talk stupidity,
or I wouldn't have rushed to bring you to my house.
TIRESIAS. Stupid I seem to you, yet to your parents   440
who gave you natural birth I seemed quite shrewd.
OEDIPUS. Who? Wait! Who is the one who gave me birth?
TIRESIAS. This day will give you birth,° and ruin too.
OEDIPUS. What murky, riddling things you always say!
TIRESIAS. Don't you surpass us all at finding out?   445
OEDIPUS. You sneer at what you'll find has brought me greatness.
TIRESIAS. And that's the very luck that ruined you.
OEDIPUS. I wouldn't care, just so I saved the city.
TIRESIAS. In that case I shall go. Boy, lead the way!
OEDIPUS. Yes, let him lead you off. Here, underfoot,   450
you irk me. Gone, you'll cause no further pain.
TIRESIAS. I'll go when I have said what I was sent for.
Your face won't scare me. You can't ruin me.
I say to you, the man whom you have looked for
as you pronounced your curses, your decrees   455
on the bloody death of Laius—he is here!
A seeming stranger, he shall be shown to be

415 *Loxias*: Apollo.   426 *Cithaeron*: reference to the mountain on which Oedipus was to be exposed as an infant.   443 *give you birth*: that is, identify your parents.

a Theban born, though he'll take no delight
in that solution. Blind, who once could see,
a beggar who was rich, through foreign lands   460
he'll go and point before him with a stick.
To his beloved children, he'll be shown
a father who is also brother; to the one
who bore him, son and husband; to his father,
his seed-fellow and killer. Go in   465
and think this out; and if you find I've lied,
say then I have no prophet's understanding!

[*Exit* TIRESIAS, *led by a* SERVANT. OEDIPUS *exits into the palace with his* ATTENDANTS.]

STASIMON 1

Strophe 1

CHORUS.   Who is the man of whom the inspired
    rock of Delphi° said
he has committed the unspeakable   470
    with blood-stained hands?
Time for him to ply a foot
mightier than those of the horses
    of the storm in his escape;
upon him mounts and plunges the weaponed   475
son of Zeus,° with fire and thunderbolts,
and in his train the dreaded goddesses
of Death, who never miss.

Antistrophe 1

The message has just blazed,
    gleaming from the snows   480
of Mount Parnassus: we must track
    everywhere the unseen man.
He wanders, hidden by wild
forests, up through caves
    and rocks, like a bull,   485
anxious, with an anxious foot, forlorn.
He puts away from him the mantic° words come from earth's
navel,° at its center, yet these live
forever and still hover round him.

---

469 *rock of Delphi*: Apollo's oracle at Delphi.   476 *son of Zeus*: Apollo.   487 *mantic*:
prophetic.   487–88 *earth's navel*: Delphi.

Strophe 2

Terribly he troubles me,   490
    the skilled interpreter of birds!°
I can't assent, nor speak against him.
    Both paths are closed to me.
I hover on the wings of doubt,
    not seeing what is here nor what's to come.   495
What quarrel started in the house of Labdacus°
or in the house of Polybus,°
    either ever in the past
    or now, I never
heard, so that . . . with this fact for my touchstone   500
I could attack the public
    fame of Oedipus, by the side of the Labdaceans
an ally, against the dark assassination.

Antistrophe 2

No, Zeus and Apollo
    understand and know things   505
mortal; but that another man
    can do more as a prophet than I can—
for that there is no certain test,
    though, skill to skill,
one man might overtake another.   510
No, never, not until
    I see the charges proved,
when someone blames him shall I nod assent.
For once, as we all saw, the winged maiden° came
against him: he was seen then to be skilled,   515
    proved, by that touchstone, dear to the people. So,
never will my mind convict him of the evil.

EPISODE 2

[*Enter* CREON *from the right door of the skene and speaks to the* CHORUS.]

CREON. Citizens, I hear that a fearful charge
    is made against me by King Oedipus!
    I had to come. If, in this crisis,   520
    he thinks that he has suffered injury
    from anything that I have said or done,

---

491 *interpreter of birds*: Tiresias. The Chorus is troubled by his accusations.   496 *house of Labdacus*: the line of Laius.   497 *Polybus*: Oedipus's foster father.   514 *winged maiden*: The Sphinx.

I have no appetite for a long life—
bearing a blame like that! It's no slight blow
the punishment I'd take from what he said: 525
it's the ultimate hurt to be called traitor
by the city, by you, by my own people!
CHORAGOS.   The thing that forced that accusation out
could have been anger, not the power of thought.
CREON.   But who persuaded him that thoughts of mine   530
had led the prophet into telling lies?
CHORAGOS.   I do not know the thought behind his words.
CREON.   But did he look straight at you? Was his mind right
when he said that I was guilty of this charge?
CHORAGOS.   I have no eyes to see what rulers do.   535
But here he comes himself out of the house.

[*Enter OEDIPUS from the palace.*]

OEDIPUS.   What? You here? And can you really have
the face and daring to approach my house
when you're exposed as its master's murderer
and caught, too, as the robber of my kingship?   540
Did you see cowardice in me, by the gods,
or foolishness, when you began this plot?
Did you suppose that I would not detect
your stealthy moves, or that I'd not fight back?
It's your attempt that's folly, isn't it—   545
tracking without followers or connections,
kingship which is caught with wealth and numbers?
CREON.   Now wait! Give me as long to answer back!
Judge me for yourself when you have heard me!
OEDIPUS.   You're eloquent, but I'd be slow to learn   550
from you, now that I've seen your malice toward me.
CREON.   That I deny. Hear what I have to say.
OEDIPUS.   Don't you deny it! You are the traitor here!
CREON.   If you consider mindless willfulness
a prized possession, you are not thinking sense.   555
OEDIPUS.   If you think you can wrong a relative
and get off free, you are not thinking sense.
CREON.   Perfectly just, I won't say no. And yet
what is this injury you say I did you?
OEDIPUS.   Did you persuade me, yes or no, to send   560
someone to bring that solemn prophet here?
CREON.   And I still hold to the advice I gave.
OEDIPUS.   How many years ago did your King Laius . . .
CREON.   Laius! Do what? Now I don't understand.
OEDIPUS.   Vanish—victim of a murderous violence?   565
CREON.   That is a long count back into the past.
OEDIPUS.   Well, was this seer then practicing his art?

CREON.   Yes, skilled and honored just as he is today.
OEDIPUS.   Did he, back then, ever refer to me?
CREON.   He did not do so in my presence ever.   570
OEDIPUS.   You did inquire into the murder then.
CREON.   We had to, surely, though we discovered nothing.
OEDIPUS.   But the "skilled" one did not say this then? Why not?
CREON.   I never talk when I am ignorant.
OEDIPUS.   But you're not ignorant of your own part.   575
CREON.   What do you mean? I'll tell you if I know.
OEDIPUS.   Just this: if he had not conferred with you
    he'd not have told about my murdering Laius.
CREON.   If he said that, you are the one who knows.
    But now it's fair that you should answer me.   580
OEDIPUS.   Ask on! You won't convict me as the killer.
CREON.   Well then, answer. My sister is your wife?
OEDIPUS.   Now there's a statement that I can't deny.
CREON.   You two have equal power in this country?
OEDIPUS.   She gets from me whatever she desires.   585
CREON.   And I'm a third? The three of us are equals?
OEDIPUS.   That's where you're treacherous to your kinship!
CREON.   But think about this rationally, as I do.
    First look at this: do you think anyone
    prefers the anxieties of being king   590
    to untroubled sleep—if he has equal power?
    I'm not the kind of man who falls in love
    with kingship. I am content with a king's power.
    And so would any man who's wise and prudent.
    I get all things from you, with no distress;   595
    as king I would have onerous duties, too.
    How could the kingship bring me more delight
    than this untroubled power and influence?
    I'm not misguided yet to such a point
    that profitable honors aren't enough.   600
    As it is, all wish me well and all salute;
    those begging you for something have me summoned,
    for their success depends on that alone.
    Why should I lose all this to become king?
    A prudent mind is never traitorous.   605
    Treason's a thought I'm not enamored of;
    nor could I join a man who acted so.
    In proof of this, first go yourself to Pytho°
    and ask if I brought back the true response.
    Then, if you find I plotted with that portent   610
    reader,° don't have me put to death by your vote
    only—I'll vote myself for my conviction.

608 *Pytho*: Delphi.   610–611 *portent reader*: Apollo's oracle or prophet.

Don't let an unsupported thought convict me!
It's not right mindlessly to take the bad
for good or to suppose the good are traitors. 615
Rejecting a relation who is loyal
is like rejecting life, our greatest love.
In time you'll know securely without stumbling,
for time alone can prove a just man just,
though you can know a bad man in a day. 620
CHORAGOS.   Well said, to one who's anxious not to fall.
Swift thinkers, Lord, are never safe from stumbling.
OEDIPUS.   But when a swift and secret plotter moves
against me, I must make swift counterplot.
If I lie quiet and await his move, 625
he'll have achieved his aims and I'll have missed.
CREON.   You surely cannot mean you want me exiled!
OEDIPUS.   Not exiled, no. Your death is what I want!
CREON.   If you would first define what envy is . . .
OEDIPUS.   Are you still stubborn? Still disobedient? 630
CREON.   I see you cannot think!
OEDIPUS.   For me I can.
CREON.   You should for me as well!
OEDIPUS.   But you're a traitor!
CREON.   What if you're wrong?
OEDIPUS.   Authority must be maintained.
CREON.   Not if the ruler's evil.
OEDIPUS.   Hear that, Thebes!
CREON.   It is my city too, not yours alone! 635
CHORAGOS.   Please don't, my Lords! Ah, just in time, I see
Jocasta there, coming from the palace.
With her help you must settle your quarrel.

[Enter JOCASTA from the Palace.]

JOCASTA.   Wretched men! What has provoked this ill-
advised dispute? Have you no sense of shame, 640
with Thebes so sick, to stir up private troubles?
Now go inside! And Creon, you go home!
Don't make a general anguish out of nothing!
CREON.   My sister, Oedipus your husband here
sees fit to do one of two hideous things: 645
to have me banished from the land—or killed!
OEDIPUS.   That's right: I caught him, Lady, plotting harm
against my person—with a malignant science.
CREON.   May my life fail, may I die cursed, if I
did any of the things you said I did! 650
JOCASTA.   Believe his words, for the god's sake, Oedipus,
in deference above all to his oath
to the gods. Also for me, and for these men!

KOMMOS°

Strophe 1

CHORUS.   Consent, with will and mind,
   my king, I beg of you!   655
OEDIPUS.   What do you wish me to surrender?
CHORUS.   Show deference to him who was not feeble in time past
   and is now great in the power of his oath!
OEDIPUS.   Do you know what you're asking?
CHORUS.   Yes.
OEDIPUS.   Tell me then.
CHORUS.   Never to cast into dishonored guilt, with an unproved   660
   assumption, a kinsman who has bound himself by curse.
OEDIPUS.   Now you must understand, when you ask this,
   you ask my death or banishment from the land.

Strophe 2

CHORUS.   No, by the god who is the foremost of all gods,
   the Sun! No! Godless,   665
      friendless, whatever death is worst of all,
   let that be my destruction, if this
      thought ever moved me!
   But my ill-fated soul
      this dying land   670
   wears out—the more if to these older troubles
   she adds new troubles from the two of you!
OEDIPUS.   Then let him go, though it must mean my death,
   or else disgrace and exile from the land.
   My pity is moved by your words, not by his—   675
   he'll only have my hate, wherever he goes.
CREON.   You're sullen as you yield; you'll be depressed
   when you've passed through this anger. Natures like yours
   are hardest on themselves. That's as it should be.
OEDIPUS.   Then won't you go and let me be?
CREON.   I'll go.   680
   Though you're unreasonable, they know I'm righteous.

                                     [Exit CREON.]

Antistrophe 1

CHORUS.   Why are you waiting, Lady?
   Conduct him back into the palace!
JOCASTA.   I will, when I have heard what chanced.   685
CHORUS.   Conjectures—words alone, and nothing based on thought.

654 *Kommos*: a dirge or lament sung by the Chorus and one or more of the chief characters.

But even an injustice can devour a man.
JOCASTA.   Did the words come from both sides?
CHORUS.   Yes.
JOCASTA.   What was said?
CHORUS.   To me it seems enough! enough! the land already troubled,   690
  that this should rest where it has stopped.
OEDIPUS.   See what you've come to in your honest thought,
  in seeking to relax and blunt my heart?

Antistrophe 2

CHORUS.   I have not said this only once, my Lord.
  That I had lost my sanity,   695
      without a path in thinking—
  be sure this would be clear
      if I put you away
  who, when my cherished land
      wandered crazed   700
  with suffering, brought her back on course.
  Now, too, be a lucky helmsman!

JOCASTA.   Please, for the god's sake, Lord, explain to me
  the reason why you have conceived this wrath?
OEDIPUS.   I honor you, not them,° and I'll explain   705
  to you how Creon has conspired against me.
JOCASTA.   All right, if that will explain how the quarrel started.
OEDIPUS.   He says I am the murderer of Laius!
JOCASTA.   Did he claim knowledge or that someone told him?
OEDIPUS.   Here's what he did: he sent that vicious seer   710
  so he could keep his own mouth innocent.
JOCASTA.   Ah then, absolve yourself of what he charges!
  Listen to this and you'll agree, no mortal
  is ever given skill in prophecy.
  I'll prove this quickly with one incident.   715
  It was foretold to Laius—I shall not say
  by Phoebus himself, but by his ministers—
  that when his fate arrived he would be killed
  by a son who would be born to him and me.
  And yet, so it is told, foreign robbers   720
  murdered him, at a place where three roads meet.
  As for the child I bore him, not three days passed
  before he yoked the ball-joints of its feet,°
  then cast it, by others' hands, on a trackless mountain.
  That time Apollo did not make our child   725
  a patricide, or bring about what Laius

705 *them*: the Chorus.   723 *ball-joints of its feet*: the ankles.

feared, that he be killed by his own son.
That's how prophetic words determined things!
Forget them. The things a god must track
he will himself painlessly reveal.   730
OEDIPUS. Just now, as I was listening to you, Lady,
what a profound distraction seized my mind!
JOCASTA. What made you turn around so anxiously?
OEDIPUS. I thought you said that Laius was attacked
and butchered at a place where three roads meet.   735
JOCASTA. That is the story, and it is told so still.
OEDIPUS. Where is the place where this was done to him?
JOCASTA. The land's called Phocis, where a two-forked road
comes in from Delphi and from Daulia.
OEDIPUS. And how much time has passed since these events?   740
JOCASTA. Just prior to your presentation here
as king this news was published to the city.
OEDIPUS. Oh, Zeus, what have you willed to do to me?
JOCASTA. Oedipus, what makes your heart so heavy?
OEDIPUS. No, tell me first of Laius' appearance,   745
what peak of youthful vigor he had reached.
JOCASTA. A tall man, showing his first growth of white.
He had a figure not unlike your own.
OEDIPUS. Alas! It seems that in my ignorance
I laid those fearful curses on myself.   750
JOCASTA. What is it, Lord? I flinch to see your face.
OEDIPUS. I'm dreadfully afraid the prophet sees.
But I'll know better with one more detail.
JOCASTA. I'm frightened too. But ask: I'll answer you.
OEDIPUS. Was his retinue small, or did he travel   755
with a great troop, as would befit a prince?
JOCASTA. There were just five in all, one a herald.
There was a carriage, too, bearing Laius.
OEDIPUS. Alas! Now I see it! But who was it,
Lady, who told you what you know about this?   760
JOCASTA. A servant who alone was saved unharmed.
OEDIPUS. By chance, could he be now in the palace?
JOCASTA. No, he is not. When he returned and saw
you had the power of the murdered Laius,
he touched my hand and begged me formally   765
to send him to the fields and to the pastures,
so he'd be out of sight, far from the city.
I did. Although a slave, he well deserved
to win this favor, and indeed far more.
OEDIPUS. Let's have him called back in immediately.   770
JOCASTA. That can be done, but why do you desire it?
OEDIPUS. I fear, Lady, I have already said
too much. That's why I wish to see him now.
JOCASTA. Then he shall come; but it is right somehow

that I, too, Lord, should know what troubles you.   775
OEDIPUS.   I've gone so deep into the things I feared
I'll tell you everything. Who has a right
greater than yours, while I cross through this chance?
Polybus of Corinth was my father,
my mother was the Dorian Meropē.   780
I was first citizen, until this chance
attacked me—striking enough, to be sure,
but not worth all the gravity I gave it.
This: at a feast a man who'd drunk too much
denied, at the wine, I was my father's son.   785
I was depressed and all that day I barely
held it in. Next day I put the question
to my mother and father. They were enraged
at the man who'd let this fiction fly at me.
I was much cheered by them. And yet it kept   790
grinding into me. His words kept coming back.
Without my mother's or my father's knowledge
I went to Pytho. But Phoebus sent me away
dishonoring my demand. Instead, other
wretched horrors he flashed forth in speech.   795
He said that I would be my mother's lover,
show offspring to mankind they could not look at,
and be his murderer whose seed I am.°
When I heard this, and ever since, I gauged
the way to Corinth by the stars alone,   800
running to a place where I would never see
the disgrace in the oracle's words come true.
But I soon came to the exact location
where, as you tell of it, the king was killed.
Lady, here is the truth. As I went on,   805
when I was just approaching those three roads,
a herald and a man like him you spoke of
came on, riding a carriage drawn by colts.
Both the man out front and the old man himself°
tried violently to force me off the road.   810
The driver, when he tried to push me off,
I struck in anger. The old man saw this, watched
me approach, then leaned out and lunged down
with twin prongs° at the middle of my head!
He got more than he gave. Abruptly—struck   815
once by the staff in this my hand—he tumbled
out, head first, from the middle of the carriage.

798 *be . . . am*: that is, murder my father.   809 *old man himself*: Laius.   813–814
lunged . . . prongs: Laius strikes Oedipus with a two-pronged horse goad or whip.

And then I killed them all. But if there is
a kinship between Laius and this stranger,
who is more wretched than the man you see? 820
Who was there born more hated by the gods?
For neither citizen nor foreigner
may take me in his home or speak to me.
No, they must drive me off. And it is I
who have pronounced these curses on myself! 825
I stain the dead man's bed with these my hands,
by which he died. Is not my nature vile?
Unclean?—if I am banished and even
in exile I may not see my own parents,
or set foot in my homeland, or else be yoked 830
in marriage to my mother, and kill my father,
Polybus, who raised me and gave me birth?
If someone judged a cruel divinity
did this to me, would he not speak the truth?
You pure and awful gods, may I not ever 835
see that day, may I be swept away
from men before I see so great and so
calamitous a stain fixed on my person!
CHORAGOS.   These things seem fearful to us, Lord, and yet,
until you hear it from the witness, keep hope! 840
OEDIPUS.   That is the single hope that's left to me,
to wait for him, that herdsman—until he comes.
JOCASTA.   When he appears, what are you eager for?
OEDIPUS.   Just this: if his account agrees with yours
then I shall have escaped this misery. 845
JOCASTA.   But what was it that struck you in my story?
OEDIPUS.   You said he spoke of robbers as the ones
who killed him. Now: if he continues still
to speak of many, then I could not have killed him.
One man and many men just do not jibe. 850
But if he says one belted man, the doubt
is gone. The balance tips toward me. I did it.
JOCASTA.   No! He told it as I told you. Be certain.
He can't reject that and reverse himself.
The city heard these things, not I alone. 855
But even if he swerves from what he said,
he'll never show that Laius' murder, Lord,
occurred just as predicted. For Loxias
expressly said my son was doomed to kill him.
The boy—poor boy—he never had a chance 860
to cut him down, for he was cut down first.
Never again, just for some oracle
will I shoot frightened glances right and left.
OEDIPUS.   That's full of sense. Nonetheless, send a man
to bring that farm hand here. Will you do it?

865

JOCASTA.   I'll send one right away. But let's go in.
        Would I do anything against your wishes?

                [*Exit OEDIPUS and JOCASTA through the central door into the palace.*]

STASIMON 2

Strophe 1

CHORUS.   May there accompany me
        the fate to keep a reverential purity in what I say,
        in all I do, for which the laws have been set forth   870
        and walk on high, born to traverse the brightest,
        highest upper air; Olympus° only
        is their father, nor was it
        mortal nature
        that fathered them, and never will   875
        oblivion lull them into sleep;
        the god in them is great and never ages.

Antistrophe 1

        The will to violate, seed of the tyrant,
        if it has drunk mindlessly of wealth and power,
        without a sense of time or true advantage,   880
        mounts to a peak, then
        plunges to an abrupt . . . destiny,
        where the useful foot
        is of no use. But the kind
        of struggling that is good for the city   885
        I ask the god never to abolish.
        The god is my protector: never will I give that up.

Strophe 2

        But if a man proceeds disdainfully
                in deeds of hand or word
        and has no fear of Justice   890
                or reverence for shrines of the divinities
        (may a bad fate catch him
                for his luckless wantonness!),
        if he'll not gain what he gains with justice
        and deny himself what is unholy,   895
        or if he clings, in foolishness, to the untouchable

872 *Olympus*: Mount Olympus, home of the gods, treated as a god.

(what man, finally, in such an action, will have strength
enough to fend off passion's arrows from his soul?),
if, I say, this kind of
    deed is held in honor—   900
why should I join the sacred dance?

Antistrophe 2

No longer shall I visit and revere
    Earth's navel,° the untouchable,
nor visit Abae's° temple,
    or Olympia,°   905
if the prophecies are not matched by events
    for all the world to point to.
No, you who hold the power, if you are rightly called
Zeus the king of all, let this matter not escape you
and your ever-deathless rule,   910
for the prophecies to Laius fade . . .
and men already disregard them;
nor is Apollo anywhere
    glorified with honors.
Religion slips away.   915

EPISODE 3

[*Enter* JOCASTA *from the palace carrying a branch wound with wool and a jar of incense. She is attended by two women.*]

JOCASTA.   Lords of the realm, the thought has come to me
    to visit shrines of the divinities
    with suppliant's branch in hand and fragrant smoke.
    For Oedipus excites his soul too much
    with alarms of all kinds. He will not judge   920
    the present by the past, like a man of sense.
    He's at the mercy of all terror-mongers.

[JOCASTA *approaches the altar on the right and kneels.*]

    Since I can do no good by counseling,
    Apollo the Lycēan!—you are the closest—
    I come a suppliant, with these my vows,   925
    for a cleansing that will not pollute him.
    For when we see him shaken we are all
    afraid, like people looking at their helmsman.

---

903 *Earth's navel*: Delphi   904 *Abae*: a town in Phocis where there was another oracle of Apollo.   905 *Olympia*: site of the oracle of Zeus.

[*Enter a* MESSENGER *along one of the Parados. He sees* JOCASTA *at the altar and then addresses the* CHORUS.]

MESSENGER.   I would be pleased if you would help me, stranger.
Where is the palace of King Oedipus?   930
Or tell me where he is himself, if you know.
CHORUS.   This is his house, stranger. He is within.
This is his wife and mother of his children.
MESSENGER.   May she and her family find prosperity,
if, as you say, her marriage is fulfilled.   935
JOCASTA.   You also, stranger, for you deserve as much
for your gracious words. But tell me why you've come.
What do you wish? Or what have you to tell us?
MESSENGER.   Good news, my Lady, both for your house and
husband.
JOCASTA.   What is your news? And who has sent you to us?   940
MESSENGER.   I come from Corinth. When you have heard my
news
you will rejoice, I'm sure—and grieve perhaps.
JOCASTA.   What is it? How can it have this double power?
MESSENGER.   They will establish him their king, so say
the people of the land of Isthmia.°   945
JOCASTA.   But is old Polybus not still in power?
MESSENGER.   He's not, for death has clasped him in the tomb.
JOCASTA.   What's this? Has Oedipus' father died?
MESSENGER.   If I have lied then I deserve to die.
JOCASTA.   Attendant! Go quickly to your master,   950
and tell him this.

                              [*Exit an* ATTENDANT *into the palace.*]

              Oracles of the gods!
Where are you now? The man whom Oedipus
fled long ago, for fear that he should kill him—
he's been destroyed by chance and not by him!

[*Enter* OEDIPUS *from the palace.*]

OEDIPUS.   Darling Jocasta, my beloved wife,   955
Why have you called me from the palace?
JOCASTA.   First hear what this man has to say. Then see
what the god's grave oracle has come to now!
OEDIPUS.   Where is he from? What is this news he brings me?
JOCASTA.   From Corinth. He brings news about your father: 960
that Polybus is no more! that he is dead!
OEDIPUS.   What's this, old man? I want to hear you say it.
MESSENGER.   If this is what must first be clarified,
please be assured that he is dead and gone.
OEDIPUS.   By treachery or by the touch of sickness?   965

---

945 *land of Isthmia:* Corinth, which was on an isthmus.

MESSENGER.   Light pressures tip agéd frames into their sleep.
OEDIPUS.   You mean the poor man died of some disease.
MESSENGER.   And of the length of years that he had tallied.
OEDIPUS.   Aha! Then why should we look to Pytho's vapors,°
    or to the birds that scream above our heads?°   970
    If we could really take those things for guides,
    I would have killed my father. But he's dead!
    He is beneath the earth, and here am I,
    who never touched a spear. Unless he died
    of longing for me and I "killed" him that way!   975
    No, in this case, Polybus, by dying, took
    the worthless oracle to Hades with him.
JOCASTA.   And wasn't I telling you that just now?
OEDIPUS.   You were indeed. I was misled by fear.
JOCASTA.   You should not care about this anymore.   980
OEDIPUS.   I must care. I must stay clear of my mother's bed.
JOCASTA.   What's there for man to fear? The realm of chance
    prevails. True foresight isn't possible.
    His life is best who lives without a plan.
    This marriage with your mother—don't fear it.   985
    How many times have men in dreams, too, slept
    with their own mothers! Those who believe such things
    mean nothing endure their lives most easily.
OEDIPUS.   A fine, bold speech, and you are right, perhaps,
    except that my mother is still living,   990
    so I must fear her, however well you argue.
JOCASTA.   And yet your father's tomb is a great eye.
OEDIPUS.   Illuminating, yes. But I still fear the living.
MESSENGER.   Who is the woman who inspires this fear?
OEDIPUS.   Meropē, Polybus' wife, old man.   995
MESSENGER.   And what is there about her that alarms you?
OEDIPUS.   An oracle, god-sent and fearful, stranger.
MESSENGER.   Is it permitted that another know?
OEDIPUS.   It is. Loxias once said to me
    I must have intercourse with my own mother   1000
    and take my father's blood with these my hands.
    So I have long lived far away from Corinth.
    This has indeed brought much good luck, and yet,
    to see one's parents' eyes is happiest.
MESSENGER.   Was it for this that you have lived in exile?   1005
OEDIPUS.   So I'd not be my father's killer, sir.
MESSENGER.   Had I not better free you from this fear,
    my Lord? That's why I came—to do you service.
OEDIPUS.   Indeed, what a reward you'd get for that!
MESSENGER.   Indeed, this is the main point of my trip,   1010
    to be rewarded when you get back home.

969 *Pytho's vapors*: the prophecies of the oracle at Delphi.   970 *birds . . . heads*: the
prophecies derived from interpreting the flights of birds.

OEDIPUS.   I'll never rejoin the givers of my seed!°
MESSENGER.   My son, clearly you don't know what you're doing.
OEDIPUS.   But how is that, old man? For the gods' sake, tell me!
MESSENGER.   If it's because of them you won't go home.   1015
OEDIPUS.   I fear that Phoebus will have told the truth.
MESSENGER.   Pollution from the ones who gave you seed?
OEDIPUS.   That is the thing, old man, I always fear.
MESSENGER.   Your fear is groundless. Understand that.
OEDIPUS.   Groundless? Not if I was born their son.   1020
MESSENGER.   But Polybus is not related to you.
OEDIPUS.   Do you mean Polybus was not my father?
MESSENGER.   No more than I. We're both the same to you.
OEDIPUS.   Same? One who begot me and one who didn't?
MESSENGER.   He didn't beget you any more than I did.   1025
OEDIPUS.   But then, why did he say I was his son?
MESSENGER.   He got you as a gift from my own hands.
OEDIPUS.   He loved me so, though from another's hands?
MESSENGER.   His former childlessness persuaded him.
OEDIPUS.   But had you bought me, or begotten me?   1030
MESSENGER.   Found you. In the forest hallows of Cithaeron.
OEDIPUS.   What were you doing traveling in that region?
MESSENGER.   I was in charge of flocks which grazed those mountains.
OEDIPUS.   A wanderer who worked the flocks for hire?
MESSENGER.   Ah, but that day I was your savior, son.   1035
OEDIPUS.   From what? What was my trouble when you took me?
MESSENGER.   The ball-joints of your feet might testify.
OEDIPUS.   What's that? What makes you name that ancient trouble?
MESSENGER.   Your feet were pierced and I am your rescuer.
OEDIPUS.   A fearful rebuke those tokens left for me!   1040
MESSENGER.   That was the chance that names you who you are.
OEDIPUS.   By the gods, did my mother or my father do this?
MESSENGER.   That I don't know. He might who gave you to me.
OEDIPUS.   From someone else? You didn't chance on me?
MESSENGER.   Another shepherd handed you to me.   1045
OEDIPUS.   Who was he? Do you know? Will you explain!
MESSENGER.   They called him one of the men of—was it Laius?
OEDIPUS.   The one who once was king here long ago?
MESSENGER.   That is the one! The man was shepherd to him.
OEDIPUS.   And is he still alive so I can see him?   1050
MESSENGER.   But you who live here ought to know that best.
OEDIPUS.   Does any one of you now present know
   about the shepherd whom this man has named?
   Have you seen him in town or in the fields? Speak out!
   The time has come for the discovery!   1055
CHORAGOS.   The man he speaks of, I believe, is the same

1012 *givers of my seed*: that is, my parents. Oedipus still thinks Merope and Polybus are his
parents.

as the field hand you have already asked to see.
But it's Jocasta who would know this best.
OEDIPUS.   Lady, do you remember the man we just
now sent for—is that the man he speaks of?   1060
JOCASTA.   What? The man he spoke of? Pay no attention!
His words are not worth thinking about. It's nothing.
OEDIPUS.   With clues like this within my grasp, give up?
Fail to solve the mystery of my birth?
JOCASTA.   For the love of the gods, and if you love your life,   1065
give up this search! My sickness is enough.
OEDIPUS.   Come! Though my mothers for three generations
were in slavery, you'd not be lowborn!
JOCASTA.   No, listen to me! Please! Don't do this thing!
OEDIPUS.   I will not listen; I will search out the truth.   1070
JOCASTA.   My thinking is for you—it would be best.
OEDIPUS.   This "best" of yours is starting to annoy me.
JOCASTA.   Doomed man! Never find out who you are!
OEDIPUS.   Will someone go and bring that shepherd here?
Leave her to glory in her wealthy birth!   1075
JOCASTA.   Man of misery! No other name
shall I address you by, ever again.

[*Exit JOCASTA into the palace after a long pause.*]

CHORAGOS.   Why has your lady left, Oedipus,
hurled by a savage grief? I am afraid
disaster will come bursting from this silence.   1080
OEDIPUS.   Let it burst forth! However low this seed
of mine may be, yet I desire to see it.
She, perhaps—she has a woman's pride—
is mortified by my base origins.
But I who count myself the child of Chance,   1085
the giver of good, shall never know dishonor.
She is my mother,° and the months my brothers
who first marked out my lowness, then my greatness.
I shall not prove untrue to such a nature
by giving up the search for my own birth.   1090

STASIMON 3

Strophe

CHORUS.   If I have mantic power
and excellence in thought,
by Olympus,
you shall not, Cithaeron, at tomorrow's

1087 *She . . . mother*: Chance is my mother.

full moon, 1095
fail to hear us celebrate you as the countryman
of Oedipus, his nurse and mother,
or fail to be the subject of our dance,
     since you have given pleasure
to our king. 1100
Phoebus, whom we summon by "iē!,"
may this be pleasing to you!

Antistrophe

Who was your mother, son?
which of the long-lived nymphs
after lying with Pan,° 1105
     the mountain roaming . . . Or was it a bride
of Loxias?°
For dear to him are all the upland pastures.
Or was it Mount Cyllēnē's lord,°
or the Bacchic god,° 1110
     dweller of the mountain peaks,
who received you as a joyous find
from one of the nymphs of Helicon,
the favorite sharers of his sport?

EPISODE 4

OEDIPUS.   If someone like myself, who never met him, 1115
    may calculate—elders, I think I see
the very herdsman we've been waiting for.
His many years would fit that man's age,
and those who bring him on, if I am right,
are my own men. And yet, in real knowledge, 1120
you can outstrip me, surely: you've seen him.

[*Enter the old* HERDSMAN *escorted by two of Oedipus's* ATTENDANTS. *At first, the* HERDSMAN *will not look at* OEDIPUS.]

CHORAGOS.   I know him, yes, a man of the house of Laius,
    a trusty herdsman if he ever had one.
OEDIPUS.   I ask you first, the stranger come from Corinth:
    is this the man you spoke of?
MESSENGER   That's he you see. 1125
OEDIPUS.   Then you, old man. First look at me! Now answer:
    did you belong to Laius' household once?

1105 *Pan*: god of shepherds and woodlands, half man and half goat.   1107 *Loxias*: Apollo.   1109 *Mount Cyllēnē's lord*: Hermes, messenger of the gods.   1110 *Bacchic god*: Dionysus.

HERDSMAN. I did. Not a purchased slave but raised in the palace.
OEDIPUS. How have you spent your life? What is your work?
HERDSMAN. Most of my life now I have tended sheep.   1130
OEDIPUS. Where is the usual place you stay with them?
HERDSMAN. On Mount Cithaeron. Or in that district.
OEDIPUS. Do you recall observing this man there?
HERDSMAN. Doing what? Which is the man you mean?
OEDIPUS. This man right here. Have you had dealings with him?   1135
HERDSMAN. I can't say right away. I don't remember.
MESSENGER. No wonder, master. I'll bring clear memory
    to his ignorance. I'm absolutely sure
    he can recall it, the district was Cithaeron,
    he with a double flock, and I, with one,   1140
    lived close to him, for three entire seasons,
    six months long, from spring right to Arcturus.°
    Then for the winter I'd drive mine to my fold,
    and he'd drive his to Laius' pen again.
    Did any of the things I say take place?   1145
HERDSMAN. You speak the truth, though it's from long ago.
MESSENGER. Do you remember giving me, back then,
    a boy I was to care for as my own?
HERDSMAN. What are you saying? Why do you ask me that?
MESSENGER. There, sir, is the man who was that boy!   1150
HERDSMAN. Damn you! Shut your mouth! Keep your silence!
OEDIPUS. Stop! Don't you rebuke his words.
    Your words ask for rebuke far more than his.
HERDSMAN. But what have I done wrong, most royal master?
OEDIPUS. Not telling of the boy of whom he asked.   1155
HERDSMAN. He's ignorant and blundering toward ruin.
OEDIPUS. Tell it willingly—or under torture.
HERDSMAN. Oh god! Don't—I am old—don't torture me!
OEDIPUS. Here! Someone put his hands behind his back!
HERDSMAN. But why? What else would you find out, poor man?   1160
OEDIPUS. Did you give him the child he asks about?
HERDSMAN. I did. I wish that I had died that day!
OEDIPUS. You'll come to that if you don't speak the truth.
HERDSMAN. It's if I speak that I shall be destroyed.
OEDIPUS. I think this fellow struggles for delay.   1165
HERDSMAN. No, no! I said already that I gave him.
OEDIPUS. From your own home, or got from someone else?
HERDSMAN. Not from my own. I got him from another.
OEDIPUS. Which of these citizens? What sort of house?
HERDSMAN. Don't—by the gods!—don't, master, ask me more!   1170
OEDIPUS. It means your death if I must ask again.
HERDSMAN. One of the children of the house of Laius.
OEDIPUS. A slave—or born into the family?

1142 *Arcturus*: a star that is first seen in September in the Grecian sky.

HERDSMAN.   I have come to the dreaded thing, and I shall say it.
OEDIPUS.   And I to hearing it, but hear I must.   1175
HERDSMAN.   He was reported to have been—his son.
   Your lady in the house could tell you best.
OEDIPUS.   Because she gave him to you?
HERDSMAN.   Yes, my lord.
OEDIPUS.   What was her purpose?
HERDSMAN.   I was to kill the boy.
OEDIPUS.   The child she bore?
HERDSMAN.   She dreaded prophecies.   1180
OEDIPUS.   What were they?
HERDSMAN   The word was that he'd kill his parents.
OEDIPUS.   Then why did you give him up to this old man?
HERDSMAN.   In pity, master—so he would take him home,
   to another land. But what he did was save him
   for this supreme disaster. If you are the one   1185
   he speaks of—know your evil birth and fate!
OEDIPUS.   Ah! All of it was destined to be true!
   Oh light, now may I look my last upon you,
   shown monstrous in my birth, in marriage monstrous,
   a murderer monstrous in those I killed.   1190

[Exit OEDIPUS, running into the palace.]

STASIMON 4

Strophe 1

CHORUS.   Oh generations of mortal men,
   while you are living, I will
      appraise your lives at zero!
   What man
   comes closer to seizing lasting blessedness   1195
   than merely to seize its semblance,
   and after living in this semblance, to plunge?
   With your example before us,
   with your destiny, yours,
      suffering Oedipus, no mortal   1200
   can I judge fortunate.

Antistrophe 1

For he,° outranging everybody,
   shot his arrow° and became the lord
      of wide prosperity and blessedness,

1202 *he*: Oedipus.   1203 *shot his arrow*: took his chances; made a guess at the Sphinx's
riddle.

oh Zeus, after destroying   1205
the virgin with the crooked talons,°
singer of oracles; and against death,
in my land, he arose a tower of defense.
From which time you were called my king
and granted privileges supreme—in mighty   1210
Thebes the ruling lord.

Strophe 2

But now—whose story is more sorrowful than yours?
Who is more intimate with fierce calamities,
with labors, now that your life is altered?
Alas, my Oedipus, whom all men know: 1215
one great harbor°—
one alone sufficed for you,
as son and father,
when you tumbled,° plowman° of the woman's chamber.
How, how could your paternal   1220
     furrows, wretched man,
endure you silently so long.

Antistrophe 2

Time, all-seeing, surprised you living an unwilled life
and sits from of old in judgment on the marriage, not a marriage,
where the begetter is the begot as well.
Ah, son of Laius . . . ,   1225
would that—oh, would that
I had never seen you!
I wail, my scream climbing beyond itself
from my whole power of voice. To say it straight: 1230
     from you I got new breath—
but I also lulled my eye to sleep.°

EXODOS

[*Enter the* SECOND MESSENGER *from the palace.*]

SECOND MESSENGER.   You who are first among the citizens,
     what deeds you are about to hear and see!
     What grief you'll carry, if, true to your birth,   1235

1206 *virgin . . . talons*: the Sphinx.   1216 *one great harbor*: metaphorical allusion to Jocasta's
body.   1219 *tumbled*: were born and had sex.   *plowman*: Plowing is used here as a sexual
metaphor.   1232 *I . . . sleep*: I failed to see the corruption you brought.

you still respect the house of Labdacus!
Neither the Ister nor the Phasis river
could purify this house, such suffering
does it conceal, or soon must bring to light—
willed this time, not unwilled. Griefs hurt worst   1240
which we perceive to be self-chosen ones.
CHORAGOS.   They were sufficient, the things we knew before,
   to make us grieve. What can you add to those?
SECOND MESSENGER.   The thing that's quickest said and quickest heard:
   our own, our royal one, Jocasta's dead.   1245
CHORAGOS.   Unhappy queen! What was responsible?
SECOND MESSENGER.   Herself. The bitterest of these events
   is not for you, you were not there to see,
   but yet, exactly as I can recall it,
   you'll hear what happened to that wretched lady.   1250
She came in anger through the outer hall,
and then she ran straight to her marriage bed,
tearing her hair with the fingers of both hands.
Then, slamming shut the doors when she was in,
she called to Laius, dead so many years,   1255
remembering the ancient seed which caused
his death, leaving the mother to the son
to breed again an ill-born progeny.
She mourned the bed where she, alas, bred double—
husband by husband, children by her child.   1260
From this point on I don't know how she died,
for Oedipus then burst in with a cry,
and did not let us watch her final evil.
Our eyes were fixed on him. Wildly he ran
to each of us, asking for his spear   1265
and for his wife—no wife: where he might find
the double mother-field, his and his children's.
He raved, and some divinity then showed him—
for none of us did so who stood close by.
With a dreadful shout—as if some guide were leading—   1270
he lunged through the double doors; he bent the hollow
bolts from the sockets, burst into the room,
and there we saw her, hanging from above,
entangled in some twisted hanging strands.
He saw, was stricken, and with a wild roar   1275
ripped down the dangling noose. When she, poor woman,
lay on the ground, there came a fearful sight:
he snatched the pins of worked gold from her dress,
with which her clothes were fastened: these he raised
and struck into the ball-joints of his eyes.°   1280
He shouted that they would no longer see
the evils he had suffered or had done,

1280 *ball-joints of his eyes*: his eyeballs. Oedipus blinds himself in both eyes at the same time.

see in the dark those he should not have seen,
and know no more those he once sought to know.
While chanting this, not once but many times   1285
he raised his hand and struck into his eyes.
Blood from his wounded eyes poured down his chin,
not freed in moistening drops, but all at once
a stormy rain of black blood burst like hail.
These evils, coupling them, making them one,   1290
have broken loose upon both man and wife.
The old prosperity that they had once
was true prosperity, and yet today,
mourning, ruin, death, disgrace, and every
evil you could name—not one is absent.   1295
CHORAGOS.   Has he allowed himself some peace from all this grief?
SECOND MESSENGER.   He shouts that someone slide the bolts and show
to all the Cadmeians the patricide,
his mother's—I can't say it, it's unholy—
so he can cast himself out of the land,   1300
not stay and curse his house by his own curse.
He lacks the strength, though, and he needs a guide,
for his is a sickness that's too great to bear.
Now you yourself will see: the bolts of the doors
are opening. You are about to see   1305
a vision even one who hates must pity.

[Enter the blinded OEDIPUS from the palace, led in by a household SERVANT.]

CHORAGOS.   This suffering sends terror through men's eyes,
terrible beyond any suffering
my eyes have touched. Oh man of pain,
what madness reached you? Which god from far off,   1310
surpassing in range his longest spring,
  struck hard against your god-abandoned fate?
Oh man of pain,
I cannot look upon you—though there's so much
I would ask you, so much to hear,   1315
so much that holds my eyes—
  so awesome the convulsions you send through me.
OEDIPUS.   Ah! Ah! I am a man of misery.
Where am I carried? Pity me! Where
is my voice scattered abroad on wings?   1320
          Divinity, where has your lunge transported me?
CHORAGOS.   To something horrible, not to be heard or seen.

KOMMOS

Strophe 1

OEDIPUS.   Oh, my cloud
  of darkness, abominable, unspeakable as it attacks me,

not to be turned away, brought by an evil wind! 1325
Alas!
Again alas! Both enter me at once:
the sting of the prongs,° the memory of evils!
CHORUS. I do not marvel that in these afflictions
you carry double griefs and double evils. 1330

Antistrophe 1

OEDIPUS. Ah, friend,
so you at least are there, resolute servant!
Still with a heart to care for me, the blind man.
Oh! Oh!
I know that you are there. I recognize 1335
even inside my darkness, that voice of yours.
CHORUS. Doer of horror, how did you bear to quench
your vision? What divinity raised your hand?

Strophe 2

OEDIPUS. It was Apollo there, Apollo, friends,
who brought my sorrows, vile sorrows to their perfection, 1340
these evils that were done to me.
But the one who struck them with his hand,
that one was none but I, in wretchedness.
For why was I to see
when nothing I could see would bring me joy? 1345
CHORUS. Yes, that is how it was.
OEDIPUS. What could I see, indeed,
or what enjoy—what greeting
is there I could hear with pleasure, friends?
Conduct me out of the land 1350
as quickly as you can!
Conduct me out, my friends,
the man utterly ruined,
supremely cursed,
the man who is by gods 1355
the most detested of all men!
CHORUS. Wretched in disaster and in knowledge:
oh, I could wish you'd never come to know!

Antistrophe 2

OEDIPUS. May he be destroyed, whoever freed the savage shackles
from my feet when I'd been sent to the wild pasture, 1360
whoever rescued me from murder

1328 *prongs*: refers to both the whip that Laius used and the two gold pins Oedipus used
to blind himself.

and became my savior—
    a bitter gift:
if I had died then,
I'd not have been such grief to self and kin.   1365
CHORUS.   I also would have had it so.
OEDIPUS.   I'd not have returned to be my father's
murderer; I'd not be called by men
my mother's bridegroom.
Now I'm without a god,   1370
    child of a polluted parent,
fellow progenitor with him
    who gave me birth in misery.
If there's an evil that
    surpasses evils, that   1375
has fallen to the lot of Oedipus.

CHORAGOS.   How can I say that you have counseled well?
Better not to be than live a blind man.
OEDIPUS.   That this was not the best thing I could do—
don't tell me that, or advise me any more!   1380
Should I descend to Hades and endure
to see my father with these eyes? Or see
my poor unhappy mother? For I have done,
to both of these, things too great for hanging.
Or is the sight of children to be yearned for,   1385
to see new shoots that sprouted as these did?
Never, never with these eyes of mine!
Nor city, nor tower, nor holy images
of the divinities! For I, all-wretched,
most nobly raised—as no one else in Thebes—   1390
deprived myself of these when I ordained
that all expel the impious one—god-shown
to be polluted, and the dead king's son!°
Once I exposed this great stain upon me,
could I have looked on these with steady eyes?   1395
No! No! And if there were a way to block
the source of hearing in my ears, I'd gladly
have locked up my pitiable body,
so I'd be blind and deaf. Evils shut out—
that way my mind could live in sweetness.   1400
Alas, Cithaeron,° why did you receive me?
Or when you had me, not killed me instantly?
I'd not have had to show my birth to mankind.
Polybus, Corinth, halls—ancestral,
they told me—how beautiful was your ward,   1405

1391–1393 *I . . . son:* Oedipus refers to his own curse against the murderer as well as his
sins of patricide and incest.   1401 *Cithaeron:* the mountain on which the infant Oedipus
was supposed to be exposed.

a scar that held back festering disease!
Evil my nature, evil my origin.
You, three roads, and you, secret ravine,
you oak grove, narrow place of those three paths
that drank my blood° from these my hands, from him   1410
who fathered me, do you remember still
the things I did to you? When I'd come here,
what I then did once more? Oh marriages! Marriages!
You gave us life and when you'd planted us
you sent the same seed up, and then revealed   1415
fathers, brothers, sons, and kinsman's blood,
and brides, and wives, and mothers, all the most
atrocious things that happen to mankind!
One should not name what never should have been.
Somewhere out there, then, quickly, by the gods,   1420
cover me up, or murder me, or throw me
to the ocean where you will never see me more!

[OEDIPUS *moves toward the* CHORUS *and they back away from him.*]

Come! Don't shrink to touch this wretched man!
Believe me, do not be frightened! I alone
of all mankind can carry these afflictions.   1425

[*Enter* CREON *from the palace with* ATTENDANTS.]

CHORAGOS.   Tell Creon what you wish for. Just when we need him
he's here. He can act, he can advise you.
He's now the land's sole guardian in your place.
OEDIPUS.   Ah! Are there words that I can speak to him?
What ground for trust can I present? It's proved   1430
that I was false to him in everything.
CREON.   I have not come to mock you, Oedipus,
nor to reproach you for your former falseness.
You men, if you have no respect for sons
of mortals, let your awe for the all-feeding   1435
flames of lordly Hēlius° prevent
your showing unconcealed so great a stain,
abhorred by earth and sacred rain and light.
Escort him quickly back into the house!
If blood kin only see and hear their own   1440
afflictions, we'll have no impious defilement.
OEDIPUS.   By the gods, you've freed me from one terrible fear,
so nobly meeting my unworthiness:
grant me something—not for me; for you!
CREON.   What do you want that you should beg me so?   1445
OEDIPUS.   To drive me from the land at once, to a place
where there will be no man to speak to me!

1410 *my blood*: that is, the blood of my father, Laius.   1436 *Hēlius*: the sun.

CREON.   I would have done just that—had I not wished
to ask first of the god what I should do.
OEDIPUS.   His answer was revealed in full—that I,   1450
the patricide, unholy, be destroyed.
CREON.   He said that, but our need is so extreme,
it's best to have sure knowledge what must be done.
OEDIPUS.   You'll ask about a wretched man like me?
CREON.   Is it not time you put your trust in the god?   1455
OEDIPUS.   But I bid you as well, and shall entreat you.
Give her who is within what burial
you will—you'll give your own her proper rites;
but me—do not condemn my fathers' land
to have me dwelling here while I'm alive,   1460
but let me live on mountains—on Cithaeron
famed as mine, for my mother and my father,
while they yet lived, made it my destined tomb,
and I'll be killed by those who wished my ruin!
And yet I know: no sickness will destroy me,   1465
nothing will: I'd never have been saved
when left to die unless for some dread evil.
Then let my fate continue where it will!
As for my children, Creon, take no pains
for my sons—they're men and they will never lack   1470
the means to live, wherever they may be—
but my two wretched, pitiable girls,
who never ate but at my table, never
were without me—everything that I
would touch, they'd always have a share of it—   1475
please care for them! Above all, let me touch
them with my hands and weep aloud my woes!
Please, my Lord!
Please, noble heart! Touching with my hands,
I'd think I held them as when I could see.   1480

[*Enter* ANTIGONE *and* ISMENE *from the palace with* ATTENDANTS.]

What's this?
Oh gods! Do I hear, somewhere, my two dear ones
sobbing? Has Creon really pitied me
and sent to me my dearest ones, my children?
Is that it?   1485
CREON.   Yes, I prepared this for you, for I knew
you'd feel this joy, as you have always done.
OEDIPUS.   Good fortune, then, and, for your care, be guarded
far better by divinity than I was!
Where are you, children? Come to me! Come here   1490
to these my hands, hands of your brother, hands
of him who gave you seed, hands that made
these once bright eyes to see now in this fashion.

[OEDIPUS embraces his daughters.]

He, children, seeing nothing, knowing nothing,
he fathered you where his own seed was plowed.   1495
I weep for you as well, though I can't see you,
imagining your bitter life to come,
the life you will be forced by men to live.
What gatherings of townsmen will you join,
what festivals, without returning home   1500
in tears instead of watching holy rites?
And when you've reached the time for marrying,
where, children, is the man who'll run the risk
of taking on himself the infamy
that will wound you as it did my parents?   1505
What evil is not here? Your father killed
his father, plowed the one who gave him birth,
and from the place where he was sown, from there
he got you, from the place he too was born.
These are the wounds: then who will marry you?   1510
No man, my children. No, it's clear that you
must wither in dry barrenness, unmarried.

[OEDIPUS addresses CREON.]

Son of Menoeceus! You are the only father
left to them—we two who gave them seed
are both destroyed: watch that they don't become   1515
poor, wanderers, unmarried—they are your kin.
Let not my ruin be their ruin, too!
No, pity them! You see how young they are,
bereft of everyone, except for you.
Consent, kind heart, and touch me with your hand!   1520

[CREON grasps OEDIPUS's right hand.]

You, children, if you had reached an age of sense,
I would have counseled much. Now, pray you may live
always where it's allowed, finding a life
better than his was, who gave you seed.

CREON.   Stop this now. Quiet your weeping. Move away, into the house.   1525
OEDIPUS.   Bitter words, but I obey them.
CREON.   There's an end to all things.
OEDIPUS.   I have first this request.
CREON.   I will hear it.
OEDIPUS.   Banish me from my homeland.
CREON.   You must ask that of the god.
OEDIPUS.   But I am the gods' most hated man!
CREON.   Then you will soon get what you want.
OEDIPUS.   Do you consent?
CREON.   I never promise when, as now, I'm ignorant.   1530

OEDIPUS.   Then lead me in.
CREON.   Come. But let your hold fall from your children.
OEDIPUS.   Do not take them from me, ever!
CREON   Do not wish to keep all of the power.
   You had power, but that power did not follow you through life.

[OEDIPUS's *daughters are taken from him and led into the palace by* ATTENDANTS. OEDIPUS
is led into the palace by a SERVANT. CREON *and the other* ATTENDANTS *follow. Only the*
CHORUS *remains.*]

CHORUS.   People of Thebes, my country, see: here is that Oedipus—
   he who "knew" the famous riddle, and attained the highest power,   1535
   whom all citizens admired, even envying his luck!
   See the billows of wild troubles which he has entered now!
   Here is the truth of each man's life: we must wait, and see his end,
   scrutinize his dying day, and refuse to call him happy
   till he has crossed the border of his life without pain.   1540

[*Exit the* CHORUS *along each of the Parados.*]

QUESTIONS

Prologue and Parados

1. What is the situation in Thebes as the play begins? Why does Oedipus want
    to find Laius's murderer?

Episode 1 and Stasimon 1

2. How does Oedipus react to Tiresias's refusal to speak? How is this reaction
    characteristic of Oedipus? What other instances of this sort of behavior can
    you find in Oedipus's story?
3. When Tiresias does speak, he answers the central question of the play and
    tells the truth. Why doesn't Oedipus recognize this as the truth?

Episode 2 and Stasimon 2

4. What does Oedipus accuse Creon of doing? How does Creon defend himself?
    Do you find Creon's defense convincing? Why?
5. What is Jocasta's attitude toward oracles and prophecy? Why does she have
    this attitude? How does it contrast with the attitude of the chorus?
6. At what point in the play does Oedipus begin to suspect that he killed Laius?
    What details make him begin to suspect himself?

Episode 3 and Stasimon 3

7. What news does the messenger from Corinth bring? Why does this news seem to be good at first? How is this situation reversed?

Episode 4 and Stasimon 4

8. What do you make of the coincidence that the same herdsman (1) saved the infant Oedipus from death, (2) was with Laius at the place where three roads meet and was the lone survivor of the attack, and (3) will now be the agent to destroy Oedipus?
9. What moral does the chorus see in Oedipus's life?

Exodos

10. Why does Oedipus blind himself? What is the significance of the instruments that he uses to blind himself?
11. Who or what does Oedipus blame for his tragic life and destruction?

GENERAL QUESTIONS

1. In *Oedipus*, the peripeteia, anagnorisis, and catastrophe all occur at the same moment. When is this moment? Who is most severely affected by it?
2. Sophocles tells the events of Oedipus's life out of chronological order. Put all the events of his life in chronological order and consider how you might dramatize them. Why does Sophocles' ordering of these events produce an effective play?
3. Each episode of the play introduces new conflicts: Oedipus against the plague, against Tiresias, against Creon. What is the central conflict of the play? Why is it central?
4. All the violent acts of this play—the suicide of Jocasta and the blinding of Oedipus—occur offstage and are reported rather than shown to the audience. What are the advantages of dealing with violence this way? What are the disadvantages?
5. Discuss the use of coincidences in the play. How do you react to them? Do they seem convincing or forced, given the plot of the play?
6. Explore the ways in which Sophocles employs dramatic irony, with reference to three specific examples.
7. Consider the extent to which *Oedipus* is a tragedy of both the individual and the state. What do you think will happen to Thebes after Oedipus is exiled?
8. Discuss the functions of the chorus and the Choragos. What do the choral odes contribute to the play?
9. Early in the play Oedipus begins a search for a murderer. How does the object of his search change as the play progresses? Why does it change?

THE THEATER OF SHAKESPEARE

In the early part of the English Renaissance, religious drama fused with rediscovered Roman drama and neoclassical European drama to produce **Tudor interludes** (the house of Tudor ruled England from 1485 to 1603). These interludes were short tragedies, comedies, or history plays that were performed by students or professional actors. The religious drama and the interludes, in turn, gave birth to the first generation of Elizabethan playwrights: Christopher Marlowe, Thomas Kyd, Robert Greene, George Peele, Thomas Lodge, and John Lyly. These were the men whose plays William Shakespeare watched and acted in when he first arrived in London from Stratford-upon-Avon in the early 1590s.

The latter part of the English Renaissance (1580–1642) was the golden age of British drama. During the reigns of Queen Elizabeth I (1558–1603) and King James I (1603–1625) the theater in England reached a pinnacle of development that began during the early Middle Ages. Greek and Roman drama were, for the most part, lost to the world for almost a thousand years from the fall of Rome in A.D. 476 until the Renaissance. As a consequence, drama was "reinvented" in England and Europe during the Middle Ages. Not surprisingly, it once again developed in a religious context. Drama was reborn in the tenth century when short dialogues (called **tropes**) were inserted into the Catholic mass to dramatize passages of the Gospel. As these tropes grew longer and more complicated, they evolved into mystery plays, miracle plays, and finally morality plays. **Mystery plays** are dramatizations of Bible stories; **Miracle plays** provide enactments of saints' lives. **Morality plays** teach the principles of Christian life and salvation. Although originally performed by the clergy, after the thirteenth century the plays were taken over by workingmen in the craft guilds (medieval unions) and, still later, by professional actors.

The Elizabethan public theater also represents the high point of a long process of development and refinement. Before 1576 plays were performed by traveling companies of professional players on temporary stages set up in inn yards or in bear-baiting or bull-baiting arenas. Plays were also performed at court, in the great halls of aristocratic houses, in the law courts, and at universities. All these locations contributed to the ultimate shape and design of the Elizabethan public theater.

The Globe Theater, (see illustration on p. 1116) most famous of the Elizabethan public theaters, was built on the south bank of the Thames River in 1599 by members of the Lord Chamberlain's Men, the acting company to which Shakespeare belonged. It was an octagonal building with a central courtyard open to the sky. The stage thrust about 30 feet out into the yard from one of the eight sides of the building. On the remaining seven sides were three floors of galleries. Spectators sat in these galleries or, for much less money, stood in the yard around the stage

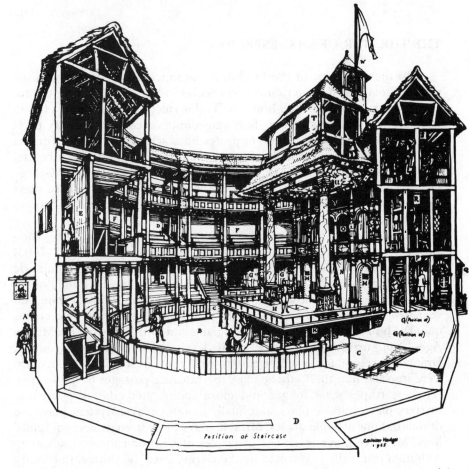

The Globe Playhouse, 1599-1613

A CONJECTURAL RECONSTRUCTION

KEY
AA Main entrance
B   The Yard
CC Entrances to lowest gallery
D   Entrances to staircase and upper galleries
E   Corridor serving the different sections of the middle gallery
F   Middle gallery ('Twopenny Rooms')
G   'Gentlemen's Rooms' or 'Lords' Rooms'
H   The stage

J   The hanging being put up round the stage
K   The 'Hell' under the stage
L   The stage trap, leading down to the Hell
MM Stage doors
N   Curtained 'place behind the stage'
O   Gallery above the stage, used as required sometimes by musicians, sometimes by spectators, and often as part of the play
P   Back-stage area (the tiring-house)
Q   Tiring-house door
R   Dressing-rooms
S   Wardrobe and storage
T   The hut housing the machine for lowering enthroned gods, etc., to the stage
U   The 'Heavens'
W   Hoisting the playhouse flag

From C. Walter Hodges, *The Globe Restored*.

(these people were called *groundlings* because they stood "on the ground"). Compared with the massive Greek theaters, the Globe was relatively small. Although it could hold as many as 2,500 spectators, no one stood or sat more than 70 feet from the action of the play.

The stage in the Globe was a *thrust stage* that extended far into the yard and was raised about five feet from the ground. The area below the stage was called the "Hell." In the center of the stage, leading to this Hell, was a trap door that was often used for the entrances and exits of devils, monsters, or ghosts. On the left and right of the stage were two pillars holding up the "Heavens," a decorated roof over the stage and a hut that concealed machinery used to lower and raise gods and goddesses. These pillars were probably used in productions to support small props and to provide hiding places for characters to observe and eavesdrop on other characters. Behind the stage was a **tiring house** and storage area where actors changed their costumes and awaited their cues. Two or three doors led from the tiring house onto the stage. In addition, there was an area at the rear of stage center where a curtained enclosure could be set up when it was necessary to indicate interior and exterior scenes at the same time. On the second floor, at the rear of the stage, was a **gallery** that was used by musicians, actors (as in the "balcony" scene in Shakespeare's *Romeo and Juliet*), or spectators.

Plays were performed at the Globe and other Elizabethan public theaters in the afternoon. As in the Greek theater, there was neither artificial lighting nor scenery. However, extensive props and elaborate costumes were used. As in Greek drama, women were excluded from the Elizabethan stage; all women's roles were played by boys. Because of these performance conditions and the physical shape of the Elizabethan theater, a number of dramatic conventions developed over time. In Chapter 25, we defined a *dramatic convention* as an implicit or understood agreement between playwrights and audiences that allows the writers to simplify and limit their material and allows the spectators to recognize and accept a number of shortcuts in staging. On the Elizabethan stage, for example, costumes were stylized to permit instant recognition of various characters. Kings always wore a robe and a crown and carried a sceptre; fools wore *motley* (multicolored) clothing; and ghosts wore leather. Since plays were performed without lights or scenery, time and place were also established through convention or dialogue. Shakespeare would indicate a night scene by having the actors carry candles or torches. Often, a character would simply state the time and place. For example, in act 2, scene 4, line 13 of *As You Like It*, the heroine says, "Well, this is the forest of Arden." In the first scene of *Hamlet*, Horatio informs the audience that it is dawn by saying, "But look, the morn in russet mantle clad / Walks o'er the dew of yon high eastward hill" (lines 166–167).

The actors in the Elizabethan public theaters used no masks. Instead, they developed a series of conventional expressions and gestures to convey various emotions. These acting conventions sometimes led to overacting. Shakespeare alludes to this in *Hamlet*, act 3, scene 2, when Hamlet advises a company of traveling actors not to "mouth" their lines "as many of your players do" and not to "saw the air too much with your hands" (lines 1–4). Hamlet goes on to condemn actors who "tear a passion to tatters, to very rags, to split the ears of the groundlings . . ." (lines 9–10).

The closeness of the spectators to the thrust stage may have led to two additional conventions of presentation that are important to Elizabethan and Shakespearean drama. One of these, called an **aside,** allows a character to make a brief remark directly to the audience or to another character without the rest of the characters on stage hearing the lines. In the other, called a **soliloquy,** a single character alone on stage speaks his or her thoughts or plans at length directly to the spectators. For example, in Hamlet's second soliloquy (act 2, scene 2, lines 524–580), the prince criticizes his emotional detachment from his father's murder and lets us in on how he plans to test Claudius's guilt. These two conventions, by giving the audience information that is withheld from the other characters, can bring about dramatic irony.

The small size of the Globe theater and the thrust of its stage made for performances that were intimate and immediate. The actors had a great deal of playing space at their disposal: the rear of the stage, the upper gallery, and also the very front of the stage. There was no barrier or separation between the audience and the actors (no orchestra and chorus) as there were in the Greek theater, and no proscenium and curtain as there are in most twentieth-century theaters. Consequently, in the Elizabethan theater there was a good deal of interaction between the actors and the spectators. The plays were performed at a very quick pace, without any intermissions or indications of changes in scene or act other than an occasional rhymed couplet. With no curtain to raise or lower and no scenery to change, shifts in scene were indicated by having one group of characters walk off one side of the stage and another group walk on from the opposite side at the same time. This type of scene change produced rapid shifts in time and place and made for great fluidity and fast pacing.

WILLIAM SHAKESPEARE, *HAMLET*

William Shakespeare, the greatest English playwright and poet, was born in 1564 in Stratford-upon-Avon. He attended the Stratford grammar school, married in 1582, had three children, and moved to London without his family sometime between 1585 and 1592. During this period he began to act in professional acting companies and to write poetry and plays; by

1595 he was recognized as a major writer of comedies and tragedies. He eventually became associated with the leading theatrical company of Elizabethan England, the Lord Chamberlain's Men, and wrote thirty-seven plays: sixteen comedies or tragicomedies, eleven tragedies, and ten historical dramas.

When Shakespeare's acting company staged *Hamlet* for the first time in 1600 or 1601 at the Globe Theater, it is more than likely that the Elizabethan audience already knew the story of the Danish prince who avenges his father's murder and is killed in the process. There is evidence that a play based on the Hamlet story, now lost, had been written and performed before 1589. If this is the case, then most of the spectators would have known that King Claudius had murdered the old King Hamlet and married the dead king's wife. Since only Claudius and Hamlet (and later Horatio) possess information about the murder, the audience knew a great deal more than most of the characters. Thus the play was open to the same kinds of dramatic irony that we find in *Oedipus the King*.

Even if the spectators did not know the Hamlet story, they would have been familiar with the traditions and conventions of **revenge tragedy.** The Elizabethans had been introduced to this type of drama in the 1570s and early 1580s, when the plays of Seneca, a Roman playwright, were translated into English and performed. The audience was also familiar with Thomas Kyd's *Spanish Tragedy* (ca. 1587), the first English revenge tragedy and the most popular play of the English Renaissance. Thus, the spectators expected to see specific key features and conventions of revenge tragedy in *Hamlet*. They expected, for example, a ghost who calls for vengeance and a revenger who pretends to be insane at least part of the time. They also expected that the revenge itself would be postponed through some twist of the plot until the end or close to the end. Above all else, the audience understood that the revenger—in this case Hamlet—would die during the conclusion. Since personal blood vengeance was forbidden by both the Church and the state, a successful revenger was automatically condemned as an outlaw. The conventions of revenge tragedy thus dictate that a revenger—no matter how good the man or how just the cause— has to die. In the light of this convention, it is possible to see Hamlet's fall partly as the result of circumstances beyond his control and partly as the result of his commitment to personal blood revenge. To make such an assertion about Hamlet, however, oversimplifies both the character and the play.

Although prepared for *Hamlet* by the traditional formulas of revenge tragedy, the Elizabethan audience could not have anticipated a protagonist of such depth and complexity. Traditionally, revengers are presented as flat characters who have a single fixation on justice through personal ven-

geance. Hamlet, however, is a much deeper character. He is acutely aware
of the political and moral corruption of the Danish court, and this awareness
leads him to reflect on the fallen state of humanity and to contemplate
suicide. In addition, Hamlet learns and changes in the course of the play.
Although he does not have the kind of dramatic and focused *anagnorisis*
that Oedipus experiences, Hamlet does learn that he must look beyond
reason and philosophy for ways of coping with the world. He also learns
to be patient and to trust in providence. In the last scene of the play he
calmly awaits the turn of events with a new understanding that "there's a
divinity that shapes our ends" (line 10) and that "the readiness is all"
(line 205).

In modern times, attempts have been made to see Hamlet as an
Aristotelian tragic protagonist, brought to his death by some aspect of his
character that leads him into error. To some scholars Hamlet's *hamartia*,
or "fatal flaw," is his tendency to overrationalize or his mother fixation
(an Oedipal complex). Most critics, however, claim that the prince's downfall
may be found in the deferring of revenge brought about by his "inability
to act." The facts in the play simply do not bear out this interpretation.
Although Hamlet chastises himself for delay, he actually wastes almost
no time at all. Once Hamlet has been urged to revenge by the ghost, he
uses both his pretended madness and "The Murder of Gonzago"—the
play-within-a-play—in an attempt to confirm the ghost's accusations against
Claudius. And once this confirmation has been gained, Hamlet acts almost
immediately. Although he cannot bring himself to kill an unarmed man
at prayers, minutes later he kills a person who he assumes is Claudius
behind the curtain in the Queen's chamber. This accidental murder of
Polonius makes Hamlet's revenge a great deal more complicated because
it turns Laertes into a revenger and also lets Claudius know that Hamlet
is trying to kill him. Hamlet's quest for revenge is further complicated
and delayed by Claudius's counterplots; the king sends Hamlet off to England immediately after the death of Polonius.

Just as Hamlet does not perfectly fit Aristotle's conception of a tragic
protagonist, so the play itself does not conform to Aristotle's description
of a tragedy (see pp. 1064–68). We may find a single motive or action in
Hamlet's desire to avenge his father's murder and cleanse the state. This
motivation, however, does not account for all the events in the play. The
story of Polonius and his family, for example, is at least partly irrelevant
to this motive. Also, Shakespeare does not follow the unities of time
and place; the play covers several months (some have suggested years),
and scenes change from place to place. Perhaps the most radical departure
from Aristotelian standards is Shakespeare's willingness to mix humorous
elements into his tragedy. Whereas Aristotle called for absolutely pure
forms of comedy and tragedy, English drama offered a mixture of elements
and modes from its beginnings. Thus, *Hamlet* presents a great deal of

humor in characters like Polonius, Osric, and the gravediggers. In addition, Hamlet's remarks are often quite witty.

Finally, we must recognize that *Hamlet*, like *Oedipus the King*, touches our lives in a significant way and raises ever-present questions about living and dying, truth and honor, art and nature, and responsibility to ourselves, our families, and the state. In the hundreds of years since Shakespeare wrote *Hamlet*, it has remained among the most popular, most moving, and most effective plays in the world. It has been translated into scores of languages, and it has successfully held the stage from Shakespeare's day to our own. Beyond its enduring stage presence, *Hamlet* has become one of the central documents of western civilization. Somehow, we all know about *Hamlet*, even if we have never read the play or seen a performance. This fact, more than anything else, testifies to Shakespeare's consummate skill as a poet and playwright.

WILLIAM SHAKESPEARE (1564–1616)

The Tragedy of Hamlet, Prince of Denmark   *ca. 1600*

Edited by Alice Griffin°

CHARACTERS

  Claudius, *King of Denmark*
  Hamlet, *Son to the former, and nephew to the present King*
  Polonius, *Lord Chamberlain*
  Horatio, *Friend to Hamlet*
  Laertes, *Son to Polonius*
  Valtemand ⎫
  Cornelius ⎪
  Rosencrantz ⎬ *Courtiers*
  Guildenstern ⎪
  Osric   ⎭
  A Gentleman
  A Priest
  Marcellus ⎫
  Barnardo ⎬ *Officers*
  Francisco, *a Soldier*
  Reynaldo, *Servant to Polonius*
  Players

Professor Griffin's text for *Hamlet* was the Second Quarto (edition) published in 1604, with modifications based on the First Folio, published in 1623. Stage directions in those editions are printed here without brackets; added stage directions are printed within brackets. We have edited Griffin's notes for this text.

Two Clowns, *gravediggers*
Fortinbras, *Prince of Norway*
A Norwegian Captain
English Ambassadors
Gertrude, *Queen of Denmark, mother to Hamlet*
Ophelia, *Daughter to Polonius*
Ghost of Hamlet's Father
Lords, Ladies, Officers, Soldiers, Sailors, Messengers, Attendants

SCENE: Elsinore]

ACT 1

Scene 1. *[A platform on the battlements of the castle]*

Enter BARNARDO *and* FRANCISCO, *two Sentinels.*

BARNARDO. Who's there?
FRANCISCO. Nay, answer me. Stand and unfold° yourself.
BARNARDO. Long live the king.
FRANCISCO. Barnardo?
BARNARDO. He.   5
FRANCISCO. You come most carefully upon your hour.
BARNARDO. 'Tis now struck twelve, get thee to bed Francisco.
FRANCISCO. For this relief much thanks, 'tis bitter cold,
And I am sick at heart.
BARNARDO. Have you had quiet guard?
FRANCISCO.   Not a mouse stirring.   10
BARNARDO. Well, good night:
If you do meet Horatio and Marcellus,
The rivals° of my watch, bid them make haste.

Enter HORATIO *and* MARCELLUS.

FRANCISCO. I think I hear them. Stand ho, who is there?
HORATIO. Friends to this ground.
MARCELLUS.   And liegemen° to the Dane.°   15
FRANCISCO. Give you good night.
MARCELLUS.   O, farewell honest soldier,
Who hath relieved you?
FRANCISCO.   Barnardo hath my place;
Give you good night.   *Exit* FRANCISCO
MARCELLUS.   Holla, Barnardo!
BARNARDO.   Say,
What, is Horatio there?
HORATIO.   A piece of him.

2 *unfold*: reveal.   13 *rivals*: partners.   15 *liegemen*: subjects.   *Dane*: King of Denmark.

BARNARDO.   Welcome Horatio, welcome good Marcellus.   20
HORATIO.   What, has this thing appeared again tonight?
BARNARDO.   I have seen nothing.
MARCELLUS.   Horatio says 'tis but our fantasy,°
      And will not let belief take hold of him,
      Touching this dreaded sight twice seen of us,   25
      Therefore I have entreated him along
      With us to watch the minutes of this night,
      That if again this apparition come,
      He may approve° our eyes and speak to it.
HORATIO.   Tush, tush, 'twill not appear.
BARNARDO.   Sit down awhile,   30
      And let us once again assail your ears,
      That are so fortified against our story,
      What we have two nights seen.
HORATIO.   Well, sit we down,
      And let us hear Barnardo speak of this.
BARNARDO.   Last night of all,   35
      When yon same star that's westward from the pole°
      Had made his course t'illume that part of heaven
      Where now it burns, Marcellus and myself,
      The bell then beating one—

Enter GHOST.

MARCELLUS.   Peace, break thee off, look where it comes again.   40
BARNARDO.   In the same figure like the king that's dead.
MARCELLUS.   Thou art a scholar, speak to it Horatio.
BARNARDO.   Looks a' not like the king? mark it Horatio.
HORATIO.   Most like, it harrows me with fear and wonder.
BARNARDO.   It would be spoke to.
MARCELLUS.   Question it Horatio.   45
HORATIO.   What art thou that usurp'st° this time of night,
      Together with that fair and warlike form,
      In which the majesty of buried Denmark°
      Did sometimes° march? by heaven I charge thee speak.
MARCELLUS.   It is offended.
BARNARDO.   See, it stalks away.   50
HORATIO.   Stay, speak, speak, I charge thee speak.   *Exit GHOST.*
MARCELLUS.   'Tis gone and will not answer.
BARNARDO.   How now Horatio, you tremble and look pale,
      Is not this something more than fantasy?
      What think you on't?   55
HORATIO.   Before my God I might not this believe,

---

23 *fantasy*: imagination.   29 *approve*: prove reliable.   36 *pole*: North Star.
46 *usurp'st*: wrongfully occupy (both the time and the shape of the dead king).
48 *buried Denmark*: the buried King of Denmark.   49 *sometimes*: formerly.

Without the sensible and true avouch°
Of mine own eyes.

MARCELLUS.   Is it not like the king?

HORATIO.   As thou art to thyself.

Such was the very armour he had on,   60
When he the ambitious Norway° combated:
So frowned he once, when in an angry parle°
He smote the sledded Polacks° on the ice.
'Tis strange.

MARCELLUS.   Thus twice before, and jump° at this dead hour,   65
With martial stalk hath he gone by our watch.

HORATIO.   In what particular thought to work, I know not,
But in the gross and scope° of mine opinion,
This bodes some strange eruption to our state.

MARCELLUS.   Good now sit down, and tell me he that knows,   70
Why this same strict and most observant watch
So nightly toils the subject° of the land,
And why such daily cast of brazen cannon
And foreign mart,° for implements of war,
Why such impress° of shipwrights, whose sore° task   75
Does not divide the Sunday from the week,
What might be toward° that this sweaty haste
Doth make the night joint-labourer with the day,
Who is't that can inform me?

HORATIO.   That can I.

At least the whisper goes so; our last king,   80
Whose image even but now appeared to us,
Was as you know by Fortinbras of Norway,
Thereto pricked on by a most emulate° pride,
Dared to the combat; in which our valiant Hamlet
(For so this side of our known world esteemed him)   85
Did slay this Fortinbras, who by a sealed compact,°
Well ratified by law and heraldy,°
Did forfeit (with his life) all those his lands
Which he stood seized° of, to the conqueror:
Against the which a moiety competent°   90
Was gagèd° by our King, which had returned
To the inheritance of Fortinbras,
Had he been vanquisher; as by the same co-mart,°
And carriage of the article designed,°

---

57 *Sensible . . . avouch*: assurance of the truth of the senses.   61 *Norway*: King of Norway.
62 *parle*: parley, verbal battle.   63 *sledded Polacks*: Poles on sleds.   65 *jump*: just.
68 *gross and scope*: general view.   72 *toils the subject*: makes the subjects toil.   74 *mart*:
trade.   75 *impress*: conscription.   *sore*: difficult.   77 *toward*: forthcoming.   83 *emulate*:
rivalling.   86 *compact*: treaty.   87 *law and heraldy*: heraldic law regulating combats.
89 *seized*: possessed.   90 *moiety competent*: equal amount.   91 *gagèd*: pledged.
93 *co-mart*: joint bargain.   94 *carriage . . . designed*: intent of the treaty drawn up.

His fell to Hamlet; now sir, young Fortinbras,   95
Of unimprovèd mettle° hot and full,
Hath in the skirts° of Norway here and there
Sharked up° a list of lawless resolutes°
For food and diet to some enterprise
That hath a stomach° in't, which is no other,   100
As it doth well appear unto our state,
But to recover of us by strong hand
And terms compulsatory, those foresaid lands
So by his father lost; and this I take it,
Is the main motive of our preparations,   105
The source of this our watch, and the chief head°
Of this post-haste and romage° in the land.
BARNARDO.   I think it be no other, but e'en so;
Well may it sort° that this portentous figure
Comes armèd through our watch so like the king   110
That was and is the question of these wars.
HORATIO.   A mote it is to trouble the mind's eye:
In the most high and palmy° state of Rome,
A little ere the mightest Julius fell,
The graves stood tenantless, and the sheeted dead   115
Did squeak and gibber in the Roman streets,
As stars with trains of fire,° and dews of blood,
Disasters° in the sun; and the moist star,°
Upon whose influence Neptune's empire stands,
Was sick almost to doomsday with eclipse.   120
And even the like precurse° of feared events,
As harbingers preceding still° the fates
And prologue to the omen° coming on,
Have heaven and earth together demonstrated
Unto our climatures° and countrymen.   125

Enter GHOST.

But soft, behold, lo where it comes again.
I'll cross° it though it blast me: *Spreads his arms.*
                              stay illusion,
If thou hast any sound or use of voice,
Speak to me.
If there be any good thing to be done   130

---

96 *unimproved mettle*: untested (1) metal (2) spirit.   97 *skirts*: outskirts.   98 *Sharked up*:
gathered up indiscriminately (as a shark preys).   *lawless resolutes*: determined outlaws.
100 *stomach*: show of courage.   106 *head*: fountainhead.   107 *romage*:
bustle (rummage).   109 *sort*: turn out.   113 *palmy*: triumphant.   117 *stars . . fire*:
meteors.   118 *Disasters*: unfavorable portents.   *moist star*: moon.   121 *precurse*:
portent.   122 *still*: always.   123 *omen*: disaster.   125 *climatures*: regions.
127 *cross*: (1) cross its path (2) spread my arms to make a cross of my body (to ward against
evil).

That may to thee do ease, and grace° to me,
Speak to me.
If thou art privy° to thy country's fate
Which happily° foreknowing may avoid,
O speak: 135
Or if thou hast uphoarded in thy life
Extorted treasure in the womb of earth,
For which they say you spirits oft walk in death,

The cock crows.

Speak of it, stay and speak. Stop it Marcellus.
MARCELLUS.   Shall I strike at it with my partisan?°   140
HORATIO.   Do, if it will not stand
BARNARDO.   'Tis here.
HORATIO.   'Tis here.
MARCELLUS.   'Tis gone.   *Exit GHOST.*
We do it wrong being so majestical,
To offer it the show of violence,
For it is as the air, invulnerable,   145
And our vain blows malicious mockery.°
BARNARDO.   It was about to speak when the cock crew.°
HORATIO.   And then it started like a guilty thing,
Upon a fearful summons; I have heard,
The cock that is the trumpet to the morn,   150
Doth with his lofty and shrill-sounding throat
Awake the god of day, and at his warning
Whether in sea or fire, in earth or air,°
Th'extravagant and erring° spirit hies°
To his confine, and of the truth herein   155
This present object made probation.°
MARCELLUS.   It faded on the crowing of the cock.
Some say that ever 'gainst° that season comes
Wherein our Saviour's birth is celebrated
This bird of dawning singeth all night long,   160
And then they say no spirit dare stir abroad,
The nights are wholesome,° then no planets strike,°
No fairy takes,° nor witch hath power to charm,
So hallowed, and so gracious is that time.

131 *grace*: (1) honor (2) blessedness.   133 *art privy*: know secretly of.   134 *happily*:
perhaps.   140 *partisan*: spear.   146 *malicious mockery*: mockery because they only imitate
harm.   147 *cock crew*: (traditional signal for ghosts to return to their confines).
153 *sea . . . air*: the four elements (inhabited by spirits, each indigenous to a particular
element).   154 *extravagant and erring*: going beyond its bounds (vagrant) and
wandering.   *hies*: hastens.   156 *made probation*: gave proof.   158 *'gainst*: just
before.   162 *wholesome*: healthy (night air was considered unhealthy).   *strike*: exert evil
influence.   163 *takes*: bewitches.

HORATIO.   So have I heard and do in part believe it.   165
But look, the morn in russet° mantle clad
Walks o'er the dew of yon high eastward hill:
Break we our watch up and by my advice
Let us impart what we have seen tonight
Unto young Hamlet, for upon my life   170
This spirit dumb to us, will speak to him:
Do you consent we shall acquaint him with it,
As needful in our loves,° fitting our duty?
MARCELLUS.   Let's do't I pray, and I this morning know
Where we shall find him most convenient.   *Exeunt.*°   175

Scene 2. [*A room of state in the castle*]

Flourish.° Enter CLAUDIUS *King of Denmark,* GERTRUDE *the Queen,* [*members of the*] *Council:
as* POLONIUS; *and his son* LAERTES, HAMLET, [VALTEMAND *and* CORNELIUS] *cum aliis.°*

KING.   Though yet of Hamlet our dear brother's death
The memory be green, and that it us befitted
To bear our hearts in grief, and our whole kingdom
To be contracted in one brow of woe,
Yet so far hath discretion fought with nature,°   5
That we° with wisest sorrow think on him
Together with remembrance of ourselves:°
Therefore our sometime° sister,° now our queen,
Th'imperial jointress° to this warlike state,
Have we as 'twere with a defeated joy,   10
With an auspicious, and a dropping eye,°
With mirth in funeral, and with dirge in marriage,
In equal scale weighing delight and dole,
Taken to wife: nor have we herein barred
Your better wisdoms,° which have freely gone   15
With this affair along—for all, our thanks.
Now follows that you know, young Fortinbras,
Holding a weak supposal of our worth,°
Or thinking by our late dear brother's death
Our state to be disjoint and out of frame,°   20
Colleaguèd° with this dream of his advantage,°

166 *russet*: reddish.   173 *needful . . . loves*: urged by our friendship.   175 stage
direction: *Exeunt*: all exit.   stage direction: *Flourish*: fanfare of trumpets.   *cum aliis*: with
others.   5 *nature*: natural impulse (of grief).   6 *we*: (royal plural).   7 *remembrance of
ourselves*: reminder of our duties.   8 *sometime*: former.   *sister*: sister-in-law.   9 *jointress*:
widow who inherits the estate.   11 *auspicious . . . eye*: one eye happy, the other tearful.
14–15 *barred . . . wisdoms*: failed to seek and abide by your good advice.
18 *weak . . . worth*: low opinion of my ability in office.   20 *out of frame*: tottering.
21 *Colleagued*: supported.   *advantage*: superiority.

He hath not failed to pester us with message
Importing the surrender of those lands
Lost by his father, with all bands° of law,
To our most valiant brother—so much for him: 25
Now for ourself, and for this time of meeting,
Thus much the business is. We have here writ
To Norway, uncle of young Fortinbras—
Who impotent and bed-rid scarcely hears
Of this his nephew's purpose—to suppress   30
His further gait° herein, in that the levies,
The lists, and full proportions are all made
Out of his subject:° and we here dispatch
You good Cornelius, and you Valtemand,
For bearers of this greeting to old Norway,   35
Giving to you no further personal power
To business with the king, more than the scope
Of these delated° articles allow:
Farewell, and let your haste commend your duty.°
CORNELIUS, VALTEMAND.   In that, and all things, will we show our duty.   40
KING.   We doubt it nothing, heartily farewell.

                   Exeunt VALTEMAND and CORNELIUS.

And now Laertes what's the news with you?
You told us of some suit, what is't Laertes?
You cannot speak of reason to the Dane
And lose your voice;° what wouldst thou beg Laertes,   45
That shall not be my offer, not thy asking?°
The head is not more native° to the heart,
The hand more instrumental to the mouth,
Than is the throne of Denmark to thy father.
What wouldst thou have Laertes?
LAERTES.   My dread lord,   50
Your leave and favour° to return to France,
From whence, though willingly I came to Denmark,
To show my duty in your coronation,
Yet now I must confess, that duty done,
My thoughts and wishes bend again toward France,   55
And bow them to your gracious leave and pardon.°
KING.   Have you your father's leave? What says Polonius?

---

24 *bands* : bonds.   31 *gait*: progress.   31–33 *levies . . . subject*: taxes, conscriptions, and
supplies are all obtained from his subjects.   38 *delated*: accusing.   39 *haste . . . duty*:
prompt departure signify your respect.   45 *lose your voice*: speak in vain.   46 *offer . . .*
asking: grant even before requested.   47 *native*: related.   51 *leave and favour*: kind
permission.   56 *pardon*: allowance.

POLONIUS.   He hath my lord wrung from me my slow leave
    By laboursome petition, and at last
    Upon his will I sealed my hard consent.°   60
    I do beseech you give him leave to go.
KING.   Take thy fair hour Laertes, time be thine,
    And thy best graces spend it at thy will.
    But now my cousin° Hamlet, and my son—
HAMLET.   [*Aside.*] A little more than kin,° and less than kind.°   65
KING.   How is it that the clouds still hang on you?
HAMLET.   Not so my lord, I am too much in the sun.°
QUEEN.   Good Hamlet cast they nighted colour° off
    And let thine eye look like a friend on Denmark,°
    Do not for ever with they vailèd° lids   70
    Seek for thy noble father in the dust,
    Thou know'st 'tis common, all that lives must die,
    Passing through nature to eternity.
HAMLET.   Ay madam, it is common.°
QUEEN.   If it be,
    Why seems it so particular with thee?   75
HAMLET.   Seems, madam? nay it is, I know not "seems."
    'Tis not alone my inky cloak good mother,
    Nor customary suits of solemn black,
    Nor windy suspiration of forced breath,
    No, nor the fruitful river in the eye,°   80
    Nor the dejected haviour° of the visage,
    Together with all forms, moods, shapes of grief,
    That can denote me truly: these indeed seem,
    For they are actions that a man might play,°
    But I have that within which passes show,   85
    These but the trappings and the suits of woe.°
KING.   'Tis sweet and commendable in your nature Hamlet,
    To give these mourning duties to your father:
    But you must know your father lost a father,
    That father lost, lost his, and the survivor bound   90
    In filial obligation for some term

---

60 *Upon . . . consent*: (1) at his request, I gave my grudging consent (2) on the soft sealing wax of his (legal) will, I stamped my approval.   64 *cousin*: kinsman (used for relatives outside the immediate family).   65 *more than kin*: too much of a kinsman, being both uncle and stepfather.   *less than kind*: (1) unkind because of: being a kin (proverbial) and taking the throne from the former king's son (2) unnatural (as it was considered incest to marry the wife of one's dead brother).   67 *in the sun*: (1) in the presence of the king (often associated metaphorically with the sun) (2) proverbial: "out of heaven's blessing into the warm sun" (3) of a "son."   68 *nighted colour*: black.   69 *Denmark*: the King of Denmark.   70 *vailed*: downcast.   74 *common*: (1) general (2) vulgar.   79–80 *windy . . . eye*: (hyperbole used to describe exaggerated sighs and tears).   81 *haviour*: behavior.   84 *play*: act.   86 *trappings . . . woe*: costumes of mourning.

To do obsequious sorrow:° but to persever
In obstinate condolement,° is a course
Of impious stubbornness, 'tis unmanly grief,
It shows a will most incorrect to heaven,   95
A heart unfortified, a mind impatient,
An understanding simple and unschooled:
For what we know must be, and is as common
As any the most vulgar thing to sense,°
Why should we in our peevish opposition   100
Take it to heart? Fie, 'tis a fault to heaven,
A fault against the dead, a fault to nature,
To reason most absurd, whose common theme
Is death of fathers, and who still° hath cried
From the first corse,° till he that died today,   105
"This must be so." We pray you throw to earth
This unprevailing° woe, and think of us
As of a father, for let the world take note
You are the most immediate° to our throne,
And with no less nobility of love   110
Than that which dearest father bears his son,
Do I impart toward you. For your intent
In going back to school in Wittenberg,
It is most retrograde° to our desire,
And we beseech you, bend you° to remain   115
Here in the cheer and comfort of our eye,
Our chiefest courtier, cousin, and our son.
QUEEN.   Let not thy mother lose her prayers Hamlet,
   I pray thee stay with us, go not to Wittenberg.
HAMLET.   I shall in all my best obey you madam.   120
KING.   Why 'tis a loving and a fair reply,
   Be as ourself in Denmark. Madam come,
   This gentle and unforced accord of Hamlet
   Sits smiling to my heart, in grace whereof,
   No jocund health that Denmark drinks today,   125
   But the great cannon to the clouds shall tell,
   And the king's rouse° the heaven shall bruit° again,
   Re-speaking earthly thunder; come away.

                              Flourish. Exeunt all but HAMLET.

92 *do obsequious sorrow*: express sorrow befitting obsequies or funerals.   93 *condolement*:
grief.   99 *As any . . . sense*: as the most ordinary thing the senses can perceive.
104 *still*: always.   105 *corse*: corpse (of Abel, also, ironically, the first
fratricide).   107 *unprevailing*: useless.   109 *most immediate*: next in succession (though
Danish kings were elected by the council, an Elizabethan audience might feel that Hamlet,
not Claudius, should be king).   114 *retrograde*: movement (of planets) in a reverse
direction.   115 *beseech . . . you*: hope you will be inclined.   127 *rouse*: toast that empties
the wine cup.   *bruit*: sound.

HAMLET. O that this too too sullied° flesh would melt,
Thaw and resolve itself into a dew,   130
Or that the Everlasting had not fixed
His canon° 'gainst self-slaughter. O God, God,
How weary, stale, flat, and unprofitable
Seem to me all the uses of this world!
Fie on't, ah fie, 'tis an unweeded garden   135
That grows to seed, things rank° and gross in nature
Possess it merely.° That it should come to this,
But two months dead, nay not so much, not two,
So excellent a king, that was to this
Hyperion° to a satyr,° so loving to my mother,   140
That he might not beteem° the winds of heaven
Visit her face too roughly—heaven and earth,
Must I remember? why, she would hang on him
As if increase of appetite had grown
By what it fed on,° and yet within a month—   145
Let me not think on't: Frailty, thy name is woman—
A little month or ere those shoes were old
With which she followed my poor father's body
Like Niobe° all tears, why she, even she—
O God, a beast that wants° discourse of reason   150
Would have mourned longer—married with my uncle,
My father's brother, but no more like my father
Than I to Hercules: within a month,
Ere yet the salt of most unrighteous° tears
Had left the flushing° in her gallèd° eyes,   155
She married. O most wicked speed, to post°
With such dexterity to incestuous° sheets:
It is not, nor it cannot come to good,
But break my heart, for I must hold my tongue.

Enter HORATIO, MARCELLUS and BARNARDO.

HORATIO. Hail to your lordship.
HAMLET.   I am glad to see you well;   160
    Horatio, or I do forget my self.
HORATIO. The same my lord, and your poor servant ever.

HAMLET.   Sir my good friend, I'll change° that name with you:
     And what make you from Wittenberg, Horatio?
     Marcellus.   165
MARCELLUS.   My good lord.
HAMLET.   I am very glad to see you: good even, sir.
     But what in faith make you from Wittenberg?
HORATIO.   A truant disposition, good my lord.
HAMLET.   I would not hear your enemy say so,   170
     Nor shall you do mine ear that violence
     To make it truster of your own report
     Against yourself. I know you are no truant,
     But what is your affair in Elsinore?
     We'll teach you to drink deep ere you depart.   175
HORATIO.   My Lord, I came to see your father's funeral.
HAMLET.   I prithee do not mock me, fellow student,
     I think it was to see my mother's wedding.
HORATIO.   Indeed my lord it followed hard upon.
HAMLET.   Thrift, thrift, Horatio, the funeral baked meats   180
     Did coldly° furnish forth the marriage tables.
     Would I had met my dearest° foe in heaven
     Or ever I had seen that day Horatio.
     My father, methinks I see my father.
HORATIO.   Where my lord?
HAMLET.   In my mind's eye Horatio.   185
HORATIO.   I saw him once, a' was a goodly° king.
HAMLET.   A' was a man, take him for all in all,
     I shall not look upon his life again.
HORATIO.   My lord, I think I saw him yesternight.
HAMLET.   Saw? Who?   190
HORATIO.   My lord, the king your father.
HAMLET.   The king my father?
HORATIO.   Season your admiration° for a while
     With an attent ear till I may deliver
     Upon the witness of these gentlemen
     This marvel to you.
HAMLET.   For God's love let me hear!   195
HORATIO.   Two nights together had these gentlemen,
     Marcellus and Barnardo, on their watch
     In the dead waste and middle of the night,
     Been thus encountered. A figure like your father
     Armed at point exactly, cap-a-pe,°   200
     Appears before them, and with solemn march,

163 *change*: exchange (and be called your friend).   181 *coldly*: when cold.   182 *dearest*:
direst.   186 *goodly*: handsome.   192 *Season your admiration*: control your wonder.
200 *at point . . . cap-a-pe*: in every detail, head to foot.

Goes slow and stately by them; thrice he walked
By their oppressed° and fear-surprisèd eyes
Within his truncheon's° length, whilst they distilled°
Almost to jelly with the act of fear, 205
Stand dumb and speak not to him; this to me
In dreadful secrecy° impart they did,
And I with them the third night kept the watch,
Where as they had delivered, both in time,
Form of the thing, each word made true and good, 210
The apparition comes: I knew your father,
These hands are not more like.
HAMLET.   But where was this?
MARCELLUS.   My lord upon the platform where we watch.
HAMLET.   Did you not speak to it?
HORATIO.   My lord I did,
But answer made it none, yet once methought 215
It lifted up it° head, and did address
Itself to motion° like as it would speak:
But even then the morning cock crew loud,
And at the sound it shrunk in haste away
And vanished from our sight.
HAMLET.   'Tis very strange. 220
HORATIO.   As I do live my honoured lord 'tis true,
And we did think it writ down in our duty
To let you know of it.
HAMLET.   Indeed indeed sirs, but this troubles me.
Hold you the watch tonight?
ALL.   We do my lord. 225
HAMLET.   Armed say you?
ALL.   Armed my lord.
HAMLET.   From top to toe?
ALL.   My lord from head to foot.
HAMLET.   Then saw you not his face.
HORATIO.   O yes my lord, he wore his beaver° up. 230
HAMLET.   What, looked he frowningly?
HORATIO.   A countenance more in sorrow than in anger.
HAMLET.   Pale, or red?
HORATIO.   Nay, very pale.
HAMLET.   And fixed his eyes upon you?
HORATIO.   Most constantly.
HAMLET.   I would I had been there. 235
HORATIO.   It would have much amazed you.

---

203 *oppressed*: overcome by horror.   204 *truncheon*: staff (of office).   *distilled*:
dissolved.   207 *in dreadful secrecy*: as a dread secret.   216 *it*: its.   216–217 *address . . .
motion*: start to move.   230 *beaver*: visor.

HAMLET.   Very like, very like, stayed it long?
HORATIO.   While one with moderate haste might tell° a hundred.
MARCELLUS, BARNARDO.   Longer, longer.
HORATIO.   Not when I saw't.
HAMLET.   His beard was grizzled,° no?   240
HORATIO.   It was as I have seen it in his life,
   A sable silvered.°
HAMLET.   I will watch tonight;
   Perchance 'twill walk again.
HORATIO.   I warr'nt it will.
HAMLET.   If it assume my noble father's person,
   I'll speak to it though hell itself should gape   245
   And bid me hold my peace;° I pray you all
   If you have hitherto concealed this sight
   Let it be tenable° in your silence still,
   And whatsoever else shall hap tonight,
   Give it an understanding but no tongue.   250
   I will requite your loves, so fare you well:
   Upon the platform 'twixt eleven and twelve
   I'll visit you.
ALL.   Our duty to your honour.
HAMLET.   Your loves, as mine to you:° farewell.   *Exeunt.*   255
   My father's spirit (in arms) all is not well,
   I doubt° some foul play, would the night were come;
   Till then sit still my soul, foul deeds will rise,
   Though all the earth o'erwhelm them, to men's eyes.   *Exit.*

Scene 3. [*Polonius's chambers*]

Enter LAERTES *and* OPHELIA *his sister.*

LAERTES.   My necessaries are embarked, farewell,
   And sister, as the winds give benefit
   And convoy° is assistant, do not sleep
   But let me hear from you.
OPHELIA.   Do you doubt that?
LAERTES.   For Hamlet, and the trifling of his favour,   5
   Hold it a fashion, and a toy in blood,°
   A violet in the youth of primy nature,°
   Forward,° not permanent, sweet, not lasting,
   The perfume and suppliance of° a minute,
   No more.

---

238 *tell*: count.   240 *grizzled*: grey.   242 *A sable silvered*: black flecked with grey.   245–
246 *though hell . . . peace*: despite the risk of hell (for speaking to a demon) warning me to
be silent.   248 *tenable*: held onto.   254 *Your loves . . . you*: offer your friendship (rather
than duty) in exchange for mine.   256 *doubt*: fear.   3 *convoy*: conveyance.   6 *toy in
blood*: whim of the passions.   7 *youth of primy nature*: early spring.   8 *Forward*:
Premature.   9 *suppliance of*: supplying diversion for.

OPHELIA.   No more but so?

LAERTES.   Think it no more.   10
    For nature crescent° does not grow alone
    In thews and bulk,° but as this temple waxes°
    The inward service of the mind and soul
    Grows wide withal.° Perhaps he loves you now,
    And now no soil nor cautel° doth besmirch   15
    The virtue of his will:° but you must fear,
    His greatness weighed,° his will is not his own,
    For he himself is subject to his birth:
    He may not as unvalued persons° do,
    Carve° for himself, for on his choice depends   20
    The sanctity and health of this whole state,
    And therefore must his choice be circumscribed
    Unto the voice and yielding° of that body
    Whereof he is the head. Then if he says he loves you,
    It fits your wisdom so far to believe it   25
    As he in his particular act and place
    May give his saying deed,° which is no further
    Than the main voice of Denmark goes withal.
    Then weigh what loss your honour may sustain
    If with too credent° ear you list° his songs,   30
    Or lose your heart, or your chaste treasure open
    To his unmast'red importunity.°
    Fear it Ophelia, fear it my dear sister,
    And keep you in the rear of your affection,
    Out of the shot and danger of desire.   35
    The chariest° maid is prodigal enough
    If she unmask her beauty to the moon.
    Virtue itself 'scapes not calumnious strokes.
    The canker galls the infants° of the spring
    Too oft before their buttons° be disclosed,   40
    And in the morn and liquid dew of youth
    Contagious blastments° are most imminent.
    Be wary then, best safety lies in fear,
    Youth to itself rebels,° though none else near.

OPHELIA.   I shall the effect° of this good lesson keep   45
    As watchman to my heart: but good my brother,

---

11 *nature crescent*: man as he grows.   12 *thews and bulk*: sinews and body.   *temple waxes*:
body grows: (1 Cor. 6:19).   14 *withal*: at the same time.   15 *cautel*: deceit.   16 *will*:
desire.   17 *weighed*: considered.   19 *unvalued persons*: common people.   20 *Carve*:
choose (as does the one who carves the food).   23 *voice and yielding*: approving vote.   26–
27 *in his . . . deed*: limited by personal responsibilities and rank, may perform what he promises.
30 *credent*: credulous.   *list*: listen to.   31–32 *your chaste . . . importunity*:
lose your virginity to his uncontrolled persistence.   36 *chariest*: most cautious.   39 *canker*
. . . *infants*: cankerworm or caterpillar harms the young plants.   40 *buttons*: buds
42 *blastments*: blights.   44 *to itself rebels*: lusts by nature.   45 *effect*: moral.

Do not as some ungracious° pastors do,
Show me the steep and thorny way to heaven,
Whiles like a puffed and reckless libertine
Himself the primrose path of dalliance treads,   50
And recks not his own rede.°

Enter POLONIUS.

LAERTES.   O fear me not,°
I stay too long, but here my father comes:
A double blessing is a double grace,
Occasion smiles upon a second leave.°
POLONIUS.   Yet here Laertes? aboard, aboard for shame,   55
The wind sits in the shoulder of your sail,
And you are stayed for: there, my blessing with thee,
And these few precepts in thy memory
Look thou character.° Give thy thoughts no tongue,
Nor any unproportioned thought his act: 60
Be thou familiar, but by no means vulgar:°
Those friends thou hast, and their adoption tried,°
Grapple them unto thy soul with hoops of steel,
But do not dull° thy palm with entertainment
Of each new-hatched unfledged° comrade. Beware   65
Of entrance to a quarrel, but being in,
Bear't that th'opposèd may beware of thee.
Give every man thy ear, but few thy voice:
Take each man's censure,° but reserve thy judgment.
Costly thy habit° as thy purse can buy,   70
But not expressed in fancy;° rich, not gaudy,
For the apparel oft proclaims the man,
And they in France of the best rank and station,
Are of a most select and generous chief° in that:
Neither a borrower nor a lender be,   75
For loan oft loses both itself and friend,
And borrowing dulls the edge of husbandry;°
This above all, to thine own self be true
And it must follow as the night the day,
Thou canst not then be false to any man.   80
Farewell, my blessing season° this in thee.
LAERTES.   Most humbly do I take my leave my lord.
POLONIUS.   The time invites you, go, your servants tend.°

---

47 *ungracious*: lacking God's grace.   51 *recks . . . rede*: does not follow his own
advice.   *fear me not*: don't worry about me.   54 *Occasion . . . leave*: opportunity favors
a second leave-taking.   59 *character*: write.   61 *vulgar*: indiscriminately friendly.
62 *adoption tried*: loyalty proved.   64 *dull*: get callouses on.   65 *new-
hatched, unfledged*: new and untested.   69 *censure*: opinion.   70 *habit*: clothing.
71 *expressed in fancy*: so fantastic as to be ridiculous.   74 *select . . . chief*:
judicious and noble eminence.   77 *husbandry*: thrift.   81 *season*: bring to maturity.
83 *tend*: attend, wait.

LAERTES.   Farewell Ophelia, and remember well
  What I have said to you.
OPHELIA.   'Tis in my memory locked,   85
  And you yourself shall keep the key of it.
LAERTES.   Farewell.   *Exit* LAERTES.
POLONIUS.   What is't Ophelia he hath said to you?
OPHELIA.   So please you, something touching the Lord Hamlet.
POLONIUS.   Marry,° well bethought: 90
  'Tis told me he hath very oft of late
  Given private time to you, and you yourself
  Have of your audience been most free and bounteous.
  If it be so, as so 'tis put on me,
  And that in way of caution, I must tell you,   95
  You do not understand yourself so clearly
  As it behoves my daughter, and your honour.
  What is between you? give me up the truth.
OPHELIA.   He hath my lord of late made many tenders°
  Of his affection to me.   100
POLONIUS.   Affection, puh, you speak like a green girl
  Unsifted° in such perilous circumstance.
  Do you believe his tenders as you call them?
OPHELIA.   I do not know my lord what I should think.
POLONIUS.   Marry, I will teach you; think yourself a baby   105
  That you have ta'en these tenders° for true pay
  Which are not sterling.° Tender yourself more dearly,°
  Or (not to crack the wind of the poor phrase,
  Running it thus°) you'll tender me a fool.°
OPHELIA.   My lord he hath importuned me with love   110
  In honourable fashion.
POLONIUS.   Ay, fashion you may call it, go to, go to.
OPHELIA.   And hath given countenance° to his speech, my lord,
  With almost all the holy vows of heaven.
POLONIUS.   Ay, springes° to catch woodcocks.° I do know   115
  When the blood burns, how prodigal the soul
  Lends the tongue vows: these blazes daughter,
  Giving more light than heat, extinct in both,
  Even in their promise, as it is a-making,°
  You must not take for fire. From this time   120

---

90 *Marry*: (a mild oath, from "By the Virgin Mary").   99 *tenders*: offers (see lines 106–
109).   102 *Unsifted*: untested.   106 *tenders*: offers (of money).   107 *sterling*: genuine
(currency).   *Tender . . . dearly*: hold yourself at a higher value.   108–109 *crack . . .
thus*: make the phrase lose its breath.   109 *tender . . . fool*: (1) make me look foolish (2)
present me with a baby.   113 *countenance*: confirmation.   115 *springes*: snares.
woodcocks: snipelike birds (believed to be stupid and therefore easily trapped).
118–119 *extinct . . . a-making*: losing both appearance, because of brevity, and substance,
because of broken promises.

Be something scanter of your maiden presence,
Set your entreatments at a higher rate
Than a command to parle;° for Lord Hamlet,
Believe so much in him that he is young,
And with a larger tether may he walk   125
Than may be given you: in few° Ophelia,
Do not believe his vows, for they are brokers°
Not of that dye which their investments° show,
But mere implorators° of unholy suits,
Breathing° like sanctified and pious bonds,°   130
The better to beguile. This is for all,
I would not in plain terms from this time forth
Have you so slander any moment leisure
As to give words or talk with the Lord Hamlet.
Look to't I charge you, come your ways.°   135
OPHELIA. I shall obey, my lord.   [*Exeunt.*]

[*Scene 4. The platform on the battlements*]

Enter HAMLET, HORATIO and MARCELLUS.

HAMLET. The air bites shrewdly,° it is very cold.
HORATIO. It is a nipping and an eager° air.
HAMLET. What hour now?
HORATIO.   I think it lacks of twelve.
MARCELLUS. No, it is struck.
HORATIO. Indeed? I heard it not: it then draws near the season,   5
Wherein the spirit held his wont to walk.

A flourish of trumpets, and two pieces [of ordnance] go off.

What does this mean my lord?
HAMLET. The king doth wake° tonight and takes his rouse,°
Keeps wassail° and the swagg'ring up-spring° reels:
And as he drains his draughts of Rhenish° down,   10
The kettle-drum and trumpet thus bray out
The triumph of his pledge.°
HORATIO.   Is it a custom?
HAMLET. Ay marry is't,
But to my mind, though I am native here
And to the manner born,° it is a custom   15

122–123 *Set . . . parle*: Don't rush to negotiate a surrender as soon as the besieger asks for a discussion of terms.   126 *few*: short.   127 *brokers*: (1) business agents (2) procurers.   128 *investments*: (1) business ventures (2) clothing.   129 *implorators*: solicitors.   130 *Breathing*: speaking softly.   *bonds*: pledges.   135 *come your ways*: come along.   1 *shrewdly*: piercingly.   2 *eager*: sharp.   8 *wake*: stay awake.   *rouse*: drinks that empty the cup.   9 *Keeps wassail*: holds drinking bouts.   *up-spring*: a vigorous German dance.   10 *Rhenish*: Rhine wine.   12 *triumph . . . pledge*: victory of emptying the cup with one draught.   15 *to . . . born*: accustomed to the practice since birth.

More honoured in the breach than the observance.°
This heavy-headed revel east and west
Makes us traduced and taxed of° other nations:
They clepe° us drunkards, and with swinish phrase
Soil our addition,° and indeed it takes   20
From our achievements, though performed at height,°
The pith and marrow of our attribute.°
So oft it chances in particular men,
That for some vicious mole of nature° in them,
As in their birth, wherein they are not guilty   25
(Since nature cannot choose his origin),
By the o'ergrowth of some complexion,°
Oft breaking down the pales° and forts of reason,
Or by some habit, that too much o'er-leavens°
The form of plausive° manners—that these men,   30
Carrying I say the stamp of one defect,
Being nature's livery,° or fortune's star,°
His virtues else be they as pure as grace,
As infinite as man may undergo,
Shall in the general censure° take corruption   35
From that particular fault: the dram of evil
Doth all the noble substance of a doubt,
To his own scandal.°

Enter GHOST.

HORATIO.   Look my lord, it comes.
HAMLET.   Angels and ministers of grace defend us:
Be thou a spirit of health, or goblin damned,°   40
Bring with thee airs from heaven, or blasts from hell,
Be thy intents wicked, or charitable,
Thou com'st in such a questionable° shape,
That I will speak to thee. I'll call thee Hamlet,
King, father, royal Dane. O answer me,   45
Let me not burst in ignorance, but tell
Why thy canonized° bones hearsèd° in death

---

16 *More . . . observance*: better to break than to observe.   18 *traduced and taxed of*: defamed
and taken to task by.   19 *clepe*: call.   19–20 *with swinish . . . addition*: blemish our
reputation by comparing us to swine.   21 *at height*: to the maximum.   22 *attribute*:
reputation.   24 *mole of nature*: natural blemish.   27 *o'er growth . . . complexion*:
overbalance of one of the body's four humors or fluids believed to determine
temperament.   28 *pales*: defensive enclosures.   29 *too much o'er-leavens*: excessively
modifies (like too much leaven in bread).   30 *plausive*: pleasing.   32 *nature's livery*:
marked by nature.   *fortune's star*: destined by chance.   35 *general censure*: public
opinion.   36–38 *the dram . . . scandal*: the minute quantity of evil casts doubt upon his
noble nature, to his shame.   40 *spirit . . . damned*: true ghost or demon from
hell.   43 *questionable*: question-raising.   47 *canonized*: buried in accordance with church
edict.   *hearsèd*: entombed.

Have burst their cerements°? why the sepulchre,
Wherein we saw thee quietly interred
Hath oped his ponderous and marble jaws,   50
To cast thee up again? What may this mean
That thou, dead corse, again in complete steel
Revisits thus the glimpses of the moon,
Making night hideous, and we fools of nature°
So horridly to shake our disposition   55
With thoughts beyond the reaches of our souls,
Say why is this? wherefore? what should we do?   *GHOST beckons HAMLET.*

HORATIO.   It beckons you to go away with it,
As if it some impartment did desire°
To you alone.

MARCELLUS.   Look with what courteous action   60
It waves you to a more removèd ground,
But do not go with it.

HORATIO.   No, by no means.

HAMLET.   It will not speak, then I will follow it.

HORATIO.   Do not my lord.

HAMLET.   Why what should be the fear?
I do not set my life at a pin's fee,°   65
And for my soul, what can it do to that
Being a thing immortal as itself;
It waves me forth again, I'll follow it.

HORATIO.   What if it tempt you toward the flood my lord,
Or to the dreadful summit of the cliff   70
That beetles o'er° his base into the sea,
And there assume some other horrible form
Which might deprive your sovereignty of reason,°
And draw you into madness? think of it,
The very place puts toys of desperation,°   75
Without more motive, into every brain
That looks so many fathoms to the sea
And hears it roar beneath.

HAMLET.   It waves me still:
Go on, I'll follow thee.

MARCELLUS.   You shall not go my lord.

HAMLET.   Hold off your hands.   80

HORATIO.   Be ruled, you shall not go.

HAMLET.   My fate cries out,
And makes each petty artire° in this body

---

48 *crements*: waxed cloth wrappings.   54 *fools of nature*: mocked by our natural limitations
when faced with the supernatural.   59 *some . . . desire*: desired to impart
something.   65 *fee*: value.   71 *beetles o'er*: overhangs.   73 *deprive . . . reason*: dethrone
your reason from its sovereignty.   75 *toys of desperation*: desperate whims.   82 *artire*:
ligament.

As hardy as the Nemean lion's° nerve;°
Still am I called, unhand me gentlemen,
By heaven I'll make a ghost of him that lets° me: 85
I say away; go on, I'll follow thee.   *Exeunt Ghost and Hamlet.*
HORATIO.   He waxes desperate° with imagination.
MARCELLUS.   Let's follow, 'tis not fit thus to obey him.
HORATIO.   Have after—to what issue will this come?
MARCELLUS.   Something is rotten in the state of Denmark.   90
HORATIO.   Heaven will direct it.
MARCELLUS.   Nay, let's follow him.   *Exeunt.*

[*Scene 5. Another part of the platform*]

Enter Ghost and Hamlet.

HAMLET.   Whither wilt thou lead me? Speak, I'll go no further.
GHOST.   Mark me.
HAMLET.   I will
GHOST.   My hour is almost come
When I to sulphurous and tormenting flames
Must render up myself.
HAMLET.   Alas poor ghost.
GHOST.   Pity me not, but lend thy serious hearing   5
To what I shall unfold.
HAMLET.   Speak, I am bound° to hear.
GHOST.   So art thou to revenge, when thou shalt hear.
HAMLET.   What?
GHOST.   I am thy father's spirit,
Doomed for a certain term to walk the night,   10
And for the day confined to fast in fires,
Till the foul crimes done in my days of nature°
Are burnt and purged away: but that I am forbid
To tell the secrets of my prison-house,
I could a tale unfold whose lightest word   15
Would harrow up thy soul, freeze thy young blood,
Make thy two eyes like stars start from their spheres,°
Thy knotted and combinèd locks to part,
And each particular hair to stand an end,
Like quills upon the fretful porpentine:°   20
But this eternal blazon° must not be
To ears of flesh and blood; list, list, O list:
If thou didst ever thy dear father love—

---

83 *Nemean lion*: (killed by Hercules as one of his twelve labors).   *nerve*: sinew.   85 *lets*:
prevents.   87 *waxes desperate*: grows frantic.   6 *bound*: obliged by duty.   12 *crimes
. . . nature*: sins committed during my life on earth.   17 *spheres*: (1) orbits (according to
Ptolemy, each planet was confined to a sphere revolving around the earth) (2) sockets.
20 *fretful porpentine*: angry porcupine.   21 *eternal blazon*: revelation about eternity.

HAMLET.   O God!

GHOST.   Revenge his foul and most unnatural murder.   25

HAMLET.   Murder?

GHOST.   Murder most foul, as in the best it is,
But this most foul, strange and unnatural.

HAMLET.   Haste me to know't, that I with wings as swift
As meditation or the thoughts of love,   30
May sweep to my revenge.

GHOST.   I find thee apt,°
And duller shouldst thou be than the fat° weed
That rots itself in ease on Lethe wharf,°
Wouldst thou not stir in this; now Hamlet hear,
'Tis given out, that sleeping in my orchard,°   35
A serpent stung me, so the whole ear of Denmark
Is by a forgèd process° of my death
Rankly abused:° but know thou noble youth,
The serpent that did sting thy father's life
Now wears his crown.

HAMLET.   O my prophetic soul!   40
My uncle?

GHOST.   Ay, that incestuous, that adulterate° beast,
With witchcraft of his wit, with traitorous gifts,
O wicked wit and gifts, that have the power
So to seduce; won to his shameful lust   45
The will of my most seeming-virtuous queen;
O Hamlet, what a falling-off was there,
From me whose love was of that dignity
That it went hand in hand, even with the vow
I made to her in marriage, and to decline   50
Upon° a wretch whose natural gifts were poor
To° those of mine;
But virtue, as it never will be moved,
Though lewdness court it in a shape of heaven,°
So lust, though to a radiant angel linked,   55
Will sate itself in a celestial bed
And prey on garbage.
But soft, methinks I scent the morning air,
Brief let me be; sleeping within my orchard,
My custom always of the afternoon,   60
Upon my secure° hour thy uncle stole
With juice of cursèd hebona° in a vial,

---

31 *apt*: ready.   32 *fat*: slimy.   33 *Lethe wharf*: the banks of Lethe (river in Hades from which spirits drank to forget their past lives).   35 *orchard*: garden.   37 *process*: account.   38 *abused*: deceived.   42 *adulterate*: adulterous.   50–51 *decline Upon*: descend to.   52 *To*: compared to.   54 *shape of heaven*: angelic appearance.   61 *secure*: unsuspecting.   62 *hebona*: poisonous sap of the ebony or henbane.

And in the porches of my ears did pour
The leperous° distilment, whose effect
Holds such an enmity with blood of man,   65
That swift as quicksilver it courses through
The natural gates and alleys of the body,
And with a sudden vigour it doth posset°
And curd, like eager° droppings into milk,
The thin and wholesome° blood; so did it mine,   70
And a most instant tetter° barked about°
Most lazar°-like with vile and loathsome crust
All my smooth body.
Thus was I sleeping by a brother's hand,
Of life, of crown, of queen at once dispatched,   75
Cut off even in the blossoms of my sin,
Unhouseled, disappointed, unaneled,°
No reck'ning° made, but sent to my account°
With all my imperfections on my head;
O horrible, O horrible, most horrible!   80
If thou hast nature in thee bear it not,
Let not the royal bed of Denmark be
A couch for luxury° and damnèd incest.
But howsomever thou pursues this act,
Taint not thy mind, nor let thy soul contrive   85
Against thy mother aught;° leave her to heaven,
And to those thorns that in her bosom lodge
To prick and sting her. Fare thee well at once,
The glow-worm shows the matin° to be near
And 'gins to pale his uneffectual fire:°   90
Adieu, adieu, adieu, remember me.   *Exit.*
HAMLET.   O all you host of heaven! O earth! what else?
And shall I couple° hell? O fie! Hold, hold my heart,
And you my sinews, grow not instant old,
But bear me stiffly up; remember thee?   95
Ay thou poor ghost, whiles memory holds a seat
In this distracted globe.° Remember thee?
Yea, from the table° of my memory
I'll wipe away all trivial fond° records,
All saws of books,° all forms, all pressures° past   100
That youth and observation copied there,

---

64 *leperous*: leprosy-causing.   68 *posset*: curdle.   69 *eager*: sour.   70 *wholesome*:
healthy.   71 *tetter*: skin eruption.   *barked about*: covered (like bark on a tree).   72 *lazar*:
leper.   77 *Unhouseled . . . unaneled*: without final sacrament, unprepared (without
confession) and lacking extreme unction (anointing).   78 *reck'ning*: (1) accounting (2)
payment of my bill (3) confession and absolution.   *account*: judgment.   83 *luxury*:
lust.   86 *aught*: anything.   89 *matin*: dawn.   90 *'gins . . . fire*: his light becomes
ineffective, made pale by day.   93 *couple*: engage in a contest against.   97 *distracted
globe*:(his head).   98 *table*: tablet, "table-book."   99 *fond*: foolish.   100 *saws of books*:
maxims copied from books.   *forms, pressures*: ideas, impressions.

And thy commandment all alone shall live
Within the book and volume of my brain,
Unmixed with baser matter, yes by heaven:
O most pernicious woman! 105
O villain, villain, smiling damnèd villain!
My tables,° meet° it is I set it down
That one may smile, and smile, and be a villain,
At least I am sure it may be so in Denmark.
So uncle, there you are: now to my word,° 110
It is 'Adieu, adieu, remember me.'
I have sworn't.

Enter HORATIO and MARCELLUS.

HORATIO. My lord, my lord!
MARCELLUS. Lord Hamlet!
HORATIO. Heaven secure° him.
HAMLET. So be it.
MARCELLUS. Illo, ho, ho, my lord! 115
HAMLET. Hillo, ho, ho, boy, come° bird, come.
MARCELLUS. How is't my noble lord?
HORATIO. What news my lord?
HAMLET. O, wonderful!
HORATIO. Good my lord, tell it.
HAMLET. No, you will reveal it.
HORATIO. Not I my lord, by heaven.
MARCELLUS. Nor I my lord. 120
HAMLET. How say you then, would heart of man once think it?
But you'll be secret?
BOTH. Ay, by heaven, my lord.
HAMLET. There's ne'er a villain dwelling in all Denmark
But he's an arrant° knave.
HORATIO. There needs no ghost my lord, come from the grave 125
To tell us this.
HAMLET. Why right, you are in the right,
And so without more circumstance° at all
I hold it fit that we shake hands and part,
You, as your business and desire shall point you,
For every man hath business and desire 130
Such as it is, and for my own poor part,
Look you, I will go pray.
HORATIO. These are but wild and whirling words my lord.
HAMLET. I am sorry they offend you, heartily,
Yes faith, heartily.

107 *tables*: see note for line 98.   *meet*: fitting.   110 *word*: motto (to guide my
actions).   113 *secure*: protect.   116 *Hillo . . . come*: (falconer's cry with which Hamlet
replies to their calls).   124 *arrant*: thoroughgoing.   127 *circumstance*: ceremony.

HORATIO.   There's no offence my lord.   135
HAMLET.   Yes by Saint Patrick, but there is Horatio,
    And much offence too: touching this vision here,
    It is an honest° ghost that let me tell you:
    For your desire to know what is between us,
    O'ermaster't as you may. And now good friends,   140
    As you are friends, scholars, and soldiers,
    Give me one poor request.
HORATIO.   What is't, my lord? we will.
HAMLET.   Never make known what you have seen tonight.
BOTH.   My lord we will not.
HAMLET.   Nay, but swear't.
HORATIO.   In faith   145
    My lord, not I.
MARCELLUS.   Nor I my lord, in faith.
HAMLET.   Upon my sword.
MARCELLUS.   We have sworn my lord already.
HAMLET.   Indeed, upon my sword,° indeed.
GHOST.   Swear.   *Ghost cries under the stage.*
HAMLET.   Ha, ha, boy, say'st thou so, art thou there, truepenny°?   150
    Come on, you hear this fellow in the cellarage,
    Consent to swear.
HORATIO.   Propose the oath my lord.
HAMLET.   Never to speak of this that you have seen.
    Swear by my sword.
GHOST. [*Beneath.*]   Swear.   155
HAMLET.   Hic et ubique?° then we'll shift our ground:
    Come hither gentlemen,
    And lay your hands again upon my sword,
    Swear by my sword
    Never to speak of this that you have heard.   160
GHOST. [*Beneath.*]   Swear by his sword.
HAMLET.   Well said old mole, canst work i'th' earth so fast?
    A worthy pioner°—once more remove,° good friends.
HORATIO.   O day and night, but this is wondrous strange.
HAMLET.   And therefore as a stranger give it welcome.   165
    There are more things in heaven and earth Horatio,
    Than are dreamt of in your philosophy.
    But come,
    Here as before, never so help you mercy,
    How strange or odd some'er I bear myself,   170
    (As I perchance hereafter shall think meet
    To put an antic disposition on°)

---

138 *honest*: true (not a devil in disguise).   148 *sword*: (the cross-shaped hilt).
150 *truepenny*: old pal.   156 *Hic et ubique*: here and everywhere.   163 *pioner*:
digger (army trencher).   *remove*: move elsewhere.   172 *put . . . on*: assume a mad or
grotesque behavior.

That you at such times seeing me, never shall
With arms encumbered° thus, or this head-shake,
Or by pronouncing of some doubtful phrase,   175
As "Well, well, we know," or "We could and if we would,"
Or "If we list° to speak," or "There be and if they might,"
Or such ambiguous giving out, to note
That you know aught of me; this do swear,
So grace and mercy at your most need help you.   180
GHOST. [*Beneath.*]   Swear.
HAMLET.   Rest, rest, perturbed spirit: so gentlemen,
With all my love I do commend me to you,°
And what so poor a man as Hamlet is,
May do t'express his love and friending to you   185
God willing shall not lack: let us go in together,
And still° your fingers on your lips I pray.
The time is out of joint: O cursèd spite,
That ever I was born to set it right.
Nay come, let's go together.   *Exeunt.*   190

ACT 2

Scene 1. [*Polonius's chambers*]

Enter old POLONIUS with his man REYNALDO.

POLONIUS.   Give him this money, and these notes Reynaldo.
REYNALDO.   I will my lord.
POLONIUS.   You shall do marvellous° wisely, good Reynaldo,
Before you visit him, to make inquire
Of his behaviour.
REYNALDO.   My lord, I did intend it.   5
POLONIUS.   Marry, well said, very well said; look you sir,
Inquire me first what Danskers° are in Paris,
And how, and who, what means, and where they keep,°
What company, at what expense, and finding
By this encompassment° and drift of question   10
That they do know my son, come you more nearer
Than your particular demands° will touch it,
Take you as 'twere some distant knowledge of him,
As thus, "I know his father, and his friends,
And in part him"—do you mark this, Reynaldo?   15

174 *encumbered*: folded.   177 *list*: please.   183 *commend . . . you*: put myself in your
hands.   187 *still*: always.   3 *marvellous*: wonderfully.   7 *Danskers*: Danes.   8 *keep*:
lodge.   10 *encompassment*: roundabout way.   12 *particular demands*: specific questions.

REYNALDO. Ay, very well my lord.
POLONIUS. 'And in part him, but,' you may say, 'not well,
    But if't be he I mean, he's very wild,
    Addicted so and so;' and there put on him
    What forgeries° you please, marry none so rank°   20
    As may dishonour him, take heed of that,
    But sir, such wanton, wild, and usual slips,
    As are companions noted and most known
    To youth and liberty.
REYNALDO.   As gaming my lord.
POLONIUS. Ay, or drinking, fencing, swearing,   25
    Quarrelling, drabbing° —you may go so far.
REYNALDO. My lord, that would dishonour him.
POLONIUS. Faith no, as you may season it in the charge.°
    You must not put another scandal on him,
    That he is open to incontinency,°   30
    That's not my meaning, but breathe his faults so quaintly°
    That they may seem the taints of° liberty,
    The flash and outbreak of a fiery mind,
    A savageness in unreclaimèd blood,°
    Of general assault.°
REYNALDO.   But my good lord—   35
POLONIUS. Wherefore° should you do this?
REYNALDO.   Ay my lord,
    I would know that.
POLONIUS.   Marry sir, here's my drift,
    And I believe it is a fetch of warrant:°
    You laying these slight sullies on my son,
    As 'twere a thing a little soiled i'th' working,°   40
    Mark you, your party in converse, him you would sound,
    Having ever seen° in the prenominate crimes°
    The youth you breathe of guilty, be assured
    He closes with you in this consequence,°
    "Good sir," or so, or "friend," or "gentleman,"   45
    According to the phrase, or the addition°
    Of man and country.
REYNALDO.   Very good my lord.
POLONIUS. And then sir, does a'° this, a' does, what was I
           about to say?

---

20 *forgeries*: inventions.   *rank*: excessive.   26 *drabbing*: whoring.   28 *season . . .*
charge: temper the charge as you make it.   30 *incontinency*: uncontrolled lechery.
31 *quaintly*: delicately.   32 *taints of*: blemishes due to.   34 *unreclaimed blood*:
unbridled passion.   35 *general assault*: attacking all (young men).   36 *Wherefore*: why.
38 *fetch of warrant*: trick guaranteed to succeed.   40 *working*: handling.
42 *Having ever seen*: if he has ever seen.   *prenominate crimes*: aforenamed sins.
44 *closes . . . consequence*: comes to terms with you as follows.   46 *addition*: title,
form of address.   48 *'a*: he.

By the mass I was about to say something,
Where did I leave?
REYNALDO.   At "closes in the consequence,"   50
At "friend, or so, and gentleman."
POLONIUS.   At "closes in the consequence," ay marry,
He closes thus, "I know the gentleman,
I saw him yesterday, or th'other day,
Or then, or then, with such or such, and as you say,   55
There was a' gaming, there o'ertook in's rouse,°
There falling out at tennis," or perchance
"I saw him enter such a house of sale,"
Videlicet,° a brothel, or so forth. See you now,
Your bait of falsehood takes this carp of truth,   60
And thus do we of wisdom, and of reach,°
With windlasses,° and with assays of bias,°
By indirections find directions out:
So by my former lecture and advice
Shall you my son; you have me, have you not?   65
REYNALDO.   My lord I have.
POLONIUS.   God bye ye, fare ye well.
REYNALDO.   Good my lord.
POLONIUS.   Observe his inclination in yourself.°
REYNALDO.   I shall my lord.
POLONIUS.   And let him ply° his music.
REYNALDO.   Well my lord.   70
POLONIUS.   Farewell.

                                        Exit REYNALDO.

Enter OPHELIA.

                    How now Ophelia, what's the matter?
OPHELIA.   O my lord, my lord, I have been so affrighted.
POLONIUS.   With what, i'th'name of God?
OPHELIA.   My lord, as I was sewing in my closet,°
Lord Hamlet with his doublet all unbraced,°   75
No hat upon his head, his stockings fouled,
Ungart'red, and down-gyvèd° to his ankle,
Pale as his shirt, his knees knocking each other,
And with a look so piteous in purport°
As if he had been loosèd out of hell   80
To speak of horrors, he comes before me.

---

56 *o'ertook in's rouse*: overcome by drunkenness.   59 *Videlicet*: namely.   61 *reach*: far-reaching knowledge.   62 *windlasses*: roundabout approaches.   *assays of bias*: indirect attempts.   68 *in yourself*: personally.   70 *ply*: practice.   74 *closet*: private room.
75 *doublet all unbraced*: jacket all unfastened.   77 *down-gyvèd*: down around his ankles (like prisoners' fetters or gyves).   79 *purport*: expression.

POLONIUS.   Mad for thy love?

OPHELIA.   My lord I do not know,
   But truly I do fear it.

POLONIUS.   What said he?

OPHELIA.   He took me by the wrist, and held me hard,
   Then goes he to the length of all his arm,°   85
   And with his other hand thus o'er his brow,
   He falls to such perusal of my face
   As° a' would draw it; long stayed he so,
   At last, a little shaking of mine arm,
   And thrice his head thus waving up and down,   90
   He raised a sigh so piteous and profound
   As it did seem to shatter all his bulk,°
   And end his being; that done, he lets me go,
   And with his head over his shoulder turned
   He seemed to find his way without his eyes,   95
   For out adoors he went without their helps,
   And to the last bended their light on me.

POLONIUS.   Come, go with me, I will go seek the king,
   This is the very ecstasy° of love,
   Whose violent property fordoes itself,°   100
   And leads the will to desperate undertakings
   As oft as any passion under heaven
   That does afflict our natures: I am sorry.
   What, have you given him any hard words of late?

OPHELIA.   No my good lord, but as you did command   105
   I did repel his letters, and denied
   His access to me.

POLONIUS.   That hath made him mad.
   I am sorry that with better heed and judgment
   I had not quoted° him. I feared he did but trifle
   And meant to wrack° thee, but beshrew my jealousy:°   110
   By heaven it is as proper to our age
   To cast beyond ourselves in our opinions,°
   As it is common for the younger sort
   To lack discretion; come, go we to the king,
   This must be known, which being kept close, might move   115
   More grief to hide, than hate to utter love.°   [*Exeunt.*]

---

85 *goes . . . arm:* holds me at arm's length.   88 *As:* as if.   92 *bulk:* body.
99 *ecstasy:* madness.   100 *Whose . . . itself:* that, by its violent nature, destroys the lover.
109 *quoted:* observed.   110 *wrack:* ruin.   *beshrew my jealousy:* curse my suspicion.
111–112 *proper . . . opinions:* natural for old people to read more into something
than is actually there.   115–116 *being kept . . . love:* if kept secret, might cause more grief
than if we risked the king's displeasure.

Scene 2. [*A room in the Castle*]

Flourish. Enter KING *and* QUEEN, ROSENCRANTZ *and* GUILDENSTERN, *cum aliis.*

KING.   Welcome dear Rosencrantz and Guildenstern.
Moreover° that we much did long to see you,
The need we have to use you did provoke
Our hasty sending. Something have you heard
Of Hamlet's transformation—so call it,   5
Sith° nor th'exterior nor the inward man
Resembles that it was. What it should be,
More than his father's death, that thus hath put him
So much from th'understanding of himself,
I cannot dream of: I entreat you both,   10
That being of so young days° brought up with him,
And sith so neighboured to his youth and haviour,
That you vouchsafe your rest° here in our court
Some little time, so by your companies
To draw him on to pleasures, and to gather   15
So much as from occasion you may glean,
Whether aught to us unknown afflicts him thus,
That opened° lies within our remedy.
QUEEN.   Good gentlemen, he hath much talked of you,
And sure I am, two men there are not living   20
To whom he more adheres. If it will please you
To show us so much gentry° and good will,
As to expend your time with us awhile,
For the supply and profit of our hope,
Your visitation shall receive such thanks   25
As fits a king's remembrance.
ROSENCRANTZ.   Both your majesties
Might be the sovereign power you have of us,
Put your dread pleasures more into command
Than to entreaty.
GUILDENSTERN.   But we both obey,
And here give up ourselves in the full bent,°   30
To lay our service freely at your feet
To be commanded.
KING.   Thanks Rosencrantz, and gentle Guildenstern.
QUEEN.   Thanks Guildenstern, and gentle Rosencrantz.
And I beseech you instantly to visit   35
My too much changèd son. Go some of you
And bring these gentlemen where Hamlet is.

---

2 *Moreover*: in addition to the fact.   6 *Sith*: since.   11 *of . . . days*: from your early
days.   13 *vouchsafe your rest*: agree to stay.   18 *opened*: discovered.   22 *gentry*:
courtesy.   30 *in the full bent*: to the utmost (in archery, bending the bow).

GUILDENSTERN.   Heavens make our presence and our practices°
   Pleasant and helpful to him.
QUEEN.   Ay, amen.

                                 Exeunt ROSENCRANTZ and GUILDENSTERN.

Enter POLONIUS.

POLONIUS.   Th' ambassadors from Norway my good lord,   40
   Are joyfully returned.
KING.   Thou still° hast been the father of good news.
POLONIUS.   Have I, my lord? Assure you, my good liege,
   I hold my duty as I hold my soul,
   Both to my God and to my gracious king;   45
   And I do think, or else this brain of mine
   Hunts not the trail of policy° so sure
   As it hath used to do, that I have found
   The very cause of Hamlet's lunacy.
KING.   O speak of that, that do I long to hear.   50
POLONIUS.   Give first admittance to th' ambassadors,
   My news shall be the fruit° to that great feast.
KING.   Thyself do grace to them, and bring them in.   [*Exit POLONIUS.*]
   He tells me my dear Gertrude, he hath found
   The head and source of all your son's distemper.   55
QUEEN.   I doubt° it is no other but the main,
   His father's death and our o'erhasty marriage.
KING.   Well, we shall sift him.

Enter POLONIUS, VALTEMAND, and CORNELIUS.

                         Welcome, my good friends.
   Say Valtemand, what from our brother Norway?
VALTEMAND.   Most fair return of greetings and desires;   60
   Upon our first,° he sent out to suppress
   His nephew's levies, which to him appeared
   To be a preparation 'gainst the Polack,
   But better looked into, he truly found
   It was against your highness, whereat grieved   65
   That so his sickness, age, and impotence
   Was falsely borne in hand,° sends out arrests
   On Fortinbras, which he in brief obeys,
   Receives rebuke from Norway, and in fine,°
   Makes vow before his uncle never more   70
   To give th'assay° of arms against your majesty:
   Whereon old Norway, overcome with joy,
   Gives him threescore thousand crowns in annual fee,

---

38 *practices*: (1) actions (2) plots.   42 *still*: always.   47 *policy*: (1) politics (2) plots.
52 *fruit*: dessert.   56 *doubt*: suspect.   61 *first*: first presentation.   67 *borne in hand*:
deceived.   69 *fine*: finishing.   71 *assay*: test.

And his commission to employ those soldiers
So levied (as before) against the Polack,   75
With an entreaty herein further shown,
That it might please you to give quiet pass°
Through your dominions for this enterprise,
On such regards of safety and allowance
As therein are set down.   *[Giving a paper.]*
KING.   It likes° us well,   80
And at our more considered time,° we'll read,
Answer, and think upon this business:
Meantime, we thank you for your well-took labour,
Go to your rest, at night we'll feast together.
Most welcome home.   *Exeunt* AMBASSADORS.
POLONIUS.   This business is well ended.   85
My liege and madam, to expostulate°
What majesty should be, what duty is,
Why day is day, night night, and time is time,
Were nothing but to waste night, day, and time.
Therefore since brevity is the soul of wit,°   90
And tediousness the limbs and outward flourishes,°
I will be brief. Your noble son is mad:
Mad call I it, for to define true madness,
What is't but to be nothing else but mad?
But let that go.
QUEEN.   More matter, with less art.   95
POLONIUS.   Madam, I swear I use no art at all:
That he is mad 'tis true: 'tis true, 'tis pity,
And pity 'tis 'tis true: a foolish figure,°
But farewell it, for I will use no art.
Mad let us grant him then, and now remains   100
That we find out the cause of this effect,
Or rather say, the cause of this defect,
For this effect defective comes by cause:
Thus it remains, and the remainder thus.
Perpend.°   105
I have a daughter, have while she is mine,
Who in her duty and obedience, mark,
Hath given me this, now gather and surmise.
[Reads.] "To the celestial, and my soul's idol, the most
beautified° Ophelia,"—   110
That's an ill phrase, a vile phrase, "beautified" is a vile
phrase, but you shall hear. Thus: *[Reads.]*
      "In her excellent white bosom, these, &c."—

---

77 *pass*: passage.   80 *likes*: pleases.   81 *at . . . time*: when time is available for
consideration.   86 *expostulate*: discuss.   90 *wit*: understanding.   91 *tediousness . . .*
flourishes: embellishments and flourishes cause tedium.   98 *figure*: rhetorical
figure.   105 *Perpend*: consider.   110 *beautified*: beautiful.

QUEEN. Came this from Hamlet to her?

POLONIUS. Good madam stay awhile, I will be faithful.   [*Reads.*]   115
    "Doubt thou the stars are fire,
      Doubt that the sun doth move,°
    Doubt° truth to be a liar,
      But never doubt I love.
O dear Ophelia, I am ill at these numbers, I have not   120
art to reckon° my groans, but that I love thee best. O
most best, believe it. Adieu.
    Thine evermore, most dear lady, whilst
      this machine° is to° him, Hamlet."
This in obedience hath my daughter shown me,   125
And more above hath his solicitings,
As they fell out by time, by means, and place,
All given to mine ear.

KING.   But how hath she
Received his love?

POLONIUS.   What do you think of me?

KING. As of a man faithful and honourable.   130

POLONIUS. I would fain prove so. But what might you think
When I had seen this hot love on the wing,
As I perceived it (I must tell you that)
Before my daughter told me, what might you,
Or my dear majesty your queen here think,   135
If I had played the desk or table-book,°
Or given my heart a winking° mute and dumb,
Or looked upon this love with idle° sight,
What might you think? No, I went round to work,
And my young mistress thus I did bespeak,   140
"Lord Hamlet is a prince out of thy star,°
This must not be:" and then I prescripts° gave her
That she should lock herself from his resort,°
Admit no messengers, receive no tokens:
Which done, she took the fruits of my advice,   145
And he repellèd, a short tale to make,
Fell into a sadness, then into a fast,
Thence to a watch,° thence into a weakness,
Thence to a lightness,° and by this declension,
Into the madness wherein now he raves,   150
And all we mourn for.

---

117 *move*: (as it was believed to do, around the earth).   118 *Doubt*: suspect.   121 *reckon*: express in meter.   124 *machine*: body.   *to*: attached to.   136 *played . . . book*: kept it concealed as in a desk or personal notebook.   137 *given . . . winking*: had my heart shut its eyes to the matter.   138 *idle*: unseeing.   141 *out . . . star*: out of your sphere (above you in station).   142 *prescripts*: orders.   143 *resort*: company.   148 *watch*: sleeplessness.   149 *lightness*: lightheadedness.

KING.   Do you think 'tis this?
QUEEN.   It may be very like.
POLONIUS.   Hath there been such a time, I would fain know that,
That I have positively said "Tis so,"
When it proved otherwise?
KING.   Not that I know.   155
POLONIUS.   Take this, from this, if this be otherwise;

[*Points to his head and shoulder.*]

If circumstances lead me, I will find
Where truth is hid, though it were hid indeed
Within the center.
KING.   How may we try° it further?
POLONIUS.   You know sometimes he walks four hours together   160
Here in the lobby.
QUEEN.   So he does indeed.
POLONIUS.   At such a time, I'll loose° my daughter to him,
Be you and I behind an arras° then,
Mark the encounter: if he love her not,
And be not from his reason fall'n thereon,   165
Let me be no assistant for a state,°
But keep a farm and carters.
KING.   We will try it.

Enter HAMLET reading on a book.

QUEEN.   But look where sadly the poor wretch comes reading.
POLONIUS.   Away, I do beseech you both away,
I'll board him presently,° O give me leave.   *Exeunt KING and QUEEN.*   170
How does my good Lord Hamlet?
HAMLET.   Well, God-a-mercy.
POLONIUS.   Do you know me, my lord?
HAMLET.   Excellent well, you are a fishmonger.°
POLONIUS.   Not I my lord.   175
HAMLET.   Then I would you were so honest a man.
POLONIUS.   Honest, my lord?
HAMLET.   Ay sir, to be honest as this world goes, is to be one
man picked out of ten thousand.
POLONIUS.   That's very true, my lord.   180
HAMLET.   For if the sun breed maggots° in a dead dog, being a good
kissing carrion°—have you a daughter?
POLONIUS.   I have my lord.

---

159 *try*: test.   162 *loose*: (1) release (2) turn loose.   163 *arras*: hanging tapestry.
166 *assistant . . . state*: state official.   170 *board him presently*: approach him
immediately.   174 *fishmonger*: (1) fish dealer (2) pimp.   181 *breed maggots*: (in the belief
so that the rays of the sun caused maggots to breed in dead flesh).   182 *kissing carrion*: piece
of flesh for kissing.

Shakespeare *The Tragedy of Hamlet, Prince of Denmark*, Act 2, Scene 2 **1155**

HAMLET.   Let her not walk i'th'sun:° conception° is a blessing, but as
your daughter may conceive, friend look to'it.   185
POLONIUS.   [*Aside.*] How say you by that? Still harping on my daughter,
yet he knew me not at first, a' said I was a fishmonger.
A' is far gone, far gone, and truly in my youth, I suffered
much extremity for love, very near this. I'll speak to him
again. What do you read my lord?   190
HAMLET.   Words, words, words.
POLONIUS.   What is the matter my lord?
HAMLET.   Between who?
POLONIUS.   I mean the matter° that you read, my lord.
HAMLET.   Slanders, sir; for the satirical rogue says here, that old men   195
have grey beards, that their faces are wrinkled, their eyes
purging thick amber and plum-tree gum,° and that they
have a plentiful lack of wit, together with most weak
hams. All which sir, though I most powerfully and
potently believe, yet I hold it not honesty° to have it thus set   200
down, for yourself sir shall grow old as I am: if like a crab
you could go backward.
POLONIUS.   [*Aside.*] Though this be madness, yet there is method
in't.
Will you walk out of the air° my lord?   205
HAMLET.   Into my grave.
POLONIUS.   [*Aside.*] Indeed that's out of the air; how pregnant°
sometimes his replies are, a happiness° that often
madness hits on, which reason and sanity could not so
prosperously° be delivered of. I will leave him, and   210
suddenly contrive the means of meeting between him
and my daughter. My honourable lord, I will most
humbly take leave of you.
HAMLET.   You cannot sir take from me anything that I will more
willingly part withal: except my life, except my life,   215
except my life.
POLONIUS.   Fare you well my lord.
HAMLET.   These tedious old fools.

Enter ROSENCRANTZ and GUILDENSTERN.

POLONIUS.   You go to seek the Lord Hamlet, there he is.
ROSENCRANTZ.   [*To Polonius.*] God save you sir.   [*Exit POLONIUS.*]   220

---

184 *Let . . . sun*: (1) (proverbial: "out of God's blessing, into the warm sun") (2) because
the sun is a breeder (3) don't let her go near me (with a pun on "sun" and "son").   *conception*:
(1) understanding (2) pregnancy.   194 *matter*: (1) content (Polonius's meaning) (2) cause
of a quarrel (Hamlet's interpretation).   197–198 *purging . . . gum*: exuding a viscous
yellowish discharge.   200 *honesty*: decency.   205 *out . . . air*: (in the belief that fresh
air was bad for the sick).   207 *pregnant*: full of meaning.   208 *happiness*: aptness.
210 *prosperously*: successfully.

GUILDENSTERN. My honoured lord.

ROSENCRANTZ. My most dear lord.

HAMLET. My excellent good friends, how dost thou Guildenstern?
Ah Rosencrantz, good lads, how do you both?

ROSENCRANTZ. As the indifferent° children of the earth. 225

GUILDENSTERN. Happy, in that we are not over-happy:
On Fortune's cap we are not the very button.°

HAMLET. Nor the soles of her shoe?

ROSENCRANTZ. Neither my lord.

HAMLET. Then you live about her waist, or in the middle of her 230
favours?

GUILDENSTERN. Faith, her privates° we.

HAMLET. In the secret parts of Fortune? O most true, she is a
strumpet.° What news?

ROSENCRANTZ. None my lord, but that the world's grown honest. 235

HAMLET. Then is doomsday near: but your news is not true. Let me
question more in particular: what have you my good
friends, deserved at the hands of Fortune, that she sends
you to prison hither?

GUILDENSTERN. Prison, my lord? 240

HAMLET. Denmark's a prison.

ROSENCRANTZ. Then is the world one.

HAMLET. A goodly one, in which there are many confines, wards,°
and dungeons; Denmark being one o'th'worst.

ROSENCRANTZ. We think not so my lord. 245

HAMLET. Why then 'tis none to you; for there is nothing either good
or bad, but thinking makes it so: to me it is a prison.

ROSENCRANTZ. Why then your ambition makes it one: 'tis too narrow for
your mind.

HAMLET. O God, I could be bounded in a nutshell, and count 250
myself a king of infinite space; were it not that I have bad
dreams.

GUILDENSTERN. Which dreams indeed are ambition: for the very substance
of the ambitious, is merely the shadow of a dream.

HAMLET. A dream itself is but a shadow. 255

ROSENCRANTZ. Truly, and I hold ambition of so airy and light a quality,
that it is but a shadow's shadow.

HAMLET. Then are our beggars bodies, and our monarchs and
outstretched heroes the beggars' shadows:° shall we to th'
court? for by my fay,° I cannot reason. 260

BOTH. We'll wait upon° you.

HAMLET. No such matter. I will not sort° you with the rest of my
servants: for to speak to you like an honest man, I am most

225 *indifferent*: ordinary.   227 *on Fortune's . . . button*: we are not at the height of our
fortunes.   232 *privates*: (1) intimate friends (2) private parts.   234 *strumpet*: inconstant
woman, giving favor to many.   243 *wards*: cells.   258–259 *Then are . . . shadows*: then
beggars are the true substance and ambitious kings and heroes the elongated shadows of
beggars' bodies (for only a real substance can cast a shadow).   260 *fay*: faith.   261 *wait
upon*: attend.   262 *sort*: class.

dreadfully attended. But in the beaten way of friendship,
what make you at Elsinore?   265
ROSENCRANTZ.   To visit you my lord, no other occasion.
HAMLET.   Beggar that I am, I am even poor in thanks, but I thank
you, and sure dear friends, my thanks are too dear a
halfpenny:° were you not sent for? is it your own inclining?
is it a free° visitation? come, come, deal justly with me,   270
come, come, nay speak.
GUILDENSTERN.   What should we say my lord?
HAMLET.   Anything but to th'purpose: you were sent for, and there
is a kind of confession in your looks, which your modesties
have not craft enough to colour: I know the good king and   275
queen have sent for you.
ROSENCRANTZ.   To what end my lord?
HAMLET.   That you must teach me: but let me conjure° you, by the
rights of our fellowship, by the consonancy of our youth,°
by the obligation of our ever-preserved love, and by what   280
more dear a better proposer can charge you withal,° be
even and direct with me whether you were sent for or no.
ROSENCRANTZ.   [*Aside to Guildenstern.*] What say you?
HAMLET.   Nay then, I have an eye of° you: If you love me,
hold not off.   285
GUILDENSTERN.   My lord, we were sent for.
HAMLET.   I will tell you why, so shall my anticipation prevent° your
discovery,° and your secrecy to the king and queen moult
no feather.° I have of late, but wherefore I know not, lost all
my mirth, forgone all custom of exercises: and indeed it   290
goes so heavily with my disposition, that this goodly
frame the earth, seems to me a sterile promontory, this
most excellent canopy the air, look you, this brave°
o'erhanging firmament, this majestical roof fretted° with
golden fire,° why it appeareth nothing to me but a foul and   295
pestilent congregation of vapours.° What a piece of work is
a man! How noble in reason, how infinite in faculties,° in
form and moving, how express° and admirable in action,
how like an angel in apprehension, how like a god: the
beauty of the world; the paragon of animals; and yet to   300
me, what is this quintessence of dust? Man delights not
me, no, nor woman neither, though by your smiling, you
seem to say so.
ROSENCRANTZ.   My lord, there was no such stuff in my thoughts.
HAMLET.   Why did ye laugh then, when I said 'man delights not me'?   305

268–269 *too dear a halfpenny*: worth not even a halfpenny (as I have no influence).   270 *free*:
voluntary.   278 *conjure*: appeal to.   279 *consonancy . . . youth*: agreement in our
ages.   281 *withal*: with.   284 *of*: on.   287 *prevent*: forestall.   288 *discovery*:
disclosure.   288–289 *moult no feather*: change in no way.   293 *brave*: splendid.
294 *fretted*: ornamented with fretwork.   295 *golden fire*: stars.   296 *pestilent . . . vapours*:
(clouds were believed to carry contagion).   297 *faculties*: physical powers.   298 *express*:
well framed.

ROSENCRANTZ. To think, my lord, if you delight not in man, what lenten
     entertainment° the players shall receive from you: we coted°
     them on the way, and hither are they coming to offer you
     service.
HAMLET. He that plays the king shall be welcome, his majesty shall   310
     have tribute of me, the adventurous knight° shall use his
     foil and target,° the lover shall not sigh gratis,° the humorous
     man° shall end his part in peace,° the clown shall make
     those laugh whose lungs are tickle o'th'sere,° and the lady
     shall say her mind freely: or the blank verse shall halt° for't.   315
     What players are they?
ROSENCRANTZ. Even those you were wont to take such delight in, the
     tragedians of the city.
HAMLET. How chances it they travel? Their residence° both in
     reputation and profit was better both ways.   320
ROSENCRANTZ. I think their inhibition comes by the means of the late
     innovation.°
HAMLET. Do they hold the same estimation they did when I was in
     the city; are they so followed?
ROSENCRANTZ. No indeed are they not.   325
HAMLET. How comes it? Do they grow rusty?
ROSENCRANTZ. Nay, their endeavour keeps in the wonted pace; but there
     is sir an aery° of children, little eyases,° that cry out on the
     top of question,° and are most tyrannically° clapped for't:
     these are now the fashion, and so berattle° the common   330
     stages° (so they call them) that many wearing rapiers° are
     afraid of goose-quills,° and dare scarce come thither.
HAMLET. What, are they children? Who maintains 'em? How are
     they escoted°? Will they pursue the quality no longer than
     they can sing°? Will they not say afterwards if they should   335
     grow themselves to common players (as it is most like, if
     their means are not better) their writers do them wrong, to
     make them exclaim against their own succession°?
ROSENCRANTZ. Faith, there has been much to-do on both sides: and the

---

306–307 *lenten entertainment*: meager treatment.   307 *coted*: passed.   311 *adventurous
knight*: knight errant (a popular stage character).   312 *foil and target*: sword blunted for
stage fighting, and small shield.   312 *gratis*: (without applause).   312–313 *humorous man*:
eccentric character with a dominant trait, caused by an excess of one of the four humours,
or bodily fluids.   313 *in peace*: without interruption.   314 *tickle o'th' sere*: attuned to
respond to laughter, as the finely adjusted gunlock responds to the touch of the trigger (fr.
hunting).   315 *halt*: limp (if she adds her own opinions and spoils the meter).
319 *residence*: i.e. in a city theatre.   321–322 *inhibition . . . innovation*: hinderance
is due to the recent novelty (of the children's companies).   328 *aery*: nest.
eyases: young hawks.   328–329 *that cry . . . question*: whose shrill voices can be heard above
all others (in the "War of the Theatres" between the child and adult companies, 1601–
1602).   329 *tyrannically*: strongly.   330 *berattle*: berate.   330–331 *common stages*:
public playhouses (the children's companies performed in private theatres).
331 *wearing rapiers*: (worn by gentlemen).   332 *goose-quills*: pens (of satirical dramatists
who wrote for the children).   334 *escoted*: supported.   334–335 *pursue . . . sing*: continue
acting only until their voices change.   338 *succession*: inheritance.

nation holds it no sin to tarre° them to controversy. There   340
was for a while, no money bid for argument,° unless the
poet and the player went to cuffs in the question.°
HAMLET.   Is't possible?
GUILDENSTERN.   O there has been much throwing about of brains.
HAMLET.   Do the boys carry it away°?   345
ROSENCRANTZ.   Ay, that they do my lord, Hercules and his load too.°
HAMLET.   It is not very strange, for my uncle is king of Denmark,
and those that would make mows° at him while my father
lived, give twenty, forty, fifty, a hundred ducats apiece
for his picture in little.° 'Sblood,° there is something in this   350
more than natural, if philosophy° could find it out.

A flourish for the Players.

GUILDENSTERN.   There are the players.
HAMLET.   Gentlemen, you are welcome to Elsinore: your hands,
come then, th'appurtenance° of welcome is fashion and
ceremony; let me comply with you in this garb,° lest my   355
extent° to the players, which I tell you must show fairly
outwards, should more appear like entertainment than
yours.° You are welcome: but my uncle-father, and aunt-
mother, are deceived.
GUILDENSTERN.   In what my dear lord?   360
HAMLET.   I am but mad north-north-west; when the wind is southerly,
I know a hawk from a handsaw.°

Enter POLONIUS.

POLONIUS.   Well be with you, gentlemen.
HAMLET.   Hark you Guildenstern, and you too, at each ear a hearer:
that great baby you see there is not yet out of his swaddling   365
clouts.°
ROSENCRANTZ.   Happily° he is the second time come to them, for they say
an old man is twice a child.
HAMLET.   I will prophesy, he comes to tell me of the players, mark
it.—You say right sir, a Monday morning, 'twas then   370
indeed.
POLONIUS.   My lord, I have news to tell you.

---

340 *tarre*: provoke.   341 *bid for argument*: paid for the plot of a proposed play.   342 *went
. . . question*: came to blows on the subject.   345 *carry it away*: carry off the prize.
346 *Hercules . . . too*: (Shakespeare's own company at the Globe Theatre, whose sign was
Hercules carrying the globe of the world).   348 *mows*: mouths, grimaces.
350 *little*: a miniature.   *'Sblood*: by God's blood.   351 *philosophy*: science.
354 *appurtenance*: accessory.   355 *comply . . . garb*: observe the formalities with you in
this style.   356 *extent*: i.e. of welcome.   357–358 *should . . . yours*: should appear more
hospitable than yours.   362 *I know . . . handsaw*: I can tell the difference between two
things that are unlike ("hawk" = (1) bird of prey (2) mattock, pickaxe; "handsaw" = (1)
hernshaw or heron bird (2) small saw).   365–366 *swaddling clouts*: strips of cloth binding
a newborn baby.   367 *Happily*: perhaps.

HAMLET.   My lord, I have news to tell you. When Roscius° was an
  actor in Rome—
POLONIUS.   The actors are come hither, my lord.   375
HAMLET.   Buz, buz.°
POLONIUS.   Upon my honour.
HAMLET.   Then came each actor on his ass—
POLONIUS.   The best actors in the world, either for tragedy, comedy,
  history, pastoral, pastoral-comical, historical-pastoral,   380
  tragical-historical, tragical-comical-historical-pastoral,
  scene individable,° or poem unlimited.° Seneca cannot be
  too heavy, nor Plautus° too light for the law of writ, and the
  liberty:° these are the only men.
HAMLET.   O Jephthah,° judge of Israel, what a treasure hadst thou.   385
POLONIUS.   What a treasure had he, my lord?
HAMLET.   Why
  'One fair daughter and no more,
      The which he lovèd passing° well.'
POLONIUS.   [Aside.] Still on my daughter.   390
HAMLET.   Am I not i'th' right, old Jephthah?
POLONIUS.   If you call me Jephthah my lord, I have a daughter that I
  love passing well.
HAMLET.   Nay, that follows not.
POLONIUS.   What follows then, my lord?   395
HAMLET.   Why
      "As by lot, God wot,"
  and then you know
      "It came to pass, as most like° it was:"
  the first row° of the pious chanson will show you more, for   400
  look where my abridgement° comes.

Enter four or five PLAYERS.

  You are welcome masters, welcome all. I am glad to see
  thee well: welcome, good friends. O my old friend, why
  thy face is valanced° since I saw thee last, com'st thou to
  beard me in Denmark? What, my young lady° and   405
  mistress? by'r lady, your ladyship is nearer to heaven than
  when I saw you last, by the altitude of a chopine.° Pray
  God your voice, like a piece of uncurrent° gold, be not

---

373 *Roscius*: famous Roman actor.   376 *Buz, buz*: (contemptuous).   382 *scene individable*:
play observing the unities (time, place, action).   *poem unlimited*: play ignoring the unities.
382–383 *Seneca, Plautus*: Roman writers of tragedy and comedy respectively.
383–384 *law . . . liberty*: "rules" regarding the unities and those exercising freedom from
the unities.   385 *Jephthah*: (who was forced to sacrifice his only daughter because of a
rash promise: Judges 11:29–39).   389 *passing*: surpassingly.   399 *like*: likely.
400 *row*: stanza.   401 *abridgement*: (the players who will cut short my song).
404 *valanced*: fringed with a beard.   405 *lady*: boy playing women's roles.   407 *chopine*:
thick-soled shoe.   408 *uncurrent*: not legal tender.

cracked within the ring.° Masters, you are all welcome:
we'll e'en to't like French falconers, fly at any thing we see:°   410
we'll have a speech straight. Come give us a taste of your
quality: come, a passionate speech.

I. PLAYER.   What speech, my good lord?

HAMLET.   I heard thee speak me a speech once, but it was never
acted, or if it was, not above once, for the play I remember   415
pleased not the million, 'twas caviary to the general,° but it
was (as I received it, and others, whose judgments in such
matters cried in the top of mine°) an excellent play, well
digested in the scenes, set down with as much modesty as
cunning.° I remember one said there were no sallets° in th   420
lines, to make the matter savoury, nor no matter in the
phrase that might indict the author of° affection, but called
it an honest method, as wholesome as sweet, and by very
much more handsome than fine:° one speech in't I chiefly
loved, 'twas Aeneas' tale to Dido, and thereabout of it   425
especially where he speaks of Priam's slaughter.° If it live in
your memory begin at this line, let me see, let me see:
     "The rugged Pyrrhus,° like th'Hyrcanian beast"°—
'tis not so: it begins with Pyrrhus—
     "The rugged Pyrrhus, he whose sable° arms,   430
Black as his purpose, did the night resemble
When he lay couchèd in th'ominous horse,°
Hath now this dread and black complexion smeared
With heraldy more dismal: head to foot
Now is he total gules,° horridly tricked°   435
With blood of fathers, mothers, daughters, sons,
Baked and impasted° with the parching° streets,
That lend a tyrannous and damnèd light
To their lord's murder. Roasted in wrath and fire,
And thus o'er-sizèd° with coagulate gore,   440
With eyes like carbuncles,° the hellish Pyrrhus
Old grandsire Priam seeks;"
So proceed you.

POLONIUS.   'Fore God, my lord, well spoken, with good accent and
good discretion.°   445

---

409 *ring*: (1) ring enclosing the design on a gold coin (to crack it within the ring [to steal
the gold] made it "uncurrent") (2) sound.   410 *fly . . . see*: undertake any difficulty.
416 *caviary . . . general*: like caviar, too rich for the general public.   418 *cried . . . mine*:
spoke with more authority than mine.   419–420 *modesty as cunning*: moderation as
skill.   420 *sallets*: spicy bits.   422 *indict . . . of*: charge . . . with.   424 *handsome than
fine*: dignified than finely wrought.   426 *Priam's slaughter*: the murder of the King of Troy
(as told in the Aeneid).   428 *Pyrrhus*: son of Achilles.   *Hyrcanian beast*: tiger noted for
fierceness.   430 *sable*: black.   432 *horse*: the hollow wooden horse used by the Greeks
to enter Troy.   435 *gules*: red.   *horridly tricked*: horribly decorated.   437 *impasted*:
coagulated.   *parching*: (because the city was on fire).   440 *o'er-sized*: covered over.
441 *carbuncles*: red gems.   445 *discretion*: interpretation.

I. PLAYER.   "Anon he finds him,
   Striking too short at Greeks, his antique° sword,
   Rebellious to his arm, lies where it falls,
   Repugnant to command;° unequal matched,
   Pyrrhus at Priam drives, in rage strikes wide,   450
   But with the whiff and wind of his fell° sword,
   Th'unnerved father falls: then senseless Ilium,°
   Seeming to feel this blow, with flaming top
   Stoops to his base; and with a hideous crash
   Takes prisoner Pyrrhus' ear. For lo, his sword   455
   Which was declining on the milky head
   Of reverend Priam, seemed i'th'air to stick;
   So as a painted° tyrant Pyrrhus stood,
   And like a neutral to his will and matter,°
   Did nothing: 460
   But as we often see, against° some storm,
   A silence in the heavens, the rack° stand still,
   The bold winds speechless, and the orb° below
   As hush as death, anon the dreadful thunder
   Doth rend the region, so after Pyrrhus' pause,   465
   A rousèd vengeance sets him new awork,
   And never did the Cyclops'° hammers fall
   On Mars's armour, forged for proof eterne,°
   With less remorse than Pyrrhus' bleeding sword
   Now falls on Priam.   470
   Out, out, thou strumpet Fortune: all you gods,
   In general synod° take away her power,
   Break all the spokes and fellies from her wheel,°
   And bowl the round nave° down the hill of heaven
   As low as to the fiends."°   475
POLONIUS.   This is too long.
HAMLET.   It shall to the barber's with your beard; prithee say on: he's
   for a jig, or a tale of bawdry, or he sleeps. Say on, come to
   Hecuba.
I. PLAYER.   "But who, ah woe, had seen the mobled° queen—"   480
HAMLET.   "The mobled queen"?
POLONIUS.   That's good, "mobled queen" is good.
I. PLAYER.   "Run barefoot up and down, threat'ning the flames
   With bissom rheum,° a clout° upon that head
   Where late the diadem stood, and for a robe,   485

---

447 *antique*: ancient.   449 *Repugnant to command*: Refusing to obey its commander.
451 *fell*: savage.   452 *senseless Ilium*: unfeeling Troy.   458 *painted*: pictured.
459 *like . . . matter*: unmoved by either his purpose or its achievement.
461 *against*: before.   462 *rack*: clouds.   463 *orb*: earth.   467 *Cyclops*: workmen of
Vulcan, armorer of the gods.   468 *for proof eterne*: to be eternally invincible.   472 *synod*:
assembly. 473 *fellies . . . wheel*: curved pieces of the rim of the wheel that fortune turns,
representing a man's fortunes.   474 *nave*: hub.   475 *fiends*: i.e. of hell.   480 *mobled*:
muttled in a scarf.   484 *bissom rheum*: binding tears.   *clout*: cloth.

About her lank and all o'er-teemèd° loins,
A blanket in the alarm of fear caught up—
Who this had seen, with tongue in venom steeped,
'Gainst Fortune's state° would treason have pronounced;
But if the gods themselves did see her then,   490
When she saw Pyrrhus make malicious sport
In mincing with his sword her husband's limbs,
The instant burst of clamour that she made,
Unless things mortal move them not at all,
Would have made milch° the burning eyes of heaven,   495
And passion in the gods."

POLONIUS.   Look whe'r° he has not turned° his colour, and has tears in's
  eyes, prithee no more.
HAMLET.   'Tis well, I'll have thee speak out the rest of this soon.
  Good my lord, will you see the players well bestowed;° do   500
  you hear, let them be well used, for they are the abstract°
  and brief chronicles° of the time; after your death you were
  better have a bad epitaph than their ill report while you
  live.
POLONIUS.   My lord, I will use them according to their desert.°   505
HAMLET.   God's bodkin° man, much better. Use every man after° his
  desert, and who shall 'scape whipping? Use them after
  you own honour and dignity: the less they deserve, the
  more merit is in your bounty. Take them in.
POLONIUS.   Come sirs.   *Exeunt* POLONIUS *and* PLAYERS.   510
HAMLET.   Follow him friends, we'll hear a play tomorrow; [*Stops the
  First Player.*] dost thou hear me, old friend, can you play
  The Murder of Gonzago?
I. PLAYER.   Ay my lord.
HAMLET.   We'll ha't tomorrow night. You could for a need° study a   515
  speech of some dozen or sixteen lines, which I would set
  down and insert in't, could you not?
I. PLAYER.   Ay my lord.
HAMLET.   Very well, follow that lord, and look you mock him not.
                                                      [*Exit First* PLAYER.]
  [*To Rosencrantz and Guildenstern.*] My good friends, I'll   520
  leave you till night, you are welcome to Elsinore.
ROSENCRANTZ.   Good my lord.   [*Exeunt.*]
HAMLET.   Ay so, God bye to you, now I am alone.
  O what a rogue and peasant slave am I.
  Is it not monstrous that this player here,   525

---

486 *o'erteemed*: worn out by excessive childbearing.   489 *state*: reign.   495 *milch*: milky,
moist.   497 *whe'r*: whether.   *turned*: changed.   500 *bestowed*: lodged.
501 *abstract*: summary (noun).   502 *brief chronicles*: history in brief.
505 *desert*: merit.   506 *God's bodkin*: God's little body, the communion wafer (an oath).
after: according to.   515 *for a need*: if necessary.

But in a fiction, in a dream of passion,°
Could force his soul so to his own conceit°
That from her working all his visage wanned,°
Tears in his eyes, distraction in his aspect,
A broken voice, and his whole function° suiting   530
With forms° to his conceit; and all for nothing,
For Hecuba
What's Hecuba to him, or he to Hecuba,
That he should weep for her? what would he do,
Had he the motive and the cue for passion   535
That I have? he would drown the stage with tears,
And cleave the general ear° with horrid speech,
Make mad the guilty and appal the free,°
Confound° the ignorant, and amaze indeed
The very faculties of eyes and ears; yet I,   540
A dull and muddy-mettled° rascal, peak°
Like John-a-dreams,° unpregnant of° my cause,
And can say nothing; no, not for a king,
Upon whose property and most dear life,
A damnèd defeat was made: am I a coward?   545
Who calls me villain, breaks my pate° across,
Plucks off my beard° and blows it in my face,
Tweaks me by the nose, gives me the lie i'th'throat
As deep as to the lungs,° who does me this?
Ha, 'swounds,° I should take it: for it cannot be   550
But I am pigeon-livered,° and lack gall
To make oppression bitter, or ere this
I should ha' fatted all the region kites°
With this slave's offal: bloody, bawdy villain,
Remorseless, treacherous, lecherous, kindless° villain!   555
O vengeance!
Why what an ass am I, this is most brave,°
That I, the son of a dear father murdered,
Prompted to my revenge by heaven and hell,
Must like a whore unpack my heart with words,   560
And fall a-cursing like a very drab,°
A scullion,° fie upon't, foh.

---

526 *dream of passion*: portrayal of emotion.   527 *conceit*: imagination.   528 *wanned*: grew
pale.   530 *function*: bearing.   531 *With forms*: in appearance.   537 *general ear*: ears
of all in the audience.   538 *free*: innocent.   539 *confound*: confuse.   541 *muddy-
mettled*: dull-spirited.   *peak*: pine, mope.   542 *John-a-dreams*: a daydreaming fellow.
unpregnant of: unstirred by.   546 *pate*: head.   547 *Plucks . . . beard*: (a way of
giving insult).   548–549 *gives . . . lungs*: insults me by calling me a liar of the worst
kind (the lungs being deeper than the throat).   550 *'swounds*: God's wounds.   551 *pigeon-
livered*: meek and uncouraged.   553 *region kites*: vultures of the upper air.   555 *kindless*:
unnatural.   557 *brave*: fine.   561 *drab*: whore.   562 *scullion*: kitchen wench.

About, my brains; hum, I have heard,
That guilty creatures sitting at a play,
Have by the very cunning of the scene   565
Been struck so to the soul, that presently°
They have proclaimed their malefactions:
For murder, though it have no tongue, will speak
With most miraculous organ: I'll have these players
Play something like the murder of my father   570
Before mine uncle, I'll observe his looks,
I'll tent° him to the quick, if a' do blench°
I know my course. The spirit that I have seen
May be a devil, and the devil hath power
T'assume a pleasing shape, yea, and perhaps   575
Out of my weakness, and my melancholy,
As he is very potent with such spirits,
Abuses me to damn me; I'll have grounds
More relative than this: the play's the thing
Wherein I'll catch the conscience of the king.   *Exit.*

[ACT 3]

[Scene 1. A room in the castle]

Enter KING, QUEEN, POLONIUS, OPHELIA, ROSENCRANTZ, GUILDENSTERN, *and Lords.*

KING.   And can you by no drift of conference°
   Get from him why he puts on this confusion,°
   Grating so harshly all his days of quiet
   With turbulent and dangerous lunacy?
ROSENCRANTZ.   He does confess he feels himself distracted,   5
   But from what cause, a' will by no means speak.
GUILDENSTERN.   Nor do we find him forward to be sounded,°
   But with a crafty madness keeps aloof
   When we would bring him on to some confession
   Of his true state.
QUEEN.   Did he receive you well?   10
ROSENCRANTZ.   Most like a gentleman.
GUILDENSTERN.   But with much forcing of his disposition.°
ROSENCRANTZ.   Niggard of question,° but of our demands

566 *presently*: immediately.   572 *tent*: probe.   *blench*: flinch.   1 *drift of conference*: turn
of conversation.   2 *puts . . . confusion*: seems so distracted ("puts on" indicates the king's
private suspicion that Hamlet is playing mad).   7 *forward . . . sounded*: disposed to be
sounded out.   12 *forcing . . . disposition*: forcing himself to be so.   13 *Niggard of question*:
unwilling to talk.

Most free in his reply.

QUEEN.   Did you assay° him
  To any pastime?   15
ROSENCRANTZ. Madam, it so fell out that certain players
  We o'er-raught° on the way: of these we told him,
  And there did seem in him a kind of joy
  To hear of it: they are here about the court,
  And as I think, they have already order   20
  This night to play before him.
POLONIUS.   'Tis most true,
  And he beseeched me to entreat your majesties
  To hear and see the matter.°
KING.   With all my heart, and it doth much content me
  To hear him so inclined.   25
  Good gentlemen, give him a further edge,°
  And drive his purpose into these delights.
ROSENCRANTZ.   We shall my lord.   *Exeunt* ROSENCRANTZ *and* GUILDENSTERN.
KING.   Sweet Gertrude, leave us too,
  For we have closely° sent for Hamlet hither,
  That he, as 'twere by accident, may here   30
  Affront° Ophelia;
  Her father and myself, lawful espials,°
  Will so bestow° ourselves, that seeing unseen,
  We may of their encounter frankly° judge,
  And gather by him as he is behaved,   35
  If't be th'affliction of his love or no
  That thus he suffers for.
QUEEN.   I shall obey you.
  And for your part Ophelia, I do wish
  That your good beauties be the happy cause
  Of Hamlet's wildness, so shall I hope your virtues   40
  Will bring him to his wonted° way again,
  To both your honours.
OPHELIA.   Madam, I wish it may.   [*Exit* QUEEN.]
POLONIUS.   Ophelia, walk you here—Gracious,° so please you,
  We will bestow ourselves—read on this book,°
  That show of such an exercise° may colour°   45
  Your loneliness; we are oft to blame in this,
  'Tis too much proved,° that with devotion's visage
  And pious action, we do sugar o'er
  The devil himself.

---

14 *assay*: tempt.   17 *o'er-raught*: overtook.   23 *matter*: i.e. of the play.   26 *give . . .
edge*:encouragehiskeeninterest.   29 *closely*:secretly.   31 *Affront*:meetfacetoface
with.   32 *espials*:spies.   33,44 *bestow*place.   34 *frankly*:freely.   41. *wonted*:
customary.   43 *Gracious*: i.e., sir.   44 *book*: (of prayer).   45 *exercise*: religious
exercise   *colour*: make appear plausible.   47 *'Tis . . . proved*: it is all too apparent.

KING.   [*Aside.*] O 'tis too true,°
How smart a lash that speech doth give my conscience.   50
The harlot's cheek, beautied with plast'ring art,
Is not more ugly to° the thing that helps it,
Than is my deed to my most painted word:°
O heavy burden!
POLONIUS.   I hear him coming, let's withdraw my lord.   *Exeunt.* 55

Enter HAMLET.

HAMLET.   To be, or not to be, that is the question,
Whether 'tis nobler in the mind° to suffer
The slings and arrows of outrageous fortune,
Or to take arms against a sea of troubles,
And by opposing, end them: to die, to sleep,   60
No more; and by a sleep, to say we end
The heart-ache, and the thousand natural shocks
That flesh is heir to; 'tis a consummation
Devoutly to be wished. To die, to sleep,
To sleep, perchance to dream, ay there's the rub,°   65
For in that sleep of death what dreams may come
When we have shuffled off this mortal coil°
Must give us pause—there's the respect°
That makes calamity of so long life:°
For who would bear the whips and scorns of time,°   70
Th'oppressor's wrong, the proud man's contumely,°
The pangs of disprized love, the law's delay,°
The insolence of office,° and the spurns
That patient merit of th'unworthy takes,
When he himself might his quietus° make   75
With a bare bodkin;° who would fardels° bear,
To grunt and sweat under a weary life,
But that the dread of something after death,
The undiscovered° country, from whose bourn°
No traveller returns, puzzles the will,   80
And makes us rather bear those ills we have,
Than fly to others that we know not of.
Thus conscience does make cowards of us all,
And thus the native hue° of resolution

49 *'tis too true*: (the king's first indication that he is guilty).   52 *to*: compared to.   51–
53 *harlot's cheek . . . word*: just as the harlot's cheek is even uglier by contrast to the makeup
that tries to beautify it, so my deed is uglier by contrast to the hypocritical words under
which I hide it.   57 *nobler in the mind*: best, according to "sovereign" reason.   65 *rub*:
obstacle.   67 *mortal coil*: (1) turmoil of mortal life (2) coil of flesh encircling the body.
68 *respect*: consideration.   69 *of so long life*: so long-lived.   70 *time*: the
times.   71 *contumely*: contempt.   72 *law's delay*: longevity of lawsuits.   73 *office*:
officials.   75 *quietus*: settlement of his debt.   76 *bare bodkin*: mere dagger.   *fardels*:
burdens.   79 *undiscovered*: unexplored.   *bourn*: boundary.   84 *native hue*: natural
complexion.

Is sicklied o'er with the pale cast of thought,   85
And enterprises of great pitch° and moment,°
With this regard° their currents turn awry,°
And lose the name of action. Soft you now,
The fair Ophelia—Nymph, in thy orisons°
Be all my sins remembered.

OPHELIA.   Good my lord,   90
How does your honour for this many a day°?

HAMLET.   I humbly thank you: well, well, well.

OPHELIA.   My lord, I have remembrances of yours
That I have longèd long to re-deliver,
I pray you now receive them.

HAMLET.   No, not I,   95
I never gave you aught.

OPHELIA.   My honoured lord, you know right well you did,
And with them words of so sweet breath° composed
As made the things more rich: their perfume lost,
Take these again, for to the noble mind   100
Rich gifts wax° poor when givers prove unkind.
There my lord.

HAMLET.   Ha, ha, are you honest°?

OPHELIA.   My lord.

HAMLET.   Are you fair°?   105

OPHELIA.   What means your lordship?

HAMLET.   That if you be honest and fair, your honesty should admit
no discourse to your beauty.°

OPHELIA.   Could beauty my lord, have better commerce than with
honesty?   110

HAMLET.   Ay truly, for the power of beauty will sooner transform
honesty° from what it is to a bawd,° than the force of
honesty can translate beauty into his likeness. This was
sometime° a paradox, but now the time gives it proof. I did
love you once.   115

OPHELIA.   Indeed my lord, you made me believe so.

HAMLET.   You should not have believed me, for virtue cannot so
inoculate our old stock, but we shall relish of it.° I loved
you not.

OPHELIA.   I was the more deceived.   120

---

86 *pitch*: height, excellence.   *moment*: importance.   87 *regard*: consideration.   *their
currents turn awry*: change their course.   89 *orisons*: prayers (referring to her prayer book).
91 *this . . . day*: all these days.   98 *breath*: speech.   101 *wax*: grow.   103 *honest*: (1)
chaste (2) truthful.   105 *fair*: (1) beautiful (2) honorable.   107–108 *admit . . . beauty*:
(1) not allow communication with your beauty (2) not allow your beauty to be used as a
trap (Hamlet may have overheard the Polonius-Claudius plot or spotted their movement
behind the arras).   112 *honesty*: chastity.   *bawd*: procurer, pimp.   114 *sometime*:
once.   118 *inoculate . . . it*: change our sinful nature (as a tree is grafted to improve it)
but we will keep our old taste (as will the fruit of the grafted tree).

HAMLET. Get thee to a nunnery,° why wouldst thou be a breeder of
sinners? I am myself indifferent honest,° but yet I could
accuse me of such things, that it were better my mother
had not borne me: I am very proud, revengeful, ambitious,
with more offences at my beck,° than I have thoughts   125
to put them in, imagination to give them shape, or time to
act them in: what should such fellows as I do, crawling
between earth and heaven? we are arrant° knaves all,
believe none of us, go thy ways to a nunnery. Where's
your father?   130
OPHELIA. At home my lord.
HAMLET. Let the doors be shut upon him, that he may play the fool
no where but in's own house. Farewell.
OPHELIA. O help him, you sweet heavens.
HAMLET. If thou dost marry, I'll give thee this plague° for thy dowry: 135
be thou as chaste as ice, as pure as snow, thou shalt not
escape calumny; get thee to a nunnery, go, farewell. Or if
thou wilt needs marry, marry a fool, for wise men know
well enough what monsters° you make of them: to a nunnery
go, and quickly too, farewell.   140
OPHELIA. O heavenly powers, restore him.
HAMLET. I have heard of your paintings too, well enough. God hath
given you one face, and you make yourselves another: you
jig,° you amble, and you lisp,° you nick-name God's
creatures, and make your wantonness your ignorance;° go to,   145
I'll no more on't, it hath made me mad. I say we will have
no moe° marriage. Those that are married already, all but
one shall live, the rest shall keep as they are: to a nunnery,
go.   *Exit* HAMLET.
OPHELIA. O what a noble mind is here o'erthrown!   150
The courtier's, soldier's, scholar's, eye, tongue, sword,
Th'expectancy and rose° of the fair state,
The glass° of fashion, and the mould of form,°
Th'observed of all observers, quite quite down,
And I of ladies most deject and wretched,   155
That sucked the honey of his music vows,
Now see that noble and most sovereign° reason
Like sweet bells jangled, out of tune and harsh,
That unmatched form and feature° of blown° youth

---

121 *nunnery*: (1) cloister (2) slang for "brothel" (cf. "bawd" above).   122 *indifferent honest*:
reasonably virtuous.   125 *beck*: beckoning.   128 *arrant*: absolute.   135 *plague*:
curse.   139 *monsters*: horned cuckolds (men whose wives were unfaithful).   144 *jig*: walk
in a mincing way.   *lisp*: put on affected speech.   145 *make your . . . ignorance*: excuse
your caprices as being due to ignorance.   147 *moe*: more.   152 *expectancy and rose*: fair
hope.   153 *glass*: mirror.   *mould of form*: model of manners.   157 *sovereign*: (because
it should rule).   159 *blown*: flowering

Blasted with ecstasy.° O woe is me,   160
T'have seen what I have seen, see what I see.

Enter KING *and* POLONIUS.

KING.   Love? his affections° do not that way tend,
    Nor what he spake, though it lacked form a little,
    Was not like madness. There's something in his soul
    O'er which his melancholy sits on brood,   165
    And I do doubt,° the hatch and the disclose°
    Will be some danger; which for to prevent,
    I have in quick determination
    Thus set it down: he shall with speed to England,
    For the demand of our neglected° tribute: 170
    Haply° the seas, and countries different,
    With variable° objects, shall expel
    This something°-settled matter in his heart,
    Whereon his brains still beating puts him thus
    From fashion of himself.° What think you on't?   175
POLONIUS.   It shall do well. But yet do I believe
    The origin and commencement of his grief
    Sprung from neglected° love. How now Ophelia?
    You need not tell us what Lord Hamlet said,
    We heard it all. My lord, do as you please,   180
    But if you hold it fit, after the play,
    Let his queen-mother all alone entreat him
    To show his grief, let her be round° with him,
    And I'll be placed (so please you) in the ear
    Of° all their conference. If she find° him not,   185
    To England send him: or confine him where
    Your wisdom best shall think
KING.   It shall be so,
    Madness in great ones must not unwatched go.   *Exeunt.*

[Scene 2. A hall in the castle.]

Enter HAMLET *and three of the* PLAYERS.

HAMLET.   Speak the speech° I pray you as I pronounced it to you,
    trippingly on the tongue, but if you mouth it° as many of
    your players do, I had as lief the town-crier spoke my
    lines. Nor do not saw the air too much with your hand

---

160 *Blasted with ecstasy*: blighted by madness.   162 *affections*: emotions, afflictions.
166 *doubt*: fear.   165–166 *on brood . . . hatch . . . disclose*: (metaphor of a hen
sitting on eggs).   170 *neglected*: (being unpaid).   171 *Haply*: perhaps.
172 *variable*: varied.   173 *something-*: somewhat-.   175 *fashion of himself*: his usual
self.   178 *neglected*: unrequited.   183 *round*: direct.   184–185 *in the ear Of*: so
as to overhear.   185 *find*: find out.   1 *the speech*: i.e., that Hamlet has inserted.
2 *mouth it*: deliver it slowly and over-dramatically.

thus, but use all gently, for in the very torrent, tempest, 5
and as I may say, whirlwind of your passion, you must
acquire and beget° a temperance that may give it smoothness.
O it offends me to the soul, to hear a robustious°
periwig-pated° fellow tear a passion to tatters, to very rags,
to split the ears of the groundlings,° who for the most part 10
are capable of° nothing but inexplicable dumb shows° and
noise: I would have such a fellow whipped for o'erdoing
Termagant:° it out-herods Herod,° pray you avoid it.

I. PLAYER.   I warrant you honour.

HAMLET.   Be not too tame neither, but let your own discretion be 15
your tutor, suit the action to the word, the word to the
action, with this special observance, that you o'erstep not
the modesty° of nature: for any thing so o'erdone, is from°
the purpose of playing, whose end both at the first, and
now, was and is, to hold as 'twere the mirror up to nature, 20
to show virtue her own feature, scorn° her own image, and
the very age and body of the time his form and pressure.°
Now this overdone, or come tardy off,° though it make the
unskilful° laugh, cannot but make the judicious grieve, the
censure of the which one,° must in your allowance° 25
o'erweigh a whole theatre of others. O there be players
that I have seen play, and heard others praise, and that
highly (not to speak it profanely) that neither having
th'accent of Christians, nor the gait of Christian, pagan,
nor man, have so strutted and bellowed, that I have 30
thought some of nature's journeymen° had made men, and
not made them well, they imitated humanity so
abominably.

I. PLAYER.   I hope we have reformed that indifferently° with us, sir.

HAMLET.   O reform it altogether, and let those that play your clowns 35
speak no more than is set down for them,° for there be of
them that will themselves laugh, to set on some quantity
of barren° spectators to laugh too, though in the meantime,
some necessary question° of the play be then to be considered:

---

7 *acquire and beget*: achieve for yourself and instill in other actors.   8 *robustious*:
boisterous.   9 *periwig-pated*: wig-wearing.   10 *groundlings*: audience who paid least and
stood on the ground floor.   11 *capable of*: able to understand.   *dumb shows*: pantomimed
synopses of the action to follow (as below).   13 *Termagant*: violent, ranting character in
the guild or mystery plays.   *out-herods Herod*: outdoes even Herod, King of Judea (who
commanded the slaughter of the innocents and who was a ranting tyrant in the mystery
plays).   18 *modesty*: moderation.   *from*: away from.   21 *scorn*: that which should be
scorned.   22 *age . . . pressure*: shape of the times in its accurate impression.   23 *come
tardy off*: understated, underdone.   24 *unskilful*: unsophisticated.   25 *one*: the
judicious.   *allowance*: estimation.   31 *journeymen*: artisans working for others and not
yet masters of their trades.   34 *indifferently*: reasonably well.   36 *speak no more . . . them*:
stick to their lines.   38 *barren*: witless.   39 *question*: dialogue.

that's villainous, and shows a most pitiful ambition   40
in the fool that uses it. Go make you ready.   *Exeunt* PLAYERS.

Enter POLONIUS, ROSENCRANTZ, *and* GUILDENSTERN.

How now my lord, will the king hear this piece of work?
POLONIUS.   And the queen too, and that presently.
HAMLET.   Bid the players make haste.   *Exit* POLONIUS.
Will you two help to hasten them?   45
ROSENCRANTZ.   Ay my lord.   *Exeunt they two.*
HAMLET.   What ho, Horatio!

Enter HORATIO.

HORATIO.   Here sweet lord, at your service.
HAMLET.   Horatio, thou art e'en as just° a man
As e'er my conversation coped withal.°   50
HORATIO.   O my dear lord.
HAMLET.   Nay, do not think I flatter,
For what advancement may I hope from thee,
That no revenue hast but thy good spirits
To feed and clothe thee? Why should the poor be flattered?
No, let the candied° tongue lick° absurd pomp,   55
And crook the pregnant° hinges of the knee
Where thrift may follow fawning.° Dost thou hear,
Since my dear soul was mistress of her choice,
And could of men distinguish her election,°
Sh'hath sealed° thee for herself, for thou hast been   60
As one in suff'ring all that suffers nothing,
A man that Fortune's buffets° and rewards
Hast ta'en with equal thanks; and blest are those
Whose blood° and judgment are so well co-mingled,
That they are not a pipe for Fortune's finger   65
To sound what stop° she please:° give me that man
That is not passion's slave, and I will wear him
In my heart's core, ay in my heart of heart,
As I do thee. Something too much of this.
There is a play tonight before the king,   70
One scene of it comes near the circumstance
Which I have told thee of my father's death.
I prithee when thou seest that act afoot,
Even with the very comment° of thy soul
Observe my uncle: if his occulted° guilt   75

---

49 *just*: well-balanced.   50 *coped withal*: had to do with.   55–57 *candied . . . fawning*:
(metaphor of a dog licking and fawning for candy).   55 *candied*: flattering.   *lick*: pay
court to.   56–57 *crook . . . fawning*: obsequiously kneel when personal profit may
ensue.   56 *pregnant*: quick in motion.   59 *election*: choice.   60 *sealed*: confirmed.
62 *buffets*: blows.   64 *blood*: passions.   66 *sound . . . please*: play whatever tune she
likes.   *stop*: finger hole in wind instrument for varying the sound.   74 *very comment*:
acutest observation.   75 *occulted*: hidden.

Do not itself unkennel° in one speech,
It is a damnèd ghost° that we have seen,
And my imaginations are as foul
As Vulcan's stithy;° give him heedful note,
For I mine eyes will rivet to his face,   80
And after we will both our judgments join
In censure of his seeming.°
HORATIO.   Well my lord,
If a' steal aught the whilst this play is playing,
And 'scape detecting, I will pay° the theft.   *Sound a flourish.*
HAMLET   They are coming to the play. I must be idle,°   85
Get you a place.

Enter Trumpets and Kettledrums, KING, QUEEN, POLONIUS, OPHELIA, ROSENCRANTZ, GUIL-
DENSTERN, and other LORDS attendant, with his GUARD carrying torches. Danish March.

KING.   How fares° our cousin Hamlet?
HAMLET.   Excellent i'faith, of the chameleon's dish: I eat the air,°
promise-crammed, you cannot feed capons so.°
KING.   I have nothing with° this answer Hamlet, these words are   90
not mine.°
HAMLET.   No, nor mine now. [*To Polonius.*] My lord, you played
once i'th'university you say?
POLONIUS.   That did I my lord, and was accounted a good actor.
HAMLET.   What did you enact?   95
POLONIUS.   I did enact Julius Caesar, I was killed i'th'Capitol, Brutus
killed me.
HAMLET.   It was a brute part of him to kill so capital a calf there. Be
the players ready?
ROSENCRANTZ.   Ay my lord, they stay upon your patience.°   100
QUEEN.   Come hither my dear Hamlet, sit by me.
HAMLET.   No, good mother, here's metal more attractive.°
POLONIUS.   [*To the King.*] O ho, do you mark that?
HAMLET.   Lady, shall I lie in your lap?
OPHELIA.   No my lord.   105
HAMLET.   I mean, my head upon your lap?
OPHELIA.   Ay my lord.

---

76 *unkennel*: force from hiding.   77 *damned ghost*: devil (not the ghost of my father).
79 *Vulcan's stithy*: the forge of the blacksmith of the gods.   82 *censure . . . seeming*: (1)
judgment of his appearance (2) disapproval of his pretending.   84 *pay*: i.e., for.   85
be idle: act mad.   87 *fares*: does, but Hamlet takes it to mean "eats" or "dines."   88 *eat*
the air: the chamelion supposedly ate air, but Hamlet also puns on "heir."   89 *you cannot*
. . . so: (1) even a capon cannot feed on air and your promises (2) like a capon stuffed with
food before being killed, I am stuffed (fed up) with your promises.   90 *nothing with*: nothing
to do with.   91 *not mine*: not in answer to my question.   100 *stay . . . patience*: await
your permission.   102 *metal more attractive*: (1) iron more magnetic (2) stuff ("mettle")
more beautiful.

HAMLET.   Do you think I meant country° matters?
OPHELIA.   I think nothing my lord.
HAMLET.   That's a fair thought to lie between maids' legs.   110
OPHELIA.   What is, my lord?
HAMLET.   Nothing.
OPHELIA.   You are merry my lord.
HAMLET.   Who, I?
OPHELIA.   Ay my lord.   115
HAMLET.   O God, your only jig-maker: what should a man do but be
      merry, for look you how cheerfully my mother looks, and
      my father died within's two hours.
OPHELIA.   Nay, 'tis twice two months my lord.
HAMLET.   So long? Nay then let the devil wear black, for I'll have a   120
      suit of sables;° O heavens, die two months ago, and not
      forgotten yet? Then there's hope a great man's memory
      may outlive his life half a year, but by'r lady° a' must build
      churches then, or else shall a' suffer not thinking on,° with
      the hobby-horse,° whose epitaph is "For O, for O, the   125
      hobby-horse is forgot."

*The trumpets sound. The Dumb Show° follows. Enter a King and a Queen, very lovingly,
the Queen embracing him, and he her. She kneels and makes show of protestation unto him.
He takes her up, and declines his head upon her neck. He lies him down upon a bank of
flowers; she seeing him asleep leaves him: anon comes in another man, takes off his crown,
kisses it, pours poison in the sleeper's ears, and leaves him: the Queen returns, finds the
King dead, and makes passionate action. The poisoner with some three or four mutes° comes
in again, seeming to condole with her. The dead body is carried away. The poisoner wooes
the Queen with gifts: she seems harsh and unwilling awhile, but in the end accepts his love.
Exeunt.*

OPHELIA.   What means this, my lord?
HAMLET.   Marry, this is miching mallecho,° it means mischief.
OPHELIA.   Belike this show imports the argument° of the play.

Enter PROLOGUE.

HAMLET.   We shall know by this fellow: the players cannot keep   130
      counsel,° they'll tell all.
OPHELIA.   Will a' tell us what this show meant?
HAMLET.   Ay, or any show that you will show him. Be not you
      ashamed to show, he'll not shame to tell you what it
      means.   135
OPHELIA.   You are naught,° you are naught, I'll mark the play.

108 *country:* rustic, sexual (with a pun on an obscene word for the female sexual organ).
121 *sables:* (1) rich fur (2) black mourning garb.   123 *by'r lady:* by Our Lady (the Virgin
Mary).   124 *not thinking on:* being forgotten.   125 *hobby-horse:* (1) character in the May
games (2) slang for "prostitute."   126 stage direction: *Dumb Show:* pantomimed synopsis
of the action to follow.   126 stage direction: *mutes:* actors without speaking parts.
128 *miching mallecho:* skulking mischief.   129 *imports the argument:* signifies the plot.
131 *counsel:* a secret.   136 *naught:* naughty, lewd.

25

PROLOGUE.   For us and for our tragedy,
   Here stooping to your clemency,
   We beg your hearing patiently.   [*Exit.*]
HAMLET.   Is this a prologue, or the posy° of a ring?   140
OPHELIA.   'Tis brief, my lord.
HAMLET.   As woman's love.

Enter Player KING *and* QUEEN.

PLAYER KING.   Full thirty times hath Phoebus' cart° gone round
   Neptune's salt wash,° and Tellus' orbèd ground,°
   And thirty dozen moons with borrowed sheen   145
   About the world have times twelve thirties been,
   Since love our hearts, and Hymen° did our hands
   Unite commutual,° in most sacred bands.
PLAYER QUEEN.   So many journeys may the sun and moon
   Make us again count o'er ere love be done,   150
   But woe is me, you are so sick of late,
   So far from cheer, and from your former state,
   That I distrust you:° yet though I distrust,
   Discomfort you, my lord, it nothing must.
   For women fear too much, even as they love,   155
   And women's fear and love hold quantity,°
   In neither aught, or in extremity:°
   Now what my love is, proof° hath made you know,
   And as my love is sized, my fear is so.
   Where love is great, the littlest doubts are fear,   160
   Where little fears grow great, great love grows there.
PLAYER KING.   Faith, I must leave thee love, and shortly too,
   My operant° powers their functions leave° to do,
   And thou shalt live in this fair world behind,
   Honoured, beloved, and haply° one as kind   165
   For husband shalt thou—
PLAYER QUEEN.   O confound the rest:
   Such love must needs be treason in my breast.
   In second husband let me be accurst,
   None wed the second, but who killed the first.
HAMLET.   [*Aside.*] That's wormwood,° wormwood.   170
PLAYER QUEEN.   The instances° that second marriage move°
   Are base respects of thrift,° but none of love.
   A second time I kill my husband dead,
   When second husband kisses me in bed.

---

140 *posy*: motto (engraved in a ring).   143 *Phoebus' cart*: chariot of the sun.   144 *wash*:
sea.   *Tellus'* . . . *ground*: the earth (Tellus was a Roman earth goddess).   147 *Hymen*:
Roman god of marriage.   148 *commutual*: mutually.   153 *distrust you*: am worried about
you.   156 *quantity*: proportion.   157 *In neither* . . . *extremity*: their love and fear are either
absent or excessive.   158 *proof*: experience.   163 *operant*: vital.   *leave*: cease.
165 *haply*: perhaps.   170 *wormwood*: bitter (like the herb).   171 *instances*:
causes.   *move*: motivate.   172 *respects of thrift*: considerations of profit.

PLAYER KING.   I do believe you think what now you speak,   175
    But what we do determine, oft we break:
    Purpose is but the slave to memory,
    Of violent birth but poor validity:°
    Which now like fruit unripe sticks on the tree,
    But fall unshaken when they mellow be.   180
    Most necessary 'tis that we forget
    To pay ourselves what to ourselves is debt:°
    What to ourselves in passion we propose,
    The passion ending, doth the purpose lose.
    The violence of either grief or joy   185
    Their own enactures° with themselves destroy:
    Where joy most revels, grief doth most lament;
    Grief joys, joy grieves, on slender accident.
    This world is not for aye,° nor 'tis not strange
    That even our loves should with our fortunes change: 190
    For 'tis a question left us yet to prove,
    Whether love lead fortune, or else fortune love.°
    The great man down, you mark his favourite flies,
    The poor advanced, makes friends of enemies:
    And hitherto doth love on fortune tend,   195
    For who not needs, shall never lack a friend,
    And who in want a hollow friend doth try,
    Directly seasons him° his enemy.
    But orderly to end where I begun,
    Our wills and fates do so contrary run,   200
    That our devices still° are overthrown,
    Our thoughts are ours, their ends none of our own.
    So think thou wilt no second husband wed,
    But die thy thoughts when thy first lord is dead.
PLAYER QUEEN.   Nor earth to me give food, nor heaven light,   205
    Sport and repose lock from me day and night,
    To desperation turn my trust and hope,
    An anchor's° cheer in prison be my scope,
    Each opposite that blanks° the face of joy,
    Meet what I would have well, and it destroy,   210
    Both here and hence° pursue me lasting strife,
    If once a widow, ever I be wife.
HAMLET.   If she should break it now.
PLAYER KING.   'Tis deeply sworn: sweet, leave me here awhile,
    My spirits grow dull, and fain° I would beguile   215
    The tedious day with sleep.   *Sleeps.*

---

178 *validity*: strength.   181–182 *Most . . . debt*: we are easy creditors to ourselves and
forget our former promises (debts).   186 *enactures*: fulfillments.   189 *aye*: ever.
192 *fortune love*: fortune lead love.   198 *seasons him*: sees him mature into.
201 *devices still*: plans always.   208 *anchor's*: hermit's.   209 *opposite that blanks*: contrary
event that pales.   211 *here and hence*: in this world and the next.   215 *fain*: gladly.

PLAYER QUEEN.   Sleep rock thy brain,
  And never come mischance between us twain.   *Exit.*
HAMLET.   Madam, how like you this play?
QUEEN.   The lady doeth protest too much methinks.
HAMLET.   O but she'll keep her word.   220
KING.   Have you heard the argument°? Is there no offence in't?
HAMLET.   No, no, they do but jest, poison in jest, no offence
  i'th'world.
KING.   What do you call the play?
HAMLET.   The Mouse-trap. Marry, how? Tropically:° this play is the   225
  image of a murder done in Vienna: Gonzago is the duke's
  name, his wife Baptista, you shall see anon, 'tis a knavish
  piece of work, but what of that? Your majesty, and we
  that have free° souls, it touches us not: let the galled jade
  winch,° our withers are unwrung.°   230

Enter LUCIANUS.

  This is one Lucianus, nephew to the king.
OPHELIA.   You are as good as a chorus,° my lord.
HAMLET.   I could interpret between you and your love, if I could see
  the puppets dallying.
OPHELIA.   You are keen my lord, you are keen.°   235
HAMLET.   It would cost you a groaning to take off mine edge.
OPHELIA.   Still better and worse.°
HAMLET.   So you mistake° your husbands. Begin, murderer. Pox,°
  leave thy damnable faces° and begin. Come, 'the croaking
  raven doth bellow for revenge.'   240
LUCIANUS.   Thoughts black, hands apt, drugs fit, and time agreeing,
  Confederate season, else no creature seeing,°
  Thou mixture rank, of midnight weeds collected,
  With Hecate's° ban° thrice blasted, thrice infected,
  Thy natural magic, and dire property,   245
  On wholesome° life usurps immediately.   *Pours the poison in his ears.*
HAMLET.   A' poisons him i'th'garden for's estate, his name's Gonzago,
  the story is extant, and written in very choice
  Italian, you shall see anon how the murderer gets the love
  of Gonzago's wife.   250
OPHELIA.   The king rises.
HAMLET.   What, frighted with false fire°?
QUEEN.   How fares my lord?

221 *argument*: plot.   225 *Tropically*: figuratively.   229 *free*: innocent.   229–230 *galled jade winch*: chafed old horse wince (from its sores).   230 *withers are unwrung*: (1) shoulders are unchafed (2) consciences are clear.   232 *chorus*: actor who introduced the action.   235 *keen*: (1) sharp (Ophelia's meaning) (2) sexually excited (Hamlet's interpretation).   237 *better and worse*: better wit but a worse meaning, with a pun on "better" and "bitter."   238 *mistake*: mis-take.   *Pox*: a plague on it.   239 *faces*: exaggerated facial expressions.   242 *Confederate . . . seeing*: no one seeing me except time, my confederate.   244 *Hecate*: goddess of witchcraft.   *ban*: evil spell.   246 *wholesome*: healthy.   252 *false fire*: discharge of blanks (not gunpowder).

POLONIUS.   Give o'er the play.

KING.   Give me some light. Away!   255

ALL.   Lights, lights, lights!   *Exeunt all but Hamlet and Horatio.*

HAMLET.   Why, let the strucken deer go weep,
      The hart ungallèd° play,°
    For some must watch while some must sleep,
      Thus runs the world away.   260
  Would not this° sir, and a forest of feathers,° if the rest of my
  fortunes turn Turk with° me, with two Provincial roses° on
  my razed° shoes, get me a fellowship° in a cry° of players?

HORATIO.   Half a share.°

HAMLET.   A whole one, I.   265
  For thou dost know, O Damon° dear,
    This realm dismantled was
  Of Jove° himself, and now reigns here
    A very very—pajock.°

HORATIO.   You might have rhymed.°   270

HAMLET.   O good Horatio, I'll take the ghost's word for a thousand
  pound. Didst perceive?

HORATIO.   Very well my lord.

HAMLET.   Upon the talk of the poisoning?

HORATIO.   I did very well note him.   275

Enter ROSENCRANTZ *and* GUILDENSTERN.

HAMLET.   Ah ha, come, some music. Come, the recorders.°
  For if the king like not the comedy,
  Why then belike he likes it not, perdy.°
  Come, some music.

GUILDENSTERN.   Good my lord, vouchsafe me a word with you.   280

HAMLET.   Sir, a whole history.

GUILDENSTERN.   The king, sir—

HAMLET.   Ay sir, what of him?

GUILDENSTERN.   Is in his retirement, marvellous distempered.

HAMLET.   With drink sir?   285

GUILDENSTERN.   No my lord, with choler.°

HAMLET.   Your wisdom should show itself more richer to signify
  this to the doctor: for, for me to put him to his purgation,°
  would perhaps plunge him into more choler.

257–258 *deer . . . play:* (the belief that a wounded deer wept, abandoned by the others).
258 *ungalled:* unhurt.   261 *this:* i.e. sample (of my theatrical talent).
feathers: plumes (worn by actors).   262 *turn Turk with:* cruelly turn against.
Provincial roses: rosettes named for Provins, France.   263 *razed:* slashed, decorated with
cutouts.   *fellowship:* partnership.   *cry:* pack, troupe.   264 *share:* divisions of profits
among members of theatre producing company.   266 *Damon:* legendary ideal friend to
Pythias.   268 *Jove:* (Hamlet's father).   269 *pajock:* peacock (associated with
lechery).   270 *rhymed:* (used "ass" instead of "pajock").   276 *recorders:* soft-toned
woodwind instruments, similar to flutes.   278 *perdy:* by God.   286 *choler:* anger.
288 *purgation:* (1) purging of excessive bile (2) judicial investigations (3) purgatory.

GUILDENSTERN.   Good my lord, put your discourse into some frame,° and   290
start not so wildly from my affair.
HAMLET.   I am tame sir, pronounce.
GUILDENSTERN.   The queen your mother, in most great affliction of spirit,
hath sent me to you.
HAMLET.   You are welcome.   295
GUILDENSTERN.   Nay good my lord, this courtesy is not of the right breed.°
If it shall please you to make me a wholesome° answer, I
will do your mother's commandment: if not, your pardon°
and my return shall be the end of my business.
HAMLET.   Sir I cannot.   300
ROSENCRANTZ.   What, my lord?
HAMLET.   Make you a wholesome answer: my wit's diseased. But
sir, such answer as I can make, you shall command, or
rather as you say, my mother: therefore no more, but to
the matter. My mother you say.   305
ROSENCRANTZ.   Then thus she says, your behaviour hath struck her into
amazement and admiration.°
HAMLET.   O wonderful son that can so stonish a mother. But is there
no sequel at the heels of this mother's admiration? Impart.
ROSENCRANTZ.   She desires to speak with you in her closet   310
ere you go to bed.
HAMLET.   We shall obey, were she ten times our mother. Have you
any further trade with us?
ROSENCRANTZ.   My lord, you once did love me.
HAMLET.   And do still, by these pickers and stealers.°   315
ROSENCRANTZ.   Good my lord, what is your cause of distemper? You do
surely bar the door upon your own liberty, if you deny
your griefs to your friend.°
HAMLET.   Sir, I lack advancement.
ROSENCRANTZ.   How can that be, when you have the voice° of the king   320
himself for your succession in Denmark?
HAMLET.   Ay sir, but 'while the grass grows'°—the proverb is
something musty.°

Enter the PLAYERS with recorders.

O the recorders, let me see one. To withdraw° with you,
why do you go about to recover the wind of me,° as if you   325
would drive me into a toil°?

---

290 *frame*: order.   296 *breed*: (1) species (2) manners.   297 *wholesome*: reasonable.
298 *pardon*: permission to depart.   307 *admiration*: wonder.   315 *pickers and stealers*:
hands (from the prayer, "Keep my hands from picking and stealing").   317–318 *deny
. . . friend*: refuse to let your friend know the cause of your suffering.   320 *voice*: vote.
322 *while . . . grows*: (the proverb ends: "the horse starves").   323 *something musty*:
somewhat too old and trite (to finish).   324 *withdraw*: speak privately.   325 *recover
. . . me*: drive me towards the wind, as with a prey, to avoid its scenting the hunter.   326 *toil*:
snare.

GUILDENSTERN.   O my lord, if my duty be too bold, my love is too
    unmannerly.°
HAMLET.   I do not well understand that. Will you play
    upon this pipe°?   330
GUILDENSTERN.   My lord I cannot.
HAMLET.   I pray you.
GUILDENSTERN.   Believe me. I cannot.
HAMLET.   I do beseech you.
GUILDENSTERN.   I know no touch of it° my lord.   335
HAMLET.   It is as easy as lying; govern these ventages° with your
    fingers and thumb, give it breath with your mouth, and it
    will discourse most eloquent music. Look you, these are
    the stops.
GUILDENSTERN.   But these cannot I command to any utt'rance of harmony,   340
    I have not the skill.
HAMLET.   Why look you now how unworthy a thing you make of
    me: you would play upon me, you would seem to know
    my stops, you would pluck out the heart of my mystery,
    you would sound me from my lowest note to the top of my   345
    compass:° and there is much music, excellent voice in this
    little organ,° yet cannot you make it speak. 'Sblood, do you
    think I am easier to be played on than a pipe? Call me what
    instrument you will, though you can fret° me, you cannot
    play upon me.   350

Enter POLONIUS.

    God bless you sir.
POLONIUS.   My lord, the queen would speak with you, and presently.
HAMLET.   Do you see yonder cloud that's almost in shape of a camel?
POLONIUS.   By th'mass and 'tis, like a camel indeed.
HAMLET.   Methinks it is like a weasel.   355
POLONIUS.   It is backed like a weasel.
HAMLET.   Or like a whale?
POLONIUS.   Very like a whale.
HAMLET.   Then I will come to my mother by and by.°
    [*Aside.*] They fool me to the top of my bent.°   360
    I will come by and by.
POLONIUS.   I will say so.   *Exit.*
HAMLET.   "By and by" is easily said.
    Leave me, friends.   [*Exeunt all but Hamlet.*]
    'Tis now the very witching time of night,   365

327–328 *is too unmannerly*: makes me forget my good manners.   330 *pipe*: recorder.
335 *know . . . it*: have no skill at fingering it.   336 *ventages*: holes, stops.   346 *compass*:
range.   347 *organ*: musical instrument.   349 *fret*: (1) irritate (2) play an instrument that
has "frets" or bars to guide the fingering.   359 *by and by*: very soon.   360 *fool me . . .*
bent: force me to play the fool to my utmost.

When churchyards yawn,° and hell itself breathes out
Contagion° to this world: now could I drink hot blood,
And do such bitter business as the day
Would quake to look on: soft, now to my mother—
O heart, lose not thy nature,° let not ever   370
The soul of Nero° enter this firm bosom,
Let me be cruel, not unnatural.
I will speak daggers to her, but use none:
My tongue and soul in this be hypocrites,°
How in my words somever she be shent,°   375
To give them seals,° never my soul consent.   *Exit.*

[Scene 3. A room in the castle.]

Enter KING, ROSENCRANTZ, *and* GUILDENSTERN.

KING.   I like him not, nor stands it safe with us
To let his madness range. Therefore prepare you,
I your commission will forthwith dispatch,°
And he to England shall along with you:
The terms of our estate° may not endure   5
Hazard so near's° as doth hourly grow
Out of his brows.°
GUILDENSTERN.   We will ourselves provide:°
Most holy and religious fear it is
To keep those many many bodies safe
That live and feed upon your majesty.   10
ROSENCRANTZ. The single and peculiar° life is bound
With all the strength and armour of the mind
To keep itself from noyance,° but much more
That spirit, upon whose weal° depends and rests
The lives of many; the cess° of majesty   15
Dies not alone, but like a gulf° doth draw
What's near it, with it. O 'tis a massy wheel
Fixed on the summit of the highest mount,
To whose huge spokes, ten thousand lesser things
Are mortised° and adjoined, which when it falls,   20
Each small annexment, petty consequence,
Attends° the boist'rous ruin. Never alone
Did the king sigh, but with a general groan.

---

366 *churchyards yawn*: graves open.   367 *Contagion*: (1) evil (2) diseases.   370 *nature*: natural affection.   371 *Nero*: (who killed his mother).   374 *My tongue . . . hypocrites*: I will speak cruelly but intend no harm.   375 *shent*: chastised.   376 *give them seals*: confirm them with action (as a legal "deed" is confirmed with a "seal").   3 *forthwith dispatch*: immediately have prepared.   5 *terms . . . estate*: circumstances of my royal office.   6 *near's*: near us.   7 *brows*: effronteries.   *provide*: prepare.   11 *peculiar*: individual.   13 *noyance*: harm.   14 *weal*: well-being.   15 *cess*: cessation, death.   16 *gulf*: whirlpool.   20 *mortised*: securely fitted.   22 *Attends*: accompanies.

KING. Arm° you I pray you, to this speedy voyage,
 For we will fetters put about this fear,   25
 Which now goes too free-footed.
ROSENCRANTZ.   We will haste us.

       Exeunt [ROSENCRANTZ *and* GUILDENSTERN.]

Enter POLONIUS.

POLONIUS. My lord, he's going to his mother's closet:
 Behind the arras I'll convey myself
 To hear the process.° I'll warrant she'll tax him home,
 And as you said, and wisely was it said,   30
 'Tis meet° that some more audience than a mother,
 Since nature makes them partial, should o'erhear
 The speech of vantage;° fare you well my liege,°
 I'll call upon you ere you go to bed,
 And tell you what I know.
KING.   Thanks, dear my lord.   *Exit* [POLONIUS.] 35
 O my offence is rank, it smells to heaven,
 It hath the primal eldest curse° upon't,
 A brother's murder. Pray can I not,
 Though inclination be as sharp as will:°
 My stronger guilt defeats my strong intent,   40
 And like a man to double business bound,
 I stand in pause where I shall first begin,
 And both neglect; what if this cursèd hand
 Were thicker than itself with brother's blood,
 Is there not rain enough in the sweet heavens   45
 To wash it white as snow? Whereto serves mercy
 But to confront the visage of offence°?
 And what's in prayer but this two-fold force,
 To be forestallèd° ere we come to fall,
 Or pardoned being down? Then I'll look up,   50
 My fault is past. But O what form of prayer
 Can serve my turn? "Forgive me my foul murder":
 That cannot be, since I am still possessed
 Of those effects° for which I did the murder:
 My crown, mine own ambition, and my queen.   55
 May one be pardoned and retain th'offence?
 In the corrupted currents of this world,
 Offence's gilded hand may shove by justice,

---

24 *Arm*: prepare. 29 *the process*: what proceeds. 31 *meet*: fitting. 33 *of vantage*: from
an advantageous position. *liege*: lord. 37 *primal . . . curse*: curse of Cain.
39 *inclination . . . will*: my desire to pray is as strong as my determination to do
so. 47 *confront . . . offence*: plead in man's behalf against sin (at the Last Judgment).
49 *forestalled*: prevented. 54 *effects*: results.

And oft 'tis seen the wicked prize itself
Buys out the law;° but 'tis not so above,   60
There is no shuffling,° there the action lies
In his true nature,° and we ourselves compelled
Even to the teeth and forehead of our faults°
To give in evidence. What then? What rests°?
Try what repentance can. What can it not?   65
Yet what can it, when one can not repent?
O wretched state! O bosom black as death!
O limèd soul, that struggling to be free,
Art more engaged;° help, angels, make assay:°
Bow stubborn knees, and heart with strings of steel,   70
Be soft as sinews of the new-born babe,
All may be well.   [*He kneels.*]

Enter HAMLET.

HAMLET.   Now might I do it pat,° now a' is a-praying,
And now I'll do't, [*Draws his sword.*] and so a' goes to heaven,
And so am I revenged: that would be scanned:°   75
A villain kills my father, and for that,
I his sole son, do this same villain send
To heaven.
Why, this is hire and salary, not revenge.
A' took my father grossly,° full of bread,°   80
With all his crimes° broad blown,° as flush° as May,
And how his audit° stands who knows save heaven,
But in our circumstance and course of thought,
'Tis heavy° with him: and am I then revenged
To take him in the purging of his soul,   85
when he is fit and seasoned° for his passage?
No.   [*Sheathes his sword.*]
Up sword, and know thou a more horrid hent,°
When he is drunk asleep, or in his rage,
Or in th'incestuous pleasure of his bed,   90
At game, a-swearing, or about some act
That has no relish° of salvation in't,
Then trip him that his heels may kick at heaven,

59–60 *wicked . . . law*: fruits of the crime bribe the judge.   61 *shuffling*: evasion.   61–
62 *action . . . nature*: (1) deed is seen in its true nature (2) legal action is sustained according
to the truth.   63 *to the teeth . . . faults*: meeting our sins face to face.   64 *rests*:
remains.   68–69 *limed . . . engaged*: like a bird caught in lime (a sticky substance spread
on twigs as a snare), the soul in its struggle to clear itself only becomes more entangled.
69 *make assay*: I'll make an attempt.   73 *pat*: opportunely.   75 *would be scanned*: needs
closer examination.   80 *grossly*: unpurified (by final rites).   *bread*: self-indulgence.
81 *crimes*: sins.   *broad blown*: in full flower.   *flush*: lusty.   82 *audit*: account.
84 *heavy*: grievous.   86 *seasoned*: ready (prepared).   88 *horrid hent*: horrible opportunity
("hint") for seizure ("hent") by me.   92 *relish*: taste.

And that his soul may be as damned and black
As hell whereto it goes; my mother stays,   95
This physic° but prolongs thy sickly days.   *Exit.*
KING. [*Rises.*]   My words fly up, my thoughts remain below,
Words without thoughts never to heaven go.   *Exit.*

[*Scene 4. The queen's closet.*]

Enter QUEEN and POLONIUS.

POLONIUS.   A' will come straight, look you lay home° to him,
Tell him his pranks have been too broad° to bear with,
And that your grace hath screened and stood between
Much heat° and him. I'll silence me° even here:
Pray you be round with him.   5
HAMLET. [*Within.*]   Mother, mother, mother.
QUEEN.   I'll war'nt you,
Fear me not. Withdraw, I hear him coming.   [*POLONIUS hides behind the arras.*]

Enter HAMLET.

HAMLET.   Now mother, what's the matter?
QUEEN.   Hamlet, thou hast thy father much offended.
HAMLET.   Mother, you have my father much offended.   10
QUEEN.   Come, come, you answer with an idle° tongue.
HAMLET.   Go, go, you question with a wicked tongue.
QUEEN.   Why, how now Hamlet?
HAMLET.   What's the matter now?
QUEEN.   Have you forgot me?
HAMLET.   No by the rood,° not so,
You are the queen, your husband's brother's wife,   15
And would it were not so, you are my mother.
QUEEN.   Nay, then I'll set those to you that can speak.°
HAMLET.   Come, come, and sit you down, you shall not budge,
You go not till I set you up a glass°
Where you may see the inmost part of you.   20
QUEEN.   What wilt thou do? Thou wilt not murder me?
Help, help, ho!
POLONIUS. [*Behind the arras.*]   What ho! help, help, help!
HAMLET.   How now, a rat? dead for a ducat,° dead.

                                        Kills POLONIUS [through the arras.]

POLONIUS.   O I am slain!
QUEEN.   O me, what hast thou done?

---

96 *physic*: (1) medicine (2) purgation of your soul by prayer.   1 *lay home*: thrust home;
speak sharply.   2 *broad*: unrestrained.   4 *heat*: anger.   *silence me*: hide in silence.
11 *idle*: foolish.   14 *rood*: cross.   17 *speak*: i.e. to you as you should be spoken
to.   19 *glass*: looking glass.   23 *for a ducat*: I wager a ducat (an Italian gold coin).

HAMLET.   Nay I know not,   25
   Is it the king?
QUEEN.   O what a rash and bloody deed is this!
HAMLET.   A bloody deed, almost as bad, good mother,
   As kill a king, and marry with his brother.
QUEEN.   As kill a king?
HAMLET.   Ay lady, it was my word.   30
   [*To Polonius.*] Thou wretched, rash, intruding fool, farewell,
   I took thee for thy better,° take thy fortune,
   Thou find'st to be too busy is some danger.
   [*To the Queen.*] Leave wringing of your hands, peace, sit you down,
   And let me wring your heart, for so I shall   35
   If it be made of penetrable stuff,
   If damnèd custom° have not brazed° it so,
   That it be proof° and bulwark against sense.°
QUEEN.   What have I done, that thou dar'st wag thy tongue
   In noise so rude against me?
HAMLET.   Such an act   40
   That blurs the grace and blush of modesty,
   Calls virtue hypocrite, takes off the rose°
   From the fair forehead of an innocent love
   And sets a blister there,° makes marriage vows
   As false as dicers' oaths, O such a deed,   45
   As from the body of contraction° plucks
   The very soul, and sweet religion makes
   A rhapsody° of words; heaven's face does glow,°
   Yea this solidity and compound mass°
   With heated visage, as against the doom,°   50
   Is thought-sick at the act.
QUEEN.   Ay me, what act,
   That roars so loud, and thunders in the index°?
HAMLET.   Look here upon this picture, and on this,
   The counterfeit presentment° of two brothers:
   See what a grace was seated on this brow,   55
   Hyperion's° curls, the front° of Jove himself,
   An eye like Mars, to threaten and command,
   A station° like the herald Mercury,
   New-lighted on a heaven-kissing hill,
   A combination and a form indeed,   60
   Where every god did seem to set his seal

---

32 *thy better*: the king.   37 *custom*: habit.   *brazed*: brass-plated (brazened).   38 *proof*: armor.   *sense*: sensibility.   42 *rose*: (symbol of perfection and innocence).   44 *blister there*: (whores were punished by being branded on the forehead).   46 *body of contraction*: marriage contract.   48 *rhapsody*: (meaningless) mixture.   *glow*: blush.   49 *solidity . . . mass*: solid earth, compounded of the four elements.   50 *against the doom*: expecting Judgment Day.   52 *index*: (1) table of contents (2) prologue.   54 *counterfeit presentment*: painted likeness.   56 *Hyperion*: Greek sun god.   *front*: forehead.   58 *station*: bearing.

To give the world assurance of a man.
This was your husband. Look you now what follows.
Here is your husband, like a mildewed ear,°
Blasting° his wholesome brother. Have you eyes?   65
Could you on this fair mountain leave to feed,°
And batten° on this moor? Ha! Have you eyes?
You cannot call it love, for at your age
The hey-day in the blood° is tame, it's humble,
And waits upon the judgment, and what judgment   70
Would step from this to this? Sense° sure you have
Else could you not have motion,° but sure that sense
Is apoplexed,° for madness would not err,
Nor sense to ecstasy was ne'er so thralled°
But it reserved some quantity of choice   75
To serve in such a difference.° What devil was't
That thus hath cozened you at hoodman-blind°?
Eyes without feeling, feeling without sight,
Ears without hands or eyes, smelling sans all,°
Or but a sickly part of one true sense   80
Could not so mope:° O shame, where is thy blush?
Rebellious hell,
If thou canst mutine in a matron's bones,
To flaming youth let virtue be as wax
And melt in her own fire. Proclaim no shame   85
When the compulsive° ardour gives the charge,°
Since frost itself as actively doth burn,
And reason pandars will.°
QUEEN.   O Hamlet, speak no more,
Thou turn'st my eyes into my very soul,
And there I see such black and grainèd° spots   90
As will not leave their tinct.°
HAMLET.   Nay, but to live
In the rank sweat of an enseamèd° bed,
Stewed in corruption, honeying, and making love
Over the nasty sty.
QUEEN.   O speak to me no more,
These words like daggers enter in mine ears,   95
No more, sweet Hamlet.

---

64 *ear*: i.e., of grain.   65 *Blasting*: blighting.   66 *leave to feed*: leave off feeding.
67 *batten*: gorge yourself.   69 *hey-day in the blood*: youthful passion.
71 *Sense*: perception by the senses.   72 *motion*: impulse.   73 *apoplexed*:
paralyzed.   74 *sense . . . thralled*: sensibility was never so enslaved by madness.   76 *in
. . . difference*: where the difference was so great.   77 *cozened . . . blind*: cheated you at
blindman's bluff.   79 *sans all*: without the other senses.   81 *so mope*: be so dull.
86 *compulsive*: compelling.   *gives the charge*: attacks.   88 *panders will*: pimps for
lust.   90 *grained*: dyed in grain, unfading.   91 *leave their tinct*: lose their color.
92 *enseamed*: greasy.

HAMLET.   A murderer and a villain,
A slave that is not twentieth part the tithe°
Of your precedent lord, a vice° of kings,
A cutpurse° of the empire and the rule,
That from a shelf the precious diadem stole   100
And put it in his pocket.
QUEEN.   No more.
HAMLET.   A king of shreds and patches—

Enter the GHOST in his night-gown.°

Save me and hover o'er me with your wings,
You heavenly guards. What would your gracious figure?
QUEEN.   Alas, he's mad.   105
HAMLET.   Do you not come your tardy son to chide,
That lapsed in time and passion° lets go by
Th'important acting of your dread command?
O say!
GHOST.   Do not forget: this visitation   110
Is but to whet thy almost blunted purpose.
But look, amazement on thy mother sits,
O step between her and her fighting soul,
Conceit° in weakest bodies strongest works,
Speak to her Hamlet.
HAMLET.   How is it with you lady?   115
QUEEN.   Alas, how is't with you,
That you do bend your eye on vacancy,°
And with th'incorporal° air do hold discourse?
Forth at your eyes your spirits° wildly peep,
And as the sleeping soldiers in th'alarm,   120
Your bedded° hairs, like life in excrements,°
Start up and stand an° end. O gentle son,
Upon the heat and flame of thy distemper
Sprinkle cool patience. Whereon do you look?
HAMLET.   On him, on him, look you how pale he glares,   125
His form and cause conjoined, preaching to stones,
Would make them capable.° Do not look upon me,
Lest with this piteous action you convert
My stern effects,° then what I have to do
Will want° true colour,° tears perchance for blood.   130

---

97 *tithe*: one-tenth part.   98 *vice*: buffoon (like the character of Vice in the morality
plays).   99 *cutpurse*: pickpocket.   102 stage direction *night-gown*: dressing gown.
107 *lapsed . . . passion*: having let time elapse and passion cool.   114 *Conceit*:
imagination.   117 *vacancy*: (she cannot see the ghost).   118 *incorporal*: bodiless.
119 *spirits*: vital forces.   121 *bedded*: lying flat.   *excrements*: outgrowths (of the
body).   122 *an*: on.   127 *capable*: i.e., of feeling pity.   128–129 *convert . . . effects*:
transform my outward signs of sternness.   130 *want*: lack.   *colour*: (1) complexion (2)
motivation.

QUEEN.   To whom do you speak this?
HAMLET.   Do you see nothing there?
QUEEN.   Nothing at all, yet all that is I see.
HAMLET.   Nor did you nothing hear?
QUEEN.   No, nothing but ourselves.
HAMLET.   Why look you there, look how it steals away,
    My father in his habit as he lived,°   135
    Look where he goes, even now out at the portal.   *Exit* [GHOST.]
QUEEN.   This is the very coinage of your brain,
    This bodiless creation ecstasy
    Is very cunning in.°
HAMLET.   Ecstasy?
    My pulse as yours doth temperately keep time,   140
    And makes as healthful music. It is not madness
    That I have uttered; bring me to the test
    And I the matter will re-word, which madness
    Would gambol° from. Mother, for love of grace,
    Lay not that flattering unction° to your soul,   145
    That not your trespass but my madness speaks,
    It will but skin and film the ulcerous place,
    Whiles rank corruption mining° all within,
    Infects unseen. Confess yourself to heaven,
    Repent what's past, avoid what is to come,   150
    And do not spread the compost° on the weeds
    To make them ranker. Forgive me this my virtue,°
    For in the fatness° of these pursy° times
    Virtue itself of vice must pardon beg,
    Yea curb and woo° for leave to do him° good.   155
QUEEN.   O Hamlet, thou hast cleft my heart in twain.
HAMLET.   O throw away the worser part of it,
    And live the purer with the other half.
    Good night, but go not to my uncle's bed,
    Assume° a virtue if you have it not.   160
    That monster custom, who all sense doth eat
    Of habits evil,° is angel yet in this,
    That to the use° of actions fair and good,
    He likewise gives a frock or livery
    That aptly° is put on. Refrain tonight,   165
    And that shall lend a kind of easiness
    To the next abstinence, the next more easy:

135 *habit. . . lived*: clothing he wore when alive.   138–139 *bodiless . . . cunning in*: madness
is very skillful in seeing hallucinations.   144 *gambol*: leap.   145 *unction*: salve.
148 *mining*: undermining.   151 *compost*: manure.   152 *virtue*: sermon on
virtue.   153 *fatness*: grossness.   *pursy*: flabby.   155 *curb and woo*: bow and plead.
him: vice.   160 *Assume*: put on the guise of.   161–162 *all sense . . . evil*: confuses the
sense of right and wrong in a habitué.   163 *use*: habit.   165 *aptly*: readily.

For use° almost can change the stamp° of nature,
And either . . . the° devil, or throw him out
With wondrous potency: once more good night,   170
And when you are desirous to be blessed,
I'll blessing beg of you. For this same lord,°
I do repent; but heaven hath pleased it so
To punish me with this, and this with me,
That I must be their scourge and minister.°   175
I will bestow° him and will answer° well
The death I gave him; so again good night.
I must be cruel only to be kind;
This bad begins, and worse remains behind.°
One word more, good lady.
QUEEN.   What shall I do?   180
HAMLET.   Not this by no means that I bid you do:
Let the bloat° king tempt you again to bed,
Pinch wanton on your cheek, call you his mouse,
And let him for a pair of reechy° kisses,
Or paddling in your neck with his damned fingers,   185
Make you to ravel° all this matter out
That I essentially am not in madness,
But mad in craft. 'Twere good you let him know,
For who that's but a queen, fair, sober, wise,
Would from a paddock, from a bat, a gib,°   190
Such dear concernings hide? who would do so?
No, in despite of sense and secrecy,
Unpeg the basket on the house's top,
Let the birds fly, and like the famous ape,
To try conclusions° in the basket creep,   195
And break your own neck down.°
QUEEN.   Be thou assured, if words be made of breath,
And breath of life, I have no life to breathe
What thou hast said to me.
HAMLET.   I must to England, you know that.
QUEEN.   Alack,   200
I had forgot: 'tis so concluded on.
HAMLET.   There's letters sealed, and my two school-fellows,
Whom I will trust as I will adders fanged,

---

168 *use*: habit.   *stamp*: form.   169 *either . . . the*: (word omitted, for which "tame,"
"curls," and "quell" have been suggested).   172 *lord*: Polonius.   175 *their . . . minister*:
heaven's punishment and agent of retribution.   176 *bestow*: stow away.   *answer well*:
assume full responsibility for.   179 *bad . . . behind*: is a bad beginning to a worse end to
come.   182 *bloat*: bloated with dissipation.   184 *reechy*: filthy.   186 *ravel*:
unravel.   190 *paddock, bat, gib*: toad, bat, tomcat ("familiars" or demons in animal shape
that attend on witches).   193–196 *Unpeg . . . down*: (the story refers to an ape that
climbs to the top of a house and opens a basket of birds; when the birds fly away, the ape
crawls into the basket, tries to fly, and breaks his neck. The point is that if she gives away
Hamlet's secret, she harms herself).   195 *try conclusions*: experiment.

They bear the mandate, they must sweep my way
And marshal me to knavery:° let it work,   205
For 'tis the sport to have the enginer°
Hoist with his own petar,° and't shall go hard
But I will delve one yard below their mines,
And blow them at the moon: O 'tis most sweet
When in one line two crafts directly meet.°   210
This man shall set me packing,°
I'll lug the guts into the neighbour room;
Mother good night indeed. This counsellor
Is now most still, most secret, and most grave,
Who was in life a foolish prating knave.   215
Come sir, to draw toward and end with you.
Good night mother.   *Exit* HAMLET *tugging in* POLONIUS.

[ACT 4]

[Scene 1. A room in the castle.]

Enter KING *and* QUEEN *with* ROSENCRANTZ *and* GUILDENSTERN.

KING. There's matter in these sighs, these profound heaves,
    You must translate, 'tis fit we understand them.
    Where is your son?
QUEEN. Bestow this place on us° a little while.

                              Exeunt ROSENCRANTZ *and* GUILDENSTERN.

    Ah mine own lord, what have I seen tonight!   5
KING. What, Gertrude? How does Hamlet?
QUEEN. Mad as the sea and wind when both contend
    Which is the mightier, in his lawless fit,
    Behind the arras hearing something stir,
    Whips out his rapier, cries "A rat, a rat,"   10
    And in this brainish apprehension° kills
    The unseen good old man.
KING.   O heavy deed!
    It had been so with us° had we been there:
    His liberty is full of threats to all,
    To you yourself, to us, to every one.   15
    Alas, how shall this bloody deed be answered?

204–205 *sweep . . . knavery*: (like the marshal who went before a royal procession, clearing the way, so Rosencrantz and Guildenstern clear Hamlet's path to some unknown evil).   206 *enginer*: maker of war engines.   207 *Hoist . . . petar*: blown up by his own bomb.   210 *in one . . . meet*: the digger of the mine and the digger of the countermine meet halfway in their tunnels.   211 *packing*: (1) i.e., my bags (2) rushing away (3) plotting. 4 *Bestow . . . us*: leave us.   11 *brainish apprehension*: insane delusion.   13 *us*: me (royal plural).

It will be laid to us,° whose providence°
Should have kept short,° restrained, and out of haunt°
This mad young man; but so much was our love,
We would not understand what was most fit,   20
But like the owner of a foul disease,
To keep it from divulging,° let it feed
Even on the pith of life: where is he gone?
QUEEN.   To draw apart the body he hath killed,
O'er whom his very madness, like some ore   25
Among a mineral of metals base,°
Shows itself pure: a' weeps for what is done.
KING.   O Gertrude, come away:
The sun no sooner shall the mountains touch,
But we will ship him hence and this vile deed   30
We must with all our majesty and skill
Both countenance° and excuse. Ho Guildenstern!

Enter ROSENCRANTZ and GUILDENSTERN.

Friends both, go join you with some further aid:
Hamlet in madness hath Polonius slain,
And from his mother's closet hath he dragged him.   35
Go seek him out, speak fair, and bring the body
Into the chapel; I pray you haste in this.   *Exeunt Gent[lemen.]*
Come Gertrude, we'll call up our wisest friends,
And let them know both what we mean to do
And what's untimely done: [so haply slander,]   40
Whose whisper o'er the world's diameter,
As level° as the cannon to his blank°
Transports his° poisoned shot, may miss our name,
And hit the woundless° air. O come away,
My soul is full of discord and dismay.   *Exeunt.*   45

[Scene 2. *Another room in the castle.*]

Enter HAMLET.

HAMLET.   Safely stowed.
    Gentlemen within: Hamlet, Lord Hamlet!
    But soft, what noise, who calls on Hamlet?
    O here they come.

Enter ROSENCRANTZ and GUILDENSTERN.

ROSENCRANTZ.   What have you done my lord with the dead body?

---

17 *laid to us*: blamed on me.   *providence*: foresight.   18 *short*: tethered by a short
leash.   *out of haunt*: away from others.   22 *divulging*: being divulged.   25–26 *ore . . .
base*: pure ore (such as gold) in a mine of base metal.   32 *countenance*: defend.   42 *As
level*: with a straight aim.   *blank*: white bullseye at the target's center.   43 *his*:
slander's.   44 *woundless*: invulnerable.

HAMLET.   Compounded it with dust whereto 'tis kin.   5
ROSENCRANTZ.   Tell us where 'tis that we may take it thence,
　　And bear it to the chapel.
HAMLET.   Do not believe it.
ROSENCRANTZ.   Believe what?
HAMLET.   That I can keep your counsel° and not mine own.° Besides,   10
　　to be demanded of° a sponge, what replication° should be
　　made by the son of a king?
ROSENCRANTZ.   Take you me for a sponge, my lord?
HAMLET.   Ay sir, that soaks up the king's countenance,° his rewards,
　　his authorities. But such officers do the king best service in   15
　　the end; he keeps them like an apple in the corner of his
　　jaw, first mouthed to be last swallowed: when he needs
　　what you have gleaned, it is but squeezing you, and
　　sponge, you shall be dry again.
ROSENCRANTZ.   I understand you not my lord.   20
HAMLET.   I am glad of it: a knavish speech sleeps in° a foolish ear.
ROSENCRANTZ.   My lord, you must tell us where the body is, and go with
　　us to the king.
HAMLET.   The body is with the king, but the king° is not with the
　　body. The king is a thing—   25
GUILDENSTERN.   A thing my lord?
HAMLET.   Of nothing, bring me to him. Hide fox, and all after.°   *Exeunt.*

[Scene 3. Another room in the castle.]

Enter KING and two or three.

KING.   I have sent to seek him, and to find the body:
　　How dangerous is it that this man goes loose,
　　Yet must not we put the strong law on him,
　　He's loved of the distracted multitude,°
　　Who like not in° their judgment, but their eyes,   5
　　And where 'tis so, th'offender's scourge° is weighed
　　But never the offence: to bear all° smooth and even,
　　This sudden sending him away must seem
　　Deliberate pause:° diseases desperate grown,
　　By desperate appliance° are relieved,   10
　　Or not at all.

Enter ROSENCRANTZ and all the rest.

　　　　　　How now, what hath befallen?

10 *counsel*: (1) advice (2) secret.   *keep . . . own*: follow your advice and not keep my own
secret.   11 *demanded of*: questioned by.   *replication*: reply to a charge.   14 *countenance*:
favor.   21 *sleeps in*: means nothing to.   24 *king . . . king*: Hamlet's father . . .
Claudius.   27 *Hide fox . . . after*: (cry in a children's game, like hide-and-
seek).   4 *distracted multitude*: confused mob.   5 *in*: according to.   6 *scourge*:
punishment.   7 *bear all*: carry out everything.   9 *Deliberate pause*: considered
delay.   10 *appliance*: remedy.

ROSENCRANTZ.   Where the dead body is bestowed my lord,
  We cannot get from him.
KING.   But where is he?
ROSENCRANTZ.   Without, my lord, guarded,° to know your pleasure.
KING.   Bring him before us.
ROSENCRANTZ.   Ho, bring in the lord.   15

Enter HAMLET (*guarded*) *and* GUILDENSTERN.

KING.   Now Hamlet, where's Polonius?
HAMLET.   At supper.
KING.   At supper? where?
HAMLET.   Not where he eats, but where a' is eaten: a certain
  convocation of politic° worms are e'en° at him. Your worm is your   20
  only emperor for diet, we fat all creatures else to fat us,
  and we fat ourselves for maggots. Your fat king and your
  lean beggar is but variable service,° two dishes but to one
  table, that's the end.
KING.   Alas, alas.   25
HAMLET.   A man may fish with the worm that hath eat of a king, and
  eat of the fish that hath fed of that worm.
KING.   What dost thou mean by this?
HAMLET.   Nothing but to show you how a king may go a progress°
  through the guts of a beggar.   30
KING.   Where is Polonius?
HAMLET.   In heaven, send thither to see. If your messenger find him
  not there, seek him i'th'other place yourself: but if indeed
  you find him not within this month, you shall nose him as
  you go up the stairs into the lobby.   35
KING. [*To Attendants.*]   Go seek him there.
HAMLET.   A' will stay till you come.   [*Exeunt.*]
KING.   Hamlet, this deed, for thine especial safety—
  Which we do tender,° as we dearly grieve
  For that which thou hast done—must send thee hence   40
  With fiery quickness. Therefore prepare thyself,
  The bark is ready, and the wind at help,°
  Th'associates tend,° and every thing is bent
  For England.
HAMLET.   For England.
KING.   Ay Hamlet.
HAMLET.   Good.
KING.   So is it if thou knew'st our purposes.   45
HAMLET.   I see a cherub° that sees them: but come, for England.
  Farewell dear mother.
KING.   Thy loving father, Hamlet.

14 *guarded*: (Hamlet is under guard until he boards the ship).   20 *politic*: (1) statesmanlike
(2) crafty.   *e'en*: even now.   23 *variable service*: a variety of courses.   29 *go a progress*:
make a splendid royal journey from one part of the country to another.   39 *tender*:
cherish.   42 *at help*: helpful.   43 *tend*: wait.   46 *cherub*: (considered the watchmen
of heaven).

HAMLET. My mother: father and mother is man and wife, man and
  wife is one flesh, and so my mother: come, for England.   *Exit.*   50
KING. [*To ROSENCRANTZ and GUILDENSTERN.*]
  Follow him at foot,° tempt him with speed aboard,
  Delay it not, I'll have him hence tonight.
  Away, for every thing is sealed and done
  That else leans on° th'affair, pray you make haste.   *[Exeunt.]*
  And England,° if my love thou hold'st at aught°—   55
  As my great power thereof may give thee sense,
  Since yet thy cicatrice° looks raw and red
  After the Danish sword, and thy free awe
  Pays homage° to us—thou mayst not coldly° set
  Our sovereign process,° which imports at full   60
  By letters congruing° to that effect,
  The present° death of Hamlet. Do it England,
  For like the hectic° in my blood he rages,
  And thou must cure me; till I know 'tis done,
  Howe'er my haps,° my joys were ne'er begun.   *Exit.*   65

[Scene 4. A plain in Denmark.]

Enter FORTINBRAS with his army over the stage.

FORTINBRAS. Go captain, from me greet the Danish king,
  Tell him that by his license, Fortinbras
  Craves the conveyance° of a promised march
  Over his kingdom. You know the rendezvous:
  If that his majesty would aught with us,   5
  We shall express our duty in his eye,°
  And let him know so.
CAPTAIN.   I will do't, my lord.
FORTINBRAS. Go softly° on.   *Exit.*

Enter HAMLET, ROSENCRANTZ, [GUILDENSTERN,] etc.

HAMLET. Good sir whose powers° are these?
CAPTAIN. They are of Norway sir.   10
HAMLET. How purposed sir I pray you?
CAPTAIN. Against some part of Poland.
HAMLET. Who commands them sir?
CAPTAIN. The nephew to old Norway, Fortinbras.
HAMLET. Goes it against the main° of Poland sir,   15
  Or for some frontier?

---

51 *at foot*: at his heels.   54 *leans on*: relates to.   55 *England*: King of England.   *my*
love . . . aught: you place any value on my favor.   57 *cicatrice*: scar.   58–59 *free . . .*
homage: awe which you, though free, still show by paying homage.   59 *coldly set*: lightly
estimate.   60 *process*: command.   61 *congruing*: agreeing.   62 *present*: immediate.
63 *hectic*: fever.   65 *haps*: fortunes.   3 *conveyance of*: escort for.   6 *in his eye*: face
to face.   8 *softly*: slowly.   9 *powers*: troops.   15 *main*: body.

CAPTAIN.   Truly to speak, and with no addition,
We go to gain a little patch of ground
That hath in it no profit but the name.°
To pay five ducats, five, I would not farm it;   20
Nor will it yield to Norway or the Pole
A ranker° rate, should it be sold in fee.°
HAMLET.   Why then the Polack never will defend it.
CAPTAIN.   Yes, it is already garrisoned.
HAMLET.   Two thousand souls, and twenty thousand ducats   25
Will not debate the question of° this straw:°
This is th'imposthume of much wealth and peace,°
That inward breaks, and shows no cause without
Why the man dies. I humbly thank you sir.
CAPTAIN.   God bye you sir.   [*Exit.*]
ROSENCRANTZ.   Will't please you go my lord?   30
HAMLET.   I'll be with you straight, go a little before.

[*Exeunt all but* HAMLET.]

How all occasions do inform against me,
And spur my dull revenge. What is a man
If his chief good and market° of his time
Be but to sleep and feed? a beast, no more: 35
Sure he that made us with such large discourse,°
Looking before and after,° gave us not
That capability and god-like reason
To fust° in us unused. Now whether it be
Bestial oblivion,° or some craven° scruple   40
Of thinking too precisely on th'event°—
A thought which quartered hath but one part wisdom,
And ever three parts coward—I do not know
Why yet I live to say "This thing's to do,"
Sith I have cause, and will, and strength, and means   45
To do't; examples gross° as earth exhort me:
Witness this army of such mass and charge,°
Led by a delicate and tender° prince,
Whose spirit with divine ambition puffed,
Makes mouths° at the invisible event,°   50
Exposing what is mortal, and unsure,
To all that fortune, death, and danger dare,
Even for an egg-shell. Rightly to be great,

19 *name*: glory.   22 *ranker*: higher (as annual interest on the total).   *in fee*: outright.   26 *debate . . . of*: settle the dispute over.   *straw*: triviality.   27 *imposthume . . . peace*: swelling discontent (inner abscess) resulting from too much wealth and peace.   34 *market*: profit.   36 *discourse*: power of reasoning.   37 *Looking . . . after*: seeing causes and effects.   39 *fust*: grow moldy.   40 *Bestial oblivion*: forgetfulness, as a beast forgets its parents.   *craven*: cowardly.   41 *event*: outcome.   46 *gross*: obvious.   47 *charge*: expense.   48 *delicate and tender*: gentle and young.   50 *mouths*: faces.   *event*: outcome.

Is not to stir without great argument,
But greatly to find quarrel in a straw   55
When honour's at the stake.° How stand I then
That have a father killed, a mother stained,
Excitements° of my reason, and my blood,
And let all sleep, while to my shame I see
The imminent death of twenty thousand men,   60
That for a fantasy and trick° of fame
Go to their graves like beds, fight for a plot
Whereon the numbers cannot try the cause,°
Which is not tomb enough and continent°
To hide the slain. O from this time forth,   65
My thoughts be bloody, or be nothing worth.   *Exit.*

[Scene 5. A room in the castle.]

Enter QUEEN, HORATIO, *and a Gentlemen.*

QUEEN. I will not speak with her.
GENTLEMAN. She is importunate, indeed distract,°
    Her mood will needs be° pitied.
QUEEN.   What would she have?
GENTLEMAN. She speaks much of her father, says she hears
    There's tricks i'th'world, and hems,° and beats her heart,   5
    Spurns enviously at straws,° speaks things in doubt°
    That carry but half sense: her speech is nothing,
    Yet the unshapèd use of it doth move
    The hearers to collection;° they aim° at it,
    And botch° the words up fit to their own thoughts,   10
    Which as her winks, and nods, and gestures yield them,
    Indeed would make one think there might be thought,
    Though nothing sure, yet much unhappily.
HORATIO. 'Twere good she were spoken with, for she may strew
    Dangerous conjectures in ill-breeding minds.   15
QUEEN. Let her come in.   *Exit Gentleman.*
    [*Aside.*] To my sick soul, as sin's true nature is,°
    Each toy° seems prologue to some great amiss,°
    So full of artless jealousy° is guilt,
    It spills itself, in fearing to be spilt.   20

53–56 *Rightly . . . stake:* the truly great do not fight without just cause ("argument"), but it is nobly ("greatly") done to fight even for a trifle if honor is at stake.   58 *Excitements:* incentives.   61 *fantasy and trick:* illusion and trifle.   63 *Whereon . . . cause:* too small to accommodate all the troops fighting for it.   64 *continent:* container.   2 *distract:* insane.   3 *will needs be:* needs to be.   5 *hems:* coughs.   6 *Spurns . . . straws:* reacts maliciously to trifles.   *in doubt:* ambiguous.   9 *collection:* inference.   *aim:* guess.   10 *botch:* patch.   17 *as sin's . . . is:* as is natural for the guilty.   18 *toy:* trifle.   *amiss:* disaster.   19 *artless jealousy:* uncontrollable suspicion.

Enter OPHELIA, *distracted.°*

OPHELIA.   Where is the beauteous majesty of Denmark?
QUEEN.   How now Ophelia?
OPHELIA.   [*Sings.*] How should I your true love know
From another one?
By his cockle hat and staff,°   25
And his sandal shoon.°
QUEEN.   Alas sweet lady, what imports this song?
OPHELIA.   Say you? nay, pray you mark.
[*Sings.*] He is dead and gone, lady,
He is dead and gone,   30
At his head a grass-green turf,
At his heels a stone.
O ho.
QUEEN.   Nay but Ophelia—
OPHELIA.   Pray you mark.
[*Sings.*] White his shroud as the mountain snow—

Enter KING.

QUEEN.   Alas, look here my lord.   35
OPHELIA.   [*Sings.*]   Larded° all with sweet flowers,
Which bewept to the ground did not go,
With true-love showers.
KING.   How do you, pretty lady?
OPHELIA.   Well, God 'ild° you. They say the owl was a baker's   40
daughter.° Lord, we know what we are, but know not what
we may be. God be at your table.°
KING.   Conceit° upon her father.
OPHELIA.   Pray you let's have no words of this, but when they ask
you what it means, say you this: 45
[*Sings.*] Tomorrow is Saint Valentine's day,
All in the morning betime,°
And I a maid at your window
To be your Valentine.
Then up he rose, and donned his clo'es,   50
And dupped° the chamber door,
Let in the maid, that out a maid,
Never departed more.
KING.   Pretty Ophelia.

20 stage direction *distracted*: insane.   25 *cockle hat and staff*: (marks of the pilgrim, the cockle shell symbolizing his journey to the shrine of St. James; the pilgrim was a common metaphor for the lover).   26 *shoon*: shoes.   36 *Larded*: trimmed.   40 *God 'ild*: God yield (reward).   40–41 *owl . . . daughter*: (in a medieval legend, a baker's daughter was turned into an owl because she gave Jesus short weight on a loaf of bread).   42 *God . . . table*: (a blessing at dinner). 43 *Conceit*: thinking.   47 *betime*: early (because the first girl a man saw on Valentine's Day would be his true love).   51 *dupped*: opened.

OPHELIA. Indeed, la, without an oath I'll make an end on't.   55
        [*Sings.*] By Gis° and by Saint Charity,
                Alack and fie for shame,
            Young men will do't, if they come to't,
                By Cock° they are to blame.
            Quoth she, Before you tumbled me,   60
                You promised me to wed.
    (He answers)
            So would I ha' done, by yonder sun,
                And thou hadst not come to my bed.
KING.   How long hath she been thus?   65
OPHELIA. I hope all will be well. We must be patient, but I cannot
    choose but weep to think they would lay him i'th'cold
    ground. My brother shall know of it, and so I thank you
    for your good counsel. Come, my coach: good night
    ladies, good night. Sweet ladies, good night, good night.   [*Exit* OPHELIA.]   70
KING.   Follow her close, give her good watch I pray you.   [*Exit* HORATIO.]
    O this is the poison of deep grief, it springs
    All from her father's death, and now behold:
    O Gertrude, Gertrude,
    When sorrows come, they come not single spies,   75
    But in battalions: first her father slain,
    Next, your son gone, and he most violent author
    Of his own just remove, the people muddied,°
    Thick and unwholesome in their thoughts and whispers
    For good Polonius' death: and we have done but greenly°   80
    In hugger-mugger° to inter him: poor Ophelia
    Divided from herself and her fair judgment,
    Without the which we are pictures or mere beasts,
    Last, and as much containing° as all these,
    Her brother is in secret come from France,   85
    Feeds on his wonder,° keeps himself in clouds,°
    And wants not buzzers° to infect his ear
    With pestilent speeches of his father's death,
    Wherein necessity, of matter beggared,
    Will nothing stick our person to arraign°   90
    In ear and ear:° O my dear Gertrude, this
    Like to a murdering-piece° in many places
    Gives me superfluous death.   *A noise within.*
QUEEN.   Alack, what noise is this?

56 *Gis*: contraction of "Jesus."   59 *Cock*: (vulgarization of "God" in oaths).78 *muddied*:
stirred up.   80 *done but greenly*: acted like amateurs. 81 *hugger-mugger*: secret haste.
84 *containing*: i.e., cause for sorrow.86 *Feeds . . . wonder*: sustains himself by
wondering about his father's death.*clouds*: gloom, obscurity.   87 *wants not buzzers*: lacks
not whispering gossips. 89–90 *Wherein . . . arraign*: in which the tellers, lacking facts,
will not hesitate to accuse me.   91 *In ear and ear*: whispering from one ear to another.
92 *murdering-piece*: small cannon shooting shrapnel, to inflict numerous wounds.

KING. Attend! *Enter a MESSENGER.*
    Where are my Switzers°? Let them guard the door.   95
    What is the matter?
MESSENGER.   Save yourself, my lord.
    The ocean, overpeering of his list,°
    Eats not the flats° with more impiteous haste
    Than young Laertes in a riotous head°
    O'erbears your officers: the rabble call him lord,   100
    And as the world were now but to begin,
    Antiquity forgot, custom not known,
    The ratifiers and props of every word,
    They cry "Choose we, Laertes shall be king!"
    Caps, hands, and tongues applaud it to the clouds,   105
    "Laertes shall be king, Laertes king!"   *A noise within.*
QUEEN. How cheerfully on the false trail they cry.
    O this is counter,° you false Danish dogs.
KING. The doors are broke.

Enter LAERTES with others.

LAERTES. Where is this king? Sirs, stand you all without.°   110
DANES. No, let's come in.
LAERTES.   I pray you give me leave.°
DANES. We will, we will.   [*They retire.*]
LAERTES. I thank you, keep the door. O thou vile king,
    Give me my father.
QUEEN.   Calmly, good Laertes.
LAERTES. That drop of blood that's calm proclaims me bastard,   115
    Cries cuckold° to my father, brands° the harlot
    Even here between the chaste unsmirchèd brows
    Of my true mother.
KING.   What is the cause Laertes,
    That thy rebellion looks so giant-like?
    Let him go Gertrude, do not fear° our person,   120
    There's such divinity° doth hedge a king,
    That treason can but peep to° what it would,
    Acts little of his° will. Tell me Laertes,
    Why thou art this incensed. Let him go Gertrude.
    Speak man.   125
LAERTES. Where is my father?
KING.   Dead.
QUEEN.   But not by him.
KING. Let him demand his fill.

---

95 *Switzers*: Swiss guards.   97 *overpeering . . . list*: rising above its usual limits.   98 *flats*:
lowlands.   99 *head*: armed force.   108 *counter*: following the scent backward.
110 *without*: outside.   111 *leave*: i.e., to enter alone.   116 *cuckold*: betrayed husband.
brands: (so harlots were punished).   120 *fear*: i.e., for. 121 *divinity*: divine protection.
122 *peep to*: strain to see.   123 *his*: treason's.

LAERTES.   How came he dead? I'll not be juggled with.
　　To hell allegiance, vows to the blackest devil,
　　Conscience and grace, to the profoundest pit.   130
　　I dare damnation: to this point I stand,
　　That both the worlds I give to negligence,°
　　Let come what comes, only I'll be revenged
　　Most throughly for my father.
KING.   Who shall stay you?
LAERTES.   My will, not all the world's:°   135
　　And for my means, I'll husband° them so well,
　　They shall go far with little.
KING.   Good Laertes,
　　If you desire to know the certainty
　　Of your dear father, is't writ in your revenge
　　That swoopstake,° you will draw both friend and foe,   140
　　Winner and loser?
LAERTES.   None but his enemies.
KING.   Will you know them then?
LAERTES.   To his good friends thus wide I'll ope my arms,
　　And like the kind life-rend'ring pelican,°
　　Repast them with my blood.
KING.   Why now you speak   145
　　Like a good child, and a true gentleman.
　　That I am guiltless of your father's death,
　　And am most sensibly° in grief for it,
　　It shall as level° to your judgment 'pear
　　As day does to your eye.
　　A noise within: Let her come in.   150
LAERTES.   How now, what noise is that?

Enter OPHELIA.

　　O heat, dry up my brains, tears seven time salt,
　　Burn out the sense and virtue° of mine eye!
　　By heaven, thy madness shall be paid with weight,°
　　Till our scale turn the beam.° O rose of May,   155
　　Dear maid, kind sister, sweet Ophelia:
　　O heavens, is't possible a young maid's wits
　　Should be as mortal as an old man's life?
　　Nature is fine in love, and where 'tis fine,
　　It sends some precious instance of itself   160
　　after the thing it loves.°

---

132 *both . . . negligence*: I care nothing for this world or the next.   135 *world's*: i.e.,
will.   136 *husband*: economize.   140 *swoopstake*: sweeping in all the stakes in a game,
both of winner and loser.   144 *pelican*: (the mother pelican was believed to nourish her
young with blood pecked from her own breast).   148 *sensibly*: feelingly.   149 *level*:
plain.   153 *sense and virtue*: feeling and power.   154 *with weight*: with equal
weight.   155 *turn the beam*: outweigh the other side.   159–161 *Nature . . . loves*: filial
love that is so refined and pure sends some precious token (her wits) after the beloved
dead.

OPHELIA.   [*Sings.*] They bore him barefaced on the bier,
                Hey non nonny, nonny, hey nonny:
                And in his grave rained many a tear—
     Fare you well my dove.   165
LAERTES.   Hadst thou thy wits, and didst persuade revenge,
     It could not move thus.
OPHELIA.   You must sing "adown adown," and you call him adown-a.
     O how the wheel becomes it.° It is the false steward that
     stole his master's daughter.   170
LAERTES.   This nothing's more than matter.°
OPHELIA.   There's rosemary,° that's for remembrance, pray you love
     remember: and there is pansies, that's for thoughts.
LAERTES.   A document° in madness, thoughts and remembrance
     fitted.°   175
OPHELIA.   There's fennel for you, and columbines.° There's rue° for
     you, and here's some for me, we may call it herb of grace°
     o'Sundays: O, you must wear your rue with a difference.°
     There's a daisy,° I would give you some violets,° but they
     withered all when my father died: they say a' made a good   180
     end;
            [*Sings.*] For bonny sweet Robin is all my joy.
LAERTES.   Thought and affliction, passion, hell itself,
     She turns to favour and to prettiness.
OPHELIA.   [*Sings.*] And will a' not come again,   185
                And will a' not come again?
                   No, no, he is dead,
                   Go to thy death-bed,
                   He never will come again.

                   His beard was as white as snow,   190
                   All flaxen was his poll,°
                   He is gone, he is gone,
                   And we cast away moan,
                   God ha' mercy on his soul.
     And of all Christian souls, I pray God. God bye you.   195

                                                   Exit OPHELIA.

LAERTES.   Do you see this, O God?
KING.   Laertes, I must commune with your grief,

---

169 *wheel becomes it*: refrain ("adown") suits the subject (Polonius's fall).   171 *more than
matter*: more eloquent than sane speech.   172 *There's rosemary*: (given to Laertes; she may
be distributing imaginary or real flowers, though not necessarily those she mentions).
174 *document*: lesson.   *thoughts . . . fitted*: thoughts of revenge matched with remembrance
of Polonius.   176 *fennel, columbines*: (given to the king, symbolizing flattery and
ingratitude).   *rue*: (given to the queen, symbolizing sorrow or repentance).   177 *herb
of grace*: (because it symbolizes repentance).   178 *with a difference*: for a different reason
(Ophelia's is for sorrow and the queen's for repentance).   179 *daisy*: (symbolizing
dissembling, she probably keeps it).   *violets*: (symbolizing faithfulness).   191 *flaxen . . .
poll*: white was his head.

Or you deny me right: go but apart,
Make choice of whom your wisest friends you will,
And they shall hear and judge 'twixt you and me;   200
If by direct or by collateral° hand
They find us touched,° we will our kingdom give,
Our crown, our life, and all that we call ours
To you in satisfaction; but if not,
Be you content to lend your patience to us,   205
And we shall jointly labour with your soul
To give it due content.
LAERTES.   Let this be so.
His means of death, his obscure funeral,
No trophy,° sword, nor hatchment° o'er his bones,
No noble rite, nor formal ostentation,°   210
Cry° to be heard as 'twere from heaven to earth,
That I must call't in question.
KING.   So you shall,
And where th'offence is, let the great axe fall.
I pray you go with me.   [*Exeunt.*]

[Scene 6. Another room in the castle.]

Enter HORATIO and others.

HORATIO.   What are they that would speak with me?
GENTLEMAN.   Seafaring men sir, they say they have letters for you.
HORATIO.   Let them come in.   [*Exit ATTENDANT.*]
    I do not know from what part of the world
    I should be greeted, if not from Lord Hamlet.   5

Enter SAILORS.

SAILOR.   God bless you sir.
HORATIO.   Let him bless thee too.
SAILOR.   A' shall sir, an't please him. There's a letter for you sir, it
    came from th'ambassador that was bound for England, if
    your name be Horatio, as I am let to know it is.   10
HORATIO. [*Reads the letter.*]   "Horatio, when thou shalt have
    overlooked° this, give these fellows some means to the king,
    they have letters for him. Ere we were two days old at sea,
    a pirate of very warlike appointment° gave us chase.
    Finding ourselves too slow of sail, we put on a compelled   15
    valour, and in the grapple° I boarded them. On the instant
    they got clear of our ship, so I alone became their prisoner.
    They have dealt with me like thieves of mercy,° but they

---

201 *collateral*: indirect.   202 *touched*: tainted with guilt.   209 *trophy*: memorial.
hatchment: tablet displaying coat of arms.   210 *ostentation*: ceremony.
211 *Cry*: cry out.   12 *overlooked*: read over.   14 *appointment*: equipment.
16 *in the grapple*: when the pirate ship hooked onto ours.   18 *of mercy*: merciful.

knew what they did. I am to do a good turn for them. Let
the king have the letters I have sent, and repair° thou to me   20
with as much speed as thou wouldest fly death. I have
words to speak in thine ear will make thee dumb, yet are
they much too light for the bore° of the matter. These good
fellows will bring thee where I am. Rosencrantz and
Guildenstern hold their course for England. Of them I   25
have much to tell thee. Farewell.
      He that thou knowest thine, Hamlet."
Come, I will give you way° for these your letters,
And do't the speedier that you may direct me
To him from whom you brought them.   *Exeunt.*   30

[Scene 7. Another room in the castle.]

Enter KING *and* LAERTES.

KING. Now must your conscience my acquittance seal,°
    And you must put me in your heart for friend,
    Sith you have heard and with a knowing ear,
    That he which hath your noble father slain
    Pursued my life.
LAERTES.   It well appears: but tell me   5
    Why you proceeded not against these feats
    So crimeful and so capital in nature,
    As by your safety, greatness, wisdom, all things else,
    You mainly were stirred up.°
KING.   O for two special reasons,
    Which may to you perhaps seem much unsinewed,°   10
    But yet to me they're strong. The queen his mother
    Lives almost by his looks, and for myself,
    My virtue or my plague, be it either which,
    She's so conjunctive° to my life and soul,
    That as the star moves not but in his sphere,°   15
    I could not but by her. The other motive,
    Why to a public count° I might not go,
    Is the great love the general gender° bear him,
    Who dipping all his faults in their affection,
    Would like the spring that turneth wood to stone,°   20
    Convert his gyves to graces,° so that my arrows,
    Too slightly timbered° for so loud a wind,

---

20 *repair*: come.   23 *bore*: size, caliber.   28 *way*: access (to the king).   1 *my acquittance seal*: confirm my acquittal.   9 *mainly . . . up*: were strongly urged.   10 *much unsinewed*: very weak.   14 *conjunctive*: closely allied.   15 *in his sphere*: (referring to the Ptolemaic belief that each planet, fixed in its own sphere, revolved around the earth).   17 *count*: accounting.   18 *general gender*: common people.   20 *the spring . . . stone*: (the baths of King's Newnham in Warwickshire were described as being able to turn wood into stone).   21 *Convert . . . graces*: regard his fetters (had he been imprisoned) as honors.   22 *slightly timbered*: light-shafted.

Would have reverted to my bow again,
And not where I had aimed them.

LAERTES. And so have I a noble father lost,   25
A sister driven into desperate terms,°
Whose worth, if praises may go back° again,
Stood challenger on mount of all the age
For her perfections.° But my revenge will come.

KING. Break not your sleeps for that, you must not think   30
That we are made of stuff so flat and dull,
That we can let our beard be shook with danger,
And think it pastime. You shortly shall hear more,
I loved your father, and we love ourself,
And that I hope will teach you to imagine—   35

Enter a MESSENGER with letters.

How now. What news?

MESSENGER.   Letters my lord, from Hamlet.
These to your majesty, this to the queen.

KING. From Hamlet? Who brought them?

MESSENGER. Sailors my lord they say, I saw them not:
They were given me by Claudio, he received them   40
Of him that brought them.

KING.   Laertes you shall hear them:
Leave us.   *Exit [MESSENGER]*
[*Reads*] "High and mighty, you shall know I am set naked°
on your kingdom. Tomorrow shall I beg leave to see your
kingly eyes, when I shall, first asking your pardon°   45
thereunto, recount the occasion of my sudden and more strange
return.   Hamlet."
What should this mean? Are all the rest come back?
Or is it some abuse,° and no such thing?

LAERTES. Know you the hand?

KING.   'Tis Hamlet's character.° "Naked,"   50
And in a postscript here he says "alone."
Can you devise° me?

LAERTES. I am lost in it my lord, but let him come,
It warms the very sickness in my heart
That I shall live and tell him to his teeth,   55
"Thus didest thou."

KING.   If it be so Laertes—
As how should it be so? how otherwise?—
Will you be ruled by me?

---

26 *desperate terms*: madness.   27 *go back*: i.e., before her madness.   28–29 *challenger . . .*
perfections: like a challenger on horseback, ready to defend against the world her claim to
perfection.   43 *naked*: without resources.   45 *pardon*: permission.   49 *abuse*:
deception.   50 *character*: handwriting.   52 *devise me*: explain it.

LAERTES.   Ay my lord,
  So you will not o'errule me to a peace.
KING.   To thine own peace: if he be now returned,   60
  As checking at° his voyage, and that he means
  No more to undertake it, I will work him
  To an exploit, now ripe in my device,°
  Under the which he shall not choose but fall:
  And for his death no wind of blame shall breathe,   65
  But even his mother shall uncharge the practice,°
  And call it accident.
LAERTES.   My lord, I will be ruled,
  The rather if you could devise it so
  That I might be the organ.°
KING.   It falls right.
  You have been talked of since your travel much,   70
  And that in Hamlet's hearing, for a quality
  Wherein they say you shine: your sum of parts°
  Did not together pluck such envy from him
  As did that one, and that in my regard
  Of the unworthiest siege.°
LAERTES.   What part is that my lord?   75
KING.   A very riband° in the cap of youth,
  Yet needful too, for youth no less becomes°
  The light and careless livery° that it wears,
  Than settled age his sables° and his weeds°
  Importing health and graveness; two months since,°   80
  Here was a gentleman of Normandy—
  I have seen myself, and served against the French,
  And they can° well on horseback—but this gallant
  Had witchcraft in't, he grew unto his seat,
  And to such wondrous doing brought his horse,   85
  As had he been incorpsed and demi-natured°
  With the brave beast. So far he topped my thought,
  That I in forgery of° shapes and tricks
  Come short of what he did.
LAERTES.   A Norman was't?
KING.   A Norman.   90
LAERTES.   Upon my life, Lamord.
KING.   The very same.
LAERTES.   I know him well, he is the brooch° indeed
  And gem of all the nation.

61 *checking at*: altering the course of (when the falcon forsakes one quarry for another).
another).   63 *ripe in my device*: already planned by me.   66 *uncharge the practice*: acquit
the plot (of treachery).   69 *organ*: instrument.   72 *your sum of parts*: all your
accomplishments.   75 *siege*: rank.   76 *riband*: decoration.   77 *becomes*: befits.
78 *livery*: clothing (denoting rank or occupation).   79 *sables*: fur-trimmed gowns.   *weeds*:
garments.   80 *since*: ago.   83 *can*: can do.   86 *incorpsed . . . natured*: made into one
body, sharing half its nature.   88 *in forgery of*: imagining.
92 *brooch*: ornament.

KING. He made confession° of you,
    And gave you such a masterly report   95
    For art and exercise in your defence,
    And for your rapier most especial,
    That he cried out 'twould be a sight indeed
    If one could match you; the scrimers° of their nation
    He swore had neither motion, guard, nor eye,   100
    If you opposed them; sir this report of his
    Did Hamlet so envenom° with his envy,
    That he could nothing do but wish and beg
    Your sudden coming o'er to play with him.
    Now out of this—
LAERTES.   What out of this, my lord?   105
KING. Laertes, was your father dear to you?
    Or are you like the painting of a sorrow,
    A face without a heart?
LAERTES.   Why ask you this?
KING. Not that I think you did not love your father,
    But that I know love is begun by time,   110
    And that I see in passages of proof,°
    Time qualifies° the spark and fire of it:
    There lives within the very flame of love
    A kind of wick or snuff that will abate it,°
    And nothing is at a like goodness still,°   115
    For goodness growing to a plurisy,°
    Dies in his own too-much. That we would do
    We should do when we would: for this "would"° changes,
    And hath abatements and delays as many
    As there are tongues, are hands, are accidents,   120
    And then this "should"° is like a spendthrift sigh,
    That hurts by easing;° but to the quick° of th'ulcer:
    Hamlet comes back, what would you undertake
    To show yourself in deed your father's son
    More than in words?
LAERTES.   To cut his throat i'th'church.   125
KING. No place indeed should murder sanctuarize,°
    Revenge should have no bounds: but good Laertes,
    Will you do this, keep close within your chamber:
    Hamlet returned shall know you are come home,
    We'll put on° those shall praise your excellence,   130
    And set a double varnish on the fame

94 *confession*: report.   99 *scrimers*: fencers.   102 *envenom*: poison.   111 *passages of proof*: examples drawn from experience.   112 *qualifies*: weakens.   114 *snuff . . . it*: charred end of the wick that will diminish the flame.   115 *still*: always.   116 *plurisy*: excess.   118 *"would"*: will to act.   121 *"should"*: reminder of one's duty.
121–122 *spendthrift . . . easing*: a sigh which, though giving temporary relief, wastes life, as each sigh draws a drop of blood away from the heart (a common Elizabethan belief).
122 *quick*: most sensitive spot.   126 *murder sanctuarize*: give sanctuary to murder.
130 *put on*: incite.

The Frenchman gave you, bring you in fine° together,
And wager on your heads; he being remiss,°
Most generous, and free from all contriving,
Will not peruse the foils, so that with ease,   135
Or with a little shuffling, you may choose
A sword unbated,° and in a pass of practice°
Requite him for your father.
LAERTES.   I will do't,
And for the purpose, I'll anoint my sword.
I bought an unction° of a mountebank°   140
So mortal,° that but dip a knife in it,
Where it draws blood, no cataplasm° so rare,
Collected from all simples° that have virtue°
Under the moon,° can save the thing from death
That is but scratched withal: I'll touch my point   145
With this contagion, that if I gall° him slightly,
It may be death.
KING.   Let's further think of this,
Weigh what convenience both of time and means
May fit us to our shape;° if this should fail,
And that our drift° look through° our bad performance,   150
'Twere better not assayed; therefore this project
Should have a back or second that might hold
If this did blast in proof;° soft, let me see,
We'll make a solemn wager on your cunnings°—
I ha't: 155
When in your motion you are hot and dry,
As make your bouts more violent to that end,
And that he calls for drink, I'll have prepared him
A chalice for the nonce,° whereon but sipping,
If he by chance escape your venomed stuck,°   160
Our purpose may hold there; but stay, what noise?

Enter QUEEN.

How, sweet queen?
QUEEN.   One woe doth tread upon another's heel,
So fast they follow; your sister's drowned, Laertes.
LAERTES.   Drowned! O where?   165
QUEEN.   There is a willow grows aslant a brook,
That shows his hoar° leaves in the glassy stream,

132 *in fine*: finally.   133 *remiss*: easy-going.   137 *unbated*: not blunted (the edges and points were blunted for fencing).   *pass of practice*: (1) match for exercise (2) treacherous thrust.   140 *unction*: ointment.   *mountebank*: quack doctor, medicine man.
141 *mortal*: deadly.   142 *cataplasm*: poultice.   143 *simples*: herbs.   *virtue*: power (of healing).   144 *Under the moon*: (when herbs were supposed to be collected to be most effective).   146 *gall*: scratch.   149 *shape*: plan.   150 *drift*: aim.   *look through*: be exposed by.   153 *blast in proof*: fail when tested (as a bursting cannon).
154 *cunnings*: skills.   159 *nonce*: occasion   160 *stuck*: thrust.   167 *hoar*: grey (on the underside).

There with fantastic garlands did she make
Of crow-flowers,° nettles, daisies, and long purples,°
That liberal° shepherds give a grosser name,   170
But our cold° maids do dead men's fingers call them.
There on the pendent boughs her coronet weeds°
Clamb'ring to hang, an envious sliver° broke,
When down her weedy trophies and herself
Fell in the weeping brook: her clothes spread wide,   175
And mermaid-like awhile they bore her up,
Which time she chanted snatches of old tunes,
As one incapable of° her own distress,
Or like a creature native and indued
Unto° that element: but long it could not be   180
Till that her garments, heavy with their drink,
Pulled the poor wretch from her melodious lay
To muddy death.
LAERTES.   Alas, then she is drowned?
QUEEN.   Drowned, drowned.
LAERTES.   Too much of water hast thou, poor Ophelia,   185
And therefore I forbid my tears; but yet
It is our trick, nature her custom holds,
Let shame say what it will; when these° are gone,
The woman will be out.° Adieu my lord,
I have a speech o' fire that fain would blaze,   190
But that this folly douts it.°   *Exit.*
KING.   Let's follow, Gertrude,
How much I had to do to calm his rage;
Now fear I this will give it start again,
Therefore let's follow.   *Exeunt.*

[ACT 5]

[Scene 1. A churchyard]

Enter two CLOWNS.°

1. CLOWN.   Is she to be buried in Christian burial,° when she wilfully
    seeks her own salvation?
2. CLOWN.   I tell thee she is, therefore make her grave straight.° The
    crowner hath sat on her,° and finds it Christian burial.

169 *crowflowers*: buttercups.   *long purples*: spikelike early orchid.   170 *liberal*:
libertine.   171 *cold*: chaste.   172 *coronet weeds*: garland of weeds.   173 *envious sliver*:
malicious branch.   178 *incapable of*: unable to understand.   179–180 *indued Unto*:
endowed by nature to exist in.   188 *these*: i.e., tears.   189 *woman . . . out*: womanly
habits will be out of me.   191 *folly douts it*: tears put it out.   stage direction *clowns*:
rustics.   1 *Christian burial*: consecrated ground within a churchyard (where suicides were
not allowed burial).   3 *straight*: straightway, at once.   4 *crowner . . . her*: coroner has
ruled on her case.

1. CLOWN.   How can that be, unless she drowned herself in her own   5
defence?°
2. CLOWN.   Why, 'tis found so.
1. CLOWN.   It must be "se offendendo,"° it cannot be else: for here lies
the point: if I drown myself wittingly, it argues an act,
and an act hath three branches, it is to act, to do, and to   10
perform; argal,° she drowned herself wittingly.
2. CLOWN.   Nay, but hear you, goodman delver.
1. CLOWN.   Give me leave: here lies the water, good. Here stands the
man, good. If the man go to this water and drown himself,
it is, will he nill he,° he goes, mark you that. But if the   15
water come to him, and drown him, he drowns not
himself. Argal, he that is not guilty of his own death, shortens not his own
life.
2. CLOWN.   But is this law?
1. CLOWN.   Ay marry is't, crowner's quest° law.   20
2. CLOWN.   Will you ha' the truth on't? If this had not been a
gentlewoman, she would have been buried out o'Christian
burial.
1. CLOWN.   Why there thou say'st, and the more pity that great folk
should have countenance° in this world to drown or hang   25
themselves more than their even-Christen.° Come, my
spade; there is no ancient gentlemen but gardeners,
ditchers and grave-makers; they hold up Adam's profession.
2. CLOWN.   Was he a gentleman?
1. CLOWN.   A' was the first that ever bore arms.°   30
2. CLOWN.   Why, he had none.
1. CLOWN.   What, art a heathen? How dost thou understand the
Scripture? The Scripture says Adam digged; could he dig
without arms? I'll put another question to thee; if thou
answerest me not to the purpose, confess thyself—   35
2. CLOWN.   Go to.
1. CLOWN.   What is he that builds stronger than either the mason, the
shipwright, or the carpenter?
2. CLOWN.   The gallows-maker, for that frame outlives a thousand
tenants.   40
1. CLOWN.   I like thy wit well in good faith, the gallows does well, but
how does it well? It does well to those that do ill. Now
thou dost ill to say the gallows is built stronger than the
church. Argal, the gallows may do well to thee.° To't
again, come.   45
2. CLOWN.   'Who builds stronger than a mason, a shipwright, or a
carpenter?

5–6 *her own defence*: (as self-defense justifies homicide, so may it justify suicide).   8 *"se offendendo"*: (he means *"se defendendo,"* in self-defense).   11 *argal*: (corruption of "ergo" = therefore).   15 *will he nill he*: will he or will he not (willy nilly).   20 *quest*: inquest.   25 *countenance*: privilege.   26 *even-Christen*: fellow Christian.   30 *arms*: (with a pun on "coat of arms").   44 *to thee*: i.e., by hanging you.

1. CLOWN.   Ay, tell me that, and unyoke.°
2. CLOWN.   Marry, now I can tell.
1. CLOWN.   To't.   50
2. CLOWN.   Mass,° I cannot tell.
1. CLOWN.   Cudgel thy brains no more about it, for your dull ass will
    not mend his pace with beating, and when you are asked
    this question next, say "a grave-maker:" the houses he
    makes last till doomsday. Go get thee to Yaughan, and   55
    fetch me a stoup° of liquor.   [*Exit 2. CLOWN.*]

Enter HAMLET and HORATIO afar off.

1. Clown.   (*Sings.*) In youth when I did love, did love,
                Methought it was very sweet,
                To contract oh the time for a° my behove,°
                O methought there a was nothing a meet.°   60
HAMLET.   Has this fellow no feeling of his business, that a'sings in
    grave-making?
HORATIO.   Custom hath made it in him a property of easiness.°
HAMLET.   'Tis e'en so, the hand of little employment hath the
    daintier sense.°   65
1. Clown.   (*Sings.*) But age with his stealing steps
                Hath clawed me in his clutch,
                And hath shipped me intil° the land,
                As if I had never been such.   [*Throws up a skull.*]
HAMLET.   That skull had a tongue in it, and could sing once: how the   70
    knave jowls° it to the ground, as if 'twere Cain's jaw-bone,°
    that did the first murder. This might be the pate of a
    politician, which this ass now o'erreaches;° one that
    would circumvent° God, might it not?
HORATIO.   It might my lord.   75
HAMLET.   Or of a courtier, which could say "Good morrow sweet
    lord, how dost thou good lord?" This might be my lord
    such-a-one, that praised my lord such-a-one's horse, when
    a'meant to beg it, might it not?
HORATIO.   It might my lord.   80
HAMLET.   Why e'en so, and now my Lady Worm's, chopless,° and
    knocked about the mazzard° with a sexton's spade; here's
    fine revolution and we had the trick° to see't. Did these
    bones cost no more the breeding, but to play at loggets°
    with them? Mine ache to think on't.   85

48 *unyoke*: unharness (your wits, after this exertion).   51 *Mass*: by the mass.   56 *stoup*:
stein, drinking mug.   59 *oh, a*: (he grunts as he works).   *behove*: benefit.   60 *meet*:
suitable.   63 *Custom . . . easiness*: being accustomed to it has made him indifferent.
65 *daintier sense*: finer sensibility (being uncalloused).   68 *intil*: into.
71 *jowls*: casts (with obvious pun).   *Cain's jaw-bone*: the jawbone of an ass with which
Cain murdered Abel.   73 *o'erreaches*: (1) reaches over (2) gets the better of.
74 *would circumvent*: tried to outwit.   81 *chopless*: lacking the lower jaw.
82 *mazzard*: head.   83 *trick*: knack.   84 *loggets*: game in which small pieces of wood
were thrown at fixed stakes.

1. Clown.   (*Sings.*) A pick-axe and a spade, a spade,
          For and a shrouding sheet,
          O a pit of clay for to be made
          For such a guest is meet.°   *[Throws up another skull.]*

HAMLET.   There's another: why may not that be the skull of a   90
lawyer? Where be his quiddities° now, his quillets,° his
cases, his tenures,° and his tricks? Why does he suffer this
rude knave now to knock him about the sconce° with a
dirty shovel, and will not tell him of his action of battery?
Hum, this fellow might be in's time a great buyer of land,   95
with his statutes,° his recognizances,° his fines,° his double
vouchers,° his recoveries:° is this the fine° of his fines, and
the recovery° of his recoveries, to have his fine pate full of
fine dirt? Will his vouchers vouch him no more of his
purchases, and double ones too, than the length and   100
breadth of a pair of indentures?° The very conveyances° of
his lands will scarcely lie in this box,° and must th'inheritor°
himself have no more, ha?

HORATIO.   Not a jot more my lord.

HAMLET.   Is not parchment made of sheep-skins?   105

HORATIO.   Ay my lord, and of calves'-skins too.

HAMLET.   They are sheep and calves which seek out assurance° in
that. I will speak to this fellow. Whose grave's this, sirrah?

1. Clown.   Mine sir:
        [*Sings.*] O a pit of clay for to be made   110
        For such a guest is meet.

HAMLET.   I think it be thine indeed, for thou liest in't.

1. CLOWN.   You lie out on't° sir, and therefore 'tis not yours; for my
part I do not lie in't, and yet it is mine.

HAMLET.   Thous dost lie in't, to be in't and say it is thine: 'tis for the   115
dead, not for the quick,° therefore thou liest.

1. CLOWN.   'Tis a quick lie sir, 'twill away again from me to you.

HAMLET.   What man dost thou dig it for?

1. CLOWN.   For no man sir.

HAMLET.   What woman then?   120

1. CLOWN.   For none neither.

HAMLET.   Who is to buried in't?

1. CLOWN.   One that was a woman sir, but rest her soul she's dead.

---

89 *meet*: fitting.   91 *quiddities*: subtle definition.   *quillets*: minute distinctions.
92 *tenures*: property holdings.   93 *sconce*: head.   96 *statutes*: mortgages.
recognizances: promissory bonds.   96–97 *fines, recoveries*: legal processes for transferring
real estate.   97 *vouchers*: persons who vouched for a title to real estate.   97 *fine*:
end.   98 *recovery*: attainment.   100–101 *length . . . indentures*: contracts in duplicate,
which spread out, would just cover his grave.   101 *conveyances*: deeds.   102 *box*: the
grave.   *inheritor*: owner.   107 *assurance*: (1) security (2) transfer of land.   113 *on*:
of.   116 *quick*: living.

HAMLET. How absolute° the knave is, we must speak by the card,° or
   equivocation° will undo us. By the Lord, Horatio, this   125
   three years I have took note of it, the age is grown so
   picked,° that the toe of the peasant comes so near the heel of
   the courtier, he galls his kibe.° How long hast thou been
   grave-maker?
1. CLOWN. Of all the days i'th'year I came to't that day that our last   130
   king Hamlet overcame Fortinbras.
HAMLET. How long is that since?
1. CLOWN. Cannot you tell that? Every fool can tell that. It was the
   very day that young Hamlet was born: he that is mad and
   sent into England.   135
HAMLET. Ay marry, why was he sent into England?
1. CLOWN. Why because a' was mad: a' shall recover his wits there, or
   if a' do not, 'tis no great matter there.
HAMLET. Why?
1. CLOWN. 'Twill not be seen in him there, there the men are as mad   140
   as he.
HAMLET. How came he mad?
1. CLOWN. Very strangely they say.
HAMLET. How strangely?
1. CLOWN. Faith, e'en with losing his wits.   145
HAMLET. Upon what ground?
1. CLOWN. Why here in Denmark: I have been sexton here man and
   boy thirty years.
HAMLET. How long will a man lie i'th'earth ere he rot?
1. CLOWN. Faith, if a' be not rotten before a' die, as we have many   150
   pocky° corses nowadays that will scarce hold the laying in,
   a' will last you some eight year, or nine year. A tanner will
   last you nine year.
HAMLET. Why he more than another?
1. CLOWN. Why sir, his hide is so tanned with his trade, that a' will   155
   keep out water a great while; and your water is a sore°
   decayer of your whoreson dead body. Here's a skull now:
   this skull hath lien you i'th'earth three-and-twenty years.
HAMLET. Whose was it?
1. CLOWN. A whoreson mad fellow's it was, whose do you think it   160
   was?
HAMLET. Nay, I know not.
1. CLOWN. A pestilence on him for a mad rogue, a' poured a flagon of
   Rhenish° on my head once; this same skull sir, was sir,
   Yorick's skull, the king's jester.   165

124 *absolute*: precise.   *by the card*: exactly to the point (card on which compass points are
marked).   125 *equivocation*: ambiguity.   127 *picked*: fastidious ("picky").
128 *galls his kibe*: chafes the sore on the courtier's heel.   151 *pocky*: rotten
(with venereal disease). 156 *sore*: grievous.   164 *Rhenish*: Rhine wine.

HAMLET. This?

1. CLOWN. E'en that.

HAMLET. Let me see. [*Takes the skull.*] Alas poor Yorick, I knew him
　　Horatio, a fellow of infinite jest, of most excellent fancy,°
　　he hath borne me on his back a thousand times: and now　　　　　170
　　how abhorred in my imagination it is: my gorge rises at it.
　　Here hung those lips that I have kissed I know not how
　　oft. Where be your gibes now? your gambols, your songs,
　　your flashes of merriment, that were wont to set the table
　　on a roar?° not one now to mock your own grinning? quite　　　175
　　chop-fallen?° Now get you to my lady's chamber, and tell
　　her, let her paint an inch thick, to this favour° she must
　　come. Make her laugh at that. Prithee Horatio, tell me one
　　thing.

HORATIO. What's that, my lord?　　　　　　　　　　　　　　　180

HAMLET. Dost thou think Alexander looked o' this fashion
　　i'th'earth?

HORATIO. E'en so.

HAMLET. And smelt so? pah.　　　　　　　　　　[*Puts down the skull.*]

HORATIO. E'en so my lord.　　　　　　　　　　　　　　　　　185

HAMLET. To what base uses we may return, Horatio. Why may not
　　imagination trace the noble dust of Alexander, til a'find it
　　stopping a bung-hole?°

HORATIO. 'Twere to consider too curiously,° to consider so.

HAMLET. No faith, not a jot, but to follow him thither with modesty°　190
　　enough, and likelihood to lead it; as thus: Alexander died,
　　Alexander was buried, Alexander returneth to dust, the
　　dust is earth, of earth we make loam,° and why of that loam
　　whereto he was converted, might they not stop a
　　beer-barrel?　　　　　　　　　　　　　　　　　　　　　195
　　　Imperious Caesar, dead and turned to clay,
　　　Might stop a hole to keep the wind away.
　　　O that that earth which kept the world in awe,
　　　Should patch a wall t'expel the winter's flaw.°
　　But soft, but soft awhile, here comes the king,　　　　　　　200
　　The queen, the courtiers.

Enter KING, QUEEN, LAERTES, [*Doctor of Divinity*], *and a coffin, with Lords attendant.*

　　　　　　　　　Who is this they follow?
　　And with such maimèd° rites? This doth betoken
　　The corse they follow did with desp'rate hand
　　Fordo it° own life; 'twas of some estate.°
　　Couch° we awhile, and mark.　　　　　　　　　[*They retire.*]　205

---

169 *fancy*: imagination.　　175 *on a roar*: roaring with laughter.　　176 *chopfallen*: (a) lacking
a lower jaw (2) dejected, "down in the mouth."　　177 *favour*: appearance.　　188 *bung-
hole*: hole in a cask.　　189 *curiously*: minutely.　　190 *modesty*: moderation.　　193 *loam*:
a clay mixture used as plaster.　　199 *flaw*: windy gusts.　202 *maimed*: abbreviated.
204 *Fordo it*: destroy its.　　*estate*: social rank.　　205 *Couch*: hide.

LAERTES.   What ceremony else?
HAMLET.   That is Laertes,
    A very noble youth: mark.
LAERTES.   What ceremony else?
DOCTOR.   Her obsequies have been as far enlarged
    As we have warranty: her death was doubtful,°   210
    And but that great command o'ersways the order,
    She should in ground unsanctified have lodged
    Til the last trumpet: for charitable prayers,
    Shards,° flints and pebbles should be thrown on her:
    Yet here she is allowed her virgin crants,°   215
    Her maiden strewments,° and the bringing home
    Of° bell and burial.
LAERTES.   Must there no more be done?
DOCTOR.   No more be done:
    We should profane the service of the dead,
    To sing sage requiem° and such rest to her   220
    As to peace-parted souls.
LAERTES.   Lay her i'th'earth,
    And from her fair and unpolluted flesh
    May violets spring: I tell thee churlish priest,
    A minist'ring angel shall my sister be,
    When thou liest howling.
HAMLET.   What, the fair Ophelia?   225
QUEEN.   [Scattering flowers.] Sweets to the sweet, farewell.
    I hoped thou shouldst have been my Hamlet's wife:
    I thought thy bride-bed to have decked, sweet maid,
    And not have strewed thy grave.
LAERTES.   O treble woe
    Fall ten times treble on that cursèd head   230
    Whose wicked deed thy most ingenious sense°
    Deprived thee of. Hold off the earth awhile,
    Till I have caught her once more in mine arms;   *Leaps in the grave.*
    Now pile your dust upon the quick° and dead,
    Till of this flat a mountain you have made   235
    T'o'ertop old Pelion,° or the skyish head
    Of blue Olympus.
HAMLET.   [Comes forward.] What is he whose grief
    Bears such an emphasis? whose phrase of sorrow
    Conjures the wand'ring stars,° and makes them stand
    Like wonder-wounded hearers? This is I,   240
    Hamlet the Dane.   *Hamlet leaps in after Laertes.*

---

210 *doubtful*: suspicious.   214 *Shards*: bits of broken pottery.   215 *crants*: garland.
216 *strewments*: flowers strewn on the grave.   216–217 *bringing home Of*: laying to rest
with.   220 *sage requiem*: solemn dirge.   231 *sense*: mind.   234 *quick*: live.
236 *Pelion*: mountain (on which the Titans placed Mt. Ossa, to scale Mt. Olympus and reach
the gods).   239 *Conjures . . . star*: casts a spell over the planets.

LAERTES.   [*Grapples with him.*] The devil take thy soul.
HAMLET.   Thou pray'st not well,
    I prithee take thy fingers from my throat,
    For though I am not splenitive° and rash,
    Yet have I in me something dangerous,
    Which let thy wiseness fear; hold off thy hand.   245
KING.   Pluck them asunder.
QUEEN.   Hamlet, Hamlet!
ALL.   Gentlemen!
HORATIO.   Good my lord, be quiet.

    [*Attendants part them, and they come out of the grave.*]

HAMLET.   Why, I will fight with him upon this theme
    Until my eyelids will no longer wag.   250
QUEEN.   O my son, what theme?
HAMLET.   I loved Ophelia, forty thousand brothers
    Could not with all their quantity of love
    Make up my sum. What wilt thou do for her?
KING.   O he is mad, Laertes.   255
QUEEN.   For love of God, forbear° him.
HAMLET.   'Swounds,° show me what thou't do:
    Woo't° weep? woo't fight? woo't fast? woo't tear thyself?
    Woo't drink up eisel?° eat a crocodile?°
    I'll do't. Dost thou come here to whine?   260
    To outface me with leaping in her grave?
    Be buried quick with her, and so will I.
    And if thou prate of mountains, let them throw
    Millions of acres on us, till our ground,
    Singeing his pate against the burning zone,°   265
    Make Ossa° like a wart. Nay, and thou'lt mouth,
    I'll rant as well as thou.
QUEEN.   This is mere° madness,
    And thus awhile the fit will work on him:
    Anon as patient as the female dove
    When that her golden couplets° are disclosed,   270
    His silence will sit drooping.
HAMLET.   Hear you sir,
    What is the reason that you use me thus?
    I loved you ever; but it is no matter.
    Let Hercules himself do what he may,
    The cat will mew, and dog will have his day.   *Exit* HAMLET.   275

---

244 *splenitive*: quick-tempered (anger was thought to originate in the spleen).
256 *forbear*: be patient with.   257 *Swounds*: corruption of "God's
wounds."   258 *Woo't*: wilt thou. 259 *eisel*: vinegar (thought to reduce anger and
encourage melancholy).   *crocodile*: (associated with hypocritical tears).   265 *burning
zone*: sun's sphere.   266 *Ossa*: (see above, line 236 n.).   267 *mere*: absolute.
270 *golden couplets*: fuzzy yellow twin fledglings.

KING.   I pray thee good Horatio, wait upon him.   [*HORATIO follows.*]
      [*Aside to Laertes.*] Strengthen your patience in our last night's speech,
      We'll put the matter to the present push°—
      Good Gertrude, set some watch over your son—
      This grave shall have a living monument:°   280
      An hour of quiet shortly shall we see,
      Till then, in patience our proceeding be.   *Exeunt.*

[*Scene 2. A hall in the castle*]

Enter HAMLET and HORATIO.

HAMLET.   So much for this sir, now shall you see the other;
      You do remember all the circumstance.
HORATIO.   Remember it my lord!
HAMLET.   Sir, in my heart there was a kind of fighting
      That would not let me sleep; methought I lay   5
      Worse than the mutines in the bilboes.° Rashly—
      And praised be rashness for it: let us know,
      Our indiscretion sometimes serves us well
      When our deep plots do pall,° and that should learn us
      There's a divinity that shapes our ends,   10
      Rough-hew them how we will—
HORATIO.   That is most certain.
HAMLET.   Up from my cabin,
      My sea-gown° scarfed about me, in the dark
      Groped I to find out them, had my desire,
      Fingered° their packet, and in fine° withdrew   15
      To mine own room again, making so bold,
      My fears forgetting manners, to unseal
      Their grand commission; where I found, Horatio—
      Ah royal knavery—an exact command,
      Larded° with many several sorts of reasons,   20
      Importing Denmark's health, and England's too,
      With ho, such bugs and goblins in my life,°
      That on the supervise,° no leisure bated,°
      No, not to stay° the grinding of the axe,
      My head should be struck off.
HORATIO.   Is't possible?   25
HAMLET.   Here's the commission, read it at more leisure.
      But wilt thou hear now how I did proceed?
HORATIO.   I beseech you.

278 *present push*: immediate test.   280 *living monument*: (1) lasting tombstone (2) living
sacrifice (Hamlet) to memorialize it.   6 *mutines . . . bilboes*: mutineers in shackles.
9 *pall*: fail.   13 *sea-gown*: short-sleeved knee-length gown worn by seamen.
15 *Fingered*: got my fingers on.   *in fine*: to finish.   20 *Larded*: embellished.   22 *bugs
. . . life*: imaginary evils attributed to me, like imaginary goblins ("bugs") meant to frighten
children.   23 *supervise*: looking over (the commission).
leisure bated: delay excepted.   24 *stay*: await.

HAMLET.   Being thus be-netted round with villainies,
Ere I could make a prologue to my brains,   30
They had begun the play.° I sat me down,
Devised a new commission, wrote it fair°—
I once did hold it, as our statists° do,
A baseness° to write fair, and laboured much
How to forget that learning, but sir now   35
It did me yeoman's° service: wilt thou know
Th'effect of what I wrote?
HORATIO.   Ay, good my lord.
HAMLET.   An earnest conjuration° from the king,
As England was his faithful tributary,
As love between them like the palm might flourish,   40
As peace should still her wheaten garland wear
And stand a comma° 'tween their amities,
And many such like "as'es"° of great charge,°
That on the view and know of these contents,
Without debatement further, more or less,   45
He should those bearers put to sudden death,
Not shriving° time allowed.
HORATIO.   How was this sealed?
HAMLET.   Why even in that was heaven ordinant,°
I had my father's signet° in my purse,
Which was the model° of that Danish seal: 50
Folded the writ up in the form of th'other,
Subscribed° it, gave't th'impression,° placed it safely,
The changeling° never known: now the next day
Was our sea-fight, and what to this was sequent
Thou knowest already.   55
HORATIO.   So Guildenstern and Rosencrantz go to't.
HAMLET.   Why man, they did make love to this employment,°
They are not near my conscience, their defeat
Does by their own insinuation° grow:
'Tis dangerous when the baser nature comes   60
Between the pass° and fell° incensed points
Of mighty opposites.
HORATIO.   Why, what a king is this!

30–31 *Ere . . . play*: before I could outline the action in my mind, my brains started to play their part.   32 *fair*: with professional skill.   33 *statists*: statesmen. 34 *baseness*: mark of humble status.   36 *yeoman's*: (in the sense of "faithful"). 38 *conjuration*: entreaty (he parodies the rhetoric of such documents).   42 *comma*: connection.
43 *as'es*: (1) the "as" clauses in the commission (2) asses.   *charge*: (1) weight (in the clauses) (2) burdens (on the asses).   47 *shriving*: confession and absolution.   48 *was heaven ordinant*: it was divinely ordained.   49 *signet*: seal.   50 *model*: replica.
52 *Subscribed*: signed.   *impression*: i.e., of the seal.   53 *changeling*: substitute (baby imp left when an infant was spirited away).   57 *did . . . employment*: asked for it.   59 *insinuation*: intrusion.   61 *pass*: thrust   *fell*: fierce.

HAMLET. Does it not, think thee, stand me now upon°—
    He that hath killed my king, and whored my mother,
    Popped in between th'election° and my hopes,   65
    Thrown out his angle° for my proper° life,
    And with such cozenage°—is't not perfect conscience
    To quit° him with this arm? And is't not to be damned,
    To let this canker of our nature° come
    In further evil?   70
HORATIO. It must be shortly known to him from England
    What is the issue of the business there.
HAMLET. It will be short, the interim is mine,
    And a man's life's no more than to say "One."°
    But I am very sorry good Horatio,   75
    That to Laertes I forgot myself;
    For by the image of my cause, I see
    The portraiture of his;° I'll court his favours:
    But sure the bravery° of his grief did put me
    Into a towering passion.
HORATIO.   Peace, who comes here?   80

Enter young OSRIC.

OSRIC. Your lordship is right welcome back to Denmark.
HAMLET. I humbly thank you sir. [*Aside to Horatio.*] Dost know this
    water-fly?
HORATIO. No my good lord.
HAMLET. Thy state is the more gracious,° for 'tis a vice to know him: 85
    he hath much land, and fertile: let a beast be lord of beasts,
    and his crib shall stand at the king's mess;° 'tis a chough,°
    but as I say, spacious in the possession of dirt.
OSRIC. Sweet lord, if your lordship were at leisure, I should
    impart a thing to you from his majesty.   90
HAMLET. I will receive it sir, with all diligence of spirit; put your
    bonnet° to his right use, 'tis for the head.
OSRIC. I thank your lordship, it is very hot.
HAMLET. No, believe me, 'tis very cold, the wind is northerly.
OSRIC. It is indifferent° cold my lord indeed.   95
HAMLET. But yet methinks it is very sultry and hot for my
    complexion.°

---

63 *stand . . . upon*: become incumbent upon me now.   65 *election*: (the Danish king was
so chosen).   66 *angle*: fishing hook.   *proper*: very own.   67 *cozenage*: deception.
68 *quit*: repay, requite.   69 *canker of our nature*: cancer of humanity.   74 *to say "One"*:
to score one hit in fencing.   77–78 *by the image . . . his*: in the depiction of my situation,
I see the reflection of his.   79 *bravery*: ostentation.   85 *gracious*: favorable.   86–87 *let
a beast . . . mess*: an ass who owns enough property can eat with the king.   87 *chough*:
chattering bird, jackdaw.   92 *bonnet*: hat.   95 *indifferent*: reasonably.   97 *complexion*:
temperament.

Shakespeare   *The Tragedy of Hamlet, Prince of Denmark*, Act 5, Scene 2   **1219**

OSRIC.   Exceedingly, my lord, it is very sultry, as 'twere, I cannot
tell how: but my lord, his majesty bade me signify to you
that a'has laid a great wager on your head. Sir, this is the
matter—   100

HAMLET.   [*Moves him to put on his hat.*] I beseech you remember—

OSRIC.   Nay good my lord, for mine ease,° in good faith. Sir, here
is newly come to court Laertes, believe me, an absolute
gentleman, full of most excellent differences,° of very soft   105
society, and great showing: indeed to speak feelingly of
him, he is the card° or calendar of gentry: for you shall find
in him the continent of what part a gentleman would see.°

HAMLET.   Sir, has definement° suffers no perdition° in you, though I
know to divide him inventorially would dozy°   110
th'arithmetic of memory, and yet but yaw neither, in
respect of his quick sail,° but in the verity of extolment,° I
take him to be a soul of great article,° and his infusion° of
such dearth and rareness, as to make true diction of him,
his semblable° is his mirror, and who else would trace° him,   115
his umbrage,° nothing more.°

OSRIC.   Your lordship speaks most infallibly of him.

HAMLET.   The concernancy° sir? why do we wrap the gentleman in
our more rawer breath?°

OSRIC.   Sir?   120

HORATIO.   Is't not possible to understand in another tongue?° You
will do't sir, really.

HAMLET.   What imports the nomination° of this gentleman?

OSRIC.   Of Laertes?

HORATIO.   His purse is empty already, all's golden words are spent.   125

HAMLET.   Of him, sir.

OSRIC.   I know you are not ignorant—

HAMLET.   I would you did sir, yet in faith if you did, it would not
much approve me.° Well, sir.

OSRIC.   You are not ignorant of what excellence Laertes is—   130

---

103 *for mine ease*: for my own comfort.   105 *differences*: accomplishments.   107 *card*:
shipman's compass card.   108 *continent . . . see*: (continuing the marine metaphor) (1)
geographical continent (2) all the qualities a gentleman would look for.   109–116 *Sir . . .
more*: (Hamlet outdoes Osric in affected speech).   109 *definement*: description.
perdition: loss.   110 *dozy*: dizzy.   111–112 *yaw . . . sail*: (1) moving in an unsteady course
(as another boat would do, trying to catch up with Laertes' "quick sail") (2) staggering to
one trying to list his accomplishments.   112 *in . . . extolment*: to praise him truthfully.
113 *article*: scope.   *infusion*: essence.   114–116 *as to make . . . more*: to describe him
truly I would have to employ his mirror to depict his only equal—himself, and who would
follow him is only a shadow.   115 *semblable*: equal.   *trace*: (1) describe (2) follow.
116 *umbrage*: shadow.   118 *concernancy*: relevance.   119 *rawer breath*: crude
speech.   121 *Is't not . . . tongue*: cannot Osric understand his own way of speaking when
used by another?   123 *nomination*: naming.   128–129 *if you did . . . me*: if you found
me to be "not ignorant," it would prove little (as you are no judge of ignorance).

HAMLET.   I dare not confess that, lest I should compare with him in
excellence, but to know a man well were to know himself.°
OSRIC.   I mean sir for his weapon, but in the imputation° laid on
him by them in his meed,° he's unfellowed.°
HAMLET.   What's his weapon?   135
OSRIC.   Rapier and dagger.
HAMLET.   That's two of his weapons—but well.
OSRIC.   The king sir, hath wagered with him six Barbary horses,
against which he has impawned,° as I take it, six French
rapiers and poniards,° with their assigns,° as girdle, hangers,°   140
and so. Three of the carriages° in faith are very dear to
fancy,° very responsive to the hilts, most delicate carriages,
and of very liberal conceit.°
HAMLET.   What call you the carriages?
HORATIO.   I knew you must be edified by the margent° ere you had   145
done.
OSRIC.   The carriages sir, are the hangers.
HAMLET.   The phrase would be more germane to the matter, if we
could carry a cannon by our sides: I would it might be
hangers till then, but on: six Barbary horses against six   150
French swords, their assigns, and three liberal-conceited
carriages—that's the French bet against the Danish. Why
is this all "impawned" as you call it?
OSRIC.   The king sir, hath laid sir, that in a dozen passes between
yourself and him, he shall not exceed you three hits°; he   155
hath laid on twelve for nine, and it would come to
immediate trial, if your lordship would vouchsafe the
answer.°
HAMLET.   How if I answer no?
OSRIC.   I mean my lord, the opposition of your person in trial.   160
HAMLET.   Sir, I will walk here in the hall; if it please his majesty, it is
the breathing time° of day with me; let the foils be brought,
the gentleman willing, and the king hold his purpose, I
will win for him an I can, if not, I will gain nothing but my
shame and the odd hits.   165
OSRIC.   Shall I re-deliver you° e'en so?
HAMLET.   To this effect sir, after what flourish your nature will.°
OSRIC.   I commend° my duty to your lordship.

---

132 *to know . . . himself*: to know a man well, one must first know oneself.   133 *imputation*:
repute.   134 *meed*: worth.   *unfellowed*: unequalled.   139 *impawned*: staked.
140 *poniards*: daggers.   *assigns*: accessories.   140 *girdle, hangers*: belt, straps attached
thereto, from which swords were hung.   141 *carriages*: hangers.   141–142 *dear to fancy*:
rare in design.   143 *liberal conceit*: elaborate conception.   145 *margent*: marginal
note.   154–155 *laid . . . three hits*: wagered that in twelve bouts Laertes must win three
more than Hamlet.   158 *answer*: acceptance of the challenge (Hamlet interprets as "reply").
162 *breathing time*: exercise period.   166 *re-deliver you*: take back your answer.
167 *after . . . will*: embellished as you wish.   168 *commend*: offer (Hamlet interprets
as "praise").

HAMLET. Yours, yours.   [*Exit OSRIC.*]
  He does well to commend it himself, there are no tongues   170
  else for's turn.°
HORATIO. This lapwing° runs away with the shell on his head.
HAMLET. A' did comply° sir, with his dug° before a' sucked it: thus
  has he—and many more of the same bevy that I know the
  drossy° age dotes on—only got the tune of the time, and   175
  out of an habit of encounter,° a kind of yeasty collection,°
  which carries them through and through the most fond
  and winnowed° opinions; and do but blow them to their
  trial, the bubbles are out.°

Enter a LORD.

LORD. My lord, his majesty commended him to you by young   180
  Osric, who brings back to him that you attend him in
  the hall. He sends to know if your pleasure hold to play
  with Laertes, or that you will take longer time.
HAMLET. I am constant to my purposes, they follow the king's
  pleasure, if his fitness speaks,° mine is ready: now or   185
  whensoever, provided I be so able as now.
LORD. The king, and queen, and all are coming down.
HAMLET. In happy time.
LORD. The queen desires you to use some gentle entertainment°
  to Laertes, before you fall to play.   190
HAMLET. She well instructs me.   [*Exit LORD.*]
HORATIO. You will lose this wager, my lord.
HAMLET. I do not think so, since he went into France, I have been in
  continual practice, I shall win at the odds; but thou
  wouldst not think how ill all's here about my heart: but it   195
  is no matter.
HORATIO. Nay good my lord—
HAMLET. It is but foolery, but it is such a kind of gaingiving° as
  would perhaps trouble a woman.
HORATIO. If your mind dislike any thing, obey it. I will forestall their   200
  repair° hither, and say you are not fit.
HAMLET. Not a whit, we defy augury;° there is special providence
  in the fall of a sparrow.° If it be now, 'tis not to come:
  if it be not to come, it will be now; if it be not now,

170–171 *no tongues . . . turn*: no others who would.   172 *lapwing*: (reported to be so
precocious that it ran as soon as hatched).   173 *comply*: observe the formalities of
courtesy.   *dug*: mother's breast.   175 *drossy*: frivolous.   176 *habit of encounter*: habitual
association (with others as frivolous).   176 *yeasty collection*: frothy assortment of phrases.
177–178 *fond and winnowed*: trivial and considered.   178–179 *blow . . . out*: blow on them
to test them and they are gone.   185 *his fitness speaks*: it agrees with his convenience.
189 *gentle entertainment*: friendly treatment.   198 *gaingiving*: misgiving.   201 *repair*:
coming.   202 *augury*: omens.   202–203 *special . . . sparrow*: ("Are not two sparrows
sold for a farthing? and one of them shall not fall on the ground without your Father":
Matthew 10:29).

yet it will come—the readiness is all. Since no man has   205
aught of what he leaves, what is't to leave betimes?° let
be.

A table prepared. Trumpets. Drums, and officers with cushions. Enter KING, QUEEN, *and
all the state,* [OSRIC], *foils, daggers, and* LAERTES.

KING.   Come Hamlet, come and take this hand from me.
        [*Puts Laertes' hand into Hamlet's.*]
HAMLET.   Give me your pardon sir, I have done you wrong,
        But pardon't as you are a gentleman.   210
        This presence knows, and you must needs have heard,
        How I am punished with a sore distraction.°
        What I have done
        That might your nature, honour, and exception°
        Roughly awake, I here proclaim was madness: 215
        Was't Hamlet wronged Laertes? never Hamlet.
        If Hamlet from himself be ta'en away,
        And when he's not himself, does wrong Laertes,
        Then Hamlet does it not, Hamlet denies it:
        Who does it then? his madness. If't be so,   220
        Hamlet is of the faction that is wronged,
        His madness is poor Hamlet's enemy.
        Sir, in this audience,
        Let my disclaiming from a purposed evil,
        Free me so far in your most generous thoughts,   225
        That I have shot my arrow o'er the house
        And hurt my brother.°
LAERTES.   I am satisfied in nature,
        Whose motive in this case should stir me most
        To my revenge, but in my terms of honour
        I stand aloof, and will no reconcilement,   230
        Till by some elder masters of known honour
        I have a voice and precedent° of peace
        To keep my name ungored:° but till that time,
        I do receive your offered love, like love,
        And will not wrong it.   235
HAMLET.   I embrace it freely,
        And will this brother's wager frankly° play.
        Give us the foils: come on.
LAERTES.   Come, one for me.
HAMLET.   I'll be your foil° Laertes, in mine ignorance

---

206 *betimes*: early (before one's time).   212 *sore distraction*: grievous madness.
214 *exception*: disapproval.   226–227 *That I have . . . brother*: (that it was
accidental).   232 *voice and precedent*: opinion based on precedent.   233 *name ungored*:
reputation uninjured.   236 *frankly*: freely.   238 *foil*: (1) the blunted sword with which
they fence (2) leaf of metal set under a jewel to make it shine more brilliantly.

Your skill shall like a star i'th' darkest night
Stick fiery off° indeed.   240
LAERTES.   You mock me sir.
HAMLET.   No, by this hand.
KING.   Give them the foils young Osric. Cousin° Hamlet,
   You know the wager.
HAMLET.   Very well my lord.
   Your grace has laid the odds o'th'weaker side.
KING.   I do not fear it, I have seen you both,   245
   But since he is bettered,° we have therefore odds.
LAERTES.   This is too heavy: let me see another.°
HAMLET.   This likes° me well, these foils have all a° length?
OSRIC.   Ay my good lord.   *Prepare to play.*
KING.   Set me the stoups° of wine upon that table: 250
   If Hamlet give the first or second hit,
   Or quit in answer of° the third exchange,
   Let all the battlements their ordnance fire.
   The king shall drink to Hamlet's better breath,
   And in the cup an union° shall he throw,   255
   Richer than that which four successive kings
   In Denmark's crown have worn: give me the cups,
   And let the kettle° to the trumpet speak,
   The trumpet to the cannoneer without,
   The cannons to the heavens, the heaven to earth,   260
   "Now the king drinks to Hamlet." Come begin.
   And you the judges bear a wary eye.   *Trumpets the while.*
HAMLET.   Come on sir.
LAERTES.   Come my lord.   *They play.*
HAMLET.   One.
LAERTES.   No.
HAMLET.   Judgment.
OSRIC.   A hit, a very palpable hit.

      Flourish. Drum, trumpets and shot. A piece° goes off.

LAERTES.   Well, again.
KING.   Stay, give me drink. Hamlet, this pearl is thine.   265
   Here's to thy health: give him the cup.
HAMLET.   I'll play this bout first, set it by a while.
   Come.   *[They play.]*
     Another hit. What say you?
LAERTES.   A touch, a touch, I do confess't.

---

240 *Stick fiery off*: show in shining contrast.   242 *Cousin*: kinsman.   246 *bettered*: either
(a) judged to be better, or (b) better trained.   247 *another*: (the unbated and poisoned
sword).   248 *likes*: pleases.   *all a*: all the same.   250 *stoups*: goblets.   252 *quit in
answer of*: score a draw in.   255 *union*: large pearl.   258 *kettle*: kettle drum.
264 stage direction *piece*: i.e., a cannon.

KING.   Our son shall win.
QUEEN.   He's fat° and scant of breath.   270
    Here Hamlet, take my napkin,° rub thy brows.   [*She takes Hamlet's cup.*]
    The queen carouses° to thy fortune, Hamlet.
HAMLET.   Good madam.
KING.   Gertrude, do not drink.
QUEEN.   I will my lord, I pray you pardon me.
KING.   [*Aside.*] It is the poisoned cup, it is too late.   275
HAMLET.   I dare not drink yet madam: by and by.
QUEEN.   Come, let me wipe thy face.
LAERTES.   [*To the King.*] My lord, I'll hit him now.
KING.   I do not think't.
LAERTES.   [*Aside.*] And yet 'tis almost 'gainst my conscience.
HAMLET.   Come for the third Laertes, you do but dally,   280
    I pray you pass° with your best violence,
    I am afeard you make a wanton of me.°
LAERTES.   Say you so? Come on.   *Play.*
OSRIC.   Nothing neither way.   [*They break off.*]
LAERTES.   Have at you now.°   [*Wounds Hamlet.*]

                              In scuffling they change rapiers.

KING.   Part them, they are incensed.   285
HAMLET.   Nay, come again.   [*The Queen falls.*]
OSRIC.   Look to the queen there, ho!

                                               [*Hamlet wounds Laertes.*]

HORATIO.   They bleed on both sides. How is it, my lord?
OSRIC.   How is't, Laertes?
LAERTES.   Why as a woodcock° to my own springe,° Osric,
    I am justly killed with mine own treachery.   290
HAMLET.   How does the queen?
KING.   She sounds° to see them bleed.
QUEEN.   No, no, the drink, the drink, O my dear Hamlet,
    The drink, the drink, I am poisoned.   [*Dies.*]
HAMLET.   O villainy! ho! let the door be locked,
    Treachery, seek it out!   295
LAERTES.   It is here Hamlet. Hamlet, thou art slain,
    No medicine in the world can do thee good,
    In thee there is not half an hour of life,
    The treacherous instrument is in thy hand,
    Unbated° and envenomed. The foul practice°   300

270 *fat*: sweating (sweat was thought to be melted body fat).   271 *napkin*: handkerchief.
272 *carouses*: drinks.   281 *pass*: thrust.   282 *make a wanton of me*: are indulging me
like a spoiled child.   285 *Have . . now*: (the bout is over when Laertes attacks Hamlet
and catches him off guard).   289 *woodcock*: snipe-like bird (believed to be foolish and
therefore easily trapped).   *springe*: trap.   291 *sounds*: swoons.   300 *Unbated*: not
blunted.   *practice*: plot.

Hath turned itself on me, lo, here I lie
Never to rise again: thy mother's poisoned:
I can no more: the king, the king's to blame.
HAMLET.   The point envenomed too:
   Then venom, to thy work.   *Hurts the King.* 305
ALL.   Treason! treason!
KING.   O yet defend me friends, I am but hurt.°
HAMLET.   Here, thou incestuous, murderous, damnèd Dane,
   Drink off this potion: is thy union here?
   Follow my mother.   *King dies.*
LAERTES.   He is justly served,   310
   It is a poison tempered° by himself:
   Exchange forgiveness with me, noble Hamlet,
   Mine and my father's death come not upon thee,°
   Nor thine on me.   *Dies.*
HAMLET.   Heaven make thee free° of it, I follow thee. 315
   I am dead, Horatio; wretched queen, adieu.
   You that look pale, and tremble at this chance,
   That are but mutes,° or audience to this act,
   Had I but time, as this fell sergeant° Death
   Is strict in his arrest, O I could tell you—   320
   But let it be; Horatio, I am dead,
   Thou livest, report me and my cause aright
   To the unsatisfied.°
HORATIO.   Never believe it;
   I am more an antique Roman° than a Dane:
   Here's yet some liquor left.
HAMLET.   As thou'rt a man,   325
   Give me the cup, let go, by heaven I'll ha't.
   O God, Horatio, what a wounded name,
   Things standing thus unknown, shall live behind me.
   If thou didst ever hold me in thy heart,
   Absènt thee from felicity awhile,   330
   And in this harsh world draw thy breath in pain
   To tell my story.   *A march afar off, and shot within.*
       What warlike noise is this?
OSRIC.   Young Fortinbras with conquest come from Poland,
   To th'ambassadors of England gives
   This warlike volley.
HAMLET.   O I die Horatio,   335
   The potent poison quite o'er-crows° my spirit,
   I cannot live to hear the news from England,
   But I do prophesy th'election° lights

---

307 *but hurt:* only wounded.   311 *tempered:* mixed.   313 *come . . . thee:* are not to be
blamed on you.   315 *free:* guiltless.   318 *mutes:* actors without speaking parts.
319 *fell sergeant:* cruel sheriff's officer.   323 *unsatisfied:* uninformed.   324 *antique
Roman:* ancient Roman (who considered suicide honorable).   336 *o'er-crows:* overpowers,
conquers.   338 *election:* (for king of Denmark).

On Fortinbras, he has my dying voice,°
So tell him, with th'occurrents more and less°   340
Which have solicited°—the rest is silence.   *Dies.*
HORATIO.   Now cracks a noble heart: good night sweet prince,
And flights of angels sing thee to thy rest.
Why does the drum come hither?

Enter FORTINBRAS and English Ambassadors, with drum, colours, and attendants.

FORTINBRAS.   Where is this sight?
HORATIO.   What is it you would see?   345
If aught of woe, or wonder, cease your search.
FORTINBRAS.   This quarry cries on havoc.° O proud death,
What feast is toward° in thine eternal cell,
That thou so many princes at a shot
So bloodily hast struck?   350
AMBASSADOR.   The sight is dismal,
And our affairs from England come too late;
The ears° are senseless that should give us hearing,
To tell him his commandment is fulfilled,
That Rosencrantz and Guildenstern are dead:
Where should we have our thanks?
HORATIO.   Not from his mouth,   355
Had it th'ability of life to thank you;
He never gave commandment for their death;
But since so jump° upon this bloody question,
You from the Polack wars, and you from England
Are here arrived, give order that these bodies   360
High on a stage be placèd to the view,
And let me speak to th'yet unknowing world
How these things came about; so shall you hear
Of carnal, bloody and unnatural acts,
Of accidental judgments, casual° slaughters,   365
Of deaths put on° by cunning and forced cause,°
And in this upshot, purposes mistook,
Fall'n on th'inventors' heads:° all this can I
Truly deliver.
FORTINBRAS.   Let us haste to hear it,
And call the noblest to the audience.   370
For me, with sorrow I embrace my fortune;
I have some rights of memory° in this kingdom,
Which now to claim my vantage° doth invite me.

339 *voice*: vote.   340 *occurrents more and less*: events great and small.   341 *solicited*: incited
me.   347 *quarry . . . havoc*: heap of dead bodies proclaims slaughter done here.
348 *toward*: in preparation.   352 *ears*: (of Claudius).   358 *jump*: opportunely.
365 *casual*: unpremeditated.   366 *put on*: prompted by.   *forced cause*: being forced to
act in self-defense.   367–368 *purposes . . . heads*: plots gone wrong and destroying their
inventors.   372 *of memory*: remembered.   373 *vantage*: advantageous position.

HORATIO. Of that I shall have also cause to speak,
And from his mouth whose voice will draw on more:°   375
But let this same° be presently performed,
Even while men's minds are wild,° lest more mischance
On° plots and errors happen.
FORTINBRAS.   Let four captains
Bear Hamlet like a soldier to the stage,
For he was likely, had he been put on,°   380
To have proved most royal; and for his passage,°
The soldiers' music and the rite of war
Speak loudly for him:
Take up the bodies, such a sight as this,
Becomes the field, but here shows much amiss.   385
Go bid the soldiers shoot.

>   *Exeunt marching: after the which a peal of ordnance are shot off.*

375 *draw on more*: influence more (votes).   376 *this same*: this telling of the story.
377 *wild*: upset.   378 *On*: on top of.   380 *put on*: i.e., the throne.   381 *passage*:
i.e., to the next world.

QUESTIONS

Act 1

1. Discuss the various ways in which the first scene of *Hamlet* shows you that something is wrong in Denmark.
2. What impression does Claudius make in scene 2? Does he seem to be a rational man? A good administrator? A competent ruler? A loving husband and uncle?
3. What does Hamlet reveal about his own mental state in his first soliloquy?
4. What attitude toward Ophelia's relationship with Hamlet do Laertes and Polonius share? What do they want Ophelia to do? Why?
5. What does the ghost tell Hamlet? What does the ghost want Hamlet to do? What does the ghost tell Hamlet not to do? Why does Hamlet need proof that the ghost is telling the truth?

Act 2

6. What does Polonius think is the cause of Hamlet's madness? What do Polonius's diagnosis and his handling of the situation show us about him?
7. What does Hamlet accuse himself of in the soliloquy that begins "O what a rogue and peasant slave am I" (act 2, scene 2, lines 524–580)? To what extent is his self-accusation justified?

Act 3

8. How do you react to Hamlet's treatment of Ophelia in the first scene of act 3? What evidence might indicate that Hamlet know that Claudius and Polonius are watching and listening to everything that occurs?

9. Hamlet sets up the performance of "The Murder of Gonzago"—the play-within-a-play—to test Claudius's guilt. What is the relationship between the events of this play-within-a-play and the events of *Hamlet*?

10. How does Claudius react to "The Murder of Gonzago"? What does this reaction tell Hamlet about Claudius? Why do you suppose Claudius did not react to the dumb show presented at the beginning of the play-within-a-play?

11. What reason does Hamlet give for not killing Claudius while the king is praying?

12. How does Hamlet treat his mother during their confrontation in her closet? Is Hamlet's behavior overly nasty or justified? Why does the ghost reappear during this confrontation?

13. What crimes or sins does Hamlet accuse Gertrude of committing?

Act 4

14. Do you think Laertes's desire to avenge his father's murder is any more or less justified than Hamlet's desire?

15. How does Claudius plan to use Laertes's desire for revenge to manipulate him? To what extent does Laertes unwittingly allow himself to be used by Claudius?

Act 5

16. The conversation between the two clowns (grave-diggers) and between Hamlet and the first clown is seen as comic relief—a humorous episode designed to ease the tension. Why is a scene of comic relief appropriate at this point?

17. How does this scene of comic relief reflect and broaden the themes of the play?

18. Why does Hamlet describe Osric as a "water-fly"? How does Shakespeare use Osric's language and behavior to characterize him?

19. Discuss the lessons that Hamlet tells Horatio he has learned about life. How does this understanding change Hamlet? Why is it ironic?

20. How is Gertrude killed? Hamlet? Laertes? Claudius? Why does Hamlet insist that Horatio not commit suicide?

GENERAL QUESTIONS

1. Discuss the character of Claudius. Do you consider him purely evil or merely a flawed human? Why? To what degree can you justify calling this play "The Tragedy of Claudius, King of Denmark"?

2. How would you characterize Horatio? Why does Hamlet admire and trust him? How is he different from Polonius or Rosencrantz and Guildenstern?

3. Describe Rosencrantz and Guildenstern. Are they round or flat characters? How does Claudius use them? Why do they cooperate with Claudius? How does Hamlet arrange their deaths? To what extent can this action be justified?

4. Evaluate Polonius's character. Is he a wise counselor? A fool? Sincere? Self-serving? Hypocritical? What are his motives? How is he like Rosencrantz and Guildenstern? How is his death like their deaths?

5. *Hamlet* is full of conflicts that oppose people to other people, to society, and to themselves. List all the conflicts you can find in the play. Decide which of these is the central conflict, and explain your choice.

6. What is the crisis of *Hamlet*? When does it occur? Whom does it affect? What is the catastrophe? The resolution?

7. In Act 4, Claudius notes that "sorrows come . . . in battalions." By the end of the play these sorrows include the deaths of Polonius, Rosencrantz, Guildenstern, Ophelia, Laertes, Gertrude, Claudius, and Hamlet. To what degree can Claudius be held responsible for all the sorrows of the play? Which sorrows are primarily Hamlet's responsibility?

8. Is *Hamlet* a tragedy of the state as well as a tragedy of the individual? In what condition is Denmark at the beginning of the play? Is the condition of Denmark better or worse at the end?

THE THEATER OF ARTHUR MILLER

When we shift to the twentieth century and the theater of Arthur Miller, we abandon the masks of the Greek theater and the soliloquies of the Elizabethan stage for drama that is a mixture of realism and nonrealism (this genre is examined in Chapter 28). By **realistic drama,** we mean plays that present an image of the world as we know it. This world is populated by salesmen, workers, bankers, housewives, lawyers, and thieves instead of kings, revengers, and soothsayers. In addition, these plays are spoken in the colloquial language of our own lives instead of in choric odes or Shakespearean blank verse.

With the movement into realism, which occurred at the end of the nineteenth century, the drama required both a theater and a stage that could accommodate plays reflecting middle-class lives and values. Thus, the theater became the now familiar darkened auditorium in which we sit in rows and face a proscenium arch and a vast curtain that separate us from the acting areas. When the curtain rises, we often see a room we might actually live in or visit. This **box set** signals an attempt to make settings look as much like the real world as possible.

Today stage settings have been embellished with the full range of sound and lighting effects available to the modern playwright or director through modern technology. This technological revolution has been especially significant in the area of lighting which is managed by a (now computerized) switchboard that can be programmed to control hundreds or even thousands of individual lights in any combination and at any intensity. Thus, lighting can be used to establish distinct times, places, moods, atmospheres, and effects. It can also divide the stage or a unit set into a number of different acting areas simply by illuminating one section and darkening the rest. As a result, lighting has almost become an element of set design, especially in plays where the dramatist uses scrim. **Scrim** is a transparent curtain on which a scene, wall, or the like may be painted. When the scrim is illuminated from the front, it appears to be solid. When lit from behind, scrim becomes transparent, and another setting or stage action may be seen through it.

More recently, playwrights and theatrical designers have moved beyond the box set to experiments with stages and sets that draw their inspiration from earlier theatrical ages. Since the 1940s, theatrical designers have often eliminated both the proscenium arch and the curtain and built stages based on classical, medieval, or Elizabethan models. Thus, we find classical Greek and Roman staging reflected in contemporary **arena stages** and medieval staging imitated in **theater in the round.** Similarly, many newer theaters offer a modified thrust stage loosely based on the model of the Elizabethan public theaters. Miller's *Death of a Salesman*, for example, utilizes elements of the traditional box set combined with a thrust stage in the form of an extended *apron* that projects from the forestage.

Realistic plays called for an acting style that was equally realistic and true to life. The ranting and gesturing of the Elizabethan actor became inappropriate, as did the declamatory and flamboyant acting of the nineteenth century. A realistic acting style was initially developed in Russia at the beginning of the twentieth century under the direction of Constantin Stanislavsky, who advocated that actors and actresses undergo a combination of traditional training and psychological preparation in rehearsing a specific role. Under the leadership of directors like Lee Strasberg, American theatrical groups like the Group Theater and The Actors' Studio developed a style based on Stanislavsky's work that is now called **method acting.** In method acting the player is asked to submerge himself or herself completely in the role and to draw on personal experiences and emotions to make the performance more psychologically realistic.

ARTHUR MILLER, *DEATH OF A SALESMAN*

Arthur Miller, one of the dominant American playwrights of the 1940s and 1950s, was born in New York City in 1915 and educated at the University of Michigan, where he wrote and staged his first plays. His early dramas include *The Man Who Had All the Luck* (1944), *All My Sons* (1947), *Death of a Salesman* (1949), *An Enemy of the People* (1951, an adaptation of a play by Henrik Ibsen), *The Crucible* (1953), and *A View from the Bridge* (1955). Many of these combine Miller's interests in family relationships and social issues. *All My Sons*, for instance, explores the relationship between Joe Keller, a war profiteer who allowed damaged engines to be put into U.S. military aircraft, and his son Chris, an army pilot returning home from World War II. The play also investigates Joe Keller's guilt and his emerging realization that the pilots who died because of his faulty engines were "all my sons." These sorts of thematic concerns reveal the extent to which Miller was influenced by Henrik Ibsen (see p. 1438). Miller's later work includes *The Misfits* (1961, a screenplay), *After the Fall* (1964), *Incident at Vichy* (1964), *The Price* (1968), and *The Archbishop's Ceiling* (1976).

Death of a Salesman, which opened on February 10, 1949 in New York City, is similar to both *Oedipus* and the traditional *well-made play* (see p. 1439) in several respects. For one thing, it dramatizes the end of a much longer story. The stage action in the present (in Acts 1 and 2) covers about twenty-four hours, from Monday evening to Tuesday evening. The story, however, goes back as far as Willy Loman's childhood, and Willy's memories of past events constantly impose themselves on the present. Additionally, at least one of the central conflicts stems from a secret known only to Willy and his son, Biff, but withheld from the rest of the characters and from us for most of the play. This secret, however, is not the linchpin of the play, as it would be in a *well-made play*.

In writing a tragedy about the struggles and failures of Willy Loman, Miller effectively redefines the nature of the tragic protagonist. In a *New York Times* essay published several weeks after the Broadway opening of the play, Miller argued that "the common man is as apt a subject for tragedy in its highest sense as kings were."[3] He asserted that tragedy springs from the individual's quest for a proper place in the world and from his readiness "to lay down his life, if need be, to secure one thing—his sense of personal dignity." Willy is certainly flawed: he is weak, dishonest, and self-deluded. But Miller links his protagonist's *hamartia* with this quest for dignity: "the flaw or crack in the character is really nothing . . . but his inherent unwillingness to remain passive in the face of what he conceives to be a challenge to his dignity, his image of his rightful status."

[3] "Tragedy and the Common Man," *The New York Times*, February 27, 1949, sec. 2, p. 1.

Willy Loman fights for status and dignity on two fronts: the family and the wider world of American business. The conflict within the family focuses on his relationship with his older son, Biff. In this conflict, the central scene is Willy's long-suppressed memory of Biff's discovery that his father is a "fake" and a "phony." This realization produces a lifetime of alienation, and leads Biff to abandon his father's dreams of success for him. The action of this conflict has a clear *anagnorisis* and resolution for both men. Biff realizes that he does not need the traditional pattern of white-collar success; he will be happy working with his hands. Similarly, Willy comes to understand that Biff actually loves him.

Willy's other struggle for dignity and status is fought in the arena of business and in the context of the success ethic and the American dream. The play presents four different versions of this American dream: the inventor-entrepreneur, the athlete-businessman, the pioneer-exploiter, and the salesman. Each of these versions is represented in the play by allusions to real people or by characters from Willy's memory. The inventor-entrepreneur, for example, is evoked by references to Thomas Edison and B. F. Goodrich, and the athlete-businessman by allusions to heavyweight boxing champion Gene Tunney and football star Red Grange. The pioneer-exploiter is embodied in Willy's distorted memories of his father and his older brother, Ben. The successful salesman version of the American dream is represented by Dave Singleman, a figure whom Willy speaks about to his boss during the crucial scene in which Willy tries to get a job in the home office of his company (p. 1272):

> Old Dave, he'd go up to his room, y'understand, put on his green velvet slippers—I'll never forget—and pick up his phone and call the buyers, and without ever leaving his room, at the age of eighty-four, he made his living. And when I saw that, I realized that selling was the greatest career a man could want.

All four versions of the American dream reduce to a single formula: dignity and status are derived from success, and success is measured by wealth. Willy, of course, fails to live up to the American dream as a father, a husband, or a businessman.

Loman's pursuit of the success ethic and the American dream through salesmanship means that he must sell himself (or an image of himself) to himself and to others. Throughout the play Willy espouses the values and techniques implicit in this American dream of selling one's way to fame and fortune. More to the point, he mistakenly attributes to himself and his sons those qualities and characteristics that he believes make for a successful salesman: attractiveness, personality, luck, telling a good story, making a good appearance, and being well liked. All these qualities—like the idea of selling itself—depend, to a large extent, on the creation of false images. This fact, in turn, suggests that the American dream itself might be illusory or corrupt.

Death of a Salesman is constructed primarily from Willy Loman's point of view. Miller originally wanted to call it "The Inside of His Head," and his initial vision was of "an enormous face the height of the proscenium arch that would appear and open up, and we would see the inside of a man's head."[4] The play contains two different types of time and action: real and remembered. Present events are enacted and described as realistically as possible. Such action, however, often triggers Willy's memory, and past events intrude on the present. Sometimes, these past events occur simultaneously with present action; thus, in Act 1 Willy can speak with his own memory of his dead brother and play cards with Charley at the same time. At other times, the images of past events take over the play completely, although Willy continues to exist in the present. Willy's past is always with him, shaping the way he reacts to the present. In addition, past events emerge from Willy's memory with the distortions and exaggerations that we would expect from such a subjective point of view. Thus, the "memory" characters—especially Ben and the Woman in Boston—are flat and symbolic rather than realistic.

Like the acting of past events, the setting of *Death of a Salesman* is symbolic and nonrealistic (see p. 1437). It is designed to allow fluid transitions between present and past and to facilitate the overlapping of current action and memory. The Loman house is a skeletal framework with three rooms (or acting areas) on three different levels: the kitchen, the sons' bedroom, and Willy's bedroom. The forestage and apron are used for all scenes away from the house and for "memory" scenes. In the present, the house is hemmed in by apartment houses and lit with an "angry glow of orange," thus suggesting that Willy's present existence is claustrophobic and urbanized. When memory takes over, however, the apartment houses disappear (a trick of lighting) and the orange glow gives way to pastoral colors and the shadows of leaves.

Death of a Salesman is very much about dreams, illusions, and self-deception. Dreams pervade Willy's life, his conversation, his family, and his house. The central dream (and illusion) is the American dream of success and wealth through selling the self. This dream is recapitulated in a series of smaller dreams (illusions, lies) that Willy and his sons build out of thin air. Throughout the play, these dreams are destroyed when confronted with reality. Willy's dream of a "New York City job" and a weekly salary, for example, collides with reality in his disastrous encounter with his younger and insensitive boss. Only Linda escapes the tyranny of dreams and "hot air." While she serves and supports Willy completely,

---

[4] Arthur Miller, "Introduction to the Collected Plays," *Arthur Miller's Collected Plays* (New York: Viking, 1957), p. 23.

Stage set for *Death of a Salesman*. Billy Rose Theatre Collection, The New York Public Library at Lincoln Center; Astor, Lenox and Tilden Foundation

she remains firmly planted in the reality of house payments, insurance premiums, and her husband's need for dignity and "attention" as his world falls apart.

We are left, at the end of the play, with a number of questions about the degree to which Willy recognizes and understands the corruption and the illusory nature of the American dream, his own dreams, and his self-image. He does achieve some flashes of insight. He understands, for example, that he has run out of lies and has nothing left to sell: "I haven't got a story left in my head." He also understands—according to Miller—his own corruption and alienation from true values:

> Had Willy been unaware of his separation from values that endure he would have died contentedly while polishing his car. . . . But he was agonized by his awareness of being in a false position, so constantly haunted by the hollowness of all he had placed his faith in, so aware, in short, that he must somehow be filled with his spirit or fly apart, that he staked his life on the ultimate assertion.[5]

Yet at the end of the play, Willy is still in the grip of delusions of glory for Biff and for himself. He imagines that his insurance money will make Biff "magnificent." Similarly, he dreams that his funeral will be massive: "They'll come from Maine, Massachusetts, Vermont, New Hampshire. All the old timers with the strange license plates—that boy [Biff] will be thunder-struck, Ben, because he never realized—I am known!" (p. 1297). Both visions

[5] *Ibid.* pp. 34–35.

are delusions: Biff has already abandoned the business world, and the funeral is attended by only five people. In the Requiem at the end of the play Biff expresses his own understanding that Willy's dreams were delusions and lies: "He had all the wrong dreams. All, all wrong" (p. 1303). Charley defends Willy: "A salesman is got to dream, boy. It comes with the territory." Only Happy remains trapped in selfishness and his own petty version of Willy's dream: "I'm gonna beat this racket! . . . The Loman Brothers! . . . He had a good dream. It's the only dream you can have— to come out number-one man."

ARTHUR MILLER   (b. 1915)

Death of a Salesman   *1949*

CHARACTERS

Willy Loman
Linda, *his wife*
Biff ⎱
Happy⎰ *his sons*
Uncle Ben
Charley
Bernard
The Woman
Howard Wagner
Jenny
Stanley
Miss Forsythe
Letta

The action takes place in WILLY LOMAN'S *house and yard and in various places he visits in the New York and Boston of today.*

ACT 1

A melody is heard, played upon a flute. It is small and fine, telling of grass and trees and the horizon. The curtain rises.

Before us is the Salesman's house. We are aware of towering, angular shapes behind it, surrounding it on all sides. Only the blue light of the sky falls upon the house and forestage; the surrounding area shows an angry glow of orange. As more light appears, we see a solid vault of apartment houses around the small, fragile-seeming home. An air of the dream clings to the place, a dream rising out of reality. The kitchen at center seems actual enough, for there is a kitchen table with three chairs, and a refrigerator. But no other fixtures are seen. At the back of the kitchen there is a draped entrance, which leads to the living-room. To the right of the kitchen, on a level raised two feet, is a bedroom furnished only with a brass bedstead and a straight chair. On a shelf over the bed a silver athletic trophy stands. A window opens onto the apartment house at the side.

Behind the kitchen, on a level raised six and a half feet, is the boys' bedroom, at present barely visible. Two beds are dimly seen, and at the back of the room a dormer window. (This bedroom is above the unseen living-room.) At the left a stairway curves up to it from the kitchen.

The entire setting is wholly or, in some places, partially transparent. The roof-line of the house is one-dimensional; under and over it we see the apartment buildings. Before the house lies an apron, curving beyond the forestage into the orchestra. This forward area serves as the back yard as well as the locale of all WILLY'S *imaginings and of his city scenes. Whenever the action is in the present the actors observe the imaginary wall-lines, entering the house only through its door at the left. But in the scenes of the past these boundaries are broken, and characters enter or leave a room by stepping "through" a wall onto the forestage.*

[From the right, WILLY LOMAN, *The Salesman, enters, carrying two large sample cases. The flute plays on. He hears but is not aware of it. He is past sixty years of age, dressed quietly. Even as he crosses the stage to the doorway of the house, his exhaustion is apparent. He unlocks the door, comes into the kitchen, and thankfully lets his burden down, feeling the soreness of his palms. A word-sigh escapes his lips—it might be "Oh, boy, oh, boy." He closes the door, then carries his cases out into the living-room, through the draped kitchen doorway.]*

*[*LINDA, *his wife, has stirred in her bed at the right. She gets out and puts on a robe, listening. Most often jovial, she has developed an iron repression of her exceptions to* WILLY'S *behavior—she more than loves him, she admires him, as though his mercurial nature, his temper, his massive dreams and little cruelties, served her only as sharp reminders of the turbulent longings within him, longings which she shares but lacks the temperament to utter and follow to their end.]*

LINDA. *[hearing* WILLY *outside the bedroom, calls with some trepidation]* Willy!

WILLY.   It's all right. I came back.

LINDA.   Why? What happened? *[slight pause]* Did something happen, Willy?

WILLY.   No, nothing happened.

LINDA.   You didn't smash the car, did you?   5

WILLY.   *[with casual irritation]* I said nothing happened. Didn't you hear me?

LINDA.   Don't you feel well?

WILLY.   I'm tired to the death. [*The flute has faded away. He sits on the bed beside her, a little numb.*] I couldn't make it. I just couldn't make it, Linda.

LINDA.   *[very carefully, delicately]* Where were you all day? You look terrible.

WILLY.   I got as far as a little above Yonkers.° I stopped for a cup of coffee.   10
Maybe it was the coffee.

LINDA.   What?

WILLY.   *[after a pause]* I suddenly couldn't drive any more. The car kept going off onto the shoulder, y'know?

Yonkers: Yonkers is immediately north of New York City, touching the city limits of the Bronx. Because Willy lives in Brooklyn, to the south, he got no more than thirty or thirty-five miles from home.

LINDA. [*helpfully*] Oh. Maybe it was the steering again. I don't think Angelo knows the Studebaker.

WILLY. No, it's me, it's me. Suddenly I realize I'm goin' sixty miles an hour and I don't remember the last five minutes. I'm—I can't seem to—keep my mind to it.

LINDA. Maybe it's your glasses. You never went for your new glasses.   15

WILLY. No, I see everything. I came back ten miles an hour. It took me nearly four hours from Yonkers.

LINDA. [*resigned*] Well, you'll just have to take a rest, Willy, you can't continue this way.

WILLY. I just got back from Florida.

LINDA. But you didn't rest your mind. Your mind is overactive, and the mind is what counts, dear.

WILLY. I'll start out in the morning. Maybe I'll feel better in the morning.   20
[*She is taking off his shoes.*] These goddam arch supports are killing me.

LINDA. Take an aspirin. Should I get you an aspirin? It'll soothe you.

WILLY. [*with wonder*] I was driving along, you understand? And I was fine. I was even observing the scenery. You can imagine, me looking at scenery, on the road every week of my life. But it's so beautiful up there, Linda, the trees are so thick, and the sun is warm. I opened the windshield and just let the warm air bathe over me. And then all of a sudden I'm goin' off the road! I'm tellin' ya, I absolutely forgot I was driving. If I'd've gone the other way over the white line I might've killed somebody. So I went on again—and five minutes later I'm dreamin' again, and I nearly— [*He presses two fingers against his eyes.*] I have such thoughts, I have such strange thoughts.

LINDA. Willy, dear. Talk to them again. There's no reason why you can't work in New York.

WILLY. They don't need me in New York. I'm the New England man. I'm vital in New England.

LINDA. But you're sixty years old. They can't expect you to keep traveling   25
every week.

WILLY. I'll have to send a wire to Portland. I'm supposed to see Brown and Morrison tomorrow morning at ten o'clock to show the line. Goddammit, I could sell them! [*He starts putting on his jacket.*]

LINDA. [*taking the jacket from him*] Why don't you go down to the place tomorrow and tell Howard you've simply got to work in New York? You're too accommodating, dear.

WILLY. If old man Wagner was alive I'd a been in charge of New York now! That man was a prince, he was a masterful man. But that boy of his, that Howard, he don't appreciate. When I went north the first time, the Wagner Company didn't know where New England was!

LINDA. Why don't you tell those things to Howard, dear?

WILLY. [*encouraged*] I will, I definitely will. Is there any cheese?   30

LINDA. I'll make you a sandwich.

WILLY. No, go to sleep. I'll take some milk. I'll be up right away. The boys in?

LINDA. They're sleeping. Happy took Biff on a date tonight.

WILLY. [*interested*] That so?

LINDA.   It was so nice to see them shaving together, one behind the other,   35
in the bathroom. And going out together. You notice? The whole house smells
of shaving lotion.

WILLY.   Figure it out. Work a lifetime to pay off a house. You finally own
it, and there's nobody to live in it.

LINDA.   Well, dear, life is a casting off. It's always that way.

WILLY.   No, no, some people—some people accomplish something. Did Biff
say anything after I went this morning?

LINDA.   You shouldn't have criticized him, Willy, especially after he just
got off the train. You mustn't lose your temper with him.

WILLY.   When the hell did I lose my temper? I simply asked him if he was   40
making any money. Is that a criticism?

LINDA.   But, dear, how could he make any money?

WILLY.   [*worried and angered*] There's such an undercurrent in him. He
became a moody man. Did he apologize when I left this morning?

LINDA.   He was crestfallen, Willy. You know how he admires you. I think
if he finds himself, then you'll both be happier and not fight any more.

WILLY.   How can he find himself on a farm? Is that a life? A farmhand?
In the beginning, when he was young, I thought, well, a young man, it's good
for him to tramp around, take a lot of different jobs. But it's more than ten years
now and he has yet to make thirty-five dollars a week!

LINDA.   He's finding himself, Willy.   45

WILLY.   Not finding yourself at the age of thirty-four is a disgrace!

LINDA.   Shh!

WILLY.   The trouble is he's lazy, goddammit!

LINDA.   Willy, please!

WILLY.   Biff is a lazy bum!   50

LINDA.   They're sleeping. Get something to eat. Go on down.

WILLY.   Why did he come home? I would like to know what brought him
home.

LINDA.   I don't know. I think he's still lost, Willy. I think he's very lost.

WILLY.   Biff Loman is lost. In the greatest country in the world a young
man with such—personal attractiveness, gets lost. And such a hard worker. There's
one thing about Biff—he's not lazy.

LINDA.   Never.   55

WILLY.   [*with pity and resolve*] I'll see him in the morning; I'll have a nice
talk with him. I'll get him a job selling. He could be big in no time. My God!
Remember how they used to follow him around in high school? When he smiled
at one of them their faces lit up. When he walked down the street . . . [*He loses
himself in reminiscences.*]

LINDA.   [*trying to bring him out of it*] Willy, dear, I got a new kind of American-
type cheese today. It's whipped.

WILLY.   Why do you get American when I like Swiss?

LINDA.   I just thought you'd like a change—

WILLY.   I don't want a change! I want Swiss cheese. Why am I always being   60
contradicted?

LINDA.   [*with a covering laugh*] I thought it would be a surprise.

WILLY.   Why don't you open a window in here, for God's sake?

LINDA. [*with infinite patience*] They're all open, dear.

WILLY. The way they boxed us in here. Bricks and windows, windows and bricks.

LINDA. We should've bought the land next door. 65

WILLY. The street is lined with cars. There's not a breath of fresh air in the neighborhood. The grass don't grow any more, you can't raise a carrot in the back yard. They should've had a law against apartment houses. Remember those two beautiful elm trees out there? When I and Biff hung the swing between them?

LINDA. Yeah, like being a million miles from the city.

WILLY. They should've arrested the builder for cutting those down. They massacred the neighborhood. [*lost*] More and more I think of those days, Linda. This time of year it was lilac and wisteria. And then the peonies would come out, and the daffodils. What fragrance in this room!

LINDA. Well, after all, people had to move somewhere.

WILLY. No, there's more people now. 70

LINDA. I don't think there's more people. I think—

WILLY. There's more people! That's what ruining this country! Population is getting out of control. The competition is maddening! Smell the stink from that apartment house! And another one on the other side . . . How can they whip cheese?

[*On* WILLY'S *last line,* BIFF *and* HAPPY *raise themselves up in their beds, listening.*]

LINDA. Go down, try it. And be quiet.

WILLY. [*turning to* LINDA, *guiltily*] You're not worried about me, are you, sweetheart?

BIFF. What's the matter? 75

HAPPY. Listen!

LINDA. You've got too much on the ball to worry about.

WILLY. You're my foundation and my support, Linda.

LINDA. Just try to relax, dear. You make mountains out of molehills.

WILLY. I won't fight with him any more. If he wants to go back to Texas, 80
let him go.

LINDA. He'll find his way.

WILLY. Sure. Certain men just don't get started till later in life. Like Thomas Edison, I think. Or B. F. Goodrich.° One of them was deaf. [*He starts for the bedroom doorway.*] I'll put my money on Biff.

LINDA. And Willy—if it's warm Sunday we'll drive in the country. And we'll open the windshield, and take lunch.

WILLY. No, the windshields don't open on the new cars.

LINDA. But you opened it today. 85

WILLY. Me? I didn't. [*He stops.*] Now isn't that peculiar! Isn't that a remarkable— [*He breaks off in amazement and fright as the flute is heard distantly.*]

LINDA. What, darling?

Thomas Edison, B. F. Goodrich: Thomas A. Edison (1847–1931) was an American inventor who developed the electric light and the phonograph. Benjamin Franklin Goodrich (1841–1888) founded the B. F. Goodrich Rubber and Tire Company. Willy points to both men as examples of successes who started late in life.

|

WILLY.   That is the most remarkable thing.

LINDA.   What, dear?

WILLY.   I was thinking of the Chevvy. [*slight pause*] Nineteen twenty-eight   90
. . . when I had that red Chevvy— [*Breaks off.*] That funny? I coulda sworn I was
driving that Chevvy today.

LINDA.   Well, that's nothing. Something must've reminded you.

WILLY.   Remarkable. Ts. Remember those days? The way Biff used to
simonize that car? The dealer refused to believe there was eighty thousand miles
on it. [*He shakes his head.*] Heh! [*to LINDA*] Close your eyes, I'll be right up. [*He
walks out of the bedroom.*]

HAPPY.   [*to BIFF*] Jesus, maybe he smashed up the car again!

LINDA.   [*calling after WILLY*] Be careful on the stairs, dear! The cheese is on
the middle shelf! [*She turns, goes over to the bed, takes his jacket, and goes out of the
bedroom.*]

[*Light has risen on the boys' room. Unseen, WILLY is heard talking to himself, "Eighty
thousand miles," and a little laugh. BIFF gets out of bed, comes downstage a bit, and stands
attentively. BIFF is two years older than his brother HAPPY, well built, but in these days
bears a worn air and seems less self-assured. He has succeeded less, and his dreams are
stronger and less acceptable than HAPPY's. HAPPY is tall, powerfully made. Sexuality is like
a visible color on him, or a scent that many women have discovered. He, like his brother, is
lost, but in a different way, for he has never allowed himself to turn his face toward defeat
and is thus more confused and hard-skinned, although seemingly more content.*]

HAPPY.   [*getting out of bed*] He's going to get his license taken away if he   95
keeps that up. I'm getting nervous about him, y'know, Biff?

BIFF.   His eyes are going.

HAPPY.   No, I've driven with him. He sees all right. He just doesn't keep
his mind on it. I drove into the city with him last week. He stops at a green light
and then it turns red and he goes. [*He laughs.*]

BIFF.   Maybe he's color-blind.

HAPPY.   Pop? Why he's got the finest eye for color in the business. You
know that.

BIFF.   [*sitting down on his bed*] I'm going to sleep.   100

HAPPY.   You're not still sour on Dad, are you, Biff?

BIFF.   He's all right, I guess.

WILLY.   [*underneath them, in the living-room*] Yes, sir, eighty thousand miles—
eighty-two thousand!

BIFF.   You smoking?

HAPPY.   [*holding out a pack of cigarettes*] Want one?   105

BIFF.   [*taking a cigarette*] I can never sleep when I smell it.

WILLY.   What a simonizing job, heh!

HAPPY.   [*with deep sentiment*] Funny, Biff, y'know? Us sleeping in here again?
The old beds. [*He pats his bed affectionately.*] All the talk that went across those two
beds, huh? Our whole lives.

BIFF.   Yeah. Lotta dreams and plans.

HAPPY.   [*with a deep and masculine laugh*] About five hundred women would   110
like to know what was said in this room.

[They share a soft laugh.]

BIFF. Remember that big Betsy something—what the hell was her name—over on Bushwick Avenue?

HAPPY. *[combing his hair]* With the collie dog!

BIFF. That's the one. I got you in there, remember?

HAPPY. Yeah, that was my first time—I think. Boy, there was a pig! *[They laugh, almost crudely.]* You taught me everything I know about women. Don't forget that.

BIFF. I bet you forgot how bashful you used to be. Especially with girls. 115

HAPPY. Oh, I still am, Biff.

BIFF. Oh, go on.

HAPPY. I just control it, that's all. I think I got less bashful and you got more so. What happened, Biff? Where's the old humor, the old confidence? *[He shakes BIFF's knee. BIFF gets up and moves restlessly about the room.]* What's the matter?

BIFF. Why does Dad mock me all the time?

HAPPY. He's not mocking you, he— 120

BIFF. Everything I say there's a twist of mockery on his face. I can't get near him.

HAPPY. He just wants you to make good, that's all. I wanted to talk to you about Dad for a long time, Biff. Something's—happening to him. He—talks to himself.

BIFF. I noticed that this morning. But he always mumbled.

HAPPY. But not so noticeable. It got so embarrassing I sent him to Florida. And you know something? Most of the time he's talking to you.

BIFF. What's he say about me? 125

HAPPY. I can't make it out.

BIFF. What's he say about me?

HAPPY. I think the fact that you're not settled, that you're still kind of up in the air . . .

BIFF. There's one or two other things depressing him, Happy.

HAPPY. What do you mean? 130

BIFF. Never mind. Just don't lay it all to me.

HAPPY. But I think if you just got started—I mean—is there any future for you out there?

BIFF. I tell ya, Hap, I don't know what the future is. I don't know—what I'm supposed to want.

HAPPY. What do you mean?

BIFF. Well, I spent six or seven years after high school trying to work myself 135
up. Shipping clerk, salesman, business of one kind or another. And it's a measly manner of existence. To get on that subway on the hot mornings in summer. To devote your whole life to keeping stock, or making phone calls, or selling or buying. To suffer fifty weeks of the year for the sake of a two-week vacation, when all you really desire is to be outdoors, with your shirt off. And always to have to get ahead of the next fella. And still—that's how you build a future.

HAPPY. Well, you really enjoy it on a farm? Are you content out there?

BIFF. *[with rising agitation]* Hap, I've had twenty or thirty different kinds of jobs since I left home before the war, and it always turns out the same. I just realized it lately. In Nebraska when I herded cattle, and the Dakotas, and Arizona, and now in Texas. It's why I came home now, I guess, because I realized it. This farm I work on, it's spring there now, see? And they've got about fifteen new colts. There's nothing more inspiring or—beautiful than the sight of a mare and a new colt. And it's cool there now, see? Texas is cool now, and it's spring. And whenever spring comes to where I am, I suddenly get the feeling, my God, I'm not gettin' anywhere! What the hell am I doing, playing around with horses, twenty-eight dollars a week! I'm thirty-four years old, I oughta be makin' my future. That's when I come running home. And now, I get here, and I don't know what to do with myself. [*after a pause*] I've always made a point of not wasting my life, and everytime I come back here I know that all I've done is to waste my life.

    HAPPY.   You're a poet, you know that, Biff? You're a—you're an idealist!

    BIFF.   No, I'm mixed up very bad. Maybe I oughta get married. Maybe I oughta get stuck into something. Maybe that's my trouble. I'm like a boy. I'm not married, I'm not in business, I just—I'm like a boy. Are you content, Hap? You're a success, aren't you? Are you content?

    HAPPY.   Hell, no!   140

    BIFF.   Why? You're making money, aren't you?

    HAPPY.   [*moving about with energy, expressiveness*] All I can do now is wait for the merchandise manager to die. And suppose I get to be merchandise manager? He's a good friend of mine, and he just built a terrific estate on Long Island. And he lived there about two months and sold it, and now he's building another one. He can't enjoy it once it's finished. And I know that's just what I would do. I don't know what the hell I'm workin' for. Sometimes I sit in my apartment—all alone. And I think of the rent I'm paying. And it's crazy. But then, it's what I always wanted. My own apartment, a car, and plenty of women. And still, goddammit, I'm lonely.

    BIFF.   [*with enthusiasm*] Listen, why don't you come out West with me?

    HAPPY.   You and I, heh?

    BIFF.   Sure, maybe we could buy a ranch. Raise cattle, use our muscles.   145 Men built like we are should be working out in the open.

    HAPPY.   [*avidly*] The Loman Brothers, heh?

    BIFF.   [*with vast affection*] Sure, we'd be known all over the counties!

    HAPPY.   [*enthralled*] That's what I dream about, Biff. Sometimes I want to just rip my clothes off in the middle of the store and outbox that goddam merchandise manager. I mean I can outbox, outrun, and outlift anybody in that store, and I have to take orders from those common, petty sons-of-bitches till I can't stand it any more.

    BIFF.   I'm tellin' you, kid, if you were with me I'd be happy out there.

    HAPPY.   [*enthused*] See, Biff, everybody around me is so false that I'm   150 constantly lowering my ideals . . .

    BIFF.   Baby, together we'd stand up for one another, we'd have someone to trust.

    HAPPY.   If I were around you—

    BIFF.   Hap, the trouble is we weren't brought up to grub for money. I don't know how to do it.

    HAPPY.   Neither can I!

    BIFF.   Then let's go!   155

HAPPY. The only thing is—what can you make out there?

BIFF. But look at your friend. Builds an estate and then hasn't the peace of mind to live in it.

HAPPY. Yeah, but when he walks into the store the waves part in front of him. That's fifty-two thousand dollars a year coming through the revolving door, and I got more in my pinky finger than he's got in his head.

BIFF. Yeah, but you just said—

HAPPY. I gotta show some of those pompous, self-important executives over 160
there that Hap Loman can make the grade. I want to walk into the store the way he walks in. Then I'll go with you, Biff. We'll be together yet, I swear. But take those two we had tonight. Now weren't they gorgeous creatures?

BIFF. Yeah, yeah, most gorgeous I've had in years.

HAPPY. I get that any time I want, Biff. Whenever I feel disgusted. The only trouble is, it gets like bowling or something. I just keep knockin' them over and it doesn't mean anything. You still run around a lot?

BIFF. Naa. I'd like to find a girl—steady, somebody with substance.

HAPPY. That's what I long for.

BIFF. Go on! You'd never come home. 165

HAPPY. I would! Somebody with character, with resistance! Like Mom, y'know? You're gonna call me a bastard when I tell you this. That girl Charlotte I was with tonight is engaged to be married in five weeks. [*He tries on his new hat.*]

BIFF. No kiddin'!

HAPPY. Sure, the guy's in line for the vice-presidency of the store. I don't know what gets into me, maybe I just have an overdeveloped sense of competition or something, but I went and ruined her, and furthermore I can't get rid of her. And he's the third executive I've done that to. Isn't that a crummy characteristic? And to top it all, I go to their weddings! [*Indignantly, but laughing*] Like I'm not supposed to take bribes. Manufacturers offer me a hundred-dollar bill now and then to throw an order their way. You know how honest I am, but it's like this girl, see. I hate myself for it. Because I don't want the girl, and, still, I take it and—I love it!

BIFF. Let's go to sleep.

HAPPY. I guess we didn't settle anything, heh? 170

BIFF. I just got one idea that I think I'm going to try.

HAPPY. What's that?

BIFF. Remember Bill Oliver?

HAPPY. Sure, Oliver is very big now. You want to work for him again?

BIFF. No, but when I quit he said something to me. He put his arm on 175
my shoulder, and he said, "Biff, if you ever need anything, come to me."

HAPPY. I remember that. That sounds good.

BIFF. I think I'll go to see him. If I could get ten thousand or even seven or eight thousand dollars I could buy a beautiful ranch.

HAPPY. I bet he'd back you. 'Cause he thought highly of you, Biff. I mean, they all do. You're well liked, Biff. That's why I say to come back here, and we both have the apartment. And I'm tellin' you, Biff, any babe you want . . .

BIFF. No, with a ranch I could do the work I like and still be something. I just wonder though. I wonder if Oliver still thinks I stole that carton of basketballs.

HAPPY. Oh, he probably forgot that long ago. It's almost ten years. You're   180
too sensitive. Anyway, he didn't really fire you.

BIFF. Well, I think he was going to. I think that's why I quit. I was never
sure whether he knew or not. I know he thought the world of me, though. I was
the only one he'd let lock up the place.

WILLY. [below] You gonna wash the engine, Biff?

HAPPY. Shh!

[BIFF looks at HAPPY, who is gazing down, listening. WILLY is mumbling in the parlor.]

HAPPY. You hear that?

[They listen. WILLY laughs warmly.]

BIFF. [growing angry] Doesn't he know Mom can hear that?   185

WILLY. Don't get your sweater dirty, Biff!

[A look of pain crosses BIFF's face.]

HAPPY. Isn't that terrible! Don't leave again, will you? You'll find a job
here. You gotta stick around. I don't know what to do about him, it's getting
embarrassing.

WILLY. What a simonizing job!

BIFF. Mom's hearing that!

WILLY. No kiddin', Biff, you got a date? Wonderful!   190

HAPPY. Go on to sleep. But talk to him in the morning, will you?

BIFF. [reluctantly getting into bed] With her in the house. Brother!

HAPPY. [getting into bed] I wish you'd have a good talk with him.

[The light on their room begins to fade.]

BIFF. [to himself in bed] That selfish, stupid . . .

HAPPY. Sh . . . Sleep, Biff.   195

[Their light is out. Well before they have finished speaking, WILLY's form is dimly seen below
in the darkened kitchen. He opens the refrigerator, searches in there, and takes out a bottle
of milk. The apartment houses are fading out, and the entire house and surroundings become
covered with leaves. Music insinuates itself as the leaves appear.]

WILLY. Just wanna be careful with those girls, Biff, that's all. Don't make
any promises. No promises of any kind. Because a girl, y'know, they always believe
what you tell 'em, and you're very young, Biff, you're too young to be talking
seriously to girls.

[Light rises on the kitchen. WILLY, talking, shuts the refrigerator door and comes downstage
to the kitchen table. He pours milk into a glass. He is totally immersed in himself, smiling
faintly.]

WILLY. Too young entirely, Biff. You want to watch your schooling first.
Then when you're all set, there'll be plenty of girls for a boy like you. [He smiles
broadly at a kitchen chair.] That so? The girls pay for you? [He laughs.] Boy, you
must really be makin' a hit.

[*WILLY is gradually addressing—physically—a point offstage, speaking through the wall of the kitchen, and his voice has been rising in volume to that of a normal conversation.*]

WILLY. I been wondering why you polish the car so careful. Ha! Don't leave the hubcaps, boys. Get the chamois to the hubcaps. Happy, use newspaper on the windows, it's the easiest thing. Show him how to do it, Biff! You see, Happy? Pad it up, use it like a pad. That's it, that's it, good work. You're doin' all right, Hap. [*He pauses, then nods in approbation for a few seconds, then looks upward.*] Biff, first thing we gotta do when we get time is clip that big branch over the house. Afraid it's gonna fall in a storm and hit the roof. Tell you what. We get a rope and sling her around, and then we climb up there with a couple of saws and take her down. Soon as you finish the car, boys, I wanna see ya. I got a surprise for you, boys.

BIFF. [*offstage*] Whatta ya got, Dad?

WILLY. No, you finish first. Never leave a job till you're finished—remember   200
that. [*looking toward the "big trees"*] Biff, up in Albany I saw a beautiful hammock. I think I'll buy it next trip, and we'll hang it right between those two elms. Wouldn't that be something? Just swingin' there under those branches. Boy, that would be . . .

[*YOUNG BIFF and YOUNG HAPPY appear from the direction WILLY was addressing. HAPPY carries rags and a pail of water. BIFF, wearing a sweater with a block "S," carries a football.*]

BIFF. [*pointing in the direction of the car offstage*] How's that, Pop, professional?

WILLY. Terrific. Terrific job, boys. Good work, Biff.

HAPPY. Where's the surprise, Pop?

WILLY. In the back seat of the car.

HAPPY. Boy! [*He runs off.*]   205

BIFF. What is it, Dad? Tell me, what'd you buy?

WILLY. [*laughing, cuffs him*] Never mind, something I want you to have.

BIFF. [*turns and starts off*] What is it, Hap?

HAPPY. [*offstage*] It's a punching bag!

BIFF. Oh, Pop!   210

WILLY. It's got Gene Tunney's° signature on it!

[*HAPPY runs onstage with a punching bag.*]

BIFF. Gee, how'd you know we wanted a punching bag?

WILLY. Well, it's the finest thing for the timing.

HAPPY. [*lies down on his back and pedals with his feet*] I'm losing weight, you notice, Pop?

WILLY. [*to HAPPY*] Jumping rope is good too.   215

BIFF. Did you see the new football I got?

WILLY. [*examining the ball*] Where'd you get a new ball?

BIFF. The coach told me to practice my passing.

WILLY. That so? And he gave you the ball, heh?

Gene Tunney: James Joseph Tunney, a boxer who won the heavyweight championship from Jack Dempsey in 1926 and retired undefeated in 1928.

BIFF.   Well, I borrowed it from the locker room. [*He laughs confidentially.*]   220
WILLY.   [*laughing with him at the theft*] I want you to return that.
HAPPY.   I told you he wouldn't like it!
BIFF.   [*angrily*] Well, I'm bringing it back!
WILLY.   [*stopping the incipient argument, to HAPPY*] Sure, he's gotta practice with a regulation ball, doesn't he? [*to BIFF*] Coach'll probably congratulate you on your initiative!
BIFF.   Oh, he keeps congratulating my initiative all the time, Pop.   225
WILLY.   That's because he likes you. If somebody else took that ball there'd be an uproar. So what's the report, boys, what's the report?
BIFF.   Where'd you go this time, Dad? Gee we were lonesome for you.
WILLY.   [*pleased, puts an arm around each boy and they come down to the apron*] Lonesome, heh?
BIFF.   Missed you every minute.
WILLY.   Don't say? Tell you a secret, boys. Don't breathe it to a soul. Someday   230
I'll have my own business, and I'll never have to leave home any more.
HAPPY.   Like Uncle Charley, heh?
WILLY.   Bigger than Uncle Charley! Because Charley is not—liked. He's liked, but he's not—well liked.
BIFF.   Where'd you go this time, Dad?
WILLY.   Well, I got on the road, and I went north to Providence. Met the Mayor.
BIFF.   The Mayor of Providence!   235
WILLY.   He was sitting in the hotel lobby.
BIFF.   What'd he say?
WILLY.   He said, "Morning!" And I said, "You got a fine city here, Mayor." And then he had coffee with me. And then I went to Waterbury. Waterbury is a fine city. Big clock city, the famous Waterbury clock. Sold a nice bill there. And then Boston—Boston is the cradle of the Revolution. A fine city. And a couple of other towns in Mass., and on to Portland and Bangor and straight home!
BIFF.   Gee, I'd love to go with you sometime, Dad.
WILLY.   Soon as summer comes.   240
HAPPY.   Promise?
WILLY.   You and Hap and I, and I'll show you all the towns. America is full of beautiful towns and fine, upstanding people. And they know me, boys, they know me up and down New England. The finest people. And when I bring you fellas up, there'll be open sesame for all of us, 'cause one thing, boys: I have friends. I can park my car in any street in New England, and the cops protect it like their own. This summer, heh?
BIFF and HAPPY.   [*together*] Yeah! You bet!
WILLY.   We'll take our bathing suits.
HAPPY.   We'll carry your bags, Pop!   245
WILLY.   Oh, won't that be something! Me comin' into the Boston stores with you boys carryin' my bags. What a sensation!

[*BIFF is prancing around, practicing passing the ball.*]

WILLY.   You nervous, Biff, about the game?
BIFF.   Not if you're gonna be there.

WILLY. What do they say about you in school, now that they made you captain?

HAPPY. There's a crowd of girls behind him everytime the classes change. 250

BIFF. [*taking WILLY's hand*] This Saturday, Pop, this Saturday—just for you, I'm going to break through for a touchdown.

HAPPY. You're supposed to pass.

BIFF. I'm takin' one play for Pop. You watch me, Pop, and when I take off my helmet, that means I'm breakin' out. Then you watch me crash through that line!

WILLY. [*kisses BIFF*] Oh, wait'll I tell this in Boston!

[*BERNARD enters in knickers. He is younger than BIFF, earnest and loyal, a worried boy.*]

BERNARD. Biff, where are you? You're supposed to study with me today. 255

WILLY. Hey, looka Bernard. What're you lookin' so anemic about, Bernard?

BERNARD. He's gotta study, Uncle Willy. He's got Regents° next week.

HAPPY. [*tauntingly, spinning BERNARD around*] Let's box, Bernard!

BERNARD. Biff! [*He gets away from HAPPY.*] Listen, Biff, I heard Mr. Birnbaum say that if you don't start studyin' math he's gonna flunk you, and you won't graduate. I heard him!

WILLY. You better study with him, Biff. Go ahead now. 260

BERNARD. I heard him!

BIFF. Oh, Pop, you didn't see my sneakers! [*He holds up a foot for WILLY to look at.*]

WILLY. Hey, that's a beautiful job of printing!

BERNARD. [*wiping his glasses*] Just because he printed University of Virginia on his sneakers doesn't mean they've got to graduate him, Uncle Willy!

WILLY. [*angrily*] What're you talking about? With scholarships to three uni- 265
versities they're gonna flunk him?

BERNARD. But I heard Mr. Birnbaum say—

WILLY. Don't be a pest, Bernard! [*to his boys*] What an anemic!

BERNARD. Okay, I'm waiting for you in my house, Biff.

[*BERNARD goes off. The LOMANS laugh.*]

WILLY. Bernard is not well liked, is he?

BIFF. He's liked, but he's not well liked. 270

HAPPY. That's right, Pop.

WILLY. That's just what I mean. Bernard can get the best marks in school, y'understand, but when he gets out in the business world, y'understand, you are going to be five times ahead of him. That's why I thank Almighty God you're both built like Adonises. Because the man who makes an appearance in the business world, the man who creates personal interest, is the man who gets ahead. Be liked and you will never want. You take me, for instance. I never have to wait in line to see a buyer. "Willy Loman is here!" That's all they have to know, and I go right through.

°*Regents*: A statewide high school proficiency examination administered in New York State.

BIFF.   Did you knock them dead, Pop?

WILLY.   Knocked 'em cold in Providence, slaughtered 'em in Boston.

HAPPY.   [*on his back, pedaling again*] I'm losing weight, you notice, Pop?   275

[*LINDA enters, as of old, a ribbon in her hair, carrying a basket of washing.*]

LINDA.   [*with youthful energy*] Hello, dear!

WILLY.   Sweetheart!

LINDA.   How'd the Chevvy run?

WILLY.   Chevrolet, Linda, is the greatest car ever built. [*to the boys*] Since when do you let your mother carry wash up the stairs?

BIFF.   Grab hold there, boy!   280

HAPPY.   Where to, Mom?

LINDA.   Hang them up on the line. And you better go down to your friends, Biff. The cellar is full of boys. They don't know what to do with themselves.

BIFF.   Ah, when Pop comes home they can wait!

WILLY.   [*laughs appreciatively*] You better go down and tell them what to do, Biff.

BIFF.   I think I'll have them sweep out the furnace room.   285

WILLY.   Good work, Biff.

BIFF.   [*goes through wall-line of kitchen to doorway at back and calls down*] Fellas! Everybody sweep out the furnace room! I'll be right down!

VOICES.   All right! Okay, Biff.

BIFF.   George and Sam and Frank, come out back! We're hangin' up the wash! Come on, Hap, on the double! [*He and HAPPY carry out the basket.*]

LINDA.   The way they obey him!   290

WILLY.   Well, that's training, the training. I'm tellin' you, I was sellin' thousands and thousands, but I had to come home.

LINDA.   Oh, the whole block'll be at that game. Did you sell anything?

WILLY.   I did five hundred gross in Providence and seven hundred gross in Boston.

LINDA.   No! Wait a minute, I've got a pencil. [*She pulls pencil and paper out of her apron pocket.*] That makes your commission . . . Two hundred—my God! Two hundred and twelve dollars!

WILLY.   Well, I didn't figure it yet, but . . .   295

LINDA.   How much did you do?

WILLY.   Well, I—I did—about a hundred and eighty gross in Providence. Well, no—it came to—roughly two hundred gross on the whole trip.

LINDA.   [*without hesitation*] Two hundred gross. That's . . . [*She figures.*]

WILLY.   The trouble was that three of the stores were half closed for inventory in Boston. Otherwise I woulda broke records.

LINDA.   Well, it makes seventy dollars and some pennies. That's very good.   300

WILLY.   What do we owe?

LINDA.   Well, on the first there's sixteen dollars on the refrigerator—

WILLY.   Why sixteen?

LINDA.   Well, the fan belt broke, so it was a dollar eighty.

WILLY.   But it's brand new.   305

LINDA.   Well, the man said that's the way it is. Till they work themselves in, y'know.

[*They move through the wall-line into the kitchen.*]

WILLY. I hope we didn't get stuck on that machine.

LINDA. They got the biggest ads of any of them!

WILLY. I know, it's a fine machine. What else?

LINDA. Well, there's nine-sixty for the washing machine. And for the vacuum   310
cleaner there's three and a half due on the fifteenth. Then the roof, you got
twenty-one dollars remaining.

WILLY. It don't leak, does it?

LINDA. No, they did a wonderful job. Then you owe Frank for the carbu-
retor.

WILLY. I'm not going to pay that man! That goddam Chevrolet, they ought
to prohibit the manufacture of that car!

LINDA. Well, you owe him three and a half. And odds and ends, comes to
around a hundred and twenty dollars by the fifteenth.

WILLY. A hundred and twenty dollars! My God, if business don't pick up   315
I don't know what I'm gonna do!

LINDA. Well, next week you'll do better.

WILLY. Oh, I'll knock 'em dead next week. I'll go to Hartford. I'm very
well liked in Hartford. You know, the trouble is, Linda, people don't seem to
take to me.

[*They move onto the forestage.*]

LINDA. Oh, don't be foolish.

WILLY. I know it when I walk in. They seem to laugh at me.

LINDA. Why? Why would they laugh at you? Don't talk that way, Willy.   320

[*WILLY moves to the edge of the stage. LINDA goes into the kitchen and starts to darn
stockings.*]

WILLY. I don't know the reason for it, but they just pass me by. I'm not
noticed.

LINDA. But you're doing wonderful, dear. You're making seventy to a hundred dollars a week.

WILLY. But I gotta be at it ten, twelve hours a day. Other men—I don't
know—they do it easier. I don't know why—I can't stop myself—I talk too much.
A man oughta come in with a few words. One thing about Charley. He's a man
of few words, and they respect him.

LINDA. You don't talk too much, you're just lively.

WILLY. [*smiling*] Well, I figure, what the hell, life is short, a couple of jokes.   325
[*to himself*] I joke too much! [*The smile goes.*]

LINDA. Why? You're—

WILLY. I'm fat. I'm very—foolish to look at, Linda. I didn't tell you, but
Christmas time I happened to be calling on F. H. Stewarts, and a salesman I
know, as I was going in to see the buyer I heard him say something about—
walrus. And I—I cracked him right across the face. I won't take that. I simply
will not take that. But they do laugh at me. I know that.

LINDA. Darling . . .

WILLY.   I gotta overcome it. I know I gotta overcome it. I'm not dressing
to advantage, maybe.
LINDA.   Willy, darling, you're the handsomest man in the world—   330
WILLY.   Oh, no, Linda.
LINDA.   To me you are. [*slight pause*] The handsomest.

[*From the darkness is heard the laughter of a woman. WILLY doesn't turn to it, but it
continues through LINDA's lines.*]

LINDA.   And the boys, Willy. Few men are idolized by their children the
way you are.

[*Music is heard as behind a scrim, to the left of the house, THE WOMAN, dimly seen, is
dressing.*]

WILLY.   [*with great feeling*] You're the best there is, Linda, you're a pal, you
know that? On the road—on the road I want to grab you sometimes and just kiss
the life outa you.

[*The laughter is loud now, and he moves into a brightening area at the left, where THE
WOMAN has come from behind the scrim and is standing, putting on her hat, looking into
a "mirror" and laughing.*]

WILLY.   Cause I get so lonely—especially when business is bad and there's   335
nobody to talk to. I get the feeling that I'll never sell anything again, that I won't
make a living for you, or a business, a business for the boys. [*He talks through THE
WOMAN's subsiding laughter; THE WOMAN primps at the "mirror."*] There's so much I
want to make for—
THE WOMAN.   Me? You didn't make me, Willy. I picked you.
WILLY.   [*pleased*] You picked me?
THE WOMAN.   [*who is quite proper-looking, WILLY's age*] I did. I've been sitting
at that desk watching all the salesmen go by, day in, day out. But you've got such
a sense of humor, and we do have such a good time together, don't we?
WILLY.   Sure, sure. [*He takes her in his arms.*] Why do you have to go now?
THE WOMAN.   It's two o'clock . . .   340
WILLY.   No, come on in! [*He pulls her.*]
THE WOMAN.   . . . my sisters'll be scandalized. When'll you be back?
WILLY.   Oh, two weeks about. Will you come up again?
THE WOMAN.   Sure thing. You do make me laugh. It's good for me. [*She
squeezes his arm, kisses him.*] And I think you're a wonderful man.
WILLY.   You picked me, heh?   345
THE WOMAN.   Sure. Because you're so sweet. And such a kidder.
WILLY.   Well, I'll see you next time I'm in Boston.
THE WOMAN.   I'll put you right through to the buyers.
WILLY.   [*slapping her bottom*] Right. Well, bottoms up!
THE WOMAN.   [*slaps him gently and laughs*] You just kill me, Willy. [*He suddenly   350
grabs her and kisses her roughly.*] You kill me. And thanks for the stockings. I love a
lot of stockings. Well, good night.
WILLY.   Good night. And keep your pores open!
THE WOMAN.   Oh, Willy!

[*THE WOMAN bursts out laughing, and LINDA's laughter blends in. THE WOMAN disappears into the dark. Now the area at the kitchen table brightens. LINDA is sitting where she was at the kitchen table, but now is mending a pair of her silk stockings.*]

LINDA.   You are, Willy. The handsomest man. You've got no reason to feel that—

WILLY.   [*coming out of THE WOMAN's dimming area and going over to LINDA*] I'll make it all up to you, Linda, I'll—

LINDA.   There's nothing to make up, dear. You're doing fine, better than—   355

WILLY.   [*noticing her mending*] What's that?

LINDA.   Just mending my stockings. They're so expensive—

WILLY.   [*angrily, taking them from her*] I won't have you mending stockings in this house! Now throw them out!

[*LINDA puts the stockings in her pocket.*]

BERNARD.   [*entering on the run*] Where is he? If he doesn't study!

WILLY.   [*moving to the forestage, with great agitation*] You'll give him the answers!   360

BERNARD.   I do, but I can't on a Regents! That's a state exam! They're liable to arrest me!

WILLY.   Where is he? I'll whip him, I'll whip him!

LINDA.   And he'd better give back that football, Willy, it's not nice.

WILLY.   Biff! Where is he? Why is he taking everything?

LINDA.   He's too rough with the girls, Willy. All the mothers are afraid of   365
him!

WILLY.   I'll whip him!

BERNARD.   He's driving the car without a license!

[*THE WOMAN's laugh is heard.*]

WILLY.   Shut up!

LINDA.   All the mothers—

WILLY.   Shut up!   370

BERNARD.   [*backing quietly away and out*] Mr. Birnbaum says he's stuck up.

WILLY.   Get outa here!

BERNARD.   If he doesn't buckle down he'll flunk math! [*He goes off.*]

LINDA.   He's right, Willy, you've gotta—

WILLY.   [*exploding at her*] There's nothing the matter with him! You want   375
him to be a worm like Bernard? He's got spirit, personality . . .

[*As he speaks, LINDA, almost in tears, exits into the living-room. WILLY is alone in the kitchen, wilting and staring. The leaves are gone. It is night again, and the apartment houses look down from behind.*]

WILLY.   Loaded with it. Loaded! What is he stealing? He's giving it back, isn't he? Why is he stealing? What did I tell him? I never in my life told him anything but decent things.

[*HAPPY in pajamas has come down the stairs; WILLY suddenly becomes aware of HAPPY's presence.*]

HAPPY. Let's go now, come on.

WILLY. [*sitting down at the kitchen table*] Huh! Why did she have to wax the floors herself? Everytime she waxes the floors she keels over. She knows that!

HAPPY. Shh! Take it easy. What brought you back tonight?

WILLY. I got an awful scare. Nearly hit a kid in Yonkers. God! Why didn't I go to Alaska with my brother Ben that time! Ben! That man was a genius, that man was success incarnate! What a mistake! He begged me to go.   380

HAPPY. Well, there's no use in—

WILLY. You guys! There was a man started with the clothes on his back and ended up with diamond mines!

HAPPY. Boy, someday I'd like to know how he did it.

WILLY. What's the mystery? The man knew what he wanted and went out and got it! Walked into a jungle, and comes out, the age of twenty-one, and he's rich! The world is an oyster, but you don't crack it open on a mattress!

HAPPY. Pop, I told you I'm gonna retire you for life.   385

WILLY. You'll retire me for life on seventy goddam dollars a week? And your women and your car and your apartment, and you'll retire me for life! Christ's sake, I couldn't get past Yonkers today! Where are you guys, where are you? The woods are burning! I can't drive a car!

[CHARLEY *has appeared in the doorway. He is a large man, slow of speech, laconic, immovable. In all he says, despite what he says, there is pity, and, now, trepidation. He has a robe over pajamas, slippers on his feet. He enters the kitchen.*]

CHARLEY. Everything all right?

HAPPY. Yeah, Charley, everything's . . .

WILLY. What's the matter?

CHARLEY. I heard some noise. I thought something happened. Can't we do something about the walls? You sneeze in here, and in my house hats blow off.   390

HAPPY. Let's go to bed, Dad. Come on.

[CHARLEY *signals to* HAPPY *to go.*]

WILLY. You go ahead, I'm not tired at the moment.

HAPPY. [*to* WILLY] Take it easy, huh? [*He exits.*]

WILLY. What're you doin' up?

CHARLEY. [*sitting down at the kitchen table opposite* WILLY] Couldn't sleep good. I had a heartburn.   395

WILLY. Well, you don't know how to eat.

CHARLEY. I eat with my mouth.

WILLY. No, you're ignorant. You gotta know about vitamins and things like that.

CHARLEY. Come on, let's shoot. Tire you out a little.

WILLY. [*hesitantly*] All right. You got cards?   400

CHARLEY. [*taking a deck from his pocket*] Yeah, I got them. Someplace. What is it with those vitamins?

WILLY. [*dealing*] They build up your bones. Chemistry.

CHARLEY. Yeah, but there's no bones in a heartburn.

WILLY.   What are you talkin' about? Do you know the first thing about it?
CHARLEY.   Don't get insulted.   405
WILLY.   Don't talk about something you don't know anything about.

[*They are playing. Pause.*]

CHARLEY.   What're you doin' home?
WILLY.   A little trouble with the car.
CHARLEY.   Oh. [*Pause*] I'd like to take a trip to California.
WILLY.   Don't say.   410
CHARLEY.   You want a job?
WILLY.   I got a job, I told you that. [*after a slight pause*] What the hell are
you offering me a job for?
CHARLEY.   Don't get insulted.
WILLY.   Don't insult me.
CHARLEY.   I don't see no sense in it. You don't have to go on this way.   415
WILLY.   I got a good job. [*slight pause*] What do you keep comin' in for?
CHARLEY.   You want me to go?
WILLY.   [*after a pause, withering*] I can't understand it. He's going back to
Texas again. What the hell is that?
CHARLEY.   Let him go.
WILLY.   I got nothin' to give him, Charley, I'm clean, I'm clean.   420
CHARLEY.   He won't starve. None a them starve. Forget about him.
WILLY.   Then what have I got to remember?
CHARLEY.   You take it too hard. To hell with it. When a deposit bottle is
broken you don't get your nickel back.
WILLY.   That's easy enough for you to say.
CHARLEY.   That ain't easy for me to say.   425
WILLY.   Did you see the ceiling I put up in the living-room?
CHARLEY.   Yeah, that's a piece of work. To put up a ceiling is a mystery to
me. How do you do it?
WILLY.   What's the difference?
CHARLEY.   Well, talk about it.
WILLY.   You gonna put up a ceiling?   430
CHARLEY.   How could I put up a ceiling?
WILLY.   Then what the hell are you bothering me for?
CHARLEY.   You're insulted again.
WILLY.   A man who can't handle tools is not a man. You're disgusting.
CHARLEY.   Don't call me disgusting, Willy.   435

[*UNCLE BEN, carrying a valise and an umbrella, enters the forestage from around the right corner of the house. He is a stolid man, in his sixties, with a mustache and an authoritative air. He is utterly certain of his destiny, and there is an aura of far places about him. He enters exactly as WILLY speaks.*]

WILLY.   I'm getting awfully tired, Ben.

[*BEN'S music is heard. BEN looks around at everything.*]

CHARLEY.   Good, keep playing; you'll sleep better. Did you call me Ben?

[BEN *looks at his watch.*]

WILLY. That's funny. For a second there you reminded me of my brother
Ben.
BEN. I only have a few minutes. [*He strolls, inspecting the place.* WILLY *and*
CHARLEY *continue playing.*]
CHARLEY. You never heard from him again, heh? Since that time?   440
WILLY. Didn't Linda tell you? Couple of weeks ago we got a letter from
his wife in Africa. He died.
CHARLEY. That so.
BEN. [*chuckling*] So this is Brooklyn, eh?
CHARLEY. Maybe you're in for some of his money.
WILLY. Naa, he had seven sons. There's just one opportunity I had with   445
that man . . .
BEN. I must make a train, William. There are several properties I'm looking
at in Alaska.
WILLY. Sure, sure! If I'd gone with him to Alaska that time, everything
would've been totally different.
CHARLEY. Go on, you'd froze to death up there.
WILLY. What're you talking about?
BEN. Opportunity is tremendous in Alaska, William. Surprised you're not   450
up there.
WILLY. Sure, tremendous.
CHARLEY. Heh?
WILLY. There was the only man I ever met who knew the answers.
CHARLEY. Who?
BEN. How are you all?   455
WILLY. [*taking a pot, smiling*] Fine, fine.
CHARLEY. Pretty sharp tonight.
BEN. Is Mother living with you?
WILLY. No, she died a long time ago.
CHARLEY. Who?   460
BEN. That's too bad. Fine specimen of a lady, Mother.
WILLY. [*to* CHARLEY] Heh?
BEN. I'd hoped to see the old girl.
CHARLEY. Who died?
BEN. Heard anything from Father, have you?   465
WILLY. [*unnerved*] What do you mean, who died?
CHARLEY. [*taking a pot*] What're you talkin' about?
BEN. [*looking at his watch*] William, it's half-past eight!
WILLY. [*As though to dispel his confusion he angrily stops* CHARLEY's *hand.*] That's
my build!
CHARLEY. I put the ace—   470
WILLY. If you don't know how to play the game I'm not gonna throw my
money away on you!
CHARLEY. [*rising*] It was my ace, for God's sake!
WILLY. I'm through, I'm through!
BEN. When did Mother die?

WILLY. Long ago. Since the beginning you never knew how to play cards. 475

CHARLEY. [*picks up the cards and goes to the door*] All right! Next time I'll bring a deck with five aces.

WILLY. I don't play that kind of game!

CHARLEY. [*turning to him*] You ought to be ashamed of yourself!

WILLY. Yeah?

CHARLEY. Yeah! [*He goes out.*] 480

WILLY. [*slamming the door after him*] Ignoramus!

BEN. [*as WILLY comes toward him through the wall-line of the kitchen*] So you're William.

WILLY. [*shaking BEN's hand*] Ben! I've been waiting for you so long! What's the answer? How did you do it?

BEN. Oh, there's a story in that.

[*LINDA enters the forestage, as of old, carrying the wash basket.*]

LINDA. Is this Ben? 485

BEN. [*gallantly*] How do you do, my dear.

LINDA. Where've you been all these years? Willy's always wondered why you—

WILLY. [*pulling BEN away from her impatiently*] Where is Dad? Didn't you follow him? How did you get started?

BEN. Well, I don't know how much you remember.

WILLY. Well, I was just a baby, of course, only three or four years old— 490

BEN. Three years and eleven months.

WILLY. What a memory, Ben!

BEN. I have many enterprises, William, and I have never kept books.

WILLY. I remember I was sitting under the wagon in—was it Nebraska?

BEN. It was South Dakota, and I gave you a bunch of wild flowers. 495

WILLY. I remember you walking away down some open road.

BEN. [*laughing*] I was going to find Father in Alaska.

WILLY. Where is he?

BEN. At that age I had a very faulty view of geography, William. I discovered after a few days that I was heading due south, so instead of Alaska, I ended up in Africa.

LINDA. Africa! 500

WILLY. The Gold Coast!

BEN. Principally diamond mines.

LINDA. Diamond mines!

BEN. Yes, my dear. But I've only a few minutes—

WILLY. No! Boys! Boys! [*YOUNG BIFF and HAPPY appear.*] Listen to this. This 505
is your Uncle Ben, a great man! Tell my boys, Ben!

BEN. Why, boys, when I was seventeen I walked into the jungle, and when I was twenty-one I walked out. [*He laughs.*] And by God I was rich.

WILLY. [*to the boys*] You see what I been talking about? The greatest things can happen!

BEN. [*glancing at his watch*] I have an appointment in Ketchikan Tuesday week.

WILLY. No, Ben. Please tell about Dad. I want my boys to hear. I want them to know the kind of stock they spring from. All I remember is a man with a big beard, and I was in Mamma's lap, sitting around a fire, and some kind of high music.

BEN. His flute. He played the flute. 510

WILLY. Sure, the flute, that's right!

[*New music is heard, a high, rollicking tune.*]

BEN. Father was a very great and a very wild-hearted man. We would start in Boston, and he'd toss the whole family into the wagon, and then he'd drive the team right across the country; through Ohio, and Indiana, Michigan, Illinois, and all the Western states. And we'd stop in the towns and sell the flutes that he'd made on the way. Great inventor, Father. With one gadget he made more in a week than a man like you could make in a lifetime.

WILLY. That's just the way I'm bringing them up, Ben—rugged, well liked, all-around.

BEN. Yeah? [*to BIFF*] Hit that, boy—hard as you can. [*He pounds his stomach.*]

BIFF. Oh, no, sir! 515

BEN. [*taking boxing stance*] Come on, get to me! [*He laughs.*]

BIFF. Okay! [*He cocks his fists and starts in.*]

WILLY. Go to it, Biff! Go ahead, show him!

LINDA. [*to WILLY*] Why must he fight, dear?

BEN. [*sparring with BIFF*] Good boy! Good boy! 520

WILLY. How's that, Ben, heh?

HAPPY. Give him the left, Biff!

LINDA. Why are you fighting?

BEN. Good boy! [*suddenly comes in, trips BIFF, and stands over him, the point of his umbrella poised over BIFF's eye.*]

LINDA. Look out, Biff! 525

BIFF. Gee!

BEN. [*patting BIFF's knee*] Never fight fair with a stranger, boy. You'll never get out of the jungle that way. [*taking LINDA's hand and bowing*] It was an honor and a pleasure to meet you, Linda.

LINDA. [*withdrawing her hand coldly, frightened*] Have a nice—trip.

BEN. [*to WILLY*] And good luck with your—what do you do?

WILLY. Selling. 530

BEN. Yes. Well . . . [*He raises his hand in farewell to all.*]

WILLY. No, Ben, I don't want you to think . . . [*He takes BEN's arm to show him.*] It's Brooklyn, I know, but we hunt too.

BEN. Really, now.

WILLY. Oh, sure, there's snakes and rabbits and—that's why I moved out here. Why, Biff can fell any one of these trees in no time! Boys! Go right over to where they're building the apartment house and get some sand. We're gonna rebuild the entire front stoop right now! Watch this, Ben!

BIFF. Yes, sir! On the double, Hap! 535

HAPPY. [*as he and BIFF run off*] I lost weight, Pop, you notice?

[*CHARLEY enters in knickers, even before the boys are gone.*]

CHARLEY.   Listen, if they steal any more from that building the watchman'll put the cops on them!

LINDA.   [*to WILLY*] Don't let Biff . . .

[*BEN laughs lustily.*]

WILLY.   You shoulda seen the lumber they brought home last week. At least a dozen six-by-tens worth all kinds a money.

CHARLEY.   Listen, if that watchman—   540

WILLY.   I gave them hell, understand. But I got a couple of fearless characters there.

CHARLEY.   Willy, the jails are full of fearless characters.

BEN.   [*clapping WILLY on the back, with a laugh at CHARLEY*] And the stock exchange, friend!

WILLY.   [*joining in BEN's laughter*] Where are the rest of your pants?

CHARLEY.   My wife bought them.   545

WILLY.   Now all you need is a golf club and you can go upstairs and go to sleep. [*to BEN*] Great athlete! Between him and his son Bernard they can't hammer a nail!

BERNARD.   [*rushing in*] The watchman's chasing Biff!

WILLY.   [*angrily*] Shut up! He's not stealing anything!

LINDA.   [*alarmed, hurrying off left*] Where is he? Biff, dear! [*She exits.*]

WILLY.   [*moving toward the left, away from BEN*] There's nothing wrong. What's   550
the matter with you?

BEN.   Nervy boy. Good!

WILLY.   [*laughing*] Oh, nerves of iron, that Biff!

CHARLEY.   Don't know what it is. My New England man comes back and he's bleedin', they murdered him up there.

WILLY.   It's contacts, Charley, I got important contacts!

CHARLEY.   [*sarcastically*] Glad to hear it, Willy. Come in later, we'll shoot a   555
little casino. I'll take some of your Portland money. [*He laughs at WILLY and exits.*]

WILLY.   [*turning to BEN*] Business is bad, it's murderous. But not for me, of course.

BEN.   I'll stop by on my way back to Africa.

WILLY.   [*longingly.*] Can't you stay a few days? You're just what I need, Ben, because I—I have a fine position here, but I—well, Dad left when I was such a baby and I never had a chance to talk to him and I still feel—kind of temporary about myself.

BEN.   I'll be late for my train.

[*They are at opposite ends of the stage.*]

WILLY.   Ben, my boys—can't we talk? They'd go into the jaws of hell for   560
me, see, but I—

BEN.   William, you're being first-rate with your boys. Outstanding, manly chaps!

WILLY.   [*hanging on to his words*] Oh, Ben, that's good to hear! Because sometimes I'm afraid that I'm not teaching them the right kind of— Ben, how should I teach them?

BEN.   [*giving great weight to each word, and with a certain vicious audacity*] William, when I walked into the jungle, I was seventeen. When I walked out I was twenty-one. And, by God, I was rich! [*He goes off into darkness around the right corner of the house.*]

WILLY. . . . was rich! That's just the spirit I want to imbue them with! To walk into a jungle! I was right! I was right! I was right!

[*BEN is gone, but WILLY is still speaking to him as LINDA, in her nightgown and robe, enters the kitchen, glances around for WILLY, then goes to the door of the house, looks out and sees him. Comes down to his left. He looks at her.*]

LINDA. Willy, dear? Willy?   565

WILLY. I was right!

LINDA. Did you have some cheese? [*He can't answer.*] It's very late, darling. Come to bed, heh?

WILLY. [*looking straight up*] Gotta break your neck to see a star in this yard.

LINDA. You coming in?

WILLY. Whatever happened to that diamond watch fob? Remember? When   570
Ben came from Africa that time? Didn't he give me a watch fob with a diamond in it?

LINDA. You pawned it, dear. Twelve, thirteen years ago. For Biff's radio correspondence course.

WILLY. Gee, that was a beautiful thing. I'll take a walk.

LINDA. But you're in your slippers.

WILLY. [*starting to go around the house at the left*] I was right! I was! [*Half to LINDA, as he goes, shaking his head*] What a man! There was a man worth talking to. I was right!

LINDA. [*calling after WILLY*] But in your slippers, Willy!   575

[*WILLY is almost gone when BIFF, in his pajamas, comes down the stairs and enters the kitchen.*]

BIFF. What is he doing out there?

LINDA. Sh!

BIFF. God Almighty, Mom, how long has he been doing this?

LINDA. Don't, he'll hear you.

BIFF. What the hell is the matter with him?   580

LINDA. It'll pass by morning.

BIFF. Shouldn't we do anything?

LINDA. Oh, my dear, you should do a lot of things, but there's nothing to do, so go to sleep.

[*HAPPY comes down the stairs and sits on the steps.*]

HAPPY. I never heard him so loud, Mom.

LINDA. Well, come around more often; you'll hear him. [*She sits down at   585
the table and mends the lining of WILLY's jacket.*]

BIFF. Why didn't you ever write me about this, Mom?

LINDA. How would I write to you? For over three months you had no address.

BIFF. I was on the move. But you know I thought of you all the time. You know that, don't you, pal?

LINDA. I know, dear, I know. But he likes to have a letter. Just to know that there's still a possibility for better things.

BIFF. He's not like this all the time, is he? 590

LINDA. It's when you come home he's always the worst.

BIFF. When I come home?

LINDA. When you write you're coming, he's all smiles, and talks about the future, and—he's just wonderful. And then the closer you seem to come, the more shaky he gets, and then, by the time you get here, he's arguing, and he seems angry at you. I think it's just that maybe he can't bring himself to—to open up to you. Why are you so hateful to each other? Why is that?

BIFF. [*evasively*] I'm not hateful, Mom.

LINDA. But you no sooner come in the door than you're fighting! 595

BIFF. I don't know why. I mean to change. I'm tryin', Mom, you understand?

LINDA. Are you home to stay now?

BIFF. I don't know. I want to look around, see what's doin'.

LINDA. Biff, you can't look around all your life, can you?

BIFF. I just can't take hold, Mom. I can't take hold of some kind of a 600
life.

LINDA. Biff, a man is not a bird, to come and go with the springtime.

BIFF. Your hair . . . [*He touches her hair.*] Your hair got so gray.

LINDA. Oh, it's been gray since you were in high school. I just stopped dyeing it, that's all.

BIFF. Dye it again, will ya? I don't want my pal looking old. [*He smiles.*]

LINDA. You're such a boy! You think you can go away for a year and . . . 605
You've got to get it into your head now that one day you'll knock on this door and there'll be strange people here—

BIFF. What are you talking about? You're not even sixty, Mom.

LINDA. But what about your father?

BIFF. [*lamely*] Well, I meant him, too.

HAPPY. He admires Pop.

LINDA. Biff, dear, if you don't have any feeling for him, then you can't 610
have any feeling for me.

BIFF. Sure I can, Mom.

LINDA. No. You can't just come to see me, because I love him. [*with a threat, but only a threat, of tears*] He's the dearest man in the world to me, and I won't have anyone making him feel unwanted and low and blue. You've got to make up your mind now, darling, there's no leeway any more. Either he's your father and you pay him that respect, or else you're not to come here. I know he's not easy to get along with—nobody knows that better than me—but . . .

WILLY. [*from the left, with a laugh*] Hey, hey, Biffo!

BIFF. [*starting to go out after WILLY*] What the hell is the matter with him? [*HAPPY stops him.*]

LINDA. Don't—don't go near him! 615

BIFF. Stop making excuses for him! He always, always wiped the floor with you. Never had an ounce of respect for you.

HAPPY. He's always had respect for—

BIFF. What the hell do you know about it?

HAPPY. [*surlily*] Just don't call him crazy!

BIFF.   He's got no character—Charley wouldn't do this. Not in his own   620
house—spewing out that vomit from his mind.

HAPPY.   Charley never had to cope with what he's got to.

BIFF.   People are worse off than Willy Loman. Believe me, I've seen them!

LINDA.   Then make Charley your father, Biff. You can't do that, can you?
I don't say he's a great man. Willy Loman never made a lot of money. His name
was never in the paper. He's not the finest character that ever lived. But he's a
human being, and a terrible thing is happening to him. So attention must be
paid. He's not to be allowed to fall into his grave like an old dog. Attention,
attention must be finally paid to such a person. You called him crazy—

BIFF.   I didn't mean—

LINDA.   No, a lot of people think he's lost his—balance. But you don't have   625
to be very smart to know what his trouble is. The man is exhausted.

HAPPY.   Sure!

LINDA.   A small man can be just as exhausted as a great man. He works
for a company thirty-six years this March, opens up unheard-of-territories to their
trademark, and now in his old age they take his salary away.

HAPPY.   [*indignantly*] I didn't know that, Mom.

LINDA.   You never asked, my dear! Now that you get your spending money
someplace else you don't trouble your mind with him.

HAPPY.   But I gave you money last—   630

LINDA.   Christmas time, fifty dollars! To fix the hot water it cost ninety-
seven fifty! For five weeks he's been on straight commission,° like a beginner, an
unknown!

BIFF.   Those ungrateful bastards!

LINDA.   Are they any worse than his sons? When he brought them business,
when he was young, they were glad to see him. But now his old friends, the old
buyers that loved him so and always found some order to hand him in a pinch—
they're all dead, retired. He used to be able to make six, seven calls a day in
Boston. Now he takes his valises out of the car and puts them back and takes
them out again and he's exhausted. Instead of walking he talks now. He drives
seven hundred miles, and when he gets there no one knows him any more, no
one welcomes him. And what goes through a man's mind, driving seven hundred
miles home without having earned a cent? Why shouldn't he talk to himself?
Why? When he has to go to Charley and borrow fifty dollars a week and pretend
to me that it's his pay? How long can that go on? How long? You see what I'm
sitting here and waiting for? And you tell me he has no character? The man who
never worked a day but for your benefit? When does he get the medal for that?
Is this his reward—to turn around at the age of sixty-three and find his sons,
who he loved better than his life, one a philandering bum—

HAPPY.   Mom!

LINDA.   That's all you are, my baby! [*To BIFF*] And you! What happened to   635
the love you had for him? You were such pals! How you used to talk to him on
the phone every night! How lonely he was till he could come home to you!

---

straight commission: refers to the fact that Willy is receiving no salary, only a commission
(percentage) on the sales he makes.

HELMER.   I promise. This evening I will be wholly and absolutely at your service, you helpless little mortal. Ah, by the way, first of all I will just——

[*Goes towards the hall door*]

NORA.   What are you going to do there?
HELMER.   Only see if any letters have come.   375
NORA.   No, no! don't do that, Torvald!
HELMER.   Why not?
NORA.   Torvald, please don't. There is nothing there.
HELMER.   Well, let me look. [*Turns to go to the letter-box.* NORA, *at the piano, plays the first bars of the Tarantella.* HELMER *stops in the doorway.*] Aha!
NORA.   I can't dance to-morrow if I don't practise with you.   380
HELMER.   [*going up to her*] Are you really so afraid of it, dear.
NORA.   Yes, so dreadfully afraid of it. Let me practise at once; there is time now, before we go to dinner. Sit down and play for me, Torvald dear; criticise me, and correct me as you play.
HELMER.   With great pleasure, if you wish me to.

[*Sits down at the piano.*]

NORA.   [*takes out of the box a tambourine and a long variegated shawl. She hastily drapes the shawl round her. Then she springs to the front of the stage and calls out.*] Now play for me! I am going to dance!

[HELMER *plays and* NORA *dances.* RANK *stands by the piano behind* HELMER *and looks on.*]

HELMER.   [*as he plays*] Slower, slower!   385
NORA.   I can't do it any other way.
HELMER.   Not so violently, Nora!
NORA.   This is the way.
HELMER.   [*stops playing*] No, no—that is not a bit right.
NORA.   [*laughing and swinging the tambourine*] Didn't I tell you so?   390
RANK.   Let me play for her.
HELMER.   [*getting up*] Yes, do. I can correct her better then.

[RANK *sits down at the piano and plays.* NORA *dances more and more wildly.* HELMER *has taken up a position beside the stove, and during her dance gives her frequent instructions. She does not seem to hear him; her hair comes down and falls over her shoulders; she pays no attention to it, but goes on dancing. Enter* MRS. LINDE.]

MRS. LINDE.   [*standing as if spell-bound in the doorway*] Oh!——
NORA.   [*as she dances*] Such fun, Christine!
HELMER.   My dear darling Nora, you are dancing as if your life depended   395
on it.
NORA.   So it does.
HELMER.   Stop, Rank; this is sheer madness. Stop, I tell you! [RANK *stops playing, and* NORA *suddenly stands still.* HELMER *goes up to her.*] I could never have believed it. You have forgotten everything I taught you.

NORA.   [*throwing away the tambourine*] There, you see.

HELMER.   You will want a lot of coaching.

NORA.   Yes, you see how much I need it. You must coach me up to the   400
last minute. Promise me that, Torvald!

HELMER.   You can depend on me.

NORA.   You must not think of anything but me, either to-day or to-morrow;
you mustn't open a single letter—not even open the letter-box——

HELMER.   Ah, you are still afraid of that fellow——

NORA.   Yes, indeed I am.

HELMER.   Nora, I can tell from your looks that there is a letter from him   405
lying there.

NORA.   I don't know; I think there is; but you must not read anything of
that kind now. Nothing horrid must come between us till this is all over.

RANK.   [*whispers to* HELMER] You mustn't contradict her.

HELMER.   [*taking her in his arms*] The child shall have her way. But to-morrow
night, after you have danced——

NORA.   Then you will be free.

[*The* MAID *appears in the doorway to the right.*]

MAID.   Dinner is served, ma'am.   410

NORA.   We will have champagne, Helen.

MAID.   Very good, ma'am.   [*Exit.*]

HELMER.   Hullo!—are we going to have a banquet?

NORA.   Yes, a champagne banquet till the small hours. [*calls out*] And a
few macaroons, Helen—lots, just for once!

HELMER.   Come, come, don't be so wild and nervous. Be my own little skylark,   415
as you used.

NORA.   Yes, dear, I will. But go in now and you too, Doctor Rank. Christine,
you must help me to do up my hair.

RANK.   [*whispers to* HELMER *as they go out*] I suppose there is nothing—she is
not expecting anything?

HELMER.   Far from it, my dear fellow; it is simply nothing more than this
childish nervousness I was telling you of.

[*They go into the right-hand room.*]

NORA.   Well!

MRS. LINDE.   Gone out of town.   420

NORA.   I could tell from your face.

MRS. LINDE.   He is coming home to-morrow evening. I wrote a note for
him.

NORA.   You should have let it alone; you must prevent nothing. After all,
it is splendid to be waiting for a wonderful thing to happen.

MRS. LINDE.   What is it that you are waiting for?

NORA.   Oh, you wouldn't understand. Go in to them, I will come in a moment.   425
[*MRS. LINDE goes into the dining-room.* NORA *stands still for a little while, as if to compose
herself. Then she looks at her watch.*] Five o'clock. Seven hours till midnight; and
then four-and-twenty hours till the next midnight. Then the Tarantella will be
over. Twenty-four and seven? Thirty-one hours to live.

HELMER. *[from the doorway on the right]* Where's my little skylark?

NORA. *[going to him with her arms outstretched]* Here she is!

ACT 3

THE SAME SCENE. *The table has been placed in the middle of the stage, with chairs round it. A lamp is burning on the table. The door into the hall stands open. Dance music is heard in the room above. MRS. LINDE is sitting at the table idly turning over the leaves of a book; she tries to read, but does not seem able to collect her thoughts. Every now and then she listens intently for a sound at the outer door.*

MRS. LINDE. *[looking at her watch]* Not yet—and the time is nearly up. If only he does not—. *[listens again]* Ah, there he is. *[Goes into the hall and opens the outer door carefully. Light footsteps are heard on the stairs. She whispers.]* Come in. There is no one here.

KROGSTAD. *[in the doorway]* I found a note from you at home. What does this mean?

MRS. LINDE. It is absolutely necessary that I should have a talk with you.

KROGSTAD. Really? And is it absolutely necessary that it should be here?

MRS. LINDE. It is impossible where I live; there is no private entrance to 5
my rooms. Come in; we are quite alone. The maid is asleep, and the Helmers are at the dance upstairs.

KROGSTAD. *[coming into the room]* Are the Helmers really at a dance to-night?

MRS. LINDE. Yes, why not?

KROGSTAD. Certainly—why not?

MRS. LINDE. Now, Nils, let us have a talk.

KROGSTAD. Can we two have anything to talk about? 10

MRS. LINDE. We have a great deal to talk about.

KROGSTAD. I shouldn't have thought so.

MRS. LINDE. No, you have never properly understood me.

KROGSTAD. Was there anything else to understand except what was obvious to all the world—a heartless woman jilts a man when a more lucrative chance turns up?

MRS. LINDE. Do you believe I am as absolutely heartless as all that? And 15
do you believe that I did it with a light heart?

KROGSTAD. Didn't you?

MRS. LINDE. Nils, did you really think that?

KROGSTAD. If it were as you say, why did you write to me as you did at the time?

MRS. LINDE. I could do nothing else. As I had to break with you, it was my duty also to put an end to all that you felt for me.

KROGSTAD. *[wringing his hands]* So that was it. And all this—only for the 20
sake of money!

MRS. LINDE. You must not forget that I had a helpless mother and two little brothers. We couldn't wait for you, Nils; your prospects seemed hopeless then.

KROGSTAD. That may be so, but you had no right to throw me over for any one else's sake.

MRS. LINDE. Indeed I don't know. Many a time did I ask myself if I had the right to do it.

KROGSTAD. [*more gently*] When I lost you, it was as if all the solid ground went from under my feet. Look at me now—I am a shipwrecked man clinging to a bit of wreckage.

MRS. LINDE. But help may be near. 25

KROGSTAD. It *was* near; but then you came and stood in my way.

MRS. LINDE. Unintentionally, Nils. It was only to-day that I learnt it was your place I was going to take in the Bank.

KROGSTAD. I believe you, if you say so. But now that you know it, are you not going to give it up to me?

MRS. LINDE. No, because that would not benefit you in the least.

KROGSTAD. Oh, benefit, benefit—I would have done it whether or no. 30

MRS. LINDE. I have learnt to act prudently. Life, and hard, bitter necessity have taught me that.

KROGSTAD. And life has taught me not to believe in fine speeches.

MRS. LINDE. Then life has taught you something very reasonable. But deeds you must believe in?

KROGSTAD. What do you mean by that?

MRS. LINDE. You said you were like a shipwrecked man clinging to some 35 wreckage.

KROGSTAD. I had good reason to say so.

MRS. LINDE. Well, I am like a shipwrecked woman clinging to some wreckage—no one to mourn for, no one to care for.

KROGSTAD. It was your own choice.

MRS. LINDE. There was no other choice—then.

KROGSTAD. Well, what now? 40

MRS. LINDE. Nils, how would it be if we two shipwrecked people could join forces?

KROGSTAD. What are you saying?

MRS. LINDE. Two on the same piece of wreckage would stand a better chance than each on their own.

KROGSTAD. Christine!

MRS. LINDE. What do you suppose brought me to town? 45

KROGSTAD. Do you mean that you gave me a thought?

MRS. LINDE. I could not endure life without work. All my life, as long as I can remember, I have worked, and it has been my greatest and only pleasure. But now I am quite alone in the world—my life is so dreadfully empty and I feel so forsaken. There is not the least pleasure in working for one's self. Nils, give me someone and something to work for.

KROGSTAD. I don't trust that. It is nothing but a woman's overstrained sense of generosity that prompts you to make such an offer of yourself.

MRS. LINDE. Have you ever noticed anything of the sort in me?

KROGSTAD. Could you really do it? Tell me—do you know all about my 50 past life?

MRS. LINDE. Yes.

KROGSTAD. And do you know what they think of me here?

MRS. LINDE. You seemed to me to imply that with me you might have been quite another man.

KROGSTAD. I am certain of it.

MRS. LINDE. Is it too late now? 55

KROGSTAD. Christine, are you saying this deliberately? Yes, I am sure you are. I see it in your face. Have you really the courage, then—?

MRS. LINDE. I want to be a mother to someone, and your children need a mother. We two need each other. Nils, I have faith in your real character—I can dare anything together with you.

KROGSTAD. [*grasps her hands*] Thanks, thanks, Christine! Now I shall find a way to clear myself in the eyes of the world. Ah, but I forgot——

MRS. LINDE. [*listening*] Hush! The Tarantella! Go, go!

KROGSTAD. Why? What is it? 60

MRS. LINDE. Do you hear them up there? When that is over, we may expect them back.

KROGSTAD. Yes, yes—I will go. But it is all no use. Of course you are not aware what steps I have taken in the matter of the Helmers.

MRS. LINDE. Yes, I know all about that.

KROGSTAD. And in spite of that have you the courage to—?

MRS. LINDE. I understand very well to what lengths a man like you might 65
be driven by despair.

KROGSTAD. If I could only undo what I have done!

MRS. LINDE. You can. Your letter is lying in the letter-box now.

KROGSTAD. Are you sure of that?

MRS. LINDE. Quite sure, but——

KROGSTAD. [*with a searching look at her*] Is that what it all means?—that you 70
want to save your friend at any cost? Tell me frankly. Is that it?

MRS. LINDE. Nils, a woman who has once sold herself for another's sake, doesn't do it a second time.

KROGSTAD. I will ask for my letter back.

MRS. LINDE. No, no.

KROGSTAD. Yes, of course I will. I will wait here till Helmer comes; I will tell him he must give me my letter back—that it only concerns my dismissal—that he is not to read it——

MRS. LINDE. No, Nils, you must not recall your letter. 75

KROGSTAD. But, tell me, wasn't it for that very purpose that you asked me to meet you here?

MRS. LINDE. In my first moment of fright, it was. But twenty-four hours have elapsed since then, and in that time I have witnessed incredible things in this house. Helmer must know all about it. This unhappy secret must be disclosed; they must have a complete understanding between them, which is impossible with all this concealment and falsehood going on.

KROGSTAD. Very well, if you will take the responsibility. But there is one thing I can do in any case, and I shall do it at once.

MRS. LINDE. [*listening*] You must be quick and go! The dance is over; we are not safe a moment longer.

KROGSTAD. I will wait for you below. 80

MRS. LINDE.   Yes, do. You must see me back to my door.

KROGSTAD.   I have never had such an amazing piece of good fortune in my life.

[*Goes out through the outer door. The door between the room and the hall remains open.*]

MRS. LINDE.   [*tidying up the room and laying her hat and cloak ready*] What a difference! what a difference! Someone to work for and live for—a home to bring comfort into. That I will do, indeed. I wish they would be quick and come— [*listens*] Ah, there they are now. I must put on my things.

[*Takes up her hat and cloak. HELMER's and NORA's voices are heard outside; a key is turned, and HELMER brings NORA almost by force into the hall. She is in an Italian costume with a large black shawl round her; he is in evening dress and a black domino which is flying open.*]

NORA.   [*hanging back in the doorway, and struggling with him*] No, no, no!— don't take me in. I want to go upstairs again; I don't want to leave so early.

HELMER.   But, my dearest Nora——   85

NORA.   Please, Torvald dear—please, *please*—only an hour more.

HELMER.   Not a single minute, my sweet Nora. You know that was our agreement. Come along into the room; you are catching cold standing there.

[*He brings her gently into the room, in spite of her resistance.*]

MRS. LINDE.   Good evening.

NORA.   Christine!

HELMER.   You here, so late, Mrs. Linde?   90

MRS. LINDE.   Yes, you must excuse me; I was so anxious to see Nora in her dress.

NORA.   Have you been sitting here waiting for me?

MRS. LINDE.   Yes, unfortunately I came too late, you had already gone upstairs; and I thought I couldn't go away again without having seen you.

HELMER.   [*taking off NORA's shawl*] Yes, take a good look at her. I think she is worth looking at. Isn't she charming, Mrs. Linde?

MRS. LINDE.   Yes, indeed she is.   95

HELMER.   Doesn't she look remarkably pretty? Everyone thought so at the dance. But she is terribly self-willed, this sweet little person. What are we to do with her? You will hardly believe that I had almost to bring her away by force.

NORA.   Torvald, you will repent not having let me stay, even if it were only for half an hour.

HELMER.   Listen to her, Mrs. Linde! She had danced her Tarantella, and it had been a tremendous success, as it deserved—although possibly the performance was a trifle too realistic—a little more so, I mean, than was strictly compatible with the limitations of art. But never mind about that! The chief thing is, she had made a success—she had made a tremendous success. Do you think I was going to let her remain there after that, and spoil the effect? No indeed! I took my charming little Capri maiden—my capricious little Capri maiden, I should say—on my arm; took one quick turn round the room; a curtsey on either side, and, as they say in novels, the beautiful apparition disappeared. An exit ought always to be effective, Mrs. Linde; but that is what I cannot make Nora understand.

Pooh! this room is hot. [*throws his domino on a chair and opens the door of his room*]
Hullo! it's all dark in here. Oh, of course—excuse me——.

[*He goes in and lights some candles.*]

NORA. [*in a hurried and breathless whisper*] Well?
MRS. LINDE. [*in a low voice*] I have had a talk with him.   100
NORA. Yes, and——
MRS. LINDE. Nora, you must tell your husband all about it.
NORA. [*in an expressionless voice*] I knew it.
MRS. LINDE. You have nothing to be afraid of as far as Krogstad is concerned;
but you must tell him.
NORA. I won't tell him.   105
MRS. LINDE. Then the letter will.
NORA. Thank you, Christine. Now I know what I must do. Hush——!
HELMER. [*coming in again*] Well, Mrs. Linde, have you admired her?
MRS. LINDE. Yes, and now I will say good-night.
HELMER. What, already? Is this yours, this knitting?   110
MRS. LINDE. [*taking it*] Yes, thank you, I had very nearly forgotten it.
HELMER. So you knit?
MRS. LINDE. Of course.
HELMER. Do you know, you ought to embroider.
MRS. LINDE. Really? Why?   115
HELMER. Yes, it's far more becoming. Let me show you. You hold the embroi-
dery thus in your left hand, and use the needle with the right—like this—with a
long, easy sweep. Do you see?
MRS. LINDE. Yes, perhaps——
HELMER. But in the case of knitting—that can never be anything but ungrace-
ful; look here—the arms close together, the knitting-needles going up and down—
it has a sort of Chinese effect—. That was really excellent champagne they gave us.
MRS. LINDE. Well,—good-night, Nora, and don't be self-willed any more.
HELMER. That's right, Mrs. Linde.   120
MRS. LINDE. Good-night, Mr. Helmer.
HELMER. [*accompanying her to the door*] Good-night, good-night. I hope you
will get home all right. I should be very happy to—but you haven't any great
distance to go. Good-night, good-night. [*She goes out; he shuts the door after her, and
comes in again.*] Ah!—at last we have got rid of her. She is a frightful bore, that
woman.
NORA. Aren't you very tired, Torvald?
HELMER. No, not in the least.
NORA. Nor sleepy?   125
HELMER. Not a bit. On the contrary, I feel extraordinarily lively. And you?—
you really look both tired and sleepy.
NORA. Yes, I am very tired. I want to go to sleep at once.
HELMER. There, you see it was quite right of me not to let you stay there
any longer.
NORA. Everything you do is quite right, Torvald.
HELMER. [*kissing her on the forehead*] Now my little skylark is speaking reason-   130
ably. Did you notice what good spirits Rank was in this evening?

NORA.   Really? Was he? I didn't speak to him at all.

HELMER.   And I very little, but I have not for a long time seen him in such good form. [*looks for a while at her and then goes nearer to her*] It is delightful to be at home by ourselves again, to be all alone with you—you fascinating, charming little darling!

NORA.   Don't look at me like that, Torvald.

HELMER.   Why shouldn't I look at my dearest treasure?—at all the beauty that is mine, all my very own?

NORA.   [*going to the other side of the table*] You mustn't say things like that to me to-night.   135

HELMER.   [*following her*] You have still got the Tarantella in your blood, I see. And it makes you more captivating than ever. Listen—the guests are beginning to go now. [*in a lower voice*] Nora—soon the whole house will be quiet.

NORA.   Yes, I hope so.

HELMER.   Yes, my own darling Nora. Do you know, when I am out at a party with you like this, why I speak so little to you, keep away from you, and only send a stolen glance in your direction now and then?—do you know why I do that? It is because I make believe to myself that we are secretly in love, and you are my secretly promised bride, and that no one suspects there is anything between us.

NORA.   Yes, yes—I know very well your thoughts are with me all the time.

HELMER.   And when we are leaving, and I am putting the shawl over your   140
beautiful young shoulders—on your lovely neck—then I imagine that you are my young bride and that we have just come from the wedding, and I am bringing you for the first time into our home—to be alone with you for the first time— quite alone with my shy little darling! All this evening I have longed for nothing but you. When I watched the seductive figures of the Tarantella, my blood was on fire; I could endure it no longer, and that was why I brought you down so early——

NORA.   Go away, Torvald! You must let me go. I won't——

HELMER.   What's that? You're joking, my little Nora! You won't—you won't? Am I not your husband—?

[*A knock is heard at the outer door.*]

NORA.   [*starting*] Did you hear——?

HELMER.   [*going into the hall*] Who is it?

RANK.   [*outside*] It is I. May I come in for a moment?   145

HELMER.   [*in a fretful whisper*] Oh, what does he want now? [*aloud*] Wait a minute! [*unlocks the door*] Come, that's kind of you not to pass by our door.

RANK.   I thought I heard your voice, and felt as if I should like to look in. [*with a swift glance round*] Ah, yes!—these dear familiar rooms. You are very happy and cosy in here, you two.

HELMER.   It seems to me that you looked after yourself pretty well upstairs too.

RANK.   Excellently. Why shouldn't I? Why shouldn't one enjoy everything in this world?—at any rate as much as one can, and as long as one can. The wine was capital——

HELMER. Especially the champagne.   150

RANK. So you noticed that too? It is almost incredible how much I managed to put away!

NORA. Torvald drank a great deal of champagne tonight, too.

RANK. Did he?

NORA. Yes, and he is always in such good spirits afterwards.

RANK. Well, why should one not enjoy a merry evening after a well-spent   155
day?

HELMER. Well spent? I am afraid I can't take credit for that.

RANK. [*clapping him on the back*] But I can, you know!

NORA. Doctor Rank, you must have been occupied with some scientific investigation to-day.

RANK. Exactly.

HELMER. Just listen!—little Nora talking about scientific investigations!   160

NORA. And may I congratulate you on the result?

RANK. Indeed you may.

NORA. Was it favourable, then?

RANK. The best possible, for both doctor and patient—certainty.

NORA. [*quickly and searchingly*] Certainty?   165

RANK. Absolute certainty. So wasn't I entitled to make a merry evening of it after that?

NORA. Yes, you certainly were, Doctor Rank.

HELMER. I think so too, so long as you don't have to pay for it in the morning.

RANK. Oh well, one can't have anything in this life without paying for it.

NORA. Doctor Rank—are you fond of fancy-dress balls?   170

RANK. Yes, if there is a fine lot of pretty costumes.

NORA. Tell me—what shall we two wear at the next?

HELMER. Little featherbrain!—are you thinking of the next already?

RANK. We two? Yes, I can tell you. You shall go as a good fairy——

HELMER. Yes, but what do you suggest as an appropriate costume for that?   175

RANK. Let your wife go dressed just as she is in everyday life.

HELMER. That was really very prettily turned. But can't you tell us what you will be?

RANK. Yes, my dear friend, I have quite made up my mind about that.

HELMER. Well?

RANK. At the next fancy dress ball I shall be invisible.   180

HELMER. That's a good joke!

RANK. There is a big black hat—have you never heard of hats that make you invisible? If you put one on, no one can see you.

HELMER. [*suppressing a smile*] Yes, you are quite right.

RANK. But I am clean forgetting what I came for. Helmer, give me a cigar—one of the dark Havanas.

HELMER. With the greatest pleasure. [*offers him his case*]   185

RANK. [*takes a cigar and cuts off the end*] Thanks.

NORA. [*striking a match*] Let me give you a light.

RANK. Thank you. [*She holds the match for him to light his cigar.*] And now good-bye!

HELMER.   Good-bye, good-bye, dear old man!

NORA.   Sleep well, Doctor Rank.   190

RANK.   Thank you for that wish.

NORA.   Wish me the same.

RANK.   You? Well, if you want me to sleep well! And thanks for the light.

[*He nods to them both and goes out.*]

HELMER.   [*in a subdued voice*] He has drunk more than he ought.

NORA.   [*absently*] Maybe. [*HELMER takes a bunch of keys out of his pocket and*   195
goes into the hall.] Torvald! what are you going to do there?

HELMER.   Empty the letter-box; it is quite full; there will be no room to
put the newspaper in to-morrow morning.

NORA.   Are you going to work to-night?

HELMER.   You know quite well I'm not. What is this? Some one has been
at the lock.

NORA.   At the lock—?

HELMER.   Yes, someone has. What can it mean? I should never have thought   200
the maid—. Here is a broken hairpin. Nora, it is one of yours.

NORA.   [*quickly*] Then it must have been the children—

HELMER.   Then you must get them out of those ways. There, at last I have
got it open. [*Takes out the contents of the letter-box, and calls to the kitchen.*] Helen!—
Helen, put out the light over the front door. [*Goes back into the room and shuts the
door into the hall. He holds out his hand full of letters.*] Look at that—look what a
heap of them there are. [*turning them over*] What on earth is that?

NORA.   [*at the window*] The letter—No! Torvald, no!

HELMER.   Two cards—of Rank's.

NORA.   Of Doctor Rank's?   205

HELMER.   [*looking at them*] Doctor Rank. They were on the top. He must
have put them in when he went out.

NORA.   Is there anything written on them?

HELMER.   There is a black cross over the name. Look there—what an uncomfortable idea! It looks as if he were announcing his own death.

NORA.   It is just what he is doing.

HELMER.   What? Do you know anything about it? Has he said anything to   210
you?

NORA.   Yes. He told me that when the cards came it would be his leave-
taking from us. He means to shut himself up and die.

HELMER.   My poor old friend. Certainly I knew we should not have him
very long with us. But so soon! And so he hides himself away like a wounded
animal.

NORA.   If it has to happen, it is best it should be without a word—don't
you think so, Torvald?

HELMER.   [*walking up and down*] He had so grown into our lives. I can't
think of him as having gone out of them. He, with his sufferings and his loneliness,
was like a cloudy background to our sunlit happiness. Well, perhaps it is best so.
For him, anyway. [*standing still*] And perhaps for us too, Nora. We two are thrown
quite upon each other now. [*puts his arms round her*] My darling wife, I don't feel
as if I could hold you tight enough. Do you know, Nora, I have often wished

that you might be threatened by some great danger, so that I might risk my life's blood, and everything, for your sake.

NORA. [*disengages herself, and says firmly and decidedly*] Now you must read your letters, Torvald. 215

HELMER. No, no; not to-night. I want to be with you, my darling wife.

NORA. With the thought of your friend's death——

HELMER. You are right, it has affected us both. Something ugly has come between us—the thought of the horrors of death. We must try and rid our minds of that. Until then—we will each go to our own room.

NORA. [*hanging on his neck*] Good-night, Torvald—Good-night!

HELMER. [*kissing her on the forehead*]. Good-night, my little singing-bird. Sleep sound, Nora. Now I will read my letters through. 220

[*He takes his letters and goes into his room, shutting the door after him.*]

NORA. [*gropes distractedly about, seizes* HELMER'S *domino, throws it round her, while she says in quick, hoarse, spasmodic whispers*] Never to see him again. Never! Never! [*puts her shawl over her head*] Never to see my children again either—never again. Never! Never!—Ah! the icy, black water—the unfathomable depths—If only it were over! He has got it now—now he is reading it. Good-by, Torvald and my children!

[*She is about to rush out through the hall, when* HELMER *opens his door hurriedly and stands with an open letter in his hand.*]

HELMER. Nora!

NORA. Ah!——

HELMER. What is this? Do you know what is in this letter?

NORA. Yes, I know. Let me go! Let me get out! 225

HELMER. [*holding her back*] Where are you going?

NORA. [*trying to get free*] You shan't save me, Torvald!

HELMER. [*reeling*] True? Is this true, that I read here? Horrible! No, no—it is impossible that it can be true.

NORA. It is true. I have loved you above everything else in the world.

HELMER. Oh, don't let us have any silly excuses. 230

NORA. [*taking a step towards him*] Torvald——!

HELMER. Miserable creature—what have you done?

NORA. Let me go. You shall not suffer for my sake. You shall not take it upon yourself.

HELMER. No tragedy airs, please. [*locks the hall door*] Here you shall stay and give me an explanation. Do you understand what you have done? Answer me? Do you understand what you have done?

NORA. [*looks steadily at him and says with a growing look of coldness in her face*] Yes, now I am beginning to understand thoroughly. 235

HELMER. [*walking about the room*] What a horrible awakening! All these eight years—she who was my joy and pride—a hypocrite, a liar—worse, worse—a criminal! The unutterable ugliness of it all! For shame! For shame! [NORA *is silent and looks steadily at him. He stops in front of her.*] I ought to have suspected that something of the sort would happen. I ought to have foreseen it. All your father's want of principle—be silent!—all your father's want of principle has come out in you. No religion, no morality, no sense of duty—. How I am punished for having winked at what he did! I did it for your sake, and this is how you repay me.

NORA.   Yes, that's just it.

HELMER.   Now you have destroyed all my happiness. You have ruined all my future. It is horrible to think of! I am in the power of an unscrupulous man; he can do what he likes with me, ask anything he likes of me, give me any orders he pleases—I dare not refuse. And I must sink to such miserable depths because of a thoughtless woman!

NORA.   When I am out of the way, you will be free.

HELMER.   No fine speeches, please. Your father had always plenty of those   240 ready, too. What good would it be to me if you were out of the way, as you say? Not the slightest. He can make the affair known everywhere; and if he does, I may be falsely suspected of having been a party to your criminal action. Very likely people will think I was behind it all—that it was I who prompted you! And I have to thank you for all this—you whom I have cherished during the whole of our married life. Do you understand now what it is you have done for me?

NORA.   [*coldly and quietly*] Yes.

HELMER.   It is so incredible that I can't take it in. But we must come to some understanding. Take off that shawl. Take it off, I tell you. I must try and appease him some way or another. The matter must be hushed up at any cost. And as for you and me, it must appear as if everything between us were just as before—but naturally only in the eyes of the world. You will still remain in my house, that is a matter of course. But I shall not allow you to bring up the children; I dare not trust them to you. To think that I should be obliged to say so to one whom I have loved so dearly, and whom I still——. No, that is all over. From this moment happiness is not the question; all that concerns us is to save the remains, the fragments, the appearance——

[*A ring is heard at the front-door bell.*]

HELMER.   [*with a start*] What is that? So late! Can the worst——? Can he ——? Hide yourself, Nora. Say you are ill.

[*NORA stands motionless. HELMER goes and unlocks the hall door.*]

MAID.   [*half-dressed, comes to the door*] A letter for the mistress.

HELMER.   Give it to me. [*takes the letter, and shuts the door*] Yes, it is from   245 him. You shall not have it; I will read it myself.

NORA.   Yes, read it.

HELMER.   [*standing by the lamp*] I scarcely have the courage to do it. It may mean ruin for both of us. No, I must know. [*tears open the letter, runs his eye over a few lines, looks at a paper enclosed and gives a shout of joy*] Nora! [*She looks at him questioningly.*] Nora!—No, I must read it once again——. Yes, it is true! I am saved! Nora, I am saved!

NORA.   And I?

HELMER.   You too, of course; we are both saved, both you and I. Look, he sends you your bond back. He says he regrets and repents—that a happy change in his life—never mind what he says! We are saved, Nora! No one can do anything to you. Oh, Nora, Nora!—no, first I must destroy these hateful things. Let me see——. [*takes a look at the bond*] No, no, I won't look at it. The whole thing shall be nothing but a bad dream to me. [*tears up the bond and both letters, throws them all into the stove, and watches them burn*] There—now it doesn't exist any longer. He says that since Christmas Eve you——. These must have been three dreadful days for you, Nora.

NORA. I have fought a hard fight these three days. 250

HELMER. And suffered agonies, and seen no way out but——. No, we won't call any of the horrors to mind. We will only shout with joy, and keep saying "It's all over! It's all over!" Listen to me, Nora. You don't seem to realise that it is all over. What is this?—such a cold, set face! My poor little Nora, I quite understand; you don't feel as if you could believe that I have forgiven you. But it is true, Nora, I swear it; I have forgiven you everything. I know that what you did, you did out of love for me.

NORA. That is true.

HELMER. You have loved me as a wife ought to love her husband. Only you had not sufficient knowledge to judge of the means you used. But do you suppose you are any the less dear to me, because you don't understand how to act on your own responsibility? No, no; only lean on me; I will advise you and direct you. I should not be a man if this womanly helplessness did not just give you a double attractiveness in my eyes. You must not think any more about the hard things I said in my first moment of consternation, when I thought everything was going to overwhelm me. I have forgiven you, Nora; I swear to you I have forgiven you.

NORA. Thank you for your forgiveness.

[*She goes out through the door to the right.*]

HELMER. No, don't go——. [*looks in*] What are you doing in there? 255

NORA. [*from within*] Taking off my fancy dress.

HELMER. [*standing at the open door*] Yes, do. Try and calm yourself, and make your mind easy again, my frightened little singing-bird. Be at rest, and feel secure; I have broad wings to shelter you under. [*walks up and down by the door*] How warm and cosy our home is, Nora. Here is shelter for you; here I will protect you like a hunted dove that I have saved from a hawk's claws. I will bring peace to your poor beating heart. It will come, little by little, Nora, believe me. Tomorrow morning you will look upon it all quite differently; soon everything will be just as it was before. Very soon you won't need me to assure you that I have forgiven you; you will yourself feel the certainty that I have done so. Can you suppose I should ever think of such a thing as repudiating you, or even reproaching you? You have no idea what a true man's heart is like, Nora. There is something so indescribably sweet and satisfying, to a man, in the knowledge that he has forgiven his wife—forgiven her freely, and with all his heart. It seems as if that had made her, as it were, doubly his own; he has given her a new life, so to speak; and she has in a way become both wife and child to him. So you shall be for me after this, my little scared, helpless darling. Have no anxiety about anything, Nora; only be frank and open with me, and I will serve as will and conscience both to you——. What is this? Not gone to bed? Have you changed your things?

NORA. [*in everyday dress*] Yes, Torvald, I have changed my things now.

HELMER. But what for?—so late as this.

NORA. I shall not sleep to-night. 260

HELMER. But, my dear Nora——

NORA. [*looking at her watch*] It is not so very late. Sit down here, Torvald. You and I have much to say to one another.

[*She sits down at one side of the table.*]

HELMER. Nora—what is this?—this cold, set face?

NORA. Sit down. It will take some time; I have a lot to talk over with you.

HELMER. [*sits down at the opposite side of the table*] You alarm me, Nora!—   265
and I don't understand you.

NORA. No, that is just it. You don't understand me, and I have never understood you either—before to-night. No, you mustn't interrupt me. You must simply listen to what I say. Torvald, this is a settling of accounts.

HELMER. What do you mean by that?

NORA. [*after a short silence*] Isn't there one thing that strikes you as strange in our sitting here like this?

HELMER. What is that?

NORA. We have been married now eight years. Does it not occur to you   270
that this is the first time we two, you and I, husband and wife, have had a serious conversation?

HELMER. What do you mean by serious?

NORA. In all these eight years—longer than that—from the very beginning of our acquaintance, we have never exchanged a word on any serious subject.

HELMER. Was it likely that I would be continually and for ever telling you about worries that you could not help me to bear?

NORA. I am not speaking about business matters. I say that we have never sat down in earnest together to try and get at the bottom of anything.

HELMER. But, dearest Nora, would it have been any good to you?   275

NORA. That is just it; you have never understood me. I have been greatly wronged, Torvald—first by papa and then by you.

HELMER. What! By us two—by us two, who have loved you better than anyone else in the world?

NORA. [*shaking her head*] You have never loved me. You have only thought it pleasant to be in love with me.

HELMER. Nora, what do I hear you saying?

NORA. It is perfectly true, Torvald. When I was at home with papa, he   280
told me his opinion about everything, and so I had the same opinions; and if I differed from him I concealed the fact, because he would not have liked it. He called me his doll-child, and he played with me just as I used to play with my dolls. And when I came to live with you——

HELMER. What sort of an expression is that to use about our marriage?

NORA. [*undisturbed*] I mean that I was simply transferred from papa's hands into yours. You arranged everything according to your own taste, and so I got the same tastes as you—or else I pretended to, I am really not quite sure which— I think sometimes the one and sometimes the other. When I look back on it, it seems to me as if I had been living here like a poor woman—just from hand to mouth. I have existed merely to perform tricks for you, Torvald. But you would have it so. You and papa have committed a great sin against me. It is your fault that I have made nothing of my life.

HELMER. How unreasonable and how ungrateful you are, Nora! Have you not been happy here?

NORA. No, I have never been happy. I thought I was, but it has never really been so.

HELMER. Not—not happy! 285

NORA. No, only merry. And you have always been so kind to me. But our home has been nothing but a playroom. I have been your doll-wife, just as at home I was papa's doll-child; and here the children have been my dolls. I thought it great fun when you played with me, just as they thought it great fun when I played with them. That is what our marriage has been, Torvald.

HELMER. There is some truth in what you say—exaggerated and strained as your view of it is. But for the future it shall be different. Playtime shall be over, and lesson-time shall begin.

NORA. Whose lessons? Mine, or the children's?

HELMER. Both yours and the children's, my darling Nora.

NORA. Alas, Torvald, you are not the man to educate me into being a proper 290 wife for you.

HELMER. And you can say that!

NORA. And I—how am I fitted to bring up the children?

HELMER. Nora!

NORA. Didn't you say so yourself a little while ago—that you dare not trust me to bring them up?

HELMER. In a moment of anger! Why do you pay any heed to that? 295

NORA. Indeed, you were perfectly right. I am not fit for the task. There is another task I must undertake first. I must try and educate myself—you are not the man to help me in that. I must do that for myself. And that is why I am going to leave you now.

HELMER. [*springing up*] What do you say?

NORA. I must stand quite alone, if I am to understand myself and everything about me. It is for that reason that I cannot remain with you any longer.

HELMER. Nora! Nora!

NORA. I am going away from here now, at once. I am sure Christine will 300 take me in for the night——

HELMER. You are out of your mind! I won't allow it! I forbid you!

NORA. It is no use forbidding me anything any longer. I will take with me what belongs to myself. I will take nothing from you, either now or later.

HELMER. What sort of madness is this!

NORA. To-morrow I shall go home—I mean, to my old home. It will be easiest for me to find something to do there.

HELMER. You blind, foolish woman! 305

NORA. I must try and get some sense, Torvald.

HELMER. To desert your home, your husband and your children! And you don't consider what people will say!

NORA. I cannot consider that at all. I only know that it is necessary for me.

HELMER. It's shocking. This is how you would neglect your most sacred duties.

NORA. What do you consider my most sacred duties? 310

HELMER. Do I need to tell you that? Are they not your duties to your husband and your children?

NORA. I have other duties just as sacred.

HELMER.   That you have not. What duties could those be?

NORA.   Duties to myself.

HELMER.   Before all else, you are a wife and a mother.   315

NORA.   I don't believe that any longer. I believe that before all else I am a reasonable human being, just as you are—or, at all events, that I must try and become one. I know quite well, Torvald, that most people would think you right, and that views of that kind are to be found in books; but I can no longer content myself with what most people say, or with what is found in books. I must think over things for myself and get to understand them.

HELMER.   Can you not understand your place in your own home? Have you not a reliable guide in such matters as that?—have you no religion?

NORA.   I am afraid, Torvald, I do not exactly know what religion is.

HELMER.   What are you saying?

NORA.   I know nothing but what the clergyman said when I went to be   320
confirmed. He told us that religion was this, and that, and the other. When I am away from all this, and am alone, I will look into that matter too. I will see if what the clergyman said is true, or at all events if it is true for me.

HELMER.   This is unheard of in a girl of your age! But if religion cannot lead you aright, let me try and awaken your conscience. I suppose you have some moral sense? Or—answer me—am I to think you have none?

NORA.   I assure you, Torvald, that is not an easy question to answer. I really don't know. The thing perplexes me altogether. I only know that you and I look at it in quite a different light. I am learning, too, that the law is quite another thing from what I supposed; but I find it impossible to convince myself that the law is right. According to it a woman has no right to spare her old dying father, or to save her husband's life. I can't believe that.

HELMER.   You talk like a child. You don't understand the conditions of the world in which you live.

NORA.   No, I don't. But now I am going to try. I am going to see if I can make out who is right, the world or I.

HELMER.   You are ill, Nora; you are delirious; I almost think you are out   325
of your mind.

NORA.   I have never felt my mind so clear and certain as to-night.

HELMER.   And is it with a clear and certain mind that you forsake your husband and your children?

NORA.   Yes, it is.

HELMER.   Then there is only one possible explanation.

NORA.   What is that?   330

HELMER.   You do not love me any more.

NORA.   No, that is just it.

HELMER.   Nora!—and you can say that?

NORA.   It gives me great pain, Torvald, for you have always been so kind to me, but I cannot help it. I do not love you any more.

HELMER.   [*regaining his composure*] Is that a clear and certain conviction too?   335

NORA.   Yes, absolutely clear and certain. That is the reason why I will not stay here any longer.

HELMER.   And can you tell me what I have done to forfeit your love?

NORA.   Yes, indeed I can. It was to-night, when the wonderful thing did not happen; then I saw you were not the man I had thought you.

HELMER. Explain yourself better—I don't understand you.

NORA. I have waited so patiently for eight years; for, goodness knows, I   340
knew very well that wonderful things don't happen every day. Then this horrible
misfortune came upon me; and then I felt quite certain that the wonderful thing
was going to happen at last. When Krogstad's letter was lying out there, never
for a moment did I imagine that you would consent to accept this man's conditions.
I was so absolutely certain that you would say to him: Publish the thing to the
whole world. And when that was done——

HELMER. Yes, what then?—when I had exposed my wife to shame and disgrace?

NORA. When that was done, I was so absolutely certain, you would come
forward and take everything upon yourself, and say: I am the guilty one.

HELMER. Nora——!

NORA. You mean that I would never have accepted such a sacrifice on
your part? No, of course not. But what would my assurances have been worth
against yours? That was the wonderful thing which I hoped for and feared; and
it was to prevent that, that I wanted to kill myself.

HELMER. I would gladly work night and day for you, Nora—bear sorrow   345
and want for your sake. But no man would sacrifice his honour for the one he
loves.

NORA. It is a thing hundreds of thousands of women have done.

HELMER. Oh, you think and talk like a heedless child.

NORA. Maybe. But you neither think nor talk like the man I could bind
myself to. As soon as your fear was over—and it was not fear for what threatened
me, but for what might happen to you—when the whole thing was past, as far as
you were concerned it was exactly as if nothing at all had happened. Exactly as
before, I was your little skylark, your doll, which you would in future treat with
doubly gentle care, because it was so brittle and fragile. [*getting up*] Torvald—it
was then it dawned upon me that for eight years I had been living here with a
strange man, and had borne him three children——. Oh, I can't bear to think of
it! I could tear myself into little bits!

HELMER. [*sadly*] I see, I see. An abyss has opened between us—there is no
denying it. But, Nora, would it not be possible to fill it up?

NORA. As I am now, I am no wife for you.   350

HELMER. I have it in me to become a different man.

NORA. Perhaps—if your doll is taken away from you.

HELMER. But to part!—to part from you! No, no, Nora, I can't understand
that idea.

NORA. [*going out to the right*] That makes it all the more certain that it must
be done.

[*She comes back with her cloak and hat and a small bag which she puts on a chair by the
table.*]

HELMER. Nora, Nora, not now! Wait till to-morrow.   355

NORA. [*putting on her cloak*] I cannot spend the night in a strange man's
room.

HELMER. But can't we live here like brother and sister——?

NORA. [*putting on her hat*] You know very well that would not last long.
[*puts the shawl round her*] Good-bye, Torvald. I won't see the little ones. I know

they are in better hands than mine. As I am now, I can be of no use to them.

HELMER.   But some day, Nora—some day?

NORA.   How can I tell? I have no idea what is going to become of me.   360

HELMER.   But you are my wife, whatever becomes of you.

NORA.   Listen, Torvald. I have heard that when a wife deserts her husband's house, as I am doing now, he is legally freed from all obligations towards her. In any case I set you free from all your obligations. You are not to feel yourself bound in the slightest way, any more than I shall. There must be perfect freedom on both sides. See here is your ring back. Give me mine.

HELMER.   That too?

NORA.   That too.

HELMER.   Here it is.   365

NORA.   That's right. Now it is all over. I have put the keys here. The maids know all about everything in the house—better than I do. To-morrow, after I have left her, Christine will come here and pack up my own things that I brought with me from home. I will have them sent after me.

HELMER.   All over! All over!—Nora, shall you never think of me again?

NORA.   I know I shall often think of you and the children and this house.

HELMER.   May I write to you, Nora?

NORA.   No—never. You must not do that.   370

HELMER.   But at least let me send you——

NORA.   Nothing—nothing——

HELMER.   Let me help you if you are in want.

NORA.   No. I can receive nothing from a stranger.

HELMER.   Nora—can I never be anything more than a stranger to you?   375

NORA.   [*taking her bag*] Ah, Torvald, the most wonderful thing of all would have to happen.

HELMER.   Tell me what that would be!

NORA.   Both you and I would have to be so changed that——. Oh, Torvald, I don't believe any longer in wonderful things happening.

HELMER.   But I will believe in it. Tell me? So changed that——?

NORA.   That our life together would be a real wedlock. Good-bye.   380

[*She goes out through the hall.*]

HELMER.   [*sinks down on a chair at the door and buries his face in his hands*] Nora! Nora! [*looks round, and rises*] Empty. She is gone. [*A hope flashes across his mind.*] The most wonderful thing of all——?

[*The sound of a door slamming is heard from below.*]

QUESTIONS

Act 1

1. What does the opening stage direction tell you about the Helmer family? About the time of year?

2. Describe the relationship between Nora and Torvald. How does Torvald treat Nora? How does she act with him?

3. Early in act 1 Torvald tells Nora: "No debt, no borrowing. There can be no freedom or beauty about a home life that depends on borrowing and debt." What general characteristic of Torvald's does this comment illustrate? What other instances of this type of behavior can you find in the play?

4. What has the economic situation of the Helmer family been in the past? Why is this situation about to change?

5. How is Mrs. Linde a parallel to Nora? A contrast? Why is it ironic that Nora helps Linde gain a position in the bank? How will this affect Krogstad? Nora?

6. How does Ibsen show you that Krogstad is a threat when he first appears?

7. Nora's scene with her children in act 1 is often cut in production. Why is the scene important? What does it show you about Nora and about the household?

8. What is Nora's secret? Her crime? Why did she commit the crime? How does she justify her actions? What new problems does she face at the close of act 1?

Act 2

9. What does the "stripped" Christmas tree at the opening of act 2 symbolize?

10. In conversation with Torvald, Nora refers to herself as "your little squirrel" and "your skylark." What does this imply about Nora's perception of her relationship to Torvald?

11. After Torvald sends Krogstad's dismissal, he tells Nora that "you will see I am man enough to take everything upon myself." How does this assertion conform to Nora's secret hopes? How is it ironic?

12. Describe Nora's relationship with Doctor Rank. Why does she flirt with him? Why is she distressed when he admits his love for her?

13. Why does Nora throw herself so wildly into the tarantella?

14. At the close of act 2 Nora asserts that "it is splendid to be waiting for a wonderful thing to happen." What is this "wonderful thing"?

Act 3

15. Why did Mrs. Linde reject Krogstad in the past? Why does she propose to join forces with him now? In what ways will this union differ from the marriage of Nora and Torvald?

16. What does Mrs. Linde decide to do about Krogstad's letter? Why?

17. How do Nora and Torvald react to the news of Doctor Rank's imminent death? How might you explain their reactions?

18. Describe Torvald's reaction to Krogstad's first letter. How does Nora respond to Torvald? How do you?

19. Explain what Nora learns about Torvald, herself, and her marriage as a result of Torvald's response to Krogstad's letter and the forgery.

GENERAL QUESTIONS

1. Which elements and aspects of *A Doll's House* are most realistic? What makes them realistic? Which are least realistic? Why?

2. Consider Ibsen's use of symbolism in the play, with specific reference to Doctor Rank, macaroons, the Christmas tree (decorated and stripped), the presents, the locked mailbox, the tarantella, Nora's black shawl, her final change of clothing in act 3, and the slamming of the door at the close of the play.

3. Discuss the extent to which Nora may be considered a victim of circumstances and society or a villain who is responsible for the problems in the play. Which view does Ibsen seem to take? What is your view? Why?

4. Describe the kinds of role-playing that characterize the Helmer marriage. To what degree does Nora play the role that Torvald expects? Is there any evidence to suggest that she knows she is playing a role? What degree of self-awareness, if any, characterizes Torvald's role-playing?

5. When Nora pleads to have Krogstad reinstated in the bank, Torvald refuses, asking, "is it to get about now that the new manager has changed his mind at his wife's bidding?" Later, when Torvald has read Krogstad's first letter, he claims that his marriage has been destroyed, but that he and Nora must "save the remains, the fragments, the appearance." Discuss Torvald's character in the light of these and similar statements. What concerns Torvald most about marriage? Life?

6. One of the themes that Ibsen explores in *A Doll's House* is the idea that weakness and corruption are passed in the blood from generation to generation. Examine this theme in connection with Krogstad and his sons, Nora and her children, Nora and her father, and Doctor Rank.

7. Discuss the ideas about individual growth, marriage, and social convention that the play explores. How are these ideas developed? How are they related? Which character most closely embodies and expresses Ibsen's ideas?

EDWARD ALBEE, *THE SANDBOX*

Edward Albee was the leading American playwright of the 1960s. His first play, *The Zoo Story*, was written in 1958, first performed in 1959 in Berlin, and published in 1960. This was followed by *The Sandbox* and *The Death of Bessie Smith* (1960), *The American Dream* (1961), and *Who's Afraid of Virginia Woolf* (1962), Albee's best-known play. This play still stands as the pinnacle of Albee's career; it had a highly successful run in New York City and was awarded the "Tony" as best play in 1963. Albee's work after

Who's Afraid of Virginia Woolf has met with mixed reactions. *Tiny Alice* (1964) was viewed as confusing and derivative, but *A Delicate Balance* (1966) and *Seascape* (1975) both won Pulitzer Prizes for drama. Other plays and adaptations have had short lives in the theater; one of Albee's more recent works, *The Lady from Dubuque* (1980), survived for only twelve performances on Broadway.

Several of Albee's early plays, including *The Sandbox*, represent the playwright's experimentation with nonrealistic staging and with Theater of the Absurd, a school of drama that evolved in Europe in the 1940s and 1950s. Dramatists of the Absurd use their plays to examine the foundations of character and existence, stripping away conventions of behavior and accidents of personality. Like the Existentialist philosophy on which the Absurdist school is based, most plays of the absurd begin with the assumption that life is irrational. In many Absurdist plays, language, action, and relationships become theatrical games in which the characters are conscious of their own fictional existence as characters in a play.

The Sandbox, written in 1959 and first performed in New York City in 1960, is an Absurdist play that deals with the emptiness of middle-class life and the American way of death. The characters are closer to types or symbols than they are to portrayals of individualized women and men. Grandma, the protagonist, is in conflict with her family, society, and death; only the last of these conflicts is resolved at the conclusion of the play. Mommy and Daddy represent Albee's vision of the American middle-class family reduced to its basic elements and patterns of behavior. Albee employs all the elements of drama to build meaning and impact into *The Sandbox*; plot, character, setting, and symbol all convey specific ideas about life and values in Albee's vision of America. The play also provides an excellent opportunity to look at the ways a playwright can use language, diction, and tone to shape meaning. Albee is a master of dialogue; his language defines the characters and directs the audience's response to the play. Repetition, parallel speech patterns, idiom, connotative words, and clichés are all skillfully employed to these ends.

EDWARD ALBEE (b. 1928)

The Sandbox

1960 (1959)

THE PLAYERS

The Young Man, 25, *a good-looking, well-built boy in a bathing suit*
Mommy, 55, *a well-dressed, imposing woman*
Daddy, 60, *a small man; gray, thin*
Grandma, 86, *a tiny, wizened woman with bright eyes*
The Musician, *no particular age, but young would be nice*

Note: When, in the course of the play, MOMMY and DADDY call each other by these names, there should be no suggestion of regionalism. These names are of empty affection and point up the pre-senility and vacuity of their characters.

The Scene: A bare stage, with only the following: Near the footlights, far stage-right, two simple chairs set side by side, facing the audience; near the footlights, far stage-left, a chair facing stage-right with a music stand before it; farther back, and stage-center, slightly elevated and raked, a large child's sandbox with a toy pail and shovel; the background is the sky, which alters from brightest day to deepest night.

At the beginning, it is brightest day; the YOUNG MAN is alone on stage, to the rear of the sandbox, and to one side. He is doing calisthenics; he does calisthenics until quite at the very end of the play. These calisthenics, employing the arms only, should suggest the beating and fluttering of wings. The YOUNG MAN is, after all, the Angel of Death.

MOMMY and DADDY enter from stage-left, MOMMY first.

MOMMY.   [*Motioning to DADDY*] Well, here we are; this is the beach.

DADDY.   [*Whining*] I'm cold.

MOMMY.   [*Dismissing him with a little laugh*] Don't be silly; it's as warm as toast. Look at that nice young man over there: *he* doesn't think it's cold. [*Waves to the YOUNG MAN*] Hello.

YOUNG MAN.   [*With an endearing smile*] Hi!

MOMMY.   [*Looking about*] This will do perfectly . . . don't you think so, Daddy?   5
There's sand there . . . and the water beyond. What do you think, Daddy?

DADDY.   [*Vaguely*] Whatever you say, Mommy.

MOMMY.   [*With the same little laugh*] Well, of course . . . whatever I say. Then, it's settled, is it?

DADDY.   [*Shrugs*] She's *your* mother, not mine.

MOMMY.   *I* know she's my mother. What do you take me for? [*A pause*] All right, now; let's get on with it. [*She shouts into the wings, stage-left.*] You! Out there! You can come in now.

[*The MUSICIAN enters, seats himself in the chair, stage-left, places music on the music stand, is ready to play. MOMMY nods approvingly.*]

MOMMY.   Very nice; very nice. Are you ready, Daddy? Let's go get Grandma.   10

DADDY.   Whatever you say, Mommy.

MOMMY.   [*Leading the way out, stage-left*] Of course, whatever I say. [*To the MUSICIAN*] You can begin now. [*The MUSICIAN begins playing; MOMMY and DADDY exit; the MUSICIAN, all the while playing, nods to the YOUNG MAN.*]

YOUNG MAN.   [*With the same endearing smile*] Hi!

[*After a moment, MOMMY and DADDY re-enter, carrying GRANDMA. She is borne in by their hands under her armpits; she is quite rigid; her legs are drawn up; her feet do not touch the ground; the expression on her ancient face is that of puzzlement and fear.*]

DADDY.   Where do we put her?

MOMMY.   [*The same little laugh*] Wherever I say, of course. Let me see . . .   15
well . . . all right, over there . . . in the sandbox. [*Pause*] Well, what are you waiting for, Daddy? . . . The sandbox!

[Together they carry GRANDMA *over to the sandbox and more or less dump her in.]*

GRANDMA. *[Righting herself to a sitting position; her voice a cross between a baby's laugh and cry]* Ahhhhhh! Graaaaa!
DADDY. *[Dusting himself]* What do we do now?
MOMMY. *[To the* MUSICIAN*]* You can stop now.

[The MUSICIAN *stops.]*

[Back to DADDY*]* What do you mean, what do we do now? We go over there and sit down, of course. *[To the* YOUNG MAN*]* Hello there.
YOUNG MAN. *[Again smiling]* Hi!

*[*MOMMY *and* DADDY *move to the chairs, stage-right, and sit down. A pause]*

GRANDMA. *[Same as before]* Ahhhhhh! Ah-haaaaaa! Graaaaaa!   20
DADDY. Do you think . . . do you think she's . . . comfortable?
MOMMY. *[Impatiently]* How would I know?
DADDY. *[Pause]* What do we do now?
MOMMY. *[As if remembering]* We . . . wait. We . . . sit here . . . and we wait . . . that's what we do.
DADDY. *[After a pause]* Shall we talk to each other?   25
MOMMY. *[With that little laugh; picking something off her dress]* Well, *you* can talk, if you want to . . . if you can think of anything to *say* . . . if you can think of anything *new.*
DADDY. *[Thinks]* No . . . I suppose not.
MOMMY. *[With a triumphant laugh]* Of course not!
GRANDMA. *[Banging the toy shovel against the pail]* Haaaaaa! Ah-haaaaaa!
MOMMY. *[Out over the audience]* Be quiet, Grandma . . . just be quiet, and   30
wait.

*[*GRANDMA *throws a shovelful of sand at* MOMMY.*]*

MOMMY. *[Still out over the audience]* She's throwing sand at me! You stop that, Grandma; you stop throwing sand at Mommy! *[To* DADDY*]* She's throwing sand at me.

*[*DADDY *looks around at* GRANDMA, *who screams at him.]*

GRANDMA. GRAAAAAA!
MOMMY. Don't look at her. Just . . . sit here . . . be very still . . . and wait. *[To the* MUSICIAN*]* You . . . uh . . . you go ahead and do whatever it is you do.

[The MUSICIAN *plays.]*
*[*MOMMY *and* DADDY *are fixed, staring out beyond the audience.* GRANDMA *looks at them, looks at the* MUSICIAN, *looks at the sandbox, throws down the shovel.]*

GRANDMA. Ah-haaaaaa! Graaaaaa! *[Looks for reaction; gets none. Now . . . directly to the audience]* Honestly! What a way to treat an old woman! Drag her out

of the house . . . stick her in a car . . . bring her out here from the city . . .
dump her in a pile of sand . . . and leave her here to set. I'm eighty-six years
old! I was married when I was seventeen. To a farmer. He died when I was thirty.
[*To the* MUSICIAN] Will you stop that, please?

[*The* MUSICIAN *stops playing.*]

I'm a feeble old woman . . . how do you expect anybody to hear me over that
peep! peep! peep! [*To herself*] There's no respect around here. [*To the* YOUNG MAN]
There's no respect around here!

> YOUNG MAN.   [*Same smile*] Hi!   35
> GRANDMA.   [*After a pause, a mild double-take, continues, to the audience*] My hus-
band died when I was thirty [*indicates* MOMMY], and I had to raise that big cow
over there all by my lonesome. You can imagine what *that* was like. Lordy! [*To
the* YOUNG MAN] Where'd they get *you*?
> YOUNG MAN.   Oh . . . I've been around for a while.
> GRANDMA.   I'll bet you have! Heh, heh, heh. Will you look at you!
> YOUNG MAN.   [*Flexing his muscles*] Isn't that something? [*Continues his calisthen-
ics*]
> GRANDMA.   Boy, oh boy; I'll say. Pretty good.   40
> YOUNG MAN.   [*Sweetly*] I'll say.
> GRANDMA.   Where ya from?
> YOUNG MAN.   Southern California.
> GRANDMA.   [*Nodding*] Figgers; figgers. What's your name, honey?
> YOUNG MAN.   I don't know. . . .   45
> GRANDMA.   [*To the audience*] Bright, too!
> YOUNG MAN.   I mean . . . I mean, they haven't given me one yet . . . the
studio . . .
> GRANDMA.   [*Giving him the once-over*] You don't say . . . you don't say. Well
. . . uh, I've got to talk some more . . . don't you go 'way.
> YOUNG MAN.   Oh, no.
> GRANDMA.   [*Turning her attention back to the audience*] Fine; fine. [*Then, once*   50
more, back to the YOUNG MAN] You're . . . you're an actor, hunh?
> YOUNG MAN.   [*Beaming*] Yes. I am.
> GRANDMA.   [*To the audience again; shrugs*] I'm smart that way. *Anyhow,* I had
to raise . . . *that* over there all by my lonesome; and what's next to her there . . .
that's what she married. Rich? I tell you . . . money, money, money. They took
me off the *farm* . . . which was real decent of them . . . and they moved me into
the big town house with *them* . . . fixed a nice place for me under the stove . . .
gave me an army blanket . . . and my own dish . . . my very own dish! So, what
have I got to complain about? Nothing, of course. I'm not complaining. [*She looks
up at the sky, shouts to someone off-stage.*] Shouldn't it be getting dark now, dear?

[*The lights dim; night comes on. The* MUSICIAN *begins to play, it becomes deepest night.
There are spots on all the players, including the* YOUNG MAN, *who is, of course, continuing
his calisthenics.*]

> DADDY.   [*Stirring*] It's nighttime.
> MOMMY.   Shhhh. Be still . . . wait.

DADDY.   [*Whining*] It's so hot.   55
MOMMY.   Shhhhhh. Be still . . . wait.
GRANDMA.   [*To herself*] That's better. Night. [*To the* MUSICIAN] Honey, do
you play all through this part?

[*The* MUSICIAN *nods.*]

Well, keep it nice and soft; that's a good boy.

[*The* MUSICIAN *nods again; plays softly.*]

That's nice.

[*There is an off-stage rumble.*]

DADDY.   [*Starting*] What was that?
MOMMY.   [*Beginning to weep*] It was nothing.
DADDY.   It was . . . it was . . . thunder . . . or a wave breaking . . . or   60
something.
MOMMY.   [*Whispering, through her tears*] It was an off-stage rumble . . . and
you know what *that* means. . . .
DADDY.   I forget. . . .
MOMMY.   [*Barely able to talk*] It means the time has come for poor Grandma
. . . and I can't bear it!
DADDY.   [*Vacantly*] I . . . I suppose you've got to be brave.
GRANDMA.   [*Mocking*] That's right, kid; be brave. You'll bear up; you'll get   65
over it.

[*Another off-stage rumble . . . louder*]

MOMMY.   Ohhhhhhhhhh . . . poor Grandma . . . poor Grandma. . . .
GRANDMA.   [*To* MOMMY] I'm fine! I'm all right! It hasn't happened yet!

[*A violent off-stage rumble. All the lights go out, save the spot on the* YOUNG MAN; *the*
MUSICIAN *stops playing.*]

MOMMY.   Ohhhhhhhhhh . . . Ohhhhhhhhhh. . . .

[*Silence*]

GRANDMA.   Don't put the lights up yet . . . I'm not ready; I'm not quite
ready. [*Silence*] All right, dear . . . I'm about done.

[*The lights come up again, to brightest day; the* MUSICIAN *begins to play.* GRANDMA *is
discovered, still in the sandbox, lying on her side, propped up on an elbow, half covered,
busily shoveling sand over herself.*]

GRANDMA.   [*Muttering*] I don't know how I'm supposed to do anything with   70
this goddam toy shovel. . . .
DADDY.   Mommy! It's daylight!

MOMMY. [*Brightly*] So it is! Well! Our long night is over. We must put away our tears, take off our mourning . . . and face the future. It's our duty.

GRANDMA. [*Still shoveling; mimicking*] . . . take off our mourning . . . face the future. . . . Lordy!

[*MOMMY and DADDY rise, stretch. MOMMY waves to the YOUNG MAN.*]

YOUNG MAN. [*With that smile*] Hi!

[*GRANDMA plays dead. (!) MOMMY and DADDY go over to look at her; she is a little more than half buried in the sand; the toy shovel is in her hands, which are crossed on her breast.*]

MOMMY. [*Before the sandbox; shaking her head*] Lovely! It's . . . it's hard to   75
be sad . . . she looks . . . so happy. [*With pride and conviction*] It pays to do things well. [*To the MUSICIAN*] All right, you can stop now, if you want to. I mean, stay around for a swim, or something; it's all right with us. [*She sighs heavily.*] Well Daddy . . . off we go.

DADDY. Brave Mommy!

MOMMY. Brave Daddy!

[*They exit, stage-left.*]

GRANDMA. [*After they leave; lying quite still*] It pays to do things well. . . . Boy, oh boy! [*She tries to sit up*] . . . well, kids . . . [*but she finds she can't.*] . . . I . . . I can't get up. I . . . I can't move. . . .

[*The YOUNG MAN stops his calisthenics, nods to the MUSICIAN, walks over to GRANDMA, kneels down by the sandbox.*]

GRANDMA. I . . . can't move. . . .

YOUNG MAN. Shhhhh . . . be very still. . . .   80

GRANDMA. I . . . I can't move. . . .

YOUNG MAN. Uh . . . ma'am; I . . . I have a line here.

GRANDMA. Oh, I'm sorry, sweetie; you go right ahead.

YOUNG MAN. I am . . . uh . . .

GRANDMA. Take your time, dear.   85

YOUNG MAN. [*Prepares; delivers the line like a real amateur.*] I am the Angel of Death. I am . . . uh . . . I am come for you.

GRANDMA. What . . . wha . . . [*Then, with resignation*] . . . ohhh . . . ohhhh, I see.

[*The YOUNG MAN bends over, kisses GRANDMA gently on the forehead.*]

GRANDMA. [*Her eyes closed, her hands folded on her breast again, the shovel between her hands, a sweet smile on her face*] Well . . . that was very nice, dear. . . .

YOUNG MAN. [*Still kneeling*] Shhhhhh . . . be still. . . .

GRANDMA. What I meant was . . . you did that very well, dear. . . .   90

YOUNG MAN. [*Blushing*] . . . oh . . .

GRANDMA. No; I mean it. You've got that . . . you've got a quality.

YOUNG MAN. [*With his endearing smile*] Oh . . . thank you; thank you very much . . . ma'am.

Grandma.   [*Slowly; softly—as the* YOUNG MAN *puts his hands on top of* GRANDMA'S] You're . . . you're welcome . . . dear.

[*Tableau. The* MUSICIAN *continues to play as the curtain slowly comes down.*]

[*Curtain*]

QUESTIONS

1. How does the setting, described at the beginning of the play, help shape your response? What props turn out to be symbolic?

2. What information does Albee provide in the opening note and stage direction that helps you understand the action and meaning of the play?

3. Why does Mommy say, "This is the beach"? Why is the line necessary? Why have the characters come to the beach? What are they waiting for?

4. Why does Albee indicate that Daddy is *whining*? What is the effect of having Daddy repeat "Whatever you say, Mommy" several times?

5. What happens to your sense of drama as the imitation of an action when Mommy tells the Musician, "You can come in now"?

6. How does Grandma "speak" to Mommy and Daddy? How does she speak to the audience and the Young Man? How do you account for this difference?

7. What does Grandma tell you directly about her relationship with Mommy and Daddy? What is her attitude toward Mommy? How is it shaped through diction and tone?

8. Albee identifies the Young Man as the Angel of Death; what else does he symbolize or represent? What is Grandma's attitude toward him? How does he treat her?

9. What does the "off-stage rumble" signify?

10. How do Mommy and Daddy react to Grandma's "death"? How would you characterize their language?

11. How does Grandma react to Mommy and Daddy's comments about her death? What does Grandma reveal about the way Mommy and Daddy deal with death?

12. What is the catastrophe of the play? The resolution?

GENERAL QUESTIONS

1. Are the characters in this play round or flat? Static or dynamic? Why don't they have names? What does each symbolize?

2. What do Mommy's calling the Musician, Grandma's cueing of the lighting technician, and Mommy's reference to an "off-stage rumble" have in common? What common effect do these events have on your perception of *The Sandbox* as a play?

3. *The Sandbox* is full of repetition; characters repeat words and even whole

lines two or three times. What is the effect of this repetition on your under-standing of character and meaning in this play?

4. How does Albee employ diction, speech patterns, connotative words, and tone to shape character and meaning?

5. How important are clichés as a device in this play? What clichés did you notice? Which characters speak most of the clichés? What effect do the clichés have on your perception of character and theme?

6. How many different generations are presented in *The Sandbox*? Which charac-ters represent each generation? To what extent do the different generations comment on different phases of American history?

THORNTON WILDER, *THE HAPPY JOURNEY TO TRENTON AND CAMDEN*

The Happy Journey to Trenton and Camden, published originally in 1931, is one of Thornton Wilder's early experiments in nonrealistic staging (see p. 1435 for a discussion of nonrealistic theater). He developed these tech-niques much more fully in later plays, including *Our Town* (1938) and *The Skin of Our Teeth* (1942). Wilder also wrote traditional realistic plays, including *The Merchant of Yonkers* (1938), which he later revised as *The Matchmaker* (1954). Ultimately, this play was adapted into the highly success-ful musical comedy, *Hello, Dolly!* (1964).

The set for *The Happy Journey* is nonrealistic and kept to a minimum. By using an empty stage instead of indicating the three separate settings of the play with scenery, Wilder calls our attention to the play's theatricality and the nature of drama as a fictional *imitation* of real life. In production, props and scenery for this play are limited to chairs, a platform, and a bed. Thus, Wilder forces us to use our imaginations to flesh out the scene. He also keeps our attention on plot, character, and dialogue; we are never distracted by elaborate sets.

The Happy Journey also exemplifies Wilder's careful construction of plot and character. At one level the plot is very simple; it involves the preparation for a trip, the journey itself, and arrival at the destination. In a very general way, these three episodes correspond to exposition, compli-cation, and finally catastrophe and resolution. We learn about the Kirby family and their world during their preparations for the journey. Conflicts and hints of the approaching catastrophe are developed during the journey. The play contains a submerged or hidden plot that deals with family life, death, and the ways people cope with sorrow. These themes are brought into focus in the third episode, the arrival at Camden and Ma's conversation with Beulah; here we find both catastrophe and resolution as Ma finds a way to deal with the details of daily life and the burdens of death and sorrow.

THORNTON WILDER   (1897–1975)

The Happy Journey to Trenton and Camden   *1931*

CHARACTERS

   Ma Kirby, *The Mother*
   Elmer Kirby, *The Father*
   Beulah Kirby, *The Older Daughter*
   Caroline Kirby, *The Younger Daughter*
   Arthur Kirby, *The Son*
   The Stage Manager

No scenery is required for this play. Perhaps a few dusty flats may be seen leaning against the brick wall at the back of the stage.

   The five members of the Kirby family and THE STAGE MANAGER *compose the cast.*

   THE STAGE MANAGER *not only moves forward and withdraws the few properties that are required, but he reads from a typescript the lines of all the minor characters. He reads them clearly, but with little attempt at characterization, scarcely troubling himself to alter his voice, even when he responds in the person of a child or a woman.*

   As the curtain rises THE STAGE MANAGER *is leaning lazily against the proscenium pillar at the audience's left. He is smoking.*

   ARTHUR *is playing marbles in the center of the stage.*

   CAROLINE *is at the remote back right talking to some girls who are invisible to us.*

   MA KIRBY *is anxiously putting on her hat before an imaginary mirror.*

   MA.   Where's your pa? Why isn't he here? I declare we'll never get started.
   ARTHUR.   Ma, where's my hat? I guess I don't go if I can't find my hat.
   MA.   Go out into the hall and see if it isn't there. Where's Caroline gone to now, the plagued child?
   ARTHUR.   She's out waitin' in the street talkin' to the Jones girls.—I just looked in the hall a thousand times, ma, and it isn't there. [*He spits for good luck before a difficult shot and mutters:*] Come on, baby.
   MA.   Go and look again, I say. Look carefully.   5

[ARTHUR *rises, runs to the right, turns around swiftly, returns to his game, flinging himself on the floor with a terrible impact and starts shooting an aggie.*]

   ARTHUR.   No, ma, it's not there.
   MA.   [*Serenely.*] Well, you don't leave Newark without that hat, make up your mind to that. I don't go no journeys with a hoodlum.
   ARTHUR.   Aw, ma!

[MA *comes down to the footlights and talks toward the audience as through a window.*]

   MA.   Oh, Mrs. Schwartz!
   THE STAGE MANAGER.   [*Consulting his script.*] Here I am, Mrs. Kirby. Are   10
you going yet?
   MA.   I guess we're going in just a minute. How's the baby?

THE STAGE MANAGER.   She's all right now. We slapped her on the back and she spat it up.

MA.   Isn't that fine!—Well now, if you'll be good enough to give the cat a saucer of milk in the morning and the evening, Mrs. Schwartz, I'll be ever so grateful to you.—Oh, good afternoon, Mrs. Hobmeyer!

THE STAGE MANAGER.   Good afternoon, Mrs. Kirby, I hear you're going away.

MA.   [*Modest.*] Oh, just for three days, Mrs. Hobmeyer, to see my married   15
daughter, Beulah, in Camden. Elmer's got his vacation week from the laundry early this year, and he's just the best driver in the world.

[*CAROLINE comes "into the house" and stands by her mother.*]

THE STAGE MANAGER.   Is the whole family going?

MA.   Yes, all four of us that's here. The change ought to be good for the children. My married daughter was downright sick a while ago——

THE STAGE MANAGER.   Tchk—Tchk—Tchk! Yes. I remember you tellin' us.

MA.   And I just want to go down and see the child. I ain't seen her since then. I just won't rest easy in my mind without I see her. [*To CAROLINE.*] Can't you say good afternoon to Mrs. Hobmeyer?

CAROLINE.   [*Blushes and lowers her eyes and says woodenly.*] Good afternoon,   20
Mrs. Hobmeyer.

THE STAGE MANAGER.   Good afternoon, dear.—Well, I'll wait and beat these rugs until after you're gone, because I don't want to choke you. I hope you have a good time and find everything all right.

MA.   Thank you, Mrs. Hobmeyer, I hope I will.—Well, I guess that milk for the cat is all, Mrs. Schwartz, if you're sure you don't mind. If anything should come up, the key to the back door is hanging by the ice box.

ARTHUR AND CAROLINE.   Ma! Not so loud. Everybody can hear yuh.

MA.   Stop pullin' my dress, children. [*In a loud whisper.*] The key to the back door I'll leave hangin' by the ice box and I'll leave the screen door unhooked.

THE STAGE MANAGER.   Now have a good trip, dear, and give my love to   25
Loolie.

MA.   I will, and thank you a thousand times. [*She returns "into the room."*] What can be keeping your pa?

ARTHUR.   I can't find my hat, ma.

[*Enter ELMER holding a hat.*]

ELMER.   Here's Arthur's hat. He musta left it in the car Sunday.

MA.   That's a mercy. Now we can start.—Caroline Kirby, what you done to your cheeks?

CAROLINE.   [*Defiant-abashed.*] Nothin'.   30

MA.   If you've put anything on 'em, I'll slap you.

CAROLINE.   No, ma, of course I haven't. [*Hanging her head.*] I just rubbed'm to make'm red. All the girls do that at High School when they're goin' places.

MA.   Such silliness I never saw. Elmer, what kep' you?

ELMER.   [*Always even-voiced and always looking out a little anxiously through his spectacles.*] I just went to the garage and had Charlie give a last look at it, Kate.

MA.   I'm glad you did. I wouldn't like to have no breakdown miles from   35
anywhere. Now we can start. Arthur, put those marbles away. Anybody'd think you didn't want to go on a journey, to look at yuh.

[*They go out through the "hall," take the short steps that denote going downstairs, and find themselves in the street.*]

ELMER.   Here, you boys, you keep away from that car.

MA.   Those Sullivan boys put their heads into everything.

[*THE STAGE MANAGER has moved forward four chairs and a low platform. This is the automobile. It is in the center of the stage and faces the audience. The platform slightly raises the two chairs in the rear. PA's hands hold an imaginary steering wheel and continually shift gears. CAROLINE sits beside him. ARTHUR is behind him and MA behind CAROLINE.*]

CAROLINE.   [*Self-consciously.*] Goodbye, Mildred. Goodbye, Helen.

THE STAGE MANAGER.   Goodbye, Caroline. Goodbye, Mrs. Kirby. I hope y'have a good time.

MA.   Goodbye, girls.   40

THE STAGE MANAGER.   Goodbye, Kate. The car looks fine.

MA.   [*Looking upward toward a window.*] Oh, goodbye, Emma! [*Modestly.*] We think it's the best little Chevrolet in the world.—Oh, goodbye, Mrs. Adler!

THE STAGE MANAGER.   What, are you going away, Mrs. Kirby?

MA.   Just for three days, Mrs. Adler, to see my married daughter in Camden.

THE STAGE MANAGER.   Have a good time.   45

[*Now MA, CAROLINE, and THE STAGE MANAGER break out into a tremendous chorus of goodbyes. The whole street is saying goodbye. ARTHUR takes out his pea shooter and lets fly happily into the air. There is a lurch or two and they are off.*]

ARTHUR.   [*In sudden fright.*] Pa! Pa! Don't go by the school. Mr. Biedenbach might see us!

MA.   I don't care if he does see us. I guess I can take my children out of school for one day without having to hide down back streets about it. [*ELMER nods to a passerby. MA asks without sharpness:*] Who was that you spoke to, Elmer?

ELMER.   That was the fellow who arranges our banquets down to the Lodge, Kate.

MA.   Is he the one who had to buy four hundred steaks? [*PA nods.*] I declare, I'm glad I'm not him.

ELMER.   The air's getting better already. Take deep breaths, children.   50

[*They inhale noisily.*]

ARTHUR.   Gee, it's almost open fields already. *"Weber and Heilbronner Suits for Well-dressed Men."* Ma, can I have one of them some day?

MA.   If you graduate with good marks perhaps your father'll let you have one for graduation.

CAROLINE.   [*Whining.*] Oh, Pa! do we have to wait while that whole funeral goes by?

[*PA takes off his hat. MA cranes forward with absorbed curiosity.*]

MA.   Take off your hat, Arthur. Look at your father.—Why, Elmer, I do believe that's a lodge-brother of yours. See the banner? I suppose this is the Elizabeth branch. [*ELMER nods. MA sighs: Tchk—tchk—tchk. They all lean forward and watch the funeral in silence, growing momentarily more solemnized. After a pause, MA continues almost dreamily:*] Well, we haven't forgotten the one that we went on, have we?

We haven't forgotten our good Harold. He gave his life for his country, we mustn't forget that. [*She passes her finger from the corner of her eye across her cheek. There is another pause.*] Well, we'll all hold up the traffic for a few minutes some day.

THE CHILDREN. [*Very uncomfortable.*] Ma! 55

MA. [*Without self-pity.*] Well I'm "ready," children. I hope everybody in this car is "ready." [*She puts her hand on* PA'S *shoulder.*] And I pray to go first, Elmer. Yes. [PA *touches her hand.*]

THE CHILDREN. Ma, everybody's looking at you. Everybody's laughing at you.

MA. Oh, hold your tongues! I don't care what a lot of silly people in Elizabeth, New Jersey, think of me.—Now we can go on. That's the last.

[*There is another lurch and the car goes on.*]

CAROLINE. "*Fit-Rite Suspenders. The Working Man's Choice.*" Pa, why do they spell Rite that way?

ELMER. So that it'll make you stop and ask about it, Missy. 60

CAROLINE. Papa, you're teasing me.—Ma, why do they say "*Three Hundred Rooms Three Hundred Baths?*"

ARTHUR. "*Miller's Spaghetti: The Family's Favorite Dish.*" Ma, why don't you ever have spaghetti?

MA. Go along, you'd never eat it.

ARTHUR. Ma, I like it now.

CAROLINE. [*With gesture.*] Yum-yum. It looks wonderful up there. Ma, make 65 some when we get home?

MA. [*Dryly.*] "The management is always happy to receive suggestions. We aim to please."

[*The whole family finds this exquisitely funny. The* CHILDREN *scream with laughter. Even* ELMER *smiles.* MA *remains modest.*]

ELMER. Well, I guess no one's complaining, Kate. Everybody knows you're a good cook.

MA. I don't know whether I'm a good cook or not, but I know I've had practice. At least I've cooked three meals a day for twenty-five years.

ARTHUR. Aw, ma, you went out to eat once in a while.

MA. Yes. That made it a leap year. 70

[*This joke is no less successful than its predecessor. When the laughter dies down,* CAROLINE *turns around in an ecstasy of well-being and kneeling on the cushions says:*]

CAROLINE. Ma, I love going out in the country like this. Let's do it often, ma.

MA. Goodness, smell that air will you! It's got the whole ocean in it.—Elmer, drive careful over that bridge. This must be New Brunswick we're coming to.

ARTHUR. [*Jealous of his mother's successes.*] Ma, when is the next comfort station?

MA. [*Unruffled.*] You don't want one. You just said that to be awful.

CAROLINE. [*Shrilly.*] Yes, he did, ma. He's terrible. He says that kind of 75 thing right out in school and I want to sink through the floor, ma. He's terrible.

MA. Oh, don't get so excited about nothing, Miss Proper! I guess we're all yewman-beings in this car, at least as far as I know. And, Arthur, you try and be a gentleman.—Elmer, don't run over that collie dog. [*She follows the dog with her eyes.*] Looked kinda peakèd to me. Needs a good honest bowl of leavings. Pretty dog, too. [*Her eyes fall on a billboard.*] That's a pretty advertisement for Chesterfield cigarettes, isn't it? Looks like Beulah, a little.

ARTHUR.   Ma?

MA.   Yes.

ARTHUR.   [*"Route" rhymes with "out".*] Can't I take a paper route with the Newark *Daily Post*?

MA.   No, you cannot. No, sir. I hear they make the paper boys get up at   80
four-thirty in the morning. No son of mine is going to get up at four-thirty every morning, not if it's to make a million dollars. Your *Saturday Evening Post* route on Thursday mornings is enough.

ARTHUR.   Aw, ma.

MA.   No, sir. No son of mine is going to get up at four-thirty and miss the sleep God meant him to have.

ARTHUR.   [*Sullenly.*]   Hhm! Ma's always talking about God. I guess she got a letter from him this morning. [*MA rises, outraged.*]

MA.   Elmer, stop that automobile this minute. I don't go another step with anybody that says things like that. Arthur, you get out of this car. Elmer, you give him another dollar bill. He can go back to Newark, by himself. I don't want him.

ARTHUR.   What did I say? There wasn't anything terrible about that.   85

ELMER.   I didn't hear what he said, Kate.

MA.   God has done a lot of things for me and I won't have him made fun of by anybody. Go away. Go away from me.

CAROLINE.   Aw, Ma,—don't spoil the ride.

MA.   No.

ELMER.   We might as well go on, Kate, since we've got started. I'll talk to   90
the boy tonight.

MA.   [*Slowly conceding.*]   All right, if you say so, Elmer. But I won't sit beside him. Caroline, you come, and sit by me.

ARTHUR.   [*Frightened.*]   Aw, ma, that wasn't so terrible.

MA.   I don't want to talk about it. I hope your father washes your mouth out with soap and water.—Where'd we all be if I started talking about God like that, I'd like to know! We'd be in the speak-easies and night-clubs and places like that, that's where we'd be.—All right, Elmer, you can go on now.

CAROLINE.   What did he say, ma? I didn't hear what he said.

MA.   I don't want to talk about it.   95

[*They drive on in silence for a moment, the shocked silence after a scandal.*]

ELMER.   I'm going to stop and give the car a little water, I guess.

MA.   All right, Elmer. You know best.

ELMER.   [*To a garage hand.*]   Could I have a little water in the radiator—to make sure?

THE STAGE MANAGER.   [*In this scene alone he lays aside his script and enters into a rôle seriously.*]   You sure can. [*He punches the tires.*] Air, all right? Do you need any oil or gas?

ELMER.   No, I think not. I just got fixed up in Newark.   100

MA. We're on the right road for Camden, are we?

THE STAGE MANAGER. Yes, keep straight ahead. You can't miss it. You'll be in Trenton in a few minutes. [*He carefully pours some water into the hood.*] Camden's a great town, lady, believe me.

MA. My daughter likes it fine,—my married daughter.

THE STAGE MANAGER. Ye'? It's a great burg all right. I guess I think so because I was born near there.

MA. Well, well. Your folks still live there? 105

THE STAGE MANAGER. No, my old man sold the farm and they built a factory on it. So the folks moved to Philadelphia.

MA. My married daughter Beulah lives there because her husband works in the telephone company.—Stop pokin' me, Caroline!—We're all going down to see her for a few days.

THE STAGE MANAGER. Ye'?

MA. She's been sick, you see, and I just felt I had to go and see her. My husband and my boy are going to stay at the Y.M.C.A. I hear they've got a dormitory on the top floor that's real clean and comfortable. Had you ever been there?

THE STAGE MANAGER. No. I'm Knights of Columbus myself. 110

MA. Oh.

THE STAGE MANAGER. I used to play basketball at the Y though. It looked all right to me. [*He has been standing with one foot on the rung of MA's chair. They have taken a great fancy to one another. He reluctantly shakes himself out of it and pretends to examine the car again, whistling.*] Well, I guess you're all set now, lady. I hope you have a good trip; you can't miss it.

EVERYBODY. Thanks. Thanks a lot. Good luck to you. [*Jolts and lurches.*]

MA. [*With a sigh.*] The world's full of nice people.—That's what I call a nice young man.

CAROLINE. [*Earnestly.*] Ma, you oughtn't to tell'm all everything about your- 115 self.

MA. Well, Caroline, you do your way and I'll do mine.—He looked kinda thin to me. I'd like to feed him up for a few days. His mother lives in Philadelphia and I expect he eats at those dreadful Greek places.

CAROLINE. I'm hungry. Pa, there's a hot dog stand. K'n I have one?

ELMER. We'll all have one, eh, Kate? We had such an early lunch.

MA. Just as you think best, Elmer.

ELMER. Arthur, here's half a dollar.—Run over and see what they have. 120 Not too much mustard either. [*ARTHUR descends from the car and goes off stage right. MA and CAROLINE get out and walk a bit.*]

MA. What's that flower over there?—I'll take some of those to Beulah.

CAROLINE. It's just a weed, ma.

MA. I like it.—My, look at the sky, wouldya! I'm glad I was born in New Jersey. I've always said it was the best state in the Union. Every state has something no other state has got.

[*They stroll about humming. Presently ARTHUR returns with his hands full of imaginary hot dogs which he distributes. He is still very much cast down by the recent scandal. He finally approaches his mother and says falteringly:*]

ARTHUR. Ma, I'm sorry. I'm sorry for what I said.

[*He bursts into tears and puts his forehead against her elbow.*]

MA. There. There. We all say wicked things at times. I know you didn't   125
mean it like it sounded. [*He weeps still more violently than before.*] Why, now, now! I
forgive you, Arthur, and tonight before you go to bed you . . . [*She whispers.*]
You're a good boy at heart, Arthur, and we all know it. [*CAROLINE starts to cry too.
MA is suddenly joyously alive and happy.*] Sakes alive, it's too nice a day for us all to
be cryin'. Come now, get in. You go up in front with your father, Caroline. Ma
wants to sit with her beau. I never saw such children. Your hot dogs are all getting
wet. Now chew them fine, everybody.—All right, Elmer, forward march.—Caroline,
whatever are you doing?

CAROLINE. I'm spitting out the leather, ma.

MA. Then say: Excuse me.

CAROLINE. Excuse me, please.

MA. What's this place? Arthur, did you see the post office?

ARTHUR. It said Lawrenceville.   130

MA. Hhn. School kinda. Nice. I wonder what that big yellow house set
back was.—Now it's beginning to be Trenton.

CAROLINE. Papa, it was near here that George Washington crossed the Dela-
ware. It was near Trenton, mama. He was first in war and first in peace, and first
in the hearts of his countrymen.

MA. [*Surveying the passing world, serene and didactic.*] Well, the thing I like
about him best was that he never told a lie. [*The CHILDREN are duly cast down.
There is a pause.*] There's a sunset for you. There's nothing like a good sunset.

ARTHUR. There's an Ohio license in front of us. Ma, have you ever been
to Ohio?

MA. No.   135

[*A dreamy silence descends upon them. CAROLINE sits closer to her father. MA puts her arm
around ARTHUR.*]

ARTHUR. Ma, what a lotta people there are in the world, ma. There must
be thousands and thousands in the United States. Ma, how many are there?

MA. I don't know. Ask your father.

ARTHUR. Pa, how many are there?

ELMER. There are a hundred and twenty-six million, Kate.

MA. [*Giving a pressure about ARTHUR's shoulder.*] And they all like to drive out   140
in the evening with their children beside'm. [*Another pause.*] Why doesn't somebody
sing something? Arthur, you're always singing something; what's the matter with
you?

ARTHUR. All right. What'll we sing? [*He sketches:*]
"In the Blue Ridge mountains of Virginia,
     On the trail of the lonesome pine . . ."
No, I don't like that any more. Let's do:
"I been workin' on de railroad
     All de liblong day.
     I been workin' on de railroad
     Just to pass de time away."

[CAROLINE *joins in at once. Finally even* MA *is singing. Even* PA *is singing.* MA *suddenly jumps up with a wild cry:*]

MA.   Elmer, that signpost said Camden, I saw it.
ELMER.   All right, Kate, if you're sure.

[*Much shifting of gears, backing, and jolting.*]

MA.   Yes, there it is. Camden—five miles. Dear old Beulah.—Now, children, you be good and quiet during dinner. She's just got out of bed after a big sorta operation, and we must all move around kinda quiet. First you drop me and Caroline at the door and just say hello, and then you men-folk go over to the Y.M.C.A. and come back for dinner in about an hour.
CAROLINE.   [*Shutting her eyes and pressing her fists passionately against her nose.*] I   145
see the first star. Everybody make a wish.
Star light, star bright,
First star I seen tonight.
I wish I may, I wish I might
Have the wish I wish tonight.

[*Then solemnly.*] Pins. Mama, you say "needles."

[*She interlocks little fingers with her mother.*]

MA.   Needles.
CAROLINE.   Shakespeare. Ma, you say "Longfellow."
MA.   Longfellow.
CAROLINE.   Now it's a secret and I can't tell it to anybody. Ma, you make a
wish.
MA.   [*With almost grim humor.*]   No, I can make wishes without waiting for   150
no star. And I can tell my wishes right out loud too. Do you want to hear them?
CAROLINE.   [*Resignedly.*] No, ma, we know'm already. We've heard'm. [*She hangs her head affectedly on her left shoulder and says with unmalicious mimicry:*] You want me to be a good girl and you want Arthur to be honest-in-word-and-deed.
MA.   [*Majestically.*]   Yes. So mind yourself.
ELMER.   Caroline, take out that letter from Beulah in my coat pocket by you and read aloud the places I marked with red pencil.
CAROLINE.   [*Working.*] "*A few blocks after you pass the two big oil tanks on your left* . . ."
EVERYBODY.   [*Pointing backward.*] There they are!   155
CAROLINE.   "*. . . you come to a corner where there's an A and P store on the left and a firehouse kitty-corner to it* . . ." [*They all jubilantly identify these landmarks.*] "*. . . turn right, go two blocks, and our house is Weyerhauser St. Number 471.*"
MA.   It's an even nicer street than they used to live in. And right handy to an A and P.
CAROLINE.   [*Whispering.*] Ma, it's better than our street. It's richer than our street.—Ma, isn't Beulah richer than we are?
MA.   [*Looking at her with a firm and glassy eye.*] Mind yourself, missy. I don't want to hear anybody talking about rich or not rich when I'm around. If people aren't nice I don't care how rich they are. I live in the best street in the world

because my husband and children live there. [*She glares impressively at* CAROLINE *a moment to let this lesson sink in, then looks up, sees* BEULAH *and waves.*] There's Beulah standing on the steps lookin' for us.

[BEULAH *has appeared and is waving. They all call out:*] Hello, Beulah—Hello. [*Presently they are all getting out of the car.* BEULAH *kisses her father long and affectionately.*]

BEULAH. Hello, papa. Good old papa. You look tired, pa.—Hello, mama.—   160
Lookit how Arthur and Caroline are growing!

MA. They're bursting all their clothes!—Yes, your pa needs a rest. Thank Heaven, his vacation has come just now. We'll feed him up and let him sleep late. Pa has a present for you, Loolie. He would go and buy it.

BEULAH. Why, pa, you're terrible to go and buy anything for me. Isn't he terrible?

MA. Well, it's a secret. You can open it at dinner.

ELMER. Where's Horace, Loolie?

BEULAH. He was kep' over a little at the office. He'll be here any minute.   165
He's crazy to see you all.

MA. All right. You men go over to the Y and come back in about an hour.

BEULAH. [*As her father returns to the wheel, stands out in the street beside him.*] Go straight along, pa, you can't miss it. It just stares at yuh. [*She puts her arm around his neck and rubs her nose against his temple.*] Crazy old pa, goin' buyin' things! It's me that ought to be buyin' things for you, pa.

ELMER. Oh, no! There's only one Loolie in the world.

BEULAH. [*Whispering, as her eyes fill with tears.*] Are you glad I'm still alive, pa? [*She kisses him abruptly and goes back to the house steps.* THE STAGE MANAGER *removes the automobile with the help of* ELMER *and* ARTHUR *who go off waving their goodbyes.*] Well, come on upstairs, ma, and take off your things. Caroline, there's a surprise for you in the back yard.

CAROLINE. Rabbits?   170

BEULAH. No.

CAROLINE. Chickins?

BEULAH. No. Go and see. [CAROLINE *runs off stage.* BEULAH *and* MA *gradually go upstairs.*] There are two new puppies. You be thinking over whether you can keep one in Newark.

MA. I guess we can. It's a nice house, Beulah. You just got a *lovely* home.

BEULAH. When I got back from the hospital, Horace had moved everything   175
into it, and there wasn't anything for me to do.

MA. It's lovely.

[THE STAGE MANAGER *pushes out a bed from the left. Its foot is toward the right.* BEULAH *sits on it, testing the springs.*]

BEULAH. I think you'll find the bed comfortable, ma.

MA. [*Taking off her hat.*] Oh, I could sleep on a heapa shoes, Loolie! I don't have no trouble sleepin'. [*She sits down beside her.*] Now let me look at my girl. Well, well, when I last saw you, you didn't know me. You kep' saying: *When's mama comin'? When's mama comin'?* But the doctor sent me away.

BEULAH. [*Puts her head on her mother's shoulder and weeps.*] It was awful, mama. It was awful. She didn't even live a few minutes, mama. It was awful.

MA. [*Looking far away.*] God thought best, dear. God thought best. We don't   180
understand why. We just go on, honey, doin' our business. [*Then almost abruptly—
passing the back of her hand across her cheek.*] Well, now, what are we giving the men
to eat tonight?

BEULAH. There's a chicken in the oven.

MA. What time didya put it in?

BEULAH. [*Restraining her.*] Aw, ma, don't go yet. I like to sit here with you
this way. You always get the fidgets when we try and pet yuh, mama.

MA. [*Ruefully, laughing.*] Yes, it's kinda foolish. I'm just an old Newark bag-
a-bones.

[*She glances at the backs of her hands.*]

BEULAH. [*Indignantly.*] Why, ma, you're good-lookin'! We always said you   185
were good-lookin'.—And besides, you're the best ma we could ever have.

MA. [*Uncomfortable.*] Well, I hope you like me. There's nothin' like being
liked by your family.—Now I'm going downstairs to look at the chicken. You stretch
out here for a minute and shut your eyes.—Have you got everything laid in for
breakfast before the shops close?

BEULAH. Oh, you know! Ham and eggs.

[*They both laugh.*]

MA. I declare I never could understand what men see in ham and eggs. I
think they're horrible.—What time did you put the chicken in?

BEULAH. Five o'clock.

MA. Well, now, you shut your eyes for ten minutes. [*BEULAH stretches out   190
and shuts her eyes. MA descends the stairs absentmindedly singing:*]
"There were ninety and nine that safely lay
In the shelter of the fold,
But one was out on the hills away,
Far off from the gates of gold. . . ."

AND THE CURTAIN FALLS

QUESTIONS

Preparation for the Journey

1. What expositional details are found in the opening stage direction? What
   additional exposition is established during the preparation for the journey?
2. What do you learn about Ma during the preparation? How would you explain
   her reaction to Arthur's missing hat and Caroline's red cheeks? What is Ma's
   relationship with her neighbors?
3. What foreshadowing of the catastrophe do you find in the exposition?
4. How are Arthur and Caroline characterized initially? How does their behavior
   on the trip reinforce or change these initial images?

5. What is Elmer Kirby like? How would you characterize his relationship to Ma?

The Journey

6. What is the effect of having the characters recite advertisements?
7. How does Ma react to the funeral? How does she react to Arthur's remark that "Ma's always talking about God. I guess she got a letter from him this morning"? What does the remark reveal about Ma? What does her reaction reveal?
8. How does Ma relate to the garage attendant? What does this tell you about her?
9. How does Ma deal with Arthur's apology and tears?
10. What does Ma like about George Washington? Why is this significant?
11. What is Ma's wish and what does it tell you about her?
12. Why is it significant that Ma spots the signpost to Camden and gets the car headed down the correct road?

The Arrival

13. What is Ma's reaction to Caroline's observation that Beulah's street is "better than our street . . . richer than our street"?
14. What has happened to Beulah? How does Ma deal with this?
15. Why does the play end with a fragment of a hymn?

GENERAL QUESTIONS

1. What is the effect of having the stage manager play all the "bit" parts (small roles) and remain on stage even when he is not in a specific role? To what extent does he become a narrator? How pervasive is his point of view?
2. How clearly does this play follow the structural pattern of exposition, complication, crisis, catastrophe, and resolution? Where is the crisis? The catastrophe? How does the play resolve?
3. Who is the protagonist? Who or what are the antagonists? What are the conflicts? Which is central?
4. Is Ma a round or flat character? Static or dynamic? To what extent is she a stereotyped or stock character?
5. To what extent does Ma hold the Kirby family together and keep it on track? How does Wilder demonstrate this in the play?
6. What is Ma's attitude toward her own life? Her family? Her home? How does she cope with day-to-day problems and the larger trials of the world?

TENNESSEE WILLIAMS, *THE GLASS MENAGERIE*

Many of Tennessee Williams's plays reflect the attitudes and customs that he encountered as he was growing up in Mississippi and Missouri. Until he was eight, his family lived in genteel poverty, mostly in Columbus, Mississippi; his father was a traveling shoe salesman who was rarely at home, while his mother, the daughter of an Episcopal clergyman, had the traditional social values and graces of a Southern belle. In 1919 the family moved to a lower-class neighborhood in St. Louis. Williams, who was bookish and sickly, tried to escape from poverty and family conflicts by writing and going to the movies. One of his few companions during those years was his shy and withdrawn sister, Rose.

Williams began college at the University of Missouri in 1931, but the Depression and family poverty forced him to drop out and go to work in a shoe warehouse. After two years of this, he suffered a nervous collapse, but finally finished college, at the University of Iowa. Williams then began wandering through the Americas, doing odd jobs, and writing. His first full-length play, *Battle of Angels*, was produced in 1940 but was unsuccessful. Williams continued to write, however, and *The Glass Menagerie* was staged in 1945; the critical and popular success of this play was the beginning of many good years in the theater. During the 1940s and 1950s Williams, along with Arthur Miller, dominated the American stage. He went on to write many one-act plays and over fifteen full-length dramas, including *A Streetcar Named Desire* (1947), *The Rose Tattoo* (1951), *Cat on a Hot Tin Roof* (1955), *Suddenly Last Summer* (1958), and *The Night of the Iguana* (1961).

The Glass Menagerie, written in 1944 and produced to rave reviews in Chicago and New York in 1945, is a highly autobiographical play which explores the family dynamics, delusions, and personalities of the Wingfields. Williams originally developed his ideas for the play in a short story called "Portrait of a Girl in Glass" and then in a screenplay for Metro-Goldwyn-Mayer entitled "The Gentleman Caller." In these, and in *The Glass Menagerie*, Laura Wingfield is modeled after Rose Williams. The least competent member of the family, she is crippled by her own insecurity and her mother's expectations. At every opportunity, Laura withdraws into a world of glass figurines and old phonograph records left by her father when he abandoned the family. Amanda Wingfield is patterned after Williams's mother; she valiantly tries to hold the family together and provide for Laura's future, but her perspectives are skewed by her romanticized memories of a gracious southern past of plantations, formal dances, and "gentleman callers." Tom, a figure based on the playwright himself, is the most desperate to escape the trap of his impoverished family; he seeks to emulate the long-missing father and move out of the drab Wingfield apartment into adventure and experience.

The play offers a fascinating mixture of realistic and nonrealistic dramatic techniques. The characters (excluding Tom when he narrates) and the language are predominantly realistic. This is especially true of Amanda's language, in which Williams skillfully recreates the cadences and characteristics of his mother's Mississippi dialect. The structure of the play and the staging, as Williams points out in his production notes and stage directions, are strikingly nonrealistic. Williams employs various devices nonrealistically, including the narrator, music, lighting, and screen projections, to underscore the emotions of his characters and to explore ideas about family and personality.

One of the most effective nonrealistic techniques in *The Glass Menagerie* is its structure as "a memory play." The characters and the action are neither real nor in the present; rather, they are memories living through Tom's mind about five years after the actual events occurred. Tom as narrator embodies the present time in the play (1944). We thus see action that probably occurred in 1939 through the "eyes" of Tom's recollections. Even Tom as a character in the Wingfield household is a memory, quite distinct from Tom as narrator. Thus, the action in the apartment cannot be considered a real or accurate recreation of life; it is reshaped and exaggerated through the distorting filter of Tom's feelings of guilt and his selective memory.

TENNESSEE WILLIAMS (1911–1983)

The Glass Menagerie   *1945*

THE CHARACTERS

Amanda Wingfield (*the mother*)
A little woman of great but confused vitality clinging frantically to another time and place. Her characterization must be carefully created, not copied from type. She is not paranoiac, but her life is paranoia. There is much to admire in Amanda, and as much to love and pity as there is to laugh at. Certainly she has endurance and a kind of heroism, and though her foolishness makes her unwittingly cruel at times, there is tenderness in her slight person.

Laura Wingfield (*her daughter*)
Amanda, having failed to establish contact with reality, continues to live vitally in her illusions, but Laura's situation is even graver. A childhood illness has left her crippled, one leg slightly shorter than the other, and held in a brace. This defect need not be more than suggested on the stage. Stemming from this, Laura's separation increases till she is like a piece of her own glass collection, too exquisitely fragile to move from the shelf.

Tom Wingfield (*her son*)
And the narrator of the play. A poet with a job in a warehouse. His nature is not remorseless, but to escape from a trap he has to act without pity.

Jim O'Connor (*the gentleman caller*)
A nice, ordinary, young man.

PRODUCTION NOTES

Being a "memory play," *The Glass Menagerie* can be presented with unusual freedom of convention. Because of its considerably delicate or tenuous material, atmospheric touches and subtleties of direction play a particularly important part. Expressionism and all other unconventional techniques in drama have only one valid aim, and that is a closer approach to truth. When a play employs unconventional techniques, it is not, or certainly shouldn't be, trying to escape its responsibility of dealing with reality, or interpreting experience, but is actually or should be attempting to find a closer approach, a more penetrating and vivid expression of things as they are. The straight realistic play with its genuine Frigidaire and authentic ice-cubes, its characters who speak exactly as its audience speaks, corresponds to the academic landscape and has the same virtue of a photographic likeness. Everyone should know nowadays the unimportance of the photographic in art: that truth, life, or reality is an organic thing which the poetic imagination can represent or suggest, in essence, only through transformation, through changing into other forms than those which were merely present in appearance.

These remarks are not meant as a preface only to this particular play. They have to do with a conception of a new, plastic theatre which must take the place of the exhausted theatre of realistic conventions if the theatre is to resume vitality as a part of our culture.

THE SCREEN DEVICE: There is *only one important difference between the original and the acting version of the play* and that is the *omission* in the latter of the device that I tentatively included in my *original* script. This device was the use of a screen on which were projected magic-lantern slides bearing images or titles. I do not regret the omission of this device from the original Broadway production. The extraordinary power of Miss Taylor's° performance made it suitable to have the utmost simplicity in the physical production. But I think it may be interesting to some readers to see how this device was conceived. So I am putting it into the published manuscript. These images and legends, projected from behind, were cast on a section of wall between the front-room and dining-room areas, which should be indistinguishable from the rest when not in use.

The purpose of this will probably be apparent. It is to give accent to certain values in each scene. Each scene contains a particular point (or several) which is structurally the most important. In an episodic play, such as this, the basic structure or narrative line may be obscured from the audience; the effect may seem fragmentary rather than architectural. This may not be the fault of the play so much as a lack of attention in the audience. The legend or image upon the screen will strengthen the effect of what is merely allusion in the writing and allow the primary point to be made more simply and lightly than if the entire responsibility were on the spoken lines. Aside from this structural value, I think the screen will have a definite emotional appeal, less definable but just as important. An imaginative

---

Miss Taylor's: The role of Amanda was first played by the American actress Laurette Taylor (1884–1946).

producer or director may invent many other uses for this device than those indicated in the present script. In fact the possibilities of the device seem much larger to me than the instance of this play can possibly utilize.

THE MUSIC: Another extra-literary accent in this play is provided by the use of music. A single recurring tune, "The Glass Menagerie,"° is used to give emotional emphasis to suitable passages. This tune is like circus music, not when you are on the grounds or in the immediate vicinity of the parade, but when you are at some distance and very likely thinking of something else. It seems under those circumstances to continue almost interminably and it weaves in and out of your preoccupied consciousness; then it is the lightest, most delicate music in the world and perhaps the saddest. It expresses the surface vivacity of life with the underlying strain of immutable and inexpressible sorrow. When you look at a piece of delicately spun glass you think of two things: how beautiful it is and how easily it can be broken. Both of those ideas should be woven into the recurring tune, which dips in and out of the play as if it were carried on a wind that changes. It serves as a thread of connection and allusion between the narrator with his separate point in time and space and the subject of his story. Between each episode it returns as reference to the emotion, nostalgia, which is the first condition of the play. It is primarily Laura's music and therefore comes out most clearly when the play focuses upon her and the lovely fragility of glass which is her image.

THE LIGHTING: The lighting in the play is not realistic. In keeping with the atmosphere of memory, the stage is dim. Shafts of light are focused on selected areas or actors, sometimes in contradistinction to what is the apparent center. For instance, in the quarrel scene between Tom and Amanda, in which Laura has no active part, the clearest pool of light is on her figure. This is also true of the supper scene, when her silent figure on the sofa should remain the visual center. The light upon Laura should be distinct from the others, having a peculiar pristine clarity such as light used in early religious portraits of female saints or madonnas. A certain correspondence to light in religious paintings, such as El Greco's,° where the figures are radiant in atmosphere that is relatively dusky, could be effectively used throughout the play. (It will also permit a more effective use of the screen.) A free, imaginative use of light can be of enormous value in giving a mobile, plastic quality to plays of a more or less static nature.

Tennessee Williams

Scene 1

The Wingfield apartment is in the rear of the building, one of those vast hive-like conglomerations of cellular living-units that flower as warty growths in overcrowded urban centers of lower middle-class population and are symptomatic of the impulse of this largest and fundamentally enslaved section of American society to avoid fluidity and differentiation and to exist and function as one interfused mass of automatism.

"*The Glass Menagerie*": original music, including this recurrent theme, was composed for the play by Paul Bowles.

El Greco: Greek painter (ca. 1548–1614) who lived in Spain; typical paintings have elongated and distorted figures and extremely vivid foreground lighting set against a murky background.

The apartment faces an alley and is entered by a fire escape, a structure whose name is a touch of accidental poetic truth, for all of these huge buildings are always burning with the slow and implacable fires of human desperation. The fire escape is part of what we see—that is, the landing of it and steps descending from it.

The scene is memory and is therefore nonrealistic. Memory takes a lot of poetic license. It omits some details; others are exaggerated, according to the emotional value of the articles it touches, for memory is seated predominantly in the heart. The interior is therefore rather dim and poetic.

At the rise of the curtain, the audience is faced with the dark, grim rear wall of the Wingfield tenement. This building is flanked on both sides by dark, narrow alleys which run into murky canyons of tangled clotheslines, garbage cans, and the sinister latticework of neighboring fire escapes. It is up and down these side alleys that exterior entrances and exits are made during the play. At the end of TOM's opening commentary, the dark tenement wall slowly becomes transparent° and reveals the interior of the ground-floor Wingfield apartment.

Nearest the audience is the living room, which also serves as a sleeping room for LAURA, *the sofa unfolding to make her bed. Just beyond, separated from the living room by a wide arch or second proscenium with transparent faded portieres° (or second curtain), is the dining room. In an old-fashioned whatnot° in the living room are seen scores of transparent glass animals. A blown-up photograph of the father hangs on the wall of the living room, to the left of the archway. It is the face of a very handsome young man in a doughboy's° First World War cap. He is gallantly smiling, ineluctably smiling, as if to say "I will be smiling forever."*

Also hanging on the wall, near the photograph, are a typewriter keyboard chart and a Gregg shorthand diagram. An upright typewriter on a small table stands beneath the charts.

The audience hears and sees the opening scene in the dining room through both the transparent fourth wall of the building and the transparent gauze portieres of the dining-room arch. It is during this revealing scene that the fourth wall slowly ascends, out of sight. This transparent exterior wall is not brought down again until the very end of the play, during TOM's final speech.

The narrator is an undisguised convention of the play. He takes whatever license with dramatic convention is convenient to his purposes.

TOM enters, dressed as a merchant sailor, and strolls across to the fire escape. There he stops and lights a cigarette. He addresses the audience.

TOM. Yes, I have tricks in my pocket, I have things up my sleeve. But I am the opposite of a stage magician. He gives you illusion that has the appearance of truth. I give you truth in the pleasant disguise of illusion.

To begin with, I turn back time. I reverse it to that quaint period, the thirties, when the huge middle class of America was matriculating in a school for the blind. Their eyes had failed them, or they had failed their eyes, and so they were

---

transparent: the wall is painted on a scrim, a transparent curtain that is opaque when lit from the front and transparent when lit from behind.

portieres: curtains hung in a doorway; in production, these may also be painted on a scrim.

whatnot: a small set of shelves for ornaments.

doughboy: popular name for an American infantryman during World War I.

having their fingers pressed forcibly down on the fiery Braille alphabet of a dissolving economy.

In Spain there was revolution. Here there was only shouting and confusion. In Spain there was Guernica.° Here there were disturbances of labor, sometimes pretty violent, in otherwise peaceful cities such as Chicago, Cleveland, Saint Louis . . . This is the social background of the play.

[*Music begins to play.*]

The play is memory. Being a memory play, it is dimly lighted, it is sentimental, it is not realistic. In memory everything seems to happen to music. That explains the fiddle in the wings.

I am the narrator of the play, and also a character in it. The other characters are my mother, Amanda, my sister, Laura, and a gentleman caller who appears in the final scenes. He is the most realistic character in the play, being an emissary from a world of reality that we were somehow set apart from. But since I have a poet's weakness for symbols, I am using this character also as a symbol; he is the long-delayed but always expected something that we live for.

There is a fifth character in the play who doesn't appear except in this larger-than-life-size photograph over the mantel. This is our father who left us a long time ago. He was a telephone man who fell in love with long distances; he gave up his job with the telephone company and skipped the light fantastic out of town . . .

The last we heard of him was a picture postcard from Mazatlan, on the Pacific coast of Mexico, containing a message of two words: "Hello—Goodbye!" and no address.

I think the rest of the play will explain itself. . . .

[AMANDA'S *voice becomes audible through the portieres.*]

[*Legend on screen:* "Où sont les neiges."°]

TOM *divides the portieres and enters the dining room.* AMANDA *and* LAURA *are seated at a drop-leaf table. Eating is indicated by gestures without food or utensils.* AMANDA *faces the audience.* TOM *and* LAURA *are seated profile. The interior has lit up softly and through the scrim we see* AMANDA *and* LAURA *seated at the table.*]

AMANDA. [*calling*] Tom?
TOM. Yes, Mother.
AMANDA. We can't say grace until you come to the table!
TOM. Coming, Mother. [*He bows slightly and withdraws, reappearing a few moments later in his place at the table.*]   5
AMANDA. [*to her son*] Honey, don't *push* with your *fingers.* If you have to push with something, the thing to push with is a crust of bread. And chew— chew! Animals have secretions in their stomachs which enable them to digest food

---

Guernica: a Basque town that was destroyed in 1937 by German planes fighting on General Franco's side during the Spanish Civil War. The huge mural *Guernica*, painted by Pablo Picasso, depicts the horror of that bombardment (see plate 5).
   "Où sont les neiges": "Where are the snows (of yesteryear)," refrain from "The Ballade of Dead Ladies" by the French poet François Villon (ca. 1431–1463).

without mastication, but human beings are supposed to chew their food before they swallow it down. Eat food leisurely, son, and really enjoy it. A well-cooked meal has lots of delicate flavors that have to be held in the mouth for appreciation. So chew your food and give your salivary glands a chance to function!

[*Tom deliberately lays his imaginary fork down and pushes his chair back from the table.*]

TOM. I haven't enjoyed one bite of this dinner because of your constant directions on how to eat it. It's you that make me rush through meals with your hawklike attention to every bite I take. Sickening—spoils my appetite—all this discussion of—animals' secretion—salivary glands—mastication!

AMANDA. [*lightly*] Temperament like a Metropolitan star!°

[*Tom rises and walks toward the living room.*]

You're not excused from the table.

TOM. I'm getting a cigarette.

AMANDA. You smoke too much.   10

[*Laura rises.*]

LAURA. I'll bring in the blanc mange.°

[*Tom remains standing with his cigarette by the portieres.*]

AMANDA. [*rising*] No, sister, no, sister° —you be the lady this time and I'll be the darky.

LAURA. I'm already up.

AMANDA. Resume your seat, little sister—I want you to stay fresh and pretty—for gentlemen callers!

LAURA. [*sitting down*] I'm not expecting any gentlemen callers.   15

AMANDA. [*crossing out to the kitchenette, airily*] Sometimes they come when they are least expected! Why, I remember one Sunday afternoon in Blue Mountain°—

[*She enters the kitchenette.*]

TOM. I know what's coming!

LAURA. Yes. But let her tell it.

TOM. Again?

LAURA. She loves to tell it.   20

[*Amanda returns with a bowl of dessert.*]

Metropolitan star: the Metropolitan Opera in New York City; opera stars are traditionally considered to be highly temperamental.

blanc mange: a bland, molded pudding or custard.

sister: In the South of Amanda's youth, the oldest daughter in a family was frequently called "sister" by her parents and siblings.

Blue Mountain: an imaginary town in northwest Mississippi modeled after Clarksville, where Williams spent much of his youth. Blue Mountain (Clarksville) is at the northern edge of the Mississippi Delta, a large fertile plain that supports numerous plantations. This is the recollected world of Amanda's youth—plantations, wealth, black servants, and gentlemen callers who were the sons of cotton planters.

AMANDA.   One Sunday afternoon in Blue Mountain—your mother received—*seventeen!*—gentlemen callers! Why, sometimes there weren't chairs enough to accommodate them all. We had to send the nigger over to bring in folding chairs from the parish house.

TOM.   [*remaining at the portieres*] How did you entertain those gentlemen callers?

AMANDA.   I understood the art of conversation!

TOM.   I bet you could talk.

AMANDA.   Girls in those days *knew* how to talk, I can tell you.   25

TOM.   Yes?

[*Image on screen: AMANDA as a girl on a porch, greeting callers.*]

AMANDA.   They knew how to entertain their gentlemen callers. It wasn't enough for a girl to be possessed of a pretty face and a graceful figure—although I wasn't slighted in either respect. She also needed to have a nimble wit and a tongue to meet all occasions.

TOM.   What did you talk about?

AMANDA.   Things of importance going on in the world! Never anything coarse or common or vulgar.

[*She addresses TOM as though he were seated in the vacant chair at the table though he remains by the portieres. He plays this scene as though reading from a script.°*]

My callers were gentlemen—all! Among my callers were some of the most prominent young planters of the Mississippi Delta—planters and sons of planters!

[*TOM motions for music and a spot of light on AMANDA. Her eyes lift, her face glows, her voice becomes rich and elegiac.*

[*Screen legend: "Ou sont les neiges d'antan?"°*]

There was young Champ Laughlin who later became vice-president of the Delta Planters Bank. Hadley Stevenson who was drowned in Moon Lake and left his widow one hundred and fifty thousand in Government bonds. There were the Cutrere brothers, Wesley and Bates. Bates was one of my bright particular beaux! He got in a quarrel with that wild Wainwright boy. They shot it out on the floor of Moon Lake Casino. Bates was shot through the stomach. Died in the ambulance on his way to Memphis. His widow was also well provided-for, came into eight or ten thousand acres, that's all. She married him on the rebound—never loved her—carried my picture on him the night he died! And there was that boy that every girl in the Delta had set her cap for! That beautiful, brilliant young Fitzhugh boy from Greene County!

TOM.   What did he leave his widow?   30

AMANDA.   He never married! Gracious, you talk as though all of my old admirers had turned up their toes to the daisies!

TOM.   Isn't this the first you've mentioned that still survives?

---

script: Here Tom becomes both a character in the play and the stage manager.
"Où sont les neiges d'antan?": Where are the snows of yesteryear? See page 1519n.

AMANDA.   That Fitzhugh boy went North and made a fortune—came to be known as the Wolf of Wall Street! He had the Midas touch,° whatever he touched turned to gold! And I could have been Mrs. Duncan J. Fitzhugh, mind you! But—I picked your *father*!

LAURA.   [*rising*] Mother, let me clear the table.

AMANDA.   No, dear, you go in front and study your typewriter chart. Or   35
practice your shorthand a little. Stay fresh and pretty!—It's almost time for our gentlemen callers to start arriving. [*She flounces girlishly toward the kitchenette.*] How many do you suppose we're going to entertain this afternoon?

[*Tom throws down the paper and jumps up with a groan.*]

LAURA.   [*alone in the dining room*] I don't believe we're going to receive any, Mother.

AMANDA.   [*reappearing airily*] What? No one?—not one? You must be joking!

[*LAURA nervously echoes her laugh. She slips in a fugitive manner through the half-open portieres and draws them gently behind her. A shaft of very clear light is thrown on her face against the faded tapestry of the curtains. Faintly the music of "The Glass Menagerie" is heard as she continues lightly:*]

Not one gentleman caller? It can't be true! There must be a flood, there must have been a tornado!

LAURA.   It isn't a flood, it's not a tornado, Mother. I'm just not popular like you were in Blue Mountain. . . .

[*Tom utters another groan. LAURA glances at him with a faint, apologetic smile. Her voice catches a little:*]

Mother's afraid I'm going to be an old maid.

[*The scene dims out with the "Glass Menagerie" music.*]

Scene 2

On the dark stage the screen is lighted with the image of blue roses. Gradually LAURA's figure becomes apparent and the screen goes out. The music subsides.

LAURA is seated in the delicate ivory chair at the small clawfoot table. She wears a dress of soft violet material for a kimono—her hair is tied back from her forehead with a ribbon. She is washing and polishing her collection of glass. AMANDA appears on the fire escape steps. At the sound of her ascent, LAURA catches her breath, thrusts the bowl of ornaments away, and seats herself stiffly before the diagram of the typewriter keyboard as though it held her spellbound. Something has happened to AMANDA. It is written in her face as she climbs to the landing: a look that is grim and hopeless and a little absurd. She has on one of those cheap or imitation velvety-looking cloth coats with imitation fur collar. Her hat is five or six years old, one of those dreadful cloche hats that were worn in the late Twenties, and she is clutching an enormous black patent-leather pocketbook with nickel

Midas touch: In Greek mythology, King Midas was given the power to turn everything he touched into gold.

*clasps and initials. This is her full-dress outfit, the one she usually wears to the D.A.R.°
Before entering she looks through the door. She purses her lips, opens her eyes very wide,
rolls them upward and shakes her head. Then she slowly lets herself in the door. Seeing her
mother's expression,* LAURA *touches her lips with a nervous gesture.*]

LAURA. Hello, Mother, I was—[*She makes a nervous gesture toward the chart
on the wall.* AMANDA *leans against the shut door and stares at* LAURA *with a martyred
look.*]

AMANDA. Deception? Deception? [*She slowly removes her hat and gloves, continuing the sweet suffering stare. She lets the hat and gloves fall on the floor—a bit of acting.*]

LAURA. [*shakily*] How was the D.A.R. meeting?

[AMANDA *slowly opens her purse and removes a dainty white handkerchief which she shakes
out delicately and delicately touches to her lips and nostrils.*]

Didn't you go to the D.A.R. meeting, Mother?

AMANDA. [*faintly, almost inaudibly*] —No.—No. [*then more forcibly:*] I did not
have the strength—to go to the D.A.R. In fact, I did not have the courage! I
wanted to find a hole in the ground and hide myself in it forever! [*She crosses
slowly to the wall and removes the diagram of the typewriter keyboard. She holds it in front
of her for a second, staring at it sweetly and sorrowfully—then bites her lips and tears it in
two pieces.*]

LAURA. [*faintly*] Why did you do that, Mother?   5

[AMANDA *repeats the same procedure with the chart of the Gregg Alphabet.*]

Why are you—

AMANDA. Why? Why? How old are you, Laura?

LAURA. Mother, you know my age.

AMANDA. I thought that you were an adult; it seems that I was mistaken.
[*She crosses slowly to the sofa and sinks down and stares at* LAURA.]

LAURA. Please don't stare at me, Mother.

[AMANDA *closes her eyes and lowers her head. There is a ten-second pause.*]

AMANDA. What are we going to do, what is going to become of us, what is   10
the future?

[*There is another pause.*]

LAURA. Has something happened, Mother?

[AMANDA *draws a long breath, takes out the handkerchief again, goes through the dabbing
process.*]

Mother, has—something happened?

AMANDA. I'll be all right in a minute, I'm just bewildered—[*She hesitates.*]—
by life. . . .

D.A.R.: Daughters of the American Revolution, a patriotic women's organization
(founded in 1890) open only to women whose ancestors aided the cause of the American
Revolution.

LAURA. Mother, I wish that you would tell me what's happened!

AMANDA. As you know, I was supposed to be inducted into my office at the D.A.R. this afternoon.

[Screen image: A swarm of typewriters.]

But I stopped off at Rubicam's Business College to speak to your teachers about your having a cold and ask them what progress they thought you were making down there.

LAURA. Oh. . . .

15

AMANDA. I went to the typing instructor and introduced myself as your mother. She didn't know who you were.

"Wingfield," she said, "We don't have any such student enrolled at the school!"

I assured her she did, that you had been going to classes since early in January.

"I wonder," she said, "If you could be talking about that terribly shy little girl who dropped out of school after only a few days' attendance?"

"No," I said, "Laura, my daughter, has been going to school every day for the past six weeks!"

"Excuse me," she said. She took the attendance book out and there was your name, unmistakably printed, and all the dates you were absent until they decided that you had dropped out of school.

I still said, "No, there must have been some mistake! There must have been some mix-up in the records!"

And she said, "No—I remember her perfectly now. Her hands shook so that she couldn't hit the right keys! The first time we gave a speed test, she broke down completely—was sick at the stomach and almost had to be carried into the wash room! After that morning she never showed up any more. We phoned the house but never got any answer"—While I was working at Famous-Barr,° I suppose, demonstrating those—

[She indicates a brassiere with her hands.]

Oh! I felt so weak I could barely keep on my feet! I had to sit down while they got me a glass of water! Fifty dollars' tuition, all of our plans—my hopes and ambitions for you—just gone up the spout, just gone up the spout like that.

[LAURA draws a long breath and gets awkwardly to her feet. She crosses to the Victrola and winds it up.°]

What are you doing?

LAURA. Oh! [She releases the handle and returns to her seat.]

AMANDA. Laura, where have you been going when you've gone out pretending that you were going to business college?

LAURA. I've just been going out walking.

AMANDA. That's not true.

20

LAURA. It is. I just went walking.

Famous-Barr: a department store in St. Louis.
winds it up: Laura is using a spring-powered (rather than electric) phonograph that had to be rewound frequently.

AMANDA. Walking? Walking? In winter? Deliberately courting pneumonia in that light coat? Where did you walk to, Laura?

LAURA. All sorts of places—mostly in the park.

AMANDA. Even after you'd started catching that cold?

LAURA. It was the lesser of two evils, Mother. 25

[*Screen image: Winter scene in a park.*]

I couldn't go back there. I—threw up—on the floor!

AMANDA. From half past seven till after five every day you mean to tell me you walked around in the park, because you wanted to make me think that you were still going to Rubicam's Business College?

LAURA. It wasn't as bad as it sounds. I went inside places to get warmed up.

AMANDA. Inside where?

LAURA. I went in the art museum and the bird houses at the Zoo. I visited the penguins every day! Sometimes I did without lunch and went to the movies. Lately I've been spending most of my afternoons in the Jewel Box, that big glass house where they raise the tropical flowers.

AMANDA. You did all this to deceive me, just for deception? [*LAURA looks down.*] Why? 30

LAURA. Mother, when you're disappointed, you get that awful suffering look on your face, like the picture of Jesus' mother in the museum!

AMANDA. Hush!

LAURA. I couldn't face it.

[*There is a pause. A whisper of strings is heard. Legend on screen: "The Crust of Humility."*]

AMANDA. [*hopelessly fingering the huge pocketbook*] So what are we going to do the rest of our lives? Stay home and watch the parades go by? Amuse ourselves with the glass menagerie, darling? Eternally play those worn-out phonograph records your father left as a painful reminder of him? We won't have a business career—we've given that up because it gave us nervous indigestion! [*She laughs wearily.*] What is there left but dependency all our lives? I know so well what becomes of unmarried women who aren't prepared to occupy a position. I've seen such pitiful cases in the South—barely tolerated spinsters living upon the grudging patronage of sister's husband or brother's wife!—stuck away in some little mousetrap of a room—encouraged by one in-law to visit another—little birdlike women without any nest—eating the crust of humility all their life!

Is that the future that we've mapped out for ourselves? I swear it's the only alternative I can think of! [*She pauses.*] It isn't a very pleasant alternative, is it? [*She pauses again.*] Of course—some girls *do marry.*

[*LAURA twists her hands nervously.*]

Haven't you ever liked some boy?

LAURA. Yes. I liked one once. [*She rises.*] I came across his picture a while ago. 35

AMANDA. [*with some interest*] He gave you his picture?

LAURA. No, it's in the yearbook.

AMANDA. [*disappointed*] Oh—a high school boy.

[*Screen image: JIM as the high school hero bearing a silver cup.*]

LAURA. Yes. His name was Jim. [*She lifts the heavy annual from the claw-foot table.*] Here he is in *The Pirates of Penzance.*°

AMANDA. [*absently*] The what?   40

LAURA. The operetta the senior class put on. He had a wonderful voice and we sat across the aisle from each other Mondays, Wednesdays and Fridays in the Aud. Here he is with the silver cup for debating! See his grin?

AMANDA. [*absently*] He must have had a jolly disposition.

LAURA. He used to call me—Blue Roses.

[*Screen image: Blue roses.*]

AMANDA. Why did he call you such a name as that?

LAURA. When I had that attack of pleurosis—he asked me what was the   45
matter when I came back. I said pleurosis—he thought that I said Blue Roses! So that's what he always called me after that. Whenever he saw me, he'd holler, "Hello, Blue Roses!" I didn't care for the girl that he went out with. Emily Meisenbach. Emily was the best-dressed girl at Soldan. She never struck me, though, as being sincere . . . It says in the Personal Section—they're engaged. That's—six years ago! They must be married by now.

AMANDA. Girls that aren't cut out for business careers usually wind up married to some nice man. [*She gets up with a spark of revival.*] Sister, that's what you'll do!

[*LAURA utters a startled, doubtful laugh. She reaches quickly for a piece of glass.*]

LAURA. But, Mother—

AMANDA. Yes? [*She goes over to the photograph.*]

LAURA. [*in a tone of frightened apology*] I'm—crippled!

AMANDA. Nonsense! Laura, I've told you never, never to use that word.   50
Why, you're not crippled, you just have a little defect—hardly noticeable, even! When people have some slight disadvantage like that, they cultivate other things to make up for it—develop charm—and vivacity—and—*charm!* That's all you have to do! [*She turns again to the photograph.*] One thing your father had *plenty of*—was charm!

[*The scene fades out with music.*]

Scene 3

[*Legend on screen: "After the fiasco—"*]

TOM *speaks from the fire escape landing.*]

TOM. After the fiasco at Rubicam's Business College, the idea of getting a gentleman caller for Laura began to play a more and more important part in Mother's calculations. It became an obsession. Like some archetype of the universal unconscious, the image of the gentleman caller haunted our small apartment. . . .

[*Screen image: A young man at the door of a house with flowers.*]

The Pirates of Penzance: a comic light opera (1879) by W. S. Gilbert and Arthur Sullivan.

An evening at home rarely passed without some allusion to this image, this specter, this hope. . . . Even when he wasn't mentioned, his presence hung in Mother's preoccupied look and in my sister's frightened, apologetic manner—hung like a sentence passed upon the Wingfields!

Mother was a woman of action as well as words. She began to take logical steps in the planned direction. Late that winter and in the early spring—realizing that extra money would be needed to properly feather the nest and plume the bird—she conducted a vigorous campaign on the telephone, roping in subscribers to one of those magazines for matrons called *The Homemaker's Companion*, the type of journal that features the serialized sublimations of ladies of letters who think in terms of delicate cuplike breasts, slim, tapering waists, rich, creamy thighs, eyes like wood smoke in autumn, fingers that soothe and caress like strains of music, bodies as powerful as Etruscan sculpture.

[*Screen image: The cover of a glamor magazine.*]

AMANDA *enters with the telephone on a long extension cord. She is spotlighted in the dim stage.*]

AMANDA. Ida Scott? This is Amanda Wingfield! We *missed* you at the D.A.R. last Monday! I said to myself: She's probably suffering with that sinus condition! How is that sinus condition?

Horrors! Heaven have mercy!—You're a Christian martyr, yes, that's what you are, a Christian martyr!

Well, I just now happened to notice that your subscription to the *Companion's* about to expire! Yes, it expires with the next issue, honey!—just when that wonderful new serial by Bessie Mae Hopper is getting off to such an exciting start. Oh, honey, it's something that you can't miss! You remember how *Gone with the Wind*° took everybody by storm? You simply couldn't go out if you hadn't read it. All everybody *talked* was Scarlett O'Hara. Well, this is a book that critics already compare to *Gone with the Wind*. It's the *Gone with the Wind* of the post-World-War generation!— What?—Burning?—Oh, honey, don't let them burn, go take a look in the oven and I'll hold the wire! Heavens—I think she's hung up!

[*The scene dims out.*]

[*Legend on screen: "You think I'm in love with Continental Shoemakers?"*]

[*Before the lights come up again, the violent voices of* TOM *and* AMANDA *are heard. They are quarreling behind the portieres. In front of them stands* LAURA *with clenched hands and panicky expression. A clear pool of light is on her figure throughout this scene.*]

TOM. What in Christ's name am I—
AMANDA. [*shrilly*] Don't you use that—
TOM. —supposed to do!   5
AMANDA. —expression! Not in my—
TOM. Ohhh!

Gone with the Wind: an extremely popular novel (1936) by Margaret Mitchell (1900–1949), set in the South before, during, and after the Civil War. Scarlett O'Hara was the heroine.

AMANDA.   —presence! Have you gone out of your senses?

TOM.   I have, that's true, *driven* out!

AMANDA.   What is the matter with you, you—big—big—IDIOT!   10

TOM.   Look!—I've got *no thing*, no single thing—

AMANDA.   Lower your voice!

TOM.   —in my life here that I can call my OWN! Everything is—

AMANDA.   Stop that shouting!

TOM.   Yesterday you confiscated my books! You had the nerve to—   15

AMANDA.   I took that horrible novel back to the library—yes! That hideous book by that insane Mr. Lawrence.°

[*TOM laughs wildly.*]

I cannot control the output of diseased minds or people who cater to them—

[*TOM laughs still more wildly.*]

BUT I WON'T ALLOW SUCH FILTH BROUGHT INTO MY HOUSE! No, no, no, no, no!

TOM.   House, house! Who pays rent on it, who makes a slave of himself to—

AMANDA.   [*fairly screeching*] Don't you DARE to—

TOM.   No, no, *I* mustn't say things! *I've* got to just—

AMANDA.   Let me tell you—   20

TOM.   I don't want to hear any more!

[*He tears the portieres open. The dining-room area is lit with turgid smoky red glow. Now we see AMANDA; her hair is in metal curlers and she is wearing a very old bathrobe, much too large for her slight figure, a relic of the faithless Mr. Wingfield. The upright typewriter now stands on the drop-leaf table, along with a wild disarray of manuscripts. The quarrel was probably precipitated by AMANDA's interruption of TOM's creative labor. A chair lies overthrown on the floor. Their gesticulating shadows are cast on the ceiling by the fiery glow.*]

AMANDA.   You *will* hear more, you—

TOM.   No, I won't hear more, I'm going out!

AMANDA.   You come right back in—

TOM.   Out, out, out! Because I'm—   25

AMANDA.   Come back here, Tom Wingfield! I'm not through talking to you!

TOM.   Oh, go—

LAURA.   [*desperately*] —Tom!

AMANDA.   You're going to listen, and no more insolence from you! I'm at the end of my patience!

[*He comes back toward her.*]

TOM.   What do you think I'm at? Aren't I supposed to have any patience   30 to reach the end of, Mother? I know, I know. It seems unimportant to you, what I'm *doing*—what I *want* to do—having a little *difference* between them! You don't think that—

Lawrence: D. H. Lawrence (1885–1930), English poet and fiction writer, popularly known as an advocate of passion and sexuality. See "The Horse Dealer's Daughter," p. 373.

AMANDA. I think you've been doing things that you're ashamed of. That's why you act like this. I don't believe that you go every night to the movies. Nobody goes to the movies night after night. Nobody in their right minds goes to the movies as often as you pretend to. People don't go to the movies at nearly midnight, and movies don't let out at two A.M. Come in stumbling. Muttering to yourself like a maniac! You get three hours' sleep and then go to work. Oh, I can picture the way you're doing down there. Moping, doping, because you're in no condition.

TOM. [*wildly*] No, I'm in no condition!

AMANDA. What right have you got to jeopardize your job? Jeopardize the security of us all? How do you think we'd manage if you were—

TOM. Listen! You think I'm crazy about the *warehouse*? [*He bends fiercely toward her slight figure.*] You think I'm in love with the Continental Shoemakers? You think I want to spend fifty-five *years* down there in that—*celotex interior*! with—*fluorescent—tubes*! Look! I'd rather somebody picked up a crowbar and battered out my brains—than go back mornings! I *go*! Every time you come in yelling that God damn *"Rise and Shine!" "Rise and Shine!"* I say to myself, "How *lucky dead* people are!" But I get up. I *go*! For sixty-five dollars a month I give up all that I dream of doing and being *ever*! And you say self—*self's* all I ever think of. Why, listen, if self is what I thought of, Mother, I'd be where he is—GONE! [*He points to his father's picture.*] As far as the system of transportation reaches! [*He starts past her. She grabs his arm.*] Don't grab at me, Mother!

AMANDA. Where are you going?

TOM. I'm going to the *movies*!

AMANDA. I don't believe that lie!

[*TOM crouches toward her, overtowering her tiny figure. She backs away, gasping.*]

TOM. I'm going to opium dens! Yes, opium dens, dens of vice and criminals' hangouts, Mother. I've joined the Hogan Gang,° I'm a hired assassin, I carry a tommy gun in a violin case! I run a string of cat houses in the Valley! They call me Killer, Killer Wingfield, I'm leading a double-life, a simple, honest warehouse worker by day, by night a dynamic *czar* of the *underworld, Mother*. I go to gambling casinos, I spin away fortunes on the roulette table! I wear a patch over one eye and a false mustache, sometimes I put on green whiskers. On those occasions they call me—*El Diablo*!° Oh, I could tell you many things to make you sleepless! My enemies plan to dynamite this place. They're going to blow us all sky-high some night! I'll be glad, very happy, and so will you! You'll go up, up on a broomstick, over Blue Mountain with seventeen gentlemen callers! You ugly—babbling old—*witch*. . . .

[*He goes through a series of violent, clumsy movements, seizing his overcoat, lunging to the door, pulling it fiercely open. The women watch him, aghast. His arm catches in the sleeve of the coat as he struggles to pull it on. For a moment he is pinioned by the bulky garment. With an outraged groan he tears the coat off again, splitting the shoulder of it, and hurls it across the room. It strikes against the shelf of LAURA's glass collection, and there is a tinkle of shattering glass. LAURA cries out as if wounded.*]

Hogan Gang: one of the major criminal organizations in St. Louis in the 1930s.
El Diablo: the devil.

35

Music.

Screen legend: "The Glass Menagerie."]

LAURA   [*shrilly*] *My glass!*—menagerie. . . . [*She covers her face and turns away.*]

[*But* AMANDA *is still stunned and stupefied by the "ugly witch" so that she barely notices this occurrence. Now she recovers her speech.*]

AMANDA.   [*in an awful voice*] I won't speak to you—until you apologize!   40

[*She crosses through the portieres and draws them together behind her.* TOM *is left with* LAURA. LAURA *clings weakly to the mantel with her face averted.* TOM *stares at her stupidly for a moment. Then he crosses to the shelf. He drops awkwardly on his knees to collect the fallen glass, glancing at* LAURA *as if he would speak but couldn't.*

"The Glass Menagerie" music steals in as the scene dims out.]

Scene 4

[*The interior of the apartment is dark. There is a faint light in the alley. A deep-voiced bell in a church is tolling the hour of five.*

TOM *appears at the top of the alley. After each solemn boom of the bell in the tower, he shakes a little noisemaker or rattle as if to express the tiny spasm of man in contrast to the sustained power and dignity of the Almighty. This and the unsteadiness of his advance make it evident that he has been drinking. As he climbs the few steps to the fire escape landing light steals up inside.* LAURA *appears in the front room in a nightdress. She notices that* TOM's *bed is empty.* TOM *fishes in his pockets for his door key, removing a motley assortment of articles in the search, including a shower of movie ticket stubs and an empty bottle. At last he finds the key, but just as he is about to insert it, it slips from his fingers. He strikes a match and crouches below the door.*]

TOM.   [*bitterly*] One crack—and it falls through!

[LAURA *opens the door.*]

LAURA.   Tom! Tom, what are you doing?
TOM.   Looking for a door key.
LAURA.   Where have you been all this time?
TOM.   I have been to the movies.
LAURA.   All this time at the movies?   5
TOM.   There was a very long program. There was a Garbo° picture and a Mickey Mouse and a travelogue and a newsreel and a preview of coming attractions. And there was an organ solo and a collection for the Milk Fund—simultaneously— which ended up in a terrible fight between a fat lady and an usher!
LAURA.   [*innocently*] Did you have to stay through everything?
TOM.   Of course! And, oh, I forgot! There was a big stage show! The headliner on this stage show was Malvolio° the Magician. He performed wonderful tricks,

---

Garbo: Greta Garbo (b. 1905), Swedish star of American silent and early sound films.
Malvolio: the name, borrowed from a puritanical character in Shakespeare's *Twelfth Night*, means "malevolence" or "ill-will."

many of them, such as pouring water back and forth between pitchers. First it turned to wine and then it turned to beer and then it turned to whisky. I know it was whisky it finally turned into because he needed somebody to come up out of the audience to help him, and I came up—both shows! It was Kentucky Straight Bourbon. A very generous fellow, he gave souvenirs. [*He pulls from his back pocket a shimmering rainbow-colored scarf.*] He gave me this. This is his magic scarf. You can have it, Laura. You wave it over a canary cage and you get a bowl of goldfish. You wave it over the goldfish bowl and they fly away canaries. . . . But the wonderfullest trick of all was the coffin trick. We nailed him into a coffin and he got out of the coffin without removing one nail. [*He has come inside.*] There is a trick that would come in handy for me—get me out of this two-by-four situation! [*He flops onto the bed and starts removing his shoes.*]

    LAURA. Tom—shhh!   10

    TOM. What're you shushing me for?

    LAURA. You'll wake up Mother.

    TOM. Goody, goody! Pay 'er back for all those "Rise an' Shines." [*He lies down, groaning.*] You know it don't take much intelligence to get yourself into a nailed-up coffin, Laura. But who in hell ever got himself out of one without removing one nail?

[*As if in answer, the father's grinning photograph lights up. The scene dims out.*]

[*Immediately following, the church bell is heard striking six. At the sixth stroke the alarm clock goes off in* AMANDA's *room, and after a few moments we hear her calling: "Rise and Shine! Rise and Shine! Laura, go tell your brother to rise and shine!"*]

    TOM. [*sitting up slowly*] I'll rise—but I won't shine.

[*The light increases.*]

    AMANDA. Laura, tell your brother his coffee is ready.   15

[LAURA *slips into the front room.*]

    LAURA. Tom!—It's nearly seven. Don't make Mother nervous.

[*He stares at her stupidly.*]

[*Beseechingly.*] Tom, speak to Mother this morning. Make up with her, apologize, speak to her!

    TOM. She won't to me. It's her that started not speaking.

    LAURA. If you just say you're sorry she'll start speaking.

    TOM. Her not speaking—is that such a tragedy?

    LAURA. Please—please!   20

    AMANDA. [*calling from the kitchenette*] Laura, are you going to do what I asked you to do, or do I have to get dressed and go out myself?

    LAURA. Going, going—soon as I get on my coat!

[*She pulls on a shapeless felt hat with a nervous, jerky movement, pleadingly glancing at* TOM. *She rushes awkwardly for her coat. The coat is one of* AMANDA's, *inaccurately made-over, the sleeves too short for* LAURA.]

Butter and what else?

AMANDA.   [*entering from the kitchenette*] Just butter. Tell them to charge it.

LAURA.   Mother, they make such faces when I do that.

AMANADA.   Sticks and stones can break our bones, but the expression on   25
Mr. Garfinkel's face won't harm us! Tell your brother his coffee is getting cold.

LAURA.   [*at the door*] Do what I asked you, will you, will you, Tom?

[*He looks sullenly away.*]

AMANDA.   Laura, go now or just don't go at all!

LAURA.   [*rushing out*] Going—going!

[*A second later she cries out. TOM springs up and crosses to the door. TOM opens the door.*]

TOM.   Laura?

LAURA.   I'm all right. I slipped, but I'm all right.   30

AMANDA.   [*peering anxiously after her*] If anyone breaks a leg on those fire-
escape steps, the landlord ought to be sued for every cent he possesses! [*She shuts
the door. Now she remembers she isn't speaking to TOM and returns to the other room.*]

[*As TOM comes listlessly for his coffee, she turns her back to him and stands rigidly facing
the window on the gloomy gray vault of the areaway. Its light on her face with its aged but
childish features is cruelly sharp, satirical as a Daumier print.°*]

The music of "Ave Maria,"° is heard softly.

TOM *glances sheepishly but sullenly at her averted figure and slumps at the table. The
coffee is scalding hot; he sips it and gasps and spits it back in the cup. At his gasp, AMANDA
catches her breath and half turns. Then she catches herself and turns back to the window.
TOM blows on his coffee, glancing sidewise at his mother. She clears her throat. TOM clears
his. He starts to rise, sinks back down again, scratches his head, clears his throat again.
AMANDA coughs. TOM raises his cup in both hands to blow on it, his eyes staring over the
rim of it at his mother for several moments. Then he slowly sets the cup down and awkwardly
and hesitantly rises from the chair.*]

TOM.   [*hoarsely*] Mother. I—I apologize, Mother.

[*AMANDA draws a quick, shuddering breath. Her face works grotesquely. She breaks into
childlike tears.*]

I'm sorry for what I said, for everything that I said, I didn't mean it.

AMANDA.   [*sobbingly*] My devotion has made me a witch and so I make myself
hateful to my children!

TOM.   *No, you don't.*

AMANDA.   I worry so much, don't sleep, it makes me nervous!   35

TOM.   [*gently*] I understand that.

AMANDA.   I've had to put up a solitary battle all these years. But you're my
right-hand bower!° Don't fall down, don't fail!

Daumier print: Honoré Daumier (1808–1879), French painter and engraver whose prints
frequently satirized his society.

"*Ave Maria*": a Roman Catholic prayer to the Virgin Mary; the musical setting called
for here is by Franz Schubert (1797–1828), an Austrian composer.

bower: an anchor at the bow (or front) of a ship.

TOM. [*gently*] I try, Mother.

AMANDA. [*with great enthusiasm*] Try and you will *succeed!* [*The notion makes her breathless.*] Why, you—you're just *full* of natural endowments! Both of my children—they're *unusual* children! Don't you think I know it? I'm so—*proud!* Happy and—feel I've—so much to be thankful for but—promise me one thing, son!

TOM. What, Mother?   40

AMANDA. Promise, son, you'll—never be a drunkard!

TOM. [*turns to her grinning*] I will never be a drunkard, Mother.

AMANDA. That's what frightened me so, that you'd be drinking! Eat a bowl of Purina!

TOM. Just coffee, Mother.

AMANDA. Shredded wheat biscuit?   45

TOM. No. No, Mother, just coffee.

AMANDA. You can't put in a day's work on an empty stomach. You've got ten minutes—don't gulp! Drinking too-hot liquids makes cancer of the stomach. . . . Put cream in.

TOM. No, thank you.

AMANDA. To cool it.

TOM. No! No, thank you, I want it black.   50

AMANDA. I know, but it's not good for you. We have to do all that we can to build ourselves up. In these trying times we live in, all that we have to cling to is—each other. . . . That's why it's so important to—Tom, I—I sent out your sister so I could discuss something with you. If you hadn't spoken I would have spoken to you. [*She sits down.*]

TOM. [*gently*] What is it, Mother, that you want to discuss?

AMANDA. *Laura!*

[*TOM puts his cup down slowly.*]

Legend on screen "Laura." Music: "The Glass Menagerie."]

TOM. —Oh.—Laura . . .

AMANDA. [*touching his sleeve*] You know how Laura is. So quiet but—still   55
water runs deep! She notices things and I think she—broods about them.

[*TOM looks up.*]

A few days ago I came in and she was crying.

TOM. What about?

AMANDA. You.

TOM. Me?

AMANDA. She has an idea that you're not happy here.

TOM. What gave her that idea?   60

AMANDA. What gives her any idea? However, you do act strangely. I—I'm not criticizing, understand *that!* I know your ambitions do not lie in the warehouse, that like everybody in the whole wide world—you've had to—make sacrifices, but—Tom—Tom—life's not easy, it calls for—Spartan endurance! There's so many things in my heart that I cannot describe to you! I've never told you but I—*loved* your father. . . .

TOM. [*gently*] I know that, Mother.

AMANDA. And you—when I see you taking after his ways! Staying out late—
and—well, you *had* been drinking the night you were in that—terrifying condition!
Laura says that you hate the apartment and that you go out nights to get away
from it! Is that true, Tom?

TOM. No. You say there's so much in your heart that you can't describe to
me. That's true of me, too. There's so much in my heart that I can't describe to
you! So let's respect each other's—

AMANDA. But, why—*why*, Tom—are you always so *restless?* Where do you   65
go to, nights?

TOM. I—go to the movies.

AMANDA. Why do you go to the movies so much, Tom?

TOM. I go to the movies because—I like adventure. Adventure is something
I don't have much of at work, so I go to the movies.

AMANDA. But, Tom, you go to the movies *entirely* too *much!*

TOM. I like a lot of adventure.   70

[AMANDA *looks baffled, then hurt. As the familiar inquisition resumes,* TOM *becomes hard
and impatient again.* AMANDA *slips back into her querulous attitude toward him.*

Image on screen: A sailing vessel with Jolly Roger.°]

AMANDA. Most young men find adventure in their careers.

TOM. Then most young men are not employed in a warehouse.

AMANDA. The world is full of young men employed in warehouses and
offices and factories.

TOM. Do all of them find adventure in their careers?

AMANDA. They do or they do without it! Not everybody has a craze for   75
adventure.

TOM. Man is by instinct a lover, a hunter, a fighter, and none of those
instincts are given much play at the warehouse!

AMANDA. Man is by instinct! Don't quote instinct to me! Instinct is something
that people have got away from! It belongs to animals! Christian adults don't
want it!

TOM. What do Christian adults want, then, Mother?

AMANDA. Superior things! Things of the mind and the spirit! Only animals
have to satisfy instincts! Surely your aims are somewhat higher than theirs! Than
monkeys—pigs—

TOM. I reckon they're not.   80

AMANDA. You're joking. However, that isn't what I wanted to discuss.

TOM. [*rising*] I haven't much time.

AMANDA. [*pushing his shoulders*] Sit down.

TOM. You want me to punch in red° at the warehouse, Mother?

AMANDA. You have five minutes. I want to talk about Laura.   85

[*Screen legend: "Plans and Provisions."*]

Jolly Roger: the traditional flag of a pirate ship—a skull and crossed bones on a field
of black.
punch in red: arrive late for work; the time clock stamps late arrival times in red on
the time card.

TOM. All right! What about Laura?

AMANDA. We have to be making some plans and provisions for her. She's older than you, two years, and nothing has happened. She just drifts along doing nothing. It frightens me terribly how she just drifts along.

TOM. I guess she's the type that people call home girls.

AMANDA. There's no such type, and if there is, it's a pity! That is unless the home is hers, with a husband!

TOM. What?   90

AMANDA. Oh, I can see the handwriting on the wall as plain as I see the nose in front of my face! It's terrifying! More and more you remind me of your father! He was out all hours without explanation! —Then *left*! *Goodbye*! And me with the bag to hold. I saw that letter you got from the Merchant Marine. I know what you're dreaming of. I'm not standing here blindfolded. [*She pauses.*] Very well, then. Then *do* it! But not till there's somebody to take your place.

TOM. What do you mean?

AMANDA. I mean that as soon as Laura has got somebody to take care of her, married, a home of her own, independent—why, then you'll be free to go wherever you please, on land, on sea, whichever way the wind blows you! But until that time you've got to look out for your sister. I don't say me because I'm old and don't matter! I say for your sister because she's young and dependent.

I put her in business college—a dismal failure! Frightened her so it made her sick at the stomach. I took her over to the Young People's League at the church. Another fiasco. She spoke to nobody, nobody spoke to her. Now all she does is fool with those pieces of glass and play those worn-out records. What kind of a life is that for a girl to lead?

TOM. What can I do about it?

AMANDA. Overcome selfishness! Self, self, self is all that you ever think of!   95

[*TOM springs up and crosses to get his coat. It is ugly and bulky. He pulls on a cap with earmuffs.*]

Where is your muffler? Put your wool muffler on!

[*He snatches it angrily from the closet, tosses it around his neck and pulls both ends tight.*]

Tom! I haven't said what I had in mind to ask you.

TOM. I'm too late to—

AMANDA. [*catching his arm—very importunately; then shyly*] Down at the warehouse, aren't there some—nice young men?

TOM. No!

AMANDA. There *must* be—*some* . . .

TOM. Mother— [*He gestures.*]   100

AMANDA. Find out one that's clean-living—doesn't drink and ask him out for sister!

TOM. What?

AMANDA. For *sister*! To *meet*! Get *acquainted*!

TOM. [*stamping to the door*] Oh, my *go-osh*!

AMANDA. Will you? [*He opens the door. She says, imploringly:*] Will you?   105

[*He starts down the fire escape.*]

Will you? *Will* you, dear?

    TOM. *[calling back]* Yes!

[AMANDA *closes the door hesitantly and with a troubled but faintly hopeful expression.*

Screen image: The cover of a glamor magazine.

The spotlight picks up AMANDA *at the phone.*]

    AMANDA. Ella Cartwright? This is Amanda Wingfield! How are you honey? How is that kidney condition?

[*There is a five-second pause.*]

Horrors!

[*There is another pause.*]

You're a Christian martyr, yes, honey, that's what you are, a Christian martyr! Well, I just now happened to notice in my little red book that your subscription to the *Companion* has just run out! I knew that you wouldn't want to miss out on the wonderful serial starting in this new issue. It's by Bessie Mae Hopper, the first thing she's written since *Honeymoon for Three.* Wasn't that a strange and interesting story? Well, this one is even lovelier, I believe. It has a sophisticated, society background. It's all about the horsey set on Long Island!

[*The light fades out.*]

Scene 5

[*Legend on the screen: "Annunciation."*

Music is heard as the light slowly comes on.

It is early dusk of a spring evening. Supper has just been finished in the Wingfield apartment. AMANDA *and* LAURA, *in light-colored dresses, are removing dishes from the table in the dining room, which is shadowy, their movements formalized almost as a dance or ritual, their moving forms as pale and silent as moths.* TOM, *in white shirt and trousers, rises from the table and crosses toward the fire escape.*]

    AMANDA. *[as he passes her]* Son, will you do me a favor?

    TOM. What?

    AMANDA. Comb your hair! You look so pretty when your hair is combed!

[TOM *slouches on the sofa with the evening paper. Its enormous headline reads: "Franco Triumphs."*°]

There is only one respect in which I would like you to emulate your father.

    TOM. What respect is that?

"Franco Triumphs": Francisco Franco (1892–1975), dictator of Spain from 1939 until his death, was the general of the victorious Falangist armies in the Spanish Civil War (1936–1939).

AMANDA.   The care he always took of his appearance. He never allowed   5
himself to look untidy.

[*He throws down the paper and crosses to the fire escape.*]

Where are you going?

TOM.   I'm going out to smoke.

AMANDA.   You smoke too much. A pack a day at fifteen cents a pack. How
much would that amount to in a month? Thirty times fifteen is how much, Tom?
Figure it out and you will be astounded at what you could save. Enough to give
you a night-school course in accounting at Washington U.!° Just think what a
wonderful thing that would be for you, son!

[*TOM is unmoved by the thought.*]

TOM.   I'd rather smoke. [*He steps out on the landing, letting the screen door
slam.*]

AMANDA.   [*sharply*] I know! That's the tragedy of it. . . . [*Alone, she turns to
look at her husband's picture.*]

[*Dance music: "The World Is Waiting for the Sunrise!"°*]

TOM.   [*to the audience*] Across the alley from us was the Paradise Dance Hall.   10
On evenings in spring the windows and doors were open and the music came
outdoors. Sometimes the lights were turned out except for a large glass sphere
that hung from the ceiling. It would turn slowly about and filter the dusk with
delicate rainbow colors. Then the orchestra played a waltz or a tango, something
that had a slow and sensuous rhythm. Couples would come outside, to the relative
privacy of the alley. You could see them kissing behind ash pits and telephone
poles. This was the compensation for lives that passed like mine, without any
change or adventure. Adventure and change were imminent in this year. They
were waiting around the corner for all these kids. Suspended in the mist over
Berchtesgaden, caught in the folds of Chamberlain's umbrella. In Spain there
was Guernica!° But here there was only hot swing music and liquor, dance halls,
bars, and movies, and sex that hung in the gloom like a chandelier and flooded
the world with brief, deceptive rainbows. . . . All the world was waiting for bombard-
ments!

[*AMANDA turns from the picture and comes outside.*]

AMANDA.   [*sighing*] A fire escape landing's a poor excuse for a porch. [*She*

Washington U: Washington University, a highly competitive liberal arts school in St.
Louis.
   "The World . . . Sunrise": popular song written in 1919 by Eugene Lockhart and Ernest
Seitz.
   Berchtesgaden . . . Guernica: The three names mentioned are all foreshadowings of
World War II. Berchtesgaden, a resort in the Bavarian Alps, was Adolf Hitler's favorite
residence. Neville Chamberlain was the British prime minister who signed the Munich Pact
with Hitler in 1938, allowing Nazi Germany to occupy parts of Czechoslovakia. Chamberlain,
who always carried an umbrella, declared that he had ensured "peace in our time." The
bombardment of Guernica during the Spanish Civil War made the name of the town synonymous with the horrors of war, and especially the killing of civilian women and children.
(See p. 1519n. and plate 5.)

spreads a newspaper on a step and sits down, gracefully and demurely as if she were settling into a swing on a Mississippi veranda.] What are you looking at?

TOM.   The moon.

AMANDA.   Is there a moon this evening?

TOM.   It's rising over Garfinkel's Delicatessen.

AMANDA.   So it is! A little silver slipper of a moon. Have you made a wish   15
on it yet?

TOM.   Um-hum.

AMANDA.   What did you wish for?

TOM.   That's a secret.

AMANDA.   A secret, huh? Well, I won't tell mine either. I will be just as mysterious as you.

TOM.   I bet I can guess what yours is.   20

AMANDA.   Is my head so transparent?

TOM.   You're not a sphinx.°

AMANDA.   No, I don't have secrets. I'll tell you what I wished for on the moon. Success and happiness for my precious children! I wish for that whenever there's a moon, and when there isn't a moon, I wish for it, too.

TOM.   I thought perhaps you wished for a gentleman caller.

AMANDA.   Why do you say that?   25

TOM.   Don't you remember asking me to fetch one?

AMANDA.   I remember suggesting that it would be nice for your sister if you brought home some nice young man from the warehouse. I think that I've made that suggestion more than once.

TOM.   Yes, you have made it repeatedly.

AMANDA.   Well?

TOM.   We are going to have one.   30

AMANDA.   *What?*

TOM.   A gentleman caller!

[*The annunciation is celebrated with music.*

AMANDA rises.

Image on screen: A caller with a bouquet.]

AMANDA.   You mean you have asked some nice young man to come over?

TOM.   Yep. I've asked him to dinner.

AMANDA.   You really did?   35

TOM.   I did!

AMANDA.   You did, and did he—*accept?*

TOM.   He did!

AMANDA.   Well, well—well, well! That's—lovely!

TOM.   I thought that you would be pleased.   40

AMANDA.   It's definite then?

TOM.   Very definite.

AMANDA.   Soon?

sphinx: a mythological monster with the head of a woman and body of a lion, famous for her riddles. See p. 789 and plate 4.

TOM.   Very soon.

AMANDA.   For heaven's sake, stop putting on and tell me some things, will   45
you?

TOM.   What things do you want me to tell you?

AMANDA.   *Naturally* I would like to know when he's *coming!*

TOM.   He's coming tomorrow.

AMANDA.   *Tomorrow?*

TOM.   Yep. Tomorrow.   50

AMANDA.   But, Tom!

TOM.   Yes, Mother?

AMANDA.   Tomorrow gives me no time!

TOM.   Time for what?

AMANDA.   Preparations! Why didn't you phone me at once, as soon as you   55
asked him, the minute that he accepted? Then, don't you see, I could have been
getting ready!

TOM.   You don't have to make any fuss.

AMANDA.   Oh, Tom, Tom, Tom, of course I have to make a fuss! I want
things nice, not sloppy! Not thrown together. I'll certainly have to do some fast
thinking, won't I?

TOM.   I don't see why you have to think at all.

AMANDA.   You just don't know. We can't have a gentleman caller in a pigsty!
All my wedding silver has to be polished, the monogrammed table linen ought to
be laundered! The windows have to be washed and fresh curtains put up. And
how about clothes? We have to *wear* something, don't we?

TOM.   Mother, this boy is no one to make a fuss over!   60

AMANDA.   Do you realize he's the first young man we've introduced to your
sister? It's terrible, dreadful, disgraceful that poor little sister has never received a
single gentleman caller! Tom, come inside! [*She opens the screen door.*]

TOM.   What for?

AMANDA.   I want to ask you some things.

TOM.   If you're going to make such a fuss, I'll call it off, I'll tell him not to
come!

AMANDA.   You certainly won't do anything of the kind. Nothing offends   65
people worse than broken engagements. It simply means I'll have to work like a
Turk! We won't be brilliant, but we will pass inspection. Come on inside.

[*TOM follows her inside, groaning.*]

Sit down.

TOM.   Any particular place you would like me to sit?

AMANDA.   Thank heavens I've got that new sofa! I'm also making payments
on a floor lamp I'll have sent out! And put the chintz covers on, they'll brighten
things up! Of course I'd hoped to have these walls re-papered. . . . What is the
young man's name?

TOM.   His name is O'Connor.

AMANDA.   That, of course, means fish° —tomorrow is Friday! I'll have that

---

fish: Amanda assumes that O'Connor is Roman Catholic. Until the 1960s, Roman
Catholics were required by the church to abstain from meat on Fridays.

salmon loaf—with Durkee's dressing! What does he do? He works at the warehouse?

TOM.   Of course! How else would I—   70

AMANDA.   Tom, he—doesn't drink?

TOM.   Why do you ask me that?

AMANDA.   Your father *did*!

TOM.   Don't get started on that!

AMANDA.   He *does* drink, then?   75

TOM.   Not that I know of!

AMANDA.   Make sure, be certain! The last thing I want for my daughter's a
boy who drinks!

TOM.   Aren't you being a little bit premature? Mr. O'Connor has not yet
appeared on the scene!

AMANDA.   But will tomorrow. To meet your sister, and what do I know
about his character? Nothing! Old maids are better off than wives of drunkards!

TOM.   Oh, my God!   80

AMANDA.   Be still!

TOM.   [*leaning forward to whisper*] Lots of fellows meet girls whom they don't
marry!

AMANDA.   Oh, talk sensibly, Tom—and don't be sarcastic! [*She has gotten a
hairbrush.*]

TOM.   What are you doing?

AMANDA.   I'm brushing that cowlick down! [*She attacks his hair with the brush.*]   85
What is this young man's position at the warehouse?

TOM.   [*submitting grimly to the brush and the interrogation*] This young man's
position is that of a shipping clerk, Mother.

AMANDA.   Sounds to me like a fairly responsible job, the sort of a job *you*
would be in if you just had more *get-up*. What is his salary? Have you any idea?

TOM.   I would judge it to be approximately eighty-five dollars a month.

AMANDA.   Well—not princely, but—

TOM.   Twenty more than I make.   90

AMANDA.   Yes, how well I know! But for a family man, eighty-five dollars a
month is not much more than you can just get by on. . . .

TOM.   Yes, but Mr. O'Connor is not a family man.

AMANDA.   He might be, mightn't he? Some time in the future?

TOM.   I see. Plans and provisions.

AMANDA.   You are the only young man that I know of who ignores the   95
fact that the future becomes the present, the present the past, and the past turns
into everlasting regret if you don't plan for it!

TOM.   I will think that over and see what I can make of it.

AMANDA.   Don't be supercilious with your mother! Tell me some more about
this—what do you call him?

TOM.   James D. O'Connor. The D. is for Delaney.

AMANDA.   Irish on *both* sides! *Gracious*! And he doesn't drink?

TOM.   Shall I call him up and ask him right this minute?   100

AMANDA.   The only way to find out about those things is to make discreet
inquiries at the proper moment. When I was a girl in Blue Mountain and it was
suspected that a young man drank, the girl whose attentions he had been receiving,
if any girl *was*, would sometimes speak to the minister of his church, or rather

her father would if her father was living, and sort of feel him out on the young man's character. That is the way such things are discreetly handled to keep a young woman from making a tragic mistake!

Tom. Then how did you happen to make a tragic mistake?

Amanda. That innocent look of your father's had everyone fooled! He *smiled*—the world was *enchanted*! No girl can do worse than put herself at the mercy of a handsome appearance! I hope that Mr. O'Connor is not too good-looking.

Tom. No, he's not too good-looking. He's covered with freckles and hasn't too much of a nose.

Amanda. He's not right-down homely, though?   105

Tom. Not right-down homely. Just medium homely, I'd say.

Amanda. Character's what to look for in a man.

Tom. That's what I've always said, Mother.

Amanda. You've never said anything of the kind and I suspect you would never give it a thought.

Tom. Don't be so suspicious of me.   110

Amanda. At least I hope he's the type that's up and coming.

Tom. I think he really goes in for self-improvement.

Amanda. What reason have you to think so?

Tom. He goes to night school.

Amanda. [*beaming*] Splendid! What does he do, I mean study?   115

Tom. Radio engineering and public speaking!

Amanda. Then he has visions of being advanced in the world! Any young man who studies public speaking is aiming to have an executive job some day! And radio engineering? A thing for the future! Both of these facts are very illuminating. Those are the sort of things that a mother should know concerning any young man who comes to call on her daughter. Seriously or—not.

Tom. One little warning. He doesn't know about Laura. I didn't let on that we had dark ulterior motives. I just said, why don't you come and have dinner with us? He said okay and that was the whole conversation.

Amanda. I bet it was! You're eloquent as an oyster. However, he'll know about Laura when he gets here. When he sees how lovely and sweet and pretty she is, he'll thank his lucky stars he was asked to dinner.

Tom. Mother, you mustn't expect too much of Laura.   120

Amanda. What do you mean?

Tom. Laura seems all those things to you and me because she's ours and we love her. We don't even notice she's crippled any more.

Amanda. Don't say crippled! You know that I never allow that word to be used!

Tom. But face facts, Mother. She is and—that's not all—

Amanda. What do you mean "not all"?   125

Tom. Laura is very different from other girls.

Amanda. I think the difference is all to her advantage.

Tom. Not quite all—in the eyes of others—strangers—she's terribly shy and lives in a world of her own and those things make her seem a little peculiar to people outside the house.

Amanda. Don't say peculiar.

Tom. Face the facts. She is.   130

[*The dance hall music changes to a tango that has a minor and somewhat ominous tone.*]

AMANDA.   In what way is she peculiar—may I ask?
TOM.   [*gently*] She lives in a world of her own—a world of little glass ornaments, Mother. . . .

[*He gets up. AMANDA remains holding the brush, looking at him, troubled.*]

She plays old phonograph records and—that's about all—[*He glances at himself in the mirror and crosses to the door.*]
AMANDA.   [*sharply*] Where are you going?
TOM.   I'm going to the movies. [*He goes out the screen door.*]
AMANDA.   Not to the movies, every night to the movies! [*She follows quickly   135
to the screen door.*] I don't believe you always go to the movies!

[*He is gone. AMANDA looks worriedly after him for a moment. Then vitality and optimism return and she turns from the door, crossing to the portieres.*]

Laura! Laura!

[*LAURA answers from the kitchenette.*]

LAURA.   Yes, Mother.
AMANDA.   Let those dishes go and come in front!

[*LAURA appears with a dish towel. AMANDA speaks to her gaily.*]

Laura, come here and make a wish on the moon!

[*Screen image: The Moon.*]

LAURA.   [*entering*] Moon—moon?
AMANDA.   A little silver slipper of a moon. Look over your left shoulder, Laura, and make a wish!

[*LAURA looks faintly puzzled as if called out of sleep. AMANDA seizes her shoulders and turns her at an angle by the door.*]

Now! Now, darling, *wish!*
LAURA.   What shall I wish for, Mother?   140
AMANDA.   [*her voice trembling and her eyes suddenly filling with tears*] Happiness!
Good fortune!

[*The sound of the violin rises and the stage dims out.*]

Scene 6

[*The light comes up on the fire escape landing. Tom is leaning against the grill, smoking. Screen image: The high school hero.*]

TOM.   And so the following evening I brought Jim home to dinner. I had known Jim slightly in high school. In high school Jim was a hero. He had tremendous

Irish good nature and vitality with the scrubbed and polished look of white china-ware. He seemed to move in a continual spotlight. He was a star in basketball, captain of the debating club, president of the senior class and the glee club and he sang the male lead in the annual light operas. He was always running or bounding, never just walking. He seemed always at the point of defeating the law of gravity. He was shooting with such velocity through his adolescence that you would logically expect him to arrive at nothing short of the White House by the time he was thirty. But Jim apparently ran into more interference after his graduation from Soldan. His speed had definitely slowed. Six years after he left high school he was holding a job that wasn't much better than mine.

[*Screen image: The Clerk.*]

He was the only one at the warehouse with whom I was on friendly terms. I was valuable to him as someone who could remember his former glory, who had seen him win basketball games and the silver cup in debating. He knew of my secret practice of retiring to a cabinet of the washroom to work on poems when business was slack in the warehouse. He called me Shakespeare. And while the other boys in the warehouse regarded me with suspicious hostility, Jim took a humorous attitude toward me. Gradually his attitude affected the others, their hostility wore off and they also began to smile at me as people smile at an oddly fashioned dog who trots across their path at some distance.

I knew that Jim and Laura had known each other at Soldan, and I had heard Laura speak admiringly of his voice. I didn't know if Jim remembered her or not. In high school Laura had been as unobtrusive as Jim had been astonishing. If he did remember Laura, it was not as my sister, for when I asked him to dinner, he grinned and said, "You know, Shakespeare, I never thought of you as having folks!"

He was about to discover that I did. . . .

[*Legend on screen: "The accent of a coming foot."*]

[*The light dims out on Tom and comes up in the Wingfield living room—a delicate lemony light. It is about five on a Friday evening of late spring which comes "scattering poems in the sky."*

AMANDA has worked like a Turk in preparation for the gentleman caller. The results are astonishing. The new floor lamp with its rose silk shade is in place, a colored paper lantern conceals the broken light fixture in the ceiling, new billowing white curtains are at the windows, chintz covers are on the chairs and sofa, a pair of new sofa pillows make their initial appearance. Open boxes and tissue paper are scattered on the floor.

LAURA stands in the middle of the room with lifted arms while AMANDA crouches before her, adjusting the hem of a new dress, devout and ritualistic. The dress is colored and designed by memory. The arrangement of LAURA's hair is changed; it is softer and more becoming. A fragile, unearthly prettiness has come out in LAURA: she is like a piece of translucent glass touched by light, given a momentary radiance, not actual, not lasting.]

AMANDA. [*impatiently*] Why are you trembling?
LAURA.   Mother, you've made me so nervous!
AMANDA. How have I made you nervous?

LAURA.   By all this fuss! You make it seem so important!   5

AMANDA.   I don't understand you, Laura. You couldn't be satisfied with just sitting home, and yet whenever I try to arrange something for you, you seem to resist it. [*She gets up.*] Now take a look at yourself. No, wait! Wait just a moment— I have an idea!

LAURA.   What is it now?

[*AMANDA produces two powder puffs which she wraps in handkerchiefs and stuffs in LAURA's bosom.*]

LAURA.   Mother, what are you doing?

AMANDA.   They call them "Gay Deceivers"!

LAURA.   I won't wear them!   10

AMANDA.   You will!

LAURA.   Why should I?

AMANDA.   Because, to be painfully honest, your chest is flat.

LAURA.   You make it seem like we were setting a trap.

AMANDA.   All pretty girls are a trap, a pretty trap, and men expect them to   15
be.

[*Legend on screen: "A pretty trap."*]

Now look at yourself, young lady. This is the prettiest you will ever be! [*She stands back to admire LAURA.*] I've got to fix myself now! You're going to be surprised by your mother's appearance!

[*AMANDA crosses through the portieres, humming gaily. LAURA moves slowly to the long mirror and stares solemnly at herself. A wind blows the white curtains inward in a slow, graceful motion and with a faint, sorrowful sighing.*]

AMANDA.   [*from somewhere behind the portieres*] It isn't dark enough yet.

[*LAURA turns slowly before the mirror with a troubled look.*

Legend on screen: "This is my sister: Celebrate her with strings!" Music plays.]

AMANDA.   [*laughing, still not visible*] I'm going to show you something. I'm going to make a spectacular appearance!

LAURA.   What is it, Mother?

AMANDA.   Possess your soul in patience—you will see! Something I've resur- rected from that old trunk! Styles haven't changed so terribly much after all. . . . [*She parts the portieres.*] Now just look at your mother! [*She wears a girlish frock of yellowed voile with a blue silk sash. She carries a bunch of jonquils—the legend of her youth is nearly revived. Now she speaks feverishly:*] This is the dress in which I led the cotillion. Won the cakewalk twice at Sunset Hill, wore one Spring to the Governor's Ball in Jackson!° See how I sashayed around the ballroom, Laura? [*She raises her skirt and does a mincing step around the room.*] I wore it on Sundays for my gentlemen callers! I had it on the day I met your father. . . . I had malaria fever all that Spring. The change of climate from East Tennessee to the Delta—weakened resis-

---

Jackson: capital of Mississippi. Amanda refers to the social events of her youth. A cotillion is a formal ball, often given for debutantes. The cakewalk is a strutting dance step.

tance. I had a little temperature all the time—not enough to be serious—just enough to make me restless and giddy! Invitations poured in—parties all over the Delta! "Stay in bed," said Mother, "you have a fever!"—but I just wouldn't. I took quinine° but kept on going, going! Evenings, dances! Afternoons, long, long rides! Picnics— lovely! So lovely, that country in May—all lacy with dogwood, literally flooded with jonquils! That was the spring I had the craze for jonquils. Jonquils became an absolute obsession. Mother said, "Honey, there's no more room for jonquils." And still I kept on bringing in more jonquils. Whenever, wherever I saw them, I'd say, "Stop! Stop! I see jonquils!" I made the young men help me gather the jonquils! It was a joke, Amanda and her jonquils. Finally there were no more vases to hold them, every available space was filled with jonquils. No vases to hold them? All right, I'll hold them myself! And then I—[*She stops in front of the picture. Music plays.*] met your father! Malaria fever and jonquils and then—this— boy. . . . [*She switches on the rose-colored lamp.*] I hope they get here before it starts to rain. [*She crosses the room and places the jonquils in a bowl on the table.*] I gave your brother a little extra change so he and Mr. O'Connor could take the service car home.

LAURA.   [*with an altered look*] What did you say his name was?   20
AMANDA.   O'Connor.
LAURA.   What is his first name?
AMANDA.   I don't remember. Oh, yes, I do. It was—Jim.

[*LAURA sways slightly and catches hold of a chair.*

Legend on screen: "Not Jim!"]

LAURA.   [*faintly*] Not—Jim!
AMANDA.   Yes, that was it, it was Jim! I've never known a Jim that wasn't   25
nice!

[*The music becomes ominous.*]

LAURA.   Are you sure his name is Jim O'Connor?
AMANDA.   Yes. Why?
LAURA.   Is he the one that Tom used to know in high school?
AMANDA.   He didn't say so. I think he just got to know him at the warehouse.
LAURA.   There was a Jim O'Connor we both knew in high school—[*Then,*   30
with effort.] If that is the one that Tom is bringing to dinner—you'll have to excuse me, I won't come to the table.
AMANDA.   What sort of nonsense is this?
LAURA.   You asked me once if I'd ever liked a boy. Don't you remember I showed you this boy's picture?
AMANDA.   You mean the boy you showed me in the yearbook?
LAURA.   Yes, that boy.
AMANDA.   Laura, Laura, were you in love with that boy?   35
LAURA.   I don't know, Mother. All I know is I couldn't sit at the table if it was him!

---

quinine: long used as a standard drug to control malaria.

AMANDA.   It won't be him! It isn't the least bit likely. But whether it is or not, you will come to the table. You will not be excused.

LAURA.   I'll have to be, Mother.

AMANDA.   I don't intend to humor your silliness, Laura. I've had too much from you and your brother, both! So just sit down and compose yourself till they come. Tom has forgotten his key so you'll have to let them in, when they arrive.

LAURA.   [*panicky*] Oh, Mother—*you* answer the door!   40

AMANDA.   [*lightly*] I'll be in the kitchen—busy!

LAURA.   Oh, Mother, please answer the door, don't make me do it!

AMANDA.   [*crossing into the kitchenette*] I've got to fix the dressing for the salmon. Fuss, fuss—silliness!—over a gentleman caller!

[*The door swings shut. LAURA is left alone.*

Legend on screen: "Terror!"

She utteres a low moan and turns off the lamp—sits stiffly on the edge of the sofa, knotting her fingers together.

Legend on screen: "The Opening of a Door!"

TOM *and* JIM *appear on the fire escape steps and climb to the landing. Hearing their approach,* LAURA *rises with a panicky gesture. She retreats to the portieres. The doorbell rings.* LAURA *catches her breath and touches her throat. Low drums sound.*]

AMANDA.   [*calling*] Laura, sweetheart! The door!

[LAURA *stares at it without moving.*]

JIM.   I think we just beat the rain.   45

TOM.   Uh-huh. [*He rings again, nervously.* JIM *whistles and fishes for a cigarette.*]

AMANDA.   [*very, very gaily*] Laura, that is your brother and Mr. O'Connor! Will you let them in, darling?

[LAURA *crosses toward the kitchenette door.*]

LAURA.   [*breathlessly*] Mother—you go to the door!

[AMANDA *steps out of the kitchenette and stares furiously at* LAURA. *She points imperiously at the door.*]

LAURA.   Please, please!

AMANDA.   [*in a fierce whisper*] What is the matter with you, you silly thing?   50

LAURA.   [*desperately*] Please, you answer it, *please*!

AMANDA.   I told you I wasn't going to humor you, Laura. Why have you chosen this moment to lose your mind?

LAURA.   Please, please, please, you go!

AMANDA.   You'll have to go to the door because I can't!

LAURA.   [*despairingly*] I can't either!   55

AMANDA.   *Why?*

LAURA.   I'm *sick*!

AMANDA.   I'm sick, too—of your nonsense! Why can't you and your brother be normal people? Fantastic whims and behavior!

[*TOM gives a long ring.*]

Preposterous goings on! Can you give me one reason—[*She calls out lyrically.*] *Coming!* Just one second!—why you should be afraid to open a door? Now you answer it, Laura!

    LAURA.   Oh, oh, oh . . . [*She returns through the portieres, darts to the Victrola, winds it frantically and turns it on.*]

    AMANDA.   Laura Wingfield, you march right to that door!   60

    LAURA.   *Yes—yes, Mother!*

[*A faraway, scratchy rendition of "Dardanella"° softens the air and gives her strength to move through it. She slips to the door and draws it cautiously open. TOM enters with the caller, JIM O'CONNOR.*]

    TOM.   Laura, this is Jim. Jim, this is my sister, Laura.

    JIM.   [*stepping inside*] I didn't know that Shakespeare had a sister!

    LAURA.   [*retreating, stiff and trembling, from the door*] How—how do you do?

    JIM.   [*heartily, extending his hand*] Okay!   65

[*LAURA touches it hesitantly with hers.*]

    JIM.   Your hand's *cold*, Laura!

    LAURA.   Yes, well—I've been playing the Victrola. . . .

    JIM.   Must have been playing classical music on it! You ought to play a little hot swing music to warm you up!

    LAURA.   Excuse me—I haven't finished playing the Victrola. . . . [*She turns awkwardly and hurries into the front room. She pauses a second by the Victrola. Then she catches her breath and darts through the portieres like a frightened deer.*]

    JIM.   [*grinning*] What was the matter?   70

    TOM.   Oh—with Laura? Laura is—terribly shy.

    JIM.   Shy, huh? It's unusual to meet a shy girl nowadays. I don't believe you ever mentioned you had a sister.

    TOM.   Well, now you know. I have one. Here is the *Post Dispatch.*° You want a piece of it?

    JIM.   Uh-huh.

    TOM.   What piece? The comics?   75

    JIM.   Sports! [*He glances at it.*] Ole Dizzy Dean° is on his bad behavior.

    TOM.   [*uninterested*] Yeah? [*He lights a cigarette and goes over to the fire-escape door.*]

    JIM.   Where are *you* going?

    TOM.   I'm going out on the terrace.

    JIM.   [*going after him*] You know, Shakespeare—I'm going to sell you a bill   80 of goods!

    TOM.   What goods?

"Dardanella": a popular song and dance tune written in 1919 by Fred Fisher, Felix Bernard, and Johnny S. Black.

Post Dispatch: The St. Louis Post Dispatch, a newspaper.

Dizzy Dean: Jerome Herman (or Jay Hanna) Dean (1911–1974), outstanding pitcher with the St. Louis Cardinals (1932–1938).

JIM.   A course I'm taking.

TOM.   Huh?

JIM.   In public speaking! You and me, we're not the warehouse type.

TOM.   Thanks—that's good news. But what has public speaking got to do   85
with it?

JIM.   It fits you for—executive positions!

TOM.   Awww.

JIM.   I tell you it's done a helluva lot for me.

[*Image on screen: Executive at his desk.*]

TOM.   In what respect?

JIM.   In every! Ask yourself what is the difference between you an' me and   90
men in the office down front? Brains?—No!—Ability?—No! Then what? Just one
little thing—

TOM.   What is that one little thing?

JIM.   Primarily it amounts to—social poise! Being able to square up to people
and hold your own on any social level!

AMANDA.   [*from the kitchenette*] Tom?

TOM.   Yes, Mother?

AMANDA.   Is that you and Mr. O'Connor?   95

TOM.   Yes, Mother.

AMANDA.   Well, you just make yourselves comfortable in there.

TOM.   Yes, Mother.

AMANDA.   Ask Mr. O'Connor if he would like to wash his hands.

JIM.   Aw, no—no—thank you—I took care of that at the warehouse. Tom—   100

TOM.   Yes?

JIM.   Mr. Mendoza was speaking to me about you.

TOM.   Favorably?

JIM.   What do you think?

TOM.   Well—   105

JIM.   You're going to be out of a job if you don't wake up.

TOM.   I am waking up—

JIM.   You show no signs.

TOM.   The signs are interior.

[*Image on screen: The sailing vessel with the Jolly Roger again.*]

TOM.   I'm planning to change. [*He leans over the fire escape rail, speaking with*   110
quiet exhilaration. The incandescent marquees and signs of the first-run movie
houses light his face from across the alley. He looks like a voyager.] I'm right at
the point of committing myself to a future that doesn't include the warehouse
and Mr. Mendoza or even a night-school course in public speaking.

JIM.   What are you gassing about?

TOM.   I'm tired of the movies.

JIM.   Movies!

TOM.   Yes, movies! Look at them— [*a wave toward the marvels of Grand Avenue*]
All of those glamorous people—having adventures—hogging it all, gobbling the
whole thing up! You know what happens? People go to the *movies* instead of *moving*!
Hollywood characters are supposed to have all the adventures for everybody in

America, while everybody in America sits in a dark room and watches them have them! Yes, until there's a war. That's when adventure becomes available to the masses! *Everyone's* dish, not only Gable's!° Then the people in the dark room come out of the dark room to have some adventures themselves—goody, goody! It's our turn now, to go to the South Sea Island—to make a safari—to be exotic, far-off! But I'm not patient. I don't want to wait till then. I'm tired of the *movies* and I am *about* to *move*!

JIM. [*incredulously*] Move?   115
TOM. Yes.
JIM. When?
TOM. Soon!
JIM. Where? Where?

[*The music seems to answer the question, while* TOM *thinks it over. He searches in his pockets.*]

TOM. I'm starting to boil inside. I know I seem dreamy, but inside—well,   120
I'm boiling! Whenever I pick up a shoe, I shudder a little thinking how short life is and what I am doing! Whatever that means, I know it doesn't mean shoes—except as something to wear on a traveler's feet! [*He finds what he has been searching for in his pockets and holds out a paper to* JIM.] Look—
JIM. What?
TOM. I'm a member.
JIM. [*reading*] The Union of Merchant Seamen.
TOM. I paid my dues this month, instead of the light bill.
JIM. You will regret it when they turn off the lights.   125
TOM. I won't be here.
JIM. How about your mother?
TOM. I'm like my father. The bastard son of a bastard! Did you notice how he's grinning in his picture in there? And he's been absent going on sixteen years!
JIM. You're just talking, you drip. How does your mother feel about it?
TOM. Shhh! Here comes Mother! Mother is not acquainted with my plans!   130
AMANDA. [*coming through the portieres*] Where are you all?
TOM. On the terrace, Mother.

[*They start inside. She advances to them.* TOM *is distinctly shocked at her appearance. Even* JIM *blinks a little. He is making his first contact with the girlish Southern vivacity and in spite of the night-school course in public speaking is somewhat thrown off the beam by the unexpected outlay of social charm. Certain responses are attempted by* JIM *but are swept aside by* AMANDA's *gay laughter and chatter.* TOM *is embarrassed but after the first shock* JIM *reacts very warmly. He grins and chuckles, is altogether won over.*

Image on screen: AMANDA *as a girl.*]

AMANDA. [*coyly smiling, shaking her girlish ringlets*] Well, well, well, so this is Mr. O'Connor. Introductions entirely unnecessary. I've heard so much about you

---

Gable: Clark Gable (1901–1960), popular American screen actor and matinee idol from the 1930s to his death.

from my boy. I finally said to him, Tom—good gracious!—why don't you bring
this paragon to supper? I'd like to meet this nice young man at the warehouse!—
instead of just hearing him sing your praises so much! I don't know why my son
is so stand-offish—that's not Southern behavior!

Let's sit down and—I think we could stand a little more air in here! Tom,
leave the door open. I felt a nice fresh breeze a moment ago. Where has it gone
to? Mmm, so warm already! And not quite summer, even. We're going to burn
up when summer really gets started. However, we're having—we're having a very
light supper. I think light things are better fo' this time of year. The same as
light clothes are. Light clothes an' light food are what warm weather calls fo'.
You know our blood gets so thick during th' winter—it takes a while fo' us to
adjust ourselves!—when the season changes . . . It's come so quick this year. I
wasn't prepared. All of a sudden—heavens! Already summer! I ran to the trunk
an' pulled out this light dress—terribly old! Historical almost! But feels so good—
so good an' co-ol, y'know. . . .

TOM.   Mother—

AMANDA.   Yes, honey?   135

TOM.   How about—supper?

AMANDA.   Honey, you go ask Sister if supper is ready! You know that Sister
is in full charge of supper! Tell her you hungry boys are waiting for it. [*To JIM.*]
Have you met Laura?

JIM.   She—

AMANDA.   Let you in? Oh, good, you've met already! It's rare for a girl as
sweet an' pretty as Laura to be domestic! But Laura is, thank heavens, not only
pretty but also very domestic. I'm not at all. I never was a bit. I never could
make a thing but angel-food cake. Well, in the South we had so many servants.
Gone, gone, gone. All vestige of gracious living! Gone completely! I wasn't prepared
for what the future brought me. All of my gentlemen callers were sons of planters
and so of course I assumed that I would be married to one and raise my family
on a large piece of land with plenty of servants. But man proposes—and woman
accepts the proposal! to vary that old, old saying a little but—I married no planter!
I married a man who worked for the telephone company! That gallantly smiling
gentleman over there! [*She points to the picture.*] A telephone man who—fell in
love with long-distance! Now he travels and I don't even know where! But what
am I going on for about my—tribulations? Tell me yours—I hope you don't have
any! Tom?

TOM.   [*returning*] Yes, Mother?   140

AMANDA.   Is supper nearly ready?

TOM.   It looks to me like supper is on the table.

AMANDA.   Let me look— [*She rises prettily and looks through the portieres.*] Oh
lovely! But where is Sister?

TOM.   Laura is not feeling well and she says that she thinks she'd better
not come to the table.

AMANDA.   What? Nonsense! Laura? Oh, Laura!   145

LAURA.   [*from the kitchenette, faintly*] Yes, Mother.

AMANDA.   You really must come to the table. We won't be seated until you
come to the table! Come in, Mr. O'Connor. You sit over there and I'll. . . . Laura?
Laura Wingfield! You're keeping us waiting, honey! We can't say grace until you
come to the table!

[*The kitchenette door is pushed weakly open and* LAURA *comes in. She is obviously quite faint, her lips trembling, her eyes wide and staring. She moves unsteadily toward the table.*

Screen legend: "Terror!"

Outside a summer storm is coming on abruptly. The white curtains billow inward at the windows and there is a sorrowful murmur from the deep blue dusk.

LAURA *suddenly stumbles; she catches at a chair with a faint moan.*]

    TOM. Laura!
    AMANDA. Laura!

[*There is a clap of thunder.*

Screen legend: "Ah!"]

[*despairingly*] Why, Laura, you *are* ill, darling! Tom, help your sister into the living room, dear! Sit in the living room, Laura—rest on the sofa. Well! [*To* JIM *as* TOM *helps his sister to the sofa in the living room.*] Standing over the hot stove made her ill! I told her that it was just too warm this evening, but—

[TOM *comes back to the table.*]

Is Laura all right now?
    TOM. Yes.
    AMANDA.   What is that? Rain? A nice cool rain has come up! [*She gives* JIM *a frightened look.*] I think we may—have grace—now . . . [TOM *looks at her stupidly.*] Tom, honey—you say grace!
    TOM.   Oh . . . "For these and all thy mercies—"

[*They bow their heads,* AMANDA *stealing a nervous glance at* JIM. *In the living room* LAURA, *stretched on the sofa, clenches her hand to her lips, to hold back a shuddering sob.*]

God's Holy Name be praised—

[*The scene dims out.*]

Scene 7

    It is half an hour later. Dinner is just being finished in the dining room, LAURA *is still huddled upon the sofa, her feet drawn under her, her head resting on a pale blue pillow, her eyes wide and mysteriously watchful. The new floor lamp with its shade of rose-colored silk gives a soft, becoming light to her face, bringing out the fragile, unearthly prettiness which usually escapes attention. From outside there is a steady murmur of rain, but it is slackening and soon stops; the air outside becomes pale and luminous as the moon breaks through the clouds. A moment after the curtain rises, the lights in both rooms flicker and go out.*]

    JIM.   Hey, there, Mr. Light Bulb!

[AMANDA *laughs nervously.*

Legend on screen: "Suspension of a public service."]

AMANDA.   Where was Moses when the lights went out? Ha-ha. Do you know the answer to that one, Mr. O'Connor?

JIM.   No, Ma'am, what's the answer?

AMANDA.   In the dark!

[*JIM laughs appreciatively.*]

Everybody sit still. I'll light the candles. Isn't it lucky we have them on the table? Where's a match? Which of you gentlemen can provide a match?

JIM.   Here.   5

AMANDA.   Thank you, Sir.

JIM.   Not at all, Ma'am!

AMANDA.   [*as she lights the candles*] I guess the fuse has burnt out. Mr. O'Connor, can you tell a burnt-out fuse? I know I can't and Tom is a total loss when it comes to mechanics. [*They rise from the table and go into the kitchenette, from where their voices are heard.*] Oh, be careful you don't bump into something. We don't want our gentleman caller to break his neck. Now wouldn't that be a fine howdy-do?

JIM.   Ha-ha! Where is the fuse-box?

AMANDA.   Right here next to the stove. Can you see anything?   10

JIM.   Just a minute.

AMANDA.   Isn't electricity a mysterious thing? Wasn't it Benjamin Franklin who tied a key to a kite? We live in such a mysterious universe, don't we? Some people say that science clears up all the mysteries for us. In my opinion it only creates more! Have you found it yet?

JIM.   No, Ma'am. All these fuses look okay to me.

AMANDA.   Tom!

TOM.   Yes, Mother?   15

AMANDA.   That light bill I gave you several days ago. That one I told you we got the notices about?

[*Legend on screen: "Ha!"*]

TOM.   Oh—yeah.

AMANDA.   You didn't neglect to pay it by any chance?

TOM.   Why, I—

AMANDA.   Didn't! I might have known it!   20

JIM.   Shakespeare probably wrote a poem on that light bill, Mrs. Wingfield.

AMANDA.   I might have known better than to trust him with it! There's such a high price for negligence in this world!

JIM.   Maybe the poem will win a ten-dollar prize.

AMANDA.   We'll just have to spend the remainder of the evening in the nineteenth century, before Mr. Edison made the Mazda lamp!°

JIM.   Candlelight is my favorite kind of light.   25

AMANDA.   That shows you're romantic! But that's no excuse for Tom. Well, we got through dinner. Very considerate of them to let us get through dinner before they plunged us into everlasting darkness, wasn't it, Mr. O'Connor?

Mazda lamp: Thomas A. Edison (1847–1931) developed the first practical incandescent lamp in 1879.

JIM. Ha-ha!

AMANDA. Tom, as a penalty for your carelessness you can help me with the dishes.

JIM. Let me give you a hand.

AMANDA. Indeed you will not!   30

JIM. I ought to be good for something.

AMANDA. Good for something? [*Her tone is rhapsodic.*] *You?* Why, Mr. O'Connor, nobody, *nobody's* given me this much entertainment in years—as you have!

JIM. Aw, now, Mrs. Wingfield!

AMANDA. I'm not exaggerating, not one bit! But Sister is all by her lonesome. You go keep her company in the parlor! I'll give you this lovely old candelabrum that used to be on the altar at the Church of the Heavenly Rest. It was melted a little out of shape when the church burnt down. Lightning struck it one spring. Gypsy Jones was holding a revival at the time and he intimated that the church was destroyed because the Episcopalians gave card parties.

JIM. Ha-ha.   35

AMANDA. And how about you coaxing Sister to drink a little wine? I think it would be good for her! Can you carry both at once?

JIM. Sure. I'm Superman!

AMANDA. Now, Thomas, get into this apron!

[*JIM comes into the dining room, carrying the candelabrum, its candles lighted, in one hand and a glass of wine in the other. The door of the kitchenette swings closed on AMANDA'S gay laughter; the flickering light approaches the portieres. LAURA sits up nervously as JIM enters. She can hardly speak from the almost intolerable strain of being alone with a stranger.*

Screen legend: "I don't suppose you remember me at all!"

At first, before JIM's warmth overcomes her paralyzing shyness, LAURA's voice is thin and breathless, as though she had just run up a steep flight of stairs. JIM's attitude is gently humorous. While the incident is apparently unimportant, it is to LAURA the climax of her secret life.]

JIM. Hello there, Laura.

LAURA. [*faintly*] Hello.   40

[*She clears her throat.*]

JIM. How are you feeling now? Better?

LAURA. Yes. Yes, thank you.

JIM. This is for you. A little dandelion wine. [*He extends the glass toward her with extravagant gallantry.*]

LAURA. Thank you.

JIM. Drink it—but don't get drunk!   45

[*He laughs heartily. LAURA takes the glass uncertainly; she laughs shyly.*]

Where shall I set the candles?

LAURA. Oh—oh, anywhere . . .

JIM. How about here on the floor? Any objections?

LAURA. No.

JIM. I'll spread a newspaper under to catch the drippings. I like to sit on the floor. Mind if I do?

LAURA. Oh, no.   50

JIM. Give me a pillow?

LAURA. What?

JIM. A pillow!

LAURA. Oh . . . [*She hands him one quickly.*]

JIM. How about you? Don't you like to sit on the floor?   55

LAURA. Oh—yes.

JIM. Why don't you, then?

LAURA. I—will.

JIM. Take a pillow!

[*LAURA does. She sits on the floor on the other side of the candelabrum. JIM crosses his legs and smiles engagingly at her.*] I can't hardly see you sitting way over there.

LAURA. I can—see you.   60

JIM. I know, but that's not fair, I'm in the limelight.

[*LAURA moves her pillow closer.*]

Good! Now I can see you! Comfortable?

LAURA. Yes.

JIM. So am I. Comfortable as a cow! Will you have some gum?

LAURA. No, thank you.

JIM. I think that I will indulge, with your permission. [*He musingly unwraps*   65
a stick of gum and holds it up.] Think of the fortune made by the guy that invented the first piece of chewing gum. Amazing, huh? The Wrigley Building° is one of the sights of Chicago—I saw it when I went up to the Century of Progress.° Did you take in the Century of Progress?

LAURA. No, I didn't.

JIM. Well, it was quite a wonderful exposition. What impressed me most was the Hall of Science. Gives you an idea of what the future will be in America, even more wonderful than the present time is! [*There is a pause. JIM smiles at her.*] Your brother tells me you're shy. Is that right—Laura?

LAURA. I—don't know.

JIM. I judge you to be an old-fashioned type of girl. Well, I think that's a pretty good type to be. Hope you don't think I'm being too personal—do you?

LAURA. [*Hastily, out of embarrassment*] I believe I *will* take a piece of gum, if   70
you—don't mind. [*clearing her throat*] Mr. O'Connor, have you—kept up with your singing?

JIM. Singing? Me?

LAURA. Yes. I remember what a beautiful voice you had.

JIM. When did you hear me sing?

Wrigley Building: Finished in 1924, this was one of the first skyscrapers in the United States.

Century of Progress: a world's fair held in Chicago (1933–1934) to celebrate the city's centennial.

[*LAURA does not answer, and in the long pause which follows a man's voice is heard singing offstage.*]

VOICE:
> O blow, ye winds, heigh-ho,
>   A-roving I will go!
>   I'm off to my love
>   With a boxing glove—
>   Ten thousand miles away!

JIM.   You say you've heard me sing?   75

LAURA.   Oh, yes! Yes, very often . . . I—don't suppose—you remember me—at all?

JIM.   [*smiling doubtfully*] You know I have an idea I've seen you before. I had that idea soon as you opened the door. It seemed almost like I was about to remember your name. But the name that I started to call you—wasn't a name! And so I stopped myself before I said it.

LAURA.   Wasn't it—Blue Roses?

JIM.   [*springing up, grinning*] Blue Roses! My gosh, yes—Blue Roses! That's what I had on my tongue when you opened the door! Isn't it funny what tricks your memory plays? I didn't connect you with high school somehow or other. But that's where it was; it was high school. I didn't even know you were Shakespeare's sister! Gosh, I'm sorry.

LAURA.   I didn't expect you to. You—barely knew me!   80

JIM.   But we did have a speaking acquaintance, huh?

LAURA.   Yes, we—spoke to each other.

JIM.   When did you recognize me?

LAURA.   Oh, right away!

JIM.   Soon as I came in the door?   85

LAURA.   When I heard your name I thought it was probably you. I knew that Tom used to know you a little in high school. So when you came in the door—well, then I was—sure.

JIM.   Why didn't you *say* something, then?

LAURA.   [*breathlessly*] I didn't know what to say, I was—too surprised!

JIM.   For goodness' sakes! You know, this sure is funny!

LAURA.   Yes! Yes, isn't it, though . . .   90

JIM.   Didn't we have a class in something together?

LAURA.   Yes, we did.

JIM.   What class was that?

LAURA.   It was—singing—chorus!

JIM.   Aw!   95

LAURA.   I sat across the aisle from you in the Aud.

JIM.   Aw!

LAURA.   Mondays, Wednesdays, and Fridays.

JIM.   Now I remember—you always came in late.

LAURA.   Yes, it was so hard for me, getting upstairs. I had that brace on   100
my leg—it clumped so loud!

JIM.   I never heard any clumping.

LAURA. [*wincing at the recollection*] To me it sounded like—thunder!

JIM. Well, well, well, I never even noticed.

LAURA. And everybody was seated before I came in. I had to walk in front of all those people. My seat was in the back row. I had to go clumping all the way up the aisle with everyone watching!

JIM. You shouldn't have been self-conscious.   105

LAURA. I know, but I was. It was always such a relief when the singing started.

JIM. Aw, yes, I've placed you now! I used to call you Blue Roses. How was it that I got started calling you that?

LAURA. I was out of school a little while with pleurosis. When I came back you asked me what was the matter. I said I had pleurosis—you thought that I said *Blue Roses*. That's what you always called me after that!

JIM. I hope you didn't mind.

LAURA. Oh, no—I liked it. You see, I wasn't acquainted with many—peo-   110
ple. . . .

JIM. As I remember you sort of stuck by yourself.

LAURA. I—I—never have had much luck at—making friends.

JIM. I don't see why you wouldn't.

LAURA. Well, I—started out badly.

JIM. You mean being—   115

LAURA. Yes, it sort of—stood between me—

JIM. You shouldn't have let it!

LAURA. I know, but it did, and—

JIM. You were shy with people!

LAURA. I tried not to be but never could—   120

JIM. Overcome it?

LAURA. No, I—I never could!

JIM. I guess being shy is something you have to work out of kind of gradually.

LAURA. [*sorrowfully*] Yes—I guess it—

JIM. Takes time!   125

LAURA. Yes—

JIM. People are not so dreadful when you know them. That's what you have to remember! And everybody has problems, not just you, but practically everybody has got some problems. You think of yourself as having the only problems, as being the only one who is disappointed. But just look around you and you will see lots of people as disappointed as you are. For instance, I hoped when I was going to high school that I would be further along at this time, six years later, than I am now. You remember that wonderful write-up I had in *The Torch*?

LAURA. Yes! [*She rises and crosses to the table.*]

JIM. It said I was bound to succeed in anything I went into!

[*LAURA returns with the high school yearbook.*]

Holy Jeez! *The Torch!*

[*He accepts it reverently. They smile across the book with mutual wonder. LAURA crouches beside him and they begin to turn the pages. LAURA's shyness is dissolving in his warmth.*]

LAURA. Here you are in *The Pirates of Penzance*!   130

JIM. [*wistfully*] I sang the baritone lead in that operetta.

LAURA. [*raptly*] So—*beautifully!*

JIM. [*protesting*] Aw—

LAURA. Yes, yes—beautifully—beautifully!

JIM. You heard me?   135

LAURA. All three times!

JIM. No!

LAURA. Yes!

JIM. All three performances?

LAURA. [*looking down*] Yes.   140

JIM. Why?

LAURA. I—wanted to ask you to—autograph my program. [*She takes the program from the back of the yearbook and shows it to him.*]

JIM. Why didn't you ask me to?

LAURA. You were always surrounded by your own friends so much that I never had a chance to.

JIM. You should have just—   145

LAURA. Well, I—thought you might think I was—

JIM. Thought I might think you was—what?

LAURA. Oh—

JIM. [*with reflective relish*] I was beleaguered by females in those days.

LAURA. You were terribly popular!   150

JIM. Yeah—

LAURA. You had such a—friendly way—

JIM. I was spoiled in high school.

LAURA. Everybody—liked you!

JIM. Including you?   155

LAURA. I—yes, I—did, too— [*She gently closes the book in her lap.*]

JIM. Well, well, well! Give me that program, Laura.

[*She hands it to him. He signs it with a flourish.*]

There you are—better late than never!

LAURA. Oh, I—what a—surprise!

JIM. My signature isn't worth very much right now. But some day—maybe—it will increase in value! Being disappointed is one thing and being discouraged is something else. I am disappointed but I am not discouraged. I'm twenty-three years old. How old are you?

LAURA. I'll be twenty-four in June.   160

JIM. That's not old age!

LAURA. No, but—

JIM. You finished high school?

LAURA. [*with difficulty*] I didn't go back.

JIM. You mean you dropped out?   165

LAURA. I made bad grades in my final examinations. [*She rises and replaces the book and the program on the table. Her voice is strained.*] How is—Emily Meisenbach getting along?

JIM. Oh, that kraut-head!

LAURA. Why do you call her that?

JIM.   That's what she was.
LAURA.   You're not still—going with her?   170
JIM.   I never see her.
LAURA.   It was in the "Personal" section that you were—engaged!
JIM.   I know, but I wasn't impressed by that—propaganda!
LAURA.   It wasn't—the truth?
JIM.   Only in Emily's optimistic opinion!   175
LAURA.   Oh—

[*Legend:* "What have you done since high school?"]

JIM lights a cigarette and leans indolently back on his elbows smiling at LAURA with a
warmth and charm which lights her inwardly with altar candles. She remains by the table,
picks up a piece from the glass menagerie collection, and turns it in her hands to cover her
tumult.]

JIM.   [*after several reflective puffs on his cigarette*] What have you done since
high school?

[*She seems not to hear him.*]

Huh?

[*LAURA looks up.*]

I said what have you done since high school, Laura?
LAURA.   Nothing much.
JIM.   You must have been doing something these six long years.
LAURA.   Yes.   180
JIM.   Well, then, such as what?
LAURA.   I took a business course at business college—
JIM.   How did that work out?
LAURA.   Well, not very—well—I had to drop out, it gave me—indigestion—

[*JIM laughs gently.*]

JIM.   What are you doing now?   185
LAURA.   I don't do anything—much. Oh, please don't think I sit around
doing nothing! My glass collection takes up a good deal of time. Glass is something
you have to take good care of.
JIM.   What did you say—about glass?
LAURA.   Collection I said—I have one— [*She clears her throat and turns away*
again, acutely shy.]
JIM.   [*abruptly*] You know what I judge to be the trouble with you? Inferiority
complex! Know what that is? That's what they call it when someone low-rates
himself! I understand it because I had it too. Although my case was not so aggravated
as yours seems to be. I had it until I took up public speaking, developed my
voice, and learned that I had an aptitude for science. Before that time I never
thought of myself as being outstanding in any way whatsoever! Now I've never
made a regular study of it, but I have a friend who says I can analyze people
better than doctors that make a profession of it. I don't claim that to be necessarily
true, but I can sure guess a person's psychology. Laura! [*He takes out his gum.*]

Excuse me, Laura. I always take it out when the flavor is gone. I'll use this scrap of paper to wrap it in. I know how it is to get it stuck on a shoe. [*He wraps the gum in paper and puts it in his pocket.*] Yep—that's what I judge to be your principal trouble. A lack of confidence in yourself as a person. You don't have the proper amount of faith in yourself. I'm basing that fact on a number of your remarks and also on certain observations I've made. For instance that clumping you thought was so awful in high school. You say that you even dreaded to walk into class. You see what you did? You dropped out of school, you gave up an education because of a clump, which as far as I know was practically nonexistent! A little physical defect is what you have. Hardly noticeable even! Magnified thousands of times by imagination! You know what my strong advice to you is? Think of yourself as *superior* in some way!

LAURA.   In what way would I think?   190

JIM.   Why, man alive, Laura! Just look about you a little. What do you see? A world full of common people! All of 'em born and all of 'em going to die! Which of them has one-tenth of your good points! Or mine! Or anyone else's, as far as that goes—gosh! Everybody excels in some one thing. Some in many! [*He unconsciously glances at himself in the mirror.*] All you've got to do is discover in *what*! Take me, for instance. [*He adjusts his tie at the mirror.*] My interest happens to lie in electro-dynamics. I'm taking a course in radio engineering at night school, Laura, on top of a fairly responsible job at the warehouse. I'm taking that course and studying public speaking.

LAURA.   Ohhhh.

JIM.   Because I believe in the future of television! [*turning his back to her*] I wish to be ready to go up right along with it. Therefore I'm planning to get in on the ground floor. In fact I've already made the right connections and all that remains is for the industry itself to get under way! Full steam—[*His eyes are starry.*] *Knowledge*—Zzzzzp! *Money*—Zzzzzp!—Power! That's the cycle democracy is built on!

[*His attitude is convincingly dynamic.* LAURA *stares at him, even her shyness eclipsed in her absolute wonder. He suddenly grins.*]

I guess you think I think a lot of myself!

LAURA.   No—o-o-o, I—

JIM.   Now how about you? Isn't there something you take more interest in   195
than anything else?

LAURA.   Well, I do—as I said—have my—glass collection—

[*A peal of girlish laughter rings from the kitchenette.*]

JIM.   I'm not right sure I know what you're talking about. What kind of glass is it?

LAURA.   Little articles of it, they're ornaments mostly! Most of them are little animals made out of glass, the tiniest little animals in the world. Mother calls them a glass menagerie! Here's an example of one, if you'd like to see it! This one is one of the oldest. It's nearly thirteen.

[*Music: "The Glass Menagerie."*]

He stretches out his hand.]

Oh, be careful—if you breathe, it breaks!

JIM.   I'd better not take it. I'm pretty clumsy with things.

LAURA.   Go, on, I trust you with him! [*She places the piece in his palm.*] There   200
now—you're holding him gently! Hold him over the light, he loves the light! You
see how the light shines through him?

JIM.   It sure does shine!

LAURA.   I shouldn't be partial, but he is my favorite one.

JIM.   What kind of a thing is this one supposed to be?

LAURA.   Haven't you noticed the single horn on his forehead?

JIM.   A unicorn, huh?   205

LAURA.   Mmmm-hmmm!

JIM.   Unicorns—aren't they extinct in the modern world?

LAURA.   I know!

JIM.   Poor little fellow, he must feel sort of lonesome.

LAURA.   [*smiling*] Well, if he does, he doesn't complain about it. He stays   210
on a shelf with some horses that don't have horns and all of them seem to get
along nicely together.

JIM.   How do you know?

LAURA.   [*lightly*] I haven't heard any arguments among them!

JIM.   [*grinning*] No arguments, huh? Well, that's a pretty good sign! Where
shall I set him?

LAURA.   Put him on the table. They all like a change of scenery once in a
while!

JIM.   Well, well, well, well—[*He places the glass piece on the table, then raises*   215
his arms and stretches.] Look how big my shadow is when I stretch!

LAURA.   Oh, oh, yes—it stretches across the ceiling!

JIM.   [*crossing to the door*] I think it's stopped raining. [*He opens the fire-escape*
door and the background music changes to a dance tune.] Where does the music come
from?

LAURA.   From the Paradise Dance Hall across the alley.

JIM.   How about cutting the rug a little, Miss Wingfield?

LAURA.   Oh, I—   220

JIM.   Or is your program filled up? Let me have a look at it. [*He grasps an*
imaginary card.] Why, every dance is taken! I'll just have to scratch some out.

[*Waltz music: "La Golondrina"°*]

Ahh, a waltz! [*He executes some sweeping turns by himself, then holds his arms*
toward LAURA.]

LAURA.   [*breathlessly*] I—can't dance.

JIM.   There you go, that inferiority stuff!

LAURA.   I've never danced in my life!

JIM.   Come on, try!   225

LAURA.   Oh, but I'd step on you!

"*La Golondrina*": a popular Mexican song (1883) written by Narciso Seradell (1843–
1910).

JIM. I'm not made out of glass.

LAURA. How—how—how do we start?

JIM. Just leave it to me. You hold your arms out a little.

LAURA. Like this? 230

JIM. [*taking her in his arms*] A little bit higher. Right. Now don't tighten up, that's the main thing about it—relax.

LAURA. [*laughing breathlessly*] It's hard not to.

JIM. Okay.

LAURA. I'm afraid you can't budge me.

JIM. What do you bet I can't? [*He swings her into motion.*] 235

LAURA.   Goodness, yes, you can!

JIM. Let yourself go, now, Laura, just let yourself go.

LAURA. I'm—

JIM. Come on!

LAURA. —trying! 240

JIM. Not so stiff—easy does it!

LAURA. I know but I'm—

JIM. Loosen th' backbone! There now, that's a lot better.

LAURA. Am I?

JIM. Lots, lots better! [*He moves her about the room in a clumsy waltz.*] 245

LAURA. Oh, my!

JIM. Ha-ha!

LAURA. Oh, my goodness!

JIM. Ha-ha-ha!

[*They suddenly bump into the table, and the glass piece on it falls to the floor. JIM stops the dance.*]

What did we hit?

LAURA. Table. 250

JIM. Did something fall off it? I think—

LAURA. Yes.

JIM. I hope that it wasn't the little glasshorse with the horn!

LAURA. Yes. [*She stoops to pick it up.*]

JIM. Aw, aw, aw. Is it broken? 255

LAURA. Now it is just like all the other horses.

JIM. It's lost its—

LAURA. Horn! It doesn't matter. Maybe it's a blessing in disguise.

JIM. You'll never forgive me. I bet that that was your favorite piece of glass.

LAURA. I don't have favorites much. It's no tragedy, Freckles. Glass breaks 260
so easily. No matter how careful you are. The traffic jars the shelves and things fall off them.

JIM. Still I'm awfully sorry that I was the cause.

LAURA. [*smiling*] I'll just imagine he had an operation. The horn was removed to make him feel less—freakish!

[*They both laugh.*]

Now he will feel more at home with the other horses, the ones that don't have horns. . . .

Jim.   Ha-ha, that's very funny! [*Suddenly he is serious.*] I'm glad to see that you have a sense of humor. You know—you're—well—very different! Surprisingly different from anyone else I know! [*His voice becomes soft and hesitant with a genuine feeling.*] Do you mind me telling you that?

[*Laura is abashed beyond speech.*]

I mean it in a nice way—

[*Laura nods shyly, looking away.*]

You make me feel sort of—I don't know how to put it! I'm usually pretty good at expressing things, but—this is something that I don't know how to say!

[*Laura touches her throat and clears it—turns the broken unicorn in her hands. His voice becomes softer.*]

Has anyone ever told you that you were pretty?

[*There is a pause, and the music rises slightly. Laura looks up slowly, with wonder, and shakes her head.*]

Well, you are! In a very different way from anyone else. And all the nicer because of the difference, too.

[*His voice becomes low and husky. Laura turns away, nearly faint with the novelty of her emotions.*]

I wish that you were my sister. I'd teach you to have some confidence in yourself. The different people are not like other people, but being different is nothing to be ashamed of. Because other people are not such wonderful people. They're one hundred times one thousand. You're one times one! They walk all over the earth. You just stay here. They're common as—weeds, but—you—well, you're—*Blue Roses!*

[*Image on screen: Blue Roses.*

The music changes.]

Laura.   But blue is wrong for—roses. . . .
Jim.   It's right for you! You're—pretty!   265
Laura.   In what respect am I pretty?
Jim.   In all respects—believe me! Your eyes—your hair—are pretty! Your hands are pretty! [*He catches hold of her hand.*] You think I'm making this up because I'm invited to dinner and have to be nice. Oh, I could do that! I could put on an act for you, Laura, and say lots of things without being very sincere. But this time I am. I'm talking to you sincerely. I happened to notice you had this inferiority complex that keeps you from feeling comfortable with people. Somebody needs to build your confidence up and make you proud instead of shy and turning away and—blushing. Somebody—ought to—*kiss* you, Laura!

[*His hand slips slowly up her arm to her shoulder as the music swells tumultuously. He suddenly turns about and kisses her on the lips. When he releases her, LAURA sinks on the sofa with a bright, dazed look. JIM backs away and fishes in his pocket for a cigarette.*

Legend on screen: "A souvenir."]

Stumblejohn!

[*He lights the cigarette, avoiding her look. There is a peal of girlish laughter from AMANDA in the kitchenette. LAURA slowly raises and opens her hand. It still contains the little broken glass animal. She looks at it with a tender, bewildered expression.*]

Stumblejohn! I shouldn't have done that—that was way off the beam. You don't smoke, do you?

[*She looks up, smiling, not hearing the question. He sits beside her rather gingerly. She looks at him speechlessly—waiting. He coughs decorously and moves a little further aside as he considers the situation and senses her feelings, dimly, with perturbation. He speaks gently.*]

Would you—care for a mint?

[*She doesn't seem to hear him but her look grows brighter even.*]

Peppermint? Life Saver? My pocket's a regular drugstore—wherever I go. . . . [*He pops a mint in his mouth. Then he gulps and decides to make a clean breast of it. He speaks slowly and gingerly.*] Laura, you know, if I had a sister like you, I'd do the same thing as Tom. I'd bring out fellows and—introduce her to them. The right type of boys—of a type to—appreciate her. Only—well—he made a mistake about me. Maybe I've got no call to be saying this. That may not have been the idea in having me over. But what if it was? There's nothing wrong about that. The only trouble is that in my case—I'm not in a situation to—do the right thing. I can't take down your number and say I'll phone. I can't call up next week and— ask for a date. I thought I had better explain the situation in case you—misunderstood it and—I hurt your feelings. . . .

[*There is a pause. Slowly, very slowly, LAURA's look changes, her eyes returning slowly from his to the glass figure in her palm. AMANDA utters another gay laugh in the kitchenette.*]

LAURA. [*faintly*] You—won't—call again?

JIM. No, Laura, I can't. [*He rises from the sofa.*] As I was just explaining, I've—got strings on me, Laura, I've—been going steady! I go out all the time with a girl named Betty. She's a home-girl like you, and Catholic, and Irish, and in a great many ways we—get along fine. I met her last summer on a moonlight boat trip up the river to Alton,° on the *Majestic*. Well—right away from the start it was—love!

[*Legend: Love!*]

LAURA *sways slightly forward and grips the arm of the sofa. He fails to notice, now enrapt in his own comfortable being.*]

Being in love has made a new man of me!

[*Leaning stiffly forward, clutching the arm of the sofa, LAURA struggles visibly with her storm. But JIM is oblivious; she is a long way off.*]

Alton: a city in Illinois about twenty miles north of St. Louis on the Mississippi River.

The power of love is really pretty tremendous! Love is something that— changes the whole world, Laura!

[*The storm abates a little and* LAURA *leans back. He notices her again.*]

It happened that Betty's aunt took sick, she got a wire and had to go to Centralia.° So Tom—when he asked me to dinner—I naturally just accepted the invitation, not knowing that you—that he—that I—[*He stops awkwardly.*] Huh— I'm a stumblejohn!

[*He flops back on the sofa. The holy candles on the altar of* LAURA'S *face have been snuffed out. There is a look of almost infinite desolation.* JIM *glances at her uneasily.*]

I wish that you would—say something.

[*She bites her lip which was trembling and then bravely smiles. She opens her hand again on the broken glass figure. Then she gently takes his hand and raises it level with her own. She carefully places the unicorn in the palm of his hand, then pushes his fingers closed upon it.*]

What are you—doing that for? You want me to have him? Laura?

[*She nods.*]

What for?

LAURA.   A—souvenir. . . .   270

[*She rises unsteadily and crouches beside the Victrola to wind it up.*

Legend on screen: "Things have a way of turning out so badly!" Or image: "Gentleman caller waving goodbye—gaily."

At this moment AMANDA *rushes brightly back into the living room. She bears a pitcher of fruit punch in an old-fashioned cut-glass pitcher, and a plate of macaroons. The plate has a gold border and poppies painted on it.*]

AMANDA.   Well, well, well! Isn't the air delightful after the shower? I've made you children a little liquid refreshment. [*She turns gaily to* JIM.] Jim, do you know that song about lemonade?
"Lemonade, lemonade
Made in the shade and stirred with a spade—
Good enough for any old maid!"
JIM.   [*uneasily*] Ha-ha! No—I never heard it.
AMANDA.   Why, Laura! You look so serious!
JIM.   We were having a serious conversation.
AMANDA.   Good! Now you're better acquainted!   275
JIM.   [*uncertainly*] Ha-ha! Yes.
AMANDA.   You modern young people are much more serious-minded than my generation. I was so gay as a girl!

Centralia: a city in Illinois about sixty miles east of St. Louis.

JIM.   You haven't changed, Mrs. Wingfield.

AMANDA.   Tonight I'm rejuvenated! The gaiety of the occasion, Mr. O'Connor! [*She tosses her head with a peal of laughter, spilling some lemonade.*] Oooo! I'm baptizing myself!

JIM.   Here—let me—   280

AMANDA.   [*setting the pitcher down*] There now. I discovered we had some maraschino cherries. I dumped them in, juice and all!

JIM.   You shouldn't have gone to that trouble, Mrs. Wingfield.

AMANDA.   Trouble, trouble? Why, it was loads of fun! Didn't you hear me cutting up in the kitchen? I bet your ears were burning! I told Tom how outdone with him I was for keeping you to himself so long a time! He should have brought you over much, much sooner! Well, now that you've found your way, I want you to be a very frequent caller! Not just occasional but all the time. Oh, we're going to have a lot of gay times together! I see them coming! Mmm, just breathe that air! So fresh, and the moon's so pretty! I'll skip back out—I know where my place is when young folks are having a—serious conversation!

JIM.   Oh, don't go out, Mrs. Wingfield. The fact of the matter is I've got to be going.

AMANDA.   Going, now? You're joking! Why, it's only the shank of the evening,° Mr. O'Connor!   285

JIM.   Well, you know how it is.

AMANDA.   You mean you're a young workingman and have to keep workingmen's hours. We'll let you off early tonight. But only on the condition that next time you stay later. What's the best night for you? Isn't Saturday night the best night for you workingmen?

JIM.   I have a couple of time-clocks to punch, Mrs. Wingfield. One at morning, another one at night!

AMANDA.   My, but you *are* ambitious! You work at night, too?

JIM.   No, Ma'am, not work but—Betty!   290

[*He crosses deliberately to pick up his hat. The band at the Paradise Dance Hall goes into a tender waltz.*]

AMANDA.   Betty? Betty? Who's—Betty!

[*There is an ominous cracking sound in the sky.*]

JIM.   Oh, just a girl. The girl I go steady with!

[*He smiles charmingly. The sky falls.*

Legend: "The Sky Falls."]

AMANDA.   [*a long-drawn exhalation*] Ohhh . . . Is it a serious romance, Mr. O'Connor?

JIM.   We're going to be married the second Sunday in June.

AMANDA.   Ohhh—how nice! Tom didn't mention that you were engaged   295
to be married.

---

shank of the evening: still early, the best part of the evening.

JIM.   The cat's not out of the bag at the warehouse yet. You know how they are. They call you Romeo and stuff like that. [*He stops at the oval mirror to put on his hat. He carefully shapes the brim and the crown to give a discreetly dashing effect.*] It's been a wonderful evening, Mrs. Wingfield. I guess this is what they mean by Southern hospitality.

AMANDA.   It really wasn't anything at all.

JIM.   I hope it don't seem like I'm rushing off. But I promised Betty I'd pick her up at the Wabash depot, an' by the time I get my jalopy down there her train'll be in. Some women are pretty upset if you keep 'em waiting.

AMANDA.   Yes, I know—the tyranny of women! [*She extends her hand.*] Good-bye, Mr. O'Connor. I wish you luck—and happiness—and success! All three of them, and so does Laura! Don't you, Laura?

LAURA.   Yes!   300

JIM.   [*taking LAURA's hand*] Goodbye, Laura. I'm certainly going to treasure that souvenir. And don't you forget the good advice I gave you. [*He raises his voice to a cheery shout.*] So long, Shakespeare! Thanks again, ladies. Good night!

[*He grins and ducks jauntily out. Still bravely grimacing, AMANDA closes the door on the gentleman caller. Then she turns back to the room with a puzzled expression. She and LAURA don't dare to face each other. LAURA crouches beside the Victrola to wind it.*]

AMANDA.   [*faintly*] Things have a way of turning out so badly. I don't believe that I would play the Victrola. Well, well—well! Our gentleman caller was engaged to be married? [*She raises her voice.*] Tom!

TOM.   [*from the kitchenette*] Yes, Mother?

AMANDA.   Come in here a minute. I want to tell you something awfully funny.

TOM.   [*entering with a macaroon and a glass of the lemonade*] Has the gentleman   305
caller gotten away already?

AMANDA.   The gentleman caller has made an early departure. What a wonderful joke you played on us!

TOM.   How do you mean?

AMANDA.   You didn't mention that he was engaged to be married.

TOM.   Jim? Engaged?

AMANDA.   That's what he just informed us.   310

TOM.   I'll be jiggered! I didn't know about that.

AMANDA.   That seems very peculiar.

TOM.   What's peculiar about it?

AMANDA.   Didn't you call him your best friend down at the warehouse?

TOM.   He is, but how did I know?   315

AMANDA.   It seems extremely peculiar that you wouldn't know your best friend was going to be married!

TOM.   The warehouse is where I work, not where I know things about people!

AMANDA.   You don't know things anywhere! You live in a dream; you manufacture illusions!

[*He crosses to the door.*]

Where are you going?

TOM.   I'm going to the movies.

AMANDA.   That's right, now that you've had us make such fools of ourselves.   320
The effort, the preparations, all the expense! The new floor lamp, the rug, the
clothes for Laura! All for what? To entertain some other girl's fiancé! Go to the
movies, go! Don't think about us, a mother deserted, an unmarried sister who's
crippled and has no job! Don't let anything interfere with your selfish pleasure!
Just go, go, go—to the movies!

TOM.   All right, I will! The more you shout about my selfishness to me the
quicker I'll go, and I won't go to the movies!

AMANDA.   Go, then! Go to the moon—you selfish dreamer!

[*TOM smashes his glass on the floor. He plunges out on the fire escape, slamming the door.
LAURA screams in fright. The dance-hall music becomes louder. TOM stands on the fire
escape, gripping the rail. The moon breaks through the storm clouds, illuminating his face.*

Legend on screen: "And so goodbye. . ."

*TOM's closing speech is timed with what is happening inside the house. We see, as though
through soundproof glass, that AMANDA appears to be making a comforting speech to LAURA,
who is huddled upon the sofa. Now that we cannot hear the mother's speech, her silliness is
gone and she has dignity and tragic beauty. LAURA's hair hides her face until, at the end
of the speech, she lifts her head to smile at her mother. AMANDA's gestures are slow and
graceful, almost dancelike, as she comforts her daughter. At the end of her speech she glances
a moment at the father's picture—then withdraws through the portieres. At the close of
TOM's speech, LAURA blows out the candles, ending the play.*]

TOM.   I didn't go to the moon, I went much further—for time is the longest
distance between two places. Not long after that I was fired for writing a poem
on the lid of a shoe-box. I left Saint Louis. I descended the steps of this fire
escape for a last time and followed, from then on, in my father's footsteps, attempting
to find in motion what was lost in space. I traveled around a great deal. The
cities swept about me like dead leaves, leaves that were brightly colored but torn
away from the branches. I would have stopped, but I was pursued by something.
It always came upon me unawares, taking me altogether by surprise. Perhaps it
was a familiar bit of music. Perhaps it was only a piece of transparent glass. Perhaps
I am walking along a street at night, in some strange city, before I have found
companions. I pass the lighted window of a shop where perfume is sold. The
window is filled with pieces of colored glass, tiny transparent bottles in delicate
colors, like bits of a shattered rainbow. Then all at once my sister touches my
shoulder. I turn around and look into her eyes. Oh, Laura, Laura, I tried to
leave you behind me, but I am more faithful than I intended to be! I reach for a
cigarette, I cross the street, I run into the movies or a bar, I buy a drink, I speak
to the nearest stranger—anything that can blow your candles out!

[*LAURA bends over the candles.*]

For nowadays the world is lit by lightning! Blow out your candles, Laura—
and so goodbye . . . .

[*She blows the candles out.*]

QUESTIONS

1. What does the setting described in the opening stage direction tell you about the Wingfields? Consider especially the adjectives Williams employs and the symbolism of the alley and the fire escape.

2. Who is the "fifth character" in the play and how is his presence established? In what ways is Tom a parallel to this character?

3. What does Amanda reveal about her past in scene 1? How does Williams reveal that Amanda often dwells on the past?

4. What happened to Laura at Rubicam's Business College? How can you account for her behavior? What plan of Amanda's did she upset?

5. What new plan for Laura's future does Amanda begin to develop in scene 2? Why is the plan impracticable? Why is the image of Jim introduced here?

6. Summarize the argument between Tom and Amanda in scene 3. What does Amanda assert about Tom? What does he claim about his life? Why is Laura spotlighted throughout the argument?

7. What sort of agreement does Amanda try to reach with Tom about Laura in scene 4?

8. What distinction between Europe and America does the narrator make in scene 5? How is the song playing at the Paradise Dance Hall ironic?

9. Which character seems to have a more accurate and realistic understanding of Laura in scene 5? Why?

10. How does Amanda react to the news of a gentleman caller? How does Laura react? What happens when Laura discovers the caller's identity? Why?

11. Describe Laura's feelings toward Jim during the conversation and the dancing in scene 7. Describe his feelings toward her. How and why do his feelings change after the kiss?

12. Explain the symbolism of the unicorn (both whole and broken). Why does Laura give it to Jim as a souvenir?

13. What is Tom's situation at the close of the play? To what degree has he achieved his dreams of escape and adventure?

14. Describe Amanda's and Laura's situations at the close of the play. What is the significance of Laura's blowing out the candles? What future can you predict for these women? Why?

GENERAL QUESTIONS

1. What are the most striking nonrealistic aspects of the play? Explain why each is nonrealistic and how each contributes to the impact and meaning of the play. Which is the most effective? Why?

2. Each of the Wingfields seeks to escape the harsh realities of existence in a different way. Discuss the method each uses.

3. Which character do you consider the protaganist of the play? Why? How might a case be made supporting the claims of each of the Wingfields? What specific details support the case for each?

4. Consider the distinction between Tom as a character and as narrator. How and why is the language of the narrator different from that of the character? What does the character dream about and strive for? What has the narrator learned about these dreams and strivings?

5. As the title suggests, Laura and her fantasy world are central to the play. Explain the reasons for Laura's inability to deal with reality. What is the significance of her glass menagerie?

6. Williams says that there is much to admire, pity, and laugh at in Amanda. What aspects of her character are admirable? Pitiable? Laughable? Which reaction is dominant for you at the close of the play? Why?

7. In his opening speech, Tom calls Jim "the most realistic character in the play." In what ways is Jim realistic? How are his dreams and goals more (or less) realistic than Tom's?

8. Discuss the ideas about family life, poverty, personality, and the ability to escape from the past explored in this play.

9. At the opening of the play, Tom (as narrator) mentions the "social background," and he remarks on it throughout. Discuss this background, especially the events occurring in Europe, and the ways it relates to the play's action.

10. Discuss the line of religious allusion and imagery that runs through the play. Consider especially Malvolio the Magician, "Ave Maria," "Annunciation," the Paradise Dance Hall, and Laura's candles.

11. Do you consider this play a comedy, tragedy, or something in between? Which characters, if any, learn or change in significant ways? To what extent do the characters succeed or fail in the goals they set for themselves?

WRITING ABOUT REALISTIC AND NONREALISTIC DRAMA

In planning and writing an essay about a realistic or nonrealistic play, your attention will naturally be focused on the traditional elements of drama—plot, character, perspective, setting, language, tone, symbol, and theme. Conventional approaches to these were discussed earlier (pp. 1009–1017); you may want to review this material. You will also be concerned, however, with the relative degrees of realism or nonrealism with which the elements are presented and developed, and the ways in which this variable affects the impact and meaning of the play.

You will be dealing with four related areas of exploration for this type of essay: (1) the elements or aspects of the play that you find most interesting, significant, and effective; (2) the feelings, ideas, and effects created or emphasized through these features; (3) the degree to which these elements or aspects may be considered realistic (or nonrealistic); and (4) the extent to which the impact or meaning of the play depends on the realism or nonrealism of the elements under consideration. The introduction of a new variable into your planning—the spectrum of realism and its impact on the play—thus creates some new ways in which you might look at the traditional elements. The following can only begin to suggest some of these.

1. *Plot.* Evaluate the relative realism or nonrealism of the plot, structure, action, and conflicts. Does the play unfold in a chronological order that imitates reality, or does it mix past and present action in any way? Is the action true to life or stylized? Are the conflicts resolved realistically, or does the playwright employ a conventional and perhaps improbable happy (or sad) ending? How does the realistic or nonrealistic development of these aspects affect the impact and meaning of the play?

2. *Character.* Are the characters presented and developed in a predominantly realistic manner? Are they symbolic, representative, or stereotyped? Round or flat? Are they motivated by lifelike considerations, or simply by the requirements of the play? In *The Glass Menagerie*, for example, Amanda's motivations are entirely realistic, but the narrator is motivated only through the theatrical demand that he speak to the audience or reader. Are the characters consistent, or do they drop in and out of character? Is their clothing and makeup (as described in the stage directions) an imitation of real life, or is it blatantly theatrical and nonrealistic? Are all the characters in the play developed in the same manner, or are there differences in the degree of realism you find in each? Is there one character who is remarkably more or less realistic than any of the others? If so, what impact does this have on the play?

3. *Perspective.* In realistic drama, the perspective or point of view tends to be completely objective; that is finally the goal of the picture-frame stage and the principle of the missing fourth wall. Characters never reveal their thoughts or emotions directly to us, and they never speak to us about other characters. Consequently, it is almost impossible to impose anything but an objective point of view on a realistic play. One of the few ways to impose a more subjective point of view is to give all or most of the lines to a single character; Eugene O'Neill uses such a device in *Before Breakfast* (see p. 1047), in which Mrs. Rowland has the only speaking part. When you encounter such a play, consider why the character is given most of the dialogue and how the device shapes or distorts your perception of the play. In nonrealistic drama, the playwright has the freedom to unfold the play through whatever perspective he or she chooses. In such a case, you might consider which characters speak directly to the audience or the reader. How extensive is such direct address? Is there a single character who does most of this talking? If so, what is he or she like? What does the character tell you about himself or herself? About the other characters in the play? The background? Plot? Action? Setting? Staging? How accurate and objective is this character? Above all else, how does this direct address shape and control your response to the play?

4. *Setting.* You might investigate the degree to which the setting is presented as realistic or nonrealistic in the stage directions. Do the playwright's directions call for the reproduction of an actual room or place in

minute detail? If less than a fully realistic setting is described, how far does the playwright go in reducing the setting to the bare stage? How much of the physical theater (brick walls, pipes, wires, lights, backstage ropes) does the playwright indicate that he or she wants you to see or imagine? To what extent do you find symbolic, impressionistic and nonrealistic devices such as transparent walls? Most important, how does the setting and its degree of realism (or nonrealism) contribute to the impact and meaning of the play? As you evaluate the setting, you might also explore other aspects of staging and presentation, as described in the stage directions, that can determine the relative realism of a play. How is lighting employed? Is it used realistically, to recreate the natural illumination in a room, or nonrealistically, to isolate and emphasize specific places, objects, characters, or actions?

5. *Language.* When you are considering language, look carefully at the diction, style, and patterns of the dialogue. Is the language colloquial and appropriate for the characters, or do you find nonrealistic devices such as verse, song, or unnatural and patterned repetition? In *A Doll's House*, for example, the dialogue is consistently imitative of real life, but in *The Sandbox* we find inarticulate noises, strings of clichés, and massive amounts of repetition. Does each character maintain a consistent style and level or diction, or do you find a single character speaking in different voices? How do these aspects of language determine the extent to which the play effectively communicates ideas and emotions to you? As you deal with language, also consider the significance of other aspects of sound indicated in the stage directions, such as sound effects or music.

6. *Symbolism.* This is one of the few elements that tend to work in the same manner whether the play is highly realistic, nonrealistic, or something in between. Since symbols can operate in life as they do in art, there is room for symbolism in the realistic plays of Glaspell and Ibsen as well as in the relatively nonrealistic dramas of Miller and Williams. Nevertheless, your investigation of symbolism can be worthwhile because symbols may be introduced through realistic or nonrealistic techniques. You can focus your exploration directly on the symbol and its meaning (the locked mailbox in *A Doll's House*) or the nonrealistic methods through which it is established (the image of the blue roses in *The Glass Menagerie*).

7. *Theme.* The exploration of theme in realistic and nonrealistic drama seeks to identify important concepts in the play *and* the ways in which they are conveyed. Here you should give special consideration to significantly realistic or nonrealistic techniques. In dealing with a realistic play like *Trifles* or *A Doll's House*, you might explore the ways in which realism in character, action, and setting contribute to the emergence of the play's ideas. Conversely, you might consider how Williams employs a strikingly nonrealistic device, such as the music or the screen projections, to convey and emphasize the themes of *The Glass Menagerie*.

Once you have investigated all these areas, created a set of working notes, and narrowed your focus to a specific group of elements and effects, begin to plan the essay in more detail. Formulate a tentative central idea and start to organize the supporting details. The central idea must provide a connection between specifically realistic or nonrealistic elements and their effect on part or all of the play. It is inadequate to assert as a central idea that "Nora is a realistic character" or that "Tom is a nonrealistic character." You cannot build an effective essay on simple descriptive sentences. A better central idea would link Nora's realistic character or Tom's nonrealistic one to the effect the character had on the play. In working on an essay about Tom, for example, you might tentatively assert: "The development of Tom as a nonrealistic narrator and realistic character unifies *The Glass Menagerie* and gives the play a coherent and subjective point of view." Although such a formulation will need a great deal of revision, it will provide the basis for an assertive essay.

The central idea may change many times as you evaluate the nature and the implications of your supporting evidence. Organize your notes into logical units; these will become the essay's central paragraphs. This material should be constantly reevaluated to ensure that it supports your ideas in the most convincing and relevant ways possible.

Organizing Your Essay

INTRODUCTION.   As in most other cases, the introduction should provide an overview and a guide to the essay. You might begin with a general statement that establishes the author, title, and dominant style of the play. The most important aspects of the introduction, however, are the central idea and the thesis or topic sentence. The central idea will normally assert a connection between a specific aspect of the play, its relative realism or nonrealism, and the impact or effect it produces. The thesis sentence should enumerate the topics that the essay will take up to support the central idea.

BODY.   The body of the essay provides the supporting details and arguments that validate your central idea. This material may be organized in any fashion that produces a logical and convincing essay. If you deal with several topics, you can treat them in sequence. If you are writing about the ways in which nonrealistic devices emphasize meaning in *The Glass Menagerie*, for example, you might treat the setting, the lighting, and the screen device in a series of paragraphs. When the essay focuses on just one element, you may organize your supporting details to reflect the order in which they occur in the play.

CONCLUSION.   The concluding paragraph should bring the essay to an assertive and convincing close. A summary of your major points is always appropriate here. You might also raise larger issues or make broader connections about the topics you discussed and the play as a whole. Finally, this is a good place to reconsider the plays' general level of realistic or nonrealistic techniques, and the impact it creates.

SAMPLE ESSAY

Realism and Nonrealism in Tom's Triple Role in *The Glass Menagerie**

[1] In *The Glass Menagerie*, Tennessee Williams combines realistic and nonrealistic elements to explore the personalities and conflicts of the Wingfield family. One of the most effective nonrealistic elements in the play is Williams's use of Tom in three different roles to unify the play's theme and to provide a subjective and overall perspective.° As realistic character within the action, nonrealistic stage manager of the action, and nonrealistic narrator of the entire play, Tom combines three functions that significantly shape our perception of the drama.□

[2] As a realistic character involved in the recollected action of the play, Tom is ensnared by the economic and emotional demands of his family and his job. In the opening description of the characters, Williams defines Tom as trapped when he notes that "To escape from a trap he [Tom] has to act without pity." In addition, the character repeatedly expresses his feelings of entrapment and the need to escape from his dull, drab life. He discusses these things with his mother in scene 3, Laura in scene 4, and, above all, with Jim in scene 6. Here, we see that Tom craves escape and adventure. He tells Jim, "I'm planning a change." And he clearly expresses his desire to move out of the prison house of the family:

> It's our turn now, to go the South Sea Island—to make a safari—to be exotic, far off! But I'm not patient. I don't want to wait till then. I'm tired of the *movies* and I am *about* to *move*! . . . . I'm starting to boil inside. I know I seem dreamy, but inside—well, I'm boiling.   (p. 1549: 114, 120)

As this passage indicates, Tom as a character repeatedly directs us to one of the central ideas in the play—the need to escape. His strivings define a major line of thought and action in *The Glass Menagerie*.

[3] Tom's realism as a character is deeply undercut by his momentary role as a stage manager in scene 1. Here, he speaks with Amanda "*as though reading from a script.*" In this same scene, "Tom *motions for music and a spot of light on* Amanda." Although this device is quickly abandoned, the image of Tom holding an imaginary script and giving cues to the musicians and the lighting technicians has a profound effect on our perception of the action.

---

* See p. 1515 for this play.
° Central idea.
□ Thesis sentence.

For one thing, the device breaks the illusion of the play as an imitation of real life and reminds us that what we are reading about or watching is a stage with actors on it. It suggests that Tom controls and directs the entire action.

Tom's part in shaping and unifying the play becomes most explicit in his nonrealistic function as narrator. In this role, he stands completely outside the action occurring in the Wingfield apartment and speaks directly to us; he introduces the characters, provides background, and supplies an ongoing retrospective commentary on the dramatized events. Most important, Tom as the narrator provides two central functions in the play, thematic unity and a subjective and overriding perspective on the action. First, the narrator speaks truths that the character has not yet learned. As a character, Tom strives for freedom and adventure. As narrator, however, he recognizes that escape

[4]   from the past is impossible. At the close of the play, he tells us that he remains trapped, even as he wanders through the streets of strange cities:

> Then all at once my sister touches my shoulder. I turn around and look into her eyes. Oh, Laura, Laura, I tried to leave you behind me, but I am more faithful than I intended to be!   (p. 1567: 323)

The narrator, unlike the character, understands that the past will always be present; he thus provides a final perspective on the central theme of escape.

The second striking aspect of Tom's function as narrator concerns his complete control of the play. Because he is the narrator, the action in *The Glass Menagerie* represents Tom's memories of events, rather than the events themselves. In his first speech, Tom tells us that "The play is memory. Being

[5]   a memory play, it is dimly lighted, it is sentimental, it is not realistic." Since the events which occur on stage from the past emerge from Tom's memory, it is he who provides an overriding unity and perspective. We see everything through his mind and from his point of view. Tom as a nonrealistic narrator thus holds the central stage action together and shapes our response to everything we experience.

Williams thus uses Tom in three distinct ways to create unity and perspective. As a realistic character, Tom embodies the theme of escape. As a nonrealistic stage manager and narrator, he offers thematic resolution, controls the action, and imposes a coherent and subjective point of view. The nonrealistic

[6]   aspects of his roles mesh perfectly with other devices that Williams employs nonrealistically, especially the music and lighting. This coming together of nonrealistic devices is perfectly captured in that single moment early in the play when Tom, as stage manager, explicitly controls both the lighting and the music.

Commentary on the Essay

This essay takes on a great deal; it discusses theme and perspective, or point of view, as they are shaped by Tom's various roles in *The Glass Menagerie*. The primary focus is on character, but a number of distinct topics are taken up in connection with this single element because the essay concerns Tom as a character, stage director, and narrator.

The introductory paragraph supplies an overview of the essay. The first sentence provides the title, identifies the author, and makes a general but relevant observation about the play. The second states the central idea; it isolates a specific element (character), identifies it as nonrealistic, and asserts an effect (unity and perspective) that the element produces. The thesis or topic sentence lists the three aspects of Tom's role that the essay will investigate.

The body of the essay (paragraphs 2–5) takes up these three roles in the order in which they are listed in the introduction. Notice that this order does not reflect the sequence in which these occur in the play. Rather, they are organized to reflect a progression from the most realistic to the most nonrealistic aspects of Tom's three different functions. Thus, paragraph 2 discusses Tom as a realistic character and connects him to one of the play's central themes—entrapment and the desire to escape.

Paragraph 3 shifts to a consideration of Tom as stage manager. It explains why such a role is nonrealistic and explores the effects produced by such a nonrealistic figure in the play. Similarly, paragraphs 4 and 5 discuss Tom as narrator. Again, the essay establishes why such a role is nonrealistic and how the role affects our perceptions of the play. Paragraph 4 also returns to the thematic concerns of paragraph 2, while paragraph 5 returns to the issues of control and perspective raised in connection with Tom as stage manager. Throughout the body, direct quotation of dialogue or action as indicated in the stage directions is employed as supporting evidence. Quotation is used sparingly, but when it does occur, it has the effect of validating a specific point.

The conclusion of the essay provides a review-summary of the three roles that Tom plays and the effects that each produces in connection with theme, unity, and perspective. In addition, it suggests a connection between the nonrealistic aspects of Tom's roles and other elements of the play that Williams employs nonrealistically and to good effect.

WRITING TOPICS FOR CHAPTER 28

1. Some critics have asserted that *A Doll's House* should be called "A Doll House" because everyone in the Helmer household leads a doll-like existence that is tested and exposed by outsiders. Write an essay arguing for or against this assertion with regard to Torvald, the Helmer children, and the servants.

2. Write an essay dealing with any or all of the following questions:
   a. Is *A Doll's House* a comedy, tragedy, or something in between?
   b. To what extent do the play's characters learn and change for the better (or worse)?
   c. Does the resolution strike you as affirmative or negative? Why?

3. Compare Mommy and Daddy in *The Sandbox* to Ma and Elmer Kirby in Wilder's *The Happy Journey to Trenton and Camden*. To what degrees are the characters realistic? Nonrealistic? Why? In what ways are they similar and different?

4. Write an essay exploring Edward Albee's characterization of Mommy, Daddy, and Grandma in *The Sandbox*, and showing how these characterizations are related to his views of the American family, the relationship of men and women in marriage, and attitudes toward old age.

5. In an essay, compare the sets described in *The Sandbox* and *The Happy Journey to Trenton and Camden*. What elements of realism are common to them? What is unrealistic about them, and why? To what extent do you think the sets would have similar effects on the audience? Why?

6. Suppose that you were a film director undertaking a film of *The Happy Journey to Trenton and Camden*, and that you had an unlimited budget to do anything you wanted. Would you honor Wilder's set directions for the film medium, or would you introduce realistic settings, vintage cars, and so on? If you made such changes, what would be their effect? Would your film represent the play as Wilder has left it for us, and how would you justify the changes, if any? Answer these questions in an essay.

7. The screen device described in Tennessee Williams's Production Notes (see pp. 1516–17) is omitted from most productions of *The Glass Menagerie*. Write an essay considering the advantages or disadvantages of including reference to this device in the printed text. How are you affected by the screen images as you read the play? How effective would they be in a stage production?

8. Write an essay investigating Williams's symbolism in *The Glass Menagerie*. To what end does Williams use symbolism? Which characters, places, objects, and actions are symbolic, and what do they symbolize? If these elements are symbolic, to what degree are they also realistic? If there were no basis in realism, how successful would they be as symbols?

9. Write two separate versions of a scene of your own. (Some possible topics: a woman confronts her boyfriend upon learning that he has been seeing someone else; a man has an interview with his boss and learns that he must be let go; an army captain tells a group of soldiers that they are about to be attacked by an army of fanatics; a woman realizes that she is the best salesperson in the firm). First, aim for total reality, and second, for total unreality. What differences do you think your differing intentions require of you as a practicing dramatist? What different requirements are made on your dialogue, on your action, on your setting, and on your costuming and suggested make-up for your actors? What elements do you think are the most unrealistic in your unrealistic version, and why do you believe you make them so unrealistic? Does the lack of realism, in your judgment, make your scene either more or less dramatic? Write an introductory essay to your two versions explaining these and other principles of your dramatic composition.

Appendix A:
Evaluating Literature

Evaluation means the act of deciding what is good, bad, or mediocre. It requires a steady pursuit of the best—to be satisfied with less is to deny the best efforts of our greatest writers. Evaluation implies that there are ideal standards of excellence by which decisions about quality can be made, but it must be remembered that these standards are flexible, and may be applicable to works of literature written in all places and ages.

An evaluation is different from an essay on what you might like or dislike in a work (see Chapter 1, pp. 39–45). While your preferences are important in your evaluation, they are not as important as your judgment, and your judgment may lead you into positions that seem contrary to your preferences. In other words, it is possible to grant the excellence of a work or writer that you personally may not like.

STANDARDS FOR EVALUATION

There is no precise answer to the problem of how to justify an evaluation. Evaluation is the most abstract, philosophical, and difficult writing about literature you will do. Standards of taste, social mores, and even morals differ from society to society and from age to age; nonetheless, some works of art have been judged as great by generation after generation in many cultures. There are many standards to help you evaluate a literary work. Some of the major ones are described below, and many have been suggested in earlier chapters.

Truth

Although *truth* or *truthful* is often used in speaking of literature to mean *realism* or *realistic*, its meaning here is carefully restricted. To speak of the truth is to imply generality and universality. Let us take a concrete illustration.

Sophocles' *Oedipus the King*, one of the oldest works in this anthology, has survived the turbulence of almost 2,500 years. It was written within social contexts that no longer exist, and it concerns circumstances that are difficult to imagine in the twentiety century. Nevertheless, it remains as true (and relevant) for our time as it was when it was first performed before the Athenian public. This is because it embodies situations that human beings have always and will always face; it reflects patterns of human error, guilt, and punishment that are as valid today as they were in Sophocles' time.

While many works have not withstood such an extended test of time, those that survive and prosper beyond their initial publication do so because they, too, embody some essential fragment of truth about the human condition. Such works measure up to basic standards we use in deciding whether a work of art is good or bad, great or mediocre.

Affirmativeness

Affirmativeness means here that human beings are worth caring about and writing about, no matter how debased their condition of living or how totally they abuse their state. All art should be affirmative. If a character like Willie Loman falls to the depths of misfortune and death, the author must demonstrate that this loss has value and meaning. Human worth is here affirmed even as a major character is destroyed. If a character is happy at the end of the work, the author must show that this character's qualities have justified such good fortune. Life is again affirmed. If an unworthy character is fortunate at the end, the author still affirms human worth by suggesting a world in which such worth may become triumphant. In short, authors may portray the use and abuse of life, the love and the hate, the heights and the depths, but their vision is always that life is valuable and worthy of respect and dignity. The best works are those that make this affirmation forcefully, without platitudes.

"The Joint Force and Full Result of All"

In his *Essay on Criticism*, Alexander Pope insists that a critic should not judge a work simply by its parts but should judge the *whole*—"the joint force and full result of all." You can profit from Pope's wisdom. Consider the total effect of the work, both as an artistic form and as a cause of impressions and emotions in yourself. Bear in mind that a great work may contain imperfections, but if the sum total of the work is impressive, the flaws assume minor importance.

By the same token, excellent technique in itself does not justify a claim for excellence. An interesting plot, a balanced and carefully handled structure, a touching love story, a valid or important moral—none of these attributes alone can support a total judgment of "good" unless everything in the work is balanced.

Another important phase of the "joint force and full result of all" is the way in which you become involved as you read. Most of what you read, if it has merit, will cause you to become emotionally involved with the characters and actions. You have perhaps observed that characters in some works seem real to you or that incidents are described so vividly that you feel as though you have witnessed them. The problem here is whether the involvement you experience was fleeting and momentary or whether it has assumed more permanence.

Vitality

A good work of literature has a life of its own and can be compared to a human being. A work can grow in the sense that your repeated experience with it will produce insights that you did not have in your previous readings. Examples of such works are poems like Shakespeare's sonnets and Gray's "Elegy Written in a Country Churchyard," stories like Poe's "The Masque of the Red Death" and Jackson's "The Lottery," and plays like Sophocles' *Oedipus the King* and Shakespeare's *Hamlet*. Readers and critics alike constantly find new insights and understanding in these works.

Beauty

Beauty is closely allied with unity, symmetry, harmony, and proportion. To discover the relationship of parts to whole—their logical, chronological, and associational functions within the work—is to perceive beauty. In the eighteenth century people believed that "variety within order" constituted beauty. The Romantic and post-Romantic periods held that beauty could be found only through greater freedom. This belief has produced such characteristics as originality for its own sake, experimentation in form, freedom of syntax, stream-of-consciousness narration, and personal diction. Despite the change of emphasis, however, the concepts of unity and proportion are still valid and applicable. Studies of style, structure, point of view, tone, and imagery are therefore all ways of determining whether works are beautiful.

WRITING AN EVALUATION ESSAY

Organizing Your Essay

In your essay you will attempt to answer the question of whether the work you have studied is good. If so, why? If not, why not? The grounds for your evaluation must be artistic. Although some works may be good pieces of political argument, or successfully controversial, your goal is to judge them as works of art.

INTRODUCTION.   In the introduction you can briefly summarize your evaluation, which will be your central idea, and list the points by which you expect to demonstrate the validity of your assessment. To assist your reader's comprehension of your ideas, you should note any unique facts or background about the work you are evaluating.

BODY.   In the body, demonstrate the grounds for your judgment; your principal points will be the positive or negative features of the work you are evaluating. Positive features include qualities of style, idea, structure, character, logic, point of view, and so on. Your discussion will analyze the probability, truth, force, or power with which the work embodies these positive aspects.

Avoid analysis for its own sake, and do not merely retell stories. If you are showing the excellence or deficiency of a character portrayal, you can include a description of the character, but remember that your discussion is to be pointed toward *evaluation*, not *description*. Therefore you must select details for discussion that will illustrate whether the work is good or bad. Similarly, if you are evaluating a sonnet of Shakespeare, you might argue that the superb imagery contributes to the general excellence. At this point you might introduce some of the imagery, but your purpose is not to analyze imagery as such; it should be used only for illustration. If you remember to keep your thematic purpose foremost, you should have little difficulty in making your discussion relate to your central idea.

CONCLUSION.   The conclusion should be a statement on the total result of the work you are evaluating. Your concern here is with total impressions. This part of evaluation should reemphasize your central idea.

SAMPLE ESSAY

An Evaluation of "The Chaser," by John Collier*

[1]   Collier's "The Chaser" contrasts the dreams of youth with the cynicism of age. Because cynicism is dominant at the end, the story might be considered too negative, too bleak, and it might be criticized for this reason. To dismiss "The Chaser" without further thought, however, would be hasty; a careful

---

* See p. 311 for this story.

reading shows that the story has genuine merit.° While a case may be made that the story is cynical and negative, a better case is that it is satirical and positive, demonstrating a corresponding excellence of technique. □

[2] The reader who considers "The Chaser" as only a grim joke has made the mistake of judging the old man as very wise as well as cynical. It is true that he has seen people like Alan Austen before. They have come to him wanting to make their sweethearts love them passionately, completely, worshipfully, and dependently. For such young people, the old man keeps a supply of inexpensive but infallible love potion. Beyond this, when they grow older and become tired of their potion-induced love, the old man also keeps an expensive and also infallible supply of untraceable poison—the "glove cleaner" or "life cleaner." The concluding words of the old man, "Au revoir," ("until we meet again"), indicate his knowledge that Austen will return someday for the poison. This cynicism, while justified in the light of Austen's character, seems too jarring a contrast to the enthusiasm of Austen's current passion for his sweetheart, Diana. If the story were to do no more than show that young love ended in boredom and hatred, it would indeed be totally negative, and therefore would deserve to be dismissed.

While one may grant that the old man's judgment is right, and that Austen will grow discontented with the woman he now most enjoys, it by no means follows that "The Chaser" is bad literature. In fact, the story should be seen positively as a satirical attack on the shortsightedness of Austen and of the view that he represents. The old man tantalizes Austen with the following description of the love he is seeking:

[3] "For indifference," said the old man, "they [women who are scornful] substitute devotion. For scorn, adoration. Give one tiny measure of this to the young lady—its flavour is imperceptible in orange juice, soup, or cocktails—and however gay and giddy she is, she will change altogether. She will want nothing but solitude and you."

This description suggests not love but enslavement—a fawning devotion that dehumanizes the woman and also makes a monster of the man who expects or demands such attention for himself. Instead of depicting Austen as a typical, model young man, Collier satirically shows him as corrupt right from the start.

[4] The technique of the story is geared toward this satirical revelation of Austen's weakness and shortsightedness. After the first few paragraphs of exposition to make the situation clear, Collier develops the rest of the story using a dramatic point of view. There is no sympathetic voice explaining Austen's emotions. Instead, Austen speaks for himself, revealing his own flawed, shallow character while the old man plays the cynical, grimly insinuating game of salesmanship upon him. Because Collier gives the old man much of the dialogue, with Austen's words being mainly in response, Austen is unable to speak of any warm personal relationships, even if he were able to conceive of them. Instead, the talk is all of control and possession. In this

° Central idea.
□ Thesis sentence.

way Collier uses technique to reveal Austen's shortcomings, and therefore to rule him out as a complete human being. The truth that Collier is stressing is symbolized by the old man's "glove cleaner," which represents the demeaning and destructive nature of the master-slave bond that Austen so earnestly seeks.

[5]   On balance, therefore, the story is a good one. As a satire, it is more affirmative than it may at first seem, for the positive basis against which Austen and the old man should be measured is a humanized love relationship entered into freely by equals. The bonding in such a relationship is not one of master-slave, but is instead one of mutual consent. Fidelity is freely given and is not extracted either by force, like that produced by the potion Austen comes to buy, or expectation. Through this means of satirical contrast, Collier's dramatic rendering of character and his attack on possessiveness make "The Chaser" true and affirmative. "The Chaser" is a fine and memorable story.

Commentary on the Essay

The strategy of this evaluative essay is to use an apparent weakness of Collier's "The Chaser" as the basis of an argument asserting the strength and quality of the story. The logic of the essay is that the value of Collier's work may be found in his use of satire. The essay therefore demonstrates the principle that all aspects of a work should be considered when one is making an evaluation. Although a number of ideas and techniques are considered in the essay, these are not used as ends in themselves, but instead are introduced as evidence in the argument for the merits of the story.

Paragraph 1, the introductory paragraph, brings up the issue that the story might be dismissed after no more than a hasty reading; it also asserts the need for an evaluation based on more thought. The points to be developed in the body are stressed in the thesis sentence.

In the body of the essay, paragraph 2 deals with the uncritical, hasty reading that would make the story seem intolerably negative. The strategy here is one of concession, namely, that if the old man were to be considered authoritative, the story would be generally untrue, and would be weak for that reason. Paragraph 3 deals with the idea that "The Chaser" is in fact a satire and that it therefore should be read as a positive work in which the main characters are not admired but attacked. Paragraph 4 demonstrates how Collier's technique complements this satiric thrust. Collier's handling of the story underscores his satiric revelation. In the light of the argument carried out in the body of the essay, the concluding paragraph emphasizes again that "The Chaser" is a good story. The basis for this conclusion is that the view of love in "The Chaser" (developed in three sentences of this last paragraph) is the opposite of what the main characters represent.

Appendix B: Comparison-Contrast and Extended Comparison-Contrast

A comparison-contrast essay may be used to compare and contrast different authors, two or more works by the same author, different drafts of the same work, or characters, incidents, and ideas within the same work or in different works. The virtue of comparison-contrast is that it enables the study of works in perspective. No matter what works you consider together, the method is effective in helping you isolate and highlight individual characteristics, for the quickest way to get at the essence of one work is to compare it with another. Similarities are brought out by comparison, and differences are shown by contrast. In other words, you can find out what a thing *is* by using comparison-contrast to discover what it *is not*.

For example, our understanding of Shakespeare's Sonnet 30, "When to the Sessions of Sweet Silent Thought," (p. 628) may be enhanced if we compare it with Christina Rossetti's lyric poem "Echo" (p. 701). We learn that both poems tell about personal recollections of past experiences, and that they feature individual speakers addressing listeners who are not intended as the general reader. Also, both poems similarly refer to persons, now dead, with whom the speaker was closely involved.

There are important differences, however. Shakespeare's speaker numbers the dead persons as friends whom he laments generally as he focuses on the speaker's present sorrow about the past, while Rossetti refers specifically to one person with whom the speaker was in love. Rossetti's topic is the sorrow of dead love, the irrevocability of the past, and the present loneliness of the speaker. Shakespeare includes the references to dead friends as a way of accounting for present sorrows, but he turns then to the present and stresses the fact that thinking about the "dear friend" being addressed is a way of recovering present composure and eliminating past "losses." To Rossetti, there is no reconciliation of past and present, and instead the speaker focuses entirely upon the sadness of the present moment. Though both poems are retrospective, then, Shakespeare's poem looks to the present while Rossetti's looks to the past.

While more could be said about both poems, this example shows how quickly the comparison-contrast method enables us to identify their similar characteristics, and also to determine what makes them separate and unique. It is often true that difficulty with one particular work may be eliminated if you can compare and contrast it with another work on a comparable subject.

CLARIFY YOUR INTENTION

Your first problem in planning a comparison-contrast essay is to decide on a goal, for you may use the method in a number of ways. One objective can be the equal and mutual illumination of two (or more) works. Thus, an essay comparing O'Connor's "First Confession" (p. 490) with Hawthorne's "Young Goodman Brown" (p. 333) might be designed (1) to compare ideas, characters, or methods in these stories equally, without stressing or favoring either. But you might also wish (2) to emphasize "Young Goodman Brown," and therefore you would use "First Confession" as material for highlighting the Hawthorne work. You might also use comparison-contrast (3) to show your liking of one work at the expense of another, or (4) to emphasize a method or idea that you think is especially noteworthy or appropriate.

A first task is therefore to decide upon an emphasis. The first sample essay in this appendix gives "equal time" to both works being considered, without any claims for the superiority of either. Unless you aim at a different rhetorical goal, this essay is a suitable model for most comparisons.

FIND COMMON GROUNDS FOR COMPARISON

The second stage in prewriting for this essay is to select a common ground for discussion. It is useless to compare dissimilar things, for the resulting conclusions will not have much value. Instead, compare like with like: idea with idea, characterization with characterization, imagery with imagery, point of view with point of view, symbols with symbols. Nothing much can be learned from a comparison of Welty's View of Courage and Chekhov's View of Love, but a comparison of The Relationship of Love to Stability and Courage in Chekhov and Welty suggests common ground, with the promise of important things to be learned through the examination of similarities and differences.

To discover common grounds, you may have to be inventive and creative. For instance, if you try to compare Maupassant's "The Necklace" with Chekhov's *The Bear*, these two works at first seem completely dissimilar. Yet a common ground can be found if you make the subject of your comparison The Treatment of Self-Deceit in these two works, or The Effects of Chance on Human Affairs, or The View of Women, and so on. Although other works may seem even more dissimilar than these, it is usually possible to find a common ground of comparison and contrast. Much of your success with this essay depends on your ingenuity in finding a workable basis—a common denominator—for comparison.

METHODS OF COMPARISON

Let us assume that you have decided on your rhetorical purpose and the basis or bases of your comparison. You have done your reading, taken notes, and know what you want to say. The remaining problem is the treatment of your material. Here are two acceptable ways:

A common method is to make your points first about one work and then about the other. This method makes your paper seem like two big lumps, and it also involves much repetition because you must repeat the same points as you treat your second subject.

A better method is to treat your main idea in its major aspects, making references to the two (or more) writers as the references illustrate and illuminate your main idea. Refer to *both* writers, sometimes within the same sentence, and also keep reminding your reader of the point of your discussion. This method works better for these reasons: (1) You do not repeat your points needlessly, for you document them as you raise them. (2) By continually referring to the two works, you make your points without requiring a reader to reread previous sections of your essay.

As a model, here is a paragraph on Natural References as a Basis of Comparison of Frost's "Desert Places" and Shakespeare's Sonnet 73, "That Time of Year Thou Mayest in Me Behold" (pp. 748 and 694).

[1] Both writers link their ideas to events occurring in the natural world. [2] Night as a parallel with death is common to both poems, with Frost speaking about it in his first line, and Shakespeare introducing it in his seventh. [3] Along with night, Frost emphasizes the onset of winter and snow as a time of death and desolation. [4] With this natural description, Frost also symbolically refers to empty, secret, dead places in the inner spirit, crannies of the soul where bleak winter snowfalls correspond to selfishness and indifference. [5] By contrast, Shakespeare uses the fall season, with the yellowing and dropping of leaves and also the flying away of birds, as a means of stressing the closeness of real death and therefore also as a means of emphasizing the need to love fully during the time remaining. [6] Both poems therefore share a sense of gloom, because in both death is final and as inevitable as the oncoming seasons of barrenness and waste. [7] Because Shakespeare's

sonnet is addressed to a listener who is also a loved one, however, it is more outgoing than the introspective poem of Frost. [8] Frost turns the snow, the night, and the emptiness of the universe inward as a means of stressing the inner bleakness of the speaker's spirit, and by extension, the bleakness of many human spirits. [9] Shakespeare instead uses the bleakness of seasons, night, and dying fires to emphasize the need for loving "well." [10] The poems thus use common and similar references to different purposes and effects.

The paragraph above links Shakespeare's use of natural references with those of Frost. Five sentences speak of both authors together; three speak of Frost alone, and two of Shakespeare alone, but all the sentences are unified topically. This interweaving of references indicates that the writer has learned both poems well enough to think of them at the same time, and it also enables the writing to be more pointed and succinct than if the works were treated separately.

Avoid the "Tennis-Ball" Method

As you make your comparison, do not confuse an interlocking method with the "tennis-ball" method, in which you bounce your subject back and forth constantly and repetitively, almost as though you were hitting observations back and forth over a net. The tennis-ball method is shown in the following example from a comparison of the characters Mathilde (in Maupassant's "The Necklace") and Miss Brill (in Mansfield's "Miss Brill"):

> Mathilde is a young married woman, while Miss Brill is single and getting on in years. Mathilde has at least some kind of social life, even though she is somewhat solitary, while Miss Brill leads a life of solitude. Mathilde's daydreams are almost directly responsible for her misfortunes, but Miss Brill's daydreams are shattered by someone from the outside. Therefore, Mathilde is made unhappy because of her own shortcomings, while Miss Brill is a helpless victim. In Mathilde's case the focus is on adversity not only causing trouble but also strengthening character. In Miss Brill's case the focus is on the weak getting hurt and being made weaker.

Imagine the effect of reading an entire essay written in this 1,2—1,2—1,2 order. Aside from the repetition and unvaried patterning of subjects, the tennis-ball method does not permit much illustrative development. You should not feel so cramped that you cannot take two or more sentences to develop a point about one writer or subject before you include comparative references to another. If you remember to interlock the subjects of comparison, however, as in the paragraph about Frost and Shakespeare, your method will give you the freedom to develop your topics fully.

THE EXTENDED COMPARISON-CONTRAST ESSAY

For a longer essay, such as a limited research paper, comprehensive exam questions, and the sort of extended essay required at the end of a semester, comparison-contrast may be used in treating subjects such as ideas, plot, structure, character, and setting in a number of works. For essays of this larger scope, you will still need to develop common grounds for comparison, although if you choose more than two works for comparison you will need to modify the method.

Let us assume that you have been assigned not just two works but five or more. You need first to find a common ground among them which you may use as your central, unifying idea. When you take your notes, sketch out your ideas, make early drafts, and rearrange and shape your materials, try to bring all the works together on your major points.

When you contrast the works, you should form groups based on variations and differences. If three or four works treat a topic in one way, while one or two do it in another, you can treat the topic itself in a straightforward contrast method, but use details from your groupings as the material to support your argument. Again, it is desirable to use the analysis of a particular point based on one work, so that you can make your essay concrete and vivid. But once you have exemplified your point, you need to refer to the other works only enough to strengthen your points. In this way—treating many works as groups of twos—you can keep your essay reasonably brief.

For illustration, the second sample essay shows how this grouping may be done. Four works are included in a general category of how love and service offer guidance and stability. This group is contrasted with another group of three works (including two characters from one of the works in the first group, in which love is shown as an escape or retreat.

DOCUMENTATION AND
THE EXTENDED COMPARISON-CONTRAST ESSAY

In the longer comparison-contrast essay you have to deal with the problem of documentation. Generally you will not need to give page number locations for references to major traits, ideas, and actions. For example, if you refer to the end of O'Connor's "First Confession," where the priest gives Jackie some candy, you may assume that your reader also knows about this action. You do not need to do any more than make the reference.

But if you quote lines or passages, or if you cite actions or characters in special ways, you may need to use parenthetical page references, as described in the *MLA Handbook for Writers of Research Papers* (see Appendix C, pp. 1611–15). If you quote lines or parts of lines of poetry, use line numbers in parentheses, as shown in the second sample essay. Be guided by this principle: If you make a specific reference that you think your reader might want to examine in more detail, supply the line or page number. If you refer to minor details that might easily be unnoticed or forgotten, supply the line or page number. Otherwise, if you refer to major ideas, actions, or characterizations, make your reference clear enough so that your reader can easily recall it from his or her own memory of the work. Then you will not need to provide line or page numbers.

WRITING COMPARISON-CONTRAST ESSAYS

Organizing Your Essay

First, narrow and simplify your subject so that you can handle it conveniently. For example, if you compare Amy Lowell and Wilfred Owen (as in the first sample essay), select one or two poems by each poet about the same or a similar topic, and write your essay about these. For the longer comparison-contrast essay, you will need no more than a single work by each author. Be wary, however, of the limitations of your selection, because generalizations made from one or two works may not apply to all works of that writer.

Once you have found an organizing principle along with the relevant works, begin to refine and focus the direction of your essay. As you study each work, note common or contrasting elements, and use these to form your central idea. At the same time, you can select the most illustrative works and classify them according to your topics, such as war (first sample essay) or love (second sample essay). At the ends of the various chapters in this book, you will find a number of suggestions to help you get started in choosing other possible comparison-contrast topics.

INTRODUCTION.   In your introduction, state the works, authors, characters, or ideas you are considering. Then show how you have narrowed the topic of comparison. Your central idea should be a brief statement highlighting the principal grounds of comparison-contrast, such as the works treat a common topic, exhibit a similar idea, use a similar form, develop a comparable attitude, and so on, and also that your conclusions about major or minor differences help to make the works unique. You may claim that one work is better than others, if you wish to make this judgment and defend it. Your thesis sentence should list the topics you plan to develop in the body.

BODY.   The body of your essay depends on the works and your basis of comparison that is, your central idea. You might discuss two or more on common grounds such as comparable ideas and themes, depictions of character, uses of setting, qualities of style, or uses of point of view. Thus you might examine a number of stories that are written in the first-person point of view. An essay based on this grouping might compare and contrast the ways each author uses this point of view to achieve similar (or distinct) effects. Or you might find and compare a group of poems that employ similar images, symbols, or ironic methods. Sometimes, the process can be as simple as identifying female (or male) protagonists, and comparing the ways each author develops them. Another approach is available through *subject* (as opposed to *theme*). You might identify works that deal with general subjects such as love, death, youth, race, or war. Such groupings provide a fruitful chance to make excellent comparisons and contrasts.

As you develop the body of your essay, remember to keep to the point of comparison-contrast. That is, your discussions of point of view, metaphorical language, or whatever should be designed not so much to explain these topics as topics, but rather to explore similarities and differences about the works you are comparing. Let us say that your topic is an idea. You will of course need to explain the idea, but only enough to make the point clear in what ways the works are either similar or different. As you develop such an essay, you might illustrate your points by referring to the authors' use of elements like setting, characterization, rhythm or rhyme, symbolism, point of view, or metaphor. When you introduce these new subjects, you will be right on target as long as you discuss them comparatively.

CONCLUSION. Here you may reflect on other ideas or techniques in the works you have compared, make observations about similar qualities, or summarize briefly the grounds of your comparison. The conclusion of an extended comparison-contrast essay should represent the final bringing together of your materials. In the body of your essay, you may not have referred to all the works in each paragraph; however, in your conclusion you should try to include them all.

If your writers belong to any "period" or "school" (information about this topic would require research in your preparation of your essay), you also might wish to show in your conclusion how they relate to these larger movements. References of this sort provide an obvious common ground for comparison-contrast.

FIRST SAMPLE ESSAY (TWO WORKS)

The Treatment of Human Responses to War in Amy Lowell's "Patterns" and Wilfred Owen's "Anthem for Doomed Youth"*

"Patterns" and "Anthem for Doomed Youth" are powerful and unique condemnations of war.° Owen's short poem speaks broadly and generally

---

* See pp. 947 and 606 for these poems.
° Central idea.

[1] about the ugliness of war and also about large groups of bereaved people, while Lowell's longer poem focuses upon the personal grief of just one person. In a real sense, Lowell's poem begins where Owen's ends, a fact that accounts for both the similarities and differences between the two works. The anti-war themes may be compared on the basis of their subjects, their lengths, their concreteness, and their use of a common major metaphor. °

[2] "Anthem for Doomed Youth" attacks war more directly than "Patterns." Owen's opening line, "What passing bells for those who die as cattle," suggests that in war human beings are depersonalized before they are slaughtered, like so much meat, while his observations about the "monstrous" guns and the "shrill, demented" shells unambiguously condemn the horrors of war. By contrast, in "Patterns" warfare is far away, on another continent, intruding only when the messenger delivers the letter stating that the speaker's fiancé has been killed (lines 63–64). Similar news governs the last six lines of Owen's poem, quietly describing the responses of those at home to the news that their loved ones have died in war. Thus, the anti-war focus in "Patterns" is the contrast between the calm, peaceful life of the speaker's garden and the anguish of her responses, while in Owen's poem the stress is more the external horrors of war which bring about the need for ceremonies honoring the dead. Both poems attack war, but in different ways.

[3] Another difference, which is perhaps something of a surprise, is that Owen's poem is less than one seventh as long as Lowell's. "Patterns" is an interior monologue or meditation of 107 lines, but it could not realistically be shorter. In the poem the speaker thinks about the present and past, and contemplates the future loneliness to which her intended husband's death has doomed her. Her final outburst, "Christ, what are patterns for?" could make no sense if she does not explain her situation as extensively as she does. On the other hand, "Anthem for Doomed Youth" is brief—a fourteen-line sonnet—because it is more general and less personal than "Patterns." Although Owen's speaker shows sympathy for individuals, he or she views the sorrows of others distantly, unlike Lowell, who goes right into the mind and spirit of the grieving woman. Owen's use, in his last six lines, of phrases like "tenderness of patient minds" and "drawing down of blinds" is a short but powerful representation of deep grief. He presents no further detail even though thousands of individual stories might be told. In contrast, Lowell tells one of these stories as she focuses on her solitary speaker's lost hopes and dreams. Thus, the contrasting lengths of the poems are governed by each poet's treatment of the topic.

Despite these differences of approach and length, both poems are similarly concrete and vivid. Owen moves from the real scenes and sounds of battlefields to the homes of the many doomed soldiers who are now dead, while Lowell's scene is a single place—the garden of the estate where the speaker has just received news of her lover's death. Her speaker walks on gravel along garden paths that contain daffodils, squills, a fountain, and a lime tree. She thinks of her clothing and her ribboned shoes, and also of

° Thesis sentence.

[4] her fiancé's boots, sword hilts, and buttons. The images in Owen's poem are equally real, but are not associated with any individuals: cattle, bells, rifle shots, shells, bugles, candles, and window blinds. While the poems thus reflect the reality of life, Owen's details are more general and public, whereas Lowell's are more personal and intimate.

[5] Along with this concreteness, the poems share a major metaphor: that cultural patterns both control and frustrate human wishes, plans, and hopes. In "Patterns" this metaphor is shown in warfare itself (line 106), which is the supremely destructive political structure, or pattern. Further examples of the metaphor are found in details about clothing (particularly the speaker's stiff, confining gown in lines 5, 18, 21, 73, and 100, but also the lover's military boots in lines 46 and 49); the orderly, formal garden paths in which the speaker is walking (lines 1, 93); her restraint at hearing of her lover's death; and her courtesy, despite her grief, in ordering that the messenger take refreshment (line 69). Within such rigid patterns, her hopes for happiness have vanished, along with the sensuous spontaneity represented by her lover's plans to make love with her on a "shady seat" in the garden (lines 85–89). The metaphor of the constricting pattern may also be seen in "Anthem for Doomed Youth," except that in this poem the pattern is the funeral, not love or marriage. Owen's speaker contrasts the calm, peaceful tolling of "passing bells" (line 1) with the frightening sounds of war represented by the "monstrous anger of the guns," "the rifles' rapid rattle," and "the demented choirs of wailing shells" (lines 2–8). Thus, while Lowell uses the metaphor to reveal the irony of hope and desire being destroyed by war, Owen uses it to reveal the irony of war's nullification and perversion of peaceful ceremonies.

[6] Though the poems in these ways share topics and some aspects of treatment, they are distinct and individual. "Patterns" is visual and kinesthetic, whereas "Anthem for Doomed Youth" is strongly auditory. Both poems conclude on powerfully emotional although different notes. Owen's poem dwells on the pathos and sadness that war brings to many unnamed people, while Lowell's expresses the most intimate thoughts of a particular woman in the first agony of sorrow. Although neither poem directly attacks the usual platitudes and justifications for war (the needs to mobilize, to sacrifice, to achieve peace through fighting, and so on), the attack is there by implication, because both poems make their appeal by stressing how war destroys those relationships that make life worth living. For this reason, despite their differences and their uniqueness, both "Patterns" and "Anthem for Doomed Youth," are parallel anti-war poems, and both are strong portrayals of human feeling.

Commentary on the Essay

This example illustrates how approximately equal time can be given to each work being compared, with the goal of explaining similarities and differences on a common ground of comparison. Because the essay shifts continually from one work to the other, particular phrases may be noticed. When the works are similar or identical, terms used are "common," "share," "and," "both," "similar," and "also." For comparative situations, words like "longer" and "more" are useful. Differences are marked by "by contrast," "while," "whereas," "different," "dissimilar," "on the other hand," "another difference," "although," and "unlike." Transitions from paragraph to paragraph are not different in this type of essay from those in other essays. Thus, "despite," "along with this concreteness," and "in these ways" are used here, but they could be used anywhere for the same purpose.

The central idea of the essay is that the poems mutually condemn war. This idea is brought out in the introductory paragraph, together with the supporting idea that the poems blend into each other because both show responses to news of battle casualties. The thesis sentence concluding the first paragraph indicates four topics to be explored in the body of the essay.

Paragraph 2, the first in the body, discusses how each poem brings out its attack on warfare. Paragraph 3 explains the differing lengths of the poems as a function of differences in perspective. Because Owen's sonnet views war and its effects at a distance, it is short, while Lowell's interior monologue, which views death intimately, needs greater detail and length. The point of paragraph 4 is that both poems are concrete and real, but that the specificity (about personal things and public ceremonies) points the poems in different directions. Paragraph 5, the last in the body, considers the similar and dissimilar ways in which the poems treat a common metaphor.

The final paragraph summarizes the central idea; it also stresses the ways in which both poems, while similar, are distinct and unique.

SECOND SAMPLE ESSAY
(EXTENDED COMPARISON-CONTRAST)

The Complexity of Love and Devoted Service as Shown in Six Works*

[1]   On the surface, at least, love and devotion are simple, and their results should be good. A person loves someone, or serves someone or something. This love may be romantic or familial, and the service may be religious or national. But love is not simple. It is complex, and its results are not uniformly good.° Love and devotion should be ways of saying "yes," but ironically they sometimes become ways of saying "no," too. This idea can be traced in a comparison of six works: William Shakespeare's Sonnet 116, Matthew Arnold's "Dover Beach," Thomas Hardy's "Channel Firing," Anton Chekhov's

---

* For the texts of these works, see the following pages: "Sonnet 116," p. 736; "Dover Beach," p. 559; "Channel Firing," p. 562; *The Bear*, p. 1024; "First Confession," p. 490; "A Worn Path," p. 124.
° Central idea.

The Bear, Frank O'Connor's "First Confession," and Eudora Welty's "A Worn Path." The complexity in these works is that love and devotion do not operate in a vacuum but rather in the context of personal, philosophical, economic, and national difficulties. The works show that love and devotion may be forces for stability and refuge, but also for harm.°

[2] Ideal and stabilizing love, along with service performed out of love, is shown by Shakespeare in Sonnet 116 and by O'Connor in "First Confession." Shakespeare states that love gives lovers strength and stability in a complex world of opposition and difficulty. Such love is like a "star" that guides wandering ships (line 7), and like a "fixed mark" that stands against the shaking of life's tempests (lines 5 and 6). A character who is similarly aware of human tempests and conflicts is the "young priest" who hears Jackie's confession in "First Confession." He is clearly committed to service, and is "intelligent above the ordinary" (p. 191). With service to God as his "star," to use Shakespeare's image, he is able to talk sympathetically with Jackie and to send the boy home with a clear and happy mind.

[3] For both Shakespeare and O'Connor, love and service grow out of a great human need for stability and guidance. To this degree love is a simplifying force, but it simplifies primarily because the "tempests" complicating life are so strong. Such love is one of the best things that happen to human beings, because it fulfills them and prepares them to face life.

[4] The desire for love of this kind is so strong that it can also cause people to do strange and funny things. The two major characters in Chekhov's comedy-farce *The Bear* are examples. At the play's start, Chekhov shows that Mrs. Popov and Smirnov are following some negative guides that people often confuse with the truth. She is devoted to the memory of her dead husband, while he is disillusioned and cynical about women. But Chekhov makes them go through hoops for love. As the two argue, insult each other, and reach the point of dueling with real pistols, their need for love overcomes all their other impulses. It is as though love happens despite everything going against it, because the need for the stabilizing base is so strong. Certainly love here is not without at least some complexity. Either seriously or comically, then, love is shown as a rudder, guiding people in powerful and conflicting currents. The three works examined thus far show that love shapes lives and makes for sudden and unexpected changes.

[5] This thought is somewhat like the view presented by Eudora Welty in "A Worn Path." Unlike Chekhov and Shakespeare, and more like O'Connor, Welty tells a story of service performed out of love. A poor grandmother, Phoenix Jackson, has a hard life in caring for her incurably ill grandson. The walk she takes along the "worn path" to Natchez symbolizes the hardships she endures because of her single-minded love. Her service is the closest thing to pure simple love that may be found in all the works examined, with the possible exception of the love in Chekhov's play.

But Phoenix's love is not without its complexity. Hardy in "Channel Firing" and Arnold in "Dover Beach" describe a joyless, loveless, insecure

---

° Thesis sentence.

[6] world overrun by war. Phoenix's life is just as grim. She is poor and ignorant, and her grandson has nowhere to go but down. If she were to think deeply about her condition, she might be as despairing as Arnold's and Hardy's speakers. But her strength lies in her ability to accept her difficult life and to ignore the grimness of it. With her service as her "star" and "ever-fixed mark," she is able to keep cheerful. Her life has meaning and dignity.

Arnold's view of love and devotion under bad conditions is different from the views of Shakespeare, Chekhov, O'Connor, and Welty. For the speaker in "Dover Beach," the public world seems to be so far gone that there is nothing left but personal relationships. Thus love is not so much a guide as a refuge, a place of sanity and safety. After describing what he considers the worldwide shrinking of the "Sea of Faith," he states:

[7]
Ah, love, let us be true
To one another! for the world, which seems
To lie before us like a land of dreams,
So various, so beautiful, so new,
Hath really neither joy, nor love, nor light,
Nor certitude, nor peace, nor help for pain;
And we are here as on a darkling plain
Swept with confused alarms of struggle and flight
Where ignorant armies clash by night.   (lines 29–37)

Here the word *true* should be underlined, as Shakespeare emphasizes "true minds" and as O'Connor's priest is a *true* servant of God. "True" to this speaker seems to involve a pledge to create a small area of certainty in the mad world like that of "Channel Firing," where there is no certainty. Love is not so much a guide as a last place of hope, a retreat where truth can still have meaning.

[8] In practice, perhaps, Arnold's idea of love as a refuge is not very different from the view that love is a guide. Once the truthful pledge is made, it is a force for goodness, at least for the lovers making the pledge, just as love works for goodness in Shakespeare, O'Connor, Chekhov, and Welty. Yet Arnold's view is weaker. It does not result from an inner need or conviction, but rather from a conscious decision to let everything else go and to look out only for the small relationship. In an extreme form, this could lead to total withdrawal. Such a passive relationship to other affairs could be harmful by omission.

[9] The idea that love and devotion as a refuge could be actively harmful is explored by O'Connor in other characters in "First Confession." Nora and Mrs. Ryan seem to think only of sinfulness and punishment. They seek the love of God out of a desire for protection. Their devotion is therefore a means to an end, not the pure goal which operates in Shakespeare, Welty, and O'Connor's own priest. As Jackie says of Mrs. Ryan:

She . . . wore a black cloak and bonnet, and came every day to school at three o'clock when we should have been going home, and talked to us of hell. She may have mentioned the other place as well, but that could only have been by accident, for hell had the first place in her heart (p. 491).

[10] Love and devotion for Mrs. Ryan and Nora take the form of observing ritual and following rules, such as being sure that all confessions are "good" (that is, complete, with no sins held back). If this obedience were only personal, it would be a force for security, as it is on the personal level in "Dover Beach." But from the safety of their refuge, Mrs. Ryan confuses children like Jackie by describing devilish, sadistic tortures, while Nora tells her father about the bread knife and thus brings down punishment (the "flaking") and a "scalded" heart on Jackie. Even though Mrs. Ryan is not a bad soul, and Nora is no more than a young girl, their use of religion is negative. Fortunately, their influence is counter-balanced by the priest.

[11] Mrs. Ryan and Nora are minor compared with those unseen, unnamed, and distant persons firing the big guns during the "gunnery practice out at sea" in Hardy's "Channel Firing" (line 10). Hardy does not treat the gunners as individuals but as an evil collective force made up of persons who, under the sheltering claim of devotion to country and obedience of orders, are "striving strong to make/Red war yet redder" (lines 13, 14). For them, love of country is a refuge, just like the love of God for Mrs. Ryan and Nora and the true pledge to love for Arnold's speaker. As members of the military they obey orders and, as Hardy's God says, they are not much better than the dead because they do nothing "for Christés sake" (line 15). They operate the ships and fill the columns of Arnold's "ignorant armies," for Hardy makes clear that their target practice takes place at night (line 1).

[12] In summary, love and devotion as seen in these various works may be compared with a continuous line formed out of the human need for love and for the stability and guidance that love offers. At one end love is totally good and ideal; at the other it is totally bad. Shakespeare, Welty, Chekhov, and O'Connor (in the priest) show the end that is good. Still at the good end, but moving toward the center, is Arnold's use of love as a refuge. On the other side of the line are Mrs. Ryan and Nora of "First Confession," while all the way at the bad end are the insensible and invisible gunners in "Channel Firing."

[13] The difficulty noted in all the works, and a major problem in life, is to devote oneself to the right, stabilizing, constructive part of the line. Although in his farce Chekhov makes love win against almost impossible odds, he shows the problem most vividly of all the authors studied. Under normal conditions, people like Mrs. Popov and Smirnov would not find love. Instead, they would continue following their destructive and false guides. They would be unhappy and disillusioned, or else they might become more like Mrs. Ryan and spread talk about their own confused ideas (as Smirnov actually does almost right up to his conversion to love). Like the military and naval forces of Arnold and Hardy, they would then wind up at the destructive end of the line.

[14] Change, opposition, confusion, anger, resignation, economic difficulty— these are only some of the forces that attack people as they try to find the benefits of love. If they are lucky they find meaning and stability in love and service, as in Sonnet 116, "First Confession," *The Bear*, "A Worn Path," and, to a small degree, "Dover Beach." If confusion wins, they are locked into harmful positions, like the gunners in "Channel Firing" and Mrs. Ryan and

Nora in "First Confession." Thus love is complicated by circumstances, and
[14] it is not the simple force for good that it should ideally be. The six works
compared and contrasted here have shown these difficulties and complexities.

Commentary on the Essay

This essay compares and contrasts six works—three poems, two stories,
and a play—on the common ground or central idea of the complexity of
love and service. The complexity is caused by life's difficulties and by bad
results. The essay develops the central idea in terms of love as an ideal
and guide (paragraphs 2–6) and love as a refuge or escape (paragraphs
7–11), with a subcategory of love as a cause of harm (9–11).

The various works are introduced as they are grouped according to
these sections. For example, Sonnet 116, "First Confession" (because of
the priest), *The Bear*, and "A Worn Path" are together in the first group—
love as an ideal and guide. Because "Dover Beach" and "Channel Firing"
are in the second group, these works are brought in earlier, during the
discussion of the first group. For this reason, both poems are used regularly
for comparison and contrast throughout the essay.

The use of the various works within groups may be seen in paragraph
7. There, the principal topic is the use of love as a refuge or retreat, and
the central work of the paragraph is "Dover Beach." However, the first
sentence contrasts Arnold's view with the four works in the first group;
the fifth sentence shows how Arnold is similar in one respect to Shakespeare
and O'Connor; and the sixth sentence shows a similarity of Arnold and
Hardy. The paragraph thus brings together all the works being studied
in the theme.

The technique of comparison-contrast used in this way shows how
the various works may be defined and distinguished in relation to the
common idea. Paragraph 12, the first in the conclusion, attempts to summarize these distinctions by suggesting a continuous line along which each
of the works may be placed. Paragraphs 13 and 14 continue the summary
by showing the prominence of complicating difficulties and, by implication,
the importance of love. Thus, the effect of the comparison of all the works
collectively is the enhanced understanding of each of the works separately.

Appendix C: Writing and Documenting the Research Essay

Research refers to using primary and secondary sources for assistance in solving a literary problem. In criticizing a work, pure and simple, you consult only the work in front of you (the *primary source*), whereas in doing research on the work, you consult not only the work but many other works that were written about it or that may shed light on it (*secondary sources*). Typical research tasks are to find out more about the historical period in which a work was written or about prevailing opinions of the times or about what modern (or earlier) critics have said about the work. It is obvious that a certain amount of research is always necessary in any critical job, or in any essay about a literary work. Looking up words in a dictionary, for example, is only a minimal job of research, which may be supplemented by reading introductions, critical articles, encyclopedias, biographies, critical studies, histories, and the like.

It is necessary that you put research in perspective. In general, students and scholars do research in order to uncover some of the accumulated "lore" of our civilization. This lore—the knowledge that presently exists— may be compared to a large cone that is constantly being filled. At the beginnings of human existence there was little knowledge of anything, and the cone was at its narrowest point. As civilization progressed, more and more knowledge appeared, and the cone thus began to fill. Each time a new piece of information or a new conclusion was recorded, a little more knowledge or lore was in effect poured into the cone, which accordingly became slightly fuller and wider. Though at present our cone of knowledge is quite full, it appears to be capable of infinite growth. Knowledge keeps piling up and new disciplines keep developing. It becomes more and more difficult for one person to absorb more than a small portion of the entire body of knowledge. Indeed, historians generally agree that the last person to know virtually everything about every existing discipline was Aristotle—2,400 years ago.

If you grant that you cannot learn everything, you can make a positive start by recognizing that research can provide two things: (1) a systematic understanding of a portion of the knowledge filling the cone, and (2) an understanding of, and ability to handle, the methods by which you might someday be able to make your own contributions to the filling of the cone.

Thus far we have been speaking broadly about the relevance of research to any discipline. Our problem here, however, is **literary research,** the systematic study of library sources in order to illuminate a literary topic.

SELECTING A TOPIC

Frequently your instructor will ask for a research paper on a specific topic. However, if you have only a general research assignment, your first problem is to make your own selection. It may be helpful to have a general notion of the kind of research paper you would find most congenial. Here are some possibilities (see also Chapter 23 for additional topics on the poetry of Donne, Dickinson and Frost):

1. *A paper on a particular work.* You might treat character (for example, "The Character of Bottom in *A Midsummer Night's Dream*," or "The Question of Whether Willy Loman is a Hero or Antihero in *Death of a Salesman*), or tone, ideas, form, problems, and the like. A research paper on a single work is similar to an essay on the same work, except that the research paper takes into account more views and facts than those you are likely to have without the research.

2. *A paper on a particular author.* The paper could be about an idea or some facet of style, imagery, tone, or humor of the author, tracing the origins and development of the topic through a number of different works by the author. An example might be "The Idea of the True Self as Developed by Frost in His Poetry before 1920." This type of paper is particularly suitable if you are writing on a poet whose works are short, though a topic like "Shakespeare's Idea of the Relationships Between Men and Women as Dramatized in *A Midsummer Night's Dream* and *Hamlet*" might also be possible.

3. *A paper based on comparison and contrast.* There are two types:
    a. *A paper on an idea of some artistic quality common to two or more authors.* Your intention might be to show points of similarity or contrast or to show that one author's work may be read as a criticism of another's. A possible subject of such a paper might be "The Theme of Ineffectuality in Behn, Eliot, Steinbeck, and Williams," or "Behn's Antimale Poems in the Context of Male Dominated Lyric Poetry of the Seventeenth Century." Consult the second sample essay in Appendix B for an example of this type.

b. *A paper concentrating on opposing critical views of a particular work or body of works.* Sometimes much is to be gained from an examination of differing critical opinions, say "The Vision of Women in *A Doll's House*," "The Interpretations of Gray's *Elegy*," or "The Question of Hamlet's Hesitation." Such a study would attempt to determine the critical climate of opinion and taste to which a work did or did not appeal, and it might also aim at conclusions about whether the work was in the advance or rear guard of its time.

4. *A paper showing the influence of an idea, an author, a philosophy, a political situation, or an artistic movement on specific works of an author or authors.* A paper on influences can be specific and to the point, as in "Details of Early Twentieth-Century Mexican American Culture as Reflected in Parédes's 'The Hammon and the Beans,'" or else it can be more abstract and critical, as in "The Influence of Early Twentieth-Century Oppression of Mexican-Americans on the Narrator of 'The Hammon and the Beans.'"

5. *A paper on the origins of a particular work or type of work.* One avenue of research for such a paper might be to examine an author's biography to discover the germination and development of a work—for example, "'The Old Chief Mshlanga' as an outgrowth of Lessing's life in Rhodesia-Zimbabwe." Another way of discovering origins might be to relate a work to a particular type or tradition: "*Hamlet* as Revenge Tragedy," or "*Love Is the Doctor* and Its Origins in the Tradition of Italian Comedy."

If you still have not decided on a topic after rereading the works you have liked, then you should carry your search for a topic into your school library. Look up your author or authors in the card or computer catalog. Usually the works written by the authors are included first, followed by works written about the authors. Your first goal should be to find a relatively recent book-length critical study published by a university press. Use your judgment here: Look for a title indicating that the book is a general one dealing with the author's major works rather than just one work. Study those chapters relevant to your primary text. Most writers of critical studies describe their purpose and plan in their introductions or first chapters, so read the first part of the book. If there is no separate chapter on the primary text, use the index and go to the relevant pages. Reading in this way should soon supply you with sufficient knowledge about the issues and ideas raised by the work to enable you to select a topic you will wish to study further. Once you have made your decision, you are ready to go ahead and develop a working bibliography.

SETTING UP A BIBLIOGRAPHY

The best way to develop a working bibliography of books and articles is to begin with major critical studies of the writer or writers. Again, go to the catalog and pick out books that have been published by university presses. These books will usually contain selective bibliographies. Be particularly careful to read the chapters on your primary work or works and to look for the footnotes or endnotes. Quite often you can save time if you record the names of books and articles listed in these notes. Then refer to the bibliographies included at the ends of the books, and select any likely looking titles. Now, look at the dates of publication of the critical books you have been using. Let us suppose that you have been looking at three, published in 1951, 1963, and 1982. The chances are that the bibliography in a book published in 1982 will be fairly complete up through about 1979 or 1980, for the writer will usually have completed the manuscript about two years before the book actually was published. What you should do then is to gather a bibliography of works published since 1979; you may assume that writers of critical works will have done the selecting for you of the most relevant works published before that time.

Bibliographical Guides

Fortunately for students doing literary research, the Modern Language Association (MLA) of America has been providing a virtually complete bibliography of literary studies for years, not just in English and American literatures, but in the literatures of most modern foreign languages. The bibliography is divided into four parts which are bound together in library editions. Most university and college libraries have a set of these bibliographies readily available on open shelves or tables. There are, of course, many other bibliographies that are useful for students doing research, such as the *Essay and General Literature Index*, the *International Index*, and various specific indexes. For most purposes, however, the *MLA International Bibliography* is more than adequate. Remember that as you progress in your reading, the notes and bibliographies in the works you consult also will constitute an unfolding bibliography.

The *MLA International Bibliography* is conveniently organized by period and author. If your author is Gwendolyn Brooks, for example, look her up under "American Literature V. Twentieth Century," the relevant listing for all twentieth-century American writers. If your author is Shakespeare, refer to "English Literature VI. Renaissance and Elizabethan." You will find most of the bibliography you need under the author's last name. As special help for students and researchers, the MLA has recently developed an exhaustive topics list that is keyed to the bibliographical entries. Using these topics you may locate important and relevant works that you might not have found with only the authors list. In the MLA bibliographies, journal references are abbreviated, but a lengthy list explaining abbreviations appears at the beginning of the volume. Using the MLA bibliographies, begin with the most recent one and then go backward to your stopping point. Be sure to get the complete information, especially volume numbers and years of publication, for each article and book you wish to consult. You are now ready to consult your sources and to take notes.

TAKING NOTES AND PARAPHRASING MATERIAL

There are many ways of taking notes, but the consensus is that the best method is to use note cards. If you have never used cards before, you might profit from consulting any one of a number of handbooks and special workbooks on research. A lucid and methodical explanation of taking notes on cards can be found in Glenn Leggett et al., *Prentice-Hall Handbook for Writers*, 10th ed., (Englewood Cliffs.: Prentice-Hall, 1988). The principal virtue of using cards is that they may be classified, numbered, renumbered, shuffled, tried out in one place, rejected, and then used in another place (or thrown away), and arranged in order when you start to write.

Taking Notes

WRITE THE SOURCE ON EACH CARD. As you take notes, write down the source of your information on each card. This may sound like a lot of bother, but it is easier than finding out when you finally begin writing your research paper that you will need to go back to the library to get the correct source. You can save time if you take the complete data on one card—a "master card" for that source—and then make up an abbreviation to be used in your notes. Here is an example. Observe that the author's last name goes first.

Donovan, Josephine, ed. Feminist Literary Criticism: Explorations in Theory. Lexington: The University Press of Kentucky, 1975.

DONOVAN

If you plan to use many notes from this book, then the name "Donovan" will serve as identification. Be sure not to lose your complete master card, because you will need it in preparing your list of works cited.

RECORD THE PAGE NUMBER FOR EACH NOTE.   It would be hard to guess how much exasperation has been caused by the failure to record page numbers of notes. Be sure to get the page number down first, *before* you begin to take your note, and, to be doubly sure, write the page number again at the end of your note. If the detail you are noting goes from one page to the next in your source, record the exact spot where the page changes, as in this example:

Heilbrun and Stimson, in DONOVAN, pp. 63–64

63 After the raising of the feminist consciousness it is necessary to develop/ 64 "the growth of moral perception" through anger and the correction of social inequity.

You may wish to use only a part of a note you have taken, and when there are two pages you will need to be accurate in your location of what goes where.

RECORD ONLY ONE FACT OR OPINION PER CARD.   Record only one thing on each card—one quotation, one paraphrase, one observation—never two or more. You might be tempted to fill up the entire card, but such a try at economy often causes trouble because you might need the same card in different places.

USE QUOTATION MARKS FOR ALL QUOTED MATERIAL. A major problem in taking notes is to distinguish copied material from your own words. Here you must be extremely cautious. Always put quotation marks around *every direct quotation you copy verbatim from a source*. Make the quotation marks immediately, before you forget, so that you will always know that the words of your notes within quotation marks are the words of another writer.

Often, as you take a note, you may use some of your own words and some of the words from your source. In cases like this it is even more important to be cautious. Put quotation marks around *every word* that you take directly from the source, even if you find yourself literally with a note that resembles a picket fence. Later, when you begin writing your paper, your memory of what is yours and not yours will become dim, and if you use another's words in your own paper but do not grant recognition, you lay yourself open to the charge of plagiarism. Statistics are not available, but it seems clear that a great deal of outright plagiarism has beeen caused not by deliberate deception but rather by sloppy notetaking habits.

Paraphrasing

When you take notes, it is best to paraphrase the sources. A paraphrase is a restatement in your own words, and because of this it is actually a first step in the writing of the essay. Chapter 2 in this book has a full treatment on making a précis or abridgment (pp. 90–95). If you work on this technique, you will be well prepared to paraphrase for your research essay.

A big problem in paraphrasing is to capture the idea in the source without duplicating the words. The best way to do this is to read and reread the passage you are noting. Turn over the book or journal and write out the idea *in your own words* as accurately as you can. Once you have this note, compare it with the original and make corrections to improve your thought and emphasis. Add a short quotation if you believe it is needed, but be sure to use quotation marks. If your paraphrase is too close to the original, throw out the note and try again in your own words. It is worth making this effort, because often you can transform much of your note directly to the appropriate place in your research paper.

Let us look at a paragraph of criticism and then see how a student doing research might take notes on it. The paragraph is by Maynard Mack, from an essay entitled "The World of Hamlet," originally published in *The Yale Review* 41 (1952) and reprinted in *Twentieth Century Interpretations of Hamlet*, ed. David Bevington (Englewood Cliffs: Prentice-Hall, 1968), p. 57:

The powerful sense of mortality in *Hamlet* is conveyed to us, I think, in three ways. First, there is the play's emphasis on human weakness, the instability of human purpose, the subjection of humanity to fortune—all that we might call the aspect of failure in man. Hamlet opens this theme in Act I, when he describes how from that single blemish, perhaps not even the victim's fault, a man's whole character may take corruption. Claudius dwells on it again, to an extent that goes far beyond the needs of the occasion, while engaged in seducing Laertes to step behind the arras of a seemer's world and dispose of Hamlet by a trick. Time qualifies everything, Claudius says, including love, including purpose. As for love—it has a "plurisy" in it and dies of its own too much. As for purpose—"That we would do, We should do when we would, for this 'would' changes, And hath abatements and delays as many As there are tongues, are hands, are accidents; And then this 'should' is like a spendthrift's sigh, That hurts by easing." The player-king, in his long speeches to his queen in the play within the play, sets the matter in a still darker light. She means these protestations of undying love, he knows, but our purposes depend on our memory, and our memory fades fast. Or else, he suggests, we propose something to ourselves in a condition of strong feeling, but then the feeling goes, and with it the resolve. Or else our fortunes change, he adds, and with these our loves: "The great man down, you mark his favorite flies." The subjection of human aims to fortune is a reiterated theme in *Hamlet*, as subsequently in *Lear*. Fortune is the harlot goddess in whose secret parts men like Rosencrantz and Guildenstern live and thrive; the strumpet who threw down Troy and Hecuba and Priam; the outrageous foe whose slings and arrows a man of principle must suffer or seek release in suicide. Horatio suffers them with composure: he is one of the blessed few "Whose blood and judgment are so well co-mingled That they are not a pipe for fortune's finger To sound what stop she please." For Hamlet the task is of a greater difficulty.

The task of taking notes forces you to shorten and interpret Mack's writing, and there are some things that can guide you in the face of the large amount of reading in your sources.

THINK OF THE PURPOSE OF YOUR RESEARCH PAPER.   You may not know exactly what you are "fishing for" when you start to take notes, for you cannot prejudge what your essay will contain. Research is a form of discovery. As you work you will develop a general topic or focus, and you should use that as your guide in all your note-taking.

For example, suppose that you have started to take notes on *Hamlet* criticism, and after a certain amount of reading you have decided to focus on "Shakespeare's Tragic Views in *Hamlet*." This decision would prompt you to take a note when you come to Mack's thought about morality and death in the passage quoted above. In this instance, the following note would suffice:

Mack, in Bevington,   57

Death and
Mortality

Mack cites three ways in which *Hamlet* stresses
death and mortality. The first (57) is an
emphasis on human shortcomings and "weakness."
Corruption, loss of memory and enthusiasm, bad
luck, misery—all suit the sense of the closeness of
death to life.   57

Let us now suppose that you wanted a fuller note in the expectation
that you would need not just the topic but also some of Mack's detail.
Such a note might look like this:

Mack, in Bevington,   57

Death and
Mortality

The first of Mack's "three ways" in which a
"powerful sense of mortality" is shown in *Hamlet*
is the illustration of human "weakness," "instability,"
and helplessness before fate. In support, Mack
refers to Hamlet's early speech on a single fault
leading to corruption, also to Claudius' speech
(in the scene persuading Laertes to trick Hamlet).
The player-king also talks about his queen's
forgetfulness and therefore inconstancy by default.
As slaves to fortune, Rosencrantz and Guildenstern
are examples. Horatio is not a slave, however. Hamlet's
case is by far the worst of all.   57

When the actual essay is being written, any part of this note would be useful. The words are almost all the note-taker's own, and the few quotations are within quotation marks. Note that Mack, the critic, is properly recognized as the source of the criticism, so that the note could be adapted readily to a research paper. The key here is that your taking of notes should be guided by your developing plan for your essay.

Note taking is part of your thinking and composing process. You may not always know whether you will be able to use each note that you take, and you will exclude many notes when you write your essay. You will always find, however, that taking notes is easier once you have determined your purpose.

TITLE YOUR NOTES.   To help plan and develop the various parts of your essay, write a title for each of your notes, in the upper right corner of the card, as in the examples in this chapter. This practice is a form of outlining. Let us assume that you have chosen to write about the Ghost in *Hamlet* and that your topic is the importance of the Ghost in the play. As you do research, you discover that there are conflicting views about how the Ghost should be understood. Here is a note about one of the questionable qualities of this character:

Prosser, 133, 134   Negative, Devilish

　　　When describing his pain and suffering as a dead spirit, the Ghost
is not specific but emphasizes the horror. He should, if a good spirit,
try to use his suffering to urge repentance and salvation for Hamlet.
This emphasis is a sign that he is closer in nature to a devil than to a
soul earning its way to redemption.   133, 134

Notice that the title classifies the topic of the note. If you use such classifications while taking notes, a number of like-titled cards could form the substance of a section in your essay about the negative qualities of the Ghost in *Hamlet*. In addition, once you decide that "Negative, Devilish" is one of the topics you plan to explore, the topic itself will guide you in further study and additional note taking.

WRITE DOWN YOUR OWN THOUGHTS AS THEY OCCUR TO YOU.   As you take notes, you will have many of your own thoughts. Do not let these go, on the chance of remembering later, but write them down immediately. Often you may notice a detail that your source does not mention, or you may get a hint for an idea that the critic does not develop. Often, too, you may get thoughts which can serve as "bridges" between details in your notes or as introductions or concluding observations. Be sure to title your comment and also to mark it as your own thought. Here is such a note, which is related to the importance of the Ghost in the structure of *Hamlet*:

My own   Structure

    Shakespeare does a superb job with the Ghost. His characterization is both full and round, and the Ghost is totally integrated in the play's structure.

SORT YOUR CARDS INTO GROUPS.   If you have taken your notes well, your essay will have been taking shape in your mind already. The titles of your cards will suggest areas to be developed as you do your planning and prewriting. Once you have assembled a stack of note cards derived from a reasonable number of sources (your instructor may have assigned the minimum number), you can sort them into groups according to the topics and titles. For the sample essay, after some shuffling and retitling, the following groups of cards were assembled:

1. Importance in the action
2. Importance in themes
3. Condition as a spirit
    a. Good signs
    b. Negative, devilish signs
4. Human traits
5. Importance in the structure
6. Effect on other characters

If you look at the major sections of the sample essay, you will see that the topics are closely adapted from these groups of cards. In other words, the arrangement of the cards is an effective means of outlining and organizing a research essay.

ARRANGE THE CARDS IN EACH GROUP. There is still much to be done with these individual groups. You cannot use the details as they happened to fall randomly in your "deal." You need to decide which notes are relevant. You might also need to retitle some cards and use them elsewhere. Of those that remain in the group, you will need to lay them out in a logical progression in which they may be used in the paper.

Once you have your cards in order, you can write whatever comments or transitions are needed to move from detail to detail. Write this material directly on the cards, and be sure to use a different color ink so that you will be able to know what was originally on the card and what you added at this stage of your composing process. Here is an example of such a "developed" note card:

Campbell, 127   Negative, Devilish.

Shakespeare's Ghost reflects the general uncertainty at the time about how ghosts were to be interpreted.   127

This may be the best way to answer the questions about the Ghost's ambiguous nature. Moreover, Shakespeare may have been trying to be more lifelike than consistent with his Ghost.

By adding such commentary to your note cards, you will facilitate the actual writing of the first draft. In many instances, the note and the comment may be moved directly into the paper with minor adjustments (this note and comment occur in paragraphs 5 and 6 of the sample essay).

BE CREATIVE AND ORIGINAL IN RESEARCH PAPERS. The major trap to avoid in a research paper is that your use of sources can become an end in itself and therefore a shortcut for your own thinking and writing. It is important to be creative and original in a research essay even though you are relying heavily on your sources. Here are four ways in which research papers may offer chances for originality:

1. Selection. In each major section of your essay you will include a number of details from your sources. To be creative you should select different but related details and avoid overlapping or repetition. The essay will be judged on the basis of the thoroughness with which you make your point with different details (which in turn will represent the completeness of your research). Even though you are relying on published materials and cannot be original on that score, your selection is original because you are bringing the materials together for the first time.

2. Development. Your arrangement of your various points is an obvious area of originality: one detail seems naturally to precede another, and certain conclusions stem out of certain details. As you present the details, conclusions, and arguments from your sources, you may also add your own original stamp by using supporting details that are different from those in your sources. You may also wish to add your own emphasis to particular points—an emphasis that you do not find in your sources.

Naturally, the words that you use will be original. Your topic sentences, for example, will all be your own. As you introduce details and conclusions, you will need to write "bridges" to get yourself from point to point. These may be introductory remarks or transitions. In other words, as you write, you are not just stringing things out but are actively tying thoughts together in a variety of creative ways. Your success in these efforts will constitute the area of your greatest originality.

3. Explanation of controversial views. In your research you may have found conflicting or differing views on a topic. It is original for you, as you describe and distinguish these views, to explain the reasons for the differences. As you explain a conflict or difference, you are writing an original analysis. To see how differing views may be handled, see paragraphs 4 and 5 of the sample essay.

4. Creation of your own insights and positions. There are three possibilities here, all related to how well you have learned the primary texts on which your research in secondary sources is based:

a. *Your own interpretations and ideas.* Remember that an important part of taking notes is to make your own points precisely when they occur to you. Often you can expand these as truly original parts of your essay. Your originality does not need to be extensive; it may consist of no more than a single insight. Here is such a card, which was written during the research on the ghost in *Hamlet*:

My Own   introductory

The Ghost is minor in the action but major in the play. He is seen twice in scene 1, but this scene is really all about him. (Also about his appearances before the play opens.) In scene 4 of act 1 he comes again and leads Hamlet off to scene 5, the biggest for him as an acting and speaking character. He speaks after this only from under the stage, and then a small appearance (but important) in 3.4, and that's all. But he is dominant because he set everything in motion and therefore his presence is felt everywhere in the play.

The originality here is built around the idea of the small role but dominant significance of the Ghost. The discovery is perhaps not startling, but it nevertheless represents original thought about *Hamlet*. When modified and adapted, the material of the card supplies much of the opening paragraph in addition to the central idea of the essay.

b. *Gaps in the sources.* As you read your secondary sources it may dawn on you that a certain, obvious conclusion is not being made, or that a certain detail is not being stressed. Here is an area which you can develop on your own. Your conclusions may involve a particular interpretation or major point of comparison, or it may rest on a particularly important but understressed word or fact. In the sample essay, for example, the writer discusses the idea that the Ghost's commands to Hamlet make it impossible for him to solve problems through negotiation or research, the ways he might have chosen as a prince and student. The commands force him instead into a pattern requiring murder. Most critics observe that Hamlet's life is changed because of the Ghost but have not quite stressed these aspects of the change. Given such a critical "vacuum" it is right to begin to fill it with your own insights. A great deal of scholarship is created in this way.

c. *Disputes with the sources.* Your sources may present certain arguments that you wish to dispute. As you develop your disagreement, you will be arguing originally, for you will be using details in a different way from that of the critic or critics whom you are disputing, and your conclusions will be your own. This area of originality is similar to the laying out of controversial critical views, except that you furnish one of the opposing views yourself. The approach is limited, because it is difficult to find many substantive points of interpretation on which there are not already clearly delineated opposing views. Paragraph 5 of the sample research essay shows a small point of disagreement (about whether Shakespeare was concerned with consistency in presenting the Ghost's spirit nature), but one that is nevertheless original.

DOCUMENTATION SYSTEMS: NOTES AND PARENTHETICAL REFERENCES

It is essential to acknowledge—to document—all sources from which you have quoted *or* paraphrased factual and interpretive information. If you do not grant recognition, you run the risk of being challenged for representing as your own the results of other people's work; this is plagiarism. As the means of documentation, there are many reference systems, some using parenthetical references, and others using footnotes or endnotes. Whatever system is used, documentation almost always includes a carefully prepared list of works cited (bibliography).

We will first discuss the list of works cited and then review the two major reference systems for use in a research paper: (1) Parenthetical references, preferred by the MLA since 1984, are described in Joseph Gibaldi and Walter S. Achtert, *MLA Handbook for Writers of Research Papers*, 3rd ed., 1988. (2) Footnotes or endnotes, recommended by the MLA before 1984, are still widely used today.

List of Works Cited (Bibliography)

The key to any reference system is a carefully prepared list of works cited that is included at the end of the essay. (In some cases where footnotes or endnotes are used to cite sources, a list of works cited may not be required; check your instructor's preference.) It is important to include all the following information in each bibliographic entry:

FOR A BOOK

1. The author's name, last name first, period.
2. Title, underlined, period.
3. City of publication, colon; publisher (easily recognized abbreviations may be used), comma; date, period.

FOR AN ARTICLE

1. The author's name, last name first, period.
2. Title of article in quotation marks, period.
3. Name of journal or periodical, underlined, followed immediately by volume number in Arabic numbers with no punctuation, followed by the year of publication, including month and day of weekly or daily issues, within parentheses, colon. Inclusive page numbers, period.

The list of works consulted should be arranged alphabetically by author, with unsigned articles being listed by title. Bibliographical lists are begun at the left margin, with subsequent lines being indented, so that the key to locating a particular work, usually the author's last name— may be easily noticed. The many complex combinations possible in the compilation of a bibliographical list, including ways to describe art works, performances, and films, are detailed extensively in the *MLA Handbook*. Here are two model entries:

BOOK: Spacks, Patricia Meyer. An Argument of Images: The Poetry of Alexander Pope. Cambridge: Harvard U.P., 1971.

ARTICLE: Miller, Rachel A. "Regal Hunting: Dryden's Influence on Windsor Forest." Eighteenth-Century Studies 13 (1979/1980): 169–188.

Parenthetical References to the List of Works Cited

Within the text of the essay, the list of works cited may be referred to parenthetically. The parenthetical reference system recommended in the *MLA Handbook* involves the insertion of the author's last name and the relevant page reference into the body of the essay. If the author's name is mentioned in the discussion, only the page number(s) are given in parentheses. Here are two examples:

Pope believed in the ideal that the universe is a whole, an entirety, which provides a "viable benevolent system for the salvation of everyone who does good" (Kallich 24).

Martin Kallich draws attention to Pope's belief in the ideal that the universe is a whole, an entirety, which provides a "viable benevolent system for the salvation of everyone who does good" (24).

For a full discussion of the types of in-text references and the format to be used, see the *MLA Handbook*.

Footnotes and Endnotes

A more formal system of documentation still preferred by some is the use of footnotes (references at the bottom of each page) or endnotes (references listed numerically at the end of the essay). If your instructor wants you to use one of these systems, do the following: The first time you quote or refer to the source, make a note with the details in this order:

FOR A BOOK

1. The author's name, first name or initials first;
2. The title: underlined for a book. If you are referring to a story or poem in a collection, use quotation marks for that, but underline the title of the book. (Use a comma after title if an editor, translator, or edition follows.)
3. The name of the editor or translator. Abbreviate "editor" or "edited by" as *ed.*; "editors" as *eds.* Use *trans.* for "translator" or "translated by."
4. The edition (if indicated) abbreviated thus: *2nd ed., 3rd ed.,* and so on.
5. The publication facts should be given in parentheses, without any preceding or following punctuation, in the following order:
   a. City (but *not* the state) of publication, colon.
   b. Publisher (clear abbreviations are acceptable, such as U.P. for University Press) comma.
   c. Year of publication.
6. The page number(s), for example, 65, 6–10. For books commonly reprinted, like *Hamlet,* and for well-known longer poems (like Milton's *Paradise Lost*), you should include the chapter, act and scene, or canto number together with line numbers, so that readers using a different edition may be able to locate and verify your quotation.

FOR AN ARTICLE

1. The author, first name or initials first, comma.
2. The title of the article, in quotation marks, comma.
3. The name of the journal or magazine underlined, no punctuation.
4. The volume number, in Arabic numerals, no punctuation.
5. The year of publication in parentheses, colon.
6. The page number(s), for example, 65, 65 f., 6–10.

For later notes referring to the same work, use the author's last name as reference. Thus, if you refer to only one work by Joseph Conrad, the name "Conrad" will be enough for all later references. But if you are using two or more works by Conrad, you will need to make a short reference to the specific works to distinguish them, such as "Conrad, *Lord Jim*," and "Conrad, *The Rescue*."

Footnotes are placed at the bottom of each page, separated from your essay by a ruled line; endnotes are included at the end of the essay in a list. Ask your instructor about the practice you should adopt.

The first lines of both footnotes and endnotes should be paragraph indented, and continuing lines should be flush with the left margin. Footnote numbers are positioned slightly above the line (like this[11]). Generally, you may single-space such notes, but check with your instructor to be sure about which method to follow.

SAMPLE FOOTNOTES.   In the examples below, book titles and periodicals, which are usually italicized in print, are shown underlined, as they would be in your typewritten paper.

[1] Joseph Conrad, The Rescue: A Romance of the Shallows (New York: Doubleday, 1960) 103.

[2] George Milburn, "The Apostate," An Approach to Literature, ed. Cleanth Brooks, John Thibaut Purser, and Robert Penn Warren, 3rd ed. (New York: Appleton-Century-Crofts, 1952) 74.

[3] Carlisle Moore, "Conrad and the Novel as Ordeal," Philological Quarterly 42 (1963): 59.

[4] Moore 61.

[5] Conrad 171.

[6] Milburn 76.

As a general principle, you do not need to repeat in a note any material that you have already incorporated into your essay. For example, if you mention the author and title of your source in the paper, then the note should merely give the data about publication. Here is an example:

In Charles Macklin: An Actor's Life, William W. Appleton points out that Macklin had been "reinstated at Drury Lane" by December 19, 1744, and that he was playing his stellar role of Shylock.[7]

---

[7] (Cambridge: Harvard U.P., 1961) 72.

Some Final Advice

As long as all that you want from a reference is the page number of a quotation or of a paraphrase, the parenthetical system is suitable and easy. It saves your reader the trouble of searching the bottom of the page or of thumbing through pages to find a reference in a long list of notes. However, you may wish use footnotes or endnotes in order to add more details or to refer your reader to other materials that you are not using directly in your essay.

Whatever method you use, remember that *it is always imperative to acknowledge your sources.* If questions about documentation arise while you are writing your essay (and they probably will), consult your instructor, who is your final authority.

ORGANIZING YOUR ESSAY

Introduction

For a research essay, the introduction may be expanded beyond the length of that for an ordinary essay because of the need to relate the problem of research to your topic. You may wish to bring in relevant historical or biographical information. You might also wish to summarize critical opinion or to describe any particular critical problems as they pertain to your topic. The idea is to lead your reader into your topic by providing interesting and significant materials that you have uncovered during your research. Obviously, you should plan on including your usual guides— your central idea and your thesis sentence.

Because of the greater length of most research essays, some instructors require a topic outline, which is in effect a table of contents. This pattern is followed in the sample essay. Inasmuch as this method is a matter of choice with various instructors, be sure that you understand whether your instructor requires it.

Body, Conclusion

Your development, both for the body and the conclusion, will be governed by your choice of topic. Please consult the relevant chapters in this book about what to include for whatever approach or approaches you select (setting, idea, character, tone, or any other).

In length, the research paper may be anywhere from five to fifteen or more pages. It seems reasonable to assume that an essay based on only one work would be shorter than one based on several. If you narrow the scope of your topic, as suggested in the approaches described above, you can readily keep your essay within the assigned length. The sample research paper below, for example, illustrates the first approach by being limited to one character in one work. Were you to write on characters in a number of other plays by Shakespeare (the second approach), you could limit your total number of pages by stressing comparative treatments and by avoiding excessive detail about problems pertaining to only one work. In short, you will decide to include or exclude materials by compromising between the importance of the materials and the limits of your assignment.

Although you limit your topic yourself in consultation with your instructor, you may encounter problems because you will be dealing not with one text alone but with many. Naturally the sources will provide you with details and also with many of your ideas. The problem is to handle the many strands without piling on too many details, and also without being led into digressions. It is important therefore to keep your central idea foremost, for the constant stressing of your central idea will help you both in selecting relevant materials and rejecting irrelevant ones.

Because of the sources, there is a problem about authority, and that problem is to quote, paraphrase, and otherwise adapt the materials of others without plagiarism. Your reader will automatically assume that everything you write is your own unless you indicate otherwise. You leave yourself open to a charge of plagiarism, however, if you give no recognition to details, interpretations, or specific language that you clearly derive from a source. To handle this problem, you must be especially careful in the use of quotation marks and in the granting of recognition. Most commonly, if you are simply presenting details and facts, you can write straightforwardly and let parenthetical references suffice as your authority, as the following sentence from the sample essay will show.

> Thus he is most emphatic that Hamlet should not kill her along with Claudius (Fisch 80), and he also voices concern about the reputation and future of Denmark (Gottschalk, "Scanning" 165).

Here the parenthetical references to secondary texts are sufficient recognition of authority beyond your own.

If you are using an interpretation that is unique to a particular writer, however, or if you are relying on a significant quotation from your source, you should grant recognition as an essential part of your discussion, as in this sentence:

> A. C. Bradley (126) suggests that these speeches indicate Shakespeare's master touch in the development of the Ghost's character.

Here the idea of the critic is singled out specially for acknowledgement. If you grant recognition in this way, no confusion can possibly arise about the authority underlying your essay.

SAMPLE RESEARCH ESSAY

The Ghost in *Hamlet**

OUTLINE

I. INTRODUCTION
   A. THE IMPORTANCE OF THE GHOST IN *HAMLET*
   B. THE GHOST'S INFLUENCE UPON THE PLAY'S THEMES
II. THE GHOST'S STATUS AS A SPIRIT
III. THE GHOST'S CHARACTER

* See p. 1121 for this drama.

IV. THE GHOST'S IMPORTANCE IN THE STRUCTURE OF THE PLAY
V. THE GHOST'S EFFECT
VI. CONCLUSION

I. Introduction

A. The Importance of the Ghost in *Hamlet*

[1]
Even though the Ghost of old Hamlet is present in only a few scenes of *Hamlet*, he is nevertheless a dominant presence throughout the play.° He is seen twice in the very first scene, and the entire scene is about the meaning of these and earlier appearances. He enters again in the fourth scene of the first act, when he beckons and leads Hamlet off stage. In the fifth scene of act 1 he finally speaks, telling Hamlet of his murder at the hands of Claudius. His call for vengeance is the cause of the rest of the play's action. After some words which he speaks from underground (that is, under the stage), he does not appear again until the fourth scene of act 3, when he reveals himself to Hamlet—but not to Gertrude—to reproach the Prince for his failure to act and his preoccupation with his mother. The Ghost is not present at the play's end, but the actions he sets in motion are concluded there, and hence his effect remains dominant throughout.

B. The Ghost's Influence Upon the Play's Themes

[2]
Not only is the Ghost a dominant figure, he is also directly linked to many of the play's themes. Jean Paris observes that *Hamlet* is one of Shakespeare's plays that reveals "an intensification of interior suffering" (85). Hamlet's anguished soliloquies, together with the pain of Ophelia and Laertes (and even that of Claudius himself) may thus be traced to the Ghost. The commands the Ghost makes to Hamlet are direct and urgent, and therefore the Ghost introduces another of the play's major themes—that of responsibility, whether personal, political, or conjugal (McFarland 15). Because Hamlet seems to delay in fulfilling the Ghost's demand for vengeance, Hamlet's hesitation, this great "Sphinx of modern Literature" (Ernest Jones 22), becomes one of the most frequently raised and constantly nagging questions about the prince's character. The Ghost's presence also poses questions about the power of superstition, terror, and fear in human life (Campbell 211). Beyond these, in terms of psychology, the Ghost has been cited as a "confirmation" of the influence of "psychic residues in governing and shaping human life" (McFarland 34).

[3]
Because the Ghost is such an important influence in the play, we hardly need to justify a study of him, however brief. His importance may be traced in his spirit nature, his influence upon the play's structure, and his effect upon Hamlet and therefore indirectly upon all the major characters in the play.□

° Central idea.
□ Thesis sentence.

II. The Ghost's Status as a Spirit

The Ghost is an apparition of questionable status. When Hamlet first sees the Ghost he raises a question about whether the vision is "a spirit of health, or goblin damned" (1.4.40). Horatio adds the idea that Hamlet is "desperate with imagination" (1.4.87), thus casting doubt upon the reality of the Ghost, even though everyone on the battlements has just seen it. Lily B. Campbell offers three options and sources about how to regard the Ghost: (1) as a real Ghost, from Catholic teaching in Elizabethan England, that held it possible for dead souls in Purgatory to return to earth for a time to communicate with the living; (2) as a demon, from the writings of King James I, who argued that the Devil himself could assume the shape of loved ones in order to lead living human beings to damnation; (3) as a vision, from scientifically oriented thinkers, who interpreted ghostly appearances as a sign of madness or deep melancholia (121). There were apparently a number of "tests" that might have enabled people to determine whether ghosts were truly genuine— that is, from Purgatory. Most of these required that the spirit in question be good, comforting, and sweet (Campbell 123).

[4]

Shakespeare's Ghost passes some of these tests but fails others. Even though he possesses some of the necessary redeeming qualities (Campbell 126), he also imposes a duty of revenge on Hamlet, something that no ghost of Purgatory would ever do (Prosser 136; McFarland 36). Although the Ghost describes the pain of a soul in Purgatory, he does so with a desire to horrify, not to urge Hamlet to commit himself to Christian repentance and salvation. Again, his description is an indication that he is closer in nature to the Devil than to a soul earning its way to redemption (Prosser 133, 134). Another sign suggesting that the Ghost is a devilish spirit is that he withholds his appearance from Gertrude when he shows himself to Hamlet in act 3, scene 4 (Campbell 124; Prosser 200). Perhaps the best answer to the conflicting signs about the Ghost is provided by Lily B. Campbell, who suggests that the ambiguity is to be seen as a reflection of general uncertainty about ghosts among Shakespeare's contemporaries (127). In other words, she grants that there was no unanimity about the nature and purposes of ghosts at the time Shakespeare wrote. Even more to the point, however, because of this lack of agreement, it is possible that Shakespeare was not even interested in the question of ghostly consistency as discussed by theorists. If one grants that he was concerned, it is more likely that he chose to reflect common attitudes and superstition rather than scholarly debate.

[5]

III. The Ghost's Character

Uncertainty aside, the likely fact is that Shakespeare as a dramatist is probably presenting a lifelike rendering of what he thought a ghost would be like. He inherited a tradition of noisy, bloodthirsty ghosts from his sources— what Harold Fisch calls a "Senecan ghost" (91). In many ways he keeps to this tradition. Shakespeare's Ghost is bloodthirsty, although ironically not as bloodthirsty as Hamlet himself (Gottschalk, "Scanning" 166). The Ghost is

[6]

also surrounded by awe and horror (DeLuca 147), and is genuinely frightening, both to the soldiers at the beginning of the play, and also to Hamlet in 3.4 (Charney 167–168). His speeches are designed to evoke grief, fear, and despair (Prosser 135).

[7]
But the Ghost is not just an imitation of the Senecan ghost. He is real, and well drawn as an individual person by Shakespeare (Alexander 30). Indeed, Shakespeare's Ghost is toned down from the ghost in an earlier anonymous version of *Hamlet,* perhaps one of Shakespeare's sources, which was seen by Shakespeare's contemporary Thomas Lodge (1558?–1625). Lodge talked about "ye ghost which cried so miserally [miserably] at ye theator . . . *Hamlet,* reuenge [revenge]." The Ghost in Shakespeare's *Hamlet* is certainly preoccupied with vengeance (Allman 243), but as a former king he is concerned about his country, and as a former loving husband he is also concerned about Gertrude. Thus he is most emphatic that Hamlet should not kill her along with Claudius (Fisch 80), and he also voices concern about the reputation and future of Denmark (Gottschalk, "Scanning" 165). Paul Gottschalk draws attention to this redeeming dimension as an indication that the Ghost is concerned with "restoration" as well as "retaliation" ("Scannings" 166).

Indeed, the Ghost has many qualities of a living human being as opposed to those of either a bad or a good spirit. He is, for example, witty, as Maurice Charney observes about the Ghost's interchange with Hamlet just at the beginning of the revelation speeches in 1.5.6–7:

HAMLET.   Speak, I am bound to hear.
GHOST.   So art thou to revenge, when thou shalt hear.

In other words, even though the Ghost may have come "with airs from heaven, or blasts from hell" (1.4.41), he is still mentally alert enough to make a pun out of Hamlet's word "bound" (Charney 118). To this quickness may be added his shrewd ability as a judge of Hamlet's character. He is clearly aware that his son may be prone to forget duty, and hence his last words in 1.5 are "remember me," and his first words in 3.4 are "Do not forget." A. C. Bradley (126) suggests that these speeches indicate Shakespeare's master touch in the development of the Ghost's character.

[9]
The Ghost also shows other human traits. He has strong feelings of remorse about the crimes and "imperfections" of which he was guilty in life, and for which his sudden murder did not give him time to atone. He also has a sense of appropriateness that extends to his dress. Thus, at the beginning he appears on the battlement dressed in full armor; this battle dress would be the garb expected for the circumstances, and also to be expected in light of his urging Hamlet to kill Claudius in revenge (Aldus 54). By contrast, in the closet scene he wears a dressing gown ("in his habit as he lived," 3.4.135), as though he is prepared for ordinary palace activities of both business and leisure (Charney 26).

IV. The Ghost's Importance in the Structure of the Play

It is Shakespeare's great strength as a dramatist that he gives the Ghost's character such round and full development and also integrates him fully within the actual structure of the play. We have noted the Ghost's importance as the instigator of revenge; Peter Alexander observes that the Ghost is "indispensable" as the mechanism of the plot and the source of communication to set things in motion (29). But the Ghost is also a director and organizer as well as an informer, a figure who keeps the action moving (Aldus 100). A

[10] careful study of his speeches to Hamlet shows that he is a manipulator, playing upon his son's emotions to remind him of his character as an avenger and of his obligation to defend the honor of Denmark. In 3.4, the Ghost's return to Hamlet to "whet thy almost blunted purpose" (line 111) is the mark of the manager who gets nervous when he sees his directions being neglected by the one entrusted to carry them out.

The Ghost is also significant as a part of some of the other major structures of the play. At the beginning of Hamlet, we see national mobilization going on in preparation for possible war against Norway. To a high degree, this note of future warfare and impending political change is a backdrop to remind the audience that the events being witnessed will have an important political

[11] outcome. Indeed, King Hamlet, when alive, had conquered the Norwegian king in single combat. Now, with the Danish state being torn by the internal anguish following Claudius's fratricide, the state lies weak and exposed—an easy prey to the Norwegians. Structurally, the beginning and ending of *Hamlet* are marked first by the expectation of war and then by the actual takeover by Young Fortinbras of Norway. Ironically, therefore, the Ghost in death is responsible for the fall of the state he so courageously defended in life.

There is an additional major structure involving the Ghost. Maurice Charney observes that the Ghost is significant in the "symmetrical" poison plots in the play (39). The first of these plots, the poisoning of King Hamlet, is described by the Ghost himself in 1.5. The poisoning of the Player King in 3.2 is a virtual reenactment of the first murder, and it occurs in approximately the middle of the action. The final poisonings—of Gertrude, Laertes, Claudius, and finally Hamlet himself—occur in 5.2, the play's last scene. These are of course actions, but they also have value as a set of symbolic frames that measure the progressive deterioration enveloping the major characters of the play.

V. The Ghost's Effect

Beyond his practical and structural importance as the inititator of the play's action, the Ghost has profound psychological influence, mainly negative, on the characters. Roy Walker describes him as a "prologue" to the "omen" of Hamlet himself, who will be the agent of the "dread purpose" of vengeance (220). Because Hamlet is already suffering depression and melancholia, this

[13] role as an agent in a cause of questionable credibility opens the wounds of his vulnerability (Campbell 127–128). Hamlet must resolve to give up everything he has ever learned, even "the movement of existence itself," so that he may carry out the Ghost's commandment (McFarland 32–33). In an invasive, overpowering manner, Hamlet's melancholy influences his love for Ophelia, his possible friendship with Laertes, and his relationship with his

mother (Kott 49; Kirsch 31). No one escapes. The effect is like waves radiating outwardly, with the Ghost at the center.

[14] These effects occur because, almost literally, Hamlet himself cannot escape the Ghost (Allman 218). In 1.5 the Ghost, unseen and below stage, follows him and hears his conversations with Horatio and the guards—an obvious symbolic representation of the Ghost's ongoing presence and pervasive power. As a result of this ever-present force, which as far as Hamlet is concerned might become visible at any moment, Hamlet is denied the healing that might normally occur after the death of a parent (Kirsch 26). The steady pressure toward vengeance disrupts any movement to mental health and creates what Kirsch calls a "pathology of depression" (26) that inhibits Hamlet's actions (Bradley 123), causes his Oedipal preoccupation with the sexuality of his parents (Kirsch 22), and brings about his desire for the oblivion that might come with suicide (Kirsch 27).

[15] It is this power over his son that gives the Ghost the greatest influence in the play. Once the Ghost has appeared, Hamlet can never be the same. He loses the dignity and composure (McFarland 38) that he has assumed as his right as a prince of Denmark and as a student in quest of knowledge. Rather than attack problems that he might have solved normally and easily with negotiations and research, he must sink into acts of murder. Is it any wonder that he hesitates? Despite all his reflection and hesitation, finally the web of vengeance woven by the Ghost closes in on everyone, and the consequence is that Hamlet becomes not only a murderer, but also a victim (Allman 254). There is no solution but the final one—real death, which is the literal conclusion of the symbolic death represented by the Ghost when he first appears on the Elsinore battlements.

VI. Conclusion

[16] The Ghost is real in terms of the action and structure of the play. He is seen by the characters on the stage, and when he speaks we hear him. He is made round and full by Shakespeare, and his motivation is direct and straightforward, even though the signs of his status as a spirit are presented somewhat ambiguously. But the Ghost is more. He has been made a Ghost by the greed and envy of Claudius, and in this respect he becomes in the play either a conscious or unwitting agent of the "unseen Fates or forces" of his own doom (Walker 220). What he brings is the unavoidable horror that seems somehow to be just beneath the surface of good, moral people, waiting for the license to reach out and destroy. Once the forces are released, there is no holding them, and the tragedy of *Hamlet* is that there is no way to win against such odds.

List of Works Cited

Alexander, Peter. Hamlet; Father and Son. Oxford: Clarendon, 1955.

Aldus, P. J. Mousetrap: Structure and Meaning in Hamlet. Toronto: U. of Toronto Press, 1977.

Allman, Eileen Jorge. Player-King and Adversary. Baton Rouge: Louisiana State U.P., 1980.

Bradley, A. C. Shakespearean Tragedy. London: Macmillan, 1950.

Campbell, Lily B. Shakespeare's Tragic Heroes: Slaves of Passion. New York: Barnes & Noble, 1959.

DeLuca, Diana Macintyre. "The Movements of the Ghost in Hamlet," Shakespeare Quarterly 24 (1973): 147–154.

Fisch, Harold. Hamlet and the Word. New York: Frederick Ungar, 1971.

Gottschalk, Paul. "Hamlet and the Scanning of Revenge." Shakespeare Quarterly 24 (1973): 155–170.

—— The Meanings of Hamlet. Albuquerque: U of New Mexico Press, 1972.

Kirsch, Arthur. "Hamlet's Grief." ELH 48 (1981): 17–36.

Kott, Jan. Shakespeare Our Contemporary, trans. Boleslaw Taborski. London: Methuen, 1967, repr. 1970.

McFarland, Thomas. Tragic Meanings in Shakespeare. New York: Random House, 1966.

Paris, Jean. Shakespeare, trans. Richard Seaver. New York: Grove Press, 1960.

Prosser, Eleanor. Hamlet and Revenge, 2nd ed. Stanford: Stanford U.P., 1971.

Walker, Roy. "Hamlet: the Opening Scene." Shakespeare: Modern Essays in Criticism, ed. Leonard F. Dean. New York: Oxford U.P., 1961.

Commentary on the Essay

This essay fulfills an assignment requiring about 2,500 words and fifteen sources. The sources were located through an examination of a library catalog, the *MLA International Bibliography*, and library bookshelves. They represent the range of materials available in a college library with a selective, not exhaustive, set of holdings. The essay is derived largely from the sources listed, with necessary thematic devices, including overall organization and transitions, to make the essay original. Additional particulars about the handling of sources and developing the essay are included in the discussion of note taking and related matters earlier in this chapter.

The central idea of the essay is the importance of the Ghost. Paragraph 1 stresses this idea, while conceding that the Ghost is only a minor character in the action. The research for this paragraph is derived not so much from secondary sources as from a close reading of the play itself. Paragraph 2, continuing the exploration of the central idea, demonstrates that the Ghost figures in the major themes of *Hamlet*. Paragraph 3 is mainly functional, being used as the location of the thesis sentence.

Part II of the essay, containing paragraphs 4 and 5, is on the topic of the Ghost's status as a spirit. Part III, with four paragraphs (6–9), actually continues part II but is concerned with the Ghost's character as an individual rather than as a spirit. Part IV, with paragraphs 10–12, deals with the significance of the Ghost in four of the major structures which dominate the play. Part V, with three paragraphs, considers the negative and inexorable influence the Ghost has upon the major figures of *Hamlet*, with the emphasis being the character of Hamlet as the transferring agent of the Ghost's destructive revenge. The concluding paragraph (16) summarizes much of the essay, with its final idea being concerned with the Ghost's influence upon the nature of *Hamlet* as a tragedy.

The list of works cited is the basis of all references in the text of the essay, in accord with the *MLA Handbook for Writers of Research Papers*, 3rd ed. By using the references included parenthetically in the essay, a reader might use this list to examine, verify, and further study any of the ideas located in these sources.

Appendix D: Taking Examinations on Literature

Taking an examination on literature is not difficult if you prepare in the right way. Preparing means (1) studying the material assigned, the comments made in class by your instructor and by fellow students, and your own thoughts; (2) anticipating the questions by writing some of your own on the material to be tested and by writing practice answers to these questions; and (3) understanding the precise function of the test in your education.

Tests are not designed to plague you or to hold down your grade. The grade you receive is in fact a reflection of your achievement at a given point in the course. If your grades are low, you can probably improve them by studying in a coherent and systematic way. Those students who can easily do satisfactory work might do superior work if they improve their method of preparation. From whatever level you begin, you can increase your achievement by improving your method of study.

Your instructor has three major concerns in evaluating your tests (1) to see the extent of your command over the subject material of the course, (2) to see how well you are able to think about the material, and (3) to see how well you can actually respond to a question or address yourself to an issue.

Many elements go into writing good answers on tests, but this last point, about responsiveness, is perhaps the most important. A major cause of low exam grades is that students really do not *answer* the questions asked. The problem is that some students do no more than retell the story, never confronting the issues in the question. Therefore, if you are asked, "Why does . . . ," be sure to emphasize the *why*, and use the *does* only to exemplify the *why*. If the question is about organization, focus on that. If a problem is raised, deal with it. In short, always *respond* directly to the question or instruction. Let us compare two answers to the same question:

ns, and think about the answers on the way to the exam. Try never
d passively or unresponsively, but always with a creative, question-
nswer goal. Think of studying as a potential writing experience.

STUDY WITH A FELLOW STUDENT. Often the thoughts of another person
help you understand the material to be tested. Try to find a fellow
dent with whom you can work. In view of the need for steady preparation
roughout a course, keep in mind that regular conversations are a good
iea. Also, you might wish to make your joint study genuinely systematic
nd thus might set aside a specific evening or afternoon for detailed work
essions.

TWO BASIC TYPES OF QUESTIONS ABOUT LITERATURE

There are two types of questions that you will find on any examination
about literature. Keep them in mind as your prepare. The first type is
factual, or *mainly objective*, and the second is *general, comprehensive, broad,*
or *mainly subjective*. In a literature course very few questions are purely
objective, except multiple-choice questions.

Factual Questions

MULTIPLE-CHOICE QUESTIONS. These are the most purely factual questions. In an introduction to literature course your instructor will most
likely reserve them for short quizzes, usually on days when an assignment
is due, to make sure that you are keeping up with the reading. Multiple
choice can test your knowledge of facts, and it also can test your ingenuity
in perceiving subtleties of phrasing in certain choices, but on a literature
exam this type of question is rare.

IDENTIFICATION QUESTION. These questions test not only your factual
knowledge but also your ability to relate this knowledge to your understanding of the work assigned. Typical examples of what you might be asked
to identify are:

1. *A character*, for example, Nora in O'Connor's "First Confession." It is necessary
   to describe briefly the character's position and main activity (that is, she is
   Jackie's older sister who gets him in trouble at home and who takes him to
   his confession). You should then go on to emphasize the character's importance
   (that is, her values help keep Jackie confused throughout most of the story,
   but by the end it is clear that O'Connor shows that it is really her values
   that are confused).

Question: How important is the setting of Poe's "The Masque of the Red
Death" to the plan and action of the story?

1

The setting of Poe's "The Masque of the Red Death" is a major element in all aspects of the story. The Prince Prospero invites a thousand of his subjects into his vast "castellated abbey" to be enter-tained while being shielded from the plague of the red death killing the people in the country. The abbey is surrounded by a high and strong wall, and the gates are all welded shut to prevent all contam-ination from the plague. The prince lays in much food and wine, and also has musicians, dancers, and other entertain-ers present and performing constantly so that time can pass well. After a short period he gives a gala, lavish masquerade ball in seven huge rooms of his abbey. Each room has a uniform color scheme—one blue, one purple, one green, one orange, one white, one violet, and one black (with red)—almost all the colors of the rainbow. Over all this a black clock in the black room hourly chimes a fright-ening, dismal sound that makes the mer-riment halt momentarily, as though it were a reminder of the brevity of life. At midnight—the ghostliest hour—Death himself appears, costumed as one of those who have died of the red death, to the horror of the guests. The prince runs after Death, into the black room, in reproach and assault. But then Prospero abruptly dies, and so do all the other guests. Everything happens within the abbey. And so the setting is all perva-sive in Poe's development of the story.

2

The setting of Poe's "The Masque of the Red Death" is a major element in all aspects of the story. As a location, Prospero's "castellated abbey" is a focus of human defiance against death. As a cause of action, the walling in of his thou-sand courtiers is, ironically, the same as insuring that they will all die when Death finally arrives. As a means of achieving probability, the laying in of provisions and entertainment makes the plans of the prince and his "light-hearted friends" seem possible and realistic. As atmosphere, the eerie black clock and the even eerier coloring and lighting of the ballrooms are a commentary on the prince's bizarre and vain attempt to avoid fate. Finally, the setting of the ball-rooms, expressively described by the nar-rator, is the place of the final assault that Prospero makes against the ghoul-ish, spectral figure of the Red Death, and where he and his followers all die. The setting is therefore all pervasive in Poe's development of the story.

While paragraph 1 relates the action to the various scenes of the
story, it does not focus on the relationship. It is also cluttered by details
that have no bearing on the question. Paragraph 2, on the other hand,
focuses directly on the connection. Because of this emphasis, 2 is shorter
than 1. That is, with the focus directly on the issue, there is no need for

irrelevant narrative details. Thus, 1 is unresponsive and unnecessarily long, while 2 is responsive and includes only enough detail to exemplify the major points.

PREPARATION

Your problem is how best to prepare yourself to be knowledgeable and ready for an examination. If you simply cram facts into your head in hopes that you will be able to adjust to whatever questions are asked, you will likely flounder.

1. Read and Reread. Above all, keep in mind that your preparation should begin not on the night before the exam but as soon as the course begins. When each assignment is given, you should complete it by the date due, for you will understand your instructor's lecture and the classroom discussion only if you know the material being discussed. Then, about a week before the exam, you should review each assignment, preferably rereading everything completely. With this preparation, your study on the night before the exam will be fruitful, for it might be viewed as a climax of preparation, not the entire preparation itself.

2. Make Your Own Questions: Go on the Attack. Rereading is effective but passive preparation. Go on the attack by trying to anticipate the specific conditions of the test. The best way to do this is to compose and answer your own practice questions. Do not waste your time trying to guess the questions you think your instructor might ask. What is of greatest importance is to arrange the subject matter by asking yourself questions that help you get things straight.

How can you make your own questions? Your instructor may have announced certain topics or ideas to be tested on the exam. You might develop questions from these. Or you might apply general questions to the specifics of your assignments, as in the following examples:

About a character: What sort of character is *A*? How does *A* grow, or change in the work? What does *A* learn, or not learn, that brings about the conclusion? To what degree is *A* the representative of any particular type?

About the interactions of characters: How does *B* influence *A*? Does a change in *C* bring about any corresponding change in *A*?

About events or situations: What relationship does episode *A* have to situation *B*? Does *C*'s thinking about situation *D* have any influence on the outcome of event *E*.

About a problem: Why is character *A* or situatio way? Is the conclusion justified by the ideas and e

About a theme: What ideas does the work explore? How Which were emphasized in class?

ADAPT YOUR NOTES TO MAKE QUESTIONS. Perhaps the be struct questions is to use your classroom notes, the fullest reco about the way the class approached the material. As you work notes, you should reread passages from the texts that were stu the class or mentioned by your instructor. Remember that it is help work not only with main ideas from your notes, but also with mai such as style, imagery, and organization.

Obviously you cannot make questions from all your notes, and you will therefore need to select from those that seem most important. As an example, here is a short but significant note from a classroom discussion about Walter Van Tilburg Clark's story "The Portable Phonograph" (p. 238): *A particularly timely and modern story. The context is the global, less localized nature of warfare, and the massive destructiveness made possible by modern weapons technology.* It is not difficult to adapt this note to make two practice questions:

(1) What effects of modern weapons technology make the post-war wasteland setting of "The Portable Phonograph" seem realistic?

(2) Why may "The Portable Phonograph" be considered as a particularly timely and modern story?

The first question applies the word *what* to the second part of the note, with the specific focus on the setting of the story. The second applies the word *why* to the phrasing of the first part of the note. Either question would guide you to focused study. The first would require an explanation of the setting of Clark's story realistically mirroring the complete destructiveness made possible by large-scale weapons. The second would emphasize the conditions of modern warfare and their possible effects, with attempts to show how the story reflects these modern conditions. If you were to spend fifteen or twenty minutes writing practice answers to these questions you could be confident in taking an examination on the material.

USE QUESTIONS EVEN WHEN TIME IS SHORT. Whatever your subject, i important that you spend as much study time as possible making answering your own questions. Of course, you will have limited time will not be able to write extensive answers indefinitely. Even so, do give up on the question method. If time is too short for full ans write out the main heads, or topics, of an answer. When time no l permits you to make even such a brief outline answer, keep think

2. *Incidents or situations.* These may be illustrated as follows: "A woman mourns the death of her husband." After giving the location of the situation or incident (Mrs. Popov in Chekhov's play *The Bear*) try to demonstrate its significance in the work. (That is, Mrs. Popov is mourning the death of her husband when the play opens, and in the course of the play Chekhov uses her feelings to show amusingly that life with real emotion is stronger than devotion or duty to the dead.)

3. *Things, places, and dates.* Your instructor may ask you to identify a container of poison (Collier's "The Chaser" or Shakespeare's *Hamlet*), a royal palace (Sophocles' *Oedipus the King*, Shakespeare's *Hamlet* or Poe's "The Masque of the Red Death"), or the dates of poems like Blake's "The Tyger" (1794) or Nikki Giovanni's "Woman" (1978). For dates, you might often be given a leeway of five or ten years if you must guess.

4. *Quotations.* Theoretically, you should remember enough of the text to identify a passage taken from it, or at least to make an informed guess. Generally, you should try to locate the quotation, if you remember it, or else to describe the probable location, and to show the ways in which the quotation is typical of the work you have read, with regard to both content and style. You can often salvage much from a momentary lapse of memory by writing a reasoned and careful explanation of your guess, even if the guess is incorrect.

TECHNICAL AND ANALYTICAL QUESTIONS AND PROBLEMS. In a scale of ascending importance, the third and most difficult type of factual question involves technique, analysis, and problems. You might be asked to discuss the *setting, images, point of view,* or *principal idea* of a work; you might be asked about a *specific problem*; you might be asked to analyze a poem that may or may not be duplicated for your benefit.

The use of technical questions will obviously depend on what you have been studying during the period for which you are being tested. If your instructor has been stressing topics like character, setting, point of view, metaphors and similes, and rhythm, you should prepare to answer questions involving these techniques. If classroom discussion has been confined to theme and idea, however, your preparation may be focused on these. Most instructors announce their intentions well in advance of the exam; if you have any uncertainties about how to prepare, however, be sure to ask your instructor.

Technical questions may be fairly long, perhaps with from fifteen to twenty-five minutes allowed for each. If you have two or more of these questions, try to space your time sensibly; do not devote 80 percent of your time to one question and leave only 20 percent for the rest.

Basis of Judging Factual Questions

IDENTIFICATION QUESTIONS. In all factual questions, your instructor is testing (1) your factual command, and (2) your quickness in relating a part to the whole. Thus, suppose you are asked about the incident "A man kills a canary." It is correct to say that Susan Glaspell's play *Trifles* (and also her story "A Jury of Her Peers") is the location of the incident, that the dead farmer Wright is the killer, and that the canary belonged to his wife, Minnie. Knowledge of these details establishes your factual command. But a strong answer must go further. Even in the brief time you have for short answers, you should try to connect the facts to (1) major causation in the work, (2) an important idea or ideas, (3) the development of the work, and (4) for a quotation, the style. Time is short, and you must be selective, but if you can move your answer from facts to significance, you will be achieving excellence. Along these lines, let us look at an answer identifying the killing of the canary:

> The action is from Glaspell's *Trifles* and also from her "A Jury of Her Peers." The man who kills the canary is John Wright, and the owner is Minnie, his wife. The killing is important because it is the final indignity in Minnie's long-developing rage, which prompts her to use a rope to strangle Wright in his sleep. It is thus the cause not only of murder but also of the investigation bringing the lawmen and their wives on stage. In fact, the wringing of the bird's neck makes the play possible because it is the wives who discover the dead bird, and it is the means by which Glaspell highlights them as the intelligent and also the major characters. Because Wright's brutal act shows the bleakness of Minnie's life with him, it dramatizes the lonely plight of women generally in a male-dominated way of life like that on the Wright farm. The discovery also raises issues of legality and morality, because at the end of both the play and the story, the two wives band together and cover up the evidence, in this way protecting Minnie from conviction and punishment.

Any of the points of this answer could be developed as a separate essay, but the paragraph is successful as a short answer because it goes beyond facts to deal with significance. Admittedly, such answers are possible at exam time only if you have already studied and given considerable thought to the works to be covered, because the more thinking and practicing you do before the exam, the better your answers will be. Remember this piece of advice: *You will not be able to write a really superior answer if your thinking originates **entirely** when you first see the question.* By studying well, however, you will be able to reduce surprise on an exam to an absolute minimum, and will be able to deal thoughtfully and skillfully with all the questions you face.

LONGER FACTUAL QUESTIONS.   The more extended factual questions also require more thoroughly developed organization. Remember that here your knowledge of essay writing is important, for your writing skills will determine a major share of your instructor's evaluation of your answers.

It is therefore best to take several minutes to gather your thoughts together before you begin to write. When the questions are before you, use a sheet of scratch paper to jot down the facts you remember and your ideas about them in relation to the question. Then put them together, phrase a thesis sentence, and use your facts to illustrate or prove your thesis.

Begin your answer pointedly; use key words or phrases from the question or direction if possible, so that your answer will have thematic focus. To be most responsive during the short time available for writing an exam, use the question as your guide for your answer. Let us suppose that you have the following question on your test: "How does Steinbeck use details in 'The Chrysanthemums' to reveal the character of Eliza?" The most common way to go astray on such a question, and the easiest thing to do, is to concentrate on Eliza's character rather than on *how* Steinbeck *uses details* to bring out her character. The word *how* makes a vast difference, and hence the best thing to do on an exam is to copy key phrases from the question to ensure that the answer will be launched in the right direction. Here is an opening sentence that uses the key words and phrases from the question to provide focus:

> Steinbeck *uses details* about gardening, farm life, and personal care as symbols *to reveal the character of Eliza* as a motherly and sexual but repressed and unhappy person.

This sentence sets aims and limits so that the subsequent material will be clearly focused and responsive to the question as it has been asked.

General or Comprehensive Questions

General or comprehensive questions are particularly important on final examinations, when your instructor is interested in testing your total comprehension of the course material. Considerable time is usually allowed for answering this type of question. They may be phrased in a number of ways:

1. A direct question asking about philosophy, underlying attitudes, main ideas, characteristics of style, backgrounds, and so on. Here are some possible questions in this category: "What use do ———, ———, and ——— make of the topic of ———?" "Define and characterize the short story as a genre of literature." "Explain the nature of the sonnet as treated in poets studied during the course." "Contrast the technique of point of view as used by ———, ———, and ———."

2. A "comment" question, often based on an extensive quotation, borrowed from a critic or written by your instructor for the occasion, about a broad class of writers, or about a literary movement, or the like. Your instructor

may ask you to treat this question broadly (taking in many writers) or else to apply the quotation to a specific writer.

3. A "suppose" question, such as "Suppose that Prince Prospero (from Poe's "The Masque of the Red Death") found himself in the place of Hamlet; what might he do when confronted with the testimony of the ghost?" or "What might Sophocles say if he saw performances of plays by Thornton Wilder and Tennessee Williams?"

Basis of Judging General Questions

When answering broad, general questions you are in fact dealing with an unstructured situation, and you must not only supply an *answer* but—equally important—you must also create a *structure* within which your answer can have meaning. You might almost say that you make up your own specific question out of the original general question. If you were asked to "Consider the role of women as expressed in plays by Ibsen, Glaspell, and Williams," for example, you would do well to structure the question by narrowing its limits. A possible way to focus such a question might be this:

> Ibsen, Glaspell, and Williams express wide-ranging views about women by dramatizing their positions in the home, their relationships with men, and their relative degrees of power and powerlessness.

With this sort of focus you would be able to proceed point by point, introducing supporting data as you form your answer.

As a general rule, the best method to adopt in answering a comprehensive question is that of comparison-contrast. The reason is that in dealing with, say, a general question on Donne, Burns, and Finch, it is too easy to write *three* separate essays rather than one. Thus, you should force yourself to consider a topic like "The treatment of departure," or "The relationship of men and women," and then to treat such a topic point by point rather than poet by poet. By developing your answer in this way, you can bring in references to each or all of the writers as they become relevant to your main idea. But if you were to treat each poet separately, your comprehensive answer would lose focus and effectiveness.

Glossary/Index

Abstract diction Language that refers to broad and unspecific qualities. Because of its wide applicability, it is more useful for discursive, philosophical topics than for narration, description, and dramatic dialogue. *265–266, 583.* See also *Concrete diction.*

Absurd, drama of A type of nonrealistic drama, often comedy, that explores the absurdities of modern existence. See *Comedy of the absurd.*

Accent See *Beat* and *Stress*

Accented rhyme See *Rising rhyme. 691*

Accentual, strong stress, or sprung rhythm Lines relying not on traditional meters but rather on numbers of strong stresses, regardless of the number of lightly stressed words and syllables. *686.* See also *Sprung rhythm.*

Actions (incidents) The things that characters do in works of literature; the events or occurrences. *57, 98*

Accumulation See *Cumulatio.*

Allegory A narrative or dramatic story which may be applied to a parallel set of situations while maintaining its own narrative integrity. *62–63, 328–329, 1016*

Alliteration The repetition of identical consonant sounds (most often the sounds beginning words) in close proximity. *689*

Allusion Unacknowledged references and quotations. Authors assume that readers will recognize the original sources, and relate their meaning to the new context. *330, 777–780, 802*

Amphibrach A three-syllable foot consisting of a light, heavy, and light stress, as in *wĭth pléa-sŭre. 685*

Amphimacer, or cretic A three-syllable metrical foot consisting of a heavy, light, and heavy stress, as in *thoúghts ŏf lóve. 685*

Anagnorisis (recognition) That point at which a dramatic character experiences increased self-knowledge and understanding. *1067*

Analysis, commentary, or interpretation See *Commentary.*

Anapaest A foot consisting of two light stresses followed by a heavy, as in *ĭn thĕ tówn. 684*

Antagonist The character opposing the protagonist. The conflict between a protagonist and a human or nonhuman force is **antagonism.** *57, 145*

Antimetabole See *Chiasmus.*

Anticipation See *Procatalepsis.*

Apostrophe The addressing of discourse to a real or imagined person who is not present; also, a speech to an abstraction. *630*

Arena stage A sunken acting area (arena) flanked on three sides by the audience, much like the ancient Greek and Roman amphitheaters. *1070, 1230*

Aside A short speech delivered by a character to another or to the audience, the convention being that the other characters on stage cannot hear it; the speaker usually reveals his or her thoughts or plans. *1013, 1118*

Assertion A statement about a subject. For example: *Love* (the subject) *is vital but also irrational* (the predicate, contains the assertion about the subject). *364*

Assonance The repetition of identical vowel sounds in different words in close proximity. *688–689*

Atmosphere (mood) The emotional aura evoked by a work, often as a result of the descriptions. *60* **Atmosphere and setting** *232–233*

Auditory images References to sounds. *605*

Authorial symbols See *Private symbols.*

Authorial voice The name given to the speaker of a story when this speaker is not otherwise identified; used to distinguish the speaker from the author. *195–196*

Bacchius, or Bacchic A three-syllable metrical foot consisting of a light stress followed by two heavy stresses, as in *the stréam's béd. 685*

Ballad A narrative poem composed of quatrains in which lines of iambic tetrameter alternate with iambic trimeter, rhyming X-A-X-A. *731*

Beast fable See *Fable.*

Beat The heavy stresses or accents in lines of poetry. The number of beats in a line usually dictates the meter of the line (five beats in a pentameter line, etc.). *682.* See also *Stress.*

Blank verse Unrhymed iambic pentameter. *727*

Blocking The grouping and movement of characters on stage in a play. *1006*

Blocking agent A circumstance, person, or attitude that obstructs the union of lovers. *1321*

Box set In the modern theater, a realistic setting of a single room from which the "fourth wall" is missing. *1230*

Buskins See *Cothurni.*

Cacophony ("bad sound") Words combining consonant sounds that do not permit an easy flow of pronunciation, but rather produce sharpness or harshness. *690*

Cadence group The pronunciation of grammatical units as rhythmical units, such as a noun phrase ("remembrance of things past") or prepositional phrase ("of parting day"). The rhythmical units are bounded by the slight but distinct pauses separating them. *686*

Caesura (pl. caesurae) In closed-form poetry, the pause separating units of rhythm. *686–687*

Carpe diem poetry   Poetry that expresses the shortness of life and the need to act in or enjoy the present. *Carpe diem* means "seize the day." *829*

Catastrophe   The "turning downward" of the dramatic plot, the fourth stage in the structure, after the climax. The dénouement of a play, in which things are explained and put into place. *1010*

Catharsis (purgation)   The stimulation and subsequent elimination of pity, sympathy, fear, and other strong emotions that, according to Aristotle, occur as one watches or reads an effective tragedy. *1066*

Cause and effect   The interaction of events and the pattern of causation producing doubt, tension, and interest in a work of literature. *57*

Central idea   (1) The thesis of an essay. *16, 21–34*   (2) The theme of a literary work. *57–58*. See also *Theme*.

Character   An extended verbal representation of a human being, the inner self that determines thought, speech, and behavior—a reasonable facsimile of a human being. *56–57, 143–193, 539–575, 1011*

Chiasmus (antimetabole)   A rhetorical pattern (usually with verbal repetition, but also with incidents or ideas) repeating in the sequence A-B-B-A, such as:

A   B   B   A

"I know she loves me, but she loves to keep me from knowing it." *270*

Choragos   The leader of the chorus in classical Greek drama. *1071*

Choric character   A character who remains detached from the action and who provides commentary. *1011*

Chorus   In classical Greek drama, a group of actors chanting or speaking in unison, probably while moving in a stately dance. The chorus introduces, responds, and comments on the action, and keeps the drama going from episode to episode. *1071*

Chronology ("logic of time")   The sequence of events in a work, with emphasis upon the complex intertwining of cause and effect. *57*

Clerihew   A humorous closed-form poem in four lines, rhyming A-A-B-B, usually about a famous person or figure. *734*

Cliché rhymes   Rhymes, such as *moon* and *June* or *trees* and *breeze*, that have been so widely used by poets and songwriters as to become trite. *691*

Climax (Greek for "ladder")   The high point in an action; the fourth stage of dramatic plot structure, in which the conflict and the consequent tension are brought out to the fullest extent; hence that point in a work in which the results of the conflict become inevitable. *101, 1010*

Closed couplet   See *Heroic couplet*.

Closed-form poetry   Poetry written in specific and traditional patterns produced through rhyme, meter, line-length, and line groupings. *726–738*

Colonnade   A line of columns installed at the Great Theater of Dionysius in ancient Athens to form a permanent scenic backdrop. *1070*

Comedy   A literary work, beginning in adversity and ending in prosperity, that describes the regeneration and success of a group or society. *1007–1008, 1320–1325*

Comedy of the absurd   A modern form of comedy dramatizing the absurdities of existence and ending ambiguously. *1325*

Comedy of manners   A form of comedy, usually high, in which the social conventions of society are examined and satirized. *1324–1325*

Commedia dell'arte Broadly humorous farce, developed in 16th-century Italy, featuring stock characters, stock situations, and improvised dialogue. *1324, 1385, 1387*

Commentary, analysis, or interpretation Passages of explanation and reflection about the meaning of actions, thoughts, dialogue, historical movements, and so on. *61*

Common ground of assent Those interests, concerns, and assumptions that the writer assumes in common with readers so that an effective and persuasive tone may be maintained. *661*

Common measure A closed poetic quatrain form, rhyming A-B-A-B, in which lines of iambic tetrameter alternate with iambic trimeter. *731*

Comparison-contrast A technique of analyzing two or more works in order to determine similarities and differences in topic, treatment, and quality. *Appendix A: 1583–1596*

Complex sentence A main clause together with a subordinate or dependent clause. *267*

Complication Following the exposition, the onset of the major conflicts in a work; the second stage in the structuring of a plot. *101, 1010*

Compound-complex sentence Two or more independent clauses with which one or more dependent clauses are integrated. *268*

Compound sentence Two simple sentences joined by a conjunction. *268*

Conceit See *Metaphysical conceit.*

Concrete diction Words that describe specific qualities or conditions, such as an ice cream sundae being "cold," "sweet," and "creamy." These words are *concrete*, while the words "good" or "neat" as applied to the sundae would be *abstract*. *264–266, 583.* See also *Abstract diction.*

Concrete poetry Poetry that draws much of its impact from its visual appearance. *741*

Conflict The opposition between two characters, between large groups of people, or between individuals and larger forces such as natural objects, ideas, modes of behavior, public opinion, and the like. Conflict may also be internal, involving choices facing a character. It is the essence of *Plot. 57, 99–100, 1009–1010.* See also *Protagonist* and *Antagonist.*

Connotation The emotional, psychological, or social overtones or implications that a word carries in addition to its *denotation. 266, 578–579*

Consonant sounds Sounds produced as a result of the touching or close proximity of the tongue or the lips in relation to the teeth or palate; contrasted with *vowel sounds. 680, 689*

Contextual symbol See *Private symbol.*

Continuant sounds Consonant sounds such as *m, n, l, r, s, f,* and *th,* produced by the steady release of the breath in conjunction with various positions of the tongue, teeth, palate, and lips. *680, 689*

Convention An accepted feature of a particular genre, such as the competence or brilliance of the detective in detective fiction, or the speeches by a lover to a sweetheart in love poetry. *1071.* See also *Dramatic convention.*

Cosmic irony (irony of fate) *Situational irony* that is connected to a pessimistic or fatalistic view of life. *304*

Costumes The clothing worn by actors, indicating the historical period and social class of the characters being represented and the type of activity in which they are engaged. *1006–1007*

Cothurni (buskins) Thick-soled boots worn by actors in ancient Greek tragedy. *1071*

Counts A method of determining characteristics of a writer's style by counting the number of words in sentences, the numbers of nouns, adjectives, prepositional phrases, etc. *267*

Couplet (1) Two successive rhyming lines of poetry, usually in the same meter. (2) The last two lines of an English sonnet. *727–728*

Cretic See *Amphimacer.*

Crisis The third stage in the dramatic plot structure, the turning point, at which the complication comes to a head and forces the protagonist to resolve the conflict, for better or worse, by making a decision and taking an action. See also *Climax.* *101, 1010*

Cultural (universal) symbols Generally or universally recognized symbols embodying ideas or emotions that the writer and the reader share in common as a result of their social and cultural heritage. *327*

Cumulatio (accumulation) The parallel massing of detail; a short and effective way of introducing a considerable amount of material. *270*

Dactyl A metrical foot consisting of a heavy stress followed by two lights, as in *míght-ĭ-ĕst. 685*

Dactylic (triple) rhyme Rhyming dactyls, such as *haughtier* and *naughtier. 691*

Decorum A quality of language and behavior that is thought to be appropriate, suitable, or fitting both to the literary medium (such as epic poetry or a detective story) and also to subject and character. *584, 1014*

Denotation The standard dictionary meaning of a word, without associations or overtones. *266, 577–578.* See also *Connotation.*

Dénouement (French for "untying") or **resolution** The final stage of plot development, in which all mysteries are explained and characters generally exit from the literary work. Usually the dénouement is done as speedily as possible. *102, 1011*

Description The exposition of scenes, actions, attitudes, and feelings. *59–60*

Deus ex machina (Latin for "God out of a machine") An extraordinary and illogical event (that may be attributed to mysterious or divine origin) that solves all the problems in a work. *1070*

Device A rhetorical figure, or a verbal strategy. *623*

Dialect The language of a particular social class, region, or group. *585, 1014*

Dialogue The speech of two or more characters in a story, play, or poem. *60, 1006*

Diction Word choice, types of words, and the level of language. *262–266, 582–586*

Diction, formal or high Proper, elevated, and elaborate language characterized by complex words and a lofty tone. *263, 583*

Diction, informal or low Relaxed, conversational, colloquial, or substandard language. *264, 584*

Diction, middle, neutral, or plain   Correct language and word order without elaborate words or a lofty tone. *263–264, 583–584*

Didactic play   A play designed to teach a specific lesson or moral. *1017*

Digraph   Two letters spelling one segment of a sound, as in *digraph*, where *ph* spells the sound *f*. *680*

Dilemma   Two choices facing a protagonist, with either one being unacceptable or damaging. *99*

Dimeter   A line consisting of two metrical feet. *682*

Dionysia   The religious festivals in ancient Greece which celebrated the god Diony-sius. Greek drama developed as a major feature of these festivals. *1069*

Diphthong   A vowel segment that begins with one vowel sound and then concludes in another, as the *y* in *fly* or *I* and the *ow* in *cow*.

Dipodic measure   (literally "two feet" combining to make one) develops when a poet submerges two normal feet, usually iambs or trochees, under a strong beat, so that a galloping or rollicking rhythm results. *685–686*

Domestic tragedy   A tragedy of domestic life usually involving middle-class charac-ters. *1068*

Donnée (French for "given")   The given situation or set of assumptions on which a work of literature is based. *55*

Double dactyl   A comic closed-form poem in two quatrains, written in dactylic dimeter. The first line must be a proper name, and the sixth or seventh a single word. *735*

Double-entendre   Deliberate ambiguity, often sexual. *303*

Double plot   Two different but related lines of action going on at the same time, usually in a play. *1009*

Double rhyme   See *Trochaic rhyme.*

Drama   (1) A play. (2) A group of plays, as in *modern drama.* (3) All literature written to be acted. *2, 1005–1019*

Dramatic convention   A traditional or customary method or device of presentation (such as the aside and the soliloquy) that is accepted by readers or audiences. *1018*

Dramatic irony   A special kind of situational irony in which a character perceives his or her plight in one way while both the reader (and audience) and one or more of the other characters understand it in greater perspective. *62, 304, 664, 1015*

Dramatic monologue   A type of poem derived from the theater, in which a speaker speaks to an internal listener or the reader at length. The form is related to the soliloquy. *544*

Dramatic (Objective) point of view   A third-person narration reporting speech and action, but rigorously excluding commentary on the action and thoughts of any of the characters. *199, 1012*

Dying rhyme   See *Falling rhyme.*

Dynamic character   A character with the capacity to adapt, change, and grow (opposed to *Static character*). *145, 1011*

Echoic words   Words echoing the actions they describe, such as *buzz, bump,* and *slap*, important in the device of *onomatopoeia. 689*

Enclosing method   See *Framing method.*

End-stopped line   A line ending in a full pause, usually indicated with a period or semicolon. *687*

English (Shakespearean) sonnet   A fourteen-line poem, in iambic pentameter, composed of three quatrains and a couplet, rhyming A-B-A-B, C-D-C-D, E-F-E-F, G-G. *730*

Enjambement (run-on line)   A line of poetry having no end punctuation but running over to the next line. *687*

Epic   Usually a long narrative poem that features heroic characters, momentous events, and elevated diction. *51–52*

Epigram   A short and witty poem, usually in couplets, that makes a humorous or satiric point. *733*

Episodia   The episodes or scenes in a Greek tragedy. *1071*

Epitaph   Lines composed to mark someone's death; a special type of epigram. *733*

Euphony ("good sound")   Words containing consonants that permit an easy and pleasant flow of spoken sound. *690*

Evaluation   The act of determining the quality of a literary work. *Appendix A: 1577–1582*

Exam, examination   A pedagogical technique designed to determine the extent and depth of a reader's comprehension of a body of material. *Appendix D: 1624–1632*

Exact rhyme   Rhyming words in which both the vowel and consonant sounds rhyme; also called *perfect rhyme*. *692*

Exodos   The final episode in a Greek tragedy, occurring after the last choral ode. *1071*

Explication   A complete and detailed analysis of a work of literature, often word-by-word and line-by-line. *523, 534–538*

Exposition   The laying out or putting forth of the materials necessary for an understanding of a work; the first stage of plot structure, in which the author supplies background and introduces characters and situations. *101, 1010*

Eye rhyme   In a position in a poem where rhyme is expected, eye-rhyming words look as though they should rhyme exactly but do not, as in *love* and *prove*. *693*

Fable   A short, pointed story illustrating a moral truth, most often associated with the ancient Greek writer Aesop. *52, 329–330*

Falling action   The action in a play after the climax—the catastrophe and resolution. *102, 1010*

Falling rhyme   Trochaic rhymes, such as *dying* and *crying*, and also dactylic rhymes, such as *flattery* and *battery*. *691*

Fantasy   The creation of events that are dreamlike or fantastic, departing from ordinary understanding of reality because of apparently illogical location, movement, causation, and chronology. *54*

Farce   Boisterous, physical, low comedy in which the focus is on improbable plot, action, and dialogue. *1008, 1324*

Feminine rhyme   See *Falling rhyme*.

Fiction   Narratives, characters, and speeches based in the imagination of the author, not in literal, reportorial facts. *51–97*

Figurative language   Expressions that conform to a particular pattern or form, such as metaphor, simile, and antimetabole. *623*

First-person point of view   The "I" narrator who may acquire authority because of close involvement in the action or because of being an observer. *59, 197–198, 201*

Flashback   A narrative or dramatic episode that presents past action (often through memory) in the present. *102–103*

Flat character   A character, usually minor, who is not individualized and rounded, but who is relatively undeveloped, static, and unchanging. The role of a flat character is not to be the center of interest, but rather to be useful and structural—a part of the scene and the background. Contrasted with *Round character*. *145–146, 1011*

Foil   A type of character who sets off or highlights aspects of the protagonist. *1011*

Form   (1) The shape, structure, or general pattern of a literary work. *726–771*. (2) In the consideration of ideas, a form is conceptual and ideal rather than real. The activity of thought, for example, to the degree that it can be remembered or imagined, is a mental *form. 363, 726–742*

Formal diction   See *Diction, formal*.

Framing (enclosing) method   The repetition of an element, such as an action, setting, or situation, at both the beginning and ending of a work so that the work itself is "framed" or "enclosed." *232*

Free verse   Poetry that, for rhythm, uses not metrical feet but rather the natural rhythms of phrases and normal pauses. *738*

Freytag pyramid   A scheme developed by Gustav Freytag to show how the five stages of dramatic plot structure go up and down like the sides of a pyramid. *1010*

Full-length play   A drama that contains either three to five separate acts or a long series of discrete scenes. *1008*

Gallery   The upper seats at the back and sides of a theater. *1117*

General language   Words referring to broad classes of persons or things. Distinguished from *Specific language*. *264–266, 583*

General symbol   See *Cultural symbol*.

Graph, graphics   The spelling, as opposed to the actual pronunciation, of words. "Graph" is a verb synonymous with "spell." "Graphics" is the study of spelling. *680–681*

Gustatory images   References to impressions of taste. *607*

Haiku   A poetic form derived from Japanese, traditionally containing three lines of 5, 7, and 5 syllables. Loosely, very short poems of two or three lines are often considered haiku. *132–133*

Half rhyme   See *Slant rhyme*.

Hamartia   A Greek word describing the error, frailty, or flaw that causes the downfall of a tragic protagonist. *1066*

Heavy stress rhyme   See *Rising rhyme*.

Heptameter ("the septenary")   A line containing seven metrical feet. *682*

Hero, Heroine The major character in a work, the protagonist, the human center of interest. Though the term implies that a character be particularly valiant, the fact that the character has a major role is sufficient cause to label him or her *hero* or *heroine*. *145*

Heroic couplet Two successive rhyming lines of iambic pentameter; the second line is commonly end-stopped. Couplets written from 1660–1800 are usually termed "heroic," regardless of their topic matter. *728*

Hexameter A line consisting of six metrical feet. *682*

High comedy Elegant comedies characterized by wit and sophistication, in which the complications grow out of character. *1323*

Hovering accent See *Spondee.*

Hymnal stanza See *Common measure.*

Hyperbole See *Overstatement.*

Iamb A metrical foot consisting of a light stress followed by a heavy stress (e.g., *the winds*). *683–684*

Idea A broad word referring to a concept, thought, opinion, or belief. Some types of ideas are justice, right and good, necessity, and causation. An idea developed throughout a work of literature is called a *theme. 363–404*

Idiom A phrase or style of speaking, characteristic of a particular group, class, region, or nation, whose meaning cannot be derived from an analysis of constituent parts. *584–585, 1014*

Image, imagery An "image" is language referring to sensory impressions, making for immediacy and vividness. "Imagery" refers to a number of images in a single work or in a number of works. *603–622*

Imitation The idea that literature is derived from life and is an imaginative duplication of life experiences; closely connected to *realism* and *verisimilitude. 54*

Imperfect foot A foot consisting of a single syllable, either stressed or unstressed. *685*

Incidents (actions) The events or occurrences in a work of literature. *57, 98*

Informal (Low) diction See *Diction, informal.*

Internal rhyme The occurrence of rhyming words within a single line of verse.

Interpretation See *Commentary.*

Invention The process of making up situations and stories out of the imagination, derived by the writer from life experiences and thought. *17, 54*

Ironic comedy A modern form of comedy in which the tone is ironic and the ending ambivalent. *1325*

Irony The use of language and situations that are widely inappropriate or opposite from what might be ordinarily expected. *61–61, 302–304, 661–664.* **Irony and setting** *233*

Italian sonnet A fourteen-line poem, in iambic pentameter, composed of two quatrains (the *octet*) and two tercets (the *sestet*). The octave rhymes A-B-B-A-A-B-B-A; the sestet can rhyme variously C-D-E-C-D-E, C-D-C-C-D-C, C-D-C-D-C-D, and so on. *730*

Jargon Words and phrases that are characteristic of a particular profession, trade, or pursuit such as medicine, football, or the military. *585–586, 1014*

Kinesthetic image Language describing human or animal motion and activity. *607*

Kinetic images Language describing general motion. *607*

Lighting The general word describing the many types, positions, directions, and intensities of artificial lights used in the theater. *1007*

Limerick A five-line poetic closed form in which two lines of anapestic trimeter are followed by two in anapaestic dimeter and a final line in trimeter, rhyming 3a-3a-2b-2b-3a, often used in comic and bawdy verse. *734*

Limited (Limited omniscient) point of view A third-person narration with the focus made on one particular character's activities and thoughts. *200*

Listener (internal audience) A character or characters imagined as the audience to whom a story or poem is spoken, and as a result one of the influences on the content of the work, as in Browning's "My Last Duchess" or Owen's "Dulce et Decorum Est." *543*

Literature Written (also spoken) compositions designed to tell stories, dramatize situations, and reveal thoughts and emotions, and also to interest, entertain, stimulate, broaden, and ennoble readers or listeners. *1, passim.*

Loose sentence A straightforward sentence with no climax and no surprises. *268*

Low comedy Crude, violent, and physical comedies, characterized by sight gags, bawdy jokes, and outrageous situations; farce. *1323, 1326*

Lyric A short poem written in a repeating stanzaic form, often designed to be set to music; a lyric usually emphasizes the thoughts and/or feelings of the speaker. *731–732*

Main plot The central and major line of causation and action in a literary work. *1009*

Masculine rhyme See *Rising rhyme.*

Meaning The combination of a poem's theme, its emotional impact, and the experience it creates for the reader. *827–858*

Mechanics of verse See *Prosody.*

Melodrama A sentimental form of tragedy with an artifically happy ending. *1008*

Metaphor Figurative language in which one thing is directly equated with another, as in "the bowing trees," where trees bending in a wind are equated with actors bowing after a performance. *60, 623–626.* See also *Simile.*

Metaphysical conceit An elaborate and extended metaphor or simile that links two apparently unrelated fields or subjects. The term is commonly used to describe the metaphorical language of a number of early seventeenth-century poets, particularly John Donne. *861*

Meter The measure, or number, of feet within a line of traditional verse, such as *iambic pentameter* referring to a line consisting of five iambs. *682*

Method acting A method of acting whereby actors probe deeply into their experience and imagination to portray character and situation in the most human and natural way possible. *1230, 1434–1435*

Metonymy A rhetorical figure in which one thing is used as a substitute for another with which it is closely identified. *631–632*

Metrical foot In closed-form poetry, a regular, repeating pattern of lightly stressed and heavily stressed syllables, such as an iamb (light-heavy) and a trochee (heavy-light). *682*

Metrics See *Prosody.*

Monologue A long speech spoken by a single character to himself or herself, to the audience, or to an off-stage character. *1006*

Mood (atmosphere) The emotional aura evoked by a work, usually as a result of the quality of the descriptions. *60.* **Mood and setting** *232–233*

Morality play A type of medieval and early Renaissance play that dramatizes the way to live a Christian life. *1006, 1115*

Mystery play Medieval drama that enacted events from the Bible, such as the killing of Abel by Cain, the problems of Noah, the anger of Herod, and so on. The word is derived from the *masters*, or leading citizens, who sponsored the plays in the towns where they were performed. *1006, 1115*

Myth, mythology A "myth" is a story that explains a specific aspect of life or a natural phenomenon, based in the religion, philosophy, and collective psychology of various groups or cultures. "Mythology" refers to a tribal or national group of myths, or to all myths collectively. *330, 802–826*

Narration The relating or recounting, usually fictional, of a sequence of events or actions. *51, 58*

Narrative ballad A poem in ballad measure telling a story. *524*

Narrative fiction See *Prose fiction*.

Near rhyme See *Slant rhyme*.

Negative connotation That connotative aspect of a word that reflects adversely on the person or object being described. *579*

Neutral (Middle) diction See *Diction, middle*.

New comedy Short, boisterous, and bawdy romantic comedies, exemplified by the plays of Plautus and Terence, both Roman playwrights. *1321*

Nonrealistic character An undeveloped and often symbolic character without full motivation or individual identity. *1012*

Nonrealistic drama Dreamlike, fantastic, symbolic, and otherwise artificial plays that make no attempt to present an imitation of everyday reality. *1433, 1435–1437*

Novel A long work of prose fiction. *53*

Octameter A line consisting of eight metrical feet. *682*

Octave (1) An eight-line stanza or unit of poetry. (2) The first eight lines of an Italian sonnet. *730*

Ode A (usually) long poem written in a complex stanzaic form that deals with elevated and philosophical topics—often including the speaker's ideals and aspirations. Ancient odes use repeating stanza patterns, while a varying stanza pattern is characteristic of many English odes. *732*

Off rhyme See *Slant rhyme*.

Old comedy Satirical comedy full of personal invective and improvisation, exemplified by the plays of the Greek comic writer Aristophanes. *1321*

Olfactory imagery Language describing smells. *606*

Omniscient point of view A third-person narrative in which the speaker not only describes the actions and speeches of all the characters, but also enters their minds to explain their thoughts. *59, 200*

One-act play A short play of one act, usually with one major scene and a continuous action. *1008*

Onomatopoeia A blending of consonant and vowel sounds designed to imitate or suggest the activity being described. *689*

Open-form poetry Poems that avoid traditional structural patterns, such as rhyme or meter, in favor of other methods of organization. *726, 738–740*

Orchestra (1) The central circle where the chorus performed in ancient Greek theaters. (2) The ground- or first-floor area in a modern theater where the audience sits. *1069*

Organic unity The interdependence of all elements of a work, including character, actions, speeches, descriptions, thoughts, and observations. The concept of organic unity presupposes that everything in a literary work is absolutely essential; to eliminate anything is to destroy the work. *57*

Overreacher See *Overstatement.*

Overstatement (hyperbole, or the overreacher) A figure which achieves emphasis through exaggeration. *303, 633*

Parable A brief narrative designed to illustrate a religious truth, most often used to describe the parables of Jesus as recorded in the Gospels. *52, 330*

Parados (1) Two aisles on each side of the orchestra in ancient Greek theaters along which actors could enter or exit. (2) The first lyrical ode chanted by the chorus in Greek tragedy. *1071*

Paradox A rhetorical figure embodying a seeming contradiction that is nevertheless true. *629–630*

Parallelism A rhetorical figure in which the same grammatical forms are repeated in two or more phrases, lines of verse, or sentences. *268–270, 588*

Paranomasia See *Pun.*

Paraphrase A brief restatement, in one's own words, of all or part of a literary work; a précis. *90–97, 523, 532–533, 1603–1606*

Pentameter A line consisting of five metrical feet. *682*

Perfect rhyme See *Exact rhyme.*

Periodic sentence A sentence arranged in an order of climax, building to the most important part of the idea, and sometimes even building to a surprise. *268*

Peripeteia A sudden reversal, when the action of a work, particularly a play, veers around quickly to its opposite. *1067, 1439*

Persona (1) The narrator or speaker of a story or poem. *59, 194–196, 540.* (2) The stylized mask worn by an actor in classical Greek tragedy. *1071*

Personification A rhetorical figure in which human characteristics are attributed to nonhuman things or abstractions. *631*

Petrarchian sonnet See *Italian sonnet.*

Phonetic, phonetics "Phonetic" refers to the sounds of words as opposed to their spelling. "Phonetics" is the study of speech sounds and their written representation. *681*

Plausibility See *Probability.*

Plot The plan or groundwork for a story or play, based in conflicting human motivations, with the actions resulting from believable and realistic human responses. It is causation, response, opposition, and interaction that make a plot out of a simple series of actions. *57, 98–112, 1009–1011*

Poem, poet, poetry Poetry is a variable literary form which is, foremost, characterized by the rhythmical qualities of language. While poems may be short (epigrams and haiku of just a few lines) or long (epics of several thousand lines), the essence of poetry is compression, economy, and force, in contrast with the expansiveness of prose. There is no bar to the topics that poets may consider, and poems may range from the personal and lyric to the public and discursive. A *poem* is one poetic work. A *poet* is a person who writes poems. *Poetry* may refer to the poems of one writer, to poems of a number of writers, to all poems generally, or to the aesthetics of poetry considered as an art. *517*

Poetic decorum See *Decorum.*

Point of view The voice of a story, the speaker who is doing the narration; the means by which the reality and truthfulness of a story are made to seem authentic; the focus or angle of vision from which things are not only seen and reported but also judged. *58–59, 194–228, 540, 1012*

Point-of-view character The central figure in a limited-point-of-view narration, the character about whom events turn, the focus of attention in the narration. *200*

Postulate (premise) The assumption on which a work of literature is based, such as a level of absolute, literal reality, or as a dreamlike, fanciful set of events. *55.* See also *Donneé.*

Précis A shortening, or cutting down, of a narrative into its essential parts, a synopsis, abridgment, paraphrase, condensation, or epitome. *90–97*

Premise See *Postulate.*

Private (contextual) symbol A symbol which is derived not from common historical, cultural, or religious materials, but which is rather developed within the context of an individual work. *327–328, 1016*

Private mythology A personal mythic system which writers develop and employ in their own works. *805*

Probability (plausibility) The standard of judgment requiring that literature should be about what is probable, common, normal, and usual. *148–149*

Problem plays See *See drama.*

Procatalepsis A rhetorical strategy whereby a writer raises an objection to his or her argument, and then argues to overcome this objection. *1308–1310*

Problem plays See *Social drama.*

Prologue In Greek tragedy, the action before the first choral ode. *1071*

Propaganda play A play designed to convince an audience that a particular ideology should be embraced. *1017*

Props, properties The objects, furniture, and the like used on stage during a play. *1006*

Proscenium (1) See *Proskenion.* (2) An arch that frames a *box set (q.v.)* and holds the curtain, thus creating the invisible fourth wall through which the audience sees the action of the play. *1006, 1071*

Proscenium stage A stage in which a proscenium arch separates the audience from the acting area; the effect is to produce a "room" with one wall missing. *1006.* See also *Proscenium* and *Box set.*

Prose fiction Novels, short stories, and shorter prose works that generally focus on one or a few characters who undergo some sort of change or development as they interact with other characters and deal with their problems. *2*

Prose poem A short work, written in prose, but employing the methods of verse, such as imagery, for poetic ends. *739*

Proskenion A raised wooden stage built in front of the skene in ancient Greek theaters. *1071*

Prosody The art of sound and rhythm in poetry. *680–725*

Protagonist The principal character in a work, the human center of interest, who is involved in the major conflict. *57, 145, 1011*. See also *Antagonist*.

Public (universal) mythology Widely known mythic systems that have been well established over a long period of time, such as Greco-Roman mythology and Germanic mythology. *804*

Pun (paranomasia) A word-play in which the writer surprisingly reveals that words with totally different meaning have similar or even identical sounds. *632–633*

Purgation See *Catharsis*.

Pyrric A foot consisting of two unstressed syllables. *684*

Quatrain (1) A four-line stanza or poetic unit. (2) In an English or Shakespearean sonnet, a group of four lines united by rhyme. *729*

Raisonneur A character who remains detached from the action and provides reasoned commentary; a choric character. *1011*

Realism (versimilitude) The use of true, lifelike, or probable situations and concerns. Also, the concept underlying the use of reality in literature. *54*

Realistic character The accurate imitation of individualized men and women. *1011–1012*

Realistic comedy See *Ironic comedy*.

Realistic drama Plays that dramatize characters and situations in line with the world as we know it. *1229–1230, 1433–1438*

Recognition See *Anagnorisis*.

Repetition Repeating the same word, phrase, sentence, or the like for impact and effect. *587*

Research The use of both primary and secondary sources (e.g., historical, biographical, and critical books and articles) in the investigation and solution of a literary problem. *Appendix C: 1597–1623*

Resolution See *Dénouement*.

Resonance The effect of emotional and/or intellectual reverberation and amplification produced by symbols, allusions, and myth. *802*

Revenge tragedy A popular type of English Renaissance drama, developed by Thomas Kyd, in which a person is called upon (often by a ghost) to avenge the murder of a loved one. Shakespeare's *Hamlet* is in the tradition of revenge tragedy. *1119*

Reversal See *Peripeteia*.

Rhetoric Broadly, the art of persuasive writing and even more broadly, the general art of writing. Short or long sentences, and devices such as parallelism, climax, simile, metaphor, irony, and symbolism are all aspects of rhetoric. *267–270*

Rhetorical substitution The manipulation of the caesura within a line to achieve the effect of metrical substitution, even though the line remains technically regular. *688*. See also *Substitution*.

Rhyme The repetition of identical or similar concluding syllables in different words, most often at the ends of poetic lines. *690–694*

Rhyme scheme The pattern of rhyming sounds in a poem, usually indicated by assigning a letter of the alphabet to each sound. *693–694*

Rhythm The movement, rises and falls, and intensities in the flow of words, phrases, and sentences in poetry. *681*. See also *Prosody*.

Rime See *Rhyme*.

Rising action The action in a play before the climax. *1010*

Rising rhyme Rhymes produced with one syllable words, like *sky* and *fly*, or with multisyllabic words in which the accent falls on the last syllable, such as *decline* and *confine*. *691*

Romance Lengthy Spanish and French stories written in the sixteenth and seventeenth centuries. Today, the word is applied to formulaic stories detailing the development of an enthusiastic love relationship. *53*

Romantic comedy Sympathetic comedy that presents the adventures of young lovers trying to overcome opposition and achieve a successful union. *1324*

Round character Usually the major figure in a work, but in fact any fictional character endowed by the author with many individual and dynamic traits. The essence of roundness is that a character undergo some sort of growth or change as a result of the experiences developed in the story. Contrasted with *Flat character*. *145, 1011*

Run-on line See *Enjambement*.

Satire An attack on human follies or vices, as measured positively against a normative religious, moral, or social standard. *664–665*

Satiric comedy A form of comedy designed to correct social and individual behavior by ridiculing human vices and follies. *1324*

Satyr play A short comic interlude performed during the Dionysian Festival in ancient Greece. *1069*. See also *Trilogy*.

Scansion The act of scanning, or determining the prevailing rhythm of a poem. *682*

Scenery The artificial environment created on-stage to produce the illusion of a specific or generalized place and time. *1006*

Scrim In the modern theater, a transparent curtain on which a scene may be painted and illuminated to seem solid or transparent. *1230*

Second-person point of view A narration employing the "you" personal pronoun. Rarely used. *198–199, 201*

Segment A sound in individual words essential to the meaningful understanding of those words, as in the word *top*, where there are three meaningful sounds— *t*, *o*, and *p*. The addition of the segment *s* makes the word plural (*tops*). *680*

Semivowel segments Midway between vowels and consonants, the semivowels are *w*, *y*, and *h*. *680*

Septenary See *Heptameter*.

Sequence (literally, a following) The events in a work as they take place in time, from beginning to end. *57*

Sestet (1) A six-line stanza or unit of poetry. (2) The last six lines of an Italian sonnet, usually containing the resolution of the poem. *730*

Sets See *Scenery*.

Setting The natural and artificial environment in which characters in literature live their lives; the sum total of references to physical and temporal objects and artifacts. *229–261*

Shakespearean sonnet See *English sonnet*.

Shaped verse Poetry written so that the lines or words of the poem form a recognizable shape, such as a pair of wings or a geometrical figure. *741*

Short story A compact, concentrated narrative that may also contain description, dialogue, and commentary. Poe used the term "brief prose tale" for the short story, and emphasized that it should create a powerful single impression. *53*

Sight rhyme See *Eye rhyme*.

Simile Figurative language in which words such as "like" or "as" are used to draw attention to similarities, as in "the trees were bent by the wind *like actors bowing after a performance*." *60, 623–626*. See also *Metaphor*.

Simple sentence A complete sentence containing one subject and one verb, together with modifiers and complements. *267*

Situational irony A type of irony emphasizing that human beings are enmeshed in forces beyond their comprehension or control, so that whatever they do, their efforts are minimal or ineffective. *303, 662–663*

Skene The building behind the orchestra in ancient Greek theaters used as dressing rooms and off-stage areas. *1069, 1070*

Slang Informal and substandard vocabulary, made up of spontaneous words and phrases which may exist for a time and then vanish, although some slang expressions also become permanent. *585, 1014*

Slant rhyme Words that almost rhyme, usually with different vowel sounds and similar consonant sounds, as in *could* and *solitude*. *692*

Slapstick comedy A type of low farce in which the humor depends almost entirely on physical actions and sight gags. *1324*

Social drama A type of problem play that deals with current social issues and the place of individuals in society. *1008*

Soliloquy A speech made by a character, alone on stage, directly to the audience, the convention being that the character is revealing thoughts and feelings. A soliloquy is to be distinguished from an *aside*, which is made to the audience (or confidentially to another character) when other characters are present. *1012–1013, 1118*

Sonnet A closed poetic form of fourteen lines written in iambic pentameter with a rhyme scheme reflecting the organization of the Italian or English sonnet. *730*

Speaker A fictitious observer, the point-of-view narrator of a story or poem, often a totally independent character who is completely imagined and consistently maintained by the author. *59, 194–196, 540–543*

Specific language References to a real thing or things that may be readily perceived or imagined; distinguished from *General language*. *264–266, 583*

Spondee (hovering accent) Two successive, equally heavy accents (e.g. *men's eyes*). *684*

Sprung rhythm A poetic rhythm developed by Gerard Manley Hopkins in which major stresses are released or "sprung" from the line through the juxtaposition mainly of one-syllable, heavily-stressed words, and also through the virtual abandonment of lightly stressed words such as articles. *686*

Stage business Expressions, gestures, and other movements and body language that keep a play production active and dynamic. *1006*

Stage convention See *Dramatic convention*.

Stage directions A playwright's instructions concerning lighting, scenery, blocking, tone of voice, action, entrances and exits, and the like. *1006*

Stanza A poetic unit made up of lines grouped together by rhyme and/or meter, most common in lyric poetry. The patterns established in the first stanza are usually repeated throughout. *726*

Stasimon A choral ode chanted by the chorus in Greek tragedy. *1071*

Static character A character, usually minor, who remains the same and undergoes no growth or change in the work. Contrasted with *Dynamic character*. See also *Flat character. 146, 1011*

Stereotype A stock character who seems to have been stamped from a mold; a highly conventionalized, unchanging character. *146, 1012.* See also *Stock character*.

Stock character A character, usually flat and static, who performs predictably in repeating situations. Examples are the foolish boss, the angry police captain, the lovable drunk, the bewildered or stubborn parent, and the prodigal son. *146, 1012*

Stop sound The consonant sound produced by the momentary stoppage and release of breath either when the lips touch each other or when the tongue touches the teeth or palate, as in *p, t, d, g,* and *k. 688–689*

Stress (accent) The strong emphasis ("strong stress" or "strong accent") or light emphasis ("light stress" or "light accent") given to a syllable through loudness, duration, isolation, or heightening of pitch. A heavy stress is marked with a prime mark or acute accent (´), and a light stress is marked with a short accent (˘). *683, 711.* See also *Beat*.

Structure The arrangement and placement of materials in a work, the actual assemblage of an entire work or part of a work. See also *Plot. 57, 100–142, 1009–1011*

Style The manipulation of language, the way in which writers tell the story, develop the argument, dramatize the play, or compose the poem; the placement of words in the service of content. *58, 262–298*

Subject The topic that a literary work addresses, such as love, marriage, war, death, and the like. *364, 827*

Subplot A secondary line of action in a literary work that often comments directly or obliquely on the main plot. *1009*

Substitution The use of a variant foot in a line of poetry that is otherwise regular, as in:

He went / to work / at the crack / of dawn.

Here the anapaest *at the crack* in the third foot is a substitute for the iamb expected. *687–688.* See also *Rhetorical substitution*.

Syllable A separately pronounced part of a word, or, in some cases, a complete word. *Word* has one syllable; *nation* has two. *682*

Symbol, symbolism A specific thing that may stand for ideas, values, persons, or ways of life; a symbol always points beyond its own meaning toward greater and more complex meaning. *60, 62–63, 326–362, 772–801, 1016*

Synecdoche A rhetorical figure in which a part stands for a whole, or a whole for a part. *631–632*

Synesthesia A rhetorical figure uniting or fusing separate sensations or feelings; the description of one type of perception or thought with words that are appropriate to another. *632*

Syntax Word order and sentence structure. A mark of style is a writer's syntactical patterning (regular patterns and variations), depending on the rhetorical needs of the literary work. *586–588*

Tactile image Language describing touching and feeling. *607*

Tenor In metaphorical language, the totality of ideas and attitudes which the author intends to express. *626*

Tercet A three-line unit or stanza of poetry, often rhyming A-A-A or A-B-A. *728*

Terza rima A three-line stanza form in which each stanza is linked with the next through repeated rhyme sounds: A-B-A, B-C-B, etc. *729*

Tetrameter A line consisting of four metrical feet. *682*

Theater in the round A modern theater arrangement, often outdoors, in which the audience totally surrounds the stage, with all actors entering and exiting along the aisles. *1230*

Theme The central idea or ideas that a literary work explores or asserts about its subject. *57–58, 363–404, 827–858*

Thesis sentence The sentence in an essay which provides a plan or groundwork connecting the central idea and the topics to be discussed. *23*

Third-person point of view A method of narration in which all things are described in the third person (*she, he, it, they, them*, etc.) and in which the narrator is not introduced as an identifiable persona. *59, 199–201*

Third-person objective point of view See *Dramatic point of view.*

Thrust stage A stage that projects into the area normally reserved for the audience. *1006*

Tone The methods used by writers to convey and control attitude about their material and their readers. *61, 299–325, 656–679, 1014*

Topic See *Subject.*

Traditional poetry Rhymically, verse which follows more or less regular or recurring patterns; closed-form poetry. *727–738*

Tragedy A literary work, most often a drama, beginning in prosperity and ending in adversity, that recounts the fall of an individual. *1007, 1064–1072*

Tragic flaw See *Hamartia.*

Tragicomedy A broad range of literary works containing a mixture of tragic and comic elements. *1008*

Trilogy A group of three literary works, usually related or unified. Ancient Athenian dramatists wrote a *trilogy* (three tragedies), together with a satyr play, for submission at the Dionysiac festival. *1069*

Trimeter A line consisting of three metrical feet. *682*

Triple rhyme See *Dactylic rhyme.*

Triplet See *Tercet.*

Trochaic rhyme Rhyming trochees such as *flower* and *shower. 691*

Trochee A metrical foot of two syllables with a heavy accent on the first (flŏw-ĕr). *683–684*

Trope A short dramatic dialogue inserted into the Catholic mass during the early Middle Ages. *1115*

Tudor interlude   A short tragedy, comedy, or history play written during the reigns of the English Kings Henry VII and Henry VIII (i.e., the first half of the sixteenth century). *1115*

Understatement   A rhetorical figure which creates emphasis through deliberate underplaying or undervaluing. *303, 633*

Unities   The unities of place, time, and action that, according to Aristotle, were observed by the dramatists of his time. Later critics held that the unities were to be observed scrupulously, but Shakespeare and subsequent critics ignored them. *1073*

Universal mythology   See *Public mythology.*

Universal symbol   See *Cultural symbol.*

Value   A standard by which ideas and customs are measured. *365*

Vehicle   In metaphorical language, the actual details of the metaphor or the simile. *626*

Verbal irony   Language stating the opposite of what is meant. *62, 303, 664*

Versification   See *Prosody.*

Versimilitude ("at one with truth") **or Realism**   A characteristic of literature whereby the characters, dialogue, actions, and outcomes in a literary work are designed to seem true, lifelike, real, probable, and believable. *148–149.* See also *Probability.*

Villanelle   A closed poetic form of nineteen lines, composed of five triplets and a quatrain. The form requires that whole lines be repeated in a specific order and that only two rhyming sounds occur throughout. *729*

Visual image   Language describing things that can be seen. *604–605*

Visual poetry   Poetry that draws much of its power from the appearance of the verse on the page. *741.* See also *Concrete verse* and *Shaped verse.*

Voice   See *Speaker.*

Vowel sounds   Continuant sounds produced by the resonation of the voice in the space between the tongue and the top of the mouth, such as the *ee* in *feel*, the *eh* in *bet*, and the *oo* in *cool*. *680, 688–689*

Well-made play   A type of play developed in nineteenth-century France in which the action begins at the climax and the conflict turns on a secret. *1439*

Credits

Index of Authors, Titles, and First Lines

INDEX OF KEY TERMS